MW01124672

# The Selected Papers of Jane Addams

VOLUME 3

CREATING HULL-HOUSE AND AN INTERNATIONAL PRESENCE, 1889–1900

# The Selected Papers of Jane Addams

VOLUME 3

# *Creating Hull-House and an International Presence, 1889–1900*

EDITED BY

MARY LYNN MCCREE BRYAN,

MAREE DE ANGURY,

AND ELLEN SKERRETT

*with the assistance of Richard R. Seidel*

UNIVERSITY OF ILLINOIS PRESS
Urbana, Chicago, and Springfield

FRONTISPIECE: Jane Addams, 1895. This photograph was taken by Alfred A. Cox of Cox and Prime, photographers, in Chicago. It first appeared as a rendering in the 12 September 1895 *Chicago Times-Herald*. During the last years of the nineteenth century, this became the iconic photograph of Jane Addams; it was the one she seemed to prefer. Alfred A. Cox (b. 1894, England) married Josephine Brillman in Chicago in 1864, became a naturalized citizen in 1896, and practiced his craft in Chicago between 1893 and 1912. During the 1893–1900 period, Jane Addams had at least four photographic sittings with Cox: 1895, ca. 1896, and twice in 1898 (UIC, JAMC, 0004 2792).


Manufactured in the United States of America
C 5 4 3 2 1
♾ This book is printed on acid-free paper.

Library of Congress Cataloging-in-Publication Data
Addams, Jane, 1860–1935.
The selected papers of Jane Addams / [edited by Mary Lynn McCree Bryan, Barbara Bair, and Maree de Angury].
v. <1–2>; ill.; 25 cm.
Includes bibliographical references and index.
Contents: v. 1. Preparing to lead, 1860–81 — v. 2. Venturing into usefulness, 1881–88
ISBN 978-0-252-03349-0 (vol. 2)
1. Addams, Jane, 1860–1935.
2. Addams, Jane, 1860–1945 —Correspondence.
3. Hull House (Chicago, Ill.)—History.
4. Women's International League for Peace and Freedom.
5. Social reformers—United States—Biography.
6. Social problems—United States.
7. Social settlements—United States.
8. Peace movements—United States.
9. Women—Education—History.
10. Chicago (Ill.)—History.
11. Illinois—History.
I. Addams, Jane, 1860–1935.
II. Bryan, Mary Lynn McCree.
III. Bair, Barbara, 1955–
IV. De Angury, Maree.
HV28.a35 a25 2003–
361.92—21 2001005638
[b]

Vol. 3 ISBN 978-0-252-04097-9 (hardcover), ISBN 978-0-252-09952-6 (e-book)

[W]ithout the advance and improvement of the whole, no man can hope for any lasting improvement in his own moral or material individual condition.

—Jane Addams, "Outgrowths of Toynbee Hall," 3 December 1890

[T]he time to extol the beauty of peace is at the moment when many people are forgetting it.

—Jane Addams to Adolphus Clay Bartlett, 3 December 1900

# *Contents*

## PART 2 *It Is the Work I Must Do Because It Is the Work I Love, 1894–96*

## PART 3 *Beginning to Preach Peace, 1897–1900*

# *Illustrations*

# *Acknowledgments*

For at least thirty-eight years, since 1975, our work, the Jane Addams Papers Project, has been identifying, gathering, organizing, and publishing the papers of Laura Jane Addams, known to history simply as Jane Addams (1860–1935). The purpose of our dedication has been to make the life, times, and accomplishments of Addams available to a broad range of students, scholars, and the general reading public, both nationally and internationally.

Lost to history shortly after the end of her life, when everyone was engaged in the cataclysm that was World War II, Jane Addams was one of the most world-famous and influential American women of her era, 1890–1935. She was the founder of Hull-House, the female leader of the social settlement movement that helped guide the progressive reform movement in the United States, 1890–1915, and she was the recognized head of the first international woman's peace movement formed at the time of World War I—for which she received the Nobel Peace Prize in 1931.

To place her in the mainstream of American history, historians required access to solid evidence of her life, her philosophy, her contributions, her mistakes, and her achievements. For the period during which Jane Addams lived, the traditional evidence from which history is developed consists of the print or visual records of individuals, including their speeches, writings, diaries and calendars, photographs, personal documents, illustrative matter, and writings by others about them during their lifetimes. As late as the 1970s, very little effort had been made to build collections of documents or materials that shed light on the contributions of women to U.S. history. To write Addams and other women leaders similar to her into the story of our country required locating and investigating the evidence.

Our project, designed to gather the papers of Jane Addams, was meant to help fill that void in the evidence. Over time we have identified, gathered, and organized the Addams papers from more than one thousand repositories and collections. We published eighty-two reels of microfilm with an estimated two thousand images on each reel revealing in all more than 150,000 documents. These materials are the bulk of the papers of Jane Addams. They were issued as *The Jane Addams Papers*, with a printed guide, by University Microfilms International (1985–86). In addition, we have indexed the correspondence of Addams by correspondent and subject and developed an extensive bibliography of Addams's writings and speeches. This has been issued as award-winning *The Jane Addams Papers: A Comprehensive Guide*, by Indiana University Press (1996).

The volume in which these acknowledgments appear is the third in another award-winning publication of our project: the printed series of *The Selected Papers of Jane Addams* being published by the University of Illinois Press. These volumes are meant to present the life of Addams primarily using her own words, supplemented with introductory essays and contextual comment by us as editors.

The result of this investment in time, commitment, and treasure offers the evidence for a much fuller and more comprehensive understanding of the life of this significant female leader, the contributions that she and the like-minded colleagues who worked with her made to the development of the United States in an era in its history that is identified with great social change. Our work has made possible the publication of new biographies of Addams and many of her close associates as well as monographs and articles about a wide variety of social and economic movements and events that characterize her era. As a result, women and their contributions are continuing to become a mainstream part of the story of the history of the United States.

None of this would have been possible without the consistent financial support provided throughout the years by public and private sources. For the Jane Addams Papers Project, it all began with two awards in 1975–76, one from the National Historical Publications Commission, soon to become the National Historical Publications and Records Commission, and one from the National Endowment for the Humanities. More than any other source, the National Historical Publications and Records Commission has been a determined and conscientious supporter of the Addams project. The Rockefeller, Ford, MacArthur, Lilly, Joyce, Dr. Scholls, and Spencer Foundations as well as H. T. Wilson and Co. and the Chicago Community Trust have also have been generous supporters of the Addams project. In addition, Addams relatives as well as ordinary readers and researchers who care to preserve the evidence of the life and times of Addams have offered encouragement and financial help.

For the first eight years, the Addams project was located at the University of Illinois in Chicago, but for the past thirty years it has been associated with, although not located at, Duke University in Durham, North Carolina. While Duke has provided accounting services, project offices have been located in the homes of its four primary editors: Mary Lynn McCree Bryan and Norwood Bryan, Maree de Angury, Nancy Slote and Michael Danko, and Barbara Bair. In addition, the Bryan Automotive Co., Fayetteville, North Carolina, and the

Bryan family have generously provided office equipment, including computers, desks, chairs, lighting and filing equipment, communication equipment, Internet support, storage, postage, and photocopy service throughout the project's years in North Carolina. Without the commitment of all who have supported the Addams project through direct financial contributions and with in-kind assistance, this project could not have been undertaken. We are extremely grateful to all.

As with all of the other publications of the Addams project, and in most respects like the production of the first two volumes of this printed edition, the third volume of *The Selected Papers of Jane Addams* is the result of close collaboration by a small team of documentary editors. We were ably backed by essential research, editorial and technical assistance, key public and private sources of support, and our publisher. Our work has been graced from its beginnings by the support of Addams's relatives and friends, who have shared their knowledge of events and personalities and lent materials for inclusion in the Addams volumes. The art of careful explication of the documents demands that voluminous information be drawn from myriad historical sources. This mass-research effort was dependent in part on responses to our queries from reference librarians, special collections curators, and archivists from public and private repositories throughout the United States and some foreign countries. We thank them for lending to our project their keen interest, kindness, intelligence, and skills. We are also grateful to all the scholars who post accurate documentary evidence and comment on the ever-expanding Internet.

The project has made considerable use of the library services of the following institutions: Duke University; the University of North Carolina, Chapel Hill; the University of Illinois at Chicago; the University of Chicago; the Harold Washington Center of the Chicago Public Library; the Chicago Historical Society located in the Chicago History Museum; the Swarthmore College Peace Collection, Swarthmore College, Swarthmore, Pennsylvania; and the Cumberland County Library and Information System and the Methodist University Library, both in Fayetteville, North Carolina. We are very grateful to all of the librarians, archivists, curators, researchers and other scholars and individuals in these settings who have been supportive of our scholarly efforts and provided excellent access to the collections in their care.

In the Chicago area, we are particularly grateful to librarians at the Harold Washington Center of the Chicago Public Library, especially Morag Walsh, senior archival specialist; Lyle Benedict, Municipal Reference Collection; William Cliff, microfilm room; and graphic artist III Marcus A. Berry, Special Collections and Preservation Division. They have been especially helpful in providing direction to special resources in their collections that are revealing of events in Chicago in the era covered by this volume. They have also provided free photocopies and helped without fee in securing useful photographs and illustrative matter for this volume. Independent researcher Julia W. Kramer helped develop information on the World's Columbian Exposition and the multiple roles that

Jane Addams had in it. Staff associated with the print and photograph collections in the Chicago History Museum Historical Society, including Ellen Keith and Lesley Martin, were always willing to go the extra mile to assist in identifying unique and era-sensitive photographs and special reference materials. In particular, we are grateful to Jerry Danzer and Russell Lewis, who helped us gain access to and use two sets of scrapbooks: those for Unity Church in Chicago and for Louise de Koven Bowen. At Chicago's Art Institute, development coordinator Laurie McGregor Carroll and academic records specialist Matthew Sams, Registration and Records, School of the Institute, were helpful in establishing school records for Edith deNancrede and helping identify the teaching commitment of Enella Benedict. At Rush University Medical Library, Archives, Chicago, assistant archivist M. Natalie Wheaton dug out information about Edith Nason, Wilfreda Brockway, and other nurses associated with the early days of the St. Luke's Nursing School. Assistant university archivist Janet C. Olson, Northwestern University, in Evanston, Illinois, helped us secure information about Emma Rogers. Adam Bohanan, assistant librarian at the Meadville Lombard Theological School of Lombard College, Illinois, made early issues of the *Unity* periodical available and eased our access to the Jenkin Lloyd Jones papers. Ralph Pugh and Catherine Bruck, archivist, both of the Illinois Institute of Technology, Chicago, did special research in the student records, publications, and photographs of the Armour Institute to establish the fact that Mary Rozet Smith was a student at the school before 1899 and provided biographical data and a photograph of Julia A. Beveridge. They also provided photographs of the Armour Mission, the Lewis Institute Building, and Frank W. Gunsaulus. Distinguished scholar and independent researcher Rima Lunin Schultz, of Oak Park, near Chicago, was particularly helpful in locating reviews from a variety of periodicals for Residents of Hull-House, *Hull-House Maps and Papers*, published in 1895. She also offered access to a photograph of Alzina Parsons Stevens. Cynthia Richardson, cofounder of Genlighten, provided information about Dr. Anna Ellsworth Blount. Heather Radke, exhibit coordinator, Jane Addams Hull-House Museum, gave us access to a photograph of Mary Keyser. Over and over, John Kimbrough, reference librarian at the Regenstein Library of the University of Chicago, was available to help with the variety of reference questions that came to the fore as we developed annotation for our Addams-related documents. In digging out material in the University of Chicago Archives about Jane Addams's nephew Stanley Linn, reference assistant Thomas Whittaker in the Special Collections Research Center of the University of Chicago Library was particularly helpful. Louise Howe, archivist at the Fourth Presbyterian Church of Chicago, helped us solve one of our most difficult research questions: "What and where was Room 48?" We are very grateful especially because the answer added considerably to our knowledge of the kind of activities in which Jane Addams was engaged as she went about the process of founding Hull-House. Nancy Weber, Highland Park Historical Society, and Jean Sogin helped us identify the Charles Mather

Smith home in Highland Park. Addams biographer Louise Knight directed us to information about the burial of Mary Rozet Smith, and Aki Lew, Graceland Cemetery, provided records of the Smith and Rozet burials at Graceland. Genealogist Pat Spears was particularly helpful in guiding us to photographic material in the region. Staff in the Cook County, Circuit Court, Archives in Chicago, including Julius Machnikowoski and Lois Travis, were particularly helpful in searching the Divorce Records for Matthew and Mary E. Murphy, neighbors of Hull-House on Halsted Street, as well as Mary Rozet Smith's brother and his wife, and for providing records associated with the estates, particularly that of Mary Rozet Smith. At the Winnetka Historical Society, curator Siera Heavner helped us with a photograph of Henry Demarest Lloyd. Access Service librarian Lisa Schoblasky, Newberry Library in Chicago, gave us access to the *Living Church*. Several librarians in the Richard J. Daley Library, University of Illinois at Chicago, were particularly helpful. In the Microform Department, we relied especially on April Pittman, library assistant. In the Manuscript Section of the Special Collections Department, we could always count on the help of associate special collections librarian Valerie Ann Harris and manuscript librarian Peggy Glowacki or any of their assistants, including Gretchen Neidhardt and Mary Diaz. When we spent several days in the Manuscript Section reviewing the Jane Addams Memorial Collection photograph collection, everyone went out of their way to help us use our time to the fullest.

In Illinois we want to especially recognize Jim Bade of the Cedarville Area Historical Society, Cedarville, for all of his help and his persistence in continuing to tend the heritage of Jane Addams and the Addams family in their hometown, where Jane Addams is buried. We are also grateful for the continuing help of Paul Fry, nephew of Mary Fry, for years the companion to Jane Addams's stepmother, Anna Hostetter Haldeman Addams. Mr. Fry has supported the development of the Addams project from its beginning and continues to provided encouragement as well as bits of Addams family lore. He was a superb host to the project when we visited Cedarville in 2012. In Freeport Cheryl Gleason and the staff of the Local History Room, Freeport Public Library, and various staff members of the Stephenson County Historical Society, also in Freeport, continue to provide valuable assistance on Addams family matters and friends. At Rockford College, now Rockford University, our longtime mainstay has been archivist Mary Pryor, who after nearly thirty years retired from her position in 2013. We are deeply indebted to her for her many years of assistance to our project. Most recently, acting librarian James E. Kelly has been of great assistance, especially in reviewing photographic files at Rockford. Our search for the marriage records of Madeleine Wallin and George C. Sikes, Hull-House residents, was successful with the help of John A. Duerk, a 2010 intern working at the Illinois Regional Archives Depository, Northern Illinois University, DeKalb. Archivist and librarian for special collections Arthur H. Miller, Donnelley and Lee Library/LIT, Lake Forest College, Lake Forest, offered special assistance in locating the student records of

Stanley Linn and for student and then teacher Enella Benedict. At the Decatur, Illinois, Genealogical Society, Michael E. Reynolds of the research staff helped us investigate a special sewing service for women in Decatur in the early 1890s. Amanda Lawrence, undergraduate assistant, who worked under the guidance of Dina A. Allen, research specialist, and Linda S. Stahnke in the University Archives, University of Illinois at Urbana-Champaign, conducted research on Harry Sands Grindly. At the Billy Graham Center Archives, Wheaton College, Wheaton, archivist Bob Shuster gave us special assistance in using the Woman's Union Missionary Records as we searched for evidence of the mission work of Julia C. Lathrop's aunt Martha and her friend Grace Rankin Ward. Director Eric Gillespie of the Col. R. R. McCormick Research Center, First Division Museum at Cantigny Park, Wheaton, helped us locate an Addams letter in the Medill Papers. Archivists at the Illinois State Archives, including Barbara Helfin, Illinois Regional Archives Depository supervisor, quickly retrieved and made available for us a number of documents in their care, especially records of incorporation for nonprofit organizations. At the Abraham Lincoln Presidential Library in Springfield, where collections of materials on Illinois history are kept, especially helpful were Library Services director Kathryn M. Harris; supervisor, reference and technical services, Jane Ehrenhart; and newspaper librarian Jan Perone.

In Massachusetts in the Archives and Special Collections of Frost Library, Amherst College, Amherst, archivist Peter Nelson provided valuable reference data about William Horace Day. Three different members of the staff at Boston College combined to guide us successfully to information about Dr. Leila G. Bedell. For their persistence and dedication to task, we want to thank especially assistant director for acquisitions Alex Rankin in the History of Nursing Archives, located in the Howard Gotlieb Archival Research Center; head of technical services and archives at the Boston University's School of Medicine Emily L. Beattie; and head of reference and interlibrary loan Joseph Harzbecker in the Boston University Medical Center. Researcher Robin Carlow, Harvard University Archives, Pusey Library, Harvard Yard, assisted us in identifying Jane Addams's "Mr. Palmer" as Charles Harvey Palmer. Librarian and executive director Margaret Bendroth of the American Congregational Association provided information on Rev. John McCord and ably assisted us in securing a photograph of a young Robert A. Woods. Archivist of the Congregational Church Archives Jessica Steytler was especially helpful in our search for information about Rev. E. A. Adams, who founded the Bethlehem Chapel in Chicago. At the Andover Newton Theological School, Newton Centre, Diana Yount of the Archives and Special Collections Department, Trask Library, made it possible for us to trace the life of Edwin A. Waldo. She also was key in our search for a photograph of Robert A. Woods as a young man. Jessica Gill, archivist, Newburyport Archives Center, and Ghlee Woodworth at the Oak Hill Cemetery, Newburyport, provided information about the death date of Anne Toppan Withington. We are grateful to former archivist Wilma R. Slaight and to assistant archivist Jane A.

Callahan, Wellesley College Archives, Margaret Clapp Library, for providing background information about Wellesley graduates who were associated with Jane Addams and Hull-House. At the Archives, Smith College, Northampton, archivist Nanci Young and in the Sophia Smith Collection, Smith College, manuscript librarian Susan Boone and curator of manuscripts Amy Hague and their colleagues have always been ready to answer our inquiries about the Ellen Gates Starr Papers and other collections in their care. Deborah A. Richards, archives specialist, Smith College, helped provide special information on Elizabeth ("Bessie") Eastman, Jean Fine Spahr, and Helen Rand Thayer. At Harvard University, Radcliffe Institute, the Arthur and Elizabeth Schlesinger Library on the History of Women in America, Cambridge, we had excellent help from Diana Carey, reference librarian, visual resources, and from curator Kathryn Jacob, and reference librarians Sarah Hutcheson, Alissa Link, and Ashley Susina were also helpful.

In New York, Vassar College archivists provided help with their college graduates who became associated with Jane Addams at Hull-House. In particular, Dean M. Rogers, special collections assistant, developed biographical data for Julia C. Lathrop, Anna Lathrop Case, and Sarah A. Sears. Katherine Collett, assistant archivist at the Hamilton College Library, Clinton, provided information about Charles Columbus Arnold. Director and university archivist Elaine Engst, Cornell University, Ithaca, helped us establish information on Agnes Rogers, who taught at Hull-House during the 1890s.

In Connecticut, public services librarian Claryn Spies of the Manuscripts and Archives Division of Yale University was particularly helpful with materials about William Kent, and Alice Hamilton biographer Barbara Sicherman provided special documentation about the Hamilton family. In Delaware, reference archivist Marjorie McNinch, Manuscripts and Archives Department, Hagley Museum and Library, Wilmington, conducted special research about Ida Wood. In Maryland, Elizabeth Nye DiCataldo, archivist, Edith Hamilton Library of the Bryn Mawr School, Baltimore, also provided information on Ida Wood. From Bar Harbor Historical Society in Maine, Deborah Dyer and Estelle Megquier led us to information about the summer cottages of Jane Addams and Mary Rozet Smith and Louise de Koven Bowen.

We could not have undertaken the Addams project without the cooperation and assistance of the curators at the Swarthmore College Peace Collection, Swarthmore, Pennsylvania. The most recent curator, Wendy E. Chmielewski, and all of the archivists, librarians, and assistants who work at the Peace Collection have made access to the holdings of their Jane Addams Collection, its books and photographs, easily available. They also have under their care related collections of peace materials, including the papers of Emily Greene Balch, the records of the Woman's Peace Party, and those of the United States Section of the Woman's International League for Peace and Freedom. All are useful in understanding the role and contribution of Jane Addams. Staff and volunteers at the Peace Collection continue to be supportive of the Addams project and generous with their time and their knowledge of all of the materials in their care. Also in Pennsylvania, assistant librarian Alicia Suchoski, Luzerne County Historical Society, Wilkes-Barre, provided great help in our search to discover information about the George Cotton Smith family, relatives of Mary Rozet Smith and her family. Nancy R. Miller of the University of Pennsylvania Archives in Philadelphia was of special assistance in our effort to gain more information on Ida Wood.

Marilyn McNitt, reference assistant at the Bentley Historical Library, University of Michigan, offered excellent service as we sought information and photographs of the Pond Brother Architects. Michael J. O'Reilly was of great assistance in our efforts to locate and verify the property that Jane Addams owned in Lakeside, Michigan. In seeking information about Hull-House resident Addison Alvord Ewing, we had superb assistance from Beth Swift, archivist at Wabash College, Crawfordsville, Indiana. Also in Indiana, Ellen Gates Starr scholar Suellen Hoy provided special information. As always, librarians at the Lilly Library, Indiana University, Bloomington, were supportive. In Ohio Jill Tatem of the Archives of Case Western University, Cleveland, helped by providing additional information about former faculty member Jennette Barbour Perry and about the Women's Department commencement where Jane Addams spoke in June 1894.

In our efforts to learn more about Alessandro Mastro-Valerio and the Italian agricultural colony he organized in Alabama, we conducted research in Daphne. We had wonderful assistance from reference librarian Deborah Norris, Daphne Public Library, and from archivist Cathy Donelson, Baldwin County Alabama Department of Archives and History. Working together in two different collections, they presented an amazing assortment of documents, information, and leads to other potential sources. In North Carolina, William Erwin Jr., retired, and research services librarian Janie Leigh C. Morris, both from the Rare Book, Manuscript, and Special Collections Library, Duke University, Durham, gave us assistance and access to the H. J. Gow Diaries and to copies of the *Chicago Daily Tribune*, 1889–95 period. Other librarians throughout the Duke University library system were also most helpful, especially those in microforms and in the music library. From Columbia, South Carolina, we had the able assistance of independent researcher Betsy Miller, who in her investigations of Fred Pelham discovered valuable information about Laura Dainty Pelham that she shared with the Addams project. She was also key in our investigation of the names, locations, and relationships to Mary Rozet Smith and the Smith family, the relatives that Jane Addams and Mary Rozet Smith visited there on several occasions.

In Wisconsin the project had special assistance from Erik Schneiderhan, at that time a doctoral student in sociology, University of Wisconsin–Madison, who alerted us to significant Addams materials among the minutes of the papers of the United Charities of Chicago in the Chicago History Museum, Chicago

Historical Society materials. The records he discovered helped us identify Jane Addams's leadership role in creating the Chicago Bureau of Charities that led to the formation of the United Charities of Chicago. Archivist Tom Winslow, Frances Donaldson Library, Nashotah House Seminary, Nashotah, developed useful biographical data on Rev. John Alma Bevington. In our effort to discover the history of the Holiday Home Camp, Lake Geneva, to which Hull-House neighborhood children were sent for summer vacation time before the settlement had its own camp facilities, we are indebted to Bill Herron of Delavan, a board member of the organization. Reference archivists Harry Miller and Lee Grady, at the Wisconsin State Historical Society, and archivist Steve Massar of the University of Wisconsin, both at Madison, helped with our inquiries about Amanda Johnson. We are also extremely grateful to Jim Ellickson, a distant relative of Amanda Johnson, who made family information about Amanda Johnson and the Johnson-Brun family available to us. At Beloit College in Beloit, Fred Burwell offered special research on early Hull-House resident Edward L. Burchard.

In Kansas Janice Scott, librarian, Kansas Heritage Center, and in Denver, Colorado, Jen Felts provided additional information about Rose Marie Gyles and her family. In California we had extraordinarily special assistance from independent researcher Alfred Strohlein, who tirelessly investigated early records of the Roman Catholic Church and sources about the history of the development of the Los Angeles and San Diego areas in our effort to identify the location of Las Fuentes de San Jorge. Archivist Jane Kenealy and photo archivist Carol Myers, San Diego History Center, also helped in that effort, as did Peter J. Blodgett, H. Russell Smith Foundation Curator of Western American History, Huntington Library, Pasadena.

On foreign soil, we are grateful for the assistance of information librarian Sonia Hope at the Women's Library, London Metropolitan University, for her help with our inquiries about Grace Balgarnie and Helen Gow. In Ireland Anthony O'Sullivan in Limerick City, Rev. Kingston in Carrickmacross, and Dr. Susan Hood, archivist/Publication Office, Church of Ireland, RCB Library, Braemor Park, Churchtown, Dublin, were particularly helpful as we searched for additional information on Josephine Carson Locke. Librarian Bernadette Archer of the Word and Image Department of the Victoria and Albert Museum provided excellent information on fashions of Liberty of London dresses during the 1896 summer season. Independent scholar Robert M. Tenuta provided valuable assistance in helping with sources in the British Library, London, concerning Jane Addams's 1896 visit to England. Professor Gillian O'Brien, Liverpool, England, offered special information about Florence Routledge Hankin. Miles Lewis, faculty member of architecture, University of Melbourne, Australia, helped identify dates of the Pond brothers' architectural practice in Chicago.

This volume of the edition could not have been done without the research assistance and dedication of two very special people. The first, Richard Reynolds Seidel, helped in the preparation of the second volume of *The Selected Papers of Jane Addams* and also worked on this volume until he became too ill in 2011 and died from brain cancer in 2013. From the beginning of the Addams project, while he was employed as the acquisitions librarian at the University of Illinois at Chicago library, he was a volunteer helper. During the last fifteen years of his life, he worked in Chicago, northern Illinois, and southern Wisconsin conducting research for the Addams project. In particular, he did a great deal of research about the family of Mary Rozet Smith, their residences, marriages, divorces, activities, and businesses. He was particularly helpful in providing information about the early connections Jane Addams made with religious leaders and organizations like Moody's Chicago Avenue Church and with early social nonprofit organizations like the Norwood, Illinois, Boys School. Many of the annotations that provide context for the letters that reveal the first two years of the development of Hull-House are based on his work.

When Richard's deteriorating health made it impossible for him to continue to assist the Addams project, we were extremely fortunate to gain the assistance of author and independent scholar Ellen Skerrett, an experienced researcher, especially in Chicago repositories and sources. She is dedicated, organized, an experienced author and editor, and an extraordinarily able sleuth. Ellen was key in the continuing development of the Addams project's website, where she drafted the Addams chronology, produced the selected bibliography of resources by and about Jane Addams, and identified leads to other appropriate websites for researchers using our Internet site. She was the lead scholar in the development of the 1897 period of this volume and investigated the contributions, events, and accomplishments of Graham Taylor in particular. She was the colleague most responsible for using Chicago repositories, collections, and connections to provide the data the project required to establish the basic context for the documentary evidence about the life of Jane Addams during the entire period covered by this volume. She also served as a verifying reader for the documents and annotation in each of the sections of the manuscript. In addition, Ellen was tasked with acquiring potential illustrations for this volume, including photographs and drawings of Jane Addams, her colleagues and friends, the development of Hull-House, and events of significance in Addams's life from throughout the United States and Europe.

The talented Fred Cuddy, our communications guru, website developer, and all-around Internet expert, was the designer of the Jane Addams Papers Project website. He incorporated sections of text for the website prepared by all of the editors, including Barbara Bair, our consulting associate editor. His time and talent have been a generous gift from Bryan Automotive Co.

It is impossible to leave these acknowledgments without a very special word about Maree de Angury, who has served as assistant to the editor for nearly twenty-eight years. In many ways, she has grown up with the Jane Addams Papers Project. A fast and accurate typist, she has helped to establish the Addams project's copyediting manual, comprising formats and forms as well as spellings, and then to "nitpick" and correct her way through the manuscripts we prepare in the hope of sending the cleanest possible manuscript to the university press. Just as important, she has become highly competent at deciphering the handwriting of Jane Addams and is skilled at producing initial draft transcriptions. She assisted with verification, has produced all of the final manuscripts that we submit to the press, helped with revisions after the copyediting process, and worked with the other Addams editors to produce the volume indexes. Maree prepared the more than six hundred two-column camera-ready pages that became *The Jane Addams Papers: A Comprehensive Guide*, published by Indiana University Press.

Once again we want to recognize and indicate our appreciation for the wise counsel of our experienced advisory committee. It has been composed of women's historian and Addams expert Anne Firor Scott, William K. Boyd Professor Emeritus, Department of History, Duke University, who was instrumental in inviting the Jane Addams Papers Project to a secure home at Duke University; David Chesnutt, professor of history emeritus and editor/coeditor of *The Papers of Henry Laurens*, Department of History, University of South Carolina, Columbia, who in the early days of our project was our primary adviser about electronic records and access to the Internet; and Allen F. Davis, professor of history emeritus, Temple University, Philadelphia, historian of the settlement house movement and biographer extraordinaire of Jane Addams. We are also grateful to other scholars, some known and some unknown to us, who have considered and reviewed our work through applications for grants from public and private foundations and who have supported our efforts. We have enjoyed pleasant and useful scholarly interaction with other documentary editors and with authors conducting research about Jane Addams or some aspect of the many movements and organizations with which she was associated. Among them have been Katherine Joslin, Victoria Brown, and Lucy Knight, who shared special information with us that often made our job easier.

We remain deeply indebted to those who became readers of the manuscript for this volume. Their direct corrections, the new perspectives they often brought to the material, and their comments, questions, and suggestions were exceedingly helpful. In particular, we want to recognize advisory committee member Allen F. Davis, who read each section of the work, introduction, documents, and annotation and then read the final and complete version of this volume. He also provided great assistance in conducting research for us in the Philadelphia area, especially at Swarthmore College in the Peace Collection. He proved a key scholarly influence in the production of this work. We also are extremely grateful to Barbara Bair of the Manuscript Division of the Library of Congress, former associate editor on the Addams project, who served as consulting associate editor on this volume. She reviewed our early selection of documents, especially those for the period 1889 to 1893. From the beginning, she encouraged us to consider a wide assortment of document types and sources in presenting these years of the Addams story. She has been one of the final readers for the manuscript. We are very grateful for the time that both of these scholars were able to give to this manuscript and the Addams project.

We continue to be grateful to the University of Illinois Press, retired director Willis G. Regier, and especially its former editor in chief and now director, Laurie Matheson, for supportive interaction with the press as we worked on the manuscript. Pressures on university presses from their host institutions to secure more operating funds and demands from the scholarly public for different types of products have led to ongoing changes in scholarly publishing. Through a number of discussions, the Addams project was encouraged to continue to prepare its manuscript for a print edition with the understanding that the work would eventually be available through Internet publication. We are especially grateful to the press's editorial board for their continuing support of this multivolume edition and for issuing and promoting other works by and about Jane Addams. The staff at the University of Illinois Press who have seen this volume through production are talented, and we thank them for sharing their experiences with us and for their dedication to excellence.

In short, we are deeply grateful to all the people who have helped us present the documents we have chosen to offer in this volume as evidence of these vital years in the life of Jane Addams.

# *Introduction*

*Creating Hull-House and an International Presence, 1889–1900*, the third volume of *The Selected Papers of Jane Addams*, presents primary documentation with editorial comment about the life experiences and goals of Jane Addams beginning in January 1889, when she arrived in Chicago determined to establish a permanent home and to create a new and meaningful life for herself and others. By the end of 1900, the young, well-educated, well-traveled, self-reliant, and independently wealthy (by her day's standards) Jane Addams had successfully established Hull-House, "the scheme" she envisioned as a social settlement.

As her life and work unfolded during this period, Addams and Hull-House became leaders in the rapidly developing social settlement movement in the United States that promoted social justice and progressive reforms in many areas of civic life. In the process, Jane Addams and the network of reformers who often worked with her established the profession of social work and promoted women as leaders in other professions. Just as important, they initiated dozens of reform organizations and campaigns that led to the regulation of child labor and the promotion of child welfare, the development of consumer protection, and support for the working poor in their search for better wages and safer work conditions. Jane Addams and her coworkers also promoted educational opportunities for citizens of all ages. They fought for safer, cleaner, and healthier urban living spaces as well as ready access to nutritious food and better medical care. They tried to help immigrants, offered access to the arts, and campaigned for woman suffrage.

Jane Addams settled in Chicago, a naive young woman who wanted to help others and in the process help herself to a more fulfilling life. As she continued her education through life experience, she matured as an intelligent, pragmatic, and articulate spokeswoman for reform. An able conduit of information between the poor and voiceless and the wealthy and powerful, Addams discovered that she could bring understanding to both groups and encourage support for

Hull-House complex, ca. 1900. Jane Addams had successfully added six structures to the original Hull home in which she started her social settlement in 1889. From left to right along Halsted Street, the Butler Art Gallery and Library Reading Room that became known as the Butler Building, the original Hull home, hidden to the left of the Children's House, sometimes called the Smith Building or the Children's Building. Continuing west along Polk Street, beginning at the Children's House, was the Coffee House and Theatre Building, followed by the old Gymnasium and Coffee House Building that was converted into the Labor Museum with Ellen Gates Starr's bookbindery and the gymnasium. The boiler house with equipment to heat and generate electricity for the entire complex was located behind the Jane Club, which was to the south of the complex and faced Ewing Street. Neither of those two buildings appears in this photograph (private collection).

beneficial change. She gained the respect and trust of her neighbors through her willingness to listen and help and by the programs she offered through the settlement. She also won the initial admiration of religious, civic, and social leaders in Chicago who were already engaged in efforts to improve conditions in their city. They saw her as one of them—but with the added benefit of a college education, without the encumbrance of husband and family, and with a willingness to work for reform and urban improvement. She became adroit at attracting allegiances and building alliances, especially among reform advocates. She also became more sophisticated about communicating with the public who could help her cause, and she sought the support of educators, journalists, and well-respected organizations already engaged in reform efforts.

By her actions and her commitment, she attracted other women and men to her causes and to Hull-House. Through these evolving friendships, she began creating a "family of friends," especially at Hull-House, several of whom became significant lifelong and personal friends. Those who came to the settlement as residents and volunteers brought their own commitment to beneficial social change, along with their energy, expertise, and experiences to share in the communal setting. With Addams they developed a synergistic force that enhanced the reputation of Hull-House and Jane Addams. As the "head resident" of Hull-House, Addams was the leader, an organizer with a collegial style, a superb fund-raiser, and an able and strategic promoter of Hull-House and the social settlement model. As she matured, she was willing to take more public risks in the name of reform. The documents in this volume reveal the fascinating journey Jane Addams made during these years as she became one of the most influential women in the United States—a powerful, committed, and compelling voice for progressive reform. In just twelve short and action-packed years, Jane Addams and the movements she fostered attained national and international fame.

Scholars from a variety of disciplines, including American studies, social work, and history, particularly in the fields of women's, family, cultural, and social history, and the history of education and social movements, including the development of social settlements and unions as well as efforts to promote child welfare, will find the documents in this third volume of the edition useful. Urban historians and those interested in the history of Chicago and Illinois will find the documents and annotation helpful. Scholars and general readers may also find the documents in this volume useful for a study of expositions, particularly the World's Columbian Exposition, 1893, and the Exposition Universelle, Paris, 1900. Readers, including high school students, college scholars, teachers, and researchers in public and university libraries who find biography fascinating, who have a major interest in the life of Jane Addams, or who especially delight in reading correspondence and speeches, will enjoy using the material in this volume.

Most of the major themes associated with the first two volumes of this edition continue in this third volume. As we indicated in the introduction to volume 2 of this edition, among them are the "dilemmas of family relations and gender roles, the history of education, the dynamics of female friendship, expanding public and professional roles for women, and the evolution of charity-philanthropy, social welfare, and reform ideas." In addition, Chicago and its development offers a major new theme, as do the evolving expansion and ever-changing programs, the physical plant, and the influence of Hull-House; the growing significance and influence of the social settlement movement; and specific efforts toward achieving a variety of social reforms.

Readers will learn of the family problems that Jane Addams and the other settlement residents discovered in their neighborhood. They will also learn of Jane Addams's family problems, especially in Cedarville, and be introduced to her new support group at Hull-House. There were Ellen Gates Starr, who helped

Hull-House neighborhood family members on stair leading to their home, ca. 1891 (HH Assn., UIC, JAMC 0192 0285).

her establish Hull-House, and those who became associated with Addams and Hull-House during this significant twelve-year period, including Julia C. Lathrop, Florence Kelley, Helen Culver, Alice Hamilton, Louise de Koven Bowen, Alessandro Mastro-Valerio, Graham Taylor, Jenkin Lloyd Jones, Richard T. Ely, Robert A. Woods, Henry Demarest Lloyd, Alzina Parsons Stevens, Mary Kenney O'Sullivan, Helena Dudley, Gertrude Barnum, Lillian D. Wald, Mary E. McDowell, and Mary Rozet Smith.

Documents also indicate the growth of Jane Addams's connections within an ever-widening assortment of women's organizations. An obvious example was the Chicago Woman's Club (CWC), whose members, beginning in the 1880s, spearheaded numerous reform efforts in Chicago on behalf of women and children. After Jane Addams joined the club, she was a willing committee member, working within the organization's established leadership, but soon she had become one of its leaders. Documents and annotation offer information on a number of other reform organizations that Jane Addams and those closely associated with her started and supported, particularly in Chicago. In addition, materials in this volume make it possible for readers to investigate the lives and contributions of other women who were leaders in philanthropic enterprise outside of the settlement, as well as the problems that poor and immigrant women faced and the women's organizations that evolved to help them.

Through the correspondence and documents in this volume, readers will be able to consider personal and intellectual female relationships. It will be possible to investigate the partnership between Jane Addams and Ellen Gates Starr that spawned Hull-House but was soon overshadowed by the blossoming and steady growth of the significant central relationship that developed between Addams and Mary Rozet Smith. Smith would become Jane's lifetime partner, financial supporter, traveling companion, and the person with whom Jane Addams shared her personal hopes, dreams, and worries.

At the start of her campaign to establish Hull-House, Jane Addams sought the approval and support of Protestant religious leaders, and they responded with positive published statements, promotion from their pulpits, and participation as volunteers at the settlement activities. Documents and annotation reveal that over time, those relationships began to erode. Readers may also learn of the relation of the settlement and its programs to its primarily Roman Catholic neighbors and their churches, to the Jewish residents of its neighborhood, and to Addams's concerns for the hopes of African Americans.

Tracing the development of the social settlement movement in the United States, investigating progress of the movement in Great Britain, and learning about the beginnings of the international social settlement effort will be possible in these documents. With annotation they highlight the actions, activities, and influence of Addams as the principal female leader and Hull-House as the model for settlement house development in the United States. Readers will find documents relating to the creation of other social settlements in Chicago and information on their leaders. Jane Addams also played a key role in the growth of the national social settlement movement as she toured the country, sparking local interest in creating social settlements as instruments for progressive social reform. The rise of local and national organizations for social settlement leaders and workers, sharing ideas and reform commitments, as well as the development of social work education are also part of the history of this period that scholars may consider through these documents.

There is information about the diverse backgrounds, experiences, and contributions of the continually increasing number of residents, volunteers, and workers attracted by the Hull-House experiment and its leaders. Readers will be able to follow the physical development of the settlement and the expansion of its programs. Among them were the Jane Club and other cooperative ventures; the Hull-House Woman's Club; the Phalanx and the Men's Clubs; special

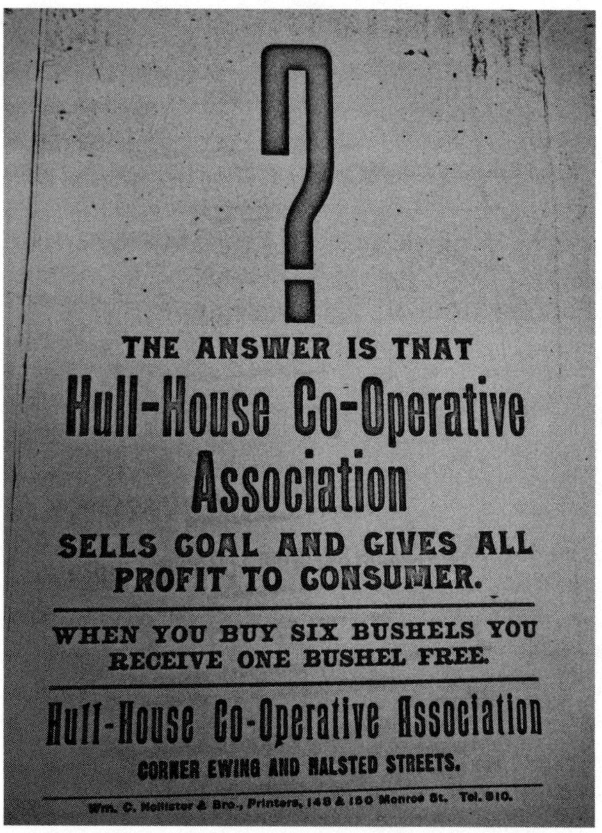


An advertising broadside from the Hull-House Co-Operative Association on behalf of its coal yard, 1894. In an effort to help their neighbors make the most of their slender resources, Jane Addams and the early Hull-House residents attempted to create a number of cooperative ventures. Among them were the cooperative living space for young working women that resulted in the formation of the Jane Club and the unsuccessful coal yard that Jane Addams hoped to expand to include grocery staples (UIC, JAMC, HH Assn.; HH Scrapbook 2:50½; *JAPM*, Addendum 10:7ff).

immigrant events; nursery and kindergarten programs for children; programs to promote improved health care, food choices, and lifestyles, especially for children and mothers; relief efforts, particularly during economic hard times; theater, music, and lectures; educational programs for children of all ages and for adults; the labor museum; the public playground; and social clubs. Not all of these efforts were successful. Documents also reveal Addams's almost constant, and sometimes frustrated, attempts to maintain financial support for the settlement's continuing development. There is also evidence of the settlement's participation in special investigations. Some of these led to beneficial social, political, and economic reforms. In many cases, the settlement and its leaders joined forces with other social settlements or other organizations to promote the reforms.

Education remains a major theme of this volume. In the beginning, the entire settlement program, formal classes as well as social clubs, had as a primary goal socialization through education. Those who were pioneers in the development of progressive education saw Hull-House as a useful laboratory leading the way to improved educational techniques and learning opportunities, especially for young children. Documents in the volume offer a view of the college extension curriculum and interaction with universities and colleges, and they identify the faculty that Hull-House developed to support these efforts. We offer evidence of the early development of special schools of art and music and opportunities for children of all ages to participate in theatrical productions and dance and to attend summer camp programs. There is information about the settlement's kindergarten training programs, food-preparation lessons, sickroom management instruction, manual training curriculum, physical education activities, and the hope that Jane Addams had for the development of the labor museum. Annotation permits readers to understand that residents and volunteers also saw their participation at the settlement as personally educational; many published articles about their Hull-House experience, and when they left the settlement they created similar programs in their new communities, building on what they had learned through their settlement experience.

The two journeys that Jane Addams made to Europe during this period of her life were significant in her continuing education. In 1896 at the invitation of Mary Rozet Smith and her family, Jane Addams spent her summer abroad with an opportunity to investigate progress in the growth of the social settlement movement in Great Britain and to widen her knowledge of social reform efforts and their leaders in Europe. This journey was a watershed event in the life of Jane Addams, for it provided her with an opportunity to meet and consider Leo Tolstoy and his philosophy in light of her own developing positions on social reform. During her visit to Paris in 1900 as a juror representing the United States at the Exposition Universelle, Addams explained the Hull-House social settlement model to an international audience of women, but even more important was the opportunity for her to continue her own education by investigating progressive ideas and activities among the countries represented at the exposition and to further develop her acquaintance among European progressive reformers.

Documents also reveal the amazing assortment of progressive reform issues in which Jane Addams and her colleagues at Hull-House were engaged, the positions they took, and the methods they used to win their reform positions.

Through these documents, readers will learn of the commitment that Addams and Hull-House leaders made to the development of labor unions, especially for women. They also sought to control the sweatshop industry; established workplace protection, especially for women and children; promoted compulsory education and the improvement of educational facilities in Chicago; and provided access to appropriate health care. They supported better legal protection for children and sought ways to control juvenile delinquency; they worked for an end to political corruption in Chicago elections, improvement in city infrastructure and the environment, immigrant protection, and improvement in state and local facilities and care options for the mentally ill and poor.

For those who are interested in the history of Chicago and Illinois during this period, there is information about the people, the institutions, and the infrastructure of the Hull-House neighborhood as well as about Chicago government and its leaders, particularly about the Nineteenth Ward. Through documents readers are able to investigate the leadership role that Addams and Hull-House workers took in helping to develop institutions useful to neighbors, including a public playground, cooperative coal yard, public bathing facilities, and model lodging facilities and work rooms for women. There are treatments of the World's Columbian Exposition, especially the international congresses associated with it. Documents also indicate the development and activities of various Chicago organizations that were created to promote civic reform or better manage civic problems. Among state and national issues that appear in documents in this edition are the Pullman strike, Illinois workplace legislation and the activities of the Office of the Chief Factory Inspector of Illinois, state legislation affecting the public education of children, and policies and legislation to improve the management of state mental institutions.

## *Selection*

Within the limits of the material available, our goal in selecting the documents for this volume has been to let Jane Addams tell her own story—helped where necessary with contextual comments. We wanted to have her present as many facets of her person as extant documents would allow. We have offered evidence about her goals and her efforts to improve the lives of those less fortunate. Capturing the personal side of Jane Addams, indicating her interactions with family and friends and the network of colleagues that began to develop around her and her activities, was also a goal.

We have tried to reveal the public Jane Addams, the development of her reform philosophy; her growth and skill as a leader, speaker, organizer, and writer; how she worked with other leaders and volunteers; and how she built support for her positions through other organizations and the development of personal and coworker friendships. We wanted to indicate the support that she established for her positions as well as the concerns and questions that arose about her positions and her leadership.

In many ways, the life of Jane Addams during these twelve years may be seen through the prism of the development of Hull-House. Her vision, her skills, and her dedication led directly to the creation of Hull-House, and that idea that became reality led to her leadership in the national social settlement movement. We have been careful to highlight the growth of the settlement, by including documents and illustrative material to reveal her central role in its development.

We believed it important to reveal the group of reform-minded friends and leaders who came into her circle of influence, some for life and some for a period of time or because of a particular issue. Those relationships offer another perspective on the life of Addams, her activities, contributions, and the person she was becoming. She influenced many of them and in return was influenced by them. Biographical treatments of those who appear in these documents offer comment on their own lives and a window on their relationship with Addams.

We wanted to be sure we provided information about significant events in this twelve years of the life of Jane Addams and the major reform efforts in which she took a leadership role, some successful, others not so successful. We have provided access to key speeches and writings through which one can begin to understand the reform issues that were important to her and to the development of her philosophy.

Providing evidence of the stresses as well as the joys in Jane Addams's personal life was an important element in our choice of documents. We hoped to offer a hint of her humor, her recreation time, her intellectual interests, and how her health affected her life. We wanted readers to explore the Addams-Haldeman-Linn family dynamic that was a constant in Jane's life. The difficulties she had with her stepmother, Anna Haldeman Addams, and Anna's Haldeman sons, as well as the concern and responsibility Jane Addams felt for her surrogate mother, her oldest sister, Mary Catherine Addams Linn, and her children; the support that she gave to her mentally ill brother, John Weber Addams, and his wife, Laura; and the troublesome but loving relationship she sought to maintain with her sister Sarah Alice Addams Haldeman are a vital part of the life story of Addams during this period. Revealing evidence that survives of Jane's special friendships with Ellen Gates Starr and Mary Rozet Smith, both central in the personal life of Addams, was also a goal.

For this twelve-year period in the life of Jane Addams, a wide variety of documentation is available from which to draw selections for this volume. Among her own papers are correspondence; diaries; drafts of speeches and statements; published essays, speeches, and statements; legal and personal documents and files; financial records; drawings and photographs; as well as newspaper and periodical clippings. There are also relevant documents available from the papers of other individuals and organizations that were associated with Jane Addams. The surviving records of Hull-House Association include early financial data, lists of contributors with their pledge amounts, legal documents, incorporation papers and lease agreements, minutes, publications, lists of various settlement

The family of Jane Addams's sister Mary Catherine Addams Linn, ca. 1889–90. *Left to right, standing*: James Weber Linn and John Addams Linn. *Seated, left to right*: Mary Catherine Addams Linn and Rev. John Manning Linn. The two younger children are Esther Margaret Linn and her brother Stanley Ross Linn (SCPC photo 00233).

club members, building plans, schedules of meetings and announcements for settlement events, descriptions of investigations, clippings, articles, cartoons, drawings, and photographs.

Throughout the volume, correspondence predominates. As Jane Addams began to create the settlement, her letters and those of her cofounding partner, Ellen Gates Starr, are very descriptive and detailed; however, in 1892, there is little extant correspondence to or from Jane Addams. Some correspondence has been lost; however, the Hull-House telephone was in place by 1892, and Addams may have called people she might previously have written. In addition, the people that Jane Addams most wanted to discuss progressive reform issues with were right there at the settlement, also obviating the need for correspondence. Correspondence about the continuing development of Hull-House appears primarily between Jane Addams and Mary Rozet Smith, who became a major settlement financial supporter. Jane Addams and Mary Smith corresponded primarily when one or the other was out of Chicago.

Most of the letters that appear in this volume were written by Jane Addams, usually to family members, Mary Rozet Smith, or a mix of progressive colleagues. To be included in this volume, letters written by others had to provide some very special and necessary evidence about Addams and her work for which there was no other documentary evidence that was written by Addams herself. Although Jane Addams gave an increasing number of speeches during this period of her life, the texts of most of them, especially those prior to 1895, have not been preserved. As Addams gained fame, newspaper coverage of her appearances and presentations increased. In many cases, the only evidence of her position on an event or issue was the "verbatim coverage" that newspapers provided for their readers. Sometimes, but not always, these presentations appeared in more than one newspaper or periodical source, as if they were circulated by a news service or Jane Addams herself provided the texts of her speeches.

To make our selections among her public statements, we evaluated extant Addams speech and essay manuscripts, essays from magazines, and versions of speeches from the large newspaper clipping file maintained by Hull-House and Jane Addams. We identified key statements Addams made in order to permit readers to understand her evolving positions on the development of Hull-House and her reform agenda. The editors did not have the space in this volume to present all of the speeches and essays that were available from this period, but researchers will find ready access to them by consulting the microfilm edition of the Addams papers.

For the initial period of the development of Hull-House and the beginning of her reform efforts, 1889–93, we have provided a selection of letters from Jane Addams primarily to Ellen Gates Starr and to Addams family members. There is also one letter that Starr wrote to Jane's family on her behalf that appears to be the first written statement authorized by Jane Addams explaining her settlement idea. No longer extant in its original form, it was sent as a circular letter first to Ellen's family and then on to Jane's sister Sarah Alice Haldeman, who copied the letter into a notebook that eventually found its way into the personal papers of Ellen Gates Starr. In addition, we have provided copies of selected newspaper clippings revealing early settlement publicity as well as Jane's first successful attempt at helping women workers arbitrate a strike. We have also included five significant speeches by Addams from this period. Three reveal her rationale for starting Hull-House and contain a description of its initial programs. Including all of these presentations permits readers to compare and contrast them. These presentations helped catapult Addams into the leadership of the budding social settlement movement in the United States. The two speeches that Addams gave at the 1892 Summer School of Applied Ethics at Plymouth, Massachusetts, were also published that year in the respected national periodical the *Forum*, and in 1893 they became chapters in the book titled *Philanthropy and Social Progress*, devoted to social welfare presentations at the summer school. Two other speeches present other Addams themes regarding progressive reform for this period. She first delivered them during the World's Columbian Exposition, held in Chicago in 1893.

In addition to the development of the Hull-House physical plant, a mix of documents that includes lists of educational opportunities and social gatherings published by the settlement house added to timely newspaper descriptions of special settlement events permits readers to view activities at the settlement. Annotation that accompanies correspondence and speeches provides researchers with the opportunity to investigate the commitment that Jane Addams made to the idea of progressive reform, especially with regard to sweatshop manufacture, child labor, her increasing visibility among religious leaders and as a member of the Chicago Woman's Club and other appropriate reform-minded organizations, her ability as a speaker in promoting the settlement idea and as a fund-raiser, the significance of her participation and leadership in helping to develop a number of international congresses held during the World's Columbian Exposition, the internal organization of the settlement and how Addams and the residents worked together on neighborhood issues, descriptions of the settlement neighborhood and its residents, interaction with neighbors, and investigations carried out through Hull-House. By presenting correspondence that Jane Addams addressed to Mary Rozet Smith, readers will see the beginning of that lifelong and significant friendship. We also present correspondence, diary entries, and annotation that permit researchers to consider the development of the Hull-House resident and volunteer group and especially identify several individuals who would remain committed lifetime colleagues and personal friends of Jane Addams.

During the midyears 1894–96, once again correspondence predominates; however, there are two legal documents of note: one identifying Jane Addams as the executor of her sister Mary Catherine Addams Linn's estate and the other the incorporation papers for Hull-House as Hull-House Association with Jane as the president and treasurer of a board of trustees. Jane's testimony about her role in the Pullman Palace Car Company strike becomes the vehicle for a discussion of that event and Jane's efforts to arbitrate it. Correspondence reveals the role Addams played in supporting the further development of the social settlement movement in the United States as well as the process of creating *Hull-House Maps and Papers*, begun in 1893, which ended with its landmark publication in 1895. Also in 1895, correspondence and newspaper clippings indicate the steps by which Jane Addams became the Nineteenth Ward garbage inspector, as well as the reaction, especially on the part of her family, the Hull-House residents, and the press, to her serious operation for appendicitis and the University of Chicago's attempts to take over the Hull-House program and the land on which it was located. It was during this period that Jane Addams realized that she could make a living though public lecturing, and correspondence, annotation, and newspaper clippings describe several of her lecture tours. The first page of the first number of the *Hull-House Bulletin*, which began publication in January 1896, presented the settlement's statement of purpose written by Addams, who usually served as the unidentified editor of the publication. Correspondence and a facsimile copy of a page from the donor book kept by Addams also highlight her fund-raising skills and her ability to keep the programs of the settlement and its reform efforts before the public. The programs and physical plant of the settlement continued to expand during this period, and correspondence indicates the role that Jane Addams had in the planning and construction of two new settlement buildings. In addition, correspondence from the minutes of the Chicago Relief and Aid Society reveal that Jane was a major leader in the development of a Chicago-wide structure for dispensing relief. A list of fellowships she was trying to provide for key residents who could not afford their own stay at the settlement indicates the commitment she made to the development and constant support of this program to successfully maintain the resident corps.

Correspondence and diary entries indicate the extent of Jane Addams's travels during the summer of 1896, the connections she fostered with reform leaders in England, and the respect with which she was received. Her own correspondence and diary entries, carefully supplemented by correspondence and recollections of her guide, Aylmer Maude, offer details of her special visit with the Leo Tolstoy family. We also highlight her commitment to the Tolstoy story after her return, providing evidence of her published comments about Tolstoy, his philosophy, and her recollections of her visit with him.

Between 1897 and 1900, Jane Addams continued her rise to national and international prominence. Correspondence, especially with Mary Rozet Smith, predominated extant Addams documents and indicated her role in developing the local and national social settlement organizations, as well as her leadership in founding additional social settlements in Chicago and throughout the country. Hull-House continued to add structures. Correspondence with Smith indicated the problems that Jane Addams encountered in the development of the Jane Club Building and the new Coffee House and Theatre Building, and moving the former Gymnasium and Coffee House to a new location as the home for the Labor Museum. An article written by Addams that originally appeared in the *Commons* indicated her vision for the Labor Museum. Among other documents in this section are articles by Addams from the *Hull-House Bulletin* that provide the background for the development of the settlement theater program.

It was during this four-year period that Addams and the Hull-House residents worked diligently and with great hope to unseat their corrupt Nineteenth Ward alderman, John Powers. Correspondence, newspaper clippings, a cartoon, snippets from the *Hull-House Bulletin*, and an Addams letter to the editor of the major Chicago newspapers as late as 1900 help tell the story of that unsuccessful effort. What Addams learned in the almost five-year struggle with corrupt Nineteenth Ward politics she presented in her essay about the experience reprinted in this volume from the original version published in the *International Journal of Ethics*.

The text of her speeches on the actions of the United States government coincident with the end of the Spanish-American War and on the Boar War raging in South Africa provides the first public hint of her developing philosophy on peace and ethnic self-determination that drew her into leadership in the international women's peace movement associated with the start of World War I. Correspondence between Florence Kelley and Jane Addams revealed more of their friendship and their plans as they prepared for the series of twelve lectures that each presented through the University of Chicago Extension Department between July and September 1899. These lectures resulted in books by both women. The year 1900 was special for Addams. Correspondence, newspaper clippings, and an official report that she submitted reveal the story of her triumphant participation as one of only three women appointed to serve as jurors at the Exposition Universelle in Paris. In addition, correspondence with annotation reveals the support Addams offered to the first African American settlement developed in Chicago. The volume ends with a description of her significance and her achievements presented in the national women's periodical *Good Housekeeping*.

The documents in the volume permit readers to follow the activities of Addams and the positions she took in support of progressive reform issues throughout the period. These included the development of unions, especially for women; promotion of child welfare as well as improvement in the neighborhood environment; delivery of relief aid; immigrant education; and political reform. A mix of documents permits the reader to follow the physical and program growth of Hull-House, the increase in the resident and volunteer support for the settlement, the significant financial supporters that Jane Addams attracted to her reform efforts, the rising visibility of Hull-House and Addams, and the development of the social settlement movement in the United States. Photographs and drawings of people, places, events, and documents in facsimile add a visual dimension to the significant documentary evidence about the life and activities of Jane Addams.

Like the first and second volumes of this edition, this third volume is the creation of a team of editors and research assistants working from various parts of the United States. We selected the documents that we thought best revealed this period of the life of Jane Addams and transcribed and verified them through at least two readings. After conducting extensive primary research to provide the historical context for the selections and to identify the people, places, organizations, events, and ideas mentioned in them, we produced the contextual materials that appear in this volume as introductions, headnotes, and annotation. Last—but by no means least—we prepared the entire manuscript; selected illustrations from among the available photographs, drawings, cartoons, broadsides, and documents; and produced the index. We hope that we have helped Jane Addams tell her story.

## *Afterword*

Through the years that followed, the name Hull-House, like that of Jane Addams, became synonymous with the idea of beneficial reform, progress, and help to a better life for those in need. Even after Jane Addams's death in 1935, the settlement continued to thrive and carry out programs responsive to the changing needs of its neighbors and the people of Chicago. It was successful in this transition and survived because of the financial commitment of board members who had become close friends of Jane Addams and wanted to carry on her vision. By the 1960s, however, private financial support could no longer keep up with program demand. Federal funds for programs designed to assist those in need began to supplant private funds and also to define settlement program. In addition, there were inadequate private funds available for Hull-House to maintain its thirteen-building complex. When the city of Chicago chose to purchase the Hull-House site for the new campus of the University of Illinois in Chicago, leaders on the settlement board were saddened, but also relieved. Hull-House would no longer be the social settlement model that Addams had created with residents and programs centralized in one location. It would continue under the name of Hull-House Association, but become a group of community centers in an increasing number of neighborhoods throughout Chicago and eventually selected suburbs. It continued to develop with a combination of increasing support provided through federal funding for special programs designed at the national level and from shrinking private support. Unfortunately, in January 2012, the Hull-House Association was forced to declare bankruptcy, its programs and operations closed, its remaining endowment used to pay outstanding bills, its federal programs taken over by other agencies. For the first time since 1889, Hull-House, the beacon of hope and positive social change for thousands of individuals, was darkened, but the memory of what had been and the example it provided shine still through the prism of history.

# *Editorial Method*

In addition to a table of contents and list of illustrations, each volume of the selected edition of the Jane Addams papers contains a list of documents presented in the volume and a list of abbreviations used by the authors of the documents and by the editors. There is an introduction for each volume. It is preceded by acknowledgments and followed by the body of the text, which is composed of selected transcribed documents with editorial annotation in the form of section introductions, headnotes, source notes, and endnotes to the documents. In addition to a bibliography and index, back matter includes an appendix containing longer biographical profiles on individuals especially important in the life of Addams.

Throughout this work, all documents are presented in chronological order. Correspondence appears in the sequence according to the date on which it was written or the date on which we believe it may have been written. Speeches usually appear in the arrangement by the date on which each was given rather than the date they were published. Published periodical articles appear at their date of publication, while unpublished essays, announcements, and assorted documents are presented by the date that appears on them or a date we are able to determine for them. When we have more than one version of a document to choose from, we will usually opt for the extant final rendition of the item and place it at the appropriate date sequence. Documents written on more than one day are placed in order according to the first date. When we include two documents of the same date, we will place them in the sequence according to the content of the documents and in consideration of the relationship of each to other documents near them in the sequence.

Documents are arranged in sections. Each section has an introduction that provides a context for the documents and annotation associated with them. Each document is identified by a title or header, which is the name of the person to whom a piece of correspondence is addressed or from whom it was received or the title of a writing or a type of document. In some cases, a headnote providing information we believe will be of benefit to readers before they read the document appears immediately under the header and before the document. Letters are presented in standardized letter form, with the salutation flush left, the place flush left, and the dateline flush right. The complimentary close is run into the last line of the text of the letter, and signatures, appearing on a separate line, are followed by any postscript, enclosures, or attachments to the letter. Diary entries are presented with the date of the entry flush left at the beginning of the text for that date. Essays, writings, speeches, announcements, and other documents are presented in straight text format, unless we present a facsimile version.

Transcriptions of all documents offered in the edition are literal, with some exceptions. We do not employ the editorial device [*sic*] to indicate errors made by the authors of the documents they present. When the misspelling of a word creates a new word that, considering its use in the context of the document text, we believe the author did not mean, we present the word as it was written by the author and suggest in an annotation the word we believe the author probably meant to use. For example, if Jane Addams wrote "who" when we believe that given the structure of the sentence she meant to write "how," we present the word "who" as Jane Addams wrote it in her text and offer our alteration in brackets or explained in an endnote. When we judge that a word is so misspelled that a reader might not be able to determine what the author meant, and if we believe we know, we correct it. If the word can be corrected by adding letters, we do so, inserting appropriate letters in brackets. If the word can be corrected only by deleting portions of it, we make our correction in an endnote. Correcting authors' spellings has been done sparingly, and so readers will find many misspellings. When an author mistakenly omits a word or words from their text, we annotate the omission and suggest the missing text in an endnote.

Jane Addams and many of her correspondents were not careful about punctuation, capitalization, and grammar in their handwritten documents. Sometimes Jane Addams ended her sentences with a period; however, sometimes her period resembled a comma. Other times she used a dash, and sometimes there was simply no sentence-ending mark. When there is a no mark or a mark other than a period and the next word begins with a capital letter and definitely denotes a new sentence, we have assumed a sentence end. We have treated the comma-like periods and dashes as periods and silently replaced them with periods in the text. When there is no punctuation at the end of a sentence, we have usually inserted a period in brackets. A reader who is interested in the sentence-ending grammar of Jane Addams may consult the microfilm edition of *The Jane Addams Papers*, which offers facsimile copies of the text for most of the documents presented in this edition.

Other punctuation throughout the document texts is presented as the authors wrote it, with two exceptions. When an author used quotation marks and omitted one set of the pair—as Jane Addams often did—we have added the missing set in brackets if we could determine where they should be placed. If we could not decide where they were meant to be placed, we used annotation to indicate that a pair is missing from the original text. In a very few instances, we have added a comma in brackets to help the reader differentiate appropriate elements in the text. This usually occurs in a string of names of people that the author and correspondent knew, but today's reader of the document may not know. For example, the author could have written "Sarah Alice Mary Catharine" with no punctuation. These could either be the names of two sisters of Jane Addams or four individuals with these first names or any combination. If we know how the names should be presented, we have added commas in brackets in appropriate places.

When writing informally and to close friends and family, Jane Addams used two methods of paragraphing. In most instances, she followed standard procedures by indenting the beginning of each new paragraph. In some instances, however, perhaps to save paper, she changed subjects in the middle of a line, by leaving a great deal of space between the end of one sentence and the start of another. We have taken these as paragraph breaks and silently standardized them as such. Any doubts the reader has may be put to rest by consulting the photocopy of the document in the microfilm edition of *The Jane Addams Papers*.

Superscripts and subscripts appear on, rather than above or below, a line. Interlineations are enclosed in angle brackets and are presented on the line and in the place where the author meant to insert them. Text written by the author on the side of the main body of the text, and sometimes perpendicular to it, has been treated as an interlineation and inserted in the text if it is clear from the author's marks where it goes. If, however, it is not possible to determine where the author meant to put it, we have placed it in an endnote. In both cases, we indicate in annotation where the marginal text appeared on the original document. Text written across or perpendicular to previously written text in a document appears as ordinary text in our transcription; however, we indicate the beginning of that text in annotation.

We have maintained the abbreviations and symbols used by Jane Addams and other authors unless we judged them to be unknown to modern readers or impossible to duplicate using modern print technology. Words underlined by the author with a single or a double line are reproduced as underlined; however, words and phrases underlined three or more times are underlined once and accompanied by a descriptive endnote. Words written by the author of a document in the Cyrillic alphabet are reproduced using letters from that alphabet and translated in an endnote. Canceled words, phrases, or paragraphs that are relevant and readable are indicated by a line drawn through the type. If necessary, they are annotated with an endnote. Single crossed-out letters or numbers, partial words, and mistakenly duplicated words are silently omitted unless particularly relevant to the content of the document. Letters, words, or phrases that we cannot decipher because of poor handwriting, crossed-out text, mutilated pages, or the like are indicated by "*[illegible]*" italicized and surrounded by italicized brackets.

We have identified enclosures or attachments and summarized their contents in annotation. In the few cases when we present the text of enclosures or attachments, the documents will be preceded by the word "Enclosure" for something sent with the letter or document or "Attachment" for something added after the document or letter was received. We handle annotations for enclosures and attachments as if they were part of the document to which they are appended.

Infrequently, and primarily to avoid repeating information already provided in previous documents or annotations, we may present only a portion of a document. When we do, we use ellipses and may indicate in a summary statement in endnote annotation the nature of the information we have omitted.

We have used square brackets to indicate to the reader that we have added information to document texts. We do this sparingly and only to clarify information. When document text is mutilated or missing and we have been able to determine with certitude what the missing elements would have been, we have inserted them in brackets where they belong. Most often we added information in the date- and place lines. When a document has a partial date or no date and we have been able to determine what the date should be, we have added the information in square brackets where the dateline should be. When the author of a document provides a date or place that is incorrect and we are aware of it, we have retained the author's information and placed the correct information in square brackets beside it. In some instances, authors wrote documents on more than one day, yet the dateline they placed on the document carries only one date. Similarly, documents may be written in more than one place. When we were aware of omissions from either the date or the place line, we added the additional information in square brackets. If there is uncertainty about an element that we supply, it appears in square brackets followed by a question mark within the brackets.

Some documents contain drawings. When we do not reproduce the drawings with the document in which they appear, we provided statements describing each drawing. The statements appear in bold italic print and within a pair of virgules, or slant lines, at the location of each drawing in the original document.

As a general rule, we do not reproduce letterheads on stationery; however, when Jane Addams wrote a letter from Hull-House and the "Hull-House" letterhead is the only place information, we used "Hull-House, [Chicago, Ill.]" as the place line. If we felt that the information contained in a letterhead was pertinent to the document, we placed it in annotation. Since the majority of the documents in the selected edition appear in the microfilm edition of *The Jane Addams Papers*, readers who wish to see letterhead information may do so by reviewing each document in it original form.

We have annotated documents in the volume to offer identifications of person, places, and events and to help clarify the narrative story of the life, times, and achievements of Jane Addams. Narrative section introductions and headnotes set documents in historical context, supply information to bridge gaps between available documents, and relate sets of documents in a given time period to one another. In addition, some documents have been treated with editorial comment in headnotes. Endnotes for the headnotes and the annotations for the documents appear with sequential numbering at the end of each document. Each document is identified by a source note that appears at the end of the document. It is composed of the physical description of the document given in abbreviated form (see "Abbreviations and Symbols") and identifies the collection and repository in which the original document will be found as well as the reel and frame number location of the document in the microfilm edition of *The Jane Addams Papers*. Other special aspects of the document may also be presented in this location.

In creating annotation, we have relied predominantly on research in primary sources. Our research has taken us to other correspondence and documents in the papers and published writings of Jane Addams. In addition, we have focused our research efforts on the manuscript collections of family and friends in a variety of repositories and in private hands; published letters and diaries; county histories, travel guides, local newspaper sources, and popular literature for the period; county records (including marriage and death records, deeds, and court records); plats and maps; state archival records (including records for the Illinois General Assembly and for the insurance department and the corporation division of the Office of the Secretary of State); city directories, advertisements, dictionaries, college catalogs, and assorted publications issued during the period; miscellaneous materials from college and university archives and manuscript repositories; historical society and public library collections; church archives; private collections; cemetery records; and census returns. We have consulted standard biographical sources and compendiums for a variety of subjects, including art, literature, and music, and consulted secondary sources on special subjects. With the exception of James Weber Linn's *Jane Addams: A Biography* and Winifred Wise's *Jane Addams of Hull-House*, biographies written with the approval and participation of Jane Addams during her lifetime, we have not relied on the work of other biographers of Jane Addams.

Because we expect that a wide audience will consult the volumes of the selected edition, we have prepared annotation to take into account the likely knowledge and context level of readers from high school through postgraduate scholars and including the general reading public. We use annotation primarily to assist readers at all levels to understand the content of the document.

As a general rule, we use annotation to identify persons, organizations, historical events, and relationships mentioned in the texts of the documents to the degree that it clarifies the importance of the document for the reader. When we have supplied information in the text of a document in square brackets, we have sometimes used annotation to explain our rationale. Annotation is also used to explain the archaic use of words and special jargon, to correct spelling errors, or to translate phrases of text in a language other than English appearing in the document. It is used to explain documentary relationships that are not immediately obvious to the reader and to provide the reader with leads to other documents and materials that might offer more information about the annotated item. Annotation also directs the reader to other documents, usually additional correspondence, personal documents, writing, or materials located in the microfilm edition of *The Jane Addams Papers*, or to other manuscript collections and repositories. We have used annotation as a cross-reference to direct the reader to other documents or appropriate annotation in this selected edition. We have also indicated in annotation the existence of documents that are mentioned in the texts of documents in the selected edition. We have provided bibliographic references for quotations, for article or book titles, and for speeches, meetings, or gatherings. Annotation is also used to note significant variations in different texts of the same document; explain aspects of the text not reproduced in the publication; describe special physical characteristics of documents, including form, spelling, grammar, punctuation, and symbols; and compare two different but similar treatments of the same subject matter by the same author. Generally, identification for people, places, organizations, events, or ideas appears at their first mention in either our annotations or the document texts.

In section introductions, biographical profiles, editors' headnotes, and endnotes of documents, we provide bibliographic citations for the source of direct quotations. We may further identify sources of information on a topic. When we quote from original correspondence, we provide the collection and repository in which the original letter is located and, if the material is in the microfilm edition of *The Jane Addams Papers*, a citation to the location of the document in the microfilm. We use a short form of all titles cited. Full bibliographic information for these titles and other sources we have consulted in the process of creating the manuscript appears in the bibliography.

# *Abbreviations and Symbols*

## *Document Descriptions*

| | |
|---|---|
| A | Autograph |
| AD | Autograph Document |
| ADS | Autograph Document Signed |
| AL | Autograph Letter |
| ALI | Autograph Letter Initialed |
| ALS | Autograph Letter Signed |
| AMs | Autograph Manuscript |
| AMsI | Autograph Manuscript Initialed |
| AMsS | Autograph Manuscript Signed |
| ANI | Autograph Note Initialed |
| ANS | Autograph Note Signed |
| D | Document |
| Dup Ms | Duplicated Manuscript |
| H | Holograph |
| HD | Holograph Document |
| HDS | Holograph Document Signed |
| HL | Holograph Letter |
| HLS | Holograph Letter Signed |
| HLSr | Holograph Letter Signed, Representation |
| HN | Holograph Note |
| I | Initialed |
| L | Letter |
| Ms | Manuscript |
| Mss | Manuscripts |
| MsS | Manuscript Signed |
| N | Note |
| PD | Printed Document |

| | |
|---|---|
| PDS | Printed Document Signed |
| S | Signed |
| TCALS | Typed Copy of Autograph Letter Signed |
| TD | Typed Document |
| TL | Typed Letter |
| TLS | Typed Letter Signed |
| TMs | Typed Manuscript |
| TMsS | Typed Manuscript Signed |
| TMsSr | Typed Manuscript Signed, Representation |

## *Manuscript Collections and Repositories*

| | |
|---|---|
| CAHS | Cedarville Area Historical Society, Cedarville, Illinois |
| CBE | Chicago Board of Education Archives, Illinois |
| CHM, CHS | Chicago History Museum, Chicago Historical Society, Chicago, Illinois |
| CHM, CHS, Sikes | Chicago History Museum, Chicago Historical Society, Madeline Wallin Sikes Papers, 1880–1950 |
| CHM, CHS, Taft | Chicago History Museum, Chicago Historical Society, Lorado Taft Papers |
| CHM, CHS, United Charities | Chicago History Museum, Chicago Historical Society, United Charities of Chicago, Records, 1867–1967 |
| CPL | Chicago Public Library, Illinois |
| CPL, WCE-CDA | Chicago Public Library, World's Columbian Exposition, C. D. Arnold Photographic Collection |
| HU | Harvard University, Cambridge, Massachusetts |
| HU, Hamilton | Harvard University, Cambridge, Massachusetts, Alice Hamilton Papers |
| HU, RI, SL | Harvard University, Cambridge, Massachusetts, Radcliffe Institute, Schlesinger Library |
| ISA | Illinois State Archives, Springfield |
| ISHL | Illinois State Historical Society, Library, Springfield |
| ITT | Illinois Institute of Technology, Chicago |
| IU, Lilly, SAAH | Indiana University, Bloomington, Lilly Library, Mrs. Sarah Alice Haldeman Mss |
| JAPP | Jane Addams Papers Project, Fayetteville, North Carolina |
| JAPP, DeLoach | Alice DeLoach Collection, Jane Addams Papers Project, Fayetteville, North Carolina |
| JAPP, Hulbert | Mary Hulbert Collection, Jane Addams Papers Project, Fayetteville, North Carolina |
| JAPP, MRS Files | Mary Rozet Smith Files, Jane Addams Papers Project, Fayetteville, North Carolina |

| | |
|---|---|
| LC, NWTUL | Library of Congress, Manuscripts Division, National Women's Trade Union League Records, 1903–50 |
| LFC | Lake Forest University, Lake Forest, Illinois, Archives |
| MIT, Swope | Massachusetts Institute of Technology, Boston, Gerard Swope Papers |
| MTS, Jones | Meadville Lombard Theological School, Chicago, Jenkin Lloyd Jones Papers and Sermons Collection |
| NYPL | The New York Public Library |
| NYPL, Kelley | The New York Public Library, Astor, Lenox, and Tilden Foundations, Manuscripts and Archives Division, Florence Kelley Papers, 1859–1932 |
| NYPL, Ordway | The New York Public Library, Manuscripts and Archives Division, Edward Warren Ordway Papers, 1893–1914 |
| NYPL, Shaw | The New York Public Library, Manuscript and Archives Division, Albert Shaw Papers |
| NYPL, Wald | The New York Public Library, Humanities and Social Science Library, Manuscripts and Archives Division, Lillian D. Wald Incoming Papers, 1889–1957 |
| RC, Archives | Rockford University, Rockford College, Rockford, Illinois, Colman Library, Archives |
| RC, Archives, Anderson | Rockford University, Rockford College, Rockford, Illinois, Colman Library, Archives, Sarah Anderson Papers |
| RC, Archives, Lathrop | Rockford University, Rockford College, Rockford, Illinois, Colman Library, Archives, Julia C. Lathrop Papers |
| RS, Denison | Radcliffe College, Cambridge, Massachusetts, Schlesinger Library, Denison House, Records, 1890–1984 |
| RS, HFP | Radcliffe College, Cambridge, Massachusetts, Schlesinger Library, Hamilton Family Papers, 1818–1974 |
| SC, Archives | Smith College, Northampton, Massachusetts, Archives |
| SC, Starr | Smith College, Northampton, Massachusetts, Sophia Smith Collection, Ellen Gates Starr Papers, 1659–1975 |
| SCPC | Swarthmore College, Swarthmore, Pennsylvania, Swarthmore College Peace Collection |
| SCPC, Balch | Swarthmore College, Swarthmore, Pennsylvania, Swarthmore College Peace Collection, Emily Greene Balch Papers |

| | |
|---|---|
| SCPC, JAC | Swarthmore College, Swarthmore, Pennsylvania, Swarthmore College Peace Collection, Jane Addams Collection |
| SHSW, Blaine | State Historical Society of Wisconsin, Madison, McCormick–International Harvester Collection, Anita McCormick Blaine Papers |
| SHSW, Ely | State Historical Society of Wisconsin, Madison, Richard T. Ely Papers, 1812–1963 |
| SHSW, Lloyd | State Historical Society of Wisconsin, Madison, Henry Demarest Lloyd Papers, 1840–1937 |
| SHSW, McCormick | State Historical Society of Wisconsin, Madison, McCormick–International Harvester Collection, Nettie Fowler McCormick Collection, 1850–1912 |
| UC, Archives | University of Chicago, Special Collections Research Center, Archives |
| UC, Jones | University of Chicago, Special Collections Research Center, Jenkin Lloyd Jones Papers, 1861–1932 |
| UC, Misc. | University of Chicago, Special Collections Research Center, Miscellaneous Manuscript Collection |
| UC, Presidents | University of Chicago, Special Collections Research Center, University Archives, Office of the President, Papers, 1899–1925 |
| UC, WCE/WCX | University of Chicago, Special Collections Research Center, World's Columbian Exposition, World's Columbian Auxiliary |
| UIC, IHS | University of Illinois at Chicago, Richard J. Daley Library, Illinois Humane Society Records |
| UIC, JAMC | University of Illinois at Chicago, Richard J. Daley Library, Jane Addams Memorial Collection |
| UIC, JAMC, Barnett | University of Illinois at Chicago, Richard J. Daley Library, Jane Addams Memorial Collection, Dame Henrietta O. Barnett Papers, 1897–1935 |
| UIC, JAMC, Detzer | University of Illinois at Chicago, Richard J. Daley Library, Jane Addams Memorial Collection, Mrs. Karl Detzer [Dorothy Detzer] Collection |
| UIC, JAMC, HH Assn. | University of Illinois at Chicago, Richard J. Daley Library, Jane Addams Memorial Collection, Hull-House Collection, Hull-House Association Records, 1889–1991 |
| UIC, JAMC, HJ | University of Illinois at Chicago, Richard J. Daley Library, Jane Addams Memorial Collection, Haldeman-Julius Family Papers, 1854–1964 |
| UIC, JAMC, Hull-Culver | University of Illinois at Chicago, Richard J. Daley Library, Jane Addams Memorial Collection, Hull-Culver Collection, 1848–1948 |

| | |
|---|---|
| UIC, JAMC, Rich | University of Illinois at Chicago, Richard J. Daley Library, Jane Addams Memorial Collection, Adena Miller Rich Papers, 1905–61 |
| UIC, JAMC—Small: Letters | University of Illinois at Chicago, Richard J. Daley Library, Small: Letters, Madeleine and George Sikes Papers, 1907–28 |
| UIC, SC, Mss. | University of Illinois at Chicago, Richard J. Daley Library, Special Collections, Manuscripts |
| UIC, Sunset | University of Illinois at Chicago, Richard J. Daley Library, Sunset Club Collection, 1873–1901 |
| UM, BHL, Mich. HC, Adams | University of Michigan, Ann Arbor, Bentley Historical Library, Michigan Historical Collection, Henry Carter Adams Papers, 1864–1924 |
| UM, BHL, Mich. HC, Pond | University of Michigan, Ann Arbor, Bentley Historical Library, Michigan Historical Collection, Pond Family Papers, 1841–1939 |
| YU, Davidson | Yale University, New Haven, Connecticut, Department of Manuscripts and Archives, Thomas Davidson Papers |

## *Individuals*

| | |
|---|---|
| AH | Anna Hostetter |
| AHH | Anna Hostetter Haldeman |
| AHHA | Anna Hostetter Haldeman Addams or Anna Haldeman Addams |
| EGS | Ellen Gates Starr |
| GBH | George Bowman Haldeman or George Haldeman |
| HWH | Henry Winfield Haldeman or Harry Haldeman |
| JA | Jane Addams or Laura Jane Addams |
| JHA | John Huy Addams or John H. Addams |
| JML | John Manning Linn or John M. Linn |
| JWA | John Weber Addams or Weber Addams |
| LSA | Laura Shoemaker Addams or Laura Addams |
| MCAL | Mary Catherine Addams Linn or Mary Linn |
| MRS | Mary Rozet Smith |
| SA | Sarah F. Anderson or Sarah Anderson or Sarah Ainsworth |
| SAA | Sarah Alice Addams |
| SAAH | Sarah Alice Addams Haldeman or Alice Haldeman |
| SH | Sarah Hostetter |
| SWA | Sarah Weber Addams or Sarah Addams (mother of Jane Addams) |

## *Frequently Cited Published Sources*

| | |
|---|---|
| *EC* | *Encyclopedia of Chicago*. Edited by James R. Grossman, Ann Durkin Keating, and Janice L. Reiff. Chicago: University of Chicago Press, 2004. |
| *HH Bulletin* | *Hull-House Bulletin*, 1896–1905. Chicago: Hull-House Association. |
| *HH Year Book* | *Hull-House Year Book, 1906– 1907, 1910, 1913, 1916, 1921, 1925, 1029, 1931, 1935*. Chicago: Hull-House Association. |
| *JAPM* | *The Jane Addams Papers*. Edited by Mary Lynn McCree Bryan et al. Microfilm, 82 reels. Sanford, N.C.: Microfilming Corporation of American; Ann Arbor, Mich.: University Microfilms International, 1985–86. |
| *NAW* | *Notable American Women, 1607–1950*. Vols. 1–3 edited by Edward T. James, Janet Wilson James, and Paul S. Boyer. Cambridge, Mass.: Harvard University Press, 1971. Vol. 4 edited by Barbara Sicherman and Carol Hurd Green. Cambridge, Mass.: Harvard University Press, 1980. |
| *NCAB* | *The National Cyclopedia of American Biography*. New York: James T. White, 1897. |
| *OED* | *The Compact Edition of the Oxford English Dictionary*. [New York]: Oxford University Press, 1971. |
| *PJA* | *The Selected Papers of Jane Addams*. Vols. 1–3. Urbana: University of Illinois Press, 2003, 2009, 2018. |
| *RSM* | *Rockford Female Seminary Magazine*. Rockford Female Seminary and Rockford Seminary, Archives, Rockford College, Rockford, Ill. |
| *WBC* | Schultz, Rima Lunin, and Adele Hast, eds. *Women Building Chicago, 1790–1990*. Bloomington: Indiana University Press, 2001. |

## *Organizations, Institutions, or Events*

| | |
|---|---|
| ACLU | American Civil Liberties Union |
| AFL | American Federation of Labor |
| AME | African Methodist Episcopal |
| ARU | American Railway Union |
| AUAM | American Union against Militarism |
| AWSA | American Woman Suffrage Association |
| CFSNH | Chicago Federation of Settlements and Neighborhood Houses |
| COS | Charity Organization Society |
| CWC | Chicago Woman's Club |
| GMA | General Managers' Association, Chicago |
| GPO | Government Printing Office, Washington, D.C. |
| HH | Hull-House, Chicago |
| HH Assn. | Hull-House Association, Chicago |

| | |
|---|---|
| ICWPP | International Committee of Women for Permanent Peace |
| IHS | Illinois Humane Society |
| IWW | Industrial Workers of the World |
| JPA | Juvenile Protective Association, Chicago |
| MIT | Massachusetts Institute of Technology, Boston |
| NAACP | National Association for the Advancement of Colored People |
| NACW | National Association of Colored Women |
| NAWSA | National American Woman Suffrage Association |
| NEA | National Education Association |
| NWSA | National Woman Suffrage Association |
| PTA | Parent Teacher Association |
| NWTUL | National Women's Trade Union League |
| RC | Rockford College, Rockford, Ill. |
| RFS | Rockford Female Seminary, Rockford, Ill. |
| RS | Rockford Seminary, Rockford, Ill. |
| SPD | Social Democratic Party, Germany |
| WBMI | Woman's Board of Missions of the Interior , Chicago, Ill. |
| WCTU | Woman's Christian Temperance Union |
| WILPF | Woman's International League for Peace and Freedom |
| WPP | Woman's Peace Party |
| WTUL | Women's Trade Union League |
| YMCA | Young Men's Christian Association |
| YWCA | Young Women's Christian Association |

## *Symbols*

| | |
|---|---|
| $ | dollar or dollars |
| " | JA's version of "th" after a number or in a date |

## *Other*

| | |
|---|---|
| Com. | Committee |
| Comm. | Commission |
| Conf. | Conference |

# Part 1

## THE BALL IS ROLLING, 1889–93

The part title is a quote from Jane Addams, 12 February 1889, presented below.

Photograph: Jane Addams, ca. 1890, by Max Platz, society and theatrical photographer in Chicago until his illness and death in 1893–94 (UIC, JAMC 0005 0014).

# *Introduction*

It was the end of January 1889 when the twenty-nine-year-old Laura Jane Addams of Cedarville, Illinois, boarded the Chicago and Northwestern train in Freeport, Illinois, with trunks in tow, to resettle herself, one of many emigrants seeking a new life in Chicago. She was a slender woman, five feet and two and a half inches tall, weighing no more than 120 pounds, with light-brown hair pulled into a bun worn low at the nape of her neck, direct gray eyes, a sallow complexion, and a generous mouth above dimpled chin. She dressed fashionably, with hat, coat, and gloves. A seasoned traveler, she was already familiar with the city, poised and sure of herself. Jane Addams, as she would be known for the rest of her life, had come to Chicago to seek a new kind of life, helping herself and others achieve a more just and open society.

The smelly, smoky, and coal-dusted city, a-roil with entrepreneurial verve and spirit, was bulging with "every race, every grade of human creature that seems to pour into that great caldron of Chicago."[1] The Great Chicago Fire, 8–10 October 1871, destroyed "practically every building in an area of three and a third square miles in the heart" of the city. "Property valued at $200,000,000 was turned into rubble, 90,000 people were left homeless, 300 lost their lives."[2] Since that disaster, Chicago had reinvented itself. The remainder of the 1870s and the 1880s was a time of continued rebuilding and industrial development in Chicago. It was also a time characterized by an increasing influx of European immigrants, labor disturbances, the growth of urban slum areas, and fear about the influence of anarchists stemming from the Haymarket Riot in 1886.[3] Chicago was soon to be recognized as the second city of the land after only New York City. Seen by the leaders of other urban areas as an upstart just seventeen years from its tragic fire of 1871, Chicago was vying successfully with New York, St. Louis, and Washington, D.C., to host what became the World's Columbian Exposition in 1893, which brought thousands of visitors from across the world to see the wonders of the "Great White City," as the exposition grounds of gleaming white structures became known, and to experience the excitement of the city itself. Chicago was expanding, too, from a city composed of 35 square miles in 1888 to one with 178 square miles in 1889 when it annexed more than 140 contiguous square miles of land. Between 1870 and 1889, Chicago's population skyrocketed from approximately 299,000 to almost 1.1 million. Of those, 450,000 were immigrants, primarily from Germany and Ireland, and another almost 400,000 were the children of foreign-born parents.

By 1889 more than 289 significant new structures, mostly brick, six to seven stories high, had replaced what had been a hodgepodge of brick and frame three- and four-story structures in the center of the city. Although the first skyscraper had been constructed in Chicago in the earlier 1880s,[4] in 1889 the city skyline boasted two major new buildings at a cost of $31 million: the twelve-story brick Tacoma building[5] and the prestigious ten-story Auditorium Theater, Hotel, and Office Building, the home of one of the largest opera houses in the world.[6] New government buildings, churches, hotels, restaurants, mercantile establishments, and manufacturing plants enhanced the environment in which wealthier Chicagoans lived. While the infrastructure in the areas damaged by the 1871 fire had improved, the housing stock outside that area was rickety, inferior, and primarily of insubstantial wood-frame construction. The majority of streets were unpaved, and much of the older housing had no central heating, no sanitation or in-house water connection, and no yard. In one of Jane Addams's earliest public descriptions of the neighborhoods untouched by the Great Fire, she offered: "The streets are inexpressibly dirty, the number of schools inadequate, factory legislation unenforced, the street-lighting bad, the paving miserable and altogether lacking in the alleys and smaller streets, and the stables defy all laws of sanitation. Hundreds of houses are unconnected with the street sewer. The older and richer inhabitants seem anxious to move away as rapidly as they can afford it. They make room for newly arrived emigrants who are densely ignorant of civic duties."[7]

Chicago stood at the nexus of rail transportation in the continental United States, with access to the East and West and with shipping traffic through the Great Lakes and on south through the Mississippi River to the world beyond. It was an ideal site for the continued development of such major industries as meatpacking; manufacture of clothing, metal goods, and agricultural implements; printing; and lumber. Many of these industries were fueled by the combination of capital provided by a growing number of wealthy Chicago industrialists, cheap labor (the result of thousands of new immigrants flooding the employment market), and few workplace restrictions. Chicago was a divided city: the very wealthy entrepreneurs and barons of industry lived in small pockets clustered near Lake Michigan on the city's Near South and North Sides, and the poor lived in slum areas housing the thousands of immigrants, often near the manufacturing and mercantile businesses, developing south and west of the city center.

The dirt streets in the Hull-House neighborhood were bordered by wooden houses in various sizes and states of repair. A peddler brought his wares into the neighborhood to sell from the back of his wagon, ca. 1891 (HH Assn., UIC, JAMC, 0190 0264).

Jane Addams's initial plan for her Chicago "scheme" was to secure a home for herself and begin to "learn of life from life itself."[8] Using London's Toynbee Hall[9] as a model, she would live among the working poor and encourage college women to join her. They would educate themselves about the problems of their neighbors, use their educations to help ameliorate those problems; and, being good neighbors, help to ease the lives of immigrants as they settled into their new country, "minister to the deep-seated craving for social intercourse that all men feel,"[10] and enrich their lives by offering them educational opportunities.

It was not until 1892 that Addams and other women and men associated with Hull-House, who were committed to the ideals of social justice for all, became unalterably and visibly committed to engaging in activities that resulted in progressive reforms. They were drawn to the need for altering the conditions and systems that promoted the status quo and stifled positive life experiences as well as progress and upward mobility for the working poor. The process by which Addams and her friends engaged in reform efforts included identifying a problem and conducting an investigation of it in order to get the facts and then presenting those facts to the general public and suggesting solutions in a simple, logical treatment with solid examples. Addams and many of her colleagues believed that the better educated and more economically secure citizens were concerned about the life conditions of all human beings and were dedicated to the development of a just and civil society. Addams was certain that if told about inequities, they would demand reform to improve conditions and right proven wrongs. In making their case, they learned to use all of the means possible to inform the public, including mass meetings, speeches, essays, interviews, and activities that would draw the attention of newspapers. They developed support from organized groups of citizens and in one-on-one meetings, most often with male decision makers. In the process, they became identified as progressive reformers.

With Ellen Gates Starr,[11] her best friend, European traveling companion, and former Rockford Female Seminary classmate, Jane Addams began her Chicago life in an upscale boardinghouse at 4 Washington Place, north of the Chicago River. Both women were anxious to bring Jane's idea to fruition. They proceeded in three directions at the same time: they looked for a suitable place and neighborhood in which to begin their project, they began to investigate other efforts in the city that had as their goal helping those who needed help, and they began to promote the plan that they hoped to develop and to secure approval of from key civic and social leaders. By the end of February 1889, they had made significant progress.

In their effort to build alliances and develop allegiances, they first sought the approval of leaders and opinion shapers that they already knew in Chicago. Ellen Gates Starr, who had been employed as a teacher for a number of years in private schools in Chicago, introduced Jane Addams to two women who were wealthy social leaders and already identified with social and civic reform efforts. Mrs. Lydia Avery Coonley-Ward[12] and Mrs. Julia Plato Harvey[13] became lifelong friends of Jane Addams and Hull-House. They participated in settlement programs and projects, provided financial and political support, offered friendship and advice, and, most important, put their stamp of approval on the social settlement idea and encouraged their friends to meet Jane Addams and support her project. Addams arrived in Chicago with at least one very important friendship. The former mayor of Chicago Colonel Roswell B. Mason[14] had been a friend of Jane Addams's father, and Jane took advantage of that friendship. She later recalled that Mason was "a warm friend to our plans."[15] Just as important, the entire Mason-Trowbridge-Miller family[16] became involved in helping to establish the settlement. They likely offered valuable advice about whom Jane should see to promote her idea. They participated in settlement activities after Hull-House opened, and they provided an assortment of furnishings for the house. They also offered Jane and Ellen a place to stay while they were preparing their home at 335 South Halsted Street for occupancy.

Jane and Ellen began to speak with younger groups of college graduates that they met through churches or women's organizations in the hope of encouraging them to join in Jane's "scheme." They made three converts to their social settlement plan from among those living in their boardinghouse and on Washington Place. Enella Benedict[17] became the Hull-House resident who created the Hull-House art program. Alexander A. McCormick,[18] also a fellow boarder, served as a volunteer at the settlement, helped provide access to newspaper coverage for the settlement, and continued over many years to provide regular financial support. Lucy Durfee Bogue,[19] a young woman who lived with her parents at 5 Washington Place, was also one of the early volunteers at the settlement.

Jane Addams also began investigating missions, self-help programs, special schools, and church-related programs created to help Chicago's working poor. She visited programs like the Clybourn Avenue Mission,[20] the Armour Mission,[21] the Boys Industrial School at Norwood,[22] an Anarchist Sunday School,[23] the Moody Church Evening School for boys,[24] and the Bohemian Mission.[25] She sought opportunities to present her ideas to their boards and participated as she could in their programs.

At the same time, she met with influential Protestant religious leaders in Chicago and won their public support. Articles about the settlement idea by many of them appeared in the public and religious press, and they offered her opportunities to speak to their congregations. Many who were impressed by her plan and her commitment helped open doors for her to other leaders in the city. The Armour Mission leadership allowed her to present her plans to their board. At least one of their board members, architect Allen B. Pond,[26] was so taken with the plan and its presenter that he became a lifelong devotee of Hull-House and Jane Addams. Allen Pond and his brother, Irving K. Pond,[27] served as the architects for most of the Hull-House renovations and additions, but even more important, Allen Pond convinced other influential Chicago friends to listen to the story that Addams was telling and to support her venture. Irving Pond recalled that Jane Addams's first public appearance in Chicago was at the home of Mrs. Mary Hawes Wilmarth[28] on Michigan Avenue, on the site of which a portion of the Congress Hotel was later built. The rooms were filled with a gathering of Chicago's high-minded, philanthropic, and generous citizens who sat fascinated as "this sweet faced, frail young woman unfolded a story of life in the slums and how she proposed to be a factor in the amelioration of such conditions. From that moment the idea in its general form was assured a backing. All that remained for Miss Addams to do was to find a proper site for a social settlement, to establish herself, and prove the metal that was in her!"[29]

Mrs. Julia A. Beveridge[30] of the Armour Mission introduced Jane to the leadership of the mission and also introduced her to Mrs. Sarah Sears[31] of the Chicago Woman's Club,[32] where Mrs. Julia Plato Harvey was also an influential member. As a result, by April 1889, Jane Addams and Ellen Starr were members of the Woman's Club, the most powerful organization of leading women in the city. Suddenly, their access to Chicago leaders and opinion makers had grown exponentially. The Woman's Club members understood the value of the program that Jane and Ellen were launching.[33]

Julia A. Beveridge, librarian and registrar at the Armour Mission, befriended Jane Addams and introduced her to other men and women who were working to improve the conditions for the working poor in Chicago (ITT, Archives/1998.270/ *Armour Engineer and Alumnus*).

From these simple beginnings, the social settlement idea began to catch the attention of other Chicago social and civic leaders. It also began to attract the interest of young men and women. While young women were slow to become residents, they did become active volunteers. Without them it would have been difficult for the two founders to develop the program that attracted so many neighbors and friends to Hull-House each week. Those educational, social, and neighborhood programs were the first trademark of the settlement.

In their search for a structure that would serve as their home in a suitable neighborhood, Addams and Starr "went about with the officers of the compulsory education department, with city missionaries and with . . . newspaper reporters."[34] The two women and their guides journeyed back and forth by horse-drawn carriage over the dirt and wood block streets in the working-class neighborhoods of Chicago. The Woman's Christian Temperance Union[35] recommended that Jane and Ellen establish their settlement on South Clark Street near the Anchorage,[36] in the center of prostitution and gambling activities in Chicago. After consulting the Mason family, Addams made her decision. She chose a neighborhood that encompassed a congested, dysfunctional, dowdy, and poverty-ridden German, Irish, and Jewish immigrant area, with a notable influx of Italian immigrants, primarily from southern Italy. The house was located at 335 South Halsted Street in the vicinity of Harrison, Polk, and Halsted streets and Blue Island Avenue, just to the west of the Chicago River and south of the city center. It had been the former home of highly successful real estate developer and philanthropist Charles J. Hull.[37] He died in February 1889 and left the property to his cousin Helen Culver,[38] who over time became one of the major benefactors of the settlement. Jane was able to gain access to the property and with the help of the Pond brothers and others to prepare it as a home for herself and her social settlement. The settlement officially opened on 18 September 1889, and because the dwelling was known in the neighborhood as Mr. Hull's house, Jane and Ellen chose the name Hull-House for their enterprise.

Addams's ideas and plans caught the attention and the rapid approval of the Chicago religious, social, cultural, and civic leadership. Aware of the unrest in their city, especially among the working poor, these leaders were seeking ways to reduce the disparity between the wealthy and the working poor. The social settlement idea could be supported by those with power and money; they did not have to participate actively unless they chose to, but could watch the process and progress from afar. In addition and perhaps more important, the idea was based on a successful program under way in London, and many of Chicago's elite were great admirers of England. Jane Addams had visited Toynbee Hall and could describe it in detail and explain its strong points that she expected to replicate.

That Jane Addams was an acceptable and nonthreatening proponent of the settlement idea was a major factor in her successful promotion of the idea. There was something about her that permitted men and women of all ages to listen to her and seriously consider her plan. She was from northern Illinois and the daughter of a recognized and admired former state political leader with a reputation for honesty. When she appeared, she was appropriately attired by the standards of proper behavior of the day. She was well educated, well read, and well traveled. She could share grand-tour experiences with those in her audiences who had also traveled extensively in Europe. She was old enough to be taken seriously, but young enough to appear idealistic. She was energetic, articulate, well organized in her presentations, and an able debater. She was serious, unfrivolous, and convincing as a speaker; she seems to have been able to judge her audiences and to tailor her presentations to meet their expectations. She presented herself as dedicated to her plan and persistent in the pursuit of her objective, even passionate about it. She was at ease with herself and her abilities, with a genuine interest in other people and a sureness of purpose that gave those who heard her confidence that she would succeed. Most of all, and most unusual, she was not asking Chicago leaders for their immediate financial support; she was willing to use her own wealth to establish her home and social settlement. She wanted their approval of the idea, their help in making it a success, because of their positions in the community as recognized leaders and opinion shapers.

It took Jane Addams and Hull-House just five years, 1889–93, to become a recognized force for progressive change in Chicago. During those years, she managed to win the trust and admiration of her neighbors, organize Hull-House as a social settlement, and secure its survival. She attracted both women and men as residents and volunteers; developed its educational, social, and reform-based programs; increased the size of the physical space of the settlement by adding buildings; and obtained financial support for Hull-House to supplement the amount she provided from her own wealth. She began to develop a number of significant friendships with like-minded reformers who became lifelong personal friends. She became a speaker increasingly in demand. She also became an author, with essays published in periodical and book form. She developed a number of significant alliances among Chicago leaders and key organizations and became the recognized leader of the budding national social settlement movement. She participated in many of the international congresses that were held at the World's Columbian Exposition in Chicago in 1893. In the meantime, she maintained her Cedarville family relationships and discovered a new personal friendship with Mary Rozet Smith,[39] who would become her lifelong best friend and companion. Among the reform issues she helped tackle were support for labor unions, especially for women. She advocated settling strikes through arbitration and improving workplace safety. She tried to provide single women with an option for safe and affordable lodging and access to improved health care, especially through medical care offered by Hull-House and through the city visiting nurse program she helped start. She opposed the sweatshop industry and fought for access to arts and culture for all people. She worked for improved child care and campaigned for better schools and compulsory education for children under the age of fourteen. At the same time, she tried to teach the educated and well-to-do what it meant to live among the working poor. In the process, she began to develop a network of like-minded colleagues, dedicated to the democratic ideal and progressive reform. Among those who emerged during these first five years were Julia C. Lathrop,[40] Florence Kelley,[41] Louise de Koven Bowen,[42] Mary E. McDowell,[43] Emily Greene Balch,[44] Robert A. Woods,[45] Helena Dudley,[46] Mary Hawes Wilmarth, Lydia Avery Coonley-Ward, John Dewey,[47] Jenkin Lloyd Jones,[48] Henry Demarest Lloyd,[49] Mary Kenney O'Sullivan,[50] and Alzina Parsons Stevens.[51]

## Notes

1. C. R. Ashbee, "Journals," 2:198–99.

2. Paul M. Angle, *The Great Chicago Fire*, 11.

3. See EGS [for JA] to Mary Houghton Starr Blaisdell [and SAAH], 23 Feb. [1889], n. 7, below.

4. The ten-story Montauk Building (1882–1902), located at 64–70 West Monroe, was the first Chicago skyscraper. However, the first building of skeleton construction was the nine-

story Home Insurance Building (1885–1931), on the southeast corner of South LaSalle and West Adams streets.

5. The Tacoma Building (1889–1929), begun in 1888, was twelve stories tall and located on the northeast corner of North LaSalle and West Madison streets.

6. The Auditorium, ten stories tall with a nineteen-story tower and designed by the architect firm of Adler and Sullivan, was completed in Dec. 1889. It was located at 431 South Wabash and the northwest corner of South Michigan Ave. and East Congress St.

7. Addams, "HH, Chicago: An Effort toward Social Democracy." See Two Essays in the *Forum*, Nov. and Oct. 1892, below.

8. Addams, *Twenty Years*, 85.

9. See *PJA*, 2:494–98; 2:508–17, nn. 131–71; and 2:624, n. 18.

10. Addams, *Twenty Years*, 109.

11. For a biographical note on EGS, see *PJA*, 1:544–61.

12. For a biographical note on Lydia Avery Coonley-Ward, see JA to MCAL, 19 [and 20] Feb. 1889, n. 11, below.

13. For a biographical note on Julia Plato Harvey, see JA to MCAL, 12 Feb. 1889, n. 28, below.

14. For biographical notes on Roswell Mason and his family, see JA to MCAL, 19 [and 20] Feb 1889, n. 19 (Alice Miller) and n. 40 (Harriet Trowbridge); EGS [for JA] to Mary Houghton Starr Blaisdell [and SAAH], 23 Feb. [1889], n. 22; and JA to MCAL, 26 Feb. 1889, n. 23, all below.

15. Addams, *Twenty Years*, 92.

16. See n. 14.

17. For a biographical note on Enella Benedict, see JA to MCAL, 19 [and 20] Feb. 1889, n. 6, below.

18. For a biographical note on Alexander A. McCormick, see JA to MCAL, 19 [and 20] Feb. 1889, n. 27, below.

19. For a biographical note on Lucy Durfee Bogue, see JA to MCAL, 12 Feb. 1889, n. 3, below.

20. See JA to MCAL, 12 Feb. 1889, nn. 10, 13–14, below.

21. See JA to EGS, 24 Jan. 1889, n. 7, below.

22. See JA to MCAL, 26 Feb. 1889, n. 10, below.

23. See EGS [for JA] to Mary Houghton Starr Blaisdell [and SAAH], 23 Feb. [1889], n. 8, below.

24. See JA to MCAL, 12 Feb. 1889, nn. 36–37, below.

25. See JA to MCAL, 19 [and 20] Feb. 1889, n. 37, below.

26. For a biographical note on Allen B. Pond, see JA to MCAL, 12 Feb. 1889, n. 22, below.

27. For a biographical note on Irving K. Pond, see JA to MCAL, 12 Feb. 1889, n. 22, below.

28. For a biographical note on Mary Hawes Wilmarth, see JA to SAAH, 8 Oct. 1889, n. 19, below.

29. Swan and Tatum, *Autobiography of Irving K. Pond*, 176. JA agreed with Pond. In her eulogy for Mary Hawes Wilmarth in *The Excellent Becomes the Permanent*, JA indicated, "One of the very first public meetings that was held for us, thirty years ago, when Hull-House was young, was convened in Mrs. Wilmarth's house. True to her belief in obtaining the widest possible background of knowledge, she invited Thomas Davidson, who was considered one of the leaders in the philosophic thought of America. Unhappily the philosopher disagreed with our theses. I recall his irritation with one of our favorite phrases that the 'things that make us alike are finer and stronger than the things that make us different.' Our hostess, however, was equal to the task of interpreting and reconciling philosophic differences, and from that early beginning she stood by the settlement movement in Chicago in its various manifestations" (103–4). JA made a similar statement on p. 90 in *Twenty Years*.

Thomas Davidson (1840–1900), born and educated in Scotland, came to the United States in 1867 and became a teacher of classics in a high school in St. Louis, Mo., before he went to Cambridge, Mass., and from there to work and study in Greece and Italy. He is identified with his philosophy called apeirotheism, which holds that God exists everywhere but certainly in each person and that one achieves their potential through self-cultivation and nurturing others. After HH was established, JA asked Davidson to present a lecture at the settlement; however, there is no indication that he ever agreed to appear.

JA also recalled that she met Lydia Avery Coonley while Coonley still lived "on Lasalle Street with young children still about her. . . . It was in that house that I first unfolded plans for founding a settlement in Chicago and met with that ready sympathy and understanding which her adventuring and facile mind was always ready to extend to a new cause she believed to be righteous" (*The Excellent*, 114). The Pond brothers had designed a new home for Mrs. Coonley at the corner of Lake Shore Dr. and Division St. It was ready in 1888–89, and Mrs. Coonley would have moved in by 1890. Both Mrs. Wilmarth and Mrs. Coonley may have held gatherings at which JA presented her HH idea. See also JA to MCAL, 12 Feb. 1889, n. 22, below.

30. For a biographical note on Julia A. Beveridge, see JA to EGS, 24 Jan. 1889, n. 6, below.

31. For a biographical note on Sarah Sears, see JA to MCAL, 12 Feb. 1889, n. 13, below.

32. See JA to MCAL, 12 Feb. 1889, n. 15, below.

33. See Address for the Chicago Woman's Club, 3 Dec. 1890, especially n. 3, below.

34. Addams, *Twenty Years*, 91.

35. See JA to MCAL, 26 Feb. 1889, nn. 28–30, below.

36. The Anchorage began in 1886 in a small house in the South Side vice-riddled district called "the Levee" near city-center Chicago. By 1893 it was located at 125 Plymouth Court, a street that paralleled Clark St. in the area. In 1895 it was moved to 1349 Wabash Ave.

37. Charles J. Hull was born in Manchester, Conn. His father died when he was a boy, and he went to live with his grandfather, the proprietor of a small hotel in central New York. There he attended school and when twenty years old became a teacher in a district school. In 1846 he went to Chicago, where he began to study law. After graduating from the law school at Harvard Univ., he returned to Chicago and began to practice law and develop a real estate business. According to the *Chicago Daily Tribune*, Hull was "one of the first to inaugurate the now general system of subdividing and platting suburban property and selling it on the installment plan" ("C. J. Hull Is Dead," 14 Feb. 1889).

By the mid-1850s, when he made arrangements to have constructed the brick mansion that later became the HH settlement, he had become a wealthy man with a wife and two children. Although the financial panic of 1857 left him at least one million dollars in debt, he managed to pay his creditors and build additional wealth. After the Civil War, he went to Savannah, Ga., and introduced his idea of selling homes through installment payments to workers, many of whom were recently freed slaves. He carried out similar plans for the working poor in Baltimore, Md.; Jacksonville, Fla.; Houston, Tex.; Lincoln, Blair, and Ashland, Nebr.; and in Cairo, Ill. Hull described his venture in a letter to a friend: "Our enterprise is not a land speculation. We are endeavoring to distribute the lands adjoining certain large cities among the poor. If I succeed in carrying our idea to its legitimate results the question of what is to be done with the pauper, the outcast, and the criminal will be solved" (quoted in "C. J. Hull Is Dead," *Chicago Daily Tribune*, 14 Feb. 1889).

Hull was known as a philanthropist. One of the founders and the first president of Chicago's Washington Home to help alcoholics, he was also a trustee and liberal donor to the first Univ. of Chicago, predecessor to the institution of the same name founded after his death, and active in the cause of prohibition. He was particularly dedicated to working for prison reform and to providing economic opportunity for the poor. Especially in Chicago and Savannah, he instituted night schools in his offices to help educate those without access to public education. He gave a weekly Sunday talk to prisoners in Chicago's Bridewell Prison, and when he was in Baltimore over a Sunday he met with prisoners there to present a message of hope and encouragement. At his death, his estate was estimated to have grown to between four and five million dollars, all of which he left to his cousin and business associate Helen Culver (see JA to AHHA, 9 May 1889, n. 9, below).

38. For a biographical note on Helen Culver, see JA to AHHA, 9 May 1889, n. 9, below.

39. For a biographical note on MRS, see Biographical Profiles: Smith, Mary Rozet, and Smith Family, below.

40. For a biographical note on Julia C. Lathrop, see Biographical Profiles: Lathrop, Julia Clifford, below.

41. For a biographical note on Florence Kelley, see Articles in the *Chicago News* and *Chicago Daily Tribune*, 29 and 30 Apr. 1892, n. 1, below.

42. For a biographical note on Louise de Koven Bowen, see Biographical Profiles: Bowen, Louise de Koven, below.

43. For a biographical note on Mary E. McDowell, see Two Essays in the *Forum*, Nov. and Oct. 1892, n. 154, below.

44. For a biographical note on Emily Greene Balch, see JA to Emily Greene Balch, 11 May 1893, n. 7, below.

45. For a biographical note on Robert A. Woods, see Robert A. Woods to JA, 20 June 1893, especially n. 8, below.

46. For a biographical note on Helena S. Dudley, see JA to SAAH, 23 Feb. 1893, n. 9, below.

47. For a biographical note on John Dewey, see John Dewey to JA, 27 Jan. 1892, especially n. 1, below.

48. For a biographical note on Jenkin Lloyd Jones, see Jenkin Lloyd Jones to JA, 30 June [1890], n. 4, below.

49. For a biographical note on Henry Demarest Lloyd, see JA to Henry Demarest Lloyd, 18 Nov. 1891, especially n. 1, below.

50. For a biographical note on Mary Kenney O'Sullivan, see JA to Henry Demarest Lloyd, 18 Nov. 1891, n. 5, below.

51. For a biographical note on Alzina Parsons Stevens, see JA to Richard T. Ely, 31 Oct. 1894, n. 10, below.

## To Ellen Gates Starr

*"I hope the Cedarville weather has been as bright as it is here and that the new year has opened as happily," Jane Addams wrote in her New Year salutation to her stepmother, Anna Addams, on 2 January 1889.[1] After spending Thanksgiving and Christmas in Girard, Kansas, with sister Sarah Alice Addams Haldeman, her husband, Harry, and their two-year-old daughter, Marcet, Jane traveled to Geneseo, Illinois, to have New Year's with her other sister Mary Catherine Addams Linn and her family.[2] "Mary and Mr Linn gave a reception yesterday afternoon and evening to their church people and neighbors. About a hundred and twenty people came and most of them stayed for several hours. It was a very easy pleasant day and I was surprised in the evening to find out how much I had enjoyed it."[3] Although Jane left for Chicago with sister Mary during the second week in January, planning to stay there to begin developing her social settlement idea, she had to return to Geneseo with her sister. Mary's youngest child, Stanley, had become dangerously ill. Once again family duty claimed Jane.*

Geneseo Ill. Jan. 24" 1889

My dear Ellen

I am dreadfully disappointed, I was quite sure I would be in Chicago Sat.[4] but simply cannot leave Stanley; the little fellow has been threatened with diphtheria and looks like a ghost. I owe so much to Mary in so many tender ways[5] that I feel now as if I ought to stay. I know you disapprove dear heart, and I appreciate your disapproval, I disapprove myself in a measure, but "God as make me so" I suppose.

I have not been idle, I have made friends with a Mrs Beveridge[6] who works in the Armour mission[7] and will do what she can for us. She is a practical philanthopist and the "scheme"[8] seems feasible to her. I have talked to my good Sister and her husband[9] until the thing is clearer in my own mind, and I have made a little advance into the literature of the subject.[10] Antoine Amiel,[11] a reformed Catholic in Paris has much the same scheme only on a "normal" plan. Have patience for a few days longer and I will work with all my might and do my best. I have been in Iowa for a few days to see a forlorn(?) Cousin and a bedridden Aunt.[12] My cousin seemed a beautiful Christian to me, there is certainly a reward in caring for the sick, and poor & young. Don't scold me, dear, I am awfully sorry about the delay, lets love each other through thick and thin and work out a salvation. Yours

Jane Addams.

I haven't Mrs McLish's address.[13] Will you drop her a postal & ask her when the Chicago Sem'y Association[14] meets I think it is the last week in Jan, & I should like to go[.]

ALS (SC, Starr; *JAPM*, 2:1005–6).

1. SCPC, JAC; *JAPM*, 2:998.

2. JA left Girard, Kans., on Thursday, 27 Dec.; stopped to visit her cousin Charles A. Young and his family in Kansas City, Mo., on 28 Dec.; and arrived in Geneseo, Ill., on 29 Dec. 1888. The Linns had four children, John Addams, James Weber, Esther Margaret, and Stanley Ross.

For biographical information on the Charles A. Young family, see *PJA*, 2:522–23, n. 4. At the time of JA's death in late May 1935, Charles A. Young wrote to offer his condolences to cousin James Weber Linn and reported of JA: "Several times we have had the pleasure of having her a guest in our home; and it is needless to say that always we enjoyed her visits" (SCPC, JAC).

3. SCPC, JAC; *JAPM*, 2:998. For biographical information on the MCAL family, see *PJA*, 1 and 2.

4. 26 Jan. 1889.

5. Family friend and former RFS teacher Sarah F. Blaisdell probably reinforced JA's dedication to sister MCAL and her family when she wrote to JA on 5 Jan. 1889 reminding her that MCAL's "heart has been very tenderly and painfully tried these later years" (SCPC, JAC; *JAPM*, 2:1001). MCAL's two youngest children had recently died: Charles Hodge in May 1887 and "Little Mary" Addams in Jan. 1888. For comments on JA's special relationship with her oldest sister, MCAL, see *PJA*, 1:21–23, 538–43.

6. Julia A. Brown Beveridge (1856–1919), born in Wisconsin, and the widow of commercial agent and widower Peter H. Beveridge (1834–85?) of the firm of Beveridge, McCausland, and Co., whom she wed in 1882, was a strong leader in the Armour Mission program created by the Plymouth Congregational Church. She became the Mission librarian in 1887, and she worked valiantly to stimulate an interest in reading. She soon realized that in order to succeed, she had to broaden the reading program to include other activities. She started with a class in clay modeling. Surprised by the results, she enlisted the services of five young men from a manual training school who taught the children wood carving, tile making, freehand and mechanical drawing, and designing. Before long she had 400 boys in the Saturday-morning classes and 350 girls in the afternoon classes, in which they learned dressmaking and millinery skills. Mrs. Beveridge may not have realized it at the time, but she was already laying the foundations for the formation of the Armour Institute, an offshoot of the mission, opened in 1893 to train boys and girls in industrial and domestic arts. There she served as assistant librarian in the Dept. of Library Science and registrar. After that department closed in 1895, she continued to serve as Armour Institute registrar until the 1900s. She died in St. Luke's Hospital in Chicago after being struck by a truck and was buried in Geneseo, Ill. See also n. 7.

7. The Armour Mission, located at 33rd and Butterfield streets, was created from a bequest of $100,000 from Plymouth Congregational Church member Joseph F. Armour (1842–81). With added gifts from meatpacking industrialist Philip D. Armour (1832–1901), said to be approximately $1 million, 144 flats were erected for income purposes, completely surrounding the block on which the mission was situated. When the main mission building was completed, Plymouth Mission, which had been created by Plymouth Church in 1874 and established in

a vacant store on 31st St., was asked to make the building its home. The Plymouth Mission transferred its operation to the new quarters and opened officially on 5 Dec. 1886 as the Armour Mission. It was a nonsectarian institution that not only sponsored Sunday School and religious services, but also provided educational opportunities, including a kindergarten, library, literary societies, lectures, free medical dispensary, kitchen garden, a sewing or workroom for women, nurseries, and bathrooms. Its Sunday School, when it opened in 1886, had a membership of 500; by 1895, there were 2,200 pupils, with 35 officers and 130 teachers, many of whom were from different churches in the city, although the largest proportion was from Plymouth Church.

Less than a year after the opening of the Armour Mission, Rev. Frank W. Gunsaulus became pastor of Plymouth Church (see JA to MCAL, 19 [and 20] Feb. 1889, n. 30, below). He immediately became interested in the Armour Mission. In a sermon he delivered early in 1890, "What I Would Do If I Had a Million Dollars," he outlined a school in which young people, rich and poor alike, might secure a practical education. Philip D. Armour heard that sermon and responded. The programs at Drexel Institute, Philadelphia, and Pratt Institute and Cooper Union, New York City, provided the model for the Armour Institute, for which Armour provided $300,000 for a building and an additional $1.4 million as endowment.

The cornerstone of the Armour Institute, located at 33rd St. and Armour Ave., was laid in 1891, and the building was completed in the winter of 1892. It opened 4 Sept. 1893 as a technical school for males and females, offering professional courses in electrical and mechanical engineering, architecture, and library science as well as programs in domestic arts, commerce, and music. There was also a Kindergarten Normal Dept., sponsored in association with the Chicago Free Kindergarten Assn., which had begun its work in 1881 and been affiliated with Armour Mission since 1892.

Eventually, departments formed for the training of women closed: library science (1895), shorthand and typing (1899), the Kindergarten Normal Dept. (1900), domestic arts (June 1901), as well as the Dept. of Music. JA was a lecturer at the institute during 1900–1901. Her topic was "Woman's Work." This speech may have been a later version of "Woman's Work for Chicago," published on pp. 502–8 in the Sept. 1898 issue of *Municipal Affairs* (*JAPM*, 46:871–75).

The Armour Institute and the Lewis Institute established on Chicago's West Side in 1895 with a curriculum in liberal arts, science, and engineering merged and in 1940 became the Illinois Institute of Technology.

8. JA and EGS often referred to their plan to create a social settlement as their "scheme."

9. JA apparently shared her ideas with sister MCAL and her Presbyterian minister husband, JML, who had years of experience with charitable work. She had also presented her ideas to former RFS teacher Sarah F. Blaisdell. See Sarah F. Blaisdell to JA, 5 Jan. 1889, SCPC, JAC; *JAPM*, 2:1001–4.

10. Among publications JA may have been referring to are articles by Samuel O. Barnett and other English leaders of the Christian Socialism movement that spawned the social settlement movement in England. She was also reading materials about a variety of urban missions and their programs.

11. JA may have learned about Antoine Amiel from Alice and William Gulick, missionaries she befriended in Spain (see *PJA*, 2:617, n. 4). She may have visited his program during the two weeks she was in Paris in the spring of 1888. There are no extant letters or diary entries for her activities in Paris in 1888.

Amelia Rowell, one of JA's traveling companions in Europe in 1888, wrote to AHHA on 17 July 1888 about JA, "I wrote you a long letter when she first left Paris—but did not send it fearing some of the things I wrote might alarm you" (IU, Lilly, SAAH). Mrs. Rowell, who expected JA to return to Cedarville as a companion for AHHA, might have been concerned by JA's interest in mission work.

*From left to right,* the brothers Irving K. and Allen B. Pond, the architects for most of the additions and renovations of the buildings in the Hull-House complex. Allen B. Pond was an early and lifelong friend of Jane Addams and served as a member of the first board of Hull-House Association (UM, BHL, Mich. HC, Pond, Family Photographs).

12. JA was visiting her invalid aunt Maria W. Hoffeditz Weber, widow of her uncle Rev. George A. Weber, who had just died in 1888. The Webers had three boys and two girls who lived to maturity. The caregiving cousin was likely either Mary or Grace Weber. See *PJA*, 1:131, n.1.

13. Martha Hillard (MacLeish) had been principal of RFS until 1888, when she wed widower Andrew MacLeish. For a biographical note, see *PJA*, 2:420–21, n. 5.

14. The RC Assn. of Chicago originated in 1874; however, a permanent organization was not established until 1885. The association was officially incorporated in 1899. In 1889 there were eighty-six members. They held an annual dinner or luncheon and two informal gatherings during each year in the homes of various members.

## To Mary Catherine Addams Linn

*The boardinghouse at 4 Washington Place where Jane Addams first lived with Ellen Gates Starr when she came to Chicago at the end of January was one of eight brick residences that faced Washington Square Park.*[1] *The small street, later renamed Delaware Place, extended west from Dearborn Avenue to Clark Street.*[2] *The house was the home of widow Sophia Rogers Durfee and her unmarried daughters.*[3]

*The three-acre tract of land known as Washington Square Park had been donated to the city in 1842. Located just south of Walton Place, it had been improved with trees, grass, and a fountain following the Chicago Fire of 1871. In 1888 the park was hailed by residents as an oasis on the North Side of the city, where it provided a secure play area and good air for neighborhood children. With its fine residences and Protestant churches,*[4] *Chicago's Washington Square neighborhood bore a remarkable resemblance to the Mount Vernon–Washington Place district where Jane Addams, stepmother Anna, and stepbrother George Haldeman had lived in Baltimore during the winters of 1885–86 and 1886–87.*[5]

*In order to keep their siblings informed of progress on the "scheme," Jane Addams and Ellen Gates Starr wrote letters home from 4 Washington Place to be shared as circulars by members of both families. Among extant letters written from the Washington Place address that Jane Addams directed to sister Mary Catherine Addams Linn are five*[6] *describing the initial activities of the Addams-Starr pair. They offered the most complete and timely account of their activities in organizing the settlement. All appear below.*

4 Washington Pl Chicago, [Ill.] Feb 12" 1889

My dear Mary:

Your kind letter[7] came Saturday morning at the same time with one from Weber[8] and one from Alice.[9] I sat down to read them and made myself late at an appointment at the Clybourn Ave. Mission[10] but they so filled my heart with happiness and good will that it was well worth being late.

So many things keep happening and the "ball is rolling at such a cheerful pace" as Ellen says, that it is hard to keep you all informed. Ellen wrote a long letter to Miss Anderson[11] last evening and I asked her <(Miss A.)> to send it to Weber, I will try to outline the same thing if you will be kind enough to send it on to Alice.

In the first place Mrs Beveridge has been exceedingly kind to me and I shall always feel indebted to her. More over she believes in the scheme. She came to lunch with me on Thursday[12] and in the afternoon we call together first on Mrs Sears[13]—whom I had met the day before at the Industrial Art Society[14] & who is quite determined to have me elected a member of the "Woman Club"[15] to "vivify them" as she says—and then we met an appointment Mrs Beveridge had made for me with Mr Smith[16] the Sup't of the Armour Mission, and Dr Hollister.[17] Dr H. is a member of the faculty of the Chicago Medical[18] and very kindly philanthropic old gentleman. He listened with the utmost sympathy and interest to the scheme, saying now and then "go on Miss Addams," altho when we finally went, there were eight people waiting in the outer office. He shook my hand warmly when we left & told me to come to him when ever I felt the need of a friend who had had some experiance in Chicago and said he would attend the meeting at the Armour Mission on Sunday. I met the entire board of the Armour Mission last Sunday[19] at four, about twenty gentlemen including some of the head teachers with Mrs Beveridge to chaperon me—Dr Hollister, himself introduced me, sat beside me and petted my shoulder encouragingly when I said any thing that pleased him.

The effect was mixed, Mr McCord[20] the old minister who presided evidently thought that I was vaporizing, talking <sheer> nonsense & Mr Smith, Mr Convers[21] and a Mr Pond[22] waxed enthusiastic—they were all young—and even began to make offers of support and help if we would start down there. Mr

Pond assurred me that I had voiced something hundreds of young people in the city were trying to express, & that he could send us three young ladies at once who possessed both money and a knowledge of Herbert Spencer's "Sociology"[23] but who were dying from inaction and restlessness. There is nothing more to be done at the Armour Mission at present but I should n't be surprised if some definite offer were made us in the future. Dr McPherson[24] opposes our going there, he says that ground is ~~alittle~~ <already> well worked, but that there are "places in the city that need it like the devil."

Mrs Sears is a great worker in the Clybourne Ave mission, there were 700 children in the industrial school there last Sat.[25] I enjoyed the morning and made a little opening there. A Mr Chapman a McCormick[26] student, is coming to see me this evening. He has charge of the boys Dep't & became interested in the "scheme" tho Mrs Sears. She—Mrs S—does not want us the adjunct of any mission but as a child of the "Woman's Club."

Her daughter in law is a Vassar graduate, she is coming to lunch next Friday[27] with Mrs McLeish (Miss Hillard) and a Mrs Harvey[28] who is a great philanthropist and immensely fond of Ellen.

Dear Mrs Benedict[29] is very good to me. Ellen insists that we are positively intimate. We went together to Room 48 Friday[30] morning (by the way I consider the meetings there very remarkable affairs) we went calling together in the afternoon and yesterday I went with her to attend Mrs Humpheries[31] bible class in the 4" Ch.[32] I have an appointment with Mrs Humphrey for next Monday morning,[33] and I mean to join her class. Her lecture was brilliant, a parallel between the Jewish Ch. under the Judges & the Christian Ch of the mediaeval ages.

Ellen has had an attack of tonsilitis and has not been out of the house since Thursday,[34] until this morning. I was dreadfully disappointed in being obliged to meet all these appointments alone, but got through very well & now have Ellen to fall back upon as a reserve force.

We take a lesson at the Industrial Art[35] rooms every Tuesday afternoon, & teach each Wednesday evening in the Moody Church school.[36] Mr Goss[37] the minister is <a> very satisfactory man. A humble Christian written on his face. We have two or three other appointments but I will write you of them later. Our heads are not in the least turned by the first flush of success & we realize that the slough of despond may be very near.

I called at Englewood[38] yesterday afternoon and enjoyed it very much altho I started so late I had n't much time to stay. I had a pleasant call one day with Laura Ely Curtis,[39] she had a dear little boy seven months old. I am going there to d[inner?] very soon and spread the "scheme" before Mr Curtis.

Write to me often as you can dear, please give my love to Mr Linn and the children, I do hope the batting will help your arm. Always Your loving Sister

Jane Addams—

ALS (SCPC, JAC; *JAPM*, 2:1008–16).

1. By 1906 the address of the house, which was constructed after 9 Feb. 1877 when the building permit was issued, was known as 65 West Delaware Place. The house is no longer standing.

2. In 1913 the Chicago City Council authorized the street name changed from Washington Place to Brenan St. and then to Delaware Place

3. Mrs. Sophia Rogers Durfee (1808–1900) was the widow of Chicago's first harbormaster, Sydney S. Durfee (d. 1873), who had moved his family to Chicago from New York State in 1845. In 1889 her unmarried daughters, Mary (1833–1910) and Charlotte ("Lottie"), lived with her. By the time of Mrs. Durfee's death, they had taken over the business of renting furnished rooms. The Durfees' third daughter, Lucy Tucker (1837–1919), married to Dr. Roswell G. Bogue (1832–93), lived at 5 Washington Place in a home constructed in 1881 (see also JA to MCAL, 19 [and 20] Feb. 1889, n. 20, below).

Among roomers at 4 Washington Place were Enella Benedict (see JA to MCAL, 19 [and 20] Feb. 1889, n. 6, below) and her brother, Sidney A. (see n. 29), and Alexander A. McCormick (see JA to MCAL, 19 [and 20] Feb. 1889, n. 27, below).

4. Among other residents on Washington Place were Julia Latham Magruder (d. 1904) and her husband, Benjamin Drake Magruder (1838–1910), elected to the Illinois Supreme Court in 1885 and served as chief justice, 1902–6, at number 7, and Dr. Junius M. Hall (d. 1919) and his wife, Henrietta Herr Hall, who lived with his mother, Emily Baldwin Hall (Mrs. Gordon) (1821–1912), at 2 Washington Place. In 1889 Henrietta Hall organized a Social and Industrial Club for Self-Supporting Women with friends from the New England Congregational Church, Grace Methodist Church, and Holy Name Cathedral, at the time a rare example of interfaith cooperation. By the spring of 1890, the club had forty-five members, one of whom was Sophia Bogue, daughter of the Bogue family at 5 Washington Place. In addition, in recovery from the Chicago Fire of 1871, the New England Congregational Church was rebuilt and rededicated at Dearborn and Delaware avenues on 14 Sept. 1873, and the Unity Church, at the southeast corner of Dearborn Ave. and Walton Place, was rededicated on 7 Dec. 1893. By 1883 the Union Club, a prestigious bachelors' club, had opened (to be disbanded in 1912) at the corner of Dearborn Ave. and Washington Place. In June 1889, the Newberry Library was making plans to build on property just to the north of Washington Square Park.

5. *PJA*, 2:387–98.

6. The extant letters JA to MCAL are dated 12, 19 [and 20], and 26 Feb.; 13 Mar.; and 1 Apr. 1889.

7. That letter is not known to be extant.

8. JWA's letter is not known to be extant. For a biographical note on JWA, see *PJA*, 1:479–83.

9. SAAH's letter to JA is not known to be extant.

10. The Clybourn Avenue Mission was established in 1886. When JA visited, it was located at 26 and 28 (later 1225 and 1227 North) Clybourn Ave., opened in June 1888 in the former National Theater building. Its founders, William Davidson, a butcher, and Peter and John Billhorn, hardware merchants, were associated with the "mission band" of Dwight L. Moody's Chicago Avenue Church. The mission was located in a poor working-class neighborhood noted for its anarchist leanings and where a number of other churches also maintained missions.

JA could have been attracted to the mission through an article, "Gospel for Anarchists: Christianity in Its Shirt-Sleeves Working in 'Little Hell,'" which appeared in the *Chicago Daily Tribune*, 3 Feb. 1889.

11. Sarah F. Anderson Ainsworth (SA), who had taught EGS and JA at RFS and became a close friend to both, had experienced Toynbee Hall with JA in June 1888. For a biographical note on SA, see *PJA*, 1:490–93; and *PJA*, 2, part 4.

SA wrote to AHHA, "I had a long letter from Miss Starr, they are certainly having a fine time, are meeting [by] appointment some of the [finest] people in Chicago, and [I] suppose in time will begin their missionary work. I have never been quite clear as to what the work was to be, but have no doubt but that what ever the plan or scheme it will settle itself into good practical work. They are two fine women, earnest and enthusiastic, and must be helpful to those they meet, and the great confidence in and enthusiasm they have for each other will be a help to them over the hard places.

"If I were not occupied in earning my own living I presume I would be doing city missionary work, only not being of inventive turn of mind my work would be a more ordinary kind. I think when a person sees and feels a lack, she is the one to try and fill it, and I believe the girls will fill a big one" (16 Feb. [1889], UIC, JAMC, HJ).

12. 7 Feb. 1889.

13. Susan A. Davis Sears (1827–1915) (erroneously recalled in published CWC literature as Sarah A. Sears) was born in Rockingham, Vt. In 1847 she wed Amos Gould Sears (1823–1920). After living in Brattleboro, Vt., where Amos Sears was a teacher, the couple moved west to Gallipolis, Ohio, where both were teachers at Gallia Academy and their only child, Nathaniel Clinton Sears, was born in 1854. In 1870 the family migrated to Elgin, Ill., where Amos Sears became principal and Susan Sears coprincipal of the Elgin Academy, founded in 1839. After successfully reviving the school from its precarious financial position and rebuilding its reputation for academic excellence, Amos and Susan Sears retired to Chicago in 1881 to live with their attorney son at 1035 (later 2316) North Clark St. While Amos Sears became a successful real estate agent, Susan Sears immersed herself in community and educational activities. In 1885 she joined the CWC and became a leader in its Education Com., later the Education Dept.

In 1886 Mrs. Sears became the director of the CWC's project to make manual training available to Chicago children through the Industrial Art Assn. (see n. 14). At the same time, she was superintendent of the sewing school at the Clybourn Avenue Mission, where her program trained seven hundred girls, ages five to twenty, to be good housekeepers and to make garments for market as a means to additional income. By 1889 she had become the chairwoman of the CWC's Education Dept., as it worked successfully to initiate kindergartens for the first time in Chicago's Brighton and Kinzie schools. With her leadership, in 1890 the CWC agreed to raise forty thousand dollars toward the cost of developing the Boys Industrial School at Norwood Park, Ill. (eventually to be named the Glenwood School), where she was selected to serve a three-year term (resigning after one year) as a member of the board of directors (see JA to MCAL, 26 Feb. 1889, n. 10, below).

By 1896 the Sears family had settled in northern Chicago in the Edgewater community, where she and her son's wife, Laura Davidson Sears, were active as founders and members of the North End Club. She died in her son's winter home in Daytona Beach, Fla.

14. The CWC (see n. 15), guided by its Education Com., formed the Industrial Art Assn. in the fall of 1886 to teach poor and disadvantaged children practical manual skills. During the initial year, twenty-five women volunteers met in the club rooms in the Art Institute Building once a week to take manual training lessons so that they could teach classes of children in at least four Chicago locations each Saturday morning. One of the locations was the Clybourn Avenue Mission that JA visited. Susan Sears directed the program and in 1891 was successful in her effort to get the Chicago Board of Education to make manual training a regular part of school curricula.

The CWC also secured the services of a sloyd instructor. Meri Toppelius (1863–96) was born at Helsingfors, Finland. She studied sloyd, a system of manual training that emphasizes skill, dexterity, and handwork, using wood carving as a means of training in the use of tools, probably at the sloyd school that had been established at Naas, Finland, or perhaps at the Sloyd Seminarium in Finland. Miss Toppelius was associated with Pauline Agassiz Shaw (1841–1917), founder of the Boston Kindergarten and a supporter of Ellen Richards's New England Kitchen program. She arrived in Chicago as early as 1886 and conducted classes beginning in 1887 under the auspices of the CWC. In 1890 she opened the Sloyd Institute, 188 (later 805 West) Madison St., just west of Halsted St., to train sloyd teachers. In addition, she taught sloyd in other communities. In 1891 she was giving instruction at Bay View Summer Univ., Bay View, Mich., a Chautauqua-like school sponsored by the Methodist Episcopal Church.

A member of Jenkin Lloyd Jones's All Souls Church, Chicago, she was an instructor in sloyd there beginning in 1891; however, by 1893 her duties conflicted with her work in the Chicago public school system, where she was beginning to introduce sloyd. Until her death, she taught at the Agassiz Elementary School, located on North Seminary Ave., Chicago.

She took an active part in the congresses associated with the World's Columbian Exposition of 1893. An official representative of Finland, she spoke at the Memorial Congress, which had as its topic "Women's Progress" and at the Women's Congress of Representative Women. In addition, she made a presentation on sloyd during the Congress on Manual and Art Education organized by EGS and at a Lutheran gathering as a member of the Lutheran Woman's Com. during the World's Parliament of Religions. After emergency surgery and brief hospitalization, she died near the end of Jan. 1896 and was cremated, and her theosophical funeral at Graceland Cemetery, Chicago, was conducted by Jenkin Lloyd Jones, 29 Jan. 1896.

By 1900 the Chicago public schools integrated manual training into their curriculum. The girls learned cooking and sewing skills and the boys wood- and metalworking. The work of the Industrial Art Assn. was supported by contributions from individuals, the CWC, and the Decorative Art Society.

15. The Chicago Woman's Club (name changed from Chicago Women's Club, 23 Oct. 1895) was founded by twenty-one women in 1876 at the instigation of Caroline M. Brown (Mrs. Frank B.) (b. 1836). It was created to promote cooperation among women and prepare them to involve themselves in the duty of improving municipal conditions. In celebrating their fortieth anniversary, the CWC claimed, "It has broadened the views of women and has tended to make them more impersonal and has widened their sympathies. They have learned to assume responsibility outside of home interests, and to consider the study of conditions in city and state as an extension of their concern—constituting as they do the larger home. The idea of practical work for the community was fundamental in the minds of the founders" (Frank and Jerome, *Annals, CWC*, 15). The club was incorporated 26 Oct. 1885. Officers were elected each year by the growing club membership. The 200-member limit in force in 1887 had been abandoned by 1893 when there were 570 members. The club carried out various community projects as agreed to by its membership, which was organized into a group of committees, eventually renamed departments. Among them, when JA and EGS were nominated 10 Apr. and elected to membership 8 May 1889, were education (for an example of a project undertaken by the education committee, see n. 8), philanthropy, and art and literature. In time there would also be home and reform committees or departments. Each department had its own chair, membership committee, and program.

The CWC became the largest and most influential women's organization in Chicago dedicated to civic welfare. As such it and its members were to prove crucial allies for JA as she promoted and pursued a reform agenda in Chicago.

16. Edwin Burritt Smith (1854–1906) was a prominent attorney and Republican active in political reform movements. A graduate of Union College of Law in Chicago (1879), he also attended Yale (1880) and began his practice in Chicago in 1881. He served as special counsel for the city on traction railway matters and was a professor at Northwestern Univ. (1894–1902). A director on the boards on several companies providing real estate title insurance, Smith was also manager of the Rosehill Cemetery Co. He and his wife, Emma J. Dauman Smith, had three children: Curtis Q., Otis E., and Emily.

All of the Smith family were members of the Plymouth Congregational Church. Smith served as assistant Sunday School superintendent at the Plymouth Mission in 1882 and continued in that capacity at the Armour Mission (1889–93). During the 1890s, he presented several lectures at HH and began to serve on the executive committee of the Municipal Voters' League. In 1894–95, he helped JA settle her sister MCAL's estate and helped draft and then submit the legal documents by which HH Assn. was created on 30 Mar. 1895 (see also Smith, Edwin Burritt to JA, 2 Feb. 1895, below).

17. John Hamilcar Hollister (1824–1911) was a graduate of Berkshire Medical Institute (1847) in New York. He practiced medicine in Grand Rapids, Mich., until 1855, when he associated himself with Rush Medical College in Chicago. In 1859 Hollister joined the group of doctors concerned with the state of medical education in Chicago to help organize the Chicago Medical School. There he served as a faculty member until 1895. Active in the American Medical Assn. from 1858, and for a number of years editor of its journal, he also served in the Illinois State Medical Society as its treasurer and president. He and his wife, Jennette Windiate of Drayton Plains, Mich., had one daughter, Isabelle. Dr. Hollister became superintendent of the Plymouth Church Mission Sunday School in 1882 and continued in that capacity after it became the Armour Mission Sunday School until 1889. He assumed that role once again beginning Jan. 1894.

18. The Chicago Medical School was organized as a department of Lind Univ. in Chicago in Mar. 1859 by a group of physicians who resigned from Rush Medical College. This group, led by Dr. Hosmer A. Johnson (1822–91), wished to improve medical education, and they established higher standards for the premedical education of their students, a longer and more rigorous curriculum, and a practitioner's, or postgraduate, course. The school became a leader in improving medical education throughout the United States. In 1869 the Chicago Medical School became a department of Northwestern Univ. and retained its own name until 1890, when it officially became the Northwestern Univ. Medical School.

19. 10 Feb. 1889.

20. John D. McCord (1834–1929), who had been pastor of the Plymouth Mission, continued in that capacity after the Plymouth Mission moved into the Armour Mission. He served at the Armour Mission from 1886 to 1890.

John McCord was born in Illinois, attended Wabash College in Indiana, and graduated from Lane Theological Seminary, Cincinnati, in 1862. Ordained a Presbyterian minister in 1863, he held pastorates in Ohio, Michigan, and Indiana until 1883, at which time he began to serve the Congregational church in northern Illinois. After leaving the Armour Mission, he led various Congregational churches in Chicago until 1904, when he moved to Iowa and was associated with a number of congregations. He died near Oberlin, Ohio.

21. Clarence Myron Converse (1856–1938) was born in Rindge, N.H., and attended Appleton Academy in New Ipswich. He arrived in Chicago in 1885 and became the western manager of the Magee Furnace Co. of Boston. After serving five years as manager of the J. L. Mott Iron Works, he manufactured radiators until 1900, when he organized and became president of the Chicago Heater and Supply Co. He was a Republican, a member of the Plymouth Congregational Church, and for many years one of the board members of the Armour Mission, where he also served as associate superintendent of the Sunday School. It is likely he was responsible for installing the first HH furnace. See EGS [for JA] to Susan Childs Starr and Caleb Allen Starr [and SAAH], 3 Nov. [1889], n. 29, below.

22. This was Allen B. Pond, a board member at the Armour Mission. The lifelong commitment of Allen Bartlit Pond (1858–1929) and his elder brother, Irving Kane Pond (1857–1939), to HH and to the social settlement movement was vital to the success of HH. They became the architects for the buildings and renovations JA added to the original Charles J. Hull home, especially between 1889 and 1908. Their structures revealed a special humanizing settlement house style that reflected the feel of the Arts and Crafts movement of their time, with only a hint of the Italianate style that was popular in Chicago from the 1850s through the 1880s. The functional, people-friendly buildings they designed provided the handsome

and welcoming environment in which the multitude of programs that became HH evolved. In the early settlement years, it is highly likely that they gave their services for architectural consulting, design, and construction oversight without fee.

Between 1890 and 1908, Pond and Pond designed and directed construction of all the additional structures that became the HH social settlement compound. Among them were the Butler Building, initial Gymnasium and Coffee House (eventually moved and renovated to provide space for the HH Labor Museum), Children's Building (sometimes referred to as the Smith Building), Boiler House, Residents' Dining Hall, Music School Building, Jane Club, Coffee House and Theatre, Apartment House, Men's Club, Woman's Club Building, Boys' Club Building, Mary Crane Nursery Building, and a bridge over an alleyway to connect two groups of the buildings. In addition, as programs changed and the number of residents increased, the Ponds renovated interiors and added wings or third stories; expanded kitchen, bathroom, and boiler house facilities; and revised exterior details to blend structures created over the period of time. In the process, they created a Chicago settlement house style.

The Pond brothers and their sister, Mary Louise (1852–1907), were born in Ann Arbor, Mich., the children of Mary Barlow Allen (1826–1915) and Elihu Bartlit Pond (1826–98). Elihu Pond was a journalist who published the *Michigan Argus*, 1854–79, and served as a member of the Ann Arbor Board of Education, where he was a strong advocate for improved public education. Between 1883 and 1885, he was warden for Michigan's Jackson State Prison. The Pond children attended local schools. Irving, in 1879, with a degree in engineering, and Allen, in 1880, with an A.B. with a major in civics, graduated from the Univ. of Michigan at Ann Arbor. Both moved to Chicago and became architects, and until Allen's death they practiced together in the firm of Pond and Pond, 1886–1925, which became Pond and Pond, Martin and Lloyd, 1925–31. Irving continued to be associated with the firm of Pond and Pond and Edgar Martin from 1931 until his death in 1939.

After the Pond brothers arrived in Chicago, both studied with architects. Irving, who arrived in Chicago several years before Allen, quickly allied himself with architect William le Baron Jenney (1832–1907) and then with S. S. Beman (1853–1914), where he was head draftsman during the construction of the town of Pullman, Ill. When Allen, who had remained in Ann Arbor for three years after graduation to teach Latin and to study contract and real estate law, arrived in Chicago, he also began work with Beman to earn his credential as an architect. It was three years later that the brothers formed their Pond and Pond partnership. They were two of a number of young architects, including Frank Lloyd Wright (1867–1959), Dwight H. Perkins (1867–1941), and Walter Burley Griffin (1876–1937), whose fascination with the Arts and Crafts movement emerged in their distinctive and famous Prairie School style of architecture and helped develop the urban ambience of Chicago during the last of the nineteenth and early twentieth centuries.

It seems likely that Allen, who met JA through his activities with the Armour Mission, where he was a board member and assistant superintendent of the Sunday School, was impressed by her and excited by the settlement scheme she proposed. JA recalled of the occasion: "Mr. Pond was the one person there who responded most quickly and most understandingly. He insisted we must try other places [to present the social settlement idea], outside of churches, which at that moment were doing all the social work that was being done in Chicago" (Addams, [Tribute to Allen B. Pond], 26; *JAPM*, 48:1157). According to JA, Allen Pond "arranged the very next evening a meeting at the home of his friend, Mrs. [Lydia Avery] Coonley, on the North Side. It was there I met a number of people who became friends of the new project" (Addams, [Tribute to Allen B. Pond], 26; *JAPM*, 48:1157. See also JA to MCAL, 19 [and 20] Feb. 1889, n. 11, below). JA recalled that Allen was faithful in accompanying EGS and her throughout the city on their search for a place to locate the settlement. Once JA had decided on the old Charles J. Hull home, Allen advised JA about needed repairs and saw to them during the summer before JA and EGS moved to the house in Sept. Years later, architect

Lawrence Perkins (1907–97), as a young man a friend to both Pond brothers, indicated that "Allen Pond was believed to have been in love with Jane Addams. Nothing came of it in the way of an alliance, but they were close friends" (Blum, Interview, 131). Allen, who never married, remained a lifelong close JA ally, active at HH, and a member of the HH Assn. board of trustees.

The Pond brothers became famous for their settlement house designs in the Chicago area, including those of HH, Northwestern Univ., Gads Hill, Henry Booth, and the Chicago Commons. They also designed an assortment of other Chicago-area structures, including apartment houses; commercial buildings like the eight-story Toll Building of the Illinois Bell Telephone Co. and the ten-story Kent building, both on Franklin St.; clubs, like Chicago's City Club on Plymouth Court and the Oak Park Club; private homes; and special-use buildings like the American School of Correspondence building located at 850 East 58th St. and Lorado Taft's Midway Studio structure, in the 6000 block of South Ingleside Ave., near the Univ. of Chicago. The Ponds also had a wide practice outside of Chicago. They were responsible for the designs of a number of university buildings at Lake Forest Univ. and the student unions at the Univ. of Michigan, Michigan State Univ., the Univ. of Kansas, and Purdue. They also designed federal buildings and at least one hospital. Both brothers were active members of the Illinois Society of Architects and were also fellows of the American Institute of Architects, which Irving served as president, 1910–11. Irving K. Pond became a member of the American Academy of Arts, Letters, and Music.

Of the two brothers, Allen, known among friends as the "deep Pond," was the most active in civic matters; Irving, perhaps the more creative of the two, was more active in architectural circles. In their practice, Allen focused on settlement houses and managed their business, while Irving became their principal designer. Like his father before him, Allen was dedicated to social reform. JA believed that he "always understood what the settlement was trying to do" and focused particularly on the "ethical aspects of social affairs" (Addams, [Tribute to Allen B. Pond], 29–30; *JAPM*, 48:1161–62). JA was not alone in her assessment of the "deep Pond." The *Chicago Daily News* also found him steadfast in his commitment to "good government, and to constructive social reform." It described him as "active in organizations that had for their respective purpose the improvement of housing in cities, the development of city zoning, the emancipation of public schools for spoils politics, the education of the metropolitan and cosmopolitan communities in the principles of democracy" (19 Mar. 1929, SCPC, JAC; *JAPM*, 68:117). Among the public organizations on which Allen served as a director were the National Housing Assn., Society for Prevention of Blindness, Civil Service Reform Assn., and Municipal Voters' League, 1896–1923, of which he was a founder. He became president of the Public Education Assn. of Chicago, was a member of the education committees of both the City Club of Chicago and the Commercial Club, and served on the Chicago Joint Com. on School Affairs. During World War I, Allen was an adviser to the Illinois fuel administrator, acted as secretary of the Chicago Union League Club's war committee, and was a special distribution agent for the U.S. Com. on Public Information. Although he became involved in the affairs of each of the settlement houses for which the Ponds designed buildings, besides HH he was particularly attached to Gads Hill Social Settlement, where he was a trustee. From 1923 until 1927, he was the first chairman of Chicago's Zoning Board of Appeals. His hobby was writing prose and poetry. He was a member of the Chicago Literary Club and was the chairman of its publication committee, 1897–99, and like JA he joined Chicago's Little Room crowd.

Irving, known as the "wide Pond," gained an international reputation as an architect. He represented the U.S. government and the American Institute of Architects at the International Congress of Architects meeting in Europe in 1911. He was a member of the Illinois Board of Art Advisors, 1917–25, and during World War I, he became an examiner for the Great Lakes District of the U.S. Shipbuilding Labor Adjustment Board. Like his brother, Allen, he was a member of the Chicago Literary Club and served as its president, 1922–23. He presented twenty-six papers at the club, published numerous articles in architectural journals, and wrote art and architectural criticism and reviews for the *Dial*, an American literary magazine established in Chicago in the 1880s. He was also one of the founders of the Cliff Dwellers and served as its president, 1934–35. Of his three books, two had a circus theme: *A Day under the Big Top* (1924) and *Big Top Rhythms* (1937). According to Lawrence Perkins, Irving once said that "when he got out of college he was equally prepared, literally, to be either an architect or a circus acrobat" (Blum, Interview). After his brother's death in 1929, Irving married Katharine L. de Nancrede (1880?–1936). She had grown up in Ann Arbor, where her father, Charles B. G. de Nancrede, was professor of surgery, 1889–1904, at the Univ. of Michigan Medical School. Her sister, Edith de Nancrede (1877–1936), was a longtime HH resident associated with the development of theater at the settlement.

In addition to consulting about and designing the structures added to HH, the brothers gave their time and attention to other aspects of the settlement. For example, on 12 Mar. 1891, Irving presented an illustrated lecture at HH entitled "Architecture." A year later, his lecture, on 28 Apr. 1892, was "Artistic Expressions in Water Color." In the fall of 1891, Allen offered a series of twelve lectures on James Russell Lowell and continued in the winter and spring of 1892 with a reading party on Lowell works. When JA formed HH Assn. in 1895, Allen became one of the original board members and served as secretary of the board until his death. He was comfortable in the settlement neighborhood with its mix of immigrants, was an adviser to JA, often negotiated with Helen Culver over real estate the settlement needed for expansion, and managed details of the treasurer's work so long as JA was both president and treasurer of the board. After a six-day illness, he died of pneumonia on 17 Mar. 1929. On Sunday afternoon, 21 Apr. 1929, JA, Graham Taylor, and several other prominent Chicago friends spoke at a memorial service held for Allen Pond at the City Club of Chicago. JA recalled her long conversations with Allen Pond about municipal corruption and especially about their mutual attempt during the 1890s to unseat John Powers, their Nineteenth Ward alderman. JA indicated that they determined a need for "decent standards, how to make the politician square a little better to accepted standards of political conduct." She described Allen as someone who felt "identified with all our moral failures" and willing to make "tough judgments" and stand by them publicly (Addams, [Tribute to Allen B. Pond], 31; *JAPM*, 48:1163). A *Chicago Daily News* editorial called him an "outspoken foe of civic treason . . . , a fighter for public advancement, a leader and an organizer of sound and beneficial reform movements" (19 Mar. 1929, SCPC, JAC; *JAPM*, 68:117).

23. The work of biologist turned philosopher Herbert Spencer (1820–1903) was well known in the United States through his many publications in periodicals and books. As a contemporary of Darwin and, like Darwin, an evolutionist, he is associated with coining the phrase "survival of the fittest" and for his development of the ideas of social evolution and liberal utilitarianism. His *The Study of Sociology* was issued by chapter in serial form in the United States in *Popular Science Monthly*. It appeared May 1872 to Oct. 1874 and was then published as one of the volumes in the International Scientific Series edited by E. L. Youmans in 1874. During the late nineteenth century, Spencer was also at work on what became three volumes titled *The Principles of Sociology*, issued by subscription between 1876 and 1896. This work became part of his monumental nine-volume *A System of Synthetic Philosophy*. Many of Spencer's ideas made their way through his journal articles and through the writings of his supporters and critics into the popular press of the day.

24. Rev. Simon John McPherson (1850–1919) was born in Mumford, Monroe Co., N.Y., the son of John Finlay McPherson and Jeanette Fraser McPherson. He graduated from Princeton (1874; M.A. 1877) and Princeton Theological Seminary (1879). In 1879 he wed Lucy Bell Harmon of Danville, Ill., and the couple had three children: Jeanette, Oscar Harmon, and Elizabeth.

Rev. McPherson began his career as a Presbyterian minister at the First Presbyterian Church of East Orange, N.J., in 1879. He moved to the Second Presbyterian Church, Chicago, in Aug. 1882, where he was pastor when JA met him. In 1899 Rev. McPherson became headmaster of Lawrenceville School, N.J. Between 1883 and 1900, he served as a director of the McCormick Theological Seminary, Chicago. He was a trustee of Princeton Univ., 1897–1919.

25. 9 Feb. 1889.

26. Frederick Leslie Chapman (1864–1925) was a student at the McCormick Theological Seminary in 1889 and received his degree there in 1891. Never ordained, he chose business and religious journalism as a profession. From 1891 to 1893, he was editor of the *Interior*, a weekly denominational magazine, published under the auspices of the Presbyterian Church, and from 1893 until 1906 he was editor and publisher of the *Ram's Horn*, a weekly religious magazine, published in Chicago. At the time of his death, he was editor of the agricultural magazine *Better Farming*.

McCormick Theological Seminary, located on North Halsted St., between Belden and Fullerton avenues, was established in Chicago in 1859 as the Theological Seminary of the Northwest through a gift of one hundred thousand dollars by Cyrus H. McCormick (1809–84). After several more generous contributions from the McCormick family, the name was officially changed in 1886 to the "McCormick Theological Seminary of the Presbyterian Church." By the early 1890s, the faculty numbered eight and the students seeking preparation for the Presbyterian ministry numbered nearly two hundred.

27. 15 Feb. 1889.

28. Julia Plato Harvey (1836–1918) came to Geneva, Ill., with her father, Judge William D. Plato, in the 1840s. She went to school and grew up in Geneva, living at the corner of 4th and South streets. In 1858 she married Joel D. Harvey (1836–1911), born in Kane Co., Ill., the son of Joel and Polly Harvey, who also attended public schools in Geneva. The Harveys had three children, two of whom, Philip and Harry, were living when Julia Harvey died; William Plato died in 1917 (see JA to EGS, 4 June 1889, n. 10, below). Until 1864, when they moved to Chicago, the Harvey couple lived in Geneva, where Mr. Harvey practiced law, specializing in real estate. Between 1876 and 1885, he served under Republican presidents as the collector of internal revenue in Chicago. Between 1876 and 1883, he was a member of the Board of Counselors of the Chicago Homeopathic College. By 1890 the couple had returned to live out their lives in the Plato home place in Geneva.

Julia Plato Harvey was active in civic affairs in both Geneva and Chicago. In Geneva she organized the Village Improvement Society, supervised the planting of hundreds of elm trees on the streets of Geneva, gathered a group of women who cared for the cemeteries, and, in general, monitored the physical health of her village. Through her efforts, Geneva built a public library and became the location for the Illinois State Training School for Girls (1893).

In Chicago she became one of the twenty-one founders of the CWC and served as its treasurer, 1881–82; vice-president, 1889–90, 1893–95; and president, 1891–92. While she was chairwoman of the club's Philanthropic Dept., beginning in 1884, she helped create the Protective Agency for Women and Children, which later merged into Chicago's Legal Aid Society. She was also successful in her effort to have the city hire a night matron for the city jail, a protective measure for women prisoners. She was a member of Unity Church, Chicago, but after the Harvey family returned to Geneva they attended the Geneva Unitarian Church. Julia Plato Harvey died in Geneva, Ill., and was buried in the Oak Wood Cemetery there.

29. Catherine Courtland Walrath Benedict (1829–1907), wife of Amzi Benedict (1826–1913), who helped found Lake Forest, Ill., where the couple made their home beginning in 1865, was the mother of Enella K. Benedict (1858–1942), longtime HH resident and director of the settlement art programs, 1893–1938. The Benedicts had four other children, two of whom, Caroline F. and Sidney A., lived to maturity. The Benedicts were staunch Presbyterians. JA and EGS may have met Mrs. Benedict through Enella and her brother Sidney Benedict

when both were living in the same boardinghouse with JA and EGS at 4 Washington Place in Chicago. See also JA to MCAL, 19 [and 20] Feb. 1889, nn. 6, 41, below.

30. 8 Feb. 1889. Between 1873 and 1900, "Room 48" was located in the McCormick Block at Randolph and Dearborn streets. It had been given to the Woman's Presbyterian Board of Missions of the Northwest rent free for the life of the donor, Cyrus H. McCormick. JA had attended a gathering of the Woman's Board of the Chicago Presbyterian Society. Organized to support mission work, it met weekly on Fridays. At the meeting on 1 Feb. 1889, Harriette L. Sykes Humphrey spoke (see n. 31). The room was a gathering place for those interested in mission works. There was a large table covered with magazines containing foreign missionary intelligence. There was also a library of books about missionary work and maps showing various Presbyterian missions as well as an opportunity to meet informally with other women interested in missionary works.

31. Harriette L. Sykes Humphrey (1832–1910), noted lecturer on the Bible, was teaching a class of fifty women at the Fourth Presbyterian Church in Chicago. JA, who attended each Monday morning class, found Mrs. Humphrey "a leader of no common power and personality" (Addams, "Course: 'Divine Plan of Redemption' Fulfilled in the Old Testament"; *JAPM*, 46:455). In an article that JA wrote about the class for the *RSM*, she indicated, "It is no light thing to begin every week under such an influence [Mrs. Humphrey]. To find it shaping each days thoughts and <reading and> even determining mutual relations and ~~friendships~~ attitudes" (Addams, "Course: 'Divine Plan of Redemption' Fulfilled in the Old Testament"; *JAPM*, 46:452). JA's article was never published in the *RSM*.

Harriette Sykes was born in Dorset, Vt., and by the time she was ten years old, the family had moved to Westfield, N.Y., where her mother died. As a young girl, she became active in the Episcopal Church. There she played the organ, trained the choir, and took care of the vestments and altar. She met Presbyterian minister Zephaniah Moore Humphrey (1824–1881) while visiting a cousin at Racine, Wis. The two were wed in 1853 and spent the first fifteen years of their marriage in the Midwest. Rev. Humphrey had churches in Racine and Milwaukee, Wis., before serving as pastor of the First Presbyterian Church, Chicago, 1859–68. While in Chicago, Harriette was active in the church as the pastor's wife and enthusiastically supported the Union cause in the Civil War, wrapping bandages and advocating Lincoln's presidency. Between 1868 and 1881, Rev. Humphrey and his family moved to Philadelphia, where he was pastor of Calvary Church, 1868–75, and then to Cincinnati, where, until his death, he was professor of Ecclesiastical History and Church Polity at Lane Theological Seminary. He had served as moderator of the Presbyterian Church beginning in 1871, and Harriette and her husband were well known by leaders throughout the denomination.

After her husband's death, Harriette returned to Chicago, made her home in Lake Forest, Ill., in a house provided by friends, and sought employment. Having worked closely with her husband, especially in the preparation of his Bible classes, she had become well versed in biblical and historical studies. During her first summer at Lake Forest, she resolved to prepare a course of lectures on Old Testament history and began teaching the class in Chicago that fall. She was an outstanding speaker, and soon she was invited to lecture in Racine and Milwaukee and in New York and Philadelphia. All of her classes were for women only. By the time JA attended her class in 1889, she had also established herself as an adviser to women on all manner of issues. Her daughter Zephine Humphrey, her mother's biographer, indicated that JA sought her opinion on the placement of the social settlement and that Harriette urged her not to locate it in the worst area of Chicago. Shortly after Zephine enrolled at Smith College, in 1892, Harriette moved to Northampton, Mass., and after her daughter's graduation in 1896, she and Harriette spent two years traveling through Europe. By the early 1900s, Harriette had retired to New Haven, Conn., and kept a summer home in Dorset, Vt. She was buried beside her husband and three of their children in Graceland Cemetery, Chicago, Ill. See *PJA*, 2:534–35, n. 2.

32. Monday, 11 Feb. 1889. The Fourth Presbyterian Church, Chicago, was formed from a combination of the North and Westminster Presbyterian churches with Prof. David Swing as pastor. After the Chicago Fire of 1871, a new church was built at the corner of Rush and Superior streets. Swing remained at the helm until he withdrew in 1875, taking approximately one-third of the congregation with him. By 1889 the pastor was Rev. M. Wolsey Stryker (1851–1929), who came from Holyoke, Mass., in Apr. 1885 and remained until 1892, when he became president of Hamilton College (1892–1917). See also EGS [for JA] to Mary Houghton Starr Blaisdell [and SAAH], 23 Feb. [1889], nn. 20–21, below.

33. 18 Feb. 1889.

34. 7 Feb. 1889.

35. Industrial Art Assn. (see n. 14) held its lessons in the rooms of the CWC in the Chicago Art Institute Building (which in 1892 became the Chicago Club) at the corner of Michigan Ave. and Van Buren St.

36. At the time JA and EGS were investigating possible sites in Chicago to establish their "scheme," Dwight L. Moody (1837–99) and the Moody Church were well known. Moody had arrived in Chicago in 1856 as a salesman. He attended the Plymouth Congregational Church, where he began his mission work with young boys from the streets. By 1858 he had founded two mission schools in Chicago. Both attracted a rapidly growing group of students. He moved the largest school to the North Market Hall and eventually constructed the Illinois Street Church nearby in 1864. Both were destroyed in the Chicago Fire of 1871. Moody built a new church and school at Chicago Ave. and LaSalle St. It was called the Chicago Avenue Church. See n. 37 and also JA to MCAL, 19 [and 20] Feb. 1889, nn. 5–6; and 1 Apr. 1889, n. 23, below.

37. Rev. Charles Frederick Goss (1852–1930) was the son of Rev. Simon S. Goss and his wife, Mary C. Weaver Goss of Meridian N.Y. He was a graduate of Hamilton College (1873) and Auburn Theological Seminary (1876). From Weatherford, Tex., where he was in charge of the Presbyterian Home Mission, he became pastor of Kendall Creek Presbyterian Church in the oil fields of Pennsylvania. By 1881 he was at the Bethany Presbyterian Church in Utica, N.Y., and in Nov. 1884, after Dwight L. Moody heard him speak, he became the first permanent pastor of Moody's Chicago Avenue Church, serving from Feb. 1885 until 1890. After taking pastorates in New York City and Cincinnati, he settled in Cincinnati, wrote books on religion and Cincinnati and became an editorial writer for the *Cincinnati Enquirer*. He was married on 30 Aug. 1876 to Rosa Houghton. The couple had at least one child, Stella C. Goss.

38. Anna J. Jones Linn (1850?–95) and James C. Linn, JML's brother and his wife, who were married in 1878 in Winnebago Co., Ill., lived at 6617 Harvard St. in Englewood, Ill.

39. Laura Ely Curtis, wife of Rev. Edwin (sometimes Edward) L. Curtis, was a RFS classmate of JA. See *PJA*, 1:295, n. 12.

## To Sarah Alice Addams Haldeman

4 Washington Pl [Chicago, Ill.] Feb. 19" 1889.

My dear Alice

I was horrified this morning to find that I had never acknowledged the draft. It came safely and I am much obliged. I merited the warning in regard to spending too much money and mean to be careful.

We were right when we decided that our temptation was to give, I see it plainly all the time, & that giving may be as much a self indulgence as any thing else.

I have become very much interested in the boys of the Moody school, I have told them a story two evening as a sort of a recess to the drawing and now they clamor whenever I appear. If you are going to lend me the magic-lantern[1] for Cedarville—and I will want it for May—couldn't you send it to me here and then I would take it right home with me, & I could use it two or three times here. That is if you are not going to use it yourself, and would like to do it, I would certainly be very much obliged.

The scheme is progressing at an astonishing pace, I will send a letter to Mary and you and then have it sent to Weber I think, simply because it takes so long to write it all out so many times.

I am so glad dear, about the Trusteeship of the church[.][2] I read a bit in Browning[3] last night which it seems to me applies in a modified sense to us both,

"There's power in me & will to dominate
Which I must exercise, they hurt me else,
In many ways I need mankind's respect
Obediance &c &c"

It seems to me almost impossible to constantly repress inherited powers and tendencies & constantly try to exercise another set.

Please give my love to Harry and kisses to dear Marcet[4]—Ellen & I talk about her a great deal. Your loving & devoted Sister

Jane Addams

ALS (JAPP, DeLoach; *JAPM*, 2:1017–19).

1. This earliest form of slide projector could project images from glass slides onto a wall, fabric scrim, or screen. Some magic lanterns displayed one image at a time; some offered the possibility of stereopticon images. This piece of equipment made illustrated lectures possible and entertaining.

2. SAAH had just been named a trustee for the Presbyterian church in Girard, Kans.

3. Robert Browning's poem "Bishop Bloughram's Apology" was first issued in *Men and Women* (1885). It portrays "an individual who is motivated by conflicting impulses" (Allen, *A Critical Edition*, 1). The bishop uses spiritual values to defend his devotion to worldly values. JA quotes lines 322–24 correctly. For line 325 she should have written, "Obedience, and the love that's born of fear" (Allen, *A Critical Edition*).

4. Anna Marcet Haldeman (Julius; Haldeman-Julius) (1887–1941) was the two-year-old daughter of SAAH and HWH.

## To Mary Catherine Addams Linn

4 Washington Pl. [Chicago, Ill.] Feb. 19" [and 20] 1889

My dear Mary—

I was very glad for your kind letter[1] last week but quite alarmed that you thought I had written the article on Toynbee Hall. It was under the Editorial Contributions,[2] but I considered it quite fortunate that it appeared just now.

The ball is still rolling at a rapid pace, it certainly cannot last but we mean to make the most of it while it does. I scarcely know where I left off the account last, but I think I have not written since I saw Dr McPherson[3]—I had to go alone as Ellen's tonsilitis has hung on in the most provoking way. He was very kind and much interested, gave his approval and said we could call upon him any time for any aid we wanted, but warned us against growing "amateurish," said that the pioneers of every movement were apt to fail and their successors on the same ideas to succeed. He was a good tonic however and promised to call this week. I saw him Wednesday afternoon,[4] and in the evening we all had a very funny experiance at the Industrial School.[5] The boys are cutting out Greek vases in colored paper, and so many can't bring scissors that we borrow from every body in the house—Wednesday in spite of all our efforts at watching, three pairs were stolen, one of Miss Benedict's[6] one of mine and one of Miss Russell,[7] Mr <Goss's> assistant. Miss Russell and Ellen were angry about it and tried to find out <u>who</u>. Miss B. and I did not interfere but we all felt very uncomfortable, and had rather a see saw evening teaching <both> the Ten Commandments and Greek art.

Thursday evening[8] we were invited to a Root Concert[9] at Central Music Hall,[10] by a Mrs Coonley[11] a friend of Ellen's but the invitation came rather through a Mr Pond of the Armour mission who has been much interested in the "scheme" and who sat with us. Ellen did not dare go out, but as Mrs Coonley called for me with her carriage and brought me back I was quite comfortable alone. Miss Root went with her and I enjoyed her very much, all the Rockford people have been her pupils from poor Carrie Hood[12] to Miss St John.[13]

The concert was very pretty, about two hundred young ladies, and the last of the programe in costume. Mr Pond[14] exerted himself and certainly succeeded in being agreeable, during the evening he brought up a Mr Bailey and introduced him as being much interested in Newsboys[15]—I did not see the connection at first, until I remembered that I was playing the role of philanthropist too—I told him so, and he said "Oh that is charming that you can forget it, if you are that kind of a person I am quite ready to listen." I insisted that I would not talk until he gave me a dose of news boys <first> and altogether we had a very jolly time.

Friday[16] was a full day and I have been somewhat tired ever since. Mr Bidwell of Freeport (the senior)[17] called in the morning and had scarcely gone when

Mrs J. D. Harvey came. She knows Ellen and came to investigate me she frankly said. She is a great power in the Woman's Club in which she has held various offices. She plunged at once into the midst of things in rather an alarming way, and at the end of about half an hour asked me if I wanted to join the "Woman's Club"—I told her I should be very glad indeed if it were possible to be elected. She said that they had 360 members, too many & that they were trying to restrict it to the election of one new member a year—"I came to see you about that, I should n't wonder if you would be the one woman."[18] I said that struck me as rather improbable as I was almost a stranger in Chicago. She said "That doesn't make any difference if I want you—I am a pretty important member of that club."

We had invited Mrs McLeish (Miss Hillard of R.F.S.) and Mrs Sears another Vassar graduate to lunch on Friday with a few girls in the afternoon at three. Most of them "took great stock" [in] the scheme, two or three did n't see it or did n't care for it. Miss Alice Miller[19] a Smith graduate liked it greatly.

In the evening four young men who live in the house, took Miss Bogue[20] Miss Benedict Miss Starr and myself down to see the Russian pictures by Verestchagin[21]—They <i.e. the young men> had asked us about a week ago and they all came down to dinner in fine array.

The pictures are very fine in point of technique and filled <with> the man's great horror of war and irreligion. It seems perfectly insupportable to him that human beings should indulge in war <& the pictures> make a powerful story.

Saturday morning[22] we received a note from a Mrs Simmons[23] chairman of the Philanthropy Committee of the Woman Club, saying the members of the Committee would drink tea at her house between three and five and asking us to come and address them. Ellen declared that it was just like Mrs Harvey to make an appointment for the very next day, no time for the grass to grow under her feet. It was rather inconvenient as Ellen had invited Miss Locke,[24] the Industrial Art teacher to lunch on Sat., but we hurried her off as soon as we decently could, and reached Mrs Simmons about four—I was almost immediately requested to begin and talked for about fifteen minutes as well as I could. Some of the older ladies cried—"surprises never cease" Ellen says—and the minute I stopped there was a general discussion of pros & cons. The chairman brought them to order and said they would hear from Mrs Starrett. She is of much weight in the Club, has written books,—"Letters to Married Daughters" &c &c[.][25] I quite trembled when this dignified personage begun and thought if she wants, she can crush the whole thing at a blow. She begun by saying that her ancestors were Quakers and that occasionally she found herself back to their point of view, she believed that just now she had felt the stirring of the Spirit, she intended to follow whither it led and she advised the other ladies to meditate on the matter which had been presented. The effect was very good for us, two or three of the other ladies made appointments for us, among them a Dr Fox,[26] a physician on the South side who was greatly taken with it.

I went to a little reception at Mrs Coonley's Sat. evening, Ellen could not go out again but Mr McCormick[27]—a young man in the house—took me on his way to teachers meeting and called for me on his way back. The main feature of the evening was a story composed by a young man who read it himself. It was on the order of Frank Stockton,[28] not quite so good but entertaining.

On Sunday[29] we went to hear Dr Gunsaulus,[30] some of the Armour Mission people brought him around after service and we made an appointment with him for Wednesday at four.[31] He had heard a great deal about the plan from Mr Smith he said—Mr Smith is superintendent of the Armour Mission S.S.[32] Ellen and I have fallen into the way of calling him "the first convert," he has proclaimed us far and wide with more zeal than ourselves—I am never quite sure that he has the idea <u>exactly</u> but we are grateful to him.

I saw Mr and Mrs Bidwell[33] after church with Mrs Clark[34] whom they are visiting. She is a sister in law to Mr John A. Clark.[35] Sunday afternoon Mr Gates[36]—an old gentleman who has for years been very active in City Missionary work here—took me down into the Bohemian quarter to see the school of a Mr Adams.[37] Mr Gates had his own carriage and it took us almost an hour to reach the place even then.

Prof. Blaisdell[38] had told me of this Mr Adams whom he considers a very remarkable man. He was a Missionary in Prague for a number of years, ten I think, and when back on a furlough was so impressed with the degradation of the Bohemians here, that he works among them in Chicago just as he did before in Prague. There are 40000 Bohemians here, & 20000 within ten blocks of Mr Adams' Chapel. The Sunday School was remarkable in its way, I had a class of boys who spoke English but hearing Bohemian all around me created just as "foreign" an atmosphere as I ever felt in Europe. I made an appointment with Mr & Mrs Adams to come to their house Tuesday evening.[39] Accordingly last evening, Miss Trowbridge[,][40] Ellen and I escorted by Mr McCormick went down. Mr McCormick bemoaned at dinner that he could not afford a sleigh for the sleighing was so good. Mr Benedict[41] suggested that if we put our feet in buckets of cold water, and jingled bells the street cars would be quite the same thing. It took us a good while to get there but it was well worth the journey. Mr Adams is one of those deeply spiritual men whom one meets about once in a life time, his wife is exceedingly pleasant and they were so glad to see us for they have "few visitors from Chicago" they said.

We enjoyed the evening very much. Mr Adams was so sympathetic and so heartily approved of the idea that we came away much fortified. Mr and Mrs Bidwell asked me to lunch with them on Monday[42] at the Palmer House,[43] I enjoyed it very much. I attended Mrs Humphries Bible Class[44] in the morning. Mrs Benedict[45] had told her that I was Mrs Linn's sister. She spoke of you so kindly and sent her best love to "dear Mrs Linn". I think you will all grow tired of journalistic letters, if they are as long as this one—I like to have you know all that happens however. We realize that the first enthusiasm won't last and that we will come to the slough soon enough. We are rather humbled by the kindness of people, than "set up." Ellen is in school or would send messages.[46] Will you please send this to Alice and ask her to send it to Weber, I can't write it off so many times.

With my best love to each member of the household, Always Your loving Sister

Jane Addams.

Can you read letters written like this? If you can't I will use ink, altho this is much easier.

ALS (SCPC, JAC; *JAPM*, 2:1020–32).

1. This letter is not known to be extant.
2. The editors have been unable to identify this article.
3. See JA to MCAL, 12 Feb. 1889, n. 24, above.
4. 13 Feb. 1889.
5. JA was teaching in the Industrial School associated with the Chicago Avenue Church (Moody Church). See n. 7 and JA to MCAL, 12 Feb. 1889, n. 36, above.
6. Enella Katherine Benedict (1858–1942) was born in Chicago to Catherine Courtland Walrath and Amzi Benedict (see JA to MCAL, 12 Feb 1889, n. 29, above; and n. 41). She was later joined by four siblings: Caroline F. (Burrell) (b. 1861), Albert (1864–81), Sidney A. (b. 1867), and Katie (1870–81). By 1865 Amzi Benedict had built a new family home in Lake Forest, Ill., a community he helped found, and the family moved from their downtown Chicago home to the new northern suburb. The Benedicts were strong Presbyterians, and Enella Benedict graduated in 1878 from Ferry Hall (founded in 1869), a girls school associated with Presbyterian-founded Lake Forest Univ. She returned to teach drawing and painting there, 1882–84, 1886–88. She became a student at Chicago's Art Institute in the 1880s and received a medal for her work there in 1887. Later she studied in New York City and in Paris. Her Paris experience, ca. 1889–91, was to prove seminal for her.

She studied at the Academy of Rodolphe Julian (1839–1907), organized in 1868 as an alternative to the renown École des Beaux-Arts in Paris. Julian's school, with about six hundred students by 1890, was becoming "the outstanding private art academy in France" (Farmer, "Overcoming All Obstacles"). It was the first art school to admit women for the same curriculum of drawing and painting using nude models that was available for men, an avant-garde practice in its day. By the time that Enella Benedict arrived, the women's section of the school was located at no. 51 rue Vivienne in the 2nd arrondissement of Paris. "Unofficial and unbureaucratic," and taught primarily by painters of note, some of whom were earlier graduates of the school, it was an atelier composed of an array of students from different ethnic backgrounds who learned in a "collegial, easygoing and mutually supportive" environment where it was "customary for new ideas to be looked over without prejudice" (Russell, "Art View: An Art School That Also Taught Life"). Among Benedict's teachers were painters Benjamin Constant (1845–1902) and Jules Lefebvre (1836–1912). On her return from Europe, she became associated with the Chicago Art Institute, where she taught drawing and painting for at least thirty-five years, during which she sometimes taught art history at the University School for Girls.

It was her thirty-five-year association with HH as the creator and manager of the settlement's art programs that permitted Enella Benedict to use her Paris education to the fullest to benefit others. At HH she could replicate her Julian Academy experience that "related as much to the conduct of life as to the use of brush and chisel" (Russell, "Art View: An Art

School That Also Taught Life") and create a welcoming, secure, and open environment for all groups to explore art and beauty together. Under her guidance, art became an integral part of everyday life in the settlement and its neighborhood.

Enella Benedict and her brother Sidney may have been introduced to JA by EGS, who was already lodged at 4 Washington Place, where the two Benedicts were also living when JA arrived at the end of Jan. 1889. JA seems to have befriended the Benedict family at that time. Benedict family correspondence indicates that while Enella was in Paris, JA and Mrs. Catherine Benedict continued their friendship and that Enella was aware of the connection between what JA and EGS were doing and programs at Toynbee Hall, London. By the fall of 1893, Enella Benedict had become a HH resident. At that time, she began teaching drawing and painting at the settlement. In Lists of Residents and Fellowships, dated Nov. 1896, JA wrote that Enella Benedict had been a HH resident for four years.

The art programs at HH grew and flourished under her leadership. While classes were held initially in the Butler Art Gallery Building, when the Music School moved to its own building, the art program replaced it on the top floor of the Children's Building. There were classes in drawing, clay modeling, painting, and etching. Through the years, printmaking, linoleum block printing, and lithography as well as mechanical drawing, lettering, commercial design, and cast modeling were added. By the 1920s, there were ceramic classes, and these led to the creation of the HH Kilns begun in 1927 and resulted in the creation of the HH Shop at 619 North Michigan Ave., where HH pottery and weaving were sold. There were classes, exhibitions, lectures, demonstrations, and tours of museums as well as adult classes in life and still-life presentation, drawing with pencil and charcoal, and pastel, oil, and watercolor painting. By the mid-1920s, an ever-increasing number of children's classes were gathered administratively into a separate Art School for Children at HH, featuring drawing, cutting shapes, modeling clay, and using colors.

Enella Benedict encouraged her students to be creative, participate in city-wide as well as national juried exhibitions, and hold their own special exhibitions. They recalled her as "a warm, friendly, understanding" person, small in stature, with "a sense of real values; patience, and an utter frankness whose tang was only heightened by her tender kindness" ("Last Rites for Enella Benedict"). She also encouraged teachers from the Art Institute to join her in teaching classes at the settlement, and by the 1920s some of the HH art teachers at the settlement were her early students who wanted to participate in the program that had given them their start.

In addition to her direction of the art program and the lessons she gave at HH and at the Art Institute where she taught daily, she participated in other settlement duties and activities. She presented lectures, served as a banker for the Provident Penny Bank savings plan for children, monitored activities in the gymnasium, and sat at the front door to greet neighbors and visitors. Two favorite personal pastimes were consulting a dictionary and learning new words and reading. Among her favorite authors were George Bernard Shaw, Bertrand Russell, and Anthony Trollop. She opened a library in the HH Boys' Club and for many years spent time encouraging youngsters who used the club to read and learn. She often cooperated with resident Edith de Nancrede, who held dancing classes, and she helped develop community theater at HH, while creating scenery for theatrical productions presented by HH drama groups. In addition, she joined Miss de Nancrede and Eleanor Smith of the settlement Music School in successfully producing the settlement's admired annual Christmas tableau featuring the Christmas story of the birth of Christ.

Enella Benedict made her living from her teaching duties away from HH and from sales of her own work. "Excellent in draftsmanship, the handling of color, in portraiture, still-life and land and seascapes, Miss Benedict was no modernist in art. But when modern art was fighting for recognition, she said: 'I don't understand it, but I see no reason to poke fun at it'" ("Last Rites for Enella Benedict"). In 1893 she exhibited three paintings at the World's Columbian

Exposition in the Women's, Fine Arts, and Illinois buildings. Before 1900 she also created a portrait of JA. She regularly entered Chicago and area exhibitions with her watercolors and oils. And her subjects sometimes reveal the journeys—Europe, South America, and the United States—she took each summer to focus on her own painting. Each year when she returned, she held an exhibition and tea at HH in the fall to show her summer's work and to welcome back her HH students.

Enella Benedict created a summer retreat for herself in 1917 when, serving as her own architect and with the help of a local carpenter, she designed and had constructed a small cottage in Westport Point, Mass., where she began spending her summers to paint. She died on 6 Apr. 1942, in Richmond, Va., after contracting meningitis. HH held a memorial service 11 Apr. 1942, in the Benedict Gallery, which had been created and dedicated to her on her retirement from settlement life in 1938. She was described as having "manifested an almost uncanny breadth of knowledge . . . tolerance and liberalism . . . loyalty to friends and to principles . . . with great humility" and praised for her "honesty in art as in human relations" (Todd, "Tribute to Enella Benedict," 1). She was buried in Rose Hill Cemetery, Chicago.

7. Nellie Naomi Russell (1862–1911) was born in Ontonagon, Mich., and after the death of her widowed mother she was raised by a Rutland, Vt., physician. She graduated in 1885 from Northfield Young Ladies' Seminary, Northfield, Mass., as president of her class and the school's missionary society. Dwight L. Moody, who had founded the school in 1874, persuaded her to join the work of his Chicago Avenue Church, and she became a member there in Oct. 1885. She lived with Rev. Goss and his family at 38 Pearson St. and immediately became active in church work as a parish visitor. With Northfield classmate Lila Peabody (Cragin), she encouraged church members to attend services. She also became involved in Sunday School work and visited the poor and sick in their homes. Lila Peabody Cragin recalled: "We would select a street and call from house to house and family to family. In these calls we would ask if the children could come to Sunday school. We would give them cards telling when and where to come. In many calls the parents could not understand us, but as the children practically lived on the street and so picked up English, we would ask them to come and tell them to bring others with them" ("Letter from Mrs. Lila Peabody Cragin").

Before long Nellie Russell had a Sunday School class of 150 boys. She also organized evening classes and secured the help of young men to teach carpentry and other manual skills. When she returned from a much-needed rest in Sept. 1888, her responsibilities continued to expand. She became a leader in the church Industrial School, which had begun operation much earlier during the Civil War period. One of her projects, initiated on 1 Feb. 1889, was a dressmaking class held on Monday evenings for girls from the church or Sunday School. Wednesday evenings at the Industrial School were devoted to work with boys. This was the work that JA, EGS, and Enella Benedict had undertaken beginning in Feb. 1889.

From 18 Jan. until 18 Aug. 1890, Nellie Russell was a student at the Bible Institute of the Chicago Evangelistic Society (Moody Bible Institute) in preparation for becoming a missionary. Probably influenced by lectures given at the Chicago Avenue Church by China missionary Mary H. Porter, Nellie Russell left for China, where she worked at the North China Mission under the auspices of the Congregational American Board of Commissioners for Foreign Missions. She died in Peking, 22 Aug. 1911.

8. 14 Feb. 1889.

9. Frederic W. Root (1846–1916), son of composer of hymns and patriotic songs George Frederick Root (1820–95), and his wife, Mary Olive Woodman Root, was a well-known and -respected music teacher in Chicago. On 15 Feb. 1889, he held his sixth annual concert at the Central Music Hall, presenting his most advanced pupils as well as performances by several well-known local musicians. Like his sister, Frances Amelia Root (see EGS [for JA] to Susan Childs Starr and Caleb Allen Starr [and SAAH], 15,[16–20?] Nov. [1889], n.

12, below), he helped JA with musical programs for the settlement. He opened the 1891 fall Thursday Lectures and Concerts series at HH on 1 Oct., when he presented "A Study of Musical Taste."

10. Central Music Hall, at Randolph and State streets, contained concert and lecture rooms, stores, and offices. It was constructed in 1879 from designs by architect Dankmar Adler. The auditorium seated two thousand. It was claimed by John J. Flinn in *Chicago . . . a Guide, 1892*, prepared for visitors to the World's Columbian Exposition of 1893, that "its acoustic properties have been pronounced perfect" (120). On Sundays the auditorium became the home for the Central Church congregation presided over by Prof. David Swing, who had left the Fourth Presbyterian Church in 1874 to develop his own following (see EGS [for JA] to Mary Houghton Starr Blaisdell [and SAAH], 23 Feb. [1889], n. 20, below).

11. When JA first met her, Lydia Arms Avery Coonley (Coonley-Ward) (1845–1924) was the widow of John Clark Coonley (1838–82), whom she married 24 Dec. 1867; she had six children; and she lived at 391 (later 1127) LaSalle St. JA made one of her earliest presentations about her "scheme" in the Coonley home. See introduction to part 1, n. 29, and JA to MCAL, 12 Feb. 1889, n. 22, both above).

Lydia Avery, born in Lynchburg, Va., was educated and grew up primarily in Louisville, Ky., where her father, Benjamin Avery, started Avery Plow Works. He and her mother, Susan Look Avery—who was active in a variety of social and political reform movements—were staunch advocates for the Union cause. Lydia, following in her mother's footsteps, became a supporter of social and educational causes in Chicago. She was a valued member of the CWC, serving as president, 1895–96, and a member of the Fortnightly Club of Chicago. She was also a member of the Cordon Club, Society of Midland Authors, the Chicago Literary Club, and Authors' Club of Boston and a participant in Chicago's Little Room.

When she married geologist and natural historian Henry August Ward (1834–1906) in 1897, they settled in her recently constructed home on Lake Shore Drive at Division St., overlooking Lake Michigan. It became a haven for "both weighty discussions on philosophy and social science conducted by famous scholars and other parties conducted by the young and frivolous, recitals and exhibits by young artists, many of them gifted, all of whom she constantly encouraged, some of them with financial aid, whether they were musicians, poets, dramatists, sculptors, painters" (Addams, *The Excellent*, 115).

Lydia Avery Coonley-Ward was not only a philanthropist and club woman, but also a writer and poet. She prepared papers for presentation and publication through the various literary societies to which she belonged, and she was a contributor to the *Chicago Daily News*; the *Home and Farm*, located in Louisville, Ky.; and the *Wyoming (N.Y.) Reporter*. Her poems were issued in three volumes in 1921 as *The Melody of Life*, *The Melody of Love*, and *The Melody of Childhood*. With Alice Kellogg Tyler and Eleanor Smith, two women often identified with HH, she created *Singing Verses for Children* (1897) for which she wrote the verses.

Lydia Coonley-Ward and JA remained lifelong friends. JA visited Lydia in her summer home in Wyoming, N.Y. She was also a sometime-traveling companion for JA. She supported HH financially and participated in settlement activities, particularly giving presentations of prose and poetry for the HH Woman's Club and the Jane Club. She was especially supportive of the music program at the settlement and often opened her home to groups of settlement neighbors for special recitals on her pipe organ. Between 1891 and 1894, she gathered funds to support settlement development through JA's Ten Account program. She was a regular contributor to JA's fellowship program and to funds supporting the settlement's kindergarten and relief efforts. She and her family also contributed regularly to specific HH projects. For example, in the early 1890s, daughter Sarah gave one hundred dollars for the Crêche, fifty dollars for the Jane Club, and two hundred dollars toward furnishings for the coffeehouse and billiard room. Sons Avery, Stuart, and Howard each gave one hundred dollars toward development of the Men's Club.

Lydia Avery Coonley-Ward died in Chicago at the home of one of her children after a long illness. JA presented a eulogy at her funeral (see Addams, "Lydia Avery Coonley-Ward," in *The Excellent*, 113–20).

12. For a biographical note on Carrie Hood, see *PJA*, 1:183, n. 42; 1:344, n. 5.

13. Adele ("Addie") St. John was a voice teacher in the Conservatory of Music for RFS, 1879–93, and in 1892 presented a concert during the HH summer school at RC. She had been a student at RFS, 1876–77.

14. See JA to MCAL, 12 Feb. 1889, n. 22, above.

15. Edward P. Bailey (1841–1925) was a board member and auditor for the Newsboys' and Bootblacks' Home located at 1418 Wabash Ave. The home began as the Chicago Industrial School in 1867. Its goal was to "assist helpless street children in Chicago" (Flinn, *Chicago . . . a Guide, 1892*, 187). It offered temporary shelter, four nights of classes to help prepare them for jobs, and assistance in locating a permanent home and employment.

Bailey, who was born in Almont, Mich., and educated there, and also in Joliet, Ill., and at Bryant and Stratton Commercial College, Chicago, held a number of positions, including clerk, bank cashier, and bookkeeper in a Knoxville, Tenn., bank before coming to Chicago in 1882 to manage the Chicago Malleable Iron works. In 1911 he became vice-president of the Chicago Trust Co. He served on several boards of directors and became president of the Young Men's Christian Assn. (YMCA) in Chicago in addition to his work with the newsboys. He was a Republican and active in the Episcopal Church, especially in its laymen's missionary movement. He had two children by his first wife, Katherine Baxter (m. 1866), and four children with his second wife, Minerva Spruance (m. 1889).

16. 15 Feb. 1889.

17. Orlando B. Bidwell (1830?–1909) was a banker and businessman from Freeport, Ill. In 1864 he helped found the First National Bank of Freeport (competitor with JHA's Second National Bank, Freeport) and served as a director until he became president in 1870, a position he held until his death. Bidwell, who had been in the wholesale rations and the lumber business, also served as a director of the Freeport Light and Fuse Co. and as treasurer of the Freeport Water Co. The Bidwell family, including Candace A. Bidwell (1829–65) and her children, one of whom was Orlando Bidwell Jr., and Orlando Bidwell's second wife, Margaret (1838–1926), and her children, were acquaintances of the Addams family.

18. About JA and EGS joining the CWC, see JA to MCAL, 12 Feb. 1889, n. 15, above. In 1889 Julia Plato Harvey, founding and life member of the CWC, was vice-president of the club. See also JA to MCAL, 12 Feb. 1889, n. 28, above.

19. Alice Mason Miller (Whitman) (1862?–1932) was the daughter of Henry G. Miller (1824–99) and Sarah Caroline Mason Miller (1833–1917), eldest daughter of the Roswell B. Masons of Chicago. Miller was an attorney who arrived in Chicago to practice law in 1851 and wed the Mason daughter in 1857. The Millers lived next door to the Masons on Delaware Place. They had three children: Harriet Hopkins (1858–60), Helen Lyman (1859–1900), and Alice Mason.

Alice Mason Miller, a student in the Collegiate Dept. of Dearborn Seminary in Chicago, graduated from Smith College in 1883. After graduation she taught at Miss Rice's School for Girls and worked in the "Little Hell" area of Chicago north of Goose Island, where she met Russell Whitman (1861–1945), whom she married in Apr. 1893. Whitman, who was an attorney and dedicated to civil service reform, had started a boys' club in this neighborhood on Larrabee St. near the Chicago River. There Alice played checkers with the boys and helped run their theatricals. She was an active member of the Chicago Branch of the Assn. of Collegiate Alumnae to whom JA gave a speech in 1889–90 about the HH idea (see Article in the *Chicago Inter Ocean*, 30 June 1892, n. 2, below).

She also quickly became a mainstay in the HH operation. Always a volunteer and not a resident, she taught in the extension program beginning in 1890, and by 1892 she was directing the settlement's College Extension Program, responsible for its organization and program offerings and for collecting fees. Her subjects were political economy, 1890–92; Latin, 1890–92; conducting reading parties, 1890–93; and American history, 1890. She taught botany in the 1892 settlement summer school at RC. She also supported HH financially by donating through the HH Ten Account program initiated by JA in the first year of the settlement. Alice Mason's article about HH, with particular emphasis on the first year of the College Extension Program, appeared in the second number of vol. 1 of *Charities Review* (Feb. 1892): 167–73 (see *JAPM*, Addendum 10:6ff).

In Mason Trowbridge's *Family Annals*, Russell Whitman observed that when Alice finally accepted his proposal of marriage, "Louis Greeley said, 'I'm glad to hear of this engagement. It will stop all this talk as to what tangible results we get out of the work in Little Hell and Hull House.'" The couple, who lived in Evanston, Ill., had four children, and Alice Whitman gave a great deal of her time to the Parent Teacher Assn. (PTA). The Whitmans were Unitarians.

20. Likely Sophia Rogers Bogue (1866–1930), who wed physician Oliver Nixon Huff of Fountain City, Ind., in 1892. She was the daughter of Dr. Roswell Griswold Bogue and his wife, Lucy Tucker Durfee Bogue (see JA to MCAL, 12 Feb. 1889, n. 3, above). In 1889 the Bogue family, including another daughter Lucy Durfee Bogue (1870–1953), lived at 5 Washington Place, near JA and EGS's rooming house at 4 Washington Place. Daughter Lucy, who sang at HH on 10 Jan. 1890, became a musician and personal friend of Mr. and Mrs. Thomas Alva Edison.

Dr. Bogue, born in Louisville, N.Y., and educated in Vermont and New York City, had come to Chicago in 1852. He was one of the founders of Cook County Hospital and the first professor of surgery at what became the Woman's Medical School at Northwestern Univ. His medical career was cut short by the onset of blindness in 1883. Mrs. Bogue was the daughter of Chicago's first harbormaster, Sydney S. Durfee, and his wife, Sophia Rogers Durfee, who came to the city in 1845.

21. Vassili Vasilievich Verestchagin (1842–1904) was a Russian soldier and artist. His exhibit at the Chicago Art Institute caused quite a stir when it opened on Friday, 1 Feb. 1889. The *Chicago Daily Tribune* described the exhibit as composed of "huge scenic compositions whose moral purpose is to make repellent brutishness, whether in war, or of social relations, or of marked sentiment; great landscapes which interpret the Hellenic spirit of art as applied to nature; architectural themes, Oriental and religious; and Oriental types of the human race" (3 Feb. 1889). Almost two weeks later, on 12 Feb. 1889, the newspaper reported that vast crowds attended the exhibit. In addition to the artwork presented in galleries decorated with draperies, there was a Russian pianist who played a classical repertoire while the exhibit was open and tea served to viewers, who were welcomed to the exhibit by costumed greeters.

22. 16 Feb. 1889.

23. Hattie Northam Bush Simmons (1856?–1931) was born in Martinsburg, N.Y. Her parents were James and Carolyn L. Hills Bush. She joined the CWC in Apr. 1885 and became a director in 1889–90 and second vice-president, 1903–4. She was a member of a Woman's City Club committee to investigate tenement conditions in the Italian neighborhood west of LaSalle St. in the summer of 1917. In the late 1880s, she was secretary of the Industrial Art Assn. and active in its work. She became a member of Chicago's Fortnightly Club in 1911. Her husband, Francis Tolles Simmons (1855–1920), whom she wed in 1883, came to Chicago in 1881 and became an importer of kid gloves and the secretary-treasurer of the Francis T. Simmons Co., as well as a director in William H. Bush and Co. A Republican and a Presbyterian, he served as a Lincoln Park commissioner, 1901–14, 1917–20, and was associated with the Civic Federation of Chicago in the mid-1890s. In 1889 Mr. and Mrs. Simmons lived at 584 (later 1510–1512) Dearborn Ave.

24. Josephine Carson Locke (1851–1919) was born in Ireland. She was a graduate of the Boston Normal Art School. Before she came to Chicago, she taught art in Boston schools and

was the supervisor of drawing in St. Louis, Mo., schools, 1882–87. By 1890 she was teaching drawing and methods of art in the Cook County Normal School, and between 1890 and 1900 she successfully led a revolution in methods of teaching art to public school children. "She displaced the formal drill exercises which had characterized courses in Art instruction in this country up to that time, substituting free experience and creative exercises in color, mass drawing, free cutting, figure drawing, illustration, design and applied design, and encouraging participation of pupils in class discussion of results" (Silke, "Josephine-Carson-Locke," 1). She was particularly devoted to bringing her ideas into the kindergarten and lower primary grade class rooms. In support of beautiful classrooms, she, along with EGS and others, helped start the Chicago Public School Art Society and personally contributed the first loan collection of foreign photographs. She was also instrumental in opening the Chicago Art Institute galleries to children and their teachers free of charge. She presented lectures on form, color, and clay modeling at the Chicago Free Kindergarten Assn., 1891–92, and also at the Ethical Humanist Society in Chicago. During the World's Congress of Representative Women, 15–22 May 1893, she participated in the session on moral and social reform. She traveled throughout the world exploring art and died in Los Angeles.

25. JA was probably referring to Helen Starrett's *Letters to a Daughter* (1882). *Letters to Elder Daughters, Married and Unmarried* was not issued until 1892. Helen Ekin Starrett (1840–1920), educator, journalist, speaker, and author, was born in Allegheny Co., Pa., to Rev. John and Esther Fell (Lee) Ekin. After graduating from high school in Pittsburgh, she wed Rev. William Aiken Starrett of Fayette Co., Pa. (1864). Member of the CWC and the Fortnightly Club of Chicago, she founded the Kenwood School for Girls Institute in 1884, and from 1893 until 1915, when she became principal emeritus, she was principal of Mrs. Starrett's Classical School for Girls.

In 1879 she moved the *Western Magazine*, which she was editing, from Omaha, Nebr., to Chicago, and in 1882 it took over the *Alliance*, an undenominational religious journal begun by David Swing in 1873. The merger of these two journals, edited by Mrs. Starrett and named the *Weekly Magazine*, had to cease publication for lack of funding after two years.

The author of numerous magazine articles, she also wrote a number of books, including *Future of Educated Women* (1880), *After College: What? For Girls* (1885), *The Future of Our Daughters, and Other Essays* (1909), and *Little Book of Good Manners in Home and School* (1919). She died in Portland, Oreg.

26. Perhaps Dr. Harriet Magee Fox (1848?–1911), a homeopathic physician born at Meadville, Pa. After graduating from Hillsdale College, Hillsdale, Mich., she enrolled in Hahnemann Medical College, Chicago, where she received her M.D. (1873?). Before her marriage to Bonham H. Fox in 1874, she established a free dispensary at the Railroad Mission sponsored by the First Presbyterian Church, Chicago. In 1892 she was treasurer of Unity Industrial School and Day Nursery, 80 Elm St., near Halsted St. on Chicago's North Side. Although she retired from practice in 1900, she remained active in civic, political, and professional organizations, including the Women's Physiological Institute, the Chicago Medical Woman's Club, and the CWC. An ardent suffragist, she took strong positions on the independence of women. In 1894 she successfully promoted two African American women for membership in Chicago's Women's Republican Club of the Fourth Ward.

27. Alexander Agnew McCormick (1863–1925), journalist and Chicago political leader, was born in Philadelphia and educated in public schools. While still in Philadelphia, and at the age of seventeen, he listed his occupation as salesman. When JA first met him, he was employed by A. C. McClurg and Co., in Chicago, 1888–95. He was general manager for the *Chicago Evening Post* and *Times-Herald* newspapers until 1901, when he became associated with the *Chicago Record Herald*. By 1904 he had become editor and publisher of the *Chicago Evening Post*. From 1906 until 1909, he published Indiana newspapers, including the *Indianapolis Star*. Active in politics, McCormick was president of the Cook County Board of Commissioners,

1912–14, and alderman of the Sixth Ward of Chicago, 1915–21. He was a leader in the Sunset Club of Chicago in 1892 when JA spoke there and served as president of the Civil Service Reform Assn. He was vice-president of the American Newspaper Publishers' Assn., 1903–4.

McCormick was an early supporter of JA and her settlement idea. He began participating in settlement activities in Dec. 1889. He joined JA making calls on HH neighbors, and on 6 Dec. JA recorded in her 1889–90 diary that "Mr. McCormick took me to musicale" (*JAPM*, 29:117). Into the fall of 1890, he was a frequent dinner guest at the settlement and helped with boys' clubs. Beginning in Jan. 1891, he was a member of the executive committee of the Working People's Social Science Club, in 1892 led a reading party on John Fisk's *The American Revolution* (2 vols., 1891), and helped organize the settlement congress that met during the World's Columbian Exposition in Chicago in 1893. He also raised money from friends to support HH programs. Surviving HH financial records indicate that McCormick raised or gave approximately one hundred dollars each year for general use of the settlement. By 1898 he had increased his giving to two hundred dollars a year, which he sustained through 1900. He also gave, when he could, to the settlement's relief and Christmas funds.

In June 1895, McCormick wed Maud I. Warner (1867–1945), who was also a settlement volunteer. She was one of five children of wholesale grocer Ezra Joseph Warner and his wife, Jane E. Remsen Warner, who lived in the Chicago area (see JA to SAAH, 28 Dec. 1894, n. 6, below). The McCormicks had three children. Their first child, Ezra Warner McCormick, died an infant in Aug. 1896. Their second son, Alexander, was born in Dec. 1897 and died in France during World War I. Their daughter, who became Mrs. Justin Sturm, survived them.

At HH Maud Warner supported the creation of the Jane Club with gifts that totaled at least seventy dollars and helped with a variety of children's and young people's clubs. In the spring of 1895, she was responsible for the Longfellow Debating Club, which met on Wednesday afternoons at four. The McCormicks also supported the Juvenile Protective Assn. (JPA) headquartered at HH. In 1938 Maud McCormick's brother Harold Warner (1880–1938) left ten thousand dollars in his estate to the HH Fresh-Air Fund and the same amount to the JPA.

28. Frank R. Stockton (1834–1902) was an American writer of mostly humorous fiction, "The Lady or the Tiger?" (short story, 1882), *Rudder Grange* (1879), and *The Rudder Grangers Abroad* (1884), among others.

29. 17 Feb 1889.

30. Frank Wakeley Gunsaulus (1856–1921), who became for Chicago what Phillips Brooks was in Boston or Henry Ward Beecher in Brooklyn, had been in Chicago as pastor of the Plymouth Congregational Church only two years when JA and EGS sought him out. Already he had attained a position as a religious and civic leader in the city, and his stature would only continue to grow. Gunsaulus was born in Chesterville, Ohio; attended public schools; received an A.B. from Ohio Wesleyan Univ.; was ordained a Methodist minister; and began preaching in Ohio. In 1879 he entered the Congregational ministry. He served in churches in Ohio and Massachusetts before becoming pastor of the Brown Memorial Presbyterian Church of Baltimore, 1885–87 (JA was in Baltimore during the winters of 1885–86 and 1886–87; though she might have made his acquaintance then, there is no evidence that she did). He served at the Plymouth Congregational Church in Chicago until 1899, when he became a preacher at the Independent Central Church also in Chicago, where he remained for the next twenty years.

Noted as a preacher and lecturer (he spoke at HH on Savonarola, 30 Oct. 1894), he collected art and rare manuscripts and books. He was a poet and prolific writer. Gunsaulus became president of the Armour Institute of Technology in Chicago (1893), serving in that capacity until his death (see also JA to EGS, 24 Jan. 1889, n. 7, above).

31. 20 Feb. 1889.

32. Edwin Burritt Smith (see JA to MCAL, 12 Feb. 1889, n. 16, above). See also JA to EGS, 24 Jan. 1889, nn. 6–7, above.

33. Likely either Mr. and Mrs. Orlando B. Bidwell (see n. 17) or their son Addison Bidwell (1854–1945), cashier of the First National Bank of Freeport, and his wife, Ada (1875–1904).

34. Elizabeth Keep Clark (1849–1934) was born in Hartford, Ohio. She married George Mark Clark (1841–1924), manufacturer of stoves and appliances, who became chairman of the board of the American Stove Co., at Oberlin, Ohio, 18 June 1872, and they settled at 401 (later 1228) North State St., where JA first met Mrs. Clark. The Clarks had two children: Alice Keep and Robert Keep. In 1888 Mrs. Clark became a member of the CWC and served in its Reform Dept. She and her husband were active members of the New England Congregational Church. The family eventually lived in Glencoe and Evanston, Ill.

35. John A. Clark (1814–81) was well known to JA and SAAH. A young attorney, he had come from Galena, Ill., to construct the first wooden bridge over the Pecatonica River at Freeport (1840) and to help JHA bring the railroad through Stephenson County at Freeport. He served twelve years as Stephenson Co.'s clerk of the circuit court beginning in 1839 and during the 1840s was also county recorder. He also served two terms as alderman of Freeport (1855–59) and was surveyor general of Utah and New Mexico in Abraham Lincoln's administration. His father, Democratic Republican Robert Clark (1777–1837), was a member of the U.S. Congress from New York, 1819–21. With his wife, Anna Jane Kyle Clark (1818–1900), John Clark had at least seven children, four of whom died in their youth.

36. Frederick Taylor Gates (1853–1929), Baptist clergyman and executive in philanthropic endeavors, was newly arrived in Chicago with his second wife, Emma Lucile Cahoon Gates of Racine, Wis. Gates had been born in Maine, N.Y., and had graduated from the Univ. of Rochester (1877) and the Rochester Theological Seminary (1881). After serving as pastor of Central Church, Minneapolis, he began successfully raising endowment for the Pillsbury Academy there.

With the organization of the American Baptist Education Society in 1888, he became its corresponding secretary in Chicago. In this capacity, he made a thorough study of Baptist educational interests throughout the country and determined there was a need for a Baptist institution of higher education in Chicago (the old Univ. of Chicago had expired in 1886). Thomas W. Goodspeed, William R. Harper, and others were of like mind and had interested John D. Rockefeller in the project. Gates secured the endorsement of the Education Society for this enterprise and did much to forward the movement for the university among Baptists.

Rockefeller was also much impressed by Gates's accomplishments, and beginning in 1893 Gates became a guiding force in many Rockefeller projects, such as iron-ore mining in Minnesota. Gates was a trustee of the Univ. of Chicago but later went to New York City to assist Rockefeller with his benevolent causes. He became a trustee and the longtime president of the General Education Board, the first of the Rockefeller foundations, which was set up to support colleges and universities throughout the United States, without regard to creed, race, or nationality. Gates had a strong commitment to medical education, especially the causes and prevention of diseases. He conceived the idea of the Rockefeller Institution for Medical Research, and from its inception he was president of its board of trustees.

37. Edwin Augustus Adams (1837–1927), Congregational clergyman and missionary, was born in Franklin, Mass., to Newell and Abigale Fales (Blake) Adams. After graduating from Amherst (A.B. 1861), attending Union Theological Seminary (1864–65), and graduating from Andover Theological Seminary (1868), he was ordained and became pastor at the North Manchester, Conn., Congregational Church, 1868–72, and served as American Board of Commissioners of Foreign Missions missionary to Prague, Bohemia, 1873–82. He returned to the United States to become pastor of the Northboro, Mass., Congregational Church, 1882–84. Called by the Chicago City Missionary Society of the Congregational Church, he became head of the Bohemian mission, 1884–1907, and Bethlehem Church (Bohemia), in Chicago, 1888–1907.

In May 1866, he wed Caroline Amelia Plimpton (1842–1929), and the couple had at least four children, all of whom became educators. Miss Plimpton was born in Walpole, Mass., and educated to become a teacher at Worcester and Abbott Female Seminary, Andover, Mass. She helped her husband in his Prague mission and at their Chicago mission was responsible for developing and guiding the industrial school, which by 1897 had 250 male and female students. "Girls learned 'cleanliness, obedience, ladylike behavior, as well as sewing.'" Boys and girls learned English (D. Smith, *Community Renewal Society*, 25). When JA visited the mission, there were one hundred children in the kindergarten in cramped quarters on South Throop St. Later in 1889, the new mission church building, begun in 1888, was opened at 710 (later 1852) South Loomis Ave. By 1902 the Sunday School had a regular attendance of six to seven hundred children.

The Adams couple retired from the mission in 1907 and returned to Walpole, Mass., where they died.

38. Rev. James Joshua Blaisdell of Beloit, Wis., helped JA with Greek while she was a student at RFS. See *PJA*, 1:185, n. 46.

39. 19 Feb. 1889.

40. Harriet Hopkins Trowbridge (1867–93) was the daughter of Presbyterian minister James Hewit Trowbridge (1820–87) and his second wife, Alice Lindsley Mason Trowbridge (1837–1912), the daughter of former Chicago mayor Roswell B. Mason and his wife, Harriet (see EGS [for JA] to Mary Houghton Starr Blaisdell [and SAAH], 23 Feb. [1889], n. 22, below). She attended Chicago's Dearborn Seminary. When JA and EGS were founding HH, Harriet Trowbridge was living with her widowed mother in the home of her Mason grandparents at 27 (later 8 West) Delaware Place in Chicago. Perhaps it is not surprising that she became an early volunteer at HH. Her grandparents the Masons, who had been friends of JHA, were supportive of the HH experiment. In addition, it is likely that she had become a friend of EGS. Harriet Trowbridge taught at Miss Kirkland's School for Girls as early as 1887–88 and may have known EGS before EGS and JA left to travel in Europe in 1887–88.

That first year of the settlement, Harriet Trowbridge spent most Friday evenings with JA and EGS, helping to entertain the young women and working girls who came to socialize after work. By 1891 she was assisting with the boys' clubs that were being formed. She was the leader of the Jolly Boys' Club, which met on Tuesday from 3:30 to 5:00 P.M. in the HH dining room to hear Roland stories. It was Miss Trowbridge to whom JA was referring when she wrote that "the young girl who organized our first really successful club of boys, holding their fascinated interest by the old chivalric tales set forth so dramatically and vividly that checkers and jackstraws were abandoned by all the other clubs on Boys' Day, that their members might form a listening fringe to 'The Young Heroes'" (Addams, *Twenty Years*, 103–4). During the second HH Summer School at RC held in 1892, Harriet Trowbridge taught botany and then traveled to Plymouth, Mass., with JA to participate in the Applied Ethics summer program and hear JA deliver two addresses on settlement work. She supported the settlement financially by giving through JA's Ten Accounts. Harriet Trowbridge died in 1893 at the age of twenty-six.

41. Probably Enella Benedict's father, Amzi Benedict, who had come to Chicago in 1849 and formed a partnership with Benjamin M. Field in the wholesale woolen dry-goods business as Field, Benedict, and Co. See also JA to MCAL, 12 Feb. 1889, nn. 6, 29, above.

42. 18 Feb. 1889.

43. The elegant Palmer House Hotel was almost completed at the direction of businessman, entrepreneur, and social and cultural leader Potter Palmer shortly before the Great Chicago Fire of 1871 in which it was destroyed. Not deterred, Palmer rebuilt the structure on the same site in 1873. Flinn's *Chicago . . . a Guide, 1892* pronounced its dining room "one of the most elegant in Chicago" and its "furnishings and fittings . . . of the first order. . . . The Palmer House is itself one of the most imposing and beautiful structures in the city" (356). The Palmer House was located at State and Monroe streets in the heart of downtown Chicago and could accommodate twenty-four hundred guests.

44. See JA to MCAL, 12 Feb. 1889, above.
45. Enella Benedict's mother, Catherine C. Benedict.
46. EGS was still teaching at Miss Kirkland's School for Girls, Chicago.

## Ellen Gates Starr [for Jane Addams] to Mary Houghton Starr Blaisdell [and Sarah Alice Addams Haldeman]

*In this seminal letter to her sister Mary Blaisdell,[1] Ellen Gates Starr described the settlement scheme that became Hull-House. It stands as the most succinct and timely explanation of what the founders hoped to do. Jane Addams may have believed that Starr's discourse on the subject was superior to anything that she herself had time to write, for there is no extant letter from Jane Addams to any of her family describing what it was that she was planning. The fact that Jane Addams asked Starr to have Blaisdell forward the letter to her three siblings seems also an indication that she approved of Starr's explanation.*

*Following Ellen Gates Starr's instructions, Mary Blaisdell must have started the letter on its way to Mary Catherine Addams Linn, John Weber Addams, and Alice Addams Haldeman. Thus, it became a circular letter similar to those that Jane Addams had written to her family during her recent European trips.[2] And like many of those letters, the original letter that Starr wrote is no longer extant. The text of the letter survived because Alice Addams Haldeman copied it into a notebook, much as she had the European circular letters. Perhaps she planned to keep a diary-like record of the progress of the "scheme."[3] The notebook in which this letter was copied contained only this letter. It was saved and given to Ellen Gates Starr.*

4. Washington Place. [Chicago, Ill.] Feb. 23rd [1889]

Dear Mary—

The thermometer is 7 degrees below zero and we have decided to stay indoors this morning. I will take part of the time to begin an account of "the scheme."

Jane intends to take a house or flat in some district which we shall determine upon with the aid of various wise persons. We are going on Wed.[4] with Dr. Gunsaulus[5] to look at one.

We should like to have it in a neighborhood where there are a good many Germans & French immigrants so as to utilize the French & German which girls learn in school & have little or no opportunity to practice. There are thousands of Italians in the city who have no mission & "No Nothin." to raise them out of their degradation & Jane leans decidedly to them; but she seems to think that Chicago is swimming in girls who speak Italian fluently, which I happen to know is not the case: whereas there are a great many girls who speak French & German.[6]

Jane also thirsts very much for the Anarchists.[7] She is going to hunt up their Sunday Schools[8] (Perhaps you dont know that there are a good many Anarchist Sunday Schools) & get a chance to teach in one if she can.

Bien![9] "We" take a house i.e. Jane takes it & furnishes it prettily. She has a good deal of furniture & she intends to spend several hundred dollars on some more & of course we put all our pictures and 'stuff' into it. Then we shall both live there naturallement & I shall make an offer to Miss. K.[10] to teach from 9:30 to 12 or some such matter. I shall try to get $5[.]00 for it & if I can <only> get $4.50 it will still be as much as I have after paying board & of course I shall have no board to pay.[11] Jane can afford after furnishing the house to expend $100.00 a month & we think by economy we can run the house on that.[12] We shall need one large room in which to have classes, lectures or whatever we may wish, & to receive people—our friends from civilization who may think us worth travelling the distance to see and our friends from the surrounding neighborhood. We shall make this as pretty as we can. Then besides our own bedroom we shall have several others with little single beds; and we desire and hope that certain young ladies will from time to time wish to come & abide with us for a season, longer or shorter as they feel disposed. If they wish to come in the day time and not stay over night, very well. But after we have been there long enough & people see that we don't catch diseases, & that vicious people do not destroy us or our property, we think we have well founded reason to believe that there are at least half a dozen girls in the city who will be glad to come & stay for a while & learn to know the people & understand them and their ways of life; to give them what they have to give out of their culture and leisure & over indulgence, & to receive the culture that comes of self denial and poverty & failure, which these people have always known. There is to be no <"organization" &> no "institution" about it. The world is overstocked with institutions and organizations; & after all, a personality is the only thing that ever touches anybody.

I pity girls so! especially rich girls who have nothing in the world to do. People get up in church & in missionary meetings & tell them about the suffering in the world & the need of relieving it, all of which they knew & it ends in their giving some money, which isn't theirs as they never earned it; & all their emotion over it & their restlessness to do something, has to end in that. Nobody ever shows them a place & says "Here <u>do</u> <u>this</u>" I <u>know</u> that girls <u>want</u> to do—I have talked with enough of them, poor little things! They are sick & tired of society, simply because as Hattie[13] said last night "Its a man's recreation, but its a womans business." If ever the ordinary girl expresses any wish to <u>do</u> anything for her less fortunate sisters her mother throws cold water on it probably says "O, my dear, I dont think it is laid upon you to put the world to rights" and then she shrivels up, & feels that she is of no use whatever, & that it was of course very foolish & presuming in her to think she could do anything.

Of course we perfectly well understand that the mothers will throw cold water on them when they wish to come to us; but a girl can tease pretty efficiently when she really wants to do a definite thing; & when they are assured of its being safe, they will probably consent, at least a few will. London is full of such things, I think the English are more Christian in spirit then we are, I wonder how many young men would be found in America to found a Toynbee Hall;[14] I do believe, however, that there are enough young women.

Jane's idea which she puts very much to the front & on no account will give up is that it is more for the <benefit of the> people who do it, than for the other class. She has worked that out of her own experience & ill health. She discovered, when recovering from her spinal trouble,[15] that she could take care of children actually lift them, & not feel worn, but better for being with them; while an effort to see people & be "up to things" used her up completely.

Then she made the discovery a second time in Baltimore among the old colored people.[16] After a lecture or social evening she would be quite exhausted & have to stay in bed, but after a morning with the colored people in the Johns Hopkins home, she was actually physically better than if she had stayed in bed & been rubbed.[17]

Nervous people do <u>not</u> crave rest, but activity of a certain kind. Doctors are taking to this wonderfully as we thought they would. They see the point & believe in it. I had no idea in my most sanguine moments, that people were going to take it up as they do. The truth is the thing is in the air. People are coming to the conclusion that if anything is to be done toward tearing down these walls—half imaginary between classes, that are making anarchists & strikers the order of the day, it must be done by actual contact & done voluntarily from the top. One thing more comes up, but a dozen like it spring up likewise. A printed letter has just reached us from a Smith College graduate who is doing practically the same thing in New York;[18] only hers is to be confined to college women & is to be an organization, which ours distinctly is not; & then I think she is less Christian than Jane is. Jane feels that it is not the Christian spirit to go among these people as if you were bringing them a great boon; that one gets as much as she gives. The Toynbee Hall men you know, quite repudiate the idea that they are making any sacrifice. They go in with their different occupations & simply live there. They get elected on the school boards, & improve the condition of things as citizens. They dont invite Tom, Dick and Harry indiscriminately there but associate with the men down there that they like, as they would at the West End,[19] and they say that they find "good fellows" with gentlemanly instincts there as elsewhere[.]

Of course the thing spreads[.] Its an influence. We dont wish the girls who come to us to feel that they are doing anything queer & extraordinary; turning themselves into sisters giving up the world or society or <cutting> themselves off from the things of the flesh or any such sentimental nonsense. We dont intend to. Of course it will be inconvenient on account of distances & will take

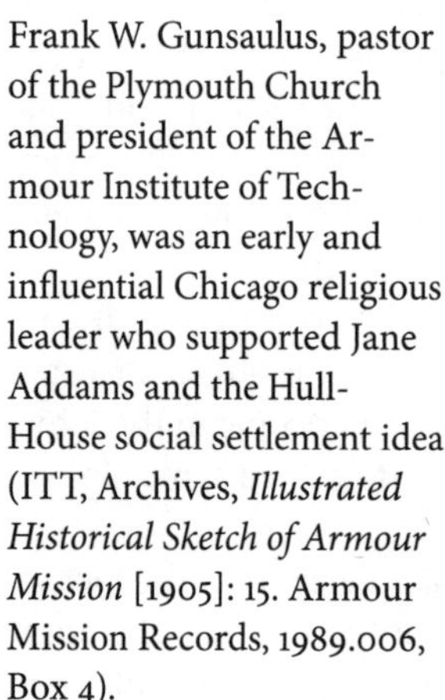

Frank W. Gunsaulus, pastor of the Plymouth Church and president of the Armour Institute of Technology, was an early and influential Chicago religious leader who supported Jane Addams and the Hull-House social settlement idea (ITT, Archives, *Illustrated Historical Sketch of Armour Mission* [1905]: 15. Armour Mission Records, 1989.006, Box 4).

a good deal of carriage hire, but it will certainly be worth that sacrifice, if we at all do what we wish. We shall go to our friends & expect them to come to us. Even the novelty will attract them, I think, & I dont mind banking on that a little; anything to get them & their interest.

We have a splendid background already[.] Dr Gunsaulus is the most popular minister in the city with the exception of Prof Swing,[20] & he is fast rivaling him & Dr. G. is unqualified & enthusiastic in his adherence[.] We had a charming conversation with him in his study. He is a brilliant man & he simply pointed out one bright thing after another. He was very clever in the way he went to work to find out what our idea was & not help us to one, or give his color to it. For instance he said "Then your idea would be perhaps to have a little training school where young ladies could be instructed how to deal with the poor" & he said it as if he thought nothing would be nicer than such a little training school. When we quite repudiated it & said we would have naught of a training school or any "institution" whatever; that we were tired of institutions; that Miss Addams & Miss Starr simply intended to live there & get acquainted with the people & ask their friends of both classes to visit them he was "tickled to death[.]" He said "good! The kingdom of heaven isnt an organization or an institution!" He was very amusing. He remarked that there were two classes to be avoided "One is made up of saintly drivellers, who go out harpooning for souls, to lug in as many as possible. For my part if I saw a man riding around me lassooing for my soul I should say 'see here; I'm looking out for this bussiness[.] Be so good as to take yourself off!' Then the other class was composed of good gentlemen who buttoned up their coats & formed a committee & met & wrote out by laws, & organized, & got money & spent a great deal of it on the organization &c &c &c.["] And Dr Gunsaulus says he's had enough of that & that as soon as there are a lot more wheels to be carted in & set up he doesn't want any thing further to do with it; but that if we want to go to the thing & do it, we may command him without limit & he knows one very wealthy girl, heiress to a million, who, he is sure will be one of our assistants from the first. She wont join an organization & she wont join an abstraction but the moment we show her definite work & ask her personal assistance she will be ready to give it. Of course our great advantage lies in not being obliged to begin by asking for money. When the thing is once under way, & we have our home & our people & want money for a lecture, or a stereoptican or a piano or some such thing, I think Dr Gunsaulus or Mr. Striker[21] of the Fourth Presbyterian (whom we met last night & Mrs Trowbridges[22] & who also gave us his hearty approval & promise of any assistance in his power[)] will get it for us. Dont you see? When we had been with Dr Gunsaulus half an hour or more, I said "Dr G we are taking a good deal of your time I'm afraid we ought to go[.]" O, my no! he exclaimed, in a tone of positive alarm. "Im in no condition to be left!" Dr G. is our strongest man yet though Dr Striker assures us that he will try to do as much for us, if we will locate on this side as the South side men can. The Armour Mission men fairly clamor for it there but I am very much against that, & Jane says she is too, & so are Dr G & Mr Striker. We should simply be swallowed in a great organization

We want now to see Prof Swing as soon as possible. I am sure he will take to it. We see Dr G. on Wed. He is to take us to a German locality & I am going to ask him if he knows Prof Swing & get him to work him up a little for us first[.] Mrs Dow[23] is going to have us meet Mr Salter,[24] the ethical culture man who is much interested in this question so you see we have a good many strings to the bow already. Dr Bedell[25] will be a tower of strength & Mrs Trowbridge, & Mrs Harvey[26] bless her! She gives her whole heart to it.

Of course the girls who come & stay with us, if they come, will pay the actual expense of their food & service if there should be enough to require an extra servant. We of course, shall need but one. These are the main points, so far & you see how large a letter I have writ unto you. It is such a physical labor for dear Jane to write that although she would do the subject far more justice than I naturally having done all the working of it out, save a little that I happen to know about girls, I am anxious to save her the fatigue. So I shall ask you to send this letter directly (as soon that is, as you have done with it,) to Mrs H. then Mrs L. & Mr A.[27]

Dr G. said another funny thing "This is delightful! I never saw anybody before who wanted to do it. Like Artemus Ward[28] I've often been ready to put down the rebellion by sending all my brothers-in-law to the front[.]"

He expressed his pleasant surprise that we werent "in the air[.]" He expected that. He said "You ladies have done a deal of solid thinking[.]" Of course I know who has done the thinking although she resents my putting myself out of it in any way. Still I am unwilling to let people suppose that I would ever have worked it out. I believe in it now, & can chatter about it. Pray heaven I may be able to do something about it. Of course my strong point is my influence over girls.

Here I positively make an end. With much love

Ellen.

HLSr in hand of SAAH ["Record Book of Copies of Letters and Articles"], 1–18 (SC, Starr).

1. EGS's sister Mary and parents, Caleb Allen and Susan Childs Starr, were supportive of the HH idea. The elder Starrs came to visit HH soon after it opened. It seems that Caleb Starr may have been more taken with the venture and its setting than his wife. EGS told her sister that their mother wished the house were in a better neighborhood (JA to AHHA, 3 June 1890, below). For biographical information on Mary Houghton Starr Blaisdell, see *PJA*, 1:239, n. 8; 2:574, n. 13.

2. On JA's circular letters, see introduction to parts 2 and 4 in *PJA*, 2. Having others write letters for her or letting the letters of her friends and cohorts stand for her reply was a practice that JA followed throughout her public life. For information on JA's letter-writing habits, see introduction to *PJA*, 1.

3. JA's sister SAAH was encouraging about the HH enterprise. JA often turned to her to confide her private doubts and share news of her activities, in effect including SAAH in the undertaking in absentia. JA also became nervous when she did not have regular communication from SAAH. Regarding the preparations to open HH, JA observed to SAAH that "people are so good about every thing, I sometimes feel completely humbled" (6 Aug. 1889, IU, Lilly, SAAH; *JAPM*, 2:1076). The following summer, JA told SAAH that "the older I get the more I think of my sisters" (6 June 1890, UIC, JAMC; *JAPM*, 2:1182). See also JA to SAAH, 8 Oct. 1889, n. 2, below.

4. 27 Feb. 1889.

5. See JA to MCAL, 19 [and 20] Feb. 1889, n. 30, above.

6. The greater HH neighborhood included many German residents and some French and French Canadians, but the latter were a minority among the more prevalent ethnic groups. Italian, Bohemian, Russian, and Polish immigrants were in greater abundance among non-English-speaking groups represented in the West Side's Nineteenth Ward, and thus different language skills were more urgently needed than the French or German that HH volunteers were most likely to have learned in formal study. Initially, JA and EGS remained interested in fostering neighborhood evenings and study clubs conducted in German and French. See also JA to MCAL, 13 Mar. 1889, nn. 3–4, below.

7. The event that became known as the Haymarket Riot or the Haymarket Affair took place on Tuesday evening, 4 May 1886, near Desplaines St. and Haymarket Square. Workers gathered there to protest the Chicago police shooting strikers at the McCormick Reaper Plant on 3 May. The crowd was addressed by several speakers, two labor leaders, and one Methodist minister, all of whom loudly commented about what was wrong with American society. By 10:00 P.M., during the last speaker's remarks, when the gathering had dwindled from an estimated 2,500 to approximately 200, 176 armed policemen began to forcefully

disperse the crowd. Some unknown person threw a dynamite bomb into the midst of the crowd, killing a policeman and injuring other people. In the resulting melee, the police shot into the crowd, killing 4 workers and injuring others, including some police. This event drew national attention, and over the next several weeks freedom of assembly and speech was curtailed in Chicago and several other cities. Members of the Knights of Labor union were blamed for the violence, and 8 men were arrested and tried, and 4 of them were hanged. Illinois governor John P. Altgeld, who took office in 1890, pardoned the remaining workers.

Anarchists rejected the idea of private property and organized government and believed in voluntary association and sharing. During the early 1880s, there were seven anarchist newspapers and more than twenty anarchist organizations in Chicago, all of which helped to create an anarchist culture. After the Haymarket Riot, their influence waned. There is no evidence in JA's papers that she was aware of the Haymarket Riot in May 1886 when it took place.

8. JA did manage a trip to an Anarchist Sunday School. "One Sunday afternoon in the late winter a reporter took me to visit a so-called anarchist sunday school, several of which were to be found on the northwest side of the city. The young man in charge was of the German student type, and his face flushed with enthusiasm as he led the children singing one of Koerner's poems. The newspaperman, who did not understand German, asked me what abominable stuff they were singing, but seemed dissatisfied with my translation of the simple words and darkly intimated that they were 'deep ones,' and had probably 'fooled' me. When I replied that Koerner was an ardent German poet whose songs inspired his countrymen to resist the aggressions of Napoleon, and that his bound poems were found in the most respectable libraries, he looked at me rather askance and I then and there had my first intimation that to treat a Chicago man, who is called an anarchist, as you would treat any other citizen, is to lay yourself open to deep suspicion" (Addams, *Twenty Years*, 91–92). Another version of JA's visit to the Anarchist Sunday School appears below. See JA to MCAL, 13 Mar. 1889, below.

9. French, *Bien!*, translates as "Well!"

10. Elizabeth Stansbury Kirkland was the founder and principal of Miss Kirkland's School for Girls in Chicago, where EGS was teaching (see *PJA*, 2:141–42, n. 7).

11. HH financial records indicate that EGS did not begin paying room and board at the settlement until Jan. 1893, and then she was responsible for paying $25 each month. When she was unable to make the payment from her lecture and bookbinding income, a HH supporter paid it for her, as if she were on a fellowship. In Apr. 1893, Lydia Avery Coonley-Ward provided the twenty-five dollars in support. Eventually, Roman Catholic convert and philanthropist Frances Crane Lillie (1869–1958) became a good friend and patroness of EGS.

12. There are no extant detailed financial records for the 1 Oct. 1889 to 1 Oct. 1891 period in the development of HH. In summary, for the first year of operation, Oct. 1889 to Sept. 1890, JA recorded that the house expenses were $1,080.33 of which she had collected only $58 for residents' board. Other large expenditures were general repairs, $3,701.68, with outside financial support of only $1,567.60, and furniture at a cost of $1,860.50. From Oct. 1889 to Oct. 1890, JA recorded direct support from financial gifts and fees of $3,617.30 against total expenses of $8,406.76. JA made up the difference of $5,016.91 from her personal financial resources in order to balance her financial accounts at the end of her financial year. See also JA to SAAH, 5 Jan. 1890, n. 1, below.

13. Probably a reference to Harriet Hopkins Trowbridge, who was very active with EGS and JA during the first years of HH's operation. In the first year of the settlement, Trowbridge spent most Friday evenings at HH. See JA to MCAL, 19 [and 20] Feb. 1889, n. 40, above.

14. On Toynbee Hall, see part 4, *PJA*, 2, especially 493–98.

15. On JA's treatment for spinal pain, see introduction to part 1, *PJA*, 2.

16. JA spent parts of the winters of 1885–86 and 1886–87 in Baltimore, where she became a volunteer in a variety of social organizations. One of them was the Shelter for Aged and Infirm Colored Persons of Baltimore (see introduction to part 3, *PJA*, 2, especially 396).

17. This may be a reference to treatment for neurasthenia by noted Philadelphia physician S. Weir Mitchell. See introduction to part 1, *PJA*, 2.

18. This printed letter, no longer extant in the papers of JA or EGS, announced the beginning of the College Settlement to be located at 95 Rivington St. near the corner of Ludlow St. in New York City's lower East Side. JA may have sent it on to her sister MCAL (see JA to MCAL, 13 Mar. 1889, especially nn. 19–20, below).

The idea for the Smith College settlement, which became known as the College Settlement, seems to have developed in 1887, when several Smith College classmates gathered for a reunion, and Vida Scudder (1861–1954), then a young instructor at Wellesley, Jean Gurney Fine (Spahr) (1861–1935), and Helen C. Rand (1863–1935) determined to pursue a settlement idea familiar to both Scudder and Rand. Between Nov. 1888 and Apr. 1889, Dr. Jane Elizabeth Robins (1860–1946) and Miss Fine lived in a tenement near the Neighborhood Guild (often counted as the first settlement founded in America, it was started in Aug. 1886 in New York City by Stanton Coit [1857–1944]), and led a girls' club. Building on that experience, the women secured a tenement and began to organize their settlement about the same time that JA and EGS began HH. In June 1889, they indicated that they had sufficient funds pledged to their venture and had lined up two permanent residents and thirty-five other residents representing Vassar, Smith, Cornell, Wellesley, Michigan, and Boston universities; Bryn Mawr; and the Harvard Annex, who, in rotating pairs, would live and work in the settlement for two months at a time.

It seems likely that the HH founders answered the Smith College letter and revealed what they planned to do in Chicago. It is also possible that JA and EGS had already seen an article about the Rivington St. plans entitled "A Women's Toynbee Hall" by Eliza Putnam Heaton for the *Kansas City (Mo.) Journal*, about 19 Apr. 1889. SAAH pasted it into the journal she had begun to keep in Mar. 1889 about the HH adventure and that she eventually gave to EGS (see JA to MCAL, 1 Apr. 1889, n. 5, below). A later article about the College Settlement that appeared in the *New York World* on 16 June 1889, and that was placed by JA and EGS in the first of several HH scrapbooks, indicates that the New York planners knew of the Chicago venture and pronounced it a copy of their own effort. "The College Settlement that is to be established here the 1st of October at No. 95 Rivington St., near the corner of Ludlow, and is to be an imitation of Toynbee Hall has already had an imitator in its turn." The article continued, "Miss Jane Addams a wealthy young Chicago woman, heard of the plan of the College Settlement and was so pleased with it that she went over to Europe a few months ago to examine the original model herself" (HH Scrapbook 1:1; *JAPM*, Addendum 10:6ff). Existing evidence does not support this version of the founding of HH.

Information presented in Robert A. Woods and Albert J. Kennedy's *Handbook of Settlements* (1911) about the date that the College Settlement was established is conflicting. In the entry for the College Settlements Assn. (organized in the spring of 1890 by representatives from Smith, Wellesley, Vassar, Bryn Mawr, and Harvard Annex), the authors quote from the fourth report of the association, which lists Oct. 1889 as the time their settlement began (2). In addition, in their chronology, Woods and Kennedy indicate that the College Settlement opened in Oct. 1889 (x). Their entry for the College Settlement gives a beginning date of 1 Sept. 1889 (193); however, that same entry indicates that the first head resident, Jean Gureny Fine, served in that capacity from Oct. 1889 until July 1892 (195). Woods and Kennedy give a start date of 18 Sept. 1889 for HH.

The women of Smith College clearly wanted to be seen as first with the settlement idea. Ironically, the untitled *New York World* article ended with the following: "The College Settlement is the first organized movement which college-bred women have made in charity, and the experiment is watched with much interest because the enemies of the higher education of women have been making the charge that women's colleges tend to foster selfishness and concentrate individual interest in narrow channels of feeling abstracted from the general life of the world." See also JA to MCAL, 13 Mar. 1889, n. 20, below.

David Swing, pastor of Central Church, wrote one of the first published essays about the settlement idea proposed by Jane Addams and Ellen Gates Starr. "A New Social Movement" appeared in the 8 June 1889 issue of the *Chicago Evening Journal* (Newton, *David Swing, Poet-Preacher*).

19. The West End, location of the homes, clubs, and shops of wealthy Londoners.

20. By the time JA and EGS arrived in Chicago to begin HH, David Swing (1830–94) had established a solid congregation for the Central Church, which he founded in Chicago in 1875. Swing had been born in Cincinnati, and grew up on a farm. After graduating from Miami Univ. (1852), he attended Lane Seminary, where he studied theology. Between 1853 and 1866, he served as principal for a preparatory school at Miami, Ohio. He became a pastor in 1866 when he was called to Chicago's Westminster Presbyterian Church (which became the Fourth Presbyterian Church in 1868). There he remained, building a following, through the Chicago Fire of 1871 and the construction of a new church building completed by 1874. In Apr. 1874, he was tried by the Chicago Presbytery and acquitted on charges that he preached that men were saved by good works and that his beliefs were similar to those of Unitarianism. He resigned his pastorate at the Fourth Presbyterian Church and, followed by a large number of his parishioners, founded his Central Church with services held in the Central Music Hall constructed for that purpose. He developed a large Sunday School, kindergarten, industrial schools, and other relief efforts.

Even before HH was opened at 335 South Halsted, David Swing published an article about it in the 8 June 1889 *Chicago Evening Journal*. In "A New Social Movement," he reported that "a moral and intellectual home is to be set up in a place where the surrounding people are living without possessing or knowing of the higher motives of life." He stated prophetically that JA and EGS, who "possess all the qualities which their task will demand," would provide "new ways of benefiting the less fortunate thousands of the large cities" (HH Scrapbook 1:1; *JAPM*, Addendum 10:6ff). He continued to watch the settlement's development, and on 4

June 1891 he presented a lecture, "Novels," in the Thursday Lectures and Concerts series for the HH College Extension Program.

21. Melancthon Woolsey Stryker (1851–1929) was born at Vernon, N.Y., the son of Presbyterian minister Isaac Pierson Stryker and Alida Livingston Woolsey Stryker. He attended school nearby at Rome, N.Y., and then spent three years at Hamilton College, Clinton, N.Y. After taking a year to work at the YMCA in New York City, he completed his baccalaureate degree at Hamilton in 1872. He graduated from Auburn Theological Seminary in 1876, the same year he married Clara Elizabeth Goss, also of Auburn, N.Y. (see also EGS [for JA] to Mary Houghton Starr Blaisdell [and SAAH], 6 Feb. [1889], n. 16, below). Her brother, Presbyterian minister Charles Frederick Goss, was also a pastor in Chicago while the Strykers lived there. His church was the evangelical and nondenominational Chicago Avenue Church associated with Dwight L. Moody (see JA to MCAL, 12 Feb. 1889, nn. 36–37, above). Before moving to Chicago, Stryker served in churches in Auburn and Ithaca, N.Y., and in Holyoke, Mass.

When only thirty-four years old, Stryker moved to Chicago as pastor of the Fourth Presbyterian Church where he served from 1886 until 1892, when he assumed the presidency of Hamilton College and the pastorate of the College Church. A poet and hymnal editor, and intellectually progressive, he quickly placed the college, which had been in a precarious financial state when he arrived, on a solid financial footing, with new buildings, an enlarged faculty, and additions to the endowment. He retired in 1917, lived nearby at Rome, and continued to serve as college trustee until his death.

Stryker was an eloquent preacher, and by the time JA and EGS sought his counsel, he and his brilliant sermons were attracting positive attention and a following that gave him growing influence in Chicago. Membership at the Fourth Presbyterian Church doubled from three hundred to six hundred during his tenure. It was also a period of physical expansion for the church. Expenditures went for projects outside the church as well. His congregation helped build the First Italian Presbyterian Church, providing fourteen thousand dollars toward its support. In addition, Stryker was aware that the neighborhood around his church was changing from a community of houses to one of rooming houses. He began to reach out to the newcomers, providing more services to help them, including activities for young people, excursions to observe various city missions, and social programs (see also JA to MCAL, 26 Feb. 1889, below).

22. Alice Lindsley Mason (1837–1912) was one of seven children of Roswell B. Mason (1805–92), engineer, railroad developer, civic leader, and mayor of Chicago during the Chicago Fire of 1871, and his wife, Harriet Lavinia Hopkins Mason (1807–91), who were wed 6 Sept. 1831 in Williamsburg, Pa. Alice Mason grew up in the New York and Connecticut area, where her father was associated with the development of the Housatonic and the New York and New Haven railroads. By 1851 the family had moved to the Midwest, where Mason was directing the construction of the Illinois Central Railroad. While the Mason family was living in Dubuque, Iowa, and after the death of his first wife in 1855, Presbyterian minister James Hewit Trowbridge fell in love with Alice Mason and married her. There were nine children, of which five survived into adulthood: George Mason (1861–1919), Harriet Hopkins (1867–93), Cornelia Rogers (1869–1936), James Rutherford (1871–1956), and Mason (1877–1962). Rev. Trowbridge held several pastorates in Chicago between the early 1860s and his death in 1887. His last was in Reunion Presbyterian Church in a poor neighborhood of Chicago, 1886–87. After his death, the widow Trowbridge moved with her five children into the home of her parents at 27 (later 8 West) Delaware Place in Chicago. In 1897 she became a member of the Fortnightly Club of Chicago.

23. Marietta Adrience Dow (1845–1927) was the mother of Jenny Dow, who began the first organized activity at HH, the kindergarten. She was born at Poughkeepsie, N.Y., and she came to Chicago from Hopewell, N.Y. She was one of the twenty-one founding members of

the CWC, active in it and in the work of the Unity Church in Chicago to which she and her husband, William Carey Dow (1822–1903), belonged. William Carey Dow had been born in Boston and arrived in Chicago in the early 1850s. He was a real estate dealer and managed the rental of downtown Chicago properties until 1900, when his health began to fail. He died in Chicago on 13 Oct. 1903, and Marietta Dow lived on initially in the family home at 473 Orchard St. She died at the North Shore Sanitarium, Kenilworth, 23 Jun. 1927. Her only grandchildren were the five born to Jenny Dow Harvey and her husband, William Plato Harvey (see JA to EGS, 4 June 1889, n. 10, below).

24. William Mackintire Salter (1853–1931), who became a special friend of the social settlement movement, was one of the leaders of the ethical culture movement (see JA to MCAL, 1 Apr. 1889, n. 10, below) in America. He was born in Burlington, Iowa, to clergyman William Salter and his wife, Mary A. Mackintire Salter. He earned his A.B. (1871) and his M.A. (1874) from Knox College, Galesburg, Ill.; attended Yale Divinity School, 1871–73; received a B.D. from Harvard in 1876; and undertook further study at the Univ. of Göttingen (1876–77) and at Columbia Univ. (1881–82). He became a lecturer for the Chicago Society for Ethical Culture in 1883 and served until 1892. In 1885 he wed Mary S. Gibbens. The couple had one child, Eliza Webb Salter, and they adopted a second child, John Randall Salter.

On 28 Jan. 1891, Salter spoke at HH to the newly formed Working People's Social Science Club on "the problem of the unemployed." Between 1892 and 1897, he was lecturer for the Society of Ethical Culture in Philadelphia and returned to Chicago in 1897 to become leader of the movement in Chicago. From 1909 to 1913, he served as special lecturer in the Dept. of Philosophy, Univ. of Chicago. He gave numerous lectures, wrote articles, and published several books on the ethical culture philosophy and movement, some in English and some in German. Toward the end of his life, he made his home in Silver Lake, N.H.

25. Dr. Leila Gertrude Bedell (1838–1914), a graduate of Boston Univ. Medical School in 1878, was from Crown Point, Ind. She became a leader in many social improvement efforts among women's organizations in Chicago. One of the early members of the CWC, she became one of its most daring and outspoken activists. In the spring of 1882, she offered a resolution that placed the CWC in a leadership role in the fight to have women matrons in charge of women prisoners in police stations. As president of the CWC, 1885–87, she led its delegation to the founding meeting and for continuing participation in Chicago's Protective Agency for Women and Children, created in early 1886. She encouraged the Reform Com. of the CWC to take up the fight for improved conditions in the Cook County Insane Asylum. During her tenure, she also promoted the formation of the Industrial Art Assn., of which she became president. It brought children from the poorer parts of Chicago to clean, warm schoolrooms on Saturdays, where they were given what was considered practical schooling in sewing and drawing.

It seems likely that the most important contribution that she believed she made while president of the CWC was not credited to her or to the organization. Realizing that there was power and force in numbers, she launched an effort to establish a general federation of women's clubs. In her address to the CWC when she took office in Mar. 1886, she outlined her idea for a federation. Articles in both the *Chicago Inter Ocean* and the *Woman's Journal* in that year credit her with the idea. She reported in a letter 25 Feb. 1911 that "as it seemed best to have one of the oldest clubs make the call for such a movement, I wrote to Mrs. Louise Thomas, then president of Sorosis and outlined the scheme and suggested starting the movement. No reply whatever came from Mrs. Thomas, but Sorosis a few months later did issue the call for the organization of a general federation" (Frank and Jerome, *Annals, CWC*, 58). Sorosis and the Woman's Club of New York took the credit for the organization that arose from their called meeting in Mar. 1889. Bedell and members of the CWC believed that their club should have had credit for beginning the movement that resulted in the creation of the General Federation of Women's Clubs. In May 1888, Bedell sought and received the

CWC's endorsement to create a Woman's League consisting of the officers of women's clubs in Chicago. At the meeting held on 23 May 1888, fifty-six women's organizations from Chicago were represented and Bedell was elected temporary leader.

In 1890 Bedell was called on once again to serve as an officer in the CWC. From 1887 through 1889, 1890 to 1891, and again from 1902 to 1903, she was one of two vice-presidents of the organization. She resigned from the club in 1903 and was made an honorary member in 1904.

She seems to have been impressed with JA and EGS and their plan. One of her responses to their idea was an article she wrote entitled "A Chicago Toynbee Hall" with a dateline of Chicago, 5 May 1889, that appeared in the *Woman's Journal* (Boston) 20 (25 May 1889), 162 (see Letter to the *Woman's Journal* [Boston], 25 May 1889, below). Between 1889 and 1893, Bedell participated in JA's Ten Account fund-raising program, providing fifty dollars each year toward HH expenses. In addition, on 16 Oct. 1892, she gave a lecture entitled "Health and Religion" for the HH Sunday Lectures series.

Bedell was also active in her chosen profession. In 1879 she helped organize the Woman's Homeopathic Medical Society. She served as its secretary-treasurer in 1879 and as its second president in 1880. The group was created to encourage higher professional attainments and to support women in the profession. In addition, she was a member of the Western Society for Psychical Research.

Dr. Bedell was married to educator Frank S. Bedell (b. 1836?), who was born in New York, and the couple lived at 354 (later 1020) North LaSalle St. Dr. Leila Bedell lived the last ten years of her life in Tryon, N.C.

26. Julia Plato Harvey. See JA to MCAL, 12 Feb. 1889, n. 28, above.

27. JA's siblings, in order, SAAH, MCAL, and JWA.

28. Artemus Ward was the pseudonym of the American humorist Charles Farrar Browne (1834–67), who contributed "Artemus Ward's Sayings" to the *Cleveland Plain Dealer* beginning in 1857. The series spoofed backwoods characters and sentimental culture and was filled with tongue-in-cheek observations of current events, misspelled words, and colloquialisms. Browne became the editor of *Vanity Fair* and a contributor to *Punch*. "Atremus Ward's Sayings" remained popular, and selections were published after Browne's untimely death in 1867.

## To Mary Catherine Addams Linn

4 Washington Place. Chicago [Ill.] Feb. 26" 1889.

My dear Mary

I seem to be reduced to writing about one long letter a week—to giving you a perfect deluge all at once. I have been writing a good deal on the scheme this week, not to publish but to clarify my own mind[1] and that with the appointments we made seems to take up all the time.

Ellen wrote a long letter to her sister on Saturday, stating about the point we have reached.[2] I asked her to have it sent around to the rest of you and that will probably give you a clearer idea than I could—as Ellen always makes everything so graphic and dramatic.

I think I wrote on last Tuesday,[3] in the evening we had the most satisfying conversation, and appreciation of what we were about—that we have encountered in all Chicago before.

I had made an appointment with Mr Adams[4] on Sunday to spend Tuesday evening at his home and Mr McCormick[5] duly escorted Miss Trowbridge[,][6] Ellen and myself thither. Mrs Adams is very pleasant and they were so glad to see us, they say that they have very few visitors "from Chicago," Mr Adams is simply the most "spiritually minded" person I have ever come into contact with, to hear him talk was a drink of water from the purest fountain, from the very Source of all. He considered the scheme "iminently Christian" which we considered high praise.

On Wednesday afternoon we saw Dr Gunsaulus of which Ellen has written at length of in her letters.[7] I will not repeat. He was extremely witty and quite the most enthusiastic convert we have made. He said that we could command him to any extent until we "organized" and commenced to print "reports." He promised us a young lady with a million dollars to begin with.

I had made an engagement for Thursday[8] with Mrs Beveridge[9] to go out to Norwood to see the "Boys Industrial School."[10] Mrs Beveridge was not at the station so I went on alone. I had met Mrs Harrison[11] the Sup't before and did not feel in the least forlorn. She is a very remarkable woman and has a wonderful power over boys.

It has been established by the Humane Society[12] and Newsboy people,[13] as a safe place where utterly homeless and forlorn boys can be retained until other places are found for them. Mrs Harrison says they come in starved and beaten and ragged but never dull—they are almost preternaturally "sharp".

Friday morning[14] we had an appointment with Mr Goss[15] minister of Moody's Church. He is young and eagar, altho forty years old perhaps, I think he is younger and rasher in spirit than either of us. He has a dream of a "working man's church" beside which our plan must seem paltry to him, but his sympathy never failed and he made all sorts of rash promises. He is a brother of Mrs Stryker,[16] and in the evening we met Mr and Mrs Stryker at a dinner at Mrs Trowbridge's.[17] Mr Stryker you know is pastor of the 4" Pres. Church, he agreed to the plan in all respects but the girls themselves, he declared that we could not get them to do it. He said he had a perfect horror of the "modern fashionable young lady" that they were the most hard hearted creatures in existence. Ellen championed them valiently and finally declared that it was time some one did some thing for them if their very pastors talked about them like that. He was anxious that we should locate on the north side but we insisted that Dr Gunsaulus has promised marvellous things for the south side. It quite put the reverend gentleman on his mettle and we took rather a wicked enjoyment in the fact.

On Saturday afternoon[18] Ellen had invited a few ladies to our room who "all took stock, every one of them my dear."

Sunday morning[19] we heard Mr Goss and in the afternoon I talked for half an hour to the Boys of Mrs Stryker's Miss. band.[20] They were the McCormick boys, Farwells'[21] &c but altho' I said almost the same things I had told the boys at Norwood[22]—the latter seemed to me the brighter boys and the more attractive. Mason Trowbridge[23] told his mother when he went home that it was "awful interesting" but Miss A. ["]didn't know nothing of Chicago mickeys."[24]

Monday afternoon[25] I talked at the training school for Home and Foreign Missions[26] to about sixty Embryo Missionaries on East London and did not mention the scheme. I told Ellen that it was a great relief to my mind to find that I could ignore the scheme when I choose.

We have positively <done> nothing in regard to urging on the cause and yet get invitations from all sides. We think it must be the "Women's Club" people. We took tea one evening with a Miss Beedy[27] whom Ellen knew slightly & who has taught here for years. She wants us to know some socialists, thinks our ideas will be incomplete until we do. I had a letter this morning from a Mrs Carse[28] Sec. of the Central W.C.T.U.[29] to meet the Board of Directors & Miss Willard[30] at an informal "Tea" next Friday[31] at their head quarters. We are invited to dinner to morrow evening[32] at Mrs McConnell's[33] to meet some wiseacres, it is very fine but probably will not last.

I called on Mrs Brawley[34] this morning and enjoyed her very much. She lives on Lake Park Ave. a beautiful part of the city. She asked Ellen and I for Sat. evening to some sort of an artists soirrèe but I declined as we are going over to the Adams sewing school in the afternoon and they are miles apart.[35] I took lunch with Mrs Strong, Addie Smith[36] one of my old room mates at Rockford. She has a dear little girl who reminded me a little of Mary. As I was in South Chicago I went over to see Mrs Beveridge. She is almost always in the reading room the Armour Mission of which she has charge. She looked a little tired and overworked.

I have n't time for more, and it is probably a good thing that I have n't. Excuse the haste of the ending and give my love to the dear Linnets.[37] If you will send this to Alice, and she sends it to Weber together with Ellen's letter you will get a pretty clear idea of us I think. Always dear Mary Your loving Sister

Jane Addams.

ALS (SCPC, JAC; *JAPM*, 2:1033–41).

1. None of JA's notes are known to be extant.
2. See EGS [for JA] to Mary Houghton Starr Blaisdell [and SAAH], 23 Feb. [1889], above.
3. See JA to MCAL, 19 [and 20], Feb. 1889, above.
4. Rev. Edwin Augustus Adams. See JA to MCAL, 19 [and 20] Feb. 1889, n. 37, above.
5. Alexander A. McCormick. See JA to MCAL, 19 [and 20], Feb. 1889, n. 27, above.
6. Harriet Hopkins Trowbridge. See JA to MCAL, 19 [and 20], Feb. 1889, n. 40, above.
7. 20 Feb. 1889. See EGS [for JA] to Mary Houghton Starr Blaisdell [and SAAH], 23 Feb. [1889], above.
8. 28 Feb. 1889.
9. Julia A. Beveridge. See JA to EGS, 24 Jan. 1889, n. 6, above.
10. The Illinois Industrial School for Boys at Norwood Park was founded in 1887 as a result of an act of the Illinois General Assembly in 1883 and known as the Norwood Park School. Its purpose "was to furnish a home and school to which boys having no proper parental or

other control might be committed, by the order of a Court of Record, or by the consent of their parents unable to control them" (*First Annual Report of the Illinois Industrial Training School for Boys at Norwood Park*, 4). On 29 June 1887, it opened in a former hotel building in Norwood Park with 10 boys sent by the Cook County court. It cared for 143 boys ages two to fourteen its first year, providing basic education and training in agriculture, mechanics, and carpentry. By 1890 it had moved to Glenwood, Ill., after the Milton George family, publishers of the *Western Rural* agricultural periodical, offered to make their farm of three hundred acres available for $40,000 for the building and equipment. By Jan. 1890, the CWC could claim that "$31,000.00 of the $40,000 had been subscribed through the . . . Club, and over $7,000.00 raised in the Club itself" (Frank and Jerome, *Annals, CWC*, 86). By 1892 the school at Glenwood was named the Illinois School of Agriculture and Manual Training for Boys and referred to as the Glenwood School, and it had given training to 820 boys. In 1900 the name was changed to Illinois Training School Farm; in 1910 it became the Glenwood Manual Training School and in 1949 the Glenwood School for Boys.

11. Ursula L. Harrison (b. 1847?) was born in New York, probably near Smithville, Chenango Co., where she spent her later years. She was married to David G. Harrison, and they had at least two sons, Walter B. Harrison (b. 1872?) and Harry Harrison (b. 1882?). She served as the first superintendent at the Illinois Industrial School for Boys, Norwood Park, from 1887 until she resigned effective 1 Nov. 1897. Previously, she had held similar posts in Indiana, Wisconsin, and in other institutions in Illinois. In an article that JA and EGS may have seen from the *Chicago Daily Tribune*, 15 Jan. 1889, journalist "Nora Marks," pseudonym for journalist Eleanor Stackhouse (see JA to SAAH, 23 Nov. 1889, n. 11, below), described the school and its superintendent. Marks found Harrison "a fair, comfortable lady in the prime of life" with "a motherly look." Harrison seems to have had some success with a program of basic education and training. "A year ago the citizens [of Norwood Park] wanted us condemned as a nuisance; now they are as proud of us as can be," Harrison reported to Marks. "We were beginning then with a dozen or so boys fresh from the streets, and it must be confessed that they swore and fought. Now there are no better nor happier boys in the village" ("Jaunts to the Country").

After leaving the school, Mrs. Harrison accepted the position of superintendent at the State Industrial School for Girls, Denver, but stayed there only briefly. By 1900 she had returned to Smithville, N.Y., where she remained for the next several years.

12. The Illinois Humane Society was chartered by the Illinois legislature in 1869 as the Illinois Society for Preventing Cruelty to Animals. Prevention of cruelty to children was added to its responsibilities and its name changed to the Illinois Humane Society in 1877. Society efforts focused on rescue and on education to promote humane treatment. Visible signs of the organization throughout Chicago were the approximately thirty fountains to supply drinking water for people and animals. It is likely that many of the directors of the Illinois Humane Society also contributed to the development of the Illinois School of Agriculture and Manual Training for boys, for their missions to care for and protect children—especially destitute children—were similar.

Oscar Little Dudley (1843?–1918), an agent for the Illinois Humane Society beginning in 1877, was also a leader in the efforts to establish the Illinois Industrial School for Boys at Norwood Park. He had been born in Vermont and went to Wisconsin at the age of sixteen. After service in the Civil War, he opened a business college in Jefferson City, Mo., and later moved to Minneapolis, where he established the Minnesota Business College. For health reasons, he left Minneapolis for Chicago in 1873. When he arrived in Chicago, the only facility that provided care for homeless boys in trouble was St. Mary's Training School for Boys in Feehansville, and he believed that the area could use a nonsectarian counterpart. In 1891 he spoke on the Illinois Training School for Boys at the eighteenth Conf. on Charities and Correction, May 13–20, in Indianapolis. He served as a Republican in the Illinois House of Representatives, 1895–97.

The Illinois Humane Society, its mission, and officers were well known to JA. She used the organization's services to try to help children in her neighborhood. As an example, see JA to Oscar L. Dudley, 15 Dec. 1890, UIC, IHS; and *JAPM*, 2:1220–21, in which JA reported that a girl "not quite fourteen is living in improper relations with her father."

13. The Newsboys' and Bootblacks' Home was located at 1418 Wabash Ave. It was incorporated in 1867 (see JA to MCAL 19 [and 20] 1889, n. 15, above). Four evenings a week, it held a night school 7:30 to 9:00 P.M., and all boys living in the home were required to attend. With three meals a day and a bed available, the home was intended as a temporary place for a boy to live while he was learning a trade or finding permanent lodging and employment or both. When JA learned of the facility, Miss Eliza W. Bowman was matron. Bowman discovered that older larger boys were more in need of help than smaller ones, and she established a program to assist them in finding employment. She also loaned them funds, to be repaid, after they got a start. Her plan met with success and became part of the ongoing program of the home. Like the Illinois Humane Society, with which the home cooperated, it also worked with the Illinois Industrial School for Boys, and many of the directors of the Newsboys' and Bootblacks' Home had supported development of the Glenwood farms under way when JA was visiting in Norwood Park.

14. 22 Feb. 1889.

15. Rev. Charles Frederick Goss, see JA to MCAL, 12 Feb. 1889, n. 37, above.

16. Clara Elizabeth Goss Stryker and Melancthon Woolsey Stryker were wed in Sept. 1876 shortly after he graduated from Auburn Theological Seminary, N.Y. The Strykers had six children, and Clara Stryker was actively engaged in church work where her husband held pastorates. See also EGS [for JA] to Mary Houghton Starr Blaisdell [and SAAH], 23 Feb. [1889], n. 21, above.

17. Alice Lindsley Mason Trowbridge. See EGS [for JA] to Mary Houghton Starr Blaisdell [and SAAH], 23 Feb. [1889], n. 22, above.

18. 23 Feb. [1889].

19. 24 Feb. 1889.

20. A mission band was usually a group of youngsters organized to instill a missionary ideal in others and to help with the missionary program of the church. Its members were expected to contribute to the missions of the church by earning through undertaking tasks like shoveling snow or giving up money given to them for the purchase of candy.

21. JA was certainly aware that some of the boys in Clara Stryker's mission band were associated with some of the most influential families in Chicago who were also members of the Fourth Presbyterian Church. Among the Chicago families represented were those of Cyrus Hall McCormick of the International Harvester Co. and the John V. Farwell family, associated with the development of merchandising and especially with Marshall Field and Co. department store.

22. A reference to JA's visit with boys at the Illinois Industrial School at Norwood Park. See n. 10.

23. Mason Trowbridge (1877–1962) was the youngest child of Alice Lindsley Mason Trowbridge and Rev. James Hewit Trowbridge. He lived with his widowed mother at the home of her parents, the Roswell B. Masons, at 27 (later 8 West) Delaware Place. Mason Trowbridge graduated from Yale Univ. (A.B. 1902; L.L.B. 1905) and became an attorney. He served as assistant district attorney for New York Co., N.Y., 1906–9, and had the same post in Nassau Co., N.Y., 1914–15, while teaching law at Yale. After acting as general counsel for Colgate and Co., Jersey City, N.J., 1916–28, he returned to Chicago to become general counsel for Colgate-Palmolive-Peet Co. beginning in 1928 and entered private practice. He lived on Delaware Place, where he had grown up, with his wife, Helen Fox Trowbridge, with whom he had six children. By 1941 he had returned to New Jersey.

24. The word "mickeys" is a derogative slang term for Irish.

25. 25 Feb. 1889.

26. This may have been the beginning of JA's almost nine-year relationship with this organization. The Chicago Training School for City, Home, and Foreign Missions opened in Oct. 1885 to train women church workers. It was the creation of Methodist lay leader Lucy Rider Meyer, and she and her husband, Josiah Shelley Meyer, became its first leaders.

Lucy Rider Meyer (1849–1922) was a graduate of Oberlin College, Ohio (A.B. 1872; M.A. 1880). She was a student at the Woman's Medical College of Pennsylvania, 1873–75, and attended Boston School of Technology (later MIT), 1877–78, in preparation for a career as a teacher of chemistry. She taught natural science at the Cook County Normal School, 1878–79; became professor of Natural Science at McKendree College, 1879–80; and was an employee of the Illinois State Sunday School Assn. in 1881. During the winter of 1884–85, she taught at Dwight L. Moody's School for Girls at Northfield, Mass. Mrs. Meyer completed her education at the Woman's Medical College, Chicago (later incorporated into Northwestern Univ.), from which she received her M.D. degree in 1887. Her husband, Josiah Shelley Meyer (1849–1926), was educated at Park College and McCormick Theological Seminary, studied business management at a commercial school and in a newspaper office, and then served as assistant secretary of the Central Dept. of the Chicago YMCA. His business acumen was perhaps his most important contribution to the Chicago Training School for City, Home, and Foreign Missions.

Initiated in a former home on West Park Ave., by 1886 the Chicago Training School was located at 114 (later 600 North) Dearborn St., at the southwest corner of Dearborn and Ohio streets. It offered a two-year program in Bible, hygiene, chemistry, and social and family relationships. Field trips to poor neighborhoods were required. There were special adjunct faculty who presented lectures on a variety of topics, from domestic science to medicine. JA was one of those.

In *Twenty Years* (81–82), JA recalled that during her first year in Chicago, she gave a course of six lectures on early Christianity based on her 1887–88 experiences as a tourist in Europe. Records indicate that JA had a continuing relationship with the school through the 1896–97 school year. In 1889–92 she was listed as teaching a ten-hour course entitled Kindergarten Principles and Clay Modeling, described as "Form study with drawing and clay-modeling color study with paper-cutting." In 1890–91 she began teaching a three-hour course listed as Early Christian Art: "Earliest Christian painting and mosaic. Churches of Ravenna and Clement of Rome. Catacombs of St. Calixtus and St. Agnes" (Chicago Training School for City, Home, and Foreign Missions, *Announcement*, 1890–91, xx–xxi). She taught her Early Christian Art course annually through school year 1896–97. At that time, the school moved to new quarters at 4949 Indiana Ave.

Lucy Rider Meyer and JA seem to have become friends. Meyer's biographer Isabelle Horton reported in her 1928 work, "A tie of real friendship existed between these two women . . . both intent upon a life devoted to the service of humanity. Miss Addams still speaks with deep feeling of Mrs. Meyer's loyal defense of the 'settlement position' when Hull House called down upon itself the anathemas of orthodox religionists for its omission of religious instruction" (*High Adventure*, 76–77).

According to one history of the Training School, Mrs. Meyer consulted JA on the best place to relocate the school when it outgrew its Dearborn site. In addition, Mrs. Meyer also sought to have JA as a member of her board of trustees. However, "Mrs. Meyer was compelled to withdraw her invitation to Miss Addams to become a trustee" because of her stance on religious instruction at HH (Horton, *High Adventure*, 182–83). Lucy Meyer retired from her position as principal of the school in 1917. In 1934 the school moved to Evanston, Ill., where it became the Women's Dept. of Garrett Biblical Institute (later Garrett-Evangelical Theological Seminary, Evanston).

27. Mary E. Beedy (1836?–1910) was born at Meadville, Pa. After attending the local schools,

she taught for several years and then entered Antioch College, Yellow Springs, Ohio, in 1857, soon after it was founded in 1853. She graduated in the class of 1860 and resumed her teaching career. She may also have returned to Antioch for further study because she listed herself as having received an M.A. degree. Leaving Antioch, she taught first in Madison, Wis., and then spent approximately eight years as a teacher at the Mary Institute of St. Louis, a high school associated with Washington Univ. While in St. Louis, she became active in the group of amateur philosophers founded and led by William Torrey Harris (1835–1909), superintendent of the St. Louis schools, 1867–80, and Henry Conrad Brokmeyer (1828–1906). The St. Louis Hegelians organized the St. Louis Philosophical Society with its own *Journal of Speculative Philosophy*. They believed in practical action for social good and education as a means of reform.

In the early 1870s, Mary Beedy spent five years in England, where she was a strong advocate for the higher education of women. She appeared in England as a successful graduate of an American college and wrote and spoke throughout England. She was an important voice in the successful campaign to open English universities to women. While she was in England, she also contributed many letters to the editor that were published in American newspapers. Her efforts in England compromised her health, and she returned to the United States to recover.

She settled in Chicago during the early 1880s and by 1886 had become a member of the CWC and served as coprincipal of the Miss Rice's School for Girls, operated by Miss Rebecca Rice, also an Antioch graduate (see *PJA*, 1:281–82, n. 6) and member of the CWC. After Miss Rice's School for Girls closed in 1898, Miss Beedy became a teacher at Kenilworth Hall, a school for girls in Kenilworth, Ill. She retired in 1901 and moved to Miller's Station, Crawford Co., Pa. During her retirement and for approximately three years, she was associated with Berea College, Berea, Ky. As her health began once again to decline, she returned to Meadville, Pa., and spent much of the remainder of her life in Spencer Hospital there, where she died.

While living in Chicago, Mary E. Beedy took a lively interest in educational and reform issues, much as she had done during her five-year sojourn in England. Her efforts were reflected in the letters she contributed to the editor of the *Chicago Daily Tribune*, *Woman's Journal* (Boston), and other periodicals. She supported women serving on school boards, compulsory education, woman suffrage, the desirability of physical exercise for schoolchildren, and the importance of settlement work with special emphasis on the College Settlement, New York City, and HH in Chicago. She also spoke frequently on reform and political science issues. In 1891 she gave a course of ten political science lectures at the Bay View Summer Univ. near Petoskey, Mich. On 19 May 1892, she presented a lecture entitled "The House of Commons, Gladstone" at HH in the Thursday Lectures and Concerts series.

28. Matilda Bradley Carse (1835–1917) was born in Ireland and emigrated to Chicago in 1858. She wed Thomas Carse, who died from tuberculosis in 1870, leaving her and their three sons with a comfortable inheritance. When Matilda's youngest son, Thomas, was killed by a drunken cart diver, she joined the WCTU and eventually served on its executive and finance committees. In 1878 she followed Frances E. Willard as WCTU president, remaining in office until 1913, after which she was honorary president until her death. During her tenure as its leader, the organization began to offer a variety of social services throughout Chicago, including day nurseries, Sunday and industrial schools, medical dispensaries, a men's lodging house, and a retreat for prostitutes and alcoholic women. While the WCTU was her primary philanthropic effort, she also participated in other organizations, including the CWC. She served on the board of Lady Managers for the World's Columbian Exposition in 1893 and was the first woman appointed to the School Board of Cook Co.

29. The Central Chicago Woman's Christian Temperance Union was established by Frances E. Willard on 8 Oct. 1874. It was the first of the WCTU organizations founded in Chicago. Frances E. Willard served as its president until 1878, when she was called to head the national efforts of the organization. Its purpose was to combat the influence of alcohol on families

and society. Its second president, Matilda Bradley Carse (see n. 28), and the organization she led saw alcoholism as a consequence of social problems in central Chicago society. The WCTU developed a diverse assortment of social improvement efforts to offer those affected by alcoholism. The organization was most active and powerful during the 1880s and 1890s. In the first part of the twentieth century, oversight of its projects was assumed by the Cook Co. WCTU established in 1901 (see also JA to MCAL, 1 Apr. 1889, n. 19, below).

JA was certainly familiar with the goals and program of the WCTU. She had been raised in a home dedicated to the ideal of temperance (see *PJA*, 1). In addition, after her return from her second European trip in the summer of 1888, she helped form a chapter of the WCTU in Stephenson Co., Ill., and the *Freeport (Ill.) Journal* announced her selection as president of the organization on 26 Sept. 1888.

30. As the leader of the WCTU, then the largest American women's organization, Frances E. Willard (1839–98) was at the peak of her power as an internationally known figure by the time JA was invited to "tea." Born in New York, young Frances moved with her parents and two siblings to Oberlin, Ohio, then to the Janesville, Wis., area, and finally to Evanston, Ill., when her father joined a Chicago banking firm. She graduated from Northwestern Female College, Evanston, in June 1859 and began teaching school. After returning from an extensive two-and-a-half-year tour of Europe and the Middle East in 1871, she became president of Evanston College for Ladies, which became part of Northwestern Univ. in 1872 with Willard as its dean. By 1874, after a disagreement with the university administration, she resigned. She firmly believed that women deserved more parity with men, a new egalitarian relationship, and that required reform. The vehicle for her effort became the WCTU with which she became involved at its creation in 1874. She got the WCTU to support woman suffrage and a broad social reform agenda that in addition to suffrage and temperance stood for women's economic and religious rights, support for the rising labor movement, and reform in institutions associated with family, home, and marriage.

In 1888 Willard had helped form the short-lived Woman's League of Chicago, a coalition of women's organizations, and also served as president of the National Council of Women. Willard was hoping that JA and EGS would join her broadband reform organization and create a program to rehabilitate fallen women on Clark St. in the heart of Chicago's red-light district. JA did investigate the possibility and provided lectures for the WCTU, probably at the Anchorage Mission in the Clark St. area, but though she became a WCTU member she chose not to bring her settlement plan under the wing of the Willard organization.

Frances Willard became ill with pernicious anemia during the 1890s and died in 1898.

31. 1 Mar. 1889.

32. 27 Feb. 1889.

33. Perhaps Jane Binney McConnell (1842?–92), the first wife of Luther William McConnell (1839–1907). Mrs. McConnell was a member of the Board of Managers at Porter Memorial Hospital, and she joined the CWC in 1888 and was an active member in the Home Dept. until her death in 1892. At the time of her death, she was treasurer of the Municipal Order League of Chicago. She also made financial contributions to the development of the HH Diet Kitchen and to the Jane Club. Her husband, who was a businessman, expert on credit, a merchant associated for thirty-four years with Marshall Field and Co., and Union League Club founder, contributed to the HH Gymnasium and Coffee House Building fund and the Steam Heating Plant Building in 1892. His obituary in the *Chicago Daily Tribune* reported that "it was at his former residence, 531 [later 1401 North] Dearborn Avenue where the Hull house was started" (15 Jan. 1907).

34. Mary Reitzell Brawley was a cousin of JA. See *PJA*, 1:136, n. 1.

35. The Brawleys lived on Chicago's South Side at 3010 Lake Park Ave. The Adams sewing school was located to the north and west of the Brawley home and at 670 South Throop St.

36. Addie M. Smith Strong was an RFS classmate. See *PJA*, 1:220–21, n. 20; 1:427, n. 4.

37. JA and EGS's pet name for the children of MCAL and JML.

## Article in the *Chicago Daily Tribune*

*Although both are described, neither Jane Addams's nor Ellen Gates Starr's names was mentioned in this first article about the settlement scheme to appear in a major newspaper in the United States. From the very beginning of the settlement project and for the remainder of her life, Jane Addams was exceedingly mindful of the power of the press and aware of the need to market and promote her idea. Until radio was readily available to the U.S. public during the 1920s, public speaking in called meetings; periodicals, including newspapers and journals, whether popular, special interest, or scholarly; and books were the major ways to communicate with the general public. Jane Addams quickly learned to use these methods to promote her reform ideas and activities.*

TO MEET ON COMMON GROUND.
A PROJECT TO BRING THE RICH AND
THE POOR CLOSER TOGETHER.

Chicago, Ill. 8 March 1889

It is probable that within a few months an interesting departure in humanitarian work will be undertaken in this city. Although its details are not yet planned as regards practical application to this field, its general scope is understood by a number of prominent people, who will give it their support.

The plan is proposed by a young lady of independent means and generous culture, who has recently come to Chicago to interest educated women in her project. If able to secure the necessary cooperation, which now promises to be hearty, the idea will take shape in the early fall. It is difficult to make a brief statement of a plan so many-sided, but it involves a mutual exchange of the advantages of wealth and poverty. It assumes that these are by no means so one-sided as is generally supposed, but that the poor have joys and opportunities for growth that would enrich the lives of the well-to-do could they be brought within their influence. The barriers of class needlessly circumscribe them. It is narrowed and dwarfed by everything that limits its experiences or shuts out universal sympathy. Women of wealth suffer in growth and capacity for enjoyment by withdrawing from the homely cares of life. Simple joys, the wit and humor of the unlearned, as well as that knowledge of common things that only contact can furnish, make a part of life whose value money cannot buy. To provide such a supplementary course of instruction for women who so often leave the higher schools of learning to enter a narrow and disappointing sphere is one phase of the work. Another is to offer in return those higher aspirations and ennobling thoughts that culture has given.

These are in general the ideas that underlie the work of Toynbee Hall and the Denison Club in London. They were founded by college men who believed that only through personal knowledge and sympathy could the dangerous gulf between classes be overcome. Their practical success in uplifting the degraded as well as in gaining broadened experiences of life is generally known. Making their homes among the poor, meeting them as friends, they have transformed some of the vilest neighborhoods of the Whitechapel district of London.

A similar plan will be adopted by the young lady in Chicago. She will take a house in some poor district, furnish it attractively, and make it a centre of helpful social life. A young lady friend will be her companion, and it is hoped that a few daughters of the rich will at all times be found in her home. Living with her for varying periods they will enter into her plans. Several have already promised assistance and a number of our leading clergymen are enthusiastic supporters of the idea.

PD (*Chicago Daily Tribune*, 8 Mar. 1889).

## To Mary Catherine Addams Linn

4 Washington Place. Chicago [Ill.] March 13" 1889

My dear Mary

I have rather a disheartening impression that it is much more than a week since I wrote last, but I have been looking up different "slums"[1] and usually when I come back am too tired to do any thing. As I do not know where I left off in the journalistic account it may be well to go backward. I spent the morning with an Italian "Attendance Agent"[2] (a man hired by the Board of Education to look up truant children) going through the Italian quarter of south Chicago.[3] It was exactly as if we were in a quarter of Naples or Rome, the parents and the children spoke nothing but Italian and dressed like Italian peasants. They were more crowded than I imagined people ever lived in America, four families for instance of six or eight each, living in one room for which they paid eleven dollars a month, and were constantly afraid of being ejected. Yet they were affectionate and gentle, the little babies rolled up in stiff bands and the women sitting about like mild eyed Madonnas. They never begged nor even complained, and in all respects were immensely more attractive to me than the Irish neighborhood[4] I went into last week with a Mrs Ester. Every thing seems to indicate South Clark as our abiding place, Dr Gunsaulus thinks it is the one spot in the city destined for us. Signor Mastrovalerio[5] who took me this morning, is an Italian of some literary note as a journalist &c[.] He has sent five hundred Italian children to school in the last three months and was delighted with my feeble Italian, poor as it was, he said that there were many young ladies in Chicago who spoke Italian but they sang or were members of the Italian Club,[6] they did not visit the Italians. It is quite incomprehensible to me, for I felt exactly as if I had spent a morning in Italy and enjoyed it just as much.

Last evening I spoke to the Young-people Missionary Club of the New England Church,[7] about seventy five young men and women who were spending the evening at a Mrs Clark's[8] house on State St. The invitation came from a young lady of the society, but Mrs Clark had called the day before, and every thing was done in conventional order. The young are usually enthusiastic and hence it is well not to count too much on the enthusiasm expressed. Miss Blatchford[9] professed herself converted to the "scheme" and its future slave, she may be valuable.

On Sunday afternoon I visited one of the Anarchist Sunday Schools.[10] I had gotten a letter of introduction to a Mr Stauber[11] "one of the leading Anarchists" which I had presented the day before. I found a gentlemanly looking man at the head of a prosperous hard-ware store. He looked as if he were bearing the burdens of all humanity, a thin and spiritual face. He was pleased that I wanted to see the Sunday School, said that "Americans never came up there, except the reporters of the capitalist newspapers and they always exaggerated." I went on Sunday afternoon, to find about two hundred children assembled in a hall back of a saloon with some young men trying to teach them "free thought without any religion or politics," the entire affair was very innocent. I was treated with great politeness and may take a class—it seems to me an opportunity to do a great deal of good—it was all in German.

I think I wrote of the W.C.T.U. experiance and the Woman's Alliance.[12] I am getting just a little tired talking about it and should quite prefer beginning a little bit. Looking up localities is certainly toward it. We discover so many similar undertakings, the "Neighborhood Guilds" in New York,[13] the "Denison Club" in London[14] &c but we still think we have a distinct idea of our own.

I had planned for a longer letter but it is dinner time and after that the boys of the Moody School,[15] so I would better get this one off.

Mr Worrall and Mary[16] went home last week, I spent one day with them, took lunch at Mr Jenkins,[17] they have their own carriage & we afterwards rode in the park &c. They were on the verge then of giving up Kansas City then. I had a letter from Clara[18] yesterday saying they had arrived in Phila. safely. I will try to write oftener next week. Always Your loving Sister

Jane Addams.

I will inclose the circular of a <similar> thing in New York.[19] We are modest enough to think that ours is better, is more distinctively Christian and less Social Science. I have been corresponding with Miss Fine,[20] she is discouraged over the few offers of service, plenty of money has come in. The little scrap is part of an article in the Chicago Tribune of March 8" you may have seen it.[21] The reporter came twice and it was only by much brow-beating that we finally got her to mention no names & keep to generalities. The first part of it I lost but it did n't amount to much. Will you please send the letter & scraps to Alice & Weber.

ALS (JAPP, DeLoach; *JAPM*, 2:1043–48).

1. The word "slum"—of English origin—was likely new to MCAL, and JA may have placed it in quotation marks because it stood for an area of working-poor dwellings and inhabitants and she knew it was derogatory.

2. Alessandro Mastro-Valerio acted as a volunteer attendance agent in the Italian neighborhood (see n. 5). The Illinois legislature enacted a law in 1883 making attendance in school compulsory for every child between the ages of eight and fourteen for not less than twelve weeks each school year. The Chicago School Board took no steps to enforce the unpopular law until 1889, when three attendance agents, or truant officers, were appointed to help enforce the act. The CWC sent a resolution to the board, mayor, and city council late in 1888 demanding that the Compulsory Education Act be enforced. The club continued to actively support the further development of a compulsory education act in Illinois, urging more weeks of schooling and broadening the request to include younger and older children. The Truant Aid Com., formed primarily by the CWC members, provided clothing for children so that they could attend school.

3. The 1890 federal census indicates 5,685 Italian-born residents living in Chicago. By 1893–94 the newspaper editor and HH resident Alessandro Mastro-Valerio, in his description of the Italian Colony in Chicago in *HH Maps and Papers* (1895), placed the Italian population of the city at twenty-five thousand. Not all Italians lived in the same area of Chicago. A large, primarily southern Italian immigrant neighborhood developed south of the Chicago loop in the area of South Clark and Polk streets. By 1910 the Taylor-Halsted area had a population of approximately twenty-five thousand of Italian ancestry, almost one-third of Chicago's Italians. There was constant movement in and out of that neighborhood, which Italians also shared with Russians and Jews, Irish, Germans, and a smattering of other national immigrant groups. The survey conducted between 6 Apr. and 15 July 1893 in the HH neighborhood, the one-third square mile bordered by Halsted and State streets and Polk and Twelfth streets, revealed that Italians were "almost solidly packed into the front and rear tenements on Ewing and Polk Streets, especially between Halsted and Jefferson, and outnumber any single class in the district" (*HH Maps and Papers*, 17). Over time this community moved west of Halsted St. and into other neighborhoods of Chicago and its suburbs.

Alessandro Mastro-Valerio recognized that most of the Italians in Chicago belonged "to the peasant class" (*HH Maps and Papers*, 134). A largely unskilled southern Italian workforce controlled by the boss, or padrone, system channeled workers to intermittent work on railroads, in construction, and in manufacturing jobs. Rag picking was an option, and women took in sewing. Children worked where and when possible to add to the family income.

Until 1899 when the national parish of Holy Guardian Angel was organized, the Italian community in Chicago was served primarily by Assumption, Blessed Virgin Mary Church, organized as a city-wide parish. The church was located north of the Chicago River, near another large settlement of Italians, but it conducted missions in the Taylor-Halsted St. area.

4. Irish immigrants had come to the United States by the thousands as a result of harsh political and social conditions in Ireland and the five potato-crop failures in Ireland beginning in 1845. By 1850 approximately one-fifth of Chicago's population was Irish, and by 1890 there were 70,028 foreign-born Irish and an additional 176,358 of Irish heritage born in Chicago. They settled throughout the city, although primarily near employment opportunities and in neighborhoods associated with Irish Catholic parishes. They created their own organizations and clubs, and, unlike many other immigrant groups, most already spoke English and shared similar customs with longtime residents of the United States. "The Irish, although pretty well sprinkled, are most numerous on Forquer Street," reported Agnes Sinclair Holbrook in her general comments on the 1893 survey conducted of the one-third square mile of the city east of HH (*HH Maps and Papers*, 17). Irish lived throughout the HH neighborhood and formed the base of support for notorious Irish politician John Powers's strength in the area from his first successful election as alderman in 1888. Even though HH hosted Italian, German, and French social evenings, it never held an Irish night; however, many Irish women attended

events at the settlement; brought their children to nursery, kindergarten, and children's clubs; and especially participated in the HH Woman's Club.

5. Alessandro Mastro-Valerio (1855–1943), journalist, sometime truant officer, and advocate for agricultural colonies for Italian immigrants, was an early supporter and periodic resident of HH and a contributor to *HH Maps and Papers* (1895). His contacts with JA and EGS were important, and as recounted in this letter to MCAL, he had taken JA on a tour of Chicago's Italian quarter some months before the opening of HH. She was not to forget his many kindnesses and supported many of his ventures.

Born at Sannocandro Garganico, in the province of Foggia, in southern Italy, Alessandro Mastro-Valerio served as an officer in the Italian navy, 1876–80, cruising most of that time on the *Regia Corvetta Governale* in the southern Atlantic. He came to the United States in 1882 and joined the editorial staff of *Progresso Italo-Americano*, New York, in 1883. In the late 1880s, he moved to Chicago, where he soon became a force in the Italian community. *L'Italia*, the primary Italian newspaper in Chicago, indicated, "He was the only man who, as Italilan interpreter and nurse, went to risk his life . . . at the bedside of the cholera-stricken Italians in Cholera Hospital at Swinburne Island, New York, in the months of October and November 1887" ("A Worthy Appointment," *Chicago Inter Ocean*, 13 Jan. 1889). In 1888 Chicago had passed an ordinance designed to limit and control beggars and rag pickers, but the expected improvements did not take place. Concerned for the plight of poor Italian immigrants with few skills to work in the labor force, he had defended them. But in 1895, he observed that the rag pickers "formed a sort of political association, and let the party in power [Democratic] understand that they . . . would vote against that party at the next election if the interference of the police in their occupation was not stopped. . . . [T]he police, by secret orders," Mastro-Valerio charged, "let the ragpickers alone," thus assuring the Democrats of continued political support from the Italian-American community (Mastro-Valerio, "Remarks upon the Italian Colony," 138–39).

Mastro-Valerio had a deep commitment to education for the immigrants. He was instrumental in having the Illinois compulsory education law passed and for many years acted as a volunteer truant officer. And with the generosity and support of George Howland, superintendent of Chicago's public schools, he played a role in the opening of five evening schools for immigrants.

In Feb. 1895, with the encouragement of JA and other civic leaders, Mastro-Valerio attempted to start l'Istituto Italiano di Chicago (the Italian Institute of Chicago), modeled after a similar organization in New York City. Its goals were to offer a free employment bureau, protection, and relief and to promote colonization in the countryside. Headquarters was HH, specifically space in the Butler Art Gallery Building. It did not succeed for lack of financial support. Mastro-Valerio taught Italian at HH when he was in residence. He also spoke in an Italian lecture series at HH in 1896, helped organize and conduct Italian nights and other social events at the settlement, and became a director in various Italian clubs at HH. On the eve of his departure in Dec. 1890 for his agricultural colony in Alabama, EGS wrote her sister Mary Blaisdell: "I don't know how we are going to get on without him, but I think he is doing just the right thing, & I want him to do it. I'm not in love with him, quite, only about half!" But then added: "If he weren't Italian I would be." EGS found him "delightfully good . . . funny . . . one of the most entertaining men . . . and most unselfish" (19 [and 21] Dec. [1890], SC, Starr).

In 1898, with Giuseppe Ronga, Mastro-Valerio founded *La Tribuna*, an Italian-language newspaper. Its name was changed in 1900 to *La Tribuna Italiana*, and in 1903, when he assumed sole ownership, the name was changed again to *La Tribuna Italiana Transatlantica*. Published weekly, the newspaper was started initially for the benefit of Italians living in the Nineteenth Ward (where HH was located). Mastro-Valerio especially sought to weaken Irish political boss John Powers's hold, where he held sway as alderman, grocery store owner, and lord of a gambling establishment. In time the newspaper developed a city-wide audience, although it continued to primarily serve the near West Side Italian community. Its circulation was fifty-five hundred by 1905 and reached twenty-five thousand by 1908 and remained at that level into the early 1920s. The Kingdom of Italy recognized *La Tribuna*'s contributions to Italian-American life; the publication received the Diploma of Merit in 1907, and in 1921 its proprietor was made a knight (*cavaliere*) of the Italian kingdom in recognition of his contributions to the community.

A populist, Mastro-Valerio was a nineteenth-century liberal whose special heroes were Giuseppe Mazzini and Giuseppe Garibaldi—liberals, nationalists, and anti-Catholics. He was himself anti-Irish and militantly anti-Catholic. *La Tribuna* carried on a perpetual war with the *New World*, the Catholic newspaper, as well as with the Irish-dominated church hierarchy, over such issues as Italian nationalism, Garibaldi, and public education. His newspaper was criticized for its sensationalism, which emphasized brief, simply written articles, illustrations, and Italian theater and music and its free use of Italian American jargon, such as "storo" for store, "bosso" for boss, and "grosseria" for grocery store.

Mastro-Valerio's special concern was the economic and social conditions of Italian common laborers. Generally, he supported labor against capital, feeling that the latter abused the former. As the solution to these problems, he was an advocate of agricultural colonies. He observed that 80 percent of Italian immigrants were peasants, but in the United States they came not to till the soil, but to settle in cities, where they met with all the evils of urban life. He suggested that Italian immigrants should be encouraged to till the soil in their new country as they had in the old and that in terms of health, they would fare better in a rural than an urban environment.

To further these aims, he founded an agricultural colony at Daphne, Ala., in 1890. This venture had the support of JA and HH residents. As early as Jan. 1891, the weekly schedule of HH programs announced: "An effort is being made to encourage country colonization among the Italian peasants; it is hoped that a permanent colonization society may be formed in Chicago, co-operating with Sig. Mastro-Valerio in the Italian colony in Daphne, Alabama" (HH Scrapbook 2:5½; *JAPM*, Addendum 10:7ff). In its attempts to establish viticulture, the colony received backing from the U.S. Dept. of Agriculture and the State Experiment Station of Alabama. The colony also successfully cultivated potatoes, wheat, corn, rice, tobacco, and vegetables and promoted the improvement of the soil by fertilizing. A second colony was established in Lamberth, Ala., three years later. Despite Mastro-Valerio's well-meaning intentions, the colonies never received widespread support and attracted relatively small numbers of settlers.

Alessandro Mastro-Valerio's wife, Amelie (or Amelia or Emilie) Nusillard (perhaps Robinson) Valerio (1863 or 1866–1946), was also a HH resident during the 1890s and early 1900s. "[V]ery tall & dark" (EGS to Mary Houghton Starr Blaisdell, 2 Jan. 1895, SC, Starr), she had been born in Glenwood, Iowa. According to her death certificate, her parents were Emma Fleury of France and Fernandio Nusillard of Alsace. She wed Mastro-Valerio in Baldwin Co., Ala., in 1891. By 1895 she was helping in the HH office where all residents paid their bills. From 1897 to 1902, she was in charge of the HH U.S. Postal Sub-Station No. 10, open 8:00 A.M. to 6:00 P.M. daily, except Sunday. She also taught Italian and French classes in the settlement's College Extension Program. She served as Coffee House director from 1902 to 1906. During that same period, she was also banker for the Chicago Penny Savings program at HH, encouraging children to save money. Later she lived at 8 West Oak St. and became an inspector for the Chicago Dept. of Health. She was buried in Mt. Carmel Cemetery, Hillside, Ill.

Mastro-Valerio returned to Italy ca. 1933, at which time his newspaper closed, and he lived on the Bay of Naples.

6. In Chicago there were a number of opportunities for women to learn the Italian language. There was an Italian school in Chicago in 1869, but many young ladies would have

learned some Italian as they took singing lessons from private teachers, the Chicago Musical College, or the Chicago Conservatory. By 1889 there were a number of Italian clubs in Chicago. Mastro-Valerio may have been referring to the Club Maria Adelaide, which was highly social and gave parties and dances but also had a section that he called the "'Italian Beneficent Society of Chicago'" (Schiavo, *Italians in Chicago*, 60).

7. The New England Congregational Church destroyed in the Chicago Fire of 1871 was rebuilt at Dearborn Ave. and Delaware Place. By the late 1880s, the congregation had grown to more than six hundred, and the church supported a well-attended mission for German immigrants at 1460 Sedgwick St.

8. See JA to MCAL, 19 [and 20] Feb. 1889, n. 34, above.

9. Manufacturer, Eliphalet Wickes Blatchford (1827–1914), a trustee of the New England Congregational Church, and his wife, Mary Emily Williams Blatchford (1834–1921), had at least seven children, three of whom were daughters. Florence (1872–74) died in infancy. Amy (1862–1941) married Rev. Howard S. Bliss, pastor of the Plymouth Church, Brooklyn, N.Y., on 7 Nov. 1889 and went to live in Brooklyn. Frances ("Fanny") May Blatchford (1865–1919) seems likely the Miss Blatchford JA was describing. In a family memoir, *Letters, Journals and Memories of E. Huntington Blatchford*, Mary Emily Williams Blatchford wrote of her daughter that "her religious life was simply and literally her whole life." She was also described as concerned for the welfare of children and young people.

The entire Blatchford family was deeply involved in the life of the Congregational Church. Not only were they pillars of the New England Church in Chicago, but they were also supporters of inner-city social work. During the Civil War, both elder Blatchfords worked on behalf of the U.S. Sanitary Comm. in Chicago.

Eliphalet Wickes Blatchford was active in the Chicago City Missionary Society of the Congregational Churches and a member of the American Board of Commissioners for Foreign Missions. He played an important role in the establishment of the mission to Bohemian residents in "Prague," Chicago's first Bohemian neighborhood community. The result of that effort was the organization of Bethlehem Church, the community center that later became Bethlehem-Howell Settlement (see also JA to MCAL, 19 [and 20] Feb. 1889, n. 37, above). The work at HH would have been an obvious extension of the Congregational mission in "Prague."

Blatchford was a significant Chicago cultural leader and philanthropist. He helped establish both the Newberry and the Crerar libraries, was a director of the Chicago Theological Seminary, and was a founder of the Chicago Manual Training School that was absorbed by the Univ. of Chicago. He also served as a trustee for Illinois College in Jacksonville, Ill., and for JA's alma mater.

10. 10 Mar. 1889. Begun by the early 1880s, the Socialist Sunday School movement in Chicago was especially successful in the late 1880s after the 1886 Haymarket Riot. Various well-known labor leaders became teachers in the schools. Curriculum consisted primarily of history, geography, and science. One of the goals was to prevent children from attending religion-based Sunday Schools and to provide a more realistic view of the world the children inhabited.

According to an article in the 28 July 1889 *New York Volks-Zeitung* titled "The Socialist Sunday School in Chicago: Its History, Its Curriculum, Its Effectiveness," the leaders indicated that "we purposefully avoid saying anything about socialism. We are convinced that children schooled in this way will automatically find the right path. Nevertheless, each week the English-language newspapers here carry articles, sometimes even illustrated with pictures, claiming that we teach the children how to make dynamite bombs and tell them that they're supposed to kill the capitalists and the police. In its lies, the local English-language press balks at nothing when it comes to pinning something on the wicked socialists ('Anarchists')."

11. Frank A. Stauber (1848–1908) and German-born G. A. Englehardt were partners in

Frank A. Stauber and Co., 718 (later 1052) Milwaukee Ave., one of the largest stores in the area, selling stoves and ranges. Stauber was born in Switzerland in 1848. He came to Chicago in 1867 and worked as a tinsmith. By 1870 he had established his own firm. He served four years, 1878–82, on the Chicago City Council, elected from his Fourteenth Ward as a Socialist Labor Party candidate, and he was a member of the Board of Education for three years. He was dedicated to improving public school attendance and supported the development of kindergarten, vocational education, instruction in foreign language, and better training for teachers. In 1872 he wed Mary A. Doll of Peru, Ill., and they had four children: Mary Antonette, Anna Hermine, Melanie Larsallea, and Else.

Stauber worked diligently for the commutation of the death sentence against the Haymarket Riot anarchists and in 1886 was the United Labor Party's candidate for treasurer of Cook Co. By 1897 he and John Knefel were partners in real estate, lending, and an insurance businesses. He continued to be active in politics, but in the Democratic Party. In 1901 he went to South Africa. He became a postmaster in a small village near Pretoria, where he died.

12. The Illinois Woman's Alliance was a coalition of women from different classes and grew out of women's concern for the well-being of working women. Corinne Stubbs Brown (1849?–1914), social reformer, club woman, and socialist, was founder. It was the successor organization to the Frances Willard and Leila G. Bedell–led Woman's League of Chicago, founded in 1888, and was a reform organization active in the Chicago area until 1894. Then conflicts between the women who worked to pursue philanthropic activities and those who supported more militant action, like strikes, to correct problems overwhelmed the organization and it disintegrated.

The organization established three principles among women that undergirded efforts toward improving society: that the status and welfare of all women, from the poorest, was vital to the welfare and status of all women; that the future civilization rested on the welfare and condition of children; and that governmental officials and funds should serve the common good of all the people.

The initial and primary goal of the alliance was to do away with sweatshops. It was one of the groups, along with HH residents and the Chicago Trade and Labor Assembly, that joined Henry Demarest Lloyd to force the Illinois General Assembly to enact the Illinois Factory and Inspection Act (Sweatshop Act) in 1893.

13. JA was referring to neighborhood guild enthusiast Stanton Coit's idea, which he explained in his book *Neighborhood Guilds* (1891). He believed that neighbors in a small district should seek one another's company and help in an organized way. He sought to bring families, neighbors, and different interests together to meet and cooperate with other reform organizations. He developed the neighborhood-guild idea after learning of Toynbee Hall, perhaps from Howard S. Bliss (1860–1932), an early American visitor there, and after spending three months himself at Toynbee Hall in early 1886. Coit began his first guild in New York City in 1886, at 146 Forsyth St. It included twenty families and grew into University Settlement in May 1891. Coit also established the Leighton Hall Neighborhood Guild in Kenthis Town, London, in 1889.

Coit was born in Columbus, Ohio, and was educated at Amherst College, Columbia Univ., and Humboldt Univ., Berlin (Ph.D.). While he was forming his neighborhood guild, he became a leader in the ethical culture movement initially as an aid to Felix Adler (1851–1933) in the Society for Ethical Culture in New York.

He returned to London in 1888 as minister to the South Place Ethical Society. Coit eventually became president of the West London Ethical Society and preached in the Queen's Road (Bayswater) Ethical Church. In 1910 he became a Labour candidate for Parliament from Wakefield. He helped organize ethical culture societies, especially in England, and wrote prolifically on ethical culture subjects. Coit was the editor of the *International Journal of Ethics*, 1893–1905.

14. The Denison Club that JA may have been referring to was formed in 1885 to discuss social issues in general. Its members met at Toynbee Hall and were drawn from various areas of London. The club was named in honor of Edward Denison (1840–70), who, because of his deep interest in the plight of the poor, settled in a tenement in Stephany for eight months in 1867 to study the conditions in which they lived. He was an original member of the London Society for Organizing Charitable Relief and Repressing Mendacity (1869), out of which the Charity Organization Society (COS) movement in England evolved (see JA to Richard T. Ely,12 Mar. 1895, n. 1, below). Denison was one of the leaders in England's efforts to investigate and ameliorate conditions of the working poor. He was a staunch proponent of self-help. "'Build school-houses, pay teachers, give prizes, frame workmen's clubs, help them to help themselves, lend them your brains; but give them no money . . . by giving alms you keep them permanently crooked'" (quoted in Woods and Kennedy, *Settlement Horizon*, 19).

15. For information on the Moody School, see JA to MCAL, 12 Feb. 1889, n. 36, above.

16. JA's cousins Peter and Mary Young Worrall from Philadelphia were visiting in Chicago and had apparently decided not to travel on to visit Mary Worrall's brother, Charles Young, who lived in Kansas City, Mo., with his family. See *PJA*, 2:192, n. 4.

17. Likely John Elias Jenkins, born in 1849. He was a dry-goods commission merchant with the firm of Jenkins, Kreer, and Co. and had been a foreign buyer for Marshall Field and Co. and its predecessor, 1873–83, and superintendent of its dress-goods department, 1883–95. It is likely that Peter Worrall, also in the dry-goods business, representing Butterworth and Co., would have been visiting him. His residence was at 2625 (later 1730) Prairie Ave., and his business was on State St. in city-center Chicago.

18. JA's cousin and Mary Young Worrall's sister was Clara Young. See *PJA*, 1:92, n. 1. Her letter is apparently not extant.

19. This circular about the College Settlement in New York City is not extant in JA's papers or in the HH Assn. records. See also EGS [for JA] to Mary Houghton Starr Blaisdell [and SAAH], 23 Feb. [1889], n. 18, above.

20. None of JA's correspondence with Jean Gurney Fine seems to be extant. Jean Fine was a good friend of Jane Elizabeth Robins, whom she joined on weekends during the winter of 1887–88 as the two women took up residence at 130 Forsyth St., New York City, and associated their efforts at helping the poor with Stanton Coit's Neighborhood Guild. Robins, who became a physician in 1890, and Fine offered women of the neighborhood classes, social opportunities, and parties. By 1889 these two Smith College alumnae had joined Vida D. Scudder (1861–1954) in an effort to establish a College Settlement for Women. Although their intent was to provide programs especially for women, through their association with the Neighborhood Guild they soon had boys' clubs and began to expand their program in a variety of ways. In 1889 their operation moved to 95 Rivington St., where Jean Fine remained head resident from Oct. 1889 to July 1892, with Dr. Jane E. Robins serving in the same capacity from July 1893 until 1 Jan. 1898.

Jean Gurney Fine Spahr was born in Chambersburg, Pa., daughter of Lambert Suydam and Mary Ely Burchard Fine. She graduated from Smith in 1883 (B.A.) and was married in July 1892 to Charles Barzillai Spahr (see JA to MRS, [10 Oct. 1898], n. 2, below), author and associate editor of *Outlook*. Their children were Margaret, Elizabeth, Mary Burchard, Jean Gurney, and Helen Thayer. After teaching school in Clinton College, Ky., 1883–85, and Brearly School, New York City, 1885–89, she became head of the College Settlement until her marriage. She eventually lived in Princeton, N.J.; was a member of the Presbyterian Church; and served as president of the Present Day Club of Princeton. She continued her dedication to Smith College, fund-raising and serving on the editorial board of the *Smith Alumnae Quarterly*, 1916–27. By 1935 she was also honorary president of the Art Workshop, New York City, successor to the College Settlement. She died of pneumonia in New York City. See also EGS [for JA] to Mary Houghton Starr Blaisdell [and SAAH], 23 Feb. [1889], n. 18, above.

21. JA is referring to the first article published in a major daily newspaper about what would become HH. The headline and initial paragraph and a half of the article were printed at the bottom of one column and the larger remainder at the top of the next column. It is likely the larger portion that JA enclosed. This article does not appear in the HH Scrapbook, 1889–94. See Article in the *Chicago Daily Tribune*, 8 Mar. 1889, above.

## To Mary Catherine Addams Linn

4 Washington Pl [Chicago, Ill.] April 1st '89

My dear Mary

Both Ellen and I were rather appalled when her letter came back from Cedarville.[1] She had quite forgotten that the first part of the letter contained so much of her private financial affairs, and I did not know what was in the letter. She had read scraps of the last part and I had supposed it was all about "the scheme." It does not make any special difference however, for the entire financial basis will probably change before next fall. Dr Gunsaulus recommended a neighborhood last Sat.[2] and when we objected to the high rents he said "Oh that doesn't make any difference, we'll see to the rent for you." Two wealthly men have offered to become "associates on the paying bills [question?]," and a Mr Hogg,[3] (an Englishman at the head of the St Andrews Guild[4] who has friends in Toynbee Hall), thinks we will have to have an association to manage the financial part of it. We are not inclined to "organize" until we know our ground and people better, but if the promises are half fulfilled we will have no trouble on the money side. The Smith College movement in New York, is languishing for lack of volunteers,[5] they raised the sum of money they asked for within the first two weeks. When we are once started and need money, I think that there will be no difficulty, at present of course we have no use for it nor authority to collect it.

I have just come from the Maurice Porter Memorial Hospital on Fullerton Ave.[6] It is a beautiful house built for fifteen sick <&> poor children, I made arrangements there the other day for a little Italian boy nine years old, he has been almost blind since he was two and is very delicate without being absolutely sick. I took him this morning, his father went with me and was delighted with the house and the assurance that the child should always have enough to eat.

This hospital was built by Mrs Porter as a memorial to her little son. It is free but they have had vacancies all Spring because no one has applied. It is a curious instance of the need of communication between the benevolent people at the one end of the city and the poverty at the other.

I called on the Curtis'[7] this morning because I was so near—Mr Curtis has been ill in bed for a week and Bessie has malarial fever. Mr Curtis has been much interested in our plan, he knows Mr Goss very well (the pastor of Moody's Church) who is one of our best friends.

Our reception on Saturday[8] was much damped by the storm, it was blowing and raging as hard as possible at eight o'clock. Almost no one came from the south side, about twenty out of the fifty put in an appearance, and we were quite sure that they were interested. More than half of them were new, so that our whilom fear of founding a "Home for single women & widows" is being allayed. Mr Salter[9] who is at the head of the Ethical Culture Society,[10] and Mr Fischer[11] who is prominent in the Charity Organization Society[12] were two very interested and interesting people, they both talked so well and gave unqualified support. Mrs McConnell's[13] house was decorated very handsomely with flowers and she had also provided a Swedish singer—a tenor—to entertain the guests, so that it was quite a festive affair. Dr McPherson[14] did not put in an appearance. Miss Alice Miller[15] a Smith graduate of '83 who is very pretty and very popular is one of our strongest supports. She did good service on Saturday evening.

We have seen Prof. Swing[16] who has promised us "money or moral support" as we needed it—whatever that may mean.

I have been devoting all my spare time lately to seeing different neighborhoods, the result would make rather a doleful theme for a journalistic letter. You asked about taking Mrs Stryker's boys down to the Bohemians.[17] It was very successful, the boys took games with them Jack straws &c and they talked and played together in the most social way. They have since started a "Boys Union"[18] here to meet in the basement of the 4" Church. The larger portion of the membership is "little mickies who steal our marbles" I have been told.

I was waited upon rather formally by a committee of the W.C.T.U. last week who asked me to undertake some social work at their "Anchorage" on Third Ave.[19] South 3d Ave & South Clark are probably the two most disreputable streets in the city and they were anxious to get hold of young girls, school girls and others who would not come to Sunday School nor "meetings." I promised to undertake to meet a club once a week if they would collect the girls. We organized last Sat.[20] "A Girl's Social Club," a Miss Dodges[21] of the south side who is a very ready musician promises to come and help every Sat. afternoon, and we hope to get other ladies interested. The material is rather unpromising but I am very glad for the experiance.

I am getting a good many definite engagement[s]. Every Friday morning I give the Industrial Art lessons at the Missionary Training School,[22] and since we are on clay modelling I have been obliged to divide the class of sixty, so that it takes two full hours & with the preparation, all the morning.

We teach every Wednesday night of course at the Moody school,[23] and each Tuesday afternoon take a three hours lesson from Miss Locke.[24] I have about three appointments a week with the Attendance Agents or Relief Officers to see the city—so that there is very little time left. I have had five or six invitations to speak to different Missionery Societies on East London Missions. I have accepted four of them because it is a good opportunity for meeting various benevolent people, but I am always rather amused when I do it, for I know very little of

East London or its Missions I am obliged to stick closely to the three or four things I do know.[25]

We take dinner this evening at Mrs McLeish's (Miss Hillard)[26] with some Rockford Sem'y people. The Chicago Association of the Sem'y meets at her house the last of the week.

I have almost given up John and Web.[27] I am sorry they did n't come in for a few days at least. With love to each member of the family[.] Always Your loving Sister

Jane Addams.

Will you please send the letter to Alice and Weber. It takes so much time to write the same thing so often. Ellen wrote a long letter to her sister yesterday but I did not dare suggest that it be "sent around."[28]

ALS (SCPC, JAC; *JAPM*, 2:1050–61).

1. This letter is not known to be extant, unless JA was referring to EGS [for JA] to Mary Houghton Starr Blaisdell [and SAAH], 23 Feb. [1889], above.

2. 30 Mar. 1889.

3. Perhaps Guy W. Hogg of the Brotherhood of St. Andrew. He came to HH in Nov. and Dec. 1889 to visit Percival Chubb and to read *Alice in Wonderland* to children assembled on Thursday evenings at 7:30 P.M.

4. The Brotherhood of St. Andrew was organized in Chicago in 1883 by twelve young men who met at St. James Episcopal Church, Chicago, for prayer and Bible study and to undertake good works. By 1886 the organization had one hundred different chapters in the United States, and by 1900 the brotherhood had become an international movement.

5. In an article written for the *Kansas City (Mo.) Journal*, about 19 Apr. 1889, Eliza Putnam Heaton described plans for the development of the College Settlement. "And when does this project go into operation?" Heaton inquired. "Not until the hottest of the summer days are over," replied Jean G. Fine. And the reporter continued, "The college girls have friends who are unwilling that they should go through a summer in tenements until they have first tried a winter and become acclimated" (SAAH, ["Record Book of Copies of Letters and Articles"], 27, Starr, SC).

A later article in the *New York World*, 16 June 1889, reported: "The College Settlement is already an established fact since more than the necessary funds have been promised, and thirty-five residents have been secured from Vassar, Smith, [Columbia?], Wellesley, Michigan and Boston Universities, Bryn Mawr, and the Harvard Annex. The whole number present at any one time will be seven remaining two months and then being free until the whole thirty-five have served in rotation" (HH Scrapbook 1:1; *JAPM*, Addendum 10:6ff). See also EGS [for JA] to Mary Houghton Starr Blaisdell [and SAAH], 23 Feb [1889], n. 18, above.

6. Maurice Porter Memorial Hospital located at 606 (later 702) Fullerton Ave. in a new building, constructed in 1886, had been opened as an eight-bed cottage hospital in 1882. It could accommodate twenty children ages three to thirteen and had no restrictions as to "race, creed, or nationality" (*Hand-Book of Chicago's Charities*, 98). Until 1926 all hospitalization was free. In 1904 it was renamed the Children's Memorial Hospital. It was begun by Mrs. Julia Foster Porter (1846–1936) in memory of her son Maurice (d. 1881), who died at age twelve.

Julia Porter, widow of Rev. Edward Clark Porter (d. 1876) of St. Luke's Church, Racine, Wis., was the daughter of Nancy Smith and prominent physician John Herbert Foster. John Foster had amassed a considerable fortune from real estate holdings by the time of his accidental death in 1874, and Julia Porter and her two sisters each inherited one-third of one-half of his estate. Nancy Smith Foster received the remainder (see Article in the *Chicago Record*, 3 Dec. 1894, n. 10, below)

By 1890 the hospital was caring for about seventy children annually. Most were referred by the Illinois Humane Society, Children's Aid Society, Home for the Friendless, Half Orphan Asylum, Glenwood Industrial School, and the Orphan Home in Andover, Ill.

When a board of nine lady managers was named in 1892, it is likely that Julia Porter was the hospital's sole support. In 1904 she agreed to donate seventy-five thousand dollars for a new hospital to be known as the Children's Memorial Hospital, and she retired from active participation in the hospital's affairs to live in Hubbard Woods, Ill.

7. JA's classmate from RFS Laura Elizabeth Ely Curtis and her husband, Edwin (Edward) Curtis, had settled in Chicago. Bessie was one of their four children. See *PJA*, 1:295, n. 12.

8. 30 Mar. 1889.

9. See EGS [for JA] to Mary Houghton Starr Blaisdell [and SAAH], 23 Feb. [1889], n. 24, above.

10. The Society for Ethical Culture was founded initially in New York City in 1876 by Felix Adler. In 1882 a second society was organized in Chicago and developed by William Salter, who arrived in 1883 as a lecturer and remained in Chicago until 1892, when he went to the society in Philadelphia (see also EGS [for JA] to Mary Houghton Starr Blaisdell [and SAAH], 23 Feb. [1889], n. 24, above).

The society promoted the importance of the ethical factor in all life relationships. It provided lectures and religious services, placed emphasis on education, and helped establish free kindergartens, settlement houses, and adult learning programs. JA had a continuing relationship with the organization's programs in Chicago and was one of the society's lecturers. One of its early programs was a district nursing service begun in New York City in 1877. In Chicago that effort became the Visiting Nurse Assn.

It was Felix Adler who convened the lecturers for the School of Applied Ethics held during the summer of 1892 in Plymouth, Mass. At that gathering, JA delivered two lectures that brought her instant notoriety as a leader among other reformers in the United States (see Two Essays in the *Forum*, Nov. and Oct. 1892, below).

11. JA was probably referring to John Visher (1852–1914), who during the early life of the Charity Organization Society in Chicago was employed as the successful manager of the North Side branch during the late 1880s and into the early 1890s. On 16 May 1888, in an article titled "Charity Organization Society: Good Results Accomplished by the North Side Branch—Some Instances," the *Chicago Daily Tribune* praised his performance: "It has been a clearing house for ridding the benevolent of caring for any able-bodied beggars who chose to apply to them for help. . . . It shows the charitable where their charity will do the most good and, in brief, does just what its name implies—organizes charity."

Born in Holland, Ottawa Co., Mich., to Geesje Vander Harr and Jan Visscher, John Visher wed Julia Emma Sargent (1857–1948) of Hopkinton, Merrimack Co., N.H., in 1879. The couple had at least five children, all born in Illinois. Active in the Illinois Conf. of Charities and Correction, Visher was the compiler of *Hand-Book of Chicago's Charities* (1892). By 1900 the family had moved to a farm in South Dakota but by 1910 had returned to Chicago to live on North Sawyer Ave. The 1910 federal census return indicates that Visher was living on his own income. One of the Vishers' children, Stephen Sargent Visher (1888–1967), a graduate of the Univ. of Chicago, became professor emeritus of geography at Indiana Univ., an author, and a nationally recognized authority on weather.

12. The Charity Organization Society movement originated in Scotland and England. Its aim was to bring all charity relief under one administrative service to avoid duplication and make better use of the available resources. The movement had arrived in the United States in the 1870s and came to Chicago in the 1880s (see JA to Richard T. Ely, 12 Mar. 1895, n. 1, below).

13. See JA to MCAL, 26 Feb. 1889, n. 33, above.

14. See JA to MCAL, 12 Feb. 1889, n. 24, above.

15. See JA to MCAL, 19 [and 20] Feb. 1889, n. 19, above.

16. See EGS [for JA] to Mary Houghton Starr Blaisdell [and SAAH], 23 Feb. [1889], n. 20, above.

17. See EGS [for JA] to Mary Houghton Starr Blaisdell [and SAAH], 23 Feb. [1889], n. 21, above. JA seemed anxious to match up the children of the well-to-do Fourth Presbyterian Church with those of the working-class Bethlehem Church under the guidance of Rev. Edwin A. Adams. See JA to MCAL, 19 [and 20] Feb. 1889, n. 37, above.

18. By 1889 the Fourth Presbyterian Church had a definite missionary focus. There was one organization for young boys and one for young girls. Both were "'exclusively missionary.'" The boys' group had been encouraged to reach out to other young boys from other areas of the city, but especially from the church neighborhood in which the housing stock was "changing from a community of homes to one of rooming houses" (Scroggs, *A Light in the City*, 50–51).

19. Matilda Carse and Frances Willard led the Chicago WCTU to establish the Anchorage Mission for "wayward" women in 1886. It was located on 4th Ave. and was under the direction of Dr. Kate Bushnell (1856–1946) and Mrs. Elizabeth Wheeler Andrew. Only women were invited to come to the mission, initially called the Woman's Reading Room, where they could find food, a place to rest, and counseling. The goal of the program was to rehabilitate young women and give them a second chance at a moral life. By 1888 the Anchorage Mission had expanded into a former residence at 125 3rd Ave., where there were overnight accommodations for thirteen women. By Jan. 1889, such had been the success of the Anchorage Mission that 4,359 lodgings had been provided during 1888. At that time, work of the mission was still expanding, with an employment bureau, a weekly mothers' meeting, and a Bible class. However, by 1892 the program had fallen on hard financial times. Its work was taken over by Charles Crittendon (1833–1909), who designated it as the Florence Crittendon Anchorage in honor of his daughter, who died when she was four years old (see also JA to MCAL, 26 Feb. 1889, nn. 28–30, above).

20. 30 Mar. 1889.

21. Probably musician Mme. Jennie B. Dodge, whose address was 4 Timmerman's Opera House, 63rd St. and Stewart Ave.

22. See JA to MCAL, 26 Feb. 1889, n. 26, above.

23. The Moody Church school newsletter, *Pen and Scissors* (6 Apr. 1889), 4, reported: "It is with the greatest regret that we are compelled to permit Mr Shane to lay down his church work. . . . His class was taught last week most acceptably by Miss Adams, one of the gifted and devoted workers in the Industrial School, and next Sunday Mr. [Alexander Agnew] McCormick, the manager of the advertising department in A. C. McClurg & Co. will assume the labors which Mr. Shane has had to lay down." See also JA to MCAL, 12 Feb. 1889, n. 36; 19 [and 20] Feb. 1889, nn. 5, 7, both above.

24. Josephine Carson Locke. See JA to MCAL, 19 [and 20] Feb. 1889, n. 24, above.

25. None of JA's speech manuscripts on missions in East London from this period are known to be extant.

26. Martha Hillard MacLeish, who had been president of RFS, 1884–88, was newly married and living in Chicago with her widower businessman husband, Andrew MacLeish. See *PJA*, 2:420–21, n. 5. The MacLeishes lived at 627 (later 1726) West Adams and had a summer home in Glencoe, Ill.

27. JA was expecting a visit from her nephews, John Addams Linn and James Weber Linn.

28. EGS's letter is not known to be extant.

## To Anna Hostetter Haldeman Addams

4 Washington Place. City [Chicago, Ill.]— May 9" 1889

My dear Mama—

Mrs Rowell and I have been corresponding about a lost Psyche[1] and she has given me occasional news of you—otherwise I should be quite bereft of information. It has been so warm the last week & I have been trying to make up calls and get affairs into shape before I leave the city, so that when I come in I feel unequal to much writing. Mrs Henrotin[2] who has a very pretty home on this side, gave a reception to about thirty young ladies Tuesday afternoon[3] and I indoctrinated them in regard to the scheme. They evinced a good deal of enthusiasm and a Wellesley girl[4] and a Smith graduate Miss Perry[5] may "take up residence" next winter with us. It has become some thing of a fashionable "fad" and of course we realize that the ardor may all disappear before next winter but hope a few will be persistent.

I saw Miss Sill[6] last Saturday afternoon[7] at Oak Park, she has had pneumonnia this winter and looks old and broken, she has also had a good deal of family trouble. She was on her way to the Sem'y and seemed anxious to be with Miss Anderson.

We have been in a great deal of uncertainly about our house for next winter, depending on the sub lease.[8] We may be obliged to take some thing else for a few months after all and there are certain advantages in beginning in a simple "flat." Miss Culver[9] who owns most of the houses in our immediate neighborhood is very much inclined to give us the choice of what she controls. Dr McPherson remarked the other day that we were not so unworldly as we looked.

I suppose Alice started for Geneseo[10] yesterday and will be at Cedarville in about a week. Please give my dearest love to Sarah[11] and believe me Always Yr affectionate daughter

Jane Addams.

ALS (UIC, JAMC; *JAPM*, 2:1064–66).

1. JA's correspondence with Amelia Rowell is apparently not extant. The two women had traveled in Italy, the Riviera, Spain, France, and England together in 1888. On that trip, JA had purchased a copy of a statue of the *Psyche of Capua* she had discovered in Naples during her previous European adventure, 1883–85 (see *PJA*, 1:594n26; 2:325n20). According to her letter to SAAH, JA valued the rendering of *Psyche* for its "beauty" (see 7 May 1884, UIC, JAMC; *JAPM*, 1:1491; *PJA*, 2:323).

2. JA had met Ellen Martin Henrotin (1847–1922) through members of the CWC, in which Henrotin was an active and influential member. She was born in Portland, Maine, the eldest of six children of Edward Byam and Susan Ellen Norris Martin, and educated primarily in England, France, and Germany. The year after the Martin family moved to Chicago, Ellen married Charles Henrotin (1843–1914), a diplomat who founded the Chicago Stock Exchange. The couple had three children who lived to maturity.

Henrotin became a reformer who worked as a writer, speaker, and leader for women's financial independence and increased civic responsibility. During the late 1880s, she was an

This earliest known photograph of Hull-House was probably taken in 1891, shortly after the Butler Building was added to the original Hull home. By 1894 Mary Rozet Smith had replaced the picket fence and the wooden walkway leading to the main entrance with a brick wall and concrete walkway. "Mary's wall" was rebuilt and straightened by her father, Charles Mather Smith, in 1899 (HH Assn., UIC, JAMC, 0132 0146).

advocate for a protective agency for women and children. A member of Chicago's Fortnightly Club (1874), CWC (1884), and the Friday Club (1887), all of which she served as president, she earned national and international recognition as the vice-president and acting director of the Woman's Branch of the 1893 World's Columbian Exposition, as she developed thirty congresses on a variety of topics important to women. She moved on to help develop the General Federation of Women's Clubs while she was its president, 1894–98.

She was a staunch supporter of the reform efforts of JA and HH. In 1891 and 1892, she presented lectures at the settlement, spoke at HH Woman's Club functions, and attended a variety of settlement events. Between 1904 and 1907, she was president of the Illinois Women's Trade Union League. Working with JA, she created the Chicago Industrial Exhibit of 1907 that provided a showcase for women's work.

For the remainder of her life, she continued to serve as a volunteer on boards of organizations with programs devoted to helping disadvantaged women and girls. She was one of two women (JA being the other) appointed to the Chicago Vice Comm. in 1910. She died destitute at her son's home in Cherry Plains, N.Y.

3. 7 May 1889.

4. If graduates and faculty of Wellesley College had a leadership role in initiating the Col-

lege Settlement in New York City, they also had good representation at HH. By 1891 at least five Wellesley graduates, all of whom had been acquainted at the college, became active at HH as teachers in the College Extension Program, although none of them became residents.

It is likely that the first Wellesley graduate to join the settlement venture was Mary Ware Howe (Straus) (1867–1950), who was born in Chicago and returned home after graduation from Wellesley (B.S. 1888) to live. At HH she taught modern history and English history until 1894. Beginning in 1893, she also taught modern English poetry and presented a class on Thomas Carlyle. During the winter and spring of 1894, she had a reading party once a week. In 1894 she wed Michael Straus, who had been Belgian art commissioner at the World's Columbian Exposition, 1893. The couple, who eventually had four sons, settled in the Chicago area, where Straus became involved in the real estate business. Mary Straus became a member of the CWC.

By 1890 the Stone sisters, Harriet (1866–1961) and Isabelle (1868–1966), were holding classes at HH. They had been born in Chicago to Leander Stone, editor of the *Chicago Times*, and his wife, Harriet Leonard Stone, an early leader in the Chicago YWCA. After both girls took a five-year course in music at Wellesley (B.A. 1889, 1890), both attended the Univ. of Chicago, where they received M.A.'s in science, and Isabelle also received her Ph.D. in physics and mathematics in 1896. While they were students at the Univ. of Chicago, and at least until 1894, Isabelle taught algebra and Harriet chemistry at HH. Isabelle also added astronomy and geometry to her settlement curricula and in 1892 also taught women's gymnastics classes.

By the end of 1896, both women had left HH and Chicago. With Harriet teaching at Forest Park Univ., St. Louis, Mo., 1897–1907, Isabelle began her career as a teacher at Vassar, 1897–1906. While she was at Vassar, she conducted scientific research at Columbia Univ. and published several papers resulting from it. Then in 1907, the sisters moved to Europe. Until the start of World War I, they operated a small school for American girls in Rome. Returning to the United States, Isabelle helped establish the Physics Dept. at Sweet Briar College in Virginia. Then in the early 1920s, the sisters opened Misses Stones' School for Girls in Washington, D.C. As a result of the Great Depression of 1929, they closed their school, after only six years of operation, and they moved to Ponce, P.R., where both made their living tutoring. When Harriet's health failed, the sisters moved to North Miami, Fla., where both sisters died.

Adaline ("Ada") Swallow Woolfolk (1869–1962), who became a social worker and teacher, was born in Helena, Mont., to Annie S. and Col. Alexander M. Woolfolk, an attorney, who lived in Evanston, Ill. Graduating from Wellesley (B.S. 1891), Ada joined her college colleagues as a HH volunteer. There she taught English composition during the fall of 1891, added rhetoric and grammar for the spring of 1892, and beginning in Jan. 1892 conducted a girls' sewing class on Monday afternoons. After teaching during the 1893 school year at the Mary Institute in St. Louis, Mo., she became associated with the college settlements in Boston and in New York City, where she conducted research in housing for the New York Tenement House Comm. and was assistant head worker at the College Settlement on Rivington St. Ada taught at Emma Willard Institute, Troy, N.Y. (1896–1903), and at Briarcliff Manor-Knox School, Briarcliff, N.Y. (1905–11). Between 1914 and 1918, she was chief probation officer in Louisville, Ky.; served the American Red Cross, 1918–22, and the Family Welfare Society, 1922–31, both in Atlanta; and also taught at Agnes Scott College and Emory Univ. By 1932 she was in charge of federal unemployment relief in Chicago. Among her special interests were preschool children in underprivileged families, civic development, and community organization. She served on numerous boards and committees in the various communities in which she worked. By 1941 she was retired and living in Charlotte, N.C.

The fifth Wellesley graduate was Vennette Sweet Crain. See JA to AHHA, 11 Aug. 1890, n. 9, below.

5. Jennette Barbour Perry (Lee) (1861–1951) was born in Bristol, Conn., the daughter of Philemon and Mary Barbour Perry. She graduated from Smith College (B.A. 1886) and from

1886 until 1890 taught philosophy, rhetoric, and composition at Grant Collegiate Institute in Chicago. There is no evidence that Miss Perry became a HH resident or volunteer. Between 1890 and 1905, she had posts as a professor of English in Vassar College (1890–93); College for Women, Western Reserve Univ., Cleveland (1893–96); and her alma mater (1901–13). In 1896 she wed author, lecturer, and editor Gerald Stanley Lee. She was the author of numerous popular novels and children's books.

6. Anna P. Sill had been principal of RFS while JA was a student there. For a biographical note, see *PJA*, 1:178–79, nn. 6, 10; 1:437, n. 4.

7. 4 May 1889.

8. JA was negotiating a lease with owner Helen Culver (see n. 9) for a portion of the house located at 335 (later 800) South Halsted St. that she had selected in which to begin her "scheme" (see also JA to EGS, 4 June 1889, n. 11, below). JA recalled, "The house was of course rented, the lower part of it used for offices and storerooms in connection with a factory that stood back of it. However, after some difficulties were overcome, it proved to be possible to sublet the second floor and what had been the large drawing room on the first floor" (*Twenty Years*, 93).

Built in 1856 by successful real estate developer and philanthropist Charles J. Hull (see introduction to part 1, n. 37, above) for his family, the house had been considered a "very fine and elegant" structure. When it was built, "the neighborhood was a comparatively pleasant one, and it was expected that other families of similar tastes and means would seek homes in the vicinity," wrote Mary H. Porter (see EGS to JA, 4 June 1889, n. 6, below). The financial crisis of 1857 ended those hopes, and by 1868 the Hull family had abandoned the house to urban development.

Writing for the WCTU's *Union Signal*, Emily A. Kellogg described the house as "a fine old mansion built in the early part of the fifties, as a suburban home, for in those days Halsted street was quite a suburban part of Chicago. It is a square two-storied . . . house, with additions at the rear and one side. The hall, running through the center, is broad, the ceilings high. Its being used as a furniture warehouse for some years past probably did it less injury than tenement occupancy would have done. The heavy mouldings of doors and windows, and the lighter ones of the ceilings are comparatively unmarred" ("HH"). See also Two Essays in the *Forum*, Nov. and Oct. 1892, nn. 93, 103, below.

Architect Allen B. Pond, who over the coming years would work on alterations to the structure, described the house as "spacious for that day and excellently built. In addition to the drawing room and the other usual apartments of a northern house of the period, there was an octagonal office in a one-story wing to the south, opening from the library and onto the veranda. The material was a purplish red brick, in texture and color not unlike the common brick of Sayre and Fisher. On three sides of the house were broad verandas, a low-gabled room covered the high attic surmounting the second story, and the wide eaves were carried by heavily molded brackets. Indeed, after the mode of the time, columns, lintels, casings, and cornices were all heavily molded; the interior door and window casing being some 12 inches wide by 8 inches deep and elaborately built up of rope and other moldings" (Comm. on Chicago Historical and Architectural Landmarks, "Jane Addams' Hull-House and Dining Hall," 5). Sayre and Fisher Brick Co., Sayreville, N.J., in existence, 1850–1970, was at one time known as the largest brick manufacturer in the United States.

Charles J. Hull reported in his autobiography, *Reflections*, that the molding surrounding the doors and windows on the first floor of the house had been created by inmates at the Bridewell Prison where Hull spoke and offered Bible study on Sundays. Unfortunately, Hull did not reveal the name of the house's designer.

After Charles Hull left what the *Chicago Times* referred to as "Hull's Folly," it became a rental property. The Little Sisters of the Poor, a Roman Catholic order of French women established in France in 1839 with a mission of caring for the old and infirm, rented the Hull home for two years for seventy-five dollars a month beginning in July 1876. By the summer of 1877, the seven sisters were soliciting funds to support their work and managing the home with thirty-two enfeebled inmates, ten of whom were men. Eventually, Chicago had three homes operated by this order. This particular house of the order eventually moved to the corner of Harrison and Throop streets.

By 1880 the Hull home had become a boardinghouse operated by Kate Kinsley, born in Ireland and age forty. She had three children living with her, all of whom had been born in Illinois, and a servant who had been born in Ireland. Her eldest, a daughter, Margaret, who was twenty-two, was a bookbinder. Among her ten boarders were a coal dealer, two dressmakers, an iron molder, a seamstress, a painter, a baker, a news agent, and a cabinetmaker.

JA later recalled that a "Chicago wit" referred to the saloon, the settlement, and the undertaking parlor as "'Knight, Death, and the Devil'" (*Twenty Years*, 94). The 1889 *Lakeside Directory* for Chicago indicated that the saloon to the south of HH was located at 343 (later 824) South Halsted and owned (on real estate leased from Helen Culver) by Matthew Murphy (1844–1924), born in Ireland. In 1880 he lived just to the south of the saloon at 363 (later 844) South Halsted with his family, wife Mary E. Pepper (1855–ca. 1927–28), born in Illinois of Irish immigrant parents, and their two children James (b. 1876) and Grace (b. 1878), both born in Illinois, and one servant Mary Gorman, also born in Illinois of Irish immigrant parents. During 1895 and 1896, the threat of divorce initiated by Mary hung over the Catholic family, but was never finalized. By 1900 the Murphys and their nine children, one of whom was born in 1898, lived in one of four apartments in a tenement that had replaced the saloon. Matthew Murphy had become a constable. Sometime before 1910, the Murphy family left the HH neighborhood. Son James was an electrician and daughter Grace a wire winder. By 1910 Grace was a bookkeeper at HH. JA and EGS befriended the Murphys, and by 1891 JA was able to secure the site of Murphy's saloon as the first gymnasium for the settlement. Mary Murphy was an early and long an active member of the HH Woman's Club.

Just to the north of the Hulls' former home and with an address of 331 (later 775) South Halsted was the undertaking and livery business of Edward J. McGeeney (1857?–1908), who operated a saloon on the east side of Halsted St. at 374 (later 903) as Kelly & McGeeney's saloon. By 1892 that saloon had also disappeared; however, eleven other saloons still operated within a block of HH. McGeeney had an undertaking establishment as early as 1885 at 306 (later 717) South Halsted. While his residence was located at 228 (later 821) West Ewing, he moved his working address to the corner of Polk and Halsted streets, where he rented from Helen Culver while JA and EGS were creating HH. McGeeney ran as a Democrat for the office of Cook County commissioner in 1896. After his first wife died, he wed widow Mary Murphy Roth (1864?–1941) in 1899, and the couple had two daughters. By 1900 McGeeney had moved his undertaking business to 353–57 (later 830–83) South Halsted and opened a branch at 1335 (later 3002) West Van Buren St. He had moved his home to 1449 (later 3144) West Jackson Boulevard. When he died, the McGeeney family was living at 2064 West End.

9. Helen Culver (1832–1925), Chicago businesswoman and philanthropist, became a staunch HH supporter and friend of JA. She was born in Little Valley, N.Y., the youngest of four children of Lyman (1803?–51) and Emeliza Hull Culver (d. 1838), sister of the father of Charles Jerold Hull (see introduction to part 1, n. 37, above). Lyman Culver believed in educating all of his children. Like her siblings, Robert, Aurelia, and Susan, Helen attended the local school and was encouraged to read and study in her father's growing library. By the age of fourteen, Helen was teaching school in her community. Sometime after her mother died, her father remarried. His second wife was Sarah Price, with whom he had two children. When Helen's father, a respected and wealthy farmer and real estate dealer, died unexpectedly, Helen and her unmarried siblings decided that their father's entire estate should go to his second wife and her children.

By 1853 Helen and her brother, Robert, were living with their grandfather Noah Culver, who had recently settled in DeKalb, Ill. There Helen, who had attended the Randolph Academy and Female Seminary, Randolph, N.Y., and had teaching experience, established a private school and taught both day and night classes in Sycamore, Ill., until 1854, when she joined her brother in Chicago.

Helen quickly became associated with the Chicago public schools, first teaching primary grades and then high school classes, 1854–61. More important, she was reacquainted with her cousin Charles Jerold Hull, whom she had known in New York, and with his family. The Hulls had recently settled in their new home at what would become 335 South and then 800 South Halsted St. Charles J. Hull's wife, Melicent A. C. Hull, died in 1860, but not before she and Helen had become best friends and Helen had promised to help rear the Hull children. Helen, "'of medium height and figure, with large gray eyes, blooming complexion, loosely curing bronze hair'" (Martha Ellen French quoted in Goodspeed, *Helen Culver*, 10–11), gave up teaching and moved into the Hull home as housekeeper and tutor to Charles M. (1847–66) and Fredrika B. Hull (1849–74). After a brief stint as a nurse for Union forces during the Civil War at the military hospital at Murfreesboro, Tenn., she returned to Chicago and settled once again with the Hull family.

By 1868 Helen Culver and the Hull family had moved from the Hull home on Halsted but retained ownership of the house and property surrounding it. The neighborhood was changing, and the two Hull children were no longer at home: Charles, who had matriculated at the first Univ. of Chicago, had died quickly and unexpectedly from typhus while a student in law school, and Fredrika, who graduated from Oberlin College, Ohio, was traveling on a multiyear European grand tour with her best friend, Martha Ellen French (1846–1918), who in later years became a full-time companion to Helen Culver. Helen Culver assumed new responsibilities associated with the Hull family. She became an assistant to cousin Charles in his growing and highly successful real estate business.

Helen Culver learned the real estate business from Hull and had a close and loving relationship with him. The two shared business dealings, family, and philanthropic ideas. She taught in the night school Hull created at his Chicago office to help educate children involved in the street trades. Both Hull and Culver were temperance advocates and believed that they were doing a public service by making housing available to the poor. Culver was supportive of Hull's efforts in Savannah, Ga. She taught in the night school they opened there, 1871–72, that eventually hosted more than three hundred students.

After Fredrika Hull's death in 1874, Hull traveled more, and Helen remained in Chicago to manage the main office and business in the city. The Hull-Culver partnership became even closer, and in 1881 Charles J. Hull completed a will that left his business and estate to Helen. When Hull became ill with nephritis in 1884, Culver cared for him at home until he died on 14 Feb. 1889—just as JA and EGS began their search for suitable quarters in which to begin the settlement.

Among the assets Helen Culver inherited from her cousin were more than two hundred lots in Chicago and over one thousand throughout other states. She continued to live in the Hull home on Ashland Ave. across from Union Park and to run the real estate business in Chicago from her West Lake St. office. She hired her brother, Robert, to manage the properties in other locales.

For the remainder of her life, Helen Culver paid increasing attention to donating Charles Hull's legacy to philanthropic endeavors that she believed he would have liked. With a gift worth at least a million dollars to the Univ. of Chicago, she established the Hull Biological Laboratories to promote and enhance the study of biology. The structures were centered around Hull Court with a statue of Charles J. Hull, whom she meant to recognize and honor with the gift. She continued to maintain a close relationship with the leadership at the university. Through the Chicago City Club, she provided funds for a study of the finances of the city of Chicago conducted by Univ. of Chicago political science professor Charles E. Merriam (1874–1953). It was published in *Report of an Investigation of the Municipal Revenues of Chicago* (1906). From the Helen Culver Fund for Race Psychology, she supported the immigration study by sociologists W. I. Thomas (1863–1947) and Florian Znaniecki (1882–1958) that resulted in the pathbreaking five-volume *The Polish Peasant in Europe and America* (1918–20). As a devoted friend of the Geographic Society of Chicago, in 1906 Culver endowed a medallion that carried her name and honored scientific achievement, and she supported the library fund of the Field Museum of Chicago. She maintained a lifelong relationship with JA, gradually selling, leasing, or donating to HH Assn. the real estate on which HH was developed.

Culver was apparently intrigued by the settlement idea and over almost twenty years helped JA develop it by providing the land on which additional settlement buildings were constructed. The first agreement JA negotiated with Culver was a sublease on a portion of the property (see JA to EGS, 4 June 1889, n. 11, below) at that time leased by Culver to the Sherwood Co., manufacturers of school desks and seats. By Mar. 1890, JA and EGS had obtained use of the entire structure. After they named their settlement HH, keeping the historical family connection, Helen Culver agreed to waive the rent (see JA to AHHA, 3 June 1890, n. 14, below), but sparred with JA over paying for repairs and refinements (see Helen Culver to JA, [9?] [Mar. 1890], n. 1, below).

Throughout the 1890s, JA and her representative Allen B. Pond conferred with Culver over real estate. Recognizing that Culver owned the surrounding property on which the growth of her settlement depended, JA determined to establish and maintain a solid relationship with Culver. As early as 19 Jan. 1891, Culver was in doubt about JA's business acumen. In a letter to her cousin Nelly, Helen Culver described JA's spending to renovate the leased HH as a "mingling of economy and lavish expenditure." But she also found JA "unselfish" and "large hearted" and only wanting "to make the world happier and better" (UIC, JAMC, Hull-Culver Collection). JA and Helen Culver crossed paths in early 1893 while both were vacationing in Florida. Writing from the Seminole Hotel, Winter Park, Fla., on 11 Jan. 1893, Culver reported to Martha French that "Miss Jane Addams is here only younger, a little brainy and slender—very sweet and winning. Her name is unknown and I have not yet made her acquaintance" (UIC, JAMC, Hull-Culver Collection). Over the years, the two women became more friendly. For her part, Culver, who felt a responsibility to carry forward her benefactor's philanthropic perspective, became fascinated with the HH programs she saw developing. Concerned that the settlement might not be permanent, in 1895 she tied a new multiyear rent-free lease on the property to a demand that HH be incorporated in order to guarantee better business practices and the settlement's continuity should JA leave for any reason. She also demanded a place on the board of trustees for herself or her appointee. For many years, she served as vice-president of the HH Assn., and when she left the board in 1920 she was replaced by her nephew Charles Hull Ewing (see JA to MRS, 22 June 1899, n. 9, below).

Culver's concern for the continuation of the HH program remained strong. At one time, she may have suggested that the relatively new Univ. of Chicago, with which she would share a large portion of Charles J. Hull's estate, manage the settlement properties and programs. After receiving an indication of Culver's suggestion from university president William Rainey Harper, JA wrote a strong defense for the independence of the settlement (see JA to William Rainey Harper, 19 Dec. 1895, below).

Culver also continued resisting JA's attempts to purchase land around the settlement, favoring instead long-term leases. However, Culver did agree to sell property on which the Children's Building and the Jane Club were built. Then in 1906, Culver gave to the HH Assn. the land on which the early HH buildings were erected, including the Hull home, and also presented the land and a $50,000 endowment for the new Boys' Club Building, constructed facing Polk St. In 1920 Culver gave between $175,000 and $250,000 to the settlement, intending it for an endowment, which was not to be spent until it reached $500,000. This was her last major gift to HH.

Helen Culver retired from business in 1900. In 1896 she invited Charles Hull Ewing (1868–1954), son of her sister, Aurelia Culver Ewing, and her husband, Robert Finley Ewing, to join her in the real estate business and to help manage her financial affairs. Her attorney, 1891–1904, W. W. Grinstead, recalled her as "absolutely fair in business transaction." She believed that "business intercourse of the right sort was a mutual thing and that it was by no means to be assumed that only one of the parties could be benefited." He recalled her as calm and given to study before making a business decision and "gifted with a wonderful memory and capacity for mastering details." She had "at all times a thorough knowledge of her business . . . [was] courteous, considerate, and easy to approach" (Goodspeed, *Helen Culver*, 14). As she went blind, she continued to be the excellent student she had been all of her life. Declaring books the "'breath of life,'" she doted on the classics in literature and poetry; she taught herself Latin, German, French, Spanish, and, after she was blind, Italian (Goodspeed, *Helen Culver*, 16). Shortly after her retirement, she established a summer home that she called "Rockwoods" on a farm west of Lake Forest, Ill. By 1913 she had established a second, or winter, home in Sarasota, Fla. She eventually became bedridden, but Martha French continued to oversee her care and act as companion. When Helen Culver died in 1925, her estate was valued at nearly $2 million, but none of it was directed to HH.

10. MCAL, JML, and their children lived in Geneseo, Ill.

11. Likely SH, with whom JA and AHHA toured Europe in 1883–84. See *PJA*, 1:531–32 and 2.

## Letter to the *Woman's Journal* (Boston)

*The first article authorized by Jane Addams and Ellen Gates Starr about the "scheme" appeared in the* Woman's Journal *(Boston), published 25 May 1889. It was written by early settlement supporter Dr. Leila G. Bedell, probably with the assistance of Ellen's friend Mary E. Beedy. Both women were Chicago contributors to the journal.*

*Jane offered her reaction to the article to Ellen on 21 May: "I am a little sorry you wrote to Miss Beedy, at any rate the worst has happened. The article was read before the Woman's Convention[1] meeting <at present> in Freeport, and copied in full in the Freeport daily.[2] . . . I positively feel my callers peering into my face to detect 'spirituality.' We have probably made a mistake not to write it ourselves from the first, but I think now we had better wait until next fall, the reports are so contradictory that they can't hurt us much."[3]*

### A CHICAGO TOYNBEE HALL.

Chicago, Ill., May 25, 1889.

There is so much in Chicago out of which to find material for letters on topics of interest to woman, that one hesitates and deliberates upon a choice of subject. The women's club alone, with its 450 earnest working women, touching civilization at so many points, is an unfailing source of interesting information about what women are doing. But at the present time a far more interesting topic presents itself—not about "what women are doing" in the larger and more collective sense, but about what two women are doing who have become thoroughly infected with the contagion of doing good while investigating, last year, the work of the Universities' Settlement in East London.[4]

London has its Toynbee Hall, with university men as residents; but Chicago is to have a similar work projected and carried on by women, and women of rare culture and refinement as well as of rare grace and personal attraction. To them it means something to forego the fascinations of fashionable society life, for which they are remarkably well adapted. The moving spirit in this novel philanthropy is Miss Addams (and you will please forbid your proof-reader's correcting my orthography of the name). She is a young lady, still quite young enough to make her choice of such a life-work, with all the sacrifices which it involves, a seven days' wonder to all who know her. It is evident to every one that she goes into the work from no desire for notoriety, for she is the physical expression of modest simplicity itself; nor as an employment for remuneration, for she gives not only her time but generously of her means, of which she possesses sufficient to place her beyond the need of remunerative occupation, and to enable her to indulge her refined tastes in the many ways most attractive to young ladies of culture. Miss Addams's rarest attraction—although possessing a generous share of physical beauty—is her wonderful spirituality. One cannot spend much time in her presence without wondering by what processes she has attained to such remarkable growth of soul; how she has at so early a period of life grown "out of her little self into her larger self," as Prof. Harris puts it.

Her associate is Miss Ellen Starr, a niece of Miss Ellen[Eliza] Starr,[5] the artist. More perfect counterparts could scarcely be imagined. Miss Starr supplements Miss Addams completely. She is full of vivacity, a rare conversationalist, and one who never loses sight of the humorous side of things. She is a great favorite in society, with young and old, men and women. Petit, graceful, brilliant, even to sparking, she adds to the combination what could be no means be left out.

Now these young ladies have taken a house in the nineteenth ward (the worst in the city, in the sense of what is forcibly described as "tough"), and they propose to live there to know the most wretched phases of poverty from actual contact; to study the needs of these people, and then to devise means for their elevation.

One recalls an expression of Mrs. Harper,[6] once made upon the platform when speaking on the "Needs of the Colored People;" she said "they want wants." And so with some classes of the poor; they are so hopelessly degraded by poverty that they "want wants;" they need aspirations.

The work which these brave young ladies have undertaken looks like a Herculean task. But they have determined to answer affirmatively with all their powers, physical and spiritual, the question which is ringing in many of our ears. "Am I my brother's keeper?" It is no time for us to interpose any objections as to it expediency, its propriety, its safety. There are no lions in the way of any such work, which cannot readily be subdued by the power of an earnest soul.

What they will do will not bear any proportion to what they will be; to the quiet influence which will spread itself on both sides of the social line, acting as a chemical force to bring about some sort of union between two elements, having some affinity for each other, but which have long lain inert for want of a suitable reagent. There will be no lack of work for these people. The influence of the new kind of home life introduced among them will be one of the agents in making them "want want." One of its chief aims will be to make it also a retreat for other young women, who need rest and change, or who desire a safe refuge from the inordinate demands of society, and in whom it is believed that a glimpse of the reverse side of life, of the poverty and struggles of half the people, will beget a broader philanthropy and a tenderer sympathy and leave less time and inclination for introspection, for selfish ambition, or for real or fancied invalidism.

These young ladies intend to wield a two-edged sword against "apathy, ignorance, isolation and selfishness in the masses, which are the powers of resistance to be vanquished before by any chance a self-governed people can become a well-governed people." Whoever has caught a single glimpse of the Golgotha of poverty, and has turned away with the memory of the vision lashing him into a ceaseless desire to rush to the rescue of humanity, can safely be trusted with the details of a work so solemnly and so heartily espoused.

Such workers are Miss Addams and Miss Starr. No one need predict a failure based upon any less cause than failure of life. And they undertake this enterprise without asking money. But be assured Chicago will come to their rescue generously, that the work may lack nothing in its power and efficiency through lack of funds to secure its greatest measure of success.

Leila G. Bedell.

PD (*Woman's Journal* [Boston] 20 [25 May 1889], 162; HH Scrapbook 1:1; *JAPM*, Addendum 10:6ff).

1. The article came out in time to be read before the Illinois district meeting of the Equal Suffrage Assn. being held 28 and 29 May 1889 in Freeport, Ill., just five miles south of JA's Cedarville hometown. According to the *Woman's Journal* (Boston) of 1 June 1889, the convention was a success.

The Illinois Equal Suffrage Assn. had been created in 1885 when the Illinois Woman Suffrage Assn. changed its name and its goal from "seeking 'political equality with men'" to securing "'political enfranchisement of women'" (Buechler, *Transformation of the Woman Suffrage Movement*, 107).

2. The local *Freeport Daily Journal* published the article on 29 May 1889 in its report about the suffrage gathering. It omitted the paragraph that began "One recalls an expression on Mrs. Harper . . ."

3. JA to EGS, 31 May [1889], SC, Starr; *JAPM*, 2:1063.

4. A reference to Toynbee Hall supported by students from Oxford and Cambridge universities.

5. Eliza Allen Starr was EGS's Chicago aunt (see *PJA*, 1:239–40).

6. Ida H. Husted Harper (1851–1931), journalist and suffragist, was a frequent contributor to the *Woman's Journal* (Boston). In 1889 she was editing the "Woman's Department" of the *Locomotive Fireman's Magazine*, official journal of the fireman's union. She became the author of *Life and Work of Susan B. Anthony* (1898 and 1908) and collaborated with Anthony on vol. 4 of *History of Woman Suffrage* (1902).

## To Ellen Gates Starr

Cedarville Ill Jun 4" 1889

Dearest—

I consider Miss Mc Avoy[1] a great thing both for the nursing and the fact that if she "resides" she may help on running expenses, I am quite impatient for the next letter and hope you secured her. Dear Miss Lyon[2] is exactly the right kind of a ally not too enthusiastic to have her words judicious and of weight.

I tried the Tribune article to-day, I am sure I will have to wait until I see you. I look at my marble Psyche[3] some times, and think of the other Soul without whom I get on so badly.

You might see Mr Medill[4] before you leave if you think it ought to come out now—I think <&> still think it well to wait, we can write under own signatures <next fall> and assume we are forced into print because of much misrepresentation. Maybe by that time we can publish a little list of the lectures &c that have been promised, make a definite bright thing out of it—instead of a moral essay.[5]

I am glad you are liking Miss Porter[6] so well. If she would "come into residence" for a little while, it would have much weight with church people and be a good object lesson for us—she embodies the best of the Missionery spirit I think. S. Valerio[7] sends me papers and pamphlets ad infinitum, his address is 348 South Clark St.
P.O box 494

I am so glad about Mrs C.'s offers and that you are certainly going east.[8] Don't be too sure of me, I do not know that I ought to afford it—but I will cherish the possibility. I will come to Durand the first week of your visit I think, and a happy lady I will be. Yours always

Jane

Be sure to send me a Journal with Prof. Swing's article.[9] Try to have Miss Mc Avoy promise some thing as Jennie Dow[10] did that we can talk about and print. Before you leave the city you might write, or ask Mr Sherwood what the prospects are for the house in Aug.[11] Tell him we want to know for curiosity.

ALS (SC, Starr; *JAPM*, 2:1068–70).

1. Miss McAvoy is not mentioned in surviving HH records.

2. Katharine Lyon (Hamill) (1869–1964) was born at her family's Chicago home at 252 Michigan Ave., the daughter of grain merchant, John B. Lyon (1829–1904), a pioneer member of the Chicago Board of Trade, and Emily Wright Lyon. She attended Miss Kirkland's School for Girls and later was involved in the work of the Kirkland Assn., a group of Kirkland School alumnae whose goal was to work with women of education, leisure, and accomplishment and "to put them up to their highest use" (Kirkland Assn. *Annual Report*, 1891–92). With the support of JA and HH residents, the Kirkland Assn. established club rooms for working girls, which provided lunch at moderate prices, a library, and a lounge. Miss Lyon was involved in serving the meals and distributing books in the library, providing lectures, and serving on the organization's executive committee until at least 1896.

In this same period, she was participating in HH activities. She was especially active as a musician at the settlement. She offered piano lessons at the settlement in 1892 and from time to time during 1891 and 1892 provided accompaniment for singers at the HH Sunday concerts. She attended the opening of the Butler Art Gallery Building with her husband, Robert W. Hamill (1863–1943), who also became active at the settlement. He conducted a reading party at HH on the French Revolution during the spring of 1891 and by Mar. 1892 had become an honorary member of the thirty-man HH Debating Club.

The Hamills had at least four children, Robert Lyon, Katharine, Emily, and Frances, and eventually moved from their residence on Lake Ave. in Chicago to Hinsdale, Ill. Katharine was a particular friend of EGS and kept up with her through visits and correspondence. She was a member of the CWC (1917) and was identified as an early leader in efforts on behalf of women's suffrage and planned parenthood.

3. While in Europe in 1888, JA had purchased a copy of the *Psyche of Capua* in Naples. See JA to AHHA, 9 May 1889, n. 1, above. See *PJA*, 2:325, n. 20.

4. Joseph Meharry Medill (1823–99), who helped organize the Republican Party in Ohio in 1864, was the publisher of the *Chicago Daily Tribune*, of which he acquired the controlling interest in 1874. He may have been known to JA through her father, John Huy Addams's Republican Party connections; however, it is more likely that JA and EGS knew the Medills through Katharine Patrick Medill (1831?–94), whom Joseph Medill wed in 1852. A founding member of the Fortnightly Club, Mrs. Medill was fascinated by politics and the newspaper business and had a reputation for being outspoken about both. She was active in relief work after the Chicago Fire of 1871, especially while her husband was mayor of Chicago, beginning in Nov. 1871. The Medills had three children: Katherine (1852–1932), who wed diplomat Robert S. McCormick in 1876, who became publisher of the *Chicago Daily Tribune*; Elinor (1855–1933); and Josephine (1866?–92).

5. JA and EGS waited too long to draft their own version of their scheme. Other reporters who heard about their idea or visited with them hastened to report on their plan. Descriptions appeared in periodicals associated with religious organizations and in newspapers.

In 1889: Leila G. Bedell, "A Chicago Toynbee Hall," *Woman's Journal* (Boston), 25 May; "A Social Reformer," *Troy (N.Y.) Daily Press*, 15 May; Mary H. Porter, "A Home on Halsted Street," *Advance*, Chicago, 11 July. In 1890: Jenny Dow, "The Chicago Toynbee Hall," *Unity* (Chicago), 15 Mar.; "They Help the Poor," *Chicago Times*, 23 Mar.; "She Gave Up Her Home," *Chicago Journal*, 17 May; "Two Women's Work," *Chicago Journal*, 19 May; "Art for the Masses," *Chicago Journal*, 27 May; "Work of Two Women," *Chicago Times*, 3 July; Rev. J. Frothingham, "The Toynbee Idea," *Interior* (Chicago), 7 July; Eva H. Brodlique, "A Toynbee Hall Experiment in Chicago," *Chautauquan*, Sept.; "Solving a Problem," *Chicago Daily Tribune*, 29 Oct.; "Hull House," *Altruistic Review*, Springfield, Ohio, Oct.; Allen B. Pond, "Personal Philanthropy," *Plymouth Review*, Nov. See n. 9.

6. Mary Harriet Porter (1846–1929) became a Congregationalist missionary to China (North China Mission), 1868–86 and 1894–1911. Born in 1846, probably in Green Bay, Wis., she was the daughter of Rev. Jeremiah Porter (1804–93), founder of the First Presbyterian Church, Chicago (1833), and Eliza Chappell Porter (1807–88), who helped establish and taught in Chicago's first public school. During the Civil War, Illinois governor Richard Yates appointed Rev. Porter chaplain of the Chicago First Light Artillery. Mrs. Porter followed him into wartime service and was associated with the Sanitary Comm., nursing the sick at various locations. Together they established the first school for freemen near Memphis, Tenn. After the war, the Porter family moved to Texas, along the Mexican border, where U.S. forces were located in order to prevent incursions by French troops under Maximilian. There they established the Rio Grande Seminary for boys and girls before they returned to Chicago in 1866.

In 1868 Mary Harriet Porter began her first tour of duty in Peking as a member of the North China Mission, under the auspices of the American Board of Commissioners for Foreign

Missions. She was the first missionary sponsored by the Woman's Board of Missions of the Interior (WBMI), headquartered in Chicago. From 1867 until 1882, she was in charge of the Bridgman School for girls in Peking and then moved with her brother, Henry Dwight Porter (1845–1916), and his wife, Elizabeth, to Pang Chuang, China, where she taught a variety of subjects primarily to women. Between 1886 and 1893, she returned to the United States to care for her aging parents. During that time, she lived primarily in Beloit, Wis., where JA had a number of friends from RFS days. After her father died, she returned to Pang Chuang, where she also took responsibility for a girls' boarding school. Fleeing to Peking because of the Boxer Rebellion (1900), she once again became associated with the Bridgman School. From 1906 until her retirement back to California in 1911, she served as principal of the Angell Memorial Bible Training School she had founded.

Miss Porter was a great friend of Methodist church leader and teacher Nellie Naomi Russell, who had befriended JA and EGS shortly after they arrived in Chicago. She compiled and published Russell's China research as *Gleanings from Chinese Folklore* by Nellie N. Russell, published by F. H. Revell in 1915. She also wrote a book about her sister-in-law: *Elizabeth Chappell Porter: A Memoir* was issued by F. H. Revell in 1892.

7. Alessandro Mastro-Valerio. See JA to MCAL, 13 Mar. 1889, n. 5, above.

8. JA may have been referring to Mrs. Lydia Avery Coonley, who had apparently invited EGS to go east with her to visit her summer home in Wyoming, N.Y.

9. David Swing's article "A New Social Movement" appeared in the *Chicago Evening Journal*, 8 June 1889. While it is among the first articles that JA and EGS pasted into the scrapbooks they began keeping as a record of the development of their settlement (see HH Scrapbook 1:1; *JAPM*, Addendum 10:6ff), JA may not have considered it an "authorized statement" on her settlement idea. She omitted it from that category in the bibliography of literature about HH that she prepared for Wood and Kennedy's *Handbook of Settlements* (1911); see especially p. 60.

10. Jenny ("Jennie") Dow (Harvey) (1866–1904) was among the first converts to the settlement "scheme." Born in Chicago, the daughter of William Carey Dow (1822–1903) and Marietta Adrience Dow (1845–1927), young Jenny attended Unity Church, Chicago, a congregation in which her parents were active. Her father served on the church building committee. He was also prominent in real estate circles and was one of the city's pioneer real estate brokers. Her mother was one of the twenty-one founding members of the CWC. The Dows, a North Side family, resided at 473 (later 2332) Orchard St.

Jenny may have learned about JA's ideas through the CWC and her mother. She may have attended some of the gatherings at which JA and EGS presented their ideas and agreed to help. She assumed responsibility for conducting the kindergarten, the first activity organized at HH, and for providing all of the furniture and supplies used by the children. She continued to direct the kindergarten program until 1892. JA attested to her abilities as teacher, noting her "exquisite enthusiasm . . . her varied gifts, her willingness and ability to become as a little child among them [the children of the poor]" (*The Excellent*, 18). In the spring of 1892, after she gave up the directorship of the kindergarten, she helped lead a storytelling club for schoolgirls on Friday afternoons at HH, beginning at 3:30 P.M., and held Kindergarten Club on Tuesday afternoons. Her article about HH entitled "The Chicago Toynbee Hall" appeared in *Unity* (Chicago), 15 Mar. 1890 (HH Scrapbook 1:1; *JAPM*, Addendum 10:6ff).

Dow took an interest in the writings of Ralph Waldo Emerson, and during the HH Summer School held at RS, 1–30 July 1891, she conducted a reading party on Emerson. At the time of Jenny Dow's death, JA remembered the "old discussions in which I pitted Marcus Aurelius against her beloved Emerson. . . . She had above all the open mind, the untrammeled, searching, ample spirit" (*The Excellent*, 21). In addition to her involvement in HH activities, Jenny Dow was a member of the CWC.

In 1893 Jenny Dow married William Plato Harvey (1860–1917), son of Joel D. Harvey and Julia Plato Harvey (see JA to MCAL, 12 Feb. 1889, n. 28, above). The young couple lived for a time in Green Bay, Wis., later moving to Geneva, Ill., and then to Chicago. By 1901 they were living in Aurora, Ill., where William Plato Harvey worked as an auditor for the Elgin, Aurora, and Southern Traction Co. Jenny Dow Harvey died at age thirty-eight on 11 May 1904. She left five children: the eldest, William Dow, born in 1894; Julia Plato; Joel D.; Grace Furness; and the youngest, John A., a baby only a few weeks old. She was buried in the Oak Hill Cemetery, Geneva, Ill. See photograph on p. 97.

11. On 11 May 1889, and with the approval of owner Helen Culver, JA brought to successful conclusion her negotiation with the Sherwood Co., which manufactured school desks and seats. She arranged to rent "the upper floor of 335 South Halsted St. and large room on north side of building on first floor and mutual use of the hall." JA and John B. Sherwood signed the sublease "Agreement between Miss Addams and Sherwood Company," which was to be in force from 1 Aug. 1889 until 30 Apr. 1890, when JA expected to have use of the entire house (Addams, Lease, 11 May 1889). JA also executed a lease with Helen Culver on 16 May 1889 (see Helen Culver to JA, [9?] [Mar. 1890], n. 1, below). The rent was thirty dollars a month.

The Sherwood brothers, Henry M. (1831–1902) and John B. (1846–1916), were born in Westport, Conn. Henry came to Chicago in the mid-1850s and joined the Holbrook School Apparatus Manufacturing Co. After selling his interest in that firm in 1864, he began his own school-supply business. By 1882 Sherwood and Co. was operating with Henry as president and John as secretary. John designed and patented a number of school desks with folding seats. In 1886 Sherwood and Co., at 319 (later 738) South Halsted St., was manufacturing and promoting the "Chief" school desk as "The Best Stationary Top Desk with Folding Seat Ever Made," the "Trump" school desk with "folding top and folding seat," and "Books and Blanks for Illinois," school supplies for school officials and teachers. After the company vacated the Hull home, it remained in the neighborhood at 244 West Polk St. until 1896, when it established new quarters at 811 (later 1856) West 14th St. at the corner of Lincoln (later Wood) and 14th streets.

## To Ellen Gates Starr

Cedarville [Ill.] June 7" 1889

My Dearest—

I think I owe you an apology for at least two things. First that I wrote to Miss Beedy after entrusting the affairs to you. I thought may be my letter would catch her before you could see her and I devoutly pray that the article was n't sent before the correction,[1] and 2d that I gave $25.00 yesterday to Beloit College. I must stop doings of that kind and save for our affair. I don't know why I am so weak and need you to keep me from my weakness. My greatest self denial will come in, in refusing to give to other things and you must make yourself a bug bear for that. I need you, dear one, more than you can realize. I have n't time for a letter, yours are so much to me. I will see you at Durand soon and am Always Your loving friend—

AL (SC, Starr; *JAPM*, 2:1071).

1. It seems likely that Mary E. Beedy planned to send the article by Dr. Leila G. Bedell to other periodicals for publication. JA may have hoped to remove the reference to her "spirituality" before it appeared anywhere else. See Letter to the *Woman's Journal* (Boston), 25 May 1889, above.

## To Sarah Alice Addams Haldeman

*The summer of 1889 was a busy time for Jane Addams and Ellen Gates Starr. By early June, Jane was in Cedarville and helping with community events while visiting family and friends.*[1] *To Ellen, whom she addressed as "My Dear One," Jane reported, "I have just come back from a picnic of children and am too tired for more" than a brief note.*[2] *And then Anna Peck Sill, principal of the Rockford Female Seminary while Jane was a student there, died 18 June 1889 and was buried two days later. After attending the funeral service held in Chapel Hall at the seminary, Jane joined Ellen in Durand, Illinois. The two women then went on to Beloit, Wisconsin, on Sunday, 23 June, where they shared their settlement plans with retired seminary teacher Sarah F. Blaisdell. They traveled back to Rockford on 24 June in time for Jane to attend the seminary board of trustees' meeting, held on 25 June. Jane had agreed to give the alumna essay at the school commencement on the morning of 26 June. It was a memorial to Anna Sill.*[3] *Jane and Ellen attended the alumnae banquet held in the school gymnasium in the afternoon, where they presented their settlement scheme.*[4]

*Throughout the summer, Jane's focus was never far from Ellen and their plans. Jane admonished Ellen for her lack of correspondence. "A day without a letter is a* blanc *as the French say of a sleepless night—I don't like such a day at all—and I have just had one."*[5]

Geneseo Ill Aug 31 '89

My dear Alice

Your little *[one word illegible]* in your letter about Marcet[6] has made me rather solemn and I have thought of the possibility of my dying while the experiment is in full sway. As Ellen has given up her regular teaching and trusts all her future to the affair, I should like her to be given $1500.00 enough to support her for a year or more until she could get back into her regular work.[7] I have never made a will[8] and see no reason why I should but I know you would see to that for me—We have just come back from Church[9] and I am too warm and tired to write. Kisses to Marcet and always untold love for her mother. Yours

Jane

ALS (UIC, JAMC; *JAPM*, 2:1079–80).

1. JA also visited Geneseo, Ill., where she consulted her sisters, SAAH, from Girard, Kans., who was visiting MCAL.

2. 14 June 1889, SC, Starr; *JAPM*, 2:1073.

3. For the text of JA's remarks, see "RS Endowment," in *Memorials of Anna P. Sill*, 70–75; *JAPM*, 46:447–50.

4. "After tea, Miss Addams and Miss Starr told to the young ladies of their work in Chicago in the poor part of the city. They are faithful Christian women, with intelligence and talent, and their works can but be good" ("Home Happenings," *RSM* 17 [June 1889]: 143).

5. 14 June 1889, SC, Starr; *JAPM*, 2:1072.

6. That letter SAAH sent to JA is apparently no longer extant. SAAH's response may have been a will. See Document from SAAH, 5 June 1890, below.

7. Until Jan. 1893, JA did support EGS as a resident at HH. By the fall of 1889, EGS had decided to give up her teaching position at Miss Kirkland's school to join JA's "scheme." Once a HH resident, she spent her time in work for the settlement, including conducting reading parties and classes, introducing visitors and potential supporters to the settlement idea, and preparing art exhibits and catalogs. She also helped develop the selection of college extension courses the settlement began to offer in the summer of 1890. She wrote HH program brochures, made speaking appearances to present the settlement idea, and participated in various neighborhood activities and in "neighboring." To earn spending money, she gave private group and individual lessons in art appreciation and literature and presented special lectures. Yet she had a very difficult time making enough money to have sufficient funds for car fare or to provide her own clothing. Understanding her plight and seeing her artistic interests, in 1896 HH advocate Mary Wilmarth provided funds for EGS to study bookbinding in England with renowned craftsman T. J. Cobden-Sanderson (1840–1922), founder and owner of the Doves Press. Wilmarth's expectation was that EGS would establish her own bindery at HH, where she could make her own living and teach others the craft. Throughout her life, EGS received additional financial help from a variety of staunch friends, the most supportive of whom was Frances Crane Lillie. In 1932 JA made arrangements for EGS, who was experiencing increasingly poor health and large medical expenses, to be paid a HH pension of seventy-five dollars a month for the remainder of her life.

8. JA did eventually make a will. The version in force at the time of her death, 23 May 1935, was dated 24 May 1934 (UIC, JAMC; *JAPM*, 27:603–11). EGS was not a beneficiary of that will.

9. Since JA and EGS were lodging with the Roswell Mason family while they readied the former Hull home for occupancy, it is likely that they attended the Fourth Presbyterian Church, where the Mason family were members. JA was already attending a seminar on the Old Testament at that church.

## From Henry Richart
## (for Cedarville Presbyterian Church, Ill.)

*Jane Addams chose to join and participate in the Ewing Street Congregational Mission Church, created from three other Congregational church programs, Harrison Street and Twelfth Street missions and the Clinton Street Church, operating in 1888 in what became the Hull-House neighborhood. It was located at 832 Ewing (later Cabrini) Street a short block from Hull-House. Jane was a founding and attending member of the Sunday School and church first established in September 1889 and served on its Prudential Committee. A new church designed by Pond and Pond architects was completed in 1891.*

*By 1895 Jane Addams had indicated that she hoped "to have the work of the church more closely cooperative with Hull-House."[1] JA joined her new church home by presenting the following letter of reference.*

September 1st 1889

This is to certify that Miss Jane Addams is a Member in good and regular standing in the Presbyterian Church of Cedarville Ill[.][2] And that upon her own request is dismissed to unite with any evangelical church where in her lot may be cast, and to the Christian fellowship of such church she is most cordially commended[.]

Done by order of Session September 1st 1889 in the Presbyterian Church of Cedarville Illinois[.]

Henry Richart[3]
"Clerk"

ADS (UIC, JAMC; *JAPM*, 28:701).

1. Ewing Street Congregational Mission Church, Chicago, Membership Survey, Feb. 1895, "Notes," [1]; *JAPM*, 28:721.
2. JA joined the Cedarville Presbyterian Church on 14 Oct. 1888. See *PJA*, 2:630.
3. For information on Henry Richart, long an Addams family friend, who lived in Cedarville, see *PJA*, 1:121, n. 1.

## To Sarah Alice Addams Haldeman

*In August Jane was in Geneseo, Illinois, with the Linn family. Her special responsibility while Ellen was in the East visiting family in Deerfield and Chicopee, Massachusetts, was overseeing architectural changes and repair of their "flat" on the second floor of the former Charles J. Hull home. Having returned on 6 August 1889 from a trip into Chicago to consult with the Pond brothers about the kitchen of their quarters, Jane wrote her sister Alice, indicating her enthusiasm for the setting. "I was perfectly delighted with [the] house, it is coming out beautifully and I know of no prettier rooms any where than our flat is going to be. The walls and ceilings are already cleaned and the first coat of paint is on, this makes the greatest possible difference; the work is going on very rapidly and it will certainly be ready for occupancy by the 20" of Aug. If Ellen is willing we will go in then and begin to get our furniture, so that we will have at least a month of quiet living in the neighborhood before any 'audiences' are needed."[1] Jane believed that she was spending about one thousand dollars to ready their rooms.[2] One of the major expenses was a new roof. "The furnishing of the house will not be very expensive, it is repairing, getting it into shape," she pronounced.[3]*

*Jane met Ellen in Chicago in early September, and the two women stayed in the home of the Roswell B. Masons while they cleaned and organized furnishings and possessions in their new home on South Halsted Street. Ellen described some of the activities to her cousin Mary Allen: "I found it very hot here when I came & you can conjecture what it is to help 'settle' our mansion. I stood about all day before yesterday, ate a cold lunch on a plate held in my hand while I directed a*

Mary Keyser joined Jane Addams and Ellen Gates Starr as the settlement's housekeeper and became the third permanent resident of Hull-House (courtesy of UIC, Jane Addams's Hull-House Museum).

*man doing the frieze, came home very late to dinner & didn't want any, but did want two glasses of iced tea, & consumed them accordingly, sought the doctor the next morning & reposed myself till after dinner. . . . I have a diarrhea & look & feel like a dish cloth. Don't tell my family. It's too soon to afford them the luxury of 'I told you so'. It has turned cool now, & we get in to stay tomorrow or next day, & can take things gradually, so I shall be all right. . . . I feel at home in Halsted St. already. It seems perfectly natural to be there. And it is so pretty!—Our home."*[4] *In the diary Jane Addams began keeping when the settlement opened, she recorded: "came into residence Sept. 18" 1889."*[5]

27 Delaware Pl [Chicago, Ill.] Sep 13" 1889

My dear Alice

The silver[6] and the quilt came yesterday, the one was put immediately into the side board drawer and the other on a bed. Our dining room is one of the prettiest things I ever saw so many people of good taste have said so, that it cannot be bias. The wall is a strong terra cotta, the frieze & ceiling a soft terra cotta,[7] the edges of the floor are painted the same with a handsome Wilton rug in the middle. Madame Mason[8] gave us an elegant old oak side-board (she was not afraid we would leave too much to servants, excuse me, dear, I don't know why

I feel so sore about that I am ashamed of it, but every body seems to trust me more than my most beloved sister)—and we indulged in a set of heavy leather covered chairs and a 16" *[one word illegible]*[9] oak table—an antique oak book case and my writing desk completes it.[10] I have n't time to describe the other rooms now, they are all just as distinguished looking and artistic as can be, by far the prettiest house I have ever lived in. People have been so good to us, I received a check for $100.00 last night from a lady whom I had never seen. If we don't succeed after all this help we will deserve to fail.

Ellen arrived on Tuesday[11] and gave me the birthday check. I will put it into the Hawthorne set[12] as we had planned, and bless you for them. The plain good looking silver pleased every body mightily, there were five or six people in the room when I unpacked it. Dear old Col. Mason[13] came down himself yesterday afternoon, we felt very much complimented. Miss Keyser[14] from Geneseo is coming to be our maid, we hope to be settled by Monday.[15] Will write then—Yrs.

Jane.

ALS (IU, Lilly, SAAH; *JAPM*, 2:1082–83).

1. JA to SAAH, 6 [7] Aug. 1889, IU, Lilly, SAAH; *JAPM*, 2:1075. JA had gone into Chicago for the architect conference on Monday afternoon, 5 Aug., and seems to have returned the next afternoon, 6 Aug. She indicated that she spent the night with the Roswell B. Mason family in Chicago. It is likely that this letter was written on 7 Aug. rather than on 6 Aug. In the text of the letter, she reported that she returned to Geneseo, Ill. "last evening."

2. According to JA's summary of accounts for Oct. 1889–Sept. 1890, repairs to the settlement building were $3,701.68, of which she paid $2,134.08. See also EGS [for JA] to Mary Houghton Starr Blaisdell [and SAAH], 23 Feb. [1889], n. 12, above.

3. JA to SAAH, 6 [7] Aug. 1889, IU, Lilly, SAAH; *JAPM*, 2:1075.

4. 15 [and 25] Sept. 1889, SC, Starr.

5. Addams, "Diary, 1889–90," 4, SCPC, JAC; *JAPM*, 29:101

6. In her letter of 6 [7] Aug. 1889 to her sister SAAH, JA had guessed that she could count on a dozen teaspoons, a half-dozen tablespoons, and a dozen forks. In addition, she wrote, "As I remember during the appraisement you had the big rocker, Mary the parlor lamp & table and I the six chairs. None of them I think were put down on the list—I should have been glad to have used the six chairs here as bed room chairs but of course it would have been quite impossible to take them. If Ma gave you the lamp I should assume it was mine until we could straighten things out. It seems cold blooded to talk in this way and I really don't care for the things at home when I think of them" (JA to SAAH, 8 Jan. 1890, IU, Lilly, SAAH; *JAPM*, 2:1147–48).

7. The words "terra cotta" are written as a ditto mark in the original text.

8. In addition to the oak sideboard that according to JA the Mason family had "used for years," Harriet Lavinia Mason also presented JA and EGS with a "Minton ware breakfast set" (JA to SAAH, 6 [7] Aug. 1889, IU, Lilly, SAAH; *JAPM*, 2:1076). For a photograph of the table, see p. 645.

9. There is a hole in the paper at this point in the text.

10. See n. 6. JA may have been describing a dining table that could be extended to reach sixteen feet. The table was used at the settlement throughout the 1890s.

11. 10 Sept. 1889.

12. For JA's 6 Sept. 1889 birthday, SAAH had sent JA funds to purchase a set of books by Nathaniel Hawthorne. JA explained to SAAH that she had an opportunity over the Christmas

Jenny Dow initiated the first Hull-House activity, a kindergarten. She provided all of the equipment for the undertaking that was held daily in the Hull-House dining area in the northwest corner of the ground floor. She also introduced her friend Mary Rozet Smith to Hull-House and Jane Addams (UIC, JAMC 0253 1404).

holidays in 1889 to begin reading them (see JA to SAAH, 8 Jan. 1890, IU, Lilly, SAAH; *JAPM*, 2:1149).

13. Roswell B. Mason.

14. Mary Keyser (1861?–97) became one of the stalwart and beloved early HH residents. She arrived at the settlement on 14 Sept. 1889 and remained until her death on 6 Jan. 1897. See *PJA*, 2:565–66, n. 4. See photograph on p. 95.

15. 16 Sept. 1889. JA and EGS determined that the official beginning of the settlement was 18 Sept. 1889.

## To Sarah Alice Addams Haldeman

335 South Halsted St Chicago [Ill.] Oct. 8" 1889

My dear Alice

Your long kind letter came a week ago[1] and I have been trying ever since, a long reply. But there is little use in trying for that until there are fewer letters to answer and fewer people to see. We have taken Saturdays afternoon and evening for our reception day, and we are trying to disseminate the fact as rapidly as possible. Until it is well known we seem obliged to receive every afternoon. I am sorry I have not written more about ourselves, I assure you it is from no "feeling" but lack of time. I was very foolish ever to have felt hurt at my dearest sister and best friend and I hope she will forgive me.[2]

I will never be quite happy about it until she comes to see us in our own home of which we are growing so fond[3]. Ellen and I live here alone with one servant.[4] Miss Dow[5] comes every morning at eight and opens to Kinder garten at nine.[6] We have twenty-four little people, about half of them Italians and the others poor children whose mothers "work out" most of the day. We have a list of a[t] least seventy more, mothers who have applied and begged for their children. Miss Dow takes lunch with us each day, and some times her two assistants come up.[7] She is so young and pretty and taking, every one is charmed with her. She gives her services of course as well as all the material used. Our piano was sent us with the rent paid for a year and an intimation that if the institution was thriving at the end of that time it would be given us.

Miss Trowbridge[8] comes every[9] night and stays until Sat morning. She has a club of little girls.[10] Miss Forstall[11] has undertaken a "Home Library Ass." every Monday aft. the books are kept at the house of one of the children with ten books and ten children in a circle. It is a Boston plan we are trying here.[12]

We have two boys clubs every Tuesday eve.[13] Miss Starr has hers down stairs and mine are in the dining room. I have twenty they are about 16—work at Fields and Walker's[14] as errand boy and wrapping parcels most of them. I have one telegraph boy & two who are in machine shops. They are all so anxious to come and very respectful. The little ragamuffins down stairs are harder to manage. Miss Starr has help for to night Mr Greeley[15] comes with his violin[.] There are so many applicants that we have started two overflow clubs for Thursday nights,[16] mine on Thursday[17] night are all Italians. Every Wed. Mr Sammons[18] has a drawing class of twelve. Mrs Wilmarth[19] pays him a regular price (a good one I imagine for he teaches at the Art Institute) for coming. We have only taken those children who knew something about drawing, some who had left the Public schools & one or two boys who were trying to keep on alone. One Italian Frank Nardi had had lessons in Italy and his great disappointment in America was that drawing lessons cost so much and he never could have any more, his delight is unbounded. We found him through our good friend the Italian editor Signor Valerio.[20] He has been of so much help to us. On Friday evening we have older girls[21] and on Sat. we are starting a Social Science club for men.[22] Mr Pond,[23] Mr Merritt Starr[24] and some rather clever men have taken hold of it so we are sure it will succeed—we ourselves have little to do with that. We have various other things started and simmering of which I will write later. Of course we are undertaking more than we ourselves can do, that is part of the idea. Miss Culver has been very much interested and is taking steps now towards a furnace.[25] The house itself is a charming old thing and we are very fond of it. Our pictures look very well and what furniture I bought was all handsome. Our dining room is very elegant and substantial. The Mason oak side board would be fine any where, our table was a great bargain and I indulged in chairs at $5.50 apiece (I put my surrey into them).[26]

Mr Linn has been here for a week attending the Moody Convention,[27] & Mr Mitchell[28] was here for three nights, it was very pleasant to see him again altho he has not exactly improved with his years. John[29] rooms in the college building alone. He entered full Freshman in the classical course, I had a very funny time getting him across the city (or rather in not getting him across) with his bicycle and his guitar. I really admire him very much, he is growing so manly—I could write on for pages if I only had time, but it is time for me to meet an appointment now. Always Yours

Jane—

The "fend"[30] sends a 1000s kisses to Marcet, we both enjoy all you write about her so much—Can't you come for Thanksgiving?[31] Love to Harry

Jane—

ALS (IU, Lilly, SAAH; *JAPM*, 2:1085–89).

1. SAAH's letter to JA is no longer extant.

2. JA was dedicated to maintaining a close, compatible relationship with her sister SAAH. She shopped for SAAH in Chicago and on her European trips, discussed family problems with her, shared her personal activities, and reported on the development of the settlement. JA wrote to her regularly and often reminded her of the importance to her of their sisterhood. JA was noticeably vexed when there was any hiatus in SAAH's letters to her or a hint of dispute (see especially JA to SAAH, 6 Mar. 1890, and 16 Feb. and 17 Mar. 1897, IU, Lilly, SAAH; *JAPM*, 2:1157–59; 3:54–59, 62–63). See also JA to SAAH, 22 Jan. 1890, n. 1; [ca. 6] [Sept. 1891]; 9 Nov. 1891; 23 Feb. 1893, n. 11; 4 Dec. 1896; 1 Mar. 1899, n. 8, and JA to MRS, 25 July 1899, n. 4, all below.

3. SAAH's first visit to HH seems to have come near Thanksgiving time at the end of Nov. 1889. See n. 31.

4. Mary Keyser.

5. Jenny Dow Harvey. See JA to EGS, 4 June 1889, n. 10, above.

6. The first organized activity at HH was a kindergarten. Created, directed, and equipped by Jenny Dow, it was held daily from 9:00 A.M. until noon, except Sunday, in the north ground floor parlor of the house, described as "large, being about 17 x 36 feet in dimensions, well lighted, has pretty walls, a great many pictures and a piano" ("She Gave Up Her Home"). The kindergarten was indeed a learning experience for the settlement residents and volunteers as well as for their charges. JA recalled in *Twenty Years* that the settlement residents were surprised to see "social distinctions even among its lambs" (103). She also related the attempt by Jenny Dow to teach "temperance principles" to the South Italian mother of one of her students who had been brought to the kindergarten "'in quite a horrid state of intoxication' from the wine-soaked bread upon which she had breakfasted" (*Twenty Years*, 102).

Experience with the children who came to kindergarten and with their families led the HH residents to offer additional services created for the benefit of babies and young children and their mothers. Among those were a nursery and well-baby clinic, instruction in diet and food preparation, additional kindergarten classes, training for potential kindergarten teachers, and a mothers' club that became the HH Woman's Club. Initially, most of these programs were located in separate apartments or buildings close by the original settlement building. In 1895, when the Children's Building was constructed and opened as an addition to the settlement complex, settlement programs for babies and young children were brought together and located there.

In the beginning, the HH kindergarten was associated with the Kindergarten College in Chicago, which had a three-year curriculum for preparing kindergarten teachers. Students used the HH kindergarten as a laboratory. Then in 1896, the Chicago Froebel Kindergarten Assn. moved its headquarters to HH and operated the kindergarten program in the Children's

Building until 1902, when the organization moved to the Fine Arts Building in Chicago. JA recalled of its director Alice H. Putnam (1841–1919), a CWC member, her "absolute devotion to children" and her dedication to training adults as teachers (Com. of Nineteen, *Pioneers of the Kindergarten in America*, 214). In addition to its regular kindergarten program, HH established a visiting kindergarten program in 1895 to check on children who were ill or housebound.

For a short while after the Mary Crane Nursery, located on Ewing St., was opened in 1907–8, the HH kindergarten was discontinued. By 1913 it had been reestablished for children in the immediate settlement neighborhood; however, by 1925 the HH kindergarten program had been folded once again into the Mary Crane Demonstration Nursery School in the Mary Crane Nursery Building.

7. During the summer of 1890, it was reported in one of the first newspaper stories about the settlement experiment, "There are three assistants in the kindergarten, one of whom is doing the volunteer work included in the course of training, the other two are paid by individuals of the Kindergarten association" ("Work of Two Women"). A pamphlet listing weekly programs of lectures, clubs, and classes in Jan. 1891 identified Wilfreda Brockway and Miss Shannon as Jenny Dow's assistants, and by the fall of 1891 Mary McDowell (for a biographical note, see Two Essays in the *Forum*, Nov. and Oct. 1892, n. 154, below) was working in the kindergarten. According to JA's first account book, McDowell received fifty dollars a month from Oct. 1891 to May 1892.

8. Harriet Hopkins Trowbridge.

9. JA probably meant to include the word "Friday" after the word "every."

10. An entry for 4 Oct. 1889 in JA's 1889–90 diary reads: "Little girls. Miss Trowbridge 20" (SCPC, JAC; *JAPM*, 29:101). This was the beginning of a growing assortment of clubs for younger girls hosted by a variety of settlement residents and volunteers. The goal was to create a pleasant environment in which to educated and socialize youngsters.

11. Miss Forstall may have been Louise Forstall (b. 1862), the daughter of Theobald Forstall (1836–90) and Annie Walton Forstall, who had eight children and lived at 440 (later 1220) Dearborn Ave., Chicago. Mr. Forstall was president of the Chicago Gaslight and Coke Co. Louise Forstall, who became a member of the prestigious Fortnightly Club in 1884, assisted with the library for only a short time; by Jan. 1891, Anna M. Farnsworth, who was then in residence at HH for the winter, was in charge (see JA to AHHA, 9 Dec. 1890, n. 6, below). In Jan. 1891, Miss Forstall conducted a class in embroidery in the HH drawing room from 7:30 to 8:30 P.M. on Monday evenings. She was not listed again among volunteers holding classes or programs at the settlement until 1894, when she taught elementary French in the spring and fall College Extension Program.

12. The Boston Children's Aid Society established the first Home Library program for children in Jan. 1887. Under the leadership of Charles W. Birtwell (1860–1932), general secretary, the society saw the Home Library as a way to place established literature in the hands of the poor and to encourage children to make reading a lifetime habit. Little bookcases containing fifteen books were placed in the homes of children who formed reading groups of ten to fifteen friends. Members of each group met once a week to discuss their books with an adult volunteer and exchange them. When all of the books had been read by each member of the group, the books were replaced by a new collection and the exchange continued. Adult volunteers were often able to identify other services that the children and their families needed and try to provide them. Emily Greene Balch, who became a noted reformer and a colleague of JA in the American women's peace movement, was a volunteer in the program and saw its benefits as promoting citizenship and teaching children about life in the United States.

13. "Oct 1 Tuesday Boys Club. 20 down stairs, 15 up" (Addams, "Diary 1889–90," [4], SCPC, JAC; *JAPM*, 29:101). These would be the first of many boys' clubs taught in the beginning by JA and EGS and quite soon by other settlement volunteers.

14. A huge retail establishment, the Marshall Field and Co. department store, located on State St., and James H. Walker and Co. at the southeast corner of Wabash Ave. and Adams St., used young males ages ten to sixteen years old to deliver goods purchased by their customers and to run errands.

15. At least two, and perhaps three, members of the Greeley family were volunteers during the early days of HH.

Louis May Greeley (1858–1939), son of Samuel Sewell Greeley and Annie Morris Larned Greeley, was active in the early days of HH. In 1889 he helped with Italian evenings. By the fall of 1890, he was teaching mathematics at the settlement on Wednesday evenings and in Jan. 1891 switched to holding ten weeks of bookkeeping classes on Tuesday evenings in the settlement's Octagon Room. During the fall of 1891 and the winter and spring of 1892, he taught Latin, in particular Caesar, on Tuesday evenings, and for twelve weeks in the fall of 1891 only, he held a class in American constitutional law. During the winter of 1892, he also directed a reading party for James Bryce's *The American Commonwealth*. His activities as teacher in the College Extension Program apparently ended in the spring of 1892, for his name appears in no further lists of settlement volunteers.

Greeley received his A.B. from Harvard College in 1880. After attending Harvard Law School for two years, he was admitted to the Illinois Bar in 1884. In 1901 he became a professor of law in the Northwestern Univ. Law School. He was also a member of the Ethical Culture Society, and his recreation was music. He gave a violin concert at HH on Sunday, 17 Jan. 1892. In 1895 he married Anna Lowell Dunbar, who became a member of the CWC in 1896. The couple had two children.

The name Morris Larned Greeley (1863–1945) does not appear in existing HH records as a settlement volunteer; however, he may have been one. In June 1892, he wed Anne S. Foote, who, along with two other settlement volunteers, had charge of the HH kitchen garden. MIT graduate Morris Greeley was a surveyor and engineer. He joined his father's firm in 1886 and in 1914 became president of the Greeley-Howard-Norlin Co. He served as vice-president of LaSalle Extension Univ., 1921–25. The couple lived in Winnetka, Ill., and had five children.

Louis May and Morris Larned Greeley's father, Samuel Sewell Greeley (1824–1916), went to HH on at least four occasions as a lecturer. By July 1890, he had spoken before the newly organized Working People's Social Science Club. On 14 May 1981, he presented a public lecture entitled "Marie Antoinette," and on 11 Feb. 1892 he appeared once again and spoke on the French metric system. He also attended the opening of the Butler Art Gallery during June 1892. A widower at the time of his involvement at the settlement, he had been married twice and had five children. A graduate of Harvard College in 1844, and Rensselaer Polytechnic Institute, Troy, N.Y., in 1846, he arrived in Chicago in 1853 and opened a surveying business. He served as city surveyor for Chicago in 1855, 1857, and 1859, and after his home and business were destroyed in the Chicago Fire of 1871, he rebuilt and in 1887 incorporated the Greeley-Howard Co., a civil engineering and surveying business. It was located in the Opera House. His firm helped create the maps for *HH Maps and Papers* (1895). He lived in Winnetka, Ill., and was a Unitarian.

16. There is no evidence in JA's 1889–90 diary, Oct.–Dec. 1889, that overflow boys' clubs met on Thursday evenings at HH.

17. The word "Thursday" is written as a ditto mark in the original text.

18. This may have been F. H. C. Sammons, who taught drawing at the HH Summer School held at RC during July and Aug. 1900 and 1901. Mr. Sammons, who also taught at the Art Institute of Chicago, began the first drawing classes at the settlement on 2 Oct. 1889; on 9 Oct., he had six students and thereafter drawing classes usually met on Wednesday evening. In her article "Chicago Toynbee Hall" published in *Unity* (Chicago), 15 Mar. 1890, Jenny Dow reported, "A drawing class has done some excellent work in charcoale." By Jan. 1891,

the drawing teacher was Mr. J. T. Beggs, followed in the fall of 1891 by Gwynne Price. Mary H. Wilmarth gave ten dollars a month to the settlement to support art instruction.

19. Mary Jane Hawes Wilmarth (1837–1919) came to Chicago in 1861, from her birthplace, New Bedford, Mass., as the bride of banker and businessman Henry Wilmarth (1836–85). Of their three daughters, only Anna Thompson (Ickes) (1873–1935), the youngest, survived her mother and like her became a social reformer and participated in politics.

Mary Wilmarth became active in civic and social affairs, especially after her husband's sudden death. A founder and two-term president of the Fortnightly Club and an active member of the CWC beginning in Feb. 1883, she was a significant force behind the creation of the Woman's City Club in Chicago and served as its first president, 1910–12. During the World's Columbian Exposition in 1893, she was the chairwoman of the Education Congress. For ten years, Mary Wilmarth was president of the fledgling Consumers League in Illinois and lobbied frequently in the Illinois legislature for improved working conditions, especially for women and for beneficial child labor legislation. Among other organizations to which she devoted time and money were the Mental Hygiene Society, Legal Aid Society, Women's Trade Union League, Henry Booth House, and the Frederick Douglass Center. She supported the Progressive Party and was a dedicated and active suffragist.

She was attracted to the work that JA and EGS proposed and was an early supporter of their reform efforts. At the settlement, she taught French and lectured on topics connected with the history of France. She was particularly supportive of the efforts of EGS to develop and promote bookbinding as an art, donated financial help for EGS, and provided an apartment in HH for her. She also helped initiate the HH Art program in 1889, the Crêche, cooking classes, and the Jane Club. By 1895 she was providing at least two hundred dollars yearly for the settlement's general operations. She also contributed generously to various HH building projects, including enlarging the Coffee House and kitchen, improving the alley behind the settlement, moving and improving the gymnasium, and building the Men's Club and the HH Apartment complex. In 1895, when HH was incorporated, she was tapped as one of the original settlement trustees. She served until her death.

JA and Mary Wilmarth shared a thirty-year friendship that developed through HH and their mutual interests in reform and progress. JA recalled that Wilmarth was one of the first women in Chicago to offer her an opportunity to explain the settlement (see also introduction to part 1, n. 28, above). JA also considered the Wilmarth home in the Congress Hotel a retreat of sorts that provided her with "a quiet spot in which to write or one combining the tools and the mood in which to try to formulate some complicated situation so often developing in . . . Chicago" (*The Excellent*, 105). When both Wilmarth and JA were delegates to the 1912 Progressive Party convention in Chicago, JA spent "the nights and days of the Progressive Convention in her rooms when the various committees, appointed with such ardent hopes, held their meetings in the Congress Hotel" (*The Excellent*, 106). For JA, Wilmarth had a "ripeness of mind," coupled with "the touch of youth. . . . She was always ready to stand by her causes, and her high-hearted attitude toward life never for a moment deserted her" (*The Excellent*, 107). Mary Wilmarth died in her summer home at Lake Geneva, Wis., shortly after breaking her hip, and was buried in Graceland Cemetery, Chicago.

20. Alessandro Mastro-Valerio.

21. The HH program announcement dated 1 Mar. 1892 indicated that the HH Social Club would meet in the drawing room on Monday between 8:00 and 10:00 P.M. "This club has a membership of thirty-girls, between the ages of sixteen and twenty, who have met every week for two years. The primary object of the club is profitable social intercourse. The first hour of each evening is devoted to reading and discussion; the second to amusement, in which they are joined by the members of the Debating Club. Dancing every fourth Monday" (HH Scrapbook 2:13; *JAPM*, Addendum 10:7ff). Members of the Debating Club, which by 1894 had changed its name to the Lincoln Club, were males.

The HH Social Club seems to have gotten its start on Wednesday evening, 12 Oct. 1889, in a gathering of sixteen girls organized by EGS. By Sept. 1890, it was referred to as the Working Girls' Club. JA described the initial gatherings in *Twenty Years*: "In the very first weeks of our residence Miss Starr started a reading party in George Eliot's 'Romola,' which was attended by a group of young women who followed the wonderful tale with unflagging interest. The weekly reading was held in our little upstairs dining room, and two members of the club came to dinner each week, not only that they might be received as guests, but that they might help us wash the dishes afterwards and so make the table ready for the stacks of Florentine photographs" (101).

22. JA and EGS may have wanted to establish a Social Science Club for men on Saturday evenings, but entries in JA's diary indicate the two women continued to host an Italian evening with refreshments, songs, readings, and dancing most Saturday evenings into the spring of 1890. It was not until Alfred Hicks, an English workingman, took up the idea that what eventually became the Working People's Social Science Club was organized (see JA to MRS, 26 Apr. 1890, n. 8, below).

23. Allen B. Pond and his friend Louis May Greeley joined EGS and JA and their Italian neighbors for dinner at HH on the evening of Friday, 12 Oct. 1889, perhaps to discuss the beginning of the Working People's Social Science Club (see JA to MRS, 26 Apr. 1890, n. 8, below).

24. Merritt Starr (1856–1931) lectured on laissez-faire at the Working People's Social Science Club at HH in Sept. 1890. Born in Ellington, N.Y., he spent his childhood in Rock Island, Ill. He received his A.B. in 1875 and his A.M. in 1878 from Oberlin, an A.B. from Griswold College in 1876, and an A.B. and LL.B. from Harvard in 1881. He married Lelia Wheelock of Cleveland in 1885 and the couple had four children. In 1882 he began to practice law in Chicago, forming Peck, Miller, and Starr in 1893, the first of at least four firms in which he was a named partner. His practice included trusts, estates, and legal issues growing out of interstate commerce and income tax laws. He was committed to public service. Starr helped organize the Civil Service League, and he helped in drafting new city, county, and state civil service laws and in promoting their passage. From 1884 until 1914, he was a member of the executive committee of the Civil Service Reform Assn. He also took an active part in encouraging the passage of laws establishing municipal and juvenile courts. Because of their mutual interests, the paths of JA and Starr crossed on several occasions throughout their lives.

25. Helen Culver was leasing HH directly to JA at this time. EGS reported the furnace installed by 3 Nov. 1889 (see EGS [for JA] to Susan Childs Starr and Caleb Allen Starr [and SAAH], 3 Nov. [1889], below).

26. The Roswell B. Mason family had given an oak sideboard to JA and EGS for their dining room. See JA to SAAH, 13 Sept. 1889, n. 29, above.

27. JML, JA's brother-in-law, was probably in Chicago to attend the formal opening of the Bible Institute for Home and Foreign Missions of the Chicago Evangelization Society, which took place on 26 Sept. 1889, and the meetings that followed. The institute was created with the leadership of Chicago evangelist Dwight L. Moody and became known as the Moody Bible Institute.

28. Rev. Lewis Henry Mitchell, who served as the Presbyterian minister in Cedarville, Ill., 1874–78 (see *PJA*, 1:110–11, n. 5).

29. JA's nephew John Addams Linn, son of MCAL and JML, was attending Lake Forest Univ. (see *PJA*, 1:79, n. 188).

30. JA.

31. According to JA's 1889–90 diary, the "family" did go to HH for Thanksgiving. The visitors were likely cousin SH and sister MCAL, her husband, JML, and their children, including John Addams, James Weber, Esther Margaret, and Stanley Ross. See also JA to SAAH, 23 Nov. 1889, n. 6, below. SAAH and perhaps Marcet did visit JA at HH between Thanksgiving and mid-Dec. 1889. See also JA to SAAH, 22 Dec. 1889, n. 2, below.

# Ellen Gates Starr [for Jane Addams] to Susan Childs Starr and Caleb Allen Starr [and Sarah Alice Addams Haldeman]

335 South Halsted Street. [Chicago, Ill.] Nov. 3rd [1889]

Dear Mother & Father,

I believe we have no broken windows this week, so, even though you thirst for the fray you will be obliged to curb your appetite for the present. Perhaps there may be some later.

Last night we had a very peaceful & successful reception evening.[1] The previous Sat. evening was characterized by the prevalence of the élite, & conspicuous for the absence of invited neighbors, as I think I related in due order.[2] A young Mr. Day,[3] whom Harriet[4] brought on that occasion, said he didnt know whether he approved of the scheme or not, but he knew he had had the most delightful evening he had enjoyed in Chicago, & that it was a charming place to go. Last night we tried the experiment of asking mothers & children, & not inviting "him." It seems to scare them to have "him" invited. They aren't used to it, apparently, & get embarrassed over it. A good many came last night. We had tables scattered about & the children played dominoes, checkers, jackstraws &c. Miss Taylor[5] played the piano & cut paper dolls for them, & the women talked & looked at pictures. We got out the megalethoscope,[6] with colored & illuminated pictures of Venice (The Masons[7] gave us that, & it has been a stand by) professedly for the children, but the women liked it just as well. Two Germans came, with whom I conversed to our mutual delight. One of them evidently intends to come regularly. In the afternoon Mrs. Dr. Isham[8] & Mrs. Medill[9] called. I would rather talk with any neighbor than with Mrs. Medill. I've "no <use"> for Mrs. M. or any of her tribe. I dare say she thought she was conferring a great honor. She asked if we wanted it put in the Tribune, & I declined with thanks.

My first lesson at the Ishams occurred on Thursday.[10] They sent the carriage for me, & back, asking me to use it on the way if I chose. I stopped at 299.[11] & found [John?] Arnold[12] there, at lunch, but of course only stayed a minute, as I was keeping the Isham carriage. I was rather glad not to be able to stay, as he hasn't been very polite to Mary & Charles.[13] There were about twenty of the nicest north & south side girls there, & more are coming. Helen Fairbank[14] took the trouble to come over & tell me that she was going to N.Y. that day, & would be away for two weeks, but was coming when she got home. I think it is going to be far the nicest class I ever had. It is the first time I could ever have a morning class, & they are always better. If twenty come I shall get $100 from it. Perhaps, there will be thirty, even. They are all from the "best families", Mother dear, & I didn't feel any fleas on myself while there, so I hope they are safe so far. Miss

Poole[15] has postponed coming into town, & doesn't begin her lessons quite yet, & I am holding the Art class over the heads of the Literature class in regard to numbers, pay, & properly magnificent treatment of me. I don't know what will come of it, but I think people are apt to treat one better if they know that "other folks" treat one handsomely. I am not going to be in too unseemly haste about that Literature class. Jane & I frequently remark to each other that we're not so innocent as we look.

I will enclose a card for our Friday evening.[16] Mr. Chubb is an English socialist, & a Unitarian.[17] He lunched with us one day. He is a very interesting fellow. Father Huntington, Bishop H's son[18] is in town. He spoke on the single tax[19] in some hall last week. I didn't hear him. Mr. Chubb did, & said it seemed to him a pity that he should be throwing away his fire & energy on a point so little vital interest. He speaks tonight on the emancipation of labor, & we are all going. I wish we could get him to speak here the same night that Mr. Chubb does. I think it would be great fun to hear two earnest young men, one an <English> Unitarian socialist & the other a ritualist American "Christian socialist" speak on the same evening. The Rev. Mr. Goss[20] is a socialist, & he is coming. I am looking forward to the gentlemanly skirmish that follows the lecture. Mrs. Wilmarth[21] pays Mr. Chubb for the lecture. Mr. Chubb is a very agreeable man. He isn't the least "bumptious:"—is as quiet & moderate in his way of asserting himself as Mr. Mason,[22] & doesn't treat one as if one were a fool or a lunatic because one doesn't see things as he does. Nevertheless he is a socialist. I said to him, after "pumping" him for half an hour "I should think you would be very much objected to in England" "O, yes," he replied "I am a very objectionable person." Don't you wish you were going to be here?

One day when the little girls were here Miss Foote[23] came down with Harriet[24] to sing & play for them. A small being eight years old wished to pay closer attention to the music than the noise in the room allowed, & expressed her sentiments in the terse—vigorous phrase "Damn the racket!" A companion remonstrated "Don't curse!" & Miss Addams reinforced her suggestion, gently, with "No, don't curse." Miss Foote interpreting something I said, later, into a criticism, & misapplying the observation of Julia Ann Enright, threatened to go home, "What with so & so & having my singing called a damned racket I don't think I'll stay any longer." Miss Foote is very bright & nice. I hope she will be able to come every Friday.[25]

We are getting on well with the "neighboring." Two young men have called voluntarily, a woman has presented us with a bottle of catsup, & another has requested to leave her baby with us one morning while she moved her household effects. Miss Blaisdell[26] took care of the creche, as we called baby Mercer. He was very good. One of the young men was very droll.[27] He is a Hebrew German by ~~birth~~ descent & Russian by birth & residence. He speaks English in the most formal manner. "In fact I have not in my experience met people so kind as—" &c &c. He informed us that he always made it a study to be as much of a gentleman as he could. He succeeds, to a certain degree, & we signified our willingness in polite terms, to give him any assistance in our power.

Send this to Chicopee <& Deerfield>, please.[28] The furnace is in.[29] Mr. Converse[30] has been awfully good. With love,

Ellen

P.S. We have two girls now <Mrs. Matz[31] & Mrs. Coonley pay No. 2>.[32]

Jane wishes this to go to Mrs. Haldeman. She will not mind my private affairs.

Our[33] appetites are simply abnormal. We have pretty good things to eat, too. We don't neglect the flesh pots.

I wish you would send me some blocks of this kind of paper.[34]

Fancy[35] our Ellen taking care of dirty Hoodlum babies while their mothers move their abiding places[.] I have received your letter[.] Will write soon.

ALS with HN (SCPC, JAC; *JAPM*, 2:1093–1108).

1. "[M]others and children successful[;] Miss Taylor [see n. 5] played for them &c," JA wrote in her 1889–90 diary for 2 Nov. 1889 (*JAPM*, 29:106–7).

2. EGS's letter relating events of Saturday evening 26 Oct. seems not to be extant. According to JA's 1889–90 diary for 26 Oct. 1889, the Saturday-evening event garnered "South side people & 'one' neighbor" (*JAPM*, 29:104–5). In 1889 many of JA and EGS's well-to-do supporters lived south of the settlement's 335 South Halsted address.

3. William Horace Day (1866–1942) was born in Bloomingdale, near Ottawa, Ill., the son of Rev. Warren Finney and Rachel Crawford Beith Day. He attended Amherst (A.B.), Yale Theological Seminary (1890–91), and Chicago Theological Seminary (1889–90, 1891–92). He was ordained in 1892 and began preaching that year at the Sedgewick Street Congregational Church in Chicago. After studying in England and Germany (1894–96), he returned to take a pastorate at the First Congregational Church in Aurora, Ill. (1896–1900).

In 1897 he wed Julia Huntington in Chicago, and he served Los Angeles (1900–17) and Bridgeport, Conn. (1917–37), from which he retired. At various times, Day was trustee at a number of schools, including Beloit College, Wis.; Pomona College Pacific Theological Seminary, Calif.; Mt. Holyoke College, Mass.; Hartford Theological Seminary, Conn.; and Elon College, N.C. He also continued to engage in community service in most of the communities in which he held churches and after his retirement. He became a national leader in the Congregational Church, serving as moderator of the National Council of Congregational Churches, 1917–20, and as president of the American Mission Assn., 1923–27.

At HH Day and Mr. Palmer agreed to assume some leadership responsibility for "'working boys,'" as JA described them in her diary entry for Tuesday, 12 Nov. 1889. Day and Palmer continued to meet with the boys that may have been JA's overflow group from the gatherings JA and EGS led on Tuesday evenings (see JA to SAAH, 8 Oct. 1889, n. 13, above). This same duo met with the children during the remainder of 1889. Day continued to visit the settlement through the spring of 1890, and in the spring of 1892 he taught American history in the settlement's College Extension Program.

If Mr. Palmer was "a Harvard man," as JA describes him, he may have been Charles Harvey Palmer (b. 1864) born in Milwaukee, Wis., of the Harvard class of 1889, who left the university in his junior year. He returned to Milwaukee to become a banker and follow his father into the insurance business. He became manager of the tax department of the Northwestern Mutual Life Insurance Co. in Milwaukee, a trustee of Milwaukee-Downer College, and a trustee and treasurer of Boys' Busy Life Club in Milwaukee.

4. Harriet Hopkins Trowbridge.

5. Likely Agnes Taylor, piano teacher whose address was 613–40 East Randolph St. in Chicago.

6. An optical apparatus through which pictures prepared as slides are viewed with a large lens with stereoptical effects.

7. The Roswell B. Masons. See also JA to SAAH, 13 Sept. 1889, n. 8, above.

8. Katherine Snow Isham (1832–1913) was the daughter of George Washington Snow, one of Chicago's pioneers. Her husband, Dr. Ralph N. Isham (1831–1904), was a founder of the Chicago Medical College that became the medical school of Northwestern Univ. He was chief surgeon for the Chicago and Northwestern Railway Co. and a consulting surgeon at Cook Co., Passavant, and Presbyterian hospitals. He also served as a surgeon at Provident Hospital and was a member of its advisory board. The Ishams had four children, George, Ralph, Katherine, and Harriet. Both girls attended Miss Kirkland's school, where they were taught by EGS. The Ishams were especially attentive to EGS in the early days of HH. Mrs. Isham was an early member (1873) of the Fortnightly Club and also an associate member of the Kirkland School Assn. In her later years, Katherine Isham was closely associated with the anti-suffrage movement as a member of the executive committees of the Anti-Woman Suffrage Assn. and the Com. of the Chicago Anti-Suffrage Society. She was also a member of the Illinois Assn. Opposed to the Extension of Suffrage to Women. She left an estate of more than two million dollars.

9. Katharine Medill. See JA to EGS, 4 June 1889, n. 4, above.

10. 31 Oct. 1889.

11. EGS had stopped to see her aunt Eliza Allen Starr, whose St. Joseph Cottage was located at 299 (later 16 East) Huron St. For biographical information, see *PJA*, 1:239–40.

12. The home of Eliza Allen Starr was a gathering place for artists in Chicago. Miss Starr's visitor may have been painter John J. Arnold (1853–1916), born in France, who lived nearby at 208 (later 123 West) Huron St.

13. Mary and Charles Blaisdell, sister and brother-in-law of EGS. For a biographical note, see *PJA*, 2:574, n. 13.

14. Helen Fairbank, who became Mrs. Benjamin Carpenter, was a student of EGS at Miss Kirkland's School for Girls. For a biographical note on Helen Fairbank, see *PJA*, 2:450, n. 9.

15. In addition to group lessons on art and literature, EGS planned to create a livelihood for herself by private tutoring. EGS had probably agreed to offer instruction to Mary Poole (1859–1932), daughter of distinguished bibliographer, historian, and librarian William Frederick Poole (1821–94), and his wife, Frances Maria Gleason Poole (1834–1904). Miss Poole eventually followed in her father's footsteps as a librarian and indexer. She is noted as the compiler, with William I. Fletcher, of the fourth and fifth supplements to her father's *Poole's Index to Presidential Literature*. She worked for a time at Chicago's Newberry Library before returning in 1904 to Massachusetts, where she been born.

16. Enclosure lacking. Percival Chubb's lecture was Friday evening, 8 Nov. 1889, at HH.

17. Percival Ashley Chubb (1860–1960), part of the group that founded the Fabian Society in England (1884), immigrated to the United States in 1889. In England he had been a member of the Progressive Assn., 1882; the London branch of the Fellowship of the New Life, a study group intent on developing models of alternative societies, 1884–89; and the Ethical Society, 1886. In the United States, after serving as a lecturer at various schools in the East, he became associate leader of the Society for Ethical Culture of New York, 1897–1910, and leader of the St. Louis Ethical Culture Society, 1911–32. He was president of the American Ethical Union, 1934–39. Always interested in theater, he became president of the Dronia League of America, 1915–20.

For his first appearance as a lecturer at HH, his topic was Arnold Toynbee. JA and EGS also heard him lecture on socialism in England on 22 Dec. 1889 at an economic conference held in Chicago (see also JA to SAAH, 22 Dec. 1889, n. 13, below). He visited HH again in 1891, when his lecture on 22 Oct. was titled "John Ruskin, and the Task of Artistic and Social Reform" and on 29 Oct. "Thomas Huxley and the Progress of the Scientific Spirit."

18. James Otis Sargent Huntington (1854–1935), known as Father Huntington, was born in Roxbury, Mass., the son of Frederic Dan Huntington (1819–1904), a Unitarian minister who joined the Episcopal Church and eventually became bishop of central New York, and his wife, Hannah Dane Sargent Huntington. Father Huntington, a graduate of Harvard Univ. (1875), studied for the Episcopalian ministry at St. Andrews Divinity School, Syracuse, N.Y., and became a priest in 1880. In 1884 with two friends, he founded the Order of the Holy Cross, an Anglican Benedictine monastic order. They began working among the poor in New York City's East Side. Father Huntington supported the development of labor unions and the single-tax movement (see n. 19).

Father Huntington had been called to Illinois in Sept. 1889 to help moderate the prolonged coal miners' strike in Spring Valley, Ill., between the miners and the Chicago and Northwestern Railroad with the Town Site Co. Huntington spoke at HH in Dec. 1889. Russian immigrant, cloak maker, labor leader, and HH attendee Abraham ("Abram") Bisno (see n. 27) recalled a speech Huntington delivered at the settlement when the subject was "how to ameliorate the conditions of the poor," which Bisno vehemently and publicly rejected. According to Bisno, the core of Huntington's message was "believe in the aid of God" and "love your neighbor as yourself" (Bisno, *Union Pioneer*, 119–20). Bisno consulted EGS, who greatly admired Father Huntington, to be sure that his attack had not been "ill-bred" (*Union Pioneer*, 120). Huntington returned to HH in Dec. 1893 when his subject was "can a free thinker believe in Christ?"

Huntington spoke several times in Chicago and at the settlement in the early 1890s (see also JA to SAAH, 22 Dec. 1889, n. 12, below). It may have been on a visit during the World's Columbian Exposition in 1893 that Huntington observed JA interacting with a member of the audience hearing a speech at HH. Apparently, JA had invited a man standing at the back of the room to remove his overcoat. "To the girl who had explained that the man in his overcoat was her coachman," JA replied, "'He may still be too warm.'" Of the exchange, EGS remarked to Huntington that "one could never be affronted at the things [that she said]." Huntington's reply EGS recorded as "'One might as well be affronted at the multiplication table.'" And EGS reported to her cousin Mary Allen to whom she was writing that Father Huntington "laughed till he nearly cried over Miss Addams," and she added, "I don't think Jane w'd be absolutely pleased with that compliment" (5 Sept. [1893], SC, Starr).

19. In *Progress and Poverty* (1879), Henry George (1839–97) theorized that land and its natural resources, the source of wealth for all, should therefore belong to and benefit all. See Address at the World's Columbian Exposition, 19 May 1893, nn. 7, 9, below.

Father Huntington, a single-tax advocate, also spoke on 31 Dec. 1889 at the Grand Pacific Hotel to the Single Tax Club, prophesying that "in seven years single tax would be the most vital issue in American politics" (*Chicago Daily Tribune*, 1 Jan. 1890).

20. Rev. Charles Frederick Goss.

21. Mary Wilmarth.

22. Roswell B. Mason.

23. By 1888 Anne S. Foote (1868–1960) was a teacher in Chicago, likely at Miss Kirkland's School for Girls. She was active at HH, 1889–91, where she was responsible for the kitchen-garden program and sang and played piano. She married Morris Larned Greeley in 1892. The couple lived in Winnetka and raised three children. She spent the last two years of her life with her daughter Louisa Greeley in Framingham, Mass., where she died (see also JA to SAAH, 8 Oct. 1889, n. 15, above).

24. Harriet Trowbridge.

25. It seems Miss Foote did continue to come to HH. JA's diary for 1889–90 mentions her attendance on Friday, 13 Dec. 1889, and 3 and 10 Jan., 1890.

26. JA may have been referring to her former RFS teacher Sarah Blaisdell, with whom JA had shared her idea for the social settlement scheme.

27. Abraham ("Abram") Bisno (1866–1929), an avowed socialist and noted labor leader, was born in Belaya Tserkof, Russia, into a family of tailors and became a tailor's apprentice at age eleven before he migrated to the United States in 1881. After short stays in Atlanta and Chattanooga, the Bisno family settled in Chicago in 1882. It was there that he became interested in trying to improve conditions for workers and became a union advocate and leader associated with the garment industry. In 1890 he was the first president of the Chicago Cloakmakers' Union, a forerunner of the International Ladies' Garment Workers' Union. He also served as chief clerk for the New York Joint Board of the Cloakmakers' Union beginning in 1911. He was strongly in favor of forced arbitration rather than conciliation to settle disputes. After 1917 he spent most of his time managing his own real estate business, but remained dedicated to supporting union activity. He died in Chicago.

Bisno found his way to HH soon after it opened and helped JA, EGS, and Florence Kelley in their early struggles to eradicate sweatshops and support the development of unions. In an effort to improve his command of English, he became a student of EGS, whom he came to admire as "sensitively honest" and "both progressive and conservative." In his autobiography, he recalled that the two became friends and spent their "time mostly in trying to convert each other. I was all charged with the burdens of the labor movement and my effort in the same. She, I believe learned a great deal more of the labor movement from me than I learned about reading and writing from her" (*Union Pioneer*, 118–19). During the early 1890s, Bisno often appeared as a speaker at mass meetings organized in support of ridding the garment industry of sweatshops, and he served as a factory inspector for Florence Kelley when she was the chief factory inspector of Illinois. Bisno, an active and vocal attendee at the Working People's Social Science gathering, was frequently at the settlement, and on 4 Apr. 1902 he presented a lecture titled "The Tailoring Trade in New York and Chicago" in a course of industrial lectures.

28. EGS's cousins Mary and Frances Allen, photographers who lived in Deerfield, Mass., and Mary Starr Blaisdell and her husband, Charles, who lived in Deerfield, Mass.

29. Landlord Helen Culver had agreed to put a furnace in HH. See JA to Helen Culver, 7 Mar. 1890, n. 4, above.

30. Clarence Myron Converse, who was western manager for the Magee Furnace Co. in Chicago, may have overseen the installation of the furnace at HH. See JA to MCAL, 12 Feb. 1889, n. 21, above.

31. Mary E. Lewis Matz (1835?–1913), one of the founders and active members of Chicago's Fortnightly Club, was married to architect Otto H. Matz (1830–1919) in 1857. She had lived since her youth in Chicago, where her mother, Mrs. Hiram Lewis, had established an early private school on Indiana Ave. At Mrs. Lewis's School, daughter Mary had been in charge of music. For the remainder of her life, she continued to play violin and piano. In 1873 Mary Matz was head of the governing board of the Mary Thompson Women's and Children's Hospital.

In 1868 Otto H. Matz, who had been an architect for the Illinois Central Railroad and an engineer for the Union cause during the Civil War, became the architect for the Chicago public school system and served as Cook County architect, 1892. In addition, he designed hospitals. The Matz couple had three children, Hermann L., Rudolph, and Evelyn.

In 1889 and 1890, Mrs. Coonley and Mrs. Matz often went to HH together and attended programs. They lectured for the HH Woman's Club in 1897.

32. Through their contributions to JA's Ten Account program, Mrs. Avery Coonley and Mrs. Otto Matz probably made it possible for JA and EGS to have a second servant to help Mary Keyser. Between 1891 and 1894, "Service" was a regular household expense charged monthly against Ten Account donations. The expense fluctuated between twenty-five and forty-five dollars a month.

33. Text beginning with "Our appetites" and ending with "kind of paper" is written per-

pendicular to the main body of text of the letter on p. 1. This statement appears in pencil in another's hand at the end of the letter.

34. The writing paper EGS wanted measured approximately nine and three-quarters inches by eight inches and when folded in the middle made a four-sided writing surface four and seven-eighths inches wide by eight inches long. The address "335 South Halsted Street" was centered on what then became the first page of the four surfaces, with the fold making the left edge of the first page.

35. This comment is written in pencil on the last page of the letter, likely by someone in the family of EGS.

## Ellen Gates Starr [for Jane Addams] to Susan Childs Starr and Caleb Allen Starr [and Sarah Alice Addams Haldeman]

335 South Halsted Street. [Chicago, Ill.] Nov. 15th,[16–20?][1] [1889]

Dear "Folks,"

I have a vile, scratchy pen again, & the epistolary world always looks hopeless to me under these circumstances, but I will do my endeavor.

Last Monday[2] night we had a droll time with Sr. V.[3] The Italian lesson lasted a long time & it grew late for supper & for his dinner, & Jane remarked as he arose to go, that we should be very glad to have Sr. V. stay, more to relieve the embarrassment of dismissing him than anything else. He said "im altra volta",[4] & I made some observation to the effect that he was waiting for "molto corraggio",[5] when, to our great surprise he said "I will stay if you wish." We rushed to kitchen & found that we had an especially scant supper—three "measly" little chops, not quite enough for <u>us</u>, & corn, which he would <u>never</u> eat, & a sticky sort of pudding which he would abhor; so we advised him kindly not to, & invited him for Sat[6]. We invited Denton J.[7] to meet him, & had Mrs. De Guido come over & cook the macaroni, & the most absurd time we had! She offered to buy the stuff for us—cheese, meat, tomatoes etc, of which we learned that the gravy was made. We thought, from her description of the process that all this stuff, (great "chunks" of meat) were to be lumped into one dish. She examined our pans for cooking, & pronounced <u>everything</u> too small. At length her eye fell on the dish pan, a huge one, & she said "This!" with a smile of content. It was scrubbed for her use. They cook the macaroni in enormous quantities of boiling water, & then take it out, & pour the gravy over it. The gravy is the important thing. I thought it would <u>never</u> be done. She boiled the meat & boiled it, till it was as hard as a rock, together with onions (she was much disgusted that we hadn't garlic) tomatoes, cheese, parsley etc. When at last it was done, Mary[8] knocked something against it & spilt about half. Mary said she was scared half to death, she thought she would be so angry, but beyond exclaiming "O, my God!" she restrained herself. There was enough left to grease it, Mary said. I liked it very well. It took so long to do it that we had to have the chicken first, & it should have come in after soup. She brought it in, & then we asked her to sit down, with us. At first she declined; but Sr. V. bade her sit down by him, & then she did. Susie & Francesco, who came with her were already partaking. Susie (Armita is her name) is the most bewitching thing you ever saw. Sr. V. says you could light a match at her eyes, & her hair is jet black & curls so tightly that it sticks straight <out.> I am going to have Jenny Dow try to get a photograph of her.[9] She wears long gold drops in her ears, like this ***/drawing of an eardrop/*** they glitter through her hair. She is four years old. We never can get a picture of those eyes—never.

Sr. V. was delightful. I don't think there are many gentlemen of a country where the caste system prevails, who would, or could, act as if it were the expected & everyday thing for a peasant woman to sit at table with him. She wouldn't have sat down if he hadn't insisted. When the macaroni was removed she ran out & got this dreadful meat, chunks as hard as a rock; you may imagine, after the juice had been cooked out of it for an hour & a half.

Jenny "et" some & pronounced it very good, & Sr. V. demanded a plate & some of the meat "cooked in Italian style by Mrs. De Guido" with which he struggled violently to little purpose.

A lot of Italians came in the evening & Mrs. Jackson & Leonora.[10] Mrs. J. sang two Italian songs & Leonora played beautifully. The Italians were delighted. They are going to give us a concert later. Sr. Urgos,[11] the kind preacher, told Mrs. J. that her voice sounded as if she were about thirty, which tickled her so that I think the entire family will come whenever we ask them.

On Thursday of this week Miss Root[12] gives a concert with her pupils.

Denton J. was fine. He talked with the Italians, scolded a man who doesn't send his daughter to school, quoted Dante to another & was very companionable. He asked us if we had a room that we could give him one evening a week to teach some Greeks.[13] There are a good many in the city, fruit-venders &c. who have no homes to speak of, & nobody does anything for them, naturally, as not many people speak modern Greek. Probably Mr. Snider is the only one in the city who does, of course we were delighted. He wants to start a library for them which we are to take care of for a time & surrender it at any moment, if he wishes to give it to the public library, as he does, if he succeeds in doing what he wishes. He has great faith in putting people in communication with the public institutions, but he says he doesn't wish to do it till he gets them on a little; that it isn't easy for him, who "speaks pretty plain English" to get himself attended there, <at the P. library>[14] & to people who speak Greek it would certainly be out of the question. I hope it won't end in smoke. It will be a very interesting thing if it can be done, & he is the only man I know who can do it. He is so intent on "chasing roots" that he finds dialects as interesting as the straight language. He speaks the Neapolitan dialect with great success. I wish I did.

To burst abruptly into polite society—Louise Kirkland is engaged to a little fellow twenty-one years old & six feet tall & more (She is 23, & comes about to my neck)[.][15] He is the son of a Concord philosopher.[16] Jenny Dow is too funny about it. (You know she loathes her.) She commiserates the "poor little young man, away from all his parents!" with the utmost fervor & naiveté;—is perfectly honest about it.

Dear Mrs. Sedgwick has been with us again.[17] She is charming, & the greatest help. She mends our clothes & Johnny Morans,[18] reads to the little girls, & takes such stock in us that it is delightful to have her about. She is very gentle & amicable to every body. One day she began to criticise somebody slightly, but stopped herself, with "But far be it from me to find fault with people I don't care much about." I told her I had suffered from that principle in the friend of my bosom & certain of my family, & she admitted that her daughters[19] sometimes said, "Mamma, I wish you didn't love me so much." We are going to have a few ladies some afternoon to meet her, & have her give a little paper on Brooke Farm.[20] I think she will like to do it.

I have never had time to tell you the whole history of Mrs. Moran. She is Irish, & one of the funniest people we know. She laughs in the midst of her tales of deepest woe. Her husband is out of the Washingtonian home[21] & sick in bed now. She considers it the greatest joke, & laughs immoderately at the idea that he has been to confession & mass, which he hasn't done for nine years, but the priest has scared him. She went to the ~~priest~~ <county agent> the other day, & he gave her a bag of flour, & it rained, & the paper broke, "I cursed a little" she acknowledged <confidentially,> "I said 'Damn poverty!'" Most people would have said 'D. the flour,' or 'D. the rain,' but Mrs. Moran goes to the root.[22]

Mr. Ryerson,[23] a new young man, is coming down tomorrow night to make calls. We find that evening is the best time to call. "He" is at home, & they are all sitting about, rather bored with each other, & glad to be amused. In the day time 'he' & all the members of the family who work for bread are away, & 'she' is doing her housework, & in some cases doesn't like to be interrupted. Besides, we think if some men call 'he' will be more apt to respond. Jane & I have made some very successful evening calls.

Jane again requests that the epistle general be forwarded to Mrs. Haldeman. With love to you all,

Ellen.

ALS (SCPC, JAC; *JAPM*, 2:1109–24).

1. The dinner EGS described in her letter took place on Saturday, 16 Nov. 1889. This letter could have been written between 16 and 20 Nov. 1889.

2. 11 Nov. 1889.

3. Alessandro Mastro-Valerio.

4. Italian, *im altra volta*, translates as "another time."

5. Italian, *molto corragio [corraggio]*, translates as "appropriate."

6. 16 Nov. 1889.

7. Denton Jacques Snider (1841–1925), born in Mt. Gilead, Ohio, was a graduate of Oberlin College (1862). He lived in St. Louis, Mo., where he became associated with the St. Louis

Philosophical Society when he was not traveling the world to expand his knowledge of other cultures and languages. A prolific writer on philosophy, art, music, history, and psychology, he authored more than fifty works. When he became involved with HH, he had just published the novel *The Freeburgers* (1889). At that time, he was particularly interested in the ideas and life of kindergarten educator Friedrich Froebel (1782–1852) and the history, leaders, and philosophy associated with Greek culture. He seemed aware that Greek men were beginning to move into the HH neighborhood, and one of his hopes, unrealized, was to start a library for Greek immigrants at the settlement. He presented a lecture on Shakespeare's *Macbeth* in the settlement's college extension Thursday Lectures and Concerts series on 5 Nov. 1891.

8. Mary Keyser.

9. The earliest extant photographs of HH and its neighborhood may have been taken by Jenny Dow Harvey. This statement seems to be the earliest written surviving evidence that the founders had access to photography to record their settlement structures and activities. It is not surprising that EGS thought of it because she saw photography as an art form and admired the work of her photographer cousins Mary and Frances Allen, who lived in Deerfield, Mass. JA's sister SAAH, also an early practitioner of photography, took early photographs of HH. Illustrations of the Hull home began to appear in newsprint in 1890. Renderings of photos of HH began to appear in the newspaper accounts of the settlement by 1891.

10. JA's 1889–90 diary entry for Saturday, 16 Nov., reads: "Italians Miss Caruthers, M'de Jackson Leonara" (SCPC, JAC; *JAPM*, 29:110–11). M'de Jackson carried out a return engagement on Saturday, 28 Dec. 1889.

Widow and musician Elizabeth Higgins Jackson arrived in Chicago with her two children, Ernest and Leonora, about 1883 and established herself as a vocal teacher. The family lived on Chicago's Near North Side and was Episcopalian. Daughter Leonora (1879–1969), who attended Miss Kirkland's school and studied violin and piano at the Chicago Musical College, eventually studied violin in Europe with a number of noted teachers. She made her highly successful concert debut as an eighteen-year-old in 1896 with the Berlin Philharmonic Orchestra and continued to perform throughout Europe. After a command performance for Queen Victoria at Windsor Castle in 1899, she returned to perform with major symphony orchestras throughout the United States, beginning with the New York Philharmonic Society in Jan. 1900. After her marriage in 1907 to Michael L. McLaughlin, a Brooklyn, N.Y., real estate entrepreneur, ended, she wed physician W. Duncan McKim (1855–1935), scion of a prominent Baltimore banking family in 1915. Shortly after 1935, she had become a concert manager, operating under the name the Leonora Jackson Concert Co. She died in Washington, D.C.

11. Francis [Francesco] D. Urgos (1831–1906), born in Nice, Italy, was a soldier in Garibaldi's army and settled initially in St. Anne, Kankakee, Ill., in 1850 after becoming a U.S. citizen in that year in New York. Sometime before 1876, he was accidentally blinded, he contended in his biography *Political Life of an Italian* (1876), by washing his face in water containing arsenic. He was adopted by Dr. Emile Labbe and his wife, Elizabeth, who lived in Kankekee, and in 1876 married their daughter Flora (1865–1902). After a brief stay in Battle Creek, Mich., where the second of their seven children was born, the couple resided in Chicago, often in the Nineteenth Ward. Urgos is listed in the 1891 and 1892 Lakeside Chicago directories as Rev. Urgos; however, for the remainder of the listings through 1900, he is identified as a teacher of languages or a linguist. It is likely that he was one of the first Italians to befriend JA and EGS and may have been partly responsible for helping to attract the Italian community around the settlement to HH. He is first mentioned in JA's 1889–90 diary on Sunday, 13 Oct. 1889, with the notation "S.S.," which may have meant Sunday School, and then again on Sunday, 27 Oct. 1889. JA recorded on Monday, 23 Dec. 1889, "Urgos tree, every thing ready," which might indicate that Urgos was hosting a Christmas gathering at HH. Her diary indicates that he called on 7 Jan. 1890, bringing two Italians with him.

12. According to JA's diary, 1889–90, the Root concert took place on Thursday, 21 Nov. 1889. Frances ("Fanny") Amelia Root (1838–1905) was the daughter of George F. Root, and his wife, Mary Olive Woodman, and sister of Frederick W. Root, who was also a music teacher and composer of note in the Chicago area. The Root family was related to the Coonley-Ward family by marriage. See JA to MCAL 19 [and 20] Feb 1889, nn. 9, 11, above. Fanny had studied piano and voice in New York and after teaching for two years at the Judson Female Institute, Marion, Ala., and one year at Maplewood Institute, Pittsfield, Mass., returned to New York to study singing. Upon arriving in Chicago, she taught singing and sang with the First, Second, and Third Presbyterian Church Choirs and as a soloist for the Apollo Club, especially during the choir's opening season in 1873. She continued to study singing in Europe and became one of Chicago's important pioneer music teachers.

For the Jan. 1891 program term at HH, Fanny Root taught music on Thursday evenings between 7:30 and 8:00 P.M., just prior to lectures. During the 1890s, Miss Root and her students gave a number of concerts at HH. Her nephew Frederic Root sang at the HH Old Settlers Party in Jan. 1898.

13. It is not surprising that Denton J. Snider was interested in Greek immigrants in Chicago. Greek heroes and culture were among his major interests, and he spoke and read Greek. A Greek community was just beginning to develop in Chicago. Greek men began coming to the city in the late 1870s and early 1880s to establish their livelihoods. They settled near their work, which was primarily at wholesale food markets at Fulton and South Water streets. A few Greek women began to follow their husbands and fathers to Chicago by the mid-1880s.

The survey that provided the data for the maps associated with the groundbreaking study of an urban neighborhood that became *HH Maps and Papers* (1895) discovered only two structures that sheltered Greeks. It was conducted between Apr. and Aug. 1893 to determine the nationality composition of a portion of the neighborhood to the south and east of HH, bordered by Halsted St. on the west, Polk St. on the north, the Chicago River on the east, and 12th St. on the south.

During the last two years of the nineteenth century, Greek immigrants began to arrive in noticeable numbers in the HH neighborhood. "In the last three years," wrote resident Alice Hamilton on 2 Apr. 1901 to her cousin Agnes, "two thousand Greeks have moved into the neighbourhood, and now there are two Greek saloons just opposite us, and two Greek groceries just a little way down. Whenever I walk down Halsted street I see from thirty to sixty congregated on the corners of Polk. The house has been much exercised about them, of course, for they are a very undesirable lot. They bring no women with them when they emigrate and so they are a great source of danger. Also they are under the protection of the politicians. We had a residents meeting about them lately and one of the men residents offered to go and interview the patriarch and persuade him to talk about clubs and classes to his people. He found a most benevolent old gentleman but when Mr. Burlingham had explained matters, the patriarch said that he knew nothing of clubs and classes he thought only of Christian matters. Clubs and classes might be good and he would advise Mr. Burlingham to see the saloon-keeper opposite Hull-House and talk to him. Which shows that the attitude of the Greek church and the Protestant churches are not very far apart. Mr. Burlingham interviewed the saloon-keeper, Denaetrakopoulos, and he came beautifully up to the mark. He invited two hundred to a party in the [HH] Auditorium and all two hundred came. He said that as many more wished to come but he allowed only those who promised to enter English classes. They were fine, the Greeks were. They sang national songs and danced national dances and enrolled themselves in classes of twenty and thirty for English lessons. So now every available resident must take a Greek class and it is not going to be easy work" (RS, HFP).

It was not until the early 1900s that Greek families began to settle near HH and then primarily near Halsted and Harrison streets and Blue Island Ave., to the west and north of HH.

However, in 1890, HH offered a course in the Greek language, and the settlement's library may have had some Greek-language literature. By the 1930s, there were approximately thirty thousand first- and second-generation Greeks in Chicago.

Frederick Wright Burlingham (1868–1924), who was a HH resident during the early 1900s and in charge of the Men's Club, became a life insurance agent. He was born in Cairo, Ill., the son of E. P. and Susan M. Burlingham, and educated at Harvard Univ. (A.B. 1891; A.M. 1894; LL.B. 1894). Between 1894 and 1900, he practiced law in Chicago. While he was living and working at HH, he was assistant manager for Charles D. Norton, general agent, Northwestern Mutual Life Insurance Co. After being in the investment business, 1904–15, he opened his own insurance business in 1915, which he operated until his death. He married Sarah McD. Breck of Claremont, N.H., in 1906, and the couple had two daughters.

14. There is no evidence that Denton J. Snider was able to establish his library for Greek immigrants; however, HH soon had a leading library. JA and EGS believed strongly in providing the tools through which people of all ages could learn. They were aware that it would be difficult to sustain college extension classes if students did not have ready access to a library. The settlement had a small library of children's books, and JA and EGS invited their students to use the *Encyclopedia Britannica* in the settlement's library, to which they planned to add other reference materials. The "HH Weekly Program of Lectures, Clubs, Classes, Etc.," which listed educational opportunities slated to begin Jan. 1891, indicated that the Working People's Social Science Club had "a small circulating library of books upon Political Economy and Social Science" and that the librarian was Ernest Geoghegan (HH Scrapbook 2:5; *JAPM*, Addendum 10:7ff). In the same program publication, JA and EGS announced that HH had been made a "station of the Public Library" (HH Scrapbook, 2:5½; *JAPM*, Addendum 10:7ff) and that HH resident Anna M. Farnsworth was in charge. When the Butler Art Gallery Building was opened in the summer of 1891, the Chicago Public Library station had its quarters on the ground floor. The library provided the equipment, books, periodicals, and two librarians to staff the facility. By the spring of 1892, the collection consisted of four hundred books and sixty periodicals (including local and foreign-language newspapers) and was open 9:00 A.M.to 10:00 P.M. daily, except Sunday, when the hours were 10:00 A.M. to 10:00 P.M. At JA's insistence, the public library also provided HH with twenty-five dollars per month to defray the costs associated with heat, light, and water. In 1894 the Chicago Public Library moved out of its Butler Art Gallery quarters but remained available to HH students and friends in a variety of nearby sequential locations until 1943, when the station was closed.

15. Louise Wilkinson Kirkland (1866–1941), daughter of Theodosia Burr Wilkinson and Joseph Kirkland, wed Victor C. Sanborn (1867–1921), son of Franklin B. and Louisa Augusta Leavitt Sanborn of Concord, Mass., on 28 May 1891. Victor Sanborn became active in real estate in the Chicago area. The couple lived in Kenilworth, Ill., and had two children, Caroline (Mrs. Morrow Krum) and Louisa Leavitt (Mrs. Boyd Hill).

16. Franklin B. Sanborn (1831–1917) was a journalist who taught at the Concord School of Philosophy, Mass., and helped found a number of national organizations, including the American Social Science Assn. and the National Conf. of Charities. He attended the second Summer School of Applied Ethics in Plymouth, Mass., in Aug. 1892, and spoke at the settlement gathering on 3 Aug.

17. Deborah W. Gannett Sedgwick (1825–1901), born in Cambridge, Mass., was the second wife and widow of Charles Baldwin Sedgwick (1815–83). Her husband, born in Onondaga Co., N.Y., had attended Hamilton College, Clinton, N.Y. After studying law, he was admitted to the bar in 1848 and practiced law for the remainder of his life in Syracuse, N.Y. He was elected as a Republican to the U.S. Congress from the 24th N.Y. District and served two terms, 1859–63. The Sedgwicks had six children, three of whom lived to maturity. Deborah Sedgwick had been a student at Brook Farm, an experiment in communal living that flourished in Massachusetts between 1841 and 1847 (see n. 20). JA recalled that Sedgwick designated herself

as the "first resident" of HH. JA found her "a charming old lady who gave five consecutive readings from Hawthorne to a most appreciative audience, interspersing magic tales most delightfully with recollections of the elusive and fascinating author." JA seemed pleased that Sedgwick "wished to live once more in an atmosphere where 'idealism ran high'" (*Twenty Years*, 101).

18. Likely EGS's slang for underwear.

19. Her daughters were Sarah White Sedgwick (1853–82), wed to John Leonard King Jr.; Katharine Maria Sedgwick (1856–1929), who wed Walter Angell Burlingame; and Dora Gannett Sedgwick (1864–1935), wed to Frederick Rowland Hazard.

20. Mrs. Sedgwick is not mentioned in JA's 1889–90 diary until 20 and 21 Dec. 1889, when she made presentations on Nathaniel Hawthorne and Brook Farm. Brook Farm, established in West Roxbury, Mass., by transcendentalists George (1802–80) and Sophia Peabody Ripley (1809–71), was a short-lived attempt to match intellectual endeavor and simple, basic living. Each member of the group shared in the manual labor required to keep the 192-acre farm successful. Author Nathaniel Hawthorne was a member. The ideas of Charles Fourier (1772–1837) associated with an ideal systematically arranged agricultural society were popular among its members. See also Two Essays in the *Forum*, Nov. and Oct. 1892, n. 42, below.

21. The Washington Home, 566 to 572 (later 1529–37) West Madison St. at the corner of Madison St. and Ogden Ave. on Chicago's West Side, had been established in 1863 for "the care, cure and reclamation of inebriates" (*Hand-Book of Chicago Charities*, 121). It was one of several Chicago "homes" established to treat the considerable problem of alcoholism. In 1891 the average daily attendance was eighty-six, each of whom stayed an average of twenty days. When able to pay, the charge was ten dollars a week; however, only about half of the inmates were able to pay anything. The Martha Washington Home located at Graceland and Western avenues was established by the Washington Home Assn. in 1881 as an auxiliary to the Washington Home. It was the female counterpart of this nonsectarian effort to curb alcoholism.

22. JA also recalled Mrs. Moran's story in *Twenty Years*: "Mrs. Moran . . . was returning one rainy day from the office of the county agent with her arms full of paper bags containing beans and flour which alone lay between her children and starvation. Although she had no money she boarded a street car in order to save her booty from complete destruction by the rain, and as the burst bags dropped 'flour on the ladies' dresses' and 'beans all over the place,' she was sharply reprimanded by the conductor, who was further exasperated when he discovered she had no fare. He put her off, as she had hoped he would, almost in front of Hull-House. She related to us her state of mind as she stepped off the car and saw the last of her wares disappearing; she admitted she forgot the proprieties and 'cursed a little,' but, curiously enough, she pronounced her malediction, not against the rain nor the conductor, nor yet against the worthless husband who had been sent up to the city prison, but, true to the Chicago spirit of the moment, went to the root of the matter and roundly 'cursed poverty'" (159).

23. JA's 1889–90 diary does not indicate that Mr. Ryerson visited on 16 Nov. 1889; however, John Albert Ryerson (1866–1910) did become a volunteer at HH. He was born in New York City and graduated from Columbia Univ. (1885) and added an LL.B. in 1887. He began practicing law in Chicago in 1887. After being associated with the insurance and publishing industries, in 1901 he organized the Victor Chemical Works and later the Ideal Electric Co., manufacturers of electric automobiles.

At HH he taught Latin (elementary and Virgil) on Tuesday evenings in the first College Extension Program during the fall of 1890. He continued teaching during the Jan. 1891 session of ten weeks and also helped direct the Young Citizens' Club of Working Boys on Tuesday evenings.

In 1905 he married Violet E. Stone, daughter of Rev. James S. Stone, rector of Chicago's St. James. At the time of his suicide death, his son, Albert, was eighteen months old.

## To Sarah Alice Addams Haldeman

*In April 1889, while Jane and Ellen were in Chicago planning for the settlement, George Haldeman unexpectedly set off by himself from Cedarville to explore the West.[1] He hoped to discover an occupation, lifestyle, and location in the West that would suit him. He recounted his adventures, which took place primarily in Colorado, in letters to his mother, Anna Addams.[2] By June his effort at establishing his independence had failed; he succumbed to the comfort of his mother and her home in Cedarville. While Jane must certainly have known about his attempt to establish himself, none of her surviving letters during the period of his effort mentions him or the family crisis he precipitated.*

*On his way back home, he visited his physician brother, Harry Haldeman, in Girard, Kans. After the brothers returned to Colorado to climb Pikes Peak together, Harry convinced George to spend time with him in Girard while he tried to help George improve his mental health[3] before returning to Cedarville.*

335 South Halsted St [Chicago, Ill.] Nov 23d 1889

My dear Alice

I had a letter from Laura[4] to-day. She said that she was worried about George, that he was blue and seemed sort of dazed—feel dreadful sorry for Ma and George, they are certainly thoroughly unhappy—at least judging from letters and it all seems so useless and purposeless.[5] It seems to me that Harry is the only person who can do any thing about it, and of course I don't know that he can. Does Ma write to you and how do you feel about her this winter.

I do so wish that you were coming for Thanksgiving,[6] I have been homesick for you all fall—I often wish that you were doing this thing instead of me, that you would do it so much better. So many things are constantly opening up that we might do and that we would like to do, if we had the room and the people. Friday <afternoons> we have little girls in every room in the house and Tuesdays we are overwhelmed with boys almost as much.[7] The working boys in the evening are harder to manage but two young men[8] come down every Tuesday evening to help us. One of them is a Harvard man and the other a theological student who sings college songs and is otherwise very taking to the boys. They have quite given up spitting tobacco or keeping on their hats—two things that we almost despaired of curing them of. We have a German evening every Monday,[9] Fl Neushäfer[10] has charge of it and it is very successful. Prof. Snyder is going to have Greeks in the dining room every Sat. evening and we will have Italians in the drawing room.[11] Our last Italian evening was a great success,[12] we had good music and many people to help. Miss Root and her pupils gave us a little concert last Thursday evening which we all enjoyed.[13] We are getting sympathy and money from a great many people and if we do not succeed it will be altogether because we ourselves fail. We are going to an Italian wedding to morrow[14]—the father of one of the kindergarten children is married in true

Italian style. We are going to the Church and the banquet. I haven't time for more, I am always sorry that my letters are so short. With many kisses to dear Marcet and love to Harry & yourself. Your loving Sister

Jane

ALS (IU, Lilly, SAAH; *JAPM*, 2:1125–28).

1. For information about GBH's journey to the West, see *PJA*, 1:504–5.

2. GBH's correspondence with AHHA appears in UIC, JAMC, HJ; and in IU, Lilly, SAAH.

3. AHHA, who anxiously awaited the hoped for improvement in GBH's health, wrote son HWH in Oct. 1889: "Please get George all the warm underware he needs—and new suits of clothes—he used to look so nicely when well, and, he loves nice clean clothes now, I am sure; His tastes have always been refined; Do try the Electricity; and, let him use the best olive oil. John Addams is getting well on oil, has used about 14 bottles" (IU, Lilly, SAAH).

4. Sister-in-law LSA's letter is apparently not extant.

5. These letters are not known to be extant.

6. JA's 1889–90 diary entry for Thursday, 28 Nov. 1889, reads "A.M. Dr McPherson, Sarah H[ostetter] etc Thanksgiving family called at Murphys" (SCPC, JAC; *JAPM*, 29:114–15). See also JA to SAAH, 8 Oct. 1889, n. 31, above.

7. In her 1889–90 diary for 3 Dec. 1889, JA commented, "too many boys" (SCPC, JAC; *JAPM*, 29:116–17).

8. The young men were William H. Day and Charles Harvey Palmer.

9. The first German evening was held on Monday, 18 Oct. 1889, a month after the settlement was officially opened. After Jan. 1890, German evening was moved to Thursday, but by the fall was scheduled on Friday evenings. JA's 1889–90 diary indicates that attendance fluctuated. On 27 Mar. 1890, the entry reads "rainy no Germans" (*JAPM*, 29:149) and on the next Thursday, 3 Apr.: "Bad evening—only 2 German women" (*JAPM*, 29:154); however, the very next week, 17 Apr., the entry read, "A great many Germans" (*JAPM*, 29:155). On 15 May, JA's notation was "large German eve about 45" (SCPC, JAC; *JAPM*, 29:162). Journalist Eva V. Curlin described what she experienced when visiting a German evening at the settlement in Feb. 1894: "The social 'evenings' are very popular with the visitors, and rightly so, to judge by one that I was fortunate enough to attend when the Germans of the neighborhood came in true 'gemuthlichkeit' for reading and song and cozy speech. Frau [*left blank by author*], who had given one evening a week for several years to this gathering, led the literary programme with one of Schiller's lyrics. How the dull faces brightened, eyes lightened and knitting-needles quickened as memories of the past and of the Fatherland were stirred!" ("The Day in Altruria").

Emma Neuschäffer (Lunt) (see n. 10) was the volunteer who made the German evenings work so well. She taught German at the settlement on Friday evenings at 7:00 P.M. beginning in the fall of 1890 and continuing through the spring of 1891. After a summer hiatus in 1891, Frl. Neuschäffer was once again directing the German evenings. "The evening is entirely social in character, music and reading of German literature, or history, occupying a part of the time. A small German library is at the disposal of the guests" ("HH A Social Settlement . . . Weekly Program Lectures, Clubs, Classes, Etc., March 1st, 1892"). Prior to the reception, held from 8:00 P.M. to 10:00 P.M., she taught advanced German in the College Extension Program beginning Jan. 1892 and continuing until summer and beginning again in the fall and continuing until the summer of 1893. Weekly German meetings at HH continued until 1896, after which they were held irregularly.

10. Emma ("Emmy") N. Neuschäffer (sometimes spelled Neushäfer, Neuschafer, or Newschafer) (Lunt) (b. June 1863) was a native of Germany, immigrated to the United States in 1884, and beginning in May 1884 taught German language in the North Division High School

of Chicago until she resigned effective Sept. 1887. In 1888 she became a co-owner with Mary Hays Withington (d. 1891) of the Withington School, a private academy with a kindergarten and a college preparatory curriculum. It had been opened by Miss Withington on Benson St., south of Church St., in Evanston, Ill., in 1886. There Emma Neuschäffer taught German language, history, and literature. After Miss Withington's death, Frl. Neuschäffer continued to operate the school for a number of years with the help of several other teachers, one of whom, Margaretta (sometimes Margaret) West (see n. 9 on p. 340), like Emma Neuschäffer, also became associated with HH.

Frl. Neuschäffer's name appears for the first time in JA's 1889–90 diary in association with the first German night at HH. She was a faithful volunteer at the settlement for at least three years (see n. 9). During the 1889–90 year, she was often a dinner guest at HH and accompanied JA making social calls on German neighbors and other settlement friends.

On 22 Mar. 1893, Emma Neuschäffer married silversmith Ernest M. Lunt (1870–1946) in Evanston, Ill., with Henry Demarest Lloyd as one of the witnesses. She continued to operate the Withington School as Mrs. Ernest M. Lunt. The Lunts had four children, three of whom were still living in 1910 when the family lived in Lisle, DuPage Co., Ill. They were Caroline, age fifteen; Ernest M. Jr., age twelve; and Benjamin, age three. By 1917 the family had moved to Mt. Vernon, N.Y., and Ernest Lunt had become vice-president of the Towel Manufacturing Co.

11. This is the earliest mention of Greeks coming to HH. JA's diary does not record Greek evenings at the settlement. In her diary, JA reported Italian gatherings at HH on Saturday evening but never mentions Denton J. Snider's effort to attract Greeks.

The first mention of Italian evenings at HH was Saturday, 12 Oct. 1889. These evenings soon became regular and well attended. "Perhaps the most picturesque time is the Italian evening," wrote Jenny Dow in her description of activities at the settlement, "when the poor souls, who have found so inhospitable a welcome in this country, are given some really good music, and see that there is such a thing as a kindly American" ("The Chicago Toynbee Hall"). Two months later, *Chicago Daily Tribune* reporter "Nora Marks," pseudonym for Eleanor Stackhouse (1863–1942), whose specialty until she left in July 1890 to marry Francis Blake Atkinson was investigative reporting on activities, needs, and institutional assistance for the working poor, visited the settlement on Italian night and wrote a lively description of the event. EGS had helped to "manage" the reporter and her visit and found the resulting article "disgustingly vulgar & horrid" (EGS to Mary Blaisdell, 18 [and 22] May 1890, SC, Starr, published in Bryan and Davis, *100 years at HH*, 20). She reported: "I think we managed the woman 'Nora Marks' pretty well, gently directing her attention to the things we wished talked about, & directing it from delicate subjects of personal relationship. She was here last night—which was a brilliant Italian night—& I can say she will spend most of her energies on that. The Italians can't read it, & won't hear of it, so that is safe. If her article is good for anything, I will send it.

"Sig. Valerio has issued a kind of manifesto in the form of a circular letter to Italians. He took this occasion of inviting them to the concert last night to make known to them several things—to explain the situation, in fact. This he sent to 228 Italians. The room was packed, & people were in the halls. It was a very good thing. Sometime when my right little finger & powers of composition are from these newspaper articles, I will translate it for you. Sig. V. has been very much depressed lately over indifference & obstinacy of his countrymen, but his spirits were greatly raised last night. The sight was very interesting. There was a great many children, babies even & some of the women wore bright kerchiefs on their heads. The rich & vulgar Italians are taking to coming, sporting diamond crosses. I hope something will come of it. We put them on the back seats, & the peasants to the front. One of the ladies of the diamond cross recited a patriotic poem with great spirit. I missed it, being engaged in struggle with Nora Marks, on the other side of the house, but Jane says it was very spirited,

& some of the people were quite moved. I was awfully glad the things went off so well. Poor Mr. V. had toiled so, & was so nervous" (EGS to Mary Blaisdell, 18 [and 22] May 1890, SC, Starr, published in Bryan and Davis, *100 Years at HH*, 19–20).

With the exception of summers, weekly Italian receptions continued into the late 1890s. In addition, other Italian clubs evolved and continued to meet at the settlement.

12. Of the successful Italian evening on 16 Nov. 1889, JA reported in her diary no superlatives, only that M'de Jackson and Leonora sang and played the piano. For the "Nora Marks" account, see n. 11.

13. According to JA's 1889–90 diary, the Root concert took place Thursday, 21 Nov. 1889.

14. JA did not report on the wedding in her 1889–90 diary on 24 Nov. 1889.

## To George Bowman Haldeman

335 South Halsted St [Chicago, Ill.] Nov 24" 1889

My dear George

I hoped very much that I should hear from Mama and yourself oftener, and am anxious to know how you both are. I think of you very often and wish you would consent to come in to see me.

We have some very interesting experiances, last Saturday evening we had an Italian dinner cooked by an Italian woman and served to Sig. Valerio Prof. Snyder Miss Dow and ourselves. Prof Snyder is a very clever man and went into the derivation and spread of macaroni with much vigor.[1]

Every Monday evening we have a German "klatch" for the women which Fl. Neushäfer[2] has charge of. She is sympathetic and simple, at the same time very capable so that that is a great success and judging by the gratitude of the poor German women very much needed.

We have regular help on our boys club[3] and are getting much interested in the shop girls near us,[4] so that our various plans are being carried out. This winter of course will be more or less experimental, so that by next year when we have all of the house,[5] we will be ready to do things more extensively. We are constantly surprised by the number of good people who express interest and give us help. One is so overpowered by the misery and narrow lives of so large a number of city people, that the wonder is that concientious people can let it alone. The movement toward Christian Socialism[6] is certainly becoming more general from the very stress of the misery. I expect Mary[7] and the children on Wednesday and Mr Linn Thanksgiving Day. I wish very much that you and Mama were coming. Please give her my love and believe me always[.] Your loving sister

Jane Addams.

ALS (UIC, JAMC, HJ; *JAPM*, 2:1129–30).

1. See also EGS [for JA] to Susan Childs Starr and Caleb Allen Starr [and SAAH], 15,[16–20?] Nov. [1889], above.

2. See JA to SAAH, 23 Nov. 1889, nn. 9–10, above.

3. See EGS [for JA] to Susan Childs Starr and Caleb Allen Starr [and SAAH], 3 Nov. [1889], n. 3; and JA to SAAH, 23 Nov. 1889, nn. 7–8, both above.

4. See JA to SAAH, 5 Jan. 1890, n. 4, below.

5. JA and EGS anticipated being able to lease the entire house from Helen Culver when the Sherwood Co. moved out in Mar. 1890. See JA to SAAH, 6 Mar. 1890, below.

6. This may be the earliest extant example of JA using the term "Christian Socialism" in writing. She and EGS seemed to be aware of social reformer William D. P. Bliss's (1856–1926) effort to promote the ideas associated with the term through the Society of Christian Socialists and its publication, the *Dawn* (1889–1900). Its credo was "'To exalt the principle that all rights and powers are gifts of God, not for the receiver's use only, but for the benefit of all'" (Bliss, *Encyclopedia of Social Reform*, 258).

The term itself seems to have been created between 1848 and 1850 as a response to the aftermath of the revolution of 1848 by a small group of concerned English clergy led by Frederick Denison Maurice (1805–72) and laymen who believed that something had to be done to ameliorate the condition and position of the workingman. Their initial example was the workers' associations created by both the Roman Catholic Church and the Protestant Church in France to address the issues festering in that country. They held "that socialism was really but a development, an outcome of Christianity, and that to be effective and true it must be grounded on a definite Christian basis" (Bliss, *Encyclopedia of Social Reform*, 251).

7. The Linn family, including John Addams Linn, a student at Lake Forest College, Ill., and SH, were with JA and EGS for Thanksgiving.

## To Sarah Alice Addams Haldeman

335 So Halsted St [Chicago, Ill.] Dec 22d 1889

My dear Alice

A draft came from Girard yesterday I am much obliged to you for seeing to it. I wrote you once to Kansas, for I supposed you there until Sarah's[1] letter came the other day. I was so sorry to know of Mama's illness and hope she is better.[2]

We have been very busy but very happy in it as every thing is going on so smoothly and well. We have no kindergarten this week and the wild thought has come to me that perhaps you and Marcet might go home this way. Miss Lanagan[3] is here for the week and we enjoy her very much. Yesterday afternoon Mrs Sedgewick[4] gave us a paper on Brook Farm, it was delightful and received with much enthusiasm. We had the kindergarten Xmas tree on Friday morning,[5] the Kenwood Kg.[6] sent two presents for each child, and Miss Dow was back for the first time. We will have an entertainment next week for each of the Clubs,[7] people have been very generous with talent and money, and we have had enough candy[8] to share with the two nearest S. Schools.[9] I wrote you of Dr Dudley's reception[10] and the kindness of Dr Andrews & Dr Davis.[11] Mary[12] and I united in a revised version for you which I fear Mary has sent to Girard. You will accept it with our love and Christmas wishes. I will send Marcet's to Cedarville with the others. We are going out this evening to hear Father Huntington, he will speak for us next week on The "Emancipation of Labor."[13] I have been interrupted and will only add my love to the entire household. (I am a little home sick for you, your visit was so very short.) always your loving Sister

Jane Addams.

ALS (UIC, JAMC; *JAPM*, 2:1135–36).

1. SH's letter is not known to be extant.

2. "The one letter from Cedarville leaves me in doubt as to whether you are now there or at home, and I am growing homesick for a word from you," JA wrote SAAH, 18 Dec. 1889 (UIC, JAMC; *JAPM*, 2:1133). SAAH who had been visiting in Illinois from Girard, Kans., was still in Cedarville nursing an ailing AHHA. The entire Haldeman family, HWH, SAAH, and Marcet remained with AHHA and GBH for Christmas. See JA to AHHA, 26 Dec. 1889, below.

3. Effie A. Lanagan was a faculty member at RC (1889–95). She was in charge of classics, taught Latin and Greek, and lectured on Greek literature and drama at the school.

4. See EGS [for JA] to Susan Childs Starr and Caleb Allen Starr [and SAAH], 15,[16–20?] Nov. [1889], n. 20, above.

5. EGS and JA trimmed the Christmas tree on Thursday evening, 19 Dec., and had it ready to delight the kindergarten children on Friday, 20 Dec.

6. The Kenwood Kindergarten, at the corner of Lake and Woodlawn avenues, was operated between 1889 and 1893 by Mrs. Olive E. Weston (1839?–1918), who was the principal. At the time, her home was located at 97 (later 1510 East) 51st St. She became a member of the CWC in 1893 and was a member of its Art and Literature Dept. By 1900 she was living in the household of her daughter Minnie, who was Mrs. Warren McArthur.

7. The gatherings mentioned in JA's 1889–90 diary for the week beginning 23 Dec. were German night on 23 Dec.; ice cream for the boys on Tuesday, 24 Dec.; reading *Alice in Wonderland* on Thursday, 26 Dec.; and on Saturday, 28 Dec., an Italian evening. Parties for children were held during the days.

8. JA later recalled, "Our very first Christmas at Hull-House, when we as yet knew nothing of child labor, a number of little girls refused the candy which was offered them as part of the Christmas good cheer, saying simply that they 'worked in a candy factory and could not bear the sight of it.' We discovered that for six weeks they had worked from seven in the morning until nine at night, and they were exhausted as well as satiated" (*Twenty Years*, 198). Some of the candy recipients must have been grateful for the special sweets. The bill for Christmas candy in 1891 was $18.25; 1892, $39.65; and 1893, $63.44.

9. One of the two Sunday Schools may have been the Bethlehem Congregational Chapel, 670 (later 1901) Throop St., which JA had visited in her search for a location to begin her settlement. Edwin A. Adams was pastor, and there were about 400 Sunday school students. The other might have been the Harrison St. Mission, which "had a Sunday school of 350 in 1889" (Smith, *Community Renewal Society*, 33).

10. In her letter of 18 Dec. 1889 to sister SAAH, JA had written, "We have been very busy between our own work and the Italian hospital. Dr Dudley asked me to come with the Italian physicians to a reception he gave the graduating class and the faculty of the Chi. Medical. There were only four ladies and hosts of Doctors so that I had a very gay time. Dr Andrews took me out to supper, and Dr and old Dr Davis were devoted to the three Italian physicians whom I felt as if I were chaperoning" (UIC, JAMC; *JAPM*, 2:1133–34).

The Italian Hospital was the predecessor of the St. Anthony Hospital, located at West 19th St. and Marshall Blvd. It had its beginnings over a bakery shop located at the corner of South Halsted and 12th streets and was founded in 1896. On 11 Apr. 1890, the *Chicago Daily*

*Tribune* reported in "For an Italian Hospital," "The efforts of the Italian residents of Chicago to raise funds for the erection of a hospital for the sick of their race have been persistent and successful. . . . The proceeds of a number of well-attended converts have been added to the money raised by subscription."

JA's 1889–90 diary for Saturday evening, 14 Dec., carried the following notation: "P.M. meeting in regard to the W. side nurses." And under the heading "Dinner and Evening" on the same date: "Dr Dudley's reception[.] Dr & Mrs. Gilmore[.] Mr. Dalstrom, Prof. Chowosky &c[.] Italians" (*JAPM*, 29:118–19).

Emelius Clark Dudley (1850–1928) was born in Westfield, Mass., and educated at Dartmouth (A.B., 1873) and at Long Island College Hospital (M.D., 1875). He arrived in Chicago in 1875 and began to practice with a specialty in gynecology. After a year in Chicago, he returned to New York for more training. Once again in Chicago, in 1878 he established the *Chicago Medical Gazette*. By 1882 he was associated with the Chicago Medical College and became a professor of gynecology at Northwestern Univ. Medical School. He also served on the staff of Mercy Hospital and was a highly respected consulting gynecologist at St. Luke's Hospital, also in Chicago.

His *Principles and Practice of Gynecology*, first published by Lea Brothers of Philadelphia in 1898, became the standard gynecological textbook and went through many editions. A Unitarian and a Republican, he served on the reform Chicago Board of Education with JA, 1901–6. Dudley wed Anna M. Titcomb in 1882; the couple had four children.

Upon retirement, Dudley spent most of 1922 and early 1923 as a visiting professor in China under the auspices of the Yale-in-China program, where he taught at the Huna-Yale Medical School, Shanghai, and the Union Medical College, Peking.

11. JA's dinner companion was Dr. Edmund Andrews (1824–1904), who received his undergraduate and medical education at the Univ. of Michigan (A.B. 1849; M.D. 1852). A pioneer in antisepsis, he was a founder and a professor of surgery at the Chicago Medical College, 1859–81. He served as a surgeon for the Union during the Civil War and was president of the Chicago Medical Society, 1879–80. He held consulting posts at the Hospital for Women and Children, Illinois Charitable Eye and Ear Infirmary, and Michael Reese Hospital. An authority on the geology of the Chicago area, he was also noted for expertise in botany and zoology. He was a founder of the State Microscopial Society and the Chicago Academy of Sciences. He and Dr. Nathan S. Davis Sr., known to JA especially through EGS and her aunt Eliza Allen Starr, were close friends. In 1856 he and the senior Dr. Davis had opened an office together. For a biographical note on the Drs. Davis, see *PJA*, 2:500–501, n. 17.

12. MCAL.

13. The Economic Conf. to which both Percival Chubb and Father J. S. Huntington were invited as speakers was sponsored by the Economic Club of Chicago and held 22–29 Dec. 1889. The focus was "economic laws and social problems" that "had occurred within the last few years." The initial audience of five hundred included "Capitalists, clergy and wage-workers, trades-unionists, Socialists, and personal liberty men"—and one fifth of those gathered were women ("Socialism in England," *Chicago Daily Tribune*, 23 Dec. 1889).

Percival Chubb opened the Economic Conf. on 22 Dec. with a speech on the accomplishments of socialism in England. Speakers during the week made their presentation in the Recital Hall of the new Auditorium Building. According to JA's 1889–90 diary, Father Huntington, whom JA heard close the Economic Conf. on Sunday, 29 Dec., in a lecture titled "Socialism and the Church," spoke at HH on 30 Dec., and his topic was titled "Emancipation of Labor." He spoke again at HH on Wednesday evening, 12 Feb. 1890, and JA recorded that "a great many people" attended (*JAPM*, 29:137). HH and Chicago Commons became hosts of annual economic conferences during the 1890s. See Two Essays in the *Forum*, Nov. and Oct. 1892, n. 170, below.

## To Anna Hostetter Haldeman Addams

335 South Halsted Street. [Chicago, Ill.] Dec. 26" 1889

My dear Mama

You were very kind to send us ten dollars. We are going to buy dinner knives, some thing the household needs very much. We have had a very happy Christmas and a generous one certainly. Our first caller on Xmas morning left three twenty dollar gold pieces, apparently waiting for the day that he might do it gracefully. We were invited to Miss Starr's[1] but I had to stay at home and poultice my thumb which threatened to develope a felon. It is still painful and sore but not serious. Please thank George for his kind letter. I will write to Alice and himself when my thumb is better. I am so glad you had Marcet for Christmas[2]—Your loving daughter

Jane Addams.

ALS (UIC, JAMC; *JAPM*, 2:1137–38).

1. Eliza Allen Starr, EGS's aunt, in Chicago.

2. GBH's letter is not known to be extant. EGS also wrote to AHHA to thank her: "It was very kind in you to include me in the Christmas check. I shall brandish the knives with a sense of ownership. Will you not come sometime & participate in their use? We are very gay this week, with festivities for the children.

"Please give my love to Mrs. Haldeman & remember me cordially to Mr. H. I am going to write to Mrs. H. soon, to take out of her mouth the bad taste I left by being so peevish & disagreeable during her visit, when I was on the way to a sore throat & very tired & nervous" (26 Dec. 1889, SC, Starr; *JAPM*, 2:1138–39).

## To Sarah Alice Addams Haldeman

335 South Halsted Street. [Chicago, Ill.] Jan 5 '90

My dear Alice

You were very kind to send the draft so promptly. I am not nearly so cramped financially now but still it will always be a great convenience to have it come in. I mean to try very hard to keep my personal expenses, clothing street car fare &c within that, so that my other income can go into the house and its plans.[1] Those plans are daily becoming dearer to me, I fear. I was sorry you couldn't stop at Geneseo[2] but perhaps it was for the best, I can't tell you how much I wished you and Marcet would come for a week, when every thing was quiet and running smoothly. The boys behaved so well last Tuesday and all the other clubs are doing so well that we are planning for more. We saw a number of girls at the Western Electrical Works[3] last weeks, and they are all so pleased and enthusiastic over coming, we mean to have a general social time for them every Friday evening,[4] and gradually form classes if the girls like, if not let them keep to the social time.

I do wish you might have heard Father Huntington last Monday night,[5] he was like a spiritual revelation to me—what might be done by simply keeping true to the best that has been given us. He does not approve of "charity" and we did not know what he would think of what we were doing. To our great pleasure he approved in a very hearty penetrating way.

What you wrote of George of course only confirms Sarah's impression,[6] I have never felt that in him, but of course there is a chance to develope almost any thing shut off to himself like that.

I will try to go to Cedarville for a few days before very long, not that I hope to do any good but I should like to <see> them.

Prof. Blaisdell[7] was here yesterday afternoon & did us a great deal of good. Ellen has just written one of her long letters which I asked to have sent to you and would be glad to have you send to Weber.[8] I have had a touch of "la grippe," but am much better to-day. Give my dearest love to Marcet, I am so sorry not to have seen her. With love to Harry I am always dearest, Yr loving Sister

AL (UIC, JAMC; *JAPM*, 2:1145–46).

1. JA had invested some of her income-producing capital with SAAH and HWH in their State Bank of Girard, Kans. With increasing frequency, JA requested that funds from those holdings be sent to her in Chicago. During the first year of HH operation, Oct. 1889 to Oct. 1890, the expenses, including repairs to the settlement building, were $8,634.21 ($229,321.99 in 2015 dollars). The statement "Pd by Jane Addams [$]5016.91" ($133,480.02 in 2015 dollars) appears in the first-year financial summary on p. 206 of the account book for Oct. 1891–Oct. 1893 and labeled by JA as "HH Acc't Oct 1st 1891" (*JAPM*, Addendum 3:1ff); $3,617.30 came from other sources. JA spent $1,860.50 ($49,500.51 in 2015 dollars) to purchase furnishings and $1,022.33 ($27,200.14 in 2015 dollars) on daily living expenses for the settlement residents, including herself and EGS. Her costliest investment was in the building itself, on which she lavished $2,134.08 ($56,779.38 in 2015 dollars). On 6 Aug. 1889, she had written SAAH requesting funds from her account. "The bills for the house will be due in a week or two, so that I think I will have my deposit made at the Metropolitan Bank at once. If you will send me the $600.00 in a draft I will have John Taylor send it there with a little money I have at home—I will also take the $115.00 in a separate draft sent here. <I want the 600 draft sent here also.> The furnishing of the house will not be very expensive, it is repairing, getting it into shape" (IU, Lilly, SAAH; *JAPM*, 2:1076–77). At the time, John Brown Taylor was cashier at the Second National Bank of Freeport, Ill., JHA's bank (see *PJA*, 2:74, n. 8). See also EGS [for JA] to Mary Houghton Starr Blaisdell [and SAAH], 23 Feb. [1889], n. 12, above.

When JA began HH, she chose to conduct her Chicago banking at the Metropolitan National Bank that was organized in 1884. At the end of 1885, it had deposits of $13,005,909 with capital of $550,000. It was located at the northwest corner of LaSalle and Madison streets. In 1902 it was absorbed into the First National Bank of Chicago, organized in 1863.

2. MCAL and JML lived with their children in Geneseo, Ill.

3. The Western Electric Works was located at 227 (later 406) South Clinton Ave. The company had been founded in 1869 in Cleveland but moved to Chicago the next year. In 1881 it became a part of the American Bell Telephone Co., and by 1882 it was producing telephones exclusively for the Bell Co. It also manufactured telegraph equipment, batteries, heat regulators, and electrical supplies. According to the *4th Annual Report of the U.S. Commissioner of Labor*, published in 1891, the average age of the women employed at the company in Chicago was eighteen. Their average annual income was $349.75 ($9,305.46 in 2015 dollars) and their living expenses estimated to be $321.13 ($8,543.99 in 2015 dollars).

4. JA's 1889–90 diary entry for Friday, 3 Jan. 1890, indicated, "went to Western Electrical Works. Saw a number of the girls" (*JAPM*, 29:124). By that time, EGS's reading party for George Eliot's *Romola* was meeting on Thursday evenings "in our little upstairs dining room," wrote JA, "and two members of the club came to dinner each week, not only that they might be received as guests, but that they might help us wash the dishes afterwards and so make the table ready for the stacks of Florentine photographs" (*Twenty Years*, 101). On Friday, 10 Jan. 1890, EGS began hosting the new club of girls. "Friday evening the working girls come in to enjoy a lecture or concert" ("Two Women's Work"). Eva H. Brodlique wrote in "A Toynbee Hall Experiment in Chicago" that "Friday evening is reserved for the Working Girls' Club, which is a delightful little affair, largely literary in its tendency." By 1891 the Working Girls' Club had been superseded by German night, and an assortment of other activities associated with the College Extension Program were under way. At least some of the young women who came to the original Friday-evening gatherings were attending classes or were members of other social clubs at the settlement.

5. 30 Dec. 1889. Father Huntington's topic was titled "Can a Free Thinker Believe in Christ?" See also EGS [for JA] to Susan Childs Starr and Caleb Allen Starr [and SAAH], 3 Nov. [1889], n. 18, above.

6. These letters from SAAH and SH about GBH's health are not known to be extant; however, JA recounts comments about him by LSA in her letter of 23 Nov. 1889, above. Despite HWH's treatments, GBH may have been exhibiting the reclusive behavior that would eventually overwhelm him and characterize the remainder of his life.

7. Perhaps Sarah Blaisdell, EGS and JA's teacher, retired from RFS (see *PJA*, 1:184–85, n. 45), or Rev. James Joshua Blaisdell, who had helped JA master Greek when she was a student at RFS (see *PJA*, 1:186, n. 46).

8. This EGS letter is not known to be extant.

## To Sarah Alice Addams Haldeman

335 South Halsted Street. [Chicago, Ill.] Jan 22 '90

My dear Alice

I have n't been down town since your letter came[1] but will get the sash curtains and have them sent to morrow. I sent my long curtains to the cleaner yesterday and will have them sent to you when they are clean. We have decided not to use them in the house and you might just as well be enjoying them. I think that they are very handsome, but am sure that the moral effect of them down here is not good.

We have had a very successful happy week. I have started my Italian girls on Monday afternoon and Miss Coonley and Miss Matz[2] two lovely girls are helping me. We had some Irish women in to tea on Thursday[3] which proved a wild success. Write to me often, dear, I am worried when I don't hear. Ellen sends her love to you, and "unutterable things" to Marcet. I join in both of them, and am always dearest sister[.] Your lovingly

Jane

ALS (IU, Lilly, SAAH; *JAPM*, 2:1150–51).

1. SAAH's letter requesting JA's help as her purchasing representative in Chicago is not known to be extant.

Without a clear understanding of the whirl of activities at HH and the time constraints JA was beginning to experience, SAAH often asked JA to run errands for her in Chicago. And JA usually tried to comply or felt guilty because she could not respond as quickly as she knew SAAH expected. See especially JA to SAAH, 5 July 1890; 6 and 28 Dec. 1891; and 30 Sept. 1892, *JAPM*, 2:1191–92, 1278–79, 1294–96, 1330. See also JA to SAAH, [ca. 6] [Sept. 1891], below.

2. On Monday, 20 Jan. 1890, JA had lunch with Evelyn Matz (1863–1958) and Mary Letchworth Coonley (1869–1912), daughters of HH supporters Mary Lewis Matz and Lydia Avery Coonley (Coonley-Ward), followed by visits to several neighborhood Italian families. In the afternoon, they started their Italian children's club with fifteen youngsters, and JA pronounced it "a beautiful time" (Addams, "Diary, 1889–90," 20 Jan. 1890; *JAPM*, 29:130). By the end of Mar. 1890, JA had enrolled herself in an Italian class offered by Alessandro Mastro-Valerio and paid $2.50 for each Monday-afternoon lesson. See also JA to MRS, 26 Apr. 1890, n. 7, below.

Evelyn Matz, teacher and school administrator, was the daughter of CWC and Fortnightly Club founder Mary Lewis Matz and German-born Otto Hermann Matz (see EGS [for JA] to Susan Childs Starr and Caleb Allen Starr [and SAAH], 3 Nov. [1889], n. 31, above). She graduated from the fledgling Univ. of Chicago (Ph.B. 1897) and took graduate studies there, 1897–99, while she was a teacher of science at the University School for Girls. Between 1900 and 1906, she was principal of the Dearborn Seminary, and after it closed she returned to the University School for Girls, where she taught physiography and became coprincipal until 1912 when she left teaching. She lived in Chicago for the remainder of her life and was active in the Fortnightly Club and with the Dearborn Seminary alumnae.

Mary Letchworth Coonley (1869–1912) became the wife of Thomas Hollis, age twenty-six and from Grand Rivers, Ky. They married in the New Jerusalem Church in Chicago in Mar. 1892. They had three sons and were living in Concord, Mass., when Mary Coonley Hollis died.

3. 16 Jan. 1890.

## To Sarah Alice Addams Haldeman

335 So Halsted St Chicago—[Ill.] March 6" 1890

My dear Alice

I have not heard from you for so long that I have grown rather unhappy about it and am afraid all is not well. I have been in the house for two weeks, first with a severe attack of the bowels and then an atrocious cold ending with rheumatism.[1] I am sure the latter will disappear as soon as the weather is warmer, we have had a deep snow and the coldest weather of the winter in the midst of which Sherwood[2] moved out, leaving the front door open hours at a time. We were very glad however to see him go and have begun repairs energetically. We will be able to move down in two or three weeks I think,[3] the expenses will not be so great as the rest of the house as Sherwood already had it in a reasonable state of repair. We will be much more comfortable and very glad to avoid the stairs. We are constantly receiving more help from energetic young people—Miss Rhea[4] was here two weeks of the time when I was sick and really did most of my work, we started a French evening very successfully while she was here—Miss Head[5] is here this week and we expect Miss Benedict[6] next week again to paint. She was delighted with the models down here—Our boys are turning out beautifully, we have n't given them games for six weeks and it works beautifully. Would n't you like your magic lantern,[7] I will send it to you any time, the slides do not fit our new one & we never use it.

I have an indistinct remembrance of your offering me your old machine. If you did we could use it now that we have more room, Mary Keezer[8] sews so well, but of course I don't want it unless you are through with it and have no use for it.

I have been interrupted so many times that I think I will give up trying to write more. Laura[9] writes that Sarah Hostetter is at Cedarville now, I am very glad. Laura had Seeley & Read[10] send me two more comforters, I am very very much obliged to you both, I think they are almost the prettiest ones I ever saw. With love to Marcet and her parents, I am Always Your loving Sister

Jane Addams

Please write to me soon—

ALS (IU, Lilly, SAAH; *JAPM*, 2:1157–59).

1. The rheumatism continued to bother JA. "My knee is still very much swollen and the Dr is a little afraid of a stiff joint. It was a very severe case and horribly painful, but after all not so bad as sciatica," JA wrote to sister SAAH, recalling her bout of illness in Italy in 1888 (23 Mar. 1890, IU, Lilly, SAAH; *JAPM*, 2:1167). JA was ill early in 1890 beginning with the flu in Jan.

2. The Sherwood Co. had decided to vacate their portion of the house before their lease was up at the end of Mar.

3. In a 23 Mar. 1890 letter to SAAH, JA reported, "We are very happy over the prospect of going downstairs, if I am able to see to things a little bit we will 'move' the middle of the week" (IU, Lilly, SAAH; *JAPM*, 2:1168).

4. Likely actress Hortense Barbe Loret, called Mlle. Rhea (1844?–99), who was born of French parents in Belgium and began to study in Paris for the stage when she was twenty years old. She made her debut playing in *Camille* in the Imperial Theatre and continued playing in various cities on the Continent until 1881, when she went to London. There she determined to learn English and shortly after that came to the United States, where her first efforts at acting were unsuccessful because of her heavy French-accented English. She continued to strengthen her ability to act in English and "attained wide popularity in such plays as 'The Widow,' 'Camille,' 'The Power of Love,' 'The American Countess,' 'Mary Stuart,' and 'Adrienne.' . . . One of her later plays was 'Josephine, Empress of the French,' the title role of which was one of her favorite parts" ("Mlle. Rhea, Actress, Dead"). In the mid-1890s, she began to experience poor health and could no longer appear onstage. She returned to Europe and settled in Montmorency, France, where she died.

Miss Rhea seems to have helped at HH for about two months, Feb. and Mar. 1890. Her name first appeared in JA's 1889–90 diary on 17 Feb., when she sang during an evening gathering for the French neighbors of HH. That same week, 20 Feb. 1890, JA hosted a dinner party for her. She sang again during the French evening on Monday, 24 Feb., and two days later on 26 Feb. helped invite French neighbors to the settlement. On Tuesday evening, 11 Mar., she attended a party at HH with Russell Whitman and Enella Benedict. The next Friday, 14 Mar., and the Friday after, 21 Mar., she helped Harriet Trowbridge with the afternoon class of little girls. JA was not well, especially during the last two weeks of Feb. and into the first week of Mar. and was very grateful for Miss Rhea's help (see JA to EGS, [4–7 Aug. 1890], below). Rhea left Chicago in time to appear at the Broadway Theater in New York City in *Josephine, Empress of the French* on 17 Mar. 1890.

5. Katharine P. Head (Breck) (b. 1870?), was one of the three daughters of banker and manufacturer Harvey Franklin Head (listed in the 1880 federal census as Franklin H. Head) (1835–1914) and his wife, Catherine P. Durkee Head (d. 1892). She attended Miss Kirkland's School for Girls and during the 1890s was active in the Kirkland School Assn., serving separately as either secretary or treasurer. In that same period, she became involved with settlement work as a volunteer and periodic settlement resident. A notation in JA's 1889–90 diary for Tuesday, 11 Feb. 1890, indicated that Miss Head came to lunch and to catalog the collection of books JA and EGS had gathered for boys to read. In Aug. 1890, JA placed Katharine Head and Alice Miller in charge of the settlement while she and EGS were away on much-needed summer vacations. By Jan. 1891, Katharine Head held library hours for boys on Tuesday afternoons. She also taught sewing to Italian girls on Monday afternoons in the spring of 1892. During this time, she lived at 2 Banks St. in Chicago. By Jan. 1903, she was teaching a class at HH in rhetoric. She eventually married artist George William Breck (1863–1920), and after living in Rome, 1904–9, the couple went to live in New York City.

6. Enella K. Benedict. See JA to MCAL, 19 [and 20] Feb. 1889, n. 6, above.

7. JA probably acquired her sister's magic lantern in the fall of 1889. See EGS [for JA] to Susan Childs Starr and Caleb Allen Starr [and SAAH], 3 Nov. [1889], above.

8. JA was requesting the use of SAAH's sewing machine for Mary Keyser.

9. LSA.

10. Seeley and Read Dept. Store, Freeport, Ill., opened in 1877. Called Freeport's "longest-lived department store" (Barrett and Keister, *History of Stephenson County 1970*, 506), it was begun by F. A. Read, who had been burned out in the Chicago Fire of 1871, and C. H. Seeley, and was still in business in Freeport in the 1970s.

## To Helen Culver

*With the signing of the sublease on the former Charles J. Hull home in the spring of 1889, Jane Addams entered a long-term association with Helen Culver. It was a business relationship that evolved into a philanthropic alliance and a respectful friendship that lasted for the remainder of Helen Culver's life. When Jane first encountered her, Helen was already an experienced and successful businesswoman and philanthropist. Initially, Helen maintained a watchful distance from Jane's developing enterprise and, testing Jane, treated their lessee-lessor relationship as a business arrangement. While Jane was not shy about asking Helen for support for the settlement, Helen was not reticent about denying her requests. When Jane wrote Helen in the expectation that she would fund additional renovations to the Hull home, Helen responded, "Instead of making a contribution to your charities in work as you suggested I send my check for $100. . . . I hope others interested in what you are trying to do will lend a hand."[1] Jane was persistent and responded.*

The support of Helen Culver, heir to the Charles J. Hull fortune and real estate business, was crucial to the development of Hull-House. An astute businesswoman, Culver pushed Jane Addams into incorporating the settlement program as Hull-House Association in the hope of ensuring its stability. She made real estate available for the development of the Hull-House and provided financial support as well (Goodspeed, "Helen Culver").

335 So. Halsted St [Chicago, Ill.] March 7" 1890

My dear Miss Culver

I am somewhat embarrassed by the receipt of the check you sent the other day. I asked for the bath rooms as a contribution to our work, but hoped you would repair the piazza and cellar in your capacity as land lord.

We have appealed to Mrs Field[2] for the bath rooms,[3] but you doubtless understand how impossible it is to ask other people to repair property which does not belong to them.

Our friends are extremely generous to us in regard to the money we use for the pleasure and benefit of our neighbors, but we found when we asked them to put in the furnace,[4] how differently they felt. Even those who gave liberally insisted that they were playing the part of landlord and not of philanthropist.

I know how futile it would be to ask money for heavy house repairs; it simply results in many questions in regard to the lease &c and a business like refusal.

Of course I am very sorry that I cannot do it myself, I put a thousand dollars on the house last fall and feel that five hundred must be my limit this spring.[5]

~~I~~ <We> shall ~~have~~ <probably> put the money you sent on the work in the cellar,[6] and probably have the piazza torn down[7] as the cheapest method of dealing with it, altho that will of course sacrifice the new roof which was put on last fall, as well as much of the character of the house. I am very sorry indeed to trouble you further and am very sincerely Yours

Jane Addams

ALS (SCPC, JAC; *JAPM*, 2:1160–62).

1. 3 Mar. 1890, SCPC, JAC; *JAPM*, 2:1156.

2. Nannie D. Scott Field (1840–96), the first wife of merchant Marshall Field (1834–1906), founder and developer of retail giant Marshall Field and Co. department store in Chicago, was one of the leaders in Chicago society. She was noted for her magnificent entertainments, rivaling those of Bertha Honoré Palmer. As a member of the First Presbyterian Church, Mrs. Field provided funds for the construction of the Railroad Chapel, a mission of the church that maintained a free kindergarten. The Marshall Fields had two children, Marshall Field Jr., and Ethel. Nannie Field was never well and began to spend more of her life in the South of France, where she lived from 1892 until her death in Nice.

3. JA and EGS did get additional bathrooms. On 3 Jul. 1890, the *Chicago Times* reported that "two extra bathrooms have been put into the house, and small urchins gently urged to make use of them. As the good work goes on the Italian youngsters become accustomed to the usual 'tubbing' and proudly run its gamut twice a week, besides bringing clean clothing to change. Stationary washtubs are also placed at the disposal of the neighbors—a wise and generous provision which no one but a woman would ever have thought of making" ("Work of Two Women"). By 1892 the *Springfield (Mass.) Republican* in "HH in Chicago" indicated that the settlement had "five bath-rooms . . . open daily." The Carter Harrison Bath, the first public bathhouse in Chicago, was opened in Jan. 1894 near HH. It was followed by twenty-one similar facilities in the city, but HH continued to make its basement tubs available, especially for children. See also Two Essays in the *Forum*, Nov. and Oct. 1892, n. 110, below.

4. The furnace that Helen Culver had agreed to install was in place and functioning by early Nov. 1889. See EGS [for JA] to Susan Childs Starr and Caleb Allen Starr [and SAAH], 3 Nov. [1889], above.

5. Repairs to the former Hull home cost $3,701.68 during the 1889–90 financial year. Of that JA contributed $2,134.08. See JA to SAAH, 5 Jan. 1890, n. 1, above.

6. See JA to Helen Culver, 11 Mar. 1890, below.

7. See JA to Helen Culver, 11 Mar. 1890, and Helen Culver to JA, 15 Mar. 1890, both below.

## From Helen Culver

[Chicago, Ill.] [9?] [Mar. 1890]

### Copy from lease dated May 16/89.[1]

"Party of the second part is to pay water tax and make all repairs."

My Dear Miss Addams:—

I regret that my benevolent purposes—represented by gifts amounting to about $350.00 have been productive only of disappointment—and judging from your note, of an impression among your acquaintances that I sustain toward your enterprise the relation of delinquent landlady. Yours Very Truly

Helen Culver.

ALS (SCPC, JAC; *JAPM*, 2:1163).

1. No copy of a lease between Helen Culver and JA on behalf of HH and dated 16 May 1889 is in the records of HH Assn., UIC, JAMC.

This was the first of several leases that JA entered into with Helen Culver for real estate on which the Hull home stood and buildings added to HH were constructed. As Culver saw the settlement develop, she became intrigued with the HH program. HH seemed to be helping improve opportunities for people and businesses that were located in the surrounding neighborhood, and Helen Culver owned additional real estate there. In addition, she may have viewed the evolving HH programs as a continuation of efforts Charles J. Hull initiated during his life to help the working poor. Culver began to support the settlement financially, providing some leases rent free and making direct financial gifts as well. She also became certain that JA was vital to the continued success of the enterprise.

Beginning in May 1892, and as she agreed to subsequent leases, Helen Culver always demanded that JA continue her "service without compensation." She further stipulated that if JA left her leadership position, she had to relinquish the settlement furnishings minus her personal belongings and fifteen hundred dollars in cash. She demanded that the name "Hull-House" continue in use and further required that the work carried out on the premises "at all times be such as will tend to the elevation and advancement of those among whom it is carried on without being antagonistic to written laws and institutions" (HH Lease between Jane Addams and Helen Culver, 10 May 1892). In addition, JA was to make all repairs to buildings and sidewalks and pay taxes and electrical, gas, and water bills. With the exception of the original house, JA could make changes in any of the structures on land that Culver was leasing to her. Should the lease be terminated, JA had only ten days to move any structures she had built on Culver property or forfeit them to Helen Culver.

On 15 Mar. 1892, JA reported to SAAH that on 14 Mar. 1892, Helen Culver agreed to provide a rent-free lease on the original Charles J. Hull home, for which she had been paying thirty dollars per month. That new lease, to be in force from May 1892 until 1900, was superseded by another agreement dated 15 Apr. 1895 between the HH Assn., rather than JA, and Helen Culver. It was to remain in effect until 30 Apr. 1920, but in 1906 Culver made a gift to the HH Assn. of all of the real estate under lease to the association at the time (see JA to AHHA, 9 May 1889, n. 9, above). See also JA to AHHA, 3 June 1890, n. 14, below.

## To Helen Culver

335 So. Halsted St [Chicago, Ill.] March. 11" 1890

My dear Miss Culver—

Our relations have always been so frank that it seemed to me possible to tell <you> just what I was able to do, and hoped you would help accomplish. I understand of course the conditions of the lease and that the repairing of the roof &c <other help,> was in no sense a legal obligation. I ~~think we have been and are~~ <certainly hope you do not think I am in> the habit of discussing our relations with other people or that their general objection to repairing property on a short lease had any thing personal in it. I gave the attitude ~~of other people~~ toward repairs because your note suggested others would help [this?] spring as well as yourself. ~~after all we have never failed~~ Doubtless my wishing to avoid a general appeal was an unneccessary scruple. The entire office of asking for money is new to me & I am afraid I do not do it well.

I delayed my reply last week waiting for the carpenters estimates—Mr Pond[1] who has been out of the city brought them in this morning. We have decided to concrete the entire cellar, & to my suggestion that the side & back of the piazza be torn down & the front converted into a sort of porch, he said that it would be necessary to have your written consent.[2] I regret being obliged to trouble once again but of course we will do nothing to the piazza until we know your pleasure concerning it.

I hope you will not consider me ungrateful for the one hundred dollars because I some what frankly showed I had hoped for some thing else—

This lette *[one word illegible]*—&c[.] Sincerely yrs[.] J. A—

ALI draft (SCPC, JAC; *JAPM*, 2:1164–65). The extant Hull-Culver Papers at UIC did not contain a sent copy of this draft.

1. Likely Allen B. Pond.
2. See Helen Culver to JA, 15 Mar. 1890, below.

## From Helen Culver

31 Ashland Boulevard [Chicago, Ill.] March 15. 1890.

My Dear Miss Addams:

I have been hesitating about sacrificing the improvements lately made at such cost—but if it will add to the comfort and pleasure of your occupancy, you may have the veranda, or any part of it, torn down. I am sorry to know that you are ill.[1] Yours Very Truly

Helen Culver.

ALS (SCPC, JAC; *JAPM*, 2:1166).

1. See JA to SAAH, 6 Mar. 1890, especially n. 1, above.

## To Mary Rozet Smith

*Jane Addams met Mary Rozet Smith[1] during the first year that Hull-House was open. Their friendship blossomed and grew into a steadfast, mutually supportive, and lifelong relationship for both women. The following is the first letter written by Jane to Mary known to remain extant.[2] Mary was a member of a well-to-do Chicago family; a graduate of Miss Kirkland's School for Girls, where Ellen Gates*

Mary Rozet Smith came to Hull-House in 1890 and began to help out in the Crêche. She became Jane Addams's closest personal lifelong friend and with her family provided major financial support for the continuing development of Hull-House. She was beloved by Hull-House residents for her many kindnesses to residents and their families and to neighborhood residents as well and for her devotion to Jane Addams (private collection).

*Starr had taught through much of the 1880s; and a friend of Jenny Dow, one of the first converts to the Hull-House idea. She came to Halsted Street to see how she might help, and she began volunteering in the kindergarten that Jenny Dow directed.*

*Over the next decade, Mary Smith developed into Jane's dearest friend, frequent traveling partner, confidante, and companion. Jane's relationship with Mary ultimately eclipsed in emotional intimacy Jane's earlier, more intellectual friendship with cofounder Ellen Gates Starr. Ellen and Mary, who were both essential to Jane as helpmates and supporters in the 1890s, were contrasts in types, means, and ages.*

*Ellen was Jane's age, and she had earned her own living for ten years. For the remainder of her life, she continued to live on very little income and to rely primarily on outside support from various patrons, including Jane and her good friends Mary Wilmarth and Frances Crane Lillie. She was a forthright dynamo of a woman, but petite, energetic, witty, opinionated, and pointedly outspoken. Helen Gow, an English visitor who spent a month at the settlement in the spring of 1897, found her "less balanced than I even thought." And she confided to her diary: "I expected to admire her next to Miss Addams . . . & it took a great many manifestations of her so different self for me to undo the expectation I had formed."*[3] *Ellen's interests evolved into a fine bookbinding practice, and she became an active and devoted participant in labor and union causes and a political activist for the Socialist Labor Party.*

*The almost-ten-years-younger, willowy, compassionate, and independently wealthy Mary Smith, by contrast, was no rabble-rouser. She became known for her serenity and for the kindness and support that she lent to Hull-House and its people. Mary, who became a member of the first board of trustees of Hull-House Association, directed her wealth, and her family's as well, to support Hull-House building projects, program development, and an assortment of other neighborhood needs. She also provided personal financial support for Jane.*

*A master at guiding interpersonal relations, Mary chose to commit herself to the care of others, including family, friends, and Jane, and quietly to other reform efforts affecting the lives of children and women. As a trio of Hull-House wits put it, "Miss Smith is so lovely and stately / and she carried herself so sedately / Her words are ne'er tart / And she has a big heart / And her charms we can't state accurately."*[4] *She doted on children, and her life was filled with Hull-House and neighborhood children as well as Jane's and her nieces and nephews and their friends. Her comfortable Walton Place home became a haven away from Hull-House for Jane, and she specialized in providing a sense of private retreat and respite for Jane's increasingly busy public lifestyle.*

335 South Halsted Street. [Chicago, Ill.] April 26' 1890

My dear Miss Smith.

Miss Trowbridge said on Friday[5] that you were ill again.[6] We are all very sorry but I hope you are not for a moment thinking of your absence from our side of it. We would rather have you occasionally for the Italian children,[7] than anyone else regularly.

I have been very busy this week inviting for a Wednesday evening club Mr Hicks[8] is starting, and so postponed the French invitations until to-day.[9] It is raining this morning and I dare not take my rheumatic knee out, so we will have to put off the French evening one week more, I am not sorry since I know you can't come, for I think you would enjoy knowing the people from the first evening.

I hope very much that you will be able to stay for the night then[10] and that we can see something of the Canadian-French quarter.[11] It is very pleasant to feel that you are going to help "work them up"—as we foolishly say.

With an assurance of affectionate sympathy I am sincerely yours—

Jane Addams

ALS (SCPC, JAC; *JAPM*, 2:1173–75).

1. On the life of MRS, see Biographical Profiles: Smith, Mary Rozet, and Smith Family.
2. On extant JA-MRS correspondence, see introduction to *PJA*, 1.

3. "Gow, Diaries, 28 Sept. 1896–13 June 1897," 26 Apr. 1897. With the death of her father in Jan. 1896, Helen Jane Gow (1860–1925) of London came into a small inheritance and decided to spend it visiting relatives in Canada and the United States and investigating relief programs in a number of settlement houses in the United States. She had met JA during JA's London visit in 1896, and in Mar. 1897, after she had arrived in the United States, Gow was invited by JA to spend ten days at HH. Her visit, 9–26 Apr. 1897, stretched to more than ten days, and before Gow left JA invited her to stay on or return later as a HH resident. JA valued Helen's experience as a relief visitor for the Charity Organization Society in London, which she shared with workers in Chicago by serving as an adviser during her HH stay. Helen debated the offer but returned to London, where she spent the remainder of her life in relief work through the Women's University Settlement that had been founded on Blackfriar's Road in 1887 by women from the women's colleges at Oxford and Cambridge. She was also a district visitor for the COS and ultimately in charge of district visitors in the Women's University Settlement area, 1900–1924. Helen Gow was also involved with the London City and District Poor Law School at Hanwell, and for twenty-three years, 1901–24, she served on the Southwark Board of Guardians.

4. Ella Waite, Jessie Luther, and Rose Gyles. "Edith Nancrede: Her Birthday Party," 14 Dec. 1901, UIC, JAMC, and quoted in Jackson, *Lines of Activity*, 171.

5. Harriet Trowbridge, 25 Apr. 1890.

6. Throughout her life, MRS was subject to repeated attacks of asthma and associated illnesses.

7. It seems likely that a large percentage of the neighborhood children who attended the settlement kindergarten were by heritage Italian. This may have been one of the reasons that JA, EGS, and some of the kindergarten teachers were investing in Italian lessons given by Alessandro Mastro-Valerio by March 1890. In addition to the kindergarten children, a club of Italian children began meeting at HH on Monday afternoons in Jan. 1890 (see JA to SAAH, 22 Jan. 1890, n. 2, above). "Monday afternoon . . . [the] drawing-room is filled with Italian girls who sew, play games, and dance, and the little ones cut out pictures and paste them in scrap-books. Sometimes they take a bath when they can be convinced of the beauty of the porcelain tubs, and clean clothes are talked about as a desideratum" (Marks, "Two Women's Work").

8. The first "Social Science Club" was begun by Alfred Hicks, an English socialist devoted to labor's cause and a friend of feminist activist, author, and lecturer Charlotte Perkins Gilman (1860–1935) when she lived at HH during 1895. By 1896 he had returned to Newcastle upon Tyne, England. He continued to write for English socialist labor periodicals. During her 1896 visit in England, JA visited his mother in Camden Town.

A note in JA's 1889–90 diary on Friday, 4 Apr. 1890, indicated that Hicks joined her for dinner at HH to plan the "Men's Club" (*JAPM*, 29:151). He sent out a letter announcing the idea for the club on 7 Apr. 1890. "There seems to be a great need for a place where such questions [as topics particularly interesting to working men] can be debated more freely than is possible in the Trades Unions where all the time is taken up by routine business," wrote Hicks as he announced the "preliminary meeting" to be held at HH on Wednesday evening, 9 Apr. at 8:30 P.M. At that meeting, the speaker was socialist and labor reformer Corinne Stubbs Brown, whom JA may have met through her work with the Illinois Woman's Alliance. At the 16 Apr. gathering, only four men were present to hear George "Schilling speak and the next week attendance had grown to nine." An announcement sent out by Hicks, serving as secretary for the club, on 20 Apr., indicated that meetings would be held every Wednesday evening for "All who are interested, working men and women especially." In particular, the flyer promoted young attorney Clarence Darrow (1857–1938) as the speaker for 23 Apr. with his topic titled "Strikes" (HH Scrapbook 2:2; *JAPM*, Addendum 10:7ff). JA's diary indicates that Darrow did not appear until a week later, on 30 Apr. The club continued to meet weekly

College Extension Classes.
AT
The Hull-House

Monday Evening

| | |
|---|---|
| History of Art | Miss Starr |
| Microscope Studies | Miss Babcock |
| Book-keeping | Miss Babcock |

Tuesday Evening

| | |
|---|---|
| Ancient History | Mr. Howland |
| Latin | Mr. Arnold |
| Greek | Mr. Arnold |
| Mathematics | |

Wednesday Evening

| | |
|---|---|
| Political Economy | Miss Miller |
| American History | Miss Miller |

Thursday Evening

| | |
|---|---|
| Physiology | Miss Morley |
| Physics | Mr. Welles. |

Friday Evening

| | |
|---|---|
| Lectures on the History and Influence of Fiction | Miss Ray ('86). |

These Classes will begin on June 2d at 7:30 P.M. Anyone wishing to join them can be enrolled as a member of any Class, for ten weeks, on payment of one dollar, at the Hull-House 335 South Halsted Street. Other Classes will be formed, if desired. The lecture method will be used in some Classes, and Lectures by well-known scholars will be given from time to time.

The first announcement of the College Extension Program at Hull-House, 1890, was handwritten and distributed as widely as possible by the settlement founders. The curriculum changed over time to reflect the needs of those who wanted to attend. By 1891 the educational programs of Hull-House were at the core of the activities that the settlement offered (UIC, JAMC, HH Assn.; HH Scrapbook 2:11; *JAPM*, Addendum 10:7ff).

through May and recommenced in the fall after a summer hiatus. By Sept. 1890, the name was firmly established as the Working People's Social Science Club, and students attending the settlement's college extension classes were encouraged to attend.

Each meeting began with a forty-five-minute topical address followed by an hour of open, spirited, and sometimes loud and confrontational discussion. The meetings were popular and drew radical audiences ready for freewheeling debate. By 1893 speakers had included Henry Demarest Lloyd, Susan B. Anthony, founder Alfred Hicks, Clarence Darrow, and HH resident Florence Kelley. Among topics were strikes, the eight-hour movement, nationalism, child labor, domestic labor, tariff reform, and profit sharing. "All the Chicago 'schools' are represented here—socialism, anarchy, single tax, trades-unionism, Christian socialism, and orthodox economy, though the representatives of this last, it must be confessed, usually come from afar, in a missionary spirit," wrote Alice Miller as she described the club ("HH," 170). Among the regular attendees was Abraham Bisno, who recalled that he "participated actively in those public discussions of the lectures given at Hull House." And he added, "There was freedom of speech over there. It was indeed free" (Bisno, *Union Pioneer*, 119). The club was active until the latter part of the 1890s when many of its active members were attracted to the Nineteenth Ward Civic Club, which had as a goal electing an honest ward alderman.

9. JA was intent on initiating an effort to attract to HH French Canadian settlers in her neighborhood. She might also have been aware that several of the wealthy women she hoped to attract as settlement volunteers spoke French and through the French evening might become more attached to HH. Her French evening was to be held on Monday following the Italian girls' gathering. According to JA's 1889–90 diary, the first French party may have been 5 May 1890, with a second one held 19 May 1890.

10. It was not uncommon for JA and EGS to invite volunteers or donors to stay at the settlement for a week at a time or to attend a special event there. For example, Jenny Dow, Harriet Trowbridge, and MRS were all invited to come for a week in June 1890. See JA to MRS, 14 June 1890, below.

11. Based on surveys done between 6 Apr. and 15 July 1893 for *HH Maps and Papers* (1895), "A few French pepper the western edge of the section, the poorer members of a large and well-to-do French colony of which the nucleus is the French church near Vernon Park" (17). Vernon Park was located two blocks west of Polk and Halsted streets and on Polk St. between Center St. on the east and Loomis St. on the west. See also JA to SAAH, 6 Mar. 1890, n. 4, above; and Two Essays in the *Forum*, Nov. and Oct. 1892, n. 98, below.

## To Anna Hostetter Haldeman Addams

*In Jane Addams's view, "a Settlement is a protest against a restricted view of education."[1] It is not surprising, then, that a fundamental element of the program that Jane and Ellen Gates Starr had in mind when they began Hull-House was providing educational opportunities for those in need in their neighborhood. Almost from the beginning, they presented a mix of social events laced liberally with educational components. There were lectures; ethnic gatherings that featured readings, speeches, and songs; a kindergarten and clubs with educational play for younger children; reading parties for working youth; and opportunities to discuss and debate for older working adults. Now the founders were ready to establish an adult classroom experience at the college or university level, very much like the program Jane Addams had seen at Toynbee Hall.*

*An article in the* Chicago Journal *on 27 May 1890 heralded "the establishment of a 'College Extension Course'" at Hull-House, "similar in motive and method to the University Extension courses so successful in England. . . . It seems certain that many people who appreciate the value of higher education, but are unable to go to college, will embrace this opportunity." Indicating that the courses would be held at 335 South Halsted St. for a small fee, likely one dollar for ten lessons, the reporter continued, "If the demand for 'college extension' is large an early effort will be made to establish connection with some college of reputation, that certificates given may have the authority of the college."[2]*

*In the fall of 1890, when college extension programs began again after the summer break at the settlement, Ellen reported, "The Literature, history & Art classes are fullest, & the drawing. I am sorry the Physiology is small. Science doesn't seem to take yet. The Thursday night lectures are going to be popular & perhaps we can get in the scientific wedge thus."*[3] *The Hull-House program announcement for classes beginning 1 Mar. 1892 revealed that so far, 182 students had taken advantage of the settlement's College Extension Program. Classes were conducted by graduates of colleges and universities with some lectures given by university professors. Fees ranged from twenty-five cents to one dollar for each usually ten-week series of classes. Jane also initiated the Hull-House Summer School in 1891. It was usually a month long and held at Rockford College. For the next ten years, excepting in 1893 when it was not held because of the World's Columbian Exposition in Chicago, the summer school was an important element in the College Extension Program.*[4]

*In the fall of 1892, the newly created University of Chicago*[5] *initiated its college extension program, and Hull-House was identified as one of its centers in Chicago. While Hull-House continued its own college extension classes and reading parties, the Lecture-Study Department of the university provided at least one lecture series at the Hull-House center each year, 1892–96,*[6] *and speakers for the settlement's Thursday-Evening Lectures series.*[7]

*By the fall of 1896, lectures were no longer scheduled by the university for Hull-House, but the settlement continued to provide its own version of college extension opportunities. For a time, this newly reorganized program was associated with the Chicago Board of Education, which awarded student certificates.*[8] *Over time the diverse, multifaceted Hull-House curriculum*[9] *evolved into a list of much simpler, more basic offerings fashioned primarily to meet the practical needs of the settlement's neighbors. "College Extension classes have been modified," wrote Jane in the* Hull-House Year Book 1906–1907, *"for while classes of a purely cultural character are still carried on . . . the residents of Hull-House feel increasingly that the educational efforts of a settlement should not be directed primarily to reproduce the college type of culture but to work out a method and an ideal adapted to adults who spend their time in industrial pursuits. They hope to promote a culture which will not set its possessor aside in a class with others like himself, but which will, on the contrary connect him with all sorts of people by his ability to understand them and by his power to supplement their present surroundings with the historic background which legitimately belongs to them."*[10] *Among advanced classes listed in the* Year Book *were German, French, Italian, elocution, mathematics, civics, Bible class, Browning, and young people's poetry class. English and U.S. history as well as Esperanto were listed as secondary-level classes. The advanced classes aimed at helping schoolteachers hone their teaching skills and expand their knowledge; secondary classes were established for those who wished more education at the high school level. Eventually, these classes were primarily English, American history, and civics; in addition, there were classes in homemaking, dressmaking and millinery, and an assortment of trades, including shoe repair, printing, and foundry work.*

335 So Halsted St. Chicago [Ill.] June 3d 1890

My dear Mama

I have not heard directly from you for a long time, but as I will see you the end of this month,[11] I hope, I do not know that writing makes so much difference.

Miss Starr's mother[12] is visiting us this week, she is so delighted with the house and our enjoyment of it, that I am sure if you came you would have some thing of the same feeling.

We were so amused this morning by her wistful sigh that she did wish this beautiful old house was in a better neighborhood, without reflecting that if it were we would not be in it.

Ellen's Aunts Miss Starr and Mrs Wellington[13] were here to lunch to-day and thought the rooms remarkably cool for this hot day. The lake breeze is sure to come up some time during the day and I think we will be comfortable all summer.

I do not think that I have written of our great piece of good fortune. Miss Culver our land lady has given us the rent for four years. That relieves our expenses of sixty dollars a month, and makes everything easier.[14] Our lastest attempt is the College Extension Classes which promise to be very successful. The Latin Class[15] started last evening with twelve public school teachers of the neighborhood.

I have not heard from Alice this week but suppose Harry is home by this time, please give my love to George and believe me Ever Your loving daughter

Jane Addams.

ALS (UIC, JAMC; *JAPM*, 2:1180–81).

1. Addams, *Twenty Years*, 428.
2. "Art for the Masses."
3. EGS to Mary Allen, Oct. [1890], SC, Starr. An article in the *Chicago Daily Tribune* in the spring 1891 indicated that 150 students had been doing "surprisingly satisfactory" work in such classes as "history of art, mathematics, Latin, English literature, Shakespeare, English history, bookkeeping, drawing, Roman history, rhetoric, zoölogy, German, French, and Italian" ("In the Butler Gallery"). Among additional lecture-study subjects presented at HH by settlement volunteers while the Univ. of Chicago extension programs were also being offered were the following: algebra, ancient history, English composition, freehand and mechanical drawing, needlework (German method), structural botany, geometry, political economy, modern history, singing, domestic hygiene, chemistry, electricity, painting and modeling in clay, constitutional law and history, physiography, microscope studies, physics, physiology, biology, astronomy, English literature, and American literature.

Called a "Faculty meeting," the residents and teaching volunteers "have a conference once in a while about the work," wrote Univ. of Chicago graduate student Madeleine Wallin, who would become a HH resident. At JA's invitation, she and some of her fellow students met with the volunteer-teachers at the settlement. "We all gathered around the long dining table (twelve or thirteen teachers and several visitors) and listened to the reports of the teachers for the past quarter. Four or five seemed to be the average attendance in the classes, but the teachers were encouraged by that. The idea there is not so much to teach them things from books as to impress them for good by social contact. The classes are more a means of getting hold of the individuals and touching their lives some way for good. . . . A delightful company of cultured men and women—most of them college graduates—are down there trying by slow and painful degrees to lift, ennoble, purify, gladden those lives, a most Christian task" (Madeleine Wallin to Mary Ellen Keyes Wallin, 15 Jan. 1893, JAMC, Sikes).

4. See JA to SA, [12?] [Aug. 1891], below.

5. The college extension movement began in England at Cambridge Univ. and quickly spread throughout the country. Richard Green Moulton (1849–1924), who had been closely associated with its development in England, was persuaded by Dr. William Rainey Harper (1856–1906), the first president of the new Univ. of Chicago, organized in 1890, to move to Chicago and direct the development of the university's Univ. Extension Division, especially its Lecture-Study Dept. JA and EGS heard Moulton speak about the college extension idea while he was visiting in Chicago from England in 1890.

6. Teachers from the Univ. of Chicago program who appeared at HH included Prof. John Dewey; Prof. Oliver J. Thatcher who spoke on the beginnings of the Middle Ages; Prof. Nathaniel Butler, whose topic was English literature; John Graham Brooks; and Edward C. Page on American history. By 1893 the Univ. of Chicago's extension program operated in a number of centers throughout the city. It could boast 122 courses with an attendance of "nearly twenty thousand people" (Goodspeed, *A History of the University of Chicago*, 265). However, by 1896 leadership at the university was beginning to have second thoughts about its commitment to the lecture-study system. The university had found that the program was "expensive. The hearers of the lectures did not become students" at the university, and it "became increasingly difficult to find suitable lecturers" (Goodspeed, *A History of the University of Chicago*, 150).

7. Among those speakers were JA friend and Beloit graduate Rollin D. Salisbury of the Geology Dept.; J. P. Giddings, professor of petrology; T. C. Chamberlain, professor of geology; S. B. Barrett, fellow, astral physics; and Moulton himself.

8. Seeking another means to continue expanding and supporting extension education for adults, HH became associated with the School House for the People program initiated by the Chicago Board of Education during the winter of 1896–97. JA was one of the twelve lecturers that the settlement provided for the program between 2 Feb. and 10 Mar. 1897 at the Medill High School auditorium, usually crowded to its five-hundred-person capacity for the lectures. Her topic was titled "The Russian Peasant and Count Tolstoi." The lectures were funded through a bequest of ten thousand dollars from former board of education member Rev. William H. Ryder (1822–96), who between 1860 and 1882 became an admired religious orator and the successful pastor of the First Universalist or St. Paul's Church, Chicago. He also served on the board of trustees for the Woman's Medical College in Chicago and the Chicago Citizen's League and became president of the board of trustees of the Chicago Hospital for Women and Children.

9. For a time in the mid-1890s, at least six students had to join or want a specific class before the residents at HH who ran their College Extension Program would attempt to find someone qualified to teach the subject.

10. See n. 8; *JAPM*, 53:883.

11. JA planned to go to Rockford and Cedarville for the Fourth of July celebration. See JA to AHHA, 4 Jul. 1890, below.

12. Susan Childs Starr seems to have mistrusted Italian friends EGS presented to the family, including Alessandro Mastro-Valerio. EGS reported to sister Mary Blaisdell that when she introduced their parents to Alessandro Mastro-Valerio, "Papa did not turn his back on him as Mamma did" (19 [and 21] Dec. 1890, SC, Starr). For biographical information on Susan Childs Starr, see *PJA*, 1:544.

13. Chicago art-appreciation lecturer Eliza Allen Starr and her sister Eunice Allen Starr Wellington (1827–1911), widow of Charles W. W. Wellington (1825?–80), who was visiting from the East.

14. "Now comes the great item of news," wrote EGS to Mary Blaisdell. "Miss Culver has

given us the house rent free for four years, amounting to $2.880, & we have decided to call the house Hull-House. Connect these two facts in any way that your refined imagination suggests. I basely observed that we were going to have 'Castoria' on our pedestal for four years. Don't give this joke publicity, although I think it bright for of course I pretend now that it seems to me the most natural & probable name imaginable, being the name by which it is already known to old residents & the neighborhood. Indeed such awful names have been suggested that this one, though not musical, &, I fear causing restlessness & grief to the shade of Matthew Arnold, seems positively refreshing from the absence of nauseating qualities. It was growing very inconvenient not to have a name, &—it is very convenient to have four years rent. It may be necessary to explain my castoria joke by stating, in case you don't know it, that the manufacturers of that article offered the nation a large sum (I have forgotten the amount) toward the pedestal of Liberty in exchange for the privilege of having Castoria on it, in huge letters, for a year. The government declined with dignity, but it's a rich government, & can afford to be dignified. Besides, Liberty hadn't been previously known by that name, which makes a difference" (18 May 1890, SC, Starr).

15. The Latin class began on 2 June 1890. It was taught by Charles Columbus Arnold (1858–1939), among the first men to become associated with HH. He was born in Constable, N.Y.; attended the Franklin Academy in Malone, N.Y.; and graduated valedictorian of his class at Hamilton College, N.Y., in 1885, where he was a member of the Emerson Literary Society. He continued to teach Latin at HH, 1891–92; arithmetic, 1891–93; algebra in 1893; geometry in 1892; and a course on Emerson, 1893–96. He became an attorney and served as a legal adviser for HH. After 1913 he was living in Riverside, Calif., and growing oranges. JA's nephew Stanley Ross Linn eventually settled near him in Riverside and also became a fruit grower. Arnold was married to Elizabeth Tittle in Johnstown, Pa., in 1894, and after her death in 1922, to Margaret Adelaide Williams in 1926. He remained a lifelong friend of JA.

## DOCUMENT

*On Alice Haldeman's thirty-seventh birthday, she presented Jane with a special gift. Should she die, she wished Jane to have responsibility for her daughter, Marcet. Alice was aware that her husband, Harry, was an alcoholic. As a married couple, they were often at odds, and she was beginning to consider him unreliable. She also knew that Anna Addams, his mother, was growing old and bitter with the care of her reclusive younger son, George. Of her own siblings, her brother, Weber, was mentally ill, his wife, Laura, struggling to manage. Her sister Mary was worn out with the care of her own large family and her health fragile. Jane seemed the most logical choice to assume the task. Over the coming years, family members, especially those in trouble or doubt, would increasingly turn to Jane for her leadership, advice, and help, making her the matriarch of her siblings and their progeny.*

Girard. Kansas. June 5th 1890.

This is to certify that in case my little daughter, Anna Marcet Haldeman, shall lose her mother,: It is my most earnest sincere desire and often expressed wish that she shall be given into the entire care of my sister Jane Addams.

S. Alice Haldeman

ADS (UIC, JAMC; *JAPM*, 27:719).

Jane Addams's sister Sarah Alice Addams Haldeman, ca. 1895 (private collection).

## To Mary Rozet Smith

Hull-House. 335 So Halsted St [Chicago, Ill.] June 14' 1890

My dear Miss Smith

Jenny Dow is to spend next week here and probably Miss Trowbridge will be here for part of the time. It would give us great pleasure to have you come on Monday[1] prepared to stay for the rest of the week—and share our "homely fare and destiny obscure."[2] Hoping very much that you can do it, I am very sincerely yours

Jane Addams

ALS (SCPC, JAC; *JAPM*, 2:1185).

1. 16 June 1890. MRS did spend the week at HH. See also JA to SAAH, [22?] [June 1890], below.

2. JA is misquoting from line 30 of English poet Thomas Gray's (1716–71) "Elegy Written in a Country Churchyard." The line is: "Their homely joys, and destiny obscure" (Thomas Gray Archive, a Collaborative Digital Collection, Univ. of Oxford, 2000–10 <info@thomasgray .org.>).

## To Sarah Alice Addams Haldeman

Hull-House. [Chicago, Ill.] [22?] [June 1890]

My dear Alice

I hope the bible and thimble reached Marcet in time for her birthday.[1] The latter is a present from her Aunt Jane. A.M.H. seemed very dignified indeed. The bible was six dollars <postage & all> I hope you like it.

I am going to Rockford to morow,[2] I find myself very loathe to leave, I grow fonder of this place all of the time. We have had such a happy week. Jenny Dow was here all week with Miss Trowbridge & Miss Smith, two charming girls. We gave the kindergarten a picnic and the Italian children a "fiesta." The North side Car Co gave us the free use of the car track & the West Side a car.[3] The college Extension classes[4] are booming. Please keep any money for me that may be paid in. I would like $200.00 at once if possible.[5] I have been helping John and doing all sorts of things, outside of the regular expenses.[6] When we once get settled down it ought to be easy to keep within our income. Give my birthday kisses to Marcet, with love to her father & mother[.] Your loving sister

Jane Addams.

ALS (IU, Lilly, SAAH; *JAPM*, 2:1250–51).

1. Anna Marcet Haldeman was born 18 June 1887.

2. JA was about to leave Chicago to attend festivities at RS centered around graduation and the annual board of trustees meeting that was held 24 June 1890. At that meeting, the sitting principal, Anna Gelston, resigned for health reasons, and JA had the pleasure of nominating her former teacher and close friend SA to replace Gelston. JA was made a member of the solicitation committee, as the school was continuing in its effort to raise fifty thousand dollars to support its further development.

3. JA was becoming adept at soliciting and receiving support from wealthy Chicago businessmen. Charles Tyson Yerkes (1837–1905) began his career as a municipal-bond broker and banker and owner of street railways in Philadelphia, where he was jailed in the 1870s for speculating with public funds. He found his way to Chicago in 1881 and by the late 1880s had earned his robber-baron reputation. He controlled most of the city's northern and western railway lines through bribery and alliances with corrupt members of the city council (see also JA to Henry Demarest Lloyd, 22 Dec. 1895, nn. 2, 4, below). He was finally thwarted in his attempt to gain a monopoly on all of the lines, including those to the south, through votes against him on the city council. By 1899 he had sold most of his Chicago transport holdings and moved first to New York and then on to London, where he was a major developer of the London railway lines.

Yerkes bought the North Chicago Railway Co. in 1886 and the Chicago West Division Railway Co. in 1887. Both companies, which operated primarily horse-drawn cars traveling on rails, had been in business for more than twenty years when Yerkes acquired them. Yerkes himself was in a generous mood, aware that he needed to improve his public image. By 1892 he had agreed to provide the new Univ. of Chicago with funds to purchase the world's largest telescope. The result was the Yerkes Observatory, located in Williams Bay, Wis.

4. See JA to AHHA, 3 June 1890, above. "About seventy-five people came each week to teach, entertain, visit, to help in any way carry on the work for which Hull-House stands,"

reported Katherine A. Jones. Attendance in the classes and clubs swelled to between eight hundred and nine hundred each week. "Most of the students are young women. . . . Naturally there are many public school teachers; there are factory girls, stenographers, seamstresses, whomsoever the classes have drawn, irrespective of occupation. There are daughters of the rich men who come from a more fashionable quarter to attend these classes because they like them" ("The Working Girls of Chicago").

5. John Addams Linn, a senior at Lake Forest Univ., seemed to be requiring more financial support than the Linn family was able to provide. In addition, JA, a member of the RS Board of Trustees' solicitation committee, was also helping raise $50,000 for the school. HH's financial records indicate that for the year Oct. 1890 through Sept. 1891, JA paid $2,013.90 and loaned $351.25 of the total settlement expenses, which were $9,123.55, the remainder coming from outside sources. For the year Oct. 1891 through Sept. 1892, JA paid $1,813.98 and loaned $603.34 of the total expenses of $12,140.02, with the remainder coming from outside sources. JA's resources were being reduced, but she was also responsible for a diminishing percentage of the expenses to keep the settlement going.

Outside sources were described in an article probably issued in late 1891 or early 1892 from an unidentified Chicago newspaper pasted on p. 13 of HH Scrapbook 1: "An income of $100 a month for janitor, gas, heat, etc. is contributed by 'tens,' the members of which pledge $5 a year for the purposes. The various departments which have grown out of the first simple housekeeping are supported by individuals who have money, faith in the work, and a desire to assist in it. More than one Chicago 'society' girl gives half of her allowance and economizes in gowns and bonnets in order that South Halsted street may be brightened and 'grow in grace'" (*JAPM*, Addendum 10:6ff).

6. JA's nephew John Addams Linn, oldest child of MCAL and JML, was enrolled as a student at Lake Forest Univ., of which, for a time in the late 1880s, his father had been a financial agent. It is difficult to know what "things, outside of the regular expenses," that JA was doing, because there are no extant detailed financial records for the settlement or JA until Oct. 1891.

## From Jenkin Lloyd Jones

*As a major component of the educational opportunities at the settlement, and following the Toynbee Hall pattern, Jane and Ellen determined to present as many lectures as possible. Almost immediately, Jane began to invite the famous and near famous to present talks at the settlement. "We hope very much that Dr. Barrows will consent to visit our Saturday evening men's Club (which is gradually being formed)[1] and talk to them upon American history. . . . Mr. French[2] gave an illustrated lecture last evening to about fifty <young> people with their parents," Jane wrote to Sarah Mole Barrows, with whom she had become acquainted through the First Presbyterian Church in Chicago, where John Henry Barrows was pastor.[3]*

*Jane quickly discovered that finding willing, appropriate, educational, and entertaining lecturers and musicians to attend her Hull-House neighbors at the settlement was an arduous task. Jenkin Lloyd Jones,[4] pastor of Unitarian All-Souls Church at Oakwood Boulevard and Langley Avenue on Chicago's South Side, was one of the early Hull-House supporters. Jane's correspondence with him may have been indicative of her efforts with other potential lecturers.*

[Chicago, Ill.] June 30th, [1890]

Dear Miss Adams:

I cannot take to the woods without sending you a word of greeting and a word of apology. I meant what I said when I said that I wanted to help you in your work there. And now let me take time by the forelock and commit myself to your service for one evening a week or one evening a fortnight as arrangements can be made, <this fall, after my return in September—> to give you a series of six, eight or ten papers on some of the great novels of the world, or as many attempts to pick a lesson from the great pictures, ancient and modern.

I could give you in the former course a study of Victor Hugo's "Les Miserables," George Eliot's "Romola" "Daniel Deronda" and "Felix Holt," Hawthorne's "Marble Faun," Dicken's "Tale of Two Cities," "The African Farm," Bellamy's "Looking Backward" and "Robert Elsmere."[5]

As for pictures I have a study of Raphel's ["]Transfiguration," the "Sistine Madonna," Millet's "Sower," "The Agnelus" Munkcasy's "Christ Before Pilate," Vibert's "Missionary Story"[6]

If your constituency would be better served (of this alone you must judge) I could give in a conversational way the interpretation of a few poems, accompanied with readings, such as Browning's "Saul," <[*4 words illegible*]> Shelley "Skylark," Tennyson's "Locksley Hall."[7]

All this I submit of course, simply with a desire of helping you, not with the desire of making work for myself or yourself, we both of us have enough of that commodity. It simply is a token of respect for the good work and the right spirit you put into it. Silver and gold have I none but such as I have I give unto thee.[8]

I also promised to see what Prof. Bastin[9] could do in your college extension work by giving a course of talks on Botany. He needs rest and must not undertake anything until the fall, but when back, then I am very sure he will be glad to fit into any plans that may be then working. You need not answer this letter and you must not try to find me till after the first of September, then if you have any designs upon me the sooner you make them known the better for you and for the plans. Regards to Miss Starr. Very cordially thine,

TL presscopy (MTS, Jones; *JAPM*, 2:1186–87).

1. The Men's Club, which was to be a regular Saturday-evening event, fizzled, and it was not revivified until Alfred Hicks successfully launched the Working People's Social Science Club in Apr. 1890. See JA to SAAH, 8 Oct. 1889, n. 22; and JA to MRS, 26 Apr. 1890, n. 8, both above.

2. William Merchant Richardson French (1843–1914), born in Exeter, N.H., was the brother of sculptor Daniel Chester French. He came to Chicago in 1867 and became associated with the *Chicago Daily Tribune* as the art editor. Elected secretary of the old Academy of Design out of which the Art Institute of Chicago (incorporated as the Academy of Fine Arts, 24 May 1879) was born, French became the institute's first director and served until his death. As

director he did much to attract people to the institute's exhibitions. Lorado Taft observed that he "never lost sight of the idea that the Institute was to be for all the people" ("Obituary"). French was also manager of the art department at the World's Columbian Exposition in 1893, wrote on a broad spectrum of art subjects, and took an active interest in prisoners-aid work, serving for ten years as president of the Central Howard Assn. in Chicago. He was also president of the American Assn. of Museums, 1907–8.

An early HH supporter, he visited the settlement during its initial years, was helpful in the development of the Butler Art Gallery, and applauded the exhibits EGS presented there. He returned to lecture at HH on 28 May 1891, when the title of his lecture was "An Hour with the Caricaturists."

3. 16 Oct. 1889 (Oberlin College Archives, Barrows; *JAPM*, 2:1091). John Henry Barrows (1847–1902), who became president of Oberlin College, Ohio, in 1899, was born in Medina, Mich., and graduated from Olivet College, Mich., 1867. He attended Yale, Union, and Andover theological seminaries as well as a seminary in Göttigen, Germany. After serving for two years as a missionary in Kansas, he spent fourteen years in pastorates in Boston and Lawrence, Mass. He arrived at the First Presbyterian Church in Chicago in 1881 and remained until 1896. An eloquent speaker, he preached social and political reform from the pulpit and was dedicated to his congregation's program of social outreach. He helped create a kindergarten and construct the new Railroad Chapel Mission, paid for in large part by Mrs. Marshall Field, and began a series of Sunday-evening services in the Central Music Hall in which William L. Tomlins, noted for his ability to develop choral singing, directed the music. He was called to organize and serve as president of the World's Parliament of Religions, held at the World's Columbian Exposition in 1893, and afterward became a lecturer and writer. His wife was Sarah Eleanor Mole Barrows (1852–1940) of Williamstown, Mass.

4. Jenkin Lloyd Jones (1843–1918) was born in Cardiganshire, South Wales. When he was an infant, the Jones family moved to Wisconsin, where they became farmers. After serving in the Union army, he graduated from Meadville Theological Seminary in 1870, the same year that he married Susan C. Barber (d. 1911). Between 1871 and 1880, he was pastor of All Souls Church in Janesville, Wis. While serving as secretary of the Western Unitarian Conf. (1875–84), he helped found and was editor of the weekly Unitarian paper *Unity* and also helped establish Unitarianism in the Midwest. In 1882 he organized and became pastor of All Souls Church in Chicago and served as director of the settlement-like Abraham Lincoln Center that he helped his church found in 1905 in Chicago.

Secretary of the World's Parliament of Religions meeting at the World's Columbian Exposition, he helped organize similar gatherings that followed in succeeding years. He was the first president of the Illinois State Conf. of Charities, 1895–97, and taught English at the Univ. of Chicago, beginning in 1893. The author of numerous books and articles, he was especially devoted to the poetry of Robert Browning. He was often a lecturer at HH, helped JA raise money among his church members, and with Jane served on the board of the COS.

5. Of these titles, Rev. Jones suggested, there is evidence that on 30 Oct. 1890 he presented "Romola" and a month later on 20 Nov. he offered "Felix Holt, the Radical." Both were presented in the Thursday Popular Lecture series associated with the settlement's college extension classes program. In May 1890, he had been one of the early speakers for the Working People's Social Science Club.

6. In the spring of 1891, Rev. Jones again helped out with a series of lectures, only one of which had an art thesis. On 12 Feb. 1891, he presented an illustrated stereoptical lecture on French painter Jean-François Millet. In the next three months, he presented one lecture each month: "The Cost of an Idea" in Mar. and Apr., and in May he offered "The Cost of a Fool."

7. On 16 July 1891, during the HH Summer School at RS, Rev. Jones presented a lecture on Emerson, and on 17 July his subject was the poetry of Robert Browning.

8. Acts 3:6.

9. Prof. E. S. Bastin (1843–97), botanist, chemist, and pharmacologist, was born on a farm in Ozaukee Co., Wis. He attended public schools in Waukesha, Wis., and pursued theological study at the first Univ. of Chicago after graduating in 1867. He took up the study and teaching of botany and chemistry and taught at the Univ. of Chicago until 1883. He was the founder of the Illinois State Microscopial Society in 1868 and president, 1884–85. He also helped found the Chicago Lantern-Slide Club in 1886 and was a faculty member of the Chicago College of Pharmacy, where he served as professor of botany, materia medica, and microscopy, 1881–86. Bastin was the author of a number of important texts on botany that were used in colleges into the early twentieth century. He spoke twice at HH during the fall of 1890. On 23 Oct., he presented "How Plants Defend Themselves," and JA reported that his lecture was "very popular among our neighbors" (JA to Jenkin Lloyd Jones, 27 Oct. 1890, UC, Jones; *JAPM*, 2:1209). He returned to HH again on 13 Nov. and spoke on the movement of plants. He joined Rev. Jones for the 1891 HH Summer School at RS and spoke on protoplasm on 9 July and the next day on the dispersion of plants.

## To Anna Hostetter Haldeman Addams

*Toward the end of June 1890, Jane Addams combined a board of trustees meeting at Rockford Seminary and a visit in northern Illinois.*[1] *It was a time to check on her farm*[2] *and to visit friends and family. What she saw of her family concerned her. "Ma looked worn and tired, she has had a girl so irregularly t[hat] it amounts to none. George [has] grown more silent than he was last summer but I think did not seem in worse health. I h[ave] the most helpless bewildered feeling about them."*[3] *Once again, the family claimed her and she began to take a leadership role in trying to improve living conditions for George and Anna.*

Hull-House 335 So Halsted St Chicago—[Ill.] July 4" 1890

My dear Mama—

I came back quite determined to find a woman who would be willing to live at Cedarville, and have been to the two places I could think of to find, but in vain. They all object to the country[4]—I have not given it up by any means, but am very much disappointed. I reached Chicago safely on Tuesday morning[5] and found the house hold peaceful and quiet—Ellen said the heat had been very prostrating but that the house had remained comparatively cool and that she had staid in it.

We are having a very peaceful day for the fourth of July, an occasional shot being the only thing to remind us of the day. Mr McCormick[6] sent down a huge box of fire works last evening. He and some friends are coming to set them off at eight o'clock but until that time all is as calm as possible, I imagined we would see much more drunkeness &c.[7]

I spent Monday evening and night at the Bartons which I enjoyed very much, the girls[8] had not yet come home.

Dr Leland[9] from the Sem'y is here for a few days, we enjoy her very much and are quite getting into last winters life of the school.

I hope I will hear from you oftener, you are in my thoughts so much of the time. Please give my best love to George and believe me Your affectionate daughter

Jane Addams

ALS (UIC, JAMC; *JAPM*, 2:1189–90).

1. See JA to SAAH, [22?] [June 1890], n. 2, above.

2. Augustus Smith was in charge of JA's farm, located southeast of Cedarville in Lancaster Twp. JA wrote to sister SAAH, who was managing some of her investments, that "money . . . paid in" be "kept and not reinvested until" she saw "how Augustus Smith turns out in the fall" (5 Jul. 1890, IU, Lilly, SAAH; *JAPM*, 2:1191).

3. JA to SAAH, 5 Jul. 1890, IU, Lilly, SAAH; *JAPM*, 2:1192.

4. After her return to HH, JA also reported her effort to her sister SAAH. "My mind has been more at Cedarville than here ever since my visit. I have tried two places to get a woman to go, in one case a trained nurse, but t[hey] all object to the country" (5 Jul. 1890, IU, Lilly, SAAH; *JAPM*, 2:1191).

5. JA arrived back at HH, 1 Jul. 1890.

6. Alexander A. McCormick. See JA to MCAL, 19 [and 20] Feb. 1889, n. 27, above.

7. "A lot of north side people brought down fireworks last evening, some very handsome ones, and set them off in our front yard to the great edification and delight of the neighborhood" (JA to SAAH, 5 Jul. 1890, IU, Lilly, SAAH; *JAPM*, 2:1191). In "Uncle Sam's Birthday," the *Chicago Times* reported that "while a trifle too cool for picnics, it was perfect weather for crackers and fire-works."

8. The Barton family had long been associated with the Addams family. Edward P. Barton was the Addams family attorney and JA's personal attorney. JA mentions the Barton daughters Alice M. and Anna E., who were away at Smith College. For biographical notes on the members of the Barton family, see *PJA*, 2:73, n. 2.

9. The administration at RS, soon to be renamed RC (1892), as well as alumnae, students, and teachers were aware of the social experiment undertaken by JA and EGS. The founders had reported to the alumnae group gathered at graduation during the summer of 1889. SA, who had just become principal of the school, was a frequent visitor to the new settlement, and retired teacher Sarah F. Blaisdell was also a supporter.

Lena C. Leland (1859?–1923) had come to investigate the settlement. She received her degree as a physician trained in allopathy and homeopathy from the Medical College of the Univ. of Michigan. She taught natural sciences, physiology, and hygiene at RC, 1885–1906, where she was also the resident college physician. During the HH Summer School at the college, she lectured on physiology and hygiene beginning in 1894. After leaving RC, she entered private medical practice with two other physicians in Rockford, where she lived for the remainder of her life.

## To [Anna Hostetter Haldeman Addams]

335 So Halsted St [Chicago, Ill.] July 17" 1890

My dear Mama

The Sanitarium of which Miss Anderson was so fond is at Kenosha, about thirty or forty miles north of Chicago on the lake.[1] It is the same place Prof Blaisdell[2] always goes when he is broken down.

If you think seriously of going I should be glad to find out about it for you. I could easily run up and make arrangements for rooms for George and yourself. It would be very nice to have you so near for I could come to see you often. May be we could persuade Alice to bring Marcet for a couple of weeks in August—the lake air is delightful. The weather has been cool and pleasant here and I am feeling very well indeed. I spent Sunday at Evanston, the lake was delightful quite as cool and wide it seemed to me as the sea shore.

With my best love to George, I am always your loving daughter

Jane Addams

ALS (UIC, JAMC; *JAPM*, 2:1193–94).

1. AHHA may have been familiar with the Pennoyer Sanitarium in Kenosha, Wis. "If used up entirely," SA wrote to AHHA, 16 Feb. [1889], "I shall flee to Kenosha. Do you know of this wonderful place? The fount of perpetual youth. It is the only place of its kind that is near enough and cheap enough for me to gain access to and so I regard it in the light of an important discovery" (UIC, JAMC, HJ). The Pennoyer Sanitarium had its beginning in 1857, when Dr. Edgar Pennoyer (1822–93) purchased a water-cure facility (established about 1840) from Dr. H. T. Seeley in Kenosha, Wis. It survived as a rest-cure resort through 1919, at which time the property became a hospital managed by Dominican Catholic sisters. In 1890, after a disastrous fire, the sanitarium was rebuilt and located on Kenosha's Lake Michigan lakefront. JA's sister MCAL died while a patient there in July 1894. See also *PJA*, 2:185–86, n. 12.
2. Rev. James Joshua Blaisdell, brother of Sarah F. Blaisdell.

## To Ellen Gates Starr

[Chicago, Ill.?] [4–7 Aug. 1890][1]

My dear One

Your letter was a little homesick.[2] Of course I miss you all the time and have never wanted you more than the last few days when every thing seemed to be moving at once. Miss McLane stays and was a great success with the boys—like Miss Rhea.[3] The nurse for the nursery has two little girls herself but we are going to take them all in because she is such a remarkable woman.[4] We have put ~~another~~ <a single> iron bed in the blue room (it has never looked so well) Mary[5] and I may take it together and another in the white room. Last night Miss Scammon[6] was here for the night[.] Miss Babcock[7] and Miss McLane, Fl[8] of course. Mary and I slept together. The lawn tennis[9] was started very successfully, and we are going to take the entire evening Club[10] to Lake Geneva to camp over Sunday![11] Affairs have fairly boomed lately.

Miss Coman[12] is coming, we may have a little reception for her of the College women in the city. I do wish you were here.

The concert last <Friday> evening was a great success & we are going to have another on Thursday Mrs Wyman of Evanston.[13] I like our Shephardess photograph so much that I would<n't> really care for an engraving, but I should like the Sistine Madonna[14] sent for. If you can think of some thing for the Bohemian Boys,[15] send for that too. I miss you every minute and want you all the time. Yrs

Jane

ALS (SC, Starr; *JAPM*, 2:1316–17).

1. This letter was originally dated [July 1892]; however, the editors have determined that it should be dated in early Aug. 1890, while EGS was away visiting family in Chicopee, Mass., and before the second week in Aug., when JA left for her vacation with Lydia Avery Coonley in Wyoming, N.Y. The women that JA mentions in the letter, namely, Miss Scammon, Miss Babcock, and Miss McLane, seem to be associated with the first year of the settlement. For example, Miss Scammon's and Miss Rhea's names appear in JA's 1889–90 diary but do not appear in any JA correspondence, HH program materials, or news clippings after the first year.

It is not clear just when lawn tennis was introduced at the settlement, but Alice Miller, an active HH volunteer, reported in her *Charities Review* article about HH published in Feb. 1892 that it was being offered at the HH Summer School during the 1891 session. The printed HH Summer School program announcement also indicated that lawn tennis was available to those attending. More pointedly, according to a 7 Dec. 1891 letter to Katharine Coman about advances in the settlement program since her previous visit, JA reported that HH had added a day nursery "in a separate little cottage." And since that day nursery opened in Mar. 1891, it is likely that Coman's visit took place during the previous warm season, summer of 1890, and when lawn tennis might have been introduced.

2. This letter is not known to be extant.

3. See JA to SAAH, 6 Mar. 1890, n. 4, above.

4. Among the earliest nursery workers were the following: Miss Elizabeth McKee, often identified as "Miss Lizzie," and Mrs. Sedonia Loosveldt (sometimes spelled Loosfelt, Losfelt, or Loosefeldt). Their names appear in the earliest accounting records relating to the Crêche beginning in Oct. 1891. Each received a monthly salary of twenty-five dollars. By early 1892, Miss McKee was identified as superintendent of the nursery and "Mrs. Losfelt" as her assistant. Sedonia Loosveldt (b. 1871?) was the wife of cabinetmaker Camille Loosveldt (1873?–1908). The couple lived at 222 (later 813) Ewing St. Their son, Morris, was active at HH and appeared as Jack-the-Giant-Killer in the children's Christmas play *Rhymeland* in Dec. 1895.

5. It is not clear whether the Mary that JA is referring to in this letter is JA's sister MCAL, who may have been visiting in Chicago; settlement worker Mary Keyser; MRS; or one of their other friends known to EGS.

It seems likely that JA was not used to sleeping alone. She had grown up sleeping in a bed with her sisters in Cedarville and seemed to continue the practice with friends. On Christmas Eve 1890, EGS wrote to her cousin Mary Allen that a neighborhood Italian child named Francesco was to stay at HH with her for a week. She reported that "I . . . took him to my bed & board the first day & night, Miss A. returning to Miss Farnsworth, whose hospitality received her" (SC, Starr). See also JA to AHHA, 9 Dec. 1890, n. 7, below.

6. Perhaps Arianna Evans Scammon (1848–98), daughter of Chicago pioneer, businessman, and attorney John Y. Scammon (1812–90) and his first wife, Mary Ann Haven Dearborn (d. 1858), whom he wed in Bath, Maine, in 1837. During the 1880s, Arianna Scammon lived in New York City. At the time of her father's death in Mar. 1890, she was living with her sister Florence Ann Dearborn Scammon Reed (Mrs. F. S.) (1844–1927) in Beaufort, S.C. Serving as the executrix of her father's estate, Arianna Scammon returned in Chicago, and from 1894 until her death she was a member of the CWC. Like her father, she was a member of the New Jerusalem Church. After a funeral at the South Side Chicago home of her sister Florence Reed, she was buried at Oakwoods Cemetery.

7. Miss Babcock seems to have been associated with Miss Margaret Warner Morley (1858–1923), who became an American biologist, educator, and author of children's books and taught physiology and hygiene at the settlement during the early 1890s. The Babcock name appears for the first time associated with JA and HH in JA's 1889–90 diary on Thursday, 15 May 1890, when Dr. Leila G. Bedell and Miss Morley spoke to fourteen women about physiology at the settlement. At the time, Morley was likely associated with the Armour Institute in Chicago as an instructor in biology. She had been educated in Brooklyn, N.Y., public schools and attended New York City Normal College and Oswego Normal School before teaching in the Oswego, N.Y.; the Milwaukee, Wis.; and the Leavenworth, Kans., normal schools. JA's diary entry indicates that Miss Morley's residential address was "c/o Mrs. Babcock, 2417 Mich Ave" (SCPC, JAC; *JAPM,* 29:163).

Miss Babcock may have been one of the daughters of Henry H. Babcock (1837?–81) and Mary P. Keyes Babcock (1843?–1916). Both were teachers. They came from New York to settle in Chicago, where they opened a school at 2417 South Michigan Ave. and raised at least four daughters. In the federal census of 1880 for Illinois, they are identified as Mabel, age eighteen; Florence, age ten; Helen, age eight; and Ethel, age four. Florence and Helen became members of the CWC. The Babcock couple were well connected in Chicago social and cultural circles. Henry Babcock was a biologist. During the 1870s, he was a leader in developing South Park, served as director of the botanical garden there, and was active in the creation of the Chicago Academy of Sciences, for which he served as president, 1878 until his death. In 1888 Mary Babcock became a member of the powerful Fortnightly Club of Chicago.

Miss Babcock's name was also joined again with Miss Morley's in JA's 1889–90 diary entry for Friday, 3 Oct. 1890, when both women spoke to a gathering in the evening at HH. During the college extension class program that began at HH during the summer of 1890, Miss Babcock, who had an A.B. degree, taught microscope studies and bookkeeping, while her friend Margaret Morley continued to teach physiology. In the fall of 1890, she switched to teaching physical geography, while Miss Morley continued to hold classes in physiology. Miss Babcock's name does not appear on HH college extension class announcements after 1890. During the fall of 1892 and the spring of 1893, Margaret Morley taught a class at the settlement on delsarte, the study of physical development and graceful motion. On 6 June 1895, she presented an illustrated lecture titled "Steps in Evolution" in the Thursday-evening lecture course offered by the Congress of HH Clubs.

8. Fl. was Frl. Emma Neuschäffer. See JA to SAAH, 23 Nov. 1889, nn. 9–10, above.

9. By introducing lawn tennis at HH, JA had placed HH in the vanguard of the sport. Lawn tennis, a version of a much older game that might have developed before the Christian era, was devised by an Englishman, Maj. Walter C. Wingfield (1833–1912) in 1874, and was introduced into the United States about the same time. Requiring a court, center net, balls, and rackets, the sport was played primarily on the East Coast throughout the 1880s by both men and women. The first tennis tournament featuring women players was held in 1887 at the Philadelphia Cricket Club, with the first official championship tournament for women held there in 1889. The HH Summer School program for 1891 proudly announced lawn-tennis lessons on Tuesdays, Thursdays, and Saturdays from 8:00 to 9:00 A.M. Lessons were also available in 1892.

10. JA was referring to the Friday evening club of working girls who came to read and hear lectures and musical presentations.

11. Lake Geneva, Wis., was becoming a summer resort site for Chicago's wealthy citizens. Just to the north and west of Chicago and in a hilly and forested area full of water sources, it could be reached by the Chicago and Northwestern Railroad. During the 1870s, an assortment of public parks and camps were developed to welcome Chicago visitors. Among them were Forest Glen Park and Camp Collie, opened in 1870, and Kayes Park, opened in 1874. By 1892 there was a movement to close all public camping sites and parks. Soon the entire

lakeshore would be dotted with the large and elegant summer homes of Chicago's business and social elite. During the 1880s, thirty new estates were added to the fewer than ten already in place or under construction. Among friends of JA and HH who had establishments on the lake were Mary Hawes Wilmarth, David Swing, R. T. Crane, Charles L. Hutchinson, N. K. Fairbank, Shelton Sturges, and Dr. Ralph Isham.

12. Katharine (sometimes Catherine) Coman (1857–1915), graduate of the Univ. of Michigan (Ph.B. 1880), a social reformer and economic historian, had been in Chicago during the late summer of 1890, in part to address the Chicago Board of the Assn. of Collegiate Alumnae on college settlements in America before starting back to teach as professor of political economy and history at Wellesley College. A strong supporter of the College Settlements Assn., she was probably interested in investigating the HH venture. An inquiry from her after her first visit apparently required JA to respond in specific terms about the development of HH (see Extracts from JA to Katharine Coman, 7 Dec. 1891, RS, Denison; *JAPM*, 2:1283–86).

Coman became a lecturer for JA during the 1892 HH Summer School at RC, where she spoke on 14 July on contemporary Russia. She was a strong supporter of Denison House in Boston's South End and continued her active participation in the College Settlements Assn. She was also devoted to progressive causes, including the Consumers' League and the Women's Trade Union League of Chicago. After she retired from Wellesley in 1913, she supported the National Progressive Service division of the Progressive Party. She wrote several books, including a popular text, *The Industrial History of the United States* (1905), and the two-volume work *Economic Beginnings of the Far West* (1912). Her brother Seymour Coman (1852–1921) became active at HH as a financial supporter and settlement auditor.

13. Julia Moran Wyman (1859?–1907) was born in Pennsylvania, the daughter of Michael Moran, an Irish immigrant, and American-born Catherine Moran. The family moved to Joliet, Ill., where Mr. Moran was a gas manufacturer. Julia studied voice and piano at the Chicago Musical College. She sang frequently as a student at concerts sponsored by the college between 1877 and 1879. Julia Moran married Walter C. Wyman, principal in the firm of Wyman Brothers Coal Co., Chicago, in New York City in Nov. 1880. The couple resided with the groom's mother and brothers at 138 Forest Ave., Evanston, Ill. At some point, Julia Wyman studied voice in Europe and returned to America to resume her career in 1888. Shortly after her appearance at HH, she appeared to acclaim with the Boston Symphony Orchestra in Boston, New York City, and New Haven, Conn. She continued to sing in major venues for the remainder of 1890 and became a successful stage recitalist. In 1896 her career was interrupted when her husband successfully sued for divorce on charges of infidelity, at which time she was denied access to her three children. She eventually kidnapped her children and took them to Europe, where she placed them in a French convent school. There is little evidence that she sang again until she presented a few concerts in New York City in 1902. She committed suicide in New York City.

14. Writing to EGS from France on 21 Feb. 1885, JA suggested, "I believe many artists could do much good by disseminating what has already been reached. Some of the copies we saw of the Sistine Madonna, (in Dresden) were so fine that it seemed culpable and careless that every town & city in America do not contain one, that people who had already been touched by it, should be so indifferent and 'unmissionary'" (*PJA*, 2:372; 2:375, n. 27). JA did have a copy of the work to share with her neighbors.

Initially, JA and EGS decorated HH with paintings, etchings, prints, photographs, and statuary, primarily of European art. JA had gathered some of the works displayed at the settlement during her 1887–88 trip to Europe. EGS and JA were especially fond of the work of John Everett Millais, William Holman Hunt, and Edward Burne-Jones, sometimes associated with the Pre-Raphaelite movement in art, and the work of Jean-François Millet and other painters often identified with the Barbizon school. The settlement founders also favored Italian art and were particularly partial to the work of Fra Angelico. They placed renderings

Ellen Gates Starr, ca. 1890 by Max Platz. It is likely that Jane Addams and Ellen Gates Starr had their photographs taken at the same time by Max Platz (UIC, JAMC 0286 0428). For his photograph of Jane Addams, see p. 1.

According to Mary Addams Hulbert, great-niece of Jane Addams, this photograph of Jane Addams may have been taken during the first year of Hull-House. The photographer might have been Max Platz, but there is no evidence to substantiate this. This front view is one of three rocking-chair poses taken at the same time that survive. The other two were left-side views (private collection).

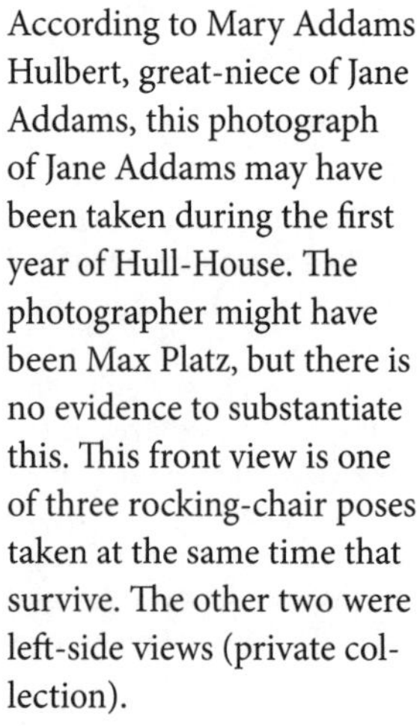

of mothers and children by classical European artists in nursery and kindergarten areas. In addition, EGS had access to the artistic photographic prints made by her Allen cousins Mary and Frances, who were amateur photographers living in Deerfield, Mass. Eventually, artists associated with the art program at HH would begin to decorate the rooms of the settlement buildings with their own works.

15. JA mentions a Bohemian Boys' Club gathering in her 1889–90 diary on 21 Apr. 1890.

## To Anna Hostetter Haldeman Addams

Hull-House. [Chicago, Ill.] Aug 11" 1890

My dear Mamma

I am going away next Wednesday[1] for two weeks and have accepted an invitation from Mrs Coonley to spend the time at her house in Wyoming New York.[2] I am feeling very well and not in the least as if the summer here were trying, but it seems the custom to go. Miss Head[3] and Miss Miller[4] will take charge of the house while we are both away and I will come back with Miss Starr the first of Sept.[5]

I hope very very much indeed that you will come for a visit in Sept.[6] I have invited Mamie and Fred Greenleaf[7] for the first week and I know you would enjoy being here with them. I am glad you have had a visit from them at Cedarville.

I was quite horrified this morning to find that I had not sent you one of my pictures,[8] which I had meant to do from the first. I do not think they are particularly good and they are certainly too smiling. Vinette Crain[9] has been here for a little while and I have enjoyed her very much. Mr Hyde and his wife[10] called one Sunday afternoon, they used to live in Freeport and sent many regards to you. Please give my best love to George and believe me Your loving daughter

Jane Addams

I hope the picture may be taken as a birthday present, as it will reach you the twelfth of Aug. I shall think of you many times tomorrow and wish you many happy returns of the day.

J.

ALS (UIC, JAMC; *JAPM*, 2:1198–99, 1184).

1. 13 Aug. 1890.

2. Wyoming, N.Y., not far from Niagara Falls, was a gaslit village where the wealthy constructed their summer homes. The highlight of the surrounding lush, wooded natural environment was the nearby six-hundred-ft.-deep gorge and waterfalls of the Genesee River, often referred to as the "Grand Canyon of the East."

3. Katharine P. Head (Breck). See JA to SAAH, 6 Mar. 1890, n. 5, above.

4. Alice Mason Miller (Whitman). See JA to MCAL, 19 [and 20] Feb. 1889, n. 19, above.

5. EGS took a vacation from HH during Aug. She visited her sister Mary Houghton Starr Blaisdell and other relatives in Mass.

6. Although JA wrote on several occasions urging AHHA to visit the settlement, AHHA resisted. Despite JA's enticements, like accompanying AHHA's favorite niece, Mary ("Mamie") Greenleaf, for her visit, AHHA probably did not visit the settlement until the end of 1890. See JA to AHHA, 9 Dec. 1890, below.

7. Mary ("Mamie") Irving Hostetter Greenleaf, at this time married to Frederick W. Greenleaf, whom she divorced and then remarried the day before he died, was a JA stepcousin. For a biographical note, see *PJA*, 1:68, n. 99.

8. JA began sitting for a photograph earlier in the summer. When JA wrote sister SAAH on 6 June 1890, the day after SAAH's birthday, JA informed her, "I thought of you all day yesterday with love and tenderness and hope you knew I did altho I apparently gave no sign. I tried to get the birthday present for you that you most wanted, but the photograph did not turn out well and I shall have to sit again" (UIC, JAMC; *JAPM*, 2:1182).

It is likely that both JA and EGS were sitting for well-known society and theatrical photographer Max Platz (1850–94), who had been born in the castle of Fetsching, near Berlin, Germany; immigrated with his family to the United States at an early age; settled initially in Racine, Wis.; and made his way to Chicago in 1867. He began his career in the photographic studio of his brother-in-law Henry Rocher, which was destroyed in the Chicago Fire of 1871, and in 1881 established his own atelier at the same address, 88 (later 507) North Clark St. He was a noted photographer of theater personalities and was also "one of the best-known photographers in the West" ("Max Platz Succumbs to Death"). He was a member of the Chicago Society of Artists, the Forty Club, the Germania Club, and the Chicago Athletic Assn. Two years before his death from kidney and heart failure, he traveled around the world.

9. Vennette Sweet Crain (Moller) (1867–1940) was born in Freeport, Ill., the daughter of Vannette Sweet Crain (1840–1935) and attorney Joseph Crain (1831–1917). When JA lived in Cedarville, she had known the Crain family. Vennette was a graduate of Wellesley College in 1888. She returned to Freeport to teach in the Mary Louise Institute, a small private school created by a group of Freeport women. In the fall of 1893, Vennette began teaching in a school in Iowa, but by Feb. 1893 she was at HH, where she started work as a Central Relief Organization visitor. By 1894 she had become head of the Central Relief Assn. dispensary operating out of HH to serve primarily the settlement neighbors living in the Seventh, Eighth, and Nineteenth wards of Chicago.

In Apr. 1894, she was a member of the HH College Extension Com. and helped organize and manage the settlement's program of classes and lectures. She taught a Shakespeare class on *Twelfth Night* on Wednesday evenings. Also in 1894, for a time, she was manager of the HH Coffee Shop. By 1895, one of the settlement's thirteen residents, in that year she taught rhetoric and letter writing, Shakespeare's *Tempest* and *Henry IV*, and also hosted the HH Shakespeare Club. On 12 May 1896, Vennette married Rev. Carl Nelson Moller. By 1900 the Mollers, who had two children, had settled in St. John's rectory, St. Louis, Mo., and in 1932, Vennette was living with her daughter Katharine Williams (Mrs. Dudley A.) in Kent, Ohio.

10. Perhaps Ebenezer H. Hyde (b. 1820?), who with his wife, Mary (b. 1824?), left Massachusetts for Freeport., Ill., in the late 1840s and established himself as a dry-goods and general merchandise dealer. He and his family lived in Freeport during the 1850s and 1860s and had at least two children, Mary E. and John. Hyde built the Plymouth block in downtown Freeport, which had stores on the ground floor, offices on the second level, and a large space called Plymouth Hall for meetings and entertainments on the third floor. By 1865 he had closed his wholesale notion business. He and his family do not appear in the 1870 or 1880 U.S. Census for Freeport.

## To Sarah Alice Addams Haldeman

*Throughout the early Hull-House years, Jane Addams kept in close communication with her siblings, especially her sister Alice. She was careful to write to Alice often, even to say that she had little time to write.*[1] *And when she did not hear from Alice, she fretted. "I have not heard from you for so long that I have grown rather unhappy about it and am afraid all is not well," she wrote to Alice early in March.*[2] *Perhaps Alice was miffed because Jane, who had been ill at the end of February and into March, had not been immediately responsive to her shopping request. Alice's reply is not extant; however, late in March, Jane commented to Alice: "I have not been able to get down town to see to Marcet's coat and hat, but I hope to go out tomorrow if it is fine."*[3] *Then as Jane was preparing to vacation with Mrs. Coonley in Wyoming, New York, she was again disturbed by the lack of a response from Alice. "It has been such a long time since I have heard from you that I am worried all the time. Do drop me just a line, dear."*[4] *Of course, some of Alice's letters may have gone astray because Alice was sending them to 338 South Halsted instead of 335 South Halsted. Jane teased her, writing, "you must reform, dear."*[5]

Wyoming New York | Aug 20' 1890

My dear Alice

Your letter came just after I had despatched mine of anxious inquiry—I had a feeling that you were sick, or some thing wrong.

You are mistaken dear about its being as far here as to Girard, the journey is ten hours shorter—and owing to reduced fare about half as expensive—which is a great point with me this summer.[6]

Every one preached rest and a cool spot at me until I finally yielded, I certainly finding both here. I will go back next week after spending Sunday with Mrs Sedgwick at Syracuse[7] where I hope to meet Miss Aria Huntington.[8]

I have never given up the hope of a long visit from you and Marcet at Hull-House, I do hope you will plan for it this fall. The idea of its not being sanitary is perfectly absurd.

Mrs McLeish (Miss Hillard) took her little baby to the country in May to avoid all danger. It died[9] the other day in spite of all her care, while our little neighbor of the same age grows bonnier and sweeter every day. Of course that proves nothing but I am more and more convinced that over care and fusiness does a child no good. I am home-sick for dear little Marcet, you know what it would be to me to have her all the time, that timidity about her mother's dying reminds me of my own childish experiances. My horrible dream every night, would be Mary's death[10] and no one to love me.

We drive and walk a great deal in this delightful mountain air and I am becoming thoroughly rested and feeling vigorous and well. Write to me often dear, and never believe that I don't love you "best of all." Your loving sister

Jane Addams

ALS (IU, Lilly, SAAH; *JAPM*, 2:1202–4).

1. See especially JA to SAAH, 8 Oct. 1889, above.
2. JA to SAAH, 6 Mar. 1890, above.
3. 23 Mar. 1890, IU, Lilly, SAAH; *JAPM*, 2:1167. See also JA to SAAH, 22 Jan. 1890, above.
4. JA to SAAH, 12 Aug. 1890, IU, Lilly, SAAH; *JAPM*, 2:1200.
5. JA to SAAH, 12 Aug. 1890, IU, Lilly, SAAH; *JAPM*, 2:1201.
6. JA had been spending her own financial resources to lease, repair, furnish, and provide household expenses for EGS, Mary Keyser, and assorted volunteers who spent time at HH. For details of the amount JA had spent, see EGS [for JA] to Mary Houghton Starr Blaisdell [and SAAH], 23 Feb. [1889], n. 12; and JA to SAAH, 5 Jan. 1890, n. 1, both above.
7. Deborah W. Gannett Sedgwick. See EGS [for JA] to Susan Childs Starr and Caleb Allen Starr [and SAAH], 15,[16–20?] Nov. [1889], n. 16, above.
8. Arria Sargent Huntington (1848–1921) was born and educated in Boston, the daughter of Hannah Dane Sargent Huntington and Episcopal bishop of central New York Frederic Dan Huntington. She became a member of the Syracuse, N.Y., Board of Education, 1898–1904; was a trustee for both the Shelter for Unprotected Girls and the Hospital of the Good Shepherd; and was also selected as the vice-president of the Syracuse YWCA. She was active in the Consumers' League, Visiting Nurse Assn., Society for Prevention of Cruelty to Children, and Church Assn. in the Interest of Advancement of Labor. As an advocate for woman suffrage, she held memberships in the Women's Political Union and the Political Equality League of Syracuse.
9. Martha Louise MacLeish (1888–90) was the first-born child of Martha Hillard MacLeish and Andrew MacLeish.
10. MCAL served as a surrogate mother to JA after SWA's death in 1862 when JA was two and a half years old and before the marriage of her widower father, JHA, to AHH in 1868. On JA's relationship with MCAL, see *PJA*, 1:21–24, 537–39.

## "Diary, 1889–90"

*Jane and Ellen returned from their vacations rested and ready to begin their second year at Hull-House. Almost immediately, two events occurred that were to prove significant in Jane's life and in the development of Hull-House.*

*"Miss Lathrop came in the evening," reads the 1 October 1890 entry in Jane's 1889–90 diary.*[1] *This is the first mention of Rockford, Illinois, native and Vassar graduate Julia Lathrop's*[2] *association with Jane Addams and Hull-House. She would spend the remainder of her life in pursuit of social justice. She became a close, lifelong friend of Jane Addams. The last book Jane Addams wrote was a partial biography of Lathrop,* My Friend Julia Lathrop, *published posthumously in 1935. Julia Lathrop's particular interests became helping to develop the field of social work education; improving conditions for the ill and infirm, especially*

Addams's lifetime friend and colleague in progressive reform, Julia C. Lathrop was photographed by Alfred A. Cox, ca. 1892. Lathrop became the first head of the U.S. Children's Bureau, the first woman to head a major division of the U.S. government (RC, Archives).

*in Illinois state institutions; and the welfare of children. The first she influenced through her pioneering work helping to develop the Chicago School of Civics and Philanthropy, the second with her pathbreaking and dedicated service as a member of the Illinois State Board of Charities, and the third as the first chief of the United States Children's Bureau.*

*In the fall of 1890, wealthy Chicago merchant Edward B. Butler*[3] *presented Jane with a major gift. Butler offered to add a new building to the settlement physical plant, which at the time consisted only of the original Hull home. The new structure was to be used primarily as an art gallery and library.*[4]

*Jane never recorded the date on which Julia Lathrop first came to the settlement or the exact date that Butler made his gift; however, she mentions both Julia Lathrop and Edward Butler for the first time in her 1889–90 diary during the first days of October 1890.*

5 and 8 October 1890

*Sunday, October 5, 1890.*

Miss Lathrop to hear Dr. Gunsaulus

Saw Mr. Pond[5] Mr. Smith[6] about Butler affair. . . .

*Wednesday, October 8, 1890.*

Dr. Bedell, Mrs. Harvey[7] &c, to dinner

Miss Smith[8] came. Very fine business meeting about Butler gallery.[9]

October 1890 entries: AD (Addams, "Diary 1889–90," 5 Oct 1890, SCPC, JAC; *JAPM*, 4:174).

1. SCPC, JAC; *JAPM*, 29:172. On 5 Oct. 1890, JA recorded in her diary that Julia Lathrop came to hear a lecture by Frank W. Gunsaulus, pastor of the Plymouth Congregational Church.

2. Julia Clifford Lathrop (1858–1932). See Biographical Profiles: Lathrop, Julia Clifford.

3. Edward Burgess Butler (1853–1928), a highly successful purveyor of general merchandise, was born in Lewiston, Maine, to Manly Orville Butler and Elizabeth Howe Butler. He attended Boston schools and worked in the wholesale dry-goods business in Boston. In 1877 with his brother George H. Butler, he founded Butler Brothers in Boston and soon also had additional stores in New York and Chicago, where he arrived in 1879 to make his home. For a time, it was the largest wholesale business in the United States and produced the first mail-order catalog in the country. He helped establish a stock-option plan for his employees before he retired from its presidency in 1914.

Butler, who in retirement became an artist, was also active in cultural and civic affairs in his adopted city. In 1893 he served as chairman for the ways and means committee of the World's Columbian Exposition. For years he was president of the Manual Training School Farm at Glenwood and was also a board member of the Chicago Orphan Asylum, Erring Woman's Refuge, RC Board of Trustees, and Art Institute of Chicago. He was also a director of the Corn Exchange National Bank. As the leader of the Chicago Commercial Club, he helped make possible Daniel Burnham's famous *Plan of Chicago* (1909). His wife, Jane Holly Butler, whom he married in 1906, was a member of the CWC.

Butler's service at HH was crucial and primarily financial. When HH was incorporated in 1895, he was selected as one of the initial seven trustees and served as a trustee until 1912. During the remainder of the 1890s, he and his firm gave at least $300 each year to defray general settlement expenses, and he continued to support the settlement financially for the remainder of his life. After providing $4,000 ($106,424 in 2015 dollars) to construct the two-story Butler Art Gallery Building for the settlement, in 1901 he provided another $2,500 ($71,799 in 2015 dollars) to add a third story to it and to remodel the entire structure to permit more flexible use of the lower two floors. In 1899 he also helped provide funds to enlarge the HH Coffee Shop and kitchen and to build the settlement theater. In 1901 he provided his largest single gift of $5,500 ($157,958 in 2015 dollars) to help construct the HH Men's Club.

4. Architects the Pond brothers designed the original Butler Art Gallery Building. It was built on the lot leased to JA by Helen Culver and located immediately to the south of the Hull home, fronting on Halsted St. "A bit of Venetian architecture on South Halsted Street!" declared the *Chicago Daily Tribune* on 31 May 1891 in an article entitled "Chicago's Toynbee Hall" about the new settlement addition. "It is a two-story structure of brick, two colors, buff and red. . . . The entrance is at the northeast corner and one passes through a small vestibule into the reading room, a large apartment—31x45—occupying the entire ground floor. . . . [T]he furniture has been especially designed for the room, and $1,500 worth of reference books will be placed on its shelves. The furniture will be of light oak, which will harmonize well with the pale lemon shades of the wainscoating, walls, and ceiling. . . . Tables and chairs to accommodate fifty people will be furnished. . . .

"The second floor is divided into two apartments. The small one occupies the rear of the building and will be the 'studio' devoted to the use of the art classes which are now conducted in Hull House. The larger front room will be a permanent class and lecture room and will also be used for loan exhibits twice a year. . . . In these rooms a very high wainscoating extends nearly to the ceiling and the whole interior will be painted the conventional dark red of the picture gallery, only in this case the shade will be somewhat lighter, for most of the visitors will judge the exhibits by gaslight.

"High diamond-paned windows give an excellent light to these airy rooms, and a large closet off the studio will receive the easels and working materials on occasions when it is desirable to throw the two rooms together. This can be easily done, as great doors as the same height and construction as the wainscoating can be swung back, virtually transforming the second floor into one large apartment." See also JA to MRS, [12?] [Apr. 1891], n. 11, below.

5. JA worked with both of the Pond brothers; however, she came to rely on Allen B. Pond for planning, estimating costs, and negotiating details for each new HH structure and on Irving K. Pond for the design of each.

6. Charles Mather Smith (1831–1912) was MRS's father. He was a member of the powerful Union League Club and the Chicago City Club. For biographical information, see Biographical Profiles: Smith, Mary Rozet and Smith Family.

7. Early JA and HH supporters Dr. Leila Gertrude Bedell and Mrs. Julia Plato Harvey.

8. MRS.

9. JA may have been seeking the support and advice of her well-connected friends about how to convince Helen Culver to lease her the property on which to construct the Butler Art Gallery Building. EGS reported the difficulty to her sister: "Miss Culver is still obdurate about land, & Mr. Butler has not yet been able to begin his Art building. We have also been unable to find anything which we could rent for a day nursery. It looks as if we might have to give it up for the present which is a great disappointment. I am awfully exasperated against Miss Culver" (SC, Starr). Before Apr. 1891, JA and EGS had located space for a day nursery or Crêche (see JA to MRS, [12?] [Apr. 1891], n. 9, below).

## To Jenkin Lloyd Jones

*In her diary for 22 October 1890, Jane recorded, "Miss Fine and Miss Dodge arrived."[1] They were coming to see what their colleague Katharine Coman had seen on her recent visit, and they were treated to a whirl of activity. Jean Gurney Fine was head worker at the College Settlement in New York City. At the time, Grace Dodge[2] was promoting cooperative working women's clubs and manual training for boys and girls. She had also initiated the kitchen-garden movement[3] in New York City. Jean Fine's visit lasted at least through 31 October 1890 and gave Jane and Ellen an opportunity to display Hull-House as well as to learn of programs and reform efforts in the East.*

*Beside the daytime settlement activities, which on Friday, 24 October, included a "pretty good" kitchen-garden gathering of young girls,[4] the visitors were treated to lectures, dinners with Helen Culver and Alice Stone Blackwell,[5] and Italian and German evenings.*

*Many local visitors also dropped by to see Jane Addams and investigate Hull-House. Many wanted details about settlement programs; some offered money or in-kind support. Jane decided that she needed to publish materials that she could use to tell the Hull-House story.*

335 South Halsted Street. Hull House [Chicago, Ill.] Nov 3d 1890

My dear Mr Jones

In the confusion of Thursday evening I did not give you the list of the college classes[6] for Mr Joiner.[7] I add a list of the other clubs &c that go on each week. He was very kind indeed to give the five dollars I have applied on a bill for easels, drawing paper &c that supplies the art classes for the winter. I am sorry to have nothing fuller to send Mr Joiner and am trying to procure several copies of "The Interior"[8] which contained a fairly good article. If I secure them I will send him one of those. We are very much obliged for the Romola lecture, the people have made some very appreciate comments.

With kindest regards to Mrs Jones in which Miss Starr joins me, I am very sincerely Yours

Jane Addams

ENCLOSURE

Kindergarten every day from 9 A.M. to 12 M—Miss Dow.

Monday aft.

Sixty Italian children who sew, model in clay &c

Monday evening

A club of working girls—music, games &c also an embroidery & cooking class.

Tuesday aft.

A hundred school boys, in "The Knights of the Round Table" club "The Jolly Boys" Club &c reading and games.

Tuesday evening

The Young Citizens Club, of Sixty working boys, between fourteen and twenty one.

Wednesday evening

The Working People's Social Science Club.

Men & a few women.

Thursday aft.

Afternoon tea and lectures for the women of the neighborhood—about twenty each time—informal. A cooking[9] of fourteen older girls.

~~Thursday~~ Friday evening.

A German evening—German families singing reading aloud in German &c

Friday aft

Kitchen garden and house keeping classes. Cooking, bed-making darning &c. A hundred & twenty school girls.

Thursday evening

College Extension lectures.

Sat. afternoon

Drawing classes—

Sat. evening.

Italian evening—Italian families come for music &c. celebration of national dates.

ALS (UC, Jones; *JAPM*, 2:1211–14).

1. SCPC, JAC; *JAPM*, 29:178. "Miss Fine of the New York College Settlement is here for a week. We are very anxious to give her a little reception and as all the evenings are full, have selected next Thursday as the easiest to arrange. The history class closes at eight, in time for the lecture, we will have it begin promptly on the hour so it will be over by nine, and the reception will be until ten. We have invited from half past eight until ten, hoping our guests will be late, or if not the first ones can be received in the south reception room," JA wrote, inviting Rev. and Mrs. Jenkin Lloyd Jones to stay after his lecture that evening. And she continued, "We are sorry to crowd the evening so much but it seems the only possible way to have the friends of Hull House see Miss Fine" (27 Oct. 1890, UC, Jones; *JAPM*, 2:1208–9). Rev. Jones was scheduled to give his lecture on Romola at 8:00 P.M. on Thursday evening, 30 Oct. 1890. After his Thursday-evening experience, Rev. Jones complimented JA, "I was delighted to see things so well at the Hull House and to believe that you are going to stand the strain and reap the blessings" (4 Nov. [1890], MTS, Jones; *JAPM*, 2:1215).

2. Grace Hoadley Dodge (1856–1914), social worker, educator, and philanthropist, was born the eldest of six children into the wealthy family that developed Phelps, Dodge, and Co. She dedicated herself to reform, especially to helping working women.

Her work as a Sunday School teacher evolved into her effort during the 1880s to help establish cooperative clubs of working women and to create a national association promoting the idea. In the fall of 1891, she returned to HH to speak about her club idea and drew a large and attentive audience. "[T]he long reception-room was filled to overflowing, the chairs were exhausted, groups of bright-faced girls were gathered about the doorways, and some were even sitting on the floor as near as possible to the woman who has so identified herself with working girls," wrote a reporter in "Clubs of Working Girls" for the *Chicago Daily Tribune* describing the gathering (13 Oct. 1891).

Among Dodge's other major interests and commitments were the Kitchen Garden Assn. and the Industrial Education Assn., which eventually, because of her continual participation and financial support, became the Teachers' College and a professional school within Columbia Univ., New York City. She also served on the National Board of the YWCA of the United States, of which she became the first president. An active and continual supporter of the Presbyterian Church and especially its organizations for young people, in 1911 Dodge became president of the Board of Trustees of the American College for Girls at Constantinople in Turkey.

3. The objective of the kitchen-garden movement "was to teach 'poor children how to make their home more comfortable'" (Huntington, *How to Teach Kitchen Garden*, 9). In the 1870s, Emily Huntington (1841–1909), matron at the Wilson Industrial School for Girls, New York City, developed the curriculum for teaching mothers and children household skills to help them improve their own homes and to prepare them to hold jobs as household servants. One of the most active instructors for the movement was Grace Dodge, who helped promote the "kitchen-garden" idea through the Kitchen Garden Assn., initially organized in 1880 in New York City.

4. Addams, "Diary, 1889–90"; *JAPM*, 29:178.

5. Alice Stone Blackwell (1857–1950), daughter of Lucy Stone and Henry Browne Blackwell, was a graduate of Boston Univ. She became a journalist for the *Woman's Journal* (Boston),

which she continued to edit until her retirement during World War I. Blackwell and JA belonged to some of the same reform organizations, including the WCTU, WTUL, NAACP, and American Peace Society. Blackwell played a pivotal role in the merger of the two major national organizations promoting woman suffrage, NAWSA and the AWSA.

6. For a list of the college extension classes for the fall of 1890, see HH Scrapbook 2:1; *JAPM*, Addendum 10:7ff). The classes included history of art, Greek, writing, English literature, arithmetic, political economy, Latin, Shakespeare, mechanical drawing, mathematics, history, German, singing (for girls), physiology, physical geography, Italian, French, and modeling. In addition, there were Thursday-Evening lectures and concerts and a lecture on Wednesdays at the Working People's Social Science Club.

7. Alvin Joiner (1848–1942) was born to Charles W. and Harriet M. Waterbury Joiner in Buffalo Grove, Ill. He was educated first in Illinois and then in Port Samilac, Mich., and the Royalton Academy, Vt. He also studied business at Hillsdale College, Mich., where Dr. Harriet M. Fox, who also had an early interest in HH, had been a student. He entered the lumbering business in Michigan, from which he retired in 1883. At that time, he settled in Polo, Ill. There and in Wisconsin, Florida, and the Dakotas, he acquired farms and operated a banking business. He and his wife, Ida P. Wood Joiner, had four children. In politics Joiner was a Republican. He served two terms as mayor of Polo, was associated with the Legislative Voters' League, and was particularly proud of attracting a Carnegie library to Polo. He also had a long association with Preston Bradley (1888–1983), pastor of the People's Church, Chicago, who promoted "Christian Unitarianism."

8. The article that JA was referring to was titled "The Toynbee Idea" and written by James Frothingham, brother of JA's RFS friend Eleanor ("Nora") Frothingham Haworth. It appeared in the *Interior* of 7 July 1890 (see HH Scrapbook 1:4; *JAPM*, Addendum 10:6ff). Frothingham also became a lecturer for the HH college extension Thursday-Evening Lectures series. On 19 Feb. 1891, his topic was Washington Irving. For information on James Frothingham, see *PJA*, 2:530, n. 9.

9. In her haste, JA seems to have omitted the word "class" after the word "cooking."

## Address for the Chicago Woman's Club

*This presentation to the membership of the influential Chicago Woman's Club is the earliest extant public statement by Jane Addams of her rationale for founding Hull-House and her hope for what it could achieve, paired with her description of the current settlement program. For most of 1890, Jane Addams had been giving versions of this speech to a number of church groups, university women, and socially and culturally significant men and women gathered in private homes.*[1] *She had the opportunity to refine and organize her thoughts and arguments so that she would be as persuasive as possible. "Miss Addams & I have been writing 'our works' lately," Ellen informed her cousin Mary Allen. "She has given a paper at the Women's Club, which has taken all the time of both of us for the last two weeks. I don't mean that I helped write it, but I did other things meanwhile. It was a remarkably good paper. If it ever 'gets itself printed' I will have you see it."*[2]

*With this particular and carefully written presentation, fashioned out of her own personal experiences, Jane was positioning Hull-House as a special, dedicated, and significant social reform organization in the city, worthy of the club's interest and financial support. Reaction of the Philanthropy Committee of the Chicago Woman's Club was enthusiastic. "Adequate praise cannot be given for the high order of philanthropic work established and being carried on by two of our members, Miss Addams and Miss Starr. Enough is not known by the Woman's Club of what these brave women are striving to accomplish. We strenuously urge all to make it a first duty to become better acquainted with their aims and methods."*[3] *During the ten years that followed, Jane Addams and Hull-House were able to count on the Chicago Woman's Club as a partner in a variety of reform efforts in the city.*[4]

Chicago, Illinois 3 December 1890

## OUTGROWTHS OF TOYNBEE HALL

Toynbee Hall,[5] as Chicago people have so often heard, is a settlement of University men in the poorest quarter of East London. They live in a handsome club house, and share their libraries and pictures, their learning and social pleasures with their neighbors.

The commercial portion of London divides the city into two parts. Broadly speaking, the West End contains the society, the wealth, the galleries and handsome houses; the people who embody the traditions and energy that make for progress. The East End contains the people who are bound over to toilsome labor, a fifth of them are buried as paupers; the remainder support themselves, but have no share in the higher products of civilization. Observers say that they tend to revert to barbarism, that they do not hold their own, much less advance. That in many families, even the traditions of truth and honesty are lost; in almost all of them the desire for learning and the higher social pleasures is extinct. The young men of Toynbee Hall were born and reared in the West End; were endowed with the best that Oxford and Cambridge could give them; but they chose to live, for the present at least, in the East End.

There are other similar settlements in London itself, several in the larger cities in the North of England and Scotland,[6] and one or two attempts in America.[7] Before proceeding, however, to these outgrowths of Toynbee Hall, or even Toynbee Hall itself, I should like to give an outline of the movement as I apprehend it, of which these various settlements are but an expression; for I should have little faith in them unless I believed them to be living apostolates, not only of conviction, but of feeling and conscience.

All later writers on social questions are fond of saying that the great word which the last century bequeathed to us was Democracy; that the history of Europe in the 18th century is a history of its struggle with the meaning of this word; an attempt to pass from the philosophical to the actual. But unfortunately the view of Democracy has been partial and the achievement has been all along one line; its leaders fancied that the franchise, that political freedom and equality would secure to all men dignity and a share in the results of civilization.

Promulgated under this theory, Democracy has made little attempt to assert itself in social affairs; so that, while in our city and national politics an effort is made to consult each citizen, there is no similar effort being made anywhere else. This is the more mortifying when we remember that social matters have always been largely under the control of women. Is it possible that with all our new advantage and liberty of action, women have failed to hear the great word of the century? In many a city ward the majority of the votes are openly sold, for drinks and dollars. Still, there is a remote pretense, at least, that a man's vote is his own. The judgment of the mass is consulted, and an opportunity for remedy given. There is not even a theory in the social order,—not a shadow answering to the polls in politics.

The social organization has been broken down thro large districts of our large cities. Most of the people living there are of the poorest. The majority of them without leisure or energy for anything but the gain of a bare subsistence. They move constantly from one wretched lodging to another; they live for the moment side by side, many of them without knowledge of each other, without fellowship, without local tradition, or public spirit; without social organization of any kind. Practically nothing is done to remedy this. The people who might do it, who have the social tact and training, the large houses and traditions of custom and hospitality, live in other parts of the city. The politician sells, one by one, to the highest bidder, all the offices in his grasp; but the time may come when he will not be considered more base in his code of morals and practice, than the woman who, year after year invites to her receptions, and shares her beautiful surroundings with those alone who bring her equal social return; who minister to a liking she has for successful social events. In doing this, she is really just as unmindful of the common weal, as unscrupulous in her use of power, as is any city "boss," who considers only the interests of the "ring." In political circles "bossism" raises a scandal; it goes on in society with scarcely a protest.

Arnold Toynbee gave his lectures on the "Industrial Revolution" thro the great manufacturing towns of northern England.[8] His soul was perplexed over the masses of inarticulate workmen who came so heavily to hear him. They were skilled weavers because they had been trained; they were organized into armies of producers, because men of executive ability and business sagacity had found it to their interest to do it. But they were not organized socially. Altho living in crowded tenements, they were left with a social organization fitted to the village. Their ideas of mutual responsibility and need of association were as unformed and simple as if each man were still treading the loom in his own thatched cottage. Their one place of meeting was the grog shop, and their only host the bar-tender. The local demagogue formed their public opinions. Men of ability and refinement, of social power, of university education, stayed away from them. The same spectacle is repeated in every large town and city. But the paradox is here:—when cultivated people do stay away from a certain portion of the population; when all these advantages are persistently with-held for years, it may be, the result itself is pointed at as a reason,—is used as an argument for the continued with-holding.

This fatal drifting apart, the dividing of a city between the rich and the poor, in itself entails much wrong. We need the thrust in the side, the lateral pressure which comes from living next door to poverty, to make over our humanitarianism of highest avail. This division would be the more justifiable, however, if the people who thus isolated themselves on certain streets and used their social ability for each other, gained thereby and added enough to the sum total of social progress to justify the with-holding of the pleasures and results of that progress from so many people who ought to have them; but they cannot accomplish this. The social spirit discharges itself in many forms, and no one form is adequate to its total expression. Nothing so deadens the sympathies and shrivels the powers of enjoyment as the persistent keeping away from great opportunities for helpfulness, and the ignoring of the starvation struggle, which makes up the life of at least half of the race. To shut oneself away from that half of our race life is to shut oneself away from the most vital part of it. It is to live out but half the humanity which we are born heirs to, and to use but half our faculties. We have all had glimpses and longings for a fuller life which should include that struggle of our ancestors and of so many of our contemporaries. It is the physical complement of the "Intimations of Immortality,"[9] on which no ode has yet been written. The glimpses come in many ways. You may remember the forlorn ache that occasionally seizes you, when you arrive, early in the morning, a stranger in a great city. The stream of laboring people goes past you as you gaze thro the plate glass window of your hotel. You see hard-worked men lifting great burdens; you see the driving and jostling of huge carts; your heart sinks with a sudden sense of futility, you long to have a little child tug at your skirts with never so simple a request. The door opens behind you, and you turn to the man who brings in your breakfast with a quick sense of human fellowship. You pray in the common parlance in which most of our genuine prayers are cast, that you may never lose your hold on it all: You mean to pray that the great mother breasts of our common humanity, with its labor and suffering and homely comforts, may never be with-held from you.

It is inevitable that those who feel most keenly this deprivation and partial living, are our young people; our so-called favored, educated young people; who have to bear the brunt of being cultivated into unnourished, over-sensitive lives. They have been shut off from the common labor by which they live; from the great sources of moral and physical health. Young girls feel it most in the first years after they leave school. In our attempt, then, to give a girl freedom from care, we succeed, for the most part, in making her pitifully miserable. She finds "life" all so different from what she expected it to be. She is besotted with innocent little ambitions, and does not understand the apparent waste of herself;—the elaborate preparation, if no work is expected of her. Her own uselessness hangs about her heavily. The sense of uselessness and impotence, Huxley[10] declares, is the severest shock the human mind can sustain, and if persistently sustained, results in atrophy of power. Doubtless many a busy woman before me whose life is full of good deeds, and whose heart is at rest, looks back upon her first year out of school as the most unhappy one of her life. There is a heritage of noble obligation which young people accept and long to perpetuate. The desire for action, the wish to right wrong and alleviate suffering haunts them daily. We smile at it indulgently, instead of making it of use to society.

The wrong to them begins even further back, when we first restrain their desire for "doing good" and tell them they must wait till they are older and better fitted; that they are now preparing for life. We intimate that social obligation begins at a fixed date, forgetting that it begins with birth itself. We treat them like children with strong growing limbs, who are allowed to use their legs, but not their arms, or whose legs are daily and carefully exercised, that, bye and bye, their arms may be put to great use. We are fortunate if their unused members in the meantime, do not atrophy and disappear. They do sometimes. There are girls who, by the time they are thus fitted, become absorbed in narrow ambitions for social success; who forget their own childish desire to help the world, and to play with the poor little girl around the corner. A Chicago woman, whose cultivation is wide, whose sympathies are broad, and whose charities are far-reaching, told me once that when she was a little girl she used to go to the over-worked women in the village and help them iron. They looked so tired, and she so loved to iron. She did this habitually. I would not like to predict the effect on that woman's character if she had been forbidden to thus iron. If she had been told that she must study and improve herself, and play, of course, that she might study more; that she was a good little girl when she thus improved herself; that she was a troublesome little girl when she went about to help people iron, I am afraid that she would not be the philanthropical and social force in the city that she now is.

There is nothing, after disease, indigence and guilt, so fatal to life itself as the want of a proper outlet for active faculties. Our young people hear in every sermon, learn in their lessons, read in their very fiction, of the great social maladjustment, but no way is provided for them to help it. They are left in the maze of indecision. They come back from college, and Europe, and Wagner operas and philosophical lectures, and wherever else culture is to be found, and some of them have a listless air that alarms you; a few of them look frankly from clear eyes and you perceive that they have had a vision. Besant[11] says that it is the vision Peter had when he saw the <great> sheet let down from Heaven, wherein was neither clean nor unclean.[12] They phrase it more modernly than Peter did, and say that the things that make us alike are stronger than the things that make us different. They say that all men are united by needs and sympathies far more radical and permanent than anything that temporarily divides and sets them in opposition to each other. Or, they may have caught another phraseology, and tell you that art for art's sake is as dead as the great Pan[13] himself; that it must be for humanity's sake, or it cannot survive; that cultivation is self-destructive when shut away from human interests and from the great mass of humanity;—and then may add rather bitterly, with the bitterness of youth, that if you expect success from the[14] them in music or art, or politics, or in whatever line your ambition for them has run, you must let them consult all of humanity, and that the largest and most vital part of it lives on the other streets. It is only the stronger young people, however, who formulate this. Many of them dissipate their energies into ill health, or are buried beneath mere mental accumulations, with lowered vitality, and discontent. This misdirected young life seems to me as pitiful as the other great mass of destitute lives. One is supplemental to the other. It is hard to tell which is the most barren but some method of communication must be devised. Each young person whose education has ignored the principle of Altruism, feels this fatal want of harmony between his thought and action, between his theory and living. Mr. Barnett,[15] the man who first urged the practical and actual Toynbee Hall, altho working in the poverty of East London, found his heart aching over this state of things among the brightest undergraduates of Oxford and Cambridge. The "bitter cry of outcaste London,"[16] started by the Pall Mall Gazette in 1881,[17] had stirred and boiled the blood of these young men, but their feelings had found expression only in foolish vaporizing or reckless giving. In the first meeting held at Cambridge to consider Mr. Barnett's propositions,[18] men like Michael Foster,[19] the physiologist, gave it as their professional opinion, that a practical outlet must be devised for all this feeling, in order that young University men might keep their self-respect;—that they might try their powers and stand on their feet. It is thus easy to understand why the Toynbee Hall movement originated in England, where the years of education are more set and definite than they are here; where the lines between rich and poor are more marked; where class distinctions are more rigid. The necessity for it was greater there, but we are fast feeling the pressure, and reaching the necessity in America. Let me say here, however, that I hope it will never be forgotten, in Chicago, at least, where Hull House feels somewhat responsible for the Toynbee Hall idea, that Toynbee Hall was first projected as an aid and outlet to educated young men. The benefit to East Londoners was then regarded as almost secondary, and the benefit has always been held, certainly by its original founders, as strictly mutual.[20]

I once heard Christine Neilson lead a chorus of four thousand voices, singing the Messiah, in the Crystal Palace at Sydenham.[21] Her voice was better trained than the others; it was correct, piercing and sweet, and could easily be distinguished above the chorus; but it was not essentially different. It was a human voice lifted in praise to its Maker, and so were the four thousand. The difference of training and cultivation were lost in the overmastering grandeur of the feeling and the unity of the purpose. This will perhaps be a weak illustration of what the "settlement" is meant to be. It aims to gather to itself, and, in a measure, lead whatever social life its neighborhood may afford, to focus, and give from to that life; to bring to bear on it the results of cultivation and training; but it receives in exchange for the music of isolated voices the volume and strength of a chorus. To do this, is to cease to resist the impulse beating at the very sources of our lives, urging us to aid the progress of the race. It is to yield to that impulse to go where the race most needs aid. But in order to ignore these differences and accentuate the likenesses, there must be the over-mastering feeling and unity of purpose. Positivism[22] insists that the very religious fervor of man can be turned into love for his race, and his desire for a future life into content to live in the echo of his deeds. This is what George Eliot[23] passionately voices. It seems simple to many of us to search for the Christ that is in each man and to found our likeness on Him,—to believe in the brother-hood of all men because we believe in His.[24]

To turn from social to professionally educational matters, we find that these, too, are more democratic in their political than in their general aspects.[25] The public schools in the poorest and most crowded wards of the city are inadequate to the number of children, and many of the teachers are illy prepared and over-worked;[26] but in each ward there is an effort to secure public education. The school house itself stands as a pledge that the city recognizes and endeavors to fulfill the duty of educating its children. But what becomes of the<se children>[27] when they are no longer ~~within its doors~~ <in the public schools>?[28] The dream of the transcendentalists that each New England village be a University, that every child taken from the common school be put into definite lines of study and mental development, had its unfulfilled beginning in the village Lyceum and lecture courses,—has its feeble representative now in the multitude of clubs for study which are so sadly restricted to educators, to the leisure class, or only to the advanced and progressive workers. The newer movement, which in one of its popular phases, is closely identified with the Toynbee Hall settlements, the "University Extension Movement,"[29] would not confine learning to those who already want it, or to those who, by making an effort, can gain it, or to those among whom professional educators are already at work, but would take it to the coal miners of Newcastle and the dock laborers of East London. It requires tact and training, love of learning and the conviction of <the> justice of its diffusion, to give it to people whose intellectual faculties are untrained and disused. But men in England are found who do it successfully, and it is believed that there are men and women in America who can do it.[30] This teaching requires distinct methods, for it is true of people who have been allowed to remain undeveloped and whose faculties are inert and sterile, that they cannot take their learning heavily. It has to be diffused in a social atmosphere. Information held in solution, a medium of fellowship and good-will, can be assimilated by the dullest. If education is, as Froebel[31] defined it, "deliverance," deliverance of the forces of the body and mind, then the untrained must first be delivered from all constraint and rigidity before their faculties can be used.

The university for working people should have its professors almost co-numerous with the students. There is an attempt to carry on a so-called social university in Philadelphia,[32] and the entire "University Extension Movement" emphasizes the social side of teaching, not only for the pleasure it gives, but that it may make learning possible. Intellectual life requires for its expansion and manifestation, the influence and assimilation of the interests and affections of others. Mazzini,[33]that greatest of all Democrats, who broke his heart over the condition of the South European peasantry, said, "Education is not merely a necessity of true life by which the individual renews his vital force in the vital force of humanity,; it is a Holy Communion with generations dead and living, by which he fecundates all his faculties. When he is with-held from this communion for generations, as the Italian peasant has been, we point our finger at him and say: 'He is like a beast of the field, he must be controlled by force.' It is absurd to educate or consult him, using, ~~as we do in social matters~~ <again>,[34] the effect as an argument for the continuance of the cause. The grandfather of Jackanapes once observed: "We are imperfect enough, all of us; we needn't be so bitter."[35]

Toynbee Hall gives a large place to university extension lectures and reading classes. It has a well-stocked library and reading-rooms. In some of its aspects it seems more like a college than a club. The work is, of necessity, done largely in the evening, but many of the young men who matriculate for the lectures, lodge in the two students' houses, Waddams and Balliol,[36] and the life there is made as much that of a college commons as possible. But the differences between this college and any other lie chiefly here: "Out of school" the relationship between the professor and student is intimately sustained. The teacher goes back to his primitive functions, which included those of friend and guide. He grapples his student by every hook possible to the fuller intellectual life which he represents, that he may over-come the tendency of his surroundings. In the long vacations at Easter and Midsummer, traveling parties are arranged, of thirty or fifty students, to the Rhine or Switzerland, or they see, under careful instruction, the pictures of Florence or the classic ruins of Rome.[37] On holidays little journeys are taken to the famous country houses, the old hunting forests, the historic and literary points of London. It would be unfair to Englishmen to omit the cricketing clubs, the tennis clubs, the athletic life of all kinds which centers about Toynbee Hall.[38] Some of the most learned and eloquent men of England have lectured courses there, for which the students are first carefully prepared.[39] There are classic concerts in the Hall, and popular concerts in the Quadrangle.[40] To the picture exhibits, spring and fall, many of the best pictures in England are brought from their ancestral walls, and Berne-Jones[41] and Watts[42] contribute, for there is a fast-growing circle of men in England who realize that the arts, certainly architecture and painting, need to be brought back to the people, for the pleasure and instruction of whom the finest products in them have been created. The cathedrals of Europe would never have been built, if all the people had not built them. They are the embodiment of the mind of them all. There is, at present, no national art, for we do not appeal to the nation. The method has not been devised of making this appeal, but we can, at least, keep fine pictures with a didactic value from being shut up in rich men's houses, and put them into popular galleries, as Toynbee Hall and the People's Palace[43] have done. Hence it is that Toynbee Hall, logically, disregards none of the results of civilization, casts aside nothing that the modern man considers beautiful or goodly. It rather stands for the fittings of a cultivated, well-ordered life, and the surroundings which are suggestive of participation in the best of the past.

To leave, however, the fascinating life at Toynbee Hall, which can be read in its reports and in many enthusiastic papers, and to come directly to the outgrowth which I know best, is to come to Chicago. There are fewer poor people here than there are in the English cities where the Toynbee Hall life is being led, or in New York, where the Neighborhood Guild and the College Settlement are so successfully establishing themselves. They are also less strictly confined to their own districts. When I thus use the expression "the poor," I did not mean people who lack much that they reasonably need. I mean that great mass of people who are SUNK in toilsome and under-paid labor; who, by the utmost efforts of their undeveloped and inefficient powers, gain but a bare subsistence; the ends of whose day's work leaves them so exhausted of nervous energy that they are gradually sinking in spirit and are worn out long before old age overtakes them. That, I consider a fair definition of the poor, of whom there are many thousands in every great city. There are fewer in Chicago than in New York, as I said, and our city offers two advantages, even in the most crowded quarters,—the sanitary condition is, as yet, much better, and the housing simpler. Many of the houses are wooden, which were originally built for one family, and are now occupied by several. The fewer brick buildings are only three or four stories high, and the little apartment houses comparatively comfortable. There is but one typical New York tenement house, that I know of, in Chicago. It is on Pacific Av., south of Polk St., occupied largely by Arabs. I never pass it nor enter it without an ominous foreboding of what Chicago will ~~be~~ present, unless a persistent effort is made at once. The right kind of a tenement house, put up now in Chicago and properly supervised, would be, I believe, a model indeed for all future tenement building here.[44] New York is struggling with the question how to rid herself of her huge houses and begin over again. We, at least have a fresh start. The little wooden houses are temporary and ready to come down. A determined effort to exclude the disagreeable New York tenement from Chicago would doubtless be successful. If the effort is not made soon, the question will be trebly complicated, for the wrong kind of house will be on the ground.

Another advantage that Chicago has over English cities, which advantage, however, it shares with New York, is the fact that many of the poorest people are foreigners. They are European peasants direct from the soil.[45] It is much easier to deal with the first generation of crowded city life, than with the second and third. It is more natural, and cast in a simpler mould. Italian and Bohemian peasants who live in Chicago, still put on their bright holiday clothes of a Sunday and go to visit their cousins. They tramp along with at least a suggestion of having once walked over plowed fields and breathed country air. The second generation of city poor have no holiday clothes, and consider their relations a "bad lot." I have heard a drunken man in the maudlin stage babble of his good country mother and sing snatches of hymns; and I knew that his little son, who laughed loud at him, would be drunk earlier in life, and have no such pious interlude to his ravings. Hospitality still survives among foreigners, altho it is buried under a false pride among the poorest Americans. We go to Europe, and consider our view incomplete if we do not see something of the peasant life of the villages, with their quaint customs and suggestive habits. We can see the same thing here. There are Germans and Bohemians and Italians and Poles and Russians and Greeks and Arabs in Chicago, vainly trying to adjust their peasant habits to the life of a large city, and coming in contact with only the most ignorant portion of that city. The more scholarship, the more historic view, the more wide humanity a settlement among them can command, the more it can do for them. Hull House found no precedent at Toynbee Hall for dealing with this foreign life, but one thing seemed clear: to conserve and keep for them whatever of value their past life contained, and to bring them in contact with a better class of Americans.

The house itself stands on the borders of several of these foreign colonies, these villages within our city. Every Saturday evening our Italian neighbors are our guests. Most of them are southern Italian peasants,—Sicilian and Neapolitan, with an occasional Lombard, Tuscan or Venetian. Perhaps the thing we hope to do for them is best illustrated by an incident. One evening a statue of Garibaldi,[46] which one of the Italian physicians had presented to the house, was unveiled while the Garibaldian hymn[47] was sung and a little ceremony of speech-making was indulged in. Some of the men had been in Garibaldi's campaigns. One of them sang, in a high, cracked, out-of-door voice, one of the campaigning songs with which Garibaldi had led them on to Naples. He had come into the house with more or less of a hang-dog look. In the opinion of the Americans, he knew, he was a "dago,"[48] unwashed and unskilled; fit only to sweep the streets and dig with the shovel. He had gone out, straightened by the memory that he had been a soldier under the most remarkable leader of modern revolutions. He had once served a noble cause; he could again become a valuable citizen. Americans had taken his hand, not with condescension, but honor. We celebrated with the same guests Washington's Birthday and the Fourth of July. But they reciprocate. They do not renounce their country, nor we ours. We call daily in their houses. The air is foul in them, as it is in their homes in Naples; but the same gaiety, family affection and gentle courtesy, is also there. We have attended their weddings, their funerals and christenings as welcomed and honored guests. We have always found them gentle and responsive; ignorant, but not brutal; dirty, but ready to use our bath-tubs themselves, and grateful when we wash their children.[49] We claim some warm friendships among them and, curiously enough, we have not yet been stabbed in the back.

Friday evening, which is devoted to the Germans, is similar <in> purpose; but owing to the superior education of our Teutonic guests, and the clever leading of a cultivated German woman,[50] we can bring out the best of that cozy social intercourse, which is found, perhaps, in its nearest perfection, in the Fatherland. The singing is in the tender unison of German folk-songs or the rousing spirit of the Rhine. But they do not sing all the time. They drink coffee, and are slowly but persistently pursuing a little course in German history and literature. The relationship by no means ends with the evening, nor does it consist merely in an interchange of social civilities. The friendships formed there have brought about radical changes in the life of more than one family, friendless in a strange land. But our evenings are by no means confined to foreigners. Every industrial neighborhood has need of a center and impetus to keep intellectual activity alive. We have found it possible to inaugurate the College Extensions Classes, to which are attracted the brightest young people of the neighborhood. With a faculty of twenty college men and women, the work done, we hope is as fine in quality as that represented by the larger University Extension Movement. Each evening these classes occupy the library, the reception and dining rooms of the house, while it is possible to reserve the large drawing room for the social or club life. Thursday evening popular lectures as well as concerts are given to the College Extension students, to which those people in the neighborhood who may enjoy them are invited, and to which the audiences have been enthusiastic. On Wednesday evening the Social Science Club meets there, composed largely of men. The opening address on a social or political topic is given by some gentleman who knows his theme, and the discussion which follows is always spirited, and sometimes valuable. The results of experience are certainly always worth careful consideration.

Tuesday evening has been appropriated to working boys. It has had a somewhat unruly record, but is fast reaching the dignity of a young citizens' club. Monday evening is more social and less club like, because we believe the girls who are our guests then need social form rather than parliamentary rule, and relaxation rather than set instruction.

Men, women and children, taken together in their family and neighborhood relation, form the life at Hull House. The time during the day is largely given to children, naturally, as the grown people are occupied.

The kindergarten goes on every morning, and in the various afternoons the older children are taught and entertained to the best of the ability of their teachers and entertainers. One afternoon the Italian children sew, read English, and sing; on another, the school-boys are formed into little clubs which make for order and quiet amusement. The girls are put into kitchen-garden, housekeeping, cooking and sewing classes, and are allowed the range of the house to teach them what it may.[51]

In all this, we have found books of the greatest use. The children have a circulating library of their own, and for the grown people there are other books and the public library, of which Hull House is a station, is accessible to them all.

We also expect a public reading room from the same source to be established in February,[52] and hope then to have the great aid of pictures and other collections when the little art exhibit building,[53] which Mr. Butler[54] is putting up, will be finished. The drawing and model classes will then be transfered there and the nucleus of an art school established. We have faith to believe that the future holds in store for us, somewhere, a little gymnasium, which would bring a much needed element into the life of working boys and girls.[55]

Of all the teaching which goes on at Hull House, the residents themselves have comparatively a small share. There are seventy-five people who come each week, by appointment, to lead, to visit, or to entertain. It would be unfair and impossible to make distinctions among them. The director of the kindergarten,[56] the secretary and promoter of the College Extension Classes,[57] the founder of the little crèche,[58] and many others of them, are members of the Women's Club. The part of the life which a "settlement" hopes to accomplish, and which the residents of Hull House care most for and try hardest to keep simple and affectionate, is that which cannot be written about, and does not occur at set hours and fixed dates. It is also the most enjoyable part. The experiences are sad and amusing, humbling and inspiring, but always genuine and never wearisome.

Hull House needs money for various enterprises, which it hopes to inaugurate and enlarge, it depends day by day upon those who are ready to impart the results of their training and cultivation, but it needs, more than anything else, residents who are willing to devote themselves to the duties of good citizenship and of the awakening of the social energies which lie so largely dormant in every neighborhood given over to Industrialism.

I remember when the Toynbee Hall statement seemed to me very radical, that the salvation of East London was the destruction of West London, but I believe now that there will be no poorer quarters in our cities at all when the conscience of each man is so touched that he prefers to live with the poorest of his brethren and not with the richest of them that his income will allow. It is easy en writing a paper to make all philosophy point one particolar moral and all history adorn one particular tale, but I hope you will forgive me for insisting that the best speculative philosophy sets forth the solidarity of the human race, that the highest moralists have taught that without the advance and improvement of the whole, no man can hope for any lasting improvement in his own moral or material individual condition.

Jane Addams.

Written for the Chicago Woman's Club, 1890.[59]

TMsSr (SCPC, JAC; *JAPM*, 46:480–97). This sixteen-page typescript may have been copied from a JA manuscript, not known to be extant, sometime after the speech was delivered (see also n. 59).

1. JA and EGS were much in demand to present their "scheme" to various groups of men and women, including church leaders, Sunday School classes, and entire congregations, and to groups invited to hear of the new undertaking gathered in private homes often at the

instigation of a hostess intrigued by what she already had heard of the plans. By the time the settlement opened, JA was taking the lead in these presentations. She was the best prepared, because of her visit to Toynbee Hall, to provide evidence of that experiment after which theirs was patterned. And her position as a graduate of the RFS gave her a certain cachet that EGS did not have.

Among the groups JA spoke before was the newly formed Chicago branch of the Assn. of Collegiate Alumnae (which became the Chicago branch of the Assn. of Univ. Women when the organization changed its name in 1921). In May 1890, JA "'gave an exhaustive account of her work'" (Talbot and Rosenberry, *History of the American Assn. of University Women*, 108), probably a version of "Outgrowths of Toynbee Hall." When the group asked how they could help, JA suggested that they offer financial support for one HH resident. In Mar. 1893, Julia C. Lathrop became their first fellow, and she was followed in 1893–94 by Jeannette C. Welch.

2. 7 Dec. [1890], SC, Starr. The paper was never published as presented to the CWC.

3. Frank and Jerome, *Annals, CWC*, 76.

4. The CWC became especially supportive of HH. The club and settlement worked together on a variety of reform efforts, including compulsory education, abolition of child labor and sweatshops, schooling for children in prison and hospital institutions, and manual training programs for public schools. For a number of years and from the founding of the Chicago Public Art Society, organized at HH in 1892 by EGS to put art into the public schools, the CWC provided financial assistance. Helping destitute women, especially those with children, find ways to achieve safe and satisfactory employment and housing was important to both organizations. In addition to assisting Florence Kelley with the HH Women's Labor Bureau, which she organized in 1892, they helped the settlement found a lodging house for women in 1893. Eventually, they assumed full responsibility for a facility located near the settlement at 253 Ewing St. HH and the CWC discovered that the women who earned fifty cents a day sewing in the New Era Building sewing workrooms provided by the CWC also needed lunch and a clean, safe place to sleep. HH provided a nutritious lunch from its Coffee Shop and, for ten cents a night, bath facilities, a clean nightgown, and a clean bed, initially at 186 West Polk St. The program continued into the twentieth century, managed by the Model Workshop and Lodging House Assn., for which JA served as one of the incorporators in 1895. During the month of Nov. 1898, 511 women stayed at the lodging house at 253 Ewing, and for the first time the sewing room was self-supporting (see also Minutes of a HH Residents Meeting, 10 Dec. 1893, n. 12, below).

5. For additional information about Toynbee Hall, London, see especially *PJA*, 2:492–97.

6. By Dec. 1891, in London and the surrounding area, there were fifteen organizations that identified themselves as settlements. Among them were Leighton Hall, Neighborhood Guild (1889), Mansfield House (1890), Mayfield House (1889), Oxford House (1884), Passmore Edwards Settlement (1891), Ruggy House (1890), St. Hilda's East, Cheltenham Ladies' College Settlement (1889), St. Margaret's House, Branch of Oxford House (1890), Trinity College Settlement (1889), Women's University Settlement (1887), and at least five missions. In Bristol, England, there was Broad Plain House (1890); in Edinburgh, Scotland, New College Settlement (1890) and Chalmer's University Settlement (1887); and in Glasgow, Scotland, Students' Settlement (1889), and Toynbee House (1888).

7. JA may have been thinking of at least three efforts. These were the Neighborhood Guild established by Stanton Coit in the lower East Side of New York City in 1886; the College Settlement developed near the Neighborhood Guild in 1889 by graduates of Smith College, Northampton, Mass.; and Andover House, which would become South End House, in Boston, begun in 1891 at the instigation of Prof. William J. Tucker of Andover Theological Seminary, Newton, Mass. In Chicago JA was also aware of the effort by Charles Zueblin and Mr. and Mrs. Clark Tisdale to found Northwestern University Settlement, which opened in Dec. 1891.

8. Between 1881 and 1882, Arnold Toynbee, for whom Toynbee Hall was named, gave three talks, "Wages and Natural Law, "Industry and Democracy," and "Are Radicals Socialists?," in Newcastle, Bradford, Bolton, Chelsea, Leicester, and Sheffield, England. He also presented a talk titled "The Education of Co-operators" at the Cooperative Congress held at Oxford Univ. in May 1882.

9. JA's reference is to "Ode: Intimations of Immortality from Recollections of Early Childhood," the work of one of her favorite poets, William Wordsworth (1770–1850). See *PJA*, 1:268, n. 11.

10. Thomas Henry Huxley (1825–95), English biologist, author, and noted advocate for Charles Darwin's theory of evolution.

11. Walter Besant. For additional information, see *PJA*, 2:625, n. 21.

12. A biblical reference to Acts 10:10–16.

13. Pan was the Greek god of pastures, herds, and herdsmen.

14. The word "the" at the end of the line seems to have been an attempt to typewrite the word "them" that ran off the page. The word "them" appears at the beginning of the next line.

15. Rev. Samuel A. Barnett.

16. A reference to the pamphlet *The Bitter Cry of Outcast London: An Inquiry into the Condition of the Abject Poor*" published in London in 1883. It became one of the major elements in the awakening of the population of England to the plight of the working poor. See *PJA*, 2:215.

17. The *Pall Mall Gazette*, edited and published by journalist William T. Stead, helped spread the message of the *Bitter Cry* to a wider audience by starting a campaign to reveal the conditions the pamphlet described. It began with the *Gazette*'s article "Is It Not Time?" that appeared in the 16 Oct. 1883 edition of the publication. JA was in England when the article appeared. See *PJA*, 2:215.

18. The gathering took place 22 May 1884 in the Guildhall of Cambridge Univ., England, after Rev. Samuel A. Barnett presented the same paper at St. John's College that he had given on 17 Nov. 1883 at Oxford.

19. Sir Michael Foster (1836–1907), English physiologist, associate of Thomas Henry Huxley, and founder of the *Journal of Physiology* and the School of Physiology at Cambridge Univ., England.

20. Rev. Samuel A. Barnett wrote, "The men who settle may either take rooms by themselves, or they may associate themselves in a Settlement. . . . They must not come as 'missioners,' they have come to settle, that is, to learn as much as to teach, to receive as much as to give. There is nothing like contact for giving or getting understanding" (quoted from *The University Review*, 1905, in Barnett, *Canon Barnett*, 1:312).

21. For JA's timely reaction to the occasion, see *PJA*, 2:382.

22. For JA's interest in Positivism see *PJA*, 2:546, 2:550–51, nn. 2–3.

23. George Eliot was one of JA's favorite authors. See *PJA*, 1:302–3, n. 13.

24. The notation "5 ½" appears in JA's hand at the beginning of the next paragraph.

25. JA has inserted a slant line by hand at the end of this sentence.

26. In 1892 Florence Kelley, JA, and other HH supporters associated with the Woman's Alliance headed by Corinne S. Brown drew attention to the inadequate public school facilities and overworked teachers in their neighborhood. According to the report of the alliance, the compulsory school-attendance laws could not reasonably be enforced because there were insufficient seats available for students between the ages of six and fourteen. "There are but nine wards in which the school sittings exceed the number of children and these are the wards where the wealthy live. It shows that in both the Ninth and Fourteenth wards the children exceed the school sittings by more than 4,500; in the Nineteenth and Thirtieth by more than 4,900; in the Fifteenth by more than 5,130 and in the Sixteenth by 7,331. The total excess of children between six and fourteen years in the city over the school sittings

provided for them is 59,878" ("Few Pupils Crowded Out"). The Chicago Board of Education denied the figures, claiming that the student excess was absorbed by private and parochial schools. The alliance responded that there should be a public school seat for each child in the community and charged poor management of the funds allotted for the development of public education in Chicago. JA and her associates at HH continued to wage a battle for more places for students and better schools for their neighbors throughout the 1890s. See also Two Essays in the *Forum*, Nov. and Oct. 1892, n. 99, below.

27. The inserted words are in the hand of JA.

28. The inserted words are in the hand of JA.

29. For information about the development of the university extension movement, see JA to AHHA, 3 June 1890, above.

30. A large right-angle bracket has been marked by JA in the margin of the text between the sentence ending "can do it" and the beginning of the next sentence.

31. Friedrich Froebel.

32. The social university idea developed out of the neighborhood guild in Philadelphia. Stanton Coit associate Morrison I. Swift (1856–1946), connected with the Johns Hopkins Univ. in 1890, took credit for getting it started. He urged a "People's University" in his article "The Working Population of Cities" in the *Andover Review*, issued in June 1890. The American Society for the Extension of University Teaching, organized in Philadelphia in 1890, was also associated with the idea. According to Edward King writing in *Charities Review* 1 (Dec. 1891): 78–79, the people's university had sixty thousand pupils after six months of operation who were taking a wide assortment of classes in science and the humanities.

33. Giuseppe Mazzini (1805–72), Italian patriot, philosopher, and politician who helped create the modern Italian state and promoted the republican idea of democracy, was admired by JHA, who shared his admiration for the leader with his daughter. JA remembered and assumed her father's respect for Mazzini, noting "his wonderful ethical and philosophical appeal to the working men of Italy" and calling it "a tower of great comfort" (*Twenty Years*, 77). Some of the Italian immigrants who lived in the HH neighborhood had been worker-soldiers in Mazzini's efforts and were comforted with the respect that HH and its leaders showed to his memory.

34. Text lined out and inserted by the hand of JA.

35. JA was quoting from Juliana Horatia Gatty Ewing's (1841–85) *Jackanapes*, a children's story of the friendship between two young men and the heroic sacrifice of life by the more able one to save the life of the other. It was originally published in 1878 in *Aunt Judy's Magazine*, but appeared as a book initially in 1883–84.

36. Two hostels were constructed by Toynbee Hall as a living, learning, and socializing space for students and teachers, a place where representatives of all classes could work "together for a better and nobler interpretation of the principles upon which English society must rest" (quoted from Toynbee Hall, *Annual Report*, 1890, 14, in Briggs and Macartney, *Toynbee Hall*, 30). The intent was to provide lodging for students and settlement residents and teachers in an attempt to replicate an important aspect of college life in a university where students and teachers shared the same living space to promote full-time learning and exchange of ideas. The first was opened in 1887 and called Wadham House, in honor of the college Rev. S. A. Barnett had attended at Oxford Univ. The second was opened in 1891 and named Balliol House, for the Oxford college that had the most direct connection with the founding of Toynbee Hall.

37. The Toynbee Travellers' Club was an enthusiastic response to Rev. Samuel A. Barnett's belief in travel as education. See *PJA*, 2:516, n. 160.

38. "Healthy physical exercise will make up for narrow surroundings," proclaimed Rev. Samuel A. Barnett (quoted in Pimlott, *Toynbee Hall*, 78). The courtyard, referred to by the Toynbee Hall residents as the Quadrangle, was paved and was the site for a variety of outdoor

events from flower shows to calisthenics and military drill. Many of the clubs associated with the settlement held their own sporting events.

39. In 1889 English economist and socialist Sidney Webb (1859–1947), still a clerk in the colonial office but destined for fame and in the process of founding the Fabian Society and writing *Socialism in England* (1890), debated Richard Burdon Haldane (1856–1928), lawyer, philosopher, and member of Parliament who in 1890 would become queen's counsel and eventually lord chancellor of Britain, on the efficacy of socialism. Webb represented socialism and Haldane radicalism. Other speakers in 1889 were English historian Samuel Rawson Gardiner (1829–1902); Edward Fry (1827–1918) of the Court of Appeals; Sydney Charles Buxton (1853–1934), who in 1890 would become undersecretary for the British colonies and eventually president of the Board of Trade; journalist, biographer, and novelist Edward Harold Spender (1864–1926); labor leaders Tom Mann (1856–1941) and Benjamin Tillett (1860–1943); statesman Herbert Henry Asquith (1852–1928), Liberal member of Parliament who within the next two years would become British home secretary; and Alexander Hugh Balfour of Burleigh (1849–1921), who in 1895 would become secretary for Scotland in the British cabinet.

40. See n. 36.

41. English painter Edward Coley Burne-Jones. See *PJA*, 2:517, n. 171.

42. George Frederic Watts (1817–1904), English painter and sculptor, noted for his portraits of famous contemporaries, among them Garibaldi, Gladstone, and Tennyson. By 1890 he had gained fame as an artist.

43. For information on the People's Palace, London, see *PJA*, 2:624, n. 19.

44. In the first issue of *Charities Review*, E. T. Potter's article titled "A Study of Some New York Tenement-House Problems" described New York tenements that took up almost the entire area of the usual 25 ft. x 100 ft. lot with the only windows for ventilation at either 25-ft. end as "squalid and repellent; dirty without, and dirty, dark, and unventilated within" (129); overcrowded, with only communal toilets for each floor; having no planned access to heat; and having running water that was likely only in the small backyard.

JA and EGS were eager for better housing for their neighbors and throughout the 1890s sought ways to create model housing projects. EGS wrote to her sister with hope: "I went to S. Clark St. this morning to show tenement houses there to a youth of wealth who is inspired by the Holy Ghost to build model tenement houses. I don't mean that he professes this inspiration, but the source is undoubtedly no less. He is a callow youth in some respects, being I should judge, not more than twenty-three or four years old, but a very serious & sensible one. Mr. Pond says his father is rich, & that he himself commands money. He had been to London to investigate the model ones, but he has evidently seen little of the worst ones; he was very much shocked by their condition. We inspected water closets (so called) together, discussed them & disreputable parts of the city with freedom. People aren't as coy as they used to be. They seem to be coming to the conclusion that if things aren't fit to be spoke of when necessary, they aren't fit to exist. This young man, Mr. Springer, is going to consult some capitalists about forming a company for the erection of model tenements, keeping the average rent what it is now, & giving good quarters & the conveniences of civilization for it. It has been found that these tenements yield a reasonable income, three, four & five percent.

"Mr. Springer's idea in his first enthusiasm was to give quarters free of rent, but he very reasonably concluded that it was better for people to pay a right & reasonable rent for their lodging. As things stand now the people who own these wretched tenements get 14 & 15 percent on their money. If he (Mr. S.), can't get any capitalists to go into this model philanthropy consisting of simple justice, he will at least put up a tenement himself. When one considers that he is young, & already thus illuminated his future career seem very promising" (EGS to Mary Houghton Starr Blaisdell, 18 May 1890, SC, Starr). George Ward Springer (1868–1947?) was newly graduated from Northwestern Univ. (B.S. 1890) and was helping with the management of an extensive estate. A son of Milton Cushing and Mary Elizabeth Ward Springer, he later was in real estate business for himself and was also associated with two insurance companies. There is no evidence that he built a model tenement in association with HH.

Among additional efforts to address neighborhood housing issues during the 1889–99 period were the creation of a model lodging house for women (see JA to Henry Demarest Lloyd, 2 Jan. 1892 [1893], n. 2; JA to Emily Greene Balch, 11 May 1893, n. 3; and Minutes of a HH Residents Meeting, 10 Dec. 1893, n. 12, all below), and the Jane Club facilities (see Article in the *Chicago Inter Ocean*, July 1892, below). In 1902 JA, with the help of Louise de Koven Bowen, constructed a twelve-apartment complex at the corner of Ewing and Halsted streets. JA was also a leader in helping to develop the City Homes Assn., which focused its energies on improving housing stock in Chicago (see JA to MRS, 18 June 1900, nn. 8–11, below).

45. In recognition of this, JA and EGS actively encouraged Italian immigrants from their neighborhood to join Alessandro Mastro-Valerio in one of the two agricultural colonies he was trying to establish in Alabama. See JA to MCAL, 13 Mar. 1889, n. 5, above.

46. Giuseppe Garibaldi (1807–82), Italian patriot and associate of Giuseppe Mazzini in efforts to unite Italy into one kingdom, was the leader of the famous thousand-strong Redshirts who attacked and successfully defeated Sicily and achieved its union with Sardinia. In 1874 he was elected deputy for Rome in the Italian parliament.

47. The war hymn is said to have been written for the Garibaldi Redshirts by a little-known Italian named Mercantini and often sung by patriots and soldiers of the effort to unite Italy. It is known by various names, including "Hymn of the Italians" and "Italia una." Its opening lines are "Va fuori d'Italia, Va fuori, o stainier!" (Baring, *Political and Literary Essays, 1903–1913*, 467).

48. A derogative term for a person of Italian descent. See also JA to AHHA, 9 Dec. 1890, n. 7, below. The derivation suggested in "Comments on the Wage-Map" in *HH Maps and Papers*, 21, is that the "nickname, 'Dago,'" is "from his characteristic occupation of digging" on railroad construction.

49. In 1890 JA and EGS added bath facilities that could be used by their neighbors. See JA to Helen Culver, 7 Mar. 1890, n. 3, above.

50. Emma Neuschäffer. See JA to SAAH, 23 Nov. 1889, nn. 9–10, above.

51. A right-angle mark appears in the left margin in the hand of JA at the beginning of the next paragraph.

52. The Chicago Public Library did establish and staff a branch library at HH on the ground floor of the Butler Art Gallery Building. See EGS [for JA] to Susan Childs Starr and Caleb Allen Starr [and SAAH], 15, [16–20?] Nov. [1889], n. 13, above.

53. By Dec. 1890, work on what would become the Butler Art Gallery Building was under way. For a description of the building and the opening ceremonies, see Addams, "Diary, 1889–90," 5 and 8 Oct. 1890, n. 4, above; JA to MRS, [12?] [Apr. 1891], n. 1; and Article in the *Chicago Inter Ocean*, 21 June 1891, both below.

54. Edward B. Butler.

55. JA was not able to take over the saloon building south of HH until late in 1891. See JA to SAAH, [ca. 6] [Sept. 1891], n. 5, below.

56. Jenny Dow.

57. Alice Miller.

58. MRS.

59. On a separate sheet of paper and at a later date, JA added the following note by hand: "'Outgrowth of Toynbee Hall' as read at the Chicago Woman's Club in 1890. J.A." (ANI, n.d., SCPC, JAC; *JAPM*, 46:497).

## To Anna Hostetter Haldeman Addams

*It is likely that while Alice and Marcet were visiting in Illinois during Thanksgiving, Anna Addams joined them for her first visit with Jane and Ellen at Hull-House.*[1] *Jane was not in the habit of sending greetings to her stepmother from friends or residents of the settlement whom Anna had not met. This is the earliest extant letter written by Jane from Hull-House to Anna Addams in which Jane sends greetings from someone associated with the settlement other than Ellen. Anna knew Ellen from Rockford Female Seminary days and visits she made to Jane at Cedarville.*

335 South Halsted Street. [Chicago, Ill.] Dec 9" 1890

My dear Mama

Your kind letter came last week[2]—I have been writing a paper for the Woman's Club[3] which seems to have taken up every minute of my spare time, and which I am very glad to have off my mind.

I am so glad that the furnace is in, and proving satisfactory. I can well imagine that the house is quiet without dear Marcet. I have had but one letter from Alice since her return,[4] that was full of her quaint little doings.

We are quietly getting ready for Christmas, we hope to have each club celebrate in a festive little way, without having anything very elaborate at any one time. Miss Dow is already beginning with the little children and their Christmas songs are sounding in my ears now.

If I am able to get off for one or two days at Christmas,[5] I shall come to Cedarville but it is hard to tell until the last minute whether it will be possible or not. Please give my love to George I want very much to see him. Ellen sends you her love and so does Miss Farnsworth,[6] who continues to be a cheerful resident, and does her duty bravely.

We had a short visit from Miss Anderson last week, and expect her in for part of her Christmas vacation. She is devoted to one of the little Italian boys and we predict that she will finally adopt him[.][7] I saw Mrs Gulick[8] whom I visited in Spain, yesterday. She is recovering from an operation at St Luke's Hospital and looks so much better than she did when I saw her. Surgery can work marvels, as Dr Dudley[9] remarked yesterday. Hoping to see George and yourself soon I am ever your loving daughter

Jane Addams.

ALS (UIC, JAMC; *JAPM*, 2:1218–19).

1. JA suggested a second visit to AHHA in her letter of 28 Dec. 1891, below.
2. The letter from AHHA is not known to be extant.
3. See Address for the Chicago Woman's Club, 3 Dec. 1890, above.
4. SAAH's letter is not known to be extant.
5. On activities during the second Christmas at HH, see JA to MRS, 19 Dec. 1890, below.
6. Anna M. Farnsworth (1862–post 1921) came to HH as a resident in Nov. 1890 and re-

Ellen Gates Starr, photographed near the entrance to Hull-House with Halsted Street in the background, ca. 1891. The child in her arms may have been the child she later identified as her favorite, Francesco [De Guido]. See also Jane Addams to Anna Hostetter Haldeman Addams, 3 June 1890, n. 11 (UIC, JAMC, 0286 3570).

mained until at least the summer of 1893. She was born in Oconto, Wis., one of four children of Diantha Wilson Farnsworth (1827–69) and George Farnsworth (1825–1913), a lumberman, and had attended Chicago's Dearborn Seminary. Farnsworth's second wife, with whom Anna did not get along, was Jane Worthington Smith (1829–1921), daughter of Mary Ann and Worthington Smith, former president of the Univ. of Vermont, Burlington, 1849–55. By the 1880s, the Farnsworth family had settled in a home in Chicago's Near North Side in the 1400 block of Astor St.

Anna Farnsworth made quite an impression on EGS, who wrote extensively about her to cousin Mary Allen: "Miss Farnsworth, our droll little society-girl resident . . . is very entertaining. Our first impression, that she came on account of some experience of her heart, was entirely off the track. Her experiences of that nature seem to have been manifold, & to set very lightly upon her. She highly disapproves the wedded state, & 'overpopulation' is her hobby. I suggested one day, in the course of conversation, that I thought the Lord intended married people to have children. In a very confidential manner peculiar to her, she said 'I don't believe he intends it as much as he did. I think he is giving people a change of heart about that. He probably sees that there's over-population!'

"You may be surprised to hear that she is a good resident. She is useful in the household—makes her bed, wipes the dishes & sweeps if there is any stress of occasion, teaches little Italians, visits in the neighborhood, hobnobs delightfully & intimately with young & old, men & women, without the least indication of patronage, &, I believe, without feeling any. (It is my conviction that no amount of good manners will conceal the feeling when it exists.) She doesn't like to go to the very sick, & when there is nothing going on, as on Sunday P.M. & evening, I have the feeling that she is lonely & bored; —that she has no special inward resources, but she seems disinclined to go to the north side to her old haunts; —goes as seldom as possible, & only on errands. She likes her compatriots to come over here to see her, but she seems to have renounced 'society' for the time being.

... "She ... is never in the way when you don't want her, & always on hand when you do: she is perfectly accommodating, & not in the least exacting, & 'catches on' perfectly to the ways of the house. She pays her board, but will always share her room or give it up without a tinge of annoyance, & we have never caught her saying an indiscreet thing to either a neighbor or a visitor. She wants to stay all winter & we want her to. If her father will let her have her board she will, & we may invite her to stay after he stops. He didn't like her coming. She & her step-mother don't 'get on.' ... I suppose the poor little thing never knew before what it was to want money. She had to spend most of what she had the first thing for a suitable dress, as the plainest one she owned wouldn't do at all to go about in, being a beautiful reddish brown broad cloth, trim[m]ed with <narrow> lines of sealskin & having a white broad cloth vest with gilt buttons & clasps across! She has asked all her friends not to give her presents at Christmas, but money to give away" (7 Dec. [1890], SC, Starr).

Anna Farnsworth was put in charge of the library at HH beginning in Jan. 1891 and conducted a Fairy Story Club on Tuesday afternoons in the HH second-floor hall. She continued to meet this club into 1893. By 1892 she was in charge of the HH Athletic Club of thirty girls, ages fourteen to sixteen. She was the first director of the Penny Provident Bank, which JA opened at the settlement in 1890 to offer neighbors a chance to save money safely and in small increments. Savers could exchange money for stamps placed on cards. The stamps were redeemable for money any time the bank was open. Contrary to the opinion of marriage she shared with EGS in 1890, she finally chose to be married. On 5 Feb. 1895, she became the wife of William A. Hay (1837?–1902), approximately twenty-five years her senior. They made their home in Montreal and New York City. By 1921 Anna Hay was a resident in Castine, Maine.

7. EGS and SA had their eye on the same child. His name was Francesco [De Guido]. EGS wrote to her cousin Mary Allen, ""I love Francesco better than any child in the world. I would like to own him if I could make enough money to buy his clothes & food. Miss Anderson wants him, too. She asked Jane if she though she could get on nicely with him at the seminary. Jane said she thought she could now, but 'if he should grow big & Horrid'—Miss A. says she doesn't see how he can grow horrid, & I certainly don't, unless he is made horrible, by other people.—We omit the small circumstance that his parents probably want him themselves. I wanted to take him home at Christmas time, but Mamma isn't anxious to receive him" (7 Dec. [1890], SC, Starr). Neither EGS nor SA adopted a HH neighborhood child.

"Mr. & Mrs. Sharkey & Mrs. & Mrs. Miller, ... are very nice people," EGS reported to her sister Mary Blaisdell. "Their children are always sweetly dressed & taken care of, & they never put on airs over the others but are always appreciative & thankful for the kg. A German parent came one morning, & demanded the removal of all the 'Italianische kinder' on account of their being so dirty, & having bugs. She explained this to us, & said that if she were in our place she wouldn't let any of them stay; that they were all that way. So we are grateful to the Sharkeys & Millers for their spirit of tolerance" (19 [and 21] Dec. [1890], SC, Starr).

EGS was also distressed by the reaction to Italian immigrants presented in the press. "Do you read the Popular Science Monthly?" she asked her cousin Mary Allen. "If so, did you read an article entitled 'What shall we do with the Dago?' It made me very mad & I answered it. After they reject it I shall send it to The Dawn which I think will take it" (7 Dec. [1890], SC, Starr). The article appeared in the Dec. 1890 issue of the popular magazine on pp. 172–79. EGS's response did not appear in *Popular Science Monthly*, which carried only one response, and that was from W. H. Larrabee in its Feb. 1891 issue on pp. 149–55, or in the

*Dawn*, a monthly magazine created and published by William D. P. Bliss as the periodical of the Society of Christian Socialists he organized in 1889.

8. JA originally met Alice Gordon Gulick in San Sebastián, Spain, in 1888, where she directed a school for girls. See *PJA*, 2:617, n. 4 .

9. Dr. Emilius C. Dudley.

## To Mary Rozet Smith

*By early December 1890, preparations for the second Christmas celebration at Hull-House were in full swing. Just before Christmas Day, as Ellen prepared to leave the city for two weeks with her family in Durand, Ill.,[1] she described the anticipated swirl of activity. "This week is mostly <be> filled with dressings & undressings & re-dressings of the festive Christmas tree. Tomorrow we have it three times; first for the kindergarten at 10 A.M. then at 3.30 P.M. for the Italian girls who come for sewing & calisthenics, & in the evening for the shop girls etc. who always come Monday evening. . . . Tuesday we have two festivities, P.M. & evening. Friday two, & Sat. one,—eight in all. In most cases we shall only give the children candy & other things to eat, & have singing &c, but the Italian children are all to have a present. The teachers of the various circles wanted to do it, & we let them. People really are growing fond of the Italians. Mary Smith is going to give her infants a tea-party in the kitchen. She always has them there. Many are very small beings—Italian beings—& they look too cunning for words, sitting around a kg. table, & making extraordinary things. All the Italian children, great & small, have made Christmas presents for their parents. The ones who sew have made aprons for their mothers—bright red, with white figures in them, & the littler ones kerchiefs, of a pretty stuff. There was a base disposition on the part of some to keep them for themselves, but I think we have persuaded them of the unholiness of that. I don't feel entitled, personally, to say much to them under that head. I did say that if I* had *made an apron for my mother I should consider it cheating her & very mean not to give it to her. The smallest Friday girls (not Italians) have made marvellous things—picture books, which they have been pasting for weeks under the direction of Mary Rozet, also needle books for their mothers, & handkerchiefs for their fathers. Mary took all the hkfs home, marked them with an initial in, ink, & washed & ironed them. Some of the girls made their picture books up, with covers, & their needle books, pin-cushions & things." And she went on to explain one difficult set of arrangements, "We have been having a desperate season over two invitations for children to go into the country. One lady wanted 25 children for Christmas* day, *& seemed to incline to Italians. I soon found that the parents didn't want to let their children go away on Christmas, & asked the hostess to change to the day after, but she wouldn't, & it ended in all the parents who had accepted withdrawing, & our scratching round to get some non-Italian children of the same age size & sex,—matching them, in fact, to fit into the list* *sent so that the rainment bought for the first list will do for the second. I feel like saying 'Diavolo!' several times. People will have to learn that the poor sometimes have the same parental feelings that they have."*[2]

Hull House [Chicago, Ill.] Dec 19" 1890

My dear Miss Smith

The little children were so happy over the presents they took home to day,—as indeed they ought to be. The little needle books were very stary and pretty and they went away in the highest good humor. It is more the Christmas spirit that we hoped the house would stand for, than anything that had been done.

The crêche is flourishing, application has been made for a baby of the tender age of seven weeks and we are all cheered, last Saturday there were fourteen children. There was no haste about the money, as Mrs Coonley and Mrs Wilmarth have paid for this month.[3]

We are both so sorry that you are ill, and are coming to call on you if such a thing is possible. Don't come over until you are well enough to make it safe, I have a great fear of your being whisked off to California if you don't improve. It would make a great difference to me whether you were in the city or out of it.

~~Mamie~~ <Susie> Doughterty said the other day "I am going to have the best Christmas this year!" On being asked what was going to happen She said, "I am going to give my father a handkerchief and ~~Susie~~ <Mamie> a scrapbook" upon mature reflection she added "Its all Miss Smith." I feel like echoing the sentiment in regard to several things that are going on. The bags[4] are approaching completion and all goes merrily towards Xmas.

The entire household sends its love to you. Always affectionately yours

Jane Addams

ALS (SCPC, JAC; *JAPM*, 2:1222–24).

1. "Miss Starr is going home for New Years and the week before and after. She combines the trip with some lectures at Rockford" (JA to JWA, 21 Dec. 1890, SCPC, JAC; *JAPM*, 2:1225–26). EGS left Chicago 30 Dec. 1890 and gave her first Rockford lecture on 8 Jan. 1891.

2. EGS to Mary Houghton Starr Blaisdell, 17 [and 21] Dec. [1890], SC, Starr.

3. There is no extant detailed accounting of individuals who supported the Crêche from Oct. 1890 to Sept. 1891, when the total income and expenses for that program were $1,053.50. By Oct. 1891, entries in JA's hand in the account book titled "HH Acc't Oct 1st 1891" reveal that among the most regular supporters of the Crêche were MRS, who gave at least $25 monthly, and Mary Wilmarth and Lydia Avery Coonley, each of whom gave at least $10 monthly. In addition, various members of the families of all three women also supported the Crêche, as did the Bradner-Smith Co. All of the gifts paid for the Crêche rent, insurance, heat, light, laundry, milk and food, and salaries for at least two nurses.

4. "We bought 200 lbs of candy for $15. Good candy, too, but broken" (EGS to Mary Houghton Starr Blaisdell 17 [and 21] Dec. [1890], SC, Starr).

The first dining room at Hull-House was located in the northwest corner of the main floor of the house. This photograph was taken in 1891, and Jane Addams sent it to her sister Sarah Alice Addams Haldeman, who recorded that she received it in March 1891 (private collection).

The first theatrical stage at the settlement was located in the north wall of the Hull home and on the first floor. It stood between the dining area and the entry parlor on the northeast side of the house. A corner of the dining table is visible in the left lower corner of the photograph. It is likely that this photograph was taken in 1893 (Residents of HH, *HH Maps and Papers*, 1st ed., opposite 218; 2nd ed., 168).

The back southeast parlor known as the Hull-House library, ca. 1893 (Residents of HH, *HH Maps and Papers*, 1st ed., opposite 208; 2nd ed., 153).

The front southeast parlor of Hull-House in 1891. Through double sliding doors was another parlor identified as the Hull-House library (private collection).

## To George Bowman Haldeman

335 So Halsted St [Chicago, Ill.] Dec 21" 1890

My dear George

Amidst the preparations for Christmas that have so occupied the week, I have been quite homesick for Cedarville and have thought of you all, a great deal of the time. I hope very much that the day will bring to you peace and comfort, as indeed thoughts on the birth of Christ ought to bring to us all.

We have seen a great deal of suffering and want this winter and the comfort of Christ's mission to the world—the need of the Messiah to the race, has been impressed upon me as never before. It seems some times as if the race life, at least the dark side would be quite unendurable if it were not for that central fact.

It has been so long since I have had a long talk with you that I do not know upon what your mind is running, but I remember a Christmas morning in Baltimore, when you said some thing of the kind, when it did not seem comprehensible to me.

I have always hoped that some time you would see the house here and what we are trying to do and represent to the neighborhood. It is not to stem the poverty nor to give them merely social pleasure, but to fortify people, who need fortitude above all others, with the best that we can procure for them. It is curious to see the helpful and warm friendships that are formed between people so diverse in circumstance and yet really alike in feeling, it is the opportunity given to both classes to form these ties, that we care most for. But this opportunity has to be given in the midst of social feeling and goodwill[.] I hope we never forget however that the entertainment is but a means.

I send a box of bon bons to Mama which I hope you will both enjoy. They represent but poorly the Christmas feeling I would send with them.[1] Please extend the Christmas greeting to Harry if he is in Cedarville, and believe me always your loving sister

Jane Addams.

ALS (JAPP, DeLoach; *JAPM*, 2:1227–29).

1. JA had sent a similar gift and apologia to her brother, JWA, and his family. "I sent a box of candy to Laura and yourself which represent my good wishes for a Merry Christmas and all the other good wishes for the season. I am sorry that they are not more adequately represented, but prudence suggests nay even necessity demands, that bon bons be my present this year" (21 Dec. 1890, SCPC, JAC; *JAPM*, 2:1225). JA also encouraged JWA and LSA to visit the settlement.

## To Mary Rozet Smith

Hull-House. [Chicago, Ill.] Feb. 3d 1891

My dear friend

The night-gown was easily identified by means of the enfolded shirt and I return it with the mingled feelings of a successful hunter and a sorrowing friend. I am mortified that I did not thank your father on Sunday[1] for the paper he so kindly gave for the programs. Please tell him that we are very much obliged, and not so indifferent to the kindness of our friends as we appear. I hope you will have a delightful winter. I am sure you know that we will miss you, not only for what you do, but for the interest and friendship which has come to mean a great deal to me.

Miss Starr and Miss Farnsworth send their love with many genuine expressions of regret and compliment which I will not repeat. Always Yours affectionately

Jane Addams

ALS (SCPC, JAC; *JAPM*, 2:1231–33).

1. 1 Feb. 1891. None of the extant printed program materials for HH during Jan. or early Feb. 1891 lists Charles Mather Smith as a speaker at the settlement. He is not listed as a presenter in the regular Thursday-Evening Lectures series or in the equally regular Working People's Social Science Club evenings. JA and EGS did not regularly schedule Sunday events at HH until later in 1891. Records of Sunday programming at the settlement for this period are scant.

## To Lorado Taft

Hull-House. 335 So Halsted St [Chicago, Ill.] Feb. 3d 1891

Mr dear Mr Taft[1]

You are very kind indeed to offer us the lectures. My delay in writing is because I waited to consult Miss Miller[2] as to times &c, she is rather at the head of the "College Extension" work before the students of which the lectures would be given.

As you will see by the inclosed program,[3] Thursday is the only evening we reserve for <literary> lectures, and the course is filled until March nineteenth.

May we not put you down for two in the next course, and also arrange for "Paris from a Mansard"[4] to be given in French during the spring vacation of the College Extension ~~course~~ <work>. We were obliged to give up our regular French evening[5] because we needed the room for other projects but we have always regretted the necessity and are grateful for an occasion which we[6] help us keep ~~on~~ a hold on our French friends until we arrange for their regular evening again—

Thanking you very much for your kindness and hoping we will have the pleasure of seeing you here soon I am very sincerely yours

Jane Addams

ALS (CHM, CHS, Taft; *JAPM*, 2:1234–35).

1. Lorado Taft (1860–1936), American sculptor of renown associated especially with Chicago and the Midwest, was born in Elmwood, Ill., to high school teacher turned professor of geology and zoology at the Univ. of Illinois, Champaign, Don Carlos Taft and his wife, Mary Lucy Foster Taft. Taft was educated in local schools and received his bachelor's degree (1879) and master's degree (1880) from the Univ. of Illinois. Between 1880 and 1883, he studied art at the École des Beaux-Arts in Paris and became a devotee of the McAll Mission program (see *PJA*, 2:225, n. 133). On his return to the United States, he settled in Chicago, established a studio and by 1886 was an instructor at the Art Institute, where he held classes until 1907. While teaching he began to establish himself as a sculptor of note and sought public commissions. His first important commission was for the Horticultural Building at the World's Columbian Exposition in 1893, where he created two sculptural groups for the entrance. He was dedicated to beautification of public space. He taught, wrote about, and promoted his ideal and sought commissions to enhance the urban landscape of Chicago. Throughout his life, he won many awards for his sculptures, two of the most famous of which are the one-hundred-ft. *Fountain of Time* associated with the campus of the Univ. of Chicago and the *Fountain of the Great Lakes* in the Art Institute of Chicago.

When Taft first sought out JA and HH, he was thirty years old and in the process of establishing himself in Chicago. During 1891 and 1892, he presented a number of lectures at HH in the Thursday Lectures and Concerts series associated with the settlement's College Extension Program and for the Sunday Lectures and Concerts series. He and his assistants, first Charles Mulligan and then Julia Brachen, taught modeling in the art program at HH. They held three twelve-week courses beginning in the fall of 1891 and continuing until the summer of 1892. By 1894 Taft had become a teacher and lecturer for the Univ. of Chicago extension program, but he returned to lecture on American sculpture at HH on Sunday evening, 22 Nov. 1903.

Taft married twice. His first wife, Carrie Scales Taft, died in 1892, after only two years of marriage, and in 1896 he married Ada Bartlett (1870?–1950), with whom he had three daughters. Taft was active in a number of Chicago cultural and reform organizations, including in the 1890s the Chicago Literary Club and the Wise Diners, a club that counted the Pond brothers, who designed Taft's South Side studio, among their members. He was also an active member of the Chicago Arts Club, the Congregational Club, and the Chicago Archaeological Society.

2. Alice M. Miller, who had been a settlement volunteer almost from the beginning in 1889, was in charge of the College Extension Program.

3. The enclosure was the flyer "HH . . . Weekly Programme of Lectures Clubs Classes, Etc. January 1891," announcing the weekly lectures 15 Jan. through 19 Mar. 189l. See HH Scrapbook 2:5; *JAPM*, Addendum 10:7ff.

4. Lorado Taft gave this illustrated lecture in the Thursday Lectures and Concerts series on 16 Apr. 1891. See HH Scrapbook 2:4; *JAPM*, Addendum 10:7ff.

5. Newspaper accounts indicate that the French evening was still being held into the summer of 1890. It is likely that regular French evenings were given up during the fall of 1890.

6. JA may have meant to write "would" instead of "we."

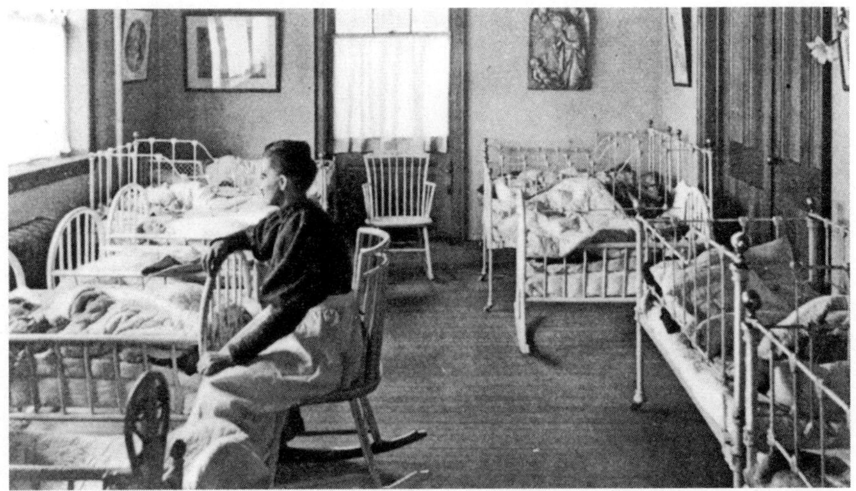

In the spring of 1891, Jane Addams rented two cottages from Helen Culver at 221 Ewing Street, near the south side of the Hull home. One served as the Diet Kitchen for cooking classes and education in sickroom food preparation. The other became the Hull-House Crêche. This photograph of one of the four rooms in the Crêche Cottage was taken prior to July 1892, when a rendering based on the photograph appeared on page 10 in *Scribner's Magazine.* (UIC, JAMC 0223 0377).

## To Mary Rozet Smith

*For Jane Addams, the late winter into spring of 1891 was filled with a search for more space in which to locate expanding Hull-House programs. Jane wanted a gymnasium, was trying to locate a suitable structure in which to resettle the Crêche, and hoping to start construction on a new settlement art gallery/library building funded by Edward B. Butler.*[1] *Helen Culver owned the property that surrounded the settlement and Jane and her supporters had been forced to negotiate with her for part of it. By late winter, Helen Culver relented and made land available for the Butler Art Gallery Building. In addition, by March 1891, Jane was able to rent two small cottages that shared the lot at 221 Ewing St. Both cottages, owned by Helen Culver, backed up to the south side of the original Hull-House building. The front cottage became the sought-after Crêche for babies several months to five years old. The smaller cottage at the back of the lot became the Hull-House Diet Kitchen.*[2] *The gymnasium would have to wait.*[3]

Hull House 335 So Halsted St Chicago—[Ill.] [12?] [Apr. 1891][4]

My dear friend

I have been literally home sick for you[5] ever since last Wednesday when we took possession of the cottage for the creche.[6] It needs a great deal of repairing but has the future of a charming dove cote if you were only here to help plan it out. We have secured, you know, one of Miss Culver's cottages, it fronts on Ewing and the back door almost opens into our back yard. Miss C. does the plumbing, we do the carpenter work, Miss C. furnishes the paper and we put it on with which business arrangment we try hard to remain content. We have torn down two partitions and made a beautifully large play room.[7] One side of it is occupied by a lounge 1 1/2 feet high, about ten long and three wide.[8] Upon this the children can roll and lie side by side when they want to sleep. I went to visit the creche on Friday.[9] There were sixteen children, two were sleeping in the cribs, two on chairs and five were profoundly slumbering on the floor. The vision of a lounge sufficiently ample for the five flashed upon me. A great many more things would flash if you were here to help talk about it and do it, and I positively long for June. I am going out to Rockford next Thursday to make the final arrangements in regard to the summer school.[10] I do hope that you can come and take your friend with you. I should like one young lady (excuse the false social distinction, a remnent of former prejudice) to at least every ten girls.

The new building is up to the top of the piazza. I send you a cut which Mr Pond made in a moment of sportiveness.[11] Some one suggested that the bow-legged boy would never be allowed to stand by the gate post but would be immediately shipped into the Maurice Porter Hospital. The little French B[ertie?]is there now and will soon die I fear. Our relations with the French on Blue Island Avenue have opened again in rather a peculiar fashion. Mr. Langois is a lover of Ida, and sweet pretty girl whom we now have in the house because we don't know exactly what to do with her. Her tale is interesting but too long for a letter.

I took a little trip this spring to visit my sister in Southern Kansas[12] I have returned feeling very ~~fell~~ <well> indeed dear Miss Starr and Miss Farnsworth are both less "chipper." We have another resident whom we hope to have room in the creche cottage.[13] She frankly acknowledges that she is "self centered", no one disputes her but I pity her from the bottom of my heart. If the children can't help her nothing human can. The house hold have all gone to church this morning save myself who am on guard over the piles of bricks, the wheel barrows &c which ornament the front yard and piazza. I have torn out so many times to remonstrate with our small neighbors, that it is now time to set the table for dinner and bring this epistle to a close. I am ashamed not to have written before and many times. I am sure you know it is not from lack of affection nor sense of loss. I can think of no one save possibly Alice Miller, whose absence from the city we would feel so much as yours. Please give my kindliest regards to your father and mother and believe me always sincerely your friend

Jane Addams.

ALS (SCPC, JAC; *JAPM*, 2:1357–60).

1. "The new Art building hasn't been begun yet," wrote EGS to her cousin Mary Allen. "The whole first floor is to be devoted to a reading room of the public library, furnished by that institution with books & periodicals & two men to take care of it. The second story will be devoted to the arts. The gymnasium has unavoidably been crowded out. Mr. Pond wants us to build one in the back yard while the other building is going up. We have a good deal of room out there, & he says he can put up one long, low building, one room only, for $1500 or $2000. As Mr. Butler not only builds the other building but, we hear proposes to pay for running it also (lighting, heating &c) we are out of that responsibility, & think of getting subscriptions for the gymnasium, which will also be used, probably for a kindergarten for the creche children (separate from the one in the house) & certainly for dramatic performances, concerts &c, for which our drawing-room is now much too small. Mrs. Coonly has bought a small pipe organ, which she says she will lend us for a year & a half, for organ recitals" (7 Dec. 1890, SC, Starr). See also Addams, "Diary, 1889–90," 5; and 8 Oct. 1890, nn. 3–4, 9, above.

2. See JA to SAAH, [ca. 6] [Sept. 1891], n. 6, below.

3. See JA to SAAH, [ca. 6] [Sept. 1891], n. 5, below.

4. The *Freeport (Ill.) Daily Democrat*, 18 Apr. 1891, cited in Barrett and Keister, *History of Stephenson County*, 354, indicated that JA had given a talk on Toynbee Hall in Freeport as part of a lecture tour that included Elgin, Geneva, and Rockford. Since JA wrote this letter on Sunday, announcing her visit to RS, the editors have dated the letter [12?] [Apr. 1891].

5. JA wrote to MRS on 14 Feb. 1891 to announce that she and EGS could not come to see her as they had planned. "We are both extremely sorry, you don't <u>know</u> how badly we feel about your going away!" (SCPC, JAC; *JAPM*, 2:1237).

6. It is likely that they took possession of what became the Crêche Cottage on Wednesday, 8 Apr. 1891. Rent payments were twenty-five dollars a month.

7. "We have been very busy this week moving our day nursery into a new cottage. The rooms are painted in babyish hues of pink and blue, and are very attractive" (JA to AHHA, 14 May 1891, UIC, JAMC; *JAPM*, 2:1243–44).

8. In the *Chicago Post* article entitled "HH Bureau" and dated 23 Jan. 1892, there is a drawing of the lounge as JA envisioned it.

9. Before JA was able to rent the cottage from Helen Culver, she established the Crêche in an apartment to the north of HH at 326 (later 745) South Halsted St. This facility was open daily except Sunday. JA may have visited the Crêche facility on 10 Apr. 1891.

10. JA went to RS on 16 Apr. 1891 to consult with SA, the new principal of the school, about the HH Summer School she wanted to hold there for a month during the summer. Toynbee Hall had established a similar summer school program for students of its classes and lectures so that they might experience the give-and-take of intellectual life in an academic setting. JA also believed that getting away from the unpleasant and unhealthy environment that many of her neighbors experienced on a daily basis would be helpful. On the HH Summer School program, see JA to SA, [12?] [Aug. 1891], below. While JA was at the school, she also presented a lecture, "Outgrowths of Toynbee Hall," likely a version of her speech to the CWC, 3 Dec. 1890. See Address for the Chicago Woman's Club, 3 Dec. 1890, above.

11. The Butler Art Gallery Building, being designed by and constructed under the direction of the Pond brothers, was progressing. The structure had reached the level of the porch roof of the Hull home. It was likely Irving K. Pond who produced the sketch of the structure

as it would look when complete that JA sent to MRS. A drawing by Irving K. Pond of the completed Butler Gallery in situ appeared in the Mar. 1891 *Inland Architect and News Record* (HH Scrapbook 2:11½; *JAPM*, Addendum 10:7ff). Similar but simpler line drawings appeared in Chicago newspapers about the time the Butler Art Gallery Building was officially opened. See especially *Chicago Daily Tribune*, 31 May 1891, for the illustration in the article entitled "In the Butler Gallery." See also Addams, "Diary, 1889–90," 5 and 8 Oct. 1890, n. 4, above.

12. JA may have visited her sister SAAH and her family in Girard, Kans., during Easter week, which in 1891 was the last week of Mar., with Easter Sunday on 29 Mar.

13. Wilfreda (or Wilfreida) ("Willie") Brockway (b. 1872) was born in Texas and probably came to Chicago with her family. At age nineteen, she began coming to HH as an assistant for Jenny Dow in the kindergarten. She first appeared in the HH rolls as a helper there in Jan. 1891, earning thirty dollars a month. By Apr. 1892, she had become a resident of the settlement and was earning forty dollars a month as the director of the Crêche kindergarten program. Her monthly stipend was fifty dollars in 1894, of which she owed twenty for board at the settlement. In 1893, when the HH residents created their committee structure, she was placed in charge of the kindergarten committee. Between 1894 and 1898, she assumed a number of additional settlement responsibilities. She was a visitor and kindergarten teacher for sick neighborhood children until 1898. From 1895 to 1897, she directed the Oriental Club and from 1896 to 1897 the Alcott Club. During 1897 and 1898, she operated the Penny Provident Bank. She was a charter member of the HH Woman's Club, founded in 1891, and remained active in it until the early part of the twentieth century.

After JA's nephew John Addams Linn graduated from Lake Forest Univ. and came to live and work at HH in 1893, John and Wilfreda fell in love. EGS delighted in their affair. "Half way down the [dinner] table sits little Sister B—who is in love with Johannes. He is in love with her, by the way. The old affair which never meant any thing, is evanished in smoke, as I knew it w'd, & this one, wh. will probably go its way, is declared, & he is packed off, on account of his health & this complication—to a ranch in Cal. & the little goose sits in the middle of the table as aforesaid, looking like doomsday, & giving herself away to the world at large. O sech times as I've had with those two infant babes! . . . Of course I'm awfully down on her because I love John best, & I know this is a bad thing for him but that is probably unjust. . . . Dr. [Bayard Taylor] Holmes thinks his nervous condition is enough to account for anything & that this won't last. He has taken him away from study, & says he must dig & sweat for a year. He, John is perfectly dignified about it. . . . It will be a bad thing if it does last & a bad thing if it doesn't. She isn't up to him. He is such a dear, & such a clever dear—& such a fool!" (EGS to Mary Allen, 21 Nov. [1893], SC, Starr). After John Addams spent his year away in California (see John Addams Linn to JA, 17 Dec. 1893, below), he returned to Chicago to attend Western Theological Seminary, and the two rekindled their relationship.

Soon Wilfreda Brockway had acquired a new suitor. His name was Frederick ("Frank") H. Deknatel (1867?–1949), an immigrant from France who was a widower (his wife, Eleanor Gardner Deknatel, had died in 1897), living at 54 North Clinton St. He was the son of Louise Schimsene and John A. Deknatel. He began volunteering at HH, primarily helping with boys' clubs. He also served infrequently as a secretary for JA, 1898–1904; was business manager for the HH Dramatic Assn. and the Junior Dramatic Assn.; and from 1900 until 1906 was HH Assn. auditor, reporting to the HH Assn. Board of Trustees.

By 1898 Wilfreda Brockway had decided to seek training as a nurse. She became a member of the first nursing class at St. Luke's Hospital. But that did not stop the settlement gossip about her two suitors. HH resident Alice Hamilton reported that Frederick H. Deknatel often escorted her from HH to St. Luke's and could be heard referring to John Linn as "that man." In a letter of 15 Sept. 1899 to her cousin Agnes Hamilton, Alice reported that "Miss Brockway and John Linn are re-engaged. It was inevitable and now they really plan to be married next summer. How that can be, I do not know, for he is not self-supporting even, I think, but I suppose they will fall back upon Miss Addams" (RS, HFP). In 1900 Alice Hamilton indicated that Wilfreda was back at HH, a "great addition," and commented further that Wilfreda added "a comfortable domestic note . . . to the house" (Alice Hamilton to Agnes Hamilton, 25 Oct. 1900, RS, HFP). In 1901, even before she graduated from nurses training in 1902, she became associated with the Visiting Nurse Assn. of Chicago and worked in a neighborhood near HH. Wilfreda's engagement to John Addams Linn ended in Oct. 1901. In 1903, after John Addams Linn wed Ethel Winthrop Storer in New York City in Sept., Wilfreda and Frederick H. Deknatel were married in Cincinnati in Dec. They returned to work at HH until they moved to LaGrange, Ill., where they were living by 1911. Frederick Deknatel became president of Mackie-Lovejoy Manufacturing Co., a small hardware manufacturing company. The couple had three children. Frederick H. Deknatel was a founding member of the City Club of Chicago and a member of the Cliff Dwellers Club in Chicago. For a biographical note on John Addams Linn, see *PJA*, 1:79, n. 188. For information on Dr. Bayard Taylor Holmes, see JA to Bayard Taylor Holmes, 15 Sept. 1892, n. 2, below.

## Article in the *Chicago Inter Ocean*

*The summer of 1891 was a busy and exciting time for the Hull-House founders. They anticipated the first Hull-House Summer School at Rockford Seminary,*[1] *and on 20 June 1891 they officially opened the first new structure that was added to Hull-House, the Butler Art Gallery Building.*[2] *Publicity surrounding the event itself and the weeklong visit of special guests and English social settlement pioneer Rev. Samuel A. Barnett and his wife, Henrietta,*[3] *must have been gratifying for both women. Almost every major Chicago newspaper carried stories about the settlement or Rev. Barnett. The* Chicago Inter Ocean *published at least three articles, one of which is presented in part below. The* Chicago Daily Tribune *actually began its coverage on 31 May and published at least five articles. The* Chicago News *had one article; the* Chicago Herald, *two; the* Chicago Globe, *one; and the* Chicago Times, *two.*[4]

*Jane understood the value of widespread and positive newspaper coverage, and she worked, her entire life, to achieve good press. The newspaper attention that this particular event created was decidedly positive. It was in part a result of the reception that "the scheme" had already received. It was also a result of the social and civic stature of those who had contributed to the creation of the Butler Art Gallery. As the* Inter Ocean *indicated in an article the day of the Butler Art Gallery Building opening, it may also have been a result of a general community perception that due to the hard work of Jane and Ellen, something beneficial was beginning to happen in a downtrodden corner of the Chicago community. "The work of the institution has attracted a great deal of attention, and the success with which it has met has made it hosts of friends. . . . Mr. Butler's attention was called to the work by some friends. He visited the place and was soon satisfied that the institution was a much-needed one. The offer to build the new gallery and extend the work came from him unsolicited."*[5]

Chicago Ill. 21 June 1891

PICTURES FOR THE POOR.

Formal Opening Yesterday of Mr. E. B. Butler's Addition to Hull House.

The Building Will Be Devoted Principally to the Display of Pictures.

Interesting Addresses on the Value and Importance of Art as an Educator.

Helping a Good Work.

A reception given last night by Misses Addams and Starr formally opened the Hull House at No. 355 South Halsted street.[6]

The mission of the Hull House is unique in Chicago. Its purpose may be learned in New York in the College Settlement and the Neighborhood Guild, and in London in the world-famed Toynbee Hall. It is neither a mission, nor a home, nor a school, nor a reformatory—yet it proposes without ostentation, to work the results wrought by all by the simply agency of social influences.

It intends bringing the people together—the children, in classes, to read or to sew or to study music; the young men and women to draw or complete subjects neglected during their school life, and the older people to become better acquainted with one another, and through means of art and literature to find matter for diversion and improvement.

Last Evening's Exercises

were more or less informal. The visitors were first shown though the different class rooms, library, and reading rooms. The halls of greatest attraction—in one of which the art loan was exhibited—are in a handsome two-story brick annex to the institute, which has been built and donated by Mr. E. B. Butler. The lower story of the building will be used by the public library, while the upper story will be devoted solely to art exhibitors and the purposes of art studies. It is through art primarily and through literature in the second place—as was learned from the address of the Rev. S. A. Barnett—that good is to be effected through this undertaking. Mr. Butler's gift will, therefore, be appreciated. This gentleman is a director of the World's Fair and a director of the Illinois Training School for Boys.

The collection of pictures exhibited was of a very high order.[7] The following were among the lenders: C. L. Hutchinson,[8] James W. Ellsworth,[9] Mrs. C. M.

In the fall of 1890, Jane Addams began planning the first new permanent structure she would add to Hull-House. It became the Butler Building, with a library reading room and art exhibition area. It was located immediately to the south of the Hull home and had an entrance on Halsted Street. The Pond brothers designed the building, Helen Culver leased the real estate to Jane Addams on which it was built, and businessman Edward B. Butler provided the money for its construction. This drawing of the structure and its site prepared by Irving K. Pond appeared in the *Inland Architect and New Record* 2 (March 1891). See UIC, JAMC, HH Assn.; HH Scrapbook 2:11½; and *JAPM*, Addendum 10:7ff.

Smith,[10] Mrs. Carpenter,[11] Mrs. Shaw,[12] Miss Kellogg,[13] A. A. Sprague,[14] and the Art Institute.

After the inspection of the art exhibit the visitors assembled in the library, where Miss Addams introduced the Rev. Samuel A. Barnett, of Toynbee Hall, London.

The Rev. Mr. Barnett

has worked in the famous Whitechapel district in London and is a most interesting speaker. Through his efforts the artists of London and the working people have been brought in touch. After Easter every year he holds an exhibition—which is contributed to by the most notable artists living. Mr. Barnett is an enthusiast in art and its mission.

He said: "Pictures are valuable because they are preachers. They make us think of other things besides ourselves. Pictures, like parables, speak to everyone, and are valuable not so much in what they say as what they suggest. But there is a wide difference between a picture and a photograph. In a photograph we see something as it is—in a picture we see it as it appears to a man of genius. A common man sees a common thing through the eyes of an uncommon man." [Applause]

The speaker then gave many interesting descriptions of interviews with the London poor. He told of incidents where the fallen and neglected were recalled to thought by the works of great masters where possible the words of preachers would have failed.

He told of the poor dock laborers of London, who had their daily toil lightened by seeing what an artistic eye could detect from the beauties of the Thames.

"A great pictorial work enlarges and elevates the mind," he said. "No man has any more right to shut up a great work of art than he does to imprison a preacher. I am glad to witness in Chicago the great work being done by Miss Addams and Miss Starr. Whatever your material prosperity may be, it is only from the elevation and cultivation of the mind that your true happiness can come."

Charles L. Hutchinson

delivered a very happy address. He said that ideals were a necessity. Otherwise we could not elevate men to high purposes. "We are told," he said, "that David and Ruth and Moses and Christ are myths. Still the virtues they typify are not mythical. In their imagery we can teach lessons where words would be useless."

Mrs. Barnett told of her working in London. She said great pictures always required some one to explain them. In their London exhibitions they had always the works of the best artists. Here, in Chicago, they would soon have the same, but young ladies of intelligence should be willing to study them and make them clear to others not equally favored in the matters of leisure and intelligence.

Mr. E. B. Butler was called on to say a few words. He said that he did not profess to know much about art, and therefore did not wish to speak about it. He always appreciated and enjoyed works of genius, he said, and should be glad if he helped others to do likewise.

Miss Addams said that whatever would be the success of the Hull House it would be due in the main to the munificence of Mr. Butler.
[Applause]

John B.[G.] Shortall[15] delivered a short and humorous address. He said that the artistic surroundings of the Hull Library were more valuable than the library itself. These ladies were making the graces of polite life compete with books, and he was compelled to admit the ladies were successful. [Applause]

After the addresses the evening was devoted to introductions, conversation, and the inspection of the institution.

Among those present were: J. S.[G.] Shortall, General McClurg, Mr. and Mrs. Strauss, A. Hammill, C. L. Hutchinson, the Rev. Floyd Tompkins, Jr., Fred Hild, General and Mrs. Chetlain, Mrs. Starkweather, Henry Bausher, Jr., Mrs. S. J. Nickerson, Dr. and Mrs. Dudley, Miss Catherine Lyon, Miss Mary Rosette Smith, Mrs. C. M. Smith, Mrs. C. Fred Smith, Miss Farnsworth, A. A. McCormick, George Schilling, Miss Culver, Mr. and Mrs. Lorado Taft, Miss Addams, and Mr. Salter.[16]

PD (*Chicago Inter Ocean*, 21 June 1891, HH Scrapbook 1:8; *JAPM*, Addendum 10:6ff).

1. See JA to SA, [12?] [Aug. 1891], below.
2. See JA to MRS, [12?] [Apr. 1891], n. 1, above.
3. Coming through the United States during the final weeks of their world tour, Samuel A. and Henrietta Barnett arrived in Chicago about 16 June 1891. "We spent ten weeks in America, ten enriching but tiring weeks, resulting in a reference for that great country and its great hodge-podge of peoples." Henrietta Barnett recalled staying with "hospitable people, including Miss Jane Addams in Chicago" (Barnett, *Canon Barnett*, 2:134). On Wednesday, 17 June, "An audience of seventy prominent people of Chicago interested in philanthropic work listened to an address by the Rev. Mr. Barnett of London, founder of Toynbee Hall at Hull House, No. 335 Halsted street.... His subject was the work of Toynbee Hall, after which Hull House is copied. He gave an interesting description of the plan on which it is managed and told of the developments that are of recent growth" ("How Toynbee Hall Is Conducted"). On Sunday, 21 June, he presented the sermon at St. James Church and at 3:00 P.M. in the afternoon spoke to young men in the church guild hall about the development of Toynbee Hall. By 23 June, the Barnetts were on their way to Cleveland.
4. For an assortment of newspaper articles about the Barnett visit and the opening of the Butler Art Gallery Building, see HH Scrapbook 1:6–8; *JAPM*, Addendum 10:6ff.
5. "A Local Toynbee Hall."
6. Not the official opening of HH but rather the official opening of the Butler Art Gallery Building, as the headlines for the article noted.
7. EGS created the printed "Catalogue of the First Loan Collection of Paintings in the Butler Gallery HH. June 20th to July 6th, 1891" for the opening exhibit. Other exhibitions followed, and most were created and described by EGS. Catalogs for the second exhibition (held in 1891), the third in 1892, and the exhibitions of 1894 and 1895, as well as for special exhibits of etchings in 1891 and another of prints of paintings associated with Public School Art Society, are in HH Scrapbook 2; *JAPM*, Addendum 10:7ff (see also JA to Jenkin Lloyd Jones, 6 Dec. 1891, n. 3, below). Information about exhibitions held at Easter in 1896 and 1897 appears in the *HH Bulletin* for those years (see *JAPM*, 53:529, 599). From the beginning, the exhibition room in the Butler Art Gallery Building was also used as a meeting place for reading parties, clubs, and classes.
8. Charles Lawrence Hutchinson (1854–1924) was one of the original members of the HH Board of Trustees. He was born in Lynn, Mass., the son of Benjamin P. and Sarah Ingalls Hutchinson, who by 1856 had settled in Chicago. He attended Chicago schools, graduated from Chicago High School in 1873, and became a grain trader and banker. In 1881 he married Frances Kinsley, who became a member of Chicago's Fortnightly Club in 1890. He served as president of the Chicago Board of Trade and as a director of the Northern Trust Co., became chairman of the fine arts committee of the World's Columbian Exposition of 1893, and was the first president of the Chicago Art Institute. He held leadership positions in the Universalist Church, Chicago Orphan Asylum, Univ. of Chicago, Rush Medical College, and South Park Comm. His primary contribution to HH was financial. He gave one hundred dollars annually to general support for the settlement. He was the recipient of honorary degrees from Tufts College and Harvard Univ.
9. James William Ellsworth (1849–1925), a businessman, bibliophile, and collector, was born in Hudson, Ohio, to Mary H. Dawes and Edgar Birge Ellsworth. He was educated in public schools in Hudson and attended the Western Reserve Prep School. At the time of the Butler Art Gallery Building opening, he was a widower. His first wife, Eva Butler, whom he married in 1874, died in 1888, and he married Mrs. Julia M. Clark Fincke in 1895. He owned and

operated coal mines and served on several for-profit boards of directors. He was a member of the South Park Comm. and was chairman of the committee on liberal arts for the World's Columbian Exposition of 1893. He received an honorary degree from Kenyon College.

10. See Biographical Profiles: Smith, Mary Rozet, and Smith Family.

11. Likely Elizabeth Curtis Greene Carpenter (1841–1905), founder of the Amateur Musical Club and a member of the influential Fortnightly Club of Chicago, which she joined in 1877, the same year that Lydia Coonley, Theodosia B. Kirkland, Rebecca S. Rice, and Dr. Sarah H. Stevenson became members. She married George B. Carpenter (1834–1912) in 1861. George Albert Carpenter, one of her four sons, all of whom were connected with their father in the ship-chandler and other businesses in Chicago, Seattle, and Anniston, Ala., would marry one of EGS's former students, Harriet Isham, in 1894. Another son, Benjamin, married EGS student Helen Graham Fairbank in 1893.

12. Likely Mrs. Gilbert B. Shaw, whose lumberman husband was by 1891 a director in the Metropolitan National Bank, where Jane did her banking.

13. Alice Kellogg. See JA to SAAH, 23 Feb. 1893, n. 13, below.

14. Albert Arnold Sprague (1835–1915) was a merchant engaged in the wholesale grocery business as the founder and president of Sprague, Warner, and Co. He had arrived in Chicago in 1862, the same year he wed Nancy Atwood. He had been born in Randolph, Vt., the son of Caroline M. and Ziba Arnold Sprague, and graduated from Yale Univ. in 1859. A director on the boards of several business and the organizer and director of the Northern Trust Co, 1873–1912, he was president of the Chicago Relief and Aid Society, 1887–90; a director of the Art Institute of Chicago; and a trustee for the Presbyterian Hospital and Rush Medical College.

15. John G. Shortall (1838–1908) served three terms as president of the Chicago Public Library. He had been born in Dublin, Ireland, to Charlotte Towson and John Shortall. He arrived in Chicago in 1854 via New York City, studied law, and was admitted to the Illinois Bar. In 1861 he married Mary Dunham Staples and also acquired a real estate abstracts business, which became exceptionally valuable after the Great Chicago Fire of 1871. He was one of the founders of the Illinois Humane Society and served as its president, 1877–1906; helped organize the American Humane Assn. in 1877; and presided over the Humane Congress of the World's Columbian Exposition, 1893. He became appraiser for school land in Chicago in 1880.

16. Two other Chicago newspapers identified attendees. They were the *Chicago Daily Tribune*, which misidentified Rev. Samuel A. Barnett as "Rev. F. O. Barnett," and the *Chicago Herald*. See HH Scrapbook 1:7; *JAPM*, Addendum 10:6ff.

## To Sarah Anderson

*By the time Jane Addams visited Toynbee Hall in London during the summer of 1888, the settlement had instituted a summer school for its neighbors at Oxford University to provide an educational and hopefully a class-shattering experience.*[1] *Jane decided to create a similar collegiate experience for Hull-House neighborhood women. It is not surprising that she selected as a venue Rockford Seminary, where she had been a student and was now a trustee.*[2]

*The Hull-House Summer School, held 1–30 July 1891, was the first of eleven summer school programs offered by the settlement until 1902. All but one was held at Jane's alma mater.*[3] *The schedule for each monthlong stay in Rockford, which attracted primarily teachers who had vacation time during the summer, was composed of classes, physical activity, and social events.*[4]

The first Hull-House Summer School was held at Rockford Seminary, Rockford, Illinois, during July 1891, and lawn tennis was a featured activity. Jane Addams is seated in the center of the photograph. On her left is her nephew Stanley Ross Linn. Behind her stands Ellen Gates Starr. To Jane's right and seated is her sister Mary Catherine Addams Linn. Her niece Esther Margaret Linn is perched on the end of the staircase wall on the far left and holding a fan. Julia C. Lathrop is standing, the second from the right (SCPC, photo 00025).

*Jane was delighted with the outcome of this first effort. "[W]e have never done any thing which gave so much enjoyment" she wrote to sister Alice.*[5] *And the financial result of this initial gathering was so positive that she was pleased to share the details with family, friends, and supporters.*[6] *To Jenkin Lloyd Jones, she pronounced that "'charity' cannot be applied to the scheme."*[7]

Rockford Seminary. Rockford, Illinois. [12?] [Aug. 1891]

My dear friend

Why I have been here for a month as your guest almost. Why I <have> thought of you each day with increasing tenderness and have had my head full of dreams for the Sem'y, without writing to you once—is more than I can tell.

The summer school has been delightful and the girls have gone away quite bewildered with the kindness of the Rockford people. Miss Stringer[8] astutely remarked that we would be expecting Mrs Cyrus McCormick[9] and Mrs Marshall Field to invite us to dinner when we got home. The month has been very rose-colored but I don't believe it has done them harm to see the goodness and kindness which most people feel toward every one else, but don't act out. I inclose a copy of the accounts, we are very much pleased with the balance— I think that we could do even better next year when I hope not to start in quite so exhausted. I feel very well now and after a week at Cedarville expect to go back in excellent trim. It has been ideal for me to combine Hull-House and Rockford Sem'y, two places I am so fond of. I hope when you come back that you will plan to stay a week in Chicago.[10] We both want so much to see you. I have had a such a good time with Miss Eastman[11] and have grown very fond of her. We had a regular lark going to Oregon & Grand Detour[12]—the latter place is very pretty.

Mrs Gregory[13] reported that you were getting rested which I devoutly hope is true. I hope we have not "marred the furniture" nor done any other harm to the dear old place, if you ever find that we have you must let us pay up. I feel very grateful to you and am always your loving friend

Jane Addams.

Have you ever read Ouida's "Bimbi,"[14] I asked Mr McC.[15] to send you a copy, it is good for vacation.

| | | | |
|---|---|---|---|
| Rec'd Rockford | 267.90 | House Ex. | 241.20 |
| " Board | 653.50 | Table Ex | 577.72 |
| " Chicago | 66.00 | Incidentals | 66.00 |
| | | | 884.92 |
| | | Balance | 102.48 |
| | $987.40 | | $987.40 |
| Table | | Gen'l Ex | |
| ice | 17.65 | service | 128.50 |
| milk | 69.28 | Fuel | 31.11 |
| meals | 138.22 | Gas | 33.32 |
| teapots | 3.00 | Washing | 42.52 |
| groc. | | | |
| veg. | | | |
| fruits | 349.57 | Paper | 5.75 |
| | $577.72 | | 241.20 |
| Bank Acct | | Incidentals | |
| Deposited | 789.43 | Excursion fund | 15.75 |
| Checks | 690.35 | linen | 27.00 |
| | 99.08 | | |
| Cash | 3.40 | lecturer's tickets | 5.00 |
| | $102.48 | students' " | 5.00 |
| | | Printing | 10.25 |
| Balance Aug. 4" | | | 66.00 |

ALS and AD (RC, Anderson; *JAPM*, 2:1253–57).

1. See *PJA*, 2:496.

2. An article by Katherine A. Jones in the Sept. 1891 issue of *Review of Reviews* reported that "The Board of Trustees [of RS] gave them the use of the buildings and grounds for July, and interested friends in the city of Rockford made themselves responsible for contingent expenses. A most sisterly interest was shown by the students of the seminary in the happiness of these summer students, and an appropriation was made by their association for the entertainment of their summer guests. Rooms were left arranged with added comfort and beauty.

"The members of the summer school were all from Chicago. Though largely public school teachers of the lower grades, all occupations were represented. Many were of Irish birth, some were German, some Jewish, and some American. All were from the crowded districts of the city, from which some had never before been separated: many had never been further than its suburbs" ("The Working Girls of Chicago"). The women who attended the summer school paid two dollars a week, which was the estimated actual cost of the food; took care of their own rooms; and gave an hour each day to the general work of the dormitory in which they stayed. While the article that Katharine A. Jones wrote indicated that the attendees numbered ninety, the brief report that JA and EGS produced for their 1 Mar. 1892 program of activities at HH indicated that the average attendance was seventy-five students, most of whom were members of the settlement's college extension courses.

3. There was no summer school held at Rockford during the World's Columbian Exposition in 1893. Instead, there were lectures and classes ongoing at the settlement throughout the summer. During the summer of 1902, the last summer the program was held, its members went to the Chautauqua Assembly in Chautauqua, N.Y., where JA was a speaker. During the summer of 1903, a few of the former summer school attendees gathered for a week to have several classes with JA in Bay View, Mich.

4. The first summer school program was varied. There were outdoor studies of birds and botany and lessons in lawn tennis. German conversation, English grammar, and composition were offered, along with reading parties in the works of Charles Lamb, Robert Browning, John Ruskin, Ralph Waldo Emerson, Victor Hugo, and "modern novelists." With singing, sketching, and German-method needlework, the arts were not neglected. There were also recitals of song and lectures on scientific and literary subjects (see "HH Summer School at RS," [Announcement]). All of the summer school teachers were volunteers. "Various garden parties, river excursions, and like entertainments were arranged by the citizens of Rockford for the students" ("The Working Girls of Chicago"). Although the HH college extension classes were coeducational, during the early years only women participated in the summer program at RS.

5. 12 Aug. 1891, IU, Lilly, SAAH; *JAPM*, 2:1259.

6. Extant JA letters indicate that she also sent a summary of the school's financial success to Lydia Avery Coonley-Ward (see 12 Aug. 1891, below), to sister SAAH (see 12 Aug. 1891, IU, Lilly, SAAH; *JAPM*, 2:1258–59), and to Jenkin Lloyd Jones (see 20 Aug. 1891, UC, Jones; *JAPM*, 2:1260–63).

7. 20 Aug. 1891, UC, Jones; *JAPM*, 2:1260.

8. Likely Mrs. Mary Stringer, who was living at 1359 (later 3039 West) Congress St. She was an early member of the HH Woman's Club and maintained an active club life until her death in 1931.

9. Nancy ("Nettie") Fowler McCormick (1835–1923), businesswoman and philanthropist, born in Brownsville, N.Y., and schooled in New York and Ohio, married reaper inventor and wealthy Chicago businessman Cyrus Hall McCormick (1809–84), twenty-six years her senior, in 1858. They had seven children, one of whom, Anita McCormick Blaine (1866–1954), became an ally of JA's in support of progressive educational reform. Despite the fact that the McCormicks spent large amounts of time away from Chicago, Nettie became a force in the city's cultural and social elite. As her husband aged and was in increasingly poor health, she became more involved in directing the McCormick Harvesting Machine Co., and she played

a major role in its consolidation in 1902 into the International Harvester Co. A conservative Presbyterian and supporter of the Fourth Presbyterian Church, like her husband she was a Democrat. She was influential in directing the family wealth to various philanthropies. She carefully investigated and then supported a number of educational institutions, orphanages, hospitals, war relief agencies, churches, and youth programs. Her goal was to make education more readily accessible, primarily because she hoped to encourage the spread of Christian ethics and religion. According to biographer Charles O. Burgess, "Her total donations to Hull House reflected her preference for personal rather than institutional giving to the poor. Over the years she gave Hull House only $2,085" (quoted from *Nettie Fowler McCormick: Profile of a Philanthropist*, 51, in Caldwell, "Nettie Fowler McCormick" *WBC*, 553).

10. SA, who had just become principal of RS, had been visiting family.

11. Elizabeth ("Bessie") Eastman (1861–1932) was born in Eastmanville, Mich., to Fanny and Calvin Eastman, an Indian agent in Grand Haven, Mich. She attended St. Johnsbury Academy in Vermont. After receiving an A.B. from Smith College (1886), she joined RFS to teach until 1898. During her tenure, she was instructor in mathematics, 1886–87, and became chair of rhetoric, 1887–92. She studied at Yale, 1892–94, and returned to Rockford in the fall of 1894. From 1898 until 1900, she was principal at the Michigan Seminary in Kalamazoo. After serving two years as principal in a New York private school, she became dean, Wilson College in Chambersburg, Pa., 1902–3; and then dean of the College for Women in Pittsburgh, Pa., 1903–5. During the HH Summer School in 1891, she taught English grammar and conducted the Charles Lamb reading party.

12. JA and Bessie Eastman were traveling in northern Illinois to the southwest of Rockford down the Rock River valley, an outstanding natural setting that attracted tourists from throughout Illinois and the Midwest. Grand Detour, located in a horseshoe bend of the river, was the small community where John Deere fashioned the first successful self-scouring steel plow. When JA visited it, it boasted a wooded environment surrounded on three sides by the river; Greek Revival, Gothic, and Victorian architecture; an Episcopal church of limestone construction with a wooden belfry erected in 1850; and perhaps Deere's original blacksmith shop that had been established in 1837.

Oregon, Ill., founded in 1839 on the Rock River, was the county seat of Ogle Co. Margaret Fuller (1810–50) found it a lovely setting. She named the bluff across the river from the community "Eagle's Nest" and wrote the poem "Ganymede to His Eagle" there during her visit in 1843. In 1898 artist and sculptor Lorado Taft made it the site of a community of Chicago artists called "Eagle's Nest Art Colony." Among the artists and writers who inhabited the separate flagstone cottages on the thirty-acre tract were poet and publisher Harriet Monroe (1860–1936), architects and writers Allen B. and Irving K. Pond, novelist Henry B. Fuller (1857–1929), composer Clarence Dickinson (1873–1969), editor and author Horace Spencer Fiske (1859–1940), and artist Charles Francis Browne (1859–1920). In 1911 Taft presented to the State of Illinois his forty-eight-ft. concrete statue of an imagined Chief Blackhawk, meant to idealize the former Native Americans of the area.

13. Sarah E. Gregory was employed at RS and RC from 1884 until 1899. She is listed as the superintendent of the Domestic Dept. from 1884 until 1887 and then as matron. She seems to have been in charge of the management of the student dormitories, where the HH Summer School students roomed. By 1905 Sarah Gregory was living with her sister in Beloit, Wis.

14. Marie Louise de la Ramée (1839–1908), pseudonym "Ouida," was an English novelist who wrote popular society romances, described Italian village life in *A Village Commune* (1881), and wrote animal and children's stories. *Bimbi: Stories for Children* was first issued in 1882.

15. JA is probably referring to Alexander A. McCormick, HH supporter who was a salesman at A. C. McClurg's bookshop. She could also have been referring to Alexander Caldwell McClurg (1832–1901), noted Chicago publisher and bookseller, who developed and became head of A. C. McClurg and Co. in 1887.

## To Lydia Avery Coonley

"Cedar Cliff." Cedarville, Ill. Aug 12" 1891

My dear Mrs Coonley

I came to my brother's[1] after the summer school closed,[2] and am having a delightful rest in this little village in which I was born and have so many associations. I hope very much indeed that I can persuade you to come out here from Chicago some time for a little visit, if only over <a> Sunday. It is really a very short distance and I wonder always why I do not insist upon my dearest friends seeing it.

Your kind letter from Wyoming[3] was very "homey" and I am so grateful to you for writing with the check.[4] The crèche has been full all summer, twenty five every day the last letters said.[5] Two of our dearest babies died that hot Sunday. Miss Wakam[6] a trained nurse who has been at the house all summer, has helped many <of> them through the teething stage. Mary[7] wrote in great despair once that they were all cutting teeth, and she did n't believe any of them were strong enough to manage it.

I inclose the financial statement of our summer school, we are very proud of it.[8] I was so determined to have the girls pay for their own food & drink—there can be no "charity" in giving concerts and lectures. I have had a good many letters asking about the finances.

The girls were all very happy, and eating, sleeping and reading with people is ~~an~~ a surer way to know them, than to entertain them over a week. I feel very grateful for the opportunity. It will make a great difference in our classes next winter. We are planning Sunday afternoon concerts for next year, historical & classical.[9] We will have six for the first term.[10] Might we have two of them, for the organ at your house?[11] Publish the programs together and with a foot note say that these would be there? Is that asking too much? The audiences are largely College Ex. students, who were so appreciative of the entertainment they received at Rockford at the different houses. Towards the last they appeared so well and were so natural and easy in manner, that we hate to have them lose it.

Please give my love to dear Mrs Matz—[12] I do hope that she will gain. With love to all your family and most of all to your dear self, I am yours always

Jane Addams.

ALS (SCPC, JAC).

1. JA went to stay with LSA and JWA in Cedarville after she and Elizabeth Eastman returned from their jaunt by horse and buggy to Grand Detour and Oregon, Ill. She arrived in Cedarville about 6 Aug. and reported to sister SAAH that "Laura and Weber are very well, and happy it seems to me. I think some times that life has for all of us stormy and calm periods, into which we emerge we scarcely know when" (12 Aug. 1891, IU, Lilly, SAAH; *JAPM*, 2:1259). JA planned to return to Chicago on 17 Aug. 1891.

2. The HH Summer School ended 30 Jul. 1891.

3. JA had vacationed with Lydia Avery Coonley at her summer home in Wyoming, N.Y., in Aug. 1890. See JA to AHHA, 11 Aug. 1890, above.

4. Lydia Avery Coonley was an early and regular financial supporter of HH. It is likely that JA was thanking her for her support for the newly established Crêche.

5. The letters are not known to be extant.

6. Emily N. Wakem (Higginson) (1864–1941) became the second wife of banker, businessman, and secretary-treasurer of Chicago's West Side Elevated Railroad Co. George Higginson Jr. (1864–1936). She was born in Chile, South America, the daughter of farmer James O. and Mary J. Nancarrow Wakem from England, who settled in Chile and then moved their large family to Lancaster Co., Nebr., by 1880. She was among the first graduates from the St. Luke's Hospital Nursing School in Chicago in the late 1880s, and she was a founder of the Visiting Nurse Assn. of Chicago. By 1891 Wakem, who began helping at the HH nursery during the summer of 1891, was identified as the head of nurses for the Visiting Nurse Assn. and living with her father and two brothers, Harold R. and J. Wallace Wakem, in Chicago. Throughout the 1890s, as a nurse, she supported Florence Kelley's efforts to close down sweatshops for health reasons, especially working with individual families. She married George Higginson Jr. in Sept. 1898. At least three children were born to the couple: George; Theresa, who became Countess Rucellai; and Emily, who was Mrs. John H. Gould. Emily Wakem Higginson continued an active life with a variety of charitable interests, but remained closely associated with the Visiting Nurse Assn. of Chicago, where she served as a director, 1902–21; first vice-president, 1905; and honorary director, 1922–41. In 1905 she became a member of Chicago's Fortnightly Club. By 1926 the Higginsons had left Chicago to retire in Lenox, Mass., where they were buried.

7. Probably Mary Keyser, housekeeper and settlement worker, who remained at HH during the summer while JA and EGS were away.

8. For enclosure, see JA to SA, [12?] [Aug.1891], above.

9. Until this time, JA and EGS had provided concerts and lectures only on Thursday evenings and maintained Sunday at the settlement as a day to attend church and rest. See also Two Essays in the *Forum*, Nov. and Oct. 1892, n. 130, below.

10. There is no extant program detailing the Sunday concerts beginning in the fall of 1891. In the announcement for weekly activities dated Mar. 1892, where the scheduled events are presented by day, an entry for Sunday appeared for the first time and with the following description: "Concerts—Drawing Room—4 to 5. . . . There have been a series of twenty concerts given by various musicians and musical clubs of the City" ("HH A Social Settlement . . . Weekly Program . . . , March 1st 1892"). The Plato Club, hosted by Julia Lathrop, also met on Sunday afternoon in the Reception Room from 5:00 to 6:00 P.M. to read philosophic essays (see also Two Essays in the *Forum*, Nov. and Oct. 1892, n. 131, below).

11. Mrs. Coonley hosted an organ recital, the first of many over several years at her home at the "South corner of Division Street and Lake Shore Drive" on Thursday evening, 17 Dec. 1891 ("[HH] Thursday Lectures and Concerts").

12. One of Mrs. Coonley's good friends was Mary E. Lewis Matz (Mrs. Otto).

## To Sarah Alice Addams Haldeman

[Chicago, Ill.] [ca. 6] [Sept. 1891]

My dear Alice

I have not heard from you <for so long,> that I am beginning to be anxious. I don't mean to be exacting and fussy but I do feel much happier when I hear from you. I had saved two of your letters,[1] the one about your dining room furniture and the one about Marcet's cloak. When I started down town the other day, I could n't find them and I should be very glad if you would write them both out again and I will see to it at once. Last Sunday was my birthday. I had a very pleasant day with George Weber[2] who was passing through from New York and spent the day with me & went into long and interesting reminiscences and was very kind and very entertaining. He has invented a rail road tie which he expects will make his fortune.

Mary[3] sent me a parcel of preserves and jelly, they are delicious and seem an appropriate present for my matronly age of thirty one.

I was very glad to have a little visit with Mrs Leonard[4] and the children. Alice made me very home sick for Marcet.

We are fitting up a gymnasium in Murphy's old saloon next door,[5] which will add a great deal to our usefulness in the neighbor hood I think, but that and the diet kitchen[6] has kept us very busy.

With kindest regards to my friends, and unchanging love to you dear, yours forever

Jane

ALS (IU, Lilly, SAAH; *JAPM*, 2:1267–70).

1. These letters are not known to be extant.

2. George Cyrus Weber (b. 1861?) was one of JA's cousins, the son of her aunt Maria W. Hoffeditz (sometimes Hoffenditz) Weber (1824–91) and uncle George Weber, brother of JA's mother, SWA (see *PJA*, 1:131, n. 1). On 1 Jan. 1887, he married Juda M. Webb (b. 1862) in Benton Co., Iowa. There is no evidence that his railroad-tie invention made his fortune.

3. MCAL.

4. Anna M. Carpenter Leonard (b. 1856?) and her husband, Joseph T. Leonard (b. 1854?), a Girard, Kans., merchant and banker, were special friends of SAAH and HWH. The Leonards had a son, Howard Carpenter (b. 1879), and a daughter, Alice (b. 1887), named for SAAH, born shortly after Marcet Haldeman was born. JA had become acquainted with the Leonards during her visits in Girard.

5. For some time, JA had her eyes on Matthew Murphy's saloon next to the settlement property to the south. The Oct. 1891 HH financial summary indicates that JA had raised $30 to help with the project of turning the saloon into a gymnasium, but spent $41.78 on the refitting. Eight months into the 1891–92 financial year, she had collected $358 and spent $347.32 on the project. By 7 Dec., she had gathered sufficient funds to create a functioning gymnasium. At that time, she reported to Katharine Coman that she had "transformed [the] saloon next door into a little gymnasium open every evening and 3 afternoons" (RS, Denison; *JAPM*, 2:1284). By June 1892, JA was aware that she was to have a new gymnasium building. A newspaper reported at that time that "a new gymnasium building is soon to be erected through the generosity of a friend of the house, on the ground in the rear of the main building" ("HH in Chicago"). See also Two Essays in the *Forum*, Nov. and Oct. 1892, n. 113, below.

6. When JA and EGS leased the lot at 221 Ewing St. from Helen Culver, it contained two cottages. At the front of the lot was the four-room cottage that became the HH Crêche, and to the back of the lot there was a smaller cottage that became the HH Diet Kitchen. JA hoped that through the cooking classes she planned to hold there, her neighbors would learn healthier and more economical ways of cooking and adopt a more nutritious diet. A series of cooking instructors presented prepared foods for sale, offered classes in food selection and preparation for the ill, and taught cooking techniques, food selection, and sanitary food handling to adult

women as well as to young females, beginning at age ten. Food prepared in the Diet Kitchen was available for purchase at cost. For the next four years, the number of classes and the class times varied greatly, depending upon the number of potential students. At the start of the program, there were six classes, held primarily from Thursdays through Saturday mornings. Theodosia Stiles (1863–1912), who married Paul A. L. Doty, 1892; moved to Paterson, N.J.; and died in St. Paul, Minn., started the cooking program on 8 Oct. 1891. As a companion class, Mrs. Mary Hinman Abel (1850–1938), who had been trained at the New England Kitchen in Boston, presented four lectures on domestic hygiene, stressing the nutritious values of various foods. Miss Stiles and Mrs. Able were soon replaced by Georgiana Allen, also a graduate of the New England Kitchen program in Boston, who taught most of the regular classes, while Edith Nason (1857–1912), who had been trained at St. Luke's Hospital (class of 1892), took over demonstrations of sickroom cooking. See Remarks on Opening the New England Kitchen, HH, 23 Aug. 1893, n. 12; and John Addams Linn to JA, 17 Dec. 1893, n. 5, both below.

After the HH Coffee House was officially opened on 23 Aug. 1893 with its new kitchen, food for sale to neighborhood residents and workers was prepared there using New England Kitchen equipment, food selections, and processes, with cooking classes continuing at the Ewing St. cottage. Jeannette (or Jeanette) ("Nettie") C. Welch (d. 1907), a graduate of Wellesley in 1889, who eventually earned a Ph.D. from the Univ. of Chicago, 1897, had attended the New York Teachers' College, joined the settlement resident corps in 1893, and until the fall of 1894 taught cooking classes, house sanitation, the science of cooking, and methods of teaching reading and arithmetic in primary grades. It was also during the early months of 1894 that she began conducting classes at 221 Ewing St. in biology and physics and using the Diet Kitchen space as a laboratory. For the remainder of the 1890s, at least one cooking class was available through HH during the fall, winter, and spring of most years. The HH Crêche Cottage and the Diet Kitchen Cottage were eventually razed.

The early attempts to inculcate among HH neighbors the ideas fostered by the New England Kitchen of Boston for providing more nourishing food options were carried out in conjunction with two dietary studies conducted in the settlement neighborhood. The first was an investigation of the types of foods eaten by various immigrant groups in the HH neighborhood. It was conducted by the U.S. Dept. of Agriculture. The second, identifying foods preferred by the nearby Italian colony, was issued by the U.S. Dept. of Labor. Both studies were conducted by Caroline L. Hunt (1865–1927) of the Bureau of Home Economics of the U.S. Dept. of Agriculture, an associate of Ellen Richards, noted home economist, and writer on matters of nutrition (see Remarks on Opening the New England Kitchen, HH, 23 Aug. 1893, n. 18, below). Despite the need these studies revealed to educate and to make cheaper and more nourishing foods available to the neighbors, JA reported that the New England Kitchen idea for teaching better preparation methods and for the sale of simple and more healthful cooked goods "has never been popular" (*HH Year Book, 1906–1907*, 40; *JAPM*, 53:915). See also Remarks on Opening the New England Kitchen, HH, 23 Aug. 1893, below.

## To Sarah Alice Addams Haldeman

Hull-House [Chicago, Ill.] Nov 9" 1891

My dear Alice

I was getting very uneasy about the second coat &c when your letter came.[1] I hope very much that the things are right—It is a great pleasure for me to get them and I hope you will always let me know. I cannot always "go at once" but I can in time.

Inclosed is the account,[2] I did not return the balance, thinking that you might want something else. I will wait until I hear from you before remitting.[3] I think about you so often, dear, and hope and pray that no harm will come to you or Marcet. It seems to me that you are a very remarkable woman.[4] I have not heard from Ma for a long time. I feel that my letters are of little comfort to her, & do not write often. Please give many kisses to Marcet and believe always & unchanging Your loving sister

Jane Addams

ALS (IU, Lilly, SAAH; *JAPM*, 2:1273–74).

1. That letter is apparently not extant. In an earlier letter, SAAH had asked JA to undertake some errands in Chicago for her. See JA to SAAH, [ca. 6] [Sept. 1891], above.
2. The enclosure is lacking.
3. SAAH seems to have given sister JA more errands to do. "If you want to get Marcet a set of dishes for Xmas, do let me select them for you. They have the cunningest set—kitchen-garden size—at Burleys that I ever saw. They quite make me wish I was a little girl again. I have looked a[t] various gauntlets but am afraid that I can do no better. I have sent the glove fasteners," JA reported to SAAH, and she continued: "Any Xmas shopping you would like me to do for you, please let me know about soon and I will be delighted to undertake it" (6 Dec. 1891, IU, Lilly, SAAH; *JAPM*, 2:1278–79). Burley and Co., located at 83 and 85 (later 531 and 533) South State St., established in 1838, were importers and purveyors of imported tablewares, glass, and ornamental lamps.
4. In her letter of 6 Dec. 1891 to SAAH, JA admitted, "I do wish you would write me oftener. I get very anxious some times. I wake up in the night with a great longing for you" (IU, Lilly, SAAH; *JAPM*, 2:1279).

## To Henry Demarest Lloyd

*Henry Demarest Lloyd,[1] independent muckraking journalist and social reformer, met Jane Addams shortly after she began her effort to found Hull-House.[2] They became colleagues in reform and personal friends.[3] Both sought a more democratic society, a "welfare democracy," as Lloyd put it.[4] Often at Hull-House as a dinner guest or speaker and once as a resident, Lloyd, and his family as well, contributed valuable access for Jane Addams to the liberal social and cultural elite of Chicago. More important, he became a settlement promoter and an Addams adviser; he helped to educate Jane to the needs of labor and provided her with introductions to labor leaders in the United States and in England.*

Hull-House 335 So Halsted St [Chicago, Ill.] Nov 18" 1891

My dear Mr Lloyd

Miss Kenny[5] has asked for the use of our drawing room Wednesday evening Dec. 2d, to form the shirt-makers into a Union.[6] She has secured a Mr. Swallow[7] to speak and on the proposal of your name, said that you would be by far the best person to do it, but that it would be utterly impossible to secure you. I

Mary Kenney, ca. 1882–87, an early labor leader, who worked to end the practice of sweatshop manufacture and helped found the Jane Club, a successful cooperative living venture for working women, became a valued Addams friend (HU, RI, SL, MC341-1-1).

promised to ask you and let Miss Kenny know if possible on Friday, so that she can issue her invitations at once.

We would be much indebted to you if you could come. We have not yet heard from Leonora Riley[8] the New York shirt-maker but hope that she may come later even if she can't come for this first meeting.[9] Very sincerely yours

Jane Addams

ALS (SHSW, Lloyd; *JAPM*, 2:1275–76).

1. Henry Demarest Lloyd (1847–1903), acclaimed journalist and devoted progressive reformer, was born in New York City to Dutch Reformed minister Aaron Lloyd and his wife, Christie Demarest Lloyd. He was educated in Pekin, Ill., and New York City, where he also worked in the Mercantile Library of New York in Clinton Hall and attended Columbia Grammar School. After graduating from Columbia College (1867), he entered Columbia Law School and two years later passed the New York Bar. In the meantime, he was employed as an assistant secretary for the American Free Trade Assn. and almost coincidentally became active in the Young Men's Municipal Reform Assn., dedicated to overthrowing corrupt mayor William Tweed.

In 1872 he joined the *Chicago Daily Tribune*. There he served first as night editor and then literary editor until 1874; was financial editor, 1874–80; and became the principal editorial writer in 1880 until 1885, when he resigned from the newspaper and established himself as a freelance journalist and activist. He also met and married Jessie Louise Bross (1844–1904),

Henry Demarest Lloyd, muckraking journalist and active socialist, became a staunch Hull-House supporter. He and his good friend Jane Addams often appeared on the same platforms to promote better working conditions and higher wages for workers (Winnetka Historical Society, Illinois).

the only surviving child of *Chicago Daily Tribune* stockholder and publisher William Bross and his wife, Mary Jane Bross (1813–1903), among Chicago's social and cultural leaders. The couple had four sons. While both Lloyds became close friends and supporters of HH and its residents, especially Florence Kelley and her children, Henry D. Lloyd and JA formed a lifelong friendship. They often found themselves participating in the same organizations, fighting for the same causes, and speaking from the same platforms. JA and other HH residents were frequent guests at the Lloyd home "Wayside," in Winnetka, Ill.

Henry D. Lloyd, who traveled widely to see other examples of what he called "welfare democracy" at work, was especially close to labor leaders and reformers in England. He supported woman suffrage; clemency for the men convicted in the Haymarket bombing; campaigns to end child labor, promote municipal reforms that would improve living conditions in Chicago, and end political corruption; a cooperative movement; the end of privately held monopolies and trusts, especially with regard to oil, coal, and transportation; organized labor, with its fight for fair wages, better working conditions, and the eight-hour day; mental hospital reform; academic freedom; peace; and basic social justice.

One of his favorite Chicago places was HH and its residents, volunteers, and neighbors. When in Chicago, he was often a visitor there and declared it "the best club in Chicago." He was among the early speakers for the Working People's Social Science Club, presenting "Conservative View of the Radical Movement" on 17 Dec. 1890. Over the following years, he appeared several times before this group. On 28 Feb. 1893, his subject was "the scab," and 4

June 1895, he spoke about "monopolies." He addressed members of the cloakmakers' union gathered at HH on 1 Apr. 1893 and the same month on the last day of the same month appeared in the Sunday Lectures series presenting "The New Conscience in Action." On 1 Mar. 1896, following the 20 Feb. gathering in the HH gymnasium at which a ward organization was formed with the goal of electing an "honest Alderman" (*HH Bulletin* 1, no. 3:4), he spoke in the settlement's free Sunday-Evening Lectures series on "the future of Chicago." Lloyd helped labor organizer Mary Kenney support strikes and organize unions in Chicago; he assisted Florence Kelly in her efforts to develop mass meetings, organize popular support, and lobby the Illinois legislature against sweatshops in her successful effort to enact the Factory Act of 1893 that established factory inspection.

As a journalist, Lloyd exposed political and business corruption. His writings appeared in a number of popular periodicals of the day. He also promoted progressive reform through his books, including perhaps his best-known works, an exposé of John D. Rockefeller and Standard Oil in *Wealth against Commonwealth* (1894); *A Strike of Millionaires against Miners* (1890), a work about the Spring Valley Coal Mine strike and treatment of miners by the mine owners and operators; *Labor Co-Partnerships* (1898), advocating cooperation of capital and labor similar to what had been established in England; and *A Country without Strikes* (1900), championing the compulsory arbitration that he had seen in his travels in Australia and New Zealand. His work *Man the Social Creator*, written during 1895 and 1896, promoting his idea of man as an ethical and creative force for progress, unpublished at his death, was edited by JA and Anne Withington, teacher, Boston settlement house worker, and reformer (see JA to Anita McCormick Blaine, 11 Dec. 1895, n. 5, below), and issued in 1906. "It cultivated the community of workers, demanded social justice based upon a balance between individualism and collectivism, and envisaged the mixed economy of the Co-operative Commonwealth. For this it offered a broad rationale. Its world-wide extension as a classless society based upon the religion of work would bring a progressive peace, Lloyd prophesied" (Destler, *Lloyd*, 431).

In 1899 Lloyd and his wife moved to Boston, but by 1903 he had returned to Chicago and reestablished ties in Winnetka. While spending three weeks at HH as a summer resident, he fought the private interests trying to secure all Chicago's traction-line franchises. At an emergency meeting of the Federation of Labor held in Chicago on 19 Sept. 1903, in part to approve a mass gathering in support of municipal ownership of the lines, he once again shared the platform with JA. Growing ill that evening, Lloyd developed pneumonia and died on 28 Sept.

2. It is difficult to know how Henry D. Lloyd and JA first met. It may have been through Lydia Coonley or the Roswell B. Masons, both of whom where known to Lloyd and to his wife.

3. Lloyd spoke at the Sunset Club on ladies' night, 4 Feb. 1892, when JA presented her version of "How Would You Uplift the Masses?" They helped one another plan for the various congresses associated with the World's Columbian Exposition in which both were participants, including the labor, cooperative, and single-tax as well as the settlement congresses. The two appeared in a series of lectures in Toledo, Ohio, organized by Samuel ("Golden Rule") Jones (1846–1904), later mayor of the city. Lloyd also gave a presentation at the Social-Economic Conf., "Social Reconstruction," held 7–12 Dec. 1896, that was planned by the Chicago Commons and HH.

4. Lloyd presented his ideas for a welfare democracy for the first time in public to the American Federation of Labor (AFL) gathered in Chicago, 12 Dec. 1893, when he pronounced that "'the *general welfare* . . . is the object of society.' Effective labor organizations must institute 'this new *democracy of human welfare*' by political action, abolishing the contract system on public work and directing 'the co-ordinated labor of all' for the general welfare" (Lloyd, "The Safety of the Future Lies in Organized Labor," in Destler, *Lloyd*, 264). In her remarks at Lloyd's memorial service held at the Auditorium Theater, 29 Nov. 1903, JA recalled his commitment "for a better social order, the hunger and thirst after social righteousness. . . . Throughout his life Mr. Lloyd believed in and worked for the 'organization of labor,' but with

his whole heart he longed for what he called 'the religion of labor,' whose mission it should be 'to advance the kingdom of God into the unevangelized territory of trade, commerce and industry'" (Addams, *The Excellent*, 39, 47).

5. Mary Kenney (O'Sullivan) (1864–1943), trade union organizer and workers' advocate, was born one of four children of Irish and Catholic railroad workers Michael (first a foreman of a tracklaying gang and then a machinist) and Mary (a cook) Kenney in Hannibal, Mo. She completed the fourth grade, and at the age of fourteen she was apprenticed to a seamstress. With the death of her father in 1878, she entered the bookbinding trade, working at the Hannibal Printing and Binding Co. in the hope of making a living to support herself and her mother, who was in poor health. Though she became expert in all facets of the binding business, was often called upon to undertake special duties because of her expertise, and eventually became a bindery foreman, her pay always lagged behind that of male coworkers in the same or even in lesser positions. In addition, she recognized that working conditions in the bindery were unsanitary, unpleasant, and unsafe. When the Hannibal bindery closed, Kenney moved, taking her mother with her, first to bindery work in Keokuk, Iowa, and finally in 1888 to Chicago, in search of better pay and safer working conditions.

In Chicago she joined the Ladies' Federal Labor Union No. 2703 (organized in 1888) and became its representative to the Chicago Trade and Labor Assembly. Allied with this large and well-established labor organization already fighting for better working conditions and reduced working hours, Kenney became an itinerant bookbinder, going from shop to shop to investigate working conditions and to encourage the approximately 450 women bindery workers in the city to join the union she was organizing. She found lodgings at the Home for Working Women, 189 (later 148 West) Huron St., and in 1890 served as its treasurer. In Dec. 1890, she began gathering members for what became on 8 Jan. 1891 the Bindery Girls' Protective Union No. 1 (later Women's Bookbinders Union No. 1). Kenney became its president and brought its meetings to HH in the fall of 1891.

As she worked to organize women workers in other industries and to help Florence Kelley carry out the struggle against sweatshops, she came to the attention of Samuel Gompers (1850–1924), leader of the AFL, who tapped her in 1892 as the federation's first official woman union organizer. By the first of May 1892, Kenney had left her mother in Chicago, lodged in the HH Jane Club (see Article in the *Chicago Inter Ocean*, 30 June 1892, below), and gone east to work in New York and Massachusetts. There she discovered that organizing women workers was not something that could be done quickly. She also found that the AFL was not dedicated to organizing women workers. Shortly after the AFL abolished her position in Sept. 1892, she was back in Chicago. Once again, joining her mother at the Jane Club, she continued work as an organizer and outspoken advocate for abolishing sweatshops and improving working conditions and worker pay. Along with Florence Kelley and Henry Demarest Lloyd, she became a featured speaker at the Feb. 1893 rally sponsored by HH and the Chicago Trade and Labor Assembly to promote protective legislation for women and children and to abolish sweatshops. She was also a featured speaker before the Congress of the Women's Trades Unions at the Congress of Representative Women held during the World's Columbian Exposition in 1893.

Early in 1893, she turned her attention to Springfield, Ill., where she actively participated in lobbying members of the legislature to pass legislation regulating sweatshops and establishing the Illinois Office of Factory Inspection to enforce the legislation. Gov. John P. Altgeld signed the Illinois Factory Inspection Act into law on 1 July 1893, and he appointed Florence Kelley as the first Illinois factory inspector. Mary Kenney became one of Kelley's eight assistant factory inspectors.

In the spring of 1894, Kenney returned to Boston and became associated with the Denison House of the College Settlement Assn., organized in 1892. Continuing her commitment to organize women workers in Boston, Kenney became an important link for Denison House to working women in Boston. She also founded and became the executive secretary of the Union for Industrial Progress to study and publicize factory conditions. On 10 Oct. 1895, Mary Kenney and John "Jack" F. O'Sullivan, journalist on labor issues for the *Boston Globe* and labor organizer, whom she had met in Boston in 1892, were married in a civil ceremony in New York City. They made their home in Boston, where they had four children, John Kenney (1897–99?), Mary Elizabeth, Mortimer, and Roger, and continued to support the cause of organized labor. After the unexpected death of Jack O'Sullivan in a transportation accident in Lynn, Mass., in Sept. 1902, Mary O'Sullivan was the sole support of her three children, ages four to several months.

Mary O'Sullivan became a real estate rental agent for the Lawrence Minot Real Estate Co. She also managed a model tenement, Ellis Memorial, in South Boston, for the Improved Dwelling Assn., where, in association with Denison House, she was able to help tenants learn English and develop housekeeping skills. From 1914 until 1934, she served as a factory inspector in the Massachusetts Dept. of Labor and Industries. Mary O'Sullivan was called upon as speaker and gained additional income from writing articles on labor topics for periodicals like the *Boston Globe* and *Survey*.

Meanwhile, she continued to work through the Boston Central Labor Union and the AFL and its affiliates to organize women's unions. In Nov. 1903, in Boston, O'Sullivan and settlement worker William English Walling (1877–1936) founded the National Women's Trade Union League (NWTUL), established to organize women workers, social workers, and women of means as a cooperating force for promoting trade unionism and protective legislation. She was a leading proponent of the organization (headquartered in Chicago with several branch organizations) for which she served as the first secretary and later as first vice-president. She resigned her position and membership over the league's decision not to support the 1912 Lawrence, Mass., textile strike led by members of the Industrial Workers of the World (IWW). Without the help of the AFL and the Boston League, but with the help of O'Sullivan, the strikers won increased wages.

O'Sullivan's friendship with JA and with other HH associates, including Julia Lathrop, MRS, and Henry Demarest Lloyd, continued throughout her life. She took classes at the settlement and became the first president of the cooperative working women's Jane Club, where she and her mother lived from its founding until they moved to Boston. In 1893, with the support of JA, who tried unsuccessfully to raise start-up capital for her, she considered organizing a cooperative bookbindery. She gained valuable experience working as an investigator, lobbyist, and factory inspector for Florence Kelley in the campaign to abolish sweatshops in Chicago. Most important, she discovered that sympathetic women from wealthy and middle-class backgrounds would work together with working-class women to support efforts to improve working conditions and pay for women. A strong advocate for Prohibition and for woman suffrage, O'Sullivan also became a peace advocate. She opposed the entry of the United States into World War I and became an active member of the Woman's International League for Peace and Freedom (WILPF). In 1926 she went to Ireland as a member of the U.S. delegation to attend the organization's Fifth International Congress, held in Dublin. She died in the home she had constructed for herself and her family in West Medford, Mass. See also Articles in the *Chicago News* and *Chicago Daily Tribune*, 29 and 30 Apr. 1892, below.

6. The Shirt Makers' Union that met at the settlement on 2 Dec. 1891 became the first of several unions to organize and then meet at HH. Shortly after their initial gathering, JA wrote to Katharine Coman in New York, "We had a very enthusiastic meeting of shirt-makers here last Wednesday <evening> who formed a <u>Trades-Union</u>. We find ourselves almost forced into the trades unions, there are very few for women in Chicago and we hope to help form them on a consentive basis" ("Extracts from a letter to Miss . . . <Coman> from Miss Addams of HH, Chicago," 7 Dec. 1891, RS, Denison; *JAPM*, 2:1285). A week later, on 15 Dec. 1891, JA informed Henry Demarest Lloyd, "I thank you very much indeed for the copies of the 'Strikes'

you so kindly sent. I have given one to Miss Kenny and the Shirt Makers who meet again here this evening, will have some of the others. Miss Ford, whom they have elected president is a very sensible girl, last week twenty more shirt-makers joined the Union, so that we feel that they are well on their feet" (SHSW, Lloyd; *JAPM*, 2:1288). JA likely made available copies of Lloyd's speech to the Sunset Club, 6 Nov. 1890, when he debated R. H. Maxton, a building contractor, on the subject "strikes and lockouts." His five-page paper was published by the club as a memorial for its twenty-third gathering. The Shirt Makers' Union continued to meet at the settlement into the early 1900s.

Other unions organized at HH were Women's Bookbinders Union No. 1, Women's Cloak-makers' Union, Cab Drivers' Union (1892, by cabman Jim Hogan), Retail Clerk Workers, Clothing Cutters Union, Tick Sewers' Union No. 7589 (1899), and Laundry Workers. The Dorcas Federal Labor Union, which took its name from Dorcas, a seamstress described in the Bible (Acts 9:36–42; she made clothing for and ministered to the poor and was revived from death by Peter's intercession through prayer), was organized at HH by Alzina Parsons Stevens (for a biographical note, see JA to Richard T. Ely, 31 Oct. 1894, n. 10, below). Its membership was open to any wage-earning woman or any woman who supported labor organization. First announced in the *HH Bulletin* of Feb. 1896, it met at HH on the first and third Wednesdays of each month. By 1900 all of its members, more than one hundred, had joined the Women's Union Label League in Chicago, effectively folding the Dorcas Federal Labor Union into that organization. See also Articles in the *Chicago News* and *Chicago Daily Tribune*, 29 and 30 Apr. 1892, n. 6, below.

7. Likely Robert T. Swallow, an active member of the Carpenters and Joiners Union, a socialist, and a leader in the Chicago Trade and Labor Assembly who was also a member of the Illinois Labor Assn. (which became the Illinois State Federation of Labor in 1896) and served in 1889 as the organization's first vice-president.

8. At this time, Leonora O'Reilly (1870–1927) was a shirtwaist worker in New York City and, though she never held a union membership, helped organize women workers. She was known as a forceful and eloquent speaker. In 1888, with the support of her good friend Louise S. W. Perkins, a teacher who had lived in Concord, Mass., and charity worker and reformer Josephine Shaw Lowell (1843–1905), she organized the Working Women's Society to support working women. Among her friends were Grace Dodge, Father James O. S. Huntington, and Margaret Dreier Robins.

O'Reilly was the daughter of Irish immigrants Winifred Rooney and John O'Reilly and educated with the help and guidance of working-class thinkers and middle-class reformers. By 1886, at the age of sixteen, she was active in the Knights of Labor. By the late 1890s, she had become connected with the settlement house movement through a short stint with Henry Street Settlement, where she helped organize a women's local of the United Garment Workers. For two years after her graduation in 1900 from Pratt Institute in Brooklyn, she served as head resident of Asacog House in the same community. From 1902 until 1909, O'Reilly was supervisor of machine sewing instruction at the Manhattan Trade School for Girls.

She helped organize both the NWTUL and its New York branch. From 1909 until 1914, she served as vice-president of the New York branch and was active picketing, fund-raising, and organizing work during strikes. At the time of the New York Triangle Shirtwaist Fire of 1911 in which 146 working girls were killed, O'Reilly was head of the New York branch's fire committee. She successfully mobilized stunned New Yorkers into demanding legislation to correct the egregious safety and sanitation abuses that the tragedy and her efforts exposed. Among her other interests were woman suffrage, the plight of blacks in America, and world peace. She was a delegate from the NWTUL to the International Congress of Women at The Hague in 1915 under the leadership of JA, out of which the Woman's Peace Party (WPP) and eventually the WILPF were formed.

9. A holograph note at the top of the first page of the letter: "Dec. 2 Miss Addams."

## To Jenkin Lloyd Jones

Hull House 335 So Halsted St [Chicago, Ill.] Dec 6" 1891

My dear Mr Jones

Jenny Dow said the other day that your good people[1] would remember our neighbors at Christmas, if you knew exactly what they wanted. There seems to be no limit to the number of good dinners and <bags of> clothing that we can dispense with and of course at Christmas time it is pleasant to tuck in some thing festive.

At Thanksgiving we sent out seventeen turkeys & other dinners, and constantly thought of people who were provided for.

Candy & little presents &c we would like to have on hand before Dec 21"[.] We have about 400 children who come regularly to the house, and last year had the tree lighted nine different times for various clubs, so that we have to begin early. We do all we can to have the children celebrate Christmas day at home, and have them weave greens &c here, to take home for decoration. So that we like any amount of decoration but like it in a shape for the children themselves to make. I am afraid that we <too> crave for our children the pleasure of giving instead of receiving. We are very much obliged to you for your offer, it is but one more to the long list of kindnesses we have received from you.[2] I wish very much indeed that you come over during our Art-Exhibit,[3] it is one of the most interesting things that we have. The attendance yesterday was 310—

With kind regards to Mrs Jones and yourself I am very sincerely yours[4]

Jane Addams

ALS (UC, Jones; *JAPM*, 2:1280–82).

1. All Souls Unitarian Church was organized in 1882 in a well-to-do neighborhood on Chicago's South Side, yet it was near an area of tenement houses full of wage-earning people. The pastor, Jenkin Lloyd Jones, was a supporter of the settlement idea. From the inception of HH, he promoted it to his church membership, who established their own settlement-like neighborhood outreach programs (see JA to Jenkins Lloyd Jones, 3 Nov. 1890, above). In 1895 this effort became the Helen Heath Settlement (later Fellowship House), located at 873 33rd Court (later 831 West 33rd Place). By May 1905, the church had reorganized its outreach work and formed the Abraham Lincoln Center, located at Oakland Blvd. and Langley Ave., with Rev. Jones as head resident.

2. According to the HH accounts for Dec. 1891, $278.44 was given to the settlement for the holiday. The large donors were Chicago's Dearborn Seminary, $37.00, and MRS, $43.35. The candy bill was $63.44. Gifts in kind were not recorded.

3. JA and EGS were determined to use their new art exhibit space as much as possible. See also Article in the *Chicago Inter Ocean*, 21 June 1891, n. 7, above.

While the Barnetts at Toynbee Hall in London mounted only one major exhibit each year at Easter, JA and EGS were planning to present an assortment of changing exhibits. The second *Loan Collection of Paintings* in the Butler Art Gallery Building, on exhibit between 29 Nov. and 14 Dec., was actually the third exhibition of art in the recently constructed gallery. For two weeks in Oct. 1891, EGS had presented an exhibit of engravings and etchings from the collection of Charles D. Hamill (1839–1905), who helped found the Chicago Symphony and served as president of the Chicago Board of Trade (1892–93) and as a trustee of the Chicago Univ. and the Art Institute. The *Catalogue* that EGS created for the third 1891 exhibit identified twenty-one paintings. It was an eclectic mix of works by Paul Rembrandt, Jan van Goyen, and Salomon van Ruysdael, as well as by Mary H. Starr Blaisdell, sister of EGS. It also featured the work of Chicago artist Alice D. Kellogg Tyler, who painted portraits of several of the women associated with HH, including MRS and JA (see JA to SAAH, 23 Feb. 1893, n. 13, below). Lenders new to the HH circle of friends were Martin A. Ryerson, Samuel M. Nickerson, Rev. Frank Milton Bristol, and Allison V. Armour.

Martin A. Ryerson (1856–1932), born in Grand Rapids, Mich., educated in Chicago, France, Switzerland, and at Harvard Univ., was a businessman and noted collector of French impressionist art. He served as president of both the Univ. of Chicago and the Art Institute Board of Trustees and was a director of the Chicago Orphan Asylum.

Samuel M. Nickerson (1830–1914), born in Chatham, Mass., reached Chicago by way of Apalachicola, Fla., in 1858, and developed businesses in alcohol, wine, and explosives. He helped develop the Chicago City Horse Railroad (1864–71), Union Stock Yards National Bank (org. 1863), and the First National Bank of Chicago (org. 1863), for which he served as vice-president, 1863–67, and president, 1867–91, 1897–1900. He traveled frequently in Europe, was a collector of fine art and books, and a trustee of the Art Institute in Chicago.

Rev. Frank Milton Bristol (1851–1932), born in Orleans Co., N.Y., graduated from Northwestern Univ. and was ordained in the Methodist Episcopal ministry in 1877. Between 1882 and 1908, he served Trinity, Grace, and Wabash Avenue churches in Chicago; First Methodist Episcopal Church in Evanston, Ill.; and Metropolitan Methodist Episcopal Church in Washington, D.C. He was a bishop in the Methodist Episcopal Church, 1908–24. Among his publications is *The Ministry of Art* (1897).

For information on Allison V. Armour, see Remarks on Opening the New England Kitchen, HH, 23 Aug. 1893, n. 4, below.

In her article "HH" in the Feb. 1892 issue of *Charities Review*, Alice Miller indicated that the Dec. exhibit attracted at least one hundred visitors each day.

4. A holograph note at the top of the first page of the document: "335 S. Halsted."

## To Anna Hostetter Haldeman Addams

Hull-House. [Chicago, Ill.] Dec. 28" 1891

My dear Mama

A very pretty little platter came the day before Christmas, for which I think I am indebted to you, and I certainly thank you very heartily. I am also very much obliged for your Christmas letter.[1] We have had a very satisfactory Christmas here. The children have never been so quiet and responsive and we have had a great deal of spontaneous help.[2]

I would have been so glad to have come home for a few days, but as the rates to Geneseo are very much reduced and as it is much longer since I have seen Mary[3] than the rest of the family, I will run down there for two days. I go to night and come back on Thursday.[4] I have thought of you so often during the Christmastide, the recollections of all the past Christmases mingle with each new one, until it sometimes <is> almost difficult to tell what is the most real.

I wish very much, that when Sarah[5] comes to Cedarville this winter, that you could come in and make another visit longer than your first one.[6] It is so easy to misinterpret letters, and lack of letters, that friends have to meet "face to face" some times to understand each other.

The salad dish I sent, I hope will remind you of Florence—that most beautiful of all cities.[7] Miss Starr went to Durand this morning, she will give a lecture at Mrs Knowlton's[8] on New Years eve, she would be much pleased if you could come. With heartiest wishes for a Happy New Year, I am your loving daughter

Jane Addams

ALS (JAPP, DeLoach; *JAPM*, 2:1292–93).

1. This letter is apparently not extant.

2. JA reported to sister SAAH that "the Christmas whirl has been some thing wonderful" (28 Dec. 1891, IU, Lilly, SAAH; *JAPM*, 2:1295). According to the financial records, JA and EGS received and spent $278.44 on Christmas at HH in 1891 and in 1892.

3. MCAL, JML, and their children were living in Geneseo, Ill. In 1892 the Linn family moved to Storm Lake, Iowa.

4. Thursday was 31 Dec. 1891.

5. AHHA's niece SH, who had been a traveling companion to JA and AHHA during the 1883–84 portion of their 1883–85 European adventure. See *PJA*, 2, especially part 2.

6. It is likely that AHHA had visited HH toward the end of 1890. See especially JA to AHHA, 9 Dec. 1890, above.

7. AHHA and JA visited Florence, Italy, together during their stay in Europe, 1883–85. See *PJA*, 2, especially part 2. JA also sent a salad dish to sister SAAH for Christmas; however, it seems that SAAH may already have had one just like it. When SAAH reported the duplication, JA responded, "I am very sorry about the salad dish. Will you please give it to Mrs Perry with my compliments, and allow me to send you something else" (JA to SAAH, 28 Dec. 1891, IU, Lilly, SAAH; *JAPM*, 2:1294). SAAH had given JA a gold thimble, and JA thanked her: "It is something I have wanted for years and I am so glad to have you give it to me" (JA to SAAH, 28 Dec. 1891, IU, Lilly, SAAH; *JAPM*, 2:1296). Mrs. Perry was likely the wife of wealthy Girard, Kans., attorney and real estate and loan businessman Theodore T. Perry. SAAH and Mrs. Sarah Chapin Perry served on the local school board together and were best friends. See *PJA*, 2:588, n. 15.

8. Mary L. Knowlton (1849–1951), wife of Dexter A. Knowlton II (1843–1903), of Freeport, Ill., was a friend of the Addams family. Dexter A. Knowlton was the son of one of the pioneer banking and merchant families of Stephenson County. His widowed mother, Austria C. Knowlton (1825–91), had met JA and AHHA in Paris while traveling in Europe in 1885.

## From John Dewey

*John Dewey's[1] 1892 visit to Hull-House[2] helped establish what would be a long friendship with Jane Addams. They often worked in support of innovative educational methods and civic reform in Chicago and, later, as fellow advocates for peace causes.[3]*

*In the 1890s, Dewey became an active supporter of Hull-House.[4] He clearly appreciated the pragmatic methods Addams and her cohorts were adopting to deal with social problems and their emphasis on direct experience. He also correctly predicted the evolutionary role that the settlement house movement would play in secularizing what would become known in future years as social work. Dewey remained very friendly with Hull-House residents and recognized early on at the settlement the new opportunities that Jane Addams and Ellen Gates Starr had created for concerned people like themselves to be of use in transformative ways as reformers and teachers. In doing so, he reaffirmed one of the goals that Addams had set, which was to open more meaningful and direct avenues of work for those educated women and men who wanted to utilize their skills to make a difference in righting the ills of society.*

15 Forest Ave Ann Arbor Mich Jan 27, 92

Dear Miss Addams

I cannot tell you how much good I got from my stay at Hull House. My indebtedness to you for giving me an insight into matters there is great. While I did not see much of any particular thing, I think I got a pretty good idea of the general spirit & methods. Every day I stayed there only added to my conviction that you had taken the right way. I am confident that 25 years from now the forces now turned in upon themselves in various church or agencies will be finding outlet very largely through just such channels as you have opened.

I hope you had a satisfactory journey to St Paul,[5] and found Miss Starr well on your return. Please remember me to the kind friends there and accept my thanks for all your hospitality. Sincerely yours

John Dewey.

ALS (RC; *JAMC*, 2:1298).

1. John Dewey (1859–1952) became the key philosopher of progressive education. He insisted that schools be child centered instead of subject oriented, and he believed that education should be flexible rather than formal. In his view, children learned best through activities rather than memorization. Dewey experimented with new educational methods and techniques, especially from his laboratory school at the Univ. of Chicago and from what he absorbed through his connections and observations at HH. In his and daughter Evelyn Dewey's (1889–1965) chapter entitled "The School as Social Settlement," 205–28, in *Schools of Tomorrow* (1915), they argued that, like HH, schools should become community centers and instruments for social reform.

John Dewey was born in Burlington, Vt., and graduated from the Univ. of Vermont (B.A. 1879) and Johns Hopkins Univ. (Ph.D. 1884). He became an instructor of philosophy at the Univ. of Michigan in 1884 and an assistant professor in 1886, the same year he married Harriet Alice Chipman (1858–1927), who became his life partner in educational theory and enterprise. After a year teaching at the Univ. of Minnesota, Dewey returned to Ann Arbor in 1889 to serve as the university's chair of philosophy and was working in that capacity when he first visited HH, perhaps at the suggestion of his wife. Two years after the visit, he moved to Chicago to become the head of the Dept. of Philosophy, Psychology, and Education at the Univ. of Chicago. He held that position from 1894 to 1904, specializing in ethics, logic, and education, and from 1902 to 1904 he also directed the university's School of Education. Beginning in 1904, and until his retirement in 1930, Dewey was a professor of philosophy at Columbia Univ. He published his first original work, *Outlines of Ethics* (1891), a year before his trip to HH. Dewey published and lectured prolifically.

2. The occasion of this visit was a lecture entitled "Psychology and History" that he presented on 21 Jan. for the HH Thursday-Evening Lectures series in connection with the settlement's College Extension Program.

3. Dewey and JA shared many concerns, and both in their later lives were very active in-

ternationally. The regard Dewey held for JA is reflected in the fact that he and his first wife named their youngest daughter, born in Chicago, Jane Mary, in honor of JA and MRS. Dewey credited JA and his visits to HH with significantly altering many of his theories and views (as an example, see Dewey to JA, 12 Oct. 1898, SCPC, JAC; *JAPM*, 3:1179). In tribute to their mutual commitment to peace causes, Dewey wrote the foreword to the 1945 reprint edition of JA's *Peace and Bread*, praising JA's conviction that means were as important ethically as ends in securing social progress.

4. Dewey's 1892 introduction to HH proved the first of many visits. Once he had moved to Chicago in 1894, he gave his time and support to the settlement, especially to its multifaceted educational programs. Shortly after he arrived in Chicago, he presented seven lectures at the settlement in the fall of 1894 on social psychology. He continued to provide occasional formal lectures there and enjoyed socializing with the settlement residents and visitors. By 1896 he was a lecturer for the Kindergarten Training School of the Froebel Assn. in Chicago that was associated with HH. Upon the death of William H. Colvin in 1896 (the same year that John and Alice Dewey organized the first laboratory school at the Univ. of Chicago of which Alice became principal and director of English), John Dewey filled his slot left vacant on the HH Board of Trustees. He served on the HH board until 1903. During his term as a trustee, Dewey published his *School and Society* (1899). He did much to publicize HH programs and bring them to the attention of educators nationally. He praised the HH educational program as a model for other educators to emulate in his 1902 speech to the National Council of Education that became the article "The School as Social Center." Among other things, in the HH system Dewey admired the stress on social psychology, the arts, and training in active problem solving and scientific method, all elements he advocated as the primary spokesperson for the progressive education movement.

5. In 1883 the RC Assn. of the Northwest had been formed in Minneapolis. The organization met periodically, alternating between St. Paul and Minneapolis. Perhaps JA was in St. Paul to continue to spread the word about the settlement venture among RFS alumnae. JA had spoken at RS in 1889, 1890, and 1891 about HH and took every opportunity offered to present the idea.

## Articles in the *Chicago News* and *Chicago Daily Tribune*

*Even before Florence Kelley[1] arrived at Hull-House in December 1891 to further spark the settlement's commitment to reform, Jane Addams and Ellen Gates Starr had become firmly enmeshed in efforts to improve working and living conditions for their neighbors. They saw that families in their area labored long hours in unhealthy conditions for little pay, and they recognized that as long as these conditions persisted, their neighbors had almost no way out of the bitter poverty of their existence.[2] In the beginning, Hull-House activities centered around investigating working conditions and wages of women and children and educational opportunities for children.*

*Jane Addams and Ellen Starr gave credit for their active commitment to labor's cause to Mary Kenney,[3] a young, feisty, street-smart woman who worked as a binder in the printing trade. Before the end of 1890, she was leading a successful effort to found the Bindery Girls' Protective Union No. 1 in 1891. It became the Women's Bookbinders Union No. 1 in Chicago and associated with the developing American Federation of Labor, established a few years earlier in 1886. Jane*

Florence Kelley, who arrived at Hull-House late in 1891 with her three children and became a force for progressive reform at the settlement, eventually led the national fight for workplace reforms through promoting consumer protection. Kelley, who became the first Illinois chief factory inspector, and Jane Addams became close personal friends and colleagues in reform (UIC, JAMC 0262 0404).

*Addams learned of Mary Kenney's efforts and, as Kenney recalled, wrote and invited her to the settlement. Of that same occasion, Jane Addams remembered that Mary Kenney doubted the good intentions of the settlement. "She came in rather a recalcitrant mood, expecting to be patronized and so suspicious of our motives," but discovered a welcoming environment and a helping hand.*[4] *That was the beginning of a long friendship as well as a more active role for Hull-House leaders in support of organizing labor.*

*Jane Addams and the residents of Hull-House aided the women binders by responding to their needs, a new experience for Kenney and the union members. "Miss Addams not only had the circulars [announcing meetings and events] distributed, but paid for them. She asked us how we want to have them worded. She climbed stairs, high and narrow. Many of the entrances were in back alleys. There were signs to 'Keep Out'. She managed to see the workers at their noon hour, and invited them to classes and meetings at Hull House."*[5] *Before 1894 the settlement could boast that it was "'on the side of unions.'" Ellen Starr reported, "Several of the women's unions have held their regular meetings at the House, two have been organized there, and in four instances, men and women on strike against reductions in wages have met there while the strike lasted." Over time the settlement also became a safe haven for other union meetings.*[6]

*Florence Kelley, determined to address the plight of workers and their families, was another powerful presence that influenced Hull-House and its founders to take a leading role in supporting efforts toward securing safer working environments and more rights for the workers.*[7] *Kelley became a trailblazer, setting the pace and defining the path of the settlement's fight to abolish sweatshops, find better paying jobs for workers, secure legislation to end child labor, and achieve improved working conditions, especially for women. Among the techniques Kelley and the settlement reformers used to bring reform were investigating working conditions and developing reports of their findings, holding mass meetings to present evidence and gain popular support, lobbying for corrective legislation, helping to organize workers, demanding that appropriate authorities uphold ameliorating legislation, offering a gathering place for discussion among workers, and in times of strike providing basic assistance with necessities.*

*If not at the head of these movements, Jane Addams was certainly at the forefront and condoned and supported these activities. She leaped into the fray as one of three members of a committee of the Chicago Woman's Club's unsuccessful attempt to encourage an arbitrated settlement of a sympathetic strike of women in a shoe factory.*[8] *Undeterred, Jane Addams stepped bravely forth again when offered an opportunity by another group of young women from her neighborhood who wanted just treatment to help settle their dispute with their employer, the Star Knitting Works.*[9] *This time she was successful, but in typical Addams fashion she later dismissed her achievement, describing the dispute at the Star Knitting Works as "hardly . . . a labor difficulty." She recalled that "the girls had never heard of a trades union and were totally unaccustomed to acting together, it was more in the nature of a 'scrap' between themselves and their foreman." Noted for his dedication to the practice of arbitration in labor disputes, Judge Murray F. Tuley's*[10] *"painstaking and just decision pleased both sides, a thing unique in my experience in labor adjudication," she reported.*[11] *The practice of settling disputes by means of arbitration suited Addams, and she promoted the practice for the remainder of her public life.*

*The successful outcome of her experience with the Star Knitting Works affair bolstered her personal preference to investigate the issues when faced with opposing positions and to seek agreement through understanding and compromise. Within the Hull-House family of residents, volunteers, and friends, there were many different levels of participation in the support of organized labor. Kelley, Kenney, Starr, and other Hull-House residents and volunteers made lifelong unequivocal commitments; they remained determined investigators of workplace abuses, inequities, and poor pay and continually sought solutions that were beneficial to workers. While dedicated to the causes of labor, Jane Addams ultimately did not offer the unquestioned loyalty to the cause of labor that many of her friends and settlement leaders exhibited throughout their lives. Her commitment to "democracy," which in 1895 she described as "giant-like and threatening as it may appear in its uncouth strength and untried applications," and her pragmatic approach to problem solving compelled her to see the labor and capital struggle as a battle in which neither was absolutely right. "The organization of society into huge battalions with syndicates and corporations on the side of capital, and trades-unions and federations on the side of labor, is to divide the world into two hostile camps, and to turn us back into class warfare and class limitations. All our experience tells us that no question of civilization is so simple as that, nor can we any longer settle our perplexities by mere good fighting. One is reminded of one's childish conception of life—that Right and Wrong were drawn up in battle array into two distinct armies, and that to join the army of Right and fight bravely would be to settle all problems."*[12]

Chicago, Ill. 29 Apr. 1892

## JUDGE TULEY AS AN ARBITRATOR.

Judge Tuley is to be requested to act as arbitrator between thirty-five girls and the proprietors of the Star knitting works. The young women in the case went on strike Tuesday noon[13] because they were fined 25 cents whenever they were late. As they work and are paid entirely by the piece they do not think a fine can rightfully be made, and they laid the matter before Miss Addams of Hull house. She sought the advice of Joseph Errant of the bureau of justice,[14] who gave as his opinion that such fines are illegal. When Miss Addams called on the proprietors of the knitting works and asked that the case be arbitrated they at first did not care to make it a subject of arbitration, but finally suggested that Judge Tuley be requested to act as arbitrator, both sides to abide by his decision.

PD (*Chicago News*, 29 Apr. 1892, HH Scrapbook 1:18; *JAPM*, Addendum 10:6ff).

Chicago, Ill. 30 Apr. 1892

## OBLIGED TO PAY BACK THE FINES. JUDGE TULEY'S DECISION IN THE CASE OF THE STAR KNITTING WORKS.

As a result of the strike of the thirty-six girls who were employed at the Star Knitting Works, No. 261 Franklin street, that firm has been obliged to pay back to such of its employés as it had fined for tardiness the amount of the fines in full. It has further been instructed by Judge Tuley, before whom the matter was brought for arbitration, that in the future whatever rules it may see fit to make for its employés must be posted on the walls of the manufactory, not merely read to the girls at uncertain intervals.

Twenty-three of the strikers are to resume work Monday with the understanding that the amount of the fines collected from them by the firm for tardiness is to be paid back to them semi-annually as prizes for good work. It is due to the fact that a small number of the girls stood firm and refused to return to work that the firm was led to make even these concessions. Had it refused to agree to the terms proposed by Judge Tuley these girls, acting on the advice of Joseph W. Errant of the Bureau of Justice stood ready to bring suit for the amount of the fines on the ground that the firm had no right to dock piece workers.

The residents of Hull House, to whom representatives from the employés went for advice directly after the strike occurred, have been active in bringing the matter to its present satisfactory conclusion.

PD (*Chicago Daily Tribune*, 30 Apr. 1892, HH Scrapbook 1:18; *JAPM*, Addendum 10:6ff).

1. "On a snowy morning between Christmas 1891 and New Years 1892," recalled Florence Kelley, "I arrived at Hull-House, Chicago, a little before breakfast time, and found there Henry Standing Bear, a Kickapoo Indian, waiting for the front door to be opened. . . . We were welcomed as though we had been invited" (Kelley, "I Go to Work," 271). Florence Molthrop Kelley (1859–1932) sought out HH on the recommendation of a representative from the WCTU and found a home for herself in Chicago. She stayed until 1 May 1899, when she left for New York City and another home at the Henry Street Settlement, where she lived for the next twenty-eight years.

When Florence Kelley arrived at HH, she was a mature woman, an avowed socialist, a dedicated and well-educated activist and social reformer, and the mother of three children, Nicholas, Margaret, and John. She was fleeing an abusive husband and broken marriage and seeking a safe place for herself and her children to live. The next day, JA took the Kelley family to "Wayside," the home of the Henry Demarest Lloyd family in Winnetka, Ill., and the Lloyds and Kelley became staunch allies in progressive reform. The Kelley children lodged safely with the Lloyds, and JA brought Kelley back to the settlement to become one of her dearest and most trusted colleagues in the variety of progressive reform movements that swirled about the settlement and on the national scene.

JA and Florence Kelley became immediate friends. Julia Lathrop reported that they "understood each other's powers" and worked together in a "wonderfully effective way" (Addams, *My Friend*, 77). After Florence Kelley died, her son Nicholas Kelley recalled that his mother "looked upon Jane Addams as her dearest and most intimate friend," and he continued: "She loved Miss Addams and admired her and approved of her unreservedly" (Linn, *Jane Addams*, 289–90). When Florence Kelley left Chicago to become the general secretary of the National Consumers' League, JA wrote to her, "I have had blows in connection with Hull-House, but nothing like this" ([June 1899], NYPL, Kelley; *JAPM*, 3:1359). A little later that same year, JA told Kelley, "Hull House sometimes seems a howling wilderness without you" (8 Nov. 1899, NYPL, Kelley; *JAPM*, 3:1470).

The two women who bonded so successfully were opposites in style: Addams calm and self-possessed, logical and determined; Kelley, outspoken, brash, and emotional. As JA's nephew James Weber Linn said of Kelley, she "hurled the spears of her thought with such apparent carelessness of what breasts they pierced" but was "full of love" and the "finest rough-and-tumble fighter for the good life for others, that Hull House every knew. Any weapon was a good weapon in her hand—evidence, argument, irony or invective" (*Jane Addams*, 138–39).

Kelley and JA shared similar early life experiences. They were almost the same age and were raised in households that pampered them as children, JA because she was the youngest sibling whose mother had died when she was not quite three and Florence because she was the last surviving daughter of the six girls who had been born to her parents. Both had been exposed to Quaker concepts: Florence Kelley through her great aunt Sarah Pugh and JA through her father, JHA, who identified himself as a Hicksite Quaker, although for neither was the Quaker faith a dominant influence. Both had grown up in families led by self-made fathers, dedicated to progressive ideas about anti-slavery and women's rights. Both fathers helped to establish the Republican Party in the United States, and both held public office, John Addams in the Illinois General Assembly, William Kelley in the U.S. Congress. Both fathers were a major influence on the education of their daughters; both encouraged their children to read from their home libraries and to seek higher education. Both became role models for their daughters. And both daughters became part of the first generation of college women. Both had traveled and lived in Europe and looked for ways to use their education to improve the world. Although Kelley's being married, then divorced, and then a single mother set her apart from JA's experiences, both women were committed to improving the life opportunities for children.

Florence Kelley was born in Philadelphia to Caroline Bartram Bonsall (1829–1903) and William Darrah Kelley (1814–90) and grew up a marginally healthy child who was mostly homeschooled at the direction of her father. She attended Cornell Univ. and graduated in 1882, a member of Phi Beta Kappa. Her published senior thesis, "Some Changes in the Legal Status of the Child Since Blackstone," revealed a determined interest in the welfare of children that would continue for the remainder of her life. When her attempt to attend graduate school at Univ. of Pennsylvania to prepare for the study of law came to naught because of her gender, she began teaching working women at the New Century Guild in Philadelphia and published another article about opportunities for women in education, philanthropy, and health.

While traveling in Europe with members of her family, Kelley discovered that the Zurich Polytechnicum admitted women, and she enrolled there as a student in 1883. Although she never graduated, the next three years were pivotal in her life. She became a dedicated socialist; translated into English for publication Friedrich Engels's *The Condition of the Working Class in England*; married a Polish socialist medical student, Lazare Wischnewetzky, 1 June 1884; and gave birth to the couple's first child, Nicholas (1885–1965). When the Wischnewetzkys returned to the United States in 1886, they settled in New York City, where Lazare attempted unsuccessfully to establish a medical practice. Much to their dismay, they were dismissed from the American Socialist Party in 1887 (but in 1912, Kelley joined the Socialist Party for a number of years). They had two additional children, Margaret (1886–1905) and John Bartram (1888–1968), but quarreled to such a degree that by 1891, Florence took their three children and left for Chicago. In March 1892, in Chicago, Florence successfully divorced her husband, resumed her maiden name, and got permanent custody of their three children.

Florence Kelley remembered that "my first activity" at HH "was conducting for a few months a small experimental employment office for working girls and women" ("I Go to Work," 272). By Feb. 1892, she spoke before the powerful CWC on the sweating system of manufacture. In 1892 and 1893, she taught adults in the Polk Street School night program and continued to lecture, primarily about the sweating system, to the assortment of clubs associated with the settlement, including the Jane Club, a study class for the Friendly Visitors, and the HH Woman's Club. She also appeared in the settlement's Sunday-Evening Lectures series and spoke throughout Chicago and its suburbs. Her friend Richard T. Ely arranged a lecture engagement for her at the Univ. of Wisconsin.

It was sometime early in 1892 that she was hired by the U.S. Dept. of Labor to carry out the Chicago portion of a federal study of slums in large cities of the United States. Using assistants who went door-to-door in 1893 throughout the square-mile area bounded by HH at Halsted and Polk streets on the north and west, the Chicago River on the east, and Twelfth St. on the south, Kelley was able to gather data on the income level and nationality mix that eventually became the source for the details presented on the maps of the area that accompanied the text for *HH Maps and Papers* (1895) by the HH residents in 1895.

Kelley investigated sweatshops, delivered speeches, and organized and conducted mass meetings to bring the sweatshop conditions in the tenements of Chicago to public attention.

Her campaign was widely covered in the newspapers and journals. She lobbied the Illinois General Assembly for protective legislation for women and children and for an end to child labor. In addition, she organized a public campaign to draw attention to the strikingly poor condition of the public schools in the neighborhood surrounding HH. There were more students who should attend school than there was classroom space for them. She initiated public campaigns to address these conditions and was at the forefront of efforts to enforce the new 1891 compulsory education legislation that had been enacted by the Illinois General Assembly. Her successful effort to make the public aware of the deplorable conditions in which men, women, and children worked long hours for paltry wages in the needle trades in poorly lighted and ventilated, and often unheated, cramped space with inadequate sanitation resulted in an investigation of sweatshop manufacture in Chicago by a committee of the Illinois General Assembly. The tour of the HH neighborhood was led by Florence Kelley and other settlement workers. The legislators were stunned by the conditions they saw, especially those in which women and children worked. One of the results, aided by the organized lobbying effort of Florence Kelley, Mary Kenney, JA, and other HH colleagues, was the Illinois Factory Inspection Act of 1893. It required inspections of workshops; no more than eight-hour workdays for women and children; and special safeguards for child workers. It provided for factory inspectors who had the power to prosecute those in violation of the law and in the interest of public safety permitted the destruction of clothing that had been produced in disease-infested workshops. In 1894 Kelley confessed to Ely, "I personally participate in the work of social reform because part of it develops along Socialist lines, and part is an absolutely necessary protest against the brutalizing of us all by Capitalism. Not because our Hull-House work alone would satisfy me" (21 June 1894).

Newly elected Illinois governor John P. Altgeld appointed Florence Kelley as the first chief factory inspector in Illinois on 12 July 1893 with a salary of fifteen hundred dollars. She had a total appropriation of twelve thousand dollars to hire ten deputies, several of whom were women connected with HH. In order to be more effective in her position, Kelley studied law at Northwestern Univ. and was admitted to the Illinois Bar in 1894. She was so successful as chief factory inspector for four years that manufacturers formed the Illinois Assn. of Manufacturers and began an effort to attack the factory inspection law. In 1895 they succeeded in getting the eight-hour provision of the law declared unconstitutional. They were also successful in 1897 in getting Gov. John R. Tanner to replace her, even though he initially had planned to reappoint her.

For the next two years, Florence Kelley continued to live and work at HH, while JA, Lillian D. Wald, and others of her progressive reformer colleagues tried to find her suitable employment. JA sought an appointment for her to teach economics at Cosmopolitan Univ. in Washington, D.C. Kelley was also nominated for a position on a national industrial commission being formed to consider labor and management problems. With Theodore Roosevelt, the newly elected governor of New York, JA and Lillian Wald also pursued a position for Kelley as chief factory inspector for the state of New York. None of these efforts was successful. In the meantime, to cover her expenses, Kelley accepted a job paying fifty dollars a month as an evening librarian at the John Crerar Library, which had been established in 1897 in Chicago as a free public library. Kelley continued to support protective legislation for women and children, an end to child labor, and an enforceable compulsory school-attendance law. She declined a position as assistant chief factory inspector, offered to her in 1901 by the newly elected Illinois governor, Richard Yates, which would have been a demotion from her former rank.

Throughout her years at HH, she wrote and published regularly. In addition to the four annual Illinois factory inspector reports and the special research papers that she wrote, she contributed two articles to *HH Maps and Papers*: "The Sweating System" and, with Alzina P. Stevens, "Wage-Earning Children." She also directed the production of the two maps showing neighborhood income levels and ethnic diversity that she fought to keep as part of the publication. Kelley published articles in German for *Archiv* magazine, presented papers to the CWC and a convention of factory inspectors in 1894, and later prepared a series of lectures that she delivered with JA during July and Aug. 1899 through the Univ. of Chicago Extension Program. In the twentieth century, she continued to publish and to speak. Her articles against child labor and in favor of protective legislation for women and children appeared in the publications of the National Conf. of Charities and Correction and in the *Survey*. Her lectures "Efficiency in Factory Inspection" and "The Street Trader under Illinois Law" became articles in *The Child in the City* (1912). Kelley also published two books, *Some Ethical Gains through Legislation* (1905), based on the lectures she had presented with JA in 1899, and *Modern Industry in Relation to the Family, Health, Education, and Morality* (1914), her analysis of how socialism might develop in the United States and how it would nationalize industry. She was delighted when *Some Ethical Gains* was used as a reference by students at Harvard, Yale, Columbia, and the Univ. of Pennsylvania.

While at HH, she became aware of the work of the Illinois Consumers' League. In her article about the settlement that appeared in 1898 in the *New England Magazine*, she credited the league with educating consumers about how they could improve the lives of workers. That may have been prophetic, for in 1899 she was offered and accepted the position of general secretary for the National Consumers' League. She moved to New York City and remained there for the rest of her life.

Kelley described the league as a way to "arouse public opinion in favor of the new legislation" to help improve and protect the working environment in industry. It "was not organized to beat down the price of groceries or dress goods. What it wanted to do was awaken responsibility for conditions under which goods were made and distributed, and through investigation, education and legislation to mobilize public opinion" (Mumford, Kelley Interview). By 1904 she had organized at least fifty-eight associated leagues in twenty-one states. Her goal was to rouse enough public sentiment to get laws passed at the state and then at the federal levels to better protect women and children in the workplace. She established standards for working conditions and created a "white label" for garments that the manufacturer declared had been "Made under clean and healthful conditions—use of label authorized after investigation." In addition, by the early years of the 1900s, Kelley became a supporter of a minimum wage. In 1911 she argued before the National Conf. of Charities and Correction that a minimum wage would eliminate poverty and the need for charity. She spoke frequently to consumers' leagues, schools, colleges, and state and national organizations, from the National Conf. of Charities and Correction to such groups as the Denver Press Club, the Ladies' Catholic Benevolent Society, and the Women's Club of Smyrna, Del.

Working with Lillian D. Wald, Kelley helped found the National Child Labor Com. to promote child welfare. The committee's influence helped to establish the U.S. Children's Bureau in 1912. Kelley and Julia C. Lathrop, the Bureau's first chief, had long been friends and partners in many progressive reform efforts, especially those identified with women and children. Kelley supported the maternity and infant care programs initiated and promoted by the Children's Bureau, compulsory education legislation, a child labor amendment to the U.S. Constitution, and a minimum wage law.

Kelley maintained her lifelong friendship with JA and with other progressive reformers. Her personal life was centered around her children. MRS and JA continued to be supportive of the Kelley children, who initially remained in Chicago when Florence first set out for New York. MRS provided financial support for Nicholas, whom she helped send to Harvard as an undergraduate and then on to law school, and for Margaret, who became a student in 1905 at Smith, where tragically she died from heart failure during her first week of school. John became a writer and his mother's constant companion for the remainder of his life.

Kelley was one of the pioneer advocates of woman suffrage, and she served as vice-president of the National American Woman Suffrage Assn. (NAWSA). Because of her stance on the need for women to have protective legislation in the workplace, she, along with most of her progressive reform friends, did not support the effort to achieve an Equal Rights Amendment to the U.S. Constitution. Like JA, in 1909 she also worked to organize and supported the NAACP. Kelley maintained an antiwar stance during World War I and like JA participated in the U.S. women's peace movement. She attended the Conf. of Women for Permanent Peace at The Hague in 1919 and became a member of the WILPF. She attended the third congress of that organization in Vienna in 1921. During World War I, she was appointed by the secretary of war to inspect factories where uniforms were made. After the war, she helped raise money and support to provide food for the starving children in Europe.

During the "red scare" in the 1920s and 1930s, Kelley, like JA and Julia Lathrop and so many of their reformer colleagues, was attacked by right-wing patriots as too radical and disloyal. The names of all three women appeared on the War Department's infamous Spiderweb chart. In addition, Florence Kelley was identified in Mrs. Elizabeth Dilling's *Red Network* as a socialist; founder and president of the Inter-collegiate Socialist Society; vice-president of League for Industrial Democracy; director of the National Child Labor Com., 1904–20, the NAACP, and the NWTUL; president of the Henry Street Settlement; and a resident at HH.

Toward the end of her life, Florence Kelley designed and had built a summer home for herself and her son John at Naskeag Point, Maine. She furnished it with Kelley family heirlooms and objects and loved to spend time there unwinding from the pressure of her National Consumers' League job. She died on 17 Feb. 1932 after several months of treatment for cancer, about which she did not tell even close friends. She was buried near her Naskeag Point home. The National Consumers' League, assisted by HH, the Henry Street Settlement, and assorted other organizations, held a memorial service in New York City for Kelley on 16 Mar. 1932. Little did Julia Lathrop know when she wrote to colleagues on 9 Mar. 1932 to plan Florence Kelley's memorial service at HH that she would actually be helping plan for their joint service, which was held at the HH on 6 May 1932 (Lathrop died on 15 April). One of the speakers on that occasion was Kelley's protégé Frances Perkins, who as secretary of labor would become the first woman to serve at the cabinet level in the U.S. government. She remembered Kelley as "explosive, hot-tempered, determined" and "no gentle saint. She spoke accusingly and passionately when moved by the sight of what she thought of as social injustice or callous unconcern." Perkins described Kelley as "a terrifying opponent" with "the voice and the presence of a great actress." She recalled Kelley as "a handsome woman" who was "witty," with a "deep maternal feeling" that "spread over all the children and helpless people of society." Frances Perkins maintained that "feeling was probably the key to her tremendous drive" for she "never ceased from toil" ("My Recollections of Florence Kelley," 18–19).

On 14 Nov. 1924, Florence Kelley was honored by the National Consumers' League at the dinner they gave to celebrate the twenty-fifth anniversary of the birth of their organization. Old friends joined the celebration: Julia Lathrop served as toast mistress, and JA and Lillian Wald spoke. After Kelly's death, the league also established an award in her honor to be given annually to someone who showed extraordinary commitment to social justice—something Florence Kelley exhibited all of her life.

2. The *Report on the Manufacturing Industries in the United States at the Eleventh Census: 1890*, pt. 2:130–45, indicated that women worked at least ten hours a day in miserable conditions, with wages from almost nothing to 80 cents a day. In addition, the labor report of 1888, published in 1889, indicated that women working in Chicago made an average of $5.74 for a six-day, ten-hour-day week (*Fourth Annual Report of the Commissioner of Labor, 1888: Working Women in Large Cities*, 69).

3. See JA to Henry Demarest Lloyd, 18 Nov. 1891, n. 5, above.

4. Addams, *Twenty Years*, 212. Mary Kenney's first meeting at the settlement may have taken place in 1891. In her autobiographical study, Kenney offered no date for the meeting, but rather explained: "One day, while I was working at my trade, I received a letter from

Miss Jane Addams. She invited me to Hull House for dinner. She said she wanted me to met some people from England who were interested in the labor movement. I had never heard of Miss Addams or Hull House. I had no idea who she was. . . .

"I decided that I would not accept the invitation. . . . No club people for me! At home I read Miss Addams' letter to Mother. She said, 'Sure, Mary, you must go and see the lady. You can't judge without knowing her and she might be different from the other club women. It's condemning you are. You wouldn't like it if someone you didn't know condemned you'" (O'Sullivan, "Autobiography," 62–63).

5. O'Sullivan, "Autobiography," 65.

6. Starr, "HH (Chicago)," 700. The same statement appears in *HH Maps and Papers*, 214. Mary Kenney O'Sullivan indicated in her autobiography that as an official organizer for the AFL, she was present during the following union gatherings at HH: "The Women's Book Binders Union 1, the Shirt Makers' Union, Men and Women's Cloakmakers' Union, Cab Driver's Union, a gathering of representatives of the Retail Clerk Workers, the strike committee of the Garment Workers, and the Clothing Cutters" (67). In 1896 the laundry workers formed a union that met on Monday evenings at the settlement for several years. The Tick Sewers' Union, with a charter membership of fifty, was organized in Oct. 1900 and continued to meet at the settlement. The Dorcas Federal Labor Union, "composed of representatives from all the unions in the city which included women in their membership," also met monthly at the settlement (Addams, *Twenty Years*, 212). See also JA to Henry Demarest Lloyd, 18 Nov. 1891, n. 6, above.

7. With the support of the CWC, Florence Kelley opened the HH Labor Bureau in Jan. 1892, primarily to help young women find safe, reliable, and better-paying household positions. It was located in rented quarters near HH at 247 (later 818) Polk St. The bureau continued to operate throughout the 1890s, often in conjunction with the settlement's relief office. By June 1892, Florence Kelley had turned over the work of the bureau to other HH residents, including, at different times, Mary Keyser, Julia Lathrop, and Amanda Johnson. Any early success had been diminished by the high unemployment rate associated with the economic depression that began in 1893 and lasted into the mid-90s.

In 1895, when EGS was asked by a reporter at Chautauqua, N.Y., what HH was doing in support of women and girls, she offered in part: "For a time we had an intelligence office in connection with the House, and the effort was made to have a regular business bargain made between the employer and employee, to have a contract signed by both parties, but the scheme was a failure, for we could not guarantee that the employee we furnished was perfectly competent in every respect we could not demand very much from the employer. In time the plan was abandoned entirely" ("Woman's Work at HH").

On 8 May 1892, a mass meeting was held at the Bricklayers' Hall, site of many trade union gatherings in Chicago, to publicly and loudly denounce the sweating system of manufacture. Rev. Jenkin Lloyd Jones chaired the gathering, and all speakers were permitted but five minutes for their comments, with the exception of Henry Demarest Lloyd, who made the primary address. However, it was remarks by Kelley that electrified the crowd. With her forceful contention that labor unions—not government—should use their collective and organized might to wipe out child labor and the hideous conditions that the sweating system permitted, she earned her leadership role in the fight to eradicate the sweating system that would engage her during the remainder of the 1890s while she lived in Chicago.

8. In Mar. 1892, women workers at Selz, Schwab, and Co., a shoe manufacturer, went out on strike to support men workers who were striking against a severe wage cut. Members of the CWC investigated and supported the women by providing money and encouragement. In addition, the club formed a committee led by Ellen Henrotin, with Emma Rogers (see Two Essays in the *Forum*, Nov. and Oct. 1892, n. 5, below) and JA as members, to try to arrange an arbitrated settlement. Even with considerable support from other unions throughout

Chicago, the arbitration attempt was unsuccessful. By the end of Apr. 1892, members of the CWC were formulating plans for an organization to create educational and social opportunities for working women. JA was not listed as a member of this committee.

9. In 1892 the Star Knitting Works was located at 261 and 263 (later 871and 873) Franklin St. It was organized by Julius Abraham (b. 1859) in 1889, who was identified as the president, five years after he arrived in Chicago from Barwalde, Germany. By 1896 the Star Knitting Works, which had moved to 250 (later 429) Clinton St., disappeared from the Chicago city directories. Abraham continued to live in Chicago and to manage other underwear garment manufacturing operations into the early twentieth century.

10. Murray Floyd Tuley (1827–1905) was born and educated in Louisville, Ky., until the age of thirteen, when he began clerking in a store there. After his widowed mother, Priscilla Buckner Tuley, remarried, he moved with her to Chicago, where he studied law in his stepfather Richard J. Hamilton's law office, 1844–46. He completed his studies at the Louisville Law Institute, 1846–47, and was admitted to the Illinois Bar in 1847. He married Catharine Edmondson of Missouri in 1851, and she became one of the influential members of the CWC. After serving in the Mexican War as a first lieutenant in the 5th Infantry Regiment, Illinois Volunteers, he practiced law in Santa Fe, 1848–54, and during that time served one term in the territorial legislature and two years as the Terr. of N.M.'s attorney general. He returned to Chicago and entered the practice of law in 1854, serving as Chicago's corporation counsel, 1869–73, during which he was instrumental in drafting and securing passage of the act under which cities in Illinois are incorporated. He was the head of the firm of Tuley, Stiles, and Lewis, 1873–79, when he first became a circuit judge in Cook Co., Ill., and served until his death at Pennoyer Sanitarium in Kenosha, Wis. He became a noted jurist and advocate of arbitration and was recognized for his fairness.

11. Addams, "Judge Murray F. Tuley," *The Excellent*, 73–74.

12. Addams, "The Settlement as a Factor in the Labor Movement," *HH Maps and Papers*, 199. For the remainder of the 1890s, JA continued to write and speak about organized labor and management. A strike at the Pullman Palace Car Co. in Pullman, Ill., in the late spring and early summer of 1894, provided JA with another learning experience. She attempted to share the experience with the public in an essay she wrote about the event. See "A Modern Tragedy: An Analysis of the Pullman Strike" (several manuscript versions all in SCPC, JAC; *JAPM*, 46:589, 647–49, 722–37; 47:611–38, unpublished until 1912).

During the United Garment Workers of America strike in Chicago between Mar. and May 1896, JA unsuccessfully promoted an arbitrated settlement, but HH provided relief for the strikers. "[A]ll great principles, especially when opposed by wealth and power, are slow in getting well lodged in the popular mind, and if this struggle results in the changed attitude of the public toward the great principles of organization and arbitration, which shall bear fruit in the next effort of organized labor for its rights, the suffering will not have been in vain" ("The Tailors' Strike," *HH Bulletin* 1, no. 5 [May 1896]: 5). See also Excerpts from Addresses, 24 Nov. 1897; JA to MRS, 25 July 1899, n. 9; and JA to MRS, [4?] [June 1900], n. 14, all below.

Among JA's other presentations about labor during the 1890s were "Testimony of Jane Addams," *Report on the Chicago Strike of June–July, 1894*, 645–48, and *JAPM*, 46:699–703 (see also Testimony, [May–June 1894] 18 Aug. 1894, below); "Significance of Organized Labor," International Assn. of Machinists, *Monthly Journal*, 551–52, and *JAPM*, 46:869–70A; and "Trades Unions and Public Duty," published in *Railroad Trainmen's Journal*, 1070–86, *American Journal of Sociology*, and 448–62; *JAPM*, 46:902–15. JA's position in support of the development of organized labor found its way into most of her public presentations. See also JA to MRS, [4?] [June 1900], n. 14, below.

13. 26 Apr. 1892.

14. Joseph W. Errant (1860–1912) was a lawyer and the founder of the Bureau of Justice in Chicago, established to help the poor who could not afford legal assistance (see Two Es-

says in the *Forum*, Nov. and Oct. 1892, n. 166, below). He was born in Lumberton, N.C., to Sigismund W. and Amalia Pohl Errant. After going to New York in 1862, the Errant family spent two years in Germany before arriving in 1874 in Chicago, where Joseph attended high school. After one year at the Univ. of Michigan, he worked at the Chicago Public Library until 1884, when he began to study law and taught in evening schools. He graduated from the Union College of Law in 1886 and in 1888 wed physician Derexa Morey; the couple had four children. Throughout his adult life, Errant was devoted to reform causes, including the Protective Agency for Women and Children, Illinois Conf. of Charities and Correction, Civil Service Comm. of Chicago, and Central Anti-Imperialist League. He was also a leader in the Sunset Club and served a term on the Chicago Board of Education.

## Article in the *Chicago Inter Ocean*

*From the beginning of the settlement, Jane Addams and Ellen Starr were hopeful that "the power of cooperation"[1] could solve some of the problems that they saw in their neighborhood. By 1892 Addams was nudging the settlement itself toward a semicooperative living model where residents shared the expenses of living together.[2] Early in the next year, she explored the possibility of creating a cooperative sewing factory in the settlement neighborhood. Addams also tried, unsuccessfully, to find sufficient capital to permit Mary Kenney and a group of women bookbinders to develop their own cooperative bindery.[3] Over the middle years of the 1890s, Addams created at least two other ventures based on the ideas of the cooperative movement.[4] These were a cooperative residence for women and a coal cooperative association that Addams expected might lead to a grocery cooperative.[5] Except for Hull-House itself, only the cooperative living residence for women was successful.*

*While Jane Addams was trying to help women workers settle differences with their employers through arbitration,[6] she was also planning a special cooperative residence for women workers in association with Hull-House. At her invitation, Grace Dodge,[7] philanthropist, social worker, and educator, spoke at Hull-House on 12 October 1891. To more than three hundred attentive listeners, Dodge explained the idea of the cooperative living club she had helped found among young working women in New York City[8] and urged a similar facility in Chicago. But it was not until 1 May 1892, with the opening reception 4 May, that Jane Addams, with the help of Mary Wilmarth, Mary Rozet Smith, and other Chicago women philanthropists,[9] was able to find appropriate quarters on Ewing Street near the settlement and a core of interested women to begin what became one of the first cooperative woman's residential clubs in the United States. Here working women could find safe, clean, and reasonably priced quarters and mutual understanding and support, especially when a strike was called.*

*The Jane Club, named in honor of its founder, Jane Addams, grew quickly. By November 1893, there were thirty-five paying members in three flats in one entire building on Ewing Street. In 1894 the club created its own constitution and bylaws and limited its membership to one hundred women.[10] It began with a housemother and two servants, with the residents helping serve meals and clean up.*

*The experiment was so successful that in 1898, a new clubhouse was constructed by Hull-House at 223 (later 814) Ewing Street, with funds supplied primarily by Mary Rozet Smith and her aunt Sarah Porter Smith.[11] The three-story brick structure, designed by the Pond brothers with English basement and situated on property sold by Helen Culver to Mary Rozet Smith, had bedroom space for thirty members, a library, a living room, and a dining room. By 1906 dues were three dollars a week. Rent the Jane Club members paid to Hull-House was earmarked to serve as an endowment for the Smith Building or Children's House of Hull-House.*

Chicago, Ill. 30 June 1892

## THE JANE CLUB
### WORKING GIRLS LIVE CHEAPLY AND PLEASANTLY ON THE CO-OPERATIVE PLAN.

Seated in a white wicker chair last night, a bright young woman was softly struming one of Audran's[12] dreamy waltzes on a guitar. A couple of other young women sat in the cozy room ostensibly reading, while in reality their feet were impatiently keeping time to the soft music furnished by the girl, with the guitar. The room was plainly used for reception purposes. The furniture was dainty, and the walls decorated with pretty etchings and water colors. Here and there were those nondescript little things which add to the beauty of an apartment and at once proclaim that they have been made by feminine hands. Altogether there was an air of home about the place that made a man wish that he had a home of his own.

The room was the reception-room of the Jane Club, a boarding club for working girls, on the co-operative plan, at Nos 249 and 253 Ewing street. While the club is the first one of the kind in this country, and is not yet six weeks old, it has two ground flats and fifteen members. The idea is that of Miss Jane Addams and Miss Wilmarth, who have done much to make it successful. When a reporter for THE INTER OCEAN called last night Miss Maggie Toomey,[13] treasurer of the club, did the honors. She is enthusiastic over the scheme, and her black eyes snapped with excitement while chatting on it.

Said she: "There are a lot of successful working girls clubs in Chicago; lunch clubs, study clubs, summer clubs, boarding clubs, and I don't know what all. But we are different from them all, in as much as we have no rules and no matron to order us around. We do as we please—in most things. Here every girl has a say in the affairs of the club. New members are elected, the stewardess appointed, bills contracted and paid by the members themselves on the co-operative basis. We have two ground flats with fourteen rooms for which we pay $45 per month rent.

"Nine of these rooms are chambers. We figure that a girl can live in a co-operative club for $3 per week. Last month we figured it out, and it cost each girl $2.61 1/2 per week for her room and board. Cheap, isn't it? And then each girl is her own mistress. If she cares to go out of an evening she does so, and lets herself in with a latch-key. Isn't that nice? By July 15 we hope to have the entire building filled with co-operative club members. Our officers are: Miss Mary E. Kenney, president; Rena Doeing, vice president; W. Kelley, recording secretary, and Maggie Toomey, treasurer."

Miss Toomey led the way through the flats, both of which were prettily furnished. Bright etchings, engravings, mezzo-tints, and water colors hung on the walls, while rugs and matting covered the floor. The bedrooms were as light and airy as the rest of the club. From all appearances the lives of the Jane Club members have fallen in pleasant places.

PD (*Chicago Inter Ocean*, 30 June 1892, HH Scrapbook 1:15; *JAPM*, Addendum 10:6ff).

1. Addams, *Twenty Years*, 133.

2. As additional residents joined the founders in the HH venture, JA could not support the enterprise on her own. The residents had to cooperate in sharing household expenses, primarily those associated with food and service. In describing the settlement residents' program in 1894, JA wrote, "The expenses of the residents are defrayed by themselves on the plan of a co-operative club under the direction of a house committee [of residents, one of which was always JA]. A limited number of fellowships has been established" (*HH Maps and Papers*, 229). By Jan. 1893, each resident, including EGS, who was to begin contributing twenty-five dollars per month, and some long-term visitors were assigned specific monthly fees. The accounts for the 1891–95 period indicate that even with this fee structure established by the residents themselves, in most months between twenty-five and forty dollars from the "ten account" funds raised by JA to meet general needs of the settlement had to be used to support resident expenses.

JA realized that several residents, central to the settlement program, might never be able to pay their expenses at the settlement. She created a "fellowship" program and sought to raise funds specifically to help these special residents. Some fellowships were provided by wealthy individuals or families, others by organizations. One of the early fellowships was offered by the Chicago chapter of the Assn. of Collegiate Alumnae, which became the Assn. of University Women. Members of the association began volunteering at HH during 1889–90. For the year 1893 their fellowship supported Julia Lathrop and for 1894 Jeannette C. Welch. EGS had help with monthly expenses from Mary Wilmarth, who also made it possible for her to secure bookbinding training from T. J. Cobden-Sanderson in 1897 and supported her 1916 campaign for alderman as a socialist. By May 1895, when JA promoted the idea of HH fellowships to graduates at RC, MRS was providing fellowship support for Dr. Harriet Rice, the settlement's first African American worker. See also JA to Anita McCormick Blaine, 11 Dec. 1895, n. 7; and Lists of Residents and Fellowships, 3 Nov. 1896, both below.

3. See JA to Henry Demarest Lloyd, 2 Jan. 1892 [1893], and notes, below. Coincident with the World's Columbian Exposition and the economic depression of the 1890s, cooperative sewing rooms were created in the HH neighborhood.

4. The successful cooperative movement began in England among the weavers of Rochdale in 1844. They promulgated several principles that when applied to a cooperative venture seemed to provide a better chance for success. These included voluntary and open membership, democratic member control and equitable economic participation, education and training for members, independence for the organization, concern for their community, and cooperation among cooperatives. By Dec. 1895, when the Cooperative Union of America was organized in Cambridge, Mass., its leaders, one of whom was JA, who became a member of

the first board, recognized that the movement in the United States had not been as successful as it was in Europe.

5. The idea for a coal yard was discussed in a HH residents' meeting in Sept. 1893. A committee of the residents was appointed to investigate the possibility. After consulting neighbors and members of the HH Woman's Club, a committee of residents recommended starting a coal business. The Nineteenth Ward Improvement Club assumed responsibility for promoting the HH Coal Co-Operative, created in Nov. 1893. The goal was to make it as easy and as inexpensive as possible for HH neighbors to obtain fuel to heat with during the winter. The organizers made arrangements to purchase coal at wholesale prices and sell it at current market prices. They expected to share the net profits, that is, the difference between the wholesale price plus expenses and the retail price, at the end of each year with those who patronized their cooperative. Initially, orders were placed and received through the HH Coffee House at 240 W. Polk St. and filled at the HH Playground. In the first ten days of operation, the cooperative collected $115 through sales. By the beginning of 1894, the coal yard was located at the corner of Ewing and Halsted streets with a telephone number of West 70. JA served as the treasurer, and she kept the accounts. "The benefit of the co-operative plan," the association stated, "cannot be over estimated. It not only gives the necessaries of life at the lowest possible price, but fosters the habit of systematic saving and teaches OBJECTIVELY the value of mutual effort." In addition, the association announced that, "It is hoped the enterprise may be so successful as to warrant the incorporation of the GROCERIES and PROVISIONS" (HH Co-Operative Assn. broadside, 15 Sept. 1894). See also Minutes of a HH Residents Meeting, 10 Dec. 1893, n. 17, below.

JA believed, "As everything is done on a cash basis, the project is practically self-sustaining from the start. On a similar plan as the coal-yard, groceries will be obtained from a wholesale house at the lowest possible figure. They will be sold in large or small quantities, as desired, at the market price. Thus the retail groceries will not be underbidden and any possible antagonism will be avoided. The benefit to the buyers will arise when the accrued profits are divided among them at stated times in proportion to their purchases. The profit will result from the savings in delivery and the extremely low price at which the goods are first bought. A system of credit checks will be adopted, by which the small buyers may have a percentage of their money refunded.

"It is the purpose of the association to confine its operations to the poor in the neighborhood of the store and the patronage of those beyond the need of such help will not be encouraged. The coming winter will be more trying to the poor than any in several years" ("Plans for the Poor").

At the end of the 1894 heating season, HH supporter William H. Colvin gave $375 to make up the coal-yard program's deficit. For the 1894–95 heating season, the association added wood to their offering of coal but had not yet branched out into acquiring and selling groceries. After another year of deficit, the Co-Operative Assn. quietly disbanded its efforts at selling fuel or groceries. JA reported that it was the "philanthropic policy" of the members of the enterprise (those who purchased coal by the ton) that spelled its demise. Voting members arranged to give those less fortunate, who could buy coal only by the basket, one basket free for every five they purchased, "because it would be a shame to keep them waiting for the dividend" at year end (Addams, *Twenty Years*, 135).

6. See Articles in the *Chicago News* and the *Chicago Daily Tribune*, 29 and 30 Apr. 1892, above.

7. For a biographical note on Grace Hoadley Dodge, see JA to Jenkin Lloyd Jones, 3 Nov. 1890, n. 2, above.

8. Association Hall in New York City was a nonresidential cooperative club for girls. It was an active educational and mutual support effort that also promoted philanthropic enterprise among its members, who paid twenty-five cents a month to maintain their quarters.

9. The account book titled "HH Acc't Oct 1st 1891" kept by JA indicated that between Apr. 1892 and Dec. 1893, the Jane Club had $2,282.14 in support, primarily from HH friends, including the Colvin and Coonley families, Mary Wilmarth, former EGS student Helen Fairbank, and MRS. JA provided nearly $500 from personal funds. Some of the money was used to purchase furnishings, but some was spent on basic club start-up expenses, including rent, food, service, and fuel.

On the second anniversary of the founding of the Jane Club, when the membership stood at fifty, the *Chicago Herald* published an article on 18 May 1894 entitled "Chicago Jane Club." It presented the following financial data as evidence of the club's financial success as a cooperative venture: "From May 1 1892, to Jan. 1, 1893 the amount received for board was $1,788.38. The expenditures were: For rent, $249; fuel, $24; wages, $264.25; gas, $108.20; ice, $26.33; groceries, $648.80; milk, $113.01; meat, $273.08 making a total bill for provisions of $1,034.89. Sundries amounted to $36.74. For the second six months Jan. 1 to July 1, 1893, increased membership ran the receipts up to $2,794.95. Rent increased to $447, fuel $140.40, wages to $373.65, gas $155.76, but ice went down to $4.60, and a watchman cost $10. Provisions rose to $1,568.46. Sundries amounted to $34.78. The club was $55.26 in debt July 1. The second half of 1893 showed receipts amounting to $2,818.82. Expenses were as follows: Rent, $415; fuel, $192.50; wages, $360; watchman, $10; gas bill, $106.65; ice, $35.95; provisions, $1,673.88; small expenses, $78.93. The club closed that year in debt to the amount of $149.94. May 1 . . . there is cash on hand of $10.41, and a debt of $65.11."

10. HH Scrapbook 2:39, *JAPM*, Addendum 10:7ff. The Jane Club was incorporated on 12 June 1895, shortly after HH was incorporated. JA was one of the incorporators and also one of the seven trustees. The club's purpose was "to secure and promote the mutual comfort and improvement of its members and to this end to provide and maintain a house or houses in the City of Chicago, at which its members may lodge and board upon the cooperative plan" (Jane Club, HH, Chicago, "Articles of Incorporation"). The club also had a constitution and bylaws.

11. On 28 Feb. 1897, JA reported to SAAH, "We are trying very hard to get money for a Jane Club building, and find it very hard these dull times" (IU, Lilly, SAAH; *JAPM*, 5:590). While she would eventually have some success, with one thousand dollars promised by Mary Wilmarth and one thousand dollars by Nancy Foster, the real fund-raising break came when MRS's maiden aunt, Sarah Porter Smith, committed ten thousand dollars to the project. When the Smith family also decided to help with acquisition of the land on which the club would be constructed, JA wrote to MRS, "I don't like the notion of the family offering a building and then being drawn into a lot as well" (29 Mar. 1898, SCPC, JAC; *JAPM*, 3:1016). But JA found that she could easily apply the Wilmarth and Foster funds to the coffeehouse and theater project for which she was raising money at the same time, and so she accepted the Smith family offer with relief.

"'Accept the offer?' said Miss Jane Addams to-day. 'Well, I should say so! This building will be right back of Hull house gymnasium and will be connected with the steam-heat and electric plants of the Hull house buildings. It will be a three-story brick structure, with what is known as an English basement, and will accommodate twenty-five girls. Work will be begun immediately.

"'Considering how little Ald. Powers admires us,' added Miss Addams, 'and how he would like to force us out of the 19th ward, this addition to our buildings and our work seems more than enjoyable, even in a political point of view. The Jane club girls are delighted with the prospect too. They have held noble to their club during these six years, despite poor quarters and discouraging circumstances, and their pleasure at this new turn in their affairs can easily be imagined'" ("Jane Club's New Home," *Chicago Daily News*, 2 Apr. 1898).

The *Chicago Daily Tribune* published the following description: "It will be three stories high and will front twenty-seven feet with a depth of seventy-eight. It is an English basement house, and will be constructed of a combination of paving and common brick. The interior will be finished in whitewood, stained and varnished, there being some hardwood in one or two of the rooms. . . . The basement will contain the dining-room, bicycle-room, lockers, and storage, and in the second story there will be the drawing, reading, and sleeping rooms. There will be about thirty-two sleeping rooms" ("Jane Club's New Home," 14 Aug. 1898). Architect's plans for the Jane Club dated June 1896 are extant; see UIC, JAMC, HH Assn.; *JAPM*, Addendum 10:3.

Helen Culver, who sold the lot to MRS on which the new Jane Club would be built, agreed to take only $3,000 for it, contributing the difference of $1,035. The Pond brothers anticipated that the building cost would be $13,000; however, JA recorded in her personal record book for 1895–1905, in which she kept a list of annual and special project donors, that the structure alone had cost $13,500. See JA to MRS, 23 Mar. 1898, below.

Sarah Porter Smith (1819–1907) was the daughter of Lucy Raney Bradner and John Smith and sister of Charles Mather Smith, John Bradner Smith, Lester Smith, and George Cotton Smith, all of whom were born and educated in Ogdensburg, N.Y. She arrived in Chicago about 1858 with her widower brother, John Bradner Smith (1816–93), with whom she made her home on LaSalle St. until his death. In 1894 she purchased two acres of property in Columbia, S.C., on Richland St. and across Lincoln St. from a home owned by her brother George Cotton Smith and his wife. On at least two occasions, once in 1894 and again in 1899, JA accompanied MRS to visit Miss Smith in Columbia. She lived there until 1899, when she sold the property to her brother George and returned to Chicago to live with the Charles Mather Smith family until her death at 19 Walton Place. She was buried in Graceland Cemetery in Chicago. See also JA to SAAH, 28 Dec. 1894, n. 3, below.

12. Edmond Audran (1842–1901) was a French composer of operettas and vaudeville pieces.

13. Margaret ("Maggie") V. Toomey (1861?–97), born in Lyndon, Wis., was the daughter of John and Margaret Toomey. She left home at the age of fifteen to work in Chicago, where she became a close friend and colleague of Mary Kenney. A bindery worker and a member of the Women's Bookbinders Union No. 1, organized by Kenney in 1891, Toomey was also associated with Kenney in an effort in 1892–93 to create a cooperative bindery, which failed when JA was unable to secure the capital they needed to start their business. Toomey was active in efforts to control sweatshop manufacture. She was among those seated on the stage at the mass meeting called by Mary Kenney through the Chicago Trade and Labor Assembly and held in the Central Music Hall on 19 Feb. 1892 to protest sweatshop manufacture and create a public awareness of the problem. In Jan. 1893, she was nominated by the cloakmakers' union as a candidate for the position of trustee for the Chicago Trade and Labor Assembly.

Toomey was among the first residents of the Jane Club in 1892. By Oct. 1894, she had given birth to a daughter, whom she named Jane in honor of JA. In Jan. 1895, with the help of MRS, she and her daughter moved to the East to keep house for Kenney. In Jan. 1897, JA began searching for a suitable place for "Little Jane," as Toomey's daughter was known at HH, because her mother was terminally ill with tuberculosis. MRS, LSA, and JWA, as well as several HH residents, seriously considered taking responsibility for "Little Jane"; however, newly married HH residents Ernest Carroll Moore and his wife, physician Dorothea Rhodes Lummis Moore (see JA to Anita McCormick Blaine, 11 Dec. 1895, n. 4, below), made arrangements to see that she grew up under their care in the home of Ernest Carroll Moore's parents, John and Martha Moore, in Coitsville Twp., Mahoning Co., Ohio. Margaret Toomey died in Chicago on 31 Jan. 1897 and was buried in Lyndon, Wis.

## To Bayard Taylor Holmes

*Initially, Jane Addams and Ellen Starr shared responsibility for arranging the classes and lectures that Hull-House offered for its neighbors. In the beginning, Ellen managed the College Extension Program, and Jane secured suitable lecturers.*[1] *When Jane wrote the following letter to Bayard Taylor Holmes,*[2] *she was in the process of organizing the Working People's Social Science Club lecture calendar for the fall of 1892.*[3] *She spent considerable effort in securing the most interesting speakers on timely topics and often used the members of established Hull-House clubs as a core group for launching other special reform efforts.*

335 S Halsted St. Hull-House. [Chicago, Ill.] Sept 15" 1892

My dear Dr Holmes.

Would it be possible for you to give a talk before our Social Science Club, Oct 18" on Tuesday evening[4]—We open the course the first Tuesday in Oct. when Dr Ware will begin[5]—We hope a series of meetings that may end in a "19th Ward improvement Club,"[6] or something similar. Could you give a talk on "The growth of Filth, Diseases, Cholera &c," I mean of course a different formulation of the topic, but that in substance. We will be very much indebted to you for this one more favor—With kindest regards to Mrs Holmes. I am very sincerely yours

Jane Addams.

P.S. I should be glad for an early reply as we are arranging our program.

ALS (Amherst College Library; *JAPM*, 2:1328–29).

1. At the start in 1890, many of the lecture topics related to history, foreign locales, literature, science, and art, but expanded to include politics and social reform. Lecturers were men and women, university professors, religious leaders, labor leaders, and buffs; lawyers, judges, and directors of public Chicago institutions were soon added. Musicians from throughout the city performed for ethnic nights and in concerts hosted on Sunday afternoons beginning in 1890.

Among frequent presenters in the early 1890s were Jenkin Lloyd Jones, Lorado Taft, John Dewey, Clarence Darrow, and Henry Demarest Lloyd. Surviving correspondence attests to JA's almost constant efforts to secure lecturers for the settlement. For example, see the following: JA to Sara Mole Barrows, 16 Oct. 1889, SCPC, JAC; *JAPM*, 2:1090; JA to Thomas Davidson, 22 Apr. 1890, YU, Davidson; *JAPM*, 2:1171–72; JA to Lorado Taft, 3 Feb. 1891, SCPC, JAC; *JAPM*, 2:1234–35; JA to Henry Demarest Lloyd, 18 Nov. 1891 and 15 Dec. 1892, SHSW, Lloyd; *JAPM*, 2:1275–77, 1342–43; JA to James Taft Hatfield, 9 Dec. 1891, Duke Univ.; *JAPM*, 2:1287; Florence Kelley [for JA] to Richard T. Ely, 30 Oct. [1892], SHSW, Ely; *JAPM*, 2:1332–33. In addition, the extant JA–Jenkin Lloyd Jones correspondence for the period provides some evidence of the kind of communication JA entered into with frequent settlement speakers and supporters before the telephone was readily available for both parties. JA to Jenkin Lloyd Jones, 20 May, 27 Oct., and 3 Nov 1890; 3 May, 20 Aug., 21 Sept., 6 Dec., and 26 Dec. 1891; *JAPM*, 2:1177–78, 1208–10, 1211–14, 1239–41, 1260–63, 1271, 1280–82, 1290–91; Jenkin Lloyd Jones to JA, 30 June, and 23 Sept. [1890]; 9 Feb., 4 May, and 21 Dec. 1891; *JAPM*, 2:1186–87, 1206, 1236, 1242, 1289.

2. Bayard Taylor Holmes (1852–1924), born in North Hero, Vt., was educated at Carleton College, Minn.; the Chicago Homeopathic College (1884); and Northwestern Univ. (1888). He began his practice in Chicago in 1886; was associated with Cook County Hospital for a number of years, where he served as secretary, 1891–95; and then became senior professor of surgery in the Medical Dept. of the Univ. of Illinois, 1892–1908. A socialist, he was a candidate for mayor of Chicago in 1895. He was the author of numerous publications, several of which concerned insanity, and between 1915 and his death he was editor of *Dementia Praecox Studies*. Holmes married Agnes Ann George in 1878. She became a member of the CWC in 1893.

3. For a listing of the entire series that JA was able to arrange, see HH Scrapbook 2:16; *JAPM*, Addendum 10:7ff.

4. Bayard Taylor Holmes presented "The Growth of Filth, Diseases, Cholera, Etc." at the Working People's Social Science Club on 18 Oct. 1892.

5. Dr. Ware opened the lecture series with an address titled "The Chicago Board of Health" on 11 Oct. 1892. Dr. Lyman Ware (1841–1916) was born in Granville, Ill., to Ralph and Lucinda A. Clark Ware. He attended Granville Academy and the Univ. of Michigan before serving as a hospital steward in the 112th Infantry Regiment Illinois Volunteers during the Civil War. He received his M.D. from the Medical Dept. of Northwestern Univ.(1866) and that of the Univ. of Pennsylvania (1868) and specialized in diseases of the eye and ear. From 1872 to 1900, he was surgeon at the Illinois Charitable Eye and Ear Infirmary. He was ophthalmic surgeon at the Cook County Hospital, 1880–88, and Presbyterian Hospital, 1880–99. He also helped treat eye and ear problems at the Chicago Orphan Asylum. In 1877 he married Elizabeth A. Law, and the couple had four daughters.

6. On 25 Oct. 1892, the topic for discussion at the Working People's Social Science Club gathering was of a Nineteenth Ward Improvement Club. This was another step in the ongoing effort of JA and the residents of HH to encourage their neighborhood residents to band together to effect change for the better in their living and working environment. The Nineteenth Ward Improvement Club was under way by late 1892 and had a constitution by 1893. Its object was "to promote the social life and municipal improvement of the neighborhood" (Nineteenth Ward Improvement Club, "Constitution."). When the constitution was adopted in early 1893, there were forty members—men and women—who signed the document. These included JA, EGS, Florence Kelley, Wilfreda Brockway, Clifford W. Barnes, Maggie V. Toomey, and JA's nephew John Addams Linn, all of whom were already active at HH. Meetings were held on alternating Saturdays but soon became monthly, and the monthly dues were ten cents. One of the first projects of the group was the creation of a cooperative coal yard, located at Ewing and Halsted streets. By 1893 responsibility for that venture was assumed by the settlement's Co-Operative Assn., created by members of the Nineteenth Ward Improvement Club. The club also assisted in the successful development of the first public baths in Chicago (see Two Essays in the *Forum*, Nov. and Oct. 1892, n. 110, below). By the fall of 1894, the active members of the club had been co-opted as members of the Nineteenth Ward Council of the Civic Federation of Chicago with the same objective as the club.

## Two Essays in the *Forum*

*The second Hull-House Summer School began at Rockford Seminary on 23 June 1892.[1] Jane Addams was there especially for the first two weeks to encourage the students who attended and to hold a reading party for them on Monday, Wednesday, and Friday afternoons. It was also the time she had reserved for drafting the two lectures*[2] *she had agreed to present during the six-week summer session of the School of Applied Ethics to be held beginning 6 July 1892, at Plymouth, Massachusetts.*[3] *Her invitation to speak had come from Henry C. Adams, professor of political economy and finance at the University of Michigan*[4] *and a colleague of Jane's admirer John Dewey. Henry Adams had been given the task of organizing the fourth week of lectures as part of the Economics Section of the school. The title he chose for the theme of lectures was "Philanthropy and Social Progress." By 25 July, when Jane Addams left Chicago for Plymouth, she carried with her the texts for the two presentations she planned to deliver.*[5]

*This was a pivotal moment in the life of Jane Addams. The occasion provided the thirty-one-year-old settlement enthusiast with a major platform from which to share her rationale and vision for the development of other social settlements throughout the country. One of five lecturers for the week beginning 27 July, Jane Addams presented "The Subjective Value of Social Settlements" to an audience of more than 150 people on 29 July, and the next day, to an even larger gathering, she presented "The Objective Value of a Social Settlement." Journalists covered both presentations, and summaries of her comments appeared in several papers, while direct quotes from "The Subjective Value of Social Settlements" appeared in the* Boston Herald *on 29 July 1892.*[6] *Although her speeches were sandwiched among remarks by Bernard Bosanquet,*[7] *Professor Franklin H. Giddings,*[8] *Robert A. Woods, and Father James O. S. Huntington, who gave two lectures, it was the presentations by Addams that captured the attention of the attendees.*[9] *Her two lectures providing a rationale for the social settlement idea, and reporting on the success of Hull-House gave voice to the hopes of those gathered to hear her and provided an exciting example of what could be done. The lectures and the response to them catapulted Addams into the leadership role in the emerging social settlement movement in America.*

*Settlement leaders and hopeful settlement founders who were there met on 3 August to discuss the social settlement idea further.*[10] *This was the first national meeting of what became regular gatherings of settlement workers and volunteers in the United States. At its end, Jane Addams and Julia Lathrop left for New York City, where, with the encouragement of Lathrop, Jane Addams made an appointment to speak with Walter Hines Page,*[11] *the bright, talented, and ambitious editor of the* Forum.[12] *During her interview with him, she offered the two papers she had presented at Plymouth for publication in the magazine. There she believed her ideas would come to national attention; Jane Addams and others of its readers regarded the* Forum *as influential and of high merit. Page not only accepted the articles and published them in the October and November 1892 issues of the periodical, but paid her for them as well. This one hundred dollars was the first money Jane Addams received for her published words. If Jane Addams had established herself as a speaker of power and import at the Plymouth summer school, it was with the publication of her articles in the* Forum *that her ability as a writer and her message came to national attention.*

*The versions of these two seminal papers by Addams that were published in the* Forum *were probably produced from the texts that she read during her presentations in Plymouth. The papers are presented below in the order in which Addams gave them at the School of Applied Ethics sessions and because they are the renderings in which her ideas were presented for the first time to the national public. Several newspapers commented on the* Forum *articles.*[13] *A version of both papers appeared in* Philanthropy and Social Progress *(1893), the volume of essays containing all seven lectures presented in the weeklong Economic Section program of the same name.*[14] *The two lead essays in the publication were by Jane Addams. This multimedia approach—lectures, periodical, and book—gave Addams's views the widest recognition available at the time to those who would be most influenced by them.*

*If Jane Addams was proud of her achievement at Plymouth and in New York City, she was careful to downplay, even to hide, it. To her sister Sarah Alice Haldeman, she carefully reported her activities after leaving Plymouth, focusing on travel and family news and omitting her extraordinary achievements: " I have not heard from you for three weeks. . . . Why don't you drop me just a line dearie? Julia Lathrop and I had a delightful trip in the White Mts and seperated in New York. She went to visit her uncle and I spent Sunday at Spring Lake with all of the Young family save Miranda who is at the Hot Springs & very wretched.*[15] *I spent one night with Aunt Elizabeth,*[16] *she has failed very much since I saw her last and is very unhappy I am afraid. It seems delightful to be at home again, altho I am head over ears in accumulated work."*[17]

## Essay in the *Forum*

*In Jane Addams's initial remarks at the School of Applied Ethics, published in the* Forum *as "A New Impulse to an Old Gospel,"*[18] *she offered a very personal rationale for her commitment to the social settlement idea. This particular paper became a central element in future Addams presentations about the social settlement movement. It is also an example of Jane Addams as editor. For its preparation, she borrowed and revised large portions of her presentation to the Chicago Woman's Club in December 1890.*[19] *She continued to rework this text for other publications, excising examples she may have believed dated and tightening text or changing tense here and there, but in large part keeping the core of this text. Most notably, a version of it appeared as a large part of chapter 6 in the first volume of her autobiography,* Twenty Years at Hull-House. *In their annotation, the editors have chosen to indicate sections of the paper that were drawn from "Outgrowths of Toynbee Hall" or were used by Jane Addams in* Twenty Years at Hull-House.

Plymouth, Mass. Nov. 1892

A NEW IMPULSE TO AN OLD GOSPEL.

"Hull House, which was Chicago's first Settlement, was established in September, 1889. It represented no association, but was opened by two women, backed by many friends, in the belief that the mere foothold of a house, easily accessible, ample in space, hospitable and tolerant in spirit, situated in the midst of the large foreign colonies which so easily isolate themselves in American cities, would be in itself a serviceable thing for Chicago. It was opened on general Settlement lines, in the conviction that along those lines many educated young people could find the best outlet for a certain sort of unexpressed activity. Hull House is neither a University Settlement nor a College Settlement: it calls itself a Social Settlement, an attempt to make social intercourse express the growing sense of the economic unity of society. It is an attempt to[20] add the social function to democracy. It was opened on the theory that the dependance of classes on each other is reciprocal; and that as the social relation is essentially a reciprocal relation, it gave a form of expression that has peculiar value." This I wrote in the FORUM for October.

I attempt in this[21] paper to treat of the subjective necessity for a Social Settlement, to analyze, as nearly as I can, the motives that underlie a movement which I believe to be based not only on conviction, but on genuine emotion. I have divided the motives which constitute the subjective pressure toward Social Settlements into three great lines: the first contains the desire to make the entire social organism democratic, to extend democracy beyond its political expression; the second is the impulse to share the race life, to bring as much as possible of social energy and the accumulation of civilization to those portions of the race which have little; the third springs from a certain renaissance of Christianity, a movement toward its early humanitarian aspects.

It is not difficult to see that although America is pledged to the democratic ideal, the view of democracy has been partial and that its best achievement thus far has been pushed along the line of the franchise. Democracy[22] has made little attempt to assert itself in social affairs. We have refused to move beyond the position of its eighteenth-century leaders, who[23] believed that political equality alone would secure all good to all men. We conscientiously followed the gift of the ballot hard upon the gift of freedom to the Negro, but we are quite unmoved by the fact that he lives among us in a practical social ostracism.[24] We hasten to give the franchise to the immigrant from a sense of justice, from a tradition that he ought to have it, while we dub him with epithets deriding his past life or present occupation and feel no duty to invite him to our houses.[25] We are forced to acknowledge that it is only in our local and national politics that we try very hard for the ideal so dear to those who were enthusiasts when the century was young. We have almost given it up as our ideal in social intercourse. In[26] many a city ward the majority of the votes are openly sold for drinks and dollars; still there is a remote pretence, at least a fiction current, that a man's vote is his own. The judgment of the voter is consulted and an opportunity for remedy given. There is not even a theory in the social order, not a shadow answering to the polls in politics. The time may come when the[27] politician who sells one by one to the highest bidder all the offices in his grasp will not be considered more base in his code of morals, more hardened in his practice, than the woman who constantly invites to her receptions those alone who bring her an equal social return, who shares her beautiful surroundings only with those who minister to a liking she has for successful social events. In doing this she is just as unmindful of the common weal, as unscrupulous in her use of power, as is any city "boss" who consults only the interests of the "ring."

In politics "bossism"[28] arouses a scandal. It goes on in society constantly and is only beginning to be challenged. Our consciences are becoming tender in regard to the lack of democracy in social affairs. We are perhaps entering upon the second phase of democracy, as the French philosophers entered upon the first, somewhat bewildered by its logical conclusions. The[29] social organism has broken down through large districts of our great cities. Many of the people living there are very poor, the majority of them without leisure or energy for anything but the gain of subsistence. They move often from one wretched lodging to another. They lived for the moment side by side, many of them without knowledge of each other, without fellowship, without local tradition or public spirit, without social organization of any kind. Practically nothing is done to remedy this. The people who might do it, who have the social tact and training, the large houses, and the traditions and custom of hospitality, live in other parts of the city. The club-houses, libraries, galleries, and semi-public conveniences for social life are also blocks away. We find workingmen organized[30] into armies of producers because men of executive ability and business sagacity have found it to their interests thus to organize them. But these workingmen are not[31] organized socially; although living in crowded tenement-houses, they are living without a corresponding social contact. The chaos is as great as it would be were they working in huge factories without foreman or superintendent. Their ideas and resources are cramped. The desire for higher social pleasure is extinct. They have no share in the traditions and social energy which make for progress. Too often their only place of meeting is a[32] saloon, their only host a bartender; a local demagogue forms their public opinion.[33] Men of ability and refinement, of social power and university cultivation, stay away from them. Personally, I believe the men who lose most are those who thus stay away. But[34] the paradox is here: when cultivated people do stay away from a certain portion of the population, when all social advantages are persistently withheld, it may be for years, the result itself is pointed at as a reason, is used as an argument, for the continued withholding.

It is constantly said that because the masses have never had social advantages they do not want them, that they are heavy and dull, and that it will take political or philanthropic machinery to change them. This[35] divides a city into rich and poor; into the favored, who express their sense of social obligation by gifts of money, and into the unfavored, who express it by clamoring for a "share"—both of them actuated by a vague sense of justice. This[36] division of the city would be the more justifiable, however, if the people who thus isolated themselves on certain streets and used their social ability for each other gained enough thereby and added sufficient to the sum total of social progress to justify the withholding of the pleasures and results of that progress from so many people who ought to have them. But they cannot accomplish this. The social spirit discharges itself in many forms, and no one form is adequate to its total expression. We are all uncomfortable in regard to the insincerity of our best phrases, because we hesitate to translate our philosophy into the deed.

It[37] is inevitable that those who feel most keenly this insincerity and partial living should be our young people, our so-called educated[38] young people who accomplish little toward the solution of this social problem, and who bear the brunt of being cultivated into unnourished, over-sensitive lives. They have been shut off from the common labor by which they live and which is a great source of moral and physical health. They feel a fatal want of harmony between their theory and their lives, a lack of co-ordination between thought and action. I think it is hard for us to realize how seriously many of them are taking to the notion of human brotherhood, how eagerly they long to give tangible expression to the democratic idea. These young men and women, longing to socialize their democracy, are animated by certain hopes. These hopes may be loosely formulated thus: that if in a democratic country nothing can be permanently achieved save through the masses of the people, it will be impossible to establish a higher political life than the people themselves crave; that it is difficult to see how the notion of a higher civic life can be fostered save through common intercourse.

The blessings which we associate with a life of refinement and cultivation can be made universal and must be made universal if they are to be permanent. The good we secure for ourselves is precarious and uncertain, its floating in mid-air, until it is secured for all of us and incorporated into our common life. These hopes are responsible for results in various directions, pre-eminently in the extension of educational advantages. We find that all educational matters are more democratic in their political than in their social aspects. The[39] public schools in the poorest and most crowded wards of the city are inadequate to the number of children,[40] and many of the teachers are ill-prepared and overworked; but in each ward there is an effort to secure public education. The school-house itself stands as a pledge that the city recognizes and endeavors to fulfil the duty of educating its children. But what becomes of these children when they are no longer in public schools? Many of them never come under the influence of a professional teacher after they are twelve. Society at large does little for their intellectual development. The[41] dream of transcendentalists[42] that each New England village would be a university, that every child taken from the common school would be put into definite lines of study and mental development, had its unfulfilled beginning in the village lyceum and lecture courses, and has its feeble representative now in the multitude of clubs for study which are so sadly restricted to educators, to the leisure class, or only to the advanced and progressive workers.

The[43] University Extension movement[44]—certainly when it is closely identified with Settlements—would not confine learning to those who already want it, or to those who, by making an effort, can gain it, or to those among whom professional educators are already at work, but would take it to the tailors of East London and the dock-laborers of the Thames. It[45] requires tact and training, love of learning, and the conviction of the justice of its diffusion to give it to people whose intellectual faculties are untrained and disused. But men in England are found who do it successfully, and it is believed there are men and women in America who can do it. I also believe that the best work in University Extension can be done in Settlements, where the teaching will be further socialized, where the teacher will grapple his students, not only by formal lectures, but by every hook possible to the fuller intellectual life which he represents. This[46] teaching requires distinct methods, for it is true of people who have been allowed to remain undeveloped and whose faculties are inert and sterile, that they cannot take their learning heavily. It has to be diffused in a social atmosphere. Information held in solution, a medium of fellow-ship and good-will can be assimilated by the dullest.

If education is, as Froebel[47] defined it, "deliverance," deliverance of the forces of the body and mind, then the untrained must first be delivered from all constraint and rigidity before their faculties can be used. Possibly one of the most pitiful periods in the drama of the much-praised young American who attempts to rise in life is the time when his educational requirements seem to have locked him up and made him rigid. He fancies himself shut off from his uneducated family and misunderstood by his friends. He is bowed down by his mental accumulations and often gets no farther than to carry them through life as a great burden. Not once has he had a glimpse of the delights of knowledge. Intellectual[48] life requires for its expansion and manifestation the influence and assimilation of the interests and affections of others. Mazzini,[49] that greatest of all democrats, who broke his heart over the condition of the South European peasantry, said: "Education is not merely a necessity of true life by which the individual renews his vital force in the vital force of humanity; it is a Holy Communion with generations dead and living, by which he fecundates all his faculties. When he is withheld from his Communion for generations, as the Italian peasant has been, we point our finger at him and say, 'He is like a beast of the field; he must be controlled by force.'"[50] Even to this it is sometimes added that it is absurd to educate him, immoral to disturb his content. We stupidly use again the effect as an argument for a continuance of the cause. It is needless to say that a Settlement is a protest against a restricted view of education, and makes it possible for every educated man or woman with a teaching faculty to find out those who are ready to be taught. The social and educational activities of a Settlement are but differing manifestations of the attempt to socialize democracy, as is the existence of the Settlement itself.

I find it somewhat difficult to[51] formulate the second line of motives which I believe to constitute the trend of the subjective pressure toward the Settlement. There is something primordial about these motives, but I am perhaps over-bold in designating them as a great desire to share the race life. We all bear traces of the starvation struggle which for so long made up the life of the race. Our very organism holds memories and glimpses of that long life of our ancestors which still goes on among so many of our contemporaries. Nothing[52] so deadens the sympathies and shrivels the power of enjoyment as the persistent keeping away from the great opportunities for helpfulness and a continual ignoring of the starvation struggle which makes up the life of at least half the race. To shut one's self away from that half of the race is to shut one's self away from the most vital part of it; it is to live out but half the humanity which we have been born heir to and to use but half our faculties. We have all had longings for a fuller life which should include the use of these faculties. These longings are the physical complement of the "Intimations of Immortality"[53] on which no ode has yet been written. To portray these would be the work of a poet, and it is hazardous for any but a poet to attempt it.

You[54] may remember the forlorn feeling which occasionally seizes you when you arrive early in the morning a stranger in a great city. The stream of laboring people goes past you as you gaze through the plate-glass window of your hotel. You see hard-working men lifting great burdens; you hear the driving and jostling of huge carts. Your heart sinks with a sudden sense of futility. The door opens behind you and you turn to the man who brings you in your breakfast with a quick sense of human fellowship. You find yourself praying that you may never lose your hold on it all. A more poetic prayer would be that the great mother breasts of our common humanity, with its labor and suffering and its homely comforts, may never be withheld from you. You turn helplessly to the waiter.[55] You feel that it would be almost grotesque to claim from him the sympathy you crave. Civilization has placed you far apart, but you resent your position with a sudden sense of snobbery. Literature is full of portrayals of these glimpses. They come to shipwrecked men on rafts; they overcome the differences of an incongruous multitude when in the presence of a great danger or when moved by a common enthusiasm. They are not, however, confined to such moments, and if we were in the habit of telling them to each other, the recital would be as long as the tales of children are when they sit down on the green grass and confide to each other how many times they have remembered that they lived once before. If that is the stirring of inherited impressions, just so surely is the other the stirring of inherited power.

There[56] is nothing after disease, indigence, and a sense of guilt so fatal to health and to life itself as the want of a proper outlet for active faculties. I have seen young girls suffer and grow sensibly lowered in vitality in the first years after they leave school.[57] In[58] our attempt then to give a girl pleasure and freedom from care we succeed, for the most part, in making her pitifully miserable. She finds "life" so different from what she expected it to be. She is besotted with innocent little ambitions and does not understand this apparent waste of herself, this elaborate preparation, if no work is provided for her. There is a heritage of noble obligation which young people accept and long to perpetuate. The desire for action, the wish to right wrong and alleviate suffering, haunts them daily. Society smiles at it indulgently instead of making it of value to itself. The wrong to them begins even farther back when we restrain the first childish desires for "doing good" and tell them that they must wait until they are older and better fitted. We intimate that social obligation begins at a fixed date, forgetting that it begins with birth itself. We treat them as we would children who, with strong-growing limbs, are allowed to use their legs but not their arms, or whose legs are daily carefully exercised that after awhile their arms may be put to high use. We do this in spite of the protest of the best educators, Locke[59] and Pestalozzi.[60] We[61] are fortunate in the mean time if their unused members do not weaken and disappear. They do sometimes. There are a few girls who, by the time they are "educated," forget their old childish desires to help the world and to play with poor little girls "who haven't playthings." Parents are often curious about this. They deliberately expose their daughters to the knowledge of the distress in the world. They send them to hear missionary addresses on famines in India and China; they accompany them to lectures on the suffering in Siberia; they agitate together over the forgotten region of East London. In addition to this, from babyhood the altruistic tendencies of these daughters are persistently cultivated. They are taught to be self-forgetting and self-sacrificing, to consider the good of the Whole before the good of the Ego. But when all this information and culture begins to show results, when the daughter comes back from college and begins to recognize her social claim to the "submerged tenth" and to evince a disposition to fulfil it, the family claim is strenuously asserted; she is told that she is unjustified, ill-advised in her efforts. If she persists the family too often are injured and unhappy, unless the efforts are called missionary, and the religious zeal of the family carry them over their sense of abuse.

We[62] have in America a fast-growing number of cultivated young people who have no recognized outlet for their active faculties. They hear constantly of the great social mal-adjustment, but no way is provided for them to change it and their uselessness hangs about them heavily. Huxley[63] declares that the sense of uselessness is the severest shock which the human system can sustain, and, if persistently sustained, it results in atrophy of function. These young people have had advantages of college, of European travel and economic study, but they are sustaining this shock of inaction. They have pet phrases, and they tell you that the things that make us[64] all alike are stronger than the things that make us different. They say that all men are united by needs and sympathies far more permanent and radical than anything that temporarily divides them and sets them in opposition to each other. If they affect art, they say that the decay in artistic expression is due to the decay in ethics, that[65] art when shut away from the human interests and from the great mass of humanity is self-destructive. They tell their elders with all the bitterness of youth that if they expect success from them in business, or politics, or whatever lines their ambition for them has run, they must let them consult all of humanity; that they must let them find out what the people want and how they want it. It[66] is only the stronger young people, however, who formulate this. Others, not content with that, go on studying and come back to college for their second degrees, not that they are especially fond of study, but they want something definite to do, and their powers have been trained in the direction of mental accumulation. Many are buried[67] beneath mere mental accumulation with lowered vitality and discontent. Walter Besant says they have had the vision that Peter[68] had when he saw the great sheet let down from heaven, wherein was neither clean nor unclean. He calls it the sense of humanity. It is not philanthropy nor benevolence. It is a thing fuller and wider than either of these. This young life, so sincere in its emotion and good phrases and yet so undirected, seems to me as pitiful as the other great mass of destitute lives. One is supplementary to the other, and some method of communication can surely be devised. Mr. Barnett,[69] who urged the first Settlement—Toynbee Hall, in East London—recognized this need of outlet for the young men of Oxford and Cambridge and hoped that the Settlement would supply the communication. It[70] is easy to see why the Settlement movement originated in England, where the years of education are more constrained and definite than they are here, where class distinctions are more rigid. The necessity of it was greater there, but we are fast feeling the pressure of the need and reaching the necessity for Settlements in America. Our young people feel nervously the need of putting theory into action and respond quickly to the Settlement form of activity.

The third division of motives[71] which I believe make toward the Settlement is the result of a certain <u>renaissance</u> going forward in Christianity. The impulse to share the lives of the poor, the desire to make social service, irrespective of propaganda, express the spirit of Christ, is as old as Christianity itself. We have no proof from the records themselves that the early Roman Christians, who strained their simple art to the point of grotesqueness in their eagerness to record a "good news" on the walls of the catacombs, considered this "good news" a religion.[72] Jesus had imposed no cult nor rites. He had no set of truths labelled "Religious." On the contrary, his doctrine was that all truth was one, that the appropriation of it was freedom. His teaching had no dogma of its own to mark it off from truth and action in general. The very universality of it precluded its being a religion. He himself called it a revelation—a life. These early Roman Christians received the Gospel message, a command to love all men, with a certain joyous simplicity. The image of the Good Shepherd is blithe and gay beyond the gentlest shepherd of Greek mythology; the hart no longer pants, but rushes to the water brooks. The Christians looked for the continuous revelation, but believed what Jesus said, that this revelation to be held and made manifest must be put into terms of action; that action is the only organ man has for receiving and appropriating truth. "If any man will do His will, he shall know of the doctrine."[73]

That[74] Christianity would have to be revealed and embodied in the line of social progress is a corollary to the simple proposition that man's action is found in his social relationships in the way in which he connects with his fellows. That his motives for action are the zeal and affection with which he regards his fellows. By this simple process was created a deep enthusiasm for humanity, which regarded man as at once the organ and object of revelation; and by this process came about that wonderful fellowship, that true democracy of the early Church, that so captivates the imagination. The early Christians were preeminently non-resistant. They believed in love as a cosmic force. There was no iconoclasm during the minor peace of the Church. They did not yet denounce, nor tear down temples, nor preach the end of the world. They grew to a mighty number, but it never occurred to them, either in their weakness or their strength, to regard other men for an instant as their foes or aliens. The spectacle of the Christians loving all men was the most astounding Rome had ever seen. They were eager to sacrifice themselves for the weak, for children and the aged. They identified themselves with slaves and did not avoid the plague. They longed to share the common lot that they might receive the constant revelation. It was a new treasure which the early Christians added to the sum of all treasures, a joy hitherto unknown in the world—the joy of finding the Christ which lieth in each man, but which no man can unfold save in fellowship. A happiness ranging from the heroic to the pastoral enveloped them. They were to possess a revelation as long as life had new meaning to unfold, new action to propose.

I believe that there is a distinct turning among many young men and women toward this simple acceptance of Christ's message. They resent the assumption that Christianity is a set of ideas which belong to the religious consciousness, whatever that may be, that it is a thing to be proclaimed and instituted apart from the social life of the community. They insist that it shall seek a simple and natural expression in the social organism itself. The Settlement movement is only one manifestation of that wider humanitarian movement which throughout Christendom, but pre-eminently in England, is endeavoring to embody itself, not in a sect, but in society itself.[75] Tolstoi has reminded us all very forcibly of Christ's principle of non-resistence. His formulation has been startling and his expression has deviated from the general movement, but there is little doubt that he has many adherents, men and women who are philosophically convinced of the futility of opposition, who believe that evil can be overcome only with good and cannot be opposed by evil. If love is the creative force of the universe, the principle which binds men together, and by their interdependence on each other makes them human, just so surely is anger the destructive principle of the universe, that which tears down, thrusts men apart, and makes them isolated and brutal.

I cannot of course speak for other Settlements, but it would, I think, be unfair to Hull House not to emphasize the conviction with which the first residents went there, that it would simply be a foolish and an unwarrantable expenditure of force to oppose and to antagonize any individual or set of people in the neighborhood; that of whatever good the House had to offer should be put into positive terms; that its residents should live with opposition to no man, with recognition of the good in every man, even the meanest. I[76] believe that this turning, this renaissance of the early Christian humanitarianism, is going on in America, in Chicago, if you please, without leaders who write or philosophize, without much speaking, but with a bent to express in social service, in terms of action, the spirit of Christ. Certain it is that spiritual force is found in the Settlement movement, and it is also true that this force must be evoked and must be called into play before the success of any Settlement is assured. There must be the overmastering belief that all that is noblest in life is common to men as men, in order to accentuate the likenesses and ignore the differences which are found among the people the Settlement constantly brings into juxtaposition. It may be true, as Frederic Harrison[77] insists, that the very religious fervor of man can be turned into love for his race and his desire for a future life into contempt to live in the echo of his deeds. How far the Positivists' formula of the high ardor for humanity can carry the Settlement movement, Mrs. Humphry Ward's house in London[78] may in course of time illustrate. Paul's formula of seeking for the Christ which lieth in each man and founding our likenesses on him seems a simpler formula to many of us.

If you have heard a[79] thousand voices singing in the Hallelujah Chorus in Handel's "Messiah,"[80] you have found that the leading voices could still be distinguished, but that the[81] differences of training and cultivation between them and the voices of the chorus were[82] lost in the unity of purpose and the fact that they were all human voices lifted by a high motive. This is a weak illustration of what a Settlement attempts to do. It[83] aims, in a measure, to lead whatever of social life its neighborhood may afford, to focus and give form to that life, to bring to bear upon it the results of cultivation and training; but it receives in exchange for the music of isolated voices the volume and strength of the chorus. It is quite impossible for me to say in what proportion or degree the subjective necessity which led to the opening of Hull House combined the three trends; first, the desire to interpret democracy in social terms; secondly, the impulse beating at the very source of our lives urging us to aid in the race progress; and, thirdly, the Christian movement toward Humanitarianism. It is difficult to analyze a living thing; the analysis is at best imperfect. Many more motives may blend with the three trends; possibly the desire for a new form of social success due to the nicety of imagination, which refuses worldly pleasures unmixed with the joys of self-sacrifice; possibly a love of approbation, so vast that it is not content with the treble clapping of delicate hands, but wishes also to hear the bass notes from toughened palms, may mingle with these.

The Settlement, then, is an experimental effort to aid in the solution of the social and industrial problems which are engendered by the modern conditions of life in a great city. It insists that these problems are not confined to any one portion of a city. It is an attempt to relieve, at the same time, the over-accumulation at one end of society and the destitution at the other; but it assumes that this over-accumulation and destitution is most sorely felt in the things that pertain to social and educational advantage. From its very nature it can stand for no political or social propaganda. It must, in a sense, give the warm welcome of an inn to all such propaganda, if perchance one of them be found an angel. The one thing to be dreaded in the Settlement is that it lose its flexibility, its power of quick adaptation, its readiness to change its methods as its environment may demand. It must be open to conviction and must have a deep and abiding sense of tolerance. It must be hospitable and ready for experiment. It should demand from its residents a scientific patience in the accumulation of facts and the steady holding of their sympathies as one of the best instruments for that accumulation. It must be grounded in a philosophy whose foundation is on the solidarity of the human race, a philosophy which will not waver when the race happens to be represented by a drunken woman or an idiot boy. Its residents must be emptied of all conceit of opinion and all self-assertion, and ready to arouse and interpret the public opinion of their neighborhood. They must be content to live quietly side by side with their neighbors until they grow into a sense of relationship and mutual interests. Their neighbors are held apart by differences of race and language which the residents can more easily overcome. They are bound to see the needs of their neighborhood as a whole, to furnish data for legislation, and use their influence to secure it. In short, residents are pledged to devote themselves to the duties of good citizenship and to the arousing of the social energies which too largely lie dormant in every neighborhood given over to industrialism. They are bound to regard the entire life of their city as organic, to make an effort to unify it and to protest against its over-differentiation.

Our philanthropies of all sorts are growing so expensive and institutional that it is to be hoped the Settlement movement will keep itself facile and unincumbered. From its very nature it needs no endowment, no roll of salaried officials. Many residents must always come in the attitude of students, assuming that the best teacher of life is life itself and regarding the Settlement as a class-room. Hull House from the outside may appear to be a cumbrous plant of manifold industries, with its round of clubs and classes, its day nursery, diet kitchen, library, art exhibits, lectures, statistical work and polyglot demands for information, a thousand people coming and going in an average week.[84] But viewed as a business enterprise it is not costly, for from this industry are eliminated two great items of expense—the cost of superintendence and the cost of distribution. All the management and teaching are voluntary and unpaid, and the consumers—to continue the commercial phraseology—are at the door and deliver the goods themselves. In the instance of Hull House, rent is also largely eliminated through the courtesy of Miss Culver, the owner.[85] Life is manifold and Hull House attempts to respond to as many sides as possible. It does this fearlessly, feeling sure that among the able people of Chicago are those who will come to do the work when once the outline is indicated. It pursues much the same policy in regard to money. It seems to me an advantage—this obligation to appeal to business men for their judgment and their money, to the educated for their effort and enthusiasm, to the neighborhood for their response and co-operation. It tests the sanity of an idea, and we enter upon a new line of activity with a feeling of support and confidence. We have always been perfectly frank with our neighbors. I have never tried so earnestly to set forth the gist of the Settlement movement, to make clear its reciprocity, as I have to them. At first we were often asked why we came to live there when we could afford to live somewhere else. I remember one man who used to shake his head and say it was "the strangest thing he had met in his experience," but who was finally convinced that it was not strange but natural. There was another who was quite sure that the "prayer-meeting snap" would come in somewhere, that it was "only a question of time." I trust that now it seems natural to all of us that the Settlement should be there. If it is natural to feed the hungry and care for the sick, it is certainly natural to give pleasure to the young and to minister to the deep-seated craving for social intercourse all men feel. Whoever does it is rewarded by something which, if not gratitude, is at least spontaneous and vital and lacks that irksome sense of obligation with which a substantial benefit is too often acknowledged. The man who looks back to the person who first put him in the way of good literature has no alloy in his gratitude.

I[86] remember when the statement seemed to me very radical that the salvation of East London was the destruction of West London; but I believe now that there will be no wretched quarters in our cities at all when the conscience of each man is so touched that he prefers to live with the poorest of his brethren, and not with the richest of them that his income will allow. It is to be hoped that this moving and living will at length be universal and need no name. The Settlement movement is from its nature a provisional one. It[87] is easy in writing a paper to make all philosophy point one particular moral and all history adorn one particular tale; but I hope you forgive me for reminding you that[88] the best speculative philosophy sets forth the solidarity of the human race, that the highest moralists have taught that without the advance and improvement of the whole no man can hope for any lasting improvement in his own moral or material individual condition. The subjective necessity for Social Settlements is identical with that necessity which urges us on toward social and individual salvation.

JANE ADDAMS.

PD ("A New Impulse to an Old Gospel," *Forum* 14 [Nov. 1892]: 345–58; *JAPM*, 46:520–34).

## Essay in the *Forum*

*Jane Addams's second speech at the Summer School of Applied Ethics was a report on the development and programs at Hull-House from the time that it opened. It provided her with an opportunity to describe the Hull-House neighborhood and her neighbors as well as the creative approaches she and her coworkers had devised for meeting their needs. This speech presents a three-year report on the growth and success of Hull-House and offers the evidence for her sobriquet "grandmother of the social settlement movement."*[89] *It was this speech Jane Addams turned to for details as she constructed the fifth chapter, "The First Days at Hull-House," for the first volume of her autobiography,* Twenty Years at Hull-House.[90]

Oct. 1892

### HULL HOUSE, CHICAGO: AN EFFORT TOWARD SOCIAL DEMOCRACY.

Hull House, Chicago's first Social Settlement, was established in September, 1889.[91] It represented no association, but was opened by two women, supported by many friends, in the belief that the mere foothold of a house, easily accessible, ample in space, hospitable and tolerant in spirit, situated in the midst of the large foreign colonies which so easily isolate themselves in American cities, would be in itself a serviceable thing for Chicago. It represents an attempt to make social intercourse express the growing sense of the economic unity of society, to add the social function to democracy. It was opened in the theory that the dependence of classes on each other is reciprocal, and that "as the social relation is essentially a reciprocal relation, it gives a form of expression that has peculiar value."[92]

Hull House stands on South Halsted Street, next door to the corner of Polk. South Halsted Street is thirty-two miles long and one of the great thoroughfares of Chicago. Polk Street crosses Halsted midway between the stock-yards to the south and the ship-building yards on the north branch of the Chicago River. For the six miles between these two dignified industries the street is lined with shops of butchers and grocers, with dingy and gorgeous saloons, and pretentious establishments for the sale of ready-made clothing. Polk Street, running west from Halsted Street, grows rapidly more respectable; running a mile east to State Street, it grows steadily worse and crosses a net-work of gilded vice on the corners of Clark Street and Fourth Avenue.

Hull House is an ample old residence, well built and somewhat ornately decorated after the manner of its time, 1856. It has been used for many purposes, and although battered by its vicissitudes, it is essentially sound and has responded kindly to repairs and careful furnishing. Its wide hall and open fires always insure it a gracious aspect.[93] It once stood in the suburbs, but the city has steadily grown up around it and its site now has corners on three or four distinct foreign colonies. Between Halsted Street and the river live about ten thousand Italians: Neapolitans, Sicilians, and Calabrians, with an occasional Lombard or Venetian. To the south on Twelfth Street are many Germans, and side streets are given over almost entirely to Polish and Russian Jews. Further south, these Jewish colonies merge into a huge Bohemian colony, so vast that Chicago ranks as the third Bohemian city in the world. To the northwest are many Canadian-French, clannish in spite of their long residence in America. On the streets directly west and farther north are well-to-do English-speaking families, many of whom own their houses and have lived in the neighborhood for years.[94] I know one man who is still living in his old farm-house. This corner of Polk and Halsted Streets is in the fourteenth precinct of the nineteenth ward. This ward has a population of about fifty thousand, and at the last presidential election registered 7,072 voters. It has had no unusual political scandal connected with it, but its aldermen are generally saloon-keepers and its political manipulations are those to be found in the crowded wards where the activities of the petty politician are unchecked.[95]

The policy of the public authorities of never taking an initiative and always waiting to be urged to do their duty is fatal in a ward where there is no initiative among the citizens. The idea underlying our self-government breaks down in such a ward. The streets are inexpressibly dirty, the number of schools inadequate, factory legislation unenforced, the street-lighting bad, the paving miserable and altogether lacking in the alleys and smaller streets, and the stables defy all laws of sanitation. Hundreds of houses are unconnected with the street sewer. The older and richer inhabitants seem anxious to move away as rapidly as they can afford it. They make room for newly arrived emigrants who are densely ignorant of civic duties. This substitution of the older inhabitants is accomplished also industrially in the south and east quarters of the ward. The Hebrews and Italians do the finishing for the great clothing-manufacturers formerly done by Americans, Irish, and Germans, who refused to submit to the extremely low prices to which the sweating system has reduced their successors. As the design of the sweating system is the elimination of rent from the manufacture of clothing, the "outside work" is begun after the clothing leaves the cutter. For this work no basement is too dark, no stable loft too foul, no rear shanty too provisional, no tenement room too small, as these conditions imply low rental. Hence these shops abound in the worst of the foreign districts, where the sweater easily finds his cheap basement and his home finishers.[96] There is a constant tendency to employ school-children, as much of the home and shop work can easily be done by children. The houses of the ward, for the most part wooden, were originally built for one family and are now occupied by several. They are after the type of the inconvenient frame cottages found in the suburbs twenty years ago. Many of them were built where they now stand; others were brought thither on rollers, because their previous site had been taken for a factory. The fewer brick tenement buildings which are three or four stories high are comparatively new. There are few huge and foul tenements. The little wooden houses have a temporary aspect, and for this reason, perhaps, the tenement-house legislation in Chicago is totally inadequate. Back tenements flourish; many houses have no water supply save the faucet in the back yard; there are no fire escapes; the garbage and ashes are placed in wooden boxes which are fastened to the street pavements. One of the most discouraging features about the present system of tenement houses is that many of them are owned by sordid and ignorant immigrants.

The theory that wealth brings responsibility, that possession entails at length education and refinement, in these cases fails utterly. The children of an Italian immigrant owner do not go to school and are no improvement on their parents. His wife picks rags from the street gutter and laboriously sorts them in a dingy court. Wealth may do something for her self-complacency and feeling of consequence; it certainly does nothing for her comfort or her children's improvement nor for the cleanliness of any one concerned. Another thing that prevents better houses in Chicago is the tentative attitude of the real-estate men. Many unsavory conditions are allowed to continue which would be regarded with horror if they were considered permanent. Meanwhile, the wretched conditions persist until at least two generations of children have been born and reared in them. Our ward contains two hundred and fifty-five saloons; our own precinct boasts of eight, and the one directly north of us twenty. This allows one saloon to every twenty-eight voters, and there is no doubt that the saloon is the centre of the liveliest political and social life in the ward. The leases and fixtures of these saloons are, in the majority of cases, owned by the wholesale liquor houses, and the saloon-keeper himself is often a bankrupt. There are seven churches and two missions in the ward.[97] All of these are small and somewhat struggling, save the large Catholic church connected with the Jesuit College on the south boundary of the ward and the French Catholic church on the west boundary.[98] There are but three out of these nine religious centres in which the service is habitually conducted in English. There are seven Catholic parochial schools in the ward, accommodating 6,244 children; three Protestant schools care for 141 children.[99] A fine manual-training school sustained by the Hebrews[100] is found in the seventh ward just south of us. In the same ward is the receiving shelter for the Jewish refugees.[101]

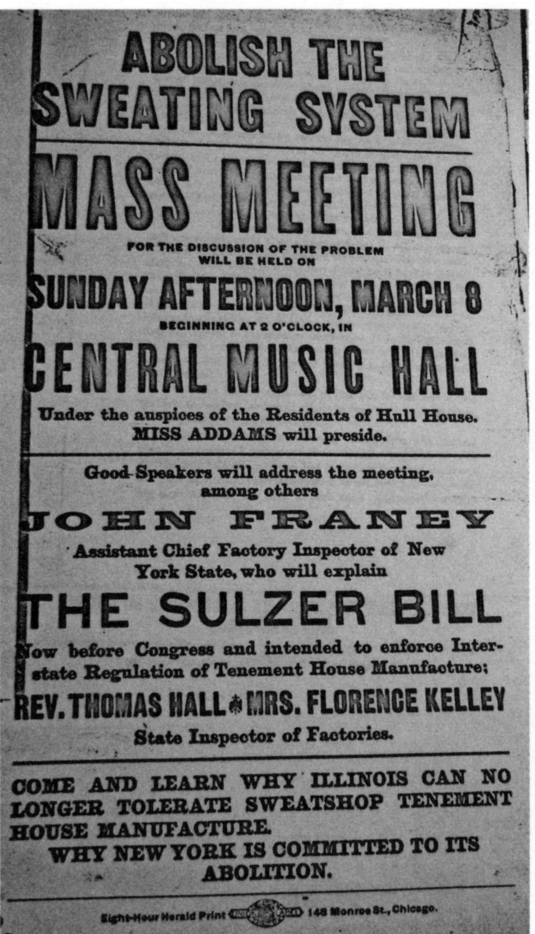


As soon as Florence Kelley settled at Hull-House, Jane Addams and other settlement residents and active volunteers began to work for the regulation of sweatshop manufacture. They continued this battle on the state and national levels for the remainder of the 1890s. This broadside announced their Chicago mass meeting on 8 March 1896, in support of the Sulzer bill in the U.S. Congress, meant to regulate tenement manufacture or sweatshops. It was not enacted (UIC, JAMC, HH Assn.; HH Scrapbook 3:88; *JAPM*, Addendum 10:8ff).

This site for a Settlement was selected in the first instance because of its diversity and the variety of activity for which it presented an opportunity. It has been the aim of the residents to respond to all sides of the neighborhood life: not to the poor people alone, nor to the well-to-do, nor to the young in contradistinction to the old, but to the neighborhood as a whole, "men, women, and children taken in families as the Lord mixes them." The activities of Hull House divide themselves into four, possibly more lines. They are not formally or consciously thus divided, but broadly separate according to the receptivity of the neighbors. They might be designated as the social, educational, and humanitarian. I have added civic—if indeed a settlement of women can be said to perform civic duties.[102] These activities spring from no preconceived notion of what a Social Settlement should be, but have increased gradually on demand. In describing these activities and their value to the neighborhood, I shall attempt to identify those people who respond to each form.

A Settlement which regards social intercourse as the terms of its expression logically brings to its aid all those adjuncts which have been found by experience to free social life. It casts aside nothing which the cultivated man regards as good and suggestive of participation in the best life of the past. It ignores none of the surroundings which one associates with a life of simple refinement. The amount of luxury which an individual indulges in is a thing which has to be determined by each for himself. It must always be a relative thing. The one test which the settlement is bound to respect is that its particular amount of luxury shall tend to "free" the social expression of its neighbors, and not cumber that expression. The residents at Hull House find that the better in quality and taste their surroundings are, the more they contribute to the general enjoyment.[103]

We have distinct advantages for Social Settlements in America. There are fewer poor people here than in England. There are also fewer people who expect to remain poor, and they are less strictly confined to their own districts. It is an advantage that our cities are diversified by foreign colonies. We go to Europe and consider our view incomplete if we do not see something of the peasant life of the little villages with their quaint costumes and suggestive habits. We can see the same thing here. There are Bohemians, Italians, Poles, Russians, Greeks, and Arabs in Chicago vainly trying to adjust their peasant life to the life of a large city and coming in contact with only the most ignorant Americans in that city. The more of scholarship, the more of linguistic attainment, the more of beautiful surroundings a Settlement among them can command, the more it can do for them.

It is much easier to deal with the first generation of crowded city life than with the second or third, because it is more natural and cast in a simpler mould. The Italian and Bohemian peasants who live in Chicago still put on their bright holiday clothes on Sunday and go to visit their cousins. They tramp along with at least a suggestion of having once walked over ploughed fields and breathed country air. The second generation of city poor have no holiday clothes and consider their cousins "a bad lot." I have heard a drunken man in a maudlin stage babble of his good country mother and imagine he was driving the cows home, and I knew that his little son, who laughed loud at him, would be drunk earlier in life, and would have no such pastoral interlude to his ravings. Hospitality still survives among foreigners, although it is buried under false pride among the poorest Americans. One thing seemed clear in regard to entertaining these foreigners: to preserve and keep for them whatever of value their past life contained and to bring them in contact with a better type of Americans. For two years, every Saturday evening, our Italian neighbors were our guests; entire families came.[104] These evenings were very popular during our first winter at Hull House. Many educated Italians helped us, and the house became known as a place where Italians were welcome and where national holidays were observed.

German night festivities at Hull-House, as rendered by Otto Henry Bacher. From its opening, Hull-House hosted separate gatherings of Italians, French, and Germans. These lively parties with music, recitations, gossip, and food provided an opportunity for social interaction among their neighbors and between the settlement residents and their neighbors. Cleveland-born American artist Otto Henry Bacher (1856–1909), who studied in Europe and was befriended by James McNeill Whistler, was noted for his etchings and impressionist-influenced paintings, and in 1890 he became an illustrator for *Scribner's Magazine*. He visited Hull-House and its neighborhood in 1892, when some of his work was exhibited in Chicago. *Scribner's Magazine* used several of his drawings and paintings of Chicago scenes, including this one, to illustrate Joseph Kirkland's article "Among the Poor of Chicago" that appeared in the July 1892 issue of the magazine (UIC, JAMC 0112 0933).

They come to us with their petty lawsuits, sad relics of the vendetta, with their incorrigible boys, with their hospital cases, with their aspirations for American clothes, and with their needs for an interpreter.

Friday evening is devoted to Germans[105] and is similar in purpose; but owing to the superior education of our Teutonic guests and the clever leading of a cultivated German woman,[106] we can bring out the best of that cozy social intercourse which is found in its perfection in the "Fatherland." They sing a great deal in the tender minor of the German folksong or in the rousing spirit of the Rhine. They are slowly but persistently pursuing a course in German history and literature. The relationship by no means ends with social civilities, and the acquaintance made there has brought about radical changes in the lives of many friendless families. I recall one peasant woman, straight from the fields of Germany. Her two years in America had been spent in patiently carrying water up and down two flights of stairs and in washing the heavy flannel suits of iron-foundry workers. For this her pay had averaged thirty-five cents a day.

Three of her daughters had fallen victims to the vice of the city. The mother was bewildered and distressed, but understood nothing. We were able to induce the betrayer of one daughter to marry her; the second, after a tedious lawsuit, supported his child; with the third we were able to do nothing. This woman is now living with her family in a little house seventeen miles from the city. She has made two payments on her land and is a lesson to all beholders as she pastures her cow up and down the railroad tracks and makes money from her ten acres. She did not need charity. She had an immense capacity for hard work, but she sadly needed "heading." She is our most shining example, but I think of many forlorn cases of German and Bohemian peasants in need of neighborly help.

Perhaps of more value than to the newly arrived peasant is the service of the settlement to those foreigners who speak English fairly well, and who have been so successful in material affairs that they are totally absorbed by them. Their social life is too often reduced to a sense of comradeship. The lives of many Germans for instance are law-abiding, but inexpressibly dull. They have resigned poetry and romance with the other good things of the Fatherland. There is a strong family affection between them and their English-speaking children, but their pleasures are not in common and they seldom go out together. Perhaps the greatest value of the Settlement to them is in simply placing large and pleasant rooms with musical facilities at their disposal, and in reviving their almost forgotten enthusiasm for Körner and Schiller.[107] I have seen sons and daughters stand in complete surprise as their mother's knitting-needles softly beat time to the song she was singing, or her worn face turned rosy under the hand-clapping as she made an old-fashioned courtesy at the end of a German poem. It was easy to fancy a growing touch of respect in her children's manner to her and a rising enthusiasm for German literature and reminiscence on the part of all the family, an effort to bring together the old life and the new, a respect for the older cultivation, and not quite so much assurance that the new was the best. I think that we have a right to expect that our foreigners will do this for us: that they will project a little of the historic and romantic into the prosaic quarters of our American cities.

But our social evenings are by no means confined to foreigners. Our most successful clubs are entirely composed of English-speaking and American-born young people. Those over sixteen meet in two clubs, one for young men and one for girls, every Monday evening.[108] Each club dispatches various literary programmes before nine o'clock, when they meet together for an hour of social amusement before going home at ten. Dancing they always prefer, although they will devise other amusements. The members of the Tuesday evening clubs are from fourteen to sixteen years old; a few of them are still in school, but most of them are working. The boys who are known as the Young Citizen's Club[109] are supposed to inform themselves on municipal affairs, as are the Hull House Columbia Guards who report alleys and streets for the Municipal Order League.[110] We have various other clubs of young people that meet weekly; their numbers are limited only by the amount of room.[111] We hold the dining-room, the reception-room, and the octagon each evening for the College Extension classes, and can reserve only the large drawing-room and gymnasium for the clubs and receptions. The gymnasium is a somewhat pretentious name for a building next door which was formerly a saloon, but which we rented last fall, repaired, and fitted up with simple apparatus.[112] A "real gymnasium" is at present being built for Hull House.[113] During the winter the old one sheltered some enthusiastic athletic classes. The evenings were equally divided between men and women. The children came in the afternoon. This may answer for a description of the formal social evenings, although there is much social life going on constantly which cannot be tabulated.

To turn to the educational effort, it will be perhaps better first to describe the people who respond to it. In every neighborhood where poorer people live, because rents are supposed to be cheaper there, is an element which, although uncertain in the individual, in the aggregate can be counted upon. It is composed of people of former education and opportunity who have cherished ambitions and prospects, but who are caricatures of what they meant to be—"hollow ghosts which blame the living men."[114] There are times in many lives when there is a cessation of energy and loss of power. Men and women of education and refinement come to live in a cheaper neighborhood because they lack the power of making money, because of ill-health, because of an unfortunate marriage, or for various other reasons which do not imply criminality or stupidity. Among them are those who, in spite of untoward circumstances, keep up some sort of an intellectual life, those who are "great for books" as their neighbors say. To such the Settlement is a genuine refuge. In addition to these there are many young women who teach in the public schools, young men who work at various occupations, but who are bent upon self-improvement and are preparing for professions. It is of these that the College Extension[115] classes are composed. The majority of the two hundred students live within the radius of six blocks from the house, although a few of them come from other parts of the city. The educational effort of Hull House always has been held by the residents to be subordinate to its social life and, as it were, a part of it. What is now known as the College Extension course, a series of lectures and classes held in the evening on the general plan of University Extension, had its origin in an informal club which, during the first winter, read "Romola" with the original residents.[116] During the last term thirty-five classes a week were in existence. The work is divided into terms of twelve weeks, and circulars are issued at the beginning of each term. Many students have taken studies in each of the seven terms of work offered.[117]

The relation of students and faculty to each other and to the residents is that of guest and hostess, and those students who have been longest in relation to the Settlement feel the responsibility of old friends of the house to new guests. A good deal of tutoring is constantly going on among the students themselves in the rooms of Hull House.[118] At the close of each term the residents give a reception to students and faculty, which is one of the chief social events of the season. Upon this comfortable social basis very good work has been done in the College Extension courses. Literature classes until recently have been the most popular.[119] The last winter's Shakespeare class had a regular attendance of forty.[120] The mathematical classes have always been large and flourishing. The faculty, consisting of college men and women, numbers thirty-five. Many of them have taught constantly at the house for two years, but their numbers are often re-enforced. During the last term a class is physics, preparatory for a class in electricity, was composed largely of workmen in the Western Electric Works, which are within a few blocks of Hull House.[121] A fee of fifty cents is charged for each course of study. This defrays all incidental expenses and leaves on hand each term fifty or seventy dollars, with which to import distinguished lecturers.[122]

It has always been the policy of Hull House to co-operate as much as possible with public institutions. The Chicago Public Library[123] has an almost unique system of branch reading-rooms and library stations. Five rooms are rented by the library in various parts of the city which are fitted up for reading-rooms, and in addition to magazines and papers they are supplied with several hundred books. There are also other stations where public-library cards can be left and to which books are delivered. Hull House was made one of these delivery stations during its second year, and when in June, 1891, the Butler Gallery was completed we offered the lower floor as a branch reading-room. The City Library supplies English magazines and papers and two librarians who are in charge. There are papers in Italian, German, Bohemian, and French. Hull House gives the room free of rent. The number of readers the first month was 1,213; during the fifth month, 2,454. The upper floor of the Butler Gallery is divided into an art exhibition room and a studio.[124] Our first art exhibit was opened in June, 1891, by Mr. and Mrs. Barnett, of St. Jude's, Whitechapel.[125] It is always pleasant to associate their hearty sympathy with that first exhibit. The pictures were some of the best that Chicago could afford, several by Corot, Watts, and Davis.[126] European country scenes, sea views, and Dutch interiors bring forth many pleasant reminiscences, and the person who is in charge of the pictures to explain them is many times more edified than edifying. We have had four exhibits during the year since the gallery was completed, two of oil-paintings, one of old engravings and etchings, and one of water-colors.[127] The average attendance at these exhibits has been three thousand. An exhibit is open from two in the afternoon until ten in the evening, and continues usually two weeks. The value of these exhibits to the neighborhood must, of course, be determined by the value one attaches to the sense of beauty and the pleasure which arises from its contemplation. Classes in free-hand drawing are held in the studio of the Butler Gallery. They have been very popular from the first and some excellent work has been done.

Every Thursday evening for three years,[128] save during the three summer months, we have had a lecture of some sort at Hull House. This has come to be an expected event in the neighborhood. These lectures are largely attended by the College Extension students, and the topics are supposed to connect with their studies, but many other people come to them and often join a class because of the interest a lecturer has awakened. This attraction is constantly in mind when these lectures are planned. For two years a summer school[129] has been held at Rockford, Ill., in connection with the College Extension classes. From one-third to one-half the students have been able to attend it, paying their board for a month and enjoying out-door study quite as much as the classes. I would recommend for imitation the very generous action on the part of the Rockford College trustees in placing at our disposal their entire educational apparatus, from the dining-room to the laboratories. On the border land between social and educational activity are our Sunday afternoon concerts,[130] and the Plato Club[131] which follows them.

The industrial education of Hull House has always been somewhat limited. From the beginning we have had large and enthusiastic cooking classes, first in the Hull House kitchen and later in a tiny cottage across the alley which has been fitted up for the purpose.[132] We have also always had sewing, mending, and embroidery classes. This leads me to speak of the children who meet weekly at Hull House, whose organization is between classes and clubs. There are three hundred of them who come on three days,[133] not counting, of course, the children who come to the house merely as depositors in the Penny Provident Fund Savings Bank.[134] A hundred Italian girls come on Monday. They sew and carry home a new garment, which becomes a pattern for the entire family. Tuesday afternoon has always been devoted to school-boys' clubs: they are practically story-telling clubs. The most popular stories are legends and tales of chivalry. The one hundred and fifty little girls on Friday afternoon are not very unlike the boys, although they want to sew while they are hearing their stories. The value of these clubs, I believe, lies almost entirely in their success in arousing the higher imagination. We have had a kindergarten[135] at Hull House ever since we have lived there. Every morning miniature Italians, Hebrews, French, Irish, and Germans assemble in our drawing-room, and nothing seems to excite admiration in the neighborhood so much as the fact that we "put up with them."

In addition to the neighbors who respond to the receptions and classes are found those who are too battered and oppressed to care for them. To these, however, is left that susceptibility to the bare offices of humanity which raises such offices into a bond of fellowship. These claim humanitarian efforts. Perhaps the chief value of a Settlement to its neighborhood, certainly to the newly arrived foreigner, is its office as an information and interpretation bureau. It sometimes seems as if the business of the settlement were that of a commission merchant. Without endowment and without capital itself, it constantly acts between the various institutions of the city and the people for whose benefit these institutions were erected. The hospitals, the county agencies, and State asylums, are often but vague rumors to the people who need them most. This commission work, as I take it, is of value not only to the recipient, but to the institutions themselves. Each institution is obliged to determine upon the line of its activity, to accept its endowment for that end and do the best it can. But each time this is accomplished it is apt to lace itself up in certain formulas, is in danger of forgetting the mystery and complexity of life, of repressing the promptings that spring from growing insight.

The residents of a Social Settlement have an opportunity of seeing institutions from the recipient's standpoint, of catching the spirit of the original impulse which founded them. This experience ought to have a certain value and ultimately find expression in the institutional management. One of the residents of Hull House received this winter an appointment from the Cook County agent as a county visitor.[136] She reported at the agency each morning, and all the cases within a radius of several blocks from Hull House were given to her for investigation. This gave her a legitimate opportunity for knowing the poorest people in the neighborhood. In no cases were her recommendations refused or her judgments reversed by the men in charge of the office. From the very nature of our existence and purpose we are bound to keep on good terms with every beneficent institution in the city. Passing by our telephone[137] last Sunday morning, I was struck with the list of numbers hung on the wall for easy reference. They were those of the Visiting Nurses' Association;[138] Cook County Hospital;[139] Women's and Children's Hospital;[140] Maxwell Street Police Station for city ambulance;[141] Health Department;[142] City Hall;[143] Cook County Agent, etc.[144] We have been on very good terms with the Hebrew Relief and Aid Society,[145] the Children's Aid,[146] the Humane Society,[147] the Municipal Order League, and with the various church and national relief associations. Every summer we send out dozens of children to the country on the "Daily News" Fresh Air Fund[148] and to the Holiday Home at Lake Geneva.[149] Our most complete co-operation has been with the Visiting Nurses' Association. One of the nurses lives at Hull House, pays her board as a resident, and does her work from there.[150] Friends of the house are constantly in need of her ministrations, and her cases become friends of the house. Owing to the lack of a charity organization society in Chicago we have been obliged to keep a sum of money as a relief fund.[151] Five bath-rooms in the rear of Hull House[152] are open to the neighborhood and are constantly in use. The number of baths taken in July was nine hundred and eighty.

The more definite humanitarian effect of Hull House has taken shape in a day nursery,[153] which was started during the second year of our residence on Halsted Street. A frame cottage of six rooms across our yard has been fitted up as a crèche. At present we receive from thirty to forty children daily. A young lady who has had kindergarten training is in charge; she has the assistance of an older woman, and a kindergarten by a professional teacher is held each morning in the play-room.[154] This nursery is not merely a convenience in the neighborhood; it is, to a certain extent, a neighborhood affair. Similar in spirit is the Hull House Diet Kitchen, in a little cottage directly back of the nursery.[155] Food is prepared for invalids and orders are taken from physicians and visiting nurses of the district. We have lately had an outfit of Mr. Atkinson's inventions,[156] in which the women of the neighborhood have taken a most intelligent interest. We sometimes have visions of a kitchen similar in purpose to the New England Kitchen of Boston,[157] but on a more co-operative plan, managed by the Hull House Woman's Club.[158] This club meets one afternoon a week. It is composed of the most able women of the neighborhood, who enjoy the formal addresses and many informal discussions. The economics of food and fuel are often discussed. The Hull House household expenses are frankly compared with those of other households. I have always felt that "friendly visiting," while of great value, was one-sided.[159] To be complete the "friendly visitor" should also be the friendly visited. It is quite possible that looking over her expense book with that of her "case" would be beneficial to her. The residents at Hull House find in themselves a constantly increasing tendency to consult their neighbors on the advisability of each new undertaking. We have lately opened a boarding club for working girls near Hull House on the co-operative plan.[160] I say advisedly that we have "opened" it; the running of it is quite in the hands of the girls themselves. The furniture, pictures, etc., belong to Hull House, and whatever experience we have is at their disposal; but it is in no sense a working-girls' "home," nor is it to be run from the outside. We hope a great deal from this little attempt at co-operative housekeeping. The club has been running three months and has twenty-five members.

In summing up the objective value of Hull House, I am sorry we have not more to present in the line of civic activities. It was through the energy of a resident[161] this spring that the fact that the public-school census recorded 6,976 school-children in the nineteenth ward and that they were provided with only 2,957 public-school sittings was made prominent just before the appropriations were voted for school buildings and sites. It was largely through her energy and the energy of the people whom she interested in it that the Board of Education was induced to purchase a site for a school building in our ward and to save and equip for immediate use a school-house about to be turned into a warehouse.[162]

During two months of this summer the reports sent in from Hull House to the Municipal Order League and through it to the Health Department were one thousand and thirty-seven. The Department showed great readiness to co-operate with this volunteer inspection, and a marked improvement has taken place in the scavenger service and in the regulation of the small stables of the ward.

Hull House has had, I hope, a certain value to the women's trades unions of Chicago.[163] It seems to me of great importance that as trades unions of women are being formed they should be kept, if possible, from falling into the self-same pits the men's unions have fallen into. Women possessing no votes and therefore having little political value will be both of advantage and disadvantage to their unions. Four women's unions meet regularly at Hull House: the book-binders', the shoemakers', the shirtmakers', and the cloakmakers'. The last two were organized at Hull House. It has seemed to us that the sewing trades are most in need of help. They are thoroughly disorganized, Russian and Polish tailors competing against English-speaking tailors, young girls and Italian women competing against both. An efficient union which should combine all these elements seems very difficult, unless it grow strong enough to offer a label and receive unexpected aid from the manufacturers. In that case there would be the hope of co-operation on the part of the consumers, as the fear of contagion from ready-made clothing has at last seized the imagination of the public.

That the trades unions themselves care for what we have done for them is shown by the fact that when the committee of investigation for the sweating system was appointed by the Trades and Labor Assembly, consisting of five delegates from the unions and five from other citizens, two of the latter were residents of Hull House.[164] It is logical that a Settlement should have a certain value in labor complications, having from its very position sympathies entangled on both sides. Last May twenty girls from a knitting factory who struck because they were docked for loss of time when they were working by the piece, came directly from the factory to Hull House.[165] They had heard that we "stood by working people." We were able to have the strike arbitrated, and although six girls lost their places, the unjust fines were remitted and we had the satisfaction of putting on record one more case of arbitration in the slowly growing list. We were helped in this case, as we have been in many others, by the Bureau of Justice.[166] Its office is constantly crowded with working people who hope for redress from the law but have no money with which to pay for it. There should be an office of this bureau in every ward. Hull House, in spite of itself, does a good deal of legal work. We have secured support for deserted women, insurance for bewildered widows, damages for injured operators, furniture from the clutches of the instalment store. One function of the Settlement to its neighborhood somewhat resembles that of the big brother whose mere presence on the play-ground protects the little one from bullies. A resident of Hull House is at present collecting labor statistics in the neighborhood for the Illinois State Bureau of Labor.[167] It is a matter of satisfaction that this work can be done from the Settlement and the residents receive the benefit of the information collected.

It is difficult to classify the Working People's Social Science Club,[168] which meets weekly at Hull House. It is social, educational, and civic in character, the latter chiefly because it strongly connects the house with the labor problems in their political and social aspects. This club was organized at Hull House in the spring of 1890 by an English workingman.[169] It has met weekly since, save during the months of summer. At eight o'clock every Wednesday evening the secretary calls to order from forty to one hundred people. A chairman for the evening is elected and a speaker is introduced who is allowed to talk until nine o'clock; his subject is then thrown open to discussion and a lively debate ensues until ten o'clock, at which hour the meeting is declared adjourned. The enthusiasm of this club seldom lags. Its zest for discussion is unceasing, and any attempt to turn it into a study or reading club always meets with the strong disapprobation of the members. Chicago is full of social theorists. It offers a cosmopolitan opportunity for discussion. The only possible danger from this commingling of many theories is incurred when there is an attempt at suppression; bottled up, there is danger of explosion; constantly uncorked, open to the deodorizing and freeing process of the air, all danger is averted. Nothing so disconcerts a social agitator as to find among his auditors men who have been through all that and who are quite as radical as he in another direction.

The economic conferences which were held between business men and workingmen during the winter of 1888–89 and the two succeeding winters doubtless did much toward relieving this state of effervescence.[170] Many thoughtful men in Chicago are convinced that if these conferences had been established earlier the Haymarket riot and all its sensational results might have been avoided. The Sunset Club[171] is at present performing much the same function. There is still need, however, for many of these clubs where men who differ widely in their social theories can meet for discussion, where representatives of the various economic schools can modify each other, and at least learn tolerance and the futility of endeavoring to convince all the world of the truth of one position. To meet in a social-science club is more educational than to meet in a single-tax club, or a socialistic chapter, or a personal-rights league, although the millennium may seem farther off after such a meeting. In addition to this modification of view there is doubtless a distinct modification of attitude. This spring the Hull House Social Science Club heard a series of talks on municipal and county affairs by the heads of the various departments.[172] During the discussion following the address on "The Chicago Police," a workingman had the pleasure of telling the chief of police that he had been arrested, obliged to pay two dollars and a half, and had lost three days' work, because he had come out of the wrong gate when he was working on the World's Fair grounds. The Chief sighed, expressed his regret, and made no defence. The speaker sat down bewildered; evidently for the first time in his life he realized that blunders cut the heart of more than the victim.

Is it possible for men, however far apart in outward circumstances, for the capitalist and the workingman, to use the common phrase, to meet as individuals beneath a friendly roof, open their minds each to each, and not have their "class theories" insensibly modified by the kindly attrition of a personal acquaintance? In the light of our experience I should say not.

In describing Hull House and in referring so often to the "residents," I feel that I may have given a wrong impression. By far the larger amount of the teaching and formal club work is done by people living outside of the House. Between ninety and one hundred of these people meet on appointment regularly each week. Our strength lies largely in this element. The average number of people who come to the House during the week is one thousand.

I am always sorry to have Hull House regarded as philanthropy, although it doubtless has strong philanthropic tendencies and has several distinct charitable departments which are conscientiously carried on. It is unfair, however, to apply the word philanthropic to the activities of the House as a whole. Charles Booth in his brilliant chapter on "The Unemployed"[173] expresses regret that the problems of the working class are so often confounded with the problems of the inefficient, the idle, and distressed. To confound thus two problems is to render the solution of both impossible. Hull House, while endeavoring to fulfil its obligations to neighbors of varying needs, will do great harm if it confounds distinct problems. Working people live in the same streets with those in need of charity, but they themselves require and want none of it. As one of their number has said, they require only that their aspirations be recognized and stimulated and the means of attaining them put at their disposal. Hull House makes a constant effort to secure these means, but to call that effort philanthropy is to use the word unfairly and to underestimate the duties of good citizenship.

JANE ADDAMS.

PD ("HH, Chicago: An Effort toward Social Democracy," *Forum* 14 [Oct. 1892]: 226–41; *JAPM*, 46:503–19).

1. The second HH Summer School lasted until 23 July 1892. "The Summer School finances are going beautifully since we have forty girls. There is something cosy about a small school," JA reported to MRS (4 July 1892, SCPC, JAC; *JAPM*, 2:1318).

2. "I have been very busy with my Plymouth lectures. I dictated the first one to a stenographer yesterday and feel as if half my burden were off" (JA to SAAH, [5?] [July 1892], SCPC, JAC; *JAPM*, 2:1315). Her stenographer may have been Edward L. Burchard, a Beloit College graduate who would later become one of the first male HH residents (see Robert A. Woods to JA, 20 June 1893, n. 12, below). JA titled the two presentations that she drafted while at Rockford "The Subjective Value of Social Settlements" and "The Objective Value of a Social Settlement."

3. The second annual Summer School of Applied Ethics, under the direction of Prof. of Hebrew and Oriental languages C. H. Toy (1836–1919) of Harvard Univ. began 6 July and lasted six weeks. It was divided into three themes of study: history of religions, economics, and ethics. During the six weeks of the school, twenty-two lecturers presented ninety-six lectures. Announcements for the summer school appeared in a variety of popular, religious, and scholarly journals.

4. Henry Carter Adams (1851–1921) was born in Davenport, Iowa, and schooled at the Johns Hopkins Univ. (Ph.D. 1878), at Heidelberg and Berlin, and in Paris. He joined the faculty at Cornell Univ., 1880–87, and moved to the Univ. of Michigan as a professor of political economy and finance beginning in 1887, where he spent the remainder of his academic career. He served as a statistician for the Interstate Commerce Comm., 1887–1911; was associate editor for the *International Journal of Ethics*; and published a number of books on economics, finance, and railroads.

5. EGS reported to her sister Mary Blaisdell that JA and Julia Lathrop left HH on 25 July, traveling together. The [5?] Aug. 1892 *Boston Transcript* also identified Harriet Trowbridge and "Miss Rogers" as attendees from HH. By 1892 Alice Trowbridge was a faithful HH volunteer; however, the editors are uncertain about the identify of Miss Rogers. No Rogers appears in the HH records as a volunteer or resident in the 1889–92 period. There are, however, two

Edward L. Burchard, often referred to as the first male resident of Hull-House, was a graduate of Beloit College in Wisconsin, where Jane Addams's brother and stepbrothers had attended school. In the early years, Burchard sometimes served as Addams's secretary (courtesy Beloit College, Wis., Archives).

women by the name of Rogers who were associated with HH and JA who could have attended the gathering. The editors have been unable to establish that either of them were at the Plymouth, Mass., meetings.

The Miss Rogers listed in a newspaper may have been Agnes Adelaide Rogers (1867?–1946), born to Eliza M. and Frederick D. Rogers, a printer in Rochester, N.Y. She was the sixth of eight daughters, many of whom became teachers, and one son born to the couple. She graduated from Cornell Univ. (Ph.B. 1888), where she was a member of Kappa Kappa Gamma social sorority and active in the Cornell Classical Assn. Between 1888 and 1895, she was a teacher in Englewood, Ill., near Chicago, where JML's brother, James Linn, and his wife, Anna, lived and JA sometimes visited. By Jan. 1894, she was teaching American history as a volunteer in the College Extension Program at HH and in the spring of 1894 continued with a course on American institutions using Bryce's *The American Commonwealth* as her text. She traveled to Europe at least twice, once in 1924 and 1934. She never married, and by 1908 she had returned to Rochester, N.Y., where she died.

It is also possible that the *Boston Transcript*, which listed the women who attended the settlement gathering from HH, may have actually meant Mrs. Rogers rather than Miss Rogers. If that is so, the likely candidate could have been Emma Ferdon Winner Rogers (1855–1922), wife of the new president of Northwestern Univ., Henry Wade Rogers (1853–1926), who officially assumed that position in Feb. 1891 and served until 1900. She had been born in Plainfield, N.J., and was a graduate of the Univ. of Michigan during the 1870s. She and Henry

Wade Rogers were married in 1876 while Rogers was a law student at the Univ. of Michigan and where he served as dean of the law school, 1883–90. With their move to Evanston, Ill., Emma Rogers became associated with several social and philanthropic efforts in the Chicago area. In 1891 she became a member of the Fortnightly Club and was also a founder of the Northwestern University Settlement, where she served a short period as the president of its board. During the spring of 1892, when women "shoe-girls" went out on strike from the Selz, Schwab, and Co., Mrs. Rogers was one of three women associated with the CWC who investigated and tried to arrange for arbitration (see Articles in the *Chicago News* and *Chicago Daily Tribune*, 29 and 30 Apr. 1892, n. 8, above). The other two members of the committee were Ellen Henrotin and JA. Emma Rogers and JA were also working together through the Municipal Order League for which Emma Rogers was the head in 1892. At the settlement conference that followed the Plymouth lectures, the attendees heard a report on Evanston House, Chicago, but there is no indication of the name of the person who presented it.

When Henry Wade Rogers went to Yale Univ., where he became dean of the law school, Emma Rogers became associated with New Haven's Model Housing Assn. and the Lowell Settlement House. She also was treasurer of the National Woman Suffrage Assn. (NWSA), active in the Women's Bureau of the Democratic National Com., and during World War I helped with the Women's Overseas Hospitals organization.

6. "Outlet for Faculties: The Subjective Necessity of a Social Settlement," *Boston Herald*. The *Boston Transcript* and the *Springfield (Mass.) Republican* also covered her remarks.

7. Bernard Bosanquet (1848–1923), British philosopher, political theorist, and social reformer, was educated at Harrow and Balliol College, Oxford Univ. (1867–70). He maintained a lifelong relationship with the COS, which his eldest brother, Charles, helped found, and he served as a member of its council (chair, 1916–17) from 1898 until his death. A prolific author, he promoted the idea that social work had to be connected with education (see also JA to EGS, 29 [and 30] May 1896, n. 7, below).

8. Franklin Henry Giddings (1855–1931), a noted sociologist, was born in Sherman, Conn., to Rev. Edward J. and Rebecca Jane Fuller Giddings. He attended Union College (A.M. 1877). He began his career as a journalist, but when he lectured at the Summer School of Applied Ethics, he was teaching at Bryn Mawr College, Penn., 1888–94, after which he became a professor of sociology at Columbia Univ. He wrote widely on his subject. His *The Principles of Sociology* (1896) was translated into several languages.

9. Bosanquet presented "The Principles and Chief Dangers of the Administration of Charity"; Robert A. Woods titled his talk "The University Settlement Idea"; Father Huntington offered "Philanthropy—Its Success and Failure" and "Philanthropy and Morality"; and Giddings presented "The Ethics of Social Progress."

10. On Wednesday, 3 Aug. 1892, many who were attending the Plymouth lectures gathered for "settlement day," which was described by the *Boston Transcript* as being "woman's day also, since the young women did most of the talking about the work, which is mostly theirs" ("The Plymouth School"). JA seems to have been the star. She was quoted summing up settlement goals as seeking "to realize the same democracy in social matters which is the ideal in politics" ("The Plymouth School"). Emily G. Balch, who would become a longtime colleague of JA in social reform and peace activities, wrote to her father about the occasion, "It is a kind of a stimulus I have not had very much of, and that I am sure is good—in moderation. Among my gains I count foremost Miss Addams" (Randall, *Improper Bostonian*, 82).

In addition to the HH contingent, among other representatives of social settlements or friends of the developing movement who met that day were Dr. Mary Damon (1842?–1902), a graduate of Vassar College (1866), who represented the College Settlement in New York City. Representing Philadelphia were Susan P. Wharton (1845–1921), Quaker, philanthropist, later a founder of the NAACP, and in 1884 founder of the St. Mary Street Library, which affiliated with the College Settlement in 1892; Ida Wood (1857–1948), Philadelphia philanthropist; and Helena S. Dudley (1858–1932), graduate of Bryn Mawr (1889), who became the first head resident of Denison House in Boston (but at that time was associated with the St. Mary Street Library). Robert A. Woods and Rev. John A. Bevington (1854–1928), Episcopal clergyman and chaplain for McLean Hospital, Somerville, Mass., attended from Andover House, which in 1895 would become South End House in Boston. Bertha Hazard (1858–1941), graduate of Vassar (1879), and Vida Scudder (1861–1954), a member of the English faculty at Wellesley College, represented the College Settlements Assn. Scudder, Katharine Coman, Emily G. Balch, Charles W. Birtwell, and Mrs. Mary Morton Kimball Kehew (1859–1913), who beginning in 1892 was president of the Women's Educational and Industrial Union in Boston, were representatives of the Boston committee of college settlements. There were reports of settlement activities from the Brooklyn Neighborhood Guild; Evanston Hall, Chicago; and East Side House in New York City. Among those who also addressed the group were Bernard Bosanquet and Franklin Benjamin Sanborn.

Robert Woods reported to his Andover Theological School mentor, Dr. William J. Tucker (1839–1939), "The Plymouth conference went off very successfully. The college settlement women were there in force. There was quite a little brush between Miss Addams, . . . and the rest of us as between the names 'social settlement' and 'University Settlement'"(quoted in E. Woods, *Robert A. Woods*, 67). All, however, agreed that they were dedicated to breaking down the "dangerous over-differentiation of rich and poor," and in doing so that condescension had to be "strictly avoided" ("The Plymouth School").

11. Walter Hines Page (1855–1918), who was born in Cary, N.C., and attended Trinity College (now Duke Univ.); Randolph-Macon College, Va., 1872–76; and the Johns Hopkins Univ., 1876–78, became a journalist and editor. He was editor of the *St. Joseph (Mo.) Daily Gazette*, 1880–81; on the staff of the *New York World*, 1882; founded and edited the *State Chronicle* (Raleigh, N.C.), 1882–83; and joined the *New York Evening Post*, 1883–87. In 1885 he was instrumental in helping to establish a school for industrial education that became North Carolina State Univ., Raleigh. He was with the *Forum*, 1887–95, where he served as the editor beginning in 1890. He became editor of the *Atlantic Monthly*, 1896–99, and the *World's Work*, 1900–13. He was a founding partner and vice-president of publishers Doubleday, Page, and Co., 1899–1913. From 1913 to 1918, he was Woodrow Wilson's decidedly pro-British ambassador to Great Britain and a force in bringing the United States into World War I.

12. The *Forum*, launched in 1885 as a monthly literary periodical, was meant to be "sufficiently dignified to attract the finest minds in America as contributors; its purpose was to exercise a profound influence in politics, literature, science, and art" (Hendrick, *Life and Letters of Walter H. Page*, 48). Under Walter Hines Page's (see n. 11) leadership, the magazine's circulation rose from very few subscribers to at least thirty thousand, "something without precedent for a publication of this character" (Hendrick, *Life and Letters of Walter H. Page*, 49). The purpose of the *Forum* "as Page explained it, was 'to provoke discussion about subjects of contemporary interest, in which the magazine is not a partisan, but merely the instrument'" (quoted in Hendrick, *Life and Letters of Walter H. Page*, 49). He saw that the publication presented articles on the ideas and events of the time, from controversy to new venture. The pages of his journal were filled with the commentary of the men of action, thought, and word of his day. Page turned the *Forum* into a moneymaking business and had to resign his position as editor in 1895 when his attempt to purchase the periodical from its owners failed. The *Forum* under different editorial direction survived until 1929, when it was merged with the *Century Monthly* (1925) to continue as the *Forum and Century*, 1930–40.

13. Comments on the two articles by JA in the *Forum* appeared in the following periodicals: *Chicago Times*, 26 Sept. 1892; *Chicago Daily Tribune*, 29 Oct. 1892; *Advance*, 20 Oct. 1892; *Toledo* (Ohio) *Journal*, Nov. 1892; *Churchman*, 24 Nov. 1892; *Religio-Philosophical Journal*, Nov. 1892 and 29 Mar. 1893; *Unity*, [Nov.? 1892]; *Review of Reviews*, Nov. 1892; and *Woman's News*, Chicago, Nov. 1892. In addition, a lengthy review quoting large sections of "HH,

Chicago: An Effort toward Social Democracy," the essay that appeared in Oct. 1892 in the *Forum*, was published in a newspaper. The article carried a New York, 24 Sept. [1892], place and dateline (HH Scrapbook 1:21, 22, 23½; *JAPM*, Addendum 10:6ff). In addition, an article entitled "HH," in which a portion of "HH, Chicago: An Effort toward Social Democracy" appeared, was published in the *RSM* for Oct. 1892, as part of a description of a visit to HH written by Rockford students.

14. *Philanthropy and Social Progress: Seven Essays by Miss Jane Addams, Robert A. Woods, Father J. O. S. Huntington, Professor Franklin H. Giddings, and Bernard Bosanquet Delivered before the School of Applied Ethics at Plymouth, Mass., during the Session of 1892*, edited by Henry C. Adams (New York: Thomas Y. Crowell, 1893).

15. JA's aunt Harriet Addams Young and uncle Nathan Young, their children and grandchildren, and Miranda Addams, sister of Harriet Addams Young.

16. Elizabeth Weber Reiff, sister of JA's mother, SWA.

17. 18 Aug. 1892, IU, Lilly, SAAH; *JAPM*, 2:1325–26.

18. The original title given this presentation by JA was "The Subjective Value of a Social Settlement." Walter Hines Page, the *Forum* editor, provided this different and more directly descriptive title. At least two extant reprints of the paper as it appeared in the *Forum* omit his chosen title as well as the first paragraph he caused to be added to the piece (see n. 20). When the paper was published in *Philanthropy and Social Progress* in 1893, it appeared as the lead essay in the volume under the title "The Subjective Necessity for Social Settlements."

19. For the text of "Outgrowths of Toynbee Hall," see Address for the Chicago Woman's Club, 3 Dec. 1890, above.

20. Walter H. Page, editor of the *Forum*, may have asked JA to draft a new opening paragraph for this article to remind readers about her HH article that appeared in the Oct. issue of the magazine. In the two reprint versions in the JAPP files (see n. 18) that reinstate JA's title "The Subjective Value of Social Settlements," the following is the lead paragraph: "A Social Settlement may be defined as an attempt to make social intercourse express the growing sense of the economic unity of society and as an effort to add the social function to democracy. It is based on the theory that the dependence of classes on each other is reciprocal; and that as the social relation is essentially a reciprocal relation, it gives a form of expression that has peculiar value. A settlement is established in the belief that the mere foothold of a house, easily accessible, ample in space, hospitable and tolerant in spirit, situated in the very midst of the industrial quarters of large cities, is in itself a serviceable thing, and that, given a starting point, many educated young people can find various outlets for a certain sort of unexpressed activity." This text may well have been the original first paragraph of the paper that Addams presented at Plymouth. The text from "to add the social function" to "gives a form of expression that has peculiar value" provides the only words in this opening paragraph that are similar to those that appear in the first paragraph of the essay as it was presented in the *Forum*.

21. From "this paper . . ." to "genuine emotion" appears in Addams, *Twenty Years*, 115.

22. "Democracy has made little attempt to assert itself in social affairs" appears in "Outgrowths of Toynbee Hall" (Address for the Chicago Woman's Club, 3 Dec. 1890, above).

23. "[W]ho believed that political equality alone would secure all good to all men" appears in "Outgrowths of Toynbee Hall" (Address for the Chicago Woman's Club, 3 Dec. 1890, above).

24. JA would attempt to right this wrong through HH. Harriet Alleyne Rice (1866–1958) arrived at HH in 1893, the first African American graduate from Wellesley (1887), a New York Infirmary for Women and Children graduate (1891), and the first African American resident at the settlement. See JA to MRS, 15 Jan. 1895, n. 21, below.

25. JA and EGS welcomed an assortment of immigrants to help with programs at HH. Among them were Julia M. E. Hintermeister (see n. 159) and Emma N. Neuschäffer (see JA to SAAH, 23 Nov. 1889, n. 10, above), both of whom served as teachers, and Alessandro Mastro-

Valerio, a conduit to the Italian community surrounding the settlement, soon identified as an independent HH resident.

26. "In many a city ward" to "the polls in politics" appears in "Outgrowths of Toynbee Hall" (Address for the Chicago Woman's Club, 3 Dec. 1890, above).

27. "[T]he politician who sells one by one" to "beginning to be challenged" appears in "Outgrowths of Toynbee Hall" (Address for the Chicago Woman's Club, 3 Dec. 1890, above).

28. *Bossism* was a nineteenth-century term that came into use in the 1870s and 1880s. It denoted a system of political control managed by a single powerful politician surrounded by a group of close supporters who did his bidding. Together the leader or boss and the supporters or gang were referred to as "the machine." In Chicago, and especially in the Nineteenth Ward in which HH was located, JA identified John Powers as the boss. He and his gang were associated with the liquor trade and saloons. JA discovered that they manipulated voters, primarily new immigrants unused to the political system in the United States, by providing for their special needs, including coal, food, lodging, jobs, and access to leniency if caught in illegal activities. See n. 95; and Minutes of a HH Residents Meeting, 10 Dec. 1893, n. 13, below.

29. "The social organism has broken" to "in other parts of the city" appears in "Outgrowths of Toynbee Hall" (Address for the Chicago Woman's Club, 3 Dec. 1890, above).

30. "[O]rganized into armies" to "found it to their interests" appears in "Outgrowths of Toynbee Hall" (Address for the Chicago Woman's Club, 3 Dec. 1890, above).

31. "[N]ot organized socially; although living in crowded tenement houses" appears in "Outgrowths of Toynbee Hall" (Address for the Chicago Woman's Club, 3 Dec. 1890, above).

32. "[A] saloon, their only host" to "stay away from them" appears in "Outgrowths of Toynbee Hall" (Address for the Chicago Woman's Club, 3 Dec. 1890, above).

33. JA had already discovered the power that saloons had in the neighborhood. She had just acquired the premises of the saloon to the immediate south of HH and had turned it into the settlement's first gymnasium. She was also becoming aware that Alderman John Powers was the neighborhood political power (see n. 95).

34. "But the paradox is here:" to "the continued with-holding" appears in "Outgrowths of Toynbee Hall" (Address for the Chicago Woman's Club, 3 Dec. 1890, above).

35. "This divides a city into rich and poor" appears in "Outgrowths of Toynbee Hall" (Address for the Chicago Woman's Club, 3 Dec. 1890, above).

36. "This division of the city" to "its total expression" appears in "Outgrowths of Toynbee Hall" (Address for the Chicago Woman's Club, 3 Dec. 1890, above).

37. "It is inevitable that" to "moral and physical health" appears in "Outgrowths of Toynbee Hall" (Address for the Chicago Woman's Club, 3 Dec. 1890, above).

38. "[E]ducated young people . . ." to "incorporated into our common life" appears in Addams, *Twenty Years*, 115–16.

39. "The public schools in the poorest" to "no longer in public schools?" appears in "Outgrowths of Toynbee Hall" (Address for the Chicago Woman's Club, 3 Dec. 1890, above).

40. See n. 99.

41. "The dream of transcendentalists" to "progressive workers" appears in "Outgrowths of Toynbee Hall" (Address for the Chicago Woman's Club, 3 Dec. 1890, above).

42. Transcendentalism, a style of thought primarily associated with a group of romantic writers in New England in the 1830s and 1840s, included Ralph Waldo Emerson, Henry David Thoreau, Margaret Fuller, Bronson Alcott, and others. They emphasized self-culture and man's capacity for good and rejected Christianity. Some of its practitioners were associated with the development of Brook Farm.

43. "The University Extension . . ." to "but would take it" appears in "Outgrowths of Toynbee Hall" (Address for the Chicago Woman's Club, 3 Dec. 1890, above). See headnote, JA to AHHA, 3 June 1890, above; and nn. 3, 5–6.

44. The University Extension movement began in England in the nineteenth century.

When JA visited Toynbee Hall, London, in the early summer of 1888, she had learned about it. JA and EGS instituted the program at HH in 1890. See headnote, JA to AHHA, 3 June 1890, above; nn. 3, 5–6; and Two Essays in the *Forum*, Oct. 1892.

45. "It requires tact and training" to "women in America who can do it" appears in "Outgrowths of Toynbee Hall" (Address for the Chicago Woman's Club, 3 Dec. 1890, above).

46. "This teaching requires distinct methods" to "before their faculties can be used" appears in "Outgrowths of Toynbee Hall" (Address for the Chicago Woman's Club, 3 Dec. 1890, above)

47. Friedrich Froebel, student of Pestalozzi (see n. 60) and German educator who developed the idea of kindergarten as a special concept in education where children could learn through creative play.

48. "Intellectual life requires" to "for a continuance of the cause" appears in "Outgrowths of Toynbee Hall" (Address for the Chicago Woman's Club, 3 Dec. 1890, above).

49. Giuseppe Mazzini. See Address for the Chicago Woman's Club, 3 Dec. 1890, n. 33, above.

50. JA is paraphrasing from chap. 7, "Duties towards Yourselves" of Giuseppe Mazzini's *The Duties of Man*, written between 1844 and 1858.

51. "[T]o formulate the . . . line of motives" to "striving of inherited power[s]" appears in Addams, *Twenty Years*, 116–18.

52. "Nothing so deadens the sympathies" to "no ode has yet been written" appears in "Outgrowths of Toynbee Hall" (Address for the Chicago Woman's Club, 3 Dec. 1890, above).

53. JA is citing one of her favorite poems by English romantic poet William Wordsworth. In its eleven stanzas, he decries the eroding as we pass into adulthood, save through memory, of the wonders and simple joys of nature and natural relationships we experienced in childhood (see *PJA*, 1:268, n. 11).

54. "You may remember the forlorn feeling" to "never be withheld from you" appears in "Outgrowths of Toynbee Hall" (Address for the Chicago Woman's Club, 3 Dec. 1890, above).

55. For an earlier description of a similar event in JA's life, see JA's experience with women workers in Saxe-Coburg, Germany, 1888, in *PJA*, 2:212–13, 2:224, n. 123; 2:297, 2:300, n. 11.

56. "There is nothing after disease" to "active faculties" appears in "Outgrowths of Toynbee Hall" (Address for the Chicago Woman's Club, 3 Dec. 1890, above). "[T]here is nothing after disease" to "zeal of the family carry them over their sense of abuse" appears in Addams, *Twenty Years*, 118–19.

57. JA seems to be recalling her own experience and that of her RFS classmates after their graduation. See especially introduction to part 1, *PJA*, 2; and pp. 5, 47–48, 50, 70–71, and 87–89.

58. "In our attempt then to give" to "arms may be put to high use" appears in "Outgrowths of Toynbee Hall" (Address for the Chicago Woman's Club, 3 Dec. 1890, above).

59. John Locke (1632–1704), English philosopher and physician, father of liberalism theory of the mind, and often associated with modern ideas of identify and the self.

60. Johann Heinrich Pestalozzi (1746–1827), Swiss educational reformer and teacher.

61. "We are fortunate" to "poor little girls" appears in "Outgrowths of Toynbee Hall" (Address for the Chicago Woman's Club, 3 Dec. 1890, above).

62. "We have in America a fast-growing" to "the Settlement from of activity" appears in Addams, *Twenty Years*, 120–22.

63. "Huxley declares that" to "atrophy of" appears in "Outgrowths of Toynbee Hall" (Speech to the Chicago Woman's Club, 3 Dec. 1890, above).

64. "[U]s all alike are stronger" to "opposition to each other" appears in "Outgrowths of Toynbee Hall" (Address for the Chicago Woman's Club, 3 Dec. 1890, above).

65. "[T]hat art when shut away from" to "consult all of humanity" appears in "Outgrowths of Toynbee Hall" (Address for the Chicago Woman's Club, 3 Dec. 1890, above).

66. "It is only the stronger young" to "who formulate this" appears in "Outgrowths of Toynbee Hall" (Address for the Chicago Woman's Club, 3 Dec. 1890, above).

67. "[B]uried beneath mere mental" to "clean nor unclean" appears in "Outgrowths of Toynbee Hall" (Address for the Chicago Woman's Club, 3 Dec. 1890, above).

68. See Address for the Chicago Woman's Club, 3 Dec. 1890, n. 12, above.

69. "Mr. Barnett, who urged the first Settlement—Toynbee Hall" appears in "Outgrowths of Toynbee Hall" (Address for the Chicago Woman's Club, 3 Dec. 1890, above). A reference to Samuel A. Barnett, Warden, Toynbee Hall, London, England.

70. "It is easy to see" to "Settlements in America" appears in "Outgrowths of Toynbee Hall" (Address for the Chicago Woman's Club, 3 Dec. 1890, above).

71. "[M]otives which I believe make toward" to "receiving and appropriating truth" appears in Addams, *Twenty Years*, 121–22. See also *PJA*, 2:554–56, 2:556, n. 3.

72. During JA's second trip to Europe, 1887–88, she indicated a considerable interest in early Christianity. See especially *PJA*, 2:xxviii; 2:551, n. 7; 2:554–55; 2:556, n. 3; 2:570, 586; and 2:587, n. 8. After founding HH, she continued to maintain that interest, giving lectures on early Christian art at the Chicago Training School for City, Home, and Foreign Missions. See JA to MCAL, 26 Feb. 1889, n. 26, above.

73. A biblical reference to John 7:17.

74. "That Christianity has to be revealed" to "embody itself, not in a sect, but in society itself" appears in Addams, *Twenty Years*, 122–24.

75. Christian socialism. See *PJA*, 2:xxxvi; 2:514, n. 154. See also JA to GBH, 24 Nov. 1889, n. 6, above.

76. "I believe that this turning, this renaissance" to "simpler formula to many of us" appears in Addams, *Twenty Years*, 124.

77. By 1888 JA had become interested in the positivist's philosophy. See *PJA*, 2:546, 551. Frederic Harrison (1831–1923) became a leader in this movement that inspired him while he was a student at Oxford Univ., 1849. A lawyer and writer, he was especially dedicated to supporting reforms helpful to working men. He served on the Trades Union Comm., 1867–69, as secretary to the commission for the digest of law, 1869–70, and as professor of jurisprudence and international law for the council of legal education, 1877–89. A liberal, he was elected to the newly formed London County Council, 1889, but resigned in 1893. JA knew him through his positivist writings, often about Auguste Comte. He was president of the English Positivist Com., 1880–1905.

78. Mary Augusta Arnold Ward (1851–1920), novelist and settlement house founder, was born in Hobart, Tasmania, Australia, and moved with her family to England in 1856. She was brought up in Oxford, where her father, Thomas Arnold, was a professor of literature. She was also a niece of Matthew Arnold. A difficult child, willful and quick to anger, Mary attended Rock Terrace School for Young Ladies at Shifnal and a school in Clifton, England. By 1871 she had accepted a proposal of marriage from her twenty-five-year-old tutor, Thomas Humphry Ward, and was married in 1872. During the remainder of the 1870s, as her children were born, 1874, 1876, and 1879, Mary began developing her talent as a writer. She and her husband moved their family to London in 1881 when he became a lead writer for the *Times*, and Mary set out in earnest on her career as a popular novelist. While her first two books were not successful, the third, *Robert Elsmere*, issued in 1888, featuring a priest who founded a sect in London's East End and preached a mixture of positivism and Christian socialism, became a best seller, with more than five hundred thousand copies sold the first year. Many of the remainder of her popular novels featured the need to help those less fortunate in society.

In 1890 she began to practice the ideas that she promoted. Her original settlement began as University Hall in Gordon Square, London, and expanded to Marchmont Hall on Marchmont St., where meetings of clubs, lectures, and concerts were held. Two ideas with which Ward's settlement was associated were helping with schooling for children with disabilities and starting Saturday play centers for young children in Marchmont Hall, an idea that spread throughout London, where by 1918–19 more than 1.5 million children participated. During JA's 1896 stay in England, she met with Ward (see JA to EGS, 29 [and 30] May 1896, n. 12; and JA to MRS, 27 June 1896, both below). By 1897 Mary Ward had opened a new settlement structure built for her programs by British journalist and philanthropist John Passmore Edwards (1823–1911). The settlement, located at 9 Tavistock Place, was named Passmore Edwards Settlement, but after Ward's death the name was changed to Mary Ward House. Ward also became a leader in the fight to block woman suffrage in England and in 1908 became the first president of the Anti-Suffrage League.

79. "[A] thousand voices singing the Hallelujah Chorus in Handel's 'Messiah,' . . . the leading voices" appears in Addams, *Twenty Years*, 124. A similar passage appears in "Outgrowths of Toynbee Hall" (Address for the Chicago Woman's Club, 3 Dec. 1890, above).

80. JA was drawing on an experience she had on her recent European trip, 1887–88, when she heard Handel's "Messiah" sung in London. See *PJA*, 2:628, n. 6; and JA to SAAH, 27 June 1888, UIC, JAMC; *JAPM*, 2:975.

81. "[T]he differences of training and cultivation between them and" appears in "Outgrowths of Toynbee Hall" (Address for the Chicago Woman's Club, 3 Dec. 1890, above).

82. "[W]ere lost in the unity of purpose" appears in "Outgrowths of Toynbee Hall" (Address for the Chicago Woman's Club, 3 Dec. 1890, above); "lost in the unity of purpose" to "to protest against is over-differentiation" appears in Addams, *Twenty Years*, 125–27.

83. "It aims, in a measure," to "strength of the chorus" appears in "Outgrowths of Toynbee Hall" (Address for the Chicago Woman's Club, 3 Dec. 1890, above).

84. For the detailed description of the HH program that JA presented as a corollary to this speech, see Two Essays in the *Forum*, especially the Oct. 1892 essay, above.

85. Helen Culver.

86. "I remember when the statement" to "that his income will allow" appears in "Outgrowths of Toynbee Hall" (Address for the Chicago Woman's Club, 3 Dec. 1890, above).

87. "It is easy in writing a paper" to "forgive me for" appears in "Outgrowths of Toynbee Hall" (Address for the Chicago Woman's Club, 3 Dec. 1890, above). "It is always easy to make all philosophy point one particular moral and all history adorn one particular tale; but I may be forgiven the reminder that the best speculative philosophy sets forth the solidarity of the human race; that the highest moralists have taught that without the advance and improvement of the whole, no man can hope for any lasting improvement in his own moral or material individual condition; and that the subjective necessity for Social Settlements is therefore identical with that necessity, which urges us on toward social and individual salvation" appears in Addams, *Twenty Years*, 127.

88. "[T]hat the best speculative philosophy" to "material individual condition" appears in "Outgrowths of Toynbee Hall" (Address for the Chicago Woman's Club, 3 Dec. 1890, above).

89. See JA to SAAH, 23 Feb. 1893, below. By 1896 F. Herbert Stead referred to her as "a fairy godmother" (24 Apr. 1896, SCPC, JAC; *JAPM*, 3:112).

90. See pp. 93, 98–101.

91. The actual date that JA and EGS later provided for the official opening of HH was 18 Sept. 1889.

92. A quote from "The Subjective Value of a Social Settlement," the first presentation that JA gave to the Summer School of Applied Ethics. See Two Essays in the *Forum*, especially the Nov. 1892 essay, above.

93. "She had all the plumbing torn out, the most approved system put in its place. Walls were cleaned and artistically papered. Beautiful etchings were hung. New floors were laid, polished, and spread with fine rugs. Book shelves were built and filled with books" ("The Lady of the House"). For other physical descriptions of HH, see JA to AHHA, 9 May 1889, n. 8, above.

94. The neighborhood in which the settlement was located was in a slow state of constant flux, with new immigrant groups settling in as those who had established themselves in their new country moved to other areas of the city.

The *Chicago Daily Tribune* reported in 1897 that the makeup of the Nineteenth Ward was changing. "It was an Irish ward in its early day" but "they have been supplanted by Italians and Jews and have moved farther westward" ("Nineteenth Ward's Crowning Glory"). See also EGS [for JA] to Mary Houghton Starr Blaisdell [and SAAH], 23 Feb. [1889], n. 6; JA to MCAL, 13 Mar. 1889, nn. 3–4; and JA to MRS, 26 Apr. 1890, n. 11, all above.

95. In July 1892, the aldermen for the Nineteenth Ward, where HH was located, were Irish saloon keeper Michael J. O'Brien (1859–1901), who served from 1891 until 1893, when he was defeated by independent Democrat Thomas F. Gallagher, and John Powers, leader of the "boodlers" in the Chicago city council, who served 1888–1904 and 1905–23. The Nineteenth Ward, described as the "Bloody Nineteenth," was even in 1892 an "office holding" ward, with "seven or eight hundred office holders connected with City Hall" ("Nineteenth Ward's Crowning Glory"). By 1894 JA and the HH residents had taken the measure of the corrupt Powers. He became the focus of attempts by HH and JA to vote him out of office and to replace him with a reform candidate (see Minutes of a HH Residents Meeting, 10 Dec. 1893, n. 13, below). O'Brien became an associate of Charles Comiskey (1859–1931) and helped him establish the White Sox in 1900 as a team in baseball's American League.

96. Florence Kelley began investigating Chicago sweatshop practices in early 1892, soon after she arrived in the city. She quickly became the leader in efforts to abolish sweatshops. Kelley appeared in numerous public meetings to decry the practice as detrimental to the well-being of the men, women, and especially children who worked in them and to the people who purchased the clothing made in them because it was often contaminated by contagious diseases. See also Articles in the *Chicago News* and *Chicago Daily Tribune*, 29 and 30 Apr. 1892, above.

97. The Community Renewal Society of Chicago, established in 1882 by the Congregational churches of the city, had two missions in the HH neighborhood. They were the Harrison Street Mission, organized in 1888 and located on Harrison St. near Halsted St., and the Twelfth Street Mission. By 1892 both had been merged into the Ewing Street Church and Mission at 241 and 243 (later 832) Ewing St. (Ewing St. became in succession Gilpin Place and then Cabrini St.), near HH.

The Ewing Street Church and Mission was constructed beginning in Jan. 1891 on property purchased from Helen Culver for seventy-two hundred dollars. It was a three-story brick structure designed by Pond and Pond Brothers Architects and ready for occupancy by Oct. 1891. Among its charter members was JA, who in 1891 moved her letter of membership in the Cedarville Presbyterian Church to the new Protestant HH neighborhood church (see Henry Richart to JA, 1 Sept. 1889, above). Members of the Keyser family, including Mary, her mother, and her brother, Frank, also joined the Ewing Street Church. Although JA and the church insisted that they hoped for a closer relationship between their two organizations, it did not materialize. The congregation remained small and struggling, in part a result of the increasingly Jewish and Roman Catholic and decreasingly Protestant population in the neighborhood it was meant to serve. With the help of the Chicago City Missionary Society, the Second Congregational Church in Oak Park, Ill., and the Butler Winfield Firman (1861–1911) family, the church survived in the neighborhood until 1 Mar. 1930, when it was destroyed by fire. The program was reestablished as Firman House and eventually relocated at 922 South Marshfield St., where it served as a center of evangelization for Mexican families in Chicago.

Other churches in the HH neighborhood were First Holland Reformed Church (Dutch Reform), located at the corner of Harrison and May streets; St. Stephen's (Episcopal) Church, located at 34 Johnson (later 1101 South Peoria) St., which became the Holy Trinity Greek Orthodox Church, dedicated 5 June 1892; Salem Church (Evangelical Assn. of North America),

The Ewing Street Congregational Church and Mission, where Jane Addams and Mary Keyser were charter members, was located within a block of Hull-House, on Ewing Street. It was designed by Hull-House architects Irving K. and Allen B. Pond and built in 1891 (Art Institute of Chicago, School of, 200101.090515 1A, Oct. 1891).

located at the corner of 12th St. and Union Ave.; Anshe Russian-Pol-Tzedek, at Clinton and 12th St.; St. Paul's Church (Methodist Episcopal), at Centre and Taylor streets; Second Church (Bohemian, Methodist Episcopal), at 12th and Halsted streets; Notre Dame de Chicago (Roman Catholic), at Vernon Park Place and Sibley (later 1324 Ada St.); Holy Family (Roman Catholic), at May and 12th streets; and St. Wenceslaus Bohemian (Roman Catholic), located at Dekoven and Desplaines streets.

98. JA was referring to St. Ignatius College, founded in 1870 by Father Arnold J. Damen, J.S., and the Church of the Holy Family, founded in 1857, located together on 12th St. near May St. Polk St. to the south branch of the Chicago River near 24th St. and then west from the Chicago River (with no western boundary because the area to the west was so sparsely settled) became a huge Irish working-class parish. By 1881 it had a church membership of 4,267 families composed of 20,230 individuals, making it the largest English-speaking parish in Chicago. In 1890 it had six schools that educated more than 4,600 boys and girls and an assortment of Catholic lay organizations. As the ethnic character of the neighborhood around it changed, the church began to reach out to the Italian Catholics in its area. The Catholic laywomen, many graduates of the Sacred Heart Academy, a parish school for girls, supported a Sunday School for Italians, and a mass for Italians was also celebrated in Holy Guardian Angel School.

St. Ignatius College was located in a brick building of thirty classrooms and boasted an auditorium that would seat 1,500, a museum, and a library. It offered a six-year comprehensive course in the classics, a four-year commercial course, a course of scientific study, and music study. In 1909 it was renamed Loyola Univ. and in 1912 began a more than ten-year move to two different locations in Chicago: one to the north of Chicago in the Rogers Park neighborhood and one to the north of Chicago's downtown Loop. Adding to its liberal arts base, it created a law school in 1908, a medical school in 1909, a social work school in 1914, and a business school in 1922.

The Church of the Holy Family, which seated 2,000, was founded in 1857 and associated with St. Ignatius College and St. Joseph's School, which by 1892 had 4,000 pupils.

Notre Dame de Chicago, founded in 1864, was a continuation of an earlier French Canadian church known as St. Louis, organized in 1850, and located at the corner of Polk and Sherman streets to serve the French Canadians who had settled in Chicago during the 1840s and into the 1850s. In addition to the church building, constructed at Vernon Park Place and Sibley (later Ada) St., there was a school and convent. The church was dedicated 1 May 1892. From 1882 the school had been under the direction of the Sisters of the Congregation of Notre Dame from Montreal, Canada, who resided in the associated convent. Before World War I, the French Canadian population of the neighborhood had dispersed primarily to the Austin and other western neighborhoods of Chicago; however, despite diminishing parish membership, the church retained its French character.

99. Although there had been a child labor law passed in Chicago in 1889 that limited the hours that children could work to between 7:00 A.M. and 6:00 P.M. and stated that manufacturers could not knowingly hire children under the age of fifteen, it had never been enforced. Children worked when they should have been in school. Florence Kelley's investigations of more than seven hundred sweatshops made her aware that the public education system overseen by the Chicago Board of Education was failing Chicago's children by not providing sufficient seats in public schools so that all children would be able to attend. A census of schools and children conducted by the Chicago Woman's Alliance in 1892 found that 60,000 students primarily in the poorer precincts of the city were without seats. Approximately 7,000 children lived in the Nineteenth Ward, but only 2,579 school seats were available for them in schools in their school district. At the time, HH and its residents and volunteers were engaged in investigating and waging war on the sweatshop businesses in their neighborhood (see n. 162; and Address for the Chicago Woman's Club, 3 Dec. 1890, n. 26, above).

In 1892 the Nineteenth Ward had three public schools: Goodrich, Dore, and Polk St. Among the Roman Catholic schools in the Nineteenth Ward were the following: Convent Academy of the Sacred Heart, opened during the fall of 1860, at 485 (later 1258) West Taylor St.; Holy Family Boys School from 1865, at 462 (later 1231) South Morgan St.; St. Ignatius College, opened in 1870 and with enrollment for young boys, at 413 (later 1076) West 12th St. (later Roosevelt Rd.); St. Aloysius School, from 1870, at 210 (later 631) West Maxwell St.; Holy Guardian Angel School, opened in 1874, at 168 (later 711) West Forquer (later Arthington) St.; St. Joseph School, from 1876, on West 13th St. near Loomis St.; Notre Dame [French] School, opened at Oregon (later Flournoy) and Sibley (later Ada) streets in 1885; St. Agnes School, 530 (later 1361) South Morgan St., opened in 1887; and Ephpheta School for the Deaf, 409 (later 1100) South May St., in operation in 1890.

In Jan. 1896, in the "Nineteenth Ward School Notes" in the *HH Bulletin*, JA still claimed: "The schools in the Nineteenth Ward are still wholly insufficient. . . . There are four public schools—the Andrew Jackson [constructed in 1894], with 918 seats and 85 children in half day divisions; the Goodrich, with 928 seats and 293 children in half day divisions; the Doré School, with 896 seats and no half day divisions; and the Polk Street School with 692 seats, 247 children in half day divisions and a night school attended by 176 men, women and children" (*JAPM*, 53:510). There were still more than 3,000 students of compulsory school age in excess of school seats available for them (see n. 162). Through the 1890s, the residents of HH continued to demand more school seats for their ward.

100. The Jewish Training School, opened 21 Oct. 1890, was located on Judd St. between Jefferson and Clinton streets. It welcomed children of all faiths between the ages of three and fifteen, and it had a kindergarten, grammar and vocational courses, and a seating capac-

ity of 800. When the doors opened for the first time, 1,100 students had been admitted. Its day-school students were children; night school was for adults. The Jewish community in Chicago became aware that the large influx of Russian Jews (under way since the pogroms began in Russia in 1881) needed education about their new country.

101. The Society in Aid of the Russian Refugees, sometimes called the Russian Refugee Charity Assn., was formed on 23 Aug. 1891 and opened an office on Jefferson St., close to the Sheltering Home at 567 (later 1404) South Halsted St., established by the Chicago Branch of the Jewish Alliance of America. Accommodations were offered at the Sheltering Home to those in need of assistance.

102. JA was reminding her listeners and readers that although as a woman she was still without the privilege of suffrage, she still had a civic responsibility.

103. "The whole arrangement of the vast building was that of an elegant, refined, and well ordered private home," wrote a reporter in an article entitled "The Lady of the House." As was the style at the time, JA and EGS came to their new home with one housekeeper Mary Keyser, who was soon counted as a settlement resident and worker. In addition, as the programs and resident body grew, HH employed cleaning women, a cook and helpers, and washerwomen to undertake housekeeping chores so that the residents could remain focused on their primary task. JA did worry that the home she had created was too "swell," for she took down and sent home to her sister SAAH the lace curtains she had originally installed in the settlement parlor (see JA to SAAH, 23 Nov. 1889, above).

104. See EGS [for JA] to Susan Childs Starr and Caleb Allen Starr [and SAAH], 15, [16–20?] Nov. [1889]; and JA to SAAH, 23 Nov. 1889, n. 11, both above.

105. See JA to SAAH, 23 Nov. 1889, n. 9; and JA to GBH, 24 Nov. 1889, both above.

106. Emma ("Emmy") N. Neuschäffer (Lunt). See JA to SAAH, 23 Nov. 1889, nn. 9–10, above.

107. German poets Karl Theodor Körner (1791–1813) and Johann Christoph Friedrich von Schiller (1759–1805).

108. JA was probably referring to two clubs that in the spring of 1892 met on Monday evening between 8:00 and 10:00 P.M. at HH. The settlement's published program for ten weeks beginning 1 Mar. 1892 identified the HH Social Club composed of thirty girls, ages sixteen to twenty, who had been meeting for two years (see n. 116). The first hour of each evening was given to reading and discussion while the second to amusement, with dancing with members of the boys HH Debating Club every fourth Monday. The HH Debating Club had a membership of thirty young men who had been meeting weekly for a year. Like the HH Social Club, the members of the Debating Club devoted the first hour of their meeting to debates, primarily on matters of national and municipal interest, and then joined the girls for the second hour of their meeting for a supervised social hour. See also JA to SAAH, 8 Oct. 1889, n. 21; and 5 Jan. 1890, n. 4, both above.

109. According to the program of HH activities beginning Mar. 1892, only one young people's club met on Tuesday evening, and that was the Young Citizens' Club, with a membership limited to thirty boys between the ages of fourteen and eighteen, most of whom had belonged to the club for two years. The club met in the gymnasium from 7:30 to 9:30 P.M. The first hour was devoted to gymnastics and the second hour to discussion of subjects of interest to the members, with an occasional party.

110. The HH Columbian Guards were twenty-five males fourteen to eighteen years of age who were organized under a constitution issued by the Municipal Order Com. of the World's Columbian Exposition Auxiliary. Their charge was to conduct themselves as good citizens and promote a clean city by helping to keep their neighborhood clear of garbage and refuse.

The all-woman Municipal Order Com. was organized early in 1891 to help clean up the city in preparation for the World's Columbian Exposition. The committee was reconstituted in Mar. 1892 as the Municipal Order League with JA serving as fourth vice-president. The league was concerned with garbage disposal and street cleaning, but quickly moved into investigating other areas of concern, including sanitary conditions in public schools, availability of public baths and drinking fountains, and ridding the city of beggars. In Mar. 1894, JA was appointed head of a committee of the league charged with seeking the cooperation of other organizations in the city that were working for an improvement in city conditions. The league pressed for hiring a woman inspector to oversee the work of Chicago's Street and Alley Cleaning Dept. On 9 Jan. 1894, the league opened the first public bath in Chicago. With its seventeen shower rooms, one tub, and a plunge tank, the four-story structure, located at Halsted and Mather streets and named the Carter Harrison Bath House, was successfully managed by the city. As many as three hundred people sometimes waited to use the facility. Men were to pay five cents and women and children three cents per bath. It was so successful that the city planned another bathhouse at Wentworth Ave. and 39th St. The league ceased operation in Apr. 1895, indicating that the recently formed Civic Federation of Chicago, composed of men and women, was a much stronger organization and could take up many of the issues that the league had identified as needing attention. In place of the Municipal Order League, a Municipal Bath League was organized. It continued to monitor the use and progress of public baths in Chicago.

111. Among other clubs in 1892 were the following: the Working People's Social Science Club, meeting on Tuesday evenings 8:00 to 10:00; the Mothers' Evening Club, which met on Wednesday evenings in the Diet Kitchen from 7:30 to 9:00; and the HH Athletic Club, meeting for two years, with a membership of thirty girls, fourteen to sixteen years of age, on Thursday evenings from 7:30 to 9:30 in the gymnasium for an hour of gymnastics and an hour of discussion. Clubs for younger children were held during the afternoons: sewing classes for Italian girls on Monday afternoons from 3:30 to 5:00; schoolboys' clubs, including Fairy Story Club, Jolly Boys' Club, Kindergarten Club, and four divisions of the Red Stars, met on Tuesday afternoons from 3:30 until 5:00; and on Friday afternoons from 3:30 to 4:00, the Pansy Club and the Story-Telling Club met. The HH Woman's Club met Thursday afternoons from 2:00 to 3:30.

112. See JA to SAAH, [ca. 6] [Sept. 1891], n. 5, above. The settlement's program brochure for six weeks of classes and clubs beginning 18 Apr. 1892 announced that College Extension Program students could have access to the gymnasium four nights a week, with classes for women on Wednesday and Saturday evenings and for men on Monday and Friday evenings.

113. Another new building was under construction at HH. It would open with a state-of-the-art New England kitchen, coffeehouse restaurant, and gymnasium in time to be shown to visitors at Chicago's World's Columbian Exposition during the summer of 1893. "The latest gift of rich men to eleemosynary institutions is that of William Colvin and Allison Vincent Armour, who have presented Hull House with $14,000. This sum will be used in defraying the cost of a gymnasium and a coffee house, which will be managed by the Hull House Men's Club. It is unnecessary to say anything in praise of the recipient, and the donors probably do not desire praise. It is enough to call attention to the facts" ("Another Praiseworthy Gift," *Chicago Post*, 27 Dec. 1892). JA and EGS opened the new building in Aug. 1893. For information on Allison Vincent Armour and William Colvin, see Remarks on Opening the New England Kitchen, HH, 23 Aug. 1893, nn. 3–4, below.

114. JA was quoting from the last two lines of essayist and poet Matthew Arnold's (1822–88) seven-stanza poem "Growing Old": "To hear the world applaud the hollow ghost / Which blamed the living man" (http://www.poetryfoundation.org/poem184057).

115. See n. 117. See also JA to AHHA, 3 June 1890, above. For listings of the classes offered through the settlement beginning in 1890, see HH Scrapbooks 2 and 3; *JAPM*, Addendum 10:7ff, 8ff; and *HH Bulletin*, 1896–1900; *JAPM*, 53:503–755.

116. JA and EGS had read George Eliot's *Romola* together while traveling in Europe. The historical novel, treating a variety of moral issues and set in Savonarola's fifteenth-century

Florence, Italy, became the focus for the first group of young women who visited JA and EGS for supper and a reading party afterward during the first weeks after HH was opened. In "The Chicago Toynbee Hall" in the 15 Mar. 1890 issue of *Unity*, Jenny Dow reported, "There is a club of working girls enjoying George Eliot's *Romola*, with beautiful Florentine photographs." See also JA to SAAH, 8 Oct. 1889, n. 21, above.

117. The College Extension Program at the settlement began 2 June 1890. Classes during the term starting in Apr. 1892 were taught by twenty-seven instructors in the following subjects: arithmetic, drawing, English grammar, English composition, rhetoric, geometry, Latin for beginners, Latin composition, American history, astronomy, algebra, needlework, singing, physiography, reading party, Shakespeare, chemistry, German, physics, French, electricity, oil painting, modeling in clay, and physical education. In addition, as part of the program, seven special lectures or concerts were held by eight different presenters on Thursday evenings. See JA to AHHA, 3 June 1890, n. 3, above.

118. Abraham Bisno recalled that his tutor was EGS. See EGS [for JA] to Susan Childs Starr and Caleb Allen Starr [and SAAH], 3 Nov. [1889], n. 27, above.

119. Julia Lathrop held a class in English literature for twelve weeks beginning in Jan. 1892; however, during the next term of classes, she took over the Shakespeare class from EGS (see n. 120).

120. EGS taught Shakespeare's *King Lear* during the fall of 1891 and followed that with *Hamlet* beginning in Jan. 1892, but by Apr. she had left HH to visit Toynbee Hall and travel in Europe with a group Samuel and Henrietta Barnett were convening and did not return until late spring. Julia Lathrop taught Shakespeare's *Midsummer Night's Dream* beginning in Apr. 1892.

121. The manufactory for Western Electric Co. was located near HH. See JA to SAAH, 5 Jan. 1890, n. 3, above. "Syllabus for a Course in Electricity" and "Course of Six Lectures on Physics" appear in HH Scrapbook 2:8, 18; *JAPM*, Addendum 10:7ff.

122. Opportunities for lecturers abounded at HH. In the 1890s, JA and EGS worked continuously to attract appropriate lecturers to their Thursday Popular Lecture series and to the Working People's Social Science Club. By 1891 the Thursday series also included concerts. In late 1891, HH began providing Sunday-afternoon concerts (see n. 130) that later in the 1890s included lectures. Lecturers also appeared in college extension classes and before various social clubs and ethnic evenings to provide educational content. See also JA to Bayard Taylor Holmes, 15 Sept. 1892, above.

123. See EGS [for JA] to Susan Childs Starr and Caleb Allen Starr [and SAAH], 15, [16–20?] Nov. [1889], n. 13, above.

124. See Addams, "Diary, 1889–90," n. 4; JA to MRS [12?] [Apr. 1891], nn. 1, 11; and Article in the *Chicago Inter Ocean*, 21 June 1891, all above.

125. Samuel A. Barnett, warden of Toynbee Hall, and Henrietta Barnett, his wife. Samuel A. Barnett was also rector of St. Jude's Parish, in which Toynbee Hall was located. See Article in the *Chicago Inter Ocean*, 21 June 1891, above.

126. JA mentioned three artists whose work appeared in the first HH exhibition of paintings with which the Butler Art Gallery was officially opened on 20 June 1891. There was a Dutch scene by Jean-Baptiste Corot (1796–1875) of France; *Time, Death and Judgement* by George F. Watts (1817–1904) of England; and a landscape by Charles Harold Davis (1856–1933) of the United States. On HH art exhibits, see Article in the *Chicago Inter Ocean*, 21 June 1891, n. 7; JA to MRS, [12?] [Apr. 1891], nn. 1, 11; and JA to Jenkin Lloyd Jones, 6 Dec. 1891, n. 3, all above.

127. EGS was in charge of producing and explaining art exhibitions. In the Butler Art Gallery, oil painting exhibitions were held 20 June–6 July and 29 Nov.–14 Dec. 1891. The engravings and etchings exhibition was available for viewing during the month of Oct. 1891. The watercolor exhibition appeared 18 Apr.–9 May 1892.

128. The free Thursday-evening lectures started at the settlement during the summer of 1890 coincident with the College Extension Program initiated by JA and EGS. By Oct. 1890, there was a firm schedule of presenters. It eventually included musical entertainments. Keeping these lecture evenings filled with educational and diverting fare was time consuming. Among the JA papers is correspondence with potential presenters. See JA to Bayard Taylor Holmes, 15 Sept. 1892, above.

129. For information about the settlement's summer school, see JA to SA, [12?] [Aug. 1891], above.

130. Sunday-afternoon concerts began at HH on 15 Nov. 1891. Until then the residents of HH had been careful to avoid scheduling programs for Sundays, which they and their neighbors reserved as a day devoted to religion and rest.

131. The Plato Club was organized in late 1891 or early 1892 by Julia Lathrop. Its members read philosophical essays and held discussions. In 1892 it met between 5:00 and 6:00 P.M., but JA recalled that it convened at 4:00 P.M. to end two hours later—or sometimes even later. Composed largely of "elderly men who had read philosophy of sorts all their lives" (Addams, *My Friend*, 50), the club survived until Jan. 1896 as a setting for late-Sunday-afternoon readings, two of which JA presented on Giuseppe Mazzini.

132. See JA to SAAH, [ca. 6] [Sept. 1891], n. 6, above; and Remarks on Opening the New England Kitchen, HH, 23 Aug. 1893, below.

133. In addition to kindergarten and nursery programs at the settlement, by mid-1892 there were an assortment of classes and clubs for young children. There were classes in sewing for Italian girls; gymnastics as well as drawing, painting, and piano lessons for girls and boys; and darning, sewing, cooking, and crocheting classes for girls. For a list of the children's clubs, see n. 111.

134. The Penny Provident Bank at HH was associated with the Penny Provident Fund, established by the COS of New York City in the late 1880s as a way to encourage savings among the working poor and their families. By 1890 JA and EGS had established a branch or "station" at the settlement and placed resident Anna M. Farnsworth in charge (see JA to AHHA, 9 Dec. 1890, n. 6, above). To record a deposit, the banker gave each depositor stamps in the denomination of the deposit, penny to one dollar, as a record of their deposit. The depositor placed the stamps on a card with thirty-six spaces for the stamps that the banker supplied, permitting the depositor to keep the record easily in one place. The money collected was deposited in the State Trust Co. The stamps were redeemable in money at the request of the depositor. After the depositor had been paid, the banker destroyed the card and stamps. "Mr. Murray, the Hull House policeman, is always in attendance to keep order if necessary, and see that the Bank is not stolen," reported a later banker (Madeleine Wallin to Alfred C. Wallin, 8 Oct. 1896, UIC, JAMC, Sikes). In 1898 the bank at HH became associated with the Chicago Penny Savings Fund. This program continued to operate through the settlement into the twentieth century.

135. See JA to SAAH, 8 Oct. 1889, n. 6, above.

136. Julia Lathrop had been serving as a "volunteer visitor in the county agent's office and was assigned for duty to the ten blocks surrounding Hull-House" (Addams, *My Friend*, 67).

137. The telephone number assigned to HH was W 70. It began appearing on HH publications during the winter of 1892. HH was not listed with a telephone number in the Feb. 1892 *Chicago City Directory*. The number associated with HH appeared for the first time in the *Chicago City Directory* of 1 June 1892. JA seemed comfortable with this informal and instantaneous means of communication. As more and more people had access to telephones, she used the convenience for local communication in preference to writing long letters.

138. The Visiting Nurse Assn. of Chicago, headquartered during the 1890s in the Masonic Temple on the northeast corner of State and Randolph streets, was incorporated in Nov. 1890 by twenty-six women, one of whom was JA. Its articles of incorporation indicate its purpose:

"[T]he benefit and assistance of those otherwise unable to secure skilled attendance in time of illness, to promote cleanliness, and to teach proper care of the sick; and to establish and maintain one or more hospitals for the sick, or a home or homes for the accommodation or training of nurses" (Visiting Nurse Assn. of Chicago, *Fifth Annual Report*, 3). Between 1891 and 1892, the *Hand-Book of Chicago's Charities* (118) reported that the organization's trained nurses cared for 1,955 different patients during 13,437 visits, each with a duration of forty minutes. The nurses could undertake physical treatments, suggest comfort measures, provide instruction, and recommend preventive measures. The demand for the service was so great that the five trained nurses who began the program in 1891 were increased to twelve by the end of 1892. Seventeen nurses worked throughout the city by 1900 and in that year helped 5,778 patients. Financial support for their efforts came from memberships, subscriptions, and entertainments. The Visiting Nurse Assn. of Chicago continued its work into the late twentieth century.

Though JA served as a director of the Visiting Nurse Assn. of Chicago only until the end of Nov. 1894, she continued to support the organization as an associate, making in-kind and financial gifts as she was able. She later identified the organization as the "only really popular charity" (Addams, *Democracy and Social Ethics*, 26). From the beginning, HH was a station for one of the nurses of the Visiting Nurse Assn. Emily N. Wakem, who became the first head nurse of the association, was at the settlement during the summer of 1891 (see also JA to Lydia Avery Coonley, 12 Aug. 1891, n. 6, above). The kindergarten that the Visiting Nurse Assn. formed in 1896 was assimilated by HH in that same year, and for a brief time in 1906 the HH Woman's Club gathered funds to support the one half of the salary of the nurse stationed at the settlement.

Among other nurses headquartered at HH during the 1890s were Beatrice Barter, Louise Salter, Anna Fryar (Hutchinson), and Jessie Blair. JA urged the Visiting Nurse Assn. to promote the idea of nurses in Chicago schools. In 1906, while she served on the Chicago Board of Education, she encouraged a five-month demonstration project in several Chicago schools to identify the benefits. On 25 Apr. 1908, when she spoke at the opening session of the National Conf. of Visiting Nurses meeting in Chicago, the subject of her presentation was the relationship of visiting nurses to public schools.

139. Cook County Hospital was the primary medical facility available to the poor and indigent. It was founded in 1865 when physicians Joseph P. Ross and George K. Amerman convinced the Cook County Board of Supervisors to take over a hospital that had been constructed before the Civil War as a city facility and used as a hospital for wounded soldiers until the end of the war. By the 1870s, the institution was enormously overcrowded, and pressures for its services were continuing to build due in large part to the number of immigrants settling in Chicago. By 1900 the hospital, located west of HH in the Harrison, Wood, Lincoln, and Polk streets area, had beds for two thousand patients. During the last years of the nineteenth century, the hospital suffered from political control and a lack of sufficient funds for food and medicine, adequate numbers of competent personnel, and a "serviceable sewerage system" (Bonner, *Medicine in Chicago*, 164). In 1905 its employees came under civil service, and conditions at the facility began to improve.

140. The Women's and Children's Hospital, founded through the efforts of Dr. Mary Harris Thompson (1829–95) in Feb. 1865, was opened the following May with fourteen beds in a house on the corner of Rush and Indiana streets. It was established "to provide (1) medical surgical aid, by women physicians, for women and children; (2) to assist women physicians by clinical and other instruction in a more thorough preparation for the practice of their profession; (3) to train nurses for the better care of the sick and wounded" (*Hand-Book of Chicago's Charities*, 39). Hospital business was conducted entirely by women and included a staff of experienced female physicians—but with a consulting staff of male doctors. Its medical school, aimed at educating female doctors, was created in 1870 and graduated its

first class of three shortly before the school and facility were burned during the Chicago Fire of 1871. Eventually, the school became associated with Northwestern Univ. In 1873 the Chicago Relief and Aid Society acquired a house at the corner of Paulina and Adams streets on the condition that the society could name the patients to be cared for free of charge in the hospital's twenty-five beds. In the mid-1880s, a new and larger hospital was erected at the same site to include as many as eighty beds, and the medical school expanded to include a nursing curriculum. A dispensary also provided prescribed drugs to patients for a small fee. After Mary Thompson's death, the hospital, which continued to expand, was renamed in her honor and was in operation until 1988, when it closed. In 1972 men were added to its all-female staff.

141. The Maxwell Street Police Station was new. It had been designed in 1888 and constructed by 1890 to serve the police department's Seventh District. It was located at 943 West Maxwell St.

142. The Health Dept. of the city of Chicago was created in 1867 and before its reorganization in 1904 "did little but look after contagious diseases, chiefly smallpox, and only in a perfunctory way did it do general sanitary inspections" (Whalen, *Biennial Report of the Dept. of Health of the City of Chicago, 1904–05*, viii–ix). The development of its activities as an investigative and regulatory agency began in 1894, and according to the department that was "caused chiefly by the excessive death rate of the previous three years, which averaged 22.5 per 1000 of population, and this was accentuated by the smallpox epidemic of that year, which cost 1190 lives before its subsidence in December, 1893, besides millions of dollars in losses of travel and traffic" (Whalen, *Biennial Report of the Dept. of Heath of the City of Chicago, 1904–05*, ix).

During the later 1890s, the department began to supervise Chicago's water supply and through its powers of inspection to promote and demand better sanitation, control the spread of contagious diseases, and make an effort to improve sanitation of the milk supply. According to the Health Dept.'s 1904–5 report, between 1894 and 1904 the death rate in Chicago dropped 26.1 percent over the previous ten years. Of the 87,275 deaths, 44,069 were infants under the age of one and 27,934 children ages one to five. While the Health Dept. calculated that in 1874 the life expectancy in Chicago at birth was fifteen years and eleven months, by 1904 it had increased to thirty-one years and ten months.

In 1892 the department was under the direction of a commissioner, appointed by the mayor, with an assistant commissioner, clerk, and secretary. There were a registrar of vital statistics, thirty-four sanitary police, eight medical inspectors, a chief, an assistant chief, thirty-four tenement house and factory inspectors, five female factory inspectors, a city physician and his assistant, and nine stockyard inspectors to regulate a city of 182 square miles and a population of approximately 1.3 million. Flinn's *Chicago . . . a Guide, 1892*, described the city's Health Dept. as having "a large and expensive corps of assistants. . . . The Health Dept. looks after our backyards, our back alleys and our back streets, where nobody else appears to be interested. It also takes a peep into our great factories, sees that work-shops are not over crowded, and protects the better classes from infection arising out of the districts occupied by the other classes" (563).

143. City Hall, destroyed in the Chicago Fire of 1871, had been rebuilt and was opened in 1885. Designed by Cook County architect James J. Egan (1839 or 1841–1914), it stood between Washington and Randolph streets and LaSalle and Clark streets in Chicago's city center until it was razed, 1906–8, and replaced. Located in it were the offices of major officials and functions of both county and city governments, including meeting halls for of the city council made up of representatives of the city's thirty-four wards in 1892 and the fourteen county commissioners.

144. The Cook County agent was in charge of managing county relief. The agent's office was responsible for maintaining records of all applications for assistance—whether from sickness,

poverty, or disease—as well as the reports of the visitors reviewing the circumstances of the requests. Into the early 1890s, benefits were usually given only to those described as "'aged indigent persons, indigent widows and orphans, old decrepit persons and cripples, and such as are physically and mentally unable to earn a living'" (Andreas, *History of Chicago*, 3:163). The agent's office also kept a list of those "deemed unworthy" of help (Andreas, *History of Chicago*, 3:163). Successful applicants were sent to the Cook County Hospital, Cook County Infirmary, or Cook County Insane Asylum for assistance. Sometimes needy families were provided with ration cards for basic food and clothing for several months. James O'Brien, former four-term alderman of the Ninth Ward, became Cook County agent in 1883.

James O'Brien (1842–1911), son of Peter and Ellen O'Brien, was born in County Wexford, Ireland, and emigrated to the United States with his parents in 1850. He attended school in Rome, N.Y., and at St. Patrick's Academy after settling in Chicago in 1857. He worked primarily as a yard master for several different railroads until 1869, when he became a saloon keeper on West Harrison St., near Desplaines St. In 1866 he married Bridget Long of Chicago, and they had nine children. In 1872 he was elected to the first of four terms as an alderman in the Chicago City Council. In 1879 he left the saloon business and became Chicago's chief sidewalk inspector until 1883, when he was appointed Cook County agent, a position he held into the 1890s. By 1900 he was gas inspector for Chicago and by 1910 was retired and living at 4118 Washington Blvd., Chicago. He died in Delavan, Wis.

145. JA was referring to the United Hebrew Relief Assn., which in Oct. 1889 had joined the United Hebrew Charities of Chicago. The relief association had been organized through the efforts of a number of Jewish organizations, including congregations, lodges, and benevolent societies, that saw a need to pool resources and coordinate charity efforts in 1859, primarily to assist the poor. Each applicant for relief help was investigated to determine need and potential job placement through services of the association-managed employment agency. The organization provided help to those in need after the Chicago Fire of 1871 and the second fire in 1874 and took the lead in building and establishing Chicago's Michael Reese Hospital, located at 29th St. and Groveland Ave., which opened in Oct. 1881. Later in the 1880s, the organization founded a dispensary and a nurses training school. According to Flinn's *Chicago . . . a Guide, 1892*, in 1889–90 the hospital's relief office helped more than sixty-five hundred people.

146. The Children's Aid Society of Chicago, located in Room 510 at 167 (later 677) Dearborn St. in 1892, was incorporated on 31 July 1890 "to improve the condition of destitute children." The organization assumed the task of placing destitute, homeless, and dependent children in permanent family homes and attempted to keep mothers and children together. By 1 Apr. 1892, the new organization had placed 316 children and 222 mothers and children in new homes. It was supported financially by voluntary contributions. In 1898 the Illinois Children's Home Society and the Children's Aid Society of Chicago merged, forming the Illinois Children's Home and Aid Society, which continued to place children and families in permanent homes and provided aid and education for families.

147. For information on the Illinois Humane Society, see JA to MCAL, 26 Feb. 1889, n. 12, above.

148. The *Chicago Daily News* Fresh Air Fund began sending children and mothers to the country for up to fourteen days in 1886, paying transportation and incidental expenses. In 1891 the number of children, working girls, mothers, and infants sent to the country was 3,352. The Lincoln Park Sanitarium built in 1889 with funds from the *Chicago Daily News* was located over water in Lincoln Park. It was open during ten weeks each summer and under the direction of physicians supplied baby carriages, food, and medicine for children in need. No children with contagious diseases were accepted, and only the very sick were kept overnight. "About two-thirds of the children brought out here are so dirty and grimy that it is hard to tell what the child's real color is," reported the matron to a *Chicago Daily News* reporter. "We provide the mother with soap, towel, bath tub and plenty of clear water,

and a person would be surprised at the changed appearance the tiny things present" ("It Is Doing a Good Thing," 1 July 1891). During 1891, 6,189 infants, 14,450 older children, and 6,021 mothers and adults attendants were treated at the sanitarium.

149. The Holiday Home Camp, one of the oldest camps in the United States accredited by the American Camp Assn. and located at 361 North Lakeshore Dr., Williams Bay, on Lake Geneva, Wis., was organized in 1887 as the Lake Geneva Fresh-Air Assn. The purpose of the organization was "constructing and maintaining at Lake Geneva, a Summer-Resort for poor children residing in or near the City of Chicago" ("Articles of Assn.," Lake Geneva Fresh-Air Assn., in "Holiday Home Camp," 1). Its founders were primarily Chicago philanthropists who had summer homes on Lake Geneva. Among the initial subscribers were Mary Delafield Sturges (Mrs. George), Edward E. Ayer, Nathaniel K. Fairbank, and R. T. Crane, all of whom gave one thousand dollars each to start the project; all became known to JA. The camp, as it approached its 125th anniversary in 2012, and almost twenty-five acres in size, was started on approximately nine acres on the lake shore. The association built a camp building, still being used in 2011, and hired Mrs. Mira Chase as the first matron. David Swing, pastor from the Central Church in Chicago, and a group of Lake Geneva clergymen led the dedicatory ceremonies on 5 July 1888. Campers were chosen by a selection committee from among those recommended by the "Relief-and-Aid-Society, Charity Organization Society, Missionaries, Bible readers, and private individuals." During the first ten weeks of the camp, which ended 13 Sept. 1888, it served 276 people. Many were the children of widows and suffered "from close confinement and lack of proper food"; some were crippled; one was mute and one blind. All had been investigated by representatives of the COS to ensure their need ("Report of the Children's Selection Com.," Lake Geneva Fresh-Air Assn., "Holiday Home Camp," 13). The camp continued as a pioneer in its field, providing age-appropriate activities in one- and two-week increments to children and families from "economically disadvantaged communities" (http://www.holidayhomecamp.org). Children from the HH neighborhood attended the camp for a number of years until HH could establish its own summer camping program. See also JA to EGS, [4–7 Aug. 1890], n. 11, above.

150. JA may have been referring to Emily N. Wakem. See n. 138.

151. Beginning in 1892, JA joined a group of Chicago social reformers in an effort to create a viable COS in the city by wresting the management of relief in the city from the powerful Chicago Relief and Aid Society. It had amassed relief dollars and a visible position in the community shortly after the Chicago Fire of 1871. See JA to Richard T. Ely, 12 Mar. 1895, below. In the meantime, HH began raising funds to help with relief efforts in its neighborhood.

The financial records for 1889–93 kept by JA in her account book titled "HH Acc't Oct 1st 1891" indicate that in the first year of the settlement, the founders had no category for gathering or dispensing relief funds. There is, however, an accounting category for miscellaneous expenditures, and some relief funds may have been allocated to that accounting designation. In the next year of operation, Oct. 1890 to Sept. 1891, HH received $468.75 to support relief efforts and gave out $493.47. For the year 1891–92, JA recorded that the settlement gathered $597.42 for relief and dispersed $665.42 throughout the year. In that year, the first in which funds gathered to support Christmas needs were separately identified, the settlement received and spent $278.44 on holiday relief. The economic depression of 1892–97 that would make itself felt in a more substantial way by 1893 and 1894 was just beginning. During Oct. 1892–Sept. 1893, the year of the World's Columbian Exposition, HH spent the same amount on Christmas needs as the previous year, but actively collected $1,615.60 during the year for relief assistance and distributed $1,549.04 that same year, an almost 60 percent increase in relief needs over the previous year.

152. See JA to Helen Culver, 7 Mar. 1890, n. 3, above.

153. For information about the day nursery or Crêche, see JA to MRS, 19 Dec. 1890, and [12?] [Apr. 1891], both above.

154. The HH announcement for programs beginning 1 Mar. 1892 identified the following workers for kindergarten and nursery duty: kindergarten, Mary McDowell, director; day nursery, Elizabeth McKee, superintendent, and Mrs. Sedonia Loosveldt, assistant (see also JA to EGS, [4–7 Aug. 1890], n. 4, above); and nursery as a daily kindergarten, Wilfreda Brockway (for a biographical note, see JA to MRS, [12?] [Apr. 1891], n. 13, above).

Mary Eliza McDowell (1854–1936), longtime friend and colleague of JA, settlement leader, and social activist, was born the oldest of six children of socially and politically well-connected Ohioans Jane Gordon and Malcolm McDowell in the Fulton area of eastern Cincinnati, on the Ohio River. Like JA, Mary McDowell adored her father, who taught tolerance for all and shared his high regard for Abraham Lincoln, and she developed an especially close relationship with him. Malcolm McDowell became an innovator in the manufacture of iron and steel as he moved his family from the Cincinnati area to Columbus, Ohio, and then to Providence, R.I., where he managed a foundry. After being invalided out of the Civil War in which he served in a staff position for his brother, General Irvin McDowell, and then as paymaster for the Army of the Tennessee, he rejoined his family in the Fulton area of Cincinnati. There Mary, who described herself as "'[n]ot being a strong girl, and being very nervous,'" began her "'rather slipshod education,'" first attending a one-room public school with children of the dockworkers and shipbuilders; then a private school in Walnut Hills, Ohio; and once again a public school. It was also in Fulton that Mary and her father left her mother's Episcopal Church to become active in the Methodist Church, particularly the McKendree Chapel, with a congregation composed of Cincinnati waterfront workers and their families. "'Ship carpenters were the pillars and saints in that church,'" and she reported "'I consider my introduction into that democratically Christian fellowship the beginning of my social education'" (Gavit, "Mary E. McDowell," 2).

In the late 1860s, the McDowells moved to Chicago, where they built a brick home on Webster Ave. on what was then the far Northwest Side of Chicago. On the outskirts of Chicago, Malcolm McDowell constructed a rolling mill that became the McDowell Steel Co., from which he retired in the mid-1890s. Mary McDowell and her father joined another working-class Methodist church in Chicago, where she successfully taught a boy's Sunday School class. During the Chicago Fire of 1871, Mary took a horse and wagon south from her home and helped people flee the fire with their belongings. After the fire, she joined her Methodist minister in distributing food and clothing until the Chicago Relief and Aid Society was established and took over those tasks. It was also in the 1870s that Mary's education continued through travel. She spent a month in Washington, D.C., with the family of newly elected president of the United States Rutherford B. Hayes, close friends of the McDowells. Later she traveled through the western United States to spend time with her uncle, Major General McDowell, at the Presidio in San Francisco.

By the late 1870s, Malcolm McDowell had moved his family to Evanston, Ill., a developing suburb just to the north of Chicago. There once again, Mary and her father became active in the Methodist church, and Mary met Frances Willard of the WCTU, also a church member. Soon Mary McDowell was active in the WCTU, helping to increase its membership and organize young women in Illinois and nearby states. By 1887 she had become the national director of that work. While giving time to the WCTU, she became interested in kindergarten work and spent the year 1889–90 studying at the Chicago Kindergarten Training School, which had been founded in 1889. During 1890 she worked in New York City as a teacher, but by early 1891 returned home to Evanston.

In the fall of 1891, Mary became the first director of the HH kindergarten. Although she was never a resident at HH, probably because her mother was ill and she was needed at home, she participated actively in the work of the settlement. One of her major lasting contributions was developing a mothers' club from among the HH kindergartners' mothers. It became a vital part of the HH program as the HH Woman's Club (see n. 158). Mary McDowell served as its initial president until Mar. 1896 and introduced club members to the procedures and power of democratic club life. After her departure as the director of the kindergarten at the end of 1893, JA wished her back: "[S]ometimes my soul longs for Miss McDowell. She has so much influence with the neighborhood, and the women are so devoted to her" (JA to MRS, 4 May 1894, SCPC, JAC; *JAPM*, 2:1537). Throughout the remainder of McDowell's life, the HH Woman's Club continued to honor her initially as their honorary president, sought her as a speaker, and always invited her to attend their anniversary gathering each Feb. At HH Mary McDowell learned about settlement life and saw a model for engaging in social and civic reform that appealed to her.

The University of Chicago Settlement was started 1 Jan. 1894 by members of the Univ. of Chicago's Christian Union and Prof. James Laurence Laughlin (1850–1933) following a meeting with JA in Dec. 1893. On the advice of JA, Mary McDowell was chosen to be the first director or head resident for the new settlement and began work in Sept. 1894. Although not funded directly by the Univ. of Chicago, the new settlement, located in what became known as "Back-of-the-Yards" to the south and east of the Chicago stockyards of the meatpacking industry, remained closely connected with the university and served as a venue for special study projects carried out by the university's graduate students in education, sociology, social work, and economics.

The forty-year-old, five-foot-five-and-a-half-inch, brown-eyed Mary McDowell, with dark brown hair turned white, who described herself as having a "retrouseé nose" (Mary McDowell's 1903 U.S. passport), began her tenure in the settlement in a small flat over a seed store at 4655 Gross Ave. (eventually renamed McDowell Ave. in honor of Mary McDowell), near Ashland Ave. In 1898 she admitted, "'I came into the settlement through my interest in children, as a kindergartner, but I believe now that even the kindergarten cannot do its legitimate work without the awakening of mothers to see that they are a social force, and in the teaching of everyone that not only can a life not live to itself, but neither can a neighborhood, a city, a nation'" (Gavit, "Mary E. McDowell," 2). One of her neighbors, Herbert E. Phillips, recalled Mary as a "new neighbor" who "welcomed everyone regardless of religion, nationality or politics," whose "wit and humor gave zest to our good times and her sympathetic, kindly manner gave dignity and understanding to our more serious discussions," and who could also be "aggressive and militant" in "her activities in the interests of our community" (Hill, comp., *Mary McDowell and Municipal Housekeeping*, 121–22). By 1906 she had succeeded in establishing the settlement in a spacious new building at 4630 Gross Ave.

In the 1890s, few streets in the neighborhood were paved, sidewalks were wooden, lamps lighted the streets at night, malodorous detritus-choked water stood in ditches, and no houses had sewer connections. Besides the stockyards associated with the odors of livestock, slaughterhouses, and a cesspool-like, stagnant refuse-filled arm of the Chicago River called "Bubbly Creek," one of the most significant physical features of the neighborhood was a large, smelly, and insect-laden city dump located at 47th and Robby streets to the immediate east of Back-of-the-Yards, where neighborhood children often played. What began as a neighborhood of working poor Irish, Scottish, and English residents by the early 1900s had become Bohemian, Pole, Slovac, Lithuanian, Gallician, Croatian, and Slovenian and by the 1920s Mexican.

Mary McDowell developed settlement programs to meet neighborhood needs. They were similar to those at HH and included a kindergarten, social clubs for neighbors of all ages, and classes in gymnastics, manual training, natural science, metalwork, cooking, sewing, music, and dancing. There was a playground, and during the summer Mary worked with fresh-air camps to send children to the countryside. After successfully establishing the small Davis Park for her neighbors, Mary helped lead the effort to establish similar small parks in neighborhoods throughout Chicago. Assisted by the CWC, of which she became a member in May 1896, Mary McDowell saw that there were library services and public baths available for her neighbors, and in 1895 she was able to add the availability of legal services as well. McDowell served as director of the settlement until 1929.

One of the struggles for which Mary McDowell was best known was her attempt to close Chicago city dumps. From the time she moved to Gross Ave. and understood the health problems and environmental issues connected with the dump in her neighborhood, her efforts to alter the way the city dealt with its refuse became steady and determined. Later referred to as the "angel of the garbage dump" (Hill, comp. *Mary McDowell and Municipal Housekeeping*, xi), in her war on municipal trash and unsanitary environments, Mary enlisted the help of the powerful CWC and the Woman's City Club, accosted politicians with her pleas, used the courts, developed petitions, held mass meetings, made speeches, and went to Europe to study treatment facilities. She served as head of the committee on city waste that was successful in having appointed a commission on city waste, on which she also served as a member, to manage and improve municipal sanitation. Eventually, the city made an initial commitment to add incinerators or reduction plants and close the dumps; however, the commitment was short-lived, and the city returned to using dumps. With the help of Upton Sinclair's *The Jungle* (1906), which exposed the misery of immigrant life and corruption in the meatpacking business to a wider public, she was more successful with the issue of "Bubbly Creek." After several unsuccessful attempts to divert it into the sewer system, "Bubbly Creek" was finally obliterated in the 1920s when it was filled in to provide more land for a street and for business development. In recognition of Mary's efforts almost single-handedly to solve the environmental headache for the entire city, JA, with humor and pride, publicly bestowed on her friend a Serbian medal of "St. George and the Dragon."

Recognizing that her settlement was located in the center of an industrial neighborhood from which many of the workers in the nearby stockyards were drawn, McDowell, in her hope for better working conditions and higher pay, was a staunch supporter of organized labor. She continually led a "campaign of education against the vicious industrial system of the stock yards, which keeps from one thousand to three thousand people on hand as surplus labor, and which disregards equally public health, the independence and spirit of men, the virtue of women, and the future of little children in the scramble for money." The University of Chicago Settlement, McDowell contended, "has always stood for the right of organization, and in the strikes since 1894 has done what it could to uphold the unions" ("University of Chicago Settlement," in Woods and Kennedy, *Handbook of Settlements*, 70). She was especially steadfast in her support of the Amalgamated Meat and Butcher Workmen in their efforts to organize workers in the meatpacking industry, and she represented them in the 1903 AFL convention in Boston. During the union's strike against the meatpacking industry in 1904, she enlisted JA to help her successfully convince industry leaders to let striking union members keep their jobs.

Mary McDowell was particularly dedicated to improving the employment conditions and pay for working women. She helped found the first woman's union in the Chicago stockyards, Local No. 183, Amalgamated Meat Cutters and Butcher Workmen of North America. In Nov. 1903, along with JA, she became one of the founders and a board member of the NWTUL and served, 1904–7, as president of the Illinois branch that she and JA started at HH on 4 Jan. 1904. JA and Mary McDowell also led an effort, begun in 1905, to have the federal government conduct the first national survey of the conditions in which women and children worked in industry. Two years of tireless lobbying finally produced adequate funds for the Dept. of Commerce and Labor to begin work on the study that was published in eight volumes between 1910 and 1913 as *Report on Conditions of Women and Child Wage-Earners in the United States*. During the early twentieth century, McDowell represented the Shorter Workday Legislative Assn. as she lobbied for improved working condition for women in Ohio, Illinois, Maryland, Pennsylvania, Massachusetts, Michigan, and Alabama. In 1913, after New York City's Triangle Shirtwaist Factory Fire, she led a successful effort in Chicago to create a Bureau of Fire Prevention. During the years of World War I, she was the chair of the League of Women Voters Com. on Women in Industry and led the Illinois committee and was a member of the subcommittee on foreign-born women of the National Council of Defense's Com. on Women in Industry. In 1919 she went to England and France for the YWCA to investigate conditions for working women. Mary McDowell was also one of the leaders in helping to establish the Women's Bureau in the U.S. Dept. of Labor.

McDowell worked with JA and other reformers to help found the Chicago Federation of Settlements and the National Federation of Settlements, of which she became president in 1914–15. She also served as president of the Chicago Woman's City Club, 1915–16. Along with other social reformers in Chicago, she became active in the Chicago School of Civics and Philanthropy that ultimately became the School of Social Service Administration of the Univ. of Chicago.

She was a staunch advocate for the idea of equal opportunity and respect for African Americans and was dedicated to working with the NAACP and the Chicago Urban League. She often invited black speakers to the settlement and encouraged the integration of women's clubs in Chicago. In the fall of 1919, as a result of the horrors she saw during the Chicago race riots, she became the leader of Chicago's Interracial Cooperative Com., composed of representatives of the city's black and white women's clubs. It was a successful effort to bring women of the two races together to consider civic matters of import to the organizations of both groups. She also served as chair of the Chicago Woman's City Club's Race Relations Com.

As a strong advocate for woman suffrage, she was a member of the Chicago Political Equality League and the Illinois Equal Suffrage Assn. She supported the Progressive Party in 1912 and in 1914, and after Illinois passed a law permitting women to vote in municipal elections, she ran on the Progressive Party ticket for a seat on the Cook County Board of Commissioners. She was unsuccessful when a judicial ruling mandated that a county election was not municipal and the votes that women submitted did not count. Nevertheless, McDowell had become increasingly involved in the political life in Chicago and had achieved recognition as a reformer who cared deeply about the conditions in which Chicago citizens lived. Chicago reform mayor William E. Dever appointed her commissioner of public welfare. She served from 1923 until 1927, and she brought the moribund city department, created in 1914, back to life. She reorganized the department, creating a Bureau of Employment and a Bureau of Social Surveys; secured a separate detention home for women offenders; reopened a lodging house for homeless men; and created an employment and social service office within the department. Her concern for the elderly poor, housing conditions, and the plight of African Americans encouraged her to plead for low-income housing and led in 1926 to a conference on housing and the establishment of Chicago's first housing commission.

At the time of World War I, she joined JA's peace efforts and became a member of the WPP and the WILPF. JA could count on her as an active colleague in attending peace parades and gatherings. A member of the Illinois League of Women Voters, she served the National League of Women Voters as the chair of its Dept. of International Cooperation to Prevent War.

McDowell was a frequent speaker but wrote sparingly. Her first published report about the development of the University of Chicago Settlement did not appear until July 1896. The more than sixty articles she authored about various aspects of her reform interests appeared in the *Commons*, *Survey*, and other journals associated with the reform organizations she helped lead. She drafted ten chapters of an autobiography during the summer of 1927, but it remained unfinished at her death after a paralytic stoke. Five of those chapters were edited and became the lead chapters in *Mary McDowell and Municipal Housekeeping*, compiled by Caroline M. Hill and privately published in McDowell's honor in 1938.

In addition to thc leadership roles she held in the variety of organizations with which she was associated, she was honored by two European governments. Lithuania presented her

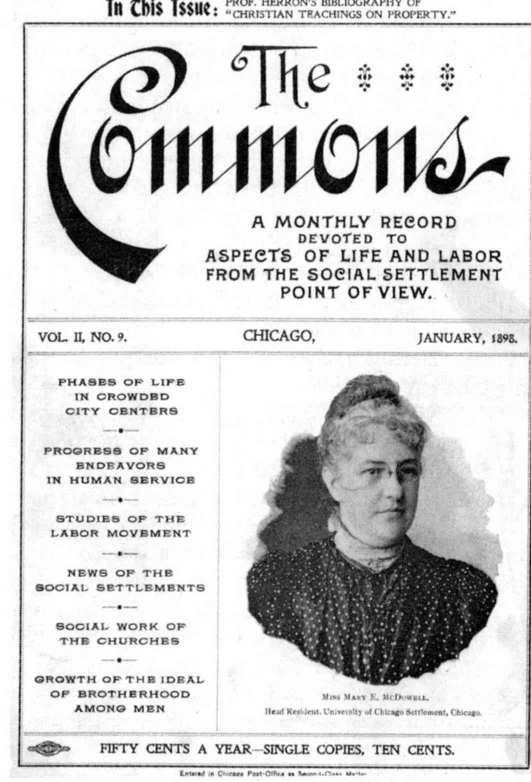

In This Issue: PROF. HERRON'S BIBLIOGRAPHY OF "CHRISTIAN TEACHINGS ON PROPERTY."

The Commons

A MONTHLY RECORD DEVOTED TO ASPECTS OF LIFE AND LABOR FROM THE SOCIAL SETTLEMENT POINT OF VIEW.

VOL. II, NO. 9. CHICAGO, JANUARY, 1898.

PHASES OF LIFE IN CROWDED CITY CENTERS

PROGRESS OF MANY ENDEAVORS IN HUMAN SERVICE

STUDIES OF THE LABOR MOVEMENT

NEWS OF THE SOCIAL SETTLEMENTS

SOCIAL WORK OF THE CHURCHES

GROWTH OF THE IDEAL OF BROTHERHOOD AMONG MEN

MISS MARY E. MCDOWELL,
Head Resident, University of Chicago Settlement, Chicago.

FIFTY CENTS A YEAR—SINGLE COPIES, TEN CENTS.

Entered in Chicago Post-Office as Second-Class Matter

Mary Eliza McDowell was a loyal Hull-House volunteer leader for the settlement's nursery and kindergarten and the founder of the Hull-House Woman's Club. Famous as the head resident of the University of Chicago Settlement, she became one of the Chicago reform leaders that Jane Addams counted on as a friend and colleague (*Commons* 2, no. 9 [Jan. 1898]: cover).

with the Order of the Grand Duke Gedeminus for her support of Lithuanian immigrants in Chicago. Mary McDowell was an adviser to Tomáš Garrigue Masaryk (1850–1937), who became president of Czechoslovakia in 1918, and to his daughter, Alice, who was the country's director of Ministry of Public Welfare. For that service, the government of Czechoslovakia presented her with the Order of the White Lion. Many times honored in Chicago, she was named by William Hard in *Everybody's Magazine* in 1906 along with JA and Julia Lathrop, Margaret Haley, and Dr. Cornelia de Bey as one of Chicago's five "Maiden Aunts."

155. For information on the HH Diet Kitchen, see JA to SAAH, [ca. 6] [Sept. 1891], n. 6, above.

156. For information about Edward Atkinson's inventions, see Remarks on Opening the New England Kitchen, HH, 23 Aug. 1893, n. 5, below.

157. JA was already in the process of planning a New England Kitchen for HH. Shortly after her return to Chicago from her trip to Plymouth, Mass., and New York City, she was trying to make arrangements to have Ellen H. Richards, the originator of the New England Kitchen program in Boston, visit HH between 17 and 22 Oct. 1892. She wanted Richards "to look over plans" for a new building and provide "suggestions" (JA to Marion Talbot, 10 Oct. 1892, UC, Talbot; *JAPM*, 2:1334). JA opened her New England Kitchen with great fanfare during the World's Columbian Exposition. See Remarks on Opening the New England Kitchen, HH, 23 Aug. 1893, below. For biographical information on Ellen H. Richards, see Remarks on Opening the New England Kitchen, HH, 23 Aug. 1893, n. 13, below.

Louise de Koven Bowen, a philanthropist and a social and civic leader in Chicago, first visited Hull-House during the early 1890s. She became one of the significant financial mainstays of the settlement, helping fund the settlement's physical expansion, serving as president of the Hull-House Woman's Club, and after the death of Jane Addams becoming treasurer and president of the board of Hull-House Association. She also became a personal Addams friend and traveling companion (UIC, JAMC 0239 0392).

158. At the suggestion of JA, the HH Woman's Club was organized by kindergarten director Mary E. McDowell in Feb. 1891. The object of the club was to hold "general discussion and investigation of, and action upon questions pertaining to household science, civics, advancement of women and care of children" ("Constitution of HH Woman's Club," 3; *JAPM*, 51:04). It was created with an initial membership of twelve women from among those who were the mothers of the children attending the HH kindergarten and who were residents of HH. Still living in 1935 were Mary E. McDowell, Mrs. Mary Heinecamp, Mrs. Rose Thornton, and Wilfreda Brockway Deknatel. Other founders were Mrs. Mary Wieherski (or Wieherska) (d. 1920–21), Mrs. Mary E. Pepper Murphy (1855–1927 or 1928), Mrs. Mary Stringer (d. 1929–30), Mrs. Lizzie Laub (d. pre-1928–29), Mrs. Josephine or Johanna McWilliams (d. 1904), Mrs. Annie McFarland (d. pre-1928–29), Mrs. Barbara Weyker (d. pre-1928–29), and Mrs. Margaret Shoemaker (d. 1910). The membership grew quickly: in 1894 it was 50; in 1895, on the third anniversary of the club's founding, it was 115; in 1897 it was 150; and by the early 1900s, the membership was near 500.

By 1898 the club had adopted a constitution, bylaws, and rules of order. Its motto was "We strive for the best." It held regular weekly meetings, and until the early twentieth century dues were fifteen cents a month. By the mid-1890s, the club had working committees, held entertainments to raise funds to support its philanthropic efforts, and had created a number of programs to help families in the neighborhood. The early leadership was supplied by Mary E. McDowell, followed by Louise de Koven Bowen (for a biographical note, see Biographical

Profiles: Bowen, Louise de Koven), Alzina Parsons Stevens (see JA to Richard T. Ely, 31 Oct. 1894, n. 10, below), and Laura Dainty Pelham (see Article in the *HH Bulletin*, 1 Dec. 1897, n. 6, below) who served as presidents of the club. A large part of their task was teaching the members how to conduct business and manage a social organization successfully.

The club's initial public effort in Sept. 1892 seems to have been producing and distributing a flyer providing information on how to prevent cholera. During the early 1890s, club members actively helped the Municipal Order League in its efforts to provide a cleaner, healthier, and safer city. They were particularly attracted to the efforts of EGS in placing art in schools and gathered enough money to secure a copy of Millet's *Knitting Shepherdess* for one of the public schools of their neighborhood. Members of the club were especially active as friendly visitors in support of relief work in their neighborhood. Because of their interest in child care, the club made it possible for one of its members to attend a series of lectures at the Kindergarten College and report to the club so that all would benefit. In 1900, to honor club president Stevens, the club created the "Alzina Parsons Stevens Linen Chest" program to gather clothing and linens and dispense them throughout each year to those in need. That particular activity was ongoing in 1935.

The club was educational and investigated a variety of subjects. For example, between 9 Oct. and 18 Dec. 1895, members participated in half-hour discussions on household economy, hospitality, education, house decoration, dress reform, temperance, religion, motherhood, fatherhood, and childhood and were treated to a speech titled "The New Woman—Has She Come?" presented by Myra Reynolds, a faculty member at the Univ. of Chicago. During the early part of 1896, among the subjects presented for club members were charity, sisterhood, kindergarten, kindness to animals, our neighborhood, purity in the home, overcome evil with good, home amusements, and patriotism. In the summer, there were outings to a number of suburban settings and to institutions like the Art Institute of Chicago, the Juvenile Court, and various social settlements. The club also met with members of other women's clubs. During the last years of the 1890s, club meetings consisted of a speaker followed by discussion and a social gathering. JA was an honorary member of the club, a frequent attendee of club activities, and often a speaker. She participated in anniversary celebrations when she was in Chicago. In Nov. 1896, JA spoke to a joint gathering of the HH and the Oak Park Woman's Club and on 8 Mar. and 24 May 1899 on Tolstoy.

The club eventually joined the General Federation of Women's Clubs and sent representatives to the meetings of the Illinois Federation. On 15 Mar. 1905, members participated in the dedication of a Woman's Club Building at HH that had been made possible through the generosity of Louise de Koven Bowen. The structure had an auditorium room that would seat 800 or could be used for large parties when the seating was removed. There was also a library. One of the highlights of the occasion was the HH Woman's Club Chorus singing the club song, "A House Stands on a Busy Street," with lyrics by JA and music by HH resident and HH Music School director Eleanor Smith. In 1935 the club was still an active and dedicated organization, with 105 members and committees to develop the program; carry out social extension work; produce publicity; develop new members; manage the Woman's Club Building and its library; carry out visiting in the neighborhood; plan receptions, outings, and entertainments; and send delegates to a variety of other organizations, among which were the State Federation, Cook County League, the Juvenile Protective League, Parent-Teachers' Assn., and HH itself. There were picnics and evening entertainments and a yearly anniversary gathering.

159. The idea of "friendly visiting" was associated with helping those in need. Almost from the start of the settlement, JA and EGS treated it as a central activity at HH. The goal was to be a helpful and supportive neighbor while trying to identify those who could benefit from the assistance of one or more of Chicago's charitable institutions. During the 1890s, JA determined that the investigative ways of the "charity visitor," represented by the Chicago Relief and Aid

Society, were disrespectful, intrusive, and degrading to those seeking help. Representatives of the Chicago Relief and Aid Society usually promoted their own ethnocentric ideas and the values and ideals of the class dispensing the charity. JA sought to substitute her "friendly visitor" model more in line with the COS visitor program (see JA to Richard T. Ely, 12 Mar. 1895, below), hoping to offer a more open and understanding and less judgmental arbiter of need. Almost from the start of HH, JA and EGS believed that HH residents and volunteers and later members of the HH Woman's Club would make the best corps of visitors. JA and EGS participated as visitors, and Mary Keyser became a favorite of the neighborhood (see *PJA*, 1:565–66, n. 4). "One of the best and most effective features of the work at Hull House is the system of family visiting. . . . It is pleasant, in spite of almost hopeless poverty with which one is confronted, to go with Miss Julia Hintermeister, herself a Swiss woman commanding most of the modern languages, among the Italians. Up rickety stairs, down dingy alleys. . . . By reporting nuisances, by giving advice about physicians and instruction in regard to hospitals, by giving more than this—sympathy and sincere affection—Miss Hintermeister has not only made these people her friends, but has been of much practical assistance to them" (article about HH in unnamed newspaper [Jan.?] [1892], HH Scrapbook 1:13; *JAPM*, Addendum 10:6ff).

Julia M. E. Hintermeister (1839–1918) was born in Zurich, Switzerland, and emigrated to the United States in 1881. She arrived in Chicago by 1890, where she became a music teacher. She lived in Chicago between 1890 and 1894 while she was most active at HH. There she taught English classes for Italians, elementary Italian, and French. In addition, she helped guide Italian evenings at HH, gave one day each week to visiting Italian families in the neighborhood, and financially supported the settlement, giving to the relief account. On 31 July 1890, during the settlement's first summer break, JA wrote to her, "I am sure you know how glad we will be to have your help next year with our Italian nights" (Library, Special Collections, Northwestern Univ.; *JAPM*, 2:1195). At All Souls Church, in which she was an active member, she held German classes. She moved her residence to Evanston, Ill., sometime in the late 1890s and by 1900 was lodging with the Willard L. Cobb family. She had become a teacher at Miss Brooks' School for Girls, a small institution that served the daughters of prominent families who lived on Chicago's West Side, with which she was associated until her death from pneumonia at the Evanston Hospital.

When Helen Gow, an experienced charity visitor associated with the COS in London, visited HH in 1896, JA saw that she had the opportunity to teach English methods of visiting. By 1897 HH was holding classes to help "friendly visitors" learn visiting techniques and became familiar with the activities and assistance that various Chicago institutions offered.

Although JA continued to support the development of the COS in Chicago with its record keeping and corps of visitors, she soon realized that the system of friendly visiting, no matter who was conducting the visits, was flawed. She revealed her awareness of the issues with that approach to handling charity matters in a lecture she presented at the Univ. of Chicago in 1899. It was published as "Charitable Effort," in *Democracy and Social Ethics* (1902): "We are learning that a standard of social ethics is not attained by travelling a sequestered byway," she wrote in the introduction to the volume, "but by mixing on the thronged and common road where all must turn out for one another, and at least see the size of one another's burdens. To follow the path of social morality results perforce in the temper if not the practice of the democratic spirit, for it implies that diversified human experience and resultant sympathy which are the foundation and guarantee of Democracy" (6–7).

160. See Article in the *Chicago Inter Ocean*, 30 June 1892, above.

161. Florence Kelley. See nn. 99, 162.

162. "There has been but one public school building (the Andrew Jackson), and but one addition to a building (the Grant-Goodrich), erected in this ward since the opening of the Goodrich school in 1890, although there have been about four thousand children in excess

of school seats throughout all these years, and the people of this ward have, therefore, been obliged either to leave their children uninstructed, as hundreds of them do, or to maintain at their own expense schools which it is the duty of the city to maintain for their children, as well as accessibly as for children in more prosperous districts" ("Petition for a New School"). The property that JA referred to in her speech was likely ground purchased on which the Chicago Board of Education planned to erect what became the Andrew Jackson School, which was opened in 1894 at 820 South Carpenter St. The Grant addition (located at 2433 Wilcox St.) to the Goodrich School, located at 915 (later 2000) West Taylor, opened in 1896, and in 1897 classes were being held in a tenement on Taylor for the overflow of children who should have been attending the Polk Street School. See n. 99.

163. See JA to Henry Demarest Lloyd, 18 Nov. 1891, nn. 5–6; and Articles in the *Chicago News* and *Chicago Daily Tribune*, 29 and 30 Apr. 1892, both above.

164. The committee of investigation for the sweating system appointed by the Chicago Trade and Labor Assembly included Mary Kenney and Abraham Bisno, both associated with HH.

165. See Articles in the *Chicago News* and *Chicago Daily Tribune*, 29 and 30 Apr. 1892, above.

166. The Bureau of Justice was formed in 1888 at the urging of the Ethical Humanist Society of Chicago and was located in rooms 6 and 7 of the Marine Building at the northeast corner of Lake and LaSalle streets. Its object was "'[t]o assist in securing legal protection against injustice for those who are unable to protect themselves; to take cognizance of the workings of existing laws and methods of procedure, and to suggest improvements; to propose new and better laws, and to make efforts toward securing their enactment'" (*Hand-Book of Chicago's Charities*, 20). Among its recommendations were making seduction an offense against the state, developing legal measures to make husbands support their wives and children, overseeing mutual benefit societies, creating a chattel mortgage loan bank, and helping those who were friendless in police court. The description of the organization in Flinn's *Chicago . . . a Guide, 1892* indicated that it handled 3,783 matters during the 1890–91 year. In addition, it brought to successful conclusion 342 out of 375 court cases and returned $10,658.45 to its clients. Supported by private donations, it eventually became the Legal Aid Society. See also Articles in the *Chicago News* and *Chicago Daily Tribune*, 29 and 30 Apr. 1892, n. 13, above.

167. Due in part to the efforts of JA, Florence Kelley had been made a special agent of the Bureau of Labor Statistics of Illinois to investigate and compose reports on two Chicago constituencies: working women and sweatshops. Her findings appeared in the bureau's seventh annual report issued in 1893. The information Kelley developed was vital in helping her argue for the regulation of sweatshops in Illinois.

168. See JA to SAAH, 8 Oct. 1889, n. 22; and JA to MRS, 26 Apr. 1890, n. 8, both above.

169. Alfred Hicks.

170. The conferences that JA referred to began as an annual event in 1888 as an antidote to the Haymarket Riot affair. It consisted of a series of lectures on Sunday evenings, primarily in the Madison Street Theatre. According to a *Chicago Daily Tribune* editorial on 22 May 1888, the purpose of the Economic Conf. was to "bring capitalists and laborers, champions of the existing order of things and Anarchists, to a better understanding of each other's positions."

In 1889 the conference was held under the auspices of the Economic Club, a group of twenty-four members, "some professional men and others drawn from industrial pursuits. It included the ultra-conservative and the ultra-radical, the lasissez-faire philosopher, and the progressive reformer." All wished to create "a great public awakening on the subject of economic laws and social problems [that] had occurred within the last few years" ("Socialism in England"). Lyman J. Gage (1836–1927), president of the First National Bank in Chicago and a national leader in banking who would become secretary of the Treasury under President

William McKinley, was the group's leader. Gage contended that the death sentences given the men convicted in the Haymarket bombing were unjust, and he worked unsuccessfully to secure executive clemency for them. He believed that better understanding between labor and capital would result in less violence, welcome dialogue, and ultimately a better use of resources for the economy. To that end, in the winter of 1889 the Economic Club presented a series of lectures held in the Auditorium Theater, offering opportunities for citizens to hear different points of view on economic issues of the day. JA and EGS attended the lectures. The first major presentation, which drew an estimated audience of five hundred men and women, was held on 22 Dec. 1889. It featured socialist Percival Chubb, who described English socialism. During his stay in Chicago, Chubb spent most of his free time at HH and lectured there as well. Another presenter was Father J. S. Huntington, who gave the presentation on 29 Dec. and also spoke at HH. Economic conferences in 1890 and 1891 followed a similar format. Later, in the 1890s, HH and the Chicago Commons assumed a leadership role in continuing the economic conferences that were held at their settlement facilities (see JA to SAAH, 6 Jan. 1897, n. 5, below).

171. The Sunset Club first met on 22 Mar. 1889. It was officially founded almost two years later, in 1891, and modeled after the Twilight Club of New York City and the Seven O'Clock Club in Washington, D.C. Its all-male membership paid two dollars a year to defray the cost of mailings and a dollar for each meal and met Thursdays at 6:30 for dinner at a hotel and a presentation from a member or guest on a matter of current interest or import, followed by discussion. The club had a significant role in informing its membership and the public, through newspaper coverage, about its activities on a wide variety of topics affecting the environment in which all lived and worked. The club ceased to exist in 1901.

JA spoke before the club members twice. On 4 Feb. 1892 at the Grand Pacific Hotel, reformer and political activist Lucy Coues Flower (1837–1921), member of the Chicago Board of Education; Jewish rabbi Dr. Emil G. Hirsch (1852–1923); labor leader, single taxer, and socialist George Schilling (1850–1936); and JA presented their answer to the question "How Would You Uplift the Masses?" It was the forty-second meeting of the club and the first time that women had been invited to attend. Six hundred people were present, and Frances Willard presided. In addition to the speakers, several friends of social reform in Chicago, including EGS and HH resident Anna M. Farnsworth, were seated at the head table. The *Chicago Times* reported that "Miss Addams received an ovation when Miss Willard introduced her. The hand clapping lasted over a minute and the heartiness and spontaneity of her reception showed the public esteem and approval of the work that she is doing in quiet" ("Invaded the Sunset Club"). The events of the evening were reported by the Chicago press. Portions of all of the speakers' presentations appeared in the *Chicago Times*, *Chicago Inter Ocean*, and *Chicago Daily Tribune* on 5 Feb. 1892. The *Chicago Advance* of 18 Feb. 1892 offered JA's presentation as "With the Masses" and boasted that it was the "paper which evidently elicited the deepest interest" ("How Would You Elevate the Masses?"). JA's version of "How Would You Uplift the Masses?" also appeared in the minutes of the Sunset Club on pp. 10–13 and in the Sunset Club *Year Book* for 1891–92 on pp. 118–21. Her second address at the Sunset Club was in answer to the presentation "What Shall We Do for Our Unemployed?" JA presented it at the sixty-fifth club meeting and on the women's night on 21 Dec. 1893 at the Sunset Club in the Grand Pacific Hotel dining room, and it was published in the Sunset Club *Year Book* for 1893–94 on pp. 81–82. This time she shared the dais with Florence Kelley and Abraham Bisno, among others. While Chicago newspapers covered the event, none chose to print her remarks or single out her comments as special (see *JAPM*, 46:498–502, 567–69).

172. The speakers were Sigmund Zeisler on 9 Feb., "Our Jury System"; Major R. W. McClaughry on 16 Feb., "The Chicago Police"; Mark Crawford on 23 Feb., "The Cook County House of Correction"; Judge M. F. Tuley on 8 Mar., "The Cook County Courts"; and Col.

Augustus Jacobson on 15 Mar., "The Municipal Control of Heat, Light, and Transportation." The series continued in the fall of 1892 (see also JA to Bayard Taylor Holmes, 15 Sept 1892, n. 3, above).

173. Charles Booth, "The Unemployed," was published in chap. 5 of vol. 1 of *Labor and Life of the People* (London: Williams and Norgate, 1889), 149–55.

## From Samuel A. Barnett

*"Permit me, though a stranger, to express my appreciation of your article in the current 'Forum.'" It is likely that William B. Thorp, a minister in the First Congregations Church, Binghamton, New York, was writing in response to the Jane Addams article "A New Impulse to an Old Gospel," which appeared in the November issue of the periodical. "I have read it with the greatest delight, and consider it the best—in fact the only adequate—statement yet made of the philosophy of the Settlement movement. . . . Your point of view in the article commands, too, an outlook so fresh and suggestive upon the social-religious situation," he told Jane Addams.[1] At issue was the role that organized religion could or should have in the social reform movement in the United States, with the social settlement movement beginning to take the van.[2] There was growing interest in a social ministry that emphasized Christian ethics and encouraged social reform at the expense of salvation, and this offered decided uncomfortableness to orthodox Protestant church members.*

*Rev. Samuel A. Barnett, warden of Toynbee Hall, whom Jane Addams respected as the leader of the settlement movement, responded to the October* Forum *article, "Hull House, Chicago: An Effort toward Social Democracy."*

St. Judes Vicarage. Commercial Street.
Whitechapel. E. [London, England] Dec. 26. 92

Dear Miss Addams.

I am taking advantage of an attack of bronchitis to write to you. For long I have had it in mind both on acct of your paper in the Forum & also on acct of my own desire for communion.

Yes. I agree with every word of the paper & I have been struck by the many new ways in wh. the offer of lives rather than of schemes meet the social needs of America. I have been especially struck by what people of knowledge may to [do] for foreign immigrants. Far better than prohibition wld be "settlement" wh. wld take the foreigner young & make him American in the truest sense before he cld talk.

It has been pleasant reading of the various activities of Hull House & our hearts warm as we think of all & of the growth of all. But if I know you, you value criticism more than praise so let me say that I think our—ie. American & English—danger is on the side of being practical.

As in metaphysics we never know how material we are so in our doings we never know how deadly practical they become. I am struck by this in repo[r]ts at home & I am struck by this in your paper. An ignorant reader might think that class rooms with leaders wld do all you describe, he wld not discover that what makes classes take & reforms go & clubs brim with good will is the fact that some of you are neighbours to the others—touching them in a 1000 ways wh. cannot be analyzed—sharing with them much more than knowledge. I don't think the value of settlement can be measured by a catalogue of deadly doing & I shld like you to have bro[ugh]t out more the value of personal service—the unselfconscious service of neighbourhood— It wld be a terrible thing if some good man were to say "Here is another machine for doing good" & forthwith begins to endow settlements to do all you describe. You, I know regard settlement as a protest agst machinery—as the offer of life for life—as the gift of friendship in faith as to what may follow— We—Americans & English—need more of the faith of our Lord—the faith wh. will bind to us a few friends & trust in love to reform the world.—We want our plans—our schemes—our results—all "doing is a deadly thing."

But I have written enough—We are grateful to you for your kindness to Mrs Hart.[3] Is she not a wonderful woman & has she not given herself to Ireland.

Personally I have all through disapproved the exhibit at Chicago.[4] I think she wld have spent her strength better in developing her mill—& I dislike all that is involved in puffing an exhibit & I doubt whether it can pay—Cholera may come & any how no Exhibit can secure trade. I am sorry she has spent herself in the matter but that does not make us less grateful for your help. We have been invited to Chatauqua in July with the offer of expenses. We incline to come if we can make it a holiday. Our idea of Chatauqua—a run by you to Niagra then by the St Lawrence back to Newport. Do you think this wld be a good summer trip giving us climate & company?[5]

Our Toynbee Report[6] is just out wh. you will like to read but how very powerless are letters in comparison with words—words themselves how poor are they. With kindest regards Ever

Saml A Barnett

ALS (SCPC, JAC; *JAPM*, 2:1348–53).

1. 7 Nov. 1892, SCPC, JAC; *JAPM*, 2:1340. William B. Thorp (1868–1952) was ordained in the Congregational ministry in 1891. After serving in Binghamton, N.Y., until 1899, he became pastor of the South Congregational Church in Chicago, 1899–1908; the First Congregational Church, San Diego, Calif., 1908–20; and the First Congregational Church, Palo Alto, Calif., 1929–39, when he retired.

2. JA found herself increasingly sought as a speaker for a variety of Protestant and Jewish congregations. Audiences were sometimes not entirely supportive because of JA's unwillingness to associate the settlement with a formal Protestant religion. After presenting "The New Philanthropy," likely a version of "A New Impulse to an Old Gospel," on 22 May 1894 to the fiftieth convention of the General Congregational Assn. of Illinois at the First Congregational Church in Oak Park, Ill., JA found herself being questioned about social reform and religion at HH. "It soon became apparent that the answers did not quite satisfy some of the more orthodox of her hearers," wrote a reporter for the Congregational periodical *Advance*.

"Among other things Miss Addams was asked if she thought the church could take such work as she had in hand and make a success of it. 'That all depends,' replied Miss Addams, 'upon what kind of people the church is composed.' 'Do you think Hull House takes the place of church?' she was asked. 'I must confess there is in my mind a little ecclesiastical confusion with regard to the meaning of the word church,' was the reply. A minister from Quincy [, Ill.] came to Miss Addams rescue with an eloquent endorsement of all the work which has been done through the agency of Hull-House and its founder. He sat down amid a storm of applause" ("Tells Ministers of HH"). Many members of orthodox Protestant denominations continued to distrust the settlement for its unwillingness to proselytize (see also Robert A. Woods to JA, 20 June 1893, n. 11, below). Catholics and Jews were wary of the draw and potential power of the settlement.

Jewish leadership in Chicago recognized the attraction that the educational opportunities at HH held especially for poorer members of their community and newly arrived immigrants. Their response was to try to emulate the HH success by creating their own social settlement. JA fostered and supported their effort by hosting a gathering at HH in the spring of 1892 to explore the possibility. The Maxwell Street Settlement was founded in Nov. 1893 and located a few blocks south of HH in an old home at 185 (later 270) Maxwell St., to the east of Jefferson St.

Leaders in the Roman Catholic Church also recognized the lure of the social settlement for immigrants of its faith. The church believed that participation in settlement programs "could be and in fact . . . [was] dangerous to . . . Catholic Americans who confused these 'proving grounds of the social spirit' with the American way of life." To many Catholic lay and church leaders, it seemed "likely that the spirit of secularization [exhibited by HH] could not only weaken the Italian American's Catholicism but cause him to fall away altogether" (Amberg, *Madonna Center*, 39). One Roman Catholic response to this dilemma was a Catholic mission initiated by Sarah Agnes Ward Amberg (d. 1919) and alumnae of the Academy of the Sacred Heart on Taylor St. in 1898. Located first in Holy Guardian Angel School and ultimately known as the Madonna Center, it was moved to St. Francis of Assisi School on Newberry St., two blocks from HH, and in 1922 to 718 and 712 Loomis St. The founder's daughter, Mary Agnes Amberg (d. 1962), served as its head resident after her mother from 1914 until her death. She recalled, "All of us had looked upon Hull-House as a challenge, yet we never experienced anything but kindness and thoughtfulness and cooperation from Jane Addams" (*Madonna Center*, 83).

3. Alice Marion Rowland Hart (b. 1848), sister of Henrietta Rowland Barnett, grew up in Bristol, England, and studied medicine in Paris and at the London School of Medicine for Women. She became the second wife of medical journalist, Oriental art collector, and children's advocate Ernest Abraham Hart (1835–97) in July 1872, and together they collaborated on several projects. Alice Hart taught physiology for Samuel and Henrietta Barnett at St. Jude's Parish in 1873, and in 1881 she presented a series of popular lectures, "Bodies and Babies," to the Toynbee mothers' meetings. In 1895 she published *Diet in Sickness and in Health* in England and the United States.

Although her Jewish husband and her sister's Christian partner shared an incompatibility in background and religious preference, they were respectful of one another's achievements and maintained a cordial relationship because the sisters remained close friends. The Harts and Barnetts traveled together in the Near and Far East, and Alice Hart was often with Henrietta at Toynbee Hall. While Henrietta Barnett described Alice Hart as "very clever, generous-minded enough to forgive injuries, humble enough to forget them, full of the passion of pity and self-forgetful enthusiasm, with a child-like confidence in everyone which none of the disappointments she had suffered ever quenches" (*Canon Barnett*, 1:149), EGS had a decidedly different view. During the spring of 1892, when she visited England to experience Toynbee Hall and travel with the Barnetts and a group of friends to Italy, she had occasion to lodge with the Harts. She found Mrs. Hart "a very strong woman" and "clever," but confided to JA, "Between you & me I don't think I like her. She is boundlessly ambitious—& conceited, & she wants to do something that will get her a name" (EGS to JA, 17 [and 19] May [1892], SC, Starr; *JAPM*, 2:1308).

Alice Hart was leading an effort to improve working opportunities for the downtrodden Irish by helping to redevelop the cottage weaving industry in Donegal. She was the founder in 1883 of the Donegal Industrial Fund and trained Irish girls in art needlework in London. She came to Chicago in the late fall of 1892 to request that the planners of the World's Columbian Exposition include the Donegal weavers and their products at the exposition. She promoted the Donegal weavers throughout her visit to the United States in Nov. and Dec. 1892, and on 5 Nov. 1892 she spoke at HH about the weavers, their products, and their lives. She also made presentations at the Lexington Hotel, Eliza Allen Starr's home, and to the CWC.

4. Alice Hart was successful in her effort to have the Donegal industries included in the exhibits at the World's Columbian Exposition. The Irish Village, admission twenty-five cents, located on the Midway Plaisance, offered a "reproduction of Donegal Castle and Drogheda gate, cottages showing different industries" (Wade and Wrenn, "*The Nut Shell*" . . . *Guide to the World's Fair*, 161). However, she had to share the spotlight with the Irish Industrial Assn., which took over her project.

5. The Barnetts were unable to accept the Chautauqua invitation and did not travel to the United States in 1893.

6. "The Eighth Annual Report of the Council on the work of Toynbee Hall has just been issued" (*Toynbee Record* 5 [Jan. 1893]: 49).

## To Henry Demarest Lloyd

Hull-House [Chicago, Ill.] Jan. 2d 1892[1893]

My dear Mr Lloyd

The conference last evening turned almost entirely upon a Halsted St factory for some sewing trade,[1] as being the trade that needed help most and Mr Colvin being anxious to have the factory near Hull-House[.][2]

We became so absorbed in this, that it was not until nearly every one had gone that we got around to Miss Kenny's plan[3] which is ready for almost immediate execution. I think that she has told you of the arrangement she has of using a numbering machine. In order to be independent of non union shops and take orders of her own she ought to have a "perforater" at $350oo and a "stitcher["] @ $100oo this with a capital of $50oo would make $500.oo[.] Of this am't she has secured $200oo from Boston at 3% interest. I should be very glad to lend $100oo at the same rate.

I have written to Mr Darrow[4] and to you to see if you could each lend 100.oo at 3%. That would make up the required amount and she could start in at once. It would really be a loan to Miss Kenny, but she would mean to make the business cöoperative. I have a great admiration for Miss Toomey and Miss Roberts the two girls who are ready to go in with her[.] Miss Kenny is very anxious to see you in regard to a mass meeting against the Sweating System,[5] but she felt somewhat embarassed to write you in regard to the money. I hope my lack of embarassment is not owing to presumption. Could you telephone or write me your decision soon so they could order the machines. She is really in an awkward position in regard to taking orders. With cordial regards to Mrs Lloyd and the compliments of the season to the household, I am sincerely yours

Jane Addams

ALS (SHSW, Lloyd; *JAPM*, 2:1362–63).

1. Continuing to develop possibilities for cooperation, on 26 Dec. 1892, and on short notice, JA arranged a meeting to discuss a cooperative sewing factory. The gathering was scheduled for the evening of 1 Jan. 1893, because that was the only evening that Ethelbert Stewart (1857–1936) could attend. Stewart, who had been born and schooled in Chicago, at the time was a special agent for the U.S. Bureau of Labor. He was familiar with a cooperative sewing venture in Decatur, Ill., and he shared his knowledge with William H. Colvin, who was planning to develop a similar program for women near HH. JA also invited Clarence Darrow, Henry Demarest Lloyd, and some "working women" to attend (JA to Henry Demarest Lloyd, 26 Dec. 1892, SHSW, Lloyd; *JAPM*, 2:1346).

2. According to JA, William H. Colvin was already committed to purchase land for a cooperative "factory for sewing women," but she hoped to give him an opportunity to understand exactly how a cooperative sewing factory could work (JA to Henry Demarest Lloyd, 26 Dec. 1892, SHSW, Lloyd; *JAPM*, 2:1346).

While Colvin did not pursue the cooperative sewing factory idea, the CWC did. Through the club's efforts, the Woman's Emergency Relief Assn. was formed by the end of 1893 and affiliated with the Children's Aid Society and Central Relief Assn. Bertha Palmer provided the initial funding of $1,000 to initiate the program, supplemented later by another $1,000 from Potter Palmer and gifts from many others in varying amounts, from 50 cents to $500.

The closest sewing room to HH was organized initially in the top or seventh floor of the New Era Building, situated where Blue Island Ave. crossed the corner of Halsted and Harrison streets. It cost $150 a day to keep the New Era room open. On 4 Jan. 1894, the *Chicago Daily Tribune* reported in an article, "Saved by the Needle," that "100 women sit sewing every day in the week from morning until night" for 50 cents a day. All had their noon meal three blocks away at HH. At least three other sewing rooms were opened in other locales in Chicago.

3. Mary Kenney, whose name JA misspelled in her letter, had hoped to establish a cooperative bindery. Unfortunately, JA was not successful at helping her raise sufficient capital to begin.

4. By this time, Clarence Darrow, like his mother, Emily Eddy Darrow, was a supporter of women's rights and suffrage. Arriving in Chicago in 1887, he became an attorney for the city of Chicago and soon a corporate lawyer for the Chicago and Northwestern Railway Co. By May 1889, the self-styled independent Democrat was speaking out in support of woman suffrage. At the request of JA's RFS classmate Catharine Waugh, who organized the program, Darrow appeared and lent his encouragement to women gathered at the state convention of the Equal Suffrage Assn. in Freeport, Ill. He worked with Illinois governor John Peter Altgeld to free the anarchist workers who had been convicted of the Haymarket Riot, and during the first years of the twentieth century he gained national fame as a labor attorney. Darrow went on to defend murderers Nathan Leopold and Richard Loeb, who killed Bobby Franks in Chicago in 1924, and John T. Scopes in 1925 for teaching the ideas of evolution in the *State of Tennessee v. Scopes*. Active at HH as a lecturer and supporter of reform causes during the 1890s, he remained a lifelong friend of JA and HH.

5. According to an article, "To Stop Sweatshops," in the *Chicago Inter Ocean*, 21 Feb. 1893, at least twenty-five hundred men and women attended the rally that Mary E. Kenney orga-

nized at Chicago's Central Music Hall on behalf of the Chicago Trade and Labor Assembly to denounce the evils associated with sweatshop manufacture and to suggest ways to remedy them. Henry Demarest Lloyd was a major participant.

## To Sarah Alice Addams Haldeman

Chicopee, Mass. Feb 23d '93

My dear Alice

Ellen forwarded your letter[1] to me here where we are spending a night and day with Mrs Blaisdell,[2] and I will find the picture when I get home.[3]

We start for Chicago tomorrow and we arrive there Sat. evening. I expect Laura to spend Sunday.[4]

The trip came about because I had an invitation to speak before the 19th Cent. Club of New York[5] on "the higher education of women" with my expenses paid. I have wanted for a long time to accept invitations from the various colleges to talk to the girls of Hull-House, so combined the two things.[6] Dear Mary Smith has been with me all the time, and we have had a beautiful trip. We were entertained at the Settlements in Phila.[7] New York[8] and Boston[9] (I find I am considered quite the grandmother of American settlements) and I have spoken at Bryn Mawr, Vassar & Wellesly, and <will speak> at Smith tonight.[10] I have enjoyed it very much and as I do not expect to be away next summer, I think that it was a good thing to break into the winter grind. I find myself looking forward to May[11] with keen pleasure and I am sure we will all have a happy time together.

Do you think that I ought to write Ma to come to the fair later?[12]

Your letters are such a pleasure to me I wish you'd send me more. Shall I engage Alice Kellogg to paint Marcet in May? My picture will cost about $300.00 you know.[13] Yours forever

Jane.

ALS (IU, Lilly, SAAH; *JAPM*, 2:1388–90).

1. SAAH's letter that EGS forwarded from Chicago is not known to be extant.

2. JA and MRS were visiting EGS's sister, Mary Houghton Starr Blaisdell, in Chicopee, Mass. JA left Chicopee on 24 Feb. and arrived the next day in Chicago.

3. A photograph of Marcet Haldeman, who would be six years old in June 1893. After a visit with LSA in Cedarville, JA had written to SAAH, "I saw a picture of Marcet when I was there that was perfectly charming—I felt a little bit hurt that you had n't sent me one, it would have been such a comfort and pleasure to me" (10 Feb. 1893, IU, Lilly, SAAH; *JAPM*, 2:1387).

4. JA had visited with JWA's wife, LSA, on 8 and 9 Feb. 1893. She had gone to console her about the condition of JWA, who had entered the Illinois Hospital for the Insane, Elgin, for the fourth time on 16 Nov. 1892. JA visited her brother, JWA, there on 4 Feb. 1893, and commented, "He is quieter but really no better and the visit was of no satisfaction to either of us" (JA to SAAH, 10 Feb. 1893, IU, Lilly, SAAH; *JAPM*, 2:1386).

Jane Addams's sister Sarah Alice Addams Haldeman contracted with Alice Kellogg, who taught art at Hull-House, to paint a portrait of Jane Addams. Before the work was sent to the Haldeman family in Girard, Kansas, Jane Addams asked Kellogg to make a copy of the work for Mary Rozet Smith. Then Alice Kellogg later painted Mary Rozet Smith at the request of Jane Addams. Both oil paintings are in the collection of the Jane Addams's Hull-House Museum, University of Illinois at Chicago (photograph of the painting of Jane Addams taken by former HH resident and *Life* magazine photographer Wallace Kirkland; private collection).

5. JA appeared as one of three presenters on the Nineteenth Century Club of New York's 16 Feb. 1893 program "The Higher Education of Women." The *New York Times* of 17 Feb. 1893 reported that Mary A. Jordan of Vassar argued that the educated woman "should be public minded, well versed in the social arts, and refined in the inner life." Mrs. Ellen H. Richards, head of the Dept. of Household Chemistry, MIT, Boston, suggested that the educated woman should become a "professional housekeeper," while JA said "she hoped that the high education of women would lead to the advancement of backward social classes—a moral necessity in the evolution of the modern race."

6. JA's topics were the responsibility of educated women and her social settlement scheme.

7. JA and MRS left Chicago for Philadelphia on Sunday evening, 12 Feb., and departed Philadelphia on Wednesday, 15 Feb. 1893. While in Philadelphia, JA saw her Young family relatives. She may also have been entertained in the St. Mary Street Neighborhood College Settlement (established 9 Apr. 1892). In addition, Neighborhood House (established 1 July 1893) was in its formative stages.

8. In New York City, JA could have visited the College Settlement on Rivington St., formed about the same time that HH opened, and the University Settlement, originally established as the Neighborhood Guild in Aug. 1886. Henry Street Settlement, a work in progress, was not established until July 1893.

9. In Boston JA and MRS visited Denison House. It was begun as Boston College Settlement, organized in Dec. 1892, under the leadership of Vida D. Scudder (see Robert A. Woods to JA, 20 June 1893, n. 3, below), but soon taken charge of by Helena S. Dudley. They also visited Andover House (in 1895 renamed South End House), founded in Oct. 1891, and led by Robert A. Woods (see also Robert A. Woods to JA, 20 June 1893, n. 8, below). JA met with Boston settlement leaders to solicit their ideas and encourage their attendance at the Congress of Social Settlements being planned for July 1893 during the World's Columbian Exposition Auxiliary gatherings in Chicago.

Helena Stuart Dudley was born in Nebraska, the only daughter of Judson H. and Carolina Bates Dudley. Her father resettled the family in Denver, where he engaged in a number of businesses that seemed to result in an unsteady income. Helena grew up in that area, received her schooling there, and with the death of her mother when Helena was nineteen began her working life there. By the time she was twenty-six years old, she had gone to Boston, where she attended MIT, 1884–85. The next year found her at Bryn Mawr College, where she studied biology, supported herself by working as a laboratory assistant, and graduated first in her class (B.A. 1889). She became a biology teacher in Brooklyn, N.Y., first at the Pratt Institute and the next year at the Packer Institute.

While she was at Bryn Mawr, she participated as a representative of the college in helping to establish the College Settlements Assn. Vida Scudder, professor of English at Wellesley, also a participant in that effort, recognized her talents and encouraged her to become more actively engaged in settlement work. The two women became lifelong best friends.

In 1892 Helena became the head worker at St. Mary's Settlement, the college settlement in Philadelphia, and by 1893 had moved as head resident to the College Settlement Assn.'s new settlement in Boston, Denison House. She remained there as head resident until 1912. She developed an assortment of settlement programs that often mirrored those at HH, and JA became a supportive friend. Denison House and Robert A. Woods' South End House often cooperated on programs. A number of unions met at Denison House, and Helena Dudley became very supportive of labor union development. For several years, she was a representative of Federal Labor Union No. 5915 of the AFL to the Boston Central Labor Union. She was one of the group of women who helped form the NWTUL and was active in the Boston branch, serving as its vice-president.

After leaving Denison House, because she feared that her labor union activities would cause it to lose support, she became engaged in the women's peace movement. She served as a member of the Boston branch of the WILPF, was a member of the Fellowship of Reconciliation, and supported the League of Nations. Like her friend Vida Scudder, she joined the Socialist Party and also like Scudder became active in the Episcopal Church's Companions of the Holy Cross. She lived the last ten years of her life with Scudder and died in Switzerland after attending the Seventh WILPF Congress in Grenoble, France. There were memorial services for Dudley at Denison House and at St. Stephen's Church in Boston, where she was a member for forty years. She left one thousand dollars from her estate to the WILPF.

Dudley and JA maintained a long and supportive friendship. Dudley saw JA and HH as an inspiration for her workers at Denison House, and JA always seemed to make time to visit that settlement and Dudley when she was in Boston. Dudley visited HH for two weeks in late Apr. 1897, and when she left her post in Denison House she once again sought JA and HH and may have visited during 1913. In 1911 Dudley was a guest of JA and MRS in Hulls Cove, Maine. For the memorial service held for Dudley on 20 Nov. 1932 at Denison House, JA sent the following statement: "Helena Dudley was a beloved member of the pioneer group responsible for the first American settlements. We all greatly admired not only her fine mind and understanding heart, but her unique ability to see our new undertaking in relation to . . . social trends and eager experiments which distinguished the contemporary period. Her lovely life ~~to the very end~~ <was consistently> dedicated to the ultimate purpose of the settlement, though often expressed through other agencies. . . . We shall always be grateful <that during this very last summer> she brought to the house of <our League> [WILPF] in Grenoble <the blessing of> her sweet and tranquil wisdom" (A and HLS telegram draft enclosed in Helen Rand Thayer to JA, 11 Nov. 1932, SCPC, JAC; *JAPM*, 24:394–95).

10. This was the first of JA's many speaking junkets to different parts of the United States throughout her life. JA probably spoke at Bryn Mawr while she was in Philadelphia. She addressed an audience at Vassar College in Poughkeepsie, N.Y., on the evening of 15 Feb. 1893. As a result of her remarks on HH, the *New York Times* suggested that "there are many Western girls in the college who, if they take up a temporary residence at any settlement, will probably answer Miss A[d]dams's appeal for residents at Hull House" (19 Feb. 1893). JA must have delivered similar messages to young women at Wellesley and also at Smith College, where she spoke on 23 Feb.

11. JA was hoping that SAAH would visit her in Chicago beginning in May for the opening of the World's Columbian Exposition, but there seems to have been a slight misunderstanding, at least on the part of SAAH. On 10 Apr. 1893, JA wrote to SAAH, "I thought you knew the Fair opened May *1st*. . . . The grounds are full of carpenters and builders of all sorts and doubtless May will seem very much unfinished. I have felt uncomfortable about not telling you of it in case you would rather go to Mary's first and come to the Fair for June, but I have been so anxious to see you that I have continued to urge May. The Fair however will not be any where nearly complete until later" (IU, Lilly, SAAH; *JAPM*, 2:1397–98). SAAH and Marcet arrived in Chicago in May to attend the fair. After visiting Cedarville relatives, where Marcet presented GBH with "a souvenier of the World's Columbian half dollar," and RC between 8 and 15 June, they returned to HH to join MCAL and her family, who arrived in Chicago on 12 June for their World's Fair venture (12 June 1893, UIC, JAMC, HJ).

12. AHHA reported to son HWH that "not the least hint of an invitation have I received [to join them]—and am glad" (12 June 1893, UIC, JAMC, HJ). Near the exposition's closing, AHHA complained to HWH, "I have not been [to the] Fair yet. Do not think I will be so fortunate—unless you should open your heart to come and go with me and—take care of me" (24 Sept. 1893, UIC, JAMC, HJ).

If AHHA did attend the exposition, it was likely not until its waning days. Paul Fry suggested in his biography of his aunt Mary Fry, who by this time was a companion to AHHA and living with her in the Cedarville Addams home, that Mary accompanied AHHA to the exposition. The fair officially closed 30 Oct. 1893. There is no evidence to indicate that they visited HH.

13. JA was having her portrait painted for SAAH by Alice Kellogg (Tyler) (1862–1900). Perhaps in an effort to mollify SAAH and dispel her seemingly hurt feelings, JA wrote, "How ~~you~~ would you like Miss Kellogg to leave a place in the canvas and put Marcet into it, when you come in May. She paints charming pictures of children and I know you would like it" (JA to SAAH, 10 Feb 1893, IU, Lilly, SAAH; *JAPM*, 2:1387). SAAH did not accept JA's offer. Instead, she engaged Alice Kellogg to paint a separate portrait of Marcet.

Kellogg painted two portraits of JA. The first, painted in 1893, was exhibited at HH before being sent with a Kellogg portrait of Marcet to the Haldeman home in Girard, Kans., in 1894. For HWH's comments on the portrait, see *PJA*, 1:514.

While the portrait was still in Chicago, Alice Kellogg began work on the copy she agreed to paint for MRS. After the death of MRS in 1934, it was returned to HH and at present is part of the collection at the Jane Addams HH at the Univ. of Illinois, Chicago.

The original portrait, a standing three-quarter view of JA, was damaged so severely in an accident that only the head portion of the painting was restored. It is in the collection of the CHM. The portrait copy at UIC is complete. See photograph on p. 302.

Alice DeWolf Kellogg was one of six daughters of Harriet Bencham Scott and homeopathic physician John Leonard Kellogg. She grew up in Chicago, attended the Unitarian Church, developed what became a lifelong interest in metaphysical subjects, and became one of the earliest students at the Academy of Fine Arts, predecessor to Chicago's Art Institute. After studying in Paris at l'Academie Julian and the Carlorossi School in 1887–89, having her work included in the 1889 Salon, and also exhibiting in the American section in the Fine Arts Pavilion at the Paris Exposition in 1889, she returned to Chicago to reestablish her own studio and teach at the Art Institute. She was a member of the Palette Club (originally the Bohemian Art Club) of female artists and was three times its president. Her work *The Mother*, sometimes call *The Mother and Child*, which she painted during her last year of study in Paris and exhibited through the Society of American Artists show in New York in 1891, earned her membership in that organization. It was featured on the cover of the Jan. 1893 *Century Magazine* and eventually found its way, along with others of her works, into the permanent collection at HH. She was an exhibitor at the Fine Arts Building at the World's Columbian Exposition. For the Illinois Building at the fair, she created a mural titled *Instruction*.

Although her subjects varied from life and still life to landscape, and included oil, watercolor, and charcoal studies, Alice Kellogg Tyler became a noted portraitist in Chicago and captured the features of many individuals who were associated with HH. In addition to JA, these included Dr. Leila G. Bedell, Jenny Dow Harvey, Edith Redding (a settlement neighbor's daughter), Marcet Haldeman, John C. Coonley, Lydia Coonley-Ward, Dr. Cornelia Barnarda de Bey, and MRS. She loved children and often painted them. She became the illustrator for Lydia Avery Coonley-Ward's book *Singing Verses for Children*, published in 1897. She was often at HH, primarily as a painter, but on Wednesday evenings from Jan. to June 1892 she became one of the first drawing teachers at the settlement. In addition, she often lent her own paintings for the Butler Art Gallery Exhibitions mounted by EGS. In 1894 she wed amateur artist Orno J. Tyler, secretary of the Story and Clark Organ and Piano Co. After a miscarriage in 1897, Alice Kellogg Tyler experienced increasingly poor health, due primarily to the effects of Bright's disease, associated with diabetes. She died 14 Feb. 1900. At her funeral, JA presented a eulogy, describing her friend as an artist offering "an impression of the openness and at the same time of the mystery of life; of a spirit of adventure and of a spirit of unusual peace; of unending vitality and of repose; of high courage and of sweet humility" (Addams, "Alice Kellogg Tyler," *The Excellent*, 57).

## To Emily Greene Balch

*The World's Columbian Exposition, meant to open in 1892, was created with the approval of the U.S. government to commemorate the four hundredth anniversary of Christopher Columbus discovering America. It opened officially in Chicago on 1 May 1893 to a crowd of almost five hundred thousand attendees, one of whom was Jane Addams. The occasion was made especially memorable for her because in the press of humanity her purse was stolen but returned to her thanks to the quick work of a policeman.*[1] *This was probably not her first visit to the "White City" on the shore of Lake Michigan. In April she had reported to sister Alice Haldeman that "every thing is very much behind and the exhibits will not be nearly all in place, but the ceremonies will be imposing I think and the buildings are beautiful."*[2]

*Even before President Grover Cleveland pressed the golden-colored telegraph key to close the electrical circuit to start the machinery that operated the fair exhibition halls, exhibits, fountains, sounds, and lights until its close six months later on 30 October, Jane Addams and her Hull-House associates were absorbed in activities associated with the spectacle. Beginning in 1891, they had helped to organize some of the gatherings of world leaders and thinkers. Called congresses, they were to take place during the fair under the auspices of the World's Congress Auxiliary to encourage unity and peace and exalt and promote progress. With the fair under way, Jane and her Hull-House friends became platform personalities, introducers and speakers during the congresses, innkeepers, hosts, and tour guides, called "toters," at the settlement. They were also tireless relief workers, as they sought to help those who came to Chicago in search of employment during the fair, which coincided with an economic depression that was to characterize the middle years of the 1890s.*[3]

*An increasing number of visitors at the exposition from across the United States and from Europe found their way to Hull-House. Among the most frequent were journalists, social settlement workers, clergy, labor leaders, and the intellectually curious who had read about the social experiment. In an article in the* Unitarian, *Eliza R. Sunderland of Ann Arbor, Michigan, reported, "There are two great attractions in Chicago this summer. . . . [T]hey are Hull House and the World's Fair."*[4]

*Recognizing an opportunity to present their fledgling enterprise in the best possible light to a great many people, Jane Addams and the settlement residents and volunteers kept Hull-House astir over the summer. To see that it was experienced by visitors as a developing program responsive to community need, Jane and Ellen maintained a more robust schedule of activities than usual for the summer months. There were free lectures, concerts, and classes.*[5] *Guests learned of the new public playground, the Jane Club, and the recently constructed gymnasium, coffeehouse, and kitchen. They also heard about efforts to abolish sweatshops, improve education, and develop better housing in the neighborhood. One of the European visitors, English journalist William T. Stead, added to the growing luster of Hull-House when he pronounced it "one of the best institutions in Chicago" in his widely read* If Christ Came to Chicago *(1893),*[6] *his scathing exposé of the corruption and immorality in the exposition city.*

*Like many other young people attracted to the developing social settlement movement, Emily Greene Balch*[7] *wanted to see Hull-House. It is likely that when Jane Addams visited Boston earlier in the year, she had promised Balch a room at Hull-House for her visit to the fair. Balch and Addams developed a lifelong friendship based on mutual interests in social justice and peace, shared friends, and respect.*

Hull-House. Chicago [Ill.] May 11" 1893

My dear Miss Balch

We have furnished another flat in the Jane Club building and would be delighted to have your sister[8] and yourself take a room there in June. I must warn you however that it will all be very simple and very far from the World's Fair, and possibly you would enjoy Hull-House more as you would see it during visits to it, than you would at such close range, without after all being in the House—as I wish you might be—if we could only stretch the walls during the summers[.] I have not in the least changed my in regard to my great desire to have you near Hull-House while you are in Chicago and our rooms are quite ready, but since I have gone to the Fair several times, I realize as I did not before, how tedious the journey is. I hope very much that you will decide only in regard to your own comfort and pleasure. Miss Lathrop enjoyed Dennison House so much and we both feel indebted for its hospitality.

Anticipating your visit to Chicago with much pleasure. I am very sincerely yours

Jane Addams

ALS (SCPC, Balch; *JAPM*, 2:1405–6).

1. Linn, *Jane Addams*, 264–65.
2. 10 Apr. 1893, IU, Lilly, SAAH; *JAPM*, 2:1397–98.
3. Between 1892 and 1897–98, there was a severe business depression in Chicago and the nation. Thousands of people came to Chicago to help construct and work on the exposition, but when it ended they were left without jobs. No statistics about unemployment were kept during the 1890s, but some economists, taking into account the more than five hundred bank failures and over sixteen thousand business bankruptcies, estimate that unemployment surged to between 10 percent and 20 percent in major urban areas. These conditions fostered labor strikes, violence, and demands that the government create jobs for the unemployed.

The HH neighborhood was especially hard-hit during the depression. JA, who was appointed a member of the Chicago Relief and Public Safety Com., sought to help her unemployed neighbors find work digging a drainage canal. When a neighbor who had been a shipping clerk whom JA had directed to the work died because he was not suited for the hard labor that was required, JA recalled that she learned a valuable lesson, "that life cannot be administered by definite rules and regulations, that wisdom to deal with a man's difficulties comes only through some knowledge of his life and habits as a whole" (Addams, *Twenty Years*,

162). Not all could work at any job; some required relief or a job suited to their health and skills. JA and the settlement residents helped create sewing rooms for women of all ages, so that families could have an opportunity to earn enough cash to purchase necessities (see JA to Henry Demarest Lloyd, 2 Jan. 1893, n. 2, above). The settlement also supported the creation of a model lodging house for women (see Minutes of a HH Residents Meeting, 10 Dec. 1893, below). HH became a place of registration for the Central Relief Assn. and received funds to support relief payments in the neighborhood. A new HH resident, Edwin A. Waldo, came from Boston to oversee that task. The records kept by JA, who served as treasurer of HH, reveal the steep increase in funds gathered and designated for relief in 1893 (see JA to MRS, 26 Aug. 1893, n. 3, below).

Edwin Augustus Waldo (1863–1930) was born in Danielson, Conn., where his father, Simon S. Waldo, was a successful wholesale merchant. He attended Andover Theological Seminary, 1891–93. As an assistant pastor, Waldo preached in Boston's Berkeley Temple and volunteered and lived at Andover House, 1892–93, before accepting an offer from JA to come to HH. In Nov. 1893, he took charge of relief registration in the HH neighborhood for the Central Relief Assn. At HH in the winter of 1894, he also began teaching arithmetic in the College Extension Program. In Mar. 1894, after attending a service at St. James Cathedral in Chicago, he disappeared and was located several days later in Jacksonville, Fla. He had no memory of how or why he was there. During the previous summer of 1893, he had experienced a similar mental blackout when he disappeared from Boston and five days later found himself at Lake George, N.Y. He returned to HH briefly, for on 7 Oct. he served as secretary at the meeting JA called to discuss founding the Chicago Federation of Social Settlements. By Feb. 1895, he had entered a sanitarium in Battle Creek, Mich., for treatment of a mental disorder. After leaving the sanitarium, he became associated with the University Settlement in New York City, but in July 1896 he again disappeared and was not heard from until Feb. 1902, when he was living in San Francisco. Waldo later indicated that "in 1905 [I] suffered [a] complete breakdown and did nothing for 9 years" and then was "acting under the C[ongretional]. H[ome]. M[ission]. S[ociety]. <6 mos in year> but, in the summer, help out small <pastorless> churches wherever I happen to be" ([Statement by Edwin A. Waldo]). According to vol. 53 of the *Year-Book of the Congregational and Christian Churches*, Waldo was ordained in Oct. 1904 through the Congregational Council, Pilgrim Church, Smyrna Park, Ceres, Calif. He served churches in Palermo and Wyandotte, Calif., in 1905; Mt. Dora and Tangerine, Fla., 1905–6; and Union Church, West Palm Beach, Fla., 1906–15; and he moved back to churches in South Pasadena and Shater, Calif., 1916–29. He died in South Pasadena, Calif.

4. "HH, Chicago," 400. Eliza Jane Read Sunderland (1865–1910) was a lecturer, educator, author, and advocate of women's rights, who after her marriage to Jabez T. Sunderland, minister of the First Unitarian Church of Ann Arbor, Mich., earned a doctorate from the Univ. of Michigan (1892). She visited Chicago as a speaker at the Women's Congress of the World's Columbian Exposition. The title of her topic was "Does the Higher Education Tend to Unfit Women for Domestic Life?"

5. For details and schedule of events, see "Plan for College Extension Classes at the HH," Summer Term, beginning 5 June 1893 (HH Scrapbook 2:29 ½; *JAPM*, 10:7ff).

6. 410.

7. Emily Greene Balch (1867–1961), born to Boston lawyer Francis Vergnies and former schoolteacher Ellen Maria Noyes Balch in Jamaica Plain, Mass., became a reformer, peace advocate, and lifelong friend to JA. For her efforts promoting peace and cooperation among peoples of the world, she was awarded the Nobel Peace Prize in 1946. Raised in a close-knit, liberal Unitarian family, Emily Balch attended Miss Catherine Ireland's School in Boston and graduated from Bryn Mawr College (A.B. 1889), after which she attended the Sorbonne in Paris, 1890–91, on her Bryn Mawr European fellowship. There she studied political economy and conducted research on public assistance for the poor of France. On her return to the

United States, she became associated with the Boston Children's Aid Society and became a friend of Mary E. Kenney and Jack O'Sullivan. In Aug. 1892, after she attended the Summer School of Applied Ethics at Plymouth, Mass., and the settlement gathering there on 3 Aug., Balch and several of her friends founded Denison House as a social settlement in the South Cove district of Boston in Dec. 1892. Balch agreed to become the head worker until Helena Dudley was free to take over in 1893, at which time Balch began to study in the Harvard Annex (later Radcliffe) program to become a teacher. In 1895 she attended the Univ. of Chicago. She spent the 1895–96 academic year at the Univ. of Berlin and then in the fall of 1896 joined Katharine Coman at Wellesley College, where she became a distinguished scholar and eventually head of the Dept. of Economics and Sociology. Although she had rejected socialism and Marxism, her extracurricular activities as a political activist and peace advocate during World War I and as an outspoken critic of class discrimination and a supporter of organized labor, resulted in her being labeled a Bolshevist during the Red Scare era immediately after World War I, which led Wellesley to dismiss her in 1919. Active in the WPP, and a participant in the unofficial peace-seeking delegation in northern Europe after the 1915 International Congress at The Hague, she became the energetic and able international secretary-treasurer of the WILPF from its founding in 1919 until 1922, when she continued her commitment to world peace as a volunteer. She was president of the WILPF, U.S. Section, 1928–33. In 1934–35 she served as the honorary WILPF international secretary-treasurer and on the death of JA became the organization's honorary international president. She favored disarmament, the use of sanctions, mediation over war, peace education, and cooperative economic and scientific efforts to bring people of different cultures together in peace. Emily Balch was a strong and dedicated ally of JA's in the struggle to promote and strengthen pacifism throughout the world. She died in a Cambridge, Mass., nursing home.

8. Emily Greene Balch had five sisters; however, by 1893 only four were living. They were Anne, Alice, Elizabeth (called Bessie), and Marion Cesares (called Maidie). Any one of them could have accompanied Emily to HH.

## Address at the World's Columbian Exposition

*Jane Addams and the Hull-House circle devoted almost all of 1893 to activities associated with the World's Columbian Exposition. Planning for their participation in the extravaganza began in earnest with the development of the World's Congress Auxiliary program in 1891. The goal of the auxiliary was to attract to the exposition world leaders expert in twenty different subject areas*[1] *in order to "establish mutual acquaintances and fraternal relations; to review in the congresses progress already achieved in the various subject areas; to define the still outstanding questions of the era; 'and to receive from eminent representatives of all interests, classes, and peoples, suggestions of the practical means by which further progress might be made and the prosperity and peace of the world advanced.'"*[2] *After the exposition had closed, the auxiliary reported, "One thousand two-hundred and eighty-three sessions were held, with 5,978 addresses or papers read by 5,822 speakers from 97 foreign nations as well as every state and territory in the United States."*[3] *Most of the congresses convened in the rooms of a new and grand structure on Michigan Avenue that would become the Art Institute of Chicago at the close of the exposition. Among the most exciting and well-attended gatherings were the*

Jane Addams attended the opening-day ceremonies of the World's Columbian Exposition on 1 May 1893. She and her reform-minded associates actively participated in the auxiliary congresses that took place during the exposition. Throughout the exposition, they promoted the social settlement idea and encouraged exposition participants to visit and experience Hull-House (CPL, WCE-CDA vol. 4, pl. 11).

*congresses on women's progress, education, labor, and religion, and Jane Addams participated in all of them.*

*The congresses offered the Hull-House leader a chance to share the stage with men and women associated with a vast array of countries, cultures, and experiences. Many of these luminaries were already well known and drew huge crowds when they spoke. Their remarks were often quoted in newspapers and periodicals, while Jane Addams was sometimes simply mentioned as a participant. Yet if this was an opportunity for Addams to meet national and even world leaders who shared her interests, it was, more important, a time for those same men and women to glimpse the slender, intelligent, organized, and articulate thirty-three-year-old Addams as she revealed a new and stark view of the lives of her neighbors; introduced her social experiment, Hull-House; and presented the budding U.S. social settlement movement to a national and international audience. "In these contacts are formed the circuits which constitute the currents of progress," wrote one reviewer of the benefits of the World's Columbian Exposition.*[4] *The congresses, especially, offered significant networking opportunities for Jane Addams.*

*Management of the local arrangements for the program of Congress of Representative Women, which met between 15 and 22 May 1893, was accomplished through volunteers organized into eight departments. Jane Addams served as the head of the conference committee for the Department of Industry. Among her committee members were Hull-House workers Florence Kelley, Ellen Gates Starr, Mary E. Kenney, and Alzina P. Stevens.*[5] *Their responsibility was to welcome attendees to the presentations associated with the department of industry, all held in Hall 21 of the still-under-construction building during the week of the congress. Some members of the committee were present each day during the hours of 9:00–10:00 A.M. and 12:30–8:00 P.M. as greeters and to help conduct informal meetings.*

*Jane Addams was active in planning for the Home Economics Congress from 1891 when she became a vice-president of the National Columbian Household Economic Association.*[6] *She helped organize the Single Tax Congress, held as part of the Social Service gathering, and at the same time as the Labor Congress.*[7] *In addition, she was a major participant in the development of the Labor Congress, when she served on the Women's Committee.*[8] *Addams was the driving force behind the Social Settlement Congress, which was held in conjunction with the Education Congress,*[9] *and she served as an advisory board member for the Congress of University Extension, also held during the Education Congress.*[10]

*Jane Addams spoke at the following congresses: Settlement,*[11] *Labor,*[12] *Representative Women,*[13] *Household Economics and Housekeepers,*[14] *Single Tax,*[15] *Religion, at gatherings of the Woman's Congregational Congress and the Evangelical Alliance Congress,*[16] *and Sunday Rest.*[17] *Most of her presentations focused on two themes. The first was a description of settlements, using Hull-House as an example. The second concerned the plight of working women and children.*

*Jane Addams's first major public solo appearance at the exposition took place during the Congress of Representative Women. According to the* Chicago Daily Tribune, *she read a "bright paper on the subject 'Domestic Service and the Family Claim'" during the morning session of the National Columbian Household Economic Association, held 19 May.*[18] *It was by relating observations from her settlement-house experiences that she hoped to interpret the working woman and to awaken among her listeners an appreciation for a working woman's point of view. This same presentation with minor changes became "Working Women in Two Related Trades," which she presented on 28 August during the first day of the Labor Congress in the session entitled "Industrial Conditions of Women and Children."*[19] *Jane Addams also used some of the same material in her remarks to the Woman's Congregational Congress on 12 September*[20] *during the Religious Congress and during the Congress of Sunday Rest, held on 30 September.*[21] *She also gave a version of this speech on 18 October at the Congress on Household Economics.*[22] *She drew on the same material once again for her remarks before the Columbian Association of Housekeepers gathered under the auspices of the auxiliary on 24 October 1893.*[23] *In addition, it became the basis for several different publications*[24] *and remained in Addams's repertoire of speeches well into the twentieth century.*[25]

*Jane Addams likely gave May Wright Sewall*[26] *the version of her address presented below. Sewall chaired the Committee on Organization of the Congress of Representative Women and was responsible for collecting the reports and papers presented at the gathering. She was the editor of the official record of the Congress of Representative Women, published in two volumes.*[27] *She tried to include "in whole or in part" all of the papers from the General Congress and at least one paper from each subordinate congress. She wrote letters to each of the speakers, requesting copies of their papers for presentation. "Many of the participants," Sewall reported, sent "their original manuscripts or carefully corrected type-written copies of them; many more, however, expressed their entire willingness to be represented by the editor's revision of the official reports of their work"*[28]

*Portions of the Jane Addams speech "Domestic Service and the Family Claim" appeared in the* Chicago Daily Tribune *on the day after Addams made the speech.*[29] *The* Tribune *account quoted two paragraphs from the presentation by Addams that are missing from the version that appeared in* The World's Congress of Representative Women, *edited by Sewall.*[30] *Jane Addams probably deleted these two paragraphs before she sent her paper to Sewall because it was text in those two paragraphs that caused the most unflattering reviews,*[31] *yet Sewall herself could also have deleted them. This version provides the most complete and earliest development of Addams's ideas on a subject she would return to again and again.*

## DOMESTIC SERVICE AND THE FAMILY CLAIM—

### ADDRESS BY JANE ADDAMS OF ILLINOIS

Chicago, Ill. 19 May 1893

Ever since we entered upon the industrial revolution of the eighteenth century, factory labor, work done in factories, has been increasingly competing in the open market with household labor—work done in private houses. Taking out of account women with little children or invalids dependent upon them, to whom both factory and household labor are impossible and who are practically confined to the sewing trades, to all untrained women seeking employment a choice is open between these two forms of labor. There are few women so dull that they can not paste labels on a box or do some form of factory work; few so dull that some perplexed housekeeper will not receive them, at least for a trial, into the household. Household labor, then, has to compete with factory labor not only in point of hours, in point of permanency of employment, in point of wages, but in point of the advantage it affords for family and social life; and all women seeking employment more or less consciously compare the two forms of labor in all these points.

The three points are easily disposed of. First: In regard to hours there is no doubt that the factory has the advantage. The average factory hours are from seven in the morning to six in the evening, with a chance of working overtime, which, in busy seasons, means until nine o'clock. This leaves most of the evenings and Sundays free. The average hours of household labor are from six in the morning to eight at night, with little difference in seasons. There is one afternoon a week, with an occasional evening, but Sunday is never wholly free.

Second: In regard to permanency of position the advantage is found clearly on the side of the household employé.

Third. In regard to wages the household is again fairly ahead, if we consider not alone the money received but also the opportunity offered for saving money. This is greater among household employés, because they do not pay board, the clothing required is simpler, and the temptation to spend money in recreation is less frequent. The average minimum wage paid an adult in household labor may be fairly put at two dollars and fifty cents a week; the maximum at six dollars, this excluding the comparatively rare opportunities for women to cook at forty dollars a month and the housekeeper's position at fifty dollars a month. The factory wages, viewed from the savings bank point of view, may be smaller in the average, but this I believe to be counterbalanced in the minds of the employés by the greater chance which the factory offers for increased wages. A girl over sixteen seldom works in a factory for less than four dollars a week, and she always cherishes the hope of being at least a forewoman with a permanent salary of from fifteen to twenty-five dollars a week. Whether she attains this or not she runs a fair chance, after serving a practical apprenticeship, of earning ten dollars a week as a skilled worker. A girl finds it easier to be content with four dollars a week when she pays for board, with a scale of wages rising toward ten dollars, than to be content with four dollars a week and board, the scale of wages rising to six dollars; and the girl well knows that there are scores of liberally paid forewomen at fifteen dollars a week for one forty-dollar cook or fifty-dollar housekeeper. In many cases this position is well taken economically, for, although the opportunity for saving may be better for the employé in the household than in the factory, her family saves more when she works in a factory and lives with them. The rent is no more when she is at home. The two dollars and fifty cents which she pays into the family fund more than covers the cost of her actual food, and at night she can often contribute toward the family labor by helping her mother wash and sew.

This brings us easily to the fourth point of comparison, that of the possibilities afforded for family life. It is well to remember that women, as a rule, are devoted to their families; that they want to live with their parents, their brothers and sisters, and kinsfolk, and will sacrifice a good deal to accomplish this. This devotion is so universal that it is impossible to ignore it when we consider women as employés. Young unmarried women are not detached from family claims and requirements as young men are, and, so far as my observation goes, are more ready and steady in their response to the needs of the aged parents and helpless members of the family. But women performing labor in households have peculiar difficulties in enjoying family life, and are more or less dependent upon their employers for possibilities to see their relatives and friends. Curiously enough, the same devotion to the family life and quick response to its claims on the part of the employer operate against the girl in household labor, and places her in the unique position of isolation. The employer of household labor, to preserve her family life intact and free from intrusion, acts inconsistently in her zeal, and grants to her cook, for instance, but once or twice a week such opportunity for untrammeled association with her relatives as the employer's family claims constantly. So strongly is the employer imbued with the sanctity of her own family life that this sacrifice of the cook's family life seems to her perfectly justifiable. If one chose to be jocose one might say that it becomes almost a religious devotion, in which the cook figures as a burnt offering and the kitchen range as the patriarchal altar.

This devotion to family life the men of the family also share. A New York gentleman who lunches at Delmonico's eats food cooked by a cook with a salary of five thousand dollars a year. He comes home hungry, and with a tantalizing memory of the lunch, to a dinner cooked by a cook who is paid at most forty dollars a month. The contrast between lunch and dinner is great and the solace of the family is needed to make the dinner endurable, but the aforesaid gentleman quiets discontent with the reflection that in eating a dinner cooked by an individual cook they are in some occult manner cherishing the sanctity of the family life, though his keen business mind knows full well that in actual money he is paying more for his badly cooked dinner than for his well-cooked lunch.

To return from the digression—this peculiar isolation of the household. In addition to her isolation from her family, a woman finds all the conditions of her social life suddenly changed when she enters the service of a household.[32] It is well to remember that the household employés for the better quarters of the city and the suburbs are largely drawn from the poorer quarters, which are nothing if not gregarious. The girl is born and reared in a tenement house full of children. She knows them almost as well as she knows her brothers and sisters, and plays with them almost as constantly. She goes to school, and there learns to march, to read, and to write in constant companionship with forty other children. If she lives at home until she is old enough to go to parties, those she goes to are mostly held in a public hall and are crowded with dancers. If she works in a factory she walks home with many other girls, in much the same spirit as she formerly walked to school with them. Most of the young men she knows are doing much the same sort of work, and she mingles with them in frank economic and social equality. If she is a cloak-maker, for instance, she will probably marry a cutter, who is a man with a good trade, and who runs a chance of some day having a shop of his own. In the meantime she remains at home, with no social break or change in her family and social life.

If she is employed in a household this is not true. Suddenly all the conditions of her life are changed. The individual instead of the gregarious instinct is appealed to. The change may be wholesome for her, but it is not easy; and the thought of the savings bank does not cheer us much when we are twenty. She is isolated from the people with whom she has been reared, with whom she has gone to school, with whom she has danced, and among whom she expects to live when she marries. She is naturally lonely and constrained.

Added to this is a social distinction, which she feels keenly, against her and in favor of the factory girls, in the minds of the young men of her acquaintance. A woman who has worked in households for twenty years told me that when she was a young and pretty nurse-girl the only young men who paid her attention were coachmen and unskilled laborers. The skill in the trades of her suitors increased as her position in the household increased in dignity. When she was a housekeeper, forty years old, skilled mechanics appeared, one of whom she married. Women seeking employment understand perfectly well this feeling, quite unjustifiable, I am willing to admit, among mechanics, and it acts as a strong inducement toward factory labor.

I have long since ceased to apologize for the views and opinions of working people. I am quite sure that, on the whole, they are just about as wise and just about as foolish as the views and opinions of other people; but that this particularly foolish opinion of young mechanics is widely shared by the employing class can be demonstrated easily.[33] It is only necessary to remind you of the number of Chicago night schools for instruction in stenography, in typewriting, telegraphy, bookkeeping, and all similar occupations, fitting girls for office work, and the meager number provided for acquiring skill in household work.

The contrast is further accentuated by the better social position of the office girls, and the advantages which she shares with factory girls, of lunch clubs, social clubs, and vacation homes, from which girls performing household labor are practically excluded by their hours of work, their geographical situation, and a curious feeling that they are not as interesting as factory girls.

PD (*World's Congress of Representative Women*, vol. 2. Edited by May Wright Sewall [Chicago: Rand McNally, 1894], 626–31).

1. The subject areas were woman's progress, public press, medicine and surgery, temperance, moral and social reform, commerce and finance, music, literature, education, engineering, art, government, general, science and philosophy, social and economic science, labor, religion, Sunday rest, public health, and agriculture. Most of these subject areas were divided into smaller, more focused areas of consideration. For example, the congress on women's progress had twenty-five divisions, education thirty-three divisions, and religion forty-six divisions. Gatherings sponsored by the divisions took place coincidentally with the congress with which they were allied and usually at the same time.

2. H. N. Higinbotham, *Report of the President to the Board of Directors of the World's Columbian Exposition* (Chicago: Rand McNally, 1895), 327–28, quoted in Burg, *Chicago's White City of 1893*, 236.

3. Johnson, *A History of the World's Columbian Exposition*, 1:6–7.

4. Hardy, "Last Impressions," 199.

5. For a biographical note on Alzina P. Stevens, see JA to Richard T. Ely, 31 Oct. 1894, n. 10, below.

6. The congress of the National Columbian Household Economic Assn. was held on 19 May 1893 during the Congress of Representative Women.

7. The Single Tax Congress was held coincidentally with the Labor Congress between 27 Aug. and 4 Sept. 1893.

It was a gathering of those who hoped to promote the ideas that Henry George had presented in his book *Progress and Poverty* (1879). The basis for George's theory was that the people of a country owned its land and all of its resources. The land could be rented by those who wanted to use it for dwelling or enterprise. The rent was to be paid to the people through government property tax. The tax had to be high enough to provide sufficient revenue for the government to operate successfully and would be the only tax, or the "single tax," because taxes on labor income and capital earnings would be eliminated. George believed that his "single tax" would promote the highest and best use of property and provide a stronger and more robust economy by encouraging work and capital investment.

8. The Labor Congress opened 28 Aug. and ended on Labor Day, Monday, 4 Sept. 1893. Planning for the Labor Congress, carried out by separate committees of men and women, began early in 1892. By the end of the year, the two committees agreed on a program of seven parts. The concentrations were to be the history of labor, present state of labor, displacement of labor by machinery and immigration, labor troubles, industrial organizations, labor legislation, and remedies for abolition of industrial warfare. The Women's Com., headed initially by Julia Plato Harvey and numbering among its members JA and HH workers Alzina P. Stevens, Julia C. Lathrop, Florence Kelley, and EGS, threatened resignation when their program plans were rejected by Charles C. Bonney, president of the auxiliary (for a biographical note on Charles C. Bonney, see Robert A. Woods to JA, 20 June 1893, n. 1, below). "We believe," they wrote, "that no adequate presentation of the labor question, which now agitates the entire civilized world, is contemplated by the controlling power of the auxiliary, and we are not willing to have any appearance of connection with what will be offered as a substitute for a real labor congress" ("Women Declare War"). Bonney backed down, and the two committees, led in large part by Henry Demarest Lloyd and JA, settled on a general program that included the following general sessions: the condition of labor, work and wages of women and children, labor statistics, literature and philosophy of the labor movement, labor legislation, arbitration and other remedies, and living questions and means of progress. The opening of the Labor Congress was described in "Congress of Labor. Formally Opened to Discuss Pressing Problems" and the program for the congress in "Men Who Lighten Labor's Burdens." In addition, events that were planned for the congress were described in *Programme of the Department of Labor* (Chicago: W. B. Conkey, 1893).

9. The Congress of Social Settlements was held 19–21 July 1893, during the Education Congress. See Robert A. Woods to JA, 20 June 1893, below.

10. Other Chicagoans serving with JA as members of the advisory council of the Congress of University Extension were William Rainey Harper, president of the Univ. of Chicago, who was president of the advisory council; Alice Freeman Palmer and Dr. Thomas Chrowder Chamberlin, both from the Univ. of Chicago; Henry Wade Rogers, president of Northwestern Univ.; and Ellen Henrotin, member of the CWC and other cultural organizations in the city. They helped the arrangements committee plan the congress.

11. See Robert A. Woods to JA, 20 June 1893, below.

12. The ceremonial beginning of the Labor Congress was held at 10:00 A.M. on 28 Aug. 1893, in the Hall of Columbus in the Art Institute Building on Michigan Ave. JA sat on the platform and made one of the welcoming addresses. Among the other welcoming speakers were Henry Demarest Lloyd, Ellen Henrotin, socialist labor leader Thomas J. Morgan, and auxiliary president Charles C. Bonney. At 11:00 A.M. that same day, JA appeared with other primarily female speakers in the Hall of Washington in the same building to present her paper "Working Women in Two Related Trades," for the session on Industrial Conditions of Women and Children. Those attending the Single Tax Congress that took place coincidentally with the Labor Congress were encouraged to attend her presentation. She had been scheduled to

speak on settlements and HH but suggested to Henry Demarest Lloyd, "If it is not too late to give the title of my paper for the Labor Congress I should like it to read—'Working women in two Related Trades.' I think that I could have it ready by Aug. 15th" (JA to Henry Demarest Lloyd, [29 July 1893], SHSW, Lloyd; *JAMC*, 2:1457–58). Chicago newspapers had trouble accurately reporting the title of JA's remarks. On 30 Aug., the *Chicago Inter Ocean* indicated that the title of JA's speech was "Working Women in Two Berated Trades." The *Chicago Daily Tribune* reported it incorrectly twice, once using the same title that the *Chicago Inter Ocean* used and once altering the title to "Working Women in Two Belated Trades."

13. JA spoke twice before the Women's Representative Congress. She presented "Domestic Service and the Family Claim" before the National Columbian Household Economic Assn., held in conjunction with the Women's Representative Congress on 19 May. On the next evening at 7:45 P.M., JA appeared as one of the speakers for the session Organization among Women as an Instrument in Promoting the Interests of Industry.

14. See n. 12. On 18 Oct. 1893, JA addressed the Congress on Household Economics. According to the *Chicago Daily Tribune* article "How to Drain Roads," 19 Oct. 1893, she "spoke upon the value of work done by specialists, thereby establishing trades and schools of household science." Later, on 24 Oct., in the Recital Hall of the Auditorium Building, and under the auspices of the woman's board of the congress auxiliary of the exposition, JA presented remarks entitled "Club Life among Employees" for the Congress of the Columbian Assn. of Housekeepers.

15. With the title of her speech incorrectly presented as "Working Women in Two Berated [Related] Trades," the *Chicago Daily Tribune* remarked with a hint of sarcasm that "Miss Addams would do away with the cook, as shoemakers and blacksmiths are done away with—namely: by having one large factory where all cooking should be done, as shoes are made at big factories instead of by individual shoemakers" ("Single Tax League Discussion"). The *Chicago Inter Ocean* also summarized her presentation: "The trades were those of sewing and domestic service. She said that the tendency of the modern home was to insolate [isolate] the servant girl and the seamstress, and therein she saw the great difficulty attending the securement of intelligent people in those employments. She believed that the house servant was to pass out of existence just as the family blacksmith had done and that cooperation would succeed present methods" ("Woman as Worker. Her Condition Discussed at the Labor Congress").

16. JA spoke before the Women's Congregational Congress on 12 Sept. 1893. In the record of the Congress of Religion presented by Rev. John Henry Barrows, who organized the congress and then served as president of Oberlin College from 1899 until his death, JA's remarks were given the following summary statement: "The Home and Labor Problem was spoken of by Miss Jane Addams, of Hull-House, Chicago, whose work enables her to speak as one having authority. The labor question was the question of the home; it could not be settled till settled right; it must be taken into the homes, and boys and girls trained to see that other boys and girls have equal rights to home and chance for growth and equitable reward for work" (Barrows, *The World's Parliament of Religions* 2:1434–35). According to the *Chicago Daily Tribune*, "Miss Jane Addams of Hull House read an address on the relation of the Christian home to the labor problem. She said the labor problem was the question of the hour. Nothing could be settled until it was settled, and the Christian home that neglected this made a great mistake" ("Beauties of the Christian Home," 13 Sept. 1893). For her appearance at the Evangelical Alliance Congress on 8 Oct. 1893, her topic was "Social Settlements."

17. At the Sunday Rest Congress, JA was scheduled to speak in the session entitled Church and Sociological Questions. In her remarks, titled "Social Relations," she presented her views "on the subject of more leisure for working-people." She stated, "Any one who has lived among the working-people realizes that the great want is the want of imagination, the want of a higherlife,—the sort of life which people take great pains to get; for which they go to college;

for which they go to Europe; for which they read and study long and wearisome hours,—to get themselves out of the humdrum life, to that wider life we find in books. Hence the desire for righteousness, which I believe is stronger in the hearts of sturdy working-people than in any other class. I believe it is a feeling after the higher and better life.

"It seems to me that the Sabbath is a sort of life-saving station for this higher life" (*The Sunday Problem: Papers Presented at the International Congress on Sunday Rest, Chicago, Sept. 28–30, 1893* [New York: Baker and Taylor, 1894], 28–29). The *Chicago Daily Tribune* offered the following description of JA's presentation: "Miss Jane Addams of Hull House spoke briefly on the desire and necessity of weekly relief from incessant work, saying that only by cooperation could Sunday rest be preserved" ("Need One Day's Rest in Seven," 30 Sept. 1893).

18. In "Home Has Its Day," the *Chicago Daily Tribune*, 20 May 1893, quoted several paragraphs of JA's remarks. See nn. 32–33.

19. The Single Tax Congress also counted JA among its speakers that day, identifying the same JA speech as part of their congress. See n. 12.

20. See n. 16.

21. See n. 17.

22. See n. 13.

23. See n. 13

24. "A Belated Industry" was published in the *American Journal of Sociology* 1 (Mar. 1896): 536–50. The *Chicago Daily Tribune* also reprised portions of JA's arguments in "Why Servants Are Scarce" on 1 Mar. 1896. *Review of Reviews* offered "The Problem of Domestic Service Viewed Scientifically" on pp. 604–5 in vol. 12, issued May 1896.

25. Later the *Chautauqua Assembly Herald* 25 (11 Aug. 1900): 7 featured "Democracy and Domestic Service," and vol. 11 of the *Journal of Home Economics* issued "A Belated Industry" (Aug. 1919): 355–64.

26. May Eliza Wright Sewall (1844–1920), educator, reformer, club woman, suffragist, and pacifist, born in Milwaukee, Wis., studied at home with her parents, Philander Montague and Mary Weeks Brackett Wright. She earned a mistress of science degree in 1866 and a master of arts in 1871 from Northwestern Female College, which became part of Northwestern Univ., Evanston, Ill. A teacher, she settled with her first husband, Edwin W. Thompson, in Indianapolis, where both taught until his death in 1875. In 1880 she remarried. Theodore Lovett Sewall, also an experienced teacher, and his new wife founded the Girls' Classical School of Indianapolis in 1882. After her second husband died in 1895, May Wright Sewall continued until 1907 as the head of the school that was focused on educating young women. She was also a leader in organizing support for woman suffrage in Indiana and was chairman of the executive committee of the NWSA, 1882–90. She served as the first recording secretary for the National Council of Women, organized in 1888, and was its president, 1897–99. An internationalist, she was a primary organizing force behind the World's Congress of Representative Women, and she traveled extensively in Europe, 1891–92, to promote the official gathering of more than three hundred women and to enlist speakers and participants. From 1899 until 1904, she was president of the International Council of Women. During the last fifteen years of her life, she became an active pacifist. In 1915, at the Panama-Pacific Exposition in San Francisco, she called for and led the International Conf. of Women Workers to Promote Permanent Peace and sailed on board Henry Ford's peace ship, *Oscar II*, as part of the attempt to avert World War I.

27. *The World's Congress of Representative Women, a Historical Resume for Popular Circulation of the World's Congress of Representative Women, Convened in Chicago on May 15, and Adjourned on May 22, 1893, under the Auspices of the Woman's Branch of the World's Congress Auxiliary* was edited by May Wright Sewall, who identified herself as chairman of the committee of organization. It was issued in two volumes, printed as one, by Rand, McNally and Co., of New York and Chicago in 1894. Vol. 1 contained chaps. 1–8 on the following topics:

introduction; preparations; education; literature and the dramatic art; science and religion; charity, philanthropy, and religion; moral and social reform; and the civil and political status of women. Vol. 2 continued chaps. 9–15 with the following topics: civil law and government; industries and occupations; the solidarity of human interests; education and literature; religion; industrial, social, and moral reform; and orders and civil and political reform. JA's article appeared in vol. 2 in chap. 10 on industries and occupations.

28. "Editor's Concluding Note," 927.

29. See n. 13.

30. See nn. 32–33.

31. See nn. 32–33.

32. In the article titled "Home Has Its Day," *Chicago Daily Tribune*, 20 May 1893, the following paragraph of JA's text, omitted by May Wright Sewall in her presentation of JA's speech, appears between the sentence that ends "when she enters the service of a household" and before the beginning of the next sentence: "It is well to remember . . .":

"The peculiar isolation of the household employé, away from her own family life, considered from the economic standpoint, is quite unique. As industrial conditions have changed the household has simplified from the medieval affair of journeymen apprentices and maidens, who spun and hewed, to the family proper—to those who love one another and live together in ties of affection and consanguinity. Were this process complete we should have no problem of household employment. But even in households comparatively humble, there is still one alien, one who is neither loved nor loving. The modern family has dropped the man who made its shoes, the woman who spun its clothes, and to a large extent the woman who washes them, but it stoutly refuses to drop the woman who cooks its food. It strangely insists that to do that would be to destroy the family itself. The cook is uncomfortable, the family is uncomfortable, but it will not drop her as all her fellow-workers have been dropped, though the cook herself insists upon it."

33. In the article titled "Home Has Its Day," *Chicago Daily Tribune*, 20 May 1893, the following paragraph of JA's text, omitted by May Wright Sewall in her presentation of JA's speech, appears after the sentence that ends: "employing class can be demonstrated easily" and before the sentence that begins "It is only necessary . . .":

"In addition to the isolations of the household employé, away from her natural family ties, she is also isolated industrially. Whether we recognize or not this isolation as a cause I think we are all ready to acknowledge that household labor has been in some way belated. There is nothing more devastating to the inventive faculties, more fatal to a flow of mind and spirits, than the constant feeling of loneliness and the absence of fellowship."

## From Robert A. Woods

*On 10 January 1893, Jane Addams wrote to Charles C. Bonney,[1] president of the World's Congress Auxiliary of the World's Columbian Exposition, to request a time and place for a gathering of people engaged in the development of the social settlement movement. "I shall be very glad," Bonney responded on 14 January, "to make a suitable assignment of rooms and definite dates for a Social Settlement Conference or Congress to be held in connection with the Educational Congress of 1893, which will commence on Monday July 12 and extend to Saturday July 29; and that your assignment will be made in compliance with your request in close connection with the University Extension Conference."[2] The dates chosen for the Congress of Social Settlements were 19 to 21 July.*

Robert A. Woods, who, in 1892, became head resident at Andover House (renamed South End House, 1895) in Boston, was one of the early leaders of the social settlement movement. He and Jane Addams often worked together organizing national meetings of settlement workers. He helped promote the settlement house movement through his writings (Andover Theological Seminary, Newton, Mass., Library).

*Jane Addams was aware of the positive benefits to Hull-House and the settlement movement that resulted from the meeting during the Summer School of Applied Ethics in 1892. She saw the exposition as an opportunity to continue the discussions begun at Plymouth, Mass., and to gain support for the new social settlement movement. She immediately formed a planning committee,[3] which she cochaired with Charles Zueblin,[4] who was in the process of helping to create Northwestern University Settlement in Chicago. The committee members corresponded frequently[5] with other settlement leaders in the United States and in Europe to seek recommendations for topics and to encourage participation and attendance. In April they sent out an official call to announce the congress for July.[6] On Jane Addams's lecturing trip to the East in February, she met with settlement leaders in Boston to gather their ideas for the congress. On 7 May and again on 1 June, the committee met at Hull-House to plan the program, events, and speakers for the congress.[7]*

*Robert A. Woods,[8] head of Andover House, Boston, made his first visit to Hull-House to attend the second committee meeting. In addition, he was there to plan the weeklong program on social settlements that he and Jane Addams were to participate in jointly at the Chautauqua encampment in New York from 10 to 16 July 1893.*

Lima, O[hio].,  June 20, 1893

My dear Miss Addams,

I have looked over the list of topics and have put down my suggestions. Perhaps you will add yours and then pass this on the Mr. Vincent.[9]

In my hurry to get my train, I forgot to say good-by to Miss Anna Lathrop and to Mrs Linn and Mrs. Haldeman.[10] Will you kindly say a goodbye for me.

I have been thinking that it would be a good thing in several ways to hold in connection with our Conference a meeting at one of the main <Chicago> churches on Sunday evening preceding for the sake of showing clearly the religious bearings of Settlement work, for the sake of showing that settlement work is in itself religious. Presented wisely I think such a suggestion would do a great deal for the idea in general ~~for settlements in general~~ and for Hull House, particularly. We want I think to claim the full power of the religious motive, with perfect freedom in putting it in action.

I would rather have the meeting in a church than in the Art Institute,—in some church where the minister is openly friendly.

I merely suggest this to you Miss Addams. It will stand or fall as you think it would ~~hinder or~~ help or hinder you at Hull House. I am thinking all the time however of the duty of the settlements to the Church and to current Christianity.[11]

I enjoyed my stay at Hull House very, very much. I believe you are doing the best piece of social work that is being done anywhere in the country, and the future of Hull House seems to me to be filed with great promise. I want you to make me a sort of non-resident resident, so that I may come whenever I can get to Chicago and stay at the Men's Settlement[12] on the same terms as the others as to tariff and as to duties to be done.

I was sorry to miss Barnes[13] as I came away, but we shall have a chance for further talks.

With good wishes to Miss Starr (who I suppose will be ready to talk some when she gets back from her silent retreat) and to all the others, Faithfully yrs

Robert. A. Woods.

Address: till June 24.
Ohio Nat. Bank
Lima, O.
after that
Hubbard, O.

ALS (SCPC, JAC; *JAPM*, 2:1438–41).

1. Charles C. Bonney (1831–1903), lawyer, judge, and teacher, was born in Hamilton, N.Y., and educated at Colgate Univ., where he received his LL.D. He moved to Peoria, Ill., and there he founded a school, became a lecturer at Peoria College, and helped establish the state school system. Admitted to the bar in 1852, he moved to Chicago in 1860 and by 1866 had become an Illinois Supreme Court judge. Active in the Illinois State Bar Assn., where he

became president in 1882, and in the American Bar Assn., where he became vice-president in 1887, he was also the author of books about insurance law and laws for railway carriers. He was best known for his role as the president of the World's Columbian Exposition Auxiliary. A member of the New Jerusalem Church, his special interest was the World's Parliament of Religions, held as a congress during the exposition. He authored two works relating to the auxiliary: *The World's Parliament of Religions* and *The World's Congress Addresses*. He died in Chicago after a three-year illness.

2. SCPC, JAC; *JAPM*, 2:1367.

3. JA asked Charles N. Zueblin (see n. 4), head of Northwestern University Settlement, the other developing social settlement in Chicago at the time and the first university settlement in the city, to share the chairmanship of the planning committee with her. In addition, the members from Chicago were EGS, Julia C. Lathrop, and Alexander A. McCormick. Vida Dutton Scudder of Wellesley and Robert A. Woods, both from the Boston area, and James Bronson Reynolds, whom JA hoped to rely on to identify and attract speakers and participants from Europe, composed the active committee.

Vida Dutton Scudder (1861–1954), settlement worker, scholar, socialist, and social reformer, was educated in private schools in the Boston area, Smith College, and Oxford Univ., after which she assumed a teaching post in the English department at Wellesley College. She was one of the organizers of the College Settlement Assn. and served from its beginning in 1889 as secretary of the electoral board of the association. A year's absence from Wellesley in 1893 gave her an opportunity to help Helena Dudley in opening Denison House, a settlement in Boston's South End. For the next almost twenty years, while she taught at Wellesley, she devoted time and behind-the-scenes leadership to the settlement. A staunch member of the Episcopal Church and the Women's Society of the Companions of the Holy Cross, in 1911 she was a founder of the Episcopal Church Socialist League, meant to encourage the blending of Christian and socialist ideas. In the same year, she joined and became active as a member of the Socialist Party. Although she supported President Wilson's decision to enter World War I, after the war she became associated with pacifist organizations, including the WILPF, for which she presented some lectures, and the Fellowship of Reconciliation. In 1928, after her resignation from Wellesley, where she was often in trouble with the administration for her radical socialism, she devoted more of her time to research and writing about religious matters and became a noted scholar of the history of the Franciscans. Among her sixteen books were works on literary, political, and religious subjects; novels; and two autobiographical volumes. She died at her home in Wellesley, Mass.

James Bronson Reynolds (1861–1924) was born in Klantone, N.Y., the son of William T. and Sarah M. Painter Reynolds. A graduate of Yale (A.B. 1884; B.D. 1888), he did postgraduate work in Paris and Berlin and was a fellow in sociology at Columbia before studying law at New York Law School in 1900. It was not surprising that JA selected him to help attract European attention to the settlement conference. Between 1889 and 1893, he served as an official representative of the College YMCA of America in Europe while he studied social reforms in England and on the Continent. In 1894 he became head worker at the University Settlement in New York City. He was active in a number of reform campaigns in New York, and in 1900 Theodore Roosevelt appointed him a member of the New York State Tenement House Comm. In the early 1900s, he headed investigations of Chicago's stockyards and industrial conditions in Panama. Between 1910 and 1913, he was district attorney for New York Co. and from 1910 to 1916 served as counsel to the American Social Hygiene Assn. He married Florence Blanchard Dike in 1898 and lived in North Haven, Conn., where he died.

4. Charles Newton Zueblin (1866–1924) (sometimes spelled Zeublin in error), who by his own definition became a publicist, was the organizer of the Northwestern University Settlement in Dec. 1891. It was the fifth social settlement formed in the United States and the second social settlement and the first university settlement to be founded in the Chicago area.

Zueblin, who was also a sociologist and trained in theology, was the son of Henrietta Follett and John E. Zueblin. He was born in Indiana and schooled in Philadelphia. He attended the Univ. of Pennsylvania (1883–85), graduated from Northwestern Univ. (Ph.B. 1887) and Yale Univ. (D.B. 1889), and concentrated on Old Testament studies at Leipzig Univ. (1889–91). On his return from Europe, Zueblin accepted an appointment from the Methodist City Mission in a section of Chicago colonized primarily by Poles, Germans, and Scandinavians. Living in the area, he became more interested in their welfare than in the evangelistic mission for which he had been hired. Influenced by Toynbee Hall and HH, he determined to found a social settlement with the help of his alma mater. In 1892 he was appointed by Univ. of Chicago president William Rainey Harper as secretary in the university's new University Extension Dept. That same year, he became an instructor in the Dept. of Sociology and ten years later achieved the rank of professor. He wrote numerous journal articles and between 1911 and 1912 was the editor of *Twentieth Century Magazine.* Among his books were *American Municipal Progress* (1902; rev. 1915) and *A Decade of Civil Development* (1905). In 1901–2 he was president of the American League for Civic Improvement and served, 1901–5, as a member of the Chicago Special Park Comm. He was married to Aurora ("Rho") Fisk in June 1892, and the couple had at least one child, Anne, who was for a time secretary for the WILPF while living at HH. "Rho" Zueblin held reading parties in the 1894 HH Summer School and at the settlement.

While he lived in Chicago, Zueblin maintained a close relationship with JA and HH. He lectured at the settlement on several occasions, speaking primarily about reform in England, and prepared a chapter, "The Chicago Ghetto," for *HH Maps and Papers* (1895). Although it is likely that JA, with the advice of James Bronson Reynolds and Robert A. Woods, actually did most of the planning for the Social Settlement Congress, 1893, Zueblin was identified in reports about the gathering as the co-convener with JA. At the conference he presented "The Settlement as a Station for Sociological Study" and was the chairman of two of the sessions.

5. Of the thirty-four pieces of known extant JA correspondence for 1893, twenty-four concern the settlement congress. The planning committee had wanted to attract at least one experienced settlement house leader from England. JA had hoped the Barnetts would come, but on 7 May 1893 Samuel Barnett wrote to JA, "We have just cabled that we must give up any hope of making America this year. . . . We are disappointed, we had pictured much new experience & much pleasure in meeting old friends" (SCPC, JAC; *JAPM*, 2:1402). Several other letters were from English settlement leaders who also indicated that they would not be able to attend. Three were from James Bronson Reynolds, and two were from Robert A. Woods about plans for the event. Additional letters concern speakers who agreed to participate and others who did not.

6. The call for the Congress on Social Settlements was sent out in the late spring of 1893. The gathering was to be held in Memorial Art Palace, 19–21 July 1893. The circular indicated there would be three general subject areas: the settlement idea, aspects of settlement work, and the importance of the settlement to industrial reform. It stated, "It is proposed to hold in connection with the World's Congress Auxiliary of the Columbian Exposition a conference of persons actively interested in the University Settlements and other similar establishments that have taken their suggestion from Toynbee Hall. . . . The Settlement stands for a new kind of effort on the part of educated men and women both toward a better understanding of the conditions of life among working people and a more complete identification with their interests, and toward bringing directly to an industrial neighborhood, in a way to quicken its own energy and self-reliance, all the better influences which the resources of modern society supply. Its method can never become rigid, for the Settlement aims at adaption to varying and developing needs rather than adherence to predetermined lines of action. Although the movement is yet very new, and may still stand only for a social experiment, yet it is believed that there are so many elements of vital consequence in the experiment that its

various phases may well be carefully considered, as they appear. It is particularly important that when there are no precedents to follow, there should be comparison of principle and action among contemporaries" (Learned, "Social Settlements in the United States," 109). The call was written by a committee composed of JA, EGS, Alexander A. McCormick, Julia C. Lathrop, and Robert A. Woods. The signers were JA, EGS, and Julia C. Lathrop, identified with HH; Vida Dutton Scudder, Wellesley College; Charles Zueblin of the Univ. of Chicago; Robert A. Woods, Andover House, Boston; Alexander A. McCormick, identified as being from Chicago, but who was extremely active at HH; and James B. Reynolds, who identified himself as being associated with the World's Fair.

7. The two planning committee meetings resulted in a program that followed the committee's announced plan. Robert A. Woods presented a paper on the history of the settlement house movement. It was followed by reports from a variety of U.S. settlements. For the next three sessions, the speakers considered the settlement and its relationship to the following subjects: university extension, universities, charitable institutions, municipal reform, tenement houses, organized social work, organized religious work, art movement, religious movement, cooperative enterprise, and sociological study. Among the speakers were Florence Kelley; Helena Dudley of Denison House, Boston; Rev. Graham Taylor, soon to found the Chicago Commons; Fannie W. McLean of the College Settlement, New York City; and R. D. Roberts, secretary of the London Society for University Extension, the only presenter who was from another country. A much larger audience attended the Thursday-evening symposium, "The Settlement in Its Relation to the Labor Movement," than the average of seventy-five people who attended the other sessions. Prof. Edward Cummings of Harvard Univ., who had written a critique of university settlements that appeared in the Apr. 1892 issue of the *Quarterly Journal of Economics*, presented a paper entitled "Weak Points in the Settlement Method." The congress ended with two papers on the subject "The Ideals of Future Society as Evolved in a Settlement." One was offered by Charles Zueblin, the other by Rev. W. D. P. Bliss of the Brotherhood of the Carpenter, Boston (read by Rev. C. W. Barnes of Chicago). JA served as the convener of two sessions and spoke, along with Henry Demarest Lloyd, Florence Kelley, Abraham Bisno, and Mary E. Kenney, as a member of the symposium on the settlement and the labor movement.

This settlement gathering, sometimes considered the first national meeting of social settlements, received almost no newspaper coverage. *Unity* presented a brief description of its events in an editorial in its 27 July 1893 issue. Henry Barrett Learned (1868–1931), a resident in the HH men's quarters and a history teacher at the University School, Chicago, provided the most extensive coverage of the occasion in his article "Social Settlements in the United States" for the *University Extension World*, Apr. 1894. When the article was published, he had just received a master's degree from the Univ. of Chicago and was to become the head of the history department of Armour Institute of Technology in Chicago, 1894–96.

Learned was active at HH. He began teaching elementary Latin in the HH College Extension Program in Jan. 1893. Over the summer of 1893, he hosted studies in American biography; read from the biographies of Webster, Clay, and Calhoun; and discussed policies these leaders helped implement. In the fall of 1894, he held a Greek history class.

Learned studied history in Germany, 1899–1900, and returned to become an instructor in history at Yale's Sheffield Scientific School while he earned a Ph.D. (1909). After two years in Washington, D.C., with the U.S. Dept. of Justice in the Bureau of Investigation, 1917–19, he taught at Stanford Univ. beginning in 1920. In 1923 and 1928, he was a delegate to the International Congress on History. He was author of studies on the presidents' cabinets. He died in Washington, D.C.

8. Robert Archey Woods (1865–1925), settlement house leader, social worker, and author, was one of the five children of Robert and Mary Hall Campbell Woods in Pittsburgh, Pa. He graduated from Amherst College (1886) and attended Andover Theological Seminary

(1886–90), where he was strongly influenced by William Jewett Tucker (1839–1926), avid proponent of the social gospel. He spent the last six months of 1890 in England living for at least three of those months in Toynbee Hall. In 1891 he began founding what in early 1892 became Andover House, soon to be renamed South End House and located at 16 Rollins St. (later 20 Union Park) in Boston. He remained its head resident and leader until his death. He helped found the National Federation of Settlements of which he was secretary, 1911–23, and then for the succeeding years and until his death was its president. He was honored as president of the National Conf. of Social Work (NCSW), 1917–18. Through his many publications, he was a major reporter and historian for the social settlement movement. Among his works are *English Social Movements* (1891), *The Neighborhood in Nation Building* (1923), and, with Albert J. Kennedy (1879–1968), *Handbook of Settlements* (1911) and *The Settlement Horizon* (1922). A lecturer at Andover Seminary on social economics, 1890–95, and at Episcopal Theological School, Cambridge, Mass., 1896–1914, he also served as president of the Boston Social Union from 1908 until his death. In 1902 he wed Eleanor Howard Bush. He received honorary degrees from Amherst College (A.M. 1908) and Harvard Univ. (1910).

9. Founder of the Chautauqua movement John H. Vincent (see *PJA*, 2:530–31, n. 14). Robert A. Woods and JA were to be major presenters for a weeklong program on social settlements at the summer encampment at Chautauqua, N.Y., which began 1 July 1893. They were in the midst of planning for their presentations and identifying additional speakers.

10. HH was full of the relatives of founders and residents who were attending the World's Columbian Exposition or planning events that took place in concert with the fair. JA's sisters were there, and so was Julia Lathrop's sister, Anna.

The second girl of five children born to Sarah Adeline Potter and successful attorney and civic leader William Lathrop, who wed in June 1857, Anna Hubbell Lathrop (1860–1944) attended Rockford schools. A graduate of Vassar College (A.B. 1883), Anna returned to Rockford, where she taught Latin in public school and served as a tutor. She taught a reading party entitled Modern Novelists at the HH Summer Schools of 1891 and 1892. When the settlement founded its New England Kitchen at the beginning of the summer, 1893, she was placed in charge by JA and became a HH resident. She had been trained in Boston in New England Kitchen methods organized through the efforts of Ellen H. Richards to "scientifically" feed the working poor (Hunt, *The Life of Ellen H. Richards*, 215). She left HH in Oct. 1894 to return to Rockford. On 5 May 1897, she married Union College graduate and Charles City, Iowa, lawyer and banker Almon G. Case (d. 1904). While her sister, Julia Lathrop, was director of the U.S. Children's Bureau, she lived with her in Washington, D.C., and in 1910–11 she and Julia toured Europe together. Back in Rockford, she served as chairwoman of Rockford's first Red Cross chapter and later helped found the Visiting Nurse Assn. in Rockford and served on its board until her death. She was a member of the Rockford Woman's Club and organized a Vassar Club in Rockford. In 1934 she provided financial assistance and access to family documents and photographs for JA and Grace Abbott as they began their biographical treatment of Julia Lathrop. *My Friend, Julia Lathrop*, written by JA, was published posthumously in Nov. 1935 with slight revisions carried out "with scrupulous care, making as few changes as possible" by Alice Hamilton (Addams, *My Friend*, vi). Anna Case spent the last eleven months of her life in a hospital in Kenilworth, Ill., where she died.

11. Woods believed that settlement work had a basis in religion and that it should be recognized. "Let us have aggressive religious propaganda," he wrote in the early 1890s, "but as long as it is necessarily socially divisive, let us keep it separate from certain other noble interests of life, as to which we can establish a genuine catholicity of sympathy" (E. Woods, *Robert A. Woods*, 73). Looking back on the early days of settlement development, he wrote in *Neighborhood in Nation Building*, published in 1923, "[W]hile a university settlement, no more than a university itself, should be committed to a theological and ecclesiastical propaganda, yet both must, if they are to have a mission to the whole of men's higher life, be ready

to meet men on the religious side of their nature. From this point of view a settlement ought to undertake its work feeling the stirring of the religious motive. It ought to be prepared to bring to the people the influences of a broad and free religious enthusiasm, which shall show the insignificance of differences compared with the unity of spirit in which every man is in some sense religious. . . . From this point of view it is an essential part of the residents' social work in the neighborhood to enter into friendly cooperation with the religious work that is being done there, especially with the hope of bringing in a greater and greater element of that religion which is pure and undefiled" (18).

Woods hoped that JA would pursue a religious connection for the Congress of Social Settlements, but the Sunday-evening gathering never materialized. Perhaps it was because, as Woods cautioned, "it would [not?] be well to have the Sunday evening meeting unless we can get some well known religious leader," and they were unable to secure an appropriate speaker (Robert A. Woods to JA, 26 June 1893, SCPC, JAC; *JAPM*, 2:1449).

In *Twenty Years*, JA wrote, "Throughout the history of Hull-House many inquiries have been made concerning the religion of the residents, and the reply that they are as diversified in belief and in the ardor of the inner life as any like number of people in a college or similar group, apparently does not carry conviction. I recall that after a house for men residents had been opened on Polk Street and the residential force at Hull-House numbered twenty, we made an effort to come together on Sunday evenings in a household service, hoping thus to express our moral unity in spite of the fact that we represented many creeds. . . . [W]e concluded at the end of the winter that this was not religious fellowship and that we did not care for another reading club" (448–49). A "diversity of creed was part of the situation in American Settlements, as it was our task to live in a neighborhood of many nationalities and faiths, and that it might be possible that among such diversified people it was better that the Settlement corp should also represent varying religious beliefs" (450).

"Robert Woods decided to change the name of Andover House in 1895 to South End House 'in order to release the settlement from certain restraints which the old name placed upon its natural progress'" (Davis, *Spearheads*, 15). While the work of HH was featured prominently in a supportive way in the publications of various denominations and religious movements, the settlement had its detractors because it was not prominently religious and did not promote Christianity with zeal. In the beginning, JA and EGS sought the approval of the Protestant religious establishment of Chicago. They saw value and coinciding interests in developing those relationships. But as time passed and the settlement developed to promote fellowship and mutual respect for all views of a higher power, the connections eroded. The diversity the settlement model attracted and the founders promoted did not fit easily with any one Christian denomination. JA's unwillingness to align the settlement with a religious organization and view lost her support among some religious leaders and groups in the city.

JA seemed to understand that HH, in its primarily Roman Catholic neighborhood, could not proselytize if it was to continue to be of service to its neighbors, yet by 1893 Protestant leaders were beginning to criticize its neutrality. *Unity* in its 27 July 1893 issue quoted the *Independent*, summarizing material from the *Living Church*, which reported that settlements "'openly and completely ignore all religious restraints;' that their 'principles are purely worldly, and that they aim at worldly results only,' and are 'necessarily antagonistic to Christianity and religion'" ("Men and Things"). In "The Mission of the Sunday School," Addams's defender Robert E. Jenkins, superintendent of the South Church Sunday School, suggested, "The aims of her work are especially social and educational, and we understand why it has not a more distinctively religious cast. She is in the midst of a Catholic community, and to them she is trying to minister. . . . [H]er message to us, is not one of neglect of religion, but of coming into touch with the people about us. She said, 'We want Christianity incarnated in man.'" At HH Edward L. Burchard (see n. 13), associated with the settlement beginning in early 1891, recalled, "Miss Addams led in evening Bible and prayer with every one on their knees"

(Edward L. Burchard to EGS, 16 Jan. 1938, Smith, Starr); however, by Nov. 1893, Sunday-evening devotion at nine was not "obligatory" for the residents but available for those who wished to attend. JA herself had joined the Ewing Street Congregational Mission Church, and she continued teaching at the Chicago Training School for City, Home, and Foreign Mission until 1896. She formed close working relationships with Protestant and Jewish leaders in Chicago, appeared before Congregational and Presbyterian congregations, and spoke in synagogues and at Chautauqua encampments. But as the questions about the absence of religious education at HH became more frequent and the comments from traditional Protestant congregations more critical, she found herself defending her stand, but not altering it. See also Samuel A. Barnett to JA, 26 Dec. 1892, n. 2, above; and Graham Taylor to JA, 26 June 1897, n. 1, below.

HH and JA continued to battle misconceptions about their position on religion. In 1898 a resident of HH reported that JA had "invited a lot of orthodox church people who never came here" as guests for luncheon to entertain missionaries from India who were visiting another HH resident. One of the visiting missionaries reported to JA that "one lady had drawn her into a corner and asked her in a whisper whether she knew that the name of God was never mentioned in this house? . . . [T]he lady said she had often heard that that was the fact" (Alice Hamilton to Agnes Hamilton, 11 Oct. 1898, Harvard, Hamilton).

12. JA indicated that there were only female residents during the first three years of the settlement. The male component of HH established itself, as JA and EGS put it in their 1894 description of the settlement, "in a cottage on Polk Street" (*HH Maps and Papers*, 229). The address was 245 (later 816) West Polk, "just opposite the coffee-house" of the settlement (Dean, "With Modest Grace").

The costs associated with establishing the Men's Settlement were borne largely by Lydia Avery Coonley, who provided $300, and by JA, who personally gave the remainder of the $1,702.69. Among the first members were Charles C. Arnold, Clifford W. Barnes, Andrew Alexander Bruce, Edward L. Burchard, Henry B. Learned, and JA's nephew John Addams Linn. Edwin A. Waldo came by Oct. 1893. By Apr. 1894, the initial male residents were joined by a group of young men associated with the Typographical Union who organized themselves cooperatively as the Phalanx Club, much like the Jane Club for young women. Both men's groups volunteered at the settlement, had access to the facilities of the newly organized Men's Club located in a front room on the second floor in the Gymnasium and Coffee House Building recently added to the settlement complex, and ate their meals at the settlement.

George Cushing Sikes described his quarters: "The house where I am reminds me considerably of the frat house in Minneapolis. It has sleeping rooms above and very pleasant parlors on the first floor" (George C. Sikes to Madeleine Wallin, 24 July 1894, UIC, JAMC, Sikes). For a biographical note on George Cushing Sikes, see Article in the *Chicago Record*, 3 Dec. 1894, n. 1, below.

Edward Lawyer Burchard (1867–1944) recalled that he went to work with JA in 1891 shortly after he graduated from Beloit College with a Ph.B. He reported that he took dictation from JA (particularly for the two seminal speeches JA presented at the Summer School of Applied Ethics, Plymouth, Mass., Aug. 1892), advertised the art exhibitions and then guarded the art displayed in the Butler Art Gallery, and accompanied EGS and JA when they had to go out at night to visit neighbors. Burchard also taught Latin in 1891 in the HH College Extension Program. He was born in Freeport, Ill., and in 1893 married Alice Barton, a friend of JA's and the daughter of the Addams family attorney Edward Barton. After serving as a chief clerk in the mines department of the World's Columbian Exposition, he was a librarian for the Field Museum of Natural History until 1898. He then went to Washington, D.C., where he was employed in the U.S. Coast and Geodetic Survey, 1898–1903, and the Library of Congress, 1903–6. From 1907 until 1909, he was the auditor of the HH Assn. He returned to Freeport and served as secretary of the Civic League, 1908–9, and 1909–14 he was director of the extension department of the Chicago School of Civics and Philanthropy. By 1917 he was associated with the National Community Center Assn.

Andrew Alexander Bruce (1866–1934), law professor and judge, was born in India, the son of Gen. Edward Archibald and Anne Young McMaster Bruce. He was educated in England and also received degrees from Univ. of Wisconsin (A.B. 1890; LL.B. 1892). From 1893 to 1895, he was attorney for the Illinois Board of Factory Inspectors. He taught bookkeeping in the fall of 1893 and Shakespeare's *Othello* in the HH College Extension Program beginning in 1894. In 1897–98, he became a lecturer for young people's classes at the settlement. After practicing law in Chicago, in 1898 he joined the law faculty at the Univ. of Wisconsin. From 1902 until 1911, he was associated with the Univ. of North Dakota Law School, where he was dean from 1904 until 1911, when he became a justice on the North Dakota Supreme Court and chief justice, 1916–19. He was a professor of law at Northwestern Univ. beginning in 1922. He was active in the American Bar Assn. and the author of many books about the law.

13. Clifford Webster Barnes (1864–1944), who became noted, especially in Chicago, as the longtime president of the Saturday Evening Club, was born in Corry, Pa., the son of businessman Joseph Barnes and Anna Webster Barnes, a granddaughter of Daniel Webster. He graduated from Yale Univ. (A.B. 1889) and its Divinity School (B.D. 1892). When his former professor of Hebrew at Yale, William Rainey Harper, invited Barnes to join him at the Univ. of Chicago, he accepted the position of a divinity fellow with the opportunity to teach in the history department.

On the advice of a Yale friend, HH was one of the first places he visited on reaching Chicago. JA invited him to work at HH and become a resident. Between 1893 and 1894, he took responsibility for developing the HH Cooperative Assn. and became a regular at the Men's Settlement at 245 West Polk St., spending at least one night a week there. During the 1893–94 year, he served as interim pastor for the Ewing Street Congregational Church. While at the settlement, he became a member of the Arnold Toynbee Club and taught courses in oratory and ancient history. He also helped JA negotiate with fellow Yale graduate William Kent to turn over to HH property that later became the HH Playground.

In 1894 the New England Congregational Church, Chicago, invited Barnes to serve as its assistant pastor, a post that included oversight for missionary activity at the Sedgwick Street Congregational Church, 388 (later 1438 North) Sedgwick St. Living on Sedgwick St., he continued to promote settlement-like activities in this North Side poor tenement district. He established boys' clubs, girls' clubs, and organizations for residents to study neighborhood problems; formed a Municipal Improvement Assn.; and helped replace a corrupt alderman.

In 1898 he married Mary Reid at Lake Forest, Ill. That same year, he studied at Oxford Univ., and in 1898–99 he served as director of the Student Christian Movement, Paris. Back in Chicago in 1899, he once again took up settlement work. He served as sociology instructor and director of university settlement work, University of Chicago Settlement, 1899–1900. It was in 1900 that he became president of Illinois College in Jacksonville, Ill. He served until 1905–6, when he became general secretary for the Religious Education Assn. of America. By 1908 he was back in Chicago, where he established the Saturday Evening Club, a nonsectarian religious organization, which provided such speakers as JA, William Jennings Bryan, William Howard Taft, Booker T. Washington, and an assortment of European leaders to audiences as large as twenty-five hundred and after radio even larger audiences.

He remained closely identified with the Chicago Church Federation and was a member of the Advisory Com., Federal Council of Church of Christ in America. He was associated with the Chicago Community Trust, Chicago Assn. of Commerce, Chicago Planning Comm., the YWCA, the Legislative Voters' League, and the Chicago Council of Social Agencies. He died in Lake Forest, Ill.

The second new structure to join the expanding Hull-House physical plant was the Pond and Pond–designed combination Gymnasium and Coffee House located on Polk Street, to the north of the original Hull home. It opened in 1893 (UIC, JAMC 0132 0148).

# Remarks on Opening the New England Kitchen, Hull-House

*On 23 August 1893, Jane Addams officially opened the New England Kitchen at Hull-House. It was "placed at the rear of and adjacent to the coffee house"[1] and on the ground floor of the combination Coffee House and Gymnasium Building,[2] the second permanent structure added to the Hull-House complex. Settlement supporters William H. Colvin[3] and Allison Vincent Armour[4] provided the major share of the funding for the building located at 240 Polk Street, just north of the original Hull home. In describing the new Pond and Pond design, the* Chicago Inter Ocean *announced on 24 August 1893, "The new kitchen has been running for two months and Miss Addams is pleased with the success.[5] Above the kitchen is a cozy little room for the men's club, with two pool tables and a billiard table.[6] Adjoining this is a gymnasium which is thrown open at specific times for men, women, boys and girls.[7] Below this is a system of baths[8] and in the rear the boys' club-room, which this summer has been used for a kindergarten."[9] Jane Addams hoped that all of the facilities in this new space would appeal to the men of the neighborhood.*

*The Men's Club would now have a gathering place of its own and responsibility—at least initially—for managing its meeting room and the gymnasium.[10] Jane*

*Addams was offering an alternative to the neighborhood saloon for socializing.*[11] *Nonalcoholic drinks would be available from a soda fountain, and food would be provided through the New England Kitchen and Coffee House.*

*Almost from the beginning of the settlement, Jane Addams and Ellen Gates Starr recognized that a generally unhealthy diet was one of the problems their neighbors faced. Consequently, the settlement leaders created programs aimed at understanding and improving neighborhood nutrition. By 1891 they had established the Diet Kitchen, located in a cottage behind the nursery at 221 Ewing Street, where trained nurses and women with cooking experience promoted the use of healthy and relatively inexpensive food, especially for those in the neighborhood who were ill.*[12] *The New England Kitchen, which the settlement leaders next added, was modeled on the one created by Ellen H. Richards*[13] *in Boston. It provided a more scientific and structured approach to the diet of the working poor and was a program that specialized in the preparation of nutritious, inexpensive foods, like beans and tough cuts of meat, using the latest in low-cost technology. The Hull-House kitchen was directed until October 1894 by Anna Lathrop,*[14] *who had trained with Mrs. Richards in Boston. At the same time, Jeannette C. Welch,*[15] *a graduate of Wellesley College and the New York College for Teachers, became a settlement resident and held cooking classes and taught physiology and house sanitation.*

*Jane Addams opened her new venture with high hopes for its success. In February 1894, while speaking to students gathered by the Household Economics Association in Chicago, she promoted the New England Kitchen idea and after its initial year at Hull-House labeled it "quite successful."*[16] *But a year later, the kitchen had closed,*[17] *and the kitchen facilities reverted to preparing coffee-house fare that would sell more easily.*[18]

*The only surviving portion of Jane Addams's speech on the occasion of the opening was printed in the* Chicago Inter Ocean, *24 August 1893.*

Chicago, Ill. 23 August 1893

"It is a part of the new philanthropy to recognize that the social question is largely a question of the stomach; temperance workers are coming to feel that they cannot make headway if they ignore the importance of proper nutriment for the body, for with monotonous food is apt to go whisky to whip up the digestion. Mission workers of all kinds are coming to feel that their weak point is the commissariat. Even with the money in hand they are unable to command such food as ought to be possible out of the abundant food material that the county affords. To all these and many more the work of which the New England kitchen has been the center offers reliable and solid help, and more and more this help is appreciated.

The New England kitchen took up one definite and very practical line of work—the collection of facts as to the food of the people. What were the food materials used, and what their nutritive value? What were the favorite dishes? Were the foods cooked at home or bought ready cooked? What relation does the food question bear to the alcohol question? What was the food of the little children whose parents worked and ate elsewhere during the day? What were the causes of the mal-nutrition observed in whole classes as in sewing women? What are the National dishes of Americans? It is astonishing how few still partake of the simple fare known as New England. It seems to be a part of the restless and hurried life of this generation in large cities to have abandoned the cheap and simple foods that need long cooking and a little skill to make them palatable. This reduces the fare to chops and steaks, and tea with bread and cakes to be picked up at the bake-shop. Are these our National foods? It would almost seem so. Certain it is that home cookery is decreasing in amount and not improving quality, more or less dependence being placed on the bake-shop and restaurant.

Now what is the result? The wage-earner is illy nourished on money that is all-sufficient, if rightly expended to buy him proper food. This is a serious question, because here there is the chance of more saving than in any other item of living, and what can so easily be saved here can be applied to better shelter, which is a more evident, if not more vital need."

PD, ("HH Kitchen Opened," *Chicago Inter Ocean*, 24 Aug. 1893. HH Scrapbook 1:40 ½; *JAPM*, Addendum 10:6ff).

1. "HH Kitchen Opened." On this opening occasion, members of the HH Woman's Club were hostesses. By 28 Aug., members of the planning committees for the Labor Congress of the World's Columbian Exposition had already toured the new kitchen.

2. On 27 Dec. 1892, the *Chicago Post* carried an article entitled "Another Praiseworthy Gift," announcing that William H. Colvin and Allison Vincent Armour had presented the settlement with $14,000 to help defray the cost of a "gymnasium and a coffee house, which will be managed by the Hull House Men's Club" (see nn. 6, 10). In addition to the new building, JA also secured funds for a new kitchen and heating and steam-producing facilities. According to the record book JA kept of financial contributions to HH programs and the physical plant between 1895 and 1905, Colvin provided $6,050 and Armour $8,500, and an assortment of other settlement friends added the remaining funds necessary to reach the $18,964.54 required to pay for the entire project.

3. William H. Colvin (1839–96) was born in Coeymans, N.Y., the son of a prominent shipper operating on the Hudson River. He began his career in a large importing house in New York City. After serving in the 7th New York Volunteer Regiment during the Civil War, he made his way to Chicago in 1867 and began to trade in coffee, tea, and sugar. In 1868 he married Susannah Burt of Dubuque, Iowa, and they had three children, William H. Jr. (b. 1871), Katharine, and Jessica ("Jessie"). The Colvins were members of the Central Church of Chicago. After the Chicago Fire of 1871, Colvin limited his trading to coffee and was said to be the largest coffee importer in the city. He retired in 1887. At his death, the *Chicago Daily Tribune* valued his estate at $750,000, primarily in real estate.

Colvin became a director of the World's Columbian Exposition Comm. in Chicago in 1890. He taught university extension courses in a downtown hall for the benefit of working men and was a trustee for the Bureau of Justice. He urged arbitration during strikes, and, according to JA, he believed that "the principle of the organization of labor must be sustained if the present industrial order is to continue" (Addams, "In Memoriam"). He was also a founder of the Municipal Voters' League, organized by reform-minded business leaders in 1896.

Colvin was a dedicated HH supporter (see also JA to Gertrude Barnam, 25 July 1896, n. 24, below). With the financial assistance of his friend Allison V. Armour (see n. 4), Colvin provided the funding for the second structure added to HH, the two-story brick Gymnasium and Coffee House Building designed by the brothers Pond. Beginning in 1895, he served as a member of the HH Assn. Board of Trustees and in particular as the auditor of the settlement's accounts. He became a successful fund-raiser for HH. JA recalled that he was "always ready to make up deficits" and "to straighten out that little matter" of money. She further reported in her praise for Colvin that when an offer of a new building for the Jane Club at the settlement was made by a man Colvin and settlement leaders considered to be of questionable business practices, he said they should not accept the gift. She reported that he "took back the message of refusal in so fair a spirit that he retained the man for his firm friend" (Addams, "In Memoriam"). JA recorded a fuller version of the incident in *Twenty Years* without naming the individuals involved. It seems likely that Colvin himself had asked a friend for the $20,000 to construct the Jane Club, but JA indicated, "When, however, he divulged the name of his generous friend, it proved to be that of a man who was notorious for underpaying the girls in his establishment and concerning whom there were even darker stories. It seemed clearly impossible" she continued, "to erect a clubhouse for working girls with such money and we at once said that we must decline the offer" (138).

At his death, his family had planned to erect a building as a memorial to him at the settlement. Daughters Jessica ("Jessie") and Katharine (sometimes Catherine) Colvin continued to support HH, but they never constructed a building at HH in his honor. They served as volunteers at the settlement in the 1890s, teaching French, assisting in the kindergarten, and directing the Clara Barton Club. JA's 1895–1905 fund-raising record book revealed that in 1899, the two sisters gave $100 toward general settlement expenses, and in 1900 Katharine Colvin gave $5,000, one of the largest single gifts, toward the $25,000 needed to build the new combination Coffee House and Theatre Building. Both sisters provided monthly support for JA's fellowship program and helped establish the Music School in the new Children's Building.

4. Allison Vincent Armour (1863–1914) was born in Chicago, the son of Barbara Allison and grain merchant George Armour. He was educated in the Harvard School in Chicago and graduated from Yale Univ. (B.A. 1884). He became an eminent yachtsman and explorer. With his schooner-rigged ship *Utowana*, he often assisted the U.S. Dept. of Agriculture in finding new plants to introduce in the United States and helped with archaeological investigations, particularly in Europe. He was often in Berlin and on occasion entertained by the kaiser. In 1885 he married Anne Louise Kelley, who died in 1890. It is likely that the Armour family's friendship with the Colvins induced Allison Armour to support the building effort. In 1895 his mother, Barbara Armour, gave $300 toward general HH expenses, while Colvin himself donated $500. Mrs. Armour did not make a gift in 1896 when Colvin's pledge was $300. In 1899 Allison Armour also gave $1,000 toward construction of the Coffee House and Theatre Building.

5. HH accounts indicate that from May to Aug. 1893, $412.85 was spent to create the "cooking plant." The kitchen had six Aladdin ovens. "These are covered with asbestos on the outside and lined with tin on the inside. The heat comes from a lamp. The sides are about an inch thick," reported the *Chicago Record*, and continued, "In addition to this there are half-jacket steam kettles and a steam plant in the yard. The soups are cooked in these kettles and none of the steam escapes. Every atom of nutrition is conserved. By this process the product can be sold very cheap. . . . Yesterday, three large kettles were filled with bean, pea, and vegetable soups. These are sold at 10 cents a quart" ("HH Kitchen Opened"). Edward Atkinson (1827–1905), American economist and financier, was the inventor of the Aladdin

The Hull-House Men's Club was located in the Gymnasium and Coffee House. This photograph of the club room reveals pool and billiard tables; there were also spittoons and a no-alcohol bar. Jane Addams hoped that the Hull-House Men's Club, with its own quarters and governance, would attract neighborhood men to the social settlement life that their families enjoyed and away from the many saloons of the neighborhood (UIC, JAMC 0111 0632).

oven. It was an insulated box placed over a kerosene lamp. The cooking process was slow and ideal for preparing foods like tough cuts of meat or beans. Atkinson saw his invention as a way to help the poor to a wholesome, affordable diet.

6. The HH Men's Club was originally developed in 1891. It paid $20 a month for space in the settlement for its meetings. The HH financial records indicate that the furnishings for its club room consisted of three billiard tables, twenty-four billiard chairs, assorted bentwood and camp chairs, a grand piano, soda fountain, and twelve cuspidors. The three largest donors were railroad car magnate George M. Pullman (1831–97), who gave $500; Sarah Coonley, daughter of Lydia Avery Coonley, $200, and a Mr. Savage, who provided $300. Emily Greene Balch, who visited the settlement during the World's Columbian Exposition and probably toured the new building, provided $10 toward the $1,215 that the furnishings cost (see n. 10).

7. By 1891 HH had acquired the use of the former saloon adjacent to the Hull home and fitted it with "crude appliances and dubbed [it] a gymnasium" ("Nobel Charity Work"). During the Oct. 1891 through Sept. 1892 financial year, JA spent $356 on the facility. Its heavy use by neighborhood children and especially male adults prompted the early development of the new Gymnasium and Coffee House Building.

8. Among the early developments at the settlement was the addition of bathtubs available for use by neighbors. They were so frequently used that more were added when the new building was designed. "There will be some twelve free bath tubs, an increase of seven. The five free bath tubs that have been an important feature of the Hull House management have

given many a young and old man in the neighborhood a chance to respect himself more because he is clean" ("Nobel Charity Work").

9. "HH Kitchen Opened."

10. In June 1893, the HH Men's Club drafted a constitution. Article II stated that the club's "object shall be to control and manage the billiard and pool room of the Hull House Gymnasium, to arouse interest in athletic and manley sports; to encourage and promote sobriety, gentlemanly behavior and good fellowship among its members." The constitution mandated regular meetings on the first and third Saturdays of each month. A membership committee vetted all candidates, who had to be proposed by at least three members of the club and elected by the entire membership. The initiation fee was one dollar and monthly dues were twenty-five cents. A member could be expelled for "disorderly and disgraceful conduct" in the club rooms (HH Scrapbook 2:47; *JAPM*, Addendum 10:7ff). Gambling was prohibited, and a sergeant-at-arms, selected by the membership, was responsible for keeping order.

11. A visitor to the settlement during the World's Columbian Exposition described the neighborhood. "In this ward are fifty thousand inhabitants, seven churches and two missions, all small and struggling save two Catholic churches, and *two hundred and fifty-five saloons*. This, upon the basis of registration for the last presidential election, gives one saloon to every twenty-eight voters. The fourteenth precinct of this ward, situated at the intersection of Polk and Halsted Street, is the exact location of Hull House. This precinct has eight saloons, and the precinct immediately north of it twenty" (Sunderland, "HH, Chicago," 400).

12. Beginning in 1891, HH held cooking classes and offered prepared food for sale at low prices. Nutritionist Mary Hinman Abel gave four lectures on nutrition at the settlement in Oct. 1891. A number of cooking teachers, some with Boston cooking-school experience and some with a nursing background, taught cooking to children and adults. Charlotte Gary began teaching in Jan. 1891. She was followed by Theodosia Stiles (Doty), Miss Clapp, Edith Nason, Fanny Gary, Georgiana Allen, Miss Kinnear, and finally Jeanette (or Jeannette) C. Welch, who arrived in 1893 and stayed through 1894 (see JA to SAAH, [ca. 6] [Sept. 1891], n. 6, above). The Diet Kitchen program continued even after the New England Kitchen was created at HH. It closed by 1895, as all of the settlement food was being prepared in the coffee-house kitchen. Eventually, the cottage itself was razed to make way for the Jane Club building.

13. Ellen Henrietta Swallow Richards (1842–1911), chemist and leader in the development of home economics, was the only child of Peter and Fanny Swallow Richards and grew up on a farm in Dunstable, Mass. She was educated primarily at home by her parents, who met while attending New Ipswich Academy in New Hampshire. When the family moved to Westford and then to Littleton, Mass., where her father opened mercantile shops, she continued her education. She also taught and prepared herself for the college education she hoped to have. At the age of twenty-five, she was finally able to enter Vassar College, where she excelled, especially in scientific studies. After graduation in 1870, she became the first woman admitted to study at MIT, albeit as a special student for the study of chemistry. In 1873 she graduated from MIT with a B.S. and at the same time from Vassar with a M.A., and she studied two more years at MIT. In 1875 she married MIT professor Robert Hallowell Richards. That same year, she received financial support to create a women's laboratory at MIT, where she continued to promote and encourage women in scientific study. Building on her own interests in housekeeping and with a background as a homemaker and helpmate for her parents, she began promoting the importance of chemistry to the homemaker. Although the MIT women's laboratory closed in 1883, in 1884 she became the instructor of sanitary chemistry in the new MIT sanitation laboratory and remained in that position until her death.

In 1890 Richards opened the New England Kitchen in Boston, where she offered scientifically prepared food for home consumption at reasonable prices and demonstrated healthy cooking techniques. During the early 1890s, her reforms seemed ideal—a way to feed the poor nutritious foods at prices they could afford. Richard's ideas were promoted at the World's

Columbian Exposition in the Rumford Kitchen, where scientifically prepared lunches were offered to visitors for thirty cents. It was in that favorable climate that the New England Kitchen at HH was opened during the exposition. Though the New England Kitchen idea failed in Boston and at HH, Richards became a well-known consultant in matters of home management. She was recognized as an expert on school lunches, helped create the field of dietetics, and was the leader in founding the American Home Economics Assn. She was a prolific writer of books and articles and sought after as a speaker. In 1910 she helped found the *Journal of Home Economics*. Ever devoted to opening more avenues of education and employment for women, in 1882 Richards was one of the founders of the Assn. of Collegiate Alumnae, later the American Assn. of University Women (AAUW), and actively supported the organization's drive to make graduate education more available to women and to promote physical education in colleges. She received an honorary degree from Smith College and was a trustee at Vassar.

14. Anna Lathrop (Case). See Robert A. Woods to JA, 20 June 1893, n. 10, above.

15. Jeanette (or Jeannette) C. Welch was placed in charge of all industrial classes at HH in early 1894; however, by Oct. 1894 she had left the settlement to attend the Univ. of Chicago. See JA to SAAH, [ca. 6] Sept. 1891], n. 6, above.

16. "Advocates Public Kitchen."

17. By Feb. 1895, JA had closed the New England Kitchen at HH. None of the other programs in the United States patterned after the Boston kitchen were successful. "'Their death knell was sounded,' to quote Mrs. Richards, 'by the woman who said, "I don't want to eat what's good for me; I'd ruther eat what I'd ruther"'" (Hunt, *The Life of Ellen H. Richards*, 220).

18. Throughout the remainder of the 1890s, JA and HH continued to look for ways to understand and improve neighborhood nutrition. See JA to William Rainey Harper, 19 Dec. 1895, nn. 12–13, below. See also JA to SAAH, [ca. 6] [Sept. 1891], n. 6, above.

## To Mary Rozet Smith

Hull-House Chicago [Ill.] Aug 26" 1893

My dear friend

You were very good to write me from Hoboken and the good letter warmed my heart.[1] Indeed it has warmed it several times after several readings. I called the other day to see your mother and inquire of your welfare. Mrs Smith[2] was unfortunately out but I was assured that you had safely landed on English soil. I miss you very much and had a positive pang of home sickness as I went up the steps.

It takes some thing of an effort these hard times to keep up one's spirits, our neighbors are so forlorn and literally flock to the house for work. To keep them from quite going under takes a good deal of effort and I have really been touched by the goodness of our neighbors to each other and their sweet attitude to us. The effort is a little like "trouble in <a> family" which draws the members together, the helplessness of the situation appeals to me very strongly. We have had one or two meetings of representatives for the various charities and I think are going to do things more systematically this winter than is usual in Chicago.[3] We are at last to have a doctor—Dr Milligan[4] a Smith graduate and a skillful

William Kent leased property that he owned on Polk Street, east of the corner of Halsted, and next to the Polk Street School, to Jane Addams. She used the space to create the first public playground in Chicago. Kent, an 1887 graduate of Yale, was a businessman and politician. He became a Cook County commissioner and eventually served in the U.S. House of Representatives from California (Yale University, Classes Photographs, Series I, Box 26, Folder 265).

and agreeable woman, she will take an office in the red brick on Polk St. Mrs Kelly[5] has the upper floor for her factory inspectors office.

Mr Stalbus'[6] cottages are filled and he is again restored to good nature, he is saving up for a pair of "new pants" and when they are at last purchased he is going to accept Mr Barnes[7] invitation to go to the Fair and be wheeled in a chair.

The Play ground[8] is a source of great pleasure in the neighborhood and we are learning to manage it much better. Miss West[9] comes the first of Oct. and is very much pleased with the idea of having general charge of the little Children's Clubs. The nursery continues to be crammed to its utmost capacity and a good many forlorn mothers and babies sleep there from time to time. We buy the food "ready cooked" from the Coffee-House which reduces the work and gives the women more time for the children, there were forty four yesterday and a few more in to dinner but by a judicious use of the rear cottage <& kindergarten room> it does not seem very crowded.

Miss Starr is having a very satisfactory visit and will not be back until the middle of next month, she is doing some work on the book "Hull-House Maps and Papers"—does n't it sound fine?[10]

Please give my love to your father, I hope the trip will be beneficial and give him some little pleasure as well. I can quite feel the breeze over the chalk downs, there are three spots I always think of with positive invigoration, the north of Wales[,] the Isle of Wight and the Valley of Wye. I wish you would have time for the latter and the little town of Ross.[11] You see I still have rural recollections. I spent last Sunday[12] at Cedarville with my brother and fanned all day Monday. Mrs Prince of the Boston Settlement[13] has just taken lunch with us, all the Boston Settlement are so disappointed not to see you when they come, they are quite sure you live here. She sends many messages who[se] purport I have forgotten. I am always your affectionate friend

Jane Addams

ALS (SCPC, JAC; *JAPM*, 2:1462–65).

1. MRS was at Hoboken, N.J., preparing to leave for England with her father. This letter is apparently no longer extant.

2. Sarah Rozet Smith, mother of MRS.

3. Five days after the World's Columbian Exposition opened on 1 May 1893, the U.S. stock market fell precipitously, providing direct evidence that the economic depression that had been building throughout Europe during 1892 had arrived in the United States. It would last until at least 1897. Even before the end of the exposition, it was evident that HH neighbors were beginning to be more economically distressed. The next years were characterized by increasingly widespread unemployment, business and bank failures and bankruptcies, major labor disputes and strikes, and reduced wages for those who were fortunate enough to be employed. Chicago's labor pool was still increasing, as immigrants continued to flood into the city. In addition, as the World's Columbian Exposition drew to a close, workers who had come to Chicago to help create and operate the extravaganza were soon unemployed and also searching the Chicago area for a way to survive. More than ever, JA and HH supporters were called upon to help their neighbors. In 1893 help provided through the settlement's relief office (established in 1893 to deal systematically with the mounting problem) nearly quadrupled from the previous year to almost twenty-five hundred dollars (see also Two Essays in the *Forum*, Nov. and Oct. 1892, n. 151, above). During the next four years, relief funds raised and granted reached more than two thousand dollars each year.

JA strongly supported the COS model operating in many U.S. cities, but not yet successfully established in Chicago (see JA to Richard T. Ely, 12 Mar. 1895, below). During this economic downturn, JA continued to work as a member of the Charity Organization Com. to harness all of the potential charitable sources in the city to provide relief. Throughout "that terrible winter after the World's Fair, when the general financial depression throughout the country was much intensified" (Addams, *Twenty Years*, 159), the committee created a new agency, the Central Relief Assn., which sought to establish a COS model to identify and meet needs. In 1895 the Central Relief Assn. was incorporated as the Bureau of Charities. See JA to Richard to Ely, 12 Mar. 1895, below.

4. Josephine Ewing Milligan, M.D. (1860–1946), was born in Jacksonville, Ill., one of five children of Dr. Harvey W. (1830–1902) and Josephine Mason Wade Milligan (1835–1911). She graduated from Smith College (A.B. 1882, M.A. 1885). She began her medical studies at the Univ. of Michigan, but transferred to the Woman's Medical College of New York Infirmary, from which she received her medical degree in 1889. Her specialty was gynecology. In 1899 she was writing medical advice associated with gynecology for the *Medical Fortnightly*, published in St. Louis, Mo., primarily for physicians west of the Mississippi River. Although Dr. Milligan devoted most of her life to private practice in Jacksonville, Ill., she lived in Chicago for a time in the early 1890s. By Oct. 1893, she had helped open the HH Dispensary at 247 West Polk St., and she continued to live as a resident at HH during 1894. She supported Florence Kelley as chief factory inspector of Illinois in her efforts to investigate and control sweatshops, and she often accompanied Kelley or her assistant inspectors as they worked.

By 1900 she had returned to Jacksonville, Ill., where she entered private medical practice, taught for four years at the Illinois State Hospital for the Deaf and Dumb, and was closely associated with the Josephine Milligan School, which provided special diet and care for delicate children. She took an active role in establishing the Morgan County Tuberculosis Sanitarium and other tuberculosis clinics. Her work in tuberculosis care and treatment earned her national recognition. After World War I, the Rockefeller Foundation sent her abroad with a small group of health care specialists to help combat tuberculosis in France. Dr. Milligan was an ardent suffragist and active member of the Illinois League of Women Voters. Like her mother, she was a longtime member of the Jacksonville Ladies Education Society and an early member of Sorosis, organized in Jacksonville by her mother in 1868. She received honorary degrees from Illinois College, Jacksonville, in 1922, and from Smith College in 1932. She retired from medical practice in 1930 and continued to live in Jacksonville for the remainder of her life.

5. Florence Kelley had become chief factory inspector of Illinois for four years beginning officially in July 1893.

6. Michael J. Stalbus (1839–1906?) was born in Germany. In 1892 he was living at 438 (later 1109) South Desplaines with his brother, John Stalbus, a wagon maker. The 1892 *Lakeside Directory of Chicago* indicated that he was in the real estate business with Lambert Caspers, who lived at 101 (later 1246 South) Newberry Ave., as Stalbus and Caspers. Stalbus apparently owned real estate in the HH neighborhood, and JA rented space from him on Polk St. for overflow programs associated with the settlement. In May 1896, he married Anna Bauer (1877–1944). They had at least three children, Bernice, John, and Adrian. By 1900 Stalbus was also in the insurance business and lived on South Albany Ave. He was an active member of the Catholic Knights of America.

7. Clifford W. Barnes.

8. In 1893 JA opened a playground at HH, "where children by the thousand" could "congregate, swinging, teeter-tautering, romping and merry-making to their hearts' content" (Onahan, "A Social Settlement"). On 11 Feb. 1893, in a newspaper article, William Kent and his family had been accused of being the slum landlords of property at 125 Ewing St. In a letter to the *Chicago Times*, published on 13 Feb., he denied the claim. According to Elizabeth T. Kent, widow and biographer of William Kent, "Florence Kelley wrote to a Chicago newspaper and criticized the unsanitary conditions of some property in the Hull House district 'owned by A. E. Kent and Son.' She called it 'a disgrace to the city and to its owners.' The property consisted of little houses which were left over from another style of living. The rapidly growing city had built up around them, and as the owners planned for future development they avoided expenses and welcomed such rental as they could get. On reading the sharp criticism by Mrs. Kelley, William Kent went at once to Hull House to talk the thing over with her and with Jane Addams. The perturbed landlord cited his problems and had a sudden idea. 'You take the property,' he said, 'put the place in order, collect the rents and make what you can of it. Tenants will steal the faucets and the door knobs — and, if you insist on cleanliness and sanitation, these people will move out. Where can they go? They pay a very small rent, but see what you can do — I give up.' The outcome was that the houses were torn down, the piece of ground cleared, and the first public playground in Chicago was opened. . . . William Kent gave approval and help, although he was disappointed not to see Jane Addams' solution of the renting problem he had wrestled with" (Kent, *William Kent*, 95–96).

William Kent (1864–1928) was born in Chicago and moved in 1871 with his parents to Marin Co., Calif., where he attended private schools. He continued his education in New Haven, Conn., first at Hopkins Grammar School, 1881–83, and then at Yale Univ., from which he graduated in 1887. In 1890 he married Elizabeth Thacher in Ojai, Calif., whom he had known in New Haven, and they settled in Chicago, where, until 1900, he helped to manage his family's real estate and livestock business. He became a member of the Chicago City

Council, 1895–97, when he helped defeat Charles T. Yerkes in his bid to secure concessions to operate rail transportation in the city for more than fifty years. Kent served as president of the Municipal Voters' League of Chicago, 1899–1900, before he returned to Marin Co., Calif. There he was elected to the U.S. Congress, 1911–17, and was a member of the U.S. Tariff Comm., 1917 until his resignation in 1920. In 1905 he and his wife purchased 611 acres of old-growth redwood forest and donated 295 acres of it to the federal government, which led to the establishment of Muir Woods National Park. Kent was an author of articles on natural science and politics. He died in Kentfield, Calif..

Sometime before Apr. 1893, William Kent gave a ten-year lease to JA on the 319 ft. x 119 ft. property located between Halsted and Desplaines streets on Polk St., near the West Polk Street School. During Apr. 1893, with Kent's permission, JA sold three houses from the property for a total of $300 to create the capital to construct the playground. She raised additional moneys and contributed $700 herself to level the lot, dump ninety-nine loads of sand on it, and build swings and an open-air shelter. The total cost of the project was $1,676.78. "The very latest addition to the Hull House beneficent activities is a play-ground for the children of the neighborhood, where boys and girls alike may enjoy various games and sports, with just enough supervision to see that fair play is had by all," reported a visitor to the settlement in the Sept. 1893 number of the *Unitarian* (Sunderland, "HH, Chicago," 401). Activities at what was referred to as the West Polk Street School Playground were monitored by residents and volunteers. In the beginning, policeman no. 1314, Mr. Murray, monitored activities in the playground. Described by one resident as having a "rich Irish brogue" and a "merry twinkle" in "his Hiberion eye," and "a very successful method of recovering stolen goods" from young male offenders, Officer Murray was a HH regular (Madeleine Wallin to Alfred C. Wallin, 8 Oct. 1896, UIC, JAMC, Sikes). He had been a sailor in the Far East, helped build swings and rope ladders for the playground, and spent some evenings teaching neighborhood boys how to weave baskets and hammocks.

Each year on or near May Day, the playground opened officially and with special fanfare. In 1895 there was a band, dancing around a May pole, races, and games, with the winners receiving flowers. The settlement also paid an organ grinder to entertain the children several times during each summer week. Kent continued to maintain the settlement's lease on the property into the early twentieth century and sometimes sent additional funds to support the settlement.

While the public playground was an important, indeed a vital, part of the HH program, JA was apparently willing to give it up or move it elsewhere if she had succeeded in enticing the Lewis Institute to the HH neighborhood. One year after the playground opened and in the midst of a successful second year, Florence Kelley wrote to Lewis Institute trustee John McLaren on JA's behalf: "We are naturally very desirous of having the Polytechnic built in our neighborhood, believing that no other one thing could contribute so much to its elevation or to the elevation of the standard of the schools as this would do. . . . [W]e know the demand that there is upon our Hull House college extension which cannot for a moment compare with the advantages offered by the projected school. And we know that there is a constituency ready for it, here, now. . . . But the main thing is . . . the stimulus that such an institution would be in a workingclass district such as this. The land in question is now used as a playground and Miss Addams holds it under a lease from Mr. Kent. But she would gladly surrender the lease as she surrendered the lease of the lot on Mather St., on which the Harrison Bath now stands" (19 July 1894, Illinois Institute of Technology, Chicago, Lewis Institute Archives, Lewis Institute Records, Box 5.1). The trustees for the plans laid out by Allen C. Lewis (1821–77) in his will secured property for construction of the school on the southeast corner of Madison and Robey (later Damen Ave.) streets, and the first school year was 1896–97.

In 1906 William Kent sold one-half of the HH Polk St. playground frontage but replaced it with additional property to make up the difference in frontage on Mather St. In the spring

The Hull-House playground opened for the first time toward the end of the summer of 1893. It was staffed by Hull-House residents, volunteers, and a city policeman. Summer activities began each year in May with a festive celebration. In winter the ground was flooded so that it could be used for winter sports. In this photograph of the play area, the building in the background is the Polk Street School (Hunter, *Tenement Conditions in Chicago*, opposite 170).

of 1906, the management and upkeep of the HH Playground became the responsibility of the Chicago Small Parks Comm. By 1910 the Polk Street Playground had been closed. The West Side Park commissioners had purchased ground connected with the Andrew Jackson School, five blocks west of HH. They created West Park No. 5 with playground equipment and access to the gymnasium of the school. In addition, West Park No. 3 was located eight blocks southwest of HH and had recreational facilities. Those two parks provided the HH neighborhood children with a public play area.

9. Margaretta (or Margaret) Stewart West (Fletcher) (1867–1921) became an influential resident of HH during the mid-1890s. She was the daughter of immigrants from Edinburgh, Scotland, James Rudeman West (1836–1921), who became a wholesale grocer in Chicago, and Agnes Johnson West (1840–1917). She was born in Montreal, Canada, but by 1870 the West family was living in suburban New Trier Twp. on Chicago's North Shore. She began working at HH in Sept. 1893. The *HH Bulletin* for Dec. 1896 reported that "Miss West has been in charge not only of the children's house but of the young people's clubs for three years, and no resident has ever had so large a circle of affectionate friends" (1, no. 7:6; *JAPM*, 53:563). In Feb. 1896, she encouraged young men and women from the young people's clubs to attend educational classes: "The question has arisen as to whether our young people are so distracted with clubs that all their time is absorbed by club affairs until neither time nor interest is left for classes or reading parties. This is perhaps the most cutting criticism on clubs that instead of leading their members to interest themselves in things of lifelong value they keep them so occupied with amusements and the smaller affairs of the day, that time glides smoothly by in easy distractions and little chance is left to store away resources for time to come" (*HH Bulletin* 1, no. 2: [7–8]; *JAPM*, 53:517–18). She recommended that young people belong to just

one club and in addition take time to attend a class of their choice. During her three years at the settlement as a single woman, she was, at the same time, children's clubs director, day nursery director, playroom director, and baby kindergarten director. She was also in charge of the HH Country Club, opened at Lakeside, Ill. (later Hubbard Woods, Ill.), on Chicago's North Shore, for the first time during the summer of 1895.

On 30 Nov. 1896, she wed Dr. John Rice Fletcher (1864–1916), an otolaryngologist from Evanston. The couple settled in Winnetka, Ill., near her parents and brother John C. West and his family. From that time until 1898, she continued her activities at the settlement on a reduced basis. She served as director of the Henry Learned Club, an association she began in Oct. 1896, and also continued to direct the HH day nursery. Her only child, Richard Pollard Fletcher, died from infection following an attack of appendicitis three months after her husband's death in Apr. 1916. In her later years, Margaretta Fletcher shared her home with her brother J. Roy West, a well-known Chicago landscape architect, and in 1930 her household expanded to include her sister, Mabel West Carpenter; her husband, Henry; and their six children. Margaretta Fletcher died on 19 Mar. 1942, shortly after a fall in her home, and her funeral was held at the Children's Chapel of the Winnetka Congregational Church.

10. EGS, who was in the East visiting family, had been at work on her article "Art and Labor," which she reworked early in 1894 for *HH Maps and Papers*, published for the first time in 1895, and recognized as the first published sociological study of a portion of any U.S. city (see JA to Richard T. Ely, 31 Oct. 1894, below). She wrote to her sister, Mary Blaisdell, on 4 Mar. [1894], "Mine article is done. I have but one—the 'Art and Labor' which is the last summer's one about entirely done over" (SC, Starr).

11. JA had visited Wales and southeastern England with AHHA and GBH in 1884. See *PJA*, 2:41–42; 2:344, nn., 6–10; and 2:345–47, n.17.

12. JA visited her brother and his family on 20 Aug. 1893.

13. Likely Lucinda Wyman Smith Prince (1862–1935), the educator sometimes referred to as the "mother of marketing education." She was born in Waltham, Mass., and educated at the Framingham Normal School and Wellesley College. She founded the Union School of Salesmanship at the Woman's Educational and Industrial Union, Boston, in 1915. It eventually became a graduate division of Simmons College. Throughout her life her major interest was the welfare of working women. She established a school to train women in sales and to train teachers to teach salesmanship. She served on numerous boards and commissions and was active in the Massachusetts Equal Suffrage Assn., the Alumnae Assn. of Wellesley, and the Twentieth Century Club, Boston. Her husband, whom she married in 1888, was author, lecturer, and educator John Tilden Prince (1844–1916).

## Minutes of a Hull-House Residents Meeting

*By the end of 1893, the number of residents at Hull-House had increased to twelve women and six, often seven, men.*[1] *There were many programs and activities, a physical plant that was constantly growing, at least two thousand visitors each week, and a much larger number of volunteers. Coordinating programs, residents, and volunteers became a struggle. Since Jane Addams, who had served as the nexus of the coordinating effort in the beginning, spent more and more of her time speaking and participating in community activities away from the settlement, it seemed logical to create an organization of the residents to help her. The residents began to meet as an organized body in January 1893. In general, the often weekly meetings followed* Robert's Rules of Order. *While the secretary of the group usually remained the same over each year and there was a committee structure, the chair for each meeting rotated among the residents and was seldom Jane Addams or Ellen Gates Starr.*[2] *The following minutes describe actions taken during the meeting of residents on 10 December 1893.*

[Hull-House, Chicago, Ill.] 10 December 1893

The meeting was called to order by Miss Addams, and Miss Holbrook[3] was elected chairman pro tem. <Minutes of the last meeting read and approved.> Present, Misses Addams, Benedict, Brockway, Browne,[4] Eaton,[5] Gyles,[6] Lathrop, Holbrook, Milligan, and Starr, and Messrs. Barnes, Bruce, Bancroft,[7] <Ewing,>[8] Waldo, and West.[9] Toting list revised. The Chair suggested that morning toters get up. The gymnasium door list was read and revised.[10]

Mr. Waldo reported that the Hull House Bureau of Labor and Charity Registration[11] was afloat, and requested that persons sending applicants known to themselves give them notes to him.

Miss Addams proposed a lodging house for women,[12] and announced that the cottage at 243 W. Polk St. was for rent at $35 a month, and could probably be heated for $10 or $15 a month.

Moved by Mr Barnes, supported by Mr. Waldo, that the Settlement favor the establishment of a lodging house for women with such labor equipments as seem feasible.

Moved by Mr. Bruce, supported by Miss Lathrop, to amend the motion by adding "which shall be organized and supported in every respect by some other person or organization." The amendment was carried. The motion as amended was carried.

Miss Addams announced that she had been honored with a visit from Alderman Powers,[13] who proposed giving some thousands of pounds of turkey and beef to the poor of the ward at Christmas, and desired Hull House to make the distribution; and that she had said that all Hull House could do would be to send him lists of needy and deserving persons. Mr. Barnes protested against the furnishing of lists to Alderman Powers.

Moved by Miss Starr, supported by Mr Barnes and Miss Lathrop, that Hull House have nothing to do with Mr. Powers and his charities.

Moved by Mr. Bruce, supported by Miss Eaton, that the motion be amended by substituting the following: that Hull House furnish Mr. Powers the lists:

By general consent it was agreed that the Chief[14] should write to Mr. Powers, as she had herself suggested, to the effect that Hull House had so much provender sent in at Christmas time that it would be well for him to distribute his turkeys through other agencies.

Moved by Miss Lathrop, supported by Mr. Bruce, that a committee of one be appointed to find out the cost of flooding the Playground and report.[15] Carried.

Concerning the matter of refreshments for the opening of the Municipal Bath House, it was moved by Miss Lathrop, supported by Mr. Bancroft, that Hull House submit its terms, and sell refreshments if it could be made to pay.[16] Carried.

Mr. Barnes reported that thro the kindness of some friends it had been made possible to purchase a coalyard, and that the business would begin on the morrow. Residents were requested to send coal purchases to the office, corner of Ewing and Halsted Streets.[17]

On motion adjourned.

Max West.

AMsS by recorder Max West (HH Residents, "Residents Meeting Reports," 1893–95, 10 Dec. 1893, UIC, JAMC, HH Assn., *JAPM*, 50:362–64).

1. The women were likely JA, EGS, Mary Keyser, Enella Benedict, Wilfreda Brockway, Jean McVicker Browne, Isabel Eaton, Rose Marie Gyles, Julia Lathrop, Agnes Sinclair Holbrook, Dr. Josephine Milligan, and Florence Kelley. The men were probably Clifford W. Barnes, A. A. Bruce, Edgar A. Bancroft, E. A. Waldo, Addison Alvord Ewing, Max West, and John Addams Linn. Meeting on 27 Aug. 1893, the residents discussed limiting their number to fifteen women and ten men. Two weeks later, they agreed that it was the "sense of the settlement that the number of settlers be limited to twelve or thirteen unless desirable for some reason to increase it beyond that number" (HH Residents, "Residents Meeting Reports," 1893–95, 10 Sept. 1893, p. 32; *JAPM*, 50:348). Over the next two years, the number of residents rose to more than twenty with the approval of the resident body.

2. Books of minutes from HH residents' meetings from 16 July 1893 until 5 Oct. 1896 are extant (UIC, JAMC, HH Assn.; *JAPM*, 50:331–424). The first thirty pages of the initial 1893 minute book are missing; however, the initial page indicates that the minutes began in Jan. 1893.

Among the committees identified in 1893 were the following: house (on which JA always served as the leader), coffeehouse, playground, college extension, relief, coal yard, Jane Club, Sunday concerts, kindergarten, children and young people's clubs, industrial classes, Butler Gallery, gymnasium, and bank. All residents served on more than one committee, and the chair as well as the membership changed frequently.

3. Agnes Sinclair Holbrook (1867–96), who was born in Marengo, Iowa, daughter of Elizabeth S. and U. Bruce Holbrook, graduated from Wellesley College in the class of 1892 (B.S.). While at Wellesley, she was a member of the Shakespeare Society, an editor of the *Prelude*, and one of two literary editors of the college's annual, *The Wellesley Ledgena for A.D. 1892*. In 1893 she was a resident at HH, where she taught a course in English poetry, emphasizing the works of Alfred Lord Tennyson. In Apr., during the spring term of the settlement's college extension classes, she offered six weeks of lectures on biology. Her subjects were man compared to lower animals, what is life, what is death, heredity, physical evolution, and evolution theory. In the summer, during the World's Columbian Exposition, she held a reading and discussion group, or "party," on Thomas H. Huxley's *Lay Sermons* (1870). She also led groups from HH and the neighborhood to popular orchestral concerts presented by Theodore Thomas (1835–1905), conductor of the Chicago Symphony, 1891–1905. She was the HH resident who assisted Florence Kelley, special agent expert in Chicago for the U.S. Dept. of Labor, in organizing the information gathered by four male investigators who canvassed the neighborhood in a square-mile area around HH about the livelihood, nationality, and living conditions of those who lived there. The data were published in *A Special Investigation*

*of the Slums of Great Cities*. The information on nationality and wages of the residents of the area was recorded by Holbrook and became the maps of *HH Maps and Papers* (1895). Her comments about the maps appear as "Map Notes and Comments," the first chapter of the work. In 1894 her article about HH was published in the *Wellesley Magazine*. In Apr. 1894, she left the settlement. She died at age thirty in Marengo, Iowa.

4. Jean McVicker Browne (Johnston) (b. 1872) came to the United States from Montreal, Canada. She began teaching dancing classes on Saturday at HH in the fall of 1893, while she was working as a stenographer and living in the HH neighborhood at 249 (later 844 West) Ewing St. In Nov. 1893, she played Mrs. Hardcastle in Oliver Goldsmith's *She Stoops to Conquer*, put on by the dramatic section of the HH Students' Assn. For the 23 May production of *A Scrap of Paper*, also presented by the dramatic section of the HH Students' Assn. and this time in the St. Rose of Lima Hall in Chicago, she played Mlle. Suzanne de Ruseville. She continued to give lessons at the settlement until July 1895, when she married William Dawson Johnston (1871–1928), who had been a student at the Univ. of Chicago and received an M.A. from Harvard Univ. in 1898. He taught history at the Univ. of Michigan, 1894–97, and at his alma mater Brown Univ., 1899–1900. He became a librarian at the Library of Congress, 1900–1901 and 1926–28; Columbia Univ., 1909–11; and St. Paul, Minn., Public Library, 1914–21. The couple had two daughters. Johnston wrote *History of the Library of Congress*, vol. 1, *1800–1864* (1904).

5. Isabel Eaton (1853–1937), who insisted on addressing JA as "Grandmother [of the settlement movement]," graduated from Smith College with an A.B. in 1888 and spent the college year 1888–89 there teaching a class in letter writing. For the next two years, until 1893, she taught school in Hyde Park, Mass. She was born in Cape Elizabeth, Maine, where she eventually had a summer home for a number of years. She was the daughter of Frances H. Webster and Daniel L. Eaton, a banker. She began a three-month stay at HH in Oct. 1893, followed by a six-month residency at the College Settlement in New York City as a Dutton fellow of the Eastern Settlements Assn. while she studied the garment trade. Her research led to the publication "Receipts and Expenditures of Certain Wage Earners in the Garments Trade," in the *American Statistical Assn. Journal,* n.s., 30 (June 1895). JA and Florence Kelley included a portion of her study they titled "Receipts and Expenditures of Cloakmakers in Chicago, Compared with Those of That Trade in New York" as a chapter in *HH Maps and Papers* (1895).

Eaton returned in 1894 to Illinois, where she taught literature at RC and continued to be active at HH. While at HH, she taught advanced algebra and geometry during the fall of 1893, but only geometry in the fall of 1894. For the HH Summer School, 10 July–10 Aug. 1894, she taught a class on Monday, Wednesday, and Friday on the outdoor study of birds, a lifelong interest. During the 1896 year, she became head resident of Hartford Settlement in Connecticut, but left to take a fellowship offered by the College Settlements Assn. and attend Columbia Univ., during which she completed her M.A. She worked with W. E. B. Du Bois on his pathbreaking study of African Americans in Philadelphia. Her contribution to his investigation was published as *A Special Report on Domestic Service* in his *The Philadelphia Negro, a Social Study* (Univ. of Pennsylvania, 1899). By 1897 she had settled at Hartley House in New York City. She continued to work on her M.A. at Columbia Univ. and Barnard College, and she taught in the primary grades in the New York public schools. By 1905 she was working at the Felix Adler School and in 1908 with Greenwood Settlement in Brooklyn, where she held a summer camp for Italian boys. In 1909 she became secretary for the Ethical Culture College in New York City and then left in 1910 to become head resident for the Robert Gould Shaw House in Boston, which served an African American community. On 2 Oct. 1911, she wrote in her letter to her Smith College classmates, "Little Robert Gould Shaw House goes on fairly well, but, truthfully, settlement work with a Negro Problem attachment is no sedentary occupation. One gyrates. One likewise does some reflecting 'on man, on nature, and on human life' and on the future in America, if the intelligent people in the country go on neglecting to inform themselves on this terrific and grisley problem—(it is that!) and thinking they 'can evolve a knowledge of ten million of human beings by casual acquaintance with a maid, a laborer, or a negro on the street.' I'm getting scared; I sure enough am!" (SC, Archives, Biographical File). After a year's rest in 1914–15, she taught at Fisk Univ., in Nashville, Tenn., but poor health caused her to leave the school in Nov. 1916. From 1917 until her resignation in 1927, she worked as a civil service employee in the U.S. Dept. of Agriculture, primarily in the office of publications in the Bureau of Plant Industry. She moved to Staffordville, Mass., where she gardened and became involved in the village community club and continued her close association with Smith College and her classmates. In 1934 she visited JA, whom she referred to as "the tallest arch-angle of the hosts," in Hadlyme, Conn. (home of Alice Hamilton), and pronounced her looking "far from well" but still "her wonderful and inspiring and singularly lovable self" (Isabel Eaton to Classmates of 1888, 17 Oct. 1934, SC, Archives, Biographical File).

6. Rose Marie Gyles (1867–1949) was born in Chicago, one of six children of Henry J. Gyles (1834–1925), an Englishman, and his German-born wife, Catherine Saurer (1835–1912). He had served in the Crimean War and emigrated to Chicago, where he established a meatpacking business that was destroyed by the Chicago Fire of 1871. By 1879 the family had resettled on a ranch near Dodge City, Kans. After attending, in the summer of 1892, physician and nineteenth-century fitness instructor D. A. Sargent's special training program at the Hemenway Gymnasium, Harvard Univ., Rose Gyles graduated in 1893 with a B.A. from RC. Sargent's training program for women provided instruction in new and improved gymnastic techniques for "most teachers now directing gymnasiums of our large colleges for women" (Sargent, "The System of Physical Training at the Hemenway Gymnasium," 69). Gyles also studied human anatomy at the Univ. of Chicago, 1895–96; spent another summer studying with Sargent; and attended the Chautauqua Summer School of Physical Education in New York and Teachers' College, Columbia Univ., New York City, in the summer of 1923.

Her first job at HH was teaching in the July 1892 Summer School at Rockford, where she held gymnastics classes daily. With the help of a fellowship of twenty-five dollars a month provided by JA, she began living at HH as a resident in 1893 and again taught in the HH Summer School in 1894. In May 1894, she appeared as Louise de la Glaciere in the HH Students' Assn. play *A Scrap of Paper*, a comedy by French dramatist Victorien Sardou published in 1860. By Jan. 1895, Gyles had become the director of all gymnasium work at the HH Gymnasium and taught classes especially for women and girls.

She introduced basketball at HH for men, women, and children. One of her great achievements was a HH woman's basketball team, which during the later 1890s had a winning record. By Apr. 1896, there were two women's teams and a group of juniors who had taken up the game. The 1 Apr. 1897 *HH Bulletin* reported that the "Young Women's team has been practicing zealously but so far has played only twice" (2, no. 4:7; *JAPM*, 53:605) and won both games. The junior team had played three times and won two of the contests. "The best game of the season was played with the Englewood High School girls' team at Hull-House on the evening of May 25. Both sides played a fast and exciting game, as both sides are equally well practiced and have had equal experience. The score was close—5 to 3—showing excellent interference on the part of the contestants" (*HH Bulletin* 2, no. 5 [June 1897]: 5; *JAPM*, 53:613). HH won.

Although offered a position at her alma mater in the early 1900s, she chose to remain at the settlement as director of the gymnasium until 1907, and for forty-five years she had charge of women's sports in the gymnasium. At the same time, she also taught at the J. Sterling Morton School; at the Jewish Training School, 1898–1901; and in 1929 she was the director of corrective gymnastics for the public schools of Cicero, Ill. At HH, beginning in the spring of 1897, she taught Sargent's and the Swedish system gymnastics for the Kindergarten Training School

The Hull-House girls basketball team in action. Physical education was an important element in the Hull-House program. Hull-House fielded one of the first girls basketball teams in Chicago. They were coached by Rose Marie Gyles, the settlement resident responsible for the physical education program (*American Home Culture*, 345).

of the Chicago Froebel Assn. established at HH, and she became the director of the Aloha-Vesperian Club of girls, who met to read stories, embroider, and host musical and literary entertainments. She also taught classes in English and citizenship. She was a member of the Cordon Club in Chicago. Each summer she traveled to Europe or around the United States. She left HH in 1938, but continued to volunteer at the Immigrants' Protective League. She died in a hospital in Denver and was buried in her family's plot in Maple Grove Cemetery in Dodge City, Kans.

7. Edgar Addison Bancroft (1857–1925) was born in Galesburg, Ill., the son of Addison N. and Catharine Blair Bancroft. He graduated from Knox College (A.B. 1878), Galesburg, Ill., and Columbia Univ. (LL.B. 1880) and practiced law in Galesburg until 1892, when he moved to Chicago as an attorney for the Atchison, Topeka, and Santa Fe Railway. By 1896, when he married Margaret Healey (1859–1923), he became general solicitor for the Chicago & Western Independent Railroad Co. and the Belt Railway Co., positions he held until he entered private practice in Chicago in 1904. From 1907 until 1920, he was general counsel for International Harvester Co. He wrote several books, among them *The Chicago Strike of 1894* (1895) and *The Destruction or Regulation of Trusts* (1907). He was associated with HH only briefly but remained a staunch supporter. When Bancroft died, he was serving as U.S. ambassador to Japan.

8. Addison Alvord Ewing (1871–1949) was born in Enfield, Mass., the son of Edward C. and Mary Alvord Ewing. He graduated from Amherst College in 1892 and became a student at the Univ. of Chicago, from which he graduated in 1896. While in Chicago, he discovered

HH and lived for a time in the Men's Settlement, 1893–94. He attended resident meetings and participated in settlement activities. In 1896 he joined the faculty at Wabash College in Crawfordsville, Ind., where the former pastor of the College Church at Amherst was president. There he helped coach football, brought golf to the college community, and served first as professor of logic and oratory and in 1898 as professor of philosophy. He was an Episcopal clergyman, who along with his wife, Elizabeth Abbott Learoyd, of Danvers, Mass., took a house in the factory district of Crawfordville and attempted, unsuccessfully, to create a social settlement. He left Wabash and Crawfordsville in 1900. He was the author of *Problems of a Preacher* (1929).

9. Max West (1870–1909), who recorded minutes for the 10 Dec. 1893 meeting of the HH residents, was born in St. Cloud, Minn. He attended the Univ. of Minnesota (1890; A.M. 1892) and Columbia Univ. (Ph.D. 1893). In 1893, while he was attending the Univ. of Chicago as an honors fellow in economics and docent in sociology, he became a resident at HH and for most of the year secretary of the HH residents' meetings. In 1894 he moved to the newly established University of Chicago Settlement and the next year to Chicago Commons Settlement. In 1894, during the Pullman railroad strike, he was a reporter for the *Chicago Herald*, and then in 1895 he became an editorial writer for the *Chicago Record*. After serving as a lecturer at Columbia Univ., 1895–96, he moved to the Division of Statistics for the U.S. Dept. of Agriculture. He was associate professor of economics at Columbia Univ., 1900–1902 and then became chief of the Bureau of Internal Revenue for the Treasury Dept. in Puerto Rico, 1903–4. He was noted for his writings on taxation.

10. Residents of HH took turns greeting visitors at the main entrance to the settlement before taking or "toting" them on a tour of the settlement. In addition, the residents monitored the activities in the gymnasium and tried to maintain order.

11. JA enticed Edwin A. Waldo to leave Boston and come to Chicago to take charge of the Labor Bureau and Relief Registration office of the settlement located at 247 West Polk St. to help JA and her reform-minded associates struggling to distribute charity fairly.

The 24 Sept. 1893 residents' minutes record the following: "The matter of co-operating with Prof. Swing's church in giving outdoor relief was discussed. It was said that systematized charitable work was not the province of the house, and had been avoided heretofore, that if this were done it should be understood that it was in view of the emergency of the present season. Upon motion it was voted to accept the assistance of Dr. Swing's church" (HH Residents, "Residents Meeting Reports," 1893–95, pp. 35–36; *JAPM*, 50:351–52).

12. After the World's Columbian Exposition closed, the need to provide secure lodging for single women did not diminish. JA moved swiftly to implement her lodging-house plans. By 14 Jan. 1894, HH had acquired buildings at two addresses, 159 Ewing and 243 Polk, for lodging houses. Both were to be financed primarily by Mrs. [Harriet Warner?] Walker. Minutes for the HH residents' meeting of 10 Mar. 1894 revealed: "'The Lodging House was opened Dec 20/93 at 159 Ewing St., with 10 cots. The expenses were defrayed by money collected by Mrs. Walker. There have been about 70 women given shelter there, some one night, some a month. Of these about 50 were houseservants who had come to Chicago to work during the Fair and were left stranded. There was 1 dressmaker, 1 factory girl, 4 laundresses, 6 who had no support, five Midway Plaisance actresses and one reporter in disguise.

"'Six were given tickets or passes home[,] six had sewing given at the New Era, some obtained certain situations, 1 was sent to a hospital, one to the Poor House, one to Brideswell.'

"An average of 8 cots are occupied each night" (HH Residents, "Residents Meeting Reports," 1893–95, p. 58; *JAPM*, 50:374).

On 24 Mar. 1894, the residents' minutes indicated that forty-four were expected in the lodging house that week. The minutes for 14 Apr. 1894 reported that the lodging house was closed. Yet during the remainder of 1894, plans for a model lodging facility and sewing room for women in the HH neighborhood progressed. It was not only presented by JA but also promoted by the Central Relief Assn. The *Chicago Record* for 6 Sept. 1894 reported, "Needy sewing-women will have a lodging house and workshop combined if the plans now under consideration are adopted. Instead of the sewing-rooms opened last winter a house is to be rented, contracts for work obtained and a model workshop started. . . . Large sewing contracts for stores will be accepted on the present plan of sweat-shops, with all the objectionable features eliminated. As soon as sufficient money is raised for the project a house will be engaged on the west side in the vicinity of Hull [H]ouse" ("To Help Seamstresses"). Throughout 1894 JA presented the plan to various charitable organizations. By Jan. 1895, the CWC had organized and maintained a model lodging-house facility. In addition, the Model Workshop and Lodging-House Assn. was incorporated in the spring of 1895 by JA and others. By 1899 the organization had become the Woman's Model Lodging-House Assn. and dropped the workshop idea, it "having been proven impracticable," and instituted in its stead "a school of domestic science" ("News of Woman's Clubs").

In the spring of 1899, the lodging house, which had been located at 243 West Polk St., was relocated to a new three-story building between Blue Island Ave. and Halsted St. at 253 Ewing St. This facility was supported by the Model Lodging-House Assn., composed of sixteen women's clubs from throughout Chicago. JA remained one of the directors of the organization. During 1898 the Woman's Lodging-House Assn. "furnished nearly 8,000 lodgings." If a lodger could not pay the fifteen-cent nightly fee for use of the home, she was provided with lodging and permitted to work two hours the next morning doing chores at the home ("News of Woman's Clubs").

13. John ("Johnny 'de Pow'") Powers, who became alderman of the Nineteenth Ward in 1888, served in that position for thirty-eight years. When his political mentor, Billy Whalen, was accidentally killed in 1891, Powers took over his position of authority as a leader among Chicago's powerful "boodler" aldermen. He devised ways to charge businessmen special fees for permitting them to establish vending rights in each street and for acquiring franchises for various means of transportation for each city block. He also helped reduce the tax assessments for the very wealthy, especially those, like Charles T. Yerkes, who were his backers. In 1893 Powers was still solidifying his power. In city elections of 1895, 1896, and 1898, JA and HH residents tried to unseat him by supporting reform candidates (see Article in the *Chicago Record*, 3 Dec. 1894, n. 1; Article in the *HH Bulletin*, Apr. 1896; Article in the *Chicago Times Herald*, 6 Mar. 1898; Essay in the *International Journal of Ethics*, Apr. 1898; JA to MRS, [3 Apr. 1898]; and Article in the *HH Bulletin*, Apr. and May 1898, all below).

Powers (1852–1913) was born in Kilkenny, Ireland, and schooled there in the common schools. He emigrated to the United States when he was twenty years old. He became a grocery clerk and then a grocery store and saloon owner on Chicago's West Side. A Democrat, he achieved political power in the Chicago aldermanic council. For years a member of the powerful finance committee, he served as its chairman in 1897 and 1898. He was also a member of the Democratic Cook County Central Com. and sometimes served as president of the Cook County Democratic Party.

14. The "Chief" was JA.

15. On the development of the HH public playground, see JA to MRS, 26 Aug. 1893, n. 8, above. In years to come, a portion of the HH Playground was flooded in the winter in the expectation that it would freeze and permit ice skating.

16. For information on the first public bathhouse in Chicago, see Two Essays in the *Forum*, Nov. and Oct. 1892, n. 110, above. JA and the HH residents supported the effort to open a large public bath facility in the city. According to Florence Kelley, JA provided the lot on which the Carter Harrison Bath House was constructed. It is unclear if HH provided refreshments for the opening on 9 Jan. 1894 (see JA to MRS, 26 Aug. 1893, n. 8, above).

17. For information on the development of the HH Coal Co-Operative, see Article from the *Chicago Inter Ocean*, 30 June 1892, n. 5, above. It is likely that Seymour T. Coman (1852–1921)

John Powers was the corrupt and powerful Nineteenth Ward alderman whom Jane Addams and the Hull-House residents tried unsuccessfully to defeat during three separate elections, 1895, 1896, and 1898 (*Prominent Democrats of Illinois*, 343).

provided at least part of the funds for leasing the property for the coal yard. The HH residents' minutes for 24 Sept. 1893 revealed that he promised one thousand to fifteen hundred dollars in support of the venture. Coman was born in Newark, Ohio, the son of Levi Parsons and Martha Seymour Coman and brother of historian and settlement resident Katharine Coman. After two years at Dartmouth College, Hanover, N.H., he took a law course at the Univ. of Michigan and came to Chicago in 1876. As a financial representative for Chicago interests, he went to Colorado in 1878 and later was in business in Texas. He returned to Chicago in 1891 and until 1913 was in the commercial paper and collateral loans business at Seymour Coman & Co. Between 1895 and 1900, he gave a total of more than two thousand dollars to the settlement. He served as auditor for HH Assn., 1897–1900. His estate established the Seymour Coman Research Fund at the Univ. of Chicago to assist medical research.

## From John Addams Linn

Las Fuentes[1] Dec 17 1893

Dear Aunt Jane.

Do you think that it is possible that a boy could become a man in one minute? It seems to me that it must be a growth.

Yet this morning as I was thinking over things as they are and as they have been suddenly the whole world seemed new to me as though I had leaped suddenly out of my past life. Do you think such a thing would be possible. Up to this time I can think of no expression of my soul which could not be exactly paralleled by what must have been in the mind of the writer of the 88th Psalm.[2] Lately I have read that over & over.

I have you know been sure that I ought to study for the ministry in the church yet there was, after all, always some lingering fear, due, perhaps, to certain opposition; that it was not perhaps the thing to do. You know I realize that in a sense it must cut me off from the family circle and I have wondered whether, after all, I ought to do it.

But today I have become certain that I could not be true to God nor to myself, if I should disregard that call. I know that I must become a minister.[3]

I talked to no one. I was thinking about my action here. When I came I faced the question as to whether I should kneel at night and pray and whether I should sit without giving thanks and I made up my mind that it would be rather a spiritual form of bravado to do it here. In consequence I have, with numerous misgivings, omitted those things. This morning I made up my mind that the question must be decided unalterably one way or the other—and at last, it seemed that my omission had really been cowardice. I know that it was not right. Then I resolved of course to resume those things in a quiet and unassuming way certainly, not at all flaunting nor definatly but none the less firmly. Then I took up the other question and decided, at last, just as surely that I ought and that I will enter the Church.

I write to you first because, in some way, I have come to consider you as [a?] second mother to me. Perhaps it is due to the fact that in the last four years, you have been nearer to me than my family. I have not consulted you as much as I should, but I have always thought of you as a sort of monitor, as the one who would back me up in any good thing or be the first to turn me from a wrong path.

I have really talked to Miss Starr more than to you and she has helped me more than she perhaps, realizes. But I always think of you rather than of her, why I do not know.

I have been determined to endure the strange surroundings here for several reasons. But I shall now go forward with a firmer confidence and a happy heart.

One other question is before me, which although I might decide now, I have determined to let go for this year, that no one may accuse me of hasty action, that my action, whatever it be, may be the only right decision. That is the question of celibacy. As you know, certain ones are sure that I should take the vow of celibacy. Certain others, who themselves are celibates, are not so sure. They say that this is a question which can only be decided by one person, the man itself. No one else can even dare to give advice. This year I shall ponder the question faithfully and I shall pray for guidance to decide it aright. I shall be glad for any opinion from any one if given to <u>me</u>, but I would ask that restriction. Certainly nothing is gained by trying to influence Miss Brockway[4] to decide the question for me. If Miss Nason[5] or Miss Starr through Miss Nason wish to express their beliefs to me, I shall think over them thankfully, happy that they interest themselves so far in me. Nothing is gained by any other course except torture and discussion where there is no need.

I should much prefer to write directly to Miss Starr, if it is she, but I have no direct information. I must assume these things from incidental allusions and from Miss Brockway's natural pain at being left to infer that she is standing in my path upward. She has not told me that it was Miss Starr. I wish that you would show this part of this letter to Miss Starr for if my suspicions are unjust, I shall be very, very happy. My real ground is that she and she alone has ever had any conversation with me upon this subject. Once, (the first time) I opened it. Well, as she knew me she never intruded.

Of my love for Miss Brockway, it is not necessary to say more than I have told you often. It deeply pains me that you cannot believe me sincere. If not in this, why is aught else?

You must realize, however, that call it by whatever name you will it has helped me to be more brave and has, I know, helped me to make the decision I made this morning. I feel far, far different in every respect but that this evening.

Whatever you believe, treat her as you would treat the woman whom you would be sure I love. [That sentence does not seem to express what I mean but you can divine that].[6]

If anything should ever happen to me, do not treat her as an outsider. Remember that I would not treat her as such.

If God should show me that I should never marry, I would still be a better man for having loved. Sometimes I have had a vague fear that I would never see another year, but I know that that must be merely the result of a headache from working in the sun. Still, God's thoughts are far above men's thoughts.

I am becoming used and hardened to the work. Always your loving nephew,

John Addams Linn.

ALS (SCPC, JAC; *JAPM*, 2:1469–74).

1. Las Fuentes de San Jorge, a site of natural springs, now in Spring Valley, San Diego Co., Calif., was named by early Spanish conquerors. The site became a ranch as early as 1856 when Augustus Ensworth acquired the property and constructed an adobe ranch house on it. In 1885 prolific historian of the American West Hubert Howe Bancroft (1832–1918) acquired the ranch, added acreage to it, and tried unsuccessfully to develop it as a farm. Over time he added rooms to the ranch house and other structures to the farm. The ranch house became a dwelling for the farm manager and the farm hands who helped work the property. Bancroft prized the area for its warm, dry climate, thought to be beneficial for those who were ill. John Addams Linn may have worked for a year on the ranch. The adobe structure survived and later became a museum identified as a U.S. national historic landmark.

2. "O LORD God of my salvation, I have cried day *and* night before thee: / 2 Let my prayer come before thee: incline thine ear unto my cry; / 3 For my soul is full of troubles: and my life draweth nigh unto the grave. / 4 I am counted with them that go down into the pit: I am as a man *that hath* no strength: / 5 Free among the dead, like the slain that lie in the grave, whom thou rememberest no more: and they are cut off from thy hand. / 6 Thou hast laid me in the lowest pit, in darkness, in the deeps. / 7 Thy wrath lieth hard upon me, and thou has afflicted

*me* with all thy waves. Selah. / 8 Thou hast put away mine acquaintance far from me; thou hast made me an abomination unto them: I *am* shut up, and I cannot come forth. / 9 Mine eye mourneth by reason of affliction: LORD, I have called daily upon thee, I have stretched out my hands unto thee. / 10 Wilt thou shew wonders to the dead? shall the dead arise *and* praise thee? Selah. / 11 Shall thy lovingkindness be declared in the grave? *or* thy faithfulness in destruction? / 12 Shall thy wonders be known in the dark? and thy righteousness in the land of forgetfulness? / 13 But unto thee have I cried, O LORD; and in the morning shall my prayer prevent thee. / 14 LORD, why castest thou off my soul? *why* hidest thou thy face from me? / 15 I *am* afflicted and ready to die from *my* youth up: *while* I suffer thy terrors I am distracted. / 16 Thy fierce wrath goeth over me; thy terrors have cut me off. / 17 They came round about me daily like water; they compassed me about together. / 18 Lover and friend hast thou put far from me, *and* mine acquaintance into darkness" (Psalms 88).

3. John Addams Linn graduated from Chicago's Western Theological Seminary in 1897 and was ordained in 1901.

4. John Addams Linn, who had come to live at HH upon graduation from Lake Forest Univ. in 1893, and HH resident Wilfreda Brockway had fallen in love. JA may have been concerned about the seriousness of their affair.

Wilfreda ("Willie") Brockway worked at HH as a nursery and kindergarten teacher from the fall of 1891. For information on the Brockway-Linn relationship, see JA to MRS, [12?] [Apr. 1891], n. 13, above. John Addams Linn was named by his aunt in her list of residents for 1893. In Oct. 1893, he was listed as teaching Latin on Tuesdays at 7:00 P.M. in the Art Exhibit Room. He was probably unable to complete his commitment. He did not teach again at the settlement until the fall of 1903, when his subject was literature.

5. Edith Nason (1857–1912) worked at HH as the teacher of the sickroom and Diet Kitchen program. She was a resident and active at the settlement, Jan. through the summer of 1892. She was an 1892 graduate of St. Luke's Hospital School of Nursing and continued to work and teach at St. Luke's Hospital while she served as a "visiting nurse" for HH (see also JA to SAAH, [ca. 6] [Sept. 1891], n. 6, above). Brockway, who became a nursing student at St. Luke's, would have known her.

According to a newspaper account, in addition to the sickroom cooking demonstrations, Nason offered each Saturday afternoon, she also "prepares special delicacies for the sick which may not be obtained on the order of any physician or accredited nurse, the prices being merely nominal. For instance gruels and porridges of various kinds are but 6 cents a pint. Soups, comprising cream tomato, cream celery, oyster or cream potato for 15 cents a quart, nutritrous broths and other dainty dishes at equally moderate prices" ("Studies at HH").

In 1897 Nason was hired by the Norfolk City Union of the King's Daughters, Norfolk, Va., to establish their Visiting Nurse Service. According to their history "Miss Nason was a brave and tireless worker who became a beloved figure in Norfolk" ("King's Daughters' History," 2). During her first year of service, she made 1,771 visits to poor families. She also helped educate families about nutrition, good hygiene, and good basic health habits. She established a diet kitchen to provide nourishing and inexpensive food. When she died, her program was so successful that there were seven other nurses working for her. She was buried in Norfolk, Va.

6. The statement in brackets and the brackets are part of the original document.

# Part 2

## IT IS THE WORK I MUST DO BECAUSE IT IS THE WORK I LOVE, 1894–96

The part title is a quote from Unidentified newspaper article, Hull-House Scrapbook, ca. 1891.

Photograph: Jane Addams, 27 June 1896. Photograph taken in London by noted society and theatrical photographer Frederick Hollyer. Jane Addams appears in the dress she had made at Liberty of London (UIC, JAMC 0003 2778).

# Introduction

Between 1893 and 1898, the United States experienced a major business depression that had begun with the financial panic of 1893. The excitement and economic benefit from hosting the World's Columbian Exposition during the summer and early fall of 1893 may have masked for Chicago the terrible events unfolding throughout the rest of the country, but by the fall of 1893, when the exposition closed, Chicago began to feel the brunt of economic collapse.

The depression of the 1890s in the United States was characterized by railroad bankruptcies, including the Reading Railroad, the Northern Pacific Railway, the Union Pacific Railroad, and the Atchison, Topeka, and Santa Fe Railroad. An estimated five hundred national, state, savings banks, loan, and trust companies as well as mortgage companies failed. There was a run on the U.S. gold reserves, approximately fifteen thousand businesses closed or at best were consolidated, and farms failed in part because there was little market for their produce. Stock prices plummeted, and wealthy citizens, especially, feared the effects of labor violence and anarchism. Unemployment and labor unrest grew at an alarming pace. In 1894 more than forty thousand workers took part in at least thirty national strikes. One of those strikes that resulted in violence and drew nationwide notice was the Pullman Palace Car strike in Chicago.[1] People could not afford the basic necessities of food and shelter unless they could find assistance from family, friends, churches, or privately based community resources. Newspapers and magazines featured the despair of the unemployed. By some estimates, during the mid-1890s at least 14 percent to 17 percent of the workforce could not find employment.

Jane Addams and her supporters launched major efforts to collect funds for the relief of their neighbors who could not find employment and needed help to survive. In addition, on behalf of the newly formed Civic Federation of Chicago,[2] Jane Addams attempted to help settle the labor disagreement at the Pullman

Palace Car Co. between owner George Pullman and his workers by arbitration.[3] She was not successful; the strike that resulted escalated and led eventually to violence and the first national railway strike in the United States. Jane Addams offered her interpretation of the lessons she learned from the experience in an essay she began writing shortly after the strike was over. She presented her ideas in speeches she gave during the remainder of the 1890s; however, the essay, which became one of her signature essays, remained unpublished because of its controversial nature until 1912, when the *Survey* published it as "A Modern Lear."[4]

At almost the same time as the Pullman strike, Mary Catherine Addams Linn, Jane's sister who had served as her surrogate mother, became ill and died.[5] Suddenly, Jane Addams found herself embroiled in family matters. Of necessity, she became the guardian for the underage Linn children and the executor of her sister's estate.[6] Meanwhile, the programs and the influence of Hull-House grew, and Jane Addams continued her efforts to raise the funds necessary to support the residents and the physical growth of the settlement.[7]

Hull-House residents increased their efforts to conduct investigations of social problems in Chicago and Illinois and to develop reform agendas. They provided a partial record of their findings in their pathbreaking sociological study of the settlement neighborhood, published as *Hull-House Maps and Papers* (1895).[8] Florence Kelley served as the Illinois chief factory inspector and worked, with other Hull-House residents and volunteers, to control sweatshop manufacture and child labor; Julia Lathrop investigated conditions in state-regulated county asylums and poorhouses, developed options for improvement, and conducted efforts to bring beneficial change. Closer to Hull-House, Jane Addams became the Nineteenth Ward garbage inspector in an effort to improve the environment, especially in the streets and alleys of her neighborhood.[9] She was a key member of a committee appointed by political leaders in Cook County to investigate facilities for the insane and poor under their jurisdiction and to recommend reforms.[10] She was also a leader in the successful effort to launch a Charity Organization Society in Cook County.[11] Recognizing that many of the reforms needed in the Nineteenth Ward could be accomplished only with the help of a committed local political leader, Hull-House residents and volunteers led by Jane Addams set out to elect an honest reform-minded alderman to the city council. Their attempts were not successful.[12]

Addams's relationship with Mary Rozet Smith and the Smith family deepened. At Hull-House, the Smiths provided the funding for construction of the Children's Building and continued to support the nursery. In 1896 Jane joined the Smith family for their summer visit to Europe. It proved a pivotal experience for Jane Addams, who found herself a noted and respected figure in Great Britain.[13] She was entertained by social settlement leaders, progressive reformers, members of Parliament, union supporters, and socialists in England, and she also developed new international friendships that would continue into the twentieth century. The high point of this trip, however, was her meeting with

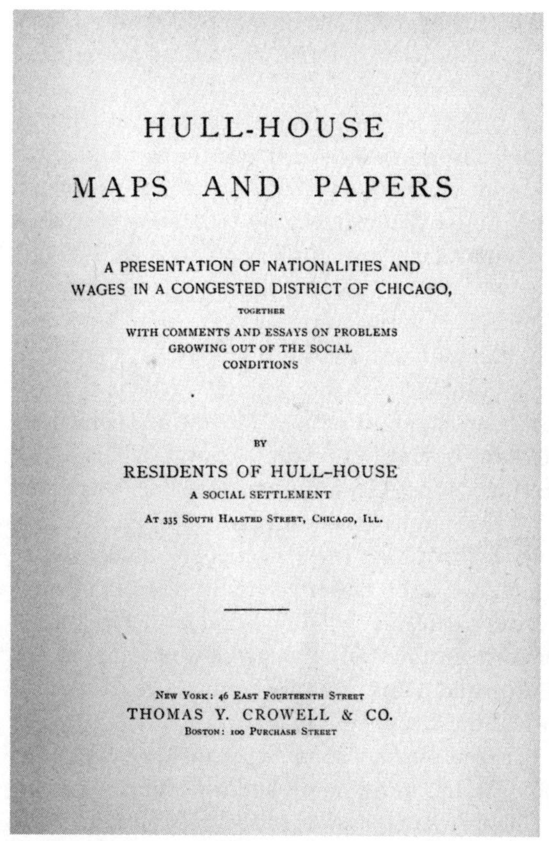

HULL-HOUSE

MAPS AND PAPERS

A PRESENTATION OF NATIONALITIES AND WAGES IN A CONGESTED DISTRICT OF CHICAGO,

TOGETHER

WITH COMMENTS AND ESSAYS ON PROBLEMS GROWING OUT OF THE SOCIAL CONDITIONS

BY

RESIDENTS OF HULL-HOUSE

A SOCIAL SETTLEMENT

AT 335 SOUTH HALSTED STREET, CHICAGO, ILL.

NEW YORK: 46 EAST FOURTEENTH STREET

THOMAS Y. CROWELL & CO.

BOSTON: 100 PURCHASE STREET

Title page for Residents of Hull-House, *Hull-House Maps and Papers*, published in 1895. As early as 1892, the residents of Hull-House, led by Florence Kelley and Jane Addams, began preparing studies for this publication, which became the first systematic social investigation of an American city. It included data gathered by Florence Kelley between 1892 and 1893 on the income levels and ethnic composition of the one-third of a square mile east and near Hull-House that constituted the study area. It was published on two foldout colored maps that helped gain the study its fame.

Leo Tolstoy and the Tolstoy family at Yasnaya Polyana, Russia.[14] In retrospect this daylong event was so significant that it influenced Jane Addams's position on social reform and peace for the remainder of her life. On her return, as one of the few people from the United States who had met Tolstoy, she became an authority on the author, his lifestyle, and his philosophy. From that time forward, many of her speeches and essays contained references to Tolstoy and his vision of the world.

Newspapers began to promote and praise Jane Addams. When she became ill in September 1895 and required a dangerous appendectomy,[15] the *Chicago Daily Tribune* announced her plight and indicated that her name by itself was "the synonym of the best type of womanhood." The *Tribune* referred to her as "universally appreciated," "unique," and a "humanitarian." It found her full of common sense, "no poser," and "perfectly genuine," with a practical perspective backed by great mental capacity. The newspaper lauded her commitment to the idea of "brotherhood" and recalled that she publicly supported the resolution approved by the Chicago Woman's Club on 23 January 1895: "Resolved, That it is the sentiment of the Chicago Women's Club that no one can be excluded from membership on race or color lines."[16]

More new residents settled at Hull-House. Some stayed for a year or two, others longer, but all were attracted by the reform spirit and the communal living arrangement. By late 1896, Addams, Starr, and Keyser were in their seventh year as residents; there were seven first-year residents and six residents in their second year at the settlement. Of the total of twenty-six residents at Hull-House, only five were men.[17]

Madeleine Wallin[18] came to Hull-House because George Sikes,[19] her fiancé, who was a key figure at the settlement as a journalist and as a leader in the Hull-House effort to elect an honest alderman in the Nineteenth Ward, was a resident. In her first year as a resident at the settlement, Madeleine Wallin often served as secretary to Jane Addams. Trying to explain the position of Jane Addams at Hull-House and the reasons for Addams's success to her father, who was a judge in North Dakota, Wallin wrote, "She is the gentlest of mortals, and far indeed from domineering over anybody. The residents are all her willing servitors, and she holds them all by reason of her very admirable qualities of mind and disposition. She is really a cosmic individual, and is able to get into relation with every sort of person by instinctively giving him what he wants and can assimilate. People of position and culture admire her because she is their equal in those lines, and has had the advantages of education and travel, and is possessed of great personal charm. Business men respect her because of her wide comprehension of principles and movements, and her almost unerring judgment in practical affairs. Literary people are impressed by her writings, and are anxious to secure them for their own publications. The poor and afflicted cling to her because of her unfailing sympathy with their troubles, and her wisdom in advising them in their difficulties; and the residents in the House are attached to her by the strongest bonds of personal regard as well as of admiration for her work. She uses the greatest consideration in all her relations with every one—trying to understand and interpret them correctly and generously, and always willing to put herself in the wrong in order to conciliate the other one. I suppose we should call it tact; and yet I am impressed with the genuineness of every such effort to establish right relations. It seems the struggle of a sensitive nature to be entirely honest with itself and with every one else, and to search its own motives and conduct constantly for fear that something not quite kindly or fair may have crept in unawares. She never drives anyone to work and is indeed most considerate in that regard. But it is impossible to live here and not feel to some extent the pressure of work to be done, and indeed one who would not share in it would have little place here. I suppose I do less than any other resident—indeed I am quite sure that I should not be so welcome to stay perhaps, if it were not for the estimation in which Mr. Sikes seem to be much thought of. Sensible men are at a premium here."[20]

Jane Addams and her progressive colleagues became adept at lobbying; developing techniques for mass communication, including organizing and promoting meetings and gaining the interest of newspapers, at the time the major means of getting the news out; and working with individuals and groups who could support their causes. Increasingly, they appeared as speakers and wrote articles for scholarly and popular journals. "Miss Addams is rapidly being recognized as a power in the sociological world. Constantly in demand to speak before gatherings of this character her addresses are widely quoted throughout the country," wrote the *Chicago Daily Tribune*.[21] By the end of 1896, Jane Addams, Hull-House, and the social settlement movement were gaining national recognition for their efforts to inform people about social problems and for successfully fighting for reforms to ameliorate the conditions they revealed.

## Notes

1. See Testimony, 18 Aug. 1894, below.
2. See Testimony, 18 Aug. 1894, n. 9, below.
3. See headnote, Testimony, 18 Aug. 1894, and nn. 10, 12, below.
4. See Testimony, 18 Aug. 1894, nn. 19–21, below.
5. See JA to SAAH, 17 Mar., 16 and 27 Apr., and 4 May 1894; JA to MRS, 29 June 1894; Document, Estate of MCAL, 13 July 1894; and JA to SAAH, 21 July 1894, all below.
6. See EGS [for JA] to SA, 8 Feb. [1895], n. 5; and JA to SAAH, 16 Feb. 1896, both below.
7. See JA to MRS, 8 Aug., and 4 [, 5, and 6] Sept. 1895, both below.
8. See JA to Richard T. Ely, 31 Oct., 27 Nov., and 4 Dec. 1894; and JA to MRS, 26 Mar., 1895, n. 3, all below.
9. See Article in the *Chicago Record*, 25 Apr. 1895, below.
10. See JA to MRS, 4 [, 5, and 6] 1895, below.
11. See JA to Richard T. Ely, 12 Mar. 1895, below.
12. See Two Essays in the *Forum*, Nov. and Oct., 1892, n. 95; Minutes of a HH Residents Meeting, 10 Dec. 1893, n. 13, both above; JA to Henry Demarest Lloyd, 22 Dec. 1895; Article in the *HH Bulletin*, Apr. 1896; Article in the *Chicago Times-Herald*, 6 Mar. 1898; and Essay in the *International Journal of Ethics*, Apr. 1898, all below.
13. See MRS to JA [ Feb. 1896]; JA to SAAH, 16 Mar. 1896; F. Herbert Stead to JA, 24 Apr. 1896; JA to EGS, 29 [and 30] May 1896; JA to Henry Demarest Lloyd, 21 June 1896; JA to Gertrude Barnum, 22 May [June] 1896; JA to MRS, 22 [24], [26 and] 27, and 27 June 1896, all below.
14. See JA to Gertrude Barnum, 25 July 1896; JA to Aylmer Maude, [30 July 1896], both below.
15. "Jane Addams Is Ill," *Chicago Daily Tribune*, 12 Sept. 1895.
16. Frank and Jerome. *Annals of the Chicago Woman's Club*, 145.
17. On 6 Nov. 1896, JA listed the following men as residents: George Hooker, two years; George C. Sikes, two years; Hervey White, one year; Mr. King, one year (HH records indicate that he may have been at the settlement for three months Nov. 1896–Jan. 1897); and Ernest C. Moore, one year. The women were EGS, seven years; Gertrude Barnum, three years; Florence Kelley, five years; Dorothea Lummis Moore, two years; Amanda Johnson, one year; Maude Gernon, two years; Edith Saluda Watson, two years; Rose Marie Gyles, four years; Wilfreda Brockway, five years; May Pitkin, one year; E. H. Johnson, one year; Ella Raymond Waite, three years; Madeleine Wallin, one year; Enella Benedict, four years; Margaret M. West, four

years; Miss Dewey (only appears as a resident in the *HH Bulletin* for Dec. 1896), one year; Mary Keyser (JA keeps writing her last name as "Keyzer"), seven years; and JA, seven years, as the other residents.

18. For a biographical note on Madeleine Wallin Sikes, see Article in the *Chicago Record*, 3 Dec. 1894, n. 1, below.

19. For a biographical note on George Cushing Sikes, see Article in the *Chicago Record*, 3 Dec. 1894, n. 1, below.

20. Madeleine Wallin Sikes to her father, 27 Oct. 1896, UIC, JAMC, Sikes.

21. "Jane Addams Is Ill," 12 Sept. 1895.

## To Mary Rozet Smith

Hotel St Angelo Los Angels—Cal. Jan 27" 1894

My dear friend

I fear this paper will remind you of the Poor & Miserable but it is good for me on that account to use it[1]—for they seem very far away. I will spare you an account of the sweet violets under the veranda where I am writing & of the rose bushes which twine about the posts & the consequent roses which scent the air—it would be nice if they could scent this paper would n't it? & distroy the association.

Alice[2] met me in Kansas City and we had a charming journey together.[3] I slept profoundly all of the nights and most of the days and am feeling quite rested out and very energetic, altho I am lounging "considerable" to live up to the climate. We spent one day in Sante Fè where I quite felt back in Spain. The Pueblo Indians[4] were very fascinating. We spent a good deal of time in one of their villages and later in a school superintended by an old friend of Alice's. I invested $33.00 of your present in spoils there, which you may behold upon your next journey to Hull-House.

We have just come back from a morning visit to the Hospital[5] where we are much cheered by John's improved appearance. He is quite fat & rosey from the "rest cure" & very anxious to be well enough to go with us to San Francisco.

Alice and I are having a very jolly journey together & a good visit. She asks me every little while if she is as good a travelling comrade as Miss Smith—I impressed her so deeply with the joys of our Green Bay trip[6] & she is going to wash my head this P.M—out of sheer emulation of your prowess.

Mr Barnes'[7] family are all out of town as his grandfather is buried to-day in Pasadena. People we know however are constantly turning up[8] & Mr Reynolds[9] sends most elegantly couched notes in regard to dining & calling, altho there are postscripts—~~and then~~ which lead me to suspect that he[10] nervous in regard to the impression the Pacific Coast is about to receive concerning Settlements. Please give my love to your father & mother & believe me always yours

Jane Addams

ALS (SCPC, JAC; *JAPM*, 2:1488–90).

1. The writing paper was without distinction and seemed to provide a difficult writing surface for JA. The first paragraph of the letter is full of lightly inked words.

2. JA and SAAH were once again headed out west. Their last trip to the western United States took place during the summer of 1886. See *PJA*, 2:458–59, n. 4.

3. From the last week in Jan. 1894 until 24 Feb. 1894, JA and SAAH traveled south from Kansas City to New Mexico and then on to Los Angeles, San Francisco, Berkeley, and Oakland, Calif., and then back to Kansas City, via Utah and Colorado. The *Rockford (Ill.) Collegian* reported that they would be going "to help organize a College Settlement on the Pacific coast" (22 Jan. 1894): 6. JA wrote to SA, "We had such a delightful impression of the Leland Stanford University and such a jolly time with the Profs their wives and the students. I spoke three times in 24 hours. I never found so responsive an audience. The University of Cal was very polite, the president gave a small reception in the evening . . . but I quite lost my heart to the other. Have you ever seen a picture of their beautiful buildings? Alice and I have had such a good visit together. We spent Sunday at Salt Lake City but this morning were obliged to part at Grand Junction thro a stupid mistake in buying our tickets. . . . In spite of a good deal of speaking, I feel rested and eager for the fray—in other words quite homesick for Hull-House" ([17 and 20] Feb. 1894, RC, Archives, Anderson; *JAPM*, 2:1495–98).

4. From the time of her youth in Cedarville, Ill., JA had been intrigued by Native Americans and their culture (see *PJA*, 1:43, 1:74, n. 154). It is likely that JA and SAAH visited the Tesuque Pueblo, nine miles north of Santa Fe, Terr. of N.M., and the closest to the town. Existing before A.D. 1200, the pueblo or village was among the smallest of all pueblos in New Mexico and one that managed to cling steadfastly to its traditions and culture despite the Spanish religious influence.

5. John Addams Linn's doctor in Chicago had ordered him to take a "rest cure." He was in a facility, which may have been a ranch, that he identified as Las Fuentes. It was located in southern California, perhaps near what is now Spring Valley, an area known earlier as Las Fuentes de San Jorge. The editors have been unable to discover any other established hospital in the area. See John Addams Linn to JA, 17 Dec. 1893, above. He did not accompany his aunts to the San Francisco area.

6. JA and MRS visited Green Bay, Wis., leaving Chicago around 7 Jan. 1894.

7. HH resident Clifford Barnes.

8. JA visited Fannie Williams McLean (1863–1919), who had shared the head-resident position at the College Settlement, New York City, with Jean Fine (Spahr), and served as head resident for the College Settlement, Philadelphia, Apr.–July 1892, but was living in Berkeley, Calif., with her mother. She had attended the Social Settlement Congress held in Chicago coincident with the World's Columbian Exposition in 1893. A graduate of the Univ. of California, Fannie became an English teacher in the Berkeley High School, 1891–1913, and wrote short stories for popular magazines. She was a director of the San Francisco Settlement Assn. and first president and then a director of the California Branch of the College Equal Suffrage League and worked tirelessly for woman suffrage.

When JA visited California, the Bethlehem Institute (Congregational), organized in 1892, existed, and in Feb. 1894 the Los Angeles Branch of the Assn. of Collegiate Alumnae was in the process of establishing its settlement. JA met with and encouraged Mary E. B. Norton and Rev. Frank E. Hinckley, who were working to create the Oakland Social Settlement in Oakland, Calif., and Fred E. Haynes, who was organizing the South Park Settlement in San Francisco and had founded the San Francisco Settlement Assn. (see Fred E. Haynes to JA, 19 Jan. 1895, UC, Misc.; *JAPM*, 2:1633–35). JA was also likely aware of the City Front Assn. of Volunteer Workers, founded in Feb. 1890, which by 1903 had become the Telegraph Hill Neighborhood Assn. in San Francisco.

9. James Bronson Reynolds.

10. JA omitted a word between "he" and "nervous."

## To Nettie Fowler McCormick

*By 1894 a great deal of Jane Addams's time was taken up with fund-raising to keep the continually expanding settlement solvent. The following letters to Nettie Fowler McCormick[1] and Katharine Medill[2] are examples of her constant attention to financial issues. Each woman already provided financial support for the settlement.[3]*

Hull-House. 335 South Halsted Street. Chicago. [Ill.] March 14" 1894

My dear Mrs McCormick

Last March you very kindly promised to give fifty dollars a year, for three years to Hull-House toward its general expenses. You have given us some money since then for other things, so that it seems almost ungrateful to collect this. But the time is here, and we should be very glad indeed to have the check. I will mark it paid on the subscription book,[4] unless you prefer to have me come with the book—I should of course be very glad to do that.

Thanking you for all your kindness to Hull-House I am very sincerely yours

Jane Addams

March 19. 1894. sent check for $50.—[5]

ALS and HN (SHSW, McCormick; *JAPM*, 2:1511–12).

1. For a biographical note on Nettie Fowler McCormick and a summary of the funds she gave to HH, see JA to SA, [12?] [Aug. 1891], n. 9, above.

2. See JA to Katharine Patrick Medill, 20 Mar. 1894, below.

3. Nettie Fowler McCormick had been a Ten Account participant and helped build the new Gymnasium and Coffee House Building. She had also provided funding for the development of the Jane Club and the Labor Bureau, organized in 1892 by Florence Kelley. Katharine Medill had made a gift in 1893 to help with relief at the settlement and then contributed ten dollars toward the furnishings for the Gymnasium and Coffee House.

4. Unfortunately, JA's "subscription book" for the first few years of the settlement is no longer extant. An example of the kind of information it may have contained has survived in the second subscription book, which JA began 1 Jan. 1895 and ended 1 Jan. 1905 (Addams, [Fund-Raising Record], 1 Jan. 1895–1 Jan. 1905). See photograph on p. 364. Initially, when JA saw donors to request support, she asked that they sign their names and indicate the amount of their pledge. As she collected their pledges, she marked the donors "Pd." By 1903 the names of most donors were written in JA's hand, perhaps indicating that by that time she may not have seen them personally but rather had written or telephoned them about their pledge.

5. Notation written by someone other than JA.

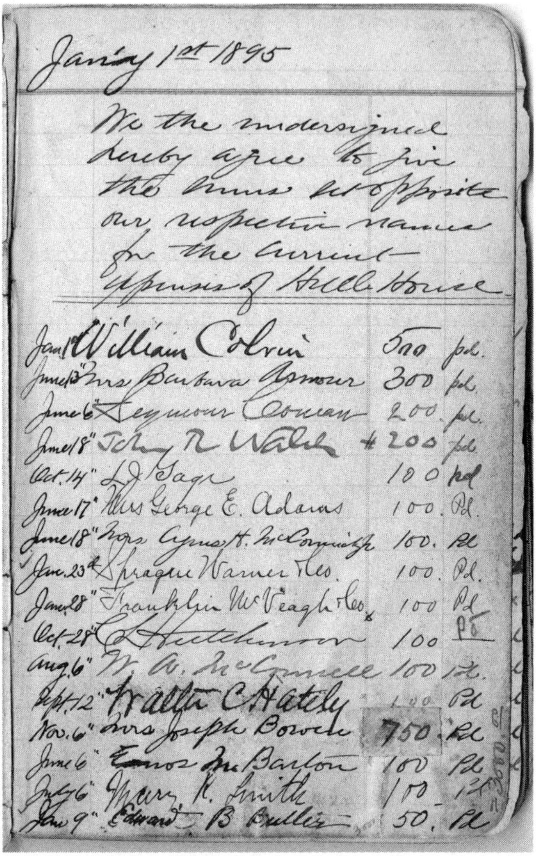
Jan'y 1st 1895

We the undersigned hereby agree to give the sums set opposite our respective names for the current expenses of Hull House

Jan 1st William Colvin 500 pd.
June 13" Mrs Barbara Armour 300 pd.
June 6" Seymour Coman 200. pd.
June 18" John R Walsh 200 pd.
Oct. 14" L J Gage 100 pd
June 17" Mrs George E. Adams 100. Pd.
June 18" Mrs Cyrus H. McCormick 100. Pd
June 23d Sprague Warner & Co. 100. Pd.
June 28" Franklin McVeagh & Co 100 Pd
Oct. 28" C L Hutchinson 100 Pd
Aug. 6" W. A. McConnell 100 Pd.
Sept. 12" Walter C Hately 100 Pd
Nov. 6" Mrs Joseph Bowen 750. Pd
June 6" Enos M Barton 100 Pd
July 6" Mary R. Smith 100
June 9" Edward B Butler 50. Pd

The first page of the 1895–1905 financial subscription book maintained by Jane Addams as her system for recording pledged and paid gifts and building expenses ([Fund Raising Record], 1 Jan. 1895–1 Jan. 1905, HH Assn., UIC, JAMC; *JAPM*, 49:1797).

## To Sarah Alice Addams Haldeman

Hull-House [Chicago, Ill.] March 17" 94

My dear Alice

The check came safely to hand, I will hand over the fifty to Miss Kellogg at the first opportunity. She is going to paint a picture of me for Mary Smith.[1]

The inclosed letter came from Mr Linn yesterday.[2] Mary Keyzer[3] will start Monday and stay with the children while Mary goes away. I want Weber to bring her here first and then later go to Girard if you want it.[4] I think that we ought to act promptly. I will gladly pay the expenses of Weber and herself to Chicago. Perhaps you could help on the [other?] trip.[5] The family claim is strong this spring is n't it? Your loving sister

Jane Addams

ALS (IU, Lilly, SAAH; *JAPM*, 2:1513).

1. JA had written to SAAH to tell her that the portraits she had commissioned by Alice Kellogg were ready. "The pictures are framed and are very magnificent. Mine is $25.00 and Marcet's is 28.50. I have just paid them" (IU, Lilly, SAAH; *JAPM*, 2:1499). In a [post–17] [Mar. 1894] note to SAAH, JA asked, "May Miss [Alice] Kellogg make a copy of my picture for Miss Smith?" (IU, Lilly, SAAH; *JAPM*, 2:1504).

2. The letter is not known to be extant. In it JML was reporting to JA about the precarious condition of MCAL's health.

3. JA frequently misspelled Mary Keyser's family name. Mary was staying with the Linn children in Grinnell, Iowa, while MCAL was seeking health care.

4. MCAL traveled to Chicago with her son James Weber Linn. JA did not favor MCAL going to Girard, Kans., for treatment by HWH. "Please do not urge it any more," JA wrote to SAAH. "I am convinced from Mary's letters that the case is very serious & that Sanitarium treatment is absolutely necessary. I have made the necessary money arrangements" ([post–17] [Mar. 1894], IU, Lilly, SAAH; *JAPM*, 2:1504). JA wanted MCAL to be treated at the Pennoyer Sanitarium in Kenosha, Wis., where SA and AHHA had been patients. See *PJA*, 2:410–11, n. 8.

5. Perhaps JA was asking SAAH to help pay expenses for JML to travel to Kenosha, Wis.

## To Nettie Fowler McCormick

Hull-House. 335 South Halsted Street. Chicago. [Ill.] March 20" 1894

My dear Mrs McCormick

Your check with the kindly note[1] came to hand this morning. I want to thank you once more for your generosity to us. Very sincerely yours

Jane Addams

ALS (SHSW, McCormick; *JAPM*, 2:1514).

1. The note is not known to be extant.

## To Katharine Patrick Medill

*"The revolution in the Coffee House under Miss Crain[1] has gone well, this month we have made a little money, and I am sure are finally on the right track altho it has been pretty tough to give up the New England Kitchen dishes."[2] Hoping to make the Coffee House a self-supporting part of her program, Jane Addams, who continued to search for a solution, had to continue her fund-raising efforts. Unfortunately, her letter to Mrs. Medill did not have the desired effect.*

Hull-House. 335 South Halsted Street. Chicago. [Ill.] March 20" 1894

My dear Mrs Medill

You have always been so much interested in our Coffee house and New England Kitchen, that I venture to write concerning a new plan we have for enlarging it. We are very anxious to do our own baking, we buy between thirty and fifty loaves of bread every day, and a goodly amount of rolls &c.

We have room for a Middlebury brick oven,[3] but to put it in complete with the necessary baking apparatus would cost about two hundred dollars, and I write to ask you whether you would be willing to contribute all or part of that sum. It sounds like a great deal of money but I think that it would do a great deal of good and I am emboldened when I remember that you contributed the first ten dollars toward the Coffee-House.[4] The winter's experiment in foods and drinks has been upon the whole very satisfactory and we are finally self sustaining but we have not enough money in the bank to take out so large a sum for an oven, altho I am convinced that we would make money if we had one. I wish that you might come to visit our Coffee House or that you might have seen the 250 women who lunched there every day from the Rooms for the Unemployed in the New Era.[5] We miss your not being in Chicago and I am sorry not to have been able to see you when I was in California. Thanking you for your many kindnesses to Hull House I am sincerely yours

Jane Addams

ALS (Col. Robert R. McCormick Research Center, Cantigny Park, Wheaton, Ill.; *JAPM*, 2:1515–17).

1. Vennette Crain. See JA to MRS, [2?] [Apr. 1894], n. 1, below.
2. JA to MRS, 3 Mar. 1894, SCPC, JAC; *JAPM*, 2:1508. Unfortunately, no financial records providing receipts and expenditures for the Coffee House are extant until 1895. See also JA to MRS, [2?] [Apr. 1894], below.
3. JA was planning to build a masonry oven constructed of Middlebury, Vt., brick in the HH kitchen. An article in *The Confectioner and Baker and American Caterer* for July 1894 indicates, "A bakery has lately been added to the equipment of the Coffee-house, and all the baking is now done on the premises" ("HH, a Social Settlement").
4. Katharine Medill's gift of ten dollars arrived on 6 Oct. 1891.
5. The sewing rooms in the New Era Building were a few blocks away from the settlement, and the women who used the rooms had their lunch at the HH Coffee House each workday. See JA to Henry Demarest Lloyd, 2 Jan. 1892 [1893], n. 2, above.

## To Mary Rozet Smith

Hull-House, 335 South Halsted Street. Chicago. [Ill.] [2?] [Apr. 1894]

My dear friend

The check came this afternoon. It gives me a lump in my throat, to think of the round thousand dollars you have put into the prosaic bakery[1] and the more prosaic debt when there are so many more interesting things you might have done and wanted to do. It grieves me a little lest our friendship (wh. is really a very dear thing to me) should be pained by all these money transactions. I had a long and warm talk with all the residents last evening, & hope we are going to be more intimate and mutually responsible on the financial side.[2] I am never going to let things get so bad again before I lay it before folks for help and suggestions. It is too bad to let it accumulate to $888.00—it is shocking.

Mr Kohlsaat[3] sent a hundred dollars this morning with a charming letter. I think that by the end of the week we will be quite "out"— I am grateful to all of them but I am more than that to you.

I will telephone you to morrow about Miss Culver for Thursday morning. Always yours affectionately

Jane Addams.

P.S.

Poor Toomey's[4] heroism on Sunday is n't lasting & she is low & veering to her old position today. The father can't be found as yet.

ALS (SCPC, JAC; *JAPM*, 2:1482–85).

1. The HH Coffee House seemed to present continuing problems for JA and the residents of the settlement. At the end of the 1892–93 year, food expenses for HH residents and their guests were $2,843.06, of which they had paid only $1,779.51, leaving a deficit of $1,063.55. The 10 Mar. 1894 minutes of the residents' meeting contained the following notation: "Coffee House. . . . First Mo. $1316.00 receipts. Bal. above receipts $88.00" (HH Residents, "Residents Meeting Reports," 1893–95, 57; *JAPM*, 50:373). Feb. 1894 must have been one of the few times the food operation at the settlement ended the month with an excess of funds over direct expenditures. While there were many people other than the residents who ate at the HH Coffee House, the residents themselves were at least part of the problem in creating the deficits. Many residents could not or would not pay their food bills. At the same residents' meeting, there was a suggestion that residents be assessed for their balances due at the Coffee House. The household account records for 1893 and 1894 indicate that it was usual for the boarding account to reflect an excess of accounts due and payable over expenses. In Apr. 1894, the household boarding account indicated a deficit of $798. See also JA to MRS, 15 Jan. 1895, n. 11, below.

JA spent considerable time and effort trying to organize the settlement's food service. There were often complaints about the quality, taste, and selection of food that the HH Coffee House served. There was also a constant turnover in Coffee House management. JA hoped that bakery offerings added to the New England Kitchen menu would produce just the right combination to make the Coffee House a financial success.

The minutes of the 25 Mar. 1894 residents' meeting indicate that JA and the residents anticipated a new oven and bakery. And by 14 Apr. 1894, the minutes reported that the "Coffee House—not actively losing money—paying bills [b]y week. Miss Daniels will come to teach baking" (HH Residents, "Residents Meeting Reports," 1893–95, 67; *JAPM*, 50:383), clearly implying that the bakery was a certain addition. In 1894 MRS gave $470 toward the purchase of the baking oven JA wanted, and JA added $100.

2. The minutes of the HH residents' meetings, 1893–95, that survived reveal a frequent effort by JA to remind residents to pay their boarding charges. On 6 Mar. 1894, the residents decided that they should receive a monthly financial statement so that they would be more aware of the amount they owed. The HH residents' minutes indicate that the 1 Apr. 1894 gathering was an "internal meeting," which could have been the one that JA described in this letter (HH Residents, "Residents Meeting Reports," 1893–95, 63; *JAPM*, 50:381).

3. Hermann Henry Kohlsaat (1853–1924), Chicago businessman, publisher, and philanthropist, was born in Albion, Edwards Co., Ill., the son of Reimer and Sarah Hill Kohlsaat. He was educated in the schools of Galena, Ill., and Skinner School, Chicago. He began his

business career in dry goods as a cash boy and then a cashier for Carson, Pirie, Scott, and Co. and then became a traveling salesman, especially for Blake, Shaw, and Co., wholesale bakers in which he became a partner in 1880. Eventually, he owned a portion of the business as H. H. Kohlsaat and Co. By 1891 he had become a part-owner of the *Chicago Inter Ocean*. In 1894 he became editor and publisher of the *Chicago Evening Post* and the *Chicago Times-Herald*, which joined with the *Chicago Record* in 1901 to form the *Record-Herald*. He retired from publishing in 1902, but repurchased the *Record-Herald* in 1910 and served as its editor until 1912. The next year, he became editor of the *Inter Ocean*. He was also an investor in Chicago real estate from the early 1900s. Shortly after JA was successfully operated on for appendicitis, he wrote to her to tell her that "it would have made you feel as if you were appreciated if you could have heard the kind expressions by newspaper writers when the papers announced your severe illness" and sent her a bouquet of roses (15 Oct. 1895, SCPC, JAC; *JAPM*, 2:1794). He was a director of the Chicago Athenaeum and the Chicago Auditorium Assn., was a trustee of the Univ. of Chicago, and presented a statue of Ulysses S. Grant to Chicago. He and his wife, Mabel Blake, whom he married in 1880, and their two daughters, Pauline and Katherine, were often donors to HH.

4. Margaret ("Maggie") Toomey.

## To Sarah Alice Addams Haldeman

*"Mary had a comfortable journey from Storm Lake but I was really shocked when I saw her. We got her across the city with the help of rolling chairs and obliging station masters, but I was much relieved to get her safely into bed at the Sanitarium. It is very delightful here and I am sure Mary will improve."[1] By 16 April 1894, Mary Catherine Addams Linn had been at well-known water and rest-cure hospital at Pennoyer Sanitarium in Kenosha, Wisconsin[2] for ten days.*

Hull-House Chicago [Ill.] April 16" 1894

My dear Alice

Mary was so much better yesterday when I spent Sunday with her,[3] that it was a pleasure to behold her. She can walk alone for a few steps and I think will soon be much better. I saw Dr Pennoyer[4] and he is hopeful for a steady recovery. There is no need to be worried, for apparently all she needs is the present treatment continued for some weeks or months. I should be very glad if you could help me on the expense, if I do not have help on the next weeks here I shall have to borrow money for it. They have been heavy so far, I will send you a statement if you care for one. Could you manage the inclosed bill for John.[5] I should be very glad to accept it for the offer you once made to pay for mine. Mary must have absolutely no worry about the bills and poor Mr Linn has been able to collect no money at all. We have known nothing like it in the history of Hull-House.[6]

It seems to me that John ought not to consider coming back to the city in June. I should think that his only chance of doing any sort of work in the fall, was in having a country summer either at Girard or Storm Lake. Mary Keyzer will stay on as long as she is needed. It seems to me that on the whole the best possible arrangements have been made—if we can manage the money part. I will write twice a week and Mary will have Miss Sullivan[7] write. Do not write to her about being worried when you do not hear. Please write or telegraph me.

With love to John and Marcet, always your loving sister

Jane Addams

ALS (IU, Lilly, SAAH; *JAPM*, 2:1525–27).

1. JA to SAAH, 8 Apr. 1894, IU, Lilly, SAAH; *JAPM*, 2:1520. After admitting MCAL to Pennoyer Sanitarium, JA returned to Chicago on the evening of 6 Apr. in order to make her 10:00 A.M. speech at the Kindergarten College on 7 Apr., after which she returned to her sister's bedside. She stayed until the evening of 8 Apr. She and James Weber Linn planned to take turns visiting MCAL.

2. Pennoyer Sanitarium was a place of rest and recovery for AHHA and SA. JA described it as "a cross between a delightful hotel and a well run hospital" (JA to SAAH, 8 Apr. 1894, IU, Lilly, SAAH; *JAPM*, 2:1523). EGS spent a week there in June 1894.

3. 15 Apr. 1894.

4. Nelson A. Pennoyer, the physician who founded the water and rest-cure institution. See *PJA*, 2:410–11, n. 8.

5. John Addams Linn, son of MCAL, spent the summer with SAAH in Girard, Kans. JA was concerned about financing MCAL's stay at Pennoyer and also about expenses associated with MCAL's children. She continued to request support from sister SAAH; however, it seems likely that she did not receive it. By the end of Apr., JA borrowed funds from the Second National Bank in Freeport (see also JA to SAAH, 27 Apr. 1894, below).

6. The economic depression that began in 1893 was in full sway in Chicago. The conditions were exacerbated by the flood of immigrants who had come to the city to work at the World's Columbian Exposition, now ended. Most were now unemployed and looking for work and a way to survive; many required help. Financial records from HH indicate that between 1 Oct. 1893 and the end of Apr. 1894, the relief office at HH provided thirty-two hundred dollars in relief, more than doubling the amount provided over the same period the previous year. The need for relief had never been so great since JA and EGS had founded HH. See also Two Essays in the *Forum*, Nov. and Oct. 1892, n. 151; JA to Emily Greene Balch, 11 May 1893, n. 3; and JA to MRS, 26 Aug. 1893, all above.

7. "The sanitarium nurse is in & out a great deal and does the actual nursing, but as long as Mary is so helpless it seems necessary to have a constant attendent. The Dr preferred some one who was not of the family and I have secured little Miss Sullivan; you may remember her as one of the sweetest girls of the Jane Club. I have offered her five dollars a week and her board will be six more, but that seems to be necessary at present" (JA to SAAH, 8 Apr. 1894, IU, Lilly, SAAH; *JAPM*, 2:1521). MCAL's room was twenty-one dollars a week. MCAL wrote to her daughter Esther Margaret Linn on 18 May 1894 that she was so much better that Miss Sullivan would return to Chicago on 21 May 1894.

## To Sarah Alice Addams Haldeman

Hull-House. 335 South Halsted Street. Chicago. [Ill.] April 27" 1894

My dear Alice

I have n't been able to get enough money ahead to send for the Phil. & So. Progress.[1] If you send me a check for twenty dollars I will send on for twenty of them at once.

I have had an attack of bowel trouble this week, inflammation of the colon Dr Holmes[2] called it. I am much better to-day and will spend Sat night with Mary.[3] She is improving so fast. Weber[4] moves down to the University to morrow, he enters full Sophomore.

I have been obliged to borrow $200.00 at Freeport. There is no need of having my note endorsed but I should be grateful for help in Marys expenses. Of course I have had the same unusual expenses this year of the Worlds Fair as that you have had.

I hope that Harry[5] is feeling better.

Miss Kellogg is copying the picture and will soon finish.[6] You have been awfully patient about it, but I could not hurry her—With much love to John and Marcet[.] Your loving sister

Jane Addams

ALS (IU, Lilly, SAAH; *JAPM*, 2:1528–30).

1. *Philanthropy and Social Progress: Seven Essays by Miss Jane Addams, Robert A. Woods, Father J. O. S. Huntington, Professor Franklin H. Giddings, and Bernard Bosanquet Delivered before the School of Applied Ethics at Plymouth, Mass., during the Session of 1892 with Introduction by Professor Henry C. Adams* was published by Thomas Y. Crowell and Co. in 1893. The price was one dollar. JA's "The Subjective Necessity for Social Settlements" and "The Objective Value of a Social Settlement" were the lead essays in the volume. The book had appeared late in 1893, and JA provided copies for such friends as MRS and the John Coonleys.

2. Dr. Bayard Taylor Holmes.

3. 28 Apr. 1894.

4. JA's nephew James Weber Linn.

5. HWH.

6. Alice Kellogg was copying for MRS the painting of JA that she had created originally for SAAH.

## To Sarah Alice Addams Haldeman

Hull-House 335 South Halsted Street Chicago [Ill.] May 4" 1894

My dear Alice

I spent yesterday afternoon with Mary at Kenosha and found her still improving.[1] I am very anxious that she should be well enough to drive. I am going to Madison next week to speak to the students,[2] I will stop at Rockford[3] and Freeport,[4] and try to write from there. Miss Starr has gone to Mass. Miss Lathrop[5] is poor housing[,] Mrs Kelley is attending the Supreme Court so that it leaves us very short handled.[6] With love to John and Marcet, always your loving sister

Jane Addams

ALS (IU, Lilly, SAAH; *JAPM*, 2:1536).

1. "Mary is better each time, she came down stairs with me and waved me good bye from the porch" (JA to SAAH, 11 May 1894; IU, Lilly, SAAH; *JAPM*, 2:1538).
2. JA was in Madison, Wis., on 9 May to speak under the auspices of the School of Economics and the Contemporary Club. She had been invited to appear by Richard T. Ely, professor and editor of Thomas Y. Crowell's Library of Economics and Politics, for which the HH residents' *HH Maps and Papers* already had been announced. That same day, she attended a reception given by Charles Kendall Adams (1835–1902), president of the Univ. of Wisconsin from 1892 until his death.
3. "May 7"—RC Students" (Addams, "Diary, 1894–95"; *JAPM*, 29:209).
4. At Cedarville JA found "Weber is so blue and depressed it quite breaks my heart" (JA to SAAH, 11 May 1894; IU, Lilly, SAAH; *JAPM*, 2:1538).
5. Julia C. Lathrop began serving on the Illinois State Board of Charities in 1893. "She visited every one of the 102 county farms or almshouses, discussing conditions with their superintendents and ameliorating for the inmates as best she might the evil effects which unjust suffering always produces," wrote JA years later about Lathrop's commitment (Addams, *My Friend*, 83).
6. In May 1894, the Illinois Supreme Court reviewed the eight-hour provision of the Illinois Sweat-Shop Act of 1893. Section 5 of the act "prohibited the employment of any female in any factory or workshop for more than eight hours in any one day or forty-eight hours in any one week" (Beckner, *A History of Labor Legislation in Illinois*, 153–54). Manufacturers and their supporters wanted that section of the law abolished. Kelley had been busy laying the groundwork for its defense and preparing the brief from which the arguments in support of that part of the law would be made. In its decision handed down 15 Mar. 1895, the Court unanimously declared that provision of the act unconstitutional primarily because it "conflicted with the constitutional guarantee that 'no person shall be deprived of life, liberty or property without due process of law' and that the 'Legislature has no right to deprive one class of persons of privileges allowed to another persons under like conditions'" (Sklar, *Florence Kelley and the Nation's Work*, 281).

## To Mary Rozet Smith

Hull-House. 335 South Halsted Street. Chicago. [Ill.] [June?] [1894]

My dearest friend

I hope that this book[1] will throw some light on the questions that vex our souls. I wish that there was some book that would express all the gratitude and affection I have for you. I fear that I will have to write one myself to get it all in. Always yours

Jane Addams

ALS (SCPC, JAC; *JAPM*, 2:1481).

1. *Philanthropy and Social Progress.*

## To Sarah Anderson

Hull-House. 335 South Halsted Street Chicago [Ill.] June 23d 1894

My dear friend

I was very much touched by your letter and the generous check[.] I am also perplexed. I do not think that I ought to accept it. I know how hard a year this has been and how many things you want for R.F.S. I have been so mean to it lately that it is still meaner to accept money that would naturally go to it, if indeed you ought to give it away at all. Our leak this year has been the huge amount given in relief to our neighbors.[1] If we had half of that money for running expenses we would have ample to pay our taxes and a few other trifles that are staring us in the face. The suffering has been & is fearful—and it is absolutely impossible to live in the midst of it and not do something about it. The Settlement will always have to face that—individual distress among personal friends—it is a pull on one's personal loyalty and affection in addition to the "cases."[2] I think that we will manage better next year, but last winter all the stray sums & friendly donations promptly went to the P. & M's[3] as we call them.

It was of course stupid—one ought to have seen that the same thing that made the poor poorer, made our donors poorer too—not to mention one's friend and 'lations.

I am wonderfully grateful to you for the sum. I sooth my conscience by thinking that when I am "easy again" I will be good to R.FS. but I probably won't ever be flush again.[4] I wish very much that you could come in for a little visit, the house is almost empty and quite cool in spots. Ellen[5] has had or is in her most charming mood. She is at Kenosha "in retreat" this week. I wish we could have some long talks together, not the professionally "long talks" that come in a short visit but some real intercourse. I had a very good time at Cleveland[6]—especially with Miss Perry[7] a friend of Miss Eastman's.

The Summer School is coming on very well.[8] So many people are applying for the little sisters &c, as the Lake Geneva is closed this summer it is pretty hard to refuse them. I have taken a few with the stipulation that "they must be kept out of doors"—Do you think that they will be dangerous to *[three words illegible]*[9] Mrs Kelley sends you her love, she is having a awful time just now with "the Dr" who is prowling about the children constantly.[10] We all need you to cheer us up. Always yours

Jane Addams

ALS (RC, Anderson; *JAPM*, 2:1544–46).

1. See JA to SAAH, 16 Apr. 1894, n. 6, above.

2. JA seems to have questioned the use of the dehumanizing word *cases* when applied to the very real and degrading plight of individuals or families who were forced to seek help through the various district offices of the Central Relief Assn.

3. "P. & M." was JA and the settlement residents' abbreviation for "poor and miserable."

4. JA was running out of funds from her legacy, but she was discovering that she could begin supporting herself through public speaking. During the months of Feb. through June, and beginning again in Sept. through Dec., 1894, JA recorded sixty-four speeches in her 1894–95 speech diary. JA did not begin keeping a record of her annual income from speaking until 1897 (see also Excerpts from Addresses, 14 July–9 Dec. 1897, n. 2, below). That year she recorded fees of $730. In 1898 she made $885; in 1899, $1,700; and in 1900, $1,590 (Addams, "Total Earnings"). She kept track of her fee income annually for thirty-seven years until Dec. 1934.

5. EGS had been in Massachusetts visiting family in May and had returned to try Pennoyer Sanitarium for a week in June.

6. "June 19" Commencement Address—Woman's Dept[.]—Western Reserve Univ., ~~Cincinnati~~ Cleveland Ohio" (Addams, "Diary, 1894–95"; *JAPM*, 29:211). For a published version of the address that JA gave on that occasion, see [Address at the commencement exercises at Western Reserve College for Women], in "The Commencement," *College Folio* 2 (June 1894): 129–31; *JAPM*, 46:643–46.

7. Elizabeth Eastman's friend was Jennette Barbour Perry (Lee ) (b. 1860), who was professor of English at the College for Women, Western Reserve Univ., from 1893 until 1896. See JA to AHHA, 9 May 1889, n. 5, above.

8. The third HH Summer School at RC was held 10 July to 10 Aug. 1894. A brochure listing the classes and events for the school was published as "Summer School at RC, Rockford, Ill. in Connection with the College Extension Classes of HH" (HH Scrapbook 1:42; *JAPM*, Addendum 10:6ff). For those attending, the settlement provided half-priced railroad tickets from Chicago to Rockford and return. Despite the death of MCAL, JA managed to attend a portion of the school. She reported to SA, "We had a delightful school and came out $74.03 ahead. This with what we had in the bank & interest for it makes our deposit $133.25" ([13?] Aug. [1894], RC, Archives, Anderson; *JAPM*, 2:1566).

9. According to RC archivist Mary Pryor, "There was a crease in the paper, and that has worn away the ink. If I were to guess, it some what looks like 'new painter.' I looked at it under a magnifying glass, and that is perhaps what the words said" (email Mary Pryor to Mary Lynn Bryan, 16 Mar. 2011, JAPP). Perhaps the words were "new paint &c."

10. In the Chicago neighborhoods where sweatshops persisted, smallpox was rampant during the summer of 1894. By May 1,407 cases of the highly contagious and dread disease had been reported. Florence Kelley was doing her best to help contain it and, at the same time, use it as a means to close sweatshops. She identified shops in which smallpox existed and used the health threat as legal means for closing the shops and destroying the clothing made in them. At the same time, she was also carefully watching the arguments before the Illinois Supreme Court in the matter of the eight-hour workday law for women and the ruling that would be issued (see JA to SAAH, 4 May 1894, n. 6, above). According to JA, she was also being harassed again by her abusive former husband, Lazare Wischnewetzky, from whom, in Chicago in Mar. 1892, she had won a divorce and full custody of her children: Nicholas ("Ko"), age nine in 1894; Margaret, age eight; and John, age six.

## To Mary Rozet Smith

*"I recived Alices Letter <this morning> telling me the sad newes of Niece Dear Mary Linns <Death.> I never new she had been sick Oh how heard it is for her family and you all for she was so loveley and good," wrote Jane Addams's aunt Elizabeth Weber Reiff,*[1] *shortly after she learned that Mary Catherine Addams Linn had died in Pennoyer Sanitarium, Kenosha, Wisconsin, on 6 July 1894.*[2] *Despite the national*

*railroad strike, which began as a rejection of the Pullman Palace Car Company policies toward its workers on 26 June and continued until at least 10 July 1894, and with the help of federal and state troops, Jane Addams and the Linn family, living in Iowa, managed to get to Mary's side before she died. Yet at the time Jane wrote this note to Mary Smith, she was still hopeful for a better outcome.*

Pennoyer Sanitarium Kenosha Wis June 29 1894

My dear friend

My sister has had a wretched week, but I left Thursday evening[3] feeling encouraged about her. Friday[4] at two I had a telephone message from Dr Dell[5] that there were symptoms of heart weakness. I came up Friday with a trained nurse and will stay until she is decidedly better. The doctors insist that there is no immediate danger but that the condition is very critical. I telegraphed the opinion to Mr Linn and Alice this morning and probably one or both of them will come.

I will certainly be here until Tuesday and longer and hope very much that you will stop on Tuesday as we planned. Whatever happens it will be a comfort to see you. Mrs Linn knows you are planning to come and hopes you will. Her mind is very active and alert and she is so pleased to have me with her that I feel like a brute when I think of the days I have n't been here. Weber[6] is a great comfort, altho [h]is round face is oddly pinched up. Please give my love to the three Harveys[7] and believe me always Yours

Jane Addams

P.S. The Cabs are always at the station & come directly here.

P.S. The heart trouble is not organic but nervous. We dread heart failure.[8]

ALS (SCPC, JAC; *JAPM*, 2:1550–51).

1. 17 July 1894, IU, Lilly, SAAH; *JAPM*, 2:1558.
2. According to MCAL's death certificate, she died of a cerebral hemorrhage.
3. 28 June 1894.
4. 29 June 1894.
5. Dr. Lillian Dell, an assistant physician at Pennoyer Sanitarium, seems to have been employed there only during the 1893–94 year.
6. James Weber Linn.
7. Joel D. and Julia Plato Harvey had three children. See JA to MCAL, 12 Feb. 1889, n. 28, above.
8. This postscript appeared at the top of the first page of the letter.

## Document

Chicago, Ill. 13 July 1894

*Mary Catherine Addams Linn died intestate on 6 July 1894, and Jane Addams became the executor of her estate. By a document executed for the Probate Court of Cook County, Illinois, on 12 July 1894, Mary's husband, Rev. John Manning*

*Linn, and her oldest son, John Addams Linn, who was legally an adult at twenty-two years of age, both of whom were eligible as executors of the estate, declined to serve in that capacity. At the time, Rev. Linn was without employment and John Addams Linn was about to become a student at Western Theological Seminary in Chicago. An inventory, listed by Rev. Linn and his son John, revealed that Mary left an estate composed primarily of real estate, which they valued at $33,600. She also had liabilities associated with that real estate of approximately $8,000 and only $73 in a bank account to meet her expenses. The estate was officially open until 22 September 1897, at which time Jane's final accounting was approved in the Cook County Probate Court and she was dismissed from her duties.*

**Know all Men by these Presents,** That we Jane Addams as principal and William H. Colvin and Theodore F. Rice as sureties of the County of Cook and State of Illinois, are held and firmly bound unto the people of the State of Illinois, in the penal sum of Five Thousand Dollars, current money of the United States, which payment well and truly to be made and performed, we and each of us bind ourselves, our heirs, executors and administrators, jointly, severally and firmly by these presents.

Witness our hands and seals, this 12th day of July A. D. 1894

**The condition of the above Obligation is such,** that if the said Jane Addams Administratrix of all and singular the goods and chattels, rights and credits of Mary C. A. Linn deceased, do make or cause to be made a true and perfect inventory of all and singular the goods and chattels, rights and credits of the said deceased, which shall come to the hands, possession or knowledge of her the said Jane Addams as Administratrix, or to the hands of any person or persons for her; and the same so made, do exhibit or cause to be exhibited in the Probate Court of the said County of Cook, agreeably to law; and such goods and chattels, rights and credits, do well and truly administer, according to law, and all the rest of the said goods and chattels, rights and credits, which shall be found remaining upon the account of the said Administratrix, the same being at first examined and allowed by the Court, shall deliver and pay unto such person or persons, respectively, as may be legally entitled thereto; and further do make a just and true account of all her actings and doings therein, when thereunto required by the said Court; and if it shall appear that any last will and testament was made by the deceased, and the same be proved in Court, and letters testamentary or of administration be obtained thereon, and the said Jane Addams do in such case, on being required thereto, render and deliver up the letters of administration granted to her as aforesaid, and shall in general do and perform all other acts which may at any time be required of her by law, then this obligation to be void; otherwise to remain in full force and virtue.

Jane Addams (SEAL)
Residence, 335 So Halsted St. Chicago Ill.
William H. Colvin (SEAL)
Residence, 4003 Ellis Ave Chicago Ill.
Theodore F. Rice (SEAL)
Residence, 5554 Woodlawn Ave Chicago Ills

APPROVED IN OPEN COURT
Jul 12 1894.
Kohlsaat
Probate Judge of Cook County, Illinois.

I do solemnly swear that I will well and truly administer all and singular the goods and chattels, rights, credits and effects of Mary C. A. Linn deceased, and pay all just claims and charges against her estate, so far as her goods, chattels and effects shall extend, and the law charge me and that I will do and perform all other acts required of me by law to the best of my knowledge and abilities.

Subscribed and sworn to before me, ROGER C. SULLIVAN Clerk of the Probate Court of Cook County, this 12 day of July A. D. 1894
Roger C. Sullivan Clerk.

Jane Addams

STATE OF ILLINOIS, } ss.
COUNTY OF COOK.

I, ROGER C. SULLIVAN, Clerk of the Probate Court of Cook County, in the State of Illinois, do hereby certify that Jane Addams William H. Colvin and Theodore F. Rice who are personally known to me to be the same persons whose names are subscribed to the foregoing instrument, appeared before me this day in person, and acknowledged that they signed, sealed and delivered said instrument, as their free and voluntary act for the uses and purposes therein set forth.

SEAL

Given under my hand and the Seal of said Probate Court, at my office, in the City of Chicago, in said County, this 12th day of July A. D. 1894
Roger C. Sullivan
Clerk of the Probate Court.

STATE OF ILLINOIS, } ss.
COUNTY OF COOK.

PROBATE COURT OF COOK COUNTY.

*THE PEOPLE OF THE STATE OF ILLINOIS,*
*To all to whom these Presents shall come, GREETING:*

**Know ye that Whereas,** Mary C. A. Linn of the County of Cook and State of Illinois, died intestate as it is said, on or about the 6th day of July A. D. 1894, having at the time of her decease personal property in this State, which may be lost, destroyed, or diminished in value, if speedy care be not taken of the same; to the end, therefore, that said property may be collected and preserved for those who shall appear to have a legal right or interest therein, we do hereby appoint Jane Addams of the County of Cook and State of Illinois, Administratrix of all and singular the goods and chattels, rights and credits which were of the said Mary C. A. Linn at the time of her decease, with full power and authority to secure and collect the said property and debts, wheresoever the same may be found in this State, and in general to do and perform all other acts, which now are or hereafter may be required of her by law.

WITNESS, ROGER C. SULLIVAN, Clerk of the Probate Court in and for the said County of Cook, and the seal of said Court, this 12th day of July A. D. 1894
Roger C. Sullivan Clerk.

SEAL

Jane Addams was the executrix for her sister Mary Catherine Addams Linn's estate and also became the guardian for her underage children, Esther Margaret and Stanley Ross Linn (P & ADS, July 1894, Records of the Estate of Mary Catherine Addams Linn, Cook Co., Ill., Clerk of the Circuit Court, Probate Records, Doc. 34, p. 307; *JAPM*, 26:734).

*During the more than three years that Jane Addams managed the estate, she, sometimes with the advice of sister Sarah Alice Haldeman, sold some of the real estate while retaining some in order to support the minor children until they reached adulthood. She also paid bills for all of the Linn children and paid Mary Linn's debts, one of which was $2,448.09 to herself for funds the estate had borrowed from her and expenses associated with Mary's last illness. Jane returned to the Linn children $448 each as the final estate distribution. Rev. Linn had rejected any claim he had against the estate in favor of his children, and Jane refused to take an executor's fee.*

*Jane and Sarah Alice continued to manage the unsold real estate from May's estate for the benefit of her children into the first years of the twentieth century.*

## To Sarah Alice Addams Haldeman

*When Jane Addams became the executor of Mary Catherine Addams Linn's estate, she also took over as surrogate mother of her sister's children. By 1896 she was recognized in the legal documents associated with the estate as guardian of the two youngest Linn children, Esther and Stanley, who had not yet reached their eighteenth birthdays.*

Hull-House 335 South Halsted Street Chicago [Ill.] July 21" 1894

My dear Alice

The inclosed letter from Mr Linn may be after all the best decision. I will talk it over with him when he comes and hope that he will decide to let me take the children for this winter. Cedarville school would be out of the question for Esther and I am not willing to have them separated if we can help it. I am sure that he could not keep house on that meagre salary in any sort of comfort.

The children are very happy and have been quite well until Stanley fished to hard yesterday and has had to stay in bed to-day. I think that he will be all right in a few hours. We have been invited up the river this afternoon and are beginning to have various festivities. It seems to me that if you would do the work of Co. Sup't[1] better than other candidates you ought to take it—it is only the work to be done that really ought to be considered. With kisses to Marcet, always your loving sister

Jane Addams

ENCLOSURE

## From John Manning Linn

CENTRAL-WEST ADVERTISING BUREAU. Chicago, Ill., July 20 1894

My dear Sister,

I have spent one day and a night in Chicago Lawn[2] and yesterday James[3] came out to the Lawn and together we looked over houses. We settled on one and told the owner I would let him know on Monday next[.][4] By that time I will know whether the salary of 1000 is surely pledged. They are at work on the subscription.[5] James and I talked the matter over in all its lights. They wanted 15 a month for the house but we got them down to 12 until May 1st[.] But the house is built on Cedar posts has no cellar but a boarded up one. The house has eight rooms and the upper story is a 3/4 story. The well is 16 ft. There is a cistern[.] There is no plumbing. It is fairly well built and could be made comfortable with stoves except lower floor would be cold.

I have made up my mind it could be a doubtful experiment to go to house keeping in that shape.

James offers me a good house near him at 15 dollars to May 1st[.] It has a furnace & all the plumbing water &c and is new & nice. But that would keep me off the field. Now if we were to drop down to living in a shell of a house on Cedar posts, the children's health would be risked.

I have made up my mind it would be too great risk & expense & that we had better provide board for the children for the winter, I think either Alice or Laura[6] wd. take them.

I will stop & see you & them on Tuesday next on my way to Storm Lake.[7] I will go out & stay over night. I expect to be away over one Sabbath, Affec Yrs. Bro.

J.M. Linn

ALS (UIC, JAMC; *JAPM*, 2:1561–64).

1. SAAH served ten terms, 1888 to 1898, as president of the Girard, Kans., Board of Education.

2. Chicago Lawn was a community in Cook Co., Ill., with a post office established 24 Dec. 1893 and disestablished 30 June 1894 when it became part of Chicago.

3. JML's brother James C. Linn and his wife, Annie, lived to the south of Chicago in Englewood, Ill., which by June 1894, when its post office was disestablished, had become annexed to Chicago. James Linn was manager of the Central-West Advertising Bureau in Chicago.

4. 23 July 1894.

5. From mid-1894 until sometime in 1895, JML was the pastor of the Chicago Lawn Presbyterian Church.

6. Neither SAAH nor LSA took the Linn children permanently. Both helped JA care for them for short periods of time. In Sept. 1894, JA wrote to SAAH, "Esther does not want to go to Englewood with her father and the plan of having her come here to school [RC] seems to me by far the best one. It would certainly be the best thing educationally and she thinks of it

The Linn children, ca. 1894–95. John Addams, James Weber, Esther Margaret, and Stanley Ross Linn photographed by William J. Root, who had a studio in Chicago between 1891 and 1900 (private collection).

enthusiastically. . . . In that case Mary K[eyser]. & I would have Stanley with us and I am sure could take good care of him. He is a dear little fellow. I grow fonder of him every day" (UIC, JAMC; *JAPM*, 2:1553–54). By 25 Sept. 1894, JA had determined that Esther would join Sarah ("Sadie") Weber Addams as a student at RC. Stanley went to stay with his aunt Annie and uncle James C. Linn in Englewood. JA also reported that John Addams Linn had just been confirmed and was about to enter seminary. Weber was a student at the Univ. of Chicago. At the end of Oct., JA wrote to SAAH: "Web and John are both here today and I have had a delightful visit with both of them. John weighs 157 lbs and is much more quiet and natural than he has been for a long time. Web is growing so handsome that is really getting to be a snare in a temptation to pride" (UIC, JAMC; *JAPM*, 2:1586–87).

7. JML had been president of Buena Vista College in Iowa and pastor of the Buena Vista Presbyterian Church, 1892–94.

## TESTIMONY

*Throughout May and June 1894, Jane Addams spoke in the Chicago area; in Madison, Wisconsin, and in Cincinnati and Cleveland,[1] and she traveled to and from Kenosha, Wisconsin, to be with her ailing sister, Mary Linn. She also became embroiled in a strike at the Pullman Palace Car Company. Jane Addams later remembered the summer of 1894 as "a time of great perplexity," when Abraham Lincoln's message "with charity towards all" seemed to resonate with her.[2]*

*More than three thousand employees of the Pullman Palace Car Company living in Pullman, Illinois,[3] the model company town developed by industrialist and company owner George M. Pullman,[4] went on strike on 11 May 1894, effectively closing the Pullman works. It became the catalyst for the first-ever national boycott and railroad strike in the United States, lasting from 26 June until 8 August 1894 and resulting in federal troops being called out to maintain order and help bring the strike to a close.*

*Since the fall of 1893, Pullman employees and their families, like most other workers caught in the business depression of the mid-1890s, had been experiencing increasing economic distress. By the spring of 1894, the Pullman Company had reduced workers' wages by an average of one-third of their 1893 level. The company was facing a declining demand for its railroad cars.[5] However, Mr. Pullman and his company administrators refused to reduce the rents he expected his workers to pay for their lodgings in his town or to see that there was a decrease in the price of necessities that he expected his workers to purchase from the town stores. The workers and their families were finding it impossible to live on what they were paid.[6] Although some business leaders in Chicago supported Pullman's actions, many of the newspapers did not. Even the* New York Times *recognized the predicament of Pullman's employees.[7]*

*One of the results of the wage-living expense disparity was increasing unionization. By April 1894, more than two thousand Pullman workers had joined the newly formed American Railway Union.[8] On 7 May and again on 9 May, a committee of at least forty workers from the nineteen unions representing Pull-*

*man employees presented a list of grievances, including wages, rents, and control over employees living in the model town, to the Pullman management. Pullman responded by firing three workers who were members of the committee and refused to arbitrate the grievances. The workers felt they had no recourse but to strike.*

*The Civic Federation of Chicago*[9] *tried to arbitrate the conflict. Leadership of the federation agreed that its Industrial Committee, of which Jane Addams was a member, form a Committee of Conciliation*[10] *to meet with disgruntled workers and with company management.*[11] *As a member of the Committee of Conciliation, Jane Addams took the lead in attempting to bring both sides to the table. She wrote several letters to Pullman management requesting a meeting,*[12] *and on 1 June she went with the Civic Federation's secretary Ralph M. Easley*[13] *to the company headquarters to try to arrange a meeting. In response to the unwillingness of George M. Pullman or his second vice-president, Thomas H. Wickes,*[14] *to meet with her, she described the strike at Pullman as "a struggle between one of the great monopolies on earth and the most powerful organization in railway labor. It is worthwhile for the Civic Federation to settle this question if it can. But Mr. Pullman . . . will not consent." And perhaps somewhat miffed at the lack of support her effort received from other conciliation committee members, she continued, "And if the Civic Federation, representing all the best elements in the community, cannot effect so desirable a result, it cannot justify its existence."*[15] *Even after George Pullman left town so that he would not be available to meet with the Civic Federation or the union representatives, Jane Addams pursued the possibility of arbitration. She described her unsuccessful efforts to achieve an arbitrated settlement on the one issue of the rents at Pullman in the following exchange with the members of the United States Strike Commission, meeting in Chicago on 18 August 1894. They were there to investigate the boycott of Pullman cars and the national strike and boycott that resulted.*[16]

*Jane Addams wrote an essay interpreting the events associated with the Pullman strike and its aftermath. She compared George M. Pullman to Shakespeare's King Lear, focusing especially on Lear's relationship with his daughter Cordelia. "After the Pullman strike I made an attempt to analyze in a paper which I called* The Modern King Lear, *the inevitable revolt of human nature against the plans Mr. Pullman had made for his employees, the miscarriage of which appeared to him such black ingratitude," she wrote in* Twenty Years at Hull-House. *"It seemed to me unendurable not to make some effort to gather together the social implications of the failure of this benevolent employer and its relation to the demand for a more democratic administration of industry."*[17] *She concluded, "The entire strike demonstrated how often the outcome of far-reaching industrial disturbances is dependent upon the personal will of the employer or the temperament of a strike leader."*[18]

*Jane Addams spent the last half of 1894 working on the essay, and intermittently for several years thereafter she polished and revised her account of the events in which she actually played only a small role. She presented her findings in numer-*

*ous speeches during the following years and asked friends to comment on her essay.*[19] *Although she offered her paper to the editors of periodicals she considered friendly to her reform perspective,*[20] *she was unable to find a publisher for it until 1912, when it was published for the first time in the* Survey.[21]

*"In the public excitement following the Pullman strike Hull-House lost many friends," Jane Addams recalled.*[22] *She discovered, "The fact that the Settlement maintained avenues of intercourse with both sides seemed to give it opportunity for nothing but a realization of the bitterness and division along class lines."*[23] *When arbitration failed, Jane Addams remained true to her belief in its efficacy and did not take sides in the Pullman struggle. Much later, her friend Alice Hamilton recalled that Jane Addams was personally stunned at the response of the public to her involvement in the strike and felt herself separated "from the great mass of her countrymen"*[24] *and also denounced by business leaders and supporters who considered her "a traitor to her class."*[25] *The perspective Jane Addams developed and presented about the events associated with the Pullman strike proved in retrospect a watershed event for her and for Hull-House. If the settlement lost its shiny image and financial appeal among business leaders and upper-middle-class supporters, Jane Addams lost her cachet as the kindly and socially acceptable spinster doing good work among the downtrodden of Chicago, but she gained a national reputation as a thoughtful and philosophical voice for reform.*

Chicago, Ill. 18 August 1894

August 18, 1894, Jane Addams, being first duly sworn, testified as follows:

1 (Commissioner Wright). State your name, residence, and occupation.—Ans. Jane Addams; live at No. 335 South Halsted street; am superintendent of the Hull House.

2 (Commissioner Wright). Are you a member of the Civic Federation?—Ans. Yes, sir; I am a member of the board of conciliation of the Civic Federation.

3 (Commissioner Wright). State briefly what your experience has been during the recent strike relative to the action of that board of which you are a member toward securing an adjustment of the difficulties.—Ans. The board met at the Auditorium[26] during the early stages of the strike, before the convention of the American Railway Union in Chicago.[27] I was asked by the gentlemen on the board to find out as near as I could the attitude of the strikers toward arbitration. The object of the board was to arrange for a board of conciliation. My first intercourse with the strikers was when Mr. Heathcoate[28] presented the case before the labor assembly committee,[29] and I made an arrangement with him to go down to Pullman. While there I took supper with some of the girls working there, and went around to see the houses with members of the relief committee;[30] also investigated as best I could the rentals, as compared with the tenement house rentals elsewhere;[31] the general committee there felt that I had better deal through the members of the American Railway Union and referred me to Mr. Howard;[32] I saw him and found he was very friendly

toward the notion of arbitration, and I reported that back to our board of conciliation. Mr. Bartlett,[33] president of the board of conciliation, and one or two other gentlemen had promised to see the Pullman committee. We found it impossible to go further with the men until we knew more about the attitude of the company.

I made arrangements with the general secretary of the association and Mr. Bartlett, the president, to go and see the company, but through a mistake in the telephone message Mr. Bartlett failed to be present; but Mr. Easley, the secretary, and myself saw the representatives of the company.[34] By this time the railway convention had assembled in Chicago, and the next time I saw Mr. Debs,[35] Mrs. Henrotin[36] went with me. This was our second call. We found Mr. Debs not only ready for arbitration, but he seemed to be eager to have the matter arbitrated. This was before the Pullman matter had been formally considered by the convention,[37] although much discussed, and Mr. Debs arranged with our committee to meet the general strike committee at Pullman that same evening.[38] He asked one of the Pullman men to go down and arrange to have a general session of the strike committee at Turner Hall, in Pullman. Mrs. Henrotin was unable to go down, and I was the only member of the committee that went to Pullman. That evening they had a meeting, at which there were present between fifty and sixty delegates from the local union, Mr. Heathcoate presiding. Some of the men at first were rather suspicious—did not know but what this attempt at arbitration was an attempt on the part of the company, and that the American Railway Union would not take up their cause—but their suspicions were quickly allayed, and after the case was presented they voted that they were ready to arbitrate any and all points, and that resolution was spread upon the minutes.

The proposition I made was the suggestion of Mr. Lyman Gage,[39] president of the Civic Federation, and also president of the First National Bank of Chicago. I had talked with him, and also with the other members of the committee. His proposition was only as to the settlement of rents. The suggestion was that three men be appointed by the real-estate board,[40] who knew more or less about suburban rents; that they make an estimate of the Pullman rents as to whether or not they were exorbitant; that that estimate be submitted to the company and to the men, and a readjustment be made on that basis. That was the proposition I made to the general strike committee at Pullman. They were anxious to have that done, but they did not wish it to appear that the rent was the only grievance, so they made their resolution general—that they were ready to arbitrate any and all points. I then came back to the city, feeling that we had made a beginning toward conciliation, and the other members of the committee went to see Mr. Pullman, I believe. . . . It was impossible to come to any understanding with the Pullman company on that proposition, and it was dropped. We considered the effort a failure.[41]

8 (Commissioner Wright). Was it the view of your committee that they ought to arbitrate the question of rents?—Ans. We hoped they would agree to

the appointment of this committee of three men from the real-estate board to arbitrate the rents alone; then we hoped, after getting that settled, other matters would be settled, and the affair would be adjusted. We knew the rent was not the only grievance.

9 (Commissioner Wright). Was it the idea of your committee that on account of a reduction in wages there should be a reduction of rents?—Ans. No. Our first notion was that the rents were higher than the rents in other suburbs around in the vicinity, and we wished to take that question by itself, irrespective of the question of wages. We held that the company had applied strong competition to wages and had cut down wages, but had had no competition on rent, and the rents had been held up, and we wished to apply competition to the rents.

PD ("Testimony of Jane Addams," 645–47. In *Report on the Chicago Strike of June–July, 1894 by the United States Strike Commission, appointed by the President July 26, 1894, under the provisions of section 6 of chapter 1063 of the laws of the United States passed October 1, 1888, with appendices containing testimony, proceedings, and recommendations* [Washington: Government Printing Office, 1895]).

1. JA went to RC on 7 May and from there to Univ. of Wisconsin at Madison to appear before the School of Economics and the Contemporary Club on 9 May. She was at the Univ. of Cincinnati and the College Club in Lincoln Club House in Cincinnati on 18 and 19 May. Back in Chicago on 20 May, she spoke to the Self-Educational Club at 572 (later 1411) South Halsted St. She went to Oak Park, Ill., to appear before the Congregational Society on 22 May and spoke twice for the Chicago public schools on 29 May.

On 3 June JA went to Ravenswood, Ill., to speak at the Third Congregational Church. She was the graduation speaker on 6 June for the Illinois Training School for Nurses, Rush Medical College, in Chicago. The next day, she was the dinner speaker for the Social Club of the University Church at the Windemere Hotel on the South Side in Chicago. On 14 June, her speaking engagement diary indicates that she met with "Pullman strikers Committee of delegates to the R.R. Convention & Strikers Committee[.] Turner Hall—Kensington [Ill.]" ("Diary, 1894–95"; *JAPM*, 29:211). Two days later in Chicago, she presented remarks before the Cook County Normal School in the morning and before the Cook County Normal School Alumni Assn. late that afternoon. And then by 19 June, she was on her way to give the commencement address for the Women's Dept. of Western Reserve Univ., Cleveland.

2. Addams, *Twenty Years*, 32.

3. The Pullman Palace Car Co. was organized in 1867 with a capital of one million dollars. By 1894, when it had paid up capital of thirty-six million dollars, it was responsible for manufacturing and the repair of railroad cars on 125,000 miles of track, for the manufacture of cars for general railroad use, and for the management of the town of Pullman, Ill., begun in 1880. The Pullman works and the town were located to the south and east of Chicago on three hundred acres beside Lake Calumet. The owner of this major industry, George M. Pullman (see n. 4), who also created the town, indicated, "The object in building Pullman was the establishment of a great manufacturing business on the most substantial basis possible, recognizing, as we did, and do now, that the working people are the most important element which enters into the successful operation of any manufacturing enterprise. We decided to build, in close proximity to the shops, homes for workingmen of such character and surroundings as would prove so attractive as to cause the best class of mechanics to seek that place for employment in preference to others. We also desired to establish the place on such a basis as would exclude all baneful influences, believing that such a policy would result in the greatest measure of success, both from a commercial point of view, and also, what was

equally important, or perhaps of greater importance, in a tendency toward continued elevation and improvement of the conditions not only of the working people themselves, but of their children growing up about them" ("Testimony of George M. Pullman," *Report on the Chicago Strike*, 529). The town had water and sewer systems, as well as paved and lighted streets. Among the pleasantly landscaped grounds were tenements for rent (see n. 6), stores and markets (leased to outside companies), a church, public schools, a library, hotels and boardinghouses, and halls for public lectures and amusements. Medical care was also available. By 1894 Pullman was legally part of the city of Chicago.

4. George M. Pullman (1831–97) was born in Brockton, N.Y., third of the ten children of Emily Caroline Minton and James Lewis Pullman. Leaving school at the age of fourteen, he learned the carpentry trade while working with his father and brother in Albion, N.Y., and helped elevate structures near the Erie Canal as it was being enlarged. He arrived in Chicago during the 1850s to undertake a similar task when the city decided to lift whole blocks of buildings to a new grade level above its swampy beginning. On his return from acting as a gold broker in Golden, Colo., between 1859 and 1863, he began remodeling railroad cars, seeking a more comfortable car configuration for long trips. His sleeping-car design known as the "Pioneer" was so successful that it led to the formation in 1867 and rapid development of the Pullman Palace Car Co. Pullman also was engaged in business in New York City, 1875–77, where he developed the Sixth Ave. and Second Ave. elevated railroads. He and his wife, Harriet Sanger (1842–1921), whom he married 13 June 1867 in Chicago, had four children. In 1893 George M. Pullman made a contribution of five hundred dollars to JA for help in furnishing the HH Men's Club, and during 1893 he gave ninety dollars toward settlement relief efforts.

5. Thomas W. Heathcoate (see n. 28) reported to the strike commissioners, "In December, 1893, I worked full time and made $22.70." After Commissioner John D. Kernan (see n. 16) asked him how much he would have earned for that same time in June 1893, Heathcoate reported, "I would have earned $48. This more than cut the wages in two; it took a little more than half the price off what it would have been in June, 1893" ("Testimony of Thomas W. Heathcoate," *Report on the Chicago Strike*, 418–19).

Before the American Railway Union (ARU) joined the Pullman strikers, Eugene V. Debs (see n. 35), president of the ARU, went to Pullman on at least two occasions to investigate conditions among the workers. "I found that the wages and the expenses of the employees," he reported, "were so adjusted that every dollar the employees earned found its way back into the Pullman coffers; that they were not only not getting wages enough to live on, but that they were daily getting deeper into the debt of the Pullman company; that it was impossible for many of them to leave there at all, even if they were disposed to quit to try and better their condition" ("Testimony of Eugene V. Debs," *Report on the Chicago Strike*, 130).

"'At the commencement of the very serious depression last year, we were employing at Pullman 5,816 men, and paying out in wages there $305,000 a month,'" reported George M. Pullman. "'Negotiations with intending purchasers of railway equipment that were then pending for new work were stopped by them, orders already given by others were canceled, and we were obliged to lay off, as you are aware, a large number of men in every department, so that by November 1, 1893, there were only about 2,000 men in all departments, or about one-third of the normal number.'" Pullman continued, "'I personally undertook the work of the lettings of cars, and by making lower bids than other manufacturers I secured work enough to gradually increase our force from 2,000 up to about 4,200, the number employed, according to the April pay rolls, in all capacities at Pullman'" ("The Strike at Pullman," *Chicago Herald*, 26 June 1894, from "Testimony of Thomas H. Wickes," *Report on the Chicago Strike*, 579). Thomas H. Wickes (see n. 11), operations manager, indicated that the company was trying to do its part to keep workers employed. "From August 1, 1893, to May 1, 1894," he told the strike commissioners, "our net loss on accepted bids was $52,069.03, and the net estimated loss on unaccepted bids was $18,303.56. We had tried to get work for our employees by bidding for work, the estimated shop cost of which was $2,775,481.81, and we only got contracts for work the estimated shop cost of which is $1,421,205.75. We had been underbid on work, the estimated shop cost of which was $1,354,276.06, notwithstanding that our bids on $1,057,355.97 of that amount not only excluded all profit, but showed a loss, based though they were on the reduced scale of wages" ("Testimony of Thomas H. Wickes," *Report on the Chicago Strike*, 577). Pullman determined that for contracts made, the percentage of loss was 3.663. For these reasons, he indicated that if the company restored wages as the committee of Pullman workers demanded, "'[I]t would be a most unfortunate thing for the men, because there is less than sixty days of contract work in sight in the shops . . . and there is absolutely no possibility, in the present condition of affairs throughout the country, of getting any more orders for work at prices measured by the wages of May, 1893'" ("The Strike at Pullman," *Chicago Herald*, 26 June 1894, from "Testimony of Thomas H. Wickes," *Report on the Chicago Strike*, 579). The company statement that Thomas H. Wickes read to the strike commissioners also contained the following note: "The selling prices of passenger, baggage, box, refrigerator and street cars in the last two years have fallen by percentages, varying in the separate classes, from 17 to 28, the average reduction, taking the five classes together, being 24 per cent" ("The Strike at Pullman," *Chicago Herald*, 26 June 1894, from "Testimony of Thomas H. Wickes," *Report on the Chicago Strike*, 579).

6. Thomas W. Heathcoate, chairman of the Pullman Co. strike committee, reported, "Whenever a man is employed in the Pullman shops he is supposed to live in a Pullman house until the Pullman houses are filled. . . . He could not live in Roseland [Ill.] unless he owned his own property. . . . I have known men who owned property in Roseland who had to leave their property not rented and come down to Pullman and hire houses in order to fill up the Pullman houses" ("Testimony of Thomas W. Heathcoate," *Report on the Chicago Strike*, 425).

Heathcoate indicated that the pay of Pullman workers came in two checks: one for the amount of the rent due the company for the worker's lodgings and one for the remainder of his or her earnings. "I have seen men with families of eight or nine children to support crying there [at the Pullman bank] because they only got 3 or 4 cents after paying their rent; I have seen them stand by the window and cry for money enough to enable them to keep their families; I have been insulted at that window time and time again by the clerks when I tried to get money enough to support my family, even after working every day and overtime. They would want to know why I could not pay my rent up when the average per capita was only 8 cents over the rent, and a man would have to keep a family for two weeks on it. If there is any woman can keep a family on 8 cents apiece, clothe themselves, and appear decent on the streets I would like to see it done" ("Testimony of Thomas W. Heathcoate," *Report on the Chicago Strike*, 426). When asked to compare what he paid for rent in Pullman for a similar dwelling outside the community, Heathcoate, who was paying seventeen dollars per month, responded: "I know a house and lot that has been built about two years. I believe the party paid $2,500 for it, and it has two tenements and is separate from any other buildings. It has a nice front yard, with as much room in it as is in my house, and much more beautifully located. That can be rented for $12 per month. . . . [I]t is in a more desirable location than the house I live in. . . . I would not give over $1,000 for the house and lot I am living in" ("Testimony of Thomas W. Heathcoate," *Report on the Chicago Strike*, 427). Heathcoate's testimony before the commission revealed that from 1 Nov. 1893 to the time of the Pullman strike, Pullman workers owed the company seventy thousand dollars in back rent.

George Pullman reported that the daily average payroll for Pullman was seven thousand dollars. The company estimated that the return on capital invested in the town of Pullman dwellings was 3.82 percent, when the company had expected a 6 percent return. "'The average rental at Pullman is at the rate of $3 per room per month. There are 1,200 tenements, of varying numbers of rooms, the average monthly rental of which is $10; of these there are 600 the average monthly rental of which is $8'" ("The Strike at Pullman," *Chicago Herald*,

26 June 1894, from "Testimony of Thomas H. Wickes," *Report on the Chicago Strike*, 580). Pullman also charged for natural gas an average of two dollars per month and four cents per one thousand gallons of water, and the company assumed the cost of garbage pickup and landscaping.

Jennie Curtis (b. 1876?), who resided in Pullman, had worked for Pullman as a seamstress in the repair shops sewing room for five years. She was head of the Girls' Union No. 269 at Pullman, had joined the ARU on 8 May 1894, and at its meeting on 14 June was selected as a member of its Com. on General Works. She led the relief effort for striking Pullman families and was probably one of the women who helped JA tour the Pullman community. She reported that her widowed father, Alexander Curtis, died in Sept. 1893 after working for the Pullman Co. for thirteen years. He was ill and unable to work for three months prior to his death. At the time of his death, he owed sixty dollars in back rent, and Jennie Curtis reported that "the company made me, out of my small earnings, pay that rent due from my father." When she was asked by Commissioner Kernan how she was to pay it back, she answered, "The contract was that I should pay $3 on the back rent every pay day; out of my small earnings I could not give them $3 every pay day, and when I did not do so I was insulted and almost put out of the bank by the clerk for not being able to pay it to them. My wages were cut so low that I could not pay my board and give them $3 on the back rent, but if I had $2 or so over my board I would leave it at the bank on the rent. On the day of the strike I still owed them $15, which I am afraid they never will give me a chance to pay back" ("Testimony of Jennie Curtis," *Report on the Chicago Strike*, 434).

7. When Lyman J. Gage (see n. 39), at the time president of the First National Bank of Chicago and also of the Civic Federation of Chicago, was approached for funds to support the families of strikers at Pullman, he refused to help. He was reported as responding that "'people who voluntarily leave good work deserve to suffer'" (quoted in "Is Deaf to Appeal: Pullman Relief Committee Meets with Rebuff: Lyman Gage Has No Sympathy with the Strikers: Says He Will Not Give a Cent: Thinks Pullman Is a Dream and Its Plutocrat a Saint: Calls Strikers Lazy Loafers," *Chicago Times*, 7 June 1894, quoted in Brown, "Advocate for Democracy," in Richard Schneirov, *Pullman Strike*, 135). As early as Dec. 1893, the *Chicago Times* reported "great dissatisfaction and suffering prevails in Pullman" (quoted in Carl Smith, *Urban Disorder*, 234). By 25 May 1894, the *Chicago Mail* was trumpeting headlines like "Grim Want in the Model Town." On 12 June 1894, even the *Chicago Daily Tribune* complained about Pullman's stubbornness in not meeting with his employees. As the national boycott and strike began, the *New York Times* offered, "It has been the policy of the Pullman Palace Car Co. to reduce the salaries of its employees until the starvation point has been reached" (28 June 1894, quoted in Vosswinkel, "Government Response to the Pullman Strike," 5).

8. The American Railway Union was founded on 20 June 1893 to create an organization to which all railroad workers could belong. Until then, workers in each craft or particular railroad job had their own organization. Its leader was Eugene V. Debs (see n. 35). By the time of its first convention, held in Chicago, 9–26 June 1894, according to Debs, it claimed 150,000 members, represented 546 local unions, and favored arbitration as a means of settling labor disputes.

The ARU gained immediate national visibility when its members began a strike and a boycott of Pullman Palace Car Co. cars. Leaders of the ARU had been unsuccessful in their attempt to meet with Pullman management on behalf of Pullman workers or to arrange for the Com. of Conciliation of the Civic Federation of Chicago (see nn. 9–10) to arbitrate workers' grievances. As a result, on 21 June delegates at the ARU convention voted to stop handling Pullman cars on 26 June unless the Pullman Co. agreed to arbitration. The Pullman Co., backed up by the General Managers' Assn. (GMA), composed of top administration officials from the twenty-four railroad companies serving Chicago, refused to arbitrate, indicating that there was nothing to arbitrate. Members of the GMA began firing workers who refused to switch or handle trains with Pullman cars, and before the strike was over the number of strikers had increased nationwide to an estimated 150,000 workers. On 2 July, President Grover Cleveland through Attorney General Richard Olney, himself a sitting director on a rail line company, asked the courts for an injunction to prevent ARU leaders from "compelling or inducing by threats, intimidation, persuasion, force or violence, railway employees to refuse or fail to perform their duties." The president called out federal troops to control the strikers and protect U.S. mail service, even though neither Illinois governor John Peter Altgeld nor Chicago mayor John Hopkins approved of the action. They arrived at the stockyards at 3:00 A.M., 3 July. On 4 July, mobs began burning and destroying property at various rail yards, including Pullman.

The violence continued to escalate, and units of the Illinois National Guard arrived on 6 and 7 July. Francis O'Neill (1848–1936), later general superintendent of police in Chicago, 1901–5, at the time of the Pullman strike was captain, commanding the stockyards district, where he and his men were in the thick of trying to keep order and protect lives and property during the strike. After the strike, he reported, "The strikers and their sympathizers became extremely active in their hostility and destructive acts on the night of July 6th. Railway cars were set on fire wherever the incendiaries could escape the vigilance of the police. Railway watchmen were powerless and the vandals, under cover of darkness, easily escaped detection. It was openly claimed that many of the fires were set by deputy United States Marshals so that their services would be viewed as necessary. In one case at least the claim appeared to be well founded." O'Neill had little use for the federal troops but indicated, "The officers and soldiers of the 2nd regiment of the Illinois National Guard willingly and faithfully cooperated with the police" (Skerrett and Lesch, *Chief O'Neill's Sketchy Recollections*, 81, 77).

As the violence continued, on 7 July ARU leader Eugene V. Debs and other officers of the ARU were arrested, indicted, and held in the Cook County Jail. When the AFL and other unions refused to approve sympathetic action in support of the striking railroaders, the strike was abandoned and declared over by 8 Aug. At that time, Pullman workers who were reemployed by the company signed pledges not to join a union, and none of the strike leaders were reinstated in their jobs. Debs received a six-month sentence in prison, and the leaders of the ARU who were arrested with him received sentences of three months. An appeal by attorneys Clarence Darrow and Lyman Trumbull before the U.S. Supreme Court in 1895 seeking to overturn the conviction of Debs for violating the federal injunction to stop the strike was unsuccessful. Debs served his sentence, which he said "was doubled because the federal judges considered me a dangerous man and a menace to society," in the McHenry County Jail, Woodstock, Ill. (Debs, *Walls and Bars*, 29).

The ARU survived until June 1897, when Debs, a newly announced socialist, held a convention of its members in Chicago, 15–17 June. At that meeting, Debs and its leaders disbanded the organization. Many of its members then joined the short-lived organization Social Democracy of America, founded under the leadership of Debs on 18, 19, and 21 June, at the same site in Chicago. Its goal was creating a socialist society.

9. In the autumn of 1886, Lyman J. Gage (see n. 39) began an effort to meld industrial and financial leaders and union leaders into an organization that might "bring justice and sense into city affairs" (Smith and Lewis, *Chicago*, 169). However, it was not until muckraking English journalist William T. Stead, who had come to Chicago to attend the World's Columbian Exposition, drew attention to the social, civic, and environmental problems plaguing the city that the movement attracted the Chicago leadership base it needed to succeed. Stead called a special conference at Central Music Hall, Chicago, on 1 Nov. 1893, at which he offered his honest evaluation of city ills and set forth the idea of a "Civic Church or Federation of all good citizens" (Stead, *If Christ Came to Chicago*, 465). His account shocked his listeners and galvanized city leaders to action. On 12 Nov. 1893, at another gathering at the Central Music Hall, these leaders formed the Civic Federation of Chicago and approved

a temporary committee of nominators to select leaders to create the organization. JA was one of the temporary committee's five members. By 17 Nov., the temporary committee had identified those, including themselves, who were to serve on the Joint Exec. Com., and in Dec. 1893 they convened to consider unemployment in Chicago and to support the formation of the Central Relief Assn. By 3 Feb. 1894, JA and fourteen others had signed and filed the organization's incorporation papers. Lyman J. Gage was selected as president, society leader Bertha Honoré Palmer became first vice-president, and labor leader John J. McGrath was named second vice-president. JA, who became a trustee of the organization, was secretary of the industrial committee, one of the organization's seven standing committees. By 1895 the federation, with its central council of one hundred, had branches in all of Chicago's thirty-four wards. The Nineteenth Ward Council of the Civic Federation was organized at HH on the evening of 8 June 1894, in the midst of the Pullman strike. JA was one of the speakers.

The Civic Federation became a strong voice for beneficial change in Chicago. It helped pass the state law that eventually brought a civil service program to city employees, led a campaign against gambling, attempted to expose corrupt politicians, helped create the Municipal Voters' League of Chicago, and throughout the 1890s continued to urge arbitration of labor disputes. As an organization, it kept the public informed about civic issues. It survived until 1941, although it was associated with the Chicago Bureau of Public Efficiency, founded in 1910.

William T. Stead went on to publish his exposé of conditions in Chicago in 1894 as *If Christ Came to Chicago*. It was issued by Laird and Lee in Chicago and printed by the *Eight-Hour Herald*. On 21 May 1894, Stead wrote to JA from London, expressing his concern for her and for HH. In his book, he had praised the settlement: "Not merely because of the humanitarian influences which it radiates around the district in which it stands, but because it will become a training ground and nursery for multitudes of similar institutions speedily to spring up in all of the great cities of America" (410). Eager to hear how his book had been received, Stead wrote, "I have often and often wondered how you were, and how you were getting on, and generally how the rumpus which has been made about my Book has effected you at Hull House. I have not heard a syllable from any person in your establishment. . . . The book has attracted a good deal of attention here, and has been criticised with extraordinary unanimity of approval. . . . What people say here is that Hull House is the only Institution in Chicago for which I have a good word to say. That is not true, but I sincerely hope that the fact that Hull House seemed to me so good will not be remembered against you for evil by my enemies." He also revealed that his editor in New York thought "very unkindly" of his Chicago book (William T. Stead to JA, 21 May 1894, SCPC, JAC; *JAPM*, 2:1540–41).

During the 1890s, membership and leadership of the Civic Federation of Chicago and its various committees changed frequently. Throughout the period, JA maintained a continuing relationship with the federation and its various reform efforts. She was also one of three members of the initial planning committee, and she served on the executive committee of the trustees beginning in 1894. She also served as a speaker and as secretary for the Congress on Industrial Conciliation and Arbitration that the federation held 13 and 14 Nov. 1894. In addition, JA was one of the signers of the federation's resolution that encouraged and supported the state law that created a "State Board and Local Boards of Arbitration for the investigation or settlement of differences between employers and their employes, and to define the powers and duties of said board" ("Industrial Dept.," in Civic Federation of Chicago, *First Annual Report*, 78). She was also part of the small committee of the federation that tried unsuccessfully in Mar. 1896 to arbitrate the strike between the garment workers in Chicago and their employers represented by the Manufacturers' Assn. By 1897 JA had become leader of the federation's standing industrial committee; however, by the end of 1898, that committee was dissolved when the federation initiated a new committee structure. Still a member of the executive committee in 1898, JA was serving as vice-president of the organization and as a member of the municipal committee.

10. The impetus for the Com. of Conciliation, announced by the *Chicago Daily Tribune* in "Board of Conciliation Named," on 8 May 1894, seems to have been the Civic Federation's industrial committee. The Com. of Conciliation, sometimes referred to as a board of conciliation, was established with the idea that it would be available to mediate any labor difficulties in the Chicago area. The first labor dispute it had to consider was the strike at the Pullman Palace Car Co. The Com. of Conciliation was composed of merchant businessman and HH supporter E. B. Butler; Baptist minister Charles Richmond Henderson (1848–1915), professor of sociology at the Univ. of Chicago; successful wholesale businessman in hardware A. C. Bartlett (see n. 33); M. J. Carroll, chairman of the Civic Federation's industrial committee and typographers' union labor leader and editor of the *Eight-Hour Herald*; Arthur Tyerson (1851–1912), an attorney who was a board member of St. Luke's Hospital and who helped found the Union League Club, and, like Stead, died in 1912 on the *Titanic*; Henry Demarest Lloyd; and JA.

11. Thomas H. Wickes reported to the strike commission, "On June 1 two members of the Civic Federation [JA and Easley] called upon me to consider some methods of conciliation and arbitration. I explained the situation to them and informed them that we did not consider there was any proper subject for arbitration. On the next day two other members of the Civic Federation called and we had a similar discussion.

"On the 15th of June 12 persons, calling themselves a committee from the American Railway Union, called upon me to request that there should be an arbitration. I informed them, in reply, that the company declined to consider any communication from the American Railway Union as representing the former employees of the company.

"On the next day a committee of six of our former employees called upon me and requested that there should be an arbitration. I informed them that we did not consider that there was any proper subject for arbitration.

"On the 22d of June Messrs. F. E. Pollans, B. W. Lovejoy, and C. A. Timlin, claiming to be a committee of three of the American Railway Union, called upon me and stated that they were instructed to notify the Pullman Company that, unless it agreed to arbitration, a boycott would be declared to stop the running of Pullman cars, taking effect at 12 o'clock noon, Tuesday, the 26th day of June. I replied to this statement that the company declined to consider any communication from the American Railway Union on the subject" ("Testimony of Thomas H. Wickes," *Report on the Chicago Strike*, 590.

Thomas H. Wickes (1846–1905) was born in Leicestershire, England. He began work with the Pullman Co. on 1 Apr. 1868. He served as assistant superintendent of the company's division in East St. Louis, Ill., 1870–73, and superintendent there in 1873. Moving to Chicago, he became general superintendent of the Western Division, 1885–86, and on 1 Jan. 1889 became second vice-president in control of the operating department until 15 Oct. 1896, when he became vice-president of the Pullman Palace Car Co., a position he held until his death in Mar. 1905. In late 1894, his wife, Laura W. Wickes, instituted divorce proceedings, charging him with extreme cruelty.

12. The *Chicago Mail* reported on 1 June 1894 that "Miss Addams has written two or three letters to the Pullman company without receiving any reply. This morning she called at the general offices in the Pullman building accompanied by Secretary Easley of the board of conciliation. Both Second Vice-President Wickes and General Superintendent [George Francis] Brown [1843–1910] were out. Mr. Wickes, when seen this afternoon, said he would refuse to treat with Miss Addams and her companion save as ordinary visitors" (Pullman Co. Archives, Secretary's Office, Strike Scrapbooks, 1894, p. 81). The letters that JA wrote to George M. Pullman or the Pullman Co. are not extant in the Pullman Co. Archives.

13. Ralph Montgomery Easley (1856–1939), journalist and political economist, was born in Frederick, Ill. He attended public schools and Johnson College in Quincy, Ill. Easley emigrated in 1875 to Hutchinson, Kans., where he taught school; founded the *Hutchinson News*, 1883–91; and served as postmaster, 1882–87. While there he wed Neva C. Cheney in 1881, with whom he had two children. After she died, in 1917 he married Gertrude Brackenridge Beeks.

Easley moved to Chicago in 1891 and for three years was associated with the *Chicago Inter Ocean* as the head of the department dealing with political and economic issues. He helped found and served as secretary for the Civic Federation of Chicago, 1893–1900. In 1900 Easley helped organize the National Civic Federation and became chairman of its executive council. During his tenure as a leader in the civic federation movement, he arranged a number of national conferences on major political and economic issues, including primary election reform, U.S. foreign policy, trusts and combinations, taxation, and immigration. In 1917 he organized and became director for the League for National Unity. Staunchly anticommunist, he wrote several books with a distinctly anti–Soviet Russia perspective.

14. See n. 11.

15. "Ready to Arbitrate: American Railway Union's Offer: Willing to Submit Its Grievances against the Pullman Company to the Civic Federation."

16. The U.S. Strike Comm. was appointed by President Grover Cleveland, 26 July 1894, to investigate causes of the boycott and national strike that began 26 June 1894 by action of the ARU and developed out of sympathy and support for workers striking at Pullman. The board heard testimony in Chicago, 15–30 Aug., and in Washington, D.C., 26 Sept., 1894. The board's members were Carroll D. Wright (1840–1909), ex-officio chairman John D. Kernan, and Nicholas E. Worthington (1836–1916). At the time, Wright was U.S. commissioner of Labor; Kernan was an attorney in Utica, N.Y., who specialized in representing railroads and had been chairman of the New York Board of Railroad Commissioners; and Worthington, an attorney who had been in the House of Representatives, 1883–87, from Peoria, Ill., was serving as circuit judge of the Tenth District of Illinois.

17. Addams, *Twenty Years*, 217.

18. Addams, *Twenty Years*, 215.

19. Among extant correspondence concerning the development of "A Modern Lear" are the following from friends who heard the paper given by JA as a speech, especially on 4 Mar. before the CWC, or read a version of the essay: JA to MRS, 17 Aug. and 4 Sept., 1895, SCPC, JAC; *JAPM*, 2:1743–46 and 1754–59; Louisa Clark to JA, [Mar.?] [1896], SCPC, JAC; *JAPM*, 3:2–5; John Dewey to JA, 19 Jan. 1896, SCPC, JAC; *JAPM*, 3:29–30; Julia P. Harvey to JA, [4 Feb. 1896], SCPC, JAC; *JAPM*, 3:41–44; JA to Henry Demarest Lloyd, 10 Feb. and 16 Feb. 1896, WSHS, Lloyd; *JAPM*, 3:49 and 60–61; Henry Demarest Lloyd to JA, 23 Feb. 1896, SCPC, JAC; *JAPM*, 3:64–65. While Henry Demarest Lloyd suggested that JA "depersonalize" her essay, John Dewey wrote, "It is one of the greatest things I ever read."

20. Among publications that refused to accept her manuscript for publication were the following: the *North American Review*, *Review of Reviews*, *Forum*, and *Atlantic Monthly*. The following is extant correspondence from publishers: Albert Shaw to JA, 18 Jan. 1896; Lloyd Bryce to JA, 6 Feb. 1896; A. E. Keet to JA, 1 Feb. 1896; and Horace Elisha Scudder to Mary Hawes Wilmarth (received by JA), 18 Apr. 1896, all SCPC, JAC; *JAPM*, 3:27–28, 39–40; 45–46; and 104–8. All had already presented stories on the strike.

Horace Elisha Scudder (1838–1902), editor of the *Atlantic Monthly* (1890–1902), indicated that he was "profoundly impressed by the skill" of JA's essay and "by the earnestness which underlies it, and by the impressiveness with which she states the principles of social morality in its relation to industrialism," but he also thought that JA "assumes throughout that Mr. Pullman was in the wrong," and he believed that "Mr. Pullman was placed in a position where a man may honestly, even if mistakenly refuse to yield," and, he added, "I cannot think the eloquence of the counsel for the weak should blind as to the judicial aspects of the case" (Horace E. Scudder to Mary Hawes Wilmarth, 18 Apr. 1896, SCPC, JAC; *JAPM*, 3:104–5, 106–8).

21. JA's "A Modern Lear" was finally published in the *Survey*, but not until 1912, almost twenty years after the events about which it was written and long after the death of George M. Pullman in 1897. See the *Survey* 29 (2 Nov. 1912): 131–37; *JAPM*, 47:611–46. At least four versions of the manuscript are extant. All are typed manuscripts; two are titled "A Modern

Tragedy" and are one and twelve pages in length; a third is fifteen typewritten pages and titled "A Modern Tragedy: An Analysis of the Pullman Strike." It is likely that the fragment one page is all that survives of an early 1894 version of the essay. JA probably developed the twelve- and fifteen-page versions in 1895 and early in 1896. JA wrote to MRS, "I have finished the 'Pullman' up to the last point which I am now writing. I will send it to you to read to your father, it may entertain him and I would like to have his opinion on it" (17 Aug. 1895, SCPC, JAC; *JAPM*, 2:1744). For his response, see JA to MRS, 4 [, 5, and 6] Sept. 1895, below.

It is likely that it was one of these two versions of her essay that JA may have shared with friends like John Dewey and Henry Demarest Lloyd. Her footnote at the bottom of the first page of the (1896?) fifteen-page manuscript reads: "The writer deplores the apparent indelicacy of making so close an analysis of the motives of the contemporary, and urge in extenuation, that the study is drawn solely from public acts" (*JAPM*, 46:723). That may have been JA's attempt to respond to Henry Demarest Lloyd's suggestion that she "depersonalize the paper, and yet retain its dramatic quality" (Henry Demarest Lloyd to JA, 23 Feb. 1896, WSHS, Lloyd; *JAPM*, 3:64). The fourth manuscript is marked for printing in a publication and is the one from which "A Modern Lear" was printed in the *Survey*. It is twenty-five typewritten pages in length. All of the manuscript versions of the essay are in SCPC, JAC. They also appear in *JAPM*, 46:589, 647–59, 722–37; 47:611–38. The essay titled "A Modern Lear: A Parenthetical Chapter" was also published as pp. 68–90 in Graham Taylor's *Satellite Cities: A Study of Industrial Suburbs* (New York: D. Appleton, 1915).

22. Addams, *Twenty Years*, 228.

23. Addams, *Twenty Years*, 214.

24. Hamilton, "Jane Addams of HH," 15.

25. Hamilton, "Jane Addams, Gentle Rebel," 34.

26. The auditorium and meeting halls of the Auditorium Building were often sites for civic gatherings.

27. The ARU met in Chicago, 9–26 June 1894. See n. 8.

28. Thomas W. Heathcoate (Heathcote) was fifty-eight years old in 1894 when he and the grievance committee he presided over voted on 10 May 1894 to lead their nineteen local unions out on strike on 11 May. He testified before the U.S. Strike Comm., "We were up all night until 5 o'clock in the morning and decided to strike against the advice of the American Railway Union. The reduction of wages was such that it was utterly impossible to sustain ourselves and families, and we had no other alternative. We had done all we possibly could with the Pullman company to have our rents cut down or give us more pay, and failed. We were not earning enough to live on and we had no other alternative than to strike" ("Testimony of Thomas W. Heathcoate," *Report on the Chicago Strike*, 433). He had been a car builder for thirty years, and at the time he had been employed at Pullman, where he and his family lived, for five years. He had become a member of the ARU along with a great many other Pullman Co. employees in Apr. and May 1894 and become president of local No. 208 as well as chairman of the central strike committee. He resigned both posts in early Sept. 1894. When the strike was over, he found himself without employment.

29. Eugene V. Debs, president of the ARU, reported to the strike commissioners: "On June 9 the delegates representing the American Railway Union, 546 local unions and about 150,000 employees, in round numbers, met in first quadrennial convention in the city of Chicago. In due course of the proceedings the matter of the Pullman trouble came up for consideration. The convention resolved itself into a committee of the whole to hear reports of committees and to take such action as in their judgment was deemed best to protect the interests of the suffering employees. . . . The result of the consideration of the convention was the appointment of a committee, consisting in part of Pullman employees that were delegates and in part of delegates who were not Pullman employees" ("Testimony of Eugene V. Debs," *Report on the Chicago Strike*, 130–31). Thomas H. Wickes recalled in his testimony before the strike

commission that the committee JA is referring to came on 15 June to attempt a meeting with the Pullman Co. (see n. 11).

30. The *Chicago Herald* of 28 May 1894 identified a committee named by the Chicago Trade and Labor Assembly and the Building Trades Council to help provide relief for the families of the Pullman strikers. The members of the committee of seven named to oversee relief efforts were Mrs. Kate Bradley; Mrs. Fanny Clarke Kavanaugh; Miss Elizabeth Alcover (Alkoffer); William Jones, vice-president of the Trade and Labor Assembly; S. A. Wilson, organizer for the Carpenters Council; Lee Hart of the theatrical workers; and Walter Groves, secretary of the Trade and Labor Assembly. William C. Hollister served as treasurer. Jennie Curtis, president of Girls' Union No. 269 of the ARU, and Thomas W. Heathcoate were leaders in hosting a special ball held at Market Hall in Pullman at which more than two thousand tickets were sold for one dollar each to help with the relief effort. The committee held other events such as dances and picnics, solicited individuals for funds, and suggested that union workers give up one day of wages to assist the Pullman strikers.

31. In its final report on the Chicago strike, the U.S. Strike Comm. found, "If we exclude the aesthetic and sanitary features at Pullman, the rents there are from 20 to 25 per cent higher than rents in Chicago or surrounding towns for similar accommodations." In addition, the commissioners found, "The company's claim that the workmen need not hire its tenements and can live elsewhere if they choose is not entirely tenable" (*Report on the Chicago Strike*, xxxv).

32. For thirty of his forty-six years, George W. Howard was a "railroad man," as he put it in testimony before the U.S. Strike Comm. on 15 Aug. 1894, p. 4. At the time he was the newly elected vice-president of the ARU under the leadership of Eugene V. Debs. His railroad experience was diverse. He served in a variety of positions, from brakeman to general superintendent, and on railroads from the Midwest to the Far West. He helped construct the streetcar system in San Diego, Calif., as he worked for the Coronado Beach Co. and worked for the Mackay railroad system in southern Indiana on several occasions, most recently in 1890 as master of transportation. He was a member of the Yardmasters' Mutual Benefit Assn. for seventeen years, a member of the Knights of Labor, and until the summer of 1894, when he resigned because of his new position with the ARU, a member of the Brotherhood of Locomotive Engineers and the Order of Railway Conductors. Initially, he became an adviser to the unions associated with the ARU as they struck at Pullman, and he advised the ARU not to call what became a national strike at their meeting of 12 June in Chicago. In 1895 Howard became president of the ARU.

33. Adolphus Clay Bartlett (1844–1922) was born in Stratford, N.Y., the son of Aaron and Delia Dibell Bartlett, and attended Dansville Academy in New York. He came to Chicago when he was nineteen and worked for Tuttle, Hibbard and Co., which became one of the largest hardware businesses in the United States. By 1882 the business was incorporated as Hibbard, Spencer, Bartlett, and Co., and in 1904 he became president of the firm. He was a trustee of Beloit College in Wisconsin and the Univ. of Chicago. A director of the Chicago Relief and Aid Society since 1873, he also served as president of the Chicago Home for the Friendless, a director of the Orphan Asylum, and as a trustee for the Art Institute of Chicago. He was a director of the Chicago Athenaeum, First National Bank, Northern Trust Co., and Globe Insurance Co., all in Chicago; the Elgin Watch Co., Liverpool and London; and the Chicago and Alton Rail Road Co. He wed three times and had at least four children.

34. JA and Easley tried to meet with Thomas H. Wickes and George Francis Brown, the general superintendent, on 1 June 1894. The *Chicago Mail* reported in a headline: "Both Second Vice-President Wickes and General Superintendent Brown were out" ("He Will Not Act," 1 June 1894, *Chicago Mail* from Newberry Library, Pullman Co. Archives, Secretary's Office, Strike Scrapbooks, p. 81). However, in his testimony before the strike commissioners, Wickes recalled that he met with JA and Ralph M. Easley.

35. Eugene V. Debs (1855–1926), labor leader and socialist, was born in Terre Haute, Ind., the son of Marguerite Marie and Jean Daniel Debs. Leaving school at age fifteen, he became a

railroad worker and by 1878 had become associate editor of the *Firemen's Magazine*, of which he became editor in 1880. He resigned his membership in the Brotherhood of Locomotive Firemen in 1892 to organize the short-lived ARU. Arrested for his activities during the national strike of the ARU and the Pullman strike in 1894, he spent six months in the McHenry County Jail in Woodstock, Ill. He became an ardent socialist and in 1897 helped found the Social Democratic Party, which became part of the Socialist Party of America. Debs helped found and for three years was a member of the IWW in 1905. During World War I, which he opposed, he was convicted for sedition under the Espionage Act and sentenced to ten years in prison for urging young men to resist the draft beginning in 1918. He was pardoned in 1921. He ran for president on the Socialist Party ticket in 1900, 1904, 1908, 1912, and 1920. He married Katherine Metzel in 1885 the same year she was elected as a Democrat to the Indiana legislature. He was the author of *Walls and Bars* (1927).

36. Ellen Henrotin (Mrs. Charles) was a member of the industrial committee of the Civic Federation of Chicago.

37. The first convention of the ARU was held in Chicago, 9–26 June 1894. Workers at Pullman and members of the ARU all favored arbitration as a solution to the issues they had raised; however, the Pullman Palace Car Co. continued to insist that there was nothing to be arbitrated.

38. JA's 1894 speaking engagement diary indicates that she met with the strike committee on 14 June 1894 (see n. 1).

39. Lyman Judson Gage (1836–1927), banker and U.S. secretary of the Treasury (1897–1902) for President William McKinley, was born in DeRuyter, N.Y., and moved to Chicago in 1853 to work as a bookkeeper. By 1858 he entered the banking business, employed by Merchants Loan and Trust Co. In 1882 he became vice-president and executive officer of the First National Bank of Chicago. He was first married to Sarah Etheridge, who died in 1874; in 1887 he wed Cornelia Lansing Washburn, who died in 1901; and in 1909 he married Frances Ada Ballou. He was selected as the president of the board of directors of the World's Columbian Exposition in Chicago. In 1890–92, he became president of the First National Bank of Chicago, 1891–97. From 1902 until he retired in 1906, he was president of the U.S. Trust Co., New York. An avid promoter of Chicago, he was always seeking ways to enhance the economic development and prestige of the city.

40. The Chicago Real Estate Board was incorporated on 21 Feb. 1883 to support and protect the real estate business. Within its first year of operation, it adopted a standard lease form that many thought was favorable to landlords. By 1892 the board had 150 members and was composed primarily of large and powerful real estate dealers, "such as Wm. D. Kerfoot & Co., E. S. Dreyer & Co., Eugene S. Pick, Dunlap Smith & Co., Bryan Lathrop, Ogden, Sheldon & Co., and H. C. Morey & Co." (Pierce, *A History of Chicago*, 3:208).

41. The editors did not include in this presentation of the JA testimony questions 4 through 7 addressed to JA by the commissioners in which they requested the names and businesses of members of the committee that went to see Mr. Pullman. In her response, JA identified them as businessman E. B. Butler, Prof. Charles R. Henderson, businessman A. C. Bartlett, and Mr. Carroll, "editor of a labor paper and a very fair-minded man" (647). In a statement to the *New York Tribune*, 14 June 1894, George M. Pullman denounced arbitration: "The demand made before quitting work was that the wages should be restored to the scale of last year, or, in effect that the actual outgoing money losses then being daily incurred by the company in car building should be deliberately increased to an amount equal to about one-fourth of the wages of the employees. It must be clear to every business man, and to every thinking workman, that no prudent employer could submit to arbitration the question whether he should commit such a piece of business folly. Arbitration always implies acquiescence in the decision of the arbitrator, whether favorable or adverse. How could I, as president of the Pullman company, consent to agree that if any body of men not concerned with the interests of the company's shareholders should, as arbitrators, for any reason seeming good to them

so decree, I would open the shops, employ workmen at wages greater than their work could be sold for, and continue this ruinous policy indefinitely; or be accused of a breach of faith? Who will deny that such a question is plainly not a subject of arbitration? Is it not, then, unreasonable that the company should be asked to arbitrate whether or not it should submit such a question to arbitration?" ("Testimony of Thomas H. Wickes," *Report on the Chicago Strike*, 585). Pullman's second-vice president, Thomas H. Wickes, consistently reiterated the refrain: "I shall refuse to arbitrate simply because I have nothing to arbitrate" ("He Will Not Act," 1 June 1894, *Chicago Mail* from Newberry Library, Pullman Co. Archives, Secretary's Offices, Strike Scrapbooks, p. 81).

## To Richard T. Ely

*Toward the end of 1894, Jane Addams, coeditor Florence Kelley, and several other Hull-House residents*[1] *were working to complete their respective portions of what would be published in 1895 by Thomas Y. Crowell*[2] *as* Hull-House Maps and Papers. *It was subtitled* A Presentation of Nationalities and Wages in a Congested District of Chicago, Together with Comments and Essays on Problems Growing Out of the Social Condition.[3] *At the urging of Richard T. Ely,*[4] *the volume was to be published in Crowell's Library of Economics and Politics series, for which Ely was general editor. The first systematic sociological study of a poor section of an American city,* Hull-House Maps and Papers *was patterned after Charles Booth's studies of portions of London.*[5]

*The idea for the volume evolved during Florence Kelley's stint as "special agent expert" in charge of the survey conducted for the U.S. Department of Labor Investigations of slum conditions in major cities.*[6] *Between April and August 1893, the slum area located to the south and east of Hull-House and between Halsted Street on the west and State Street on the east and Polk Street on the north and Twelfth Street on the south became the site of the investigation in Chicago. As survey takers working for Kelley went door-to-door, they cataloged dwelling conditions as well as family data, including names, nationality, citizenship, schooling, ability to speak English, health, profession, employment, and earnings.*[7] *Kelley obtained permission from her employer to keep copies of the surveys, with the idea of publishing the data on maps colored to reveal the mix of earnings, population density, housing stock, and nationality of residents in the area.*

*These maps became the centerpiece around which the remainder of the volume was developed.*[8] *The Hull-House residents drafted ten chapters on sweatshops; child labor; cloakmakers; Jewish, Bohemian, and Italian people in Chicago and the settlement area; Cook County charities; art; and the labor movement. The appendix was a summary of programs and activities at Hull-House that Ellen Gates Starr and Jane Addams had written and first published in 1894.*[9] *Jane Addams wrote the volume preface and "The Settlement as a Factor in the Labor Movement," and her coeditor presented "The Sweating System" and, with assistant Illinois factory inspector Alzina P. Stevens*[10] *as coauthor, "Wage-Earning Children." However, the maps became a major problem, affecting the publication of the work.*

Chicago, Ill. Oct 31st, '94.

My dear Mr. Ely:—

. . . [11] Your letter[12] in regard to Mr. Crowell's estimate on the maps came this morning. We will, of course, make no conditions in regard to royalty, as we have thought little about the financial gain, but we are very anxious indeed that the book should be published as quickly as possible. We have letters every week asking about it. Prof. Small[13] told me the other day that he could not "get on" any longer without it, and we feel that the matter will be so old and out of date if we wait much longer. Mrs. Kelly's office is already making great changes in the condition of the sweater shops in the neighborhood, the Jewish population is rapidly moving Northward, and all the conditions are of course, more or less, unlike what they were July 1st, 1893, when the data for the maps was finished.

Would it be a breach of courtesy to our editor to ask Mr. Woods[14] of the Andover House, in Boston, to go to see Mr. Crowell, or for us to take any steps in the matter? We will of course, be glad to keep the book on sale at the house,[15] and McClurg[16] will do what he can to push it. There are really many inquiries for it now from people who have seen the maps here.

We are just finishing our first six lectures on the Social Reformers.[17] The course has been very successful, and we are anxious to print the programme for the next six by Nov. 13th. Would it be possible for you to give us your lecture on the Earl of Shaftsbury,[18] some Tuesday in November or December? We would be very grateful to you if you could spare us that much time.

Regretting all the delay and trouble you are having about the book, I am Very sincerely yours,

Jane Addams.

TLS (SHSW, Ely; *JAPM*, 2:1588–90).

1. In addition to JA and Florence Kelley, the following identified as HH residents wrote essays for the volume: Agnes Sinclair Holbrook, Alzina P. Stevens, Isabel Eaton, Charles Zueblin, Josefa Humpal-Zeman, Alessandro Mastro-Valerio, Julia C. Lathrop, and EGS. In her "Prefatory Note" to the volume, written in Jan. 1895, JA reminded readers: "The residents of Hull House offer these maps and papers to the public, not as exhaustive treatises, but as recorded observations which may possibly be of value, because they are immediate, and the result of long acquaintance. All the writers have been in actual residence in Hull House, some of them for five years; their energies, however, have been chiefly directed, not toward sociological investigation, but to constructive work" (*HH Maps and Papers*, vii–viii).

Josefa Veronika Humpal-Zeman (1870?–1906) was a journalist, publisher, and reformer supporting woman's rights. She was born in Sušice, Bohemia, to Anna Srnka and Josef Humpal, who brought their family to the United States in 1874 and settled in Chicago. There Josefa Humpal attended a Czech-English school until she was nine years old, when she began attending public school. Between 1881 and 1884, the family returned to Bohemia, where she attended high school. Returning to Chicago, Josefa became a fabric cutter and amateur actress. She married Chicago teacher Robert Zeman, and the couple moved to Cleveland. Their marriage was short-lived, and their one child, Benjamin, born in Aug. 1888, lived just over a year.

Hull-House resident Alzina Parsons Stevens was a labor leader who worked tirelessly on behalf of female workers and at Hull-House led the Hull-House Woman's Club (courtesy Rima Lunin Schultz).

Humpal-Zeman remained in Cleveland, where she joined the Presbyterian Church and enrolled in the Women's College of Western Reserve Univ. In addition to becoming active in philanthropic endeavors among Bohemian women, she formed a chapter of the WCTU for Bohemian women and was a frequent speaker for women's groups. In 1892 Zeman was elected vice-president of the Western Reserve's Women's Christian Assn. She edited the college newspaper *College Folio* and contributed articles to Slavic journals throughout the Midwest.

Beginning in 1892, when she went to Chicago to encourage Bohemian women to form their own WCTU chapter, she worked for representation of Bohemian women during the World's Columbian Exposition in Chicago and served as secretary of the Bohemian women's committee to create an exhibit at the exposition. After a trip to California to visit Bohemian settlements there, she returned to Chicago to work at HH and officially become a resident on 6 Mar. 1894. She studied at the Univ. of Chicago and with Karla Máchova founded a Bohemian women's newspaper, one of the first Bohemian weekly periodicals in the world. The first number of *Ženské Listy* (Women's Gazette) appeared on 15 June 1894. The periodical featured Czech culture. Though attacked by other Czech papers, which saw her effort as competition, her publication succeeded. In 1896 she was chosen as secretary of the all-male Union of Slovenian Journalists, and in 1900 she founded the Bohemian Women's Publishing Co., with a workforce of fifty women.

It was also in 1894 that she organized a gathering of more than two thousand men and women who heard leaders of the English-speaking and Czech community in Chicago promote advancement for women through education. She also encouraged support for the new Illinois factory legislation, for joining the women's club movement, and for promoting better health care for women. At the gathering on 1 Jan. 1895, JA spoke on the settlement movement and its support for the growing immigrant populations of cities. "As to the social settlement idea, it is simple. The people who need a wider life and more education are brought face to face with the great problems of the day. To me Hull House will be a great disappointment if the impression exists that it belongs to one kind of people or one nationality. I know you have a hunger for better things, particularly in the improvement of women. With your cooperation greater things will be accomplished" ("All Meet as Sisters").

By 1895 Zeman left the newspaper that she founded and resettled in Prague. She acted as a foreign correspondent for the *Chicago Daily News* and eventually founded another women's newspaper, *Šťastný Domov* (Happy Home) in Prague. In late 1896, she returned to Chicago, where she served as a truant officer for the Chicago Board of Education, lectured at HH in the early spring on Bohemia and truancy, and helped attract Bohemian neighbors to the settlement for Bohemian evenings. By late 1897, she had returned to Prague.

In addition to the essay she wrote about the Bohemian community in Chicago for *HH Maps and Papers*, she wrote an article entitled "Bohemia: A Stir of Its Social Conscience" that appeared in the July 1904 issue of the *Commons*. During the last two years of her life, under the pen name Josephine Zeman, she wrote two novels in English, *My Crime* and *The Victim Triumphs: A Panorama of Modern Society*. After suffering a disabling stroke in 1905, she continued in ill health until her death at age thirty-six. She is buried in Prague's Olšany Cemetery.

2. An obituary in the *New York Times*, 30 July 1915, indicated that Thomas Y. Crowell (1836–1915) was born in West Dennis, Cape Cod, Mass. In the early 1860s, he began a bookbinding business in Boston. In 1876 he started a publishing house in New York City and in 1900 combined both businesses in New York. His sons, Jeremiah and Irving, eventually succeeded to the business, which survived until 1968 and became part of Harper & Row.

3. The title page of *HH Maps and Papers: A Presentation of Nationalities and Wages in a Congested District of Chicago, Together with Comments and Essays on Problems Growing Out of the Social Conditions* indicates that the authors of the work were "Residents of HH, a Social Settlement at 335 South Halsted St., Chicago." JA and Florence Kelley correspondence from the 1894 period reveals that they were the moving force behind the volume. The work had originally been promised for 1894, but was finally issued in 1895 in two editions. The smaller deluxe edition bound in olive-green cloth had a separate pouch to hold the maps that were backed with linen. The general edition was bound in blue cloth and had pockets on either end-board that contained the maps that were not linen backed. Fewer than one thousand books were printed, and according to JA the edition sold out within two years. When Crowell complained about the number and speed of sales, JA responded that the HH residents would encourage sales of the book at the settlement (see n. 15). The volume was not reissued by Crowell or by any other publisher during JA's lifetime.

4. Richard Theodore Ely (1854–1943), American economist and leader in progressive reform, became a lifelong friend of JA. Ely believed in the application of Christian social ethics to economics. He and JA shared similar reform ideas that evolved in part from that perspective: an end to child labor, abolition of sweatshops, development of labor unions, consumer protection, improved factory working conditions, better and more accessible education, increased wages and reduced working hours, and tax reform. Introduced to JA by Florence Kelley, Ely became responsible for the publication of JA's first three books, while she helped him find jobs for his students and raise money and support for his projects. It was largely through his efforts that she received her first honorary LL.D. at the Univ. of Wisconsin in 1904 and taught in the university's summer school in 1905.

Ely was born in Ripley, N.Y., the eldest of three children of Harriet Gardner Mason and Ezra Sterling Ely. After basic education at Fredonia, N.Y., he entered Dartmouth College, but transferred to Columbia Univ., from which he graduated in 1876. Three years later, he earned a Ph.D. at the Univ. of Heidelberg. Returning to the United States, from 1881 until 1892 he was associated with the Johns Hopkins Univ. as head of the Dept. of Political Economy. While there in 1885, he became one of the founders of the American Economic Assn. After serving as its first secretary, 1885–92, he was selected as its president, 1899–1901.

In 1892 Ely became the director of the School of Economics, Political Science, and History at the Univ. of Wisconsin. It was in 1894 that Ely was charged with promoting "socialistic" ideas, but he was exonerated by the Board of Regents, which dramatically defended academic freedom. As a result, he remained at the Univ. of Wisconsin for the next twenty years. He moved to Northwestern Univ. in Evanston, Ill., in 1925, and remained there until 1933, when he retired to Old Lyme, Conn., where he died. Ely was twice married. His first wife was Anna Morris Anderson, who died in 1923 and with whom he had four children. His second wife was Margaret Hahn, whom he wed in 1931 and with whom he had two children.

In 1907–8 he was the first president of the American Assn. for Labor Legislation. Ely was also the founder and president of the Economic Institute for Research, Inc. (originally referred to by Ely in 1905 as the American Bureau of Industrial Research). He wrote numerous articles and was the editor of two different publication series promoting a reform agenda. *HH Maps and Papers* became vol. 5 of Crowell's Library of Economics and Politics, for which Ely served as general editor. In 1899 he changed publishers and became the general editor of the Citizen's Library of Economics, Politics, and Sociology at the Macmillan Co. He published JA's next two books, *Democracy and Social Ethics* (1902) and *Newer Ideals of Peace* (1907), in his new series. He was a frequent visitor and lecturer at HH.

5. Charles Booth was an English author who presented conditions in the slums of London in great detail in his famous work *Life and Labour of the People in London*. See *PJA*, 2:512–13, n. 146. JA's personal copy of the 1891 edition titled *Labour and Life of the People*, published in London and Edinburgh by Williams and Norgate, and with JA's signature on the front endpaper, is located in UIC, JAMC. Only the first volume of the two-volume edition and map appendix survives in that collection. Also in the same collection is the complete work entitled *Life and Labour of the People in London* by Charles Booth in seventeen volumes and published by Macmillan and Co. in London and New York between 1902 and 1903, the first four volumes of which are a revision of the *Labour and Life of the People*. It was part of the HH Library.

6. C. Wright, *Seventh Special Report of the Commissioner of Labor*.

7. The schedules that Florence Kelley and the four men, who went door-to-door in the district, used to gather information are published in *HH Maps and Papers* prior to the first page of "Map Notes and Comments," beginning on p. 3. They were "Tenement Schedule" and "The Home," with a combined twenty-six questions. The second schedule, "Family Schedule," had forty-three questions.

8. It seems likely that from the time Florence Kelley began gathering and organizing the data, she hoped to display it in map form. On 23 July 1893, as the survey effort was winding down, the HH residents discussed the possible publication of the results in their residents' meeting. Under the heading "Maps," the following notes appear: "Miss Holbrook's need for completing records before publication. Schedules, on nationalities & wages to be verified or filled. Comments on wage-nationality & sanitary maps to be published. Prof. Ely's offer. Ownership map (proposed by Mrs. Kelley thro Miss Addams). General object to use of names of property owners; Sanitary Township Maps to be made" (HH Residents, "Residents Meeting Reports," 1893–95], 23–24; *JAPM*, 50:339–40). It also seems likely that Ely had made an offer to publish the maps with information about the survey. Florence Kelley and the HH residents hoped to issue several maps, including information on the sanitary conditions. None of these maps was produced. On 27 Aug. 1893, at a later HH residents' meeting, the discussion about the maps continued. The minutes of that meeting contain only this comment: "Map—Publications—What is to go with the maps?" (HH Residents, "Residents Meeting Reports," 1893–95, 29; *JAPM*, 50:345). From the beginning, the maps were the driving force behind the publication. HH financial records indicate that the $100 JA received for her articles in the *Forum*, plus interest of $12.80 and a supplement of $9.23 provided by JA, was used to defray costs associated with preparing the manuscript and maps for publication.

9. After hosting hundreds of people who visited HH during the World's Columbian Exposition, JA and EGS believed that they needed to have a publication that would explain the development of the settlement and its program. Late in 1893, JA and EGS created "HH: A Social Settlement at 335 South Halsted St., Chicago. An Outline Sketch," which was privately printed on 1 Feb. 1894. It was thirty-eight pages in length and based on a manuscript dated 1 Jan. 1894. Both manuscript and its published version are at SCPC, JAC; *JAPM*, 46:591–617, 618–642. For the appendix to *HH Maps and Papers*, labeled "Outline Sketch Descriptive of HH," and presented on pp. 205–30 of the volume, JA updated the publication but kept the same organization.

10. Alzina Parsons Stevens was not yet a HH resident when she coauthored "Wage-Earning Children" with Florence Kelley; however, she would become one early in 1897. Alzina Ann Parsons Stevens (1849–1900), labor activist and reformer, printer and journalist, and a founder of the Juvenile Court of Cook County, was born in Parsonsfield, Maine, the youngest of several children of Louisa Page and Enoch Parsons, who was a farmer and carpenter. She attended school in Somersworth, N.H., and after the death of her father in 1864 began her career as a working woman.

Her first job was in a textile plant, where an accident left her with permanent damage to her right hand. In 1871 she arrived in Chicago with her sister and brother-in-law and found employment as a proofreader in the nonunion printing firm of Otaway and Colbert. It was also in Chicago that she met Francis Harold Stevens, who lived in the same rooming house that she did and was a bookkeeper in the same company where she worked. Their marriage on 13 July 1876 was short-lived. Mrs. Stevens had one child. It was also while living in Chicago that she became the president of the Working Women's Union No. 1 when it was founded in 1878. The goal of the union, affiliated with the Chicago Council of Trades and Labor Unions and the Socialist Labor Party, was to encourage working women to support unionization. By 1879 she was a skilled printer and a member of the Chicago Typographical Union.

In 1881 she moved to Toledo, Ohio, and became a journalist. She worked as a copy editor and proofreader for H. H. Hardesty, a book publisher, and began to write for labor publications, including *John Swinton's Paper*, and the *Toledo Bee*. During her years in Toledo, she remained engaged in labor union activities. A leader in the Knights of Labor, which she joined in 1883, she worked for cooperation between the Toledo Knights of Labor and the Federation of Labor and led the Joan of Arc Assembly, an organization of working women associated with the Knights of Labor.

A delegate to the 1892 national convention of the Populist Party, she was coeditor of the Populist Party newspaper the *Vanguard*, founded in 1892 and published in Chicago. Back in Chicago once again and with her sister and brother-in-law, she served as a member of the Women's Labor Com., helping to plan the Labor Congress associated with the Congress Auxiliary of the World's Columbian Exposition. She also participated in one of the programs on women's trade unions. Along with Florence Kelley and Mary Kenney, she lobbied for the successful passage of the Factory and Workshop Inspection Act in 1893 and served as assistant factory inspector until 1897, when she was dismissed by the new governor of Illinois. She worked tirelessly to contain the smallpox epidemic in 1894. Her efforts and findings were issued by the Illinois factory inspector's office in 1894 as "Small Pox in the Tenements and Sweatshops of Chicago." In 1899 Alzina Stevens lobbied in support of legislation to create the Juvenile Court of Chicago and to authorize the Board of Education in Cook Co. to build and operate a truant school.

On 6 Nov. 1897, she and JA shared the same platform at the Chicago Political Equality League. There Stevens argued, "The organized working woman believes that the ballot is her right, and that it would be her duty to exercise it" ("Talk Equal Rights"). In May 1895, she spoke to the HH Social Science Club, where she presented arguments in favor of unrestricted immigration. While a resident of HH, she had several positions related to trade unions. She was president of the Chicago Working Women's Council, 1896–97; helped organize and lead the Dorcas Federal Labor Union, for which she was president, 1896–97, and then secretary, 1898–99; and was the manager of trade union gatherings at HH, 1897–99. Active in the HH Woman's Club, she became its president in 1899 and served for a year, during which she instituted the Linen Chest, which was later called the Mrs. Stevens Linen Chest in her honor, to help provide household supplies and clothing for those in need. In the meantime, she became a lecturer for HH clubs on the labor movement, and for a time in 1897 she was the director of the Tennyson Literary and Social Club at HH. Stevens had long been involved in trying to abolish child labor. She worked for improved compulsory education laws and, while stationed at HH, was the Juvenile Court of Cook County's first probation officer in 1899. According to the *HH Bulletin*, "[A]t one time [she] had in her charge over 150 boys and girls who were wards of the court" (4, no. 3 [Autumn 1900]: 11; *JAPM*, 53:750). Stevens's article about her HH experiences, "Life in a Social Settlement," appeared in *Self Culture* in the spring of 1899. She was active in the Every Day Club and in the Social Economic and Municipal Science clubs. She was a diabetic and died unexpectedly at HH on 3 June 1900. After a funeral at the settlement, her body was cremated.

Her obituary was published in several Chicago newspapers. The *Chicago Daily Tribune* hailed her, as did others, as "one of the best known sociologists in Chicago" ("Mrs. A. P. Stevens Dead"). Stevens was much beloved by the HH Woman's Club, whose members published a resolution in her honor, stating in part, "Her life work has opened large possibilities to the club women of Chicago. The Vacation school, the Parental school, the Juvenile court, better industrial conditions for women and children—these she loved and for these she worked—these she has left to us. We can best express our appreciation of her life work by pursuing the work she opened up, and in which she enlisted our first efforts as a club" ("Resolutions on the Death of Mrs. Alzina Parsons Stevens by the HH Women's Club," in "In Memoriam Mrs. Alzina Parsons Stevens"). Members of the HH Woman's Club were unsuccessful in their efforts to have the new school for truants named for her.

11. The editors have omitted the first paragraph of JA's letter to Ely. In it JA agreed to cut the length of Isabel Eaton's essay and to clarify the contents. She reported to Ely that "Mrs. Kelly and I have gone over it very carefully, and I think it is now clearer, and the general arrangement much better."

12. Richard T. Ely's letter to JA is not extant.

13. Albion Woodbury Small (1854–1926) had come to the Univ. of Chicago in 1892 as professor and head of the new graduate department of sociology he was hired to establish. He was born in Buckfield, Maine, the son of Thankful Woodbury and Rev. Albion K. P. Small. Educated at Colby College (A.B. 1876; M.A. 1879), Newton Theological Institution (1876–79), Univ. of Berlin and Univ. of Leipzig (1879–81), and the Johns Hopkins Univ. (Ph.D. 1889), he taught history and political economy at Colby from 1881 through 1888. He was a reader in history at the Johns Hopkins Univ. for the year 1888–89, before becoming president of Colby College, 1889–92. He spent the remainder of his scholarly career at the Univ. of Chicago, where he also became dean of the Graduate School of Arts and Literature in 1905. He helped establish the profession of sociology; was a charter member of the American Sociological Society, which he served twice as president; and founded the *American Journal of Sociology* in 1895, where he served for the remainder of his life as its editor. He was the author of several books; among the most influential was the textbook *An Introduction to the Study of Society* (1894), which he wrote with his student George E. Vincent (1864–1941). Small was married in Berlin, Germany, in 1881, to Valeria von Massow.

Small found his way to HH almost as soon as he arrived in Chicago. On 20 Nov. 1892, he gave a lecture entitled "The Social Philosophy of Jesus" and repeated it again on 15 Jan. 1893 in the Sunday Lectures and Concerts series. JA and Small worked together on establishing the Civic Federation of Chicago, and JA published at least four of her essays as articles in his

*American Journal of Sociology*. He was a strong proponent of attaching HH to the Univ. of Chicago and when that failed worked diligently to help establish the University of Chicago Settlement. He offered JA a part-time appointment in his department of sociology in 1913, which she declined, and he promoted her unsuccessfully in 1907 for an honorary degree at the Univ. of Chicago. Their reform interests were similar until World War I, when he disagreed with her peace activities.

14. Robert Woods wrote to JA, "I saw Mr. Crowell to-day. . . . He says he is willing to bring out part of the edition with linen-mounted maps but must have most of the edition without linen mounting in order to have the price low enough to secure a good sale" (3 Jan. 1894 [1895], SHSW, Ely; *JAPM*, 2:1622).

15. Six months after the volume was issued, JA wrote to Richard Ely to indicate that the semiannual report about sales was discouraging and that she planned to push sales, stating, "I think I will put aside any false sentiment, and pursue that course" (22 Aug. 1895, SHSW, Ely; *JAPM*, 2:1748). On 3 Jan. 1911, she wrote to Ely, remarking that she was embarrassed by her statement about Crowell in *Twenty Years* that he did not think the book worth a second edition. She admitted that Crowell lost money on the book and probably could not afford a second edition. She also recognized that Ely gave up some of his editor's pay to publish the book and that the maps were very costly. She indicated that she was still proud of the volume (SHSW, Ely; *JAPM*, 5:1444–46).

16. A. C. McClurg was a notable bookshop in Chicago.

17. The list of the first six lectures, 2 Oct. to 13 Nov. 1894, appears in HH Scrapbook 1:49; *JAPM*, Addendum 10:7ff. A list of the second series, which began 11 Dec. 1894 with a talk on Giuseppe Mazzini and lasted until 5 Feb. 1895 when the topic was John Ruskin, does not contain the name of Richard T. Ely.

18. Undoubtedly Anthony Ashley Cooper (1801–85), Seventh Earl of Shaftesbury, English philanthropist, who supported the ten-hour law for factory workers, which passed in 1847; acted to stop child labor in coal mines and employing children as chimney sweeps; worked to improve conditions of lodging houses; and helped bring about the erection of model tenements.

## To Richard T. Ely

*Completing the manuscript and publication of the maps for* Hull-House Maps and Papers *continued to be at the forefront of the efforts of Jane Addams, Florence Kelley, and the settlement residents during November. Publisher Crowell, obviously recognizing that the large colored maps would be an expensive undertaking, urged series editor Richard T. Ely to talk the Hull-House editors out of presenting the maps. After he made that suggestion, an angry and frustrated Florence Kelley wrote the following reply: "But the disappointment over the delay is trivial in comparison with the dismay, which I felt when you suggested cutting the maps. This I positively decline to permit.*

*"The charts are mine to the extent that I not only furnished the data for them but hold the sole permission from the U.S. department of labor to publish them. I have never contemplated, and do not now contemplate, any form of publication except as two linen-backed maps or charts, folding in pockets in the cover of the book, similar to Mr. Booth's charts.*

*"If Crowell and Co. do not contemplate this, it will be well to stop work at once, as I can consent to no use of my charts in any other form."*[1] *A very perturbed Ely shared his concerns with Crowell and with Jane Addams, who wrote the following two letters to mollify Ely and to ensure that the volume would be published as it was in March 1895.*

Hull-House 335 South Halsted Street Chicago [Ill.] Nov. 27th. 1894.

My dear Mr. Ely:—

It seemed to us well to have the titles of the writers at the head of the chapters, as well as in the table of contents, but we have decided not to attempt an index. We have sent back all of the first proof, and have been very conservative about corrections in the page proof. One of the residents, Mr. Sykes,[2] is "reader" for the Chicago Tribune, and we, of course, have found his aid invaluable.

I have just come back from Detroit, and found your long and kind letter of explanation awaiting me.[3] I am very sorry indeed that you were subjected to any annoyance for I assure you that we all appreciate very highly the generous amount of time and care you have given to the editing of the work. Mrs. Kelly has been getting out her annual report[4] and has been very much driven by her work. In addition to this she is having her annual struggle with the small pox[5] and the apathy of the manufacturers in regard to it. I have no doubt that accumulated annoyances appeared in her letter to you, which I regret more than I can say. She was consternated at the prospect of having the maps divided,[6] realizing that they are already difficult for the average reader, but I assure you that our feeling of gratitude to our Editor has never changed. It would doubtless have been impossible to have induced Crowell, or any other publisher to take the book without your name and aid. We of course, all of us realize this. I had hoped to see you in Milwaukee last Tuesday.[7] I heard a great deal of admiration expressed for your address given the night before, and regretted very much that I had not been able to hear it.

Trusting that you may have no further annoyance in regard to the book and assuring you that there will be none from the Hull House end of the line, I am, Very sincerely yours,

Jane Addams

TLS (SHSW, Ely; *JAPM*, 2:1596–98).

1. Florence Kelley to Richard T. Ely, 14 Nov. 1894, SHSW, Ely, in Sklar and Palmer, eds. *Selected Letters of Florence Kelley*, 78.

2. See Article in the *Chicago Record*, 3 Dec. 1894, n. 1, below.

3. JA had agreed to speak before an RFS, RS, and RC alumnae gathering in Detroit on 24 Nov. 1894. Ely's letter to JA does not appear to be extant in the papers of JA.

4. Florence Kelley's first report as chief Illinois factory inspector was published early in 1894. By late 1894, she was once again engaged in beginning to draft her second report, which came out in early 1895 as *Second Annual Report of the Factory Inspector of Illinois for the Year Ending December 15, 1894*. It was published in Springfield, Ill., by the state printer

(see *JAPM*, 54:161–280, 283–347). She had just completed a special report on the summer smallpox epidemic and its effect on clothing manufacturing (see n. 5).

In this typed letter to Richard T. Ely and the one dated 31 Oct. 1894 (see above), JA did not correct the typist's misspelling of Florence Kelley's family name.

5. During the summer of 1894, the newspapers of Chicago were full of warnings about the smallpox epidemic raging in the city. Florence Kelley wrote to Gov. John P. Altgeld describing the conditions in Chicago slums: "For a little more than two months past, the State factory inspectors have worked almost exclusively in that tenement house section of this city where manufacture of clothing and the small-pox epidemic have been in progress together" (22 June 1894 in Sklar, *Florence Kelley and the Nation's Work*, 267). A result of her efforts to publicize the conditions and warn citizens about the danger of infected clothing was the *First Special Report of the Factory Inspectors of Illinois, on Small-Pox in the Tenement House Sweat-Shops of Chicago, July 1, 1894*, which was published in Springfield, Ill., by H. W. Rokker, State Printer and Binder, in 1894.

6. The basic map of the area in which the social survey had been conducted identified streets and indicated the location of structures on lots. It was produced free of charge by HH supporter Samuel Sewell Greeley and his surveying and engineering firm, Greeley and Carlson. In order to present all of the information that Florence Kelley and JA hoped to offer, the publisher found it necessary to produce two different versions of the map. One version featured the distribution of eighteen national groups throughout the surveyed area. The other map offered data on the wages, occupations, and housing conditions of all of the people surveyed.

7. JA attended and spoke at the Wisconsin State Board of Charities meeting on 20 Nov. 1895. Ely spoke the day before.

## Article in the *Chicago Record*

*Throughout 1894 Jane Addams continued to work on developing the Hull-House physical plant to absorb the settlement's expanding programs. By year's end, she could anticipate the major changes reported in an article that settlement resident George Sikes[1] wrote for the* Chicago Record *where he was an editor there.*

*Securing the funds to add to the original Hull home, build additions to the already completed gymnasium/coffeehouse, and create a new structure for the nursery and kindergarten program were easy compared to securing the real estate on which to build a new "Children's Building."[2] Negotiations with Helen Culver, owner of the property that surrounded Hull-House, began early in 1894. On 3 March, Jane reported to her friend Mary Rozet Smith: "Mr. Pond[3] and I had another of our long conversations with Miss Culver this morning. She put a price on the Ewing St. lots—but so high that she might as well not have done it. She offers fifty feet along the alley—i.e. just west of the present nursery[4] for $200.00 a foot. On my objecting to the price being as great as Polk St she contended that it was valuable because it had an alley in the rear and on the side that she would sell through to the west alley for the same price. She will not sell any thing on Halsted St."[5] And two months later, on 1 May, Jane reported: "I think that we would better plan nothing further about the various lots for the nursery until your return,[6] a resolution is going on in the mind of Miss Culver, whether 'for or agin' us we are* *not quite sure, but she is at last going to submit 'a definite proposition.' The tale of the Revolution is long and hangs much on details which I cannot write but long to tell you. Mr. Arnold is very hopeful for a favorable decision this spring,[7] so that we look at the smoky walls of the present habitat with a faint ray of hope."[8] Later in 1894, when the funeral parlor/livery stable had moved and the corner of Halsted and Polk streets became vacant, Addams thought of placing the addition to the coffeehouse there, with men's residence quarters on the second floor and the possibility of a kindergarten room as well. That plan changed when the lot became available for Hull-House, and the new building was designed especially for children's activities.*

[Chicago, Ill.] 3 Dec. 1894

### ADDITIONS TO HULL HOUSE.
### PLANS FOR A DISTINCT ENLARGEMENT OF THE SOCIAL SETTLEMENT.

Hull house, the social settlement at 335 South Halsted street, has secured an extension of lease until 1920. Two new buildings are to be erected at once, with a third in prospect. William Colvin, who put up the building containing the coffee house and men's club-room, will furnish money for one addition and will put a third story over the whole building. One addition, on the first floor, will have a large dining-room, which may be used for club meetings. The rooms on the second floor will afford additional facilities for the Hull House Men's club. The space on the third floor will be made into sleeping-rooms for men.

A three-story building, to be known as the "Children's House," for the use of the kindergarten and day nursery, will be erected either in Ewing or Polk street, near Halsted.[9] This will be built by Charles Mather Smith, in the name of his daughter, Miss Mary Rozett [Rozet] Smith, who has long been responsible for the maintenance of the nursery. On the first floor will be the children's dining-room and club-rooms; on the second floor, the kindergarten and nursery; on the third floor, a music-room and sleeping-rooms for some of the residents whose work is with the children especially.

A third story is also to be built on Hull house itself in order to afford greater accommodations for residents. The money for this improvement is provided by Mrs. Nancy Foster, whose name is borne by one of the women's dormitories at the University of Chicago.[10]

The facilities of the settlement have increased with the field of usefulness, until now almost all of the block in which it is located is under the control of Hull house. Beside Hull house itself and the building containing the coffee house and men's club, already mentioned, there is the Butler gallery, a two-story building in Halsted street, the gymnasium, the cooperative coal yard, which has an office at the corner of Halsted and Ewing streets, and the nursery. In

Ewing street is the building occupied by the Jane club, a cooperative boarding club of fifty young women. The three-story brick flat at 247 Polk street is also used by the settlement.[11] At 245 Polk street, property also under the control of Miss Addams, there is a club of printers.[12] The block in Polk street just east of Halsted has been secured as a play ground for children.[13]

PD (3 Dec. 1894, *Chicago Record* from HH Scrapbook 1:60, UIC, JAMC; *JAPM*, Addendum 10:6ff. A holograph note written on the clipping attributes the article to George Sykes [Sikes]).

1. George Cushing Sikes, journalist and municipal reformer, was born in Dodge Center, Minn., the son of Henry Chauncey and Eleanor Sikes. He was a graduate of the Univ. of Minnesota (B.A. 1892) and the Univ. of Chicago (Ph.M. 1894). While at the Univ. of Minnesota, he learned the printers trade and became president of the Minneapolis Typographical Union. When he graduated from the Univ. of Chicago, he found newspaper work initially at the *Chicago Daily Tribune* and lodged at HH beginning in July 1894 as part of the Phalanx Club, started by a group of nine men, most of whom were associated with the Typographical Union, at 245 (later 816) West Polk St. (see also Robert A. Woods to JA, 20 June 1893, n. 12, above). It reminded him "of the frat house in Minneapolis. It has sleeping rooms above and very pleasant parlors on the first floor" (George C. Sikes to Madeleine Wallin, 24 July 1894, CHM, CHS, Sikes).

Between 1895 and 1900, he was a correspondent covering the Illinois legislature and an editorial writer for the *Chicago Record*. Beginning in 1900, he held a number of positions in municipal government and organizations: secretary of the Chicago Street Railway Comm., 1900–1902; assistant secretary, 1903–5, and then secretary, 1906–8, of the Municipal Voters' League, Chicago; special investigator for the Chicago Harbor Commissioner, 1908–9; secretary, Chicago Bureau of Public Efficiency, 1910–15; director of the Policemen's Annuity and Benefit Fund of Chicago, 1923–26; and secretary of the Chicago Pension Comm., until 1927. He was an advocate for consolidation of local governments in Chicago and Cook Co. and in Los Angeles, Calif. For a number of years, he was an editorial and special articles writer for the *Chicago Daily News*.

At HH Sikes became a key JA aide, especially when it came to local politics. He was secretary of the Nineteenth Ward Council of the Civic Federation and helped JA and the settlement residents in their fight against Alderman John Powers and his lieutenants. In 1896 JA first approached Sikes about running for alderman in the Nineteenth Ward. "I told you when I last wrote you, that Miss Addams wanted me to run for alderman," he wrote to Madeleine Wallin, whom he would later marry. JA was so intent on having him as a candidate that she met with Victor Lawson, owner of the *Chicago Record*, to seek his help and his permission for the young journalist to become a candidate. At first Lawson agreed, but having second thoughts indicated that he "was afraid it might possibly compromise the paper in some way" (29 Feb. 1896, CHM, CHS, Sikes). Sikes led the HH effort to find a suitable candidate and guided the election strategy to a successful win (see Article in the *HH Bulletin*, Apr. 1896, below). At HH he lectured on community political issues and focused efforts on raising political awareness of issues. On 16 Feb. 1896, he spoke on "Municipal Franchises." He was also instrumental in promoting the settlement through the *Chicago Record*.

On 6 Feb. 1897, he and Madeleine Wallin were married in Elgin, Ill. JA invited the young couple to have their reception at HH. Madeleine Wallin came to HH in the summer of 1896 first as a volunteer and then as a resident and to be near her husband-to-be.

Madeleine Wallin (1863–1955) was born in St. Peter, Minn., the only child of attorney and justice on the North Dakota Supreme Court Alfred C. Wallin and his wife, Ellen Keyes Wallin, who had grown up in Elgin, Ill., and had been a teacher in Brooklyn, N.Y. Madeleine attended public school in Fargo, N.D., and graduated from Elgin Academy, Ill., in 1887, as valedictorian of her class. After two years at Smith College, 1888–90, she graduated from the Univ. of Minnesota (B.L. 1892). At the Univ. of Minnesota, she met her future husband while both wrote and were board members for its student publication *Ariel*. One of the articles she wrote for the publication was about the College Settlement in New York City. In the fall of 1892, she became a fellow in political science at the Univ. of Chicago, and she earned a master's degree the next year. While at the Univ. of Chicago, she was active on the philanthropic committee of the Christian Union, which helped found the University of Chicago Settlement, where she was a volunteer in its first year. She became an assistant in history at Smith College, 1894–96.

At HH Madeleine Wallin became JA's secretary. "I write some of Miss Addams letters and put other matter in type; and they have given me the keeping of the records, i.e., the names and addresses of the members of clubs and classes, the residents, and some other material of like nature. It was arranged according to a system, and the man who first put it in order was here the other night and explained the working of the system to me, but there was no one to keep it in order, apparently, unless I took care of it. I was glad to do so, because I like that kind of work" (Madeleine Wallin to Alfred C. Wallin, 8 Oct. 1896, UIC, JAMC, Sikes). While she was taking a course in cooking and sewing at the Lewis Institute, Madeleine also taught hand sewing, helped manage the Penny Provident Bank, and was a "toter" at HH.

The Sikes had two children, Alfred Wallin, who became a chemical engineer and metallurgist, and Eleanor Shepard Sikes, who became a physical education teacher at Bradley Univ., Peoria, Ill. Like her husband, Madeleine Sikes became active in civic affairs and worked tirelessly for improved compulsory education laws. She supported woman suffrage and campaigned for the abolition of child labor.

In 1899 she joined the Chicago branch of the Assn. of Collegiate Alumnae and in 1900 was the chairwoman of its committee studying education legislation and child labor. She helped organize and spoke on compulsory education at a major conference held in Chicago in Apr. 1902 to explore ways to improve the lives of children and prevent juvenile delinquency. In Dec. 1902, she became a member of the CWC and served in its Philosophy and Education Dept. She was chairwoman of the education committees of the League of Cook County Clubs, Illinois Federation of Women's Clubs, and General Federation of Women's Clubs and in 1909–11 was president of the Chicago Assn. of Collegiate Alumnae. In 1910 Madeleine Sikes became a founding member of the Woman's City Club of Chicago and served on its board of managers, 1917–20.

After the Sikes moved to Austin, Ill., Madeleine Sikes was active in the Austin Woman's Club, serving it in a number of capacities and as president, 1911–13. Also in Austin, she was chairwoman of the Austin Civic League, 1914–15; the Austin Defense League, 1917–18; and the press and publicity committee of the Austin Red Cross, 1917–18. She became an active member of the Illinois League of Women Voters and also served on the council and executive committee of the Cook County League of Women Voters, 1928–31. Between 1924 and 1926, she was chairwoman of the Joint Com. on Public School Affairs of Chicago and between 1932 and 1937 taught English and citizenship through the Adult Dept. of the Chicago public schools. In her older years, she moved to San Antonio, Tex., and supported the development of universal health care in the United States.

Madeleine Sikes was a frequent public speaker before such groups as the PTA, League of Women Voters, and other women's clubs. Her *Summary of Child Labor and Compulsory Education Laws of U.S.* was first published by the Chicago Assn. of Collegiate Alumnae in 1901. It was then reissued by the U.S. government as "Summary of Laws Relating to Compulsory Education and Child Labor in the United States" in *Report of the Commissioner of Education, 1899–1900*, vol. 2, pp. 2590–2602. With Josephine Goldmark, she coauthored *Child Labor Legislation Handbook* (1904), which was published by the National Consumers' League.

2. The Children's Building, or Smith Building, was a four-story redbrick structure located on the corner of Halsted and Polk streets. It was designed by the Pond brothers and built beginning 17 July 1895. It was finished and opened in Dec. 1895. A newspaper description indicated, "On the first floor are two pretty rooms, which are used for the meeting of clubs in the mornings or evenings, and in the afternoon the back room is used for the 'baby kindergarten' of children under 4 years of age, who are too young for the regular kindergarten on the third floor, and the front room for the precocious children of 6 years or thereabouts, who are enough advanced to be prepared for the public schools. . . . On the second floor are the nursery, kitchen, and sleeping rooms for the 'creche' ladies. . . . On the third floor is one large room for the use of the kindergarten. . . . The studio is on the fourth floor. . . . The music room is on the same floor" ("Built for Children"). Architectural plans for the Children's Building, 1895, are at UIC, JAMC, HH Assn.; *JAPM*, Addendum 10:3.

3. Allen Pond.

4. The nursery was located in a cottage at 223 (later 814) Ewing St.

5. JA to MRS, 3 Mar. 1894, SCPC, JAC; *JAPM*, 2:1505–6.

6. MRS was away visiting at an unknown site with her mother.

7. HH resident Charles C. Arnold. Miss Helen Culver did not make a commitment to sell or lease the real estate at the corner of Halsted and Polk streets until the late spring of 1895.

8. JA to MRS, 1 May 1894, SCPC, JAC; *JAPM*, 2:1532–33.

9. JA, Helen Culver, and the Charles Mather Smith family still had not agreed to terms for the purchase or lease of the corner lot at Halsted and Polk streets.

10. Nancy Smith Foster (1807?–1901) was born near Peterborough, N.H., to Deacon John Smith and his wife and raised on their farm, "Elm Hill." She wed Dr. John H. Foster (d. 1874), and in 1840 the couple arrived in Chicago. After moving several times in the young and growing city, the Fosters settled at Belden and Clark streets in a home that became perhaps the last house on the far North Side of the city consumed in the Chicago Fire of 1871. After her husband's death, she made her home with her daughter, Julia Foster Porter (who created the Maurice Porter Hospital for Children [see also JA to MCAL, 1 Apr. 1889, n. 6, above]), on Fullerton Ave., and, experiencing increasingly poor health, became virtually housebound. She continued an avid interest in her community and its needs. In 1892 she gave the Univ. of Chicago fifty thousand dollars for what became Nancy Foster Hall, its first dormitory for women. She also gave twenty thousand dollars in 1900 to enlarge the dormitory and then throughout the years spent untold amounts to furnish it. In addition to providing the funds for adding the third story to the original Hull home, she also pledged one thousand dollars in 1899 to the new coffeehouse, a larger kitchen, and the theater building.

11. Located in that property were the HH dispensary, the labor bureau, and the relief office.

12. A June 1895 description of the Phalanx Club indicated that the building was a "two-story frame dwelling." It was composed of sleeping rooms, "[t]wo large sitting rooms provided with lounges, easy arm chairs, rugs, and a piano; a large round table supplied with Chicago dailies and current magazines. . . card, desk and checker tables and smokers outfits galore." Their simple constitution demanded that all indebtedness incurred be promptly paid and the club run on a cash basis. No liquor was allowed. "The personnel of the club largely consists of newspaper compositors on three leading dailies, but there are also an attorney, an electrician, a Y.M.C.A. physical director, a proofreader, and a newspaper correspondent." A housemother lived in a few rooms at the back of the building ("Twelve Jolly Bachelors in a Bun[ch?]").

13. The editors have omitted the last paragraph of the article that contains a listing of the contents of the soon-to-be-printed *HH Maps and Papers*.

## To Richard T. Ely

Hull-House. 335 South Halsted Street. Chicago. [Ill.] Dec 4" 1894

My dear Dr Ely—

The page proof is all carefully corrected and returned I hope very much that it will be found to be quite right.

I cannot tell you how sorry I am about Mrs Kelley's[1] letter. I understood perfectly that you had written to secure our ideas and wishes in regard to the maps and I asked Miss Holbrooke[2] to write you in regard to it. She talked it over with all of us including Mrs Kelley, but the latter swears to have fallen into a panic later and to have written very hastily and unwisely. I am sure that you will understand that the action was hasty and hers quite alone.

The residents as a whole have known nothing about it, and I assure you that we are all most grateful and appreciative of what you have done for us. I hope the book will justify your efforts, there have been two or three very good notices of it lately.[3] Very sincerely yours

Jane Addams

ALS (SHSW, Ely; *JAPM*, 2:1601–3).

1. See headnote, 27 Nov. 1894, above.
2. Agnes Sinclair Holbrook.
3. One of the references had appeared the previous day. See Article in the *Chicago Record*, 3 Dec. 1894, n. 13, above.

## To Sarah Alice Addams Haldeman

*With the stress-filled task of completing the manuscript for* Hull-House Maps and Papers *behind her, Jane Addams looked forward to a restful few days. "I have accepted an invitation from Mary Smith to go to South Carolina with her father and herself for a few weeks," she wrote sister Alice Haldeman. "We will start Friday evening Dec 7" and I will get back in time for Christmas, by the time ~~they~~ <the children> come home for their vacations."[1] After her return on 23 December, she reported, "I had a delightful and restful trip. We went to St Augustine on to Palatka,[2] and came home from Columbia[3] via Asheville[4] where we spent twenty four hours—it is a heavenly spot."[5]*

*In her note of thanks to Mary Smith, she reported, "The House seems full of Christmas cheer—and every thing is going on with great zeal. One hundred & thirty turkeys have been sent in. A bunch of cranberries, one of apples and Mr Warner[6] has sent a large share of his store full of groceries—so that all is going 'merry as merry as can be.' Every one is much impressed with my improved appearance and I have many compliments, which I smilingly receive."[7]*

Hull-House 335 South Halsted Street Chicago [Ill.] Dec. 28" 1894

My dear Alice

We had really a beautiful Xmas day—the children were not in the least sad and I am sure really enjoyed it. They were all here including Mr Linn from the Saturday before and the boys and Esther will be here for the week of course. I am quite rested and fat from my trip and am going to be better all winter for it. Thank you very much for the package[8] I am too hurried for more but wish that you would come. Always your loving sister

Jane

ALS (UIC, JAMC; *JAPM*, 2:1614).

1. 4 Dec. 1894, UIC, JAMC; *JAPM*, 2:1604. JML joined his children, John, Weber, Esther, and Stanley, at HH for Christmas. John was studying at seminary in Chicago; Weber was a student at the Univ. of Chicago; and Esther was in school at RC. Stanley had been staying with James and Annie Linn in Englewood and attending school there.

2. St. Augustine and Palatka, noted winter vacation venues for the wealthy in northern Florida, were near Green Cove Springs, where JA's stepmother, AHHA, had sometimes wintered. See *PJA*, 1:137, n. 5.

3. Charles Mather Smith and his daughter were on their way to visit his sister and MRS's aunt Sarah Porter Smith, who, in Feb. 1894, had purchased a home in Columbia, S.C., near her brother George Cotton Smith (1828–1915) and his wife, Elizabeth Virginia Laning Smith (1832–1910). In 1899 Sarah Porter Smith sold her home to the George Cotton Smiths. Known as the "Boylston House," it eventually became one of the structures within the Governor's Green, the residence for the governors of South Carolina. See also Article in the *Chicago Inter Ocean*, 30 June 1892, n. 11, above.

4. Asheville, N.C., was becoming a noted vacation retreat for the wealthy. George Washington Vanderbilt II was building his mountain mansion known as the Biltmore Estate, begun in 1889 and completed in 1895. By 1894 the railway system reaching the community in the pristine natural setting of the Blue Ridge Mountains was operated by the Southern Railway system.

5. JA to SAAH, [23 Dec. 1894], UIC, JAMC; *JAPM*, 2:1609.

6. Ezra Joseph Warner (1841–1910), a merchant, was the father of HH volunteer Maud Warner (see also JA to MCAL, 19 [and 20] Feb. 1889, n. 27, above). He had been born in Middlebury, Vt., to Joseph and Jane Meech Warner and graduated from Middlebury College in 1861. In 1863 he became associated in the wholesale grocery business with A. A. Sprague as Sprague and Warner and later as Sprague, Warner & Co. He also became involved in the insurance business, serving as a director of the Liverpool and London and Globe Insurance Co. and as chairman in 1889. He was active in the Chicago community, especially as a member of the board of the Art Institute. In 1861 he married Jane E. Remsen, and the couple had at least five children. By 1905 the Warners lived in Lake Forrest, Ill., but also spent time in Pasadena, Calif.

7. 23 Dec. 1894, SCPC, JAC; *JAPM*, 2:1611–12.

8. One of the Christmas gifts that was in the package that SAAH sent to JA was from Marcet Haldeman. "I am going to keep the pin cushion on my new desk and think of you all day long as I look at it," JA wrote to her niece ([ca. 25 Dec. 1894], IU, Lilly, SAAH; *JAPM*, 2:1613).

## To Mary Rozet Smith

Second National Bank of Freeport, Illinois. Freeport, Ill. Jan. 15" 1895

My dear friend

I am waiting here for Laura[1] to come with the sleigh to take me to Cedarville and will write while I wait.

I have made Herculean efforts to bring up the nursery account but as yet no one has subscribed by the month. Mrs Bowen[2] gave $100.oo which paid up the coal bills (50.oo) and paid Mary[3] & Mrs Hensen[4] to Feb. 1st. I have made one or two futile attempts at the kindergarten but may be more successful upon my return.[5]

Mr Barrett[6] has paid up Rose Gyles' salary to June 1st and Mr Colvin made up our yearly deficiency[7] so that we are quite square and a little ahead in certain directions.

The Stalbus case comes up in the Supreme Court in March ~~1st~~.[8] In the mean time Mr Pond and I are guilty working on Miss Culver's feeling, she may yet part with the corner on Ewing & Halsted.[9]

Mrs Foster[10] 2500.oo is in the bank and we will begin to build as soon as the weather moderates—seven single rooms with two bath rooms is what the present plan calls for—it fills our hearts with joy. We are having a general overhauling of the Coffee House and may part with the lady Nourse.[11]

I feel a little like a battered old business agent but it is quite time we had this general housecleaning. Our trip, dear friend, gave me a perspective which was most valuable and I feel soberer and calmer than I have felt for a year.[12] It is one more thing to thank you for.

I have ordered from McClug's Warner's book on "American Charities"—it is very interesting. I am enjoying it greatly.[13] Shaw sent me a copy of his new book,[14] it is n't on the market yet but I will send you one when it is. M. West[15] is growing in grace and power day by day the household is simply enthusiastic over her. We would have made a fatal mistake if we had let her go—the same sort of a serious loss to the House that G. Barnum[16] would be. Mary Kenney O'Sullivan is making us a visit, we gave her a reception on Sat—that was very jolly. She is going to take Toomey and little Jane back to her flat to keep house for her. Sister T. was over at the reception and danced and joked with the girls in a way to break your heart. I told Mrs O'Sullivan that I thought you would help on the ticket to Boston. Evidently it is going to be an awfully heavy price for her to buy it.[17]

I will write you later when the K'g plans come out better. Vennette Crain[18] is doing so well with the Relief office and we are making attempts to secure the Central Church money for another year.[19] Mr Waldo[20] is wretched and may go away for a trip & rest. I continually receive compliments on my health which I complacently enjoy.

Dr Rice[21] has an awful cold which has hung on for weeks and is perfectly miserable, she is also desperate about her financial situation, she has no practice save the Jane Club & H.H. Sister Lathrop has taken her life in her hand and is trying to induce her to go to the colored hospital.[22] She said that I might find her in fragments upon my return.

Please give my love to your dear father and mother and kindliest remembrances to the good kinsfolk. I spent last night with Miss Guiteau—who has just on[23] to school. She lost her mother during our trip in St Augustine. She is much broken and full of remorse. She is coming in for her Spring vacation.

I am always, dearest sister, yours in hoops of steel

Jane Addams

I am filled with woe lest you can't read this—I can't very well.

ALS (SCPC, JAC; *JAPM*, 2:1624–29).

1. LSA.

2. See Biographical Profiles: Bowen, Louise de Koven.

3. Mary Connelly (or Connolly), known at HH through more than fifty years as "Miss Mary," began working at the settlement in the nursery in May 1895. She earned twenty-five dollars a month as a nurse. A list of residents issued about 1920 identified her as part of the settlement's administrative staff. When she died in July 1950, at the age of ninety, the *Chicago Daily News* reported that she was one of the last of the early HH volunteers, known and beloved by four generations of children who had played at HH.

4. Mrs. Marie Hensen (or Hansen) began work as a nurse in the HH nursery Oct. 1895. She was paid twenty-five dollars a month. In the early 1900s, she also helped at HH summer camps. She was named in the "In Memoriam" section of "List of HH Residents—1889–1929," issued for the fortieth anniversary celebration of the founding of HH; however, there is no evidence that she actually lived at the settlement. In the 1920 list of individuals closely associated with the settlement, Marie Hensen was identified as coming to the HH Music School.

5. During the economic depression that began in earnest in 1893 and lingered into the late 1890s, JA found that she had difficulty raising funds to support even the nursery and kindergarten. JA reported to MRS during the week of 21–26 Jan. 1895, "The Friday Club and some S[outh]. side girls have been appealed to in regard to the K'g. No one has yet assumed it but we are cherishing hopes" (SCPC, JAC; *JAPM*, 2:1658–59). Continuing in the same vein, on 27 Jan. 1895, JA reported to MRS: "I haven't yet got anyone to take the K'g. altho a club at Hyde Park is considering. I have never been so 'balked' about any money I have tried to 'raise,' they are all rather cheerful in regard to next year and vague withal in regard to this year" (SCPC, JAC; *JAPM*, 2:1637). Her small but public role in attempting to arbitrate the Pullman Palace Car strike may also have adversely affected her access to financial support from Chicago business leaders. By Feb. the Smith family had begun to help. "Please thank your good father for the one hundred he is going to give, that will take the crèche through until April 1st by that time some of the seed I have been sewing in regard to the K'g ought to take effect" (JA to MRS, 3 Feb. 1895, SCPC, JAC; *JAPM*, 2:1648–49). JA continued to seek supporters for the nursery and kindergarten.

6. Samuel E. Barrett (1834–1912) was born in Cambridgeport, Mass., educated in Boston public schools, and settled in Chicago in 1857. After service in the Union army during the Civil War, he returned to Chicago and reestablished his business. He was the president and general manager of Barrett Manufacturing Co. and a member of the advisory board of

Chicago's Civic Federation. He gave regularly to support general operations at HH into the 1890s and provided fellowship support for Rose Marie Gyles.

7. It is difficult to know exactly to which deficit JA is referring. Many of the settlement programs operated at a deficit. In addition, during 1894 and 1895, the settlement initiated a new bookkeeping system, primarily at the insistence of Helen Culver, and the surviving records are not clear. The deficit in Dec. 1894 may have been $720. Page 160 of the "HH Cash Book, 1 Jan. 1894–30 June 1895" indicates a special deposit by William Colvin in that amount on 5 Jan. 1895.

8. The editors were unable to locate evidence of any legal matters in the city, county, or state court systems that involved JA's neighbor Michael J. Stalbus and JA. Perhaps the matter, which likely involved real estate, was settled out of court.

9. JA and Allen Pond had been negotiating with Helen Culver since early 1894 for land on which to construct the building the Smith family planned to give for expanding the HH nursery and kindergarten programs (see Article in the *Chicago Record*, 3 Dec. 1894, above; and Edwin Burritt Smith to JA, 2 Feb. 1895, n. 1, below). On 27 June 1895, JA reported to MRS, "We are having long visits with Miss Culver each week now" (SCPC, JAC; *JAPM*, 2:1639). By the time that HH was officially incorporated as HH Assn., creating the legal entity that Helen Culver demanded, perhaps in exchange for access to more of her real estate, Culver had agreed to offer the corner of Halsted and Polk streets to JA and the association so that the HH Children's Building could be started.

10. Mrs. Nancy Foster provided funds to add a third floor to the original Hull home, thus making the original settlement building a three-story structure. On 16 Feb. 1895, JA reported to MRS, "The third floor is going on fast" (SCPC, JAC; *JAPM*, 2:1667).

11. Management of the HH Coffee House was a continual problem for JA. She could never seem to find a manager who could keep receipts in line with expenditures. "We are overhauling the Coffee House and Mrs Nourse leaves Feb. 2d we have great plans for running it cheaper. Mr Colvin helps and suggests like the saint that he is" (JA to MRS, [21–26 Jan. 1895], SCPC, JAC; *JAPM*, 2:1658).

HH residents and volunteers remained perpetually busy, rushing to manage a variety of programs in an expanding mix of locations within the developing physical plant of the settlement complex. The best time to get together to share experiences, personal histories, and perspectives and exchange ideas on reform and what they were learning was mealtime or during a late-evening gathering in the coffee shop over hot chocolate. Madeleine Wallin, who would become a HH resident, described a HH teatime to her mother, Mary Ellen Keyes Wallin: "'Tea' was brought on the table as we sat around it—some cold meat placed ~~around~~ by one of the men who cut it. Buttered bread was passed by a trim little maid, and tea was made at the table. We had sauce and cake besides. All was prepared in the kitchen and whisked on to the table in no time. We ate off beautiful blue plates—I have no doubt of fine ware. . . . Miss Addams puts $100 a month of her own means into running of the house and the rest is met by the board of residents, $5.00 a week" (15 Jan. 1893, UIC, JAMC, Sikes). Almost from the start of the settlement, the dining room and the coffee shop were major social and business settings for the HH residents and volunteers. Helen Gow, a visitor from England, wrote of her arrival at HH on 9 Apr. 1897: "I was received by Miss Addams, My Diary, but she is ill & tired looking beyond all the tired Settlement-workers I have seen. She took me up to her room to wash, & then conducted me thro' dining-room back-passages and kitchens to the coffee-house where the residents it appears always have their breakfast." Lunch took place in the dining room, and sometimes breakfast was served there also. During Gow's visit at HH, at the end of the evening filled with activities, often about 9:00 P.M., Gow found herself going "into the pantry for supper" or for an after-supper get-together with other residents. She recalled being "drawn into" discussions. On one occasion, Gow, EGS, and George Hooker took up the question of servants and reported that they "sat till 11:30." (Gow, "Diaries," 9 and 11 Apr. 1897).

As the resident body grew, JA had to enlarge the dining room so that the residents could share their meals there and she could entertain the increasing number of visitors who came to see her and the settlement. Most of the residents wanted to meet her visitors and hear what they had to say. As Alice Hamilton wrote, "Percy Alden, of Mansfield House, you know, was here at first. I didn't fancy him a bit. Then we had a pair of very nice missionaries [of the Woman's Union Missionary Society] from India, Miss Lathrop's aunt [Martha Clifford Lathrop (1837–1912) of Allahabad] and a Miss [Grace Rankin] Ward [(1845?–1922)] of Kanpur. Miss Lathrop was perfectly delightful, just an older edition of her niece and she took the house so beautifully and naturally that it warmed all our hearts" (Alice Hamilton to Agnes Hamilton, 11 Oct. 1898, RS, HFP).

12. JA went with MRS to visit Smith family relatives in Columbia, S.C., during Dec. 1894. See JA to SAAH, 4 Dec. 1894, above.

13. JA had ordered Amos G. Warner's *American Charities: A Study in Philanthropy and Economics*, published by Thomas Y. Crowell and Co. in 1894, from one of Chicago's premier bookstores, McClurg and Co., located at Wabash and Madison streets. The book was composed of chapters on causes of poverty; a consideration titled "The Dependent Classes," including discussions of the insane, destitute, sick, unemployed, homeless, and dependent children; a presentation on the financing of public and private charities, endowments, and public subsidies to private charities; and a description of supervisory agencies.

Warner (1861–1900) was born in Elkander, Iowa. He graduated from the Univ. of Nebraska in 1885 and received a Ph.D. from the Johns Hopkins Univ., 1888. He became general agent of the COS in Baltimore in 1887. From 1889 to 1891, he was a lecturer on economics at the Univ. of Nebraska. In 1891 he returned east to become the superintendent of charities in the District of Columbia. He became professor of economics and social science at Leland Stanford Univ., Palo Alto, Calif., in 1893, a position he held until his death. He was the author of several works on economic subjects.

14. Albert Shaw (1857–1947) had just published *Municipal Government in Great Britain* (New York: Century, 1895). On 30 Jan. 1895, he wrote to JA, thanking her for the letter she had written to him about his book, and he requested her permission to quote from it. "I was greatly pleased to have so heartily appreciative a note from you about the volume" (NYPL, Shaw; *JAPM*, 2:1640).

Shaw was born in Shandon, Ohio, the son of the Dr. Griffin M. Shaw family. He graduated from Iowa College (now Grinnell College) in 1879 and in 1881 became a student at the Johns Hopkins Univ., where he completed his Ph.D. While at Iowa College, he became a journalist and worked with the *Grinnell Herald*. By 1883 he had joined the staff of the *Minneapolis Tribune*. In 1890 he was elected professor of international law and political institutions at Cornell Univ., but left after a year to accept William T. Stead's invitation to establish a U.S. edition of Stead's *Review of Reviews*. He remained in that position until it ceased publication in 1937.

15. Margaretta Stewart West.

16. Gertrude Barnum (1866–1948), who became a social worker and labor leader, arrived at HH in 1894 just as Agnes Sinclair Holbrook was leaving. Barnum was born in Chester, Ill., the second of four children of William Henry and Clara Letitia Hyde Barnum (see also JA to MRS, 22 June 1899, n. 10, below). Her father became a respected Chicago attorney and eventually a circuit court judge. Gertrude attended Evanston Twp. High School beginning in 1883 and by Sept. 1891 was at the Univ. of Wisconsin, where she took a course in English but stayed only until the end of her first school year.

At HH she quickly became an experienced worker and ultimately acted as an assistant to JA in the management of HH. JA organized a twenty-five-dollar-a-month fellowship for her so that she could become a settlement resident. Although from a well-to-do family, she had apparently displeased her parents by leaving the Univ. of Wisconsin after only one year and by refusing to become a debutante. She initially lacked their support in establishing herself as an independent woman.

At HH Barnum assisted with the Lincoln Club in 1895, was director of the Arlington Club of young male debaters in the fall of 1896 and into early 1897, and until 1898 was in charge of older people's clubs. She became the HH cashier through whom all bills were paid and also in 1896 was in charge of the school extension program, created to provide educational opportunities for those with at least a sixth grade education and no high school training. When it became time for Mary McDowell to relinquish leadership of the HH Woman's Club, Gertrude Barnum served for a year as the club president, beginning in Feb. 1896. At the same time, she also taught U.S. history and in 1897 and 1898 offered travel talks to any club that needed a speaker. While JA and MRS were away in Europe during the summer of 1896, Barnum was in charge of the settlement. She gave up her HH activities in 1899, but remained a settlement resident until the fall of 1900, when her name disappeared from the HH roster of residents.

After serving as head worker at Henry Booth House, Jan. 1902–June 1903, she went to work for the newly formed NWTUL and helped establish leagues in Chicago and New York. In 1905 she explained her move: "I myself have graduated from the Settlement into the trade union. As I became more familiar with the conditions around me, I began to feel that while the Settlement was undoubtedly doing a great deal to make the lives of working people less grim and hard, the work was not fundamental. It introduced into their lives books and flowers and music, and it gave them a place to meet and see their friends or leave their babies when they went out to work, but it did not raise their wages or shorten their hours" (*Weekly Bulletin of the Clothing Trades*, 24 Mar. 1905, p. 2, in Dye, *As Equals and as Sisters*, 41–42).

In 1905 she became the first national secretary of the NWTUL. In her capacity as national organizer and corresponding secretary, she compiled the official report of the organization for 1905–6. When the league abolished her position in 1906, she worked for the International Ladies' Garment Workers Union. She helped manage strikes and served as special agent in charge of publicity, 1911–16, to attract support to their cause from educated, wealthy, and social and civic leaders. She helped manage strikes of female textile workers in Fall River, Mass.; laundry workers in Troy, N.Y.; and corset workers in Aurora, Ill. During 1914 she became a special agent for the U.S. Comm. on Industrial Relations, created by President Woodrow Wilson. She then worked for the U.S. Dept. of Labor as assistant director of investigation services, 1918–19.

While she lived in New York, Barnum became a member of the Woman's Municipal League, and in 1909 she began a demonstration project for a model tenement house for working women. She rented several flats at 416 East 65th St. and invited working women to pay the small amount of rent she charged and live together sharing expenses. The *Survey* reported on 11 Sept. 1909, "Groups of working women are already availing themselves of these advantages and Miss Barnum is 'at home' in one of these model flats every Thursday afternoon and evening, for the purpose of showing the Sixty-fifth street tenements and furnishing information to wage-earning house-hunters regarding model tenements in other parts of New York" ("Housing Question for Working Women").

Barnum supported woman suffrage and spoke out on its behalf. She also wrote articles for labor periodicals, including the *Weekly Bulletin of the Clothing Trades*, *Ladies' Garment Worker*, the *Outlook*, *Charities and the Commons*, and the *Survey*. Retiring from union activities in 1919, she moved to California, first to Berkeley and then to Los Angeles, where she died and was buried.

17. Mary Kenney O'Sullivan did take her Chicago friend Margaret Toomey and her daughter Jane with her to Boston. JA commented to MRS: "The hundred dollars was most generous, it sent Sister Toomey off to Boston in fine style and has already paid debts to the Relief Acc't"

([21–26 Jan. 1895], SCPC, JAC; *JAPM*, 2:1656). JA reiterated to MRS on 3 Feb. 1895: "The money for Toomey and the Relief raised peons of joy all around." She also admitted that she missed Mary O'Sullivan "dreadfully" (SCPC, JAC; *JAPM*, 2:1647, 1649).

18. Vennette Crain had taken over the HH Relief Office when Edwin A. Waldo could no longer perform his duties. "Mr. Waldo has gone to the Sanitarium at Battle Creek and Sister Lathrop is struggling with his office, things are really in a bad way—he grew over confident at the end—and elaborated more than the town was ready to sustain. He did not actually break down but we all felt that it was better for him to go away" ([21–26 Jan. 1895], SCPC, JAC; *JAPM*, 2:1656–57). It is likely that JA asked Julia Lathrop, with her experience in bookkeeping and managing business affairs, to try to straighten out the Relief Office financial records before Vennette Crain began to direct the relief operations.

19. In 1893 the HH residents had decided to accept the Central Church offer of help with relief funds. See Minutes of a HH Residents Meeting, 10 Dec. 1893, n. 11, above. The need for help with the relief effort undertaken by HH was apparently so great that the residents were now actively seeking support from other institutions.

20. Edwin A. Waldo. See JA to Emily Greene Balch, 11 May 1893, n. 3, above.

21. Harriet Alleyne Rice (1866–1958) was born in Newport, R.I., the third daughter of African American parents, Lucinda Webster and George Addison Rice. She attended local schools, including the integrated Rogers High School, and became the first African American to attend and graduate from Wellesley College, 1887. After a year as a medical student at Univ. of Michigan, she dropped out to undergo two operations, perhaps to correct problems resulting from an accident she suffered during her final year at Wellesley. In the fall of 1890, she matriculated at the Woman's Medical College of the New York Infirmary for Women and Children, from which she received her M.D. in 1891. After a year's internship at Boston's New England Hospital for Women and Children, she did postgraduate work in Philadelphia. By 1893 she had arrived in Chicago and become associated with HH as an independent resident.

At HH her first job was working with Dr. Josephine Milligan to establish and operate a medical clinic and dispensary for the settlement's neighbors. At the end of the year, when Dr. Milligan left to return to her home in Jacksonville, Ill., JA must have assumed that Dr. Rice would continue to operate the facility, but she declined to continue with that work. It is likely that she was subjected to racism and forced to deal with a clientele to which she may have had difficulty relating. Through a fellowship stipend of twenty-five dollars a month from MRS, JA provided a position for her in the HH library. "I do not know what to do for her or about her," JA reported to MRS. "She is still working on the library but by the time she pays her room rent and her coal probably does not eat enough. She has not the settlement spirit (if there is such a thing) and makes . . . the rest of us, indignant by her utter refusal to do any thing for the sick neighbors even when they are old friends of the House. I am constantly perplexed about her" (3 Feb. 1895, SCPC, JAC; *JAPM*, 2:1653–54). Julia Lathrop was unable to convince Rice to take a position at Provident Hospital, where black and white doctors practiced together on patients of both races. Instead, she chose to enter private practice with HH supporter Sarah Hackett Stevenson and work part-time once again at the settlement dispensary until it closed in June 1896. At that time, Rice became employed by the Illinois Board of Charities on a special project to organize and report on the records of the public Cook Co. institutions serving the poor. New HH resident Madeleine Wallin found Rice "one of the most lady-like and unobjectionable people" at the settlement (Madeleine Wallin to Ellen Keyes Wallin, 23 Sept. 1896, CHM, CHS, Sikes). From 1897 until it closed in 1898, Rice was the only doctor at the Chicago Maternity Hospital and Training School for Nursery Maids. After an illness for which she went to Newport, R.I., she returned to Chicago in 1901 to do relief work for the HH office of the Chicago Bureau of Charities. After a very brief stint as the settlement cashier, she left HH in 1904, never to return as a resident.

For the remainder of her life, she found employment in the East and in Europe. In 1910 she was an assistant in a pathology laboratory at the Boston Dispensary. During World War I, she volunteered as a medical intern in France and in 1919 received the bronze medal of Reconnaissance Françaises for her service there from Jan. 1915 to Oct. 1918. After her sister in Newport, R.I., died in 1925, she became associated with St. Mary's School in the Germantown section of Philadelphia and by 1933 was employed in a laboratory at Columbia Univ. Medical Center in New York City, a job she held until at least 1935.

She was a member of the Episcopal Church and had been active in the Providence, R.I., chapter of the Society of the Companions of the Holy Cross, a lay organization of primarily well-educated, reform-minded women of the church. The life of a well-educated physician for which she had prepared herself so carefully was never hers, and she blamed her disappointment on her race and her sex. She died in Worcester, Mass., and was buried after an Episcopal service in Newport in the common grounds then allotted to African Americans.

22. There were approximately fifteen thousand African Americans living in Chicago by 1891, and while there were physicians to serve them, there were few hospitals that would take them as patients. No hospitals in Chicago at that time admitted African American physicians to practice. To correct that lack, Provident Hospital for Negroes was organized, primarily at the urging of African American physician Daniel Hale Williams (1858–1931), who is credited with performing the first successful open-heart surgery in the United States in 1893. By 1898 the hospital, originally located at 29th and Dearborn streets, had a new building. It also had a nursing school and a loose affiliation with the Northwestern Univ. Medical School until 1930, when it became affiliated with the Univ. of Chicago Medical School. Both white and African American physicians practiced at Provident Hospital on patients of all races.

23. JA may have inadvertently omitted the beginning "g" and ending "e" of the word *gone.* Flora Guiteau was JA's childhood friend from Freeport. For a biographical note, see *PJA*, 2:27–28, n. 11.

## From Edwin Burritt Smith

First National Bank Building Chicago [Ill.] February 2, 1895.

Dear Miss Addams:

In respect to a corporation to acquire and manage the work carried on at Hull-house, I have to report as follows:

I. I am of opinion that a corporation is desirable, especially to take the lease from Miss Culver from 1900 to 1920.[1] I am also of opinion that it should be of the class of corporations known in this State as "not for pecuniary profit". Whether it should acquire and conduct all of the branches of the work at ~~the~~ Hull-house, or whether some of them should be independent organizations, does not affect the main organization.

2. "Corporations not for pecuniary profit may be organized as societies, corporations and associations." I suggest as an appropriate name "Hull House Association". "Three or more persons, citizens of the United States," may unite to organize such a corporation. I suggest that you have five persons,[2] and believe it best that two of them, including yourself, should be directly connected with the work. This will make it easy to obtain a quorum and ~~for~~ <has> the advantage of having two persons thoroughly familiar with the work from the inside, and in touch with the field.

The persons organizing the corporation may be called, "trustees, directors or managers," and may be named in the certificate of incorporation as such for the first year of its existence. I do not know that there is any special choice in the term to be used.

3. I understand that Miss Culver very properly desires a representative in the corporation. She is a woman of such ability and good judgment that I should regard it very desirable if you can persuade her to act as her own representative. A corporation cannot make any valid contract as to its membership. However, I regard it practica<ble> for the lease to contain some such provision as this: <3 1/2/> "This lease is made and accepted, and said term is granted upon the express condition, that the lessor is at all times during said term, entitled to be represented by herself or some other legally qualified person to be named by her, on the Board of Trustees (Directors or Managers) of the lessee corporation. If this right of the lessor shall at anytime be denied by the refusal or failure of the members of said corporation to elect the lessor, or such representative as she shall nominate for such position, on said Board to the end that she may at all times during said term be represented thereon, this lease shall thereupon, at the option of the lessor, cease and determine; but the refusal or failure of the lessor to serve on said Board or to nominate a representative to fill any vacancy in her representation thereon shall not be construed as entitling her to determine this lease."</>[3]

4. I suggest that the articles of incorporation state its purpose as follows:

"To conduct educational, settlement and benevolent work in the City of Chicago, Illinois".[4]

The lease can specify the same in describing the use to be made of the demised premises.

If you decide to incorporate, kindly advise me as to the names of the incorporators. The by-laws[5] can provide that they shall serve for such period as may be desired. Their terms should expire at different times so that their successors can be chosen from time to time by those remaining. It may be well to have the term of one expire each year.[6] I should prefer this to an irregular arrangement.

I am aware that the above suggestions are not all strictly of a legal nature, but have assumed you wish my opinion generally for what it may be worth. Yours very truly,

Edwin Burritt Smith

TLS with H insertions (UIC, JAMC; *JAPM*, 2:1644–46).

1. Helen Culver planned to provide JA and HH with a new and extended lease. Culver was demanding more structure in the organization of HH and seeking to enhance stability. She wanted to be certain that her investment in long-term leases had the backing of an established legal entity rather than that of an individual who might become ill and be unable to function or leave. JA commented to MRS, "Miss Culver is just getting over a severe attack of pneumonia—she is too ill to do anything in regard to the trusteeship and we are too scared to push anything that will take time. The new lease will be made out to me as before with a

provision for incorporating whenever she or we desire it. That is after all the quickest thing" (3 Feb. 1895, SCPC, JAC; *JAPM*, 2:1649).

2. The initial trustees were seven in number: Helen Culver, JA, William H. Colvin, Allen B. Pond, Edward B. Butler, Mary H. Wilmarth, and MRS.

3. This paragraph did appear in all of the extant leases between HH and Helen Culver.

4. Despite Smith's recommendation, the purpose of the organization was as follows: "The object for which it is formed is to provide a center for a higher civic and social life, to initiate and maintain educational and philanthropic enterprises and to investigate and improve the conditions in the industrial districts of Chicago" ([HH Assn., Incorporation Certificate], 30 Mar. 1895, Springfield, Ill., p. 2, Illinois Secretary of State, Corp. Dept., Box 702, No. 32966).

5. For a copy of the original HH Assn. bylaws, see UIC, JAMC, HH Assn.; *JAPM*, 49:125–28, 1005–7, 1022–24, 1050–53.

6. As Smith had recommended, trustee terms were regularly staggered. So long as each was alive and agreed to serve, they were chosen as their own successors by the remaining serving trustees.

# Documents

Chicago, Ill. 28 and 30 Mar. 1895

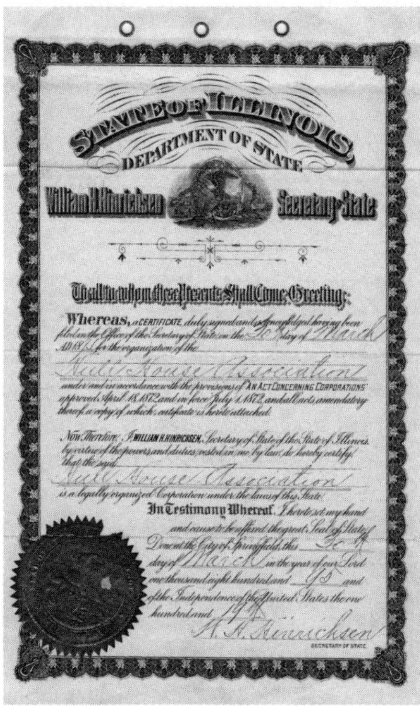

STATE OF ILLINOIS, DEPARTMENT OF STATE

William H. Hinrichsen Secretary of State

To all to whom these Presents Shall Come, Greeting:

Whereas, a CERTIFICATE, duly signed and acknowledged having been filed in the Office of the Secretary of State on the 30th day of March AD 1895 for the organization of the Hull House Association under and in accordance with the provisions of "AN ACT CONCERNING CORPORATIONS" approved April 18, 1872 and in force July 1, 1872, and all acts amendatory thereof, a copy of which certificate is hereto attached.

Now Therefore, I, WILLIAM H. HINRICHSEN, Secretary of State of the State of Illinois, by virtue of the powers and duties vested in me by law, do hereby certify that the said Hull House Association is a legally organized Corporation under the laws of this State.

In Testimony Whereof, I hereto set my hand and cause to be affixed the great Seal of State. Done at the City of Springfield, this 30th day of March in the year of our Lord one thousand eight hundred and 95 and of the Independence of the United States the one hundred and 19th.

W. H. Hinrichsen
SECRETARY OF STATE.

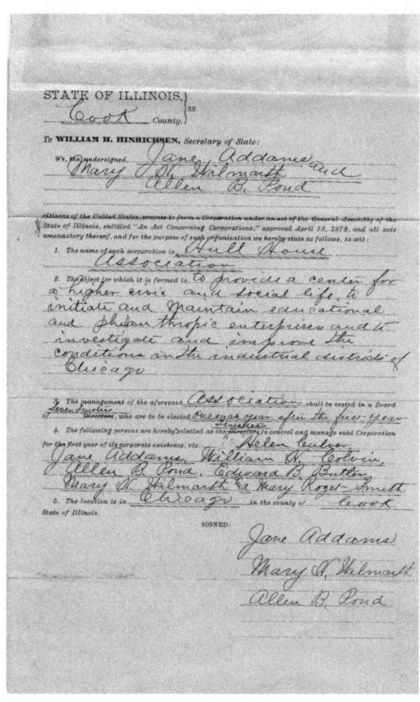

STATE OF ILLINOIS, Cook County. ss.

To WILLIAM H. HINRICHSEN, Secretary of State:

We, the undersigned, Jane Addams Mary H. Wilmarth and Allen B. Pond citizens of the United States, propose to form a Corporation under an act of the General Assembly of the State of Illinois, entitled "An Act Concerning Corporations," approved April 18, 1872, and all acts amendatory thereof, and for the purpose of such organization we hereby state as follows, to-wit:

1. The name of such corporation is Hull House Association

2. The object for which it is formed is to provide a center for a higher civic and social life, to initiate and maintain educational and philanthropic enterprises and to investigate and improve the conditions in the industrial districts of Chicago

3. The management of the aforesaid Association shall be vested in a Board of Seven Trustees ~~Directors~~, who are to be elected One each year after the first year

4. The following persons are hereby selected as the Trustees ~~Directors~~ to control and manage said Corporation for the first year of its corporate existence, viz: Helen Culver, Jane Addams, William H. Colvin, Allen B. Pond, Edward B. Butler, Mary H. Wilmarth & Mary Rozet Smith

5. The location is in Chicago in the county of Cook State of Illinois.

SIGNED: Jane Addams
Mary H. Wilmarth
Allen B. Pond

On the left, the application for incorporation submitted to the Illinois secretary of state by Jane Addams, Mary H. Wilmarth, and Allen B. Pond for the Hull-House Association (28 Mar. 1895, State of Illinois, Secretary of State, Corporations, Dissolved Domestic Corporation Charters, 1849–1963; *JAPM*, 49:1013). On the right, the certificate of incorporation issued by the Illinois secretary of state for the Hull-House Association (P and HD, 30 Mar. 1895, UIC, JAMC, HH Assn.; *JAPM*, 49:1010).

## From Ellen Gates Starr [for Jane Addams] to Sarah Anderson

Hull-House 335 South Halsted Street Chicago Feb. 8 [1895]

Sarah dear.

It falls to me, in the line of secretary's duty this morning, to write to you, which seems quite pleasant & friendly. "The chief"[1] bids me say that she will speak to Mr. Higginbotham[2] & Mr. Butler,[3] notwithstanding the hardness of the times. She will let you know ere long about the commencement.[4] She has made a resolution, she says, not to speak so much in public unless she can take time to prepare more. But she w'd like very much to do this. The subject she will write in a few days if she decides to do it.

About Esther,[5] Jane says she has had a slight attack of grip, but has also evidently had a prolonged attack of constipation. She wishes me also to say that Esther is such a child that it is almost necessary to put the medicine into her mouth. She cannot at all be relied upon to take it. Jane thinks her dizziness is as much a consequence of billiousness & constipation as of her eye trouble, & she begs that Dr. Leland[6] will keep an eye on that. She will be well enough to go back on Monday.

---

That is the end of the secretary's letter.

I feel very bad that I do not see you any more, to speak of, & that our vacations never come together, apparently, so that it seems likely that we shall cease to associate intimately. Do you feel bad? I hope you do. But you are a much-to-be-relied-upon Sarai, so if this road ever turns we can pick it up where we dropped it, I hope. Always devotedly yours,

Ellen.

ALS (RC, Archives, Anderson; *JAPM*, 2:1382–85).

1. JA. Florence Kelley also referred to JA as "the chief."

2. It seems likely that SA and JA were trying to identify new and wealthy trustees for RC.

Harlow Niles Higinbotham (1838–1919), who served as president of the World's Columbian Exposition, was born in Joliet, Ill.; educated at Lombard Univ. in Galesburg, Ill.; and in the Commercial College in Chicago. He began his working career as a clerk in a store and later in a bank in Joliet. Before he was in the Mercantile Battery of Chicago in the Civil War, he was bookkeeper in the dry goods firm of Cooley, Farwell, and Co. Returning to Chicago after the war, he went to work for Field, Palmer, and Leiter and by 1868 had become a partner in the firm. Beginning in 1881, he was associated with Marshall Field and Co., which he served for several years. A director of the Northern Trust Co., he was also president of the National Portland Cement Co. and associated with several other business firms. From 1897 until 1909, he was president of the board of the Field Museum of Natural History. Among his other interests were the News Boys and Boot Blacks Assn., of which he was president; Free Kindergarten Assn.; Chicago Home for Incurables; and the Municipal Sanitarium for Tuberculosis.

Higinbotham befriended JA and became a HH supporter. In particular, he chose to be publicly identified with the HH People's Songs Contest devised by William L. Tomlins (1844–1930) and JA. Higinbotham provided prize money offered for the best original words and the best music.

William L. Tomlins was born in London, the son of William and Sarah Lawrence Tomlins. He had been director of the Chicago Apollo Music Club (oldest volunteer choir in the United States and formed in 1872), trained fifteen hundred children selected to sing at the World's Columbian Exposition, and established a Working People's Chorus program at HH, where he taught singing to adults and children. Tomlins believed that there existed "a deplorable dearth of appropriate music, especially good songs which in character are distinctively American" for his choral groups to sing. He wanted "songs of the fireside and of the family, and especially songs which dignify labor and express its hopes of emancipation" ("People's Songs," 1 May 1895). It was with that goal in mind that the HH People's Songs Contest was devised. Tomlin also prepared teachers to go into other settlements and missions to found similar choral groups. Between 1898 and 1902, Tomlins trained schoolteachers throughout the United States to teach choral music. In 1903 he organized the National Training School for School Music Teachers in Chicago and helped establish choral music for children in the Chicago public schools.

3. E. B. Butler became an RC trustee in June 1895.

4. JA spoke at the RC commencement on 19 June 1895. Her title was "Claim on the College Woman." For her text, see *Rockford (Ill.) Collegian* 23 (June 1895): 59–63; *JAPM*, 46:711–16. JA's address to the graduate women at Western Reserve Univ., Cleveland, June 1894, was similar (see JA to SA, 23 June 1894, n. 6, above).

5. Esther Margaret Linn's behavior seems to have been a continuing and vexing problem for her aunt JA. In the fall of 1894, JA had enrolled Esther at RC, where her cousin Sarah Weber Addams was also a student, but Esther seemed to have such continuing health problems with her eyes or her digestive system that it was necessary for her to leave school for a stay with her aunt at HH. Late in Jan. 1895, JA reported to MRS that "Esther is better and I hope that she can stay [at school] during the year" ([21–26 Jan. 1895], SCPC, JAC; *JAPM*, 2:1660). On 3 Feb., Esther was back with JA and "in bed with the grip" (JA to MRS, 3 Feb. 1895, SCPC, JAC; *JAPM*, 2:1852). Mary Keyser told SAAH, "Miss Addams is thoroughly convinced that she has been too indulgent with Esther and we've talked it over to-gether and she is so grateful for your help. She said the best thing in the world for Esther would be to have her under your care for a year or two. She told Esther she intended to take a different course unless she was very much improved by Christmas" (16 Oct. 1895, IU, Lilly, SAAH; *JAPM*, 2:1791).

By 31 Oct. 1895, as JA was recovering from surgery to remove her appendix, she told SAAH that Esther "is trying very hard to be 'good'" (UIC, JAMC; *JAPM*, 2:1800). Mary Keyser commented to SAAH, "Esther is coming on Friday [20 Dec. 1895] her Aunt [Jane] is still very much puzzled what to do with her" (18 Dec. 1895, IU, Lilly, SAAH). See also JA to MRS, 17 Apr. 1898, below.

JA became more attached to her nephew Stanley, who was living with the James Linn family at 7130 Webster Ave. (later South Princeton Ave.) in the Englewood section of Chicago. "[H]e is lonely since his father has gone to Quincy, [Ill.], he does n't want to go back after his Sunday visits—my heart will melt some day and I will keep him here" (JA to MRS, 3 Feb. 1895, SCPC, JAC; *JAPM*, 2:1652). He was taking violin and dancing lessons at HH. In contrast to Esther, "Stanley is so well and such a joy to me," JA reported to MRS, adding that Stanley's violin teacher indicated that Stanley "has my musical tone perceptions" (16 Feb. 1895, SCPC, JAC; *JAPM*, 2:1667). JA seems to have been tone-deaf (see *PJA*,1:34).

While JA was recovering from her surgery for appendicitis (see AHHA to HWH and EGS to JWA, 13 Sept. 1895, below), the reliable Mary Keyser cared for Stanley. Anna ("Annie") Linn, who had been his surrogate mother during most of the year, had a baby. Thinking all was well, "Stanley came in high glee about the baby," Mary reported to SAAH, "but the Dr. tells us it is dead." And she continued, "I have not told Miss Addams but intend to go out with

## Hull-House Choral

Mr. WM. L. TOMLINS, the well-known choral director, will personally conduct a singing class for working people at the Hull-House Gymnasium, corner Halsted and Polk Streets (240 Polk Street), Friday evenings at 8 o'clock.

The course of lessons will begin Friday evening, November 2, 1894, and will continue until the end of March, 1895.

**Five Hundred Voices Wanted.**

Mr. Tomlins is the musical director of the Chicago Apollo Club and the originator of the repetition concerts given by that celebrated society for several winters in the Auditorium. In pursuance of the same plan he is now establishing choral societies throughout the industrial districts of Chicago.

The instruction is free, but a charge of twenty-five cents a month is made for the purchase of new music.

**Regularity of Attendance is Insisted Upon.**

Names will be enrolled in the order in which they are received until the class membership is full.

Application may be made at Hull-House, or in writing to

MISS JANE ADDAMS,
335 SOUTH HALSTED STREET

Music held a special place in Hull-House programming. There were concerts presented by students and teachers associated with the Hull-House Music School, outings to hear music in Chicago, and group and private lessons. During the 1890s, music educator William L. Tomlins taught choral music at the settlement. This broadside announced the program (Addams, "Hull-House Choral," [1894], UIC, JAMC, HH Assn.; HH Scrapbook 2:50; *JAPM*, Addendum 10:7ff).

Stanley in the morning and get some of his clothes, and keep him here until she is better" ([5?] Oct. 1895, IU, Lilly, SAAH; *JAPM*, 2:1777–78). The baby died on 4 Oct. 1895, and Mrs. Linn did not improve and died on 8 Oct. 1895. On 10 Oct. 1895, EGS wrote to SAAH to tell her that "Mrs. James Linn died under an operation which was the last hope for her life. She died before it was finished. It seems very terrible" (IU, Lilly, SAAH; *JAPM*, 2:1783). Soon, Stanley had a new surrogate mother. "Mrs. Linn's sister Mrs. Bets has moved into the house and the two families will live to-gether this winter. Mrs. Bets is willing to try Stanley which is very kind of her" (Mary Keyser to SAAH, 16 Oct. 1895, IU, Lilly, SAAH; *JAPM*, 2:1790). A week later, Mary Keyser reported that Stanley "seems happier there than before" (Mary Keyser to SAAH, 28 Oct. 1895, IU, Lilly, SAAH; *JAPM*, 2:1797).

On Mother's Day, 10 May 1925, Stanley wrote to remind JA of the significant position she had in his life: "Legally and sentimentally and practically you have been my 'Mother' for some thirty-four years" (SCPC, JAC; *JAPM*, 17:428). Stanley grew up playing at HH, especially with Florence Kelley's children in his younger years, and attending the primary grades under the care of his father's brother James C. Linn and his family. Frank Keyser (brother of Mary Keyser who went to HH with JA and EGS), who had known Stanley as a child in Geneseo, Ill., and who became the settlement's buildings' superintendent in 1894, was a key caregiver in Stanley's youth. After Stanley graduated from Lake Forest Academy in 1903, he entered the Univ. of Chicago in the College of Literature, but in 1904 transferred to the College of Commerce. In 1905 he became the shortstop and was captain of Coach Alonzo Stagg's baseball team. He was inducted into the Chicago chapter of Alpha Delta Phi fraternity in 1908, the same organization that his brother James Weber Linn had joined several years earlier.

For the next several years, Stanley Linn tried to find work that suited him. It may have been in 1906–7 that he spent time working on the Stanley McCormick ranch in New Mexico to improve his health. He also worked on a ranch in Wyoming while hoping for a job in the Denver area. By the summer of 1910, Stanley was living in Matagorda, Tex., and trying to make a living in the real estate business; however, toward the end of that year, he was living in a boardinghouse in La Crosse, Wis., and working as a surveyor for the Chicago, Burlington, and Quincy Railroad.

By 1914 Stanley was living in the Corona, Calif., area and learning the fruit-growing business. It was in that year that he began courting Myra Harriet Reynolds (1890–1973), daughter of Harriet Youmans (1866–1938) and Baptist minister Francis Wayland Reynolds (1861–1921) and the niece of Myra Reynolds (1853–1936), who was professor of English at the Univ. of Chicago, 1902–23. Myra Harriet Reynolds, called "Doone," graduated from the Univ. of Chicago in 1913 and began a career in teaching. For two years, she trained as a Montessori teacher in Washington, D.C., and served as a companion for Graham and Barbara Fairchild, grandchildren of the Alexander Graham Bells. It was when she returned home to Corona, after she had completed her training, that she met Stanley. The two were married 12 June 1915 by her father at the little ranch house that Stanley lived in as part of his pay from the Corona Foothill Lemon Co., where he worked. The Linns began their married life in that house.

In 1916, with their first child about to be born, JA visited the Linns. She agreed to provide six thousand dollars for the purchase of eight acres for a grove and an irrigation system so that the young trees she bought could grow successfully into a lemon orchard. Her gift also included funds for a small house to be constructed on the property (for a drawing of the house plan, see SCPC, JAC, *JAPM*, 38:747). The Linns eventually had four children, one of whom was stillborn (1918). The children who survived were Jane Addams Linn (Morse) (1916–2007), Myra Reynolds (Peck) (1921–2013), and Mary Melissa Linn (Wallace) (b. 1923).

Stanley was ill with typhoid fever early in Jan. 1917 and was unable to work for six months. During that time and for most of the remainder of her life, with help from MRS, JA supported the Linn family with monthly cash gifts of between $25 and $100, as well as money for special purchases. These included a piano, vacations, and two Ford cars, one in 1916 and one in 1934. JA often sent Myra dresses and hats for herself as well as clothing and books for the children.

When the United States entered World War I, Stanley took a job with the YMCA as a physical trainer and was sent to France in Mar. 1918. He returned at war's end and tried to expand his own orchard, but, as JA explained, there was not enough capital to develop his plan. He returned to work in the fruit-packing industry and continued to tend his orchard.

By 1925 he reported to JA that he had taken a salary of $125 to $140 a month for the past eight years, and he was able to get his living and grove expenses out of it. He expected that he would be debt free by 1926. He was ready to stand on his own. "I can honestly now say," he wrote JA, "that I pretty much know the value of money and have developed considerably more valuable character assets than I ever had before. Myra was perfect at the beginning, but even her perfection has added an extra polish & shine. We have three finest babies in the world and for it's size as good a producing and looking ranch as there is in this state of fine places. Therefore you can say to yourself, that when you started us out here, you did the best thing for your boy and his wife that you could have done. What more could a mother want?" (10 May 1925, SCPC, JAC; *JAPM*, 17:431).

By the time the Great Depression began to affect economic conditions in the United States, JA was once again helping the Linns with monthly checks to supplement what Stanley made as a grove operator and a fruit packer. He wrote to JA that he feared that Lobingiers, the fruit-packing company where he worked, would let him go. If that happened, Stanley planned to sell his ranch and live on the proceeds. In 1931 he reported that his loss from the lemon grove was $1,500. In response JA wrote Stanley on 31 Aug. 1931, "I will help until another job turns up. You are getting too middle aged for such laborious work" (SCPC, JAC; *JAPM*, 22:881).

Stanley recognized the central role that JA had played in his life. In a birthday greeting to her, he wrote that he had "jumped from pillar to post and from one frying pan into another until she just naturally had to grow arms long enough . . . just to yank him out of holes." He saw her as the "ideal towards which one strains" ([ca. 6 Sept] [1934?], SCPC, JAC; *JAPM*, 26:212).

Myra wanted to begin teaching again, primarily to help the family. The Linn children were growing up, and she wanted them to attend college. At the end of 1932, she reported to JA that she had the chance of a teaching job in Corona, Calif. If Myra took it, JA offered to make up the difference between her salary and what the family needs were. By Aug. 1933, Myra had a position at the Edgewood School in Connecticut that paid $1,500 a year and included a place for her two youngest girls to attend school. Even though it would be a continent away from Stanley, she took the position because, with JA's help, it provided the money to send Jane Addams Linn to college. All of this time, JA continued to send $100 each month to Stanley, who was at home alone. After being at home for a visit with Stanley, Myra wrote to JA on 4 July 1934, "I am touched to the core by the lonely and comfortless and graceless life Stanley has had. It makes me sick! So far we have talked very little about the future. It is not going to be easy and all the things it seems wise to do involved such hardness of heart" (SCPC, JAC; *JAPM*: 26:5–6). Returning to Connecticut, Myra wrote to Stanley, "I was thinking last night in the night how wonderful you have been . . . to let us come way off here like this—not many men would have done it with the spirit or under the conditions you have" (UIC, JAMC). It was a difficult time for the entire family. After not hearing from Myra for three weeks, Stanley wrote to JA shortly before she died: "I have worked unsuccessfully but very hard. . . . I now come to the age of almost fifty two feeling mentally, physically and spiritually almost a complete failure" (22 April 1935, SCPC, JAC; *JAPM*: 26:1373). With the $6,000 inheritance that Stanley received from JA's estate, future financial support from JA ceased. Myra became the primary breadwinner for the family. She served six years as a school principal at Ojai, Calif., and returned to Riverside, where she was a school principal for fifteen additional years. A park and an elementary school in the La Sierra area of Riverside, where the Linn ranch was located, were named in her honor. Stanley Linn died in Riverside from a ruptured gallbladder and was buried in the Corona Sunnyslope Cemetery, Riverside Co., Calif.

6. Dr. Lena C. Leland.

## To Nettie Fowler McCormick

Hull-House 335 South Halsted Street[1] Chicago Feb. 8" 1895

My dear Mrs McCormick

You have always been so generous to us[2] that I find myself hesitating when I write to make an appointment about still another matter; lest I may be imposing upon you.

You have seen our old house, so you know that while it is large and commodious in many respects, the number of bed rooms is limited. During the last two years the number of residents has grown very large[3] and we are obliged to take rooms outside of the House. This is not very comfortable for the young ladies themselves and their parents seriously object to their crossing the street late at night. To obviate this we are planning to add a third floor to our house. Mrs Nancy Foster has given us $2500.oo toward this project but we still lack about $800.oo according to the architects estimate.[4] I am now writing for permission to come to see you, to talk over these plans and our needs, and of course while I shall be most grateful if you can help us out, I will certainly understand if you are too burdened with other things to do it.

It seems a little strange, when there is so much suffering among our neighbors during this severe weather,[5] to ask for money for our comfort so to put it. But after all if we are to help them we must have an abiding place large enough to contain us all, and doubtless an endowment of a building for settlement purposes is in the same line as an endowment of a building for educational purposes. I am writing too long a letter—but I shall be very happy to meet any appointment you may make. Very sincerely yours

Jane Addams

ALS (SHSW, McCormick Papers; *JAPM*, 2:1663–65).

1. At the top margin of the first page of the letter is the following holographic notation: "Pamphlet and HH . . . a Social Settlement Jan. 15 1895 and note answered." JA and EGS had revised and updated their published description of the settlement program that first appeared as "HH: A Social Settlement at 335 South Halsted Street. Chicago. An Outline Sketch," in 1894. It was likely a reprint of the same version that was issued as the last pages of *HH Maps and Papers* (see JA to Richard T. Ely, 31 Oct. 1894, n. 9, above). At least four versions of this work are extant. Copies are in SCPC, JAC and UIC, JAMC (see also *JAPM*, 46:591–617, which is a TMs, 618–42, 660–88). A copy of the reprint of the version published as pp. 205–30 in *HH Maps and Papers* has AI annotation by JA, apparently in preparation for the publication of a version to be issued in 1896 (SCPC, JAC; *JAPM*, 46:756–78); however, that version was never published. It is likely that the *HH Bulletin* began publication instead.

2. Through 1905 Nettie Fowler and Cyrus Hall McCormick usually gave at least one hundred dollars each year to the general expenses of HH.

3. The resident body at HH was characterized by constant change, as newcomers replaced departing residents. Some left because of poor health, some to take other jobs, some to marry, and some to seek relief from the exciting but demanding and often emotionally and physically sapping HH experience. JA and EGS were the only two residents who remained at HH

from 1889 through 1900. By 1892 the HH residents consisted of eight women. In 1893 the resident group increased to twelve women. JA also counted six male settlers who resided at 245 Polk St. The Mar. 1894 list of residents revealed thirteen women and two men, while the Nov. 1894 list contained the names of seventeen women and four men. The Jan. 1895 list of residents identified fourteen women living at HH, one independent female resident living at 217 Ewing St., three men in the men's settlement quarters, and one male resident at 245 Polk St. In addition, two married couples were listed as residents and lived away from the settlement. The Nov. 1896 list composed by JA indicated eighteen women and five men as residents. The 1900 federal census return for 335 South Halsted St. listed twenty residents, fourteen women and six men.

4. JA's request to Mrs. McCormick was not successful. The HH accounting record, p. 41, for Oct. 1894–May 1895 contained the expenses and sources of funds associated with the addition of the third floor on the original Hull home. The total cost of the addition was $3,217.93. Mrs. Nancy Foster provided $2,500.00, William H. Colvin added $862.02. In addition, $5.34 in interest was credited to the project and JA added $30.57.

5. According to pp. 80–81 of Cox and Armington's *The Weather and Climate of Chicago*, for twenty-nine days between 22 Jan. and 19 Feb. 1895 the temperature in Chicago remained at or below freezing.

## To Richard T. Ely

*Since late in 1891, Jane Addams, as a representative of the Chicago Woman's Club, had been working with the Committee on Charity Organization, which had been created by representatives of the Chicago Woman's Club, United Hebrew Relief Assn., and the remnants of Chicago's initial Charity Organization Society*[1] *to establish a viable COS model in Chicago.*[2] *The committee hoped to work with the Chicago Relief and Aid Society, created by special act of the Illinois General Assembly in 1857, noted for its response to citizens after the Chicago Fire of 1871, and still the "foremost of the charitable agencies of the city."*[3] *Its power was in its wealthy and well-connected board, in its history of response immediately after the 1871 fire, and in the funds that it continued to receive and hold. It saw relief as charity based primarily on the judgment of its staff about the morals of the person or persons seeking help and with little systematic consideration of coordinating other relief available.*

*In an effort to get the Chicago Relief and Aid Society to adopt a "more scientific" approach to the distribution of charity throughout the city, the Committee on Charity Organization, accompanied by members of the press from the* Chicago Herald, Chicago Post, *and the* Inter Ocean, *presented their suggestions for improved charity management in person and in a letter dated 4 January 1895 to the board of the Chicago Relief and Aid Society. With their chairman, William J. Onahan,*[4] *they proposed "[t]hat your Society co-operate in the formation of a Charity Organization Society to the extent of allowing the latter to assume the burden of investigation and registration, and of reserving for your own Society the actual administration of relief." They suggested "[t]hat the Relief and Aid Society itself become a Society for organizing the charity of Chicago, placing at the head of this work, some one who thoroughly understands the theory and practice of charity organization, who is fully in sympathy with the movement, and who has both the tact and determination to make it a success."[5] In its response to the committee's communication, the Chicago Relief and Aid Society defended its position. Its leaders believed that their approach to managing relief in the city followed some but not all of the COS best practices. The society board maintained a centralized structure with only three branch offices rather than a "complete district and friendly [visiting] organization," which they thought was far too expensive to manage with sufficient funds remaining to distribute among those needing relief. The directors of the society were convinced "that a new organization, with its necessary machinery and expense, is not a necessity, and that in general the principles and methods of the Chicago Relief and Aid Society are the best that can be devised and maintained under existing conditions."[6] Onahan's committee, including Jane Addams, wrote a scathing reply, addressing the flaws in each point the society made about the efficacy of its operation. The committee indicated that "the most glaring inconsistency between bona fide organized charity and your claim to have been the earliest exponent of the principles . . . lies in your explicit renunciation of the underlying principles in this noble movement expressed in its motto 'not alms but a friend'" and continued that the "gravest charge to be laid at the door" of the society was "its exclusiveness." In addition, the committee indicated that without a change in the Chicago Relief and Aid Society's position, they planned to organize the COS. "[I]f your Society will not accept the responsibility of joining in the inauguration of Charity Organization in Chicago, we hold ourselves ready to move in this direction fortified as we are by the earnest sympathy and co-operation of nearly two hundred churches and charitable agencies."[7] With that threat in mind, the leadership of the Chicago Relief and Aid Society sent a more conciliatory response on 7 March 1892. In addition to responding to the criticisms outlined by the Committee on Charity Organization, the Chicago Relief and Aid Society leadership proposed that the two groups begin to work together by sharing information on relief cases and to "co-operate with any and all institutions in any effort to put a stop to fraud and imposture. . . . Let us see if with the co-operation of the hundreds of organizations whose interests you say you have enlisted some positive advance may be made along lines which will commend themselves to the conservative as well as to the enthusiastic mind." They believed that cooperation on a basic level was better than a new and potential competing organization. They also requested that the committee refrain "for the present from further statements in the Press."[8]*

*When it became evident that the Chicago Relief and Aid Society with its central approach to relief could not deal with the magnitude of the help that was needed to combat the results of the economic depression that began for the Chicago area in 1893 and lasted into the late 1890s, the Civic Federation of Chicago created the Central Relief Association on 19 December 1893. Jane Addams became one of its leaders, and the new organization attempted to address relief issues by further developing a system of districts to go along with the record-keeping Department of Registration, which was being maintained with the cooperation and support of the Chicago Relief and Aid Society in its offices. When the Central Relief Association disbanded in April 1894, its registration department and the district organizations continued to function, and a committee that included Jane Addams was enlisted to determine what should happen to the organization. Early in 1895, the Chicago Relief and Aid Society indicated that it "had decided to have no further connection with the Bureau [of Registration, beginning to be referred to as Chicago Bureau of Charities]."[9] One of the responses was the creation of the Chicago Bureau of Charities by Jane Addams with the help of John McLaren[10] on 7 May 1895. The certificate of incorporation described the purpose of the organization: "To register and co-ordinate the work of the public and private charities of Chicago; to rid its streets of tramps and beggars; to protect the public from impostors and to stimulate to orderly effort the philanthropic impulses of the citizens of Chicago and to discover and efficiently aid the worthy poor throughout said city."[11] The Chicago Relief and Aid Society and the Chicago Bureau of Charities had merged as the Chicago Bureau of Charities and in 1909 became the United Charities of Chicago. Jane Addams continued as a board member for the new organization.*

Hull-House 335 South Halsted Street Chicago March 12" 1895

My dear Dr Ely—

The cause of Charity Organization is having such a hard time here that it has occurred to us that possibly better than so much speaking and raising of money, <would be> the presentation of some carefully collected facts.

Right here in the 19th ward are many people who are receiving duplicated aids from the R. & A.[12] the County agent &c. The Catholic Societies are very well organized here, but get rid of all the charity they can. We are on friendly terms with the priest who has charge of St Vincent de Paul Society,[13] and in many ways we are well situated to make a careful investigation of the 19th Ward.

Have you a student who would like to put three months work on it this summer, we could then have a definite example to place before the Chicago public in the fall. We have unfortunately no money nor even a fellowship, altho I should make a strong effort to secure the latter if it was necessary. Miss Crain[14] and other residents could give much valuable help if the work were undertaken. I write this merely as a suggestion that you may have it in mind if you are planning work for your students—it would be most helpful to us. Very sincerely yours

Jane Addams

ALS (SHSW, Ely; *JAPM*, 2:1677–79).

1. The Charity Organization Society concept had developed first in Scotland in the early 1800s and then, led by Edward Denison, in London, in 1869, with the formation of the London Society for Organizing Charitable Relief and Repressing Mendacity. Denison and others believed that too many alms available to the poor might promote their need for relief rather

than staunch it and help develop successful independence. They emphasized establishing a relationship with the needy based on investigation, understanding, and good record keeping. The London organization was successful and became popularly known as the Charity Organization Society. Among the major goals of the COS were to promote cooperation and coordination of relief among all charitable agencies of a given locality, to develop and maintain accurate knowledge of all cases handled in a specific locality, and to attempt to find prompt and adequate relief for all that should have it. The movement spread quickly throughout England and by 1877 was started in the United States, initially in major cities on the East Coast and primarily through the work of Stephen Humphreys Gurteen (1840–98). Educated at Cambridge, Gurteen settled for a time in East London as a protégée of Edward Denison. He immigrated to New York City, where he tutored and began to write. Eventually, he attended Hobart College; there he became committed to a religious life. When he was an assistant at St. Paul's Church in Buffalo, N.Y., in 1877, he initiated the first COS in the United States. He also helped start COS organizations in Boston, Baltimore, Philadelphia, and Chicago. He produced several publications about charity organizations, including a *Handbook of Charity Organizations* (1882).

The original Chicago COS had been formed in Nov. 1883 with Gurteen's assistance. By 1887 the fledgling organization had been absorbed by the older, better established, and more powerful Chicago Relief and Aid Society, which gave lip service to the goals of the COS, but continued to distribute relief according to its own unscientific and rather narrow definition of those "morally upright poor" who "deserved" charity.

2. Among the leaders of the Com. on Charity Organization were William James Onahan (1836–1919), city comptroller, 1887–91, banker, distinguished Catholic layman and eventual member of the Chicago Board of Education; Anthony F. Seeberger (1829–1901), president of the Inter-State Industrial Exposition, 1886; Francis Kiss (1824–1901) and Henry L. Frank (1839–1926), significant leaders in the Jewish community, both of whom were associated with the United Hebrew Relief Assn. of Chicago; William Robert Stirling (1851–1918), steel manufacturer committed to civil service reform, an Episcopalian active in the Brotherhood of St. Andrew; Bishop Charles Edward Cheney (1836–1916), Reformed Episcopal missionary and churchman; Dr. Henry M. Scudder, who had been pastor of the Plymouth Church, 1882–85; William M. Salter; Lucy Louisa Coues Flower, an active member of the CWC, a board member of several Chicago charities, a founder of the Illinois Training School for Nurses in 1880, and the first female member of the Chicago Board of Education, 1891–94 (see JA to MRS, 4 [, 5, and 6] Sept. 1895, n. 8, below); Julia Plato Harvey; and JA.

3. William J. Onahan to Board of Directors, Chicago Relief and Aid Society, [4 Jan. 1892], Minute Book, 1887–1909, Chicago Relief and Aid Society, 108, CHM, CHS, United Charities.

4. See n. 2.

5. William J. Onahan to Board of Directors, Chicago Relief and Aid Society, [4 Jan. 1892], Minute Book, 1887–1909, Chicago Relief and Aid Society, 108, CHM, CHS, United Charities.

6. Exec. Com. of the Board of Directors of the Chicago Relief and Aid Society to William J. Onahan, 1 Feb. 1892, Minute Book, 1887–1909, 113–14, CHM, CHS, United Charities.

7. A. F. Seeberger et al. to President and Exec. Com. of the Chicago Relief and Aid Society, n.d. [1 Feb.–7 Mar. 1892], Minute Book, 1887–1909, 127–28, CHM, CHS, United Charities.

8. John McClaren [McLaren], President, Board of Directors, Chicago Relief and Aid Society, to A. F. Seeberger, Chairman, 7 Mar. 1892, Minute Book, 1887–1909, 132–33, CHM, CHS, United Charities.

9. Lucy L. Flower, Sarah Hackett Stevenson, and JA to Board of Directors of the Chicago Relief and Aid Society, [ca. Apr. 1895], Minute Book, 1887–1909, 250, CHM, CHS, United Charities.

10. John McLaren (1836–1916) was born in Edinburgh, Scotland, the son of William and Helen Hume McLaren, educated in Scotland, and arrived in the United States with his family

in 1852. An apprentice carpenter in the building trade in Chicago, he enlisted as a private in the Union army during the Civil War and when mustered out in 1863 was adjutant of his regiment. He became a bookkeeper for Col. John Mason Loomis and was soon a partner in the lumber firm of John Mason Loomis and Co. By 1885 the firm had become McLaren and Morris. Until 1894, when he became president of the Leather National Bank, which by 1900 had become part of the First National Bank of Chicago, he was a director of the Industrial Bank of Chicago and the Milwaukee Avenue State Bank. He served as director of the Chicago Relief and Aid Society and as its president, 1891–92, and was a member of the Chicago Board of Education, 1887–93. In 1894 he was appointed a trustee for the Allen C. Lewis trust fund, established to oversee the creation of the Lewis Institute in Chicago, and he was also a trustee for the Mary Thompson Hospital. Beginning in 1901, he became president of the International Audit Co. His wife, Harriet A. Studley, whom he married in 1868, became a member of the CWC in 1902 and served in the Home Dept.

11. Chicago Bureau of Charities, Certificate of Incorporation for, ISA, Dept. of State. Corp. Records, 7 May 1895.

Phillip Wheelock Ayres (1861–1945) was born at Winterset, Iowa, the son of Elias and Cordelia Wheelock Ayres. He was a friend of Richard T. Ely and became the first secretary of the Chicago Bureau of Charities. Lured away from a similar position in Cincinnati, he began his duties in Chicago on 18 Nov. 1895. With his Johns Hopkins Ph.D., he had become an expert in dispensing "scientific charity." In 1899 he married Alice Stanley Taylor. By 1901 he had become the chief forester for the newly formed Society for the Protection of New Hampshire Forests and was instrumental in the creation of the White Mountains National Forest. He held that position for more than thirty years. He died in New York City and was buried in Franconia, N.H.

12. "R. & A." was JA's shorthand for Chicago Relief and Aid Society.

13. St. Vincent De Paul Society was founded in Paris in 1833 as an organization of Roman Catholic laymen dedicated to charity work. Rev. Dennis Dunne (1827–68), pastor of St. Patrick's Church (and the uncle of Finley Peter Dunne, creator of Chicago's "Mr. Dooley" stories), brought the organization to Chicago during the depression of 1847 to help his parishioners. It soon spread to other parishes in Chicago and cooperated with other charitable organizations, like the Chicago Relief and Aid Society and the COS.

By 1895 the priest who was in charge of the society in Chicago was Rev. Father Peter J. Muldoon (1863–1927), born in Columbia, Calif. After attending school in Stockton, Calif., he entered St. Mary's in Kentucky and four years later went to St. Mary's Seminary in Baltimore. He was ordained in 1886 and made pastor at St. Pius's Church in Chicago. By 1888 he had been appointed chancellor of the archdiocese of Chicago and secretary to Archbishop Feehan. He also became director of the St. Vincent De Paul Society for the archdiocese. During the World's Columbian Exposition, he served as secretary of the Roman Catholic exhibit. By Nov. 1896, he had become the head of the parish in which he built the Church of St. Charles Borromeo, located at Twelfth St. and Cypress/Hoyne Ave., within walking distance of HH. Mary Kenney was one of his parishioners, a member of the Sodality, and went to confession to Muldoon each Saturday she was in Chicago. On 15 Dec. 1908, Muldoon was installed as the first bishop of a new diocese led from Rockford, Ill.

During the early years of the twentieth century, he promoted the growth of Roman Catholicism in his new diocese and "played a large role in the American Catholic scene" (Fry, *The Story of a Parish*, 37). In 1917 he was chairman of the National Catholic Welfare Council, focused on social justice. In 1925, while in St. Louis, he underwent emergency surgery for a ruptured appendix. He never fully recovered, spent days in a hospital in St. Louis, and then was bedridden in his Rockford home, where he died Oct. 1927.

14. Vennette Crain was in charge of the HH Relief Office.

## To Mary Rozet Smith

Hull-House 335 South Halsted Street Chicago [Ill.] March 26" 1895

My dear Sister

Will you consent to be one of our "trustees"— the fatal moment has arrived when we must incorporate. I want very much to have you.

When are you coming home.[1] We are postponing some very important decisions for your arrival. I am so disappointed that you are not coming here but am sure you will relent when you see the third floor.[2]

The "book"[3] is out at last, I have n't sent you one because you are coming so soon. My best love to your family. Always yours

Jane Addams

ALS (SCPC, JAC; *JAPM*, 2:1688–89).

1. MRS was in Columbia, S.C., with her parents, visiting her aunt and uncle the George C. Smith family and her aunt Sarah Porter Smith.

2. JA hoped that MRS would become a resident of HH.

3. *HH Maps and Papers* had just been published, and on 19 Mar. 1895 the publisher, Thomas Y. Crowell and Co., sent JA fifteen copies of the $2.50 edition and fifteen copies of the $3.50 edition. Except for five free copies, JA was also sent a bill for all of them with a 4 percent discount. See JA to Richard T. Ely, 22 Aug. 1895; *JAPM*, 2:1748. Crowell sent review copies to the "five large dailies of Chicago" and "all the important papers throughout the country" (T. Y. Crowell and Co. to JA, 25 Mar. 1895, SCPC, JAC; *JAPM*, 2:1687).

Reviews of *HH Maps and Papers* appeared in periodicals throughout the United States, including Detroit, Boston, and San Francisco. All were positive. On 16 June 1895, the *New York Times* labeled the work "this admirable publication," and the *Brooklyn (N.Y.) Eagle* on 14 Apr. 1895 called it "a remarkable book." Chicago newspapers, including the *Herald* (26 Mar. 1895), *Post* (6 Apr. 1895), *Evening Post* (22 June 1895), and *Standard* (11 Apr. 1895), all offered reviews, and so did the religious press, including the *Christian Advocate* (10 Apr. 1895), *Presbyterian Herald* (17 Apr. 1895), *Living Church* (15 June 1895), and *Christian Work* (18 Apr. 1895).

## To Mary Rozet Smith

Hull-House 335 South Halsted Street Chicago [Ill.] April 20" 1895

My dear Miss Smith

There will be a meeting of the Hull-House trustees next Friday afternoon (April 26") at four o'clock in the library at Hull-House.[1] We hope very much that that hour will be convenient for you as it is important that the first meeting of the board should be a full one. Very sincerely yours

Jane Addams

ALS (SCPC, JAC; *JAPM*, 2:1699).

1. On Thursday afternoon, 25 Apr. 1895, JA, Helen Culver, William H. Colvin, Mary H. Wilmarth, MRS, and Allen B. Pond gathered in the office of attorney Edwin Burritt Smith to organize HH Assn. JA served as the temporary chairman and Allen B. Pond as the temporary secretary. By the end of the meeting, the following officers had been identified to serve during the first year: president, JA; vice-president, Mary H. Wilmarth; secretary, Allen B. Pond; treasurer, JA; auditor, William H. Colvin; and assistant treasurer, Gertrude Barnum. The second board meeting was held on 20 May 1895. No meeting of the board was held 26 Apr. 1895. The board meetings scheduled for 9 July and 8 Oct. 1895 were canceled due to the illness of JA.

## Article in the *Chicago Record*

*"I wonder if your father would be cheered by an account of my garbage investigations?" wrote Jane Addams to Mary Rozet Smith, who was visiting with her parents in Columbia, South Carolina. "The Contracts are let next week and if I am going to get the 19th Ward my bid must go in next week. Seymour Coman, Sig. Valerio and myself have spent days investigating and estimating. We find that the contractor bid $1150.00 a mo. when it would properly take 1500.00 a mo. then he actually spends about $500.00. If we bid what would clean it—we can't get it, if we bid low enough to get it we probably can't keep it clean—so here we are!"[1] Although unsuccessful in her quest for the contract, she was proud to be named as the garbage inspector for the Nineteenth Ward of Chicago. She spent her annual salary of one thousand dollars to employ an assistant and pay for expenses associated with their duties.[2] In April 1896, she resigned her position in favor of her assistant Amanda Johnson.[3]*

Chicago, Ill. 25 April 1895

JANE ADDAMS WEARS A STAR.

APPOINTED TO THE FORCE OF GARBAGE INSPECTORS

BY COMMISSIONER KENT.

Miss Jane Addams called on Commissioner Kent[4] yesterday. When she went away she wore a policeman's star.[5] It indicated that she was a member of the sanitary police force for the 19th ward. She went to luncheon wearing her star, and the Hull house colony was in high glee. It was thought there that the appointment of Miss Addams as garbage inspector would do almost as much to better the condition of the garbage boxes and alleys[6] as if she had been awarded the garbage contract for which she put in a bid a few weeks ago,[7] as she will inspect the work of the man who got the contract,[8] and will see that he does his work properly.

Miss Addams said little about her appointment, or about the details of her plan of action. She means to have a horse and buggy, and she will spend most of her time driving about the ward.[9] She will be assisted by Miss Julia C. Lathrop

It is likely that Jane Addams posed for this photograph by Alfred A. Cox sometime in early 1896, perhaps after her recovery from surgery to remove her appendix (UIC, JAMC 0003 0020).

and other residents of Hull house.[10] The alleys in some parts of the ward are very filthy, and the garbage boxes have been neglected for weeks at a time. Hull house is looking for a change.[11]

It is new for a woman to be appointed garbage inspector for the city of Chicago, although Mrs. Paul[12] has been doing similar work for the Civic Federation. In New York there are two women acting as city inspectors. This is Miss Addams first official appointment. She takes the place of J. M. Burns, who has been removed by the department of public works.[13]

PD (*Chicago Record*, 25 Apr. 1895; HH Scrapbook 3:2; *JAPM*, Addendum 10:8ff).

1. 24 Feb. 1895, SCPC, JAC; *JAPM*, 2:1669–70.

2. The Oct. 1894 through May 1895 HH account book (UIC, JAMC, HH Assn.; *JAPM*, Addendum 3:0004), on p. 295 indicated that JA received $83.33 each month from the city and paid Amanda Johnson $60 a month as her assistant (see n. 3). JA spent $55 for her horse and harness and $27 a month for its upkeep.

3. Amanda Marie Johnson (1871–1949), who identified herself as a social worker, was born in Christiana, Wis., the daughter of Peter N. and Anna Folkedahl Johnson. She was a graduate of Albion Academy in Wisconsin and an 1893 graduate of the Univ. of Wisconsin, where she was enrolled in the "ancient classical course" and took special instruction from Richard T. Ely. She was a prizewinning orator during her junior year at the university and served on the yearbook editorial board.

According to her sister Claudine Johnson Teige, Amanda was a "brilliant student" who was "asked . . . to join Phi Beta Kappa twenty years after she graduated." Teige recalled her as "'dynamic and sociable,'" a friend of Clarence Darrow, and someone who "worked for several newspapers." Teige also recalled that Amanda was independent, promoted "'advanced ideas about women,'" and "the only woman who would get off the bus in Stoughton wearing red stockings or smoking cigarettes" (Krouse, "Educated Daughters and Sisters," 96). Amanda Johnson arrived at Kingsley House, Pittsburgh, in Jan. 1894, shortly after it opened. She seems to have come to Kingsley after a brief stay at HH. At Kingsley she was one of the first three residents and established an interest in clean streets and alleys. Her special responsibility was as a "visitor" in the neighborhood. Shortly after Kingsley House expanded from its original site at 1707 Penn Ave., she agreed to settle in the satellite facility at 1725 Penn Ave.; however, by May 1895, she had resigned her position at Kingsley and had returned to HH, where she became JA's assistant garbage inspector for the Nineteenth Ward.

The *Chicago Daily Tribune* reported Johnson, who worked six days a week from 6:00 A.M. until at least 4:00 P.M., was a "young and prepossessing . . . college-bred woman" ("Wage War on Dirt"). When JA resigned her position as garbage inspector in Apr. 1896, Amanda Johnson took the newly established civil service examination for the post and won it with her high marks. Johnson continued to live and work at HH.

By the end of Dec. 1896, the *Chicago Record* reported, "Miss Johnson's work as inspector has won her admiration in the ward, and from Superintendent Rhode of the street and alley cleaning department as well. Old residents of the ward say that never before in their memory have the alley and garbage boxes been kept in so good condition. . . . The 19th ward, which used to be one of the dirtiest in the city, . . . is now one of the most cleanly as regards its alleys and garbage collection" ("HH," 2 Dec. 1896). During the summer of 1897, she was transferred from the Nineteenth Ward to be garbage inspector for the Thirty-fourth Ward for political reasons; however, she was returned to the Nineteenth Ward (see also JA to MRS, [3 Apr. 1898], n. 13, below).

On 2 June 1898, HH resident Alice Hamilton wrote to her cousin Agnes, that Johnson was "quite broken down" and had gone off to "some watering-place for the summer" (RS, HFP). Later, she reported that "Miss Johnson is studying law in the Northwestern University law-school and incidentally managing the [HH] labor bureau, managing it very well, too, for she goes to see the people and finds out whether or not they take the jobs. You know you always thought a good deal could be made out of it, if only somebody took it up systematically" (Alice Hamilton to Agnes Hamilton, 11 Oct. 1898, RS, HFP). A month later, Hamilton wrote, "Miss Johnson has gone over to Catholicism as far as she can without actually being confirmed. She told Mrs. Kelley that she had promised her mother not to do that during the latter's lifetime. But she goes to confession—can you imagine that independent, hard-headed girl confessing?—and she goes regularly to mass. She has very little to do with anyone in the house except the Valerios, indeed she seems very much changed" (Alice Hamilton to Agnes Hamilton, 26 Nov. 1898, RS, HFP).

During the municipal elections campaign in Jan. 1898, Amanda Johnson found her likeness and actions presented in the *Chicago Daily Tribune* as a thorn in the side of boodler Alderman John Powers, who was running for reelection in the Nineteenth Ward. Powers claimed that she was actively trying to defeat him. Even though the residents of HH were campaigning against Powers, JA responded, "'I think Mr. Powers has been misinformed . . .

for I am sure Miss Johnson would not do such a thing.'" Powers responded: "'I have always given the women my support. . . . She is a good inspector and has kept the ward clean. I would not raise a finger against her if she would stick to her work, but when it comes to going from house to house and talking against me in my own ward, it is a different thing'" ("Miss Amanda Johnson, Nineteenth Ward Sanitary Inspector," 17 Jan. 1898). In Feb. 1898, she found herself out of a job as garbage inspector when the Chicago Council voted to abolish the Street and Alley Cleaning Dept. and place its duties under the Street Dept.

Johnson began to investigate fraud in the new civil service system in 1899, and Hamilton reported that Amanda Johnson was "deep in Civil Service frauds and is getting herself all mixed up with the [Carter H. ]Harrison [Jr.] and [former Illinois governor John Peter] Altgeld parties. You see Altgeld is running against Harrison for mayor and Altgeld uses Miss Johnson's statistics on the Civil Service cheats in his campaign speeches, and then the City Hall comes down on Miss Johnson and it gets into the papers and we have reporters and interviews and feel as if we were in the campaign again. . . . She is the most remarkable young woman—only twenty seven, just think! She makes me feel feeble and ineffectual whenever I look at her" (Alice Hamilton to Agnes Hamilton, 24 and 28 Feb. 1899, RS, HFP).

Both Harrison and Altgeld were Democrats; however, Altgeld supported immediate municipal ownership of city transportation, while Harrison favored letting the private monopolies continue to operate city transportation for a period of twenty years with the option of eventual municipal ownership. There were other issues associated with the mayoral race, and it was also clear that Harrison was not an ardent supporter of civil service. "At the election in April [1899], Altgeld received 47,169 votes, as against 148,496 for Harrison and 107,437 for [Republican Party candidate Zina R.] Carter" (Browne, *Altgeld*, 309).

By 1900 Amanda Johnson was no longer a law student. She was also no longer a settlement resident, but still an active participant and visitor. She had become the manager of a four-story and basement model tenement house designed by architect Dwight H. Perkins. The twenty-four apartments with a monthly rental of thirteen dollars had been erected for "the benefit of the better and more prosperous class of tenement dwellers" at the southeast corner of Desplaines and Bunker streets for the trustees of the James Robbins Langdon (1812?–95) estate (Colson, "A Home in the Tenements"). Through 1910 Johnson remained a resident of Chicago, living in the 600 block of Bunker (later Grenshaw) St. In July 1917, she entered the Wisconsin Hospital for the Insane at Mendota, Wis., where she was diagnosed with manic depression. By 1926 she had left the Mendota hospital and in 1930 was living in Madison, Wis. From 1948 until her death from heart failure, she resided in Ft. Atkinson, Wis. She was buried in West Koshkonong Cemetery in Pleasant Springs, Dane Co., Wis.

4. JA's friend William Kent had just been elected to the Chicago City Council in Apr. 1895 and had become commissioner of public works.

5. JA was not obliged, however, to wear the jacket and trousers uniform that male garbage inspectors wore.

6. Each city lot was equipped with a wooden box where residents were to place their refuse. Often the boxes, which made good firewood, were entirely missing or so destroyed by citizens seeking fuel that they could not hold garbage or were overflowing to the point that it was difficult to collect the garbage. In some cases, refuse was too large to fit in the boxes and was simply discarded in the alley. JA discovered better containers made of iron during her brief trip to New York City, 3–6 May, 1895, when she investigated the city's scavenger system and attended a settlement conference. She also visited Philadelphia but did not leave adequate time for a visit to Boston.

JA was aware that unless alleys were paved, they were exceedingly difficult to keep clean. She was pleased with her success in getting five alleys in the Nineteenth Ward paved and printed a list of her accomplishments in the first number of the *HH Bulletin*, which began publication in Jan. 1896.

Jane Addams, garbage inspector for the Nineteenth Ward of Chicago, and her permanent assistant Amanda Johnson were intent on making the alleys like this one in the Hull-House neighborhood clean (Hunter, *Tenement Conditions in Chicago*, 39).

7. The Topeka, Kans., *Journal* reported of her bid: "Her plan involved the offering of a cent a bushel as a prize for clean ashes, unmixed with garbage. The ashes then can be sold to railroads for ballast. The public dump can thus be supplanted by the garbage crematory, where all the refuse may be burned. The *Chicago Daily Tribune* says: 'Miss Addams' is so practical and so businesslike that her bid should be accepted forthwith. The character of her opponents, the present scavengers, may be judged from the fact that last summer Hull House lodged 700 complaints for failure to empty garbage boxes'" ("Miss Addams as Scavenger," 28 May 1895; HH Scrapbook 3:7; *JAPM*, Addendum 10:8ff).

8. On 27 Mar. 1895, the *Chicago Times-Herald* listed J. Bradley as the man who was awarded a ten-thousand-dollar scavenger contract for the Nineteenth Ward.

9. Garbage was to be picked up by the contractors three times a week. "Every morning at 6 o'clock the low covered buggy drawn by the sturdy grey nag comes to the door of Hull House and Miss Addams and her assistant start on their rounds. They come back for an 8 o'clock breakfast and then are off again until 11 o'clock" ("Doing a Good Work"). In addition to the daily inspections and issuing orders, sustained in court, for residents to clean their garbage boxes and alleys, JA kept records of where she had been, to whom she had given tasks, and what was expected. And she followed up to be sure that what she had ordered was done. By the fall of 1895, she was considered a model inspector: "Miss Addams proves that a woman makes an excellent public official when she minds her official business in this admirable way" ("Miss Addams a Good Model"). She called for wagons from the city to remove what the contractor did not have to take by law, that is, manure and dead animals. She insisted that residents were responsible for disposing of rubbish that the garbage contractor was not obliged to handle and used the courts to enforce that position.

JA also worked with Chicago's Civic Federation to clean streets and alleys. She enlisted the aid of the HH Woman's Club and organized children from clubs at the settlement to keep an eye on the alleys near their homes. "Every afternoon the urchins arrive, one club each day in the week, so that their energy may not be overtaxed, and with a teacher at their head they start out for savory precincts of such alleys as Tilden, Ewing, Forquer and Maxwell. There they run the gauntlet of angry ragpickers and objurgating peddlers and set to work gathering all the cans and papers into a heap and making them handy for collectors." The children were organized as a brigade, with each club a company with its own captain and sergeants, and all had badges ("Young Ones at Work").

10. Julia C. Lathrop or other HH residents accompanied JA until Amanda Johnson came on 1 May.

11. An article, "Doing a Good Work," in the *Chicago Times-Herald* reported on 5 July 1895 that JA had been given eight teams of horses and wagons to help her remove refuse that did not strictly fall under the definition of garbage. By 1 June, she had seen that 1,245 cubic feet of nongarbage had been removed, and by the end of June an additional 2,076 cubic feet were taken away. The newspaper further enthused: "Two months ago, a reporter for the Times-Herald accompanied her on her rounds, and saw the fifth and dirt that prevailed in the alleys. Two months have worked a wonderful change."

12. A. Emmogene (or Emogene) Paul (1843?–1912) may have been born in Rockford, Ill., where she was also buried. The U.S. Census of 1900 lists 1850 as her birth date; however, her death certificate indicates that she was sixty-nine years old at her death from chronic nephritis. She was married from 1863 to 1890 when, according to the U.S. Census of 1900, she was divorced—although her Illinois death certificate indicates that she was widowed. She had two children.

By 1894 Mrs. A. E. Paul was a member of the Municipal Order League and in Aug. 1894 reported to the Civic Federation of Chicago on the cost of garbage pickup in the city and identified boardinghouses, hotels, and restaurants as places from which garbage contractors were not obliged to remove refuse. By late 1894 and early 1895, she was an official of the Chicago Health Dept., charged with inspecting conditions in bakeries, and she was also identified as "one of the sanitary inspectors for the Civic Federation." Mrs. Paul knew that JA planned to bid for the contract for garbage removal in the Nineteenth Ward. According to "Many Bids Opened," an article in the *Chicago Inter Ocean*, 23 Mar. 1895, "Among the crowd which gathered outside the railing of the commissioner's office to see the bids opened was Mrs. Paul, who had presented a bid for Miss Jane Addams, of Hull House. . . . Mrs. Paul prepared a bid and it was turned in with the others. . . . [I]t was not even filed for consideration." As JA became the garbage inspector for the Nineteenth Ward, the *Chicago Daily Tribune* reported on 4 May 1895 that Mrs. Paul of the Civic Federation "wears a silver star thus inscribed: 'Sanitary Police, No. 94'" ("Tour of the Alleys"). She was to supervise the cleaning of an area of the city that included homes of the wealthy and reported there was more raw garbage in the rear of the mansions of the rich than in JA's ward. She praised JA's work in the Nineteenth Ward. During the summer of 1897, she organized a Clean City League among the children attending a Univ. of Chicago summer school. On 10 Oct. 1897, the *New York Times* published a photo of Mrs. Paul and reported that she had been appointed for a term of three years to oversee the "street-cleaning work of the business district of Chicago" with twenty-five men under her command. The *Outlook* identified her as a "woman of marked executive ability" ([Mrs. A. E. Paul's Appointment as Inspector of Street Cleaning], 352). In 1898, she lost her position as garbage inspector when the department in which she worked was abolished by the Chicago Council.

13. The editors have omitted the remainder of the article, which is a list of other inspectors appointed.

## To Mary Rozet Smith

*The summer of 1895 offered little rest for Jane Addams. In addition to continuing the daily alley inspections, she had to monitor the new construction at the settlement with the Children's Building going up at the corner of Polk and Halsted streets and renovations to the original Hull home, the coffeehouse, kitchen, and dining area. She also had an increasing number of speaking engagements. On 3 May, Jane Addams was in New York City to speak before the Conference of the College Settlements Association, where she presented her version of the Pullman strike. She visited Kingsley House, a social settlement in Pittsburgh, on 14 May and followed with an address on 28 May in Lewistown, Ill. Toward the end of June, she spoke on the causes of poverty and proposed remedies before the convention called by the School of Christian Sociology at Oberlin College in Ohio. On 20 July, Jane lectured at the Pan-American Congress of Religion and Education held in Toronto, 18–25 July 1895, and by 27 July Jane and Mary Rozet Smith, accompanied by Louis Greeley, were at Chautauqua, New York, where Ellen Gates Starr was offering a series of lectures on art history. After a few days at Bar Harbor, Maine, Jane was back in Chicago. There on 23 August, she lectured on working women at All Souls Church, and that evening she participated on a panel at the Chicago Commons Social Economics Summer School, considering the "Social Renewal of the Seventeenth Ward."*

Hull-House 335 South Halsted Street Chicago Aug. 8th, 1895.

Dear Sister:—

I have spent all of two days getting the new room[1] in order. It is by far the handsomest room in the house, and ~~it is a great deal to prize about H.H.~~ <by far the the most imposing.> We invited the Women's Club[2] to see it yesterday. <At the end> They all insisted upon standing in the hall and looking at it through telescopes made out of their hands, because they ~~all~~ said it was so like a <">beautiful picture.<"> They were quite horrified that we were going to have clubs upon that <">beautiful floor<">, but signified a great desire to have their monthly refreshments served in it. In the afternoon about 50 women came from the University,[3] and we served ~~our~~ <the> lemonade there, and it seem~~s~~<ed> quite like a house warming. To-night the Jane Club and the Phalanx Club are coming to the opening. Altogether it ~~seems~~ <we feel as> if we had had a new addition <wh> ~~I~~ <i>ndeed it is.

To tell the truth the drawing room looks a little empty, in spite of all my efforts to fill it up with furniture from every part of the house. I cannot tell you how grateful I am for the sofa and the table, which have not yet come, but which I place in my mind's eye in two ver<y> delightful spots.[4] It was very good of you to think about them, and it will make a vast difference in the room, <do you remember the moral remarks in "Beggars all"[5] when the two bought the piano for his wife's mother?>

Hull-House was becoming a group of imposing brick structures on the corner of Halsted and Polk Streets, yet the business and housing stock surrounding it was little changed from the assortment of small emporiums and saloons that made up the community in 1889. In this photograph of Halsted Street (ca. 1896), the Murphy store was still next door to the Butler Building (UIC, JAMC 0133 0899).

The two checks came and we have acknowledged them <u>both</u> to Bradner, Smith & Co. You see about how the nursery account stands. It comes partly because Mrs. Orr has been engaged for the month while Mary and Mrs. Hansen have their vacation.[6] Mary is going to Lakeside the first of the week with a friend of hers. The Lakeside house is a great success.[7] Quantities of people are applying all the time who are willing and able to pay their board. We could fill up cottages all along the lake if we had them. Miss West[8] was here last night and most enthusiastic about it. I inclose a letter[9] which I received at Rockford, which does not half compare with one that was read by Agnes Dwyer in the Henry Learned Club,[10] and two o~~r~~<f> th~~ree~~ read from members of the Women's Club yesterday. They all consider it a perfect paradise, and see the moon rise on the Lake as a nightly performance with almost religious fervor. I think Miss West is doing splendidly. They discuss the meals and the accounts all together, and there is a great feeling of regard to her, and none of the petty criticisms usually incident upon "cheap board". She has gone off this morning to the Fair[11] where she buys groceries at phenomenally low prices.

We talked over the question of permanent book-cases for the club rooms, long and earnestly, and it really seems to us both much better not to build any until we are sure what we want. For the present we can move in the two red wardrobes which are really very good looking, and one bookcase for the two rooms would be ample I think, as we would only keep the children's books there. I really think that it would be better not to build anything into the lower rooms.

Mr. Pond[12] has also sent over in regard to speaking tubes bells, &c. It does not seem to me that we need either of them. The main staircase will have to be more or less open like the staircase to an apartment house, and statement will have to be made below as to which floor contains which, but I see no need of speaking tubes, unless perhaps there might be one between the dining room of the Nursery and the Kindergarten room. Miss Colvin[13] is still out of town, but I will see her about the nursery kindergarten. I spoke about it in a general way to her father, who seemed much pleased.

I think your father's plan in regard to the employes is delightful, and nothing would please me more than to co-operate in such. The pillars to the porch seems at present perfectly huge, as if they were striding all over the yard, but Mr. Pond insists it is because they are only half done, and that they will not be out of proportion.[14] I send you the inclosed picture to show you that the proportion is correct.[15]

You are awfully good to go to see my aunt.[16] Alice will be there by the 20th of August. She is now in Cedarville.

The Lincoln Club[17] row is by no means ended yet, although I am sure there is not the least danger of physical fighting. Both sides are thoroughly ashamed, and it has really been a triumph for non-resistence, I think, but the Executive Committee are much affronted that we did not side altogether with them, and will probably refuse to meet at the house any longer. I do think that self-righteousness is the hardest thing in the world to deal with. <I am sure it is for me.>

I am going to write oftener now that I am back to where it does not mean long hours of toil.[18]

Mrs. Stetson[19] arrived last night. She is very interesting but my opinion of her is as yet much mixed. We are going to have a house full of people the third week in August. The author of the Experiment in Altruism[20] has applied to make a three day's visit. I am not sure that we can take her in, but I am going to make an effort to do so. She wrote a very meek little note.

Mrs. Kelley is off on her vacation. Miss Johnson[21] insists that it will be utterly impossible for her to take one, and works on like a hero. The ward is really cleaner.

With love to your father and mother, I am, Very sincerely yours <& affectionately & many other things besides>

Jane Addams

T and ALS (SCPC, JAC; *JAPM*, 2:1721–24).

1. HH was again in a renovation phase. JA was referring to the new dining room. The *Chicago Times-Herald*, 19 July 1895, described the changes that had taken place getting ready for the new Children's Building that began construction on 17 July 1895. "The old kitchen and laundry have been thrown into one room, which in future is to serve as a dining-room. It has four south and two north windows, which unfortunately look out upon nothing but a waste of brick and mortar. The room of very fine proportions which has been used as a dining-room will now become the drawing-room of the house, the former drawing-room to be used as a reception room" ("New HH Annex").

2. HH Woman's Club.

3. Univ. of Chicago.

4. "The sofa is the most delightful piece of furniture I ever beheld, and my old longings for the sham Empire affair at Tobys are forever at rest and more than satisfied. The table also is fine but the sofa defies competition and completes the room by itself—it will always be a joy and pride. It is wonderful the amount of satisfaction I get from a thing like that, I am almost ashamed of it!" (JA to MRS, 17 Aug. 1895, SCPC, JAC; *JAPM*, 2:1743–44).

5. *Beggars All: A Novel* was written by Lily Dougall (1858–1923) and published by Longmans, Green, and Co. in 1891. JA may have been remembering the following statement: "Where one gives much more perforce, to give a little more is to make all the gift lovely to the recipient, to make the giver irresistibly dear" (230).

6. The nursery account was often quite low, but MRS and her family were available to make up the deficit. Mrs. Orr had come to give Mary Connelly and Mrs. Marie Hensen some vacation time. Surviving HH financial records indicate that in 1895, members of the Smith family gave at least $150 a month to support the nursery.

7. For Aug. 1895, JA had arranged to rent a fourteen-room house at Lakeside, Ill., north of Chicago, near what eventually became part of Winnetka, Ill. This was the beginning of HH-sponsored summer camping outside of Chicago. Children and their mothers could sign up to spend time there so long as they purchased their own food. Children alone could attend for $1.50 a week. JA continued to have summer camp at Lakeside until the Bowen Country Club was established in 1912 at Waukegan, Ill. (see JA to Gertrude Barnum, 22 May [June] 1896, n. 17, below).

It was not until July 1910 that JA, Eleanor Smith, and Ruth N. Hamilton purchased property that included a house in Lakeside, Mich., from William and Caroline D. Westervelt, who lived in Honolulu, Terr. of Hawaii. JA and HH music teacher and resident Eleanor Smith each gave $1,800 toward the purchase price, while Ruth N. Hamilton provided $1,616. JA may have discovered the area about 1900 through mutual friends who owned or rented cottages there. Among them were Dr. Bayard Holmes and Gertrude Smith. When property owners formed the Chikaming Club in Oct. 1911 to promote social intercourse, safe amusements, and outdoor sports in the community, JA was issued the first membership certificate.

8. Margaretta S. West was placed in charge of the camp.

9. The enclosure is apparently not extant.

10. Agnes Dwyer, a young neighborhood woman, was a member of the Henry Learned Club at HH. Limited to sixty members, it met one evening a week at 8:00 P.M. The first and third weeks of the month, members were treated to a literary program, the second and fourth weeks a social event. The club gave a number of plays, and the proceeds from those performed during the winter of 1896 were directed toward purchasing a stove for the Lakeside camp venue. By Mar. 1896, the young people who had been to the HH Country Club at Lakeside had formed a Lakeside Club that initially met at HH one night each week. Agnes Dwyer became secretary of the club; by 1898 she was serving as its president.

11. The Fair Store was a discount department store that operated on a cash basis. It was founded in 1874 in Chicago by Ernst J. Lehmann (1849–1900) and located at the corner of State and Adams streets.

12. Probably Irving K. Pond, the primary architect on the project.

13. JA was likely referring to Miss Jessie Colvin, one of William H. Colvin's two daughters. She joined MRS in providing an endowment for the HH music program, located in the Children's Building. The editors do not know what Charles Mather Smith's suggested plan for the employees was.

14. For JA's later reaction to the pillars, see JA to MRS, 4 [, 5, and 6] Sept. 1895, below.

15. The enclosure is not known to be extant.

16. JA had three aunts still living in 1895. They were Harriet C. Young, Susan Jane Mull, and Elizabeth Weber Reiff. Harriet C. Young and Elizabeth Weber Reiff lived in the Philadelphia area. Mrs. Reiff died in Dec. 1895; Mrs. Young died in June 1897.

17. The Lincoln Club, No. 135 of the Lyceum League of America, began meeting at HH by at least 4 Jan. 1894. The Lyceum League of America had been organized in Oct. 1891 by *Youths Companion* magazine to encourage the use of debate about issues facing the United States and to promote patriotism. By 1893 the average age of its all male members was twenty years. Each chapter of the league was part of an affiliated brotherhood with a constitution and rituals that were meant to teach and encourage good citizenship. During 1894 the club, with its twenty male members and, unusually, a similar number of female members, met weekly at HH on Monday evenings. They presented at least two public events each year that included piano and vocal solo music, recitation, and debate. At the event held 4 Jan. 1894, debate on the issue "Resolved. That Grover Cleveland's policy toward Hawaii is unjustifiable" (HH Scrapbook 2:33; *JAPM*, Addendum 10:7ff) was followed by an address by JA. In Apr. 1895, Gertrude Barnum was the club's HH liaison.

Margaretta West described the ending results of a "row" the club experienced in a letter that she wrote to JA from Lakeside on 2 Aug 1895, shortly after she opened HH Country Club. This altercation took place at HH and seems to have been adjudicated by a committee representing the HH Congress of Clubs. "The girls have had a meeting with the committee, and after much talk on both sides, they sent in formal resignations, which were accepted gracefully by the side triumphant.

"The boys are in a much more lenient state of mind, and even show some vague doubts as to whether their side is entirely in the right. We had a funny time the other night when the girls were closeted in one room declaring they never would resign, and the boys in the other saying no action could be taken until the girls resigned. I flitted from one room to the other until they came together and after two hours talk we all separated pretty good friends. Mr Gillan is the problem at present, the committee wishes to expel him, unless he apologizes for stirring up a row, he talks at length about the awfulness of his act, to me privately, but unless he struggles with his conscience and grows into more light we will hear no apology, he is coming for one more talk next week when I go in to meet him, at his own request" (SCPC, JAC; *JAPM*, 2:1717–19). The HH Congress of Clubs, organized during the mid-1890s, was a body that set rules for clubs at HH and was composed of a representative from each of the clubs.

JA offered her own description of the events in *Twenty Years*, revealing that the young men "had grown much irritated by the frivolity of the girls during their long debate, and had finally proposed that three of the most 'frivolous' be expelled." After the girls appealed to some of their friends in the HH Men's Club, a quarrel between the young men and the HH Men's Club became "so bitter that at length it led to a shooting" (343), which left no one injured. The club ceased to meet at HH.

18. JA may have been referring to her responsibilities at the HH Summer School that was held at RC 6 July to 3 Aug. 1895.

19. Charlotte Anna Perkins Stetson Gilman (1860–1935) arrived at HH on 7 Aug. 1895. She had become well known in California as a writer and feminist. She was a leading member of the Pacific Coast Woman's Press Assn., which established the California Woman's Congresses

of 1894 and 1895. In articles on 25 July 1895, newspapers in Los Angeles, San Francisco, and Sacramento noted that Charlotte Stetson was leaving the state to become a resident at HH. All informed their readers that she had learned of JA and HH through one of her best friends, Mrs. Helen Campbell (1839–1918) (see also JA to MRS, 4 [, 5, and 6] Sept. 1895, n. 17, below).

Charlotte Perkins Gilman, who became a leading intellectual of the feminist movement, was born in Hartford, Conn., to Mary A. Fitch Westcott and Frederic Beecher Perkins, who left his wife and two surviving children shortly after his daughter's birth. Mary Perkins became the family's primary breadwinner and distanced herself from her children to such a degree that Charlotte experienced a lonely childhood. While the small family was living in Providence, R.I., Charlotte attended the Rhode Island School of Design and began to support herself as a commercial artist. Although she considered herself a tomboy and seemed to shun traditional feminine roles, she did marry Charles Walter Stetson, a young artist, in May 1884. Depression followed the birth in Mar. 1885 of Katharine, their only child. The rest-cure regimen prescribed by Dr. S. Weir Mitchell, whom she consulted in Philadelphia, seemed to push her only further into depression. On a trip to California in 1885, away from her husband, she improved and decided to move permanently to California with her daughter and mother, but without her husband. The Stetsons were finally divorced in 1894, and Charles Stetson promptly wed Grace Ellery Channing (1862–1938), who was one of Charlotte's best friends. Charlotte remained friends with the new couple, and when she went to Chicago she left her daughter, Katharine, in California in the care of her father and his new bride. In 1900 Charlotte married her cousin George Houghton Gilman, seven years her junior, and they lived in Norwich, Conn.

In California, Charlotte Perkins Stetson (Gilman) began her career as a poet, writer, publisher, and lecturer on her vision of the place of women in society. She was an ardent feminist and supporter of women's rights, suffrage, and total independence of women from the traditions associated with family life and motherhood. Among her short stories, the most famous remains "The Yellow Wall-Paper," an autobiographical rendering of her own breakdown after the birth of Katharine, published in the Jan. 1892 issue of the *New England Magazine*. An attractive person and an able and persuasive speaker, she supported herself primarily with lecture fees and through her writings.

While in Chicago during the fall of 1895, Charlotte Stetson gave six lectures to the Social Science Club at HH, beginning on Tuesday, 1 Oct. The subjects she addressed were the labor movement, the advance of woman, childhood, the social organism, the body of humanity, and social ethics. Like other HH residents and supporters, she attended rallies in support of the Sulzer bill before the U.S. Congress to regulate tenement-house manufacture. At the meeting called by JA and HH on 8 Mar. 1896 at the Central Music Hall, Stetson and Helen Campbell, who was head resident of Unity Settlement in Chicago (later Eli Bates House), Nov. 1895–June 1896, sat with the honored guests on the stage, while the more than one thousand gathered voted to demand that the Illinois congressional delegation support passage of the legislation. In addition, while Charlotte was in Chicago, she considered joining Helen Campbell in opening a social settlement in the "Little Hell" area of the city, north and west of Chicago's downtown. She gave up that plan, as once again she was engulfed by depression. Stetson left Chicago in June and set out to attend the International Socialist and Labor Congress in London, 26 July–1 Aug. 1896. She returned to speak at HH before the Women's Socialist Club in Oct. 1900. Never a member of the Socialist Party, she was influenced by socialist ideas and by nationalist Edward Bellamy, the Fabians, and the sociologist Lester Frank Ward. In 1898 she published *Women and Economics* in which she argued for female economic independence. Judged her most significant work, it was widely read and translated into seven languages. Other books in which she continued to define her feminist ideas followed. Among them were *Concerning Children* (1900), *The Home* (1903), *Human*

*Work* (1904), and *Man-Made World* (1911). She spoke before the International Council of Women meeting in London (1899) and in Berlin (1904) as well as at the International Suffrage Convention in Budapest (1913). She was among the founders of the WPP, but never took a leadership role. After the death of her second husband in 1934, she moved to Pasadena, Calif., to be near her daughter's family. When it was clear that the breast cancer discovered in 1932 could no longer be treated successfully, she committed suicide, was cremated, and her ashes scattered.

20. Margaret Pollock Sherwood (1864–1955), who became a professor of English literature at Wellesley College, wrote *An Experiment in Altruism* about a social settlement in England. It was published by Macmillan Co. in 1895.

21. JA's deputy garbage inspector for the Nineteenth Ward, Amanda Johnson.

## From Robert A. Woods

Boston, [Mass.] Sept. 4, 1895.

My dear Miss Addams:

I hardly know what formality to use in saying how much I enjoyed my visits at Hull House. And Hull House is chiefly a matter of persons too. I was very glad of the opportunity to get better acquainted with all of you. I should like sometime to take a hand in the work of the House when it is in full swing, so as to get a perfectly clear impression as to what the activity of the House means.

It is very impressive however that there is too much activity and not enough repose and that you and all the older residents are spending creative vitality upon mechanical details to a rather large extent. It is of course necessary to do this in the first stages of such an enterprise. But I have a feeling that the time has now come for the more experienced residents to give up just as far as possible the notion that they are members of an emergency corps subject to call or bound to guard duty.

You have a remarkable opportunity at Hull House to develop some of the higher possibilities of social effort that can be got at only by talent and genius given freedom for definite action and repose for definite thought, duty, and rest. I don't think the fear of snobbishness counts for anything in this matter. And the daily demand of the neighborhood ought not to be allowed to prevent. There are times when the greater love must even leave the starving to starve. The suffering that we <u>see</u> may be even as alluring as the joy that we <u>see</u>.

I received the documents which you kindly sent. Please remember that we are holding that promise to come to Boston against you. Ever truly yours

Robt. A. Woods.

ALS (SCPC, JAC; *JAPM*, 2:1760–63).

## To Mary Rozet Smith

*On 9 August 1895, George Pucik,[1] a new patient at the Cook County Hospital for the Insane, referred to as Dunning and located at Dunning, Ill.,[2] died as a result of treatment he received from two hospital attendants.[3]*

*At that time, and at the direction of Daniel D. Healy,[4] head of the Cook County Board of Commissioners, members of the hospital staff were examined for employment in the civil service system being instituted in Cook County. Employees of the hospital who held their positions because of their political connections hoped to keep their jobs under this new system. Although all of the commissioners were members of the Republican Party, patronage employees associated with some of the commissioners who had been in power previously had been ousted from their positions by the protégées of the new power bloc on the commission headed by Healy. Five members of the Cook County Board of Commissioners called for an investigation of conditions at the facility.[5] To keep control of the investigation, Commissioner Healy, appointed all of the members of the board to the investigating committee and added seven citizens representing community organizations.[6] Jane Addams agreed to serve as one of the community members. Her brother John Weber Addams was often confined to a state insane asylum,[7] giving her an empathy for the mentally ill, and Julia Lathrop encouraged her to serve. The investigations took place during the last two weeks of August and into early September 1895.*

*At the start, the* Chicago Daily Tribune *labeled the committee "unwieldy" in its size and "heterogenous," yet contended that the "people" who wanted "abuses corrected" had "confidence" in at least two of the committee members, Jane Addams and Lucy Flower.[8] "There are charges of murder, of violent abuse, of boodling, of maladministration at the asylum," the newspaper pronounced, that were to be investigated by the whole committee, with "special committees to investigate the present condition of patients as to physical injuries and specific charges of mismanagement of any kind."[9]*

*During the investigation, Jane Addams served as the committee's secretary and on two subcommittees of the committee of the whole. These committees were charged with investigating the condition of inmates in the women's wards and reporting on the education of children in the poorhouse. Jane visited all of the wards at Dunning on behalf of the subcommittees of the committee. Her reports to the full committee indicated that the 559 female patients she saw were generally in good condition, that boys should be removed from the ward of the older male patients to a ward of their own, and that all fifty-five children she saw should be evaluated and when possible placed in foster homes outside the institution. In fact, the members of the committee of the whole found no brutality, but also decided that "there is a degree of harshness exhibited toward patients, especially in the men's wards," and that there were "more accidents and injuries than ought to occur."[10] When the full committee chose not to include the recommendations of Lucy Flower, especially related to food and clothing, Jane Addams and Lucy Flower decided to offer a minority report. The committee of the whole led by Commissioner Healy and Dr. Harold N. Moyer voted not to include the minority report with their final report. In response, Jane Addams and Lucy Flower made their report available to Chicago newspapers.*

*Among their findings reported in the* Chicago Record *were that the hospital suffered from no continuity of oversight, since the governing body, the Cook County Board of Commissioners, changed annually. There was inadequate and untrained service for inmates because of the frequent changes in personnel, "'their employment and dismissal largely on political lines . . . what words can freely express the utter demoralization that must follow a system of patronage that apportions the various appointments by lot among the different members of the county board!'" Jane Addams and Lucy Flower found the medical service was "'entirely inadequate.'" They recommended a trained medical director with authority to direct all medical care and the addition of two physicians. All physicians and all attendants and their training were to be under the control of the medical director. "'We are strongly impressed with the fact that ability to conduct a ward primary is the worst possible recommendation for an asylum attendant.'"[11] The two women and many Chicago newspapers labeled the investigation's outcome a whitewash. Jane Addams pointed out that "'such an investigation'" of "'daily conditions . . . can have little value'" when the institution to be investigated is "'forewarned.'"[12] Jane Addams had gotten caught up in a political struggle between the so-called "honest" commissioners and the "boodlers" who wanted to control the outcome of the investigation and maintain the option of employment at the hospital for patronage positions, and the "boodlers" had won. The report of the committee of the whole indicated "no evidences of systematic cruelty"[13] but cited irregularities in food purchase and preparation and did not deal with the larger administrative issues that Addams and Flower identified. The official report "'earnestly recommends' the recognition of the civil-service law," revealed a committee "impressed with the 'vicious system' by which the insane asylum was conducted," yet held "no one responsible for the abuses which crept in under it."[14] Here was more evidence for Jane Addams that the civil service law that went into effect in Illinois on 1 July 1895 was sorely needed.*

HH [Chicago, Ill.] Sept 4"[, 5, and 6,] 1895

My dear friend

We have had two "prophets" sojourning with us for a week[.] Mr Woods[15] & Mr Herron[16] were quite remarkable in their effect upon each other and the household. Helen Campbell[17] and Mrs. Stetson were here at the same time and but for the fact that I was at Dunning for days & nights during the sojourn, I found it most edifying. Mr Herron has a most charming personality, a deep religious life which one feels all the time one is near him. He is coming often, he says, and I hope you will know him. I still think that his denunciation is a mistake — Keir Hardie[18] was here yesterday, he and Mr Smith[19] his friend, are going on to California, but you will probably be here when they come back, so that you will meet them then, he too has a religious message in spite of all the remarks of the Chicago press. I am sorry that Tolstoi gives you such a hard time with your principles, I had an awful time the two years before I came to H-H.[20] I do not like it now when my farmer pays his rent but—I do not believe that Tolstoi's position is tenable, a man cannot be a Xtain by himself.[21]

I have been distressed over the big pillars but they look smaller each day as the building is higher & altho they will always look rather larger, they are well proportioned & the building as a whole is really fine![22]

It is such a satisfaction to have one building all of red brick and goodly to look upon!

The Kindergarten started last Monday and the singing wafts into the octagon now, Miss Paine[23] comes two afternoons a week to meet the students of which there seems to be a goodly number. I am very hopeful of all the new plans. As soon as you get back we are going to have a lunch ~~of~~ with Dr Parker[24] & other residents to discuss the opening we have before us. I go to Denver to speak Sunday evening Sept 15",[25] I also have an engagement in Kansas City Sept 17"[26] but I refused almost any thing for Sept. & Oct. as I am very anxious to get affairs into shape for the winter.

We have had a fearful time with the "Unemployed" all summer, the "Relief & Aid," the "United Hebrew Charites", & all the "offices" of the Central Relief has been closed up, so that pitiful cases have come to us from all over town. Miss Gernon[27] is a fine visitor & it has been done with some care but at fearful cost. I have collected about one hundred dollars <since I came from Rockford>[28] but we are still almost two hundred dollars behind. I don't know what to do, there seemed to be nothing between what we do now and Miss Gernon's absolute repression.

I am glad your father enjoyed the Pullman,[29] I will be glad to have you keep the copy. Bro. Woods after inciting me to elaborate it, rather went back on it after it was finished. I read it one day at The Commons[30] where it certainly excited great interest—and I think that I will publish it, it is certainly a candid opinion.

I am so glad that you are all coming back so soon. I delayed asking Mr & Mrs. Smith to dine waiting to get hold of someone interesting to meet them & when Dr Bruce[31] turned up Mrs Smith had gone to Wisconsin.

I am awfully sorry, it was mostly the Dunning investigation which cut out ten days from my ordinary existence.

With love to your family always from

Jane Addams.

Please excuse this paper & this pencil. I began the other evening when it was twilight. I am finishing this on my birthday, thirty five is pretty aged!

ALS (SCPC, JAC; *JAPM*, 2:1754–59).

1. George Pucik entered the hospital 8 Aug. 1895 and was uninjured when he arrived at Dunning. He made "no violent manifestations" while being examined by the newly appointed Dr. Frederick Abner McGrew, official physician for the male wards. At Pucik's death, McGrew was called to examine his body and reported, "I believe that Pucik had been killed by the attendants," one of whom struck him and kicked him while he was down. And he added, "I knew both attendants well. I did not trust either of them. On my judgment as a physician I would have discharged both of them long ago if I had had the power to do so. They were not fit men to be attendants" ("What a Patient Saw"). McGrew (b. 1866), a graduate of Rush Medical College (1893), had just been appointed head physician at Dunning, a position he resigned in Jan. 1896. By 1901 he and his wife were living in La Porte, Ind., where he earned a reputation as a fine surgeon.

2. In 1851 Cook Co. selected a site seventeen miles northwest of the Chicago city center to create a poor farm. By 1870 when an asylum for the insane was added, the complex was referred to as Dunning for the name of the town that Andrew Dunning had created near the facility after the Civil War. The institution continued to operate under Cook Co. control until 1912, when the state of Illinois purchased it and it became the Chicago State Hospital. By the end of the twentieth century, the hospital was closed and the property acquired by the Chicago-Read Mental Health Center.

3. George ("Goff") Gough, who had been employed at Dunning for four months by 14 Aug. 1895, and John P. Anderson, who had been employed at the hospital from 1 July 1895, had been identified as the attendants who struck and killed the patient. At first, Anderson confessed, but later both men declared their innocence. The *Chicago Daily Tribune* reported that Dr. Frederick A. McGrew had recently seen "Anderson in one of the wards just as he struck a patient in the face, knocked him down and kicked him" ("Anderson and Gough Proven Unfit for Attendants").

4. Daniel D. Healy (1847–1910), born in Co. Kerry, Ireland, was a politician and coal dealer in Chicago. Educated at St. Mary's on the Lake and public schools in Cook Co., he began his working life as an engineer in the Chicago Fire Dept., 1871–82, and began serving the Assn. of Paid Fire Dept. as its president and director. He then rose as bailiff of the Circuit Court of Cook Co., 1882–86; comptroller of Cook Co., 1886–94; and president of the Cook County Board of Commissioners, 1894–98. During 1899–1900, he served as superintendent of public services for the county, and between 1900 and 1902 he was warden of the Cook County Hospital. In 1902 he formed D. D. Healy and Co., dealers in coal.

5. Commissioners Kunstman, John Ritter, Theodore W. Jones, Charles Burmeister, and Henry J. Beer demanded the investigation. The *Chicago Times-Herald* reported that Commissioner Gustav W. Kunstman "regards the staffs as composed of people unfit for the positions, through either incompetency or drunkenness. There are no rules which may not be broken, and for years, he says, the sole reason for appointment has been the politics of the appointee" ("Grand Jury the Only Remedy"). Commissioner Ritter added: "'If ever there was a hell hole, it is at Dunning. That place is a disgrace to our county'" ("Dunning a County Disgrace"). In the same edition of the same newspaper, Commissioner Healy was reported to have discovered on a visit to Dunning that "Drunkenness and lack of discipline were making Dunning insane asylum a scandal. . . . Employees would not work and tried to do little else but draw their salaries, and then spend them in the saloons catering specially to the attendants at the county institution. . . . He learned of many disgraceful episodes and many drunken orgies, due entirely to the utter lack of proper discipline" ("President Healy's Statement").

6. According to the 31 Aug. 1895 *Chicago Daily Tribune*, besides Daniel D. Healy the members of the investigating committee of the whole were as follows: Commissioners John A. Linn, Thomas J. McNichols, Louis H. Mack, David Martin, James M. Munn, George D. Unold, Henry J. Beer, Theodore W. Jones, John Ritter, George Struckman, Gustav W. Kunstman, John N. Cunning, Charles Burmeister, and public members Dr. Harold N. Moyer,

Dr. Florence Hunt, Mrs. Lucy Flower, Thomas J. Elderkin, Dr. Frank N. Lawther, Mrs. Kate Bradley, Thomas N. Johnson, and JA.

7. For information on JWA's stays in state insane asylums, see *PJA*, 1:479–83.

8. Lucy Louisa Coues Flower (1837–1921) was an orphan, probably born in the Boston area. She was adopted by Samuel Elliot Coues and his second wife, Charlotte Haven Ladd Coues, and received her schooling primarily in Portsmouth, N.H. For a short time before she moved to Madison, Wis., in 1859, she worked in the U.S. Patent Office. In Madison she taught high school students and, between 1862 and 1863, operated her own private school. In 1862 she married James Monroe Flower, a young Madison attorney. Before the couple moved to Chicago in 1873, they had three children.

Lucy Flower became active in civic enterprise in Chicago primarily to help children and the working poor. From serving on the charity committee of St. James Episcopal Church, she branched out to become a member of the board of the Half-Orphan Asylum and the Home for the Friendless. During the late 1880s, she was a founder of the Chicago Protective Agency for Women and Children and the Lake Geneva Fresh-Air Assn. An active and dedicated member of the CWC from 1883, she served the club as its president, 1890–91. From 1891 until 1894, she was the first woman to be appointed to the Chicago Board of Education, and by 1896 she had become the first woman to win elective office in Illinois when she won a seat on the Board of Trustees of the Univ. of Illinois. She was instrumental, along with other Chicago women, in founding the Illinois Training School for Nurses in 1880 and served that board as a member for twenty-eight years, eleven of which she was president. Flower and JA worked on several reform projects together. The Dunning investigation was one, and founding the juvenile court for Cook Co. was another. In 1902 Flower and her husband moved to Coronado, Calif., where he died in 1909. She continued to live there until her death.

9. "The Dunning Investigation."

10. "Harshness Was Used."

11. JA and Lucy Flower, "Report of the Sub-Committee," in "Harshness Was Used."

12. JA, "Report," in "D. D. Healy as a Czar."

13. "The Two Reports from Dunning."

14. "Whitewashed."

15. For Woods's comments on his visit, see Robert A. Woods to JA, 4 Sept. 1895, above. Woods had been staying at HH and like JA, participating in the Chicago Commons School of Social Economics, 22–29 Aug. 1895.

16. George D. Herron (1862–1925), clergyman, writer, Christian Socialist, and lecturer, was visiting Chicago to speak at the Chicago Commons School of Social Economics on 23 Aug. 1895, in a speech titled "Sociality of Religion." Herron was born in Montezuma, Ind., the son of Isabella David and William Herron. After being apprenticed to a printer, he enrolled at Ripon College, Wis. In 1883 he married Mary Everhard, with whom he eventually had five children. About the same time, he also became a Congregationalist minister. Before moving to a church in Burlington, Iowa, he served a congregation in Lake City, Minn., 1890–91, where he established his reputation as an outspoken enemy of the wealthy and their excesses. Mrs. Elizabeth D. Rand was impressed by his message and his determination and eloquence. She endowed a new chair in "applied Christianity" for him at Iowa College (later Grinnell), beginning in 1893. At the same time, Mrs. Rand's daughter, Carrie Rand, became dean of women at the school. Despite the fact that he was married, Herron and Carrie Rand became lovers, and Herron left his wife. His outspoken socialistic views and his illicit love affair gave his enemies an opportunity to force him to resign his teaching position. In 1901 his wife, Mary Everhard Herron, divorced him and in the settlement received Carrie Rand's personal fortune of sixty thousand dollars as restitution. After Herron wed Carrie Rand in May 1901, he was expelled from the Congregational Church ministry, and shortly after that the couple, who had two children of their own, escaped to Italy. By 1895, when Herron visited HH, rumblings

about his personal life, his political position as a socialist, and his philosophical arguments on the need for the wealthy to share with the poor were probably known to JA.

JA was aware of Herron's leadership in the social gospel movement as well as his continuing commitment to consolidate various socialist groups throughout the United States. He participated in the merger of the Socialist Labor Party and Chicago's Social Democratic Party into the Socialist Party of America, which finally took place during the summer of 1901. When Mrs. Rand died in 1905, Herron and his wife were made trustees of a fund, established with two hundred thousand dollars, to promote socialist education and the Rand School of Social Science was born.

When Carrie Herron died in 1914 on the eve of World War I, George Herron, a pacifist, socialist, and internationalist, moved to Geneva, Switzerland. He supported the Allied cause by passing them information that he gleaned because of his respected position among European academics and leaders. Although he was disappointed with the 1919 Paris Peace Conf. and the Treaty of Versailles, he supported Woodrow Wilson and his position and the treaty, even though he found it inadequate.

He was an exciting and able speaker and gave numerous addresses in support of his positions. He also wrote a great many books between 1891 and 1922. By the time he visited HH, Thomas Y. Crowell had published *A Plea for the Gospel* (1892), *The New Redemption: A Call to the Church to Reconstruct Society according to the Gospel of Christ* (1893), and *The Christian State: A Political Vision of Christ—a Course of Six Lectures Delivered in Churches in Various American Cities* (1895).

17. Helen Stuart Campbell became a close friend of Charlotte Perkins Stetson Gilman while the two shared editorial duties for the West Coast Press Assn.'s publication. They came to Chicago together in Aug. 1895, and Campbell served from Nov. 1895 until June 1896 as the first head resident of Unity House (later Eli Bates House), located at 621 Elm St. and an outgrowth of an industrial school for girls, begun in 1876. Mrs. Campbell was born in Lockport, N.Y., the daughter of New York attorney Homer H. Stuart and his wife, Jane E. Campbell Stuart. She was educated in public and private schools and near the opening of the Civil War wed Grenville Mellen Weeks, a physician who served until 1871 in the U.S. Army. They eventually divorced during the 1870s. She began her career as a writer of children's stories and novels in 1862 and by the late 1870s was participating in the fledgling home economics movement. In 1878 she taught cooking in the Raleigh (N.C.) Cooking School and wrote a textbook, *The Easiest Way in House-Keeping and Cooking* (1881); helped found a mission cooking school in Washington, D.C.; and was an organizer of the National Household Economics Assn., 1893.

During the 1880s, she published a series of books and articles, primarily about the plight of the working poor. Among them were *The Problem of the Poor: A Record of Quiet Work in Unquiet Places* (1882) and *Prisoners of Poverty: Women Wage-Workers, Their Trades and Their Lives* (1889). In 1891 her "Women Wage-Earners" article received an award from the American Economic Assn. and brought her to the attention of Richard T. Ely at the Univ. of Wisconsin, with whom she studied for a year. In 1893 Ely wrote a foreword for her book *Women Wage Earners*. In the following year, she presented two course offerings at the Univ. of Wisconsin: Women Wage-Earning and Domestic Science. With the publication of her *Household Economics: A Course of Lectures in the School of Economics at the Univ. of Wisconsin* in 1897, she was appointed professor of home economics at Kansas State Agricultural College. She resigned in Mar. 1898 to resume her career as a writer and lecturer. During the early years of the 1900s, she was once again reconnected with Charlotte Perkins Gilman in New York. She was also converted to the Baha'i religion. Campbell lived the last six years of her life in Boston, where she died.

18. James Keir Hardie (1856–1915), Scottish born, self-educated, mineworker, labor leader, and socialist, became the first Labour member of Parliament as the representative from West Ham South and served from 1892 until he was defeated in 1895. In 1900 Hardie organized

a meeting of trade unions and socialist groups to form the Labour Representation Com., which became the Labour Party in Great Britain in 1906. The same year, Hardie was once again elected to Parliament from Merthyr Tydfil and Aberdare in the South Wales Valleys, a position he held until his death. In 1908 he resigned as leader of the Labour Party and spent the remainder of his life supporting pacifism, woman suffrage, self-rule for India, and an unsegregated South Africa.

In 1895 he and socialist and newspaper editor Frank Smith (see n. 19), made a speaking tour of the United States. Hardie's visit to Chicago, shortly after he had been defeated for Parliament, was occasioned by an invitation to speak before the Chicago Labor Congress. Henry D. Lloyd, who met with Hardie in New York and invited him to be a guest in his home during his Chicago stay, encouraged him to visit JA and HH. Hardie spoke at HH on 8 Sept. and lunched with JA and the residents while he was visiting the settlement neighborhood. He returned the favor when JA and MRS were in London in 1896. See JA to Gertrude Barnum, 22 May[June] 1896, n. 4, below.

19. Frank Smith (1854–1940), who was Keir Hardie's traveling companion on this visit to the United States, was a Christian socialist. He was a British newspaper editor, politician, and early activist in the Salvation Army. After helping organize the Salvation Army movement in the United States, he returned to England to write, with Salvation Army founder and leader William Booth, *In Darkest England and the Way Out* (1890). Smith became a founding member of the Independent Labour Party and helped publish the socialist newspaper *Labour Leader*. Smith also became a leader on the London County Council, where he served from the early 1890s until 1913. He stood for Parliament as a Labour Party member eleven times before he was finally elected in 1929, but he served only until 1931.

20. Surviving documents from the two years before JA founded HH reveal little of the inner turmoil she refers to here. For extant evidence that survives, see *PJA*, 2.

21. JA's fascination with Tolstoy and his teachings continued throughout her life. Her interest peaked during 1896 when she had an opportunity to visit him at his home in Russia and especially during 1897 as she tried to explain her experience to a wide audience in the United States. See JA to Gertrude Barnum, 25 July 1896, n. 23, below.

22. See JA to MRS, 8 Aug. 1895, above.

23. Bertha Payne (Newell) (1867–1953) taught at the Kindergarten Training School of the Chicago Froebel Assn., the organization that was holding training classes with the HH Kindergarten. During the fall of 1895, she taught weaving at HH. By 1896, when the Froebel Assn. planned to move its teaching program to HH, Payne was teaching classes on Wednesdays and Thursdays at HH in occupations, nature study, and games. She continued to teach at HH until the summer of 1898. In 1899 Col. Francis Parker selected her to direct the kindergarten for the "slum school" that he and Anita McCormick Blaine had planned to open for children of the poor, but was never developed (see n. 24) (see also JA to MRS, 22 June 1899, nn. 11–12, below). Bertha Payne eventually married and moved to North Carolina, where she died.

24. Col. Francis Wayland Parker (1837–1902), son of Robert and Mille Rand Parker, was born in Bedford, N.H., and grew up on a farm and attended local schools in New Hampshire. He began teaching school there when he was sixteen years old. At the age of twenty-two, he served as principal of a school in Carrolton, Ill. During the Civil War, Parker joined the 4th Regiment of the New Hampshire Volunteers as a private and was mustered out in 1865 as a lieutenant-colonel. He returned to teaching after the war. He became principal of a grammar school in Manchester, N.Y., and in 1868 moved to the Normal School in Dayton, Ohio. Between 1872 and 1875, he attended King William's Univ. in Berlin, Germany, and began to develop his ideas about educating the whole person. He favored new methods of pedagogy and was one of the fathers of progressive education. Between 1875 and 1880, he served as superintendent of schools for Quincy, Mass., where he successfully tried out some of his

progressive ideas. After a stint as supervisor of schools for Boston, 1880–83, he moved to Chicago to head up the Cook County Normal School. He served until 1896, when he became principal of the Chicago Normal School.

While in Chicago, his ideas about child-centered education came to the attention of wealthy Chicago widow Anita McCormick Blaine (see JA to Anita McCormick Blaine, 11 Dec. 1895, n. 2, below)), daughter of Cyrus Hall and Nettie Fowler McCormick, who became fascinated by the educational ideas and process that Parker promoted. She encouraged him to begin his own training school with laboratory schools that she agreed to support financially on a massive scale. "[T]here will have to be a teacher training school with a practice school attached to it on the North Side, as well as a slum school in the tenement district which would 'show what education may do for poor children.'" And he continued, "It must have 'an assembly hall for the people, parents, lectures, lessons that may unite home and school,' and a place for social gatherings 'like Hull House.' Second, he said, there must be 'manual training, the moving center of education, handwork and artwork, cooking, sewing, housekeeping—all correlated with the other teaching.' Third, a kindergarten 'to take the children early from the streets and make a little heaven for them.' Fourth, a playground, green grass, a few flowers. Fifth, gymnasium and bathrooms. Six, classrooms. Seventh, a library for 'sweet, good literature.' Above all, 'the very best teachers'" (Harrison, *Timeless Affair*, 89–90). The outcome was the Francis Parker School on Chicago's North Side, founded in 1901, and the Chicago Institute, created in 1899 and open for students in the fall of 1900, where he was principal and which by 1901 was folded into the Univ. of Chicago to establish its School of Education. The "slum school," which may have been planned for a site on Chicago's Milwaukee Ave., was never funded or established (see also JA to MRS, 22 June 1899, nn. 11–12, below). Parker published five books on education, including *Talks on Pedagogies* (1894). He died at Pass Christian, Miss., where he had gone to recover from poor health.

25. JA was scheduled to speak on Sunday evening, 15 Sept. 1895, at the annual congress of the National Prison Assn. of the United States, meeting in Denver, 14–18 Sept. 1895. Her subject title was to be "Methods for the Prevention of Crime." No text for a speech by that title has been located in the Addams papers.

26. JA was unable to speak in Kansas City. See AHHA to HWH and EGS to JWA, 13 Sept. 1895, below.

27. Maud Gernon (Yeomans) (1864–1920), the daughter of Mary Ellen Sargeant and George Gernon, was born in New York and attended the Univ. of Wisconsin as a special advanced student, 1887–88. By 1895 she was a HH resident and a "visitor" for the newly created Chicago Bureau of Charities, while she also helped operate the HH Relief Bureau. The *HH Bulletin* announced in Oct. 1897 that the Relief Bureau at the settlement had been closed and that all inquiries were to be made at the West District Office of the Chicago Bureau of Charities, located at 181 West Madison St. She was also the director of the Drexel Club (disbanded Dec. 1902 because many of its members had married and had different interests), composed of young men and women organized for social and educational purposes. During the summers of 1896 and 1897, she helped place mothers and children in a variety of weeklong camps in the country available to HH neighbors. JA reported that in 1896: "Ninety-five persons went from Hull-House to the Lake Geneva Holiday House during the summer. Fourteen children went to Darien, Wis.; twelve to Fox Lake, Wis.; eleven to Blue Island, Ill.; and ten others were the guests of Mr. Weaver of Lake Forest" (*HH Bulletin* 1, no. 5 [15 Oct. 1896]: 5). In Apr. 1898, in the midst of the settlement's effort to defeat Alderman John Powers, Gernon took a six-month leave to travel to Europe. She seemed to be a pivotal leader in preparing and distributing literature for the HH candidate. Resident Alice Hamilton pronounced: "What we are to do nobody knows" (Alice Hamilton to Agnes Hamilton, 3 Apr. 1898 in Sicherman, *Alice Hamilton*, 121). Despite Gernon's leave,

she remained identified as a HH resident, and in the fall of 1899 she became director of the social clubs at HH, a position she held until 1907.

During the summer of 1902, Maud Gernon was one of the HH residents who helped carry out a special neighborhood investigation. The following was reported in the *HH Bulletin* 5 (Semi-Annual, 1902): 14–15: "Hull-House was the center of the typhoid fever epidemic of the past summer. The nineteenth ward, with only one thirty-sixth of the population of the city within its limits, had between one-sixth and one-seventh of all the deaths from this disease. As the water supply to this part of the city is the same as that for all the region between Lake and 47th Sts., Canal St. and Western Ave., it seemed probable that there were some local conditions which accounted for the concentration of the typhoid fever in this particular region. In order to discover what these conditions were, a careful investigation of the drainage and sewage disposal was made by Miss [Gertrude] Howe and Miss Gernon, who found that the number of typhoid cases was largest in those streets in which was the smallest amount of modern plumbing. As this discovery suggested the possibility of the infection having been conveyed by means of flies which had crawled, first upon typhoid discharges and then upon eatables in the houses and shops, a bacteriological examination was made of the flies, caught in adjacent yards and rooms of typhoid patients. The examination was made by Miss [Alice] Hamilton in the laboratory of the Memorial Institute for Infectious Diseases. . . . A detailed report of this examination and of the conditions in the neighborhood has been published." In 1902–3, Maud Gernon also began serving as secretary for the HH Dramatic Assn., an activity she continued until she left the settlement. She was also the president of the Seeley Club of young women that met once a week for social interaction. From 1902 until 1904, a club of young people called themselves the Gernon Club in her honor.

On 1 May 1907, Maud Gernon married Charles Yeomans (1877–1959), who became a HH resident in 1902. He was an active participant in the HH Dramatic Assn., gave vocal music performances, and became the director of the Hiawatha Glee and Dramatic Club during 1903–4. After Maud and Charles were married, he became involved in his family's pump manufacturing business as the secretary-treasurer. Maud Gernon Yeomans died in Chicago.

28. JA helped conduct the fourth HH Summer School. It was held at RC, 29 June to 31 July 1895.

29. JA's letter of 17 Aug. 1895 to MRS revealed that she shared the essay she wrote about the Pullman Palace Car strike of 1894 with Charles Mather Smith (see Testimony, 18 Aug. 1894, n. 21, above).

30. JA may have shared her Pullman paper with people attending the Chicago Commons social settlement School of Social Economics, held in Aug. 1895.

31. Andrew Alexander Bruce.

## Anna Hostetter Haldeman Addams to Henry Winfield Haldeman and Ellen Gates Starr to John Weber Addams

*"Jane is in bed, & threatened with what two doctors think is typhoid, & one thinks appendicitis," Ellen Gates Starr wrote to Alice Haldeman on 10 September 1895. "Dr. Holmes[1] and Dr. Stahmen (if that is the way to spell it)[2] have decided on the operation for appendicitis, & it is to be performed this* P.M.*"[3] Alice Haldeman came to Chicago immediately to help with nursing. Newspapers in Chicago and in the*

*eastern United States informed their readers that Jane Addams was ill.*[4] *Ellen Gates Starr also wrote to Weber to inform him about Jane's condition, but only after the appendectomy was completed successfully. She did not write to Anna Addams, who was more miffed at receiving the information second hand through her stepson, Weber, than concerned about the condition of her stepdaughter. Anna Addams copied the letter Ellen Starr wrote to Weber and sent it to her son Henry Haldeman.*

Cedarville, [Ill.] Sept 13enth 1895

My Dear Son Harry

Will copy a letter that Weber gave me to read from Miss Star (verbatum)

Chicago "Sept 11enth 1895[.]"

"Dear Mr Addams, I am attending to Jane's cares this morning, as she is ill. She was worn-out with the long investigation at —— hospital (or poor house),[5] the heat and the weariness of committies. Her old ~~trouble of the~~ intestine ~~trouble~~ weakness culminated in appendicitis for which as you perhaps know an operation is necessary, which if taken in time is comparitively simple. It was taken in time and every thing is going well.[6] Dr Holme's nurse stayed last night and Miss Fryer,[7] the dear little nurse who has lived with us ~~so long~~ is coming in to take care of her to day. Dr. Holmes did the operation Dr Haterman[8] of the Presbyterian hospital assisting. Dr. Holmes thinks two weeks will see her out of her room. Dr H. thought it safer not to move her and it was done here. I will write you again very soon. With love to Mrs Addams and Sadie Very Sincerely Yours

Ellen G. Starr"

Dear Harry[:] Weber gave me the letter this morning which I have written you word for word. Tis only the beginning of the end that, you have long prophicied any-selfish ind. no matter how it takes the form of an "angle of light" meets its down fall—surely it was no fault of ours if they saw the wind and reap the whirl-wind. I am so broken in health and spirits all for want of a little help that was my due—for the help and love I gave when they were young—and I could extend my powers and put my whole mind into their interests—all to be spurned—and neglected in old age. If only you and George can bury me quietly and no hypocritical hands laid upon me, I will feel that all is well. . . .[9] [A]nd hope you will come the 23rd as you promised; what do you hear of Alice and Marcet I hope they will get home safely and keep well, and be kinder and happier for the long summer indulgence of their caprices away from home Your loving Mother always and aye

Anna H H Addams[10]

ALS with HLSr copy embedded (IU, Lilly, SAAH; *JAPM*, 2:1769–70).

1. JA's friend and settlement supporter Dr. Bayard Taylor Holmes.

2. EGS did not spell the name correctly. In 1892 Dr. Henry B. Stehman (1852–1918) became the clinical professor of obstetrics at Rush School of Medicine. He also served for fifteen years as the medical superintendent and financial secretary for Presbyterian Hospital, which had been organized in 1883. He resigned in 1900 due to poor health and moved to Pasadena, Calif., where he died.

3. IU, Lilly, SAAH; *JAPM*, 2:1764, 1770.

4. As evidence of JA's growing public stature, newspapers in Dayton, Ohio; Poughkeepsie, N.Y.; Boston; Buffalo, N. Y.; and Rockford, Ill., reported her illness. In Chicago the *Journal, Chronicle, Dispatch, Times-Herald,* and *Daily Tribune* all carried stories about her condition.

5. The long blank line in AHHA's version of the letter was likely the word *Dunning* in EGS's missive. AHHA may have been unable to decipher it.

6. The surgery was performed at HH. "Dr. Holmes operates, Dr. Stahmen, Dr. Stevenson & Dr. Rice are present, & a trained nurse. Dr. H— thinks there will be very little surgical nursing necessary but she will have to stay in bed about two weeks" (EGS to SAAH, 10 Sept. 1895, IU, Lilly, SAAH; *JAPM*, 2:1770).

Dr. Stevenson was Sarah Ann Hackett Stevenson (1841–1909), who was an early supporter of JA and HH. Born in Buffalo Grove (later Polo), Ill., she was educated at Mt. Carroll Seminary and the State Normal School, Normal, Ill.; taught school for a time; and then actively sought medical education in both the Woman's Hospital Medical College of Chicago, from which she graduated in 1874, and in London. She entered private practice in Chicago in 1875 and with the help of male mentors became the first woman member of the American Medical Assn., 1876, and active long before other women were admitted in 1915. She became a faculty member and chair of physiology at her alma mater in 1875, joined the staff of Chicago's Cook County Hospital in 1881, and was the first woman appointed to the Illinois State Board of Health in 1893. A consulting physician at Woman's and Provident hospitals in Chicago and at Bellevue Hospital in Batavia, Ill., and an attending physician at the Mary Thompson Hospital, she was also one of the founders of the Illinois Training School for Nurses, which opened in 1881, with Stevenson on the board and a member of the faculty.

Stevenson became active in the WCTU in 1881 and was soon appointed the first superintendent of the WCTU's department of hygiene. With the founding of the Frances E. Willard National Temperance Hospital in 1886, she became president of the medical staff. During 1893 she was a leader in the World's Columbian Exposition as co-convener of the Medical and Surgery Congress, vice-president of the Congress of Medico-Climatology, and the creator of a woman's hospital at the exposition. Joining the CWC in 1877, she became president of the organization, 1892–94. She worked with the Chicago Municipal Order to create public baths in Chicago and with the CWC and HH to found a lodging house for women near HH. She was also responsible for nominating and promoting the first African American woman for membership in the CWC in 1894. Stevenson wrote two successful high school texts: *Boys and Girls in Biology* (1875) and *The Physiology of Women* (1881). Stevenson ceased practicing medicine in 1903 after suffering a stroke. She died, a Methodist turned Catholic, in St. Elizabeth's Hospital and was buried in St. Boniface Cemetery, Chicago.

7. Anna ("Annie") Fryar (1867–1922), born in Banbridge, Coventry Down, Ireland, became Mrs. Dr. Edward Buel Hutchinson (1867–1951) in a HH wedding 12 Oct. 1895. JA was in her room at HH recovering from surgery and unable to attend the festivities. EGS reported to SAAH on 10 Oct. [1895] that "Miss Fryar, even is getting excited over it. She is too dear about her things. She loves them all so much, & thinks people are so unexpectedly good to her. Mr. Murray, our policeman, sent her a large piece of peat, tied up in a green ribbon, which quite won her heart. Mr. Murray is a man of sentiment. I think the desk heads the list of her affections" (IU, Lilly, SAAH, *JAPM*, 2:1782–83). The *HH Bulletin* of Apr. 1897 announced the birth of a daughter for the Hutchinsons. Annie Fryar, like Wilfreda Brockway,

was a graduate of St. Luke's Hospital School of Nursing, and by fall of 1894 she represented the Visiting Nurse Assn. of Chicago in the southwest district of the city while living at HH. In 1902 Annie Hutchinson was elected president of the Illinois State Graduate Nurses' Assn. and worked for Illinois legislation to require state examinations and registration for nurses. The Hutchinsons had three children. Annie died in Chicago and was buried in Madison, Wis. Dr. Hutchinson practiced medicine in the Univ. of Chicago neighborhoods until 1934, when he retired to Arizona, where he died.

8. AHHA apparently had difficulty reading EGS's handwriting. The physician's name was Stehman rather than Haterman.

9. The editors have omitted the midportion of the letter in which AHHA reports that the heat is so severe that GBH did not leave his bed except to have it made. She also recalled that 9 Sept. was the forty-eighth anniversary of her marriage to HWH and GBH's father, indicated that she was ready to die, and scolded HWH for not writing often enough.

10. Perpendicular to the main text and in the left margin of the second page of her letter, AHHA wrote: "No message to me you notice."

## To Anita McCormick Blaine

*Although Jane Addams had planned to launch "a comprehensive fellowship <scheme>" with the development of Hull-House, she was eventually "obliged to abandon" it. She reported to Henry Carter Adams at the University of Michigan, "It is extremely difficult to secure money for fellowships unless it is done through friends of the individual."[1] Yet she was willing to try when there was a special reform need. By 20 December 1895, she had a positive response from Anita McCormick Blaine.[2]*

Hull House, 335 South Halsted Street. Chicago, Ill. Dec. 11th, 1895.

My dear Mrs. Blaine:—

I had a long conversation with Dr. Thos Hall[3] last week in regard to a phase of the neighborhood life concerning which we are constantly becoming more anxious.

He suggested my writing to you in regard to it, feeling quite sure you would be interested in it, and that you might possibly be able to help us.

We have never had anything which might be called direct "rescue work"[4] in connection with Hull-House, although we are constantly getting hold of young girls who are beginning to go the wrong way, and making an endeavor to substitute simple pleasures and a safer social life for the questionable ones. This fall quite a number of peculiar and atrocious cases have come under our notice, which might have been prevented if some one person had been able to give her full time to it, and had known more about the workings of the two neighboring Police Stations. We hope very much to have a resident detailed solely to this sort of work, who shall go two days a week to the Maxwell St and the Desplaines St. Station, who shall put herself in connection with all the Refuges and Anchorages of the city, and keep her evenings free to attend the balls and parties of the neighborhood where much of the "procuring" is done. Miss Anne Withington,[5] who has worked at the House more or less, and who at one time had charge of the Model Lodging House,[6] which has been established near us, I am quite sure could do this work exceptionally well. She is a girl of rather unusual advantages, who has travelled and seen enough of different sorts of people to make her judgment lenient and at the same time penetrating, and who has an unfailing spring of sympathy. Perhaps her distinguishing trait is her ability of interpretation. She is obliged to be self-supporting, and could not possibly give her time for less than $50.00 a month. It would cost her about $25.00 a month to live at the house, and as her mother is partially dependent upon her, she could not come for less.

Several people,—Mrs. Coonley, Mrs. Wilmarth, Miss Mary Rozet Smith, and Miss Colvin,— pay sums of $50.00 a month, which are known as fellowships.[7] The person receiving these sums devotes herself to a special sort of work and reports to me, of course, but directly to the person giving the money.

Mrs. Hall McCormick[8] has recently established a fellowship of $25.00. The young lady holding it, Miss Brockway, devotes her time to reading to the sick children. She has some income of her own and is able to do it for the sum named, which pays her expenses at the house.

If you would be willing to consider a fellowship, I should be very glad indeed to talk with you further about it, and to assure you of the value I believe such a work would be.

So much of the rescue work of the city is made so unattractive, and stripped so largely of social features, which, in the beginning draw many a lonely girl. I have several theories which I should be glad to work out in conjunction with so sympathetic a person as Miss Withington. Miss Withington is at present in Newburyport, Mass., and I have not yet heard from her definitely as to whether she would accept such a position, but we talked about it a great deal last summer, and she was then very anxious indeed to undertake something of the kind. I do not like to write to her until I have something definite to offer.

If the plan strikes you as in the least feasible or valuable, could you make an appointment, so that I may come and talk it over with you. Dr. Hall said he would be very glad to discuss it with you, if you cared to.

Hoping that I am not presuming on your unfailing kindness to Hull-House, and feeling that the urgency and importance of the matter is my excuse for so long a letter, I am, Yours very sincerely,

Jane Addams.

TLS (SHSW, Blaine; *JAPM*, 2:1820–22).

1. Henry Carter Adams had written to JA, hoping she could provide fellowship support at HH for one of his students. JA recognized that other settlements had fellowship programs associated with nearby universities. She had never tried that kind of arrangement but had "no doubt it would be a valuable thing" (JA to Henry Carter Adams, 28 June 1895, UM, BHL, Mich. HC, Henry Carter Adams; *JAPM*, 2:1714).

2. Anita Eugenie McCormick Blaine (1866–1954), social reformer, philanthropist, and peace activist was born in Manchester, Vt., to Cyrus Hall and Nettie Fowler McCormick. Educated at home and abroad, she also attended the Miss Kirkland's School for Girls in Chicago, from which she graduated in 1884. After making her social debut in 1887, the wealthy young woman, heiress to the McCormick Reaper Manufacturing Co. fortune, wed Emmons Blaine in 1889. Blaine was born in 1857, the son of senator from Maine and presidential candidate James G. Blaine and his wife, Harriet Stanwood Blaine. Two years after their own child, Emmons Jr. (1890–1918), was born, Emmons Blaine died in 1892. A young widow with her son to educate, Anita McCormick began to investigate educational opportunities. She was captivated by the ideas of John Dewey and Col. Francis Parker, both of whom championed child-centered education based on practical experience rather than rote learning. After learning more about Parker's methods at the Chicago Normal School, which she attended briefly, in 1899 she helped him establish the Chicago Institute, Academic and Pedagogic, to train teachers in his methods. It opened in the fall of 1900. She also provided funds to establish two laboratory schools. The one near her home on the North Side became a private school, eventually named for Col. Parker. A free school for poor children or "slum school," in which JA was vitally interested, was never established. With the financial support of Anita Blaine ($750,000 to be matched by the Univ. of Chicago), who had already established a College for Teachers in 1898 at the Univ. of Chicago, the Chicago Institute became the Univ. of Chicago's School of Education in 1901.

Between 1905 and 1907, Blaine served along with JA on the reform-minded Chicago Board of Education. In 1900 she and JA were leaders in organizing the City Homes Assn., focused on investigating tenement conditions in Chicago and working for improvements. She also supported other social reform organizations, including the Consumers' League, Chicago Playground Assn., National Child Labor Com., Chicago School of Civics and Philanthropy, Municipal Voters' League, Chicago's Bureau of Charities and then United Charities, and NWTUL. She often found herself on the board of these organizations, supporting them financially, lobbying for legislation they espoused, or heading up one of their most significant committees. In addition, she also supported individuals who needed her help.

A serious, thoughtful woman who also had to assume family responsibility for her siblings and eventually her mother, she continued to educate herself and to become more active in politics and international affairs. At the time of World War I, she actively supported the idea of world peace and world organization. She joined in the peace movement and supported Woodrow Wilson's plan for a League of Nations, campaigned for the United States' entry into the league, and provided financial support for the League of Nations Assn. She also continued to support President Franklin D. Roosevelt's vice-president, 1940–44, Henry Wallace (1888–1965) as a candidate for president on the Progressive Party ticket beginning in 1948, despite his party's communist connections. At the start of World War II, she favored a declaration of war against the Axis powers. She approved the United Nations idea and gave generously to the American Assn. for the United Nations, and she helped the Nationalist Chinese cause and organized the Foundation for World Government.

During her lifetime, she gave more than ten million dollars to individuals and organizations whose causes she joined. Her will established the New World Foundation Trust with assets of twenty million dollars.

3. JA was referring to Thomas Alonzo Hall (1849–1911), an office-building manager who was born in Richmond, Vt.; educated in public schools in Oberlin, Ohio; and a graduate of Oberlin College (A.B. 1872). Prior to becoming involved in the real estate business in Chicago in 1888, he served in a number of capacities associated with the mining of marble and copper. From 1893 until 1899, he was president of the Hyde Park Protective Assn., and in the late 1890s he also was a member of the morals committee of the Civic Federation of Chicago.

4. HH did not immediately establish a highly visible special program aimed at saving young women; however, JA did create a "social purity" fellowship with the financial support

of Blaine. On 20 Dec. 1895, JA wrote to Anita McCormick Blaine to thank her for agreeing to fund the fellowship. She indicated that Anne Withington had declined to take the position and that she hoped to encourage "Dr. Loomis," who had "spent several weeks at the house, and has had experience in settlement work in New York," to take it. JA hoped to find "the person who can do it best. It is such a delicate experiment, fraught with so many possibilities of failure" (SHSW, Blaine; *JAPM*, 2:1827). JA consulted her friend Julia Plato Harvey, who was then president of the board of the Girls' Industrial School at Geneva, Ill. Mrs. Harvey indicated the school would cooperate with the HH effort and provide a place to stay for the girls who were helped through the HH effort. The settlement residents also continued to work to improve the environment that they saw as contributing to the need for "rescue work."

Dorothea Rhodes Lummis Moore (1860–1942) was born in Chillicothe, Ohio, to Josiah H. and Sarah Crosby Swift Rhodes. When she was sixteen, she became a student at Portsmouth Female College in Ohio and graduated as class salutatorian. She studied music at Mme. Emma Seller's conservatory of music in Philadelphia and at the New England Conservatory of Music in Boston. In 1880 she secretly wed journalist, writer, and editor Charles F. Lummis (1859–1928) and entered medical school at Boston Univ., where she graduated in 1884 and began to practice medicine in Los Angeles, Calif. She also became dramatic editor and music critic for *the Los Angeles Times* and active in the Pacific Coast Press Assn. She wrote articles and stories for a variety of periodicals, helped found a humane society, and served until she left California in 1896 as treasurer for the California State Homeopathic Medical Society. The Lummis couple had one son.

By late 1895, Dorothea Lummis, who had divorced her husband, was teaching physiology and hygiene at the Univ. of Tugaloo, Miss., and there, on 17 Feb. 1896, she married Ernest Carroll Moore (1871–1955). He had been born in Youngstown, Ohio, the son of John and Martha Jane Forsythe Moore, and attended Ohio Normal Univ. (A.B.1892) and Columbia Univ. (A.M. 1896). During his time in New York City, he worked at the University Settlement (organized 1891, from former Neighborhood Guild), where Dorothea was living while she investigated the tenement houses during the winter of 1894–95. The newlywed couple lived at HH, where Dorothea began her duties on 1 Apr. 1896, and Ernest, who was a student of John Dewey, began work on his Ph.D. (1898) at the Univ. of Chicago and taught classes and held reading parties at HH. JA described Dorothea Moore as "a woman whom I admire very much" who was "very bright," with "great originality and initiative" (JA to Anita McCormick Blaine, 8 Jan. 1896, SHSW, Blaine; *JAPM*, 3:17). At HH she was JA's liaison with the Chicago police stations in the settlement neighborhood. She also taught physiology.

Unfortunately, not everyone at HH was so taken with the Moores. Alice Hamilton wrote her cousin Agnes that "the Moores are going pretty soon. They are going to have a settlement all of their own over in Maxwell Street, among the Jews. Can you imagine it? The Ethical Culture people are to support it. Somehow they both have so little really human in them that one wonders why or how they will do the work. I rather think the House is relieved, very few of the residents like them" ([22 Jan. 1898], HU, Hamilton). The Moores returned to California. Dorothea Moore became head of South Park Settlement in San Francisco, and Ernest began teaching at the Univ. of California at Berkeley, first as an instructor in philosophy and from 1901 to 1906 as assistant professor of education. He served as superintendent of schools for Los Angeles, 1906–10, before going to Yale Univ. as professor of education. In 1913 he moved to Harvard Univ., where he remained four years, until he returned to California as president of the Los Angeles State Normal School. He was a leader in turning the Normal School into the Univ. of Southern California, which he served as vice-president and provost. In 1936 he returned to teaching as professor of philosophy and education. He retired in 1941.

By 1910 JA had amassed sufficient evidence of the "social evil," as she termed prostitution, to write about it. In her book *A New Conscience and an Ancient Evil*, she defined the term as designating "the sexual commerce permitted to exist in every large city, usually in a segregated district, wherein the chastity of women is bought and sold" (Addams, *A New Conscience*, 9). Most of the seven chapters of her book, published in Apr. 1912 and in several more editions, was originally published in *McClure's Magazine* and gleaned from the records of the Juvenile Protective Assn. while she was chairwoman of its publication committee. The data on which she based her narrative were gathered through "a series of special investigations . . . on dance halls, theatres, amusement parks, lake excursion boats, petty gambling, the home surroundings of one hundred Juvenile Court children and the records of four thousand parents" as well as "the personal histories of two hundred department-store girls, of two hundred factory girls, of two hundred immigrant girls, of two hundred office girls, and of girls employed in one hundred hotels and restaurants" (Addams, *A New Conscience*, ix–x).

5. Anne Toppan Withington (1867–1933) was the daughter of Nathan Noyes Withington (1828–1914) and Elizabeth Little Withington (1828–1912). She was born in Newburyport, Mass., and among her siblings were Lothrop, David, Arthur, and Mary. The Withington children were cousins of Emily Greene Balch. In Oct. 1892, Lothrop (1856–1915), who became a noted genealogist, historian, and editor, married Caroline ("Caro") Augusta Lloyd, a sister of Henry Demarest Lloyd. Anne Withington soon found herself included within the Lloyd circle of friends.

Withington did not return to HH, but remained in the Boston-Newburyport area and became associated with social settlements in Boston. She cowrote the chapter "Life's Amenities" in one of the district studies done by residents and associates at South End House, *Americans in Process: A Study of the North and West Ends*, published in 1903 by Houghton, Mifflin, and Co. While in Boston, she continued her friendship with the Lloyds. Withington became active in the struggle of organized labor for recognition. She opposed the entrance of the United States into World War I, and she became a member of the WPP and the WILPF. Withington edited two books containing the works of Henry Demarest Lloyd, both issued posthumously. Withington and JA coedited *Man, the Social Creator*, published by Doubleday, Page, and Co. in 1906. With Lloyd's longtime secretary, Caroline Stallbohm, Withington edited *Men, the Workers*, a collection of Lloyd's articles and speeches, issued by Doubleday, Page, and Co. in 1909.

6. The model lodging house program was created in 1893 (see Minutes of a HH Residents Meeting, 10 Dec. 1893, n. 12, above).

7. JA had long hoped to have an active fellowship program to support financially those residents who were part of the settlement program but unable to finance their participation themselves, either from their own wealth or through regular daily employment. She actually promoted the idea as early as 1890 in a speech to the Chicago branch of the Assn. of Collegiate Alumnae. The organization responded by providing one of the earliest HH fellowships (see Article in the *Chicago Inter Ocean*, 30 June 1892, n. 2, above). The HH financial records for 1894 indicate that the faithful financial supporters of the fellowship program were Lydia Avery Coonley, MRS, and Mary Wilmarth, who gave regularly each month, usually fifty dollars each. William H. Colvin helped out by making up any deficit in the program. Among the regular fellowship recipients in 1894 and 1895 were EGS, Gertrude Barnum, Dr. Harriet Rice, Rose Marie Gyles, and Mary Keyser.

By 1896 Anita McCormick Blaine and Sara Lord McCormick, as well as Jessie Colvin and Sarah Porter Smith, had become fellowship supporters, and Wilfreda Brockway, Dorothea Lummis Moore, and Margaretta West were added to the list of recipients. See also Lists of Residents and Fellowships, 3 Nov. 1896, below.

8. Mrs. Hall McCormick began giving fellowship support in Aug. 1895 and gave twenty-five dollars each month for the remainder of the year. She continued to support the settlement fellowship program sporadically into 1898. Two women of the McCormick family could have been Mrs. Hall McCormick. They were Mrs. Cyrus Hall McCormick Jr., née Harriet ("Hattie") Bradley Hammond (1862–1921), who was married to the son of Cyrus Hall McCormick

and Nettie Fowler McCormick in 1889; and Mrs. Robert Hall McCormick, née Sara Lord (1850–1922), who was married to the son of Henrietta and Leander J. McCormick in 1871.

This was likely Mrs. Robert Hall McCormick, whose husband was referred to as R. Hall McCormick. She was born in New York and after her marriage came to live in Chicago, first in the Leander McCormick home, which was destroyed by the Chicago Fire of 1871, and after 1874 in a residence on Rush St., where she died. She was a member of the Fourth Presbyterian Church, Chicago's Fortnightly Club, and Colonial Dames. Four daughters and one son survived her.

## To William Rainey Harper

*Young, bold, a bit brash, innovative, and backed by John D. Rockefeller's millions, William Rainey Harper*[1] *arrived in Chicago in 1891 intending to build the new University of Chicago*[2] *into a powerful institution to rival those in the eastern United States. Aided by Thomas W. Goodspeed,*[3] *who served as secretary of the board of trustees, financial manager, fund-raiser, and Rockefeller connection, he began hiring faculty and constructing buildings. By 1895 he had hired 120 faculty, primarily by enticing them with large salaries. Among those he hired were a dozen former college presidents, many from eastern schools. He also constructed ten buildings, and he was not finished.*

*Harper also planned to add laboratories for the biological sciences in support of the expanding science curriculum. During the 1894 summer convocation, he identified these laboratories as "the greatest need of the University," and concluded his remarks by saying, "'The laboratory can be erected for $100,000. Who will build it?'"*[4] *Helen Culver must have heard his plea. She began negotiations with him toward the end of 1895 to provide sufficient support in the guise of real estate holdings she valued at one million dollars to meet Harper's need and her three goals. These were to "develop the work now represented in the several biological departments of the University of Chicago by the expansion of their present resources," to develop "an inland experimental station and. . . a marine biological laboratory," and to provide "University Extension Lectures on the West Side of Chicago."*[5] *Harper and Albion Small,*[6] *the new head of the fledgling Department of Sociology, who viewed Hull-House as a perfect laboratory for his department, may also have seen this as an opportunity to bring the highly successful and very visible settlement operation into the university fold. Helen Culver, who wanted to select "'the strongest guaranties of permanent and efficient administration'"*[7] *for any gift she made, may well have encouraged Harper to investigate making Hull-House part of the university, for she recognized that her investment in Hull-House would be more secure and offer improved protection for the real estate that she owned in the Hull-House area if it was connected with an institution backed by someone like Rockefeller.*

*On Sunday, 15 December 1895, the* Chicago Daily Tribune *headlined the Culver gift: "Gives It a Million. Miss Helen Culver's Present to Chicago University. For*

*Use in Lectures. Extension Work to Be Pursued on the West Side. Includes Hull House Land. Donation Made in Memory of Charles J. Hull." Contained in the article was the following comment: "Included in the gift is the land on which Hull House stands. This is owned by Miss Culver, but it will be given to the university, which, in a measure, will, therefore, establish a sort of a protectorate over that famous institution. Dr. Small said last night Dr. Harper was the authority for the statement Hull House's land was in the gift, but Dr. T. W. Goodspeed, Secretary of the Board of Trustees, said it was not included." And so did Jane Addams publicly the next day: "'I knew there must be some mistake when I read that the property given to the university by Miss Culver included the Hull House land. This block is not included in her gift. . . . I did not believe the report, and this morning I ascertained for myself that no part of this block is to be included in the gift. . . . Such an organization as this must remain independent to do its work in the community.'"[8] So that there would be no mistake about her position, she followed her comment in the press with the letter below.*

Hull House, 335 South Halsted Street. Chicago, Ill. Dec. 19th, 1895.

My dear Dr. Harper:—

Your courteous letter giving an explanation in regard to the rumor of the transfer of the Hull-House property to the University has been received, for which I thank you very much indeed.[9]

Of course, we must feel that any absorption of the identity of Hull-House by a larger and stronger body could not be other than an irreparable misfortune, even although it gave it a certain very valuable assurance of permanency. Its individuality is the result of the work of a group of people, who have had all the perplexities and uncertainties of pioneers. This group are living in the 19th Ward, not only as students, but as citizens, and their methods of work must differ from that of an institution established elsewhere, and following well defined lines. An absorption would be most unfair to them, as well as to their friends and supporters, who believe that the usefulness of the effort is measured by its own interior power of interpretation and adjustment.

I personally, of course, realize that the mere transference of the fee would not necessarily work an intrinsic change in our relation before 1920. Yet that the statements in the Tribune Sunday morning should have called forth the comments of the press as well as so many letters and messages, makes plain the popular impression that this transference would give the University an authoritative influence over Hull-House. Such an impression would work most disastrously to our institution, and require constant explanation which would be embarrassing for the sociological department of the University as well as for ourselves.

While I feel thus strongly that the best work of Hull-House will be done as an independent body, I am sure you know that we are very grateful for the help that the University has always tendered Hull-House. Only this winter we have had from the University Extension department, free of charge, a lecture course by Dr. Gould.[10] I should be very glad of co-operation in the proposed West Side Lectureships,[11] not only on the subjects you name, but upon any others which you may be able to establish on this side of the city.

We have undertaken Food Investigation[12] under the direction of Mr. Atwater[13] of the United States Department of Agriculture, and o[f]ten come, both to the end of our laboratory resources and of our chemical knowledge. A careful and persistent research should be made in the foods of the foreign colonies.

I certainly congratulate you most heartily in the increased work which you will be able to do through Miss Culver's very generous gift, and I rejoice that Mr. Hull's estate, like that of the Peabody may be associated, not only with practical working class problems, but with institutions of learning.

It would give me great pleasure to have a conference with you, and I shall be glad to meet any appointment which you may name. Very sincerely yours,

Jane Addams

TLS (UC, Presidents' Papers, 1899–1925; *JAPM*, 2:1824–25).

1. William Rainey Harper (1856–1906) was born in New Concord, Ohio, the son of Samuel and Ellen Rainey Harper. Homeschooled, he received his initial college degree from Muskingum College, New Concord, Ohio, in 1870 and his Ph.D. in languages from Yale Univ. in 1875 at the age of eighteen. Through a number of academic positions, he became an eminent Hebrew scholar, and by 1879 he was in Chicago at the Baptist Union Theological Seminary in Morgan Park, Ill., teaching Hebrew and the Old Testament. He was a professor of Semitic languages at Yale, 1886–91. He also served at the Chautauqua College of Liberal Arts, 1885–91. By 1890 Harper had decided to leave Yale to create a university in the Midwest that he expected would one day rival Yale. Harper arrived at the second Univ. of Chicago in 1892 and served as its first president and also as professor of Semitic languages and literature. He was a scholarly leader with vision and determination, and he built the university quickly. It was to be primarily a graduate school producing serious and creative scholars and researchers, influenced by both Christian ethic and scientific inquiry. Buildings and quality faculty were his aim, and so was expanding educational opportunities outside of the campus through the creation of an extension program, which became a benefit for programs at HH. Very quickly, he began to make himself known in Chicago as an educational entrepreneur and creative force. From 1896 to 1898, he was a member of the Chicago Board of Education. In addition to developing the Univ. of Chicago, Harper wrote numerous works about Semitic languages as well as about various books of the Bible. He served as editor for the *Biblical World*, the *American Journal of Theology*, and the *American Journal of Semitic Languages and Literature*.

2. The first Univ. of Chicago had been established by U.S. senator Stephen A. Douglas from Illinois as a Baptist mission school in 1857. Located on ten acres at Cottage Grove Ave. near 35th St., it provided college-level classes and was home to the Baptist Union Theological Seminary, which moved to the Chicago suburb of Morgan Park in 1877. When the university could not meet its growing debt load, it had to close its doors in 1886. The new Univ. of Chicago was incorporated 9 Sept. 1890 and opened in 1892 under the auspices of the American Baptist Education Society.

3. Thomas W. Goodspeed (1842–1927), Baptist clergyman and educator, had been associated with the first Univ. of Chicago and through his fund-raising skills tried to save it from closure in 1886. He was instrumental in saving the Baptist Union Theological Seminary and moving it to Morgan Park in 1877. He secured a gift of $30,000 from millionaire John D. Rockefeller, founder of the Standard Oil Co., and established a lifetime relationship with him that resulted

in millions of dollars for the development of the new Univ. of Chicago. Goodspeed was a tireless fund-raiser and supporter of the university. He became secretary of the board of trustees, 1890–1913, and also served as university registrar, 1897–1913. In 1916 he was made university historian and served in that capacity until his death. He wrote and published a number of biographies of early university luminaries and an early history of the school.

4. Goodspeed, *Helen Culver*, 19.

5. Goodspeed, *Helen Culver*, 19. Four laboratories were erected, costing $1.1 million and serving zoology, anatomy, physiology, and botany. They formed a quadrangle connected by a cloister and became known as the Hull Biological Laboratories. The laboratories were built and occupied by the spring of 1897. Over the next several years, Helen Culver added to her gift to the Univ. of Chicago, including endowment funds to equip and maintain the laboratories.

6. Albion Small's hopeful expectation was reflected in this comment: "Hull House is a part of the property Miss Culver gives the university and our former interest in that institution will be greatly increased. This gift will give the greatest facilities possible for work in which all sociologists will be interested" ("Gives It a Million").

7. Goodspeed, *Helen Culver*, 19.

8. "Miss Culver's Rich Gift."

9. No copy of the letter that William Rainey Harper sent to JA appears to be extant.

10. Elgin Ralston Lovell Gould (1860–1915), born in Ottawa, Ontario, graduated from the Univ. of Toronto (B.A. 1881) and immigrated to the United States to attend Johns Hopkins Univ. He played football at Johns Hopkins and coached the school's first official lacrosse team. While working on his Ph.D. at Johns Hopkins, he became an assistant to economist and statistician Carroll D. Wright in the Dept. of Labor, Washington, D.C. After receiving his degree in 1886, he continued to work for Wright by gathering social statistics, especially concerning sanitation and housing, in Europe. In 1892 he returned to teach social sciences at Johns Hopkins until 1897. He was at the Univ. of Chicago as a professor in 1895–96, but he moved to New York City and became involved in efforts to found the good-government organization Citizens Union, aimed at ridding the city of the Tammany Hall political machine. His best-known published work was *The Housing of the Working People* (1895).

11. Although it was clearly Helen Culver's intention, it is likely that the special West Side Lectureships never materialized as a separate program.

12. HH did undertake a food investigation. One of the studies resulted in *Dietary Studies in Chicago in 1895 and 1896* (1898), published by the U.S. Dept. of Agriculture. It included the results of an investigation of the dietary habits of Italian, French Canadian, orthodox and liberal Russian Jews, and Bohemian and American families. The purpose was "to obtain information regarding the conditions of living and the pecuniary economy of the food of the poor of different nationalities residing in the worst congested districts of Chicago" (Atwater and Bryant, *Dietary Studies in Chicago*, 7). Caroline L. Hunt (1865–1927), then a graduate student at Northwestern Univ. and a HH resident between 1893 and 1896, carried out the study, collecting information in the HH neighborhood during 1893 and 1894. For the survey questions, see "College Settlement Survey," HH Scrapbook 2:28½; *JAPM*, Addendum 10:7ff; and *JAPM*, 54:661–77; for a copy of the study, see *JAPM*, 54:678–754. Hunt taught at Chicago's Lewis Institute, 1896–1902, and became the first professor of home economics at the Univ. of Wisconsin in 1903. After she resigned her position at the Univ. of Wisconsin, she became coeditor with Belle LaFollette (1859–1931) of the women's page of *LaFollette's Weekly*. She also wrote pamphlets for the U.S. Dept. of Agriculture and in 1912 published *The Life of Ellen H. Richards*. JA participated with Harry Sands Grindley (1864–1955) of the Univ. of Illinois in bringing out *A Study of the Milk Supply in Chicago*, carried out under the auspices of HH with the direct assistance of HH resident Alice Hamilton. This study was an effort to identify problems with providing safe, clean milk to children in Chicago. It was issued as Univ. of Illinois Agricultural Experiment Station Circular No. 13 in Dec. 1898 (*JAPM*, 54:983–1000).

Harry Sands Grindley was born in Mahomet, Ill., and graduated from Champaign High School (1884), Univ. of Illinois (1888), and Harvard Univ. (Ph.D. 1894). He joined the chemistry faculty at the Univ. of Illinois and rose to the rank of professor. He was the author of more than one hundred articles, circulars, and books.

13. Wilbur Olin Atwater (1844–1907) grew up in New England. He received a liberal arts undergraduate degree from Wesleyan Univ., Middletown, Conn., in 1865, and earned a Ph.D. in agricultural chemistry from Yale in 1869. After postgraduate study in Germany, he became the first professor of chemistry at Wesleyan, 1875–77, where he became the head of the first agricultural experiment station in the United States. His interest began to change from agriculture to human nutrition, in particular discovering a diet that would be economical and nutritious for the working poor. He eventually became the first director of the Office of Experiment Stations in Washington, D.C. By 1893 he was operating the first calorimeter in the United States at Wesleyan Univ., where he continued to investigate and compare the relative values in terms of energy values and digestibility of different foods. Until a disabling stroke in 1904, he continued to encourage nutritional studies funded primarily by the U.S. Dept. of Agriculture in many states.

## To Henry Demarest Lloyd

Hull-House, 335 South Halsted Street. Chicago. Dec. 22nd, 1895.

My dear Mr. Lloyd:—

We are very anxious to open a vigorous campaign against our Alderman, John<ny> Powers[1] about the middle of January. We are planning it on a very broad line, to attack Powers as the tool of the corporations, making a great deal of the fact that we have poor street car service in the 19th Ward because Yerkes, through the Council has robbed us of our rights. We will probably begin in the most sensational manner with placards: Yerkes and Powers, the Briber and the Bribed <&c.>[2] Do you think that Mayor Pingree[3] would be willing to come and open the campaign with a speech on his street car plans &c. I can think of no one else who would bring out an audience of the 19th Ward and start things up generally. Would you be willing to write to him for me urging our great desire to have him come<?> I really believe that if we could get an in~~vesti~~<di>g<n>ation in the 19th Ward, against our corporation Aldermen,[4] it might extend to the entire city. If you have not time to write to Mayor Pingree I should be very grateful for a letter of introduction which I could inclose to him with the invitation which I mean to write.

We hope to have steriopticon slides and all sorts of popular lectures during the campaign, and I would like very much to talk it over with you, if I could see you some time.

Our copy of Carlyle's Past and Present[5] has been lent, and I will save your letter for the reference as soon as it comes.

It is only occasionally that I can get a glimpse of the chivalry of labor. So much of the time it seems so sordid. Will you please tell Mrs. Lloyd that Miss Withington's fellowship is arranged for. Mrs. Emmons Blaine promised to assume $50.00 a month for a year. I have now had the great disappointment of hearing from Miss Withington that she cannot come this winter.[6]

With love to Mrs. Lloyd in which Mrs. Kelley joins, and with very vivid and charming remembrance of my visit at the Wayside, I am, Very sincerely yours,

Jane Addams

TLS (SHSW, Lloyd; *JAPM*, 2:1829–30).

1. Alderman of the Nineteenth Ward, 1888–1904, 1905–23. For information on the first of three campaigns HH undertook to rid the Nineteenth Ward of John Powers, see Article in the *HH Bulletin*, Apr. 1896, below.

2. It was common knowledge that Charles Tyson Yerkes regularly bribed a group of "boodler" aldermen who controlled the Chicago City Council to support his efforts to obtain city contracts for utilities, including streetcar lines throughout the city. Yerkes was attempting to get monopoly control of public transportation in Chicago. In addition, he wanted to obtain franchise agreements from the city that extended for at least fifty years on all of those lines.

3. Hazen S. Pingree (1840–1901) was a reform four-term Republican mayor of Detroit, serving from 1889 until elected governor of Michigan, 1896–1901. He was a cobbler by training and after service in the Civil War settled in Detroit and established a very successful shoe manufacturing business with partners. Pingree was known for his challenges to the private utility monopolies. In his fight with the owner of the Detroit City Railway Co. to get fares on the system lowered three cents, he was barred by the constitution of Michigan from forming a competing municipally owned transportation company. He also created municipally owned companies to challenge privately held electric and gas monopolies. During the early years of the economic depressions of the mid-1890s, he developed public welfare programs, created public works jobs for the unemployed, and promoted the use of vacant city land for gardens to help feed the city's poor.

4. JA was referring to those aldermen representing the Nineteenth Ward who consistently accepted bribes from Yerkes. John Powers was the leader of the Yerkes faction in the city council. He was sometimes aided there by Thomas ("Gray Tom") Gallagher. Gallagher (1850–1930) was born in Concord, N.H., the son of John and Margaret Tighe Gallagher, and moved to Chicago in 1866. After attending public schools, he learned the iron molder trade while employed at the N. S. Boulton and Co. In 1878 he became a clerk in the Leonard Brothers store at 258 (later 531) South Halsted St. and by 1880 had started his own hat business as Gallagher and Beegan at 228 (later 612) South Halsted St. By the late 1880s, he had moved his hat business to 250 (later 921) West Madison St. A Roman Catholic and a union man, Gallagher also joined the Democratic Party. In his first elective office, he served the Nineteenth Ward as alderman, 1893–97.

Gallagher was part of the group of aldermen who had interests in saloons and gambling, yet the Municipal Voters' League supported his reelection in their 1897 report. They insisted, "During his first term many obnoxious ordinances were passed, all of which he opposed, except the Chicago Metropolitan Gas Ordinance." They found that he "has consistently voted for all amendments demanding compensation for valuable franchises in public property; is active in efforts to secure lower street car fare; voted for North Chicago Electric, West Chicago Extension on final passage, but supported compensation amendments introduced while these ordinances were under consideration" (Municipal Voters' League, "Nineteenth Ward—Thomas Gallagher"). No matter, Gallagher was defeated by the HH candidate, independent Democrat Frank Lawler (see also Article in the *HH Bulletin*, Apr. 1896, below).

5. Thomas Carlyle's *Past and Present* was initially published in 1843. It was a response to the economic crisis of the 1840s in England and focused on the development of slums and

the plight of the poor and questioned the role of business leaders who were doing nothing to solve these problems.

6. JA reported to Anita McCormick Blaine that Anne Withington had declined the offer. See also JA to Anita McCormick Blaine, 11 Dec. 1895, above.

## *Hull-House Bulletin*

*Hull-House was not unique among social settlements in its efforts to communicate its mission and programs to a broad spectrum of the public, but it did take a leadership role. In their* Handbook of Settlements, *Robert A. Woods and Albert J. Kennedy provided bibliographic entries for the publications of the 413 social settlements in existence when their work was published in 1911. A review of the number of publication entries and the variety and spectrum of popular to scholarly publications listed under each settlement's name indicates that Jane Addams and the Hull-House residents were one of the most successful at widely publicizing their mission and programs.*

*Ever conscious of the need to inform their neighbors of the activities at Hull-House, Jane Addams and Ellen Gates Starr relied on written and published communications as well as word of mouth to promote their programs and efforts. They understood that continual communication with all of their public—from their neighbors to those who might support their venture, including the wealthy and philanthropically inclined; political, civic, and social leaders and reform organizations; potential settlement residents and volunteers; other settlement leaders; and the press—was vital to the success of their enterprise.*

*Major daily Chicago newspapers as well as the neighborhood ethnic press carried stories about events at the settlement, but Jane Addams and Ellen Gates Starr knew they needed something more specific and easily available for those they wished to reach. By 1890 the two women began to publicize the classes, clubs, and events at Hull-House by issuing broadsides, flyers, and pamphlets, sometimes handwritten and sometimes printed, distributed throughout the settlement neighborhood and available at the settlement itself.*[1] *Addams and Starr advertised their lineup of college extension classes, citing all professors and the times and places of classes. They produced separate broadsides for lecture and concert schedules, and they sometimes printed a syllabus for a special course. As activities at the settlement increased in number and variety, the publications the founders produced were issued more frequently and with more variety of format. By January 1891, they were providing a quarterly Hull-House calendar of college extension classes in multiple-page pamphlet format, while they still advertised social club meetings, lectures, concerts, exhibits, and other events through flyers and broadsides. When this arrangement became too unwieldy, the founders expanded the number of pages and added a prose description of the settlement's activities. They titled their new publication "Hull-House, a Social Settlement."*[2] *They gave it away to encourage financial support or sold it to visitors at the settlement for five cents a copy.*

*At the end of 1895, to reach the public in a more timely manner, Jane and the Hull-House residents designed a new publication, the* Hull-House Bulletin, *which listed all of the activities at Hull-House for a specific period of time.*

*Issued between January 1896 and 1906,*[3] *it was meant to keep those interested in Hull-House informed about the settlement's progress and activities and to serve as a platform from which the residents of Hull-House could address their neighbors on various reform issues, especially those relating specifically to the neighborhood, including political reform, union activities, environmental issues, and Hull-House investigations. On the first page of the first issue of the* Hull-House Bulletin, *Jane Addams presented her rationale for the settlement and her hope for the publication.*

*Hull-House Bulletin* January 1896

# HULL-HOUSE BULLETIN.

Published at Hull-House, a Social Settlement,
No. 335 South Halsted Street.

**Object of Hull-House, as Stated in Its Charter:**

To provide a center for a higher civic and social life; to initiate and maintain educational and philanthropic enterprises; and to investigate and improve the conditions in the industrial districts of Chicago.

During the past year there has been some difficulty in establishing satisfactory communication among the members of the various societies, clubs and classes meeting at Hull-House. Without this communication the advantage of coming to a social and educational center such as Hull-House is largely lost.

As a student in a large school becomes interested in studies and methods outside his own pursuits, so at a settlement each member should learn to know other characters, thoughts and feelings. It has been said that "the cultivation of social life and manners is equal to a moral impulse, for it works to the same end. . . . It brings men together, makes them feel the need of one another, be considerate to one another, understand one another."

It has therefore been decided to publish a Hull-House Bulletin the first of each month if found feasible, announcing in advance the public lectures, concerts and readings, and giving so far as they are prepared the programs of the clubs and classes. It is hoped that these notices may prove suggestive and stimulate the clubs not only to a greater interest in each others' pursuits but toward a more generous co-operation. With the same end in view comments will appear upon the work of the preceding month.

Short items will occasionally be given upon civic, industrial and school matters connected with the Nineteenth Ward.

The objects of the Hull-House Bulletin may be thus succinctly stated:

1. To secure a wider advertisement of the public meetings held at Hull-House.

2. To promote co-operation in the efforts of the various societies and clubs, meeting not only at Hull-House, but in the immediate neighborhood.

3. To stimulate an interest in the public affairs of the Nineteenth Ward, and secure more unity of action towards their improvement.

JANE ADDAMS.

*Hull-House Bulletin.*

PD (*HH Bulletin* 1, no. 1 [Jan. 1896]: 1, UIC, JAMC, HH Assn.; *JAPM*, 53:503).

1. The most complete collection of these publications, 1889–1910, is in HH Assn. at UIC, JAMC. Most of these publications were preserved in HH scrapbooks begun by JA and EGS in 1889. A record of the documents as they appeared in the scrapbooks may be seen on *JAPM*, Addendum 10:6ff, 7ff, and 8ff, and Addendum 1:234ff.

2. For information on "HH: A Social Settlement at 335 South Halsted St., Chicago. An Outline Sketch," see JA to Nettie Fowler McCormick, 8 Feb. 1895, n. 1, above.

3. In their meeting on 14 Jan. 1896, the HH residents approved the monthly publication of the *HH Bulletin*. Although JA meant to publish the bulletin monthly during the fall, winter, and spring seasons of each year, almost from the first number she was unable to do so. The publication came out with increasing irregularity and with an inconsistent mixture of issue numbers and dates. From an initial eight-page version in Jan. 1896, the publication grew into a twenty-four-page offering by 1906. All of the issues of the bulletin are extant in UIC, JAMC, HH Assn., and in *JAPM*, 53:503–873. Vol. 1, nos. 1–7, were published for Jan.–May, Oct., and Dec. 1896. Vol. 2, nos. 1–4, were issued for Jan.–Apr.; no. 5, June; and nos. 6–8, Oct.–Dec. 1897. In 1898, with the publication of vol. 3, JA began to produce double issues. Nos. 1 and 2, Jan. and Feb., were one issue; issue 3 for Mar. was published separately, and nos. 4 and 5 for Apr. and May 1898 came out together; Oct. 1898 was published separately as issue 6, and Nov. became issue 7; Jan. and Feb. 1899, nos. 8 and 9; Apr. and May 1899, nos. 10 and 11; and Nov. and Dec., no. 12. Vol. 4 began with an issue labeled Midwinter 1900 as no. 1. There was no issue no. 2, but issue no. 3 was identified as Autumn, with no. 4 issued with the date 1 Jan. to 1 May 1901. Vol. 5 for 1902 had only two numbers. Both were identified as appearing semiannually. There were also only two issues of vol. 6, with the Midwinter 1903–4 issue as no. 1 and Autumn 1904 as no. 2. The last issue of the *HH Bulletin* was published as no. 1 of vol. 7 and dated 1905–6. Beginning in 1906–7, the *HH Bulletin* was expanded and reformatted as the *HH Year Book*. It was never issued annually but during JA's life was published in the following years: 1906–7, 1910, 1913, 1916, 1921, 1925, 1929, 1931, and 1935 (UIC, JAMC, HH Assn.; *JAPM*, 53:874–1498). JA and other HH residents wrote the text for the *HH Bulletin* and the *HH Year Book*. It is likely that JA served as the general editor, planning and approving each issue of both publications.

## From Mary Rozet Smith

[Chicago, Ill.] [Feb. 1896]

My dear Miss Addams

Will you go on a nice little "tour" with the Smiths in May? You can go for as long or short a time as you like, go anywhere you please and view Settlements and philanthropists to your hearts content. If you will go we will take the quickest and steadiest steamer there is. You can come home in time for part of the Summer School[1] and soon after Stanley's school is over.[2] Mother and Father are going to abide quietly in one or two spots[3] and I am prepared to go anywhere from the North Cape to Greece as occasion may offer. This is a very fine plan and you'd better consider it. I will offer <you> bribes to the extent of my fortune—I'll even build a third floor on the Butler Gallery[4] if you'll come—Otherwise I won't.

Thank you for the cheque.[5]

If its more convenient you might come over with Miss Smith and Miss Hannig[6] and bring Stanley.[7]

The trip would be very edifying for him. If you'll come this time I will stop being injured about the time you would 'nt[8] and I will promise to be a[9] gentle as a dove. Always yours

Mary R.S.

ALS (SCPC, JAC; *JAPM*, 3:35–38).

1. HH Summer School in 1896 was held at RC between 29 June and 31 July.
2. Stanley Ross Linn, JA's nephew, was attending a public school in Chicago, which closed during the summer months, beginning in June.
3. MRS's parents planned to spend time in England and on the Continent, especially in France, where Sarah Rozet Smith had relatives.
4. The third floor of the Butler Art Gallery Building was constructed in 1896 while JA was away in Europe with MRS. Chicago building permit SW411 to add the thirty-by-forty-by-eight-ft.-tall third story to the Butler Art Gallery Building was dated 23 Apr. 1896.
5. The enclosure is not known to be extant.
6. JA and MRS did see Eleanor Smith (for biographical information, see JA to SAAH, 16 Mar. 1896, n. 3, below) and Amalie Hannig (for biographical information, see JA to SAAH, 16 Mar. 1896, n. 4, below) while both were in Europe during the summer of 1896. See JA to MRS, [26 and] 27 June 1896, nn. 1–2, below.
7. Stanley Linn did not accompany JA to Europe; however, he did accompany his aunt on her trip to the eastern United States between 27 Mar. and 4 Apr. 1896. She spoke in Buffalo, Elmira, and Syracuse, N.Y., and in Philadelphia.
8. Previously, MRS had asked JA to accompany her to Europe in Aug. 1893, while JA was involved with the World's Columbian Exposition, in Chicago.
9. MRS probably meant to write "as" instead of "a."

## To Sarah Alice Addams Haldeman

Hull-House, 335 South Halsted Street. Chicago. [Ill.] Feb. 16" 1896

My dear Alice

What is in your mind and why are your letters[1] so reproachful? I cannot imagine why you should say "that I fear that the children and finances are cutting you off from your natural sister." Why do you feel cut off? It seems to me that I deserve an explanation. The forgetting that John's notes[2] were left in my care can be explained by the fact that my mind was far from alert when they were left with me. I have found them and John can send his in at once and write you.

You know of course that Mr Linn[3] has no claim on the Cedarville farm.[4] I do not see how Harry's buying it would affect your relations to him on the Dakota matter. I should of course be glad to have Harry[5] or any one else pay cash for the Cedarville farm,[6] but I do not see how Mr Linn could be brought into that, after he has relinquished his claim. If you think that it can be done, I am quite willing to do what is possible.

I had nothing to do with the arrangement you made with Mr Linn about the Dakota matter[7] nor yet with your arrangement with John, I don't know why your letter should be so reproachful to me.

I am sorry that the children show this lack of tenderness,[8] no one could have been more shocked by the manifestation of it on both sides than I was last summer, and no one could deplore it more.

Mr Linn's address is Inwood Iowa,[9] he has a church there.

I spent a day and a night with Esther at Rockford, we are going to go on until the Spring vacation at least. Of course I am fearfully worried but it seems to me a little ungenerous to reproach me with my "guardian" duties when I most need your counsel and sisterly help.

Why don't you come out for a week's visit, and let us see what we can do together toward straightening out the Dakota and other affairs. I think that you need to get away and it is certainly very difficult to write satisfactory letters.

I think that it is quite possible that Mr Linn would sell his insurance policy and take up his notes. He is coming about March 17th, do come at the same time.[10] I probably will not go east until March 27th.

My first appointment is at Buffalo March 28".[11] Always your loving sister

Jane Addams

ALS (IU, Lilly, SAAH; *JAPM*, 3:54–59).

1. The letters from SAAH that JA mentions are not known to be extant.

2. It is unclear to which "notes" associated with John Addams Linn that JA and SAAH are referring. According to the accounts JA kept for the estate of MCAL, John Addams Linn owed SAAH $260 for funds she had advanced him between Aug. 1894 and Mar. 1895. JA paid it back through her executor's account in Oct. 1895.

3. MCAL's husband, JML.

4. MCAL's Cedarville farm was composed of 223.55/100 acres in Lancaster Twp., Stephenson Co., Ill.

5. HWH.

6. JA had been trying unsuccessfully to sell MCAL's Cedarville, Ill., working farm that was being rented by August Kaiser. In the initial estate listing compiled by JML and JWA, the farm was valued at $65 an acre, or $14,300. The property was finally sold in June 1897 (see JA to SAAH, 28 Feb. 1897, nn. 1–2, below).

7. MCAL's estate also included 1,920 acres of land near Ellendale, Terr. of N. Dak., that the Linns had probably purchased when JML was attempting to establish a college at Groton, Terr. of S. Dak. In the statement of assets made by JML and JWA shortly after MCAL's death, the property was valued at $5 an acre, or a total of $9,600. HWH and SAAH were claiming that property in exchange for money that they had given JML, John Addams Linn, and Esther Margaret Linn (see JA to SAAH, [Aug.? 1896], IU, Lilly, SAAH; *JAPM*, 3:54–59; and SAAH to JA, 22 Jan. 1900, SCPC, JAC; *JAPM*, 3:1500–1501).

At the end of 1900, real estate that had been in MCAL's estate consisted of properties in Lake Forest and Englewood, Ill., and in Storm Lake, Iowa. JA and SAAH were continuing to manage this real estate to produce income to support the Linn children as they grew to maturity. The Storm Lake, Iowa, property, the home that the Linns had built when JML became president of Buena Vista College, finally sold in Mar. 1901 for $2,419.90. After JA and SAAH repaid themselves funds they had advanced to the estate to pay for repairs and taxes on the properties, each Linn child received $455.23 as their share of the sale.

Later, JA reminded SAAH, "I have paid out this month $52.43 and 26.50 on the Lake Forest lot, all of which I have had to earn—but I supposed that is what we meant to do, to help the children out with their property as best we could" (24 Feb. 1904, IU, Lilly, SAAH; *JAPM*, 4:769). JA also advanced funds to John Addams Linn when he went to New York City to find employment in 1899. In addition, for $1,000 JA bought out James Weber Linn's share of any return expected from the sale of the Lake Forest and Englewood properties so that he could visit Europe in 1901.

The sisters were not always in agreement about how to manage the assets of the estate. After a disagreement about how to pay a slightly more than $500 bill for replacing a sidewalk at the Lake Forest lot, SAAH wrote to JA, "I wish I could do more to help you, I assure you I do the best I can—though it seems otherwise at times to you I know. Surely we do not know each others difficulties even if we are loving sisters" (11 Dec. 1900, SCPC, JAC; *JAPM*, 3:1711).

8. JWA wrote to JA on 28 Feb. 1896, telling her how very pleased he was that she had "accepted the kind invitation of Mr. and Mrs. Smith to spend a few months abroad with them." So that she could go to Europe without worry, JA had to make arrangements for the care of MCAL's two youngest children, for whom she was legal guardian. Her brother and his wife, LSA, volunteered to care for them. "Would be more than pleased to have Stanley stay with us while you are away and think would have him as brown as a little Indian by Fall. . . . I think it would be better than taking violin lessons twice a week all Summer." Of Esther he wrote, "Laura says I shall tell you to send Esther to her for the Summer, as she thinks she could get along with her—and by no means send her to Alice. . . . Marion Clark was home last Sunday and she said that Esther showed her Alice's letter and told her 'that she would die before she would go and live with her Aunt Alice.' Am sorry for the girl. . . . [She] seems to think she has no one to go to if her Aunt Jane would turn her over to her Aunt Alice and hope you will think favorably of Laura trying to see what she can do for her" (SCPC, JAC; *JAPM*, 3:68–70).

9. JML was a minister at a church in Inwood, Iowa, from 1896 until 1900.

10. SAAH did not come to visit JA during 1896. A measure of JA's concern over SAAH's "reproachful" letter is the fact that JA wrote another letter to SAAH the next day, in part stating, "Why are you so suspicious of me. . . . Don't you believe that it would be better for you to come on before affairs take a settled turn. I want to apologize if I have hurt your feelings, but I feel that a frank letter from you will be so much better for both of us. In three letters you have referred to 'cutting off' or something of that sort, while I am not in the least conscious of any change either in feeling thought or deed. I am thoroughly at a loss" (17 Feb. 1896, IU, Lilly, SAAH; *JAPM*, 3:62–63). No further exchanges are apparently extant.

11. While staying at Westminster House, established Oct. 1895 in Buffalo, N.Y., with head resident Emily S. Holmes, JA spoke on 28 Mar. 1896 at the Concert Hall on "The Social Settlement Idea."

## To Sarah Alice Addams Haldeman

Hull-House, 335 South Halsted Street. Chicago. [Ill.] March 16" 1896

My dear Alice

I cannot understand why you did not get my letter in regard to my trip with the Smiths. I wrote to you and Weber both late one night and remember the letter perfectly well.[1] It ought to come back as it had the Hull-House stamp in the corner, in case it went astray. I wrote a long and minute letter because I was much concerned about leaving the children for four months. I feel much better on that point however, as Laura and Weber have been so cordial about having Esther and Stanley there for the summer—I think that they will have a happy time. Weber will be at the University and John will probably have a church in Central Ill.[2]

Mr & Mrs Smith and Mary and myself are the party, altho Eleanor Smith[3] and Fl. Hannig[4] will be abroad in the mid summer, the Colvin family[5] and the Jenkins,[6] we are going to meet all of them at Beireuth for the operas.[7] We sail April 29th on the City of St Paul of the American Line. We land at Southampton, will be on the Isle of Wight & South England most of May, in London during the last of May and all of June (where I hope to learn many things of the recent social movements) we will then go north to Norway & Sweden with a little trip into Russia coming down into Germany about Aug 1st for Beireuth. After the week there it will be Switzerland or some other loafing spot until we sail for home Sept. 12th[.] That is as far as it is planned.[8]

Stanley and I are going to Buffalo Friday night March 27" I speak in[9]

| | | |
|---|---|---|
| Buffalo | March | 28" |
| Elmira | " | 29 |
| Syracuse | " | 30 P.M |
| " | " | 31 A.M. |
| Phila | April | 1st P.M. |
| " | " | 2d A.M. |

Will come back April 3d or 4th. That will be my last set of engagements, of course I am going to Cedarville for a little visit between that and the end of the month. I am feeling well but[10] nearly so strong as usual, and hope great results from this trip.

With love to Marcet always your loving sister

Jane Addams

ALS (IU, Lilly, SAAH; *JAPM*, 3:82–85).

1. "Your long letter of the 27th was received this morning," wrote JWA in his letter back to JA on 28 Feb. 1896 (SCPC, JAC; *JAPM*, 3:68).

2. On arrangements that JA made for the two younger Linn children, see JA to SAAH, 16 Feb. 1896, n. 8, above. Weber Linn remained a student at the Univ. of Chicago until 1897,

when he graduated with an A.B. degree. John Addams Linn was nearing the end of his studies at Western Theological Seminary and by 1897 would have his first assignment as at First Trinity Church, Petersburg, Ill.

3. Eleanor Sophia Smith (1858–1942), founder of the HH Music School and a nationally recognized music educator and composer, was born in Atlantic, southern Illinois. She was the second of seven children born to Willard Newton and Matilda Jasperson Smith. In her youth, Eleanor became a self-taught musical talent. During the 1880s, she studied voice with Fanny Root and composition with Frederic Grant Gleason (1848–1903) and attended the Hershey School of Music in Chicago. She also graduated from the Cook County Normal School, after which she studied voice, composition, and piano in Berlin, Germany. While she was in Germany, she met and befriended Amalie Hannig, a pianist at the Klindworth Conservatory, who came with her to the United States and settled in Chicago.

By 1891 Eleanor Smith had discovered HH. With the upright piano that HH had been given as a starting point, Eleanor and Amalie Hannig began offering instruction in singing, piano, and reading and writing music. The first extant published notice of Eleanor Smith at HH is a singing class she taught at the settlement on Wednesday evenings during the fall of 1891. At the same time, Amalie Hannig taught German and eventually German embroidery and piano at the settlement. During the HH Summer School in July 1891, Smith gave vocal performances on Monday and Tuesday evenings during each week, with emphasis on the classical canon and on music for children. In the fall of 1891 and into the spring of 1892, Smith began to give regular concerts at the settlement and continued to offer singing classes on Wednesday evenings. Once again, she performed for the HH Summer School students in July 1892. Smith and Hannig helped attract to HH other Chicago musicians and music teachers who offered concerts at the settlement. It was not long before Smith and Hannig's students began to give concerts at HH. In 1893 the two friends started the HH Music School, the first community music school in a settlement in the United States. From the start, it was funded primarily by MRS, who helped support Eleanor Smith but was not related to her.

Smith and Hannig gave private as well as group lessons. They hoped "to give thorough musical instruction to those children showing the greatest aptitude, and to foster in a much larger group the cultural aspects of a musical education" ("HH Music School"). They taught children of all ages and emphasized the importance of excellent technique achieved through practice and the development of an emotional connection with music. The music program continued to grow at the settlement, and by 1895 the HH Music School had its own quarters on the fourth floor of the new Children's Building, erected by the family of MRS. In 1907 the school moved into new quarters in six rooms over the Residents' Dining Hall, overlooking the HH quadrangle to the south and west of the original Hull home.

The school gave at least six concerts each year at HH and presented Sunday-afternoon concerts there every week, Nov. through May. Among the offerings were solo instrumental and voice presentations as well as choral, orchestral, and chamber music performances. Many of the students from the school found work in the music profession. There were famous musicians like Benny Goodman, who was a member of the HH Boys Band in 1922, and jazz pianist Art Hodes, who recalled his early music training at HH. There were also those who became music teachers and continued to promote the kind of musical education that Smith favored. For example, in early 1940, the Francis Parker School in Chicago had at least four HH Music School students on their music faculty.

Eleanor Smith developed a number of special Christmas programs for HH that included groups of singers of all ages and nationalities. In 1906–7, groups of children "acted and sang descriptions in verse of the Christmas customs in various lands," including German, French, Russian, Italian, Bohemian, Sweden, and Syria (*HH Year Book, 1906–1907*, 34). These eventually became the fabled and beloved HH tableaux, or "Living Pictures." This special HH program, given starting in 1911 on the Sunday before Christmas, continued to be given into the mid-twentieth century. It consisted of choral music appropriate for the story of the Christ child, often Engelbert Humperdink's Christmas cantata "The Star of Bethlehem," punctuated with other song material—sometimes her own compositions—selected by Eleanor Smith, which was illustrated by static pictures or tableaux presented by live performers presenting vignettes of the Christmas story. The neighborhood people who were the actors in the pictures "were grouped so as to reproduce well-known paintings of old masters" (*HH Year Book, 1 Jan. 1913*, 35). Throughout the years, the Music Program, with the help of the leaders in the HH theater program, also presented a number of musical plays, cantatas, and operettas. Many were written by Eleanor Smith.

By 1897 Eleanor Smith was singled out by Francis W. Parker of the Chicago Normal School as someone with significant new ideas about how to teach music. Parker, who liked her student-centric approach to teaching music, hired Smith to lead his Dept. of Vocal Music. By 1902 John Dewey had also discovered Smith and selected her to teach music to teachers at the Univ. of Chicago School of Education and to help him create a more appropriate curriculum for teachers to take into their classrooms. During the same period, Smith also taught her methods and her song material for the Froebel Kindergarten College and for the Chicago Kindergarten College, both of which had strong connections with HH.

To aid in the promotion of her philosophy of music education, Eleanor Smith compiled books of songs for children of all ages and manuals for the teachers who would help children learn them. She often included songs she composed in these collections. Her published works helped alter the way musical education was managed in schools throughout the United States. Smith's first published work was *Songs for Little Children* (1887). She published continually during the later 1890s and into the first twenty years of the twentieth century. Two major collections of music for children stand out. *A Primer of Vocal Music*, the first textbook in the Modern Music Series, was issued by Scott, Foresman, and Co. in 1898. The series, Smith wrote, "instead of requiring children to advance through exercises which confine their activities to purely mechanical processes, furnishes an opportunity for practice of the highest order, and at the same time gives the children pure melody at each step" (4). In 1908 Smith initiated another series, the *Eleanor Smith Music Course*, offering more advanced selections for voice. Other Smith works that were identified as significant for the development of music education were two volumes of *Songs of a Little Child's Day* (1910 and 1915), *Twelve Songs for Twelve Boys* (1896), *Song Pictures* (1891), and *Songs of Life and Nature* (1898).

Smith was a prolific composer. She frequently selected some words or a poem to put to music. For children she composed the music for *The Trolls' Holiday* (1905) with words by poet Harriet Monroe. It was presented at HH in May 1905. She and her sister Gertrude Madeira Smith wrote the music and Caroline Foulke Urie the words for *A Fable in Flowers* (1918), an operetta also presented at HH. *The Merman's Bride* (1928) was another cantata composed by Smith and based on the Matthew Arnold poem "Forsaken Merman." It was presented at HH in the late 1920s. Many of the songs she composed are in the Eleanor Sophia Smith Collection of her papers at the Univ. of Illinois at Chicago.

Eleanor Smith often partnered with other HH residents and volunteers to produce her songs or her cantatas and operettas. For example, in producing the Christmas tableaux, she worked cooperatively with Enella Benedict, who designed the sets and costumes, and Edith de Nancrede, who helped to prepare the actors who were in each tableaux. Along with JA, who wrote the words, Eleanor Smith composed the music for the HH Woman's Club song. "A House Stands on a Busy Street" was presented at the dedication of the HH Woman's Club Building in Mar. 1905. Again, partnering with JA, she wrote the music for JA's poem "A Birthday Song for Mary" in honor of MRS. Smith also often collaborated with HH supporter Lydia Avery Coonley-Ward, who sometimes wrote the words for Smith's music. Among those songs are "After the Rain" and "O Day of Days! Wedding March." Together they worked on a book of poetry and music entitled *Singing Verses for Children* (1897).

Smith wrote the music for a number of songs relating to HH reform issues. These were issued in 1915 as *HH Songs*, in part to celebrate the twenty-fifth anniversary of the founding of HH. In the preface for the pieces, JA wrote, "Four of the songs were written at various times in response to public efforts in which the residents of Hull-House were much absorbed—the protection of sweat-shop workers ["The Sweat-Shop," with words by Morris Rosenfeld], the abolition of child labor ["The Shadow Child," with words by Harriet Monroe], the relief of the anthracite coal miners during a great strike ["Land of the Noonday Night," with words by Ernest Howard Crosby], and the movement for granting votes to women ["Suffrage Song," with words by James Weber Linn and dedicated to JA and Louise de Koven Bowen]. We believe that all of the songs in this collection fulfill the highest mission of music, first in giving expression to the type of emotional experience which quickly tends to get beyond words, and second in affording an escape from the unnecessary disorder of actual life into the wider region of the spirit which, under the laws of a great art, and be filled with an austere beauty and peace." JA continued, "The last song, a prayer ["Prayer," words from "Stagirius," by Matthew Arnold] to be saved from the eternal question as to whether in any real sense the world is governed in the interest of righteousness, voices the doubt which so inevitably dogs the footsteps of all those who venture into the jungle of social wretchedness" ([2]).

Eleanor Smith had never been physically strong. Her eyes were particularly weak, almost at times to the point of blindness. She struggled with that problem all of her life. Fortunately, she found in MRS a willing supporter and friend. She became a companion for MRS, supported by a regular stipend from MRS, whom she often served as a traveling partner. Together, they visited Europe, relatives of MRS in South Carolina, Quebec, Canada, California, Colorado, Arizona, and New Hampshire. Eleanor became a resident at HH in 1897, but by 1924 she was living permanently with MRS—and continued to live in her home until MRS died in 1934, at which time Eleanor received $5,750 from the estate of MRS. Eleanor Smith returned to live at HH until she retired as director of the HH Music School in 1936, when her sister Gertrude Madeira Smith, who studied in Berlin and Paris and had taught piano at HH for twenty-five years, took over the school's leadership, until she retired in 1940. Eleanor Smith went to live with relatives on a farm in Midland, Mich. She died there from pneumonia she contracted after breaking her hip in a fall. She was cremated and her ashes placed with those of other members of her family in a cemetery near Annapolis, Md.

HH held a memorial service for Eleanor Smith on 3 Oct. 1942 and dedicated two rooms in the HH Music School in her memory. During that service, educator Flora J. Cooke (1864–1953), a former principal of Francis Parker School, Chicago, 1901–34, reminded her audience that Smith had "rare, sensitive musical taste" and a "long successful experience in selecting excellent music for use in American schools" ("Service to Honor the Memory of Eleanor Smith," 4). Cooke recalled that Smith "loved people, young and old," and she set high standards and was a perfectionist. William L. Chenery (1884–1970), who attended HH as a youth and became the editor of *Colliers Magazine*, 1925–43, spoke at the memorial service. He recalled Smith as a very special educator who wanted those who were her students and those who heard what her students presented to be moved and enlightened by music. He remembered that she sought to give everyone an appreciation for the significance of music in all lives. "She had great gifts, prodigious energy, patience and determination that drove her onward," he reminded his audience. "Her interests were extensive and her mind ranged in many fields. She had time and the energy for friendship. Her light step and graceful carriage, the quizzical smile that so often seemed to be provoked by something she saw from behind her glasses . . . her gay wit and the penetrating comment" were all part of his memory of Smith. He identified Eleanor Smith as "[a] composer who brought the creative spirit of the poet to beautiful words that needed signing. A teacher who looked about eagerly for talent that might be nurtured and trained and enabled to do something good for its possessor and for others, too. A friend to be trusted and enjoyed and missed" ("Service to Honor the Memory of Eleanor Smith," 16–17). For JA, Eleanor Sophia Smith was one of the "creative geniuses" of HH.

4. Amalie Hannig (b. 1857) was born and educated in Germany. By the late 1880s, she was a piano instructor at the Klindworth Conservatory in Berlin, founded in 1883. In 1892, when it became the Klindworth-Scharwenka Conservatory, she emigrated to Chicago with Eleanor Smith, with whom she had become acquainted when she taught Smith piano at the conservatory. In Chicago, along with Eleanor Smith, Hannig became associated with HH and helped Smith found the HH Music School in 1893. She taught piano at the settlement for a number of years; helped establish the Christmas concerts at HH, which she described in an article that she wrote for the *Ladies' Home Journal*, published in Dec. 1911; and taught German language and German embroidery in the settlement classes. By the fall of 1899, she was living at HH and remained a resident until at least 1918. She was an avid birder and became involved in promoting the identification and study of birds through her membership in the Illinois Audubon Society. For a number of years, and until 1918 when she resigned, she served the organization as its treasurer. By 1920 she was living on the North Side of Chicago as a music teacher with private pupils, but still teaching at the settlement. Before 1929 she returned to Europe and settled in Rome.

5. JA may have been referring only to Jessie and Katharine Colvin, daughters of William H. Colvin, for William Colvin died in Chicago on 7 July 1896 and both of his daughters were out of the country. JA seems to have attended the festival, arriving at Bayreuth, Germany, on 1 Aug.

6. JA's diary for 1896 lists a "Mrs Chas Jenkins," who spent part of the summer at "160 Karsenstrasse, Frieburg im Bade" ("Cash Account. Feb.," [395]; *JAPM*, 29:299).

7. The annual Bayreuth Festival, Germany, featuring the operas of Richard Wagner, was initiated at the urging of his second wife, Cosima, in 1876. *Der Ring des Nibelungen*, with which the festival debuted, was to be performed again at the 1896 festival for the first time since its 1876 beginning. JA had been introduced to opera by her stepmother during their tour of Europe, 1883–85. See *PJA*, 2:626; 2:631, n. 19.

8. JA and the Smiths left New York on 29 Apr. and returned 12 Sept., as planned. During the time abroad, JA visited England, where she and MRS spent 6 through 8 May touring southeastern England and then settled for several days, beginning 9 May, on the Isle of Wight. JA arrived in London on 19 May and remained there, taking special side trips to Bristol to see the Samuel A. Barnetts and to Oxford and Cambridge, until she and MRS left for Hull, England, to catch the S.S. *Eldorado* of the Wilson Line to reach Bergen, Norway. They arrived there on 2 July after a very difficult crossing, during which JA was "very wretched" and "Went to bed—cold and miserable" (Addams, "Diary, 1896," 1 July, [202a–3a]; *JAPM*, 29:272). They left Stockholm, Sweden, on 10 July by boat and arrived in St. Petersburg, Russia, on 12 July. After three days there, they went by train to Moscow, arriving 16 July. Between 19 and 21 July, they went to Nizhni Novgorod and returned to Moscow by 22 July. Their visit at Yasnaya Polyana took place on 24 July, and after returning to Moscow overnight they left on Sunday, 26 July, for Warsaw, which they reached on 27 July. After part of a day in Warsaw, they took a train to Berlin, where they arrived 29 July, and JA visited Clara Steiniger, a friend from JA's first European trip (see *PJA*, 2:355, n. 6). Another train took them to Bayreuth, Germany, on 1 Aug. for the start of the Bayreuth Festival, which lasted a week. Although JA may have gone to Switzerland and visited George Herron, there is no firm evidence except a letter that Herron addressed to her that indicates he might have seen her. There are no diary entries extant for Aug. 1896; however, a letter JA penned to her sister SAAH indicates that she was in Weisbaden, Germany, where she may have spent most of Aug. JA reported, "We have had just three weeks of a quiet lazy life, and I have enjoyed the reading—more than I have

done steadily for years" (JA to SAAH, 29 Aug. 1896, UIC, JAMC; *JAPM*, 3:444). They left the Continent by way of Paris, arriving in London by 5 Aug. On 12 Sept., they sailed from Southampton on the S.S. *St. Louis* of the American Line and arrived in New York after a difficult crossing on 18 Sept. JA was back in Chicago on 21 Sept.

9. JA's article "A Belated Industry," a considerably expanded version of her first speech on this topic in 1893, as "Domestic Service and the Family Claim" (see Address at the World's Columbian Exposition, 19 May 1893, above), had just appeared in the Mar. 1896 issue of the first volume of *American Journal of Sociology* and was summarized in newspapers across the United States. She had accepted a number of invitations to lecture from settlement leaders, women's organizations, and schools in New York and Pennsylvania. Her tour provided her with an opportunity to emphasize the ideas about household servants she had presented in the article as well as to discuss the social settlement idea, her position as a garbage collection inspector in Chicago, and HH in general. Being questioned after one of her two presentations in Syracuse, N.Y., she simply suggested, "Eliminate the element of servant altogether and make the relation one of employer and employee" ("HH, Chicago," *Syracuse [N.Y.] Post*). On 27 Mar., she spoke in Rochester, N.Y., at the annual gathering of the Central WCTU meeting at Willard Hall. In Buffalo the next day, she presented "The Social Settlement Idea." The *Buffalo (N.Y.) Courier* praised her, stating, "Her practical methods and good judgment have made Hull House a famous institution" ("Miss Jane Addams"). At Syracuse, N.Y., she spoke at the Woman's Union Hall on 30 Mar. and the next morning at Syracuse Univ., before traveling on to Philadelphia and returning to Chicago. Emily S. Holmes, the head resident of Westminster House, wrote to JA, "We were glad to hear of your safe arrival in Chicago. How you were to fill all your engagements in so short a time and not be worn out was a great mystery to me. If your other engagements were as pleasing to the people as yours was here then you surely must take great satisfaction in the success of the entire trip" (16 Apr. 1896, SCPC, JAC; *JAPM*, 3:98–99).

10. JA may have been writing so quickly that she neglected to include the word "not" before the word "nearly."

## Article in the *Hull-House Bulletin*

*Jane Addams and the Hull-House residents believed that to achieve many of the reforms their Nineteenth Ward neighborhood needed, they would have to join forces with a ward alderman. Of their two aldermanic representatives,[1] one, John Powers,[2] seemed perennially to be corrupt, bribe taking, the leader of the boodlers. He was not an option; their only hope seemed to be electing a fair, honest, and reform-minded alderman who might present their reform perspective in the local political arena.*

*In 1895 Jane Addams and the Hull-House residents and volunteers set out to elect a representative who would work with them to clean up their ward and provide adequate schools. They decided to support one of the members of the Hull-House Men's Club. His name was Frank Lawler, and he had considerable political experience as a former alderman and member of the U.S. Congress.[3] Lawler was successful, winning as an independent Democrat over the sitting alderman, Thomas Gallagher,[4] who represented the regular Democratic Party and was a sometime henchman of John Powers. Unfortunately, their hopes were quickly dashed, for in the brief time that Lawler served, he joined the Powers clique.*

*Preparing for the 1896 aldermanic election, the Hull-House residents were even more determined to support a reform candidate and organize to achieve success.*

Chicago, Ill. April 1896

## HONEST ALDERMAN

At the time of going to press the campaign for an honest Alderman in the Nineteenth Ward is in full swing. Headquarters have been opened at No. 105 Blue Island avenue[5] under the auspices of the Nineteenth Ward Voters' League.[6] As the candidates indorsed by the League, William Gleeson[7] and Thomas Gallagher,[8] are both the Nineteenth Ward candidates of the People's party and also of the Republican party, a unified and determined effort is being made for their election. It will be a great triumph if we succeed in placing two honest men in the City Council as representatives of the ward. We may be able to refute the statement made by Judge Tuley, "that there are not enough public spirited citizens in the Nineteenth Ward to defeat the prince of boodlers."

It is peculiarly fitting that the candidate for this industrial district should be distinctively a workingman. Mr. Gleeson has been identified with the Bricklayers' Union for many years; and we take pleasure in quoting the following from the indorsement of Mr. M. R. Grady,[9] whose word certainly should carry weight with working people. He states "that Mr. Gleeson is a man who has been a consistent trades unionist to his own knowledge since 1879. In 1884 he was President of the Bricklayers' Union. During his term as President he exhibited the best kind of executive ability; was firm in all his decisions, treating all the elements of the society with exact justice. He it was who put into execution the economical policies of the union which finally led to the securing of its present realty. He is a man of firm and determined character. He would, as his friends know, sacrifice position and power if necessary for right and justice. He is a native of Ireland and is a man of fair education, and thoroughly understands American institutions and takes an intelligent view thereof. Being so largely identified with the working people, he would know the wants and necessities of their conditions in the Nineteenth Ward."

Mr. Gleeson has squarely taken his stand against the contract system in the various city departments; as he has been in a position to see something of the inefficiency and corruption incident to the system.

PD (*HH Bulletin* 1, no. 4 [Apr. 1896]: 4; *JAPM*, 53–532).

1. Each of the thirty-four wards that composed the Chicago political divisions had two representatives who were elected for two-year terms in alternate years.

2. For biographical information on John Powers, see Minutes of a HH Residents Meeting, 10 Dec. 1893, n. 13, above.

3. Frank Lawler (1842–96) was born in Rochester, N.Y., and arrived in Chicago with his parents in 1884 with a public grade school education. He built a mixed work experience that included time as a railroad news agent and brakeman, a shipbuilder, postal worker, and

liquor merchant. He served as president of the Ship Carpenters and Caulkers' Assn. and became active in union work and in the regular Democratic Party in Chicago. He served in the Chicago City Council, 1876–85, and in the U.S. Congress, 1885–91. He was unsuccessful in his attempts to become sheriff of Cook Co. in 1891 and to return to the U.S. Congress in 1895.

4. According to Allen F. Davis, in *Spearheads for Reform,* 287, Lawler, as an independent, polled 3,044 votes; Thomas Gallagher, as a regular Democrat, 2,842 votes; with 1,724 votes going to the Republican candidate, and 319 for the People's Party candidate.

5. Later 824 Blue Island Ave.

6. The Nineteenth Ward Voters' League was associated with the Municipal Voters' League of Chicago, formed in 1896 through the efforts of the Civic Federation of Chicago. It was organized primarily to work for the ouster of the "Gray Wolves," a group of corrupt city council members who used their positions for personal gain, displaying a "gross disregard of public interests" (Municipal Voters' League, "Official Records of Retiring Aldermen"). Led by entrenched aldermen and saloon keepers John ("Bathhouse John") Coughlin (1860–1938) and Michael ("Hinky Dink") Kenna (1858–1946) of the First Ward and John ("Johnny 'de Pow'") Powers of the Nineteenth Ward, the group had been taking bribes from businessmen as payment for voting to give city franchises for public services, like transportation, gas, and electricity, to select private businesses that gave them "kickbacks" without demanding remuneration for the city.

The league began by reviewing all of the Chicago City Council actions since 1890 and considering the votes of the sixty-eight members in 1896, identifying those who had been bilking the city through their actions. With the help of Chicago newspapers and through their own publications, the league presented these records to Chicago citizens and urged voters not to reelect council members who had been "boodling." In addition, the league sought responsible candidates to run in each ward.

In the late 1890s, the league made great strides in altering the complexion of the Chicago City Council. It sought candidates who were honest, supported the civil service system, and demanded or would demand proper compensation for the city for franchises and voting privileges. In 1898, as it promoted candidates for the aldermanic election, the league reported on its earlier success: "The League has participated in two Aldermanic campaigns. Of the Aldermen elected in 1895, but seven were found whose records could be commended. Twenty-seven were pronounced by the League upon their records as unworthy of re-election. Only two of these were re-elected in 1897. Of fifty-nine members of the notorious Council of 1895, who were shown unworthy of re-election by the League in its two campaigns, but seven are now members of the Council. The defeat of men whose records are bad is of great value, even if their successors are untried" (Municipal Voters' League, "Official Records of Retiring Aldermen").

7. In this article, JA, the probable editor of this issue, consistently spelled William Gleason's family name as "Gleeson," the way it sounded. *Gleason* is the correct spelling. JA's original choice as a reform candidate from the Nineteenth Ward was HH volunteer and journalist George Sikes. When he was unable to run, he helped identify another candidate (see Article in the *Chicago Record*, 3 Dec. 1894, n. 1, above). The reformers, who identified themselves as the People's Party and members of the Republican Party, settled on William Gleason (1844–1916) as their candidate. He had been born in Ireland, the son of Margaret and Patrick Gleason, and arrived in Chicago in the mid-1870s. He was a member of the HH Men's Club, a bricklayer, and a union man, and he lived at 518 South Morgan St. The Municipal Voters' League urged his election, stating that his "record shows him to be an aggressively honest and capable man" (Cole, "[statement about candidates for] 19th Ward," 23 Mar. 1896). In addition, Gleason signed a statement indicating that he would treat his "office as a public trust and will act in accordance with the spirit of the [Municipal Voters' League's] . . . declaration

of principles" (Gleason, "The Objects of the League are the following: . . . ," [Mar. 1896]). A disappointed JA quickly discovered that Gleason could not resist the power of "boodle" and did not prove to be the reform candidate she had hoped for.

8. In the aldermanic election of 1896, the Municipal Voters' League also supported Thomas F. Gallagher, whom they identified as "a very satisfactory alderman" (Cole, "[statement about candidates for] 19th Ward," 24 Mar. 1896). See JA to Henry Demarest Lloyd, 22 Dec. 1895, n. 4, above.

9. Michael R. Grady (1857–1916), whose parents were born in Ireland, was born in Illinois. He was a member of Bricklayers' International Union No. 21, Illinois, and active in developing bricklayers' unions in the state. In 1896 Grady was listed as the secretary of the National Accident and Adjustment Co. He had been president, 1895, and was secretary, 1896, of the United Order of American Bricklayers and Stonemasons, which joined the AFL in Feb. 1896 and the Bricklayers' International Union in 1897. He attended the national bricklayers convention, held in Rochester, N.Y., in Jan. 1900, and returned to Chicago as the western organizer for the International Bricklayers' Union. Embroiled in union disagreements, he was brutally attacked in June 1900 with a trowel by union members who disagreed with his stance on union organization and activities. In reporting the incident, the *Chicago Chronicle* called him "not only prominent in the field of labor, but is also well known among business men, and upon all occasions of strife has the reputation of being extremely quiet and unaggressive" ("Is Stabbed with a Trowel").

## From F. Herbert Stead

*Jane Addams set out on her third journey to Europe, hoping to establish support for an international organization of settlements. The seeds for her commitment to international action—a commitment she would continue to develop and nurture for the remainder of her life, especially as a pacifist—had been sown in her early life. She had grown up understanding that her father admired and held dear the commitment and ideals of Italian republican Giuseppe Mazzini. She had read the great European and American political and literary classics and while touring Europe, absorbing its history, art, music, and culture, established a comfortable relationship with its countries and its people. She had found her vocation in England and seemed committed to recognizing and maintaining a special relationship with those who had given her a template of what she might do with her life. She believed that beneficial reform practices would come from continuing to share ideas in the same way that she experienced excitement and hope in the exchange of ideas among world leaders during the congresses at the World's Columbian Exposition of 1893. And after six years of living among the mix of neighbors surrounding Hull-House, she was aware that people of different nationalities could learn from one another to the benefit of all. This would be her first international effort, and it was not successful.[1] It would not be until 1922 that the first international conference of settlements, organized by Henrietta Barnett, took place at Toynbee Hall in London. It resulted in the organization of the Continuation Committee, with Jane Addams, who was not in attendance, being selected to lead the organization and to plan the next gathering.[2]*

*Jane Addams prepared for her travel in Europe by requesting letters of introduction from colleagues who knew reformers there and by writing letters to those she already knew.*[3] *For an example in the following letter, she announced her arrival to F. Herbert Stead,*[4] *brother of journalist William T. Stead, who had lauded Hull-House, which he visited during the World's Columbian Exposition in 1893, while he wrote a scathing review of the evils of Chicago in* If Christ Came to Chicago.

Settlement House.
82 Camberwell Road
London April 24. 1896.

Dear Miss Addams,

We were delighted to get your letter[5] and to know that we might expect to see you so soon in London. I hope that this note will reach you before you leave Chicago.

In your previous letter you spoke of the possibility of forming an International Union of Settlements. If we may book you for Browning Hall[6] on Thursday May 28th,[7] we shall be very glad to invite members of the other London Settlements[8] to meet you to talk over the scheme. Perhaps you can let us have word in time to make arrangmenets before you arrive.

I cannot tell you the pleasure with which we look forward to seeing you here and receiving on our infant Settlement the blessing of such a fairy godmother.

We were very glad to hear of the success of the Civic Federation.[9] I have not seen my brother since your letter; came;—he is at present recruiting by the sea side; but he will be very happy to receive your messages and to see you should he be at home while you are here.[10]

Mrs Stead[11] joins me in wishing you a warm welcome in advance to our land. Yours most sincerely,

F. Herbert Stead

TLS (SCPC, JAC; *JAPM*, 3:112).

1. JA's appearances at various social settlements in London may have had some beneficial influence in U.S.-British relations among settlement leaders. As U.S. citizens in London celebrated the 4th of July, a recognition of a sort also took place at an English settlement house. In an article titled "The Fourth of July; American Celebrations in London," the *Lloyd's Weekly* in London reported on 5 July 1896, "[A]nother friendly demonstration [was] organized at the Robert Browning Hall, York-street, Walworth, by those whose desire is the 'unity of the English-speaking world.' Mr. W. T. Stead presided, and was supported by Sir Walter Besant, Dr. Simon Gilbert (of Chicago), the Hon. W. P. Reeves (Agent-General for New Zealand), and other gentlemen. . . . Mr. Stead, after expressing the great pleasure it gave him to preside over such a meeting in favor of our world-scattered race, said the American Independence anniversary was a continual reminder of the way we ought to walk. On this side there lingered no longer a trace of ill-feeling against America."

2. Although settlement leaders from England were usually invited to national settlement meetings in the United States, it was not until after World War I that the first international conference of settlements took place, 8–15 July 1922. Henrietta Barnett, who in 1921 had been

president of the National Federation of Settlements in America, was the organizer and the initial president of the International Conf. of Settlements. Delegates came from every country in Europe, the United States, Canada, and Japan. There were eighty-six delegates from Great Britain, twenty-eight from the United States, and sixty-three from all of the other countries combined. Mary McDowell was the only delegate to attend from Chicago. The attendees established the International Conf. of Settlements Continuation Com., charged with planning the next meeting, which they expected to hold in 1925. The secretariat of the organization was to reside in London, Henrietta Barnett and JA were to act as ex-officio members of the committee, and JA was invited to serve as chairman. JA accepted the leadership position and helped to organize the second gathering, which did not take place until 30 June–5 July 1926 in Paris. JA helped plan the meeting and did attend as the organization's leader. This international group of settlement leaders became the International Assn. of Settlements and held conferences in 1929 and 1932, neither of which JA attended.

3. JA received letters of introduction from Henry Demarest Lloyd, Elise M. Fuog (HH volunteer teacher of German and reading), EGS, George E. Hooker (see JA to EGS, 29 [and 30] May 1896, n. 19, below), Florence Kelley, and others. For letters still extant that she did not use, see JA correspondence, 25–27 Apr. 1896, SCPC, JAC; *JAPM*, 3:113–28. Once in England, F. Herbert Stead and William T. Stead, Henrietta and Samuel A. Barnett, Herbert Burrows, Percy Alden, J. C. Kenworthy, John A. and Florence Edgar Hobson, and Sidney and Oona Ball, as well as other leaders in the social reform, socialist, and labor union movements, helped introduce her to other leaders she hoped to meet.

4. Francis Herbert Stead (1857–1928) was born in Howden, England. He was the son of a Congregational minister, and he became a Congregational minister after studying at Glasgow Univ. and in Germany. He served as a minister in Leicester, 1884–90. During that time, he married Bessie Macgregor, with whom he had four children. He became editor of the *Independent and Nonconformist* and, influenced by the early Christian Socialists, became committed to finding ways to help the working poor. Following the example of Toynbee Hall and Mansfield House, he began work at Browning Hall, as a facility connected to the York Street Congregational Chapel. It was located in a southeastern quadrant of London, home to a great many working poor. The name Robert Browning was chosen for the settlement because the York Street Chapel was where Browning was baptized and attended church as a youngster. Stead, who was the warden of the settlement for twenty-seven years, tried to stress the "'promotion of the labour movement in religion'" (*Bibliography of College, Social, University and Church Settlements*, 4th ed., 53). He worked to achieve state pensions for the elderly. In addition, Browning Hall helped to promote the legal development of old-age homes in England. Stead wrote a number of books about the political struggles for these laws, about the development and programs of Browning Hall, and about social Christianity.

5. JA seems to have written to settlement and labor leaders she knew in England to announce her arrival. The letter she wrote to F. Herbert Stead is not known to be extant.

6. Robert Browning Hall, located at 82 Camberwell Road, Walworth, London, was officially opened 15 Dec. 1894. Its first warden was F. Herbert Stead (see n. 4), who led the settlement until the end of World War I. Decidedly not a university settlement, its primary goal was offering friendship and help to its neighbors in every way possible. There were clubs, adult education classes, a nonalcoholic tavern, and summertime trips to the country. The settlement sought old-age pensions and the development of old-age housing.

7. According to her 1896 diary, JA's first meeting with the F. Herbert Steads was on 23 May, when she commented in her diary about their "sitting & dining rooms combined" (*JAPM*, 29:250). See also JA to EGS, 29 [and 30] May 1896, n. 4, below.

8. By May 1896, London had eleven settlement houses: Canning Town Women's Settlement (founded Jan. 1892); Gonville and Caius College Mission and Settlement (founded in 1887); Mansfield House (founded in 1890); Oxford House (founded in 1884); Passmore Edwards Settlement (University Hall) (founded in 1891); Robert Browning Settlement (founded

in 1894); St. Hilda's East, Cheltenham Ladies' College Settlement (founded in 1889); St. Margaret's House (branch of Oxford House) (founded in 1889); Toynbee Hall (founded in 1884); Trinity College Settlement (founded in 1889); and Women's University Settlement (founded in 1887).

9. See Testimony, 18 Aug. 1894, n. 9, above.

10. On 30 May 1896, William T. Stead wrote to JA, inviting her to visit the Stead family in their cottage at Hayling Island, England, and telling her that he would be in London on 1 and 2 June 1896. A note from F. Herbert Stead to JA, 1 June 1896, identified a possible meeting time for his brother and JA as 1 June at 3:00 P.M. JA did not note a meeting on that date with either of the Stead brothers in her diary. For a biographical note on William T. Stead, see *PJA*, 2:227, n. 142.

11. Bessie Macgregor Stead also contributed to the success of Robert Browning Hall. An early settlement visitor described the couple: "'Mr. and Mrs. Stead are peculiarly bright and able people. Few are more cultured, and few represent in themselves a finer type of life'" ("London Settlements," 13).

## To Ellen Gates Starr

*Jane Addams, Mary Rozet Smith, and the Smith family arrived in London from their vacation on the Isle of Wight on 19 May 1896 and lodged initially at the Craven Hotel, 44–46 Craven Street.[1] They began a round of visits to social settlements; meetings with British churchmen, socialists, and reformers; speaking engagements; and teas, luncheons, and dinners, all interspersed with sightseeing adventures. London was ready for Jane Addams, and she relished her reception. "We have been here for ten days," she wrote to her nephew John Addams Linn, "and have seen and learned a great deal of 'social movements.' I have been amazed at the hospitality of English people, we have been entertained most hospitably not only by settlement people but by the various distinguished folk whom we have entertained at Hull-House. It is a different side of London of course than I have ever seen before."[2]*

1 Crown Street Strand London, [England] May 29 [and 30], 1896.

My dear—I am very glad for three Hull House letters tonight,[3] I am not homesick, but the sight of an H.H. Envelope has a magic beyond any other. We have been in London for ten days and have so many invitations and general attentions[4] that it is quite bewildering.

The Barnetts are in Bristol[5] or I would accuse them of having set the ball rolling—as it is I attribute it to the various visitors H.H has lunched & been good to.

We dined at Oxford house on Friday evening,[6] with the Bosinqults yesterday[7]—take tea with Mr Clark[8] and his sister tomorrow—with the Hobsons next day[9]—in fact have only one free evening left before I go to Bristol the Sixth.[10]

I will visit the Barnetts,[11] while the Smiths are in Somerset. Mary will spend one night with me, and we will come back to town the eleventh, while Mr & Mrs Smith finish their visit there.

Our most dazzling array of engagements is next Thursday[12] & I copy it truthfully from the engagement book but I am bound to say that it is not strictly typical.

| | |
|---|---|
| 4.30 | Meet Sir John Gorst<br>At the House of Commons. |
| 6.00 | Tea with Miss Toynbee[13]<br>(Arnold Toynbee's sister)<br>in Dorset Square. |
| 8.00 | Dine at Lady Dilkes.[14] |

The last invitation I think is directly tracable to sister Kelley's reports—Miss Neckwell,[15] Lady Dilkes neice is enthusiastic over them.

It is perfectly delightful to go about with M. Smith, she is so improving & fine[.]

We have only been once to Toynbee Hall[16] to see the plantation.

Mr Aves[17] has given two invitations to dinner, when we were engaged. He also suggested a Reception and really could not have been more cordial.

I am learning a lot, in all kinds of ways, I spent the afternoon talking with John Moore,[18] the man who founded the "Labor Churches", and am really quite uplifted. His health is poor and he is living 25 miles out of town whither I journeyed.

Please tell Mr Hooker,[19] that I had a most inspiring time with Tom Mann[20] and that we will meet the Socialists en Masse at a reception given at the Avelings to Liebrunecht next Wed.[21]

By the way Tom Mann as well as the other Labor leaders I have met, speak well of Mansfield House,[22] it is about the only Settlement they really care for—and I do not think that it is solely because it is the only openly Socialistic one—it is really and truly much more democratic than any of the six others[23] I have so far seen.

Mr. Alden[24] got me a delegate's tickets to the "Congress of Co-operators at Woolich"[25] and is ready to do anything. He gives a little reception to us the 13" to which he has invited the "Sockers[26] Officers of the famous Union."[27] The Maets[28] have been very active in our behalf.

I speak at Browning Hall tomorrow afternoon, and they arrange a reception for the eleventh. I feel a little absurd over it, but it is really the best way to see a good many people at once.[29]

We buy a good deal of literature and "Cram up" before we meet the folks who have written the books.[30] I have not met Mrs Hobson,[31] but she has sent several people to call, among them a Miss Moseshead[32] who knows many "ropes."

We get in a few other institutions besides Settlements and even John Burnt[33] has graciously made a change to get at some of the municipal improvements from the inside. We will have to be hospitable at H.H. forever more to all Britishers. Between reading up and making a few notes I seem to have little time for writing home—but I will do more from Bristol. I can tell some entertaining tales of Settlements, as Mr Smith remarks "they are always Greece seen from the outside."

I hope the Summer School plans are coming on, I am sorry you have had such a time in persuit of Science teachers. Miss Wilmarte[34] will make all well however, if she goes.

I have just written to Miss Johnson[35] to congratulate her with great rejoicing. Long before this reaches U.S.A. I hope, that the resignation[36] has been put in, and that she is officially inspector, as she has been so long in truth.

I sent for the Zeublin's[37] address but it has not yet reached me. It is a little awkward as Mr. Woods [h]as sent me the money for the Burinth tickets.[38]

My love to the household, which I love best. Always Yours lovingly

Jane Addams.

Please show this to all the good folks to whom I owe letters, and tell them I care much for their communications.

HLSr in hand of SAAH (["Record Book of Copies of Letters and Articles"], SC, Starr; *JAPM*, 3:204–8).

1. After her return from visiting Samuel A. and Henrietta Barnett in Bristol, England, JA and MRS settled at the Arundel Hotel, 2–4 Arundel St., London.

2. JA to John Addams Linn, 1 June 1896, SCPC, JAC; *JAPM*, 3:233. Leaders in Great Britain were aware of the growth and development of HH in Chicago and certainly knew JA's name. As an example, Sir John Gorst, who had become enamored of settlements and what they could achieve for the underclass of his country, provided a discourse on their benefits in the speech he delivered when he was installed as Lord Rector of Glasgow Univ. in Scotland. His remarks gained full newspaper coverage, with a slightly different version appearing as the introductory essay in *The Universities and the Social Problem: An Account of the University Settlements in East London*, edited by John M. Knapp, Oxford House, Bethnal Green, and issued by Rivington, Percival and Co., in 1895. Gorst called attention to JA as the founder of HH, described the settlement's educational offerings, presented its investigations of child labor and sweatshops and the successful effort to secure legislation regulating the work of women and children, identified the Nineteenth Ward Improvement Club, and reported on efforts to clean up the neighborhood and build a public bathhouse. The *Glasgow Herald*, the *Aberdeen Weekly Journal*, and the *London Daily News* all published extensive versions of the speech. A newspaper account of the contents of *The Universities and the Social Problem* offered the following from Sir John Gorst's speech, which became the introduction for the volume: "He gives an extremely interesting account of Hull House, Chicago, a Settlement founded five years ago, and managed by women under the leadership of Miss Jane Addams. It is entirely owing to the action of the Settlement that the Illinois Legislature has been induced to regulate the hours and conditions of women and children's labour. The Legislature has appointed Miss Addams Inspector of Factories in the State. A club founded by this Settlement has been the means of establishing municipal sanitation in the ward where the club exists" ("University Settlements in East London"). Although the *Daily News* made some errors of fact, what it offered—giving Florence Kelley's position to JA—may have given JA extra cachet with labor leaders and reformers in England.

Sir John Eldon Gorst (1835–1916), attorney and politician in England, was born in Preston in Lancashire and educated at St. John's College, Cambridge. He served as solicitor-general in 1885 before becoming undersecretary of state for India, 1886–91. For almost a year, in 1891–92, he was financial secretary to the Treasury, becoming vice-president of the Com. on Education, serving from 1895 until Aug. 1902. In the House of Commons, he was a Conservative from Chatham and later from Cambridge. He had active interests in poor housing, care and education of children, and social reform generally.

3. None of those letters is known to be extant.

4. JA's diary for the period reveals that her London visit began with sightseeing on Wednesday, 20 May, at the National Gallery and the Royal Academy. Her first call on the reformers she hoped to meet took place on 21 and 22 May, when she met with Edward R. Pease (1857–1955), founding member and secretary of the Fabian Society; visited Stanton Coit at his neighborhood guild facility at Leighton Hall; and looked in on John Russell, warden of University Hall, during the evening. She called on Herbert Stead and his wife, Bessie (see F. Herbert Stead to JA, 24 Apr. 1896, above), at their Camberwell Rd. address on 23 May, where they "talk[ed] of Russia." She pronounced the experience a "very charming call" (Addams, "Diary, 1896," 23 May; *JAPM*, 29:250). That same afternoon, she visited Trinity College Settlement at 131 Camberwell Rd., which was in the process of becoming Cambridge House, operated by men from colleges of Cambridge Univ. There the deaconess, associated with the sisters and nurses working at the settlement, showed JA and MRS through their facilities. These included the sister house, mission hall and rectory, boys' gym and club room, girls' club, and "beautiful play ground" (Addams, "Diary, 1896," 23 May; *JAPM*, 29:250). The next day, Sunday, 24 May, after attending church, JA went to Mansfield House (see n. 22) and had a "very impressive afternoon meeting of men 800" that included a speaker and brass band. She had tea with women residents and attended a women's meeting. At 6:30 P.M., she heard Percy Alden (see n. 24) speak on cooperation (Addams, "Diary, 1896," 24 May; *JAPM*, 29:250). Among other aspects of Mansfield House that she observed were a hospital, boys' club, cooperative club, workhouse for elderly women, and three houses for women residents. To her nephew John Addams Linn, she echoed a comment made by Ben Tillett (see Ben Tillett to JA, 6 June 1896, SCPC, JAC; *JAPM*, 3:265): "Mansfield House is by far the most democratic of all of them [the settlements], the dockers come to the meetings—the night I spoke they smoked and kept their hats on and really seemed to be the genuine working men" (1 June 1896, SCPC, JAC; *JAPM*, 3:336). A reception was held at Mansfield House for JA on 13 June 1896 (see n. 27). On 26 May, Stanton Coit took JA and MRS to the National Portrait Gallery and lunch. In the afternoon, JA received calls from Bessie Macgregor Stead and also from Herbert Burrows (see JA to Henry Demarest Lloyd, 21 June 1896, n. 12, below), whom she knew from a visit he had made to Chicago. JA and MRS attended the Cooperative Congress at Woolich on 27 May and during the evening heard Tom Mann (see n. 20) speak on socialism. JA pronounced his remarks a "powerful address" (Addams, "Diary, 1896," 27 May; *JAPM*, 29:252). The next day, she met Tom Mann at 11:30 A.M. and wrote that he "[s]aid Canon B[arnett] had spirituality but not spiritual force" (Addams, "Diary 1896," 28 May; *JAPM*, 29:252). She reported that "Tom Mann is a speaker of much force and spirituality" (JA to John Addams Linn, 1 June 1896, SCPC, JAC; *JAPM*, 3:336–37). JA also received invitations from William Clarke and sister Jessie, Florence Edgar Hobson, John Trevor, Helen L. Hood of the National British Women's Temperance Assn., Ernest Aves of Toynbee Hall, Percy Alden, Gertrude Toynbee, Gertrude Tuckwell, and Margaret Sewell of the Women's University Settlement. Some of the invitations were in response to letters JA wrote, but some were a result of communications from JA's friends who wrote to their friends, suggesting they might want to make JA and MRS welcome.

5. Henrietta Barnett had written to JA on 19 May 1896 from Bristol, England, to indicate that she and her husband would be there until 3 July. "Will you come to us here? When? . . . We shall be delighted to have you," she wrote (SCPC, JAC; *JAPM*, 3:147–48).

6. Friday was 29 May 1896; however, according to JA's diary, she had dinner at Oxford House in Bethnal Green at 7:00 P.M., on 28 May 1896. She was guided through the facilities by A. F. Winnington Ingram (1858–1946), who served as head of Oxford House, 1889–97,

and eventually became archbishop of London, 1909–39. He told JA and MRS about the University Club with its cooperative store, the Webb Institute for boys, and the Repton Club, a boys' club with an emphasis on boxing. She called at the Woman's Settlement associated with Oxford House and met its leader, Beatrice Cecilia Harington (d. 1936), daughter of Rev. Dr. Richard Harington and his wife, Mary, who attended Oxford Univ. and became the first head of the settlement. She continued to lead the program after it became St. Margaret's House in 1899 and remained in charge into at least 1919. The Oxford House men's club had nine billiard tables from which the settlement received revenue, and she saw the boys' club in an old renovated factory. "Oxford men dined in the lecture hall & served themselves. House rather dreary," she recorded ("Diary, 1896," 27 and 28 May; *JAPM*, 29:252). To John Addams Linn, she reported, "We took dinner at Oxford House the other evening and went all over the Bethnal Green district afterward. They own various houses scattered about the neighborhood and have the people come comparatively little into the actual Settlement house—the English Settlements are much more patronizing to their neighbors than we are" (1 June 1896, SCPC, JAC; *JAPM*, 3:335).

7. Although JA indicated that she was with the Bernard Bosanquets on 28 May, it was for Friday, 29 May, that the couple invited her to their home, and JA recorded in her 1896 diary: "to dine with Bosanquets at 7:30" (*JAPM*, 29:253). JA had met Bernard Bosanquet when they lectured during the same week in Aug. 1892 at the School of Applied Ethics held in Plymouth, Mass., for the theme week Philanthropy and Social Progress (see Two Essays in the *Forum*, Nov. and Oct. 1892, n. 7, above). Bosanquet was married to Helen Dendy (1860–1925), a social worker and reformer, who became a leader on England's Comm. on Poor Laws (1905–9), in 1895. At this time, he was active in promoting adult education. Between 1897 and 1900, he joined the London School of Ethics and Social Philosophy. During his later life, he taught in Scotland and wrote at least twenty books and 150 articles.

8. William Clarke (1852–1901), socialist pioneer and early member of the Fabian Society, invited JA "for early tea at a little after four & stop for supper" on Sunday, 31 May. Clarke told her, "I really know very little of what the Socialists are doing," and added that he doubted that she could "see William Morris, as he takes very little part in propaganda now" (William Clarke to JA, 23 May 1896, SCPC, JAC; *JAPM*, 3:167). He urged JA to check the newspapers for lectures and addresses she might attend. His sister, Jessie G. Clarke, decided to meet JA at the Robert Browning Settlement, where JA was speaking at 3:00 P.M. that day, and conduct her to tea at their home. Herbert Burrows was also a guest of the Clarke's at tea. In her diary, JA wrote, "famous discussion with Mr Clark and Mr Burrows" ("Diary, 1896," 31 May; *JAPM*, 29:254), but left no record of what was said. JA did visit the William Morris factory, but not Morris himself. See JA to MRS, 22[24] June 1896, n. 5, below.

9. JA's 1896 diary for Wednesday, 3 June, has the following notation: "tea at 4 o'clock Mr and Mrs Hobson— met Miss Routledge & Mr Kenworthy" (*JAPM*, 29:255). This meeting began a lifelong friendship between the Hobsons and JA. Florence Edgar Hobson (1860?–1946?), who was from New York, and John A. Hobson (1858–1940), educated at Oxford, met and married in Exeter, England, in 1886, while John Hobson was teaching school there. After a six-month trip to the United States in 1888, the couple returned to London, where he was employed as a journalist and lectured for Oxford Extension, 1888–96. While Florence Hobson became a novelist and playwright, her husband wrote more than fifty books and several hundred articles, pamphlets, and public letters, many of which supported the practice of ethics in politics. These works established his reputation as both a social and an economic theorist. Among his best-known publications, *Imperialism: A Study* was issued in 1902. JA's personal copy of his *Work and Wealth: A Human Valuation* (1914) is extant at UIC, JAMC. In 1896 the couple were already well connected among liberals and Fabian socialists and helped introduce JA to reformers, social workers, and other socialists.

Florence Routledge (1859–1944), who married playwright St. John Emile Clavering Hankin (1869–1909) in 1901, was half sister of publisher Edmund Routledge (1843–99). She was an ardent suffragist and in 1889 began serving as honorary secretary of the Women's Trade Union League, organized in 1874, and first called the Protective and Provident League. John Coleman Kenworthy (1863–1948), leader of the Croydon Brotherhood Church, founded in 1894, was associated with the Brotherhood Church movement, which began in 1887. The church philosophy was based on the ideas of Leo Tolstoy and rejected war and promoted cooperation and nonviolence. It espoused the standards of human interaction described in the Sermon on the Mount (but denied the divinity of Christ) and accepted people of all faiths into its congregation. Kenworthy provided JA with at least one letter of introduction, perhaps to his friend Aylmer Maude, for her visit to Russia. See J. C. Kenworthy to JA, 13 June 1896, SCPC, JAC; *JAPM*, 3:288. Discussing the Croyden Brotherhood and Kenworthy on her return from Europe, JA reported that she found him "an ardent disciple of Tolstoi and a trifle fanatical" ("Miss Addams on London Social Reforms").

10. Before JA left for her visit with Canon Samuel and Henrietta Barnett in Bristol, England, she and MRS had a day of sightseeing on Monday, 1 June. They visited Westminster Abby and had a "drive in the Park. Went to bed early" (Addams, "Diary, 1896"; *JAPM*, 29:254).

11. About her visit with the Barnetts, JA confessed to her nephew John Addams Linn, who was about to graduate from seminary, that "I don't know how I am going to get on in an 'ecclesiastical circle' and dread it a little" (1 June 1896, SCPC, JAC; *JAPM*, 3:237). While in Bristol, she attended religious services and visited several churches. In addition, she discussed with Canon Barnett the problem of "'tainted money,'" an issue that had been much on her mind.

HH trustee William H. Colvin found a prospective donor willing to provide twenty thousand dollars for a new Jane Club for working women. JA decided she had to "decline the offer," when she learned that the man "was notorious for underpaying the girls in his establishment and concerning whom there were even darker stories" (Addams, *Twenty Years*, 138). Other reformers in the United States were apparently facing similar dilemmas as the use of "tainted money" became a subject of debate among reformers. After JA discussed the matter with Canon Barnett, she recorded in her diary for 8 June: "Saw St. Mary Radcliffe Church with Canon Barnett . . . St. Mary Radcliffe founded by merchant with slave money. Had a talk with Canon Barnett on "'tainted money[.]' Said he thought that to determine ahead of the courts was like taking private vengeance instead of the law" ("Diary, 1896"; *JAPM*, 29:258). JA summarized his position in *Twenty Years* where she wrote that Canon Barnett "showed me a beautiful little church which had been built by the last slave-trading merchant in Bristol, who had been much disapproved of by his fellow townsmen and had hoped by this transmutation of ill-gotten money into exquisite Gothic architecture to reconcile himself both to God and man. . . . Canon Barnett did not pronounce judgment on the Bristol merchant. He was, however, quite clear upon the point that a higher moral standard for industrial life must be embodied in legislation as rapidly as possible, that it may bear equally upon all, and that an individual endeavoring to secure this legislation must forbear harsh judgment" (139–40). St. Mary Radcliffe in Bristol was one of the largest English Gothic Anglican parish churches in England. Most of the structure was built prior to 1500 A.D. See also JA to Gertrude Barnum, 22 May[June] 1896, n. 10, below.

In 1900 JA was engaged in another discussion of "tainted money" with her friends Vida D. Scudder and Helena Dudley. On 21 Mar. 1900, the *New York Times* announced that Wellesley College had received the pledge of one hundred thousand dollars from John D. Rockefeller to be used to initiate an endowment after the college raised sufficient funds to pay off its approximately ninety-six-thousand-dollar debt. Vida D. Scudder wrote to JA, "I feel deeply grieved—so grieved that I can not keep silence. Of course, I do not assert that the charges against the Standard Oil Trust are true—indeed I understand that evidence favorable to the Trust is soon forth-coming. But the money lies under grave suspicions. . . . I think the Colleges are in danger of forfeiting their power to bear effective witness to the principles of national honour and social justice, in proportion as they become beneficiaries of the great modern robber-barons" (2 Apr. 1900, SCPC, JAC; *JAPM*, 3:1537). JA's response indicated her position: "I very much admire the attitude you have taken in regard to the Standard Oil money altho of course the position is vulnerable from many points. . . . Personally I am <not> so clear as you are in regard to this particular money" (25 Apr. 1900, Wellesley College Library, Wellesley College Archives, Scudder; *JAPM*, 3:1559). For a biographical note on Vida D. Scudder, see Robert A. Woods to JA, 20 June 1893, n. 3, above. For a biographical note on Helena Dudley, see Two Essays in the *Forum*, Nov. and Oct. 1892, n. 10, above.

12. Thursday was 4 June 1896. Before meeting Sir John Eldon Gorst (see n. 2) at 4:30 P.M., where they "took tea on the terrace" and Sir John "toured us thro the House [of Commons]," JA and MRS had an appointment for a dress fitting at Liberty of London at 10:30 A.M. Sir John Gorst was responding to a letter that JA sent to him as well as to a suggestion from Henrietta Barnett that he entertain JA (see Henrietta Barnett to JA, 31 May 1896, SCPC, JAC; *JAPM*, 3:224–25). He wrote to JA, "It will give me the greatest pleasure to show you and Miss Smith as much as I can of the H. of Commons" (29 May 1896, SCPC, JAC; *JAPM*, 3:210). Next, at Arnold Toynbee's sister Gertrude Toynbee's (see n. 13) invitation, they had tea at 6:00 P.M. at 8 Balcombe St., Dorset Square, N.W. JA pronounced her "very cordial." There, they also saw "pictures of Arnold Toynbee & her father[.]" JA and MRS gave up an opportunity to visit with Lady Henry Somerset at her industrial farm home at Duxhurst on 4 June in order to join Sir Charles and Lady Emilia Francis Strong Dilke (see n. 14) at their home. After their dinner with the Dilkes was postponed until 5 June at 8:00 P.M., JA went to Marchmont Hall, where the social activities associated with Mary Ward's University Hall (later Passmore Edwards Settlement) were located. JA spoke after Mary Ward made a presentation about the salt tax in Italy. "I thought it so good of you to speak last night, and much admired, if I may say so, the ease and skill with which you accomplished it," Mary Ward wrote to JA on 5 June 1896 to thank her for her appearance (SCPC, JAC; *JAPM*, 3:262–63).

After returning to Chicago, JA recalled that Ward's "'settlement was particularly interesting'" to her and likened it to "'the end of Mrs. Ward's novel of "Robert Elsmere."'" And, JA continued, "'One might also call it a biblical exegesis of Jesus. It holds him up, bereft of his divinity, as the Perfect man.'" JA reported that she found Mary Ward "'charming. Of all the reformers I met abroad she seems to care the most'" ("Miss Addams on London Social Reforms"). In 1898 when Mary Ward visited HH, JA recalled for a newspaper reporter her 1896 evening with Mrs. Ward and her guests (see "Mrs. Humphrey Ward at Home").

13. Gertrude Toynbee (1848–1925), "Geddy" to her physician father, Joseph Toynbee (1815–66), and mother, Harriet Holmes Toynbee (b. 1823), and to the larger assortment of sisters and brothers that included Arnold Toynbee, for whom Toynbee Hall was named, edited a book of letters to and from her father and her brother, *Reminiscences and Letters of Joseph and Arnold Toynbee* (1910?). According to census returns from England, she lived in London for the remainder of her life.

14. Lady Emilia Francis Strong Dilke (1840–1904), author known as "Mrs. Mark Pattison" (she was first married to Mark Pattison, rector of Lincoln College, Oxford, who died in 1884) and noted art historian, married second husband Sir Charles Wentworth Dilke (1843–1911) in 1885. It was a second marriage for both. From the 1870s, she had supported woman suffrage and technical education for women. Sir Charles Dilke became the leader of the radical wing of the Liberal Party, and the couple continued to be active in labor politics and to support social reforms. Gertrude Tuckwell (1861–1951) (see n. 15), Lady Dilke's niece, arranged the gathering, which she and Miss May Abraham also attended (see n. 15).

15. Gertrude Tuckwell was secretary for the Women's Trade Union League and editor of the *Little League Review*. She and May Abraham (1869–1946) had planned to take JA to a Women's Trade Union League Com. meeting after dinner. May Abraham was born in Dublin

and became England's first factory inspector. She was also active in the Women's Trade Union League and served as its treasurer. JA declined their invitation because she hoped to hear German socialist political leader Wilhelm Liebknecht (1826–1900) at Exeter Hall, a meeting place in London associated with efforts to promote anti-slavery and the cause of oppressed nationalities. JA's diary for the evening reported "arrived too late" (Addams, "Diary, 1896," 5 June; *JAPM*, 29:256).

Friend of Russian revolutionary Karl Marx, Wilhelm Liebknecht, a member of the Reichstag, was visiting England. He was much in demand as a celebrity guest among Russian émigrés and English social reformers for his outspoken opposition to war as well as his support of the working man. In 1891 Liebknecht became editor of *Vorwärts* (Forward), the Social Democratic Party's (SPD) publication, and promoted a Marx-inspired program as a leader in the party.

16. JA and MRS visited Toynbee Hall for the first time between 11:00 A.M. and 12:00 noon on 29 May. Unfortunately, Ernest Harry Aves (see n. 17), who was in charge of the settlement while the Barnetts were in Bristol, was not there to greet them (Ernest Harry Aves to JA, 29 May 1896, SCPC, JAC; *JAPM*, 3:209). In a letter to JA of 27 May, Aves had invited them to visit for dinner on 29 May 1896, but JA had already accepted an invitation to dine with the Bernard Bosanquets. While JA was in London, Aves wrote to her at least three times, apologizing on two occasions for the lack of activities at Toynbee Hall in which she might be interested, but nevertheless inviting her to visit. Although he hoped to have a reception for her at the settlement, it never happened. On 17 June, JA did find an occasion to share dinner with the residents (see JA to Gertrude Barnum, 22 May[June] 1896, n. 14, below).

17. Ernest Harry Aves (1857–1917), born in Cambridge and educated at Llandaff House and Trinity College, became a resident of Toynbee Hall in 1886 and left the settlement in 1897 when he married Eva Mary Maitland. He became subwarden of Toynbee in 1890 and also served until 1907 as secretary of the Universities' Settlements' Assn. He was an associate of Charles Booth and helped in gathering data for and producing Booth's monumental work on the working people of London (see *PJA*, 2:512–13). An attorney, he spent his life in civil service in positions where he could help promote legislation beneficial to workers. He served as a commissioner for compulsory arbitration, as a statistical investigator, and as chief administrator of the Trade Boards Act.

18. It seems likely that SAAH interpreted JA's writing incorrectly as John Moore. JA's 1896 diary indicated that she visited John Trevor on the afternoon of 30 May at "Harpenden . . . charming little village—cottage in . . . a row." JA recorded: "Belief in the Labor movement ~~if~~ <is> a morale of religious expression—as an expression of service. Very interesting man, delicate cannot sleep in town. JA found new feeling in regard to the companionship at H.H." (30 May; *JAPM*, 29:253).

John Trevor (1855–1930) was born in Liverpool and raised by his material grandmother, who was a strict Baptist. He became a Unitarian minister before founding the Labor Church in Manchester in 1891 in an effort to support the working classes, something he believed traditional churches were not doing. Before 1900 there were twenty-five other Labor Churches, located primarily in Yorkshire and Lancashire. Trevor developed a monthly publication, *Labour Prophet*, from which he resigned as editor in 1896 because of ill health. He hoped to bring a spiritual dimension to the effort to give labor more power, but he was not successful in convincing the Labour Party or other churches that this was necessary. By the early twentieth century, the Labor Church idea had begun to disappear.

19. George Ellsworth Hooker (1861–1932), born in Peacham, Vt., the son of William Davenport and Esther H. Bickford Hooker, excelled in civic work and city planning. He was educated at Amherst (A.B. 1883), Columbia Univ. Law School (LL.B. 1885), Union Theological Seminary, N.Y. (1887–88), and Yale Divinity School (B.D. 1890). After practicing law in New York City, 1885–87, he became a Congregational pastor in the state of Washington for the

Home Missionary Society, 1890–93. He began traveling in the United States and in Europe to examine urban problems, 1894–97, a practice he continued throughout his life. He made friends throughout the world. While he was in England, he became a resident of Toynbee Hall, May 1894 until Jan. 1895.

He became a resident at HH in 1895 and lived the remainder of his life at the settlement. Throughout his life, he spent a great deal of time investigating urban and transportation conditions for various entities and serving as a reporter for a number of publications. In 1898 he served as secretary to the special street-railway committee of the Chicago City Council and as a result produced *Report on Street Railway Franchises of Chicago* (1898). An editorial writer for the *Chicago Daily Tribune*, 1899–1902 and 1904–5, in 1903 he became one of the founders and civic secretary (1903–19) of the City Club of Chicago, an organization of civic and business leaders in Chicago committed to positive urban development and reform. He was a member of the Chicago Planning Comm. and, after investigating European railroad terminals, wrote *Through Routes for Chicago Steam Railroads* (1914). He investigated inland water transportation, 1919–21, for the U.S. Dept. of Commerce. He also served on the Comm. to Investigate Illinois Pension Laws, 1915, and was reappointed in 1917. As a reporter for the U.S. labor press corps, he attended the fifth through the seventh assemblies of the League of Nations, 1924–26 and 1928–29, as well as the World Economics Conf. in Geneva, Switzerland, and the Pan American Conf. in Havana, Cuba, both in 1928. During World War I, he served as the chairman of the Local Exemption Board for Division 43, Chicago, 1917–19. In 1912 he was a Progressive Party member. He also served as a member of the American City Planning Institute, 1918–28.

At HH, in 1896, he led a reading party for men on *Merrie England* (1893), by socialist and journalist Robert Blatchford (1851–1943), during the early months of the year and on 23 Feb. presented a lecture on "Municipal Progress in Glasgow" in the Sunday-Evening Lecture series. His lecture "compared the figures of the Glasgow city baths with that of the Chicago Public Bath on Mather Street" (*HH Bulletin* 1, no. 3 [Mar. 1896]: 4; *JAPM*, 53:522). By Mar. he had taken over the task of keeping up the correspondence for the settlement, a job he continued until Madeleine Wallin took over the task in the late summer. During that same period, he also served as secretary of the Nineteenth Ward Council of the Civic Federation of Chicago. In time for the summer of 1896, he organized, wrote, and published the *HH Recreation Guide* entitled "A List of Pleasant Places for Nineteenth Warders to Go. Arranged in Order of Cost for Round Trip." New York City was the subject of a stereopticon lecture he gave on 14 Apr. 1896, and on 26 Apr. he was chairman of the Sunday-evening lecture in which Robert A. Woods discussed the position and future of organized labor. In Nov. 1896, he addressed the Dorcas Federal Labor Union on the labor movement in Belgium. Speaking before the Chicago Working Women's Council in Feb. 1897, Hooker's subject was England's labor movement. For the Jan. 1897 number of the *HH Bulletin*, he wrote a short article about the social economic conference that had taken place during the second week of Dec. 1896 at the Chicago Commons and HH. George E. Hooker participated at the settlement less frequently as the pace of his life and commitments increased, but he always seemed available to share his expertise with JA and other settlement residents.

20. JA's appointment with Tom Mann (1856–1941) was at 11:30 A.M. on 28 May 1896, the day after she heard him speak in Richmond Park (see n. 4). When JA first heard him speak in England, Mann was serving as general secretary of the Independent Labour Party, which he helped found. He was born near Coventry, England, and began work at age ten in a coal mine. After his family moved to Birmingham, he completed an engineering apprenticeship. When he moved to London to work in 1877, he sought more education and began his dedication to socialism and the union movement. He joined the Amalgamated Society of Engineers in 1881 and the Social Democratic Federation in 1885. He was a leader in the Bryant and May match-factory strike that took place during the summer of 1888 while JA was visiting

Toynbee Hall for the first time. His commitment to unionizing unskilled labor led to his role as a leader in the London dockers' strike of 1889. Mann was selected as president of the Dock, Wharf, Riverside, and General Labourers' Union formed after the strike. He became president of the International Transport Workers' Federation, 1893–96, and was a founding member of the Independent Labour Party. He was a devoted Anglican and once considered becoming a priest. In 1901 he emigrated to Australia to encourage the development of trade unions and became an organizer for the Australian Labor Party. On his return to England in 1910, he was active once again in the labor movement and led several strikes. He was a dedicated pacifist and opposed Britain's entry into World War I. He was elected general secretary of the Amalgamated Engineering Union and served 1919–21. In 1917 he joined the British Socialist Party and in 1920 was a founder of the Communist Party in Great Britain. In his later life, he continued to support the growth and further development of socialism, communism, and the cooperative movement.

21. JA did indeed attend the gathering on Wednesday, 3 June, at Eleanor Marx (1855–98) and Edward Aveling's (1849–98) home in Sydenham. She did not identify individuals she met, but Liebknecht was there and JA found "Mr & Mrs Aveling very charming" (Addams, "Diary, 1896," 3 June; *JAPM*, 29:255). Years later when she described the occasion in *Twenty Years*, JA recalled Liebknecht as an "old fashioned orthodox Socialist" (264).

Edward Bibbins Aveling was the son of a Congregationalist minister. He earned a B.S. in zoology in 1870 from University College London, taught biology at King's College London, and lectured on anatomy and biology at London Hospital. A leading member of the National Secular Society, in 1884 he joined the Socialist League. For a short period of time, he edited *Commonweal*, the league's journal, and also helped prepare the first volume of Karl Marx's *Das Kapital* for publication. At the same time, he and Eleanor Marx, the youngest daughter of Karl Marx, became a common-law couple and began to work together to support socialist activities. Two years later, they both left the league, and in 1886 they traveled in the United States, making appearances with Wilhelm Liebknecht for the SPD. Returning to England, Edward Aveling joined Friedrich Engles in attempting, unsuccessfully, to organize a new Marxist working-class party. Eleanor and Edward were active in helping with strikes—most notably the match-makers' strike in 1888 and the dockers' strike in 1889. By 1897 both had rejoined the Social Democratic Federation. Eleanor helped prepare her father's papers for publication, remained engaged in socialist circles, and also became active in theater work as a translator of plays and briefly as an actress. At the same time, Edward joined the theatrical world as a playwright and producer. Acknowledged among his fellow socialists as brilliant and an excellent speaker, Edward Aveling was disliked among British socialist leaders who knew him as untrustworthy with money and a philanderer. He left his first wife, heiress Isabel Campbell Frank, in 1875 after two years of marriage, and he married again after her death in 1892. Although still living with Eleanor Marx, who had nursed him through his first brush with death from kidney disease in 1895, he secretly wed young actress Eva Frye in 1897. Eleanor continued to nurse him after a surgery in 1897 and in his declining health until her suicide 31 Mar. 1898, which many of the socialist leaders believed he caused. Four months later, he died, in August 1898.

22. Mansfield House was a settlement organized through the efforts of Mansfield College, Oxford Univ., and the nearby Congregational church in Aug. 1890. Its warden was Percy Alden (see n. 24).

23. According to JA's diary, by 29 [and 30] May 1896, in addition to Mansfield House and its companion women's settlement, she had visited the following settlement programs: University Hall, Leighton Hall, Trinity College Settlement, Oxford House, Oxford House Woman's Settlement, and Toynbee Hall.

24. Percy Alden (1865–1944) became a British social worker and politician dedicated to

social reform. He was born in Oxford and attended Balliol College, Oxford, from which he graduated in 1888. He began studying for the Congregational ministry and by 1891 had become the first warden of Mansfield House in Canning Town, London, a post he held until 1901. During his tenure at Mansfield House, he supported the Independent Labour Party but was not a member and actively participated in municipal political life. From 1892 until 1901, he served on the West Ham Borough Council in one of the poorest areas of London. In 1899 he wed Margaret Pearse, physician of the Canning Town Medical Mission Hospital; they had three daughters.

From 1906 until 1918, he was a member of Parliament from Tottenham. A member of the Fabian Society and the Liberal Party, he often supported the positions of labor in Parliament. During World War I, he was opposed to conscription and supported conscientious objectors. By the mid-1920s, he had left elective politics and devoted himself to charitable enterprise as chairman of the Save the Children Fund and overseeing a number of educational trusts for children of the working poor. He wrote a number of books, supported the garden-city movement, and encouraged people to leave cities for farm colonies. He died from a German flying bomb blast during World War II.

25. The first of the continuing Co-operative Congresses was held in 1869 to promote the cooperative movement. The 1896 congress that JA attended boasted nine hundred delegates; the proceedings were published shortly after the congress ended.

26. JA meant the word "Dockers," not the word "Sockers." In copying JA's letter into the notebook, SAAH transcribed the word incorrectly.

27. Those who were associated with Mansfield House knew of JA before she spoke. William Horace Day, who spoke at Mansfield House in Jan. 1895, wrote to JA that he described HH and "when your name was mentioned such a storm of applause broke out, it would have been a pleasure to you to have rec'd such a token of the earnest interest which those dockers and laborers in Canning Town take in your work in Chicago. They voted on the spot to ask me to convey to you their great sympathy in your work at Hull House" (19 Jan. 1895, UC, Misc. Manuscripts; *JAPM*, 2:1631).

A report of JA's visit to Mansfield House that was issued in the *Mansfield House Magazine* also appeared in the *Chicago Commons* in July 1896. "'One of the most interesting meetings ever held in Canning Town was the reception of Miss Jane Addams, of Hull House, Chicago, on Saturday June 13. It was held in the Recreation Ground . . . and there present were Mr. J. Spencer Curwen, Mrs. Keir Hardie, Mr. Alderman Ben Tillett, Mr. [M. L. C.] Trenwith, head of the labour party in the Victorian Parliament, Tom McCarthy, Herbert Burrows, and a large number of people interested in the labour movement. . . . Miss Addams received a great ovation from the men and women of Mansfield House, three rousing cheers startling the neighbourhood for a considerable distance round the garden. . . . Miss Addams made a strong appeal to the leaders of the labour movement to assist all honest attempts put forth by the settlements, and the high tone of her remarks gave the key to the rest of the meeting'" (13). The "famous union" was the Dock, Wharf, Riverside, and General Labourers' Union (1889–1922), which merged into the Transport and General Workers Union in 1922. Ben Tillett was the first general secretary of the union and Tom Mann the first president.

On 20 June 1896, the *Express* of East Ham offered the following summary of JA's comments: "[U]nfortunately in America the Constitution stood in the way of many much needed reforms. The efforts of Hull House had been directed largely to empowering the condition of the women workers, and they had succeeded in establishing three or four little unions. They also passed an eight hour law, but that was declared to be unconstitutional, and was, therefore, inoperative. For some reason or other the labor movement in America was not so strong as it was in England, and she did not think there was any prospect of getting such state legislation as was needed until the workers were organized and strong enough to demand it. . . . She would go back to the States much impressed by what she had seen in England." She mentioned the bricklayers' union in Chicago as strong and then indicated, "Hull House settlement was situated in the centre of the sewing trade in Chicago, and she regretted to say that the union in the trade was weak, though the influence of Hull House had been to strengthen it considerably" ("Miss Jane Addams at Canning Town"). Other speakers were Keir Hardie and Herbert Burrows, who quoted John Burns as saying that Chicago was "'A pocket edition of hell,' but Hull House was the other side of the picture."

28. SAAH, who copied JA's original letter into the notebook that she gave to EGS, decided that JA had written the word "Maets." JA may have written *Steads*, meaning the brothers F. Herbert and William T. Stead, who knew that she would be in England.

29. JA may have begun her letter on 29 May; however, she must have continued it on 30 May because she spoke at Robert Browning Hall at 3:00 P.M. on 31 May rather than 30 May 1896, according to her diary. She was indeed back at Browning Hall once again on Thursday evening, 11 June 1896, at 8:00 P.M. for the reception. She had just returned from her visit in Bristol with the Barnetts. Of the reception at Browning Hall, she commented that the attendees were "mostly Mansfield House Bermondsey Settlement" ("Diary, 1896," 11 June; *JAPM*, 29:259). For information on Robert Browning Hall, see F. Herbert Stead to JA, 24 Apr. 1896, n. 6, above.

30. Shortly after JA returned to Chicago from Europe, she was interviewed by a reporter from the *Chicago Inter Ocean* who discovered that JA had returned with "a large trunk . . . half full of circulars, pamphlets, and books, all sorts of reading matter . . . pertaining to the various social movements abroad" ("Miss Addams on London Social Reforms," 27 Sept. 1896).

31. Florence Edgar Hobson (see n. 9).

32. Perhaps Miss Annie Catharine Fullarton Muirhead (1864–1911), born in Scotland, a musician, teacher, and poet. She seems to have been a friend of socialist labor journalist Alfred Hicks and his mother, whom JA visited at 3 Wilmot Place, Camden Town, on 20 June 1896 (see also JA to MRS, 26 Apr. 1890, n. 8, above). Miss Muirhead lived at 10 Leighton Crescent, NW, in London, near Leighton Hall, and was likely active in Stanton Coit's neighborhood guild. She planned to take JA and MRS back to her home for dinner and a garden party at Leighton Hall. According to JA's diary for the date, she and MRS returned to their hotel at 9:30 P.M.

33. John Elliot Burns (1858–1943), English labor leader, activist, socialist, antiracist, and pacifist, was born in Lambeth, Scotland, and like his father became an engineer. He joined the Amalgamated Society of Engineers in 1879 and worked for two years for the United Africa Co., where he became radicalized over the treatment of Africans by the company. In 1881 he formed a branch of the Social Democratic Federation in Battersea and joined its executive council. Active in a number of strikes during the 1880s, he participated as a leader in the dock strike of 1889. In the elections for the first London County Council, he was selected to represent Battersea. A member of Parliament (1892–1918) as a representative of Battersea, he was aligned with the Independent Labour Party, 1892–95, and with the Liberal Party, 1895–1918. He was a cabinet member as the president of the Local Government Board, 1905–14, and became president of the Board of Trade in 1914, but resigned because of his opposition to Britain's entry into World War I. For the remainder of his life, he eschewed political life for investigating London history.

Burns reached out to JA. He invited her to call on him in early June at the House of Commons, but she was unable to do so. JA's 1896 diary entry for 1 June revealed both "~~Mrs. Bosenquet~~," "~~drive in the park~~,"and "~~P. M. John Burns House of Commons at 6~~" deleted and replaced with "A.M. Westminster Abbey all morning[,] drive in the park. Drive in the Park[.] went to bd early" (*JAPM*, 29:254). It was not until 16 June that JA and Burns met face-to-face and attended a meeting of the London County Council, of which JA recorded, "[E]xciting debate in County Council, asked the head of Police to resign. Attack by John Burns ("Diary,

1896," 16 June; *JAPM*, 29:262). He also showed her Battersea "the plant turning street sweepings into cement pavement, the technical school teaching boys brick laying and plumbing, and the public bath" (Addams, *Twenty Years*, 263). Burns had invited her to come to his home in Battersea for a visit on 19 June, but she was to be in Oxford on that day. In May 1915, when JA was on her way through England as part of the International Com. of Women for Permanent Peace (ICWPP) in an attempt to stop World War I, she and Burns met. Of the occasion, Burns wrote, "For two hours we had an interesting interview with a really good woman direct, practical, sentimental" (British Library, London, Dept. of Manuscripts, John Elliot Burns Papers, #46337, 92:93).

34. JA was referring to one of Mary Hawes Wilmarth's daughters, who did not help with the HH Summer School to be held at RC, 29 June to 31 July 1896. According to the *HH Bulletin*, "Stress is laid upon the outdoor study of botany and birds" (1, no. 5 [May 1896]: 1; *JAPM*, 53:539). Physician, expert on eugenics, and dedicated suffragist Anna Ellsworth Blount (1872–1953), with her husband, conservationist, teacher, and minister Ralph E. Blount, who married in June 1893, taught the classes. He presented lessons in birds while she offered studies in botany.

35. Amanda Johnson, who took over JA's position as garbage inspector of the Nineteenth Ward of Chicago, was recognized by John C. W. Rhode, superintendent of street and alley cleaning for Chicago, as "being the best of all 34 Inspectors." And he reported to JA that "Miss Johnson has now the regular appointment from the Civil Service Commission and will remain Inspector of the 19th Ward hereafter" (John C. W. Rhode to JA, 26 May 1896, SCPC, JAC; *JAPM*, 3:181).

36. JA's resignation as garbage inspector for the Nineteenth Ward was accepted and noted in a letter to her by John C. W. Rhode, 26 May 1896 (see n. 35).

37. In 1896 Charles and Rho Zueblin lived at 6052 Kimbark Ave., Chicago

38. Robert A. Woods had enlisted JA's help in securing tickets to the Bayreuth Festival that she would attend 1 Aug. 1896.

## To Henry Demarest Lloyd

London— [England] June 21" 1896

My dear Mr Lloyd

Your two letters—the one to Mr. Trevor[1] and the one to Mr Hobson have both been so satisfactory that I am ashamed not to have written to you before.

The Hobsons[2] have been kindness itself—first they invited us to a little tea where we met Kenworthy[3] the disciple of Tolstoi who is both devoted and genuine in his non-resistance, and, Miss Routledge[4] sec'y of the Writers Club with other other interesting folk. Then they gave a dinner at which we almost ate ambrosia—so high was the talk and the fellowship. No one there how ever was so clever nor more interesting that[5] Mr Hobson himself. He is very enthusiastic over Wealth versus Common-Wealth[6] and I think that if he accepts the invitation from the University of Chicago to give a course of lectures, it will be mostly the desire of meeting you which determines him. Mr Trevor is a theme for a letter by himself so that I think I will save him until I see you. This great town has many wise men in it, but no one more impressive than the labor men themselves—Burns,[7] Tillett[8] and Mann[9] are three curiously distinct personalities.

Jane Addams and Mary Rozet Smith were befriended by an assortment of settlement, labor, and socialist leaders while they were in England in May and June 1896. The energetic Mary Ward, who founded Passmore Edwards Social Settlement, especially impressed Jane Addams, who often spoke about Ward's settlement after she returned to Chicago (courtesy Somerville College, Oxford, England).

I have gained a new impression of what <English> hospitality means, we have n't a single disengaged evening for dinner until we leave for Russia on Saturday. We have met Socialists of all varieties from Liebnecht[10] himself to the Fabian who has gone to sleep.

Mr Clark[11] is in wretched health and very pessimistic. Mr Burrows[12] plans to be in New York Sept. 1st so that you will probably see him before I am back. Please give my love to Mrs Lloyd[13] and tell her that I am coming to finish out my convalescent visit soon after my return & to discuss the "English situation." Thanking your letters and the good friendship which prompted them I am sincerely yours,

Jane Addams

ALS (SHSW, Lloyd; *JAPM*, 3:346–47).

1. For a biographical note on John Trevor, see JA to EGS, 29 [and 30] May 1896, n. 18, above.
2. For a biographical note on John A. Hobson and his wife, Florence Edgar Hobson, see JA to EGS, 29 [and 30] May 1896, n. 9, above.

3. For a biographical note on John C. Kenworthy, see JA to EGS, 29 [and 30] May 1896, n. 9, above.

4. For a biographical note on Florence Routledge, see JA to EGS, 29 [and 30] May 1896, n. 9, above.

5. JA probably meant to write *than*.

6. *Wealth against Commonwealth*, by Henry Demarest Lloyd, was first published by Harper Brothers in 1894. As an argument against monopoly and specifically taking John D. Rockefeller and Standard Oil to task, it became one of Lloyd's best-known and most influential works.

7. For a biographical note on John Burns, see JA to EGS, 29 [and 30] May 1896, n. 33, above.

8. Benjamin Tillett (1860–1943), English socialist, labor leader, and politician, was born in Bristol, England, and had a variety of jobs from the age of eight that included working in a brickyard and for a boot maker. After a stint as a sailor on a fishing vessel and in the navy and the merchant marine, he and his wife, Jane Tompkins, settled in Bethnal Green in London, and he became a docker. In 1887 he was key in forming the Tea Operatives and Labourers' Union that became the Dock, Wharf, Riverside, and General Labourers' Union. He was a leader during the 1889 London dock strike and in strikes that followed in 1911 and 1912. In 1910 he helped form Great Britain's National Transport Workers' Federation. In the Transport and General Workers' Union created in 1922, he served as international and political secretary until 1931. A member of the Fabian Society and one of the founders of the Independent Labour Party, he eventually joined the Social Democratic Federation and during the 1880s became a member of the Bristol Socialist Society.

While JA was visiting England, he was an alderman on the London County Council, 1892–98. It was not until 1917 that he became a Labour Party member of Parliament. He served until 1924 and again from 1929 to 1931. He was an outspoken supporter of Great Britain's entry into World War I. His *A Brief History of the Dockers Union* was published in 1910, *A History of the Transport Workers' Strike* issued in 1911, and his autobiographical *Memories and Reflections* in 1931.

JA visited with Ben Tillett and his family on 22 June 1896. In *Twenty Years*, she reported that he took her "in a rowboat down the Thames on a journey made exciting by the hundreds of dockers who cheered him as we passed one wharf after another on our way to his home in Greenwich" (263). There she took tea with his wife and two daughters. For JA's thank-you gift, Jane Tillett wrote to JA, "I almost envy you going into Russia and seeing Tolstoi himself give him a look and a handshake for some of his admirers here" (30 June 1896, SCPC, JAC; *JAPM*, 3:412). Tillett visited JA and HH in Dec. 1901 and presented "Reform Movements in England."

9. For a biographical note on Tom Mann, see JA to EGS, 29 [and 30] May 1896, n. 20, above.

10. For a biographical note on William Liebknecht, see JA to EGS, 29 [and 30] May 1896, n. 15, above.

11. For a biographical note on William Clarke, see JA to EGS, 29 [and 30] May 1896, n. 8, above.

12. JA had written Herbert Burrows to let him know she was in London. He recalled meeting her in Chicago, probably during the World's Columbian Exposition in 1893, and called on her almost immediately. He was very attentive and introduced her to socialist leaders, escorted her to gatherings, and attended at least one of her public presentations.

Herbert Burrows (1845–1922) was born in Redgrave, Suffolk, and studied briefly at Cambridge Univ. In 1877 he moved to London and became a member of the National Secular Society; in 1881 he was a founding member of the Social Democratic Federation and represented the organization on the executive body of the Law and Liberty League. A key figure in organizing the London match girls' strike of 1888, he then became the treasurer of the Union of Women Matchmakers. He was also a member of the Rainbow Circle, a group of Liberal, Fabian, and socialist leaders who began meeting in 1893 to see how they might work together to advance a reform agenda; the Theosophical Society; the International Arbitration and Peace Assn.; and the International Arbitration League.

13. Jessie Louise Bross Lloyd. See JA to Henry Demarest Lloyd, 18 Nov. 1891, n. 1, above.

## To Gertrude Barnum

London [England] May[June] 22, 1896.[1]

My dear Friend

I have never thanked you for the Russian letters which from what I can learn from several sources promises to be the most interesting letters we have. How ~~did~~ <were> you so lucky as to know Miss Thomas?[2]

Dont you worry a minute about the Barnetts, they were much impressed with your "Nobility" and the things you said about England. The unhappy incident was referred to very lightly. I will tell you about it. I had a beautiful visit with them.[3] We still go on seeing interesting folk day by day[4] and I am filled with awfully interesting impressions.

We are engaged to dinner every evening[5] until we leave next Saturday[6] and even had to refuse an invitation from the Nobility because we were "full up."[7] I went to Oxford on Thursday[8] and Mary came up the next morning. We stayed with the Sydney Balls (it was in his rooms that Mr Barnett read the first paper looking toward settlements).[9] They took no end of pains to have interesting people drop in. We went to a lawn party in the afternoon.[10] Miss Toynbee came to lunch.[11] The Canils[12] (The man who wrote that essay on Lincoln, I like so much) were very satisfactory, and if we hadnt gone to a student's debate and a vive voce[13] examination of degrees, I would think that Oxford was filled with the Wise and Great.

We had a charming evening at Toynbee the other evening.[14] I never saw anything simpler or more genuine than the relations of the Residents to the "Ions of Rhoenix,"[15] whom they were entertaining, nor any thing much prettier than the lighted quadrangle.

I attended a lawn party at the Neighborhood Euice[16] last night which was very pretty, they do know how to use out of doors.

I am so pleased about "Lake Side."[17] And the lectures of the summer-School appears to me quite dazzling.[18] We have seen a lot of Girls Clubs,—but nothing approaching the Jane Club—and no fresh air schemes as good and simple as ours I think. I have lots to write—but little time for writing[.]

Please give my undying love to the household. Always Yours

Jane Addams

HLSr in hand of SAAH (["Record Book of Copies of Letters and Articles"], SC, Starr; *JAPM*, 3:154–56).

1. According to JA's diary, the events that JA described in this letter happened in June 1896. For that reason the editors have altered the date. SAAH could have inserted the incorrect month when she copied the letter into the notebook that she later gave to EGS. It is now part of the Starr papers at SC.

2. Elizabeth H. Thomas (1856–1949) was born in Union Springs, N.Y., one of three daughters of J. John and H. Mary Thomas. She identified herself as a Quaker. She lived in England and traveled on the Continent for a year in 1895, when she may have visited Russia and met reformers there. By 1896 she was in Chicago, where she taught English to Russian immigrants at HH. She returned to New York City in mid-1898 and lodged with her widowed mother and two sisters for a time. In July 1901, she was one of eight female delegates in Indianapolis at the founding meeting of the Socialist Party of America. She settled in Milwaukee, where she was president of the Socialist Democratic Publishing Co., which published the *Milwaukee Leader*; was an associate of socialist and editor Victor L. Berger (1860–1929); and served as a popularly elected socialist member of the Milwaukee Board of Education during World War I. She favored woman suffrage, but saw it as a class issue and did not favor supporting it through the NAWSA.

The letters that Gertrude Barnum's friend Elizabeth H. Thomas provided were certainly helpful to JA. Alexandra Steven of Tablonka, Russia, wrote to JA to invite her to visit: "Both your letters, with Miss Thomas' letter . . . reached me only today" (11 [23] July 1896, SCPC, JAC; *JAPM*, 3:428). JA made attempts before she reached Russia to acquire letters of introduction to reform leaders there. In addition to Thomas, the following provided JA with suggestions for people she should see in Russia and in some cases letters of introduction to them: J. C. Kenworthy and Thomas Thornton of 23 Egerton Gardens in South Kensington, London, who was a friend of Toynbee Hall resident Edward Alexander Coles McCurdy (1871–1957) and reported to JA that settlement leaders were at the heart of reform in Russia.

3. On JA's visit with Rev. Samuel A. Barnett and Henrietta Barnett, see JA to EGS, 29 [and 30] May 1896, n. 11, above.

4. Among the "interesting folk" that JA had seen were the following: On Sunday, 14 June 1896, after sharing breakfast with Kier Hardie, who had visited HH in 1895 (see JA to MRS, 4 [, 5, and 6] Sept. 1895, n. 18, above), JA was treated to a tour of London by Tom Mann (see JA to EGS, 29 [and 30] May 1896, n. 20, above) and Kier Hardie that included "I[ndependent]. L[abour]. P[arty].[,] Gospel meetings. Secularist meeting[.] Salvation Army all thru the streets, very interesting and impressive" (Addams, "Diary, 1896," 14 June; *JAPM*, 29:261). The next day, 15 June, at 10:00 A.M., she was interviewed at the *London Illustrated* office, had lunch at the South Kensington Work House, and sat for photographs at Hollyer's studio (see JA to MRS, 27 June 1896, n. 11, below). That evening she joined the Bosanquets once again for dinner (see JA to EGS, 29 [and 30] May 1896, n. 7, above). The Hobsons were also guests, and a garden party afterward included additional guests. On 16 June, JA met with John Burns and Ben Tillett and visited the Soho Club at 59 Greek St., the Honor Club at 9 Fitzroy St., the College for Working Women, and the Girls Jewish Club in the East End. On 17 June, JA was a guest at Toynbee Hall. She visited with Alfred Hicks's mother on 20 June and attended a garden party at Leighton Hall and a meeting of the Woman's Industrial Council. JA "much impressed with Miss [Clementina] Black's knowledge of the East end" when she visited her on 21 June (Addams, "Diary, 1896," 21 June; *JAPM*, 29:264).

In addition to the *London Illustrated*, JA was also interviewed by journalist Frederick McKenzie (1869–1931) for the London *Daily News*. His story, titled "HH: The American Toynbee Hall," appeared 3 June 1896. After JA described the development and program of HH, McKenzie asked for her views of "London charities." In response, JA indicated that she had come "to learn from them, not to criticize." However, McKenzie quoted her "tentative criticism: 'It seems to me . . . that your London settlements and charities are not nearly so democratic as ours. The people who come seem to have less control in the management, and the workers sometimes appear to regard the people merely as material to be operated on.'" When asked how she "managed in Chicago," JA responded, "'Well, we do not look on the people as material, but try to make friends with them. Our great aim is to understand life from their point of view, to see things as they see them and to really understand their aims and wants.'"

5. On 23 June, JA had dinner with Methodist minister, educator, and reformer Scott Lidgett (1854–1953) at Bermondsey Settlement; on 24 June, she attended the Southwark Settlement Assn. (see JA to MRS, 22 [24] June, 1896, below); on 25 June, JA had dinner without MRS at the home of B. F. C. Costelloe (see JA to MRS, [26 and] 27 June 1896, n. 10, below); on 26 June, her engagement was at 8:00 P.M. with the Humphrey Wards (see JA to MRS, 27 June 1896, below); on 27 June, JA did not reach her hotel until 1:00 A.M. from the Eighty Club dinner; on 28 June, she returned late from sightseeing at Hampton Court and Richmond; and on 29 June, she attended the Woman's Industrial Council meeting.

6. On Tuesday, 30 June, JA and MRS left London for Hull, England, to board the S.S. *Eldorado* of the Wilson Line to journey to Bergen, Norway. In her diary, JA recorded "rough after supper, ill" (30 June 1896; *JAPM*, 29:269).

7. JA may have been referring to a luncheon invitation from Lady Emilia Francis Strong Dilke for Thursday, 25 June, or Friday, 26 June.

8. On Thursday, 18 June, JA arrived in Oxford by herself; MRS joined her on Friday, 19 June. Before they returned to London on 19 June, they lunched with Charlotte Toynbee (see n. 11) and visited Maudlin and Christ Church colleges at Oxford.

9. In her diary on 19 June, JA wrote that she went to St. John's College and "saw the room in wh [Samuel A. Barnett] read his first settlement paper" on 17 Nov. 1883 that led to the founding of the settlement movement (*JAPM*, 29:263). It is likely that Sidney and Oona Ball had recently occupied those quarters. Sidney Ball (1857–1918), born in Pershore, Worcester, England, and educated at Wellington and Oriel colleges, became a fellow at St. John's College in 1887. He wed Oona Howard (Butlin) (1867–1941) in Dec. 1891, and the couple settled at Oxford, where, by 1896, Ball had risen to the position of tutor and senior proctor in St. John's College. During the 1880s, he joined the Fabian Society and was instrumental in creating the Oxford branch in 1895. A noted political radical and university reformer, according to his wife he was "the recognized head of university socialism" at Oxford (Ball, *Sidney Ball*, 288). At Oxford he organized a Social Science Club. Its goal was "to find a way to the solution of social difficulties by practical investigation" (Collini, *Liberalism and Sociology*, 58). He was the first president of Barnett House, founded in 1914 and associated with Oxford for the advancement of economic and social studies connected with the work of university settlements, and he was a leader in creating the Workers' Educational Assn. He authored a number of publications. Oona Ball published memoirs of her husband, several volumes of her own prose and poetry, and a guidebook to Oxford. During JA's visit, she was instrumental in making introductions for JA among the British socialist community. JA's evening reading on 18 June was Sidney Ball's *The Moral Aspects of Socialism*, published in 1896 as Fabian tract 72, and as pp. 290–322 of vol. 6 of the *International Journal of Ethics*.

10. The lawn party was given by the master of "Waddam's" [Wadham] College at Oxford. It is likely that JA mistook the sound of "Wadham" for "Waddam," a name with which she was familiar. It remains the name of one of the townships in her home county of Stephenson in Illinois.

After the lawn party, JA and the Balls had dinner with Rev. John Carter of the Christian Social Union and quizzed him about "tainted money." She recorded in her diary that he "said same thing as Mr Barnett" (18 June 1896; *JAPM*, 29:263) (see JA to EGS, 29 [and 30] May 1896, n. 11, above). Rev. John Carter (1861–1944) was born in Toronto and educated in Canada and at Exeter College, Oxford. He was ordained and served as curate of Limehouse Parish Church, 1887–89, when he became librarian of Pusey House until 1921. He became honorary secretary of the Christian Social Union, a social gospel organization of the Church of England founded in 1889 and dedicated to remedying poverty and establishing social justice. He served as vice-president of the organization in 1910. From 1891 until 1914, he was editor of the *Economic Review*. He was mayor of Oxford, 1925–26, and an alderman, 1913–32.

11. JA's diary revealed that Oona Ball took her to visit Arnold Toynbee's widow, Charlotte Maria Atwood Toynbee, at 10 Norham Gardens on 18 June. The next day, JA and MRS had lunch with Mrs. Toynbee. Charlotte Atwood (1841–1931) was born in Muswell Hill and educated in English and French schools. She met Arnold Toynbee in 1873, and despite the eleven-year difference in their ages, they were married in 1879 while he was a tutor at Balliol College. After her husband's death, she edited his *Lectures on the Industrial Revolution in England* and continued her interest in his work through her ongoing relationship with Toynbee Hall. In 1883 she became the honorary house treasurer of Lady Margaret Hall for the education of women and kept its accounts until 1920. Charlotte Toynbee became the first woman elected as guardian of the poor in Oxford, a position she held from 1893 for thirty years. Though not in favor of woman suffrage or opening baccalaureate degrees to women, she did believe that women should have a voice in issues touching their natural spheres of interests. She argued for pension reform and self-help opportunities, especially for women.

12. SAAH had difficulty reading JA's writing and often misspelled proper names. She misspelled *Caird* as *Canils.*

On their last afternoon in Oxford, JA and MRS were entertained by Edward and Caroline Frances Wylie Caird. JA recalled that Caird had provided a "fine analysis of Abraham Lincoln" and added that he "spoke of the great American 'who was content merely to dig the channels through which the moral life of his countrymen might flow.'" JA pointed out that Caird's discussion of Lincoln helped her discover her own relationship to her immigrant neighbors. "In the unceasing ebb and flow of justice and oppression we must all dig channels as best we may . . . vision and wisdom as well as high motives must lie behind every effective stroke in the continuous labor for human equality" (Addams, *Twenty Years*, 40–41). Edward Caird (1835–1908), a Scottish-born philosopher, left the professorship of moral philosophy of Univ. of Glasgow, 1866–93, to become master of Balliol, Oxford, 1893–1907. A leader in Britain's idealist movement, 1870–1900s, he was a progressive and liberal, believed women should be educated, and supported the settlement movement, particularly Mansfield House. Among his most significant publications was *Essays on Literature and Philosophy*, published in 1892.

On Saturday evening, 5 Oct. 1895, Edward Caird presented a lecture on Abraham Lincoln for Toynbee Hall. A report in the *Times* (London) indicated that Caird argued that Lincoln "became great by discovering for himself and for others what the people really wanted, and by providing the channels in which the growing moral force of their life would flow," someone who "could believe in men without being duped by them." Lincoln proved that "it was possible to be a real ruler of men, and yet only to move along with the general sentiment of those ruled by him" and "to abolish the distinction between leading and following; to discern what was deepest and best in the popular sentiment" and "to act only when the real power and sympathy of the nation was behind him" (7 Oct. 1896).

13. SAAH translated JA's text as "vive voce" when it should have been "viva voce," meaning orally. In her 1896 diary, JA termed the debate "very poor" (18 June; *JAPM*, 29:263).

14. JA's visit to Toynbee Hall on Wednesday, 17 June, was the result of an invitation from Edward A. C. McCurdy that arrived while she was visiting Samuel and Henrietta Barnett in Bristol, England. JA and MRS attended dinner at 6:30 P.M. Edward McCurdy indicated that he expected "a good supply of residents" to be in attendance (Edward A. C. McCurdy to JA, 9 June 1896, SCPC, JAC; *JAPM*, 3:272).

15. JA and MRS also attended a meeting of the Sons of the Phoenix (SAAH transcribed this as "Ions of Rhoenix" when she copied JA's letter), which took place at Toynbee Hall after their dinner (see n. 14). The temperance organization began as the Grand Order of the Total Abstinent Sons of the Phoenix in England about 1870. With chapters primarily in London

and southeastern England, the organization may have become associated with Toynbee Hall in 1896.

16. If this letter should have been dated 22 June 1896, the night before would have been Sunday, 21 June 1896. JA's diary for that date indicated that she wrote letters during the morning and at 3:00 P.M. took a train from Victoria Station and reached South Croydon at 3:26. There she visited novelist, Fabian member, and leader in the Women's Industrial Counsel, 1889–1909, Clementina Black (1854–1922), at 19 South End, and recorded "charming little house & garden . . . 10 ½ miles ride home on the omnibus" (21 June 1896; *JAPM*, 29:264). There is no mention of a lawn party in her diary entry.

17. "Lakeside," a summer camping venue for children at Lake Side, Ill., began 1 Aug. 1895 (see JA to MRS, 8 Aug. 1895, n. 7, above). "The Hull-House Country Club opened for its second season on June 15 and closed Sept. 28, 1896. During this time, a little over three months, 220 people were entertained, and including bicyclists who dropped in to take Sunday dinner and rest, or visitors who came to spend a day with friends at the club, besides the Hull-House Women's Club, the Lowell Social, the Henry Learned and the College Extension students, who made the club grounds headquarters for their respective picnics.

"A distinctive feature of the house this summer was that it took a number of the Visiting Nurses' patients, convalescents who were too ill to grow strong in Chicago and needed the bracing air, sun and good country milk, and in every case went away greatly improved. These delicate ones were watched over by the whole club, who accepted the extra care with the best spirit of sympathy and helpfulness. . . . One source of daily entertainment was the club baby, who was born at the Club House June 25 and became a prominent resident from the very first" (*HH Bulletin* 1, no. 6 [Oct. 1896]: 4; *JAPM*, 53:552). The *HH Bulletin* for May 1896 indicated that Margaretta West and Ella Waite would be in charge and that the "Terms, per week, $4, for adults, $1.50 for children. Commutation tickets will be kept at Hull-House; by using these guests can have round-trip passage on the Chicago and Northwestern Railroad for 50 cents. . . . Children or adults unable to pay the necessary expenses for a week in the country will apply to Miss Gernon, who will try to arrange for as many as possible through the Lake Geneva Holiday House, Michigan farmers and other country week agencies" (1, no. 5: 1; *JAPM*, 53:539).

18. The fifth HH Summer School was held at RC, 29 June through 31 July 1896.

## To Mary Rozet Smith

Women's University Settlement
44. Nelson Square, Blackfriars Road, S.E.
[London, England] June 22d[24] 1896[1]

Dear Sister[2]

. . . The meeting of the Southwark Settlement[3] was interesting but powerful cold and scholarly "the poor" might have been another name for microbes. They asked me to speak but I did n't dare say what was on my tongue & so only made a brief remark.

But Red Cross Hall and the Gardens with the rows of mediaveal cottages at one side was charming.[4] I want to drive down there with you Monday evening[5] it is the prettiest little spot I have seen in a London slum—not excepting the quadrangle of Toynbee. Miss Hill[6] was very nice & toted me around the outside of the cottages & a big block—but she said that it was quite impossible to go in unless it were collecting day. There is an half ~~an~~ hour before dinner and I am put into a room <“>to rest” and then we go to Morley College.[7] Yours always

Jane Addams

ALS (SCPC, JAC; *JAPM*, 3:353–56).

1. It is likely that the date of 22 June 1896 on this letter is incorrect. On that date, JA spent most of the day from lunch until 7:00 P.M. with Benjamin Tillett and his family. According to her diary, JA "shopped all morning[;] went to steam boat office" (see n. 2) on 24 June 1896 (Addams, "Diary, 1896"; *JAPM*, 29:266).

2. The editors have omitted the first portion of the first paragraph of this document. In it JA reported to MRS, who was in France with her parents, that after visiting the Atlantic Transportation Co. on Fenchurch St., she learned that Eleanor Smith and Amalie Hannig were on their way to England and due shortly to arrive on the S.S. *Manitoba*, which had sailed from New York on 11 June 1896.

3. In her 1896 diary, JA reported, "[S]poke today at meeting of Southwark Settlement Assn." (24 June; *JAPM*, 29:266) in Red Cross Hall. The Southwark Settlement Assn. was associated with the Women's University Settlement (later called Blackfriars Settlement), organized in 1887 by the women's colleges associated with Oxford and Cambridge universities. By 1896 it was located at 44–46 Nelson Square. Associated with the settlement were rental homes developed under the guidance of Octavia Hill (see n. 6) and managed by the settlement. In addition, there were classes, clubs, and programs, especially for children.

4. Red Cross Hall and the cottages that surrounded it had been designed by English architect Elijah Hoole at the instigation of Octavia Hill (see n. 6). See also *PJA*, 2:512, n. 142.

5. JA's diary for Monday, 29 June 1896, when she expected MRS to return from France, indicated the following: "A. M. bank, St. Pauls, shopping. [W]ent to Wm Morris' factory. [M]eeting of the Woman Industrial Council. [M]et M. R. S. at Station" (*JAPM*, 29:268).

6. Octavia Hill (1838–1912), English social reformer, was devoted especially to nongovernment housing reform, improving the lives of people who lived in London, and saving open spaces for poor people. She began working when she was fourteen years old as a glass painter placed in charge of a cooperative guild workroom for distressed women. She was a disciple of art critic, social reformer, and philanthropist John Ruskin and was a copiest for him in the Dulwich Art Gallery and the National Gallery. Ruskin, who was impressed by her ability and her philosophy of self-reliance and concern for the working poor, purchased the leases of three cottages in Paradise Place, Marylebone, in London and placed them in Hill's care. Their goal was to produce a 5 percent annual return from rents after repairs, with any excess reinvested in the properties for the benefit of the tenants. She was successful and by 1874 had fifteen housing areas with almost three thousand tenants under her management and a coterie of assistants who helped her with the enterprise. Hill insisted on managing the tenants as well as the houses. She did not tolerate rents in arrears and with her assistants collected rents in person weekly while checking on tenants and their welfare. Above all, Hill encouraged personal responsibility among her tenants.

7. Morley College, London, was begun in the early 1880s and by 1889 opened as the Morley Memorial College for Working Men and Women. It was an adult education facility associated with the Royal Victoria Coffee and Music Hall and provided plays, concerts, and lectures as special entertainment. During the 1890s, one of Octavia Hill's associates, Emma Cons (1838–1912), was primarily responsible for its development and operation. JA reported that Morley College had a "charming Common Room, . . . the atmosphere very social." She continued that "no one can be a member of a club without joining a class" ("Diary 1896," 24 June; *JAPM*, 29:266).

The editors have omitted the text of the last two paragraphs of the letter. In the first paragraph, JA reported that she had purchased "a stout 2d hand" trunk for "14s." In the second, JA reported on her search for photographs of London sites and indicated, "I hope the rain did n't make the crossing perfectly horrid. I have thought about you all day it is needless to say that. I have missed you."

## To Mary Rozet Smith

Arundell Hotel [London, England] June [26 and] 27" 1896[1]

My dear Sister

E. Smith & Miss Hannig[2] landed at eleven yesterday morning[3] and I found them at the hotel when I came back for lunch[.] They are going to spend a few days in London and will certainly stay until they see you on Monday— It is powerful fine to have them here— <We went to Toynbee yesterday afternoon.>

I had a long morning in Whitechapel yesterday[.] People's Palace[,][4] Wilke's lodging house[5] (the one I have been hunting with the big kitchen—altho the one for women was closed because of difficulties)[,] a large Salvation Army Shelter & food depot,[6] a fine Tee To Tum[7] & Charringtons Hall[8] with its many attachments. They were all very interesting & suggestive. The Tee To Tum does n't seem so grocery store like once inside. It has billiard rooms, dance halls, but I was told upon inquiry that "of course it does n't pay in such a drinking neighborhood" that "none of the East End one's are self sustaining."[9] The Salvation Army fed a 1000 a day even in summer, coffee at ha'penny a cupa but they can only make the food pay with a thousand, all the food researches are discovering from the Coffee House outlook, & our food is much better than theirs which they acknowledge to be the cheapest possible. I have an appointment at twelve with Mr Went who is in charge of all the Tee To Tum, he maybe encouraging.

The dinner at Mr Costelloes[10] was very interesting, I kept wishing for you all the time. Only the Webbs[11] were at dinner, it was most easy & delightful. There was a little reception afterward of about twenty people—apparently all distinguished for something.[12] The former chairman of the Co. Council—who held it for six yeas—was delightful and he[13] & another Councillor[14] with Mr Ward[15] (the Toynbee man) got into a discussion over the model dwellings wh was most illuminating. I wish I had a chance to tell it to your father while it is fresh in my mind. There are apparently two sides to every thing. The children's letters[16] are so funny that I think I will send them after all. Yours has just come,[17] I wish I could express all the tender thoughts I feel.

The two ladies send their love to you all. They will be in Paris the day after you leave. They had some storms but insisted that their big boat was steadier than the usual ones & the cabin fine. They have just started out for a long day.

With love to Mr & Mrs Smith <my regards to Mrs Broadhead> Always yours

Jane Addams

ALS (SCPC, JAC; *JAPM*, 3:397–402).

1. It is likely that JA began this letter on 26 June 1896. In her 1896 diary on 25 June, she recorded that "Miss E. Smith & Miss Hannig arrived at 12 noon" (*JAPM*, 29:266). In addition, she also reported that on the morning of 25 June, she visited the People's Palace, Wilke's lodging house, Charrington Hall, the Salvation Army shelter, and the Tee-To-Tum and office.

2. Eleanor Smith and Amalie Hannig, in charge of the newly formed HH Music School, were traveling in Europe during the summer. JA was happy to have their company; MRS had gone to Paris with her parents on Wednesday, 24 June, and did not return until the following Monday, 29 June. To EGS JA reported, "I had expected to be alone until Monday but fortunately E. Smith & Miss Hennig came on Thursday and we have been having a very jolly time together. I have been out to dinner every night this week, and am uncommon well" (27 June 1896, SC, Starr; *JAPM*, 3:403). The text for this letter survives only in the hand of SAAH, who translated JA's handwriting incorrectly for the spelling of the names of JA's two friends.

3. See n. 1.

4. JA had also visited the People's Palace on Saturday, 6 June, when she recorded in her 1896 diary, "P.M. Saw Prince of Wales at the opening of the People's Palace Ex. The Princess & the daughters Maud and Victoria" (*JAPM*, 29:257). The occasion had been the opening of the East London Trades, Industries and Arts Exhibition held at the People's Palace. For information on the People's Palace, see *PJA*, 2:624, n. 19.

5. By 1896 Augustus Wilke served as the chief administrative officer or warden for at least two different shelters or boardinghouses for men. Both were called the Victoria Home for Working Men and could house and feed 450 men each. Both were located in London's East End: the first to be established was at 39 and 41 Commercial St., and the other, founded in 1890, was at 177 Whitechapel Road. Both served food for a small charge and provided bed, bath, and laundry facilities by the night or by the week for various fees. In addition, men could bring their own food and cook it in the kitchen, congregate in space provided in each facility, use a quiet room in which to write or the library, and attend religious services twice weekly, with at least one additional evening a week for Bible study in the six-hundred-seat auditorium. Seen as a slightly better place than the boarding facilities operated by the Salvation Army, the shelter's clientele was composed of "those who were formerly merchants, doctors, master-builders, lawyers, undergraduates of Oxford and Cambridge, besides artisans, working-men out of work, day labourers, costermongers, discharged soldiers—in fact, men of every sort and condition. All are poor, some by misfortune, some by vice," wrote Mrs. Charles Garnett when she described the facility at 39 and 41 Commercial St. ("In Whitechapel"). Wilke, who tried to help his boarders find employment, indicated that the facilities were self-sustaining so long as there were sufficient donations of dollars and used clothing.

6. JA may have visited the City Colony Headquarters of the Salvation Army at 272 Whitechapel Rd. It served as a food depot for other army facilities and, in addition to its large kitchen and dining hall, also had a dormitory for 270 men, "each person occupying an oblong box" or "'bunk'" with mattress and covers. Also in the Whitechapel district, there was a "women's shelter in Hanbury-street" with 290 beds and across the street from it workshops for 270 men who were lodged in the "'Lighthouse Métrople' in Quaker-street" ("The Salvation Army").

7. Tee-To-Tum was the title given to a group of temperance clubs founded in London for working men. JA may have visited the Tee-To-Tum in the East End. According to the *London Guardian*, 19 Mar. 1890, it was "a large, neat building of two or three stores, very attractive outside and cozy and brilliant within as any Continental café. The first floor is a public restaurant, scrupulously clean and homelike, where one can get for his money the best of tea, coffee, cocca, soup, meats, vegetables, puddings and buns. In one corner is a counter where tea is sold in packages, and the sales average some 7,000 pounds a week. The second floor is a network of apartments for the use and accommodation of the members; a smoking room for lounging, a newsroom, a café, classrooms for the benefit of students, chess and draft-

rooms, a spacious billiard room, and a hall with seats for 500 people, with a stage at one end, from which addresses are made on Sundays and where . . . performances are rendered every Saturday ("The Tee-To-Tum," *Ogden (Utah) Standard*, 12 Dec. 1891).

P. R. Buchanan, who helped organize the clubs based on a successful University Club created for and operated by working men in Bethnal Green, explained the name: "The institutions were to be temperance places, so 'tea' suggested itself. Tee-to-tum is the word for 'tea house' in the language of Ceylon and seemed to fill all the requirements, so we adopted it." He went on to explain: "I didn't see why tea merchants shouldn't help us out. . . . I made the suggestion to some of the London importers, and now the Tee-to-tums hire their buildings from them for a rent that covers gas, taxes, and everything. Besides that, the merchants have counters in the co-operative stores [associated with the Tee-To-Tums] at which their teas, coffees, and sugars are sold, and they are the only articles of the kind used by the establishments themselves" (quoted in "An American Tee-To-Tum," *New York Times*, 22 Jan. 1893). The Tee-To-Tums had members who used the club regularly, but they also served meals to the general public. According to Mr. Buchanan, in 1893 three thousand dollars was required to establish a Tee-To-Tum. He estimated that the annual income and expenditure was more than five thousand dollars. P. R. Buchanan, whom the *New York Times* called "P. G. Buchanan," was a city merchant in London who served as secretary and managing agent for the East India and Ceylon Tea Co. He and his family lived in Bethnal Green.

8. The Great Assembly Hall in Mile End Rd. was opened in 1886. Constructed by Frederick Nicholas Charrington (1850–1936), with the help of other wealthy supporters, it could seat five thousand people and was the home of Charrington's evangelical and temperance efforts, which began in 1870 when Charrington founded the Tower Hamlets Mission. Charrington, heir to a brewery fortune, rejected his inheritance and worked "to spread the word of Christ, to check the torrent of alcohol and to make Britain in general and East London in particular a 'purer' place to live in" (Bermant, *London's East End*, 99).

9. Of her visit with Mr. Went, who managed the Tee-To-Tums, JA wrote in her 1896 diary: "[S]aid each Billiard table ought to bring in $5.00 a wk. The Te To Tums not self sustaining save in connection with a good club of men even Oxford House Club does not pay all its [way?]" (26 June; *JAPM*, 29:267).

10. Of the evening at "Mr Costelloe's," JA reported to EGS, "On Friday evening at the Costelloe's, I met Mr & Mrs Sydney Webb. There was a little reception after dinner of some very interesting folk—four County Councellors, got into a discussion which was most illuminating. One of them was the Toynbee Mr Ward" (27 June 1896; *JAPM*, 3:403–4). For biographical information on Henry Ward, see *PJA*, 2:515–16, n. 157. JA's 1896 diary indicated that the dinner took place on Thursday, 25 June 1896 (*JAPM*, 29:266).

Benjamin Francis Conn (B. F. C.) Costelloe (1855–99) was a longtime close friend of Rev. Samuel Barnett and his wife. Henrietta Barnett described him as "a Roman Catholic, an open exhibitioner of Balliol and a double first of Oxford, holding also a Glasgow degree. He had a soul that worshiped, a mind that grasped at all things, an ambition that vaulted above himself, and manners that were very trying. His talk was by turns provocative, persuasive, poetical, practical and preposterous" (Barnett, *Canon Barnett*, 1:149). She also indicated that Rev. Barnett thought favorably of him. He began coming to help the Barnetts in St. Jude's Parish even before Toynbee Hall was created. After graduation from Oxford, he joined several other classmates in living and working in the East End, where they converted a former beer shop on Leman St. into quarters and called it "The Friary." Costelloe vacationed with the Barnetts; entered into all manner of philosophical discussions with them and an ever-increasing assortment of friends; helped out at Toynbee Hall, especially lecturing at men's clubs; continued with scholarly inquiry; and was devoted to helping London's working poor. Studies he pursued during the late 1880s and early 1890s resulted in *First Report of the Royal Commission on Market Rights and Rolls* (1888) and a speech, "London Taxation," which he gave at Toynbee Hall in 1893. In 1898 he was elected from Bethnal Green to the London County Council and served until his death. He wrote several pamphlets and cotranslated and edited one book. In 1884 the Com. on Irish Affairs published his forty-page pamphlet, *Notes and Statistics Concerning the Irish Franchise*, and during the 1880s and into the 1890s he was a member of the Catholic Truth Society Com. It issued a number of his speeches and tracts, one of which was "The Church Catholic," an address delivered in Feb. 1888 at South Place Institute to a primarily non-Catholic audience. When Henrietta Barnett created the State Children's Assn. in Nov. 1896, he became a member of its governing committee.

11. When JA met Sidney Webb (1859–1947) and Martha Beatrice Potter Webb (1858–1943), they had been married since 1892. Beatrice was born in Standish, Gloucestershire, the daughter of Laurencina Heyworth and Richard Potter. She was self-taught, took up social work like her sister Catherine, assisted Charles Booth in his studies in London, and served as a rent collector for the East End Dwellings Co. She met her husband in 1891 while she was conducting research on England's cooperative movement. Sidney Webb was born in London and at the age of sixteen became an office clerk and studied at the Univ. of London until he qualified to join the Civil Service, where he served 1878–91. In 1885 he joined the Fabian Society and became a leader of the group established to investigate and report on a number of timely social issues. In 1892 he was a successful candidate from Deptford for the London County Council, a position he held for eighteen years. As the chairman for the Technical Instruction Com., he became known as the minister of public education for London. He and his wife were instrumental in founding the London School of Economics and Political Science in 1895. In the 1890s, the Webbs worked on at least two books together: *The History of Trade Unionism* (1894) and *Industrial Democracy* (1897). Both believed strongly in government regulation of the economy to promote a more equitable distribution of wealth. They favored not revolution but rather social change through a more efficient operation of the economy. Both totally disapproved of the Poor Law system in England. In 1905, when the British government established a royal commission to investigate the Poor Law system, Beatrice Webb was asked to serve. The Webbs prepared and published a minority report when Beatrice disagreed with the findings of most of the other commission members. None of their recommendations, including doing away with the Poor Law, creating a national employment bureau, and improving education and health services for all, was accepted. By 1915 Sidney Webb had become active in the Labour Party. In 1923 he won a seat in the House of Commons, where he remained until 1929, when he transferred to the House of Lords as First Baron Passfield. He served Ramsay MacDonald in the first Labour Party cabinet as president of the Board of Trade; in the second Labour Party cabinet, he was secretary of state for the colonies, 1929–31. The Webbs were impressed with changes they saw in Russia after the Soviet revolution and wrote two books about it. They also wrote a number of other works and helped found the Labour Party's weekly periodical *New Statesman* in 1913.

The Webbs visited HH in 1898 during their whirlwind tour of the United States. Beatrice Webb recorded in her diary that JA was "an interesting combination of the organiser, the enthusiast and the subtle observer of human characteristics." She also described her as a "charming personality, gentle and dignified" and indicated that JA "excels in persistency of purpose and unflinching courage." Of HH itself, she was less impressed, recalling that as special guests, they "underwent a terrific ordeal" that included the "exhausting business" of an "uncomfortable" dinner as well as "a reception, preceding a lecture and a severe heckling." She also commented on the "unappetising food of the restaurant, the restless movements of the residents from room to room, the rides over impossible streets littered with unspeakable garbage" (from *Beatrice Webb's American Diary*, 1895, in Davis and McCree, *Eighty Years at HH*, 66).

12. JA's diary for 25 June 1896 reads: "Mr Dickinson —Dep'ty Chairman of the Co. Council for six years. Mr Harris, Mr Ward Chair of Board of Works very important—apparently" (*JAPM*, 29:266). See n. 10.

Willoughby Hyatt Dickinson (1859–1943), a progressive associated with the British Liberal Party, served as one of the twelve aldermen selected by the 118 councillors of the London County Council to help run the council. He was deputy chairman of the London County Council from 1892 until 1896 and became the chairman of the council, 1900–1901. Mr. Harris was likely George David Harris, known as a moderate, who served as a councillor from South Paddington from 1889 until 1901, when he was elevated to the position of alderman. At his death in 1902, Sir Harris still had five more years to serve on his six-year term. Toynbee Hall's Henry Ward served as the vice-chairman of the London County Council, 1906–7.

13. In her 1896 diary, JA mentioned only three members of the London County Council by name: Mr. Dickinson, Mr. Harris, and Mr. Ward (see n. 12). None of the three was a "former chairman" of the council. In 1896 that would have been Sir John Hutton, who served in that capacity, 1892–95. She may have been referring to Willoughby Hyatt Dickinson and simply misunderstood his position on the council.

14. Likely George David Harris (see n. 12).

15. Henry Ward. See *PJA*, 2:515–16, n. 157.

16. The Linn children: John, Weber, Margaret, and Stanley. JA had been serving as guardian for Margaret and Stanley.

17. MRS's letter to JA is not known to be extant.

## To Mary Rozet Smith

Arundel Hotel.
Victoria Embankment. London. W.C. [England] June 27" 1896

My dear Sister

The dinner at Mrs <Humphrey> Ward's[1] was a great success. I sat next to Mr Bryce who was very delightful. He and Mrs Bryce[2] tried afterward <to arrange> to have me lunch with them, but as they are out of town for <over> Sunday it was impossible. Mr Birrill scintillated for about quarter of an hour at the end of that dinner in a most marvellous manner—almost as good as his essays.[3] Mrs Ward was a very gracious hostess. She really cares a great deal about the East End—showed a simple and natural emotion when she talked of it. The plan of her new Settlement is enough to make one's mouth water—a Greek frieze across the front of it, 400 ft frontage of gardens &c[.][4] They have all the money on hand and are just beginning. Miss Smith & Fl.[5] are out for the day but we meet at four. I have called of Mrs. Stead[6] (who was out of town) and on Mrs Hobson.[7] Yesterday I saw the County Council tenements in Bethnal Green,[8] they are a little disappointing after reading the enthusiastic descriptions.

I got a good deal of light from Mr Went the head of the "Tee To Tums"—as a whole they do not pay but are an enthusiasm of Mr Buchanan's[9] who supplies the deficit.

I am going to lunch with Mr & Mrs Sidney Webb[10]—I think that the invitation was genuine this time[.]

Please give my love to the dear family and believe <me> forever yours

J. A___

P.S. My Liberty gown was none too fine.[11] I was the only "lady" out of the eight who was not decollette.

ALI (SCPC, JAC; *JAPM*, 3:393–96).

1. For a biographical note on Mary Augusta Arnold Ward (Mrs. Humphry), see Two Essays in the *Forum*, Nov. and Oct. 1892, n. 78, above. See also JA to EGS, 29 [and 30] May 1896, n. 12, above.

2. JA was familiar with the work and reputation of James Bryce before she met him and his wife, Elizabeth Marion Ashton, whom he wed in 1889. James Bryce (1838–1922) was born in Belfast, Ireland, the son of James and Margaret Brice. He was educated primarily in Glasgow, the Univ. of Heidelberg, and Trinity College, Oxford, and became a fellow of Oriel College, Oxford, and practiced law in London for a number of years. From 1870 until 1893, he was Regius Prof. of Civil Law at Oxford and also taught at Owen's College in Manchester. He was first elected to Parliament as a Liberal, the party with which he was associated for the remainder of his life, from the Tower Hamlets in London in 1880 and remained a member of Parliament until 1907. He served in a number of government positions during the 1880s and into the early twentieth century. Among them were chairman of the Royal Comm. on Secondary Education, undersecretary of state for foreign affairs, chancellor of the Duchy of Lancaster, and president of the Board of Trade—all prior to 1896. From 1907 until 1913, he was Britain's ambassador to the United States. He had already gained fame as a historian, most particularly for *The American Commonwealth* (1888), an examination of the institutions of the United States. He became Viscount Bryce in 1914 and joined the House of Lords. During World War I, he reported on German atrocities in Belgium and the Armenian genocide in the Ottoman Empire. In the last years of his life, he served at the International Court at The Hague, approved of the League of Nations, but did not favor woman suffrage. He wrote many books and essays during his life and received many honors.

In her letter of 27 June 1896, JA requested that EGS "ask Mrs Kelley to send me[Mr?] Bryse c/o the House of Commons, A copy of the Eight Hour Law, and of the Supreme Court decision—He seemed so amazed that it should have been unconstitutional under the Illinois Constitution" (SC, Starr; *JAPM*, 3:404; this letter is extant only as a copy in the hand of SAAH). On 30 June, James Bryce wrote to JA to thank her for "the copy you so kindly promise me of the decision of the Court of Illinois. It will be full of interest to me." And he further indicated that "I am extremely sorry that your departure from London has prevented my wife & myself from seeing more of you, as we should have liked to do" (SCPC, JAC; *JAPM*, 3:408–9). See also "Mrs. Humphrey Ward at Home."

3. Augustine Birrell (1850–1933), professor of comparative law at Univ. College, London (1896–99), had been educated at Amersham Hall and Trinity Hall, Cambridge. In addition to being a lawyer; president of the Board of Education, 1905–7; chief secretary for Ireland, 1907–16; and lord rector of Glasgow Univ., 1911–14, he was a Liberal Party member of Parliament, 1889–1900, 1906–18. JA knew him as a writer. The essays she would have been familiar with were *Obiter Dicta* (1885), *Res Judicatae: Papers and Essays* (1892), and *Essays about Men, Women, and Books* (1895). When JA met him, his wife was Eleanor Tennyson, daughter of the widow of Lionel Tennyson, son of poet Alfred, Lord Tennyson. See also "Mrs. Humphrey Ward at Home."

4. The new settlement would become Passmore Edwards Settlement, which opened on Tavistock Place in Oct. 1897. It was designed as a brick Arts and Crafts–style structure by the newly formed architectural partnership of Arnold Dunbar Smith (1866–1933) and Cecil Claude Brewer (1871–1918). The activities of University Hall were centered in the new building.

5. Eleanor Smith and Amalie Hannig.

6. Bessie Macgregor Stead.

7. Florence Edgar Hobson had been very helpful to JA, especially arranging a meeting for JA with Charlotte Toynbee. See JA to EGS, 29 [and 30] May 1896, n. 9, above.

8. The County Council Building was located in Bethnal Green. JA had apparently been listening to the discussion about housing that she called "most illuminating" at B. F. C. Costelloe's dinner party (see JA to MRS, [26 and] 27 June 1896, n. 10, above). She went to see for herself what could be seen of the first public housing in England. "In London there is great opposition to the 'block' dwelling in any form. . . . This aversion to congregate living is shared by those who work among the poor, and by the great mass of working people. Many philanthropic workers think that the block dwellings have a bad effect on the people socially, and morally, but the chief objection is the crowding on space." While the government favored block housing, reformers favored a cottage-type housing for the poor, resulting in "a mass of chimney-potted small cottages. In the more crowded sections, these cottages are sub-let and sub-let until often each room has its family" ("Housing Problem in London," 6–7). No doubt JA heard some version of these two positions while listening to the London County Council members discuss housing in Bethnal Green. According to "Another New Model Lodging House," appearing in the *London Daily News*, 15 Aug. 1895, the housing that the council developed was located near Drury Lane.

9. P. R. Buchanan.

10. JA had lunch at 1:30 P.M. with the Webbs on Saturday, 27 June 1896. The only extant correspondence from the Webbs to JA for 1896 is a letter Sidney Webb wrote to JA, 13 June 1896: "Mrs. Webb and I are very sorry that we have no opportunity of meeting you at Mansfield House, or elsewhere; and we trust that you will allow us the privilege of making personal acquaintance. Canon Barnett tells us that you will be here for another two or three weeks, and we should be very pleased if you would come to lunch with us at 1.30 P.M.—either next Friday, 19th inst. or any day you might choose in the week following (22nd–29th). This house is within ten minutes walk of Westminster Abbey" (SCPC, JAC; *JAPM*, 3:289–90). The Webbs were at 41 Grosvenor Rd., Westminster Embankment, London.

11. JA's 1896 diary indicated that she and MRS shopped at Liberty of London on at least three occasions in the process of purchasing gowns of Liberty fabric and design. JA's account of what she bought with SAAH's money lists a Liberty dress that cost $8.50 ("Diary, 1896," "Cost Account," *JAPM*, 29:304). On 30 May, JA recorded in her diary, "[S]hopping Liberty dress etc." On Thursday, 4 June 1896, she recorded "10.30 app at Liberty's." On Friday, 12 June 1896, JA's notation reads, "A.M. Libertys," and on the next line, "Hairdressers Regent St Polytechnic." On Monday, 15 June 1896, JA reported "photographs taken at Hollyer" (*JAPM*, 29:261).

Frederick Hollyer (1838–1933) was an English photographer, known for his photographic skill in his day and especially for his reproductions of paintings and drawings, particularly on the work of the Pre-Raphaelite artists. He also became noted for his studio portraits and his photographs of houses. Among those who sat for his portraits were artists Walter Crane, William Morris, G. F. Watts, and Burne-Jones, and writers John Ruskin, H. G. Wells, and George Bernard Shaw. He did not favor formal poses and sought to have his subjects pose themselves. Hollyer was a member of the Royal Photographic Society, of which he became a fellow in 1895, and was a founding member of the Professional Photographers' Assn. in 1901.

## To Gertrude Barnum

*Between 1 and 13 July, Jane Addams and Mary Rozet Smith traveled through Norway and Sweden and past Finland into the St. Petersburg, Russia, harbor. Along the way, they investigated natural scenery, native peoples, costumes, cul-*

*tures, and art. In St. Petersburg, which Jane thought "a typical capital, French and thoroughly imitative,"[1] they explored an outdoor recreation area with a children's theater,[2] the Hermitage,[3] St. Isaac Cathedral,[4] the islands on which the city had been constructed,[5] the Alexander Nevsky Monastery,[6] Smolny Church,[7] the cottage of Peter the Great,[8] the Winter Palace,[9] and the fortress of St. Peter and St. Paul,[10] and they spent some time shopping before taking the train to Moscow.[11]*

*Jane Addams reported to sister Sarah Alice that after "but two days in the picturesque old city" of Moscow, she and Mary had "quite lost our hearts to it."[12] They visited the "Kremlin by moonlight"[13] and St. Basil's Cathedral,[14] a large bazaar, and ventured forty-four miles north of Moscow to Troitsa-Sergieva Lavra, to see the tomb of Russia's patron saint, Sergius of Radonezh, on his saint's day, 17 July.[15] Of the visit, Jane reported: "It was an excellent opportunity to see the peasantry, with straw shoes on their bound up feet and the simple peasant dress. The Greek Church is a very impressive institution in Russia, with its elaborate ritual and gem laden icons." She also reported, "We . . . have a letter to a friend of Tolstoi's and hope to reach him."[16] While Jane and Mary had been unsuccessful in reaching most of the people for whom they had letters of introduction in St. Petersburg because they "were out of town,"[17] in Moscow they did reach Aylmer Maude, who with his wife, Louise Shanks Maude,[18] and her family became friends to both women and provided their introduction to Leo Tolstoy, whom Jane Addams longed to meet.*

*That one-day visit to the Tolstoy family estate at Yasnaya Polyana,[19] on 24 July 1896, along with her two months in England became the highlights of her 1896 European vacation. Even in shock at the unexpected death of Hull-House mainstay trustee William H. Colvin and writing to commiserate with Gertrude Barnum, who was managing Hull-House while she was away,[20] Jane could not resist a brief and timely description of her visit with the Leo Tolstoy family. She would later describe that day's events in more detail in her autobiographical* Twenty Years at Hull-House.[21]

*On her return to the United States, Jane Addams was recognized as someone who could present the philosophy and intent of Tolstoy's ideas, especially because she had the experience of meeting him personally.[22] His name and ideas often found their way into her public presentations.[23]*

Moscow Russia. July 25. 1896—

My dear Friend,

Miss Smith had a letter from her brother this morning containing the news of Mr Colvins death,[24] with a clipping from the Times-Herald which left no manner of doubt that it was our Mr Colvin. Of course you know as well as I what a blow it is to H.H. and what a genuine personal sorrow it is as well.

I am so sorry for you. I know that you must feel perfectly bereft, and as if the prop had fallen out, as I do here, only that immediate problems are pressing you as they are not on me.

It is really hard to go on being interested over here for seven or eight weeks longer, in the shadow of such a calamity, when one cares so much more to be at home.

I have not had a letter from Hull House for ten days, and find myself getting a little fussy. During that time I have had one from Miss Waite,[25] written from Lakeside[26] but containing no H.H. news. I am hoping so much to have one written since Mr Colvins death. Did you go to see him, or did no one know how sick he was? Has he been over often this summer? Mrs Kelley wrote me of one evening.[27]

We have just come back from a visit to Tolstoi on his country place.[28] An Englishman, Mr Maude who has lived in Moscow for many years and an ardent friend and disciple took us, so that it was all made easy.

We were entertained to supper—taken at ten oclock out doors under the porches, and were almost as much fascinated by his family as himself.[29]

One of the daughters had been working in the field all day. They took us over their village to make calls &c and were charming in every way.[30] Tolstoi himself is one of the gentlest and kindest of human creatures I ever saw. He was tired so that the actual conversation did not amount to so much as his presence and Spirit.[31.]

We have been to Neissen,[32] and I started a letter to Mrs Kelley apropo of the "Komise"[33] which I now have no heart to finish. I am sure you will see the Colvin Girls[34] as soon as they come home—I am so sorry for them. I wish they might have telegraphed me, it was the week we were in Norway.[35] Please give my love to all the residents at home—I am always your loving friend

Jane Addams

HLSr copy in hand of SAAH (["Record Book of Copies and Letters and Articles"], SC, Starr; *JAPM*, 3:432–34).

1. JA to SAAH, 18 July 1896; *JAPM*, 3:420.

2. It seems likely that one of the most significant venues JA saw in St. Petersburg was "a large recreation ground for working people. . . . The Open Air Theaters were very successful, one of them for Children with children actors. The 2000 people there as everywhere are very gentle and quiet. The big slav fathers carry their children about with great tenderness" (JA to Gertrude Barnum, [ca. 17 July 1896]; *JAPM*, 3:418). In her 1896 diary, JA recorded of the occasion: "[T]ook a drosky to recreation grounds 5 miles out of city. . . . Mr. [Vagunine?] —very attentive, showed us the little theaters &c 'snow maiden' very pretty play. Childrens theater Artizan quarter" (12 July; *JAPM*, 29:278). Recreation, including theatricals for workers, was supported by industrialists who wanted happier and more productive factory workers. JA may have met a member of the Vargunin family, former peasants who had become entrepreneurs and seemed dedicated to supporting programs that would aid the working class. Among their efforts were schools for children and adults, housing, libraries, and recreation areas. They were among the leaders of the Nevsky Society for Public Amusements Arrangement, or Nevskoe Public Entertainment Co., a nongovernmental group of manufacturers, which V. P. Vargunin headed to provide educational opportunities and entertainments for their workers. The society was dissolved in 1919.

3. JA and MRS visited the Hermitage, founded as a museum by Catherine the Great in 1764. Located in six buildings, its collection of art, one of the largest in the world, was opened to the public in 1852 in the Small Hermitage building and over time spilled into four other structures. Only a small portion of the collection was on display when JA visited.

4. St. Isaac Cathedral, constructed between 1818 and 1858, was the largest Greek Orthodox Cathedral in Russia. It was dedicated to St. Isaac of Dalmatia, patron saint of Russian tsar Peter the Great, who was born on St. Isaac's saint's day, 9 June (O.S. 30 May) 1672.

5. St. Petersburg, Russia, was developed on the shore of Neva Bay and on the islands in the delta of the Neva River.

6. Alexander Nevsky Monastery of the Holy Spirit was founded by Tsar Peter the Great in 1710, seven years after the founding of St. Petersburg itself. Its Tikhvin Cemetery is home to some of the greats of Russian culture, including musicians Tchaikovsky, Mussorgsky, Rimsky-Korsakov, and Glinka and writer Dostoyevsky.

7. The "Smolni Church," as JA spelled it in her diary on 14 July 1896, was the central church of the monastery built as a home for Peter the Great's daughter Elizabeth (1709–62), who, in 1741, rejected life as a nun to become empress of Russia. Begun in 1748 by Italian architect Francesco Bartolomeo Rastrelli (1700–1771), who also created the Winter Palace and other significant church and government structures, the Smolny Church and its surrounding structures were not completed until 1835.

8. The first residence constructed in St. Petersburg was the wooden house or cabin of Tsar Peter the Great. He lived in the small wooden home between 1703 and 1708. JA and MRS probably saw his original belongings in the living room, bedroom, and study.

9. The Winter Palace was the official residence of Russian monarchs. The last Russian tsar, Nicholas II, had just been coronated. JA and MRS were certainly aware of the tragic events associated with the coronation celebrations, which occurred on 30 May when the royal family held a banquet at Fhodynka Field to distribute gifts to workers and peasants. By some estimates, 500,000 people gathered early in the morning, anticipating the event and, fearful that there would not be enough food and presents for all, rioted in an attempt to get a share of the gifts. The result left 1,389 people dead and a blot on the coronation events, especially when the tsar and his wife attended the coronation ball that evening. The French had planned and funded the ball, and the new tsar was fearful that not attending would have been taken by the French as a slight and adversely affect relations between the two countries. Leo Tolstoy wrote an exposé of the events, translated by Aylmer Maude and published in England as *The Tsar's Coronation* (see JA to Aylmer Maude, [30 July 1896], n. 4, below).

10. The Fortress of St. Peter and St. Paul was constructed by Peter the Great in 1703 on an island in the delta of the Neva River, primarily to protect his new city from Swedish invasion. It served as a high-security political jail into the early twentieth century. It was also the site of the Cathedral of St. Peter and St. Paul, burial place for Russian tsars from Peter the Great through Alexander III.

11. In her 1896 diary on 15 July, JA wrote "took a train at 9 P.M. for Moscow—very comfortable sleeping compt" (*JAPM*, 29:279). JA and MRS arrived in Moscow on Thursday, 16 July, at 11:00 A.M.

12. JA to SAAH, 18 July 1896, UIC, JAMC; *JAPM*, 3:420.

13. On 23 July 1896, JA and MRS had dinner with Aylmer and Louise Maude and finished the evening with a drive through Moscow. A week earlier, JA had also visited the Kremlin's famous walled fortress, begun in 1147, which was the center of the development of Moscow. She was impressed by its churches, palaces, and size.

14. St. Basil's Cathedral, officially known as the Cathedral of the Intercession of the Virgin by the Moat, was begun in 1552 and completed in 1560 at the insistence of Tsar Ivan the Terrible to commemorate the 1552 capture of Kazan from Mongol forces. Initially, it was painted

white with golden domes, but that color scheme was replaced with a multicolored version by the 1860s.

15. The Trinity Monastery of St. Sergius was founded in 1340 by Sergius of Radonezh (1314–92), considered the patron saint of Russia. Recognized by some as the heart of religious Russia, in medieval times the site became the center of a small community that was eventually enclosed by brick walls, much as the Kremlin. It contained churches, cathedrals, and tombs.

16. JA to SAAH, 18 July 1896, UIC, JAMC; *JAPM*, 3:420.

17. JA to SAAH, 18 July 1896, UIC, JAMC; *JAPM*, 3:421.

18. "One day in Moscow, in July, 1896, I received a note from Miss Addams, enclosing a letter of introduction from a friend in England, expressing a hope that I should be able to take her to see Tolstoy," wrote Aylmer Maude ("A Talk with Miss Jane Addams and Leo Tolstoy," 203). JA and MRS accompanied Maude to his first in-person meeting with Leo Tolstoy.

Aylmer Maude (1858–1938) and Louise Shanks (1855–1939) were married in 1884 in an Anglican ceremony at the British vice-consulate in Moscow. Both became noted as the English translators of Tolstoy's works, and Aylmer Maude later wrote the authorized biography of the famous Russian writer, philosopher, and reformer.

Maude was the son of Church of England clergyman F. H. Maude, who in his later years became an Anglo-Catholic, and his wife, Lucy Thorp. He was educated in England and between 1874 and 1876 studied at the Moscow Lyceum, where he was a tutor, 1877–80. Becoming known in the British community in Moscow, he was employed by one of his chess partners, Scottish-born Archibald Mirrielees (1861–1923), whose family operated the Scottish-owned department store Muir & Mirrielees. Maude, successful as a merchant, became the business manager and then director of the Anglo-Russian Carpet Co. It was in the British community in Moscow that he met Louise Shanks, one of eight children of James Steuart Shanks, the primary proprietor of Shanks and Co., Magasin Anglais (the English Shop), Moscow, which sold a variety of goods, from handbags to carpets. Mary Shanks (1866–ca. 1939), an artist and one of the sisters of Louise, was one of the illustrators for Tolstoy's *Where Love Is, God Is*. However, it was through Dr. Peter Alekseyev (1849–1913), married to Louise's sister Lucy, that Aylmer was introduced to Tolstoy in 1888, four years after he and Louise were married. Tolstoy befriended the Maudes: they visited him for tennis, chess, and long philosophical discussions; he visited them and became close to their five children. Even after the Maudes settled in England in 1897, the friendship continued through correspondence and occasional visits to Russia, especially by Aylmer Maude. It was in 1902 that Tolstoy gave his permission for Maude to write his biography.

Although Aylmer Maude did not always agree with Tolstoy's philosophy, he was steadfast in his friendship for the writer and a devoted disciple. By 1902 he could see that "drawing practical conclusions from . . . theory" might not "work out right when submitted to the test of experience" (Maude, "A Talk with Miss Jane Addams and Leo Tolstoy," 215–16). It was not until 1931 that Maude could admit to JA, "I always remember your kindness to me when at Hull House, when I was, as I now see, a very opinionated and over-confident Tolstoyan" (Aylmer Maude to JA, 12 Dec. 1931, SCPC, JAC; *JAPM*, 22:1588).

When the Maudes arrived in England, they settled near the Brotherhood Church, first in Croydon and then a little later at Wickham's Farm in Bicknacre, a commune that came to an end in 1899. In 1898 Maude led the Doukhobors, a group of Christian peasants who rejected the Russian monarchy and Orthodox church, rejected a literal interpretation of the Bible, and adopted pacifism and renounced militarism and who were persecuted in Russia and supported by Tolstoy, to resettle in Canada, and on that occasion in Oct. 1898 he visited JA and HH. Maude wrote a book about them entitled *A Peculiar People: The Dukhobórs* (1904).

By the turn of the century, the Maudes were living in Great Baddow, near Chelmsford, and were members of the Fabian Society, active in the Anglo-Russian Society of Russian Freedom, and involved in England's cooperative movement. From 1907 to 1912, Aylmer Maude was a member of the Fabian national executive committee; he also lectured and wrote pamphlets for the society. During World War I, he traveled to Archangel with the British Expeditionary Force as an interpreter and liaison officer and gave lectures for the YMCA there.

The Maudes began translating Tolstoy's works even before they left Russia and continued producing translations for the remainder of their lives. While Aylmer Maude translated the philosophical writings, Louise Maude became Tolstoy's fiction translator.

Aylmer Maude, whom JA termed "a very charming man" (JA to Wilber (*sic*) Olin Atwater, 9 July 1897, Cornell, Atwater), maintained a lifelong correspondence with JA. In 1902 he received her permission to issue portions of a letter JA wrote to him about Tolstoy and his philosophy shortly after she first met and spoke with Tolstoy in 1896 (see JA to Aylmer Maude, [30 July 1896], below). He made a gift to HH in 1904 from the Resurrection Fund, established from the proceeds of Tolstoy's novel *Resurrection*, and praised JA's *Newer Ideals of Peace* in 1907. In 1926, in preparation for the celebration of Tolstoy's one hundredth birthday, Maude, serving as honorary organizing secretary, helped create the Tolstoy Society with the aim of publishing "a readable, reliable, and complete edition of Tolstoy's works in English" (Aylmer Maude to JA, 8 Mar. 1926, SCPC, JAC; *JAPM*, 17:1538). JA became a vice-president of the society and agreed to write the introduction for *What Then Must We Do?* She delivered the manuscript for her introduction in Feb. 1928, and she received proof to review in Nov. 1933. The work was translated by Aylmer Maude and issued by Oxford Univ. Press in 1934 as one of the twenty-one volumes in the Centenary Edition of Tolstoy's works published between 1928 and 1937.

19. In her 1896 diary for 24–25 July, JA wrote, "Mr Maude called for us. went to little village beyond Toula. drove to see Tolstoy's estate. Countess reception daughters took us to the village. supper with the Count. drove to station at 11 P.M." On Saturday, 25 July 1896, JA recorded, "A.M. arrived [at Moscow] at 8 o'clock" (*JAPM*, 29:284).

The estate, the name of which translates as "Clear Glen" or "clearing," was located approximately 130 miles south of Moscow. The day that JA and MRS visited, they took the train from Moscow to Yesanki, followed by a 10-mile ride in a horse-drawn conveyance. The estate came into the Tolstoy family at the end of the eighteenth century when Leo Tolstoy's grandfather Nikolai Volkonskiy purchased it. When JA visited the Tolstoy family, their estate was a working farm of approximately four thousand acres composed of forest, four lakes, tilled fields, houses for approximately 350 peasant workers, and the thirty-two-room estate home in which the Tolstoy family lived.

20. While JA was in Europe, Gertrude Barnum counted on William H. Colvin as a sounding board and supporter concerning HH financial affairs.

21. JA devoted chapter 12 of the first volume of her autobiography, *Twenty Years at HH*, to a description of her one-day visit to Yasnaya Polyana and to the significance for her of Tolstoy and his philosophy.

22. After her return from Europe, JA found herself an interpreter of the Russian writer, his undertakings, and his philosophy to audiences in the United States. Tolstoy became a living hero for JA and a revered icon as a moral guide in her adult life. JA was not a total disciple of Tolstoy and did not agree with his philosophy of "bread labor"—especially after she tried it for a time. She was, however, an admirer of his willingness to speak out on behalf of the Russian downtrodden and through his actions to make their plight known. She wrote and spoke frequently about him (see n. 23). Numerous photographic treatments of Tolstoy

were scattered throughout HH. Madeleine Wallin, who served as JA's secretary, reported to her father that when JA returned from her visit to Tolstoy in Europe, she "brought home an excellent photograph of him, also a picture of him in his study and another of him at the plow" (8 Oct. 1896, CHM, CHS, Sikes). When the auditorium in the HH Coffee House and Theatre Building was decorated, one wall, painted by John Duncan, was devoted to a mural depicting Tolstoy as a peasant. Another portrait of Tolstoy by Russian painter Ilya Repin (1844–1930) showed him barefoot and dressed in peasant working clothes. The painting, not available in Russia, found a place of honor at HH. Tolstoy's philosophical writings became a permanent part of JA's personal library. See JA to Aylmer Maude [30 July 1896], n. 5, below.

23. Comments by JA on Leo Tolstoy and his philosophy are in the following: *Democracy and Social Ethics* (1902), *Twenty Years at HH* (1910), and *Newer Ideals of Peace* (1911). Among her extant speeches, periodical materials, and poems are the following: "Count Tolstoy" and "Tolstoy's Theory of Life," both in *Chautauqua (N.Y.) Assembly Herald* (July 1902); "A Visit to Tolstoi," *Woman's Journal* (1910); "A Visit to Tolstoy," *McClure's Magazine* (1911), both excerpts from *Twenty Years at HH*; [Tolstoy and the Russian Soldiers], a manuscript version, and "Tolstoy and the Russian Soldiers," *New Republic* (1917); four similar manuscripts with the following titles: [Notes on Tolstoy and the Russian Revolution], [Remarks on Tolstoy and the Russian Revolution], "The Russian Complication in the Light of Tolstoy's Teachings," and "Three Efforts of Contemporary Russia to Break through Current Abstractions" (1918); "A Book That Changed My Life," *Christian Century* (1927) and a manuscript by the same title, both of which relate to Leo Tolstoy's *What Then Must We Do?* (1928), material that JA used in preparing two extant versions of her manuscript for the [introduction] for Aylmer Maude's translation of the work *What Then Must We Do?* (1934); "Tolstoy, Prophet of Righteousness," *Unity* (1928); "Tolstoy and Gandhi," *Christian Century* (1931), with four manuscript versions by the same name; and "To 'Sasha' Tolstoy—on Her Fiftieth Birthday—July 1st, 1934," in two manuscript versions. In the year following her brief visit with the Tolstoy family and for the remainder of her life, JA spoke and wrote often about her experience with the Tolstoy family and about Leo Tolstoy's philosophy (see JA to SAAH, 11 Feb. 1897, n. 1, below). See also Excerpts from Addresses, 14 July–9 Dec. 1897, below.

24. The article that MRS received, likely from her brother Charles Frederic ("Fred") Mather Smith, carried the headline "W. H. Colvin Is Dead." It appeared in the 8 July 1896 issue of the *Chicago Times Herald*. In part it reported, "He preferred, when it was possible, to work for the public good without departing from the path of the private citizen. An example of this characteristic of Mr. Colvin is to be found in the interest he took in the welfare of Hull House. This institution had no warmer friend than Mr. Colvin. It was his especial pride, a source of constant pleasure. He was ever ready to give it his encouragement in any form and was relied on from the very start of the institution as a steadfast champion. Mr. Colvin's benefactions to Hull House can never be measured in dollars and cents. He was a steady giver and a valuable adviser, but went about his work so quietly that few knew how deeply he was concerned. His chief contribution, joined to that of another friend of Hull House, built the coffee-house and gymnasium."

25. Ella Raymond Waite's letter to JA is not known to be extant. By the summer of 1896, Ella Waite (1861?–1925) was in her third year as a resident of HH. She began her journey to HH by helping to oversee the lodging house for women that HH operated after the World's Columbian Exposition. She reported to the HH residents on activities at the lodging house in Mar. 1894 and was listed as a visitor in the 1 Mar. tally of settlement residents. She reported on the closing of the lodging operation in Apr. 1894 and by Nov. 1894 was identified as a HH resident.

Ella Waite was born in Chicago, the daughter of Horace F. and Jane Garfield Waite. Horace F. Waite was a successful attorney who was elected to the Illinois House of Representatives from Cook Co., 1871–72, and the Illinois Senate from Chicago, 1873–75. The Waite family were members of the Fourth Presbyterian Church, but Horace Waite spoke on behalf of David Swing at Swing's trial (see EGS [for JA] to Mary Houghton Starr Blaisdell [and SAAH], 23 Feb. [1889], n. 20, above).

Her first task at HH was managing the Coffee House, but by 1896 she had asked to be released by the residents from the "catering" responsibility. She taught embroidery and served as director of the Children's House, 1896–97, and also ran the Penny Provident Bank. During the 1890s, she was in charge of the HH Country Club operations and into the early 1900s was in charge of the HH shop, especially the textile room. Ella Waite was a painter who belonged to the Artists Guild and the Arts Club and one of the first members and a life member of the Chicago Public School Art Society. In 1897 she was one of the founders and supporters of the Chicago Arts and Crafts Society and a long-serving secretary for the organization (see Article in the *HH Bulletin*, 1 Dec. 1897, below). She was also a member of the Friday Club and the Woman's City Club and indicated her support for woman suffrage. Still listed as a resident in 1921, she lived in an apartment at HH for most of her life.

26. See JA to Gertrude Barnum, 22 May[June] 1896, n. 17, above.

27. Florence Kelley's letter to JA is apparently not extant.

28. Aylmer Maude reported that the last train to Moscow from the Kozlovka Zaseka left at 11:00 P.M. He accompanied JA and MRS to the station and returned to Yasnaya Polyana to spend several days with the Tolstoys. JA and MRS did not reach Moscow until the next morning. That evening, 25 July, they made a farewell visit to the Shanks family, and on 26 July they rested, packed, and got ready to board their train at 5:00 P.M. for Warsaw, Poland.

29. Maude reported that they arrived at the Tolstoy estate while the family was "having afternoon tea under the shade of a tree." Count Tolstoy was not at home, and Maude explained that there was a "particularly awkward moment" when he tried to explain about his guests, JA and MRS, whom he had invited without letting the Tolstoys know they were coming. The travelers were asked, apparently with reluctance, by the Countess Tolstoy to share their tea. "It was not long before they had quite won" Countess Tolstoy's "heart, and she and her daughters were talking to them as if they had known them for years." Leo Tolstoy appeared a "little later" and welcomed them "cordially." When Tolstoy indicated that he wanted to bathe, the party "set out to walk together down to the little river that lies at some distance from the house." And that walk was the occasion for Tolstoy to learn something of his visitors.

Both MRS and JA were fashionably dressed in the style of the day. The "Ladies Page" of the 29 Aug. 1896 issue of *Illustrated London News* not only offered quotes by JA, but also two illustrations of current fashion that mirrored the clothes JA and MRS wore, with long swinging skirts, fitted waists, high collars, and large puffy sleeves between shoulder and elbow with fitted sleeves, elbow to wrist. After Tolstoy understood where JA worked and the kind of public she interacted with on a daily basis, he "gently took hold of the loose, puffy, silk shoulder of her fashionable dress . . . and smilingly asked, 'And what is this for?'" And he continued, "You should not like to be dressed differently from them." JA indicated that with all of the different ethnic groups she dealt with daily, "she could not dress in all their different costumes! To which Tolstoy made answer: 'All the more reason why you should choose some cheap and simple dress that any of them could adopt, and not cut yourself off by your dress from those you wish to serve'" (Maude, "A Talk with Miss Jane Addams and Leo Tolstoy," 208–10). After Tolstoy and the visitors returned to the house, "there was supper out in the open air with a large gathering of people; the Tolstoy family and others" (Maude, "A Talk with Miss Jane Addams and Leo Tolstoy," 212).

30. Maude does not report on this portion of the visit; neither does JA in her chapter "Tolstoyism," in *Twenty Years*. JA did, however, mention her experience in the village in her speech before the Matheon Club, a group of young Chicago women, on 2 Oct. 1897. The *Chicago Post* reported that JA "described a Russian village. They are all alike. The houses are usually of wood, some are of brick. There are but two rooms. One, the outer, shelters the cattle. The inner room is for the family. There is the great stove at the right—the center of Russian life; some stools, a bench, a table at which they stand while eating. But there is no bed. Above the table is an icon—a representation of the Madonna and Child. This is the sole gleam of light in the hopeless darkness of the peasant's life. . . .

"One day Count Tolstoy took the American visitors to the cottages of the peasants. In one family was an old woman who had once learned to read. She was quite famous because of it, and people thought she knew almost everything. But twenty years ago she had forgotten how to read. Yet they did not know. So when the visitors came one of the family said to the old woman: 'But you read, and you said to us the Americans were black.' The clever old poser said quickly: 'Some are black and some are yellow. And there'—indicating Miss Addams and her friends—'are the yellow ones'" ("Lecture on Tolstoi"; *JAPM*, 55:325).

31. JA indicated that in addition to the travelers from Germany, England, and the United States, the long table held the adult Tolstoy daughters, the younger children and their governess, and the countess, who "presided over the usual European dinner served by men." While they had "more elaborate food," Tolstoy and his "daughter who had worked in the field most of the day ate only porridge and black bread and drank only kvas" (Addams, *Twenty Years*, 272). Maude reported, "Miss Addams, if I am not mistaken, sat near the Count, but I do not know what they talked about" ("A Talk with Miss Jane Addams and Leo Tolstoy," 212). In *Twenty Years*, JA offered some tantalizing suggestions of what their conversation might have included. At least a portion of the conversation may have involved Tolstoy's query to JA about "who 'fed' me, and how did I obtain 'shelter'?" After telling him that she relied on money made from a farm near Cedarville, JA reported that he made her feel uncomfortable with his "next scathing question: 'So you are an absentee landlord?'" (208). JA had to admit that was so.

In addition, those in attendance also discussed the fate of a young man who was sent to Siberia for having in his possession a copy of one of Tolstoy's manuscripts, forbidden the people of Russia by the government. Tolstoy had written an open letter to a Moscow newspaper pointing out the "unjust" action of the state in punishing the young man who had the manuscript rather than the man who created it. As a result of the discussion of nonresistance that was associated with the tale, JA recalled, "I was disappointed in Tolstoy's position in the matter. It seemed to me that he made too great a distinction between the use of physical force and that moral energy which can override another's differences and scruples with equal ruthlessness" (Addams, *Twenty Years*, 273).

Maude reported that the countess, near whom MRS was seated, chided her about not being married. "Miss Smith pleaded as an excuse for herself that she had never been asked, but the Countess pooh-poohed the suggestion." Maude also reported that the countess, who found JA and MRS "'charming American ladies,'" had asked them to stay until the next day (Maude, "A Talk with Miss Jane Addams and Leo Tolstoy," 212). JA's version of her day with Tolstoy mirrors in part Maude's description of that special day as recalled in "A Talk with Miss Jane Addams and Leo Tolstoy," in the Oct. 1902 issue of the *Humane Review*. See especially Addams, *Twenty Years*, 267–74.

32. While JA's sister SAAH seems to have transcribed JA's writing as "Neissen," it is likely that what JA wrote was *Nizhni*, which JA spells in her diary as "Nishni," meaning Nizhni Novgorod. MRS and JA had journeyed to the East of Moscow by train in mid-July to visit that trade center of Russia. On 20 July 1896, they saw a mosque and an art exhibit and attended a play by Tolstoy. The next day, they went to the Makeryev Fair, an exposition held annually in July in the city since at least 1820. JA commented in her 1896 diary, "Peasants exhibit very interesting" (21 July; *JAPM*, 29:282). JA and MRS returned to Moscow that evening.

33. Although SAAH interpreted what JA wrote as "Komise," the most likely word that JA may have written *Promise*.

34. The daughters of William H. Colvin, Jessie and Katharine, were traveling in Europe when their father died in Chicago. JA and MRS were to meet them in Bayreuth for the 1896 Wagner opera cycle. For biographical information on the Colvin daughters, see Remarks on Opening the New England Kitchen, HH, 23 Aug. 1893, n. 3, above.

35. According to JA's 1896 diary, she and MRS were in Norway 2–9 July 1896.

## To Aylmer Maude

*Thursday, 30 July 1896, was a rainy day in Berlin and according to Jane Addams "not very satisfactory."[1] Still on JA's mind was her visit with Leo Tolstoy and his family and the discussions she shared with Aylmer Maude and Mary Rozet Smith as they journeyed to Yasnaya Polyana on 24 July 1896. Maude recalled that they spoke specifically of "Tolstoy's economic teaching"[2] and of "non-resistence."[3] Perhaps in an attempt to bring clarity to her own position with regard to Tolstoy's philosophy, she wrote the following letter to Aylmer Maude. A number of years later, Maude had occasion to reconsider his own perspective on Tolstoy's philosophy in light of the positions that Jane Addams had taken then and continued to take, and he found them so compelling that he published a large portion of her letter with his comments in "A Talk with Jane Addams and Leo Tolstoy" in the* Humane Review *in 1902.*

[Berlin, Germany] [30 July 1896]

"The glimpse of Tolstoy has made a profound impression upon me—not so much by what he said as the life, the gentleness, the Christianity in the soul of him. . . .

"A radical stand such as Tolstoy has been able to make throws all such effort as that of settlements into the ugly light of compromise and inefficiency—at least so it seemed to me—and perhaps accounts for a certain defensive attitude I found in myself.

"Our effort at Hull House has always been to seize upon the highest moral efforts we could find in the labour movement or elsewhere, and help them

Leo Tolstoy, ca. 1894. No person that Jane Addams met during her European tour in 1896 influenced her more than Russian novelist and social thinker Leo Tolstoy. Her brief one-day visit with him and his family at Yasnaya Polyana became a life-changing event for her. Jane Addams always displayed a likeness of Tolstoy at Hull-House (*Commons* 2, no. 2 [June 1897]: cover).

forward. To conserve the best which the community has achieved and push it forward along its own line when possible.

"We have always held strongly to the doctrine of non-resistance, selecting the good in the neighbourhood and refraining from railing at the bad. Gradually I have come to believe even farther than that in non-resistance—that the expectation of the opposition and martyrdom, the holding oneself in readiness for it, was in itself a sort of resistance and worked evil or at best was merely negative.

"No doubt a Christian who preached against the holding of private property would arouse much opposition on the part of the property holders; he might give up his own in a way which would work as a constant source of irritation to them. But I can imagine the thing being done in a way which would make it merely incidental to the great wave of fellowship and joy which would swallow it—the coming of the spirit was so great an event to the followers in Jerusalem that the division of goods received but little comment.

"So I would imagine the new Social Order (if it could come ideally) would gather to itself all that was best and noblest in the Old, all the human endeavour which has been put into it in the right direction, and which has become sacred because it is so human and pathetic; that its joy and righteousness would sweep men into it.

"The *ideal* is always admired, it is only when it begins to work itself out and to compromise with the world and circumstances that it becomes hated and misunderstand.

"This is doubtless inevitable, but it is a great pity to consider the hate essential, to confuse the result which the imperfect presentation of the ideal makes upon men, with the effect which the ideal might have.

"This belief has come to be part of my method of living, and I should have to start quite over again and admit the value of resistance if I gave it up.

"I should be very grateful if you could find time to write to me occasionally as your plans work out.[4] I am sure you will understand my saying that I got more of Tolstoy's philosophy from our conversations than I had gotten from Tolstoy's books.[5] I believe so much of it that I am sorry to seem to differ so much."

PD ("Extracts of a Letter to Aylmer Maude," *Humane Review* 3 [June 1902]: 216–17; *JAPM*, 3:435).

1. Addams, "Diary, 1896," 30 July; *JAPM*, 29:287.

2. "My view of Tolstoy's economic teaching," wrote Aylmer Maude, "was that the use of money obscures our vision. Men produce and consume food, clothing, shelter, &c., and if one takes more than he or she makes, the result is always that someone else has to do that much extra work. By means of money the many are enslaved to the few." JA countered that "some people have talents for organizing, for inventing, for teaching, or for healing, which are more valuable than their power of manual labor" ("A Talk with Miss Jane Addams and Leo Tolstoy," 214–15). She seemed to feel uncomfortable because her practical experience after living and working with the poor prevented her from agreeing wholeheartedly with Tolstoy's doctrinaire position, which she believed could not work in reality. Yet when she reached home again and for a brief period of time, JA spent two hours each day devoting herself to making bread, something she had learned to do as a child, until she realized how "utterly preposterous . . . it doubtless was" (Addams, *Twenty Years*, 276). JA later recalled of the evening with Leo Tolstoy, "The conversation at dinner and afterwards, although conducted with animation and sincerity, for the moment stirred vague misgivings within me. Was Tolstoy more logical than life warrants? Could the wrongs of life be reduced to the terms of unrequited labor and all be made right if each person performed the amount necessary to satisfy his own wants?" (Addams, *Twenty Years*, 274).

3. According to Maude, the three travelers also "discussed non-resistence, and the family and social friction produced by reformers and reform movements in general, and by Tolstoy in particular" ("A Talk with Miss Jane Addams and Leo Tolstoy," 215).

4. The Maudes were on the verge of leaving Russia for England to settle in and support a Tolstoy-inspired farming commune associated with the Brotherhood Church. Even the infusion of financial support and labor by the Maudes could not save the effort, and by the late 1890s the experiment had collapsed.

Maude did not respond to JA's letter of 30 July 1896 until 16 Oct. 1896. He reported that he had delayed in order to wait for the publication of Tolstoy's 136-page work *The Tsar's Coronation as Seen by "De Monto Alto" Resident in Moscow*, that he had translated. It was issued by the Brotherhood Publishing Co., with a publication date of Jan. 1896. It was Tolstoy's response to the panic of an estimated five hundred thousand people in fear of not being fed as anticipated that occurred on the fourth day of Tsar Nicholas II's coronation (see JA to Gertrude Barnum, 25 July 1896, n. 9, above). He also asked JA, "Please tell Miss Smith that everybody at Yasnaya Poliana, the day after your visit, sang the praises of the 'charmantes Americaines'" (SCPC, JAC; *JAPM*, 3:469).

"The view you are anxious to insist on is one which I think I can appreciate in theory," Maude wrote to JA, " however grievously I offend against it often in practice. Is it not something like this: 'Beware of losing your own sweetness, in your anxiety to give other people light.' No doubt a fiery prophet (like Tolstoy)—& still more his 2nd & 3rd rate followers (like myself) are apt to go too far—'to rush at a benighted man, & give him two black eyes for being blind,'" wrote Maude. And he continued, "[A]ll you say is most wholesome doctrine for me personally & I have been weighing in my mind since we met.

"So far as I see it is all a question of character and method, and does not in any way infringe on the fundamental truth of Tolstoy's conceptions & teaching, though it indicates (what he himself has often admitted) that he is too fierce in some of his writings. . . . I am grateful for the opportunity I had to exchange ideas with you" (SCPC, JAC; *JAPM*, 3:468–69).

5. Some of the books by Tolstoy that JA owned survive in the SCPC, JAC, and in the UIC, JAMC. There is no guarantee that the books from her library that are extant with her signature or annotation (or both) in them were her entire collection of Tolstoy titles. Among the volumes by Tolstoy at UIC, JAMC, are *The Christian Teaching*, trans. V. Tchertkoff (1898) with her signature; *My Confession* (1887); *What I Believe*, trans. Constantine Popoff (1885), a gift from MRS; *A Great Iniquity,* trans. V. Tchertkoff and I. F. M. (1906); *What to Do?* ([1888?]), a gift from MRS, Aug. 1896; and *What Then Must We Do?*, trans. Aylmer Maude, with an introduction by JA (1934) with her signature. There are two of Tolstoy's books at SCPC, JAC, that were gifts from JA: *Christianity and Patriotism* (1905) and *Toil* (1890), neither of which carries her signature. None of the books that JA gave to RC over the years was written by Tolstoy.

In addition, the UIC, JAMC, collection also holds JA's personal copy of Ernest Howard Crosby's *Tolstoy and His Message* (1904). *I Worked for the Soviet* (1934), by Countess Alexandra Tolstoy, carries the inscription "To Miss Jane Addams with her devoted love from Sasha Tolstoy, September 20 1934. Hadlam, Conn." It is also in UIC, JAMC. Alexandra L. Tolstoy (1884–1979) was the youngest daughter of Leo Tolstoy and his wife, worked as his secretary and executor of his estate, and settled in the United States in 1931. See also JA to Gertrude Barnum, 25 July 1896, n. 23, above.

## Lists of Residents and Fellowships

*Hoping that Enos M. Barton (1842–1916), who was president of Western Electric Co., 1887–1908, and chairman of the board of directors, 1908–16, would provide some financial support for Hull-House, Jane Addams drew up two lists to present to him when she and Gertrude Barnum met him for lunch on 10 Nov. 1896. One list indicated the resident body, the other fellowship costs. The third document (not in Jane Addams's hand) on Western Electric Co. letterhead was notes taken about Hull-House operating expenses during the luncheon meeting.*

[Chicago, Ill.] 3 Nov. 1896

The fellowship program at Hull-House was crucial to the development and stability of the settlement's resident body. These three documents, two of which were written by Jane Addams, reveal the names of donors and fellowship recipients, residents' length of service, and some of the costs associated with the fellowship program (A & HD, RC, Archives; *JAPM*, 3:493–95. Enclosures for ALS, JA to Enos M. Barton, 6 Nov. 1896, *JAPM*, 3:492).

## From Mary Rozet Smith

19 Walton Place. [Chicago, Ill.] [Dec. 1896?]

Dearest Lady

I came home with quite a glow in my heart and <even> feeling mildly resigned to Southern wastes.

You can never know what it is to me to have had you and to have you now—I only hope I am thankful enough. I'm given to turning sentimental at this season, as you know, and I feel quite a mush of emotion when I think of you. I have been having another bad time with my conscience (about my "wealth") and I've been in the depths of gloom until yesterday when the sight and sound of you cheered me. I do'nt feel any more righteous now, but a good deal less stormy and not wanting the earth to swallow me so much as I did—I wonder how it would feel to escape from the "conviction of sin" for about 10 minutes—I do hope that dying does that for one—I seem to be relapsing into melancholy, but I'm really hilariously cheerful—comparatively speaking—and full of gratitude to you and overflowing with affection. I'll put in the January cheque—to lend a practical air to this sentimental missive—and I'll try not to turn morbid and intense "on you." Father hopes to go to the party and is much pleased with the [pressing?] invitation. I found every one quite well and cheerful.

Do come to Geneva on Monday if you can manage it. Yours always

Mary RS.

ALS (SCPC, JAC; *JAPM*, 3:512–15).

## To Sarah Alice Addams Haldeman

*On 15 November 1896, Jane Addams wrote begging sister Sarah Alice Haldeman to come for a visit at Christmastime. She had apparently had a disturbing letter*[1] *from her sister and responded, "There are so many things that I want to say to you, and we ought to have a visit together. . . . I simply can't write a reply to your letter, there is so much that I want to say but it must be said and not written. . . . [Y]ou ought to see more of the children, it would do you good and I can't bear to have you so far away from us all. My heart aches for you and I am home sick to see you."*[2] *Despite Jane's letter of 4 December, she was forced to write Alice, "I am so sorry that you are not coming for Xmas."*[3]

Chicago [Ill.] Dec. 4" 1896

My dear Alice

I have had an attack of my old bowel trouble—evidently the removal of the appendix[4] did not make me over—and have come over to Miss Smith's to recuperate. Laura was in for more than a week at Thanksgiving time, Flora and Luther Guiteau[5] were in for a day or two, and of course all of the children except for Stanley were there for the day. Sarah is doing so well at the University,[6] and Esther is improving each month.[7]

I am trying very hard to get well fast because I want to take Weber home next Saturday.[8] He has improved very rapidly for the last ten days and has been quite himself since last Sunday—Laura went home yesterday to get the house open and in order, she ~~left~~ felt that it would be dreary to have him come home to an empty house. This makes ~~the~~ <Weber's> attack about two weeks shorter than the last one, and as the interval was four years—it seems to me that we have every reason to be encouraged. If the case were growing chronic the attacks would be longer and the intervals shorter. He has written such good dear letters that one cannot help feeling that out of it all he is obtaining a Christian character. I wish for so many reasons that you and Marcet would come for the holidays. It seems to me that it would be worth the journey and trouble. You know Geo. Eliot says that we have to take pains with our affections and friendships as we do with our other treasures. [I]t is already more than a year since we have seen each other and I really think that that is long enough. Do write you are coming!

I am going to ask Miss Smith to send you her picture which she could n't do last summer. She is so good to me that I would find life a different thing without her. Please give my love and kisses to Marcet and do write that you are coming. Always your loving sister

Jane Addams.

ALS (IU, Lilly, SAAH; *JAPM*, 3:518–20).

1. The letter that SAAH wrote to JA is not known to be extant.

2. JA to SAAH, 15 Nov. 1896, IU, Lilly, SAAH; *JAPM*, 3:499–500.

3. JA to SAAH, 11 Dec. 1896, UIC, JAMC; *JAPM*, 3:523. JA later reported to SAAH, "Esther went to Cedarville for the first part of her vacation and Stanley did not come, so that I was quite bereft of children" over Christmas (27 Dec. 1896; IU, Lilly, SAAH; *JAPM*, 3:527).

4. JA had surgery to remove her appendix in the fall of 1895. See AHHA to HWH and EGS to JWA, 13 Sept. 1895, above.

5. JA's childhood friend Flora Guiteau and her brother Luther. See especially *PJA*, 2:27–28.

6. Sarah Weber Addams, daughter of LSA and JWA, had entered the Univ. of Chicago in 1898.

7. JA's niece Esther Linn was a student at RC.

8. "I took Weber home last Saturday [5 Dec. 1896] and spent Sunday at Cedarville," JA reported to SAAH on 11 Dec. 1896. "He is quite restored and I feel as if a great sorrow was gone. I am so much happier when he is at home" (UIC, *JAMC*; *JAPM*, 3:523).

# Part 3

## BEGINNING TO PREACH PEACE, 1897–1900

The part title is a quote from Jane Addams to Adolphus Clay Bartlett, 3 December 1900.

Photograph: Jane Addams, 1899–1900, by J. Edgar Waters, Chicago photographer, 1889–1900. "Faithfully yours, Jane Addams" became the public signature that she used for the remainder of her life, especially on photographs that were distributed in response to requests (UIC, JAMC, 0006 1627).

# *Introduction*

In 1897 Chicago and the rest of the United States began to recover from the economic depression of the mid-1890s. Once again, Jane Addams could turn more of her energies away from gathering funds to provide relief for her neighbors and toward the continued development of Hull-House and its programs and to national progressive reform efforts. During the last four years of the nineteenth century, Addams pressed her reform agenda especially through public speaking and writing.[1] Two lecture tours, one in 1897 and one in 1899, during which she often spoke twice a day, in major cities and universities of the East, gave her an opportunity to explain and promote Hull-House, the social settlement movement, woman suffrage, the importance of education, the need to understand and support the labor union movement, and concern for child labor as well as for women workers. Political corruption and the views of immigrant communities and her experience with Leo Tolstoy and his philosophy also became major themes of her public addresses. Newspaper coverage of her appearances increased. In many instances, large segments of her remarks appeared simultaneously in multiple big-city newspapers. Newspapers in smaller communities picked up the same material or a summary of it, thus carrying her name and her ideas to a much broader public.

Jane Addams and Florence Kelley made a series of lectures in the late summer of 1899 through the University of Chicago extension program.[2] Jane Addams also presented versions of these lectures in other venues and then published them in a variety of periodicals. Eventually, they became the texts for Addams's first published book, *Democracy and Social Ethics*, issued in 1902. Jane's essay "Ethical Survivals in Municipal Corruption" in the *International Journal of Ethics* won national acclaim. It was based on her experiences in Chicago's Nineteenth Ward as she fought to remove political corruption from her neighborhood.[3]

Jane Addams never supported the Spanish-American War[4] of 1898, but she approved its quick ending. She was dismayed by the U.S. government's treatment of the indigenous people of the Philippine Islands in the war's aftermath. In defending the expectations of the island people for a safe and independent life as a nation, she was beginning to forge positions that she would continue to develop as she moved toward her commitment to an international woman's peace movement. A year later, in 1899, she registered her disappointment in what she saw as American imperialism. In a speech in Chicago, she supported efforts to provide humanitarian support for the South African Boers against Great Britain in the Second Boer War.[5]

During the last years of the nineteenth century, Jane Addams continued to expand the programs and the physical plant of Hull-House. With the help of the trustees, she raised funds for new construction at the settlement. In 1898 Addams built an electric plant for lighting the settlement buildings and the Jane Club. She collected $25,000 from a variety of donors for a new Coffee House and Theatre Building, which opened in time for the tenth anniversary of the founding of Hull-House, celebrated in October 1899.[6] In 1898 the Charles Mather Smith family provided the support Addams needed to build a permanent residence for the Jane Club, the single women's cooperative living facility and organization.[7] Although securing the $19,000 necessary to move and refurbish the old Gymnasium and Coffee House Building for another use was difficult, she had the pledges in hand by the end of 1900, and work on the building was set to begin in 1901. It was also at the end of 1900 that Jane Addams received a special gift that led to further settlement development in the first year of the twentieth century. "Miss Culver has given her, for her use only, all the land between Hull-House and Ewing Street and there are buildings to be planned, money to be raised, interviews without end."[8] Addams would add an apartment building to the Hull-House complex in 1902. Just as important, Jane Addams also managed to keep adequate financial support for the day-to-day operations at the settlement. She secured $4,250 in 1897, $4,730 in 1898, $5,185 in 1899, and $4,980 in 1900. Many of the same people gave for general support each year.

What began in 1889, shortly after Jane Addams and Ellen Gates Starr opened Hull-House, as a reading club for young working women had developed by 1900 into myriad educational and social programs to support the hopes and aspirations of neighborhood families. Public entertainments consisted of Sunday-afternoon concerts, a lecture series on Monday and Tuesday evenings, and throughout each week a variety of entertainments in the auditorium that included receptions, plays, dances, musicales, and socials. Educational opportunities encompassed advanced courses in various languages, history, literature, and economics. There were basic classes in English and arithmetic as well as art and technical classes specializing in drawing, painting, clay modeling, embroidery, millinery, dressmaking, cooking, baking, and even basket weaving. Manual training featured simple carpentry, wood carving, mechanical drawing, and sloyd. There were choral classes; dancing classes; gymnastic classes for men, women, and children; and special classes associated with the music school. An assortment of clubs promoted socialization and friendship among the adults and youth of the settlement neighborhood. In particular, the Jane Club, the Woman's Club, and the Men's Club were thriving organizations. There was a Shakespeare Club, Henry Clay Club, Medinah Club, Drexel Club, Rose Leaf Pleasure Club, Irving Club, Gertrude Howe Club, Oriole Club, Women's Socialist Club, and People's Friendly Club. Alumni from the Medill and Goodrich schools met regularly at the settlement, and so did an assortment of labor union–related organizations (the Textile Workers' Association, Tick Sewers' Union No. 7589, and Dorcas Federal Labor Union). The Hull-House Dramatic Association, the Chicago Arts and Crafts Society, as well as the Hull-House Guild held their regular gatherings and programs at the settlement. Numerous clubs for children were primarily after-school gatherings and promoted social interaction as well as education. There were play clubs, reading clubs, sewing clubs, song and games clubs, cooking-class clubs, and weaving and sewing clubs. In addition to the settlement nursery and kindergarten programs, there were both a visiting kindergarten program and, associated with all of the kindergarten programs, the Kindergarten Training School of the Chicago Froebel Assn. Also located at the settlement was a probation officer and a representative of the Visiting Nurse Assn. For the convenience of the neighbors there was a post office, and for children a penny provident banking operation. And the public, settlement residents, and volunteers made constant use of the Coffee House as a gathering place and source of inexpensive, nutritious food. In addition to the Hull-House Playground, the settlement continued its practice of holding a monthlong summer school at Rockford College. There were receptions for special settlement guests, picnics, excursions, and camping opportunities as well.

As the composition of the Hull-House neighborhood changed from primarily German, Irish, and French Canadian with a growing number of Italian newcomers to one composed largely of Italian immigrants from agrarian backgrounds with an increasing number of Greek settlers, the focus of the program changed. Some programs suitable for any immigrant flourished; others, particularly those directed to a particular ethnic group, bloomed for a while and then were disbanded when their constituency left the neighborhood. Programs that did not attract an audience or did not achieve their hoped-for goals were abandoned, to be replaced by other organizations and program efforts. All were developed by the assortment of men and women who came to be associated with Hull-House as volunteers and residents. Jane Addams encouraged all to find activities that they wanted to develop and lead for the benefit of the neighbors.

The two new special programs that Jane Addams added to the panoply of Hull-House offerings during this four-year period were a theater program[9] and the Labor Museum.[10] For some time, various youth and adult clubs had been presenting theatrical productions. With the addition of the new combination Coffee House and Theatre Building,[11] they had larger and better facilities that offered the possibility for longer and more complex productions. What began as an effort to help organize the emerging thespian productions of a mix of Hull-House clubs quickly became an association that led to the development of the near-professional company of actors, the Hull-House Players. It joined other programs already in place for art and music.[12] Addams designed the Labor Museum to promote the idea of the importance of work and to identify changes that technology had brought to manufacturing through the years. She expected that it would promote understanding between immigrant parents, familiar with the "old ways" of doing tasks, primarily by hand, and their children, who were aware of modern technological advances.

Jane Addams was always ready to support the cause of organized labor, even when it adversely affected a project at the settlement.[13] With her dedication to arbitration, she always encouraged the parties involved in a major work-related disagreement to arbitrate before resorting to a strike. In addition to providing a secure place for unions to organize and meet, Addams and the settlement offered relief to striking workers. She continued to publicly support legislation, programs, and agencies that would promote child welfare and protection for women and children in the labor force. She often appeared before legislative bodies to campaign for progressive reform solutions to societal problems. Jane Addams continued to encourage settlement residents to investigate and reveal conditions that required reform. During the 1897–1900 period, residents of Hull-House conducted investigations of neighborhood saloons and housing conditions. Addams herself helped with the housing investigation[14] and undertook a study of the milk supply of Chicago.[15]

The effort that Addams and settlement workers made to unseat the corrupt aldermen in their Nineteenth Ward in 1896 intensified in 1897 and 1898,[16] when other organizations in Chicago also campaigned to rid the city council of similar politicians representing other wards. After Hull-House residents and volunteers, led by Addams, were unsuccessful in their attempts to elect a reform candidate in the Nineteenth Ward in those years, they continued to monitor aldermanic campaigns. In 1900 they did not offer their own candidate for the position, but they did publicly offer objection to the sitting alderman who was continuing to seek election.[17] Their efforts became a learning experience, and Addams wrote and spoke about the lessons she learned during her lecture tours.

By century's end, the Hull-House residents were a well-established and growing group. The 1900 federal census return recorded on 2 June 1900 listed twenty residents living at 335 South Halsted Street; there were six men and fourteen women. The autumn 1900 edition of the *Hull-House Bulletin* identified twenty-four residents. One of those residents was Ellen Gates Starr,[18] whose role in the early development of the settlement was not forgotten but whose current interests turned to arts and crafts and fine bookbinding in particular, which she practiced and taught at the settlement. Although Florence Kelley had gone from the settlement to direct the work of the National Consumers' League, she was still active in Chicago, and at her request she was still identified as a resident.[19]

Alice Hamilton arrived at Hull-House in 1897 and stayed to become Jane Addams's primary physician for the remainder and a close personal friend and colleague. Hamilton became a noted investigator of industrial diseases and the first woman member on the Harvard University medical faculty (HU, RI, SL, MC384-16-3).

Early settlement workers Enella Benedict, Wilfreda Brockway, Julia Lathrop, and Rose Marie Gyles were still in residence. During the last five years of the nineteenth century, they were joined by a new group of residents, many of whom maintained a lifelong connection with the settlement, its programs, and particularly with Jane Addams. Alice Hamilton,[20] who arrived in 1897, became one of the close circle of progressive reformers whom Jane Addams could count on for support. She often served as Addams's personal physician and sometime traveling companion. George Hooker[21] lived at Hull-House, and it became his base of operations, from which he continued his urban planning and reform efforts throughout the world. Others who supplanted former settlement residents were Mary Hill and Gerard Swope,[22] who later married, and Victor and Rachelle Yarros.[23] Throughout the entire eleven-year period, Alessandro Mastro-Valerio and his wife, Amalie, were often residents, sometimes as a couple and sometimes individually.

Besides increasing the number of her speaking engagements, continuing to serve as the chief fund-raiser for Hull-House,[24] and promoting new settlement programs, Jane Addams strengthened her friendship with Mary Rozet Smith and the entire Smith family.[25] When Mary Smith was not traveling away from Chicago in the hope of improving her own health or traveling in support of other family members, she and Jane Addams were often together in Chicago or traveling for Jane's speaking engagements or for their vacations together. It was during this period that Mary Smith investigated alternatives for her own life's work, including kindergarten education and social settlement living in a venue other than Hull-House, yet she willingly chose to maintain her commitment as nurturing helpmate to Jane Addams. In the process, she became a beloved friend to Hull-House residents and continued to serve as a financial backer for the settlement.

Jane Addams experienced a number of health problems during these eleven years.[26] Her energy level was sometimes sapped by rheumatism, colds or flu-like symptoms, bowel attacks, and "woman problems." The emergency appendectomy that she underwent during the fall of 1895 kept her in recovery mode for two months. During that time, her friends and Sarah Alice Haldeman, her sister who had some medical experience as a nurse, provided her care. In 1897 she fell getting off a streetcar in front of Hull-House, hit her head, and, briefly unconscious, had to be carried into the settlement. After a minimum time of bed rest, she recovered. Beginning in the mid-1890s and continuing for the reminder of their lives together, Mary Smith became the primary caregiver for Jane Addams. Returning from her summer visit in Europe in 1896, Jane Addams reported that she made the trip "because my health demanded a change, and I have come back greatly benefitted. In fact I was never so fat in my life as I am now."[27] As the years unfolded, more and more Jane Addams found her energy level deserting her. In 1900 Alice Hamilton reported: "I heard Miss Addams speak this morning at the Woman's Club on Trades Unions. She speaks with a good deal of animation and much more quickly than she used to, and when she sits down at the end she is gray and haggard. But . . . this afternoon . . . [she was] looking very bright and well after her nap. . . . [W]e know now she has a slow form of Brights' Disease, the kind that brings heart trouble with it. She is trying to be careful, but you can imagine how successful it is."[28]

By 1900 Jane Addams had given up on trying to maintain a close relationship with her stepmother, Anna Addams, and her reclusive stepbrother, George Haldeman. She continued to help her mentally ill brother, John Weber Addams, and his wife, Laura, and visited them in Cedarville when she had time and especially when they needed her help. Her relationship with her sister Alice Haldeman was often troubled, yet the two women had family duties that they shared, most notably managing their sister Mary Catherine Addams Linn's estate for the benefit of the four Linn children. Jane Addams found herself the matriarch of her three nephews and a niece, all of whom brought their personal problems to her, involving her in their personal lives for the remainder of her life.[29]

While Jane Addams and her reform efforts still garnered positive coverage in newspapers throughout the United States, her image among some leaders in Chicago became a bit tarnished. Jane Addams and Hull-House were no longer new or unique. Newspaper coverage and her own efforts as speaker and writer brought her and her activities and philosophy to the attention of more people; there was more to applaud as well as more to criticize. Many politicians found her attempts to quell the influence of her Nineteenth Ward alderman worrisome. Members of traditional religious congregations complained about the settlement's unwillingness to proselytize in support of the Christian religion. Addams and Hull-House were also seen by business leaders as promoting the development and activities of labor unions that they opposed. Some of Chicago's social leaders also questioned the support that Jane Addams offered to African American leaders and their organizations.[30]

In 1900 Paris hosted the Exposition Universelle, and with the help of Chicago supporters Jane Addams was selected as one of only three women from the United States to serve as jurors for exhibits at the fair.[31] In addition, Addams became the only woman to win a place in the gathering of jurors selected for participation in the final level of judging. She was also recognized as one of the presenters at the women's congress. There she spoke about the development and significance of Hull-House and returned to the United States from the experience an even more visible representative of successful women in the larger international arena. Toward the end of 1900, in recognition of her growing fame as a leader of women and because of her achievements in progressive reform, Jane Addams was featured in a lead article in *Good Housekeeping*, an up-and-coming national woman's magazine.[32] This would be the first of many such national tributes she would receive in a multitude of national and international publications.

By the end of 1900, Jane Addams had become a national, even international, figure. From a young, relatively unknown Cedarville, Illinois, woman with passion for an idea, she had become a recognized leader for progressive reform in the United States. Jane Addams was positioned to pursue a reform agenda during the first years of the twentieth century.

## Notes

1. See especially JA to SAAH, 11 Feb. 1897; Excerpts from Addresses, 14 July–9 Dec. 1897; Article in the *Chicago Times-Herald*, 6 Mar. 1898; Essay in the *International Journal of Ethics*, Apr. 1898; JA to MRS, 6 Oct. 1898; JA to MRS, [10 Oct. 1898]; JA to SAAH, 1 Mar. 1899; Address before the Chicago Liberty Meeting, 30 Apr. 1899; JA to Henrietta O. Barnett, 30 May 1899; JA to MRS, 22 June 1899; Statement in the *St. Louis Post-Dispatch*, 27 Jan. 1900; JA to MRS, 18 June 1900; Essay in the *Commons*, 30 June 1900; and Harris Weinstock to JA, 19 Oct. 1900, all below.

2. See JA to MRS, 22 June 1899, below.

3. See Essay in *International Journal of Ethics*, Apr. 1898, below.

4. See JA to MRS, [3 Apr. 1898], n. 2; JA to MRS, 21 Oct 1898; and Address before the Chicago Liberty Meeting, 30 Apr. 1899, all below.

5. See Statement in the *St. Louis Post-Dispatch*, 27 Jan. 1900, below.

6. See Article in the *Commons*, 31 Oct. 1899, below.

7. See JA to MRS, 23 Mar. 1898, below.

8. Alice Hamilton to Agnes Hamilton, 1 Dec. 1900, RS, HFP.

9. See Article in the *HH Bulletin*, 1 Dec. 1897; Article in the *Evening Gazette*, 10 Aug. 1898; and Article in the *Commons*, 31 Oct. 1899, all below.

10. See Essay in the *Commons*, 30 June 1900, below.

11. See Article in the *Evening Gazette*, 10 Aug. 1898; JA to MRS, 25 July 1899; and Article in the *Commons*, 31 Oct. 1899, all below.

12. See Article in the *HH Bulletin*, 1 Dec. 1897; and JA to MRS, 6 Oct. 1898, both below.

13. See Graham Taylor to JA, 26 June 1897, n. 2; JA to MRS, 25 July 1899, n. 9; JA to MRS, [4?] [June 1900]; and JA to MRS, 18 June 1900, n. 5, all below.

14. See JA to MRS, 18 June 1900, nn. 8–11, below.

15. See JA to William Rainey Harper, 19 Dec. 1895, n. 12, above.

16. See JA to Madeleine Wallin Sikes, 6 Mar. 1897, n. 5; Article in the *Chicago Times-Herald*, 6 Mar. 1898; Essay in the *International Journal of Ethics*, Apr. 1898; JA to MRS, [3 Apr. 1898]; and Article in the *HH Bulletin*, Apr. and May 1898, all below.

17. See Letter to the Editor, 20 Feb. 1900, below.

18. See JA to MRS, 21 Feb. 1897, n. 8; and Essay in the *Commons*, 30 June 1900, nn. 3, 10, both below.

19. See JA to MRS, 31 Aug 1897; JA to MRS, 25 July 1899, n. 5; JA to Florence Kelley, 13 Sept. 1899; and JA to SAAH, [ca. 18 May 1900], all below.

20. Alice Hamilton (1869–1970) became a resident at HH in 1897. She was the founder of the field of occupational health and a leading pioneer in industrial toxicology and medicine. She also became one of the lifelong friends of Jane Addams, her personal physician, and her colleague in seeking social justice and progressive reform. The second of four girls born to Montgomery (1843–1909) and Gertrude Pond Hamilton (1840–1917), Alice with her sisters, Edith (1867–1963), Margaret (1871–1969), and Nora (1873–1945), were joined eventually by Arthur (1886–1967), called Quint. Alice, who was born in New York City, and her siblings grew up in Fort Wayne, Ind., in a family compound that included her paternal grandmother and cousins. The Hamiltons stressed reading from their home library and especially studying languages, literature, and history as preparation for higher education. Between 1886 and 1888, Alice attended Miss Porter's School for Young Ladies in Farmington, Conn.

All of Alice's siblings were talented. None of the sisters married. Edith became a noted classicist, writer, and educator at Bryn Mawr College. Margaret was also an educator who became headmistress at Bryn Mawr School in Baltimore. Nora, the illustrator for JA's *Twenty Years at HH*, struggled with mental illness. Alice chose medicine as a career. Perhaps she was attracted to the life of independence and usefulness that it could offer. After studying at the Fort Wayne College of Medicine, she received her M.D. from the Univ. of Michigan in 1893. Between 1893 and 1894, Alice interned at Northwestern Hospital for Women and Children in Minneapolis and at the New England Hospital for Women and Children in Boston. From 1894 until 1897, she continued her education, specializing in pathology and bacteriology at the Univ. of Michigan, the Johns Hopkins Medical School, and in Europe at the universities of Leipzig and Munich.

During the summer of 1897, Alice Hamilton accepted a position to teach pathology and conduct her own research at the Woman's Medical School of Northwestern Univ. in Chicago. She hoped to live at HH. While rejected as a trial resident to begin with, she was notified by JA at summer's end that there would be a room for her if she still chose to come. Later she discovered that Florence Kelley, whom she did not know at the time, had interceded on her behalf and was largely responsible for JA's change of mind.

Hamilton began her trial as a HH resident at the end of the summer in 1897. Six weeks later, on 3 Nov. 1897, she became a full resident. With breaks for family matters, her own health, her teaching, and conducting national and state investigations, Alice made HH her home for nearly the next forty years. She found HH exhilarating and mind opening, but challenging in its demands—especially in light of her full-time teaching position. In the summer of 1899, as she looked back on her two years at the settlement, and in an unusually contemplative mood, she wrote to her cousin Agnes Hamilton: "At Hull-House I really never think. I just live on in a condition of what I suppose the physiologist would call 'reflex activity', that is, responding always to outward stimuli, not originating ones springs of activity from within" (18 June 1899, RC, SL, HFP). In her first two HH years, Alice Hamilton established significant lifetime friendships among the residents, especially with Florence Kelley, Julia C. Lathrop, Mary Kenney O'Sullivan, MRS, and, of course, JA.

Hamilton's letters to members of her family from the 1897–1900 period reflect the pace of activity required by the settlement and reveal personalities, relationships, peccadilloes, and contributions, as well as the fun that the assortment of residents and volunteers experienced. Alice described residents or visitors that she liked as well as those for whom she had little respect, and she wrote in some detail about the interpersonal relationships and romances that evolved at the settlement. She also described how the settlement functioned, and she sometimes wrote about the musical chair–like changes in the sleeping arrangements at the settlement.

For Alice, one of the decided benefits of living at HH was her access to JA. Writing to her cousin Agnes Hamilton (1868–1961) on Halloween 1897, Alice admitted: "Miss Addams still rattles me, indeed more so all the time, and I am at my very worst with her. I really am quite school-girly in my relations with her. . . . I know when she comes into the room. I have pangs of idiotic jealously toward the resident whom she is intimate with. She is—well she is quite perfect" (RC, SL, HFP). Two years later, she informed the same cousin: "To know Miss Addams and Miss Lathrop is gain enough to make the two years seem worth while, Agnes. Miss Addams is more wonderful than ever, she really is, and I believe I shall always go on finding her more and more so no matter how long I stay with her" (18 June 1899, RC, SL, HFP). How prophetic Alice's words were. Her respect for JA never wavered, not during the 1897–1900 period nor in their continuing friendship, which grew stronger over the first thirty-five years of the twentieth century to end only in JA's death.

JA came to rely more and more on Alice for friendship, as a sounding board, and for her skills as a physician. From almost the beginning of their relationship, Alice Hamilton watched over JA through her many health problems. As early as 1900, Alice recognized that JA had health issues that would require increased vigilance. On 1 Dec. 1900, she wrote to her cousin Agnes Hamilton about JA's beginning heart trouble (see introduction to part 3, above). In 1923 when JA had an unexpected mastectomy in Japan, Alice went to Japan to oversee her care and returned with her. In 1934, after JA had experienced another serious heart attack, Alice was at her bedside on the second floor in the home of MRS when MRS was dying from pneumonia on the first floor. Alice watched her friend carefully after that, monitoring JA's declining health and continuing to keep her nieces and nephews informed. In 1934 JA stayed for a period of time with the Hamilton sisters in their retirement home in Hadlyme, Conn., and when JA required surgery to remove a bowel obstruction in May 1935, Alice was there to oversee the procedure, report to family, and help make end-of-life decisions for her friend.

The friendship that Alice Hamilton and JA enjoyed began at HH. Alice Hamilton's first duty there was as director of the men's Fencing and Athletic Club, a responsibility she continued for several years. She taught classes in art anatomy, physiology, and English. She held a well-baby clinic on Tuesdays and Saturdays, especially for Italian women and their babies, hoping to encourage them to feed their children a healthier diet. In addition, she gave three evenings a week to the settlement: one tending the door, a job most residents disliked; one for a class on hygiene; and "one extra for whatever comes up" (Alice Hamilton to Agnes Hamilton, 5 or 6 Nov. 1899, RC, SL, HFP). She helped with the 1898 HH campaign for Simeon Armstrong in his effort to unseat John Powers and become the Nineteenth Ward alderman in his place. She recalled that the "campaign literature business was lengthy and dreadful" (Sicherman, *Alice Hamilton*, 120). The HH volunteers addressed envelopes and sent information about their candidate to twelve thousand registered voters in their ward, and Alice recalled working into the night to get the literature out in time for the vote.

When the Northwestern Univ. Woman's Medical School closed at in 1902, Alice Hamilton lost her job, but readily found another as a bacteriologist at the new John McCormick Memorial Institute for Infectious Diseases. It was directed by Dr. Ludvig Hektoen (1863–1951), a noted pathologist. He encouraged Alice to continue her work as a research pathologist and to conduct investigations and describe her findings in papers and presentations. Alice struggled to both keep her work at HH and conduct research as a scientist in her chosen field. She needed aspects of both careers. It may have been through a series of investigations that Alice conducted in the HH neighborhood over the next eight years using her scientific training as a researcher, bacteriologist, and pathologist that she began to discover how to blend her two interests and make a satisfying and cohesive life for herself.

Starting in 1902, she began an investigation of a typhoid fever epidemic in the HH neighborhood. She discovered that the disease seemed the most prevalent where the sanitation was inadequate. She believed that the disease was carried to other sections of the neighborhood by flies from the contaminated areas. Her report on the discovery appeared in the prestigious *Journal of the American Medical Assn.* and gained her instant recognition. In addition, Chicago made an attempt to improve its Sanitation Bureau and fired a number of sanitation inspectors.

In 1903, with the Visiting Nurse Assn., she helped organize and then served as secretary for the Com. on the Prevention of Tuberculosis. The results of the study she conducted in the HH neighborhood revealed a close connection between the prevalence of the disease and the conditions in which those who became ill worked. Her findings were published in 1905 by the City Homes Assn. as *A Study of Tuberculosis in Chicago*. A summary of her study also appeared in several other publications, and with JA she presented a paper on the study to the Sixth International Congress of Tuberculosis, held in Washington, D.C., 28 Sept.–3 Oct. 1908.

By 1904 Alice was engaged in an investigation of the illegal use of cocaine in the HH neighborhood. In 1907 it resulted in legislation that placed more stringent penalties on pharmacists who sold the drug illegally. Even though the new legislation was eventually overturned, publicity about the problems brought more awareness and some help in the settlement area. In 1905 Alice served on a committee established by the Chicago Medical Society and HH to investigate midwife practices in Chicago. One of the results was an effort to establish improved standards for practitioners and develop additional regulations for their oversight. "The Midwives of Chicago" appeared in the *Journal of the American Medical Assn.*, 25 Apr. 1908. In 1909 Alice Hamilton conducted a study of sixteen hundred Chicago families that led to a correlation between high birthrates and high infant mortality rates. She did not favor abortion and saw birth control as the only means of limiting this problem, and she supported the work of the birth control program promoted in Chicago by HH resident Rachelle Yarros.

Illinois governor Charles S. Deneen appointed Hamilton a member of the Illinois Comm. on Occupational Diseases in 1908. Two years later, she directed a specialized study of lead poisoning in industrial processes and its results. Her findings led to the passage of an Illinois law to control the use of lead by workers in industrial settings. Alice joined the Bureau of

Labor Statistics in the U.S. Dept. of Labor in 1911 and undertook a nationwide study of the use and effects of white lead in industry. During World War I, she investigated conditions in munitions plants. All of these studies required her to travel a great deal, but she still found time for HH. In addition, she sometimes took HH colleagues with her during her investigations.

In 1919 as an assistant professor of industrial medicine, Alice Hamilton became the first female faculty member in the Harvard Medical School. She was able to arrange to teach one half of the year and spend the other half at HH. While at Harvard, her fame as a leading authority on lead poisoning continued to grow. She published two textbooks, *Industrial Poisons in the United States* (1925), the first textbook on the subject in the United States, and *Industrial Toxicology* (1934). She continued to encourage more study of industrial diseases and to promote public efforts to improve industrial conditions, and she also alerted the public to new industrial poisons, among them tetraethyl lead in 1925 and radium in 1928. She also continued to raise money from foundations and private sources for special field studies and for her research and reform efforts.

Hamilton joined JA in her commitment to peace during World War I. She attended the International Conf. of Women held at The Hague in 1915 and was JA's companion on her tour of the capitals of the warring parties in the unsuccessful effort to promote a negotiated end to hostilities. Along with JA and Emily G. Balch, Alice Hamilton was one of the authors of *Women at The Hague*, issued by Macmillan in 1916 to describe their efforts. At war's end, Hamilton also accompanied JA to Zurich for the gathering of women after the war that led to the founding of the WILPF. She and JA toured the devastated European countries. They joined others in raising funds to provide famine relief. Between 1924 and 1930, Alice served on the Health Com. of the League of Nations, and after Adolf Hitler's rise to power in Germany, she joined an effort to help many in danger from his regime escape to the United States. In 1935 she joined JA and other friends as an author of *Why Wars Must Cease*, issued by the Macmillan Co. She chose to support the war efforts of the United States during World War II, but was against America's participation in the Vietnam War.

When JA died, the residents of HH asked Alice Hamilton to become their new head resident, but she declined. Instead, after her age-forced retirement from Harvard, she became a consultant for the U.S. Dept. of Labor, where she worked part-time, and spent more time in the Hadlyme, Conn., home that she shared with her sister Margaret Hamilton and former HH resident Clara Landsberg. Between 1944 and 1949, she served as president of the National Consumers' League.

Throughout her career, Alice Hamilton wrote numerous articles about HH and about her work in occupational health. She also traveled widely in the United States and was often in Europe to investigate conditions there or to attend conferences. Between 1930 and 1932, she was the only woman on the President's Research Com. on Social Trends, composed of a small group of social scientists charged with reviewing various aspects of life in the United States. McGraw-Hill published their findings in 1933 about twenty-nine fields of endeavor as *Recent Social Trends in the United States*.

In 1943 Alice Hamilton published her autobiography, *Exploring the Dangerous Trades*. In it she attempted to provide, as she wrote, "something of the impressions" that JA had made on her. "She had intellectual integrity. . . . She never sentimentalized over the poor, or labor, or the half-baked young radicals, or the conscientious objectors. . . . She never refused to listen to damaging evidence. . . . She was a pragmatist . . . holding that anything one had learned in college and from travel must be tried out in actual life. . . . [S]he had had more than her fill of theoretical knowledge; it made her rather impatient. She turned from it eagerly to practical application, in the field of action. . . . [H]er complete absence of personal pride, made her ready to try out a new scheme and equally ready to drop it if it proved a failure. . . . She never took a stand for the sake of consistency; she was no slave to her own theories. . . . She had two conflicting traits which sometimes brought her great unhappiness: she was very dependent on a sense of warm comradeship and harmony with the mass of her fellowmen, but at the same time her clear-sighted integrity made it impossible for her to keep in step with the crowd in many a crisis. . . . Nor did she ever fall into the mire of self-pity or take refuge in a sense of self-righteousness. She simply suffered from the spiritual loneliness which her farsighted vision had imposed on her" (65–67).

Alice Hamilton lived to be 101. She died from a stroke in her Hadlyme home and was buried nearby with other family members. Her legacy was her pioneering and continuing effort to improve the conditions in which industrial workers labored, as well as the example she set for those who followed in her footsteps. Barbara Sicherman, her biographer and the editor of a selection of her letters, has characterized her as "calm and gracious but also forceful on behalf of her beliefs (though never for herself). With her aristocratic and mellow voice, and her sure sense of the ridiculous, she could gently deflate even the most seasoned opponent. Her self-sufficiency made her seem a little remote to some; others admired her serenity. . . . But spirited and open as she was in most respects, she had a deep reticence about herself that intrigued the discerning observer" (*Alice Hamilton*, 6).

After the death of JA, Alice Hamilton continued to be supportive of JA's legacy and her memory. She wrote two articles about JA. "Jane Addams, Gentle Rebel" appeared in *Political Affairs* in 1960, and "Jane Addams of Hull-House" was issued in the June–Aug. 1953 number of *Social Service*. When JA died, she had almost completed her part of the biography of Julia C. Lathrop that she and Grace Abbott planned to publish about their friend. Alice Hamilton wrote that JA "had not yet made the final revision" of her work. "It has fallen to me to do this and I have carried out the task with scrupulous care, making as few changes as possible" (Addams, *My Friend*, vi). Near the end of her life, JA had honored Alice with the dedication of *The Excellent Becomes the Permanent*: "To Alice Hamilton whose wisdom and courage have never failed when we have walked together so many times in the very borderland between life and death."

21. See JA to EGS, 29 [and 30] May 1896, n. 19, below.

22. See JA to MRS, [10 Oct. 1898], n. 5, below.

23. See JA to MRS, 6 Oct. 1898, n. 8, below.

24. See especially JA to SAAH, 28, Feb. 1897; JA to MRS, 23 Mar 1898; Article in the *Evening Gazette*, 10 Aug. 1898; JA to MRS, 22 June 1899; and JA to MRS, 25 July 1899, all below.

25. See JA to MRS, [22 July 1897]; JA to MRS, [3 Apr. 1898]; JA to MRS, 6 Oct. 1898; JA to MRS, [10 Oct. 1898]; JA to MRS, 31 May 1899; and JA to MRS, 22 June 1899, all below.

26. JA to MRS, [3 Apr. 1898], below.

27. "JA at Home," *Buffalo (N.Y.) News*, 25 Sept. 1896; *JAPM*, 55:207.

28. Alice Hamilton to Agnes Hamilton, 1 Dec. 1900, RS, HFP.

29. See JA to SAAH, 28 Feb. 1897, nn. 5–6; JA to MRS, 17 Apr. 1898; JA to SAAH, 31 Dec. 1898; JA to SAAH, 1 Mar. 1899, nn. 6, 8; JA to MRS, 25 July 1899; and JA to Florence Kelley, 13 Sept. 1899, n. 3, all below.

30. See also Harris Weinstock to JA, 19 Oct. 1900, below. On 14 Aug. 1899, the National Assn. of Colored Women (NACW) began meeting in Chicago to conduct business and elect new officers. Among their speakers from Chicago associated with the woman's club movement and social reform efforts were Corinne S. Brown and Mary E. McDowell. JA also participated, but in a more social way. Under the heading "Colored Club Women Entertained at Hull House," the *Chicago Times-Herald* reported: "The 'color line' was given another good rub yesterday by Miss Jane Addams of Hull House, who entertained at luncheon a party of colored women. The guests included in this little 'social departure' were for the most part the prominent out-of-town delegates to the convention of the National Association of Colored Women, which has just closed in this city. The invitation having been extended by Miss Addams, the arrangements, as far as the colored women were concerned were carried out by Mrs. Ida Wells-Barnett. There were thirteen guests. . . . After luncheon at which Hull

House residents were also present, another party of twenty-five colored women came to inspect this social settlement. . . . This is the first time in Chicago that the colored women have been given decided recognition in a social way by a woman of the lighter skin" (18 Aug. 1899). Among JA's guests were Mary Church Terrell, who had been reelected as the president of the NACW for another two-year term, and her newly elected vice-president, Josephine B. Bruce.

Mary Church Terrell (1863–1954), daughter of former slaves Robert Reed Church and Louise Ayers, was born in Memphis, Tenn. She was educated at the Antioch College Model School, Yellow Springs, Ohio; graduated from Oberlin College (B.A. 1884; M.A. 1888); and studied two years in Europe. She became a teacher, educator, and community woman's leader in Washington, D.C., and served on the District of Columbia Board of Education, 1895–1906. In 1891 she married Robert Heberton Terrell, a lawyer who became the first African American municipal judge in the District. In the later 1890s, she was beginning her more than fifty-year career as an African American activist for civil rights, desegregation, and suffrage. Along with Ida B. Wells-Barnett, she was one of the two African American women who were asked to sign the "call" in 1910 (as did JA) to attend the founding meeting of the NAACP. She was an internationally recognized speaker and journalist and in 1940 issued her autobiography, *A Colored Woman in a White World*.

Josephine Beall Willson Bruce (1853–1923) was a teacher, club woman, and civil rights activist who was born in Philadelphia to dentist Dr. Joseph Willson and Elizabeth Harnett Willson. The family moved in 1884 to Cleveland, where Josephine Willson was educated. In 1878 she married the U.S. senator from Mississippi Blanche K. Bruce, Republican Party political leader and the only African American in the U.S. Congress. She took an active role in efforts in Washington, D. C., to improve and promote the interests of African American women and became a leader in the NACW. After her husband's death, she became dean of women at Tuskegee Institute.

31. See JA to SAAH, [ca. 18 May 1900]; JA to MRS, [4?] [June 1900]; and JA to MRS, 18 June 1900, all below.

32. See Article in *Good Housekeeping*, Nov. 1900, below.

## To Sarah Alice Addams Haldeman

19 Walton Place [Chicago, Ill.] Jan, 6" 1897

My dear Alice

I have a New England mortgage which was due last spring for $ 1800.00 I am very anxious indeed to have some money and wonder if you could take this mortgage for security, or rather buy it from me.

The New England Loan and Trust Company[1] continue to pay the interest regularly at 7% and will pay the principal in two years from the time it <~~was~~> is due—I would like very much to have five hundred dollars advanced on it but could manage with less it you could n't do so much. If you could consider it I should be glad to send it to you to investigate, but if it is n't convenient I can make an arrangement with the Freeport bank.[2] I do not want to borrow from the Girard bank[3] but to sell you a mortgage on the plan of installment payments.

We have a sick friend whom dear Mary Smith has taken in for a few weeks,[4] I am spending the night with her so am writing from the North side. All our Christmas affairs went off very nicely[5] and we are going on with much good cheer. M. Smith sends her love to you and Marcet. Always your loving sister

Jane Addams.

P.S. Will you write me as soon as you can so that I may know what to do in the matter.

ALS (IU, Lilly, SAAH; *JAPM*, 3:544–45).

1. Investments with the New England Loan and Trust Co. do not appear among those listed by JA before she went to Europe in 1887 (see *PJA*, 2:537). The company with which JA had invested funds was organized on 21 Sept. 1882, under the laws of Iowa, with a capitalization of $875,000. Its principal business consisted of lending money on farming properties in the western and southern United States. JA tried to sell her note at a very good time. The company entered receivership on 1 Oct. 1897.

2. JA continued to maintain a personal banking account in the Second National Bank of Freeport, the bank that had been organized and run by her father, JHA, during his life.

3. In 1886 HWH purchased the Bank of Girard. HWH, and later SAAH as the first woman bank president in Kansas, directed the affairs of the bank. JA did not have a personal account there.

4. Margaret V. Toomey. See Article in the *Chicago Inter Ocean*, 30 June 1892, n. 13, above.

5. "The Christmas parties and entertainments held at Hull-House during the past two

weeks were all well attended and carried out with the good cheer of the season," reported the *HH Bulletin* in Jan. 1897. "They started off with a very credible exhibition of the gymnastic classes, and the enthusiasm engendered by the victory of the Hull-House basket ball team over the University of Chicago team, seems to have lingered in the gymnasium throughout the holidays." The report continued: "The Christmas play this year, 'Longfellow's Golden Legend,' was given three times to various audiences and the scenes from the miracle play oftener" ("Christmas Entertainments"). During the second week in Dec., HH and the Chicago Commons sponsored a series of "economic conferences" held at both settlements. In his report, George E. Hooker wrote that "in scope and variety of standpoint," these events proved "the most diversified intellectual exchange that has occurred in Chicago perhaps since the congresses of the World's Fair." Most of the speakers were from Chicago, and the "audiences contained pretty much all sorts and conditions of people—ministers, teachers, students, philanthropists, employers, employes, co-operators, and on one occasion at least an Alderman." Hooker reported that "the liveliest interest centered in the pleas of Count Tolstoy on nonresistence of evil and its logical result in doing away with war on the one hand, and with courts, prisons and policemen on the other." As a result of the gatherings, JA "voiced a feeling shared by many . . . that this method of conferences might well be applied next to some of the concrete problems of our city life" (Hooker, "Social Economic Conf.").

From 4 Oct. until 7 Oct. 1897, another economic conference was held in Chicago and hosted by the same two settlements. Among the speakers were Samuel M. Jones of Toledo, Ohio; the future prime minister of Great Britain J. Ramsay MacDonald, who lodged at HH with his wife for several days in Oct.; Edwin Burritt Smith, associated with the Civic Federation of Chicago's battle for civil service reform; Charles Zueblin; and George E. Hooker. An article in the *Commons* 2, no. 5 (Sept. 1897): 6, reported, "Open discussions are the feature of the conferences."

## To Sarah Alice Addams Haldeman

Bellevue Hotel Boston [Mass.] Feb. 11" 1897

My dear Alice

Miss Smith and I arrived in Boston Tuesday evening and will be here for ten days.[1] We are having a very jolly time at this little hotel and go forth to dinners and lunches &c with great regularity.

I spoke last evening before the XX Cent. Club[2] and to night out at Brookline.[3] We are meeting some very interesting folk and are quite ready to admit that Boston is older and gentler than most cities.

Is there any thing you would like me to get for Marcet and yourself, the shops here are very inticing.

I have been interrupted twice and will give up this letter. M. Smith sends her love to you both. Always your loving sister

Jane Addams.

ALS (IU, Lilly, SAAH; *JAPM*, 3:561–62).

1. JA accompanied by MRS left Chicago on 9 Feb. for a lecture tour in the East, using Boston as a central location. They saw old friends and received a heady mixture of honors and receptions reported with great fanfare in newspapers of the area. Their round of activities began on

Wednesday, 10 Feb., when they met Robert Woods and Mary Kenney O'Sullivan for a tour of the Boston Public Library and lunch at the Industrial Union. JA's speech that evening at the Twentieth Century Club (see n. 2) was followed by a reception in her honor. The next day, Robert Woods joined JA and MRS to tour MIT. Before JA left for her evening lecture titled "The Social Obligation of Citizenship" in the Brookline (Mass.) Union Hall, she had lunch with Mary O'Sullivan and met with Felix Adler. On Friday, 12 Feb., JA and MRS took lunch at Denison House, and during the afternoon JA spoke about settlement work with special emphasis on kindergarten development for Elizabeth Peabody House (formed in Apr. 1896). Of her appearance, the *Boston Globe* reported, "She looks a bit worn and bears some traces of the anxiety and hard work she had done" (13 Feb. 1897; *JAPM*, 55:243). The *Boston Transcript* wrote that JA "had more to say about the ideas advanced by settlement workers than of the actual programme as carried out at Hull House" ("Miss Addams Speaks on College Settlement Idea"). On Saturday JA's diary indicated that she had "callers galore" ("Diary, 1897, 10–18 Feb." SCPC, JAC; *JAPM*, 29:379), and after having dinner at Wellesley College, where she spoke on Tolstoy, JA attended a South End House, Boston, gathering. On Sunday she gave a presentation titled "Ethical Survivals in City Immorality" at Mrs. Ole Bull's home in Cambridge (see Essay in the International Journal of Ethics, Apr. 1898, n. 1, below). Monday, 15 Feb., was a day of visits, including one with RFS's former music teacher Prof. Daniel N. Hood, with Walter Page, and once again with Mary Kenney O'Sullivan. That afternoon Mr. and Mrs. Robert Treat Paine gave a reception in JA's honor, and in the evening she lectured in Lynn, Mass., for the COS. The highlight of her Boston sojourn was the reception arranged for her by the Massachusetts Woman Suffrage Assn., where more than one thousand attendees greeted her and heard her "bright five-minute speech" in which she said in part that "what was wanted was equality of consideration and recognition. 'It is hard to expect devotion from those who had no sense of responsibility'" ("Reception to Miss Addams") (see also Excerpts from Addresses, 6 Nov. 1897, n. 17, below). Among the members of the host committee were Julia Ward Howe, Mary A. Livermore, William Lloyd Garrison, Mrs. Ole Bull, Mrs. Mary Schlesinger, and John Graham Brooks. That evening, according to JA's diary notes, she spoke on Tolstoy at Denison House. Wednesday, 17 Feb., the day began at 9:30 A.M. with a visit to the New England Kitchen program, followed by lunch and a visit at the Episcopal Theological School, a dinner and reception in the private home of Mr. and Mrs. Robert Treat Paine, an address at the Industrial Union, and a visit with Graham Wallas. On 18 Feb., after meeting friends in the morning, she and MRS took a train to Amesbury, Mass., where JA lectured at the Elizabeth H. Whittier Club on college settlements and returned to Boston for a reception given by the O'Sullivans. On 20 Feb., JA returned to Chicago and HH, leaving MRS in the East to visit family.

Sara Chapman Thorp Bull (1851–1911), wife of the famous Norwegian violin virtuoso Ole Bull (1810–80), was born in upstate New York, the daughter of Joseph G. and Amelia Chapman Thorp, and educated in Madison, Wis., where her father was in the lumber business and a member of the state legislature. She wed widower Bull when she was twenty years old and he sixty, first in a secret ceremony in Bergen, Norway, and then shortly after that in Madison, Wis. Their only child, Olea, was born in 1871. Mrs. Bull, her child, and her mother settled in Cambridge, Mass., where she continued to live after her husband died. She was a member of the Bernard Club of New York and the Sesame Club of London. She wrote *Ole Bull: A Memoir*, which was published in 1882. In 1890 her father built her a home at 168 Brattle St., in Cambridge, where she lived for the remainder of her life. She became part of Boston society and between 1897 and 1899 funded and helped direct the Cambridge Conferences, gatherings of intellectual and cultural leaders who met to discuss philosophical, cultural, and religious topics. In her later years, she became fascinated by Eastern religions and eventually joined the Vedanta Society and at her death left it most of her half-million-dollar estate.

Robert Treat Paine (1855–1929), whose great-grandfather of the same name was one of the signers of the Declaration of Independence, was born in Boston, Mass., the son of Charles

Cushing and Fannie Cabot Jackson Paine. He was educated at Harvard Univ. (A.B. 1855; M.A. 1856). He retired from the practice of law in 1870 and became an active philanthropist. Among his interests were the Wells Memorial Workingmen's Institute, which he organized in 1879 and served as president; the Workingmen's Cooperative Bank, where he was president, 1886–1903; the Associated Charities of Boston, president, 1878–1907; the Episcopal Theological School, trustee; and the American Peace Society, trustee from 1891. In 1862 he married Lydia Williams Lyman (1837–97), who became the mother of his six children. JA and John Graham Brooks shared the platform with Robert Treat Paine before the Nineteenth Century Club of New York on 13 Dec. 1897. JA spoke about the limitations of systematic charity, and Brooks defended it. Paine's speech was titled "Chronic Pauperism in Connection with Early Marriage."

2. JA lectured at the Twentieth Century Club on the evening of Wednesday, 10 Feb., where her topic was titled "Ethical Survivals in City Immorality." It was an early version of what became one of her signature essays and was published in its entirety in the Apr. 1898 issue of the *International Journal of Ethics* as "Ethical Survivals in Municipal Corruption" (see Essay in the *International Journal of Ethics*, Apr. 1898, below). In it JA recounted the lessons she had learned and her reactions to the unsuccessful efforts she and the HH residents and volunteers made to unseat corrupt alderman John Powers and his gang in the Nineteenth Ward of Chicago in 1896. She gave a similar presentation at Mrs. Ole Bull's home on 14 Feb.

3. See n. 1.

## To Mary Rozet Smith

Hull-House 335 South Halsted Street Chicago [Ill.] Feb. 21" 1897

My Ever Dear

I have been homesick since I went down stairs at the Bellevue[1] and left you behind. I had a very comfortable and sleepy journey and find myself quite adjusted once more to H.H.[2]—if you were here. I called on your family[3] this afternoon, the Grants[4] were just leaving after having been to dine and the family next door[5] came in before I left. Sarah Rozet[6] inquired for you and pensively remarked that she wished you were here:—a sentiment shared by her elders I opined. They were looking well and like the residents of H.H. declare that I look well and rested—I have had many compliments since my return.

The casts came & are all up looking as fine as possible. We put the Greek one in the library on the door over the bookcase, and the one it dispossessed in the C.H.[7]

Ellen is very well and altogether absorbed in the her books—quite happiest when she is showing them & they are really imposing.[8]

When you get back we will talk over a plan that is in my mind. I did nt say what I wanted to in the confessional the other night because I did n't feel sure enough of myself—but if you ever doubt my desire to be with you—I wish you could see at the bottom of my mind—you would certainly be reassured—

With kindliest regards to all your Uncle's household, Always your unchanging friend

Jane Addams

ALS (SCPC, JAC; *JAPM*, 3:567–69).

1. JA and MRS had lodged at the Bellevue Hotel at 21 Beacon St., opposite the Massachusetts State House and overlooking the Common, while they were in Boston, 10–18 Feb. 1897.

2. JA arrived back at HH on 20 Feb. 1897.

3. JA went to see MRS's mother and father at 19 Walton Place, Chicago.

4. The Grants might have been William Arthur Grant (b. 1872) and his wife, Maud Elizabeth Carpenter Grant, who married in Chicago, 30 Jan. 1895. William Grant came to Chicago in 1892, and by 1896 he was president of the Marsh & Grant Co., Printers. He continued in that line of business during the early part of the 1900s.

5. By 1897 MRS's brother, Charles Frederic ("Fred") Mather Smith, and his wife, Kathleen McDonald Smith, who were married in June 1892, were living in the house near the elder Smiths at 11 Walton Place.

6. Sara (or Sarah) Rozet Smith, the almost four-year-old daughter of Charles Frederic ("Fred") Mather and Kathleen Smith, was born 25 May 1893 at 11 Walton Place.

7. It is likely that JA and MRS purchased at least two plaster casts for display at HH while they were in Boston. JA may have placed one in the main HH building, likely in the southeast parlor, which served as a library at the settlement, and moved the one it displaced to the Children's House, also called the Smith Building.

8. EGS, who had become focused on learning fine-bookbinding skills, was already producing bindings to order. With the financial backing of her patron, Mary H. Wilmarth, EGS honed her fine-binding skills as an apprentice to the famous English fine binder T. J. Cobden-Sanderson (see *PJA*, 1:553–54). She left her duties at HH, where she was in charge of the art exhibits and the college extension and concert programs, to live and study with him in England for a year, beginning in Oct. 1897. She was expected back at HH on 1 Nov. 1898 to take up her settlement duties in charge of evening courses. She established the HH Bookbindery, where she taught students fine binding and crafted fine bindings to order for sale (see also Essay in the *Commons*, 30 June 1900, n. 10, below).

## To Sarah Alice Addams Haldeman

Cedarville [Ill.] Feb 28" 1897

My dear Alice

We sold the farm[1] at the Freeport Court House yesterday. I regret to say that it brought only $58.00 an acre. We have been trying for more than a year to get 60.00 and it has been advertised at that figure in the county papers for a number of times.

We were all discouraged about it and finally concluded to take $58.00. Mr Phillips (of the Damascus family)[2] pays $3000.00 two weeks from Sat. and the balance in a year assuming of course the mortgage for 7500.00

The 3000.00 will pay the note at the bank, Mrs Graves'[3] claim and the other pressing debts. The Englewood on the Hill people are pushing me for $195.00[4]

It will be a great relief to get it settled up soon altho there is no prospect of an income from what is left.

I wished very much that you had been here yesterday to consult with, why cant you come in April to see Weber Linn graduate (Lady Aberdeen gives the address)[5]—it would do Marcet good to have a Spring vacation whether the schools have one or not, John is ordained in April[6] and our two newys thus start forth. Newspaper seems the only opening for Weber altho I do not like the prospect very well.[7]

Laura has gone to Sunday School and Weber is taking his bath, the house is very peaceful and attractive filled with the fragrance of hyacinth, I some times think that it is the most attractive house I know. I have not yet been down below,[8] but we will journey thither after dinner—I have had a very busy week since my return from Boston with affairs naturally accumulated. We are trying very hard to get money for a Jane Club building,[9] and find it very hard these dull times.

I hope you will write me frankly about the price of the farm, I feel dubious about it but we certainly could not have done any better yesterday. It took about an hour of vigorous pushing to get beyond $56.00

With love to Marcet and yourself, Always your loving sister

Jane Addams

ALS (IU, Lilly, SAAH; *JAPM*, 3:587–90).

1. JA and SAAH were continuing to manage MCAL's estate on behalf of the Linn children (see also JA to SAAH, 16 Feb. 1896, above). JA was about to sell MCAL's Cedarville farm located in Lancaster Twp., Stephenson Co., just north of the one that JA owned to the south of Cedarville on the road between Cedarville and Freeport (see also JA to SAAH, 16 Feb. 1896, n. 4, above). Because there had been no bids on the property as advertised, JA was selling it at public auction from the Stephenson County Courthouse steps.

2. Later in the year, JA wrote to SAAH: "We are having a dreadful time getting the sale of the farm settled. I have no estate money to pay taxes with and altogether things are not in a very cheerful state" ([Apr.?] [1897]; *JAPM*, 3:635). Although JA did not receive the $60 an acre for MCAL's farm in Stephenson Co. that she hoped for, she did eventually receive $5,465.90 in one cash settlement after a public auction on 10 June 1897. The buyer was Charles N. Phillips, likely the son of James M. Phillips, who also had farms in the area around Cedarville.

According to a report in the Circuit Court, Probate Division, 10 July 1897, JA was able to sell MCAL's farm on which she had borrowed $7,500 from the Second National Bank of Freeport in 1894. In addition, JA's estate account book indicated that on behalf of MCAL's estate, JA also borrowed $1,275 from the same bank.

3. The final payment to Delia Graves of Ellendale, N. Dak., was $412.05 and included principal and interest.

4. MCAL and JML owned four lots in Englewood-on-the-Hill in Illinois, and JA was continuing to pay taxes on them until they could be sold. See also JA to SAAH, 16 Feb. 1896, n. 7, above.

5. James Weber Linn graduated from the Univ. of Chicago, 2 Apr. 1897, and began work at the *Chicago Record* shortly thereafter. Ishbel Maria Majoribanks Gordon (1857–1939), Marchioness of Aberdeen and Temair (beginning in 1915), was the convocation speaker. A noted British social worker, feminist, and author, Lady Aberdeen was president of the Canning Town Women's Settlement (1890–1939) and was married in 1877 to John Campbell Gordon (1847–1934), who was at the time of her visit to Chicago the governor-general of Canada, 1893–98. On 2 Apr. 1897, JA was among the one thousand guests who greeted Lady Aberdeen during a three-hour reception held by the university in Haskell Hall. She was identified by the Univ. of Chicago as "the first official woman great" to visit and speak there. At that time, she was president of the National Council of Women of Canada, 1893–99, and also president of the International Council of Women, 1893–1936. She had previously visited HH, and on the occasion of this visit to Chicago, JA had invited her to come to HH again, but she wrote

on 10 and 20 Mar. 1893 that she was unable to do so. JA and Gordon later worked together as both urged their various governments to appoint women as delegates and committee members to the League of Nations.

6. John Addams Linn graduated from the Western Theological Seminary and moved to Petersburg, Ill., where, until 1898, he served as the pastor of the First Trinity Church. He was ordained as a priest in the Episcopal Church in New York in 1901. For a biographical note on John Addams Linn, see *PJA*, 1:79.

7. For a biographical note on James Weber Linn, see *PJA*, 1:80–81.

8. JA meant that she had not yet been to visit AHHA and GBH in the Cedarville Addams home place to the south of JWA's home and across Cedar Creek.

9. For JA's efforts to establish and fund the Jane Club, see JA to MRS, 23 Mar. 1898, below, as well as Remarks on Opening the New England Kitchen, HH, 23 Aug. 1893, n. 3; and Article in the *Chicago Inter Ocean*, 30 June 1892, both above.

## To Madeleine Wallin Sikes

Hull-House 335 South Halsted Street Chicago [Ill.] March 6th 1897

My dear Mrs Sikes

We were very glad to have your letter, for our imaginations had followed your wedding journey and we had often spoken of you both.[1]

I am eagar to see you in your quarters at the Leland[2] and shall doubtless have that pleasure when we come to Springfield to work on our Child Labor bill—H.H. is very much interested in these bills this winter[3] and I am afraid that I cannot escape some lobbying.[4] Perhaps in Springfield we will have time for a more uninterrupted visit than we were ever able to secure here.

Please tell Mr Sikes that we are much bewildered by the array of poor candidates which the 19th ward are contemplating for alderman[5] and that we miss him sorely.

I am sure you will pardon my delayed reply,[6] we had hoped to see you during the recess of the Legislature—With most cordial good wishes I am very sincerely yours

Jane Addams

ALS (UIC, JAMC, Sikes; *JAPM*, 3:599–601).

1. Madeleine Wallin and George Sikes, who had been HH residents, were married in Elgin, Ill., on 6 Feb. 1897, and their wedding reception was held at HH. On their wedding trip through the East, the Sikes visited Washington, D.C.

Initially, Madeleine Wallin argued that HH was the best place to have the wedding, too. She reported to her mother that JA thought "the effect on the neighborhood of so 'human' a thing as a wedding very good" (Madeleine Wallin to Ellen Keyes Wallin, 5 Nov. 1896, CHM, CHS, Sikes). In her letter of 27 Oct. 1896 to her father, Alfred C. Wallin, she indicated that she and her fiancé, George Sikes, thought, "A Hull House wedding will be . . . a distinct social advantage. A very nice circle of people is connected with the House, and this affair would give us considerable prestige. It would be quite a distinguished thing to do I do not know of any way in which we could command as much social attention as we could command in this way. George regards his connection with the House as valuable to him in both a business and a social way and would like to emphasize it. It would of course be quite unique, and would be I am sure, a very interesting affair" (CHM, CHS, Sikes).

2. The five-story Leland Hotel was built in 1866 and opened 1 Jan. 1867 at the corner of Sixth and Capitol streets, Springfield, Ill. It became the unofficial political headquarters for the Republican Party when the Illinois General Assembly was in session, the home away from home for legislators, journalists, and lobbyists. The building was destroyed by fire in 1908 and replaced by a larger eleven-story structure, which survived as a hotel until 1970, when it became an office building.

3. There were at least two bills on child welfare that JA would have supported before the Illinois General Assembly. One was drawn by Lucy Flower and had the endorsement of the CWC. It proposed twelve weeks of consecutive compulsory education at the beginning of each school year for every child under the age of fourteen and provided penalties for lack of compliance. According to the 1 Mar. 1897 *HH Bulletin*, another bill, prepared at HH by a group representing labor unions, was meant to apply to "'all children who work for wages at any gainful occupation'" ("For Working Children"). Its primary provisions were prohibition from employing any child under fourteen years of age and from employing children between the ages of fourteen and sixteen more than ten hours in any one day, or in dangerous work, or who could not read and write English.

4. JA; Florence Kelley; MRS (representing the CWC); Mrs. M. E. Metzger of Moline, Ill.; George Perkins, president of the International Cigar-Makers Union; and James O'Connell, grand master of the International Assn. of Machinists, appeared before the House of Representatives' Com. on Labor and Industrial Affairs of the Illinois General Assembly in support of "farther protection for working children." On 22 Mar. 1897, the *Chicago Daily Tribune* reported that the leadership of the committee told JA "that her advocacy of any bill would be sure to obtain the endorsement of the committee at any time" ("Of Interest to the Gentler Sex"). The bill received the unanimous support of the House committee. The legislation did pass. Factory inspectors were directed to enforce the law and to prosecute violations, which could mean the application of a fine of up to one hundred dollars for each offense.

5. In 1897, when HH was not involved in the aldermanic campaign in the Nineteenth Ward, the following were candidates: Louis P. Cardwell, who lived at 252 (later 1040) West Congress; Rocco V. Romano of 380 (later 911 South) Halstead; Patrick Morris at 130 (later 573 West) Forquer; Patrick J. Meaney, who lived at 285 (later 612) South Jefferson; Joseph A. Haberkorn, who gave his address as a saloon at Polk and Center (later Racine) streets; Moses Touvin, of 417 (later 1132) West Taylor; and Rinaldo Rossi, of 104 (later 559 West) Ewing St. Joseph A. Haberkorn was the top vote getter, with 3,438 voters supporting him.

6. The letter that Madeleine Sikes wrote to JA is not known to be extant.

## From Graham Taylor

Madison. S Dakota. June 26. 1897.

My dear Friend Miss Addams.

I find that I cannot reach home from this out-of-the-world country[1] until Thursday morning, July 1st, and will hold that evening open to attend your Industrial Committee meeting,[2] if you, still think it worth while to call it when I can be in town—Kindly let me know what to expect on my arrival at the Commons.[3] <marking your reply "personal"> I expect to be in Chicago again

Graham Taylor, founder and head resident of the Chicago Commons. Taylor and Jane Addams often joined forces to support reform issues, especially in Chicago; their settlements cooperated in presenting public programs and on organizing settlement gatherings. Taylor became an international spokesman for social settlements and was recognized as the founder of the Chicago School of Civics and Philanthropy, which became the social work school of the University of Chicago (*Commons* 2, no. 4 [Aug. 1897]: cover).

Wednesday evg July 7—on my way to Iowa and could meet an appointment for that date if preferable. In any event I want so much to see you, for I have much to tell you and confer with you about. You will I know be interested in the Social propaganda, <the large opportunity for> which <is afforded me by> these great Summer Assemblies of earnest and eager Western folk, who think for themselves, want to learn from others, and are not afraid to act upon what they think and learn.[4] Is it not inspiring to find last year's words[5] transmuted into sweet-spirited, serving deeds in all kinds of lovely ministries, here and there? I want to tell you of it all, for I deeply feel my everlasting debt of gratitude to you for inspiring and encouraging me to much of such service,—which is its own exceeding great reward. Far better than you know, or will ever admit, have you built these Hull-House years. Into many lives, far beyond the sight or sound of you, has the leaven of your life been entering to lift or level them toward the ideal. In my own life's hard struggle for reality, simple honesty, and ingenuousness in religious and social relationships, in thinking and living, you have helped me more than any other, by the simplicity and single-heartedness which you have attained—or, I suspect, always have had—And I really need to see or hear from you about every so often, to test things by the touch-stone of your judgment or experience, at so many points where you have been tested as I am being.

My struggle is by no means ended, as I full well know yours is not. But <my> spiritual vision is so much less clear and incisive than yours, and the attitude I am as yet able to take on many open issues, upon which the Social pressure bears most heavily, is so much more tentative and dualistic than yours, that I long for the peace which I know you would be glad to have me share with you. I cannot endure much longer the "moral dualism" between the clear Ethical ideals of the Christian law of love—and the tacit acknowledgment of the necessity of and the open participation in the "competitive order"; which seems to be irresistibly forced upon every one not willing to secede from the whole life of his -day or desert the service to that life. It is coming to be nothing less than the moral self-stultification of the individual and collective Christian Conscience; and, is, I believe, the very paralysis of the churchs' forever. What shall we think and do? Will you not let me have a quiet hour with you somewhere, Thursday afternoon or evening or Friday morning or afternoon?[6] You will not regard me as presuming upon our friendship in such confidences. Not am <I> myself am more grateful for the help you are and may be to me—and to her—that is Mrs Taylor, who is as helpless as I, but is less restive in admitting the present necessity for this dualism, and not so hopeful of finding any way out. If you realized the good your interviews and correspondence do me, and through me others, you would rate them among the services, if not, <in> the pleasure of your all too largely shared life—Faithfully Your Friend

Graham Taylor.

I missed your Sister Mrs Alderman so much at Ottawa, but learned she had gone East.[7]

I often think of your burden in trying to mother your other Sister's children, and wonder how you are [bearing?] it.[8]

ALS (SCPC, JAC; *JAPM*, 3:704–7).

1. Graham Taylor (1851–1938), founder and first warden of Chicago Commons settlement (see n. 3), was participating in the Lake Madison Chautauqua Assembly and Summer School in Madison, S.D. Patterned after the original Chautauqua in New York, the gathering, held on the northwest shore of Lake Madison, flourished from 1891 until 1933. While "the Great Assembly of the Northwest" primarily drew participants from North and South Dakotas, Iowa, and Minnesota, it also attracted visitors from Illinois, Wisconsin, and Michigan who traveled on the Chicago, Milwaukee & St. Paul Railroad. Taylor had planned to be in South Dakota between 25 and 28 June 1897.

Born into a family of Dutch-reformed ministers, Graham Taylor grew up in Schenectady, N.Y., and graduated from Rutgers College, N.J., in 1870. He enrolled at the Theological Seminary of the Reformed Church in America, New Brunswick, N.J., and was ordained in 1873.

Joining him at his first pastorate at the Reformed Church in Hopewell, Dutchess Co., N.Y., was his wife, Leah Demarest (1849–1918), whom he married in 1878. She was the daughter of New Brunswick Seminary theology professor Rev. David D. Demarest.

In 1880 Taylor accepted the call of the Fourth Congregational Church in Hartford, Conn. Once a prominent congregation that had taken courageous stands against slavery and in favor of woman suffrage, the church on Main St. was a shadow of its former self. Its wealthy members had moved away, effectively distancing themselves from newly arrived immigrants, many of whom worked in the Pratt and Whitney Colt firearms factory. Little more than two hundred members worshipped in a church with a seating capacity of twelve hundred.

Taylor's outreach to the poor had dramatic results and caught the attention of the president of Hartford Seminary. In 1888 Rev. Chester Hartranft invited Taylor to join his faculty, but Taylor agreed only on the condition that he could continue his innovative ministry at Fourth Church. Although conservative members of the faculty opposed him, his base of support among the students remained strong. In 1892 the *Chicago Daily Tribune* hailed Taylor's decision to chair a new Dept. of Social Economics at the Chicago Theological Seminary at Ashland Blvd. near Washington St. as "a significant 'new movement in theological education,' and encouraged him to organize a seminary settlement." He continued to be associated with the Chicago Theological Seminary for the remainder of his life and served it at different times as teacher, administrator, or professor emeritus. Graham Taylor Assembly Hall, built in 1928, was named for him. From 1903 until 1906, Taylor also held an appointment in the Dept. of Sociology at the Univ. of Chicago.

One of the stipulations that Taylor made when he moved to the Chicago Theological Seminary was that he be free to create and live in a social settlement. He later recalled that although he had been influenced by Toynbee Hall, it was actually JA and HH that "interpreted the settlement spirit and service more impressively." Taylor patterned the development of his settlement after that of HH and credited JA with encouraging him to begin Chicago Commons. "Her brooding like a mother over the homes and homeless all about her demonstrated what the gentle strength and wisdom of our own home's motherhood might be and do within the settlement household and throughout the neighborhood" (Taylor, *Pioneering on Social Frontiers*, 7). Taylor established his settlement in 1894 on Chicago's North Side and was its leader until he relinquished its helm in 1922 to his daughter Lea, who was trained as a social worker.

Although Graham Taylor was the acknowledged leader of Chicago Commons, he remained dedicated to lecturing and teaching. One of the results was the development, beginning in 1903, of what was to become in 1908 the Chicago School of Civics and Philanthropy, directed by Taylor until 1920, when it was taken over by the Univ. of Chicago. It offered courses in social work and developed a research focus in social problems that was led by Julia Lathrop, assisted by Sophonisba Breckinridge (1866–1948), who became a noted social reformer and teacher of social workers but at the time was a new instructor in political economy at the Univ. of Chicago. The *Chicago Commons*, the publication Taylor created to promote the Chicago Commons Settlement, first issued in Apr. 1896 (renamed the *Commons* beginning Apr. 1897), grew in number of pages, in number of readers, and in scope of content and eventually published information about other social settlements and social work in general. In 1905 it was combined with the journal of the New York COS and became *Charities and the Commons*, and by 1909 the *Survey*, a major publication focused on the field of social work. Taylor continued as associate editor, 1909–19.

Graham Taylor participated in various civic endeavors and also wrote several books, among them his autobiography, *Pioneering on Social Frontiers* (1930), and *Chicago Commons through Forty Years* (1936), and numerous articles. He traveled throughout the United States and Europe, lecturing on social work. From 1902 he wrote a weekly column for the *Chicago Daily News* in which he presented comments about current events from a settlement leader's point of view.

Graham Taylor and JA became colleagues in social reform and developed a deep mutual respect for one another. Taylor recalled that "the mistress of Hull-House" supported the Taylor family when they arrived in Chicago and introduced them through "her personal friendship, and through it to her understanding knowledge of this great city wilderness then so strange to me" (Taylor, "JA the Great Neighbor," 340, 339). JA served on the board of trustees for the Chicago Commons, 1895–1935, and was identified by Taylor as "the most helpful and continuous trustee" (Taylor, "JA the Great Neighbor," 340). The two settlement founders often worked together on civic projects and combined their resources to present programs that promoted reform in Chicago. Graham Taylor followed JA as president of the Chicago Federation of Settlements. On the national level, they were active together in the National Federation of Social Settlements and in the National Conf. of Charities and Correction (later called the National Conf. of Social Work), where both served as president. Four years after the death of Leah Demarest Taylor on 22 July 1918, Graham Taylor married widow Isabella Bishop McClintock of New York.

Toward the end of her life and on 3 May 1934 during the Chicago Commons' fortieth anniversary celebration, JA complimented Taylor: "When Hull-House was opened in September, 1889, it encountered much criticism on the simple ground it was not a mission, and our explanation that we were trying 'to serve God for naught' was considered inadequate. Our first real vindication came five years later when an orthodox clergyman, who was also a professor in a theological seminary, took the same line in opening a house in another river ward of Chicago.

"As years went by the Settlements, domiciled within the shadow of hardship and racial confusion, found themselves strangely initiated into the industrial unrest all about them and into the aspirations for a better social order. Their advocacy of free discussion among men of different theories and of alien experiences inevitably brought new criticisms, and perhaps only Graham Taylor's valiant defense of free speech saved the Settlements from defeat in performing what seemed to them an important function. . . .

"Graham Taylor has been successful in such understanding because he posses the essential equipment: trust in god, unresting search for knowledge combined with tolerance, and, above all, he has undaunted courage and irrepressible good will to his fellowmen" (Taylor, *Chicago Commons*, 302–3).

2. In an article titled "Civic Federation Monthly Meeting," the *Chicago Chronicle* reported on 21 May 1897 that JA would try to settle the ongoing tanners' strike by working through the Industrial Com. of the Chicago Civic Federation.

The Chicago tanners' strike in 1897 began on 17 Feb. when two thousand tanners and curriers sought resolution through the Illinois Board of Arbitration of their disagreement over wages and hours with the factory owners. The effort ended unsuccessfully on 23 Mar., and on 30 Mar. the workers went out on strike. The tannery owners, who insisted on a ten-hour workday, a reduction of ten cents in wages, and refusal to recognize the union, brought in nonunion tanners to work. The strike was over on 22 May. Only half of the workers who went out on strike were rehired. The ten-hour day was instituted, and workers' pay was reduced by five cents rather than ten cents.

3. Graham Taylor opened the Chicago Commons Social Settlement in Nov. 1894 in a rented old brick home near the intersection of Milwaukee Ave. and 140 North Union St., about two miles north of HH. Like the settlement founded by JA and EGS, Chicago Commons also aimed to "provide a center for higher civic and social life . . . and to investigate and improve conditions in the industrial districts of Chicago" (Taylor, *Pioneering on Social Frontiers*, 9). But there were significant differences: From the beginning, Taylor forged close ties with the Tabernacle Church at Grand Ave. and Morand St., the only English-speaking Protestant church in the Seventeenth Ward. Moreover, settlement residents included "family

groups" with children as well as single men and women. Taylor and his first wife, Leah, raised four children while living at the Commons: Helen, who became Mrs. George Wallace Carr; Graham Romeyn; Lea Demarest (1883–1975); and Katharine.

In selecting "Chicago Commons" as the settlement's name, Taylor expressed the hope that it "might be a community center where all people, without distinction of class, color, race or sect, could meet and mingle as fellowmen," bound together by personal bonds of "friendship, neighborship and fellow-citizenship" which he believed "alone can save our body politic" (Taylor, *Chicago Commons*, 15). JA supported Taylor's ambitious plans at Chicago Commons and was a featured speaker at his first Summer School of Social Economics, in Aug. 1895. Typical of the cordial relations that existed between the two settlements and their leaders was the Christmas gift of a rendering of the Sistine Madonna sent by HH residents later that same year. Not only did JA and Graham Taylor often appear as speakers on the same civic programs, as an example the Improved Housing Conf. held at Northwestern University Settlement, 1–2 Feb. 1897, when JA's speech was "Small Parks and Cottages" and Taylor offered "The Relation of the Home to Family Life," but they also collaborated in hosting social reformers, especially in Dec. 1896 and again in Oct. 1897 for their social economic conferences on city government. Taylor and JA were also sometime speakers for each other's settlement programs. When JA declined reelection as president of the Federation of Chicago Settlements in Mar. 1896, Graham Taylor was elected to the post.

Many of the programs, educational and outreach, that evolved at the Commons mirrored those initiated in HH. When the Commons required larger quarters, Graham Taylor hired the noted architectural firm of Pond and Pond, close HH friends and designers of the HH complex. A new brick building for Chicago Commons, located at 955 West Grand Ave. on the site of the old Tabernacle Church, was officially opened in July 1901. Taylor also initiated the monthly publication of the *Chicago Commons* shortly after JA issued the first number of *HH Bulletin* in Jan. 1896.

4. In an article titled "The Social Propaganda" and published in *Chicago Commons*, July 1896, Graham Taylor recounted, "So great was the demand for teaching on social topics at the Chautauqua Assembly that the writer's eighteen appointments grew to thirty during the ten days of his visit" (2).

5. Among the "lovely ministries" in which Graham Taylor was engaged in 1897 was his busy speaking schedule in Chicago and the Midwest and his growing reputation as an authority on urban life. Following his presentation "The Social Settlement and the Labor Movement" at the National Conf. of Charities and Correction in Grand Rapids, Mich., in June 1896, he was invited to deliver a course of lectures titled "The Condition of Labor, Past and Present" at Chautauqua, N.Y., in July 1897. In addition, he served as chairman of a subcommittee on Homeless Men and Lodging Houses, organized by the Philanthropic Com. of the Civic Federation of Chicago in the fall of 1896.

6. It is difficult to know if JA and Graham Taylor met as he hoped on 8 or 9 July. According to JA's 1897 diary, she was speaking at the Burlington, Iowa, Chautauqua on Friday, 2 July; moved on to Milwaukee by 7 July; and was in Geneva, Ill., on 8 July. Her calendar is blank for 9 July, and on 11 July she started for the National Conf. of Charities and Correction in Toronto, where, like Taylor, she was a speaker.

7. Statement written across corner of p. 1. Graham Taylor had apparently expected to see SAAH in Ottawa, Ill. Although JA had suggested that SAAH go with her to Toronto, she headed to Philadelphia to visit Addams and Weber relatives.

8. Statement written on top left corner of third page.

## To Mary Rozet Smith

*Mary Rozet Smith was trying to decide what to do with her life. She was facing a dilemma similar to that which Jane Addams struggled with after graduation from Rockford Female Seminary. In* Twenty Years at Hull-House, *Jane Addams recalled, "'Weary of myself and sick of asking / What I am and what I ought to be.'"[1] Jane Addams hoped to share wisdom she had gained from her experience with her friend.*

Hull-House 335 South Halsted Street Chicago [Ill.] [22 July 1897]

Darling—

I suppose that one of the hardest things one has to learn in life is that ones experiences (even the bitterest ones) are of no use to any one else. But I do find it hard that you insist upon repeating the self same mistakes I made over <and over> again until I caught a clue at H.H.

The Medical College,[2] the summer I did all the house work at Cedarville[,][3] my sheep farming,[4] my studying languages and "art" in Europe,[5] my drawing lessons in Baltimore to use my hands,[6] would really seem less bitter to me to remember if I felt they had been of use to the person I love best. I really don't think you ought to put aside all my experiance as of no avail—I could make a wild plea if you would only let me—and I don't think "withdrawing from the influence" is the more logical way of settling it. Of course "every-body approves" just as they would approve your staying at home or any other <thing> which was conventional or approximated it—but the heart knowest its own bitterness—and if you would just let me guide you and love you and coöperate with you I know I could be of use.

It is n't the endowment[7] nor the Armour Institute[8] which I resent, it is the fact that you are going the wrong track—That one cannot go to school with content at 28 one begins to grapple with the thing itself or is unhappy.

Do believe me, darling, and let me help you for once really & truly.

I am not cross nor anything but longing to do for you perhaps the one thing I am but able to do. I am always & unchanging your

J.A.

ALI (SCPC, JAC; *JAPM*, 3:737–41).

1. On p. 78 of the first edition of *Twenty Years*, JA recalled her own dismay in deciding a life course and quoted the first two lines from one of her favorite poems, Matthew Arnold's "Self-Dependence."

2. JA attended the Woman's Medical College of Pennsylvania, in Philadelphia, 1881–82. On her experiences, see *PJA*, 2:3, 9–10, 12–13, 16; 2:35, n. 45; 2:76; 2:78–79, n. 12; 2:80, 83–84, 87, 92, 409.

3. JA spent the summer of 1885, shortly after she and AHHA returned from Europe, in Cedarville. During the summer of 1886, JA visited her sister and toured the U.S. West. In

1887 JA spent most of the summer in support of SAAH, who gave birth to Anna Marcet Haldeman, her only child, in July 1887.

4. In *Twenty Years*, JA recalled her unpleasant brief experience with sheep farming: "I bought a farm near my native village and also a flock of innocent-looking sheep. . . . This pastoral enterprise still seems to me to have been essentially sound, both economically and morally, but perhaps one partner depended too much upon the impeccability of her motives and the other [a student who was trying to finish college] found himself too preoccupied with study to know that it is not a real kindness to bed a sheepfold with straw. . . . [T]he sight of two hundred sheep with four rotting hoofs each, was not reassuring to one whose conscience craved economic peace." The quick "sales of mutton, wool, and farm enabled the partners to end the enterprise without loss" (80–81).

5. JA studied languages and art during her first European journey. On art, see *PJA*, 2:205, 208; 2:220, n. 57; 2:371; on French language study, see *PJA*, 2:218, n. 22; 2:354, 361, 370, 371; 2:373, n. 16; 2:378, n. 3; and on German language study, see *PJA*, 2:205, 206; 2:217, n. 9; 2:222, 274, 277, 281; 2:283, nn. 10–11; 2:284, 353–54; 2:355, n. 6; 2:356, n. 12; 2:361. See also *PJA*, 2: index entry for JA, Baltimore, 1885–87.

6. See especially *PJA*, 2:473–74, n. 3.

7. MRS may have been considering using her wealth to create a foundation.

8. She was also apparently considering attending the Armour Institute, Chicago, and eventually she did take classes at the school between the fall of 1897 and 1899. The Armour Institute yearbook, *Integral*, for 1899 indicates that MRS was a student in the senior class of the Chicago Free Kindergarten Assn., held at the school (183).

## To Mary Rozet Smith

Hull-House 335 South Halsted Street Chicago [Ill.] Aug. 31" 1897

Dearie

I heard the bad news of Mrs Kelley and came in Monday afternoon.[1] I have spent to-day looking up various possible openings but am somewhat discouraged by the outlook.[2] Mrs Kelley has another plan and will know of it to morrow.[3]

I had a note from Miss French saying that Saturday would be quite convenient and that they would meet me at twelve at the North Western.[4]

Mr Pond wants to know the size of the safe which we will build into the new Post Office.[5] I dislike to bother your father about it but with his permission will ask at the office on Monroe St.

Mrs Valerio and I were serious in this morning—it had quite a solemn performance[6]

Don't return Mr Maude's letter[7] I can get it when I come out. With love to the family I am always yours

Jane Addams.

ALS (SCPC, JAC; *JAPM*, 3:774–75).

1. JA received the news on Monday, 30 Aug. 1897. Gov. John R. Tanner's ouster of Florence Kelley as chief factory inspector for Illinois on 28 Aug. 1897 caught Kelley by surprise and ignited a firestorm of controversy. Although Tanner had removed most of the minor officials

in the Factory Inspection Bureau after he defeated John Peter Altgeld as governor on 3 Nov. 1896, he had assured Kelley that he planned to keep her in her position. Florence Kelley and her friends were devastated. Dr. Julia Holmes Smith (1839–1930), first female appointed as a trustee of the Univ. of Illinois and three-time president of the CWC, joined Lucy Flower in her outspoken criticism of Tanner's replacement appointment for the post. Even the *New York Times* recognized the "blow to the interests of children" the dismissal of Kelley and new appointment would be ("Tribulations of Chicago"). The new chief factory inspector was Louis Arrington (1837?–1911), born in Fairfax, Va., a Civil War veteran, glass blower by trade, and for many years an employee of the Alton Glass Co. JA immediately began to try to find alternative employment for Kelley, who was a close personal friend and colleague reformer and who had three children and herself to support.

2. One of the possibilities that JA explored for Kelley was an appointment "as a teacher of economics in the Cosmopolitan University" being financed by *Cosmopolitan* magazine to be established by Dr. Benjamin Andrews (1844–1917), former president of Brown Univ., who by July 1898 would become superintendent of the Chicago Public Schools. Although it did not succeed, the university was meant to be a correspondence school, providing a free liberal course of studies for adults who could not afford to enroll in established universities. Into 1899 JA kept trying to assist Kelley in finding appropriate employment. In 1898 she went to Washington, D.C., to present Kelley and her credentials to President William McKinley as a candidate eminently qualified for an appointment to the newly established U.S. Industrial Comm. JA and Kelley waited in vain through the summer, only to discover that Kelley's name did not appear among those who received appointments. JA also made a determined effort in 1899, along with other social workers and friends, to obtain Kelley an appointment through Gov. Theodore Roosevelt for the position of chief factory inspector of New York, but Roosevelt declined to make the appointment and indicated he would have a difficult time hiring someone who had worked for former Illinois governor Altgeld.

3. In 1897 Florence Kelley managed to get a job paying only fifty dollars a month as an assistant periodicals librarian, working primarily at night in the Crerar Library, Chicago, which had been established in 1894 to specialize in developing collections relating to economics, science, and medicine. That position gave her more time to spend at HH and to work on reform issues.

4. JA planned to visit Helen Culver and her life's companion, Martha Ellen French (1846–ca. 1916), in Winnetka, Ill., on Saturday, 4 Sept. 1897. French had been a friend of Culver's cousin Frederika Hull at Oberlin College, where she received an L.B. in 1870.

5. JA's concern about the post office safe was justified. The U.S. postmaster had just named JA postmistress of substation No. 10, which he designated as HH. She was to be paid two hundred dollars (by June 1900 JA was receiving nine hundred dollars) annually for the job. The safe and post office were to be lodged in the Children's Building, and the Pond brothers were in the process of creating the office.

6. HH resident Amelie Valerio was in charge of the HH post office until May 1901.

7. In his letter of 14 Aug. 1897, Aylmer Maude reported on his recent visit with Tolstoy and recalled that a year before, he had accompanied JA and MRS on their visit with the famous author. Maude referred to JA's letter to him of [30 July] 1896, and indicated: "I do not know how the economic level I tried to impart to you [during their journey by train to and from their visit in Yasnaya Polyana] has acted, but your message of mildness & kindness has not left my heart (however absent it may often have been from my words & actions) . . . have greatly helped me" (Aylmer Maude to JA, SCPC, JAC; *JAPM*, 3:767–68).

## Excerpts from Addresses

*By the fall of 1896, Jane Addams had established a successful career as a public speaker, especially on reform issues. In November 1896, she began keeping a diary of the speeches she gave and fees she received.*[1] *While she did not charge for all of her appearances, by the end of 1897 she could boast that she had made $805 that year from her speaking engagements.*[2]

*She made numerous appearances outside of Chicago, visiting communities in Iowa, Kansas, Kentucky, Michigan, New Jersey, Indiana, Wisconsin, Pennsylvania, New York, and Massachusetts. Between those out-of-state jaunts, she spoke in Illinois, primarily in the Chicago area. Mirroring in part the variety of topics she covered during her ten-day visit in the Boston and Philadelphia areas in February, in her repertoire were the following topics: Hull-House and the settlement movement,*[3] *social obligations of citizenship,*[4] *Tolstoy,*[5] *and lessons she had learned from her experience in Chicago politics.*

*More and more newspapers were beginning to quote Jane Addams and describe her appearances. Even an interview that she gave to a reporter for the* Chicago Chronicle *in early April was repeated in other papers, one of which was the* State Journal *of Topeka, Kansas, on 7 April.*[6] *The speech she made on woman suffrage to the Chicago Political Equality League in November was also widely quoted.*[7]

*On 14 June she gave the missionary address at Rockford College, focusing on efforts to change society growing out of Christian efforts in England and in Russia, with special attention to Tolstoy, and two days later presented the commencement address at Freeport High School, Illinois, urging the graduates to be good citizens and to help others.*

*On the evening of 14 July, she appeared before a large gathering of attendees at the National Edcuation Association (NEA) in Milwaukee, where twenty thousand educators were expected. There she presented "Foreign Born Pupils in the Primary Grades."*[8] *In her remarks, she provided new insight based upon her neighborhood experiences about obstacles to learning faced by the children of immigrants. The* Chicago Daily Tribune *offered major coverage of the occasion and printed large portions of her remarks, which were also published in the* Journal of Proceedings and Addresses *of the organization as well as later summarized in the* School Journal, *published in New York for educators.*[9] *Even before her appearance in Milwaukee, Addams was being promoted, although unsuccessfully, for membership on the Chicago Board of Education.*[10] *Toward the end of July, she traveled to Toronto to give her first address before the National Conference of Charities and Correction during its twenty-fourth annual gathering. When published it was titled simply "Social Settlements."*[11] *She saw her task as presenting the arguments for the social settlement approach to helping the poor. Using examples from her neighborhood experiences to support her position as she presented differences between the social settlement and charity approaches to assisting the poor.*

*In October and November, Jane Addams argued against speaking on Tolstoy with Ernest Crosby*[12] *for a program that the Nineteenth Century Club of New York was planning for its December meeting. Although she considered "Mr. Crosby the most eminent, and certainly the most sincere Tolstoyan in the country,"*[13] *she did "not altogether agree with Mr. Crosby's presentation of Count Tolstoy's views. It would be a sad spectacle—would it not?—two non-resistent disciples wrangling over their master's doctrines."*[14] *When 9 December came, Jane Addams gave a speech that was similar to her talk at the National Conference of Charities.*[15] *Before and after her New York presentation, she made appearances at the Ethical Society of Philadelphia. On 5 December, she gave a version of what she planned to deliver in New York, but for her return engagement on 12 December, she decided to once again try out her essay titled "Ethical Survivals in City Immorality."*[16]

*The following are excepts from some of her 1897 speeches. It seems likely that for many of her appearances, she had no written text, no manuscript from which to read. For those occasions, the only surviving evidence of her arguments is contained in the quotations from her speeches preserved in newspapers and periodicals.*

## SOCIAL SETTLEMENTS

National Conference of Charities, Toronto, Canada — 14 July 1897

I feel a little apologetic at being here at all. The settlements are accused of doing their charity work very badly. They pretend not to do it at all; and then they become overwhelmed with the poor and the needy, and they do it, not as trained people should do it, but as neighbors do it one for the other, which is not scientifically. In spite of that, however, settlements are, I believe, valuable to charities. . . .

But, after all, the settlement does stand for something unlike that which the charity visitor stands for. You are bound, when you are doing charitable work, to lay stress upon the industrial virtues. You are bound to tell a man he must be thrifty, in order to keep his family; that his first duty is to keep at work, and support them. You must tell him that he is righteous and a good citizen when he is self-supporting, that he is unrighteous and not a good citizen when he receives aid. You must continually press upon him the need of the industrial virtues, and you have very little time for going out into the broader and more social qualities of life. Now the settlement does not ignore, I hope, those virtues; but it does not lay perpetual and continual stress upon them. . . .

Perhaps the settlement aims to change the social ideals of its neighborhood more than any other one thing. . . .

This is, I think, the only message which a settlement has for a conference like this,—that they do see people from the point of view of the recipients of the charity which is extended. I do not wish to underestimate the friendly visitor. I often say that the people who constantly visit the poor often know more about them than the people who should be content to live in settlements and should not visit them.

It is nonsense to say that one cannot know the poor who does not live with them. You know the poor, if you take pains to know them; and you do not know the poor, if you do not take pains to know them. But what I would like to say is that, living eight years as I have, and seeing them early in the morning and all day long and late at night, and not being able to get away simply because one is caught with his sympathies, with his imagination, with his desires, with his interests, he does get a point of view which, I think, comes only to us on any subject when we give it continuous attention. And, after the settlements have given this attention, they would indeed be very stupid to minimize the people who are engaged in charitable and correctional work. We need them at every possible point. . . .

I have not that great fear of pauperizing people which many of you seem to have. It is the feeling with which you give a piece of bread or the feeling with which you take it which determines whether the transaction shall be a pauperizing one. We have all accepted our bread from somebody, at least until we were fourteen; and we have help all the time from all sorts of people. If we can only make the medium of giving friendly enough, if we can only make a real fellowship, it does not make any difference whether you give an old Latin Grammar or a pair of shoes. I should feel very much ashamed if my neighbor next door did not come to me when she wants money for her taxes, and borrow it from me as she would from any other friend. I should feel that I had been a failure as a friendly neighbor. Money is not so different from the rest of life, and shoes and soup need not be so different from books and pictures. You can transfigure and transform them in the feeling of friendliness and kindness. But you cannot do it wholesale. You cannot do it unless you really know people, and unless your feeling is genuine.

This may be the only right view the settlement has at such a conference,—that its feeling for the poor is genuine, and that it gets a glimpse of charity from their point of view.

PD ("Social Settlements," National Conf. of Charities and Correction, *Proceedings* [1897]: 338–39, 344–46; *JAPM*, 46:806–7, 812–14).

## LECTURE ON TOLSTOI

Matheon Club, Chicago, Ill. 2 Oct. 1897

I was in Russia a year ago, and studied the man of whom I had read, whose books had been so much to me. Of course, as I could not speak Russian, my opportunities were limited, but I learned what I could. One of the first lessons I learned was that Tolstoi must be understood personally, and that one must make a personal application of his precepts. If it is not personal it is nothing.

His doctrine may be divided into three sections. First is his attitude toward the government and toward the church—an attitude of nonresistence. Second, each must labor to feed and clothe himself. Third is his view of art. Some people say he would lead us back to barbarism. . . .

Tolstoi, . . . impresses one first as wonderfully keen, then as great. He has squared his life by his conscience. It is perhaps the grandest view the world can present—a strong man doing absolutely what he believes to be right. I don't just accept all his views, but I do appreciate the completeness of his sacrifice. And if there are any of us—as probably there are—who are at times uncomfortable, may we not hope that a better understanding of that man's actions, and a truer measuring of our lives by what our consciences tell us is right—may not this bring us peace?

PD ("Lecture on Tolstoi," *Chicago Post*, 2 Oct. 1897; *JAPM*, 55:324–25).

## THE WORKINGWOMAN'S NEED OF THE BALLOT

Chicago Political Equality League 6 Nov. 1897

I am not one of those who believe—broadly speaking—that women are better than men. We have not wrecked railroads, nor corrupted legislatures, nor done many unholy things that men have done; but then we must remember that we have not had the chance. But my understanding of the matter is that woman should have the ballot, because without this responsibility she cannot best develop her moral courage. . . . I believe everybody should have the franchise, and qualification not be based on education or property, but representation.[17]

PD ("The Workingwoman's Need of the Ballot," in *Public Opinion* 23 [9 Dec. 1897]: 749, SCPC, JAC; *JAPM*, 46:839; 55:376) .

## SOCIAL OBLIGATIONS OF CITIZENSHIP

Federation of Clubs, Kansas City, Mo. 24 Nov. 1897

A citizen owes it to the community to place himself in such a position that he can know and understand all classes of people. . . . We must respect the poor. We must not undervalue them. Do not take away their pride and their self respect. . . .

What our charities in America need most . . . is socialization. There is nothing now that is free and real about the relation between the giver and receiver. If we could only know the poor people before they became poor, we would better understand their needs. We see people now only when they are on the verge of starvation and we get wrong ideas about them. It is the same with trades unions. We see trades unions only in strikes and we get false notions about them. We hastily condemn them. We do not see them in their quiet moments, but only in their violent moments. We do not seem to realize that the labor movement is really the onward movement of the century. We should meet this great labor movement half way. We should not hang back; we should come forward. There is no reason why we should not meet it.

PD ("Poor House Shocks Her," *Kansas City [Mo.] Star*, 25 Nov. 1897, SCPC, JAC; *JAPM*, 55:369).

## SETTLEMENTS: ONE OF THE EXPRESSIONS OF THE SOCIAL OBLIGATIONS OF CITIZENSHIP

Ethical Society of Philadelphia. Pa. Sunday Morning, 5 Dec. 1897

The great necessity is the knowledge of the condition of others, so that when want and misery come there will be those who know us and from which charity it can be received with a less stinging pang. We should by all means have more social intercourse between different classes. The weak point of the friendly visitor is the fact that he never meets his client until he is needy. Another fault in the present social life is our attitude towards trade unionism. We know little or nothing of it, until a strike is announced in the newspapers. If we knew them and saw their efforts to preserve unity, their feeble attempts to have lectures for their educational advancement, their touching care of those in need, their horror of bossism, we might see trade unionism as it is.

PD ("Miss Addams Lectures," *Philadelphia Times*, 6 Dec. 1897, SCPC, JAC; *JAPM*, 55:379).

## WHY IS SYSTEMATIC CHARITY DISLIKED?

Nineteenth Century Club of New York 9 Dec. 1897

"Who are those friendly visitors as a rule? . . . Women, yes, too many women, who have been reared in luxury, who have never earned a penny in their lives by hard work, whose hands are white and soft, whose tastes are dainty, and whose lives have been spent in colleges and homes of ease and leisure. They come to teach the poor wretches industry and thrift. Are they competent to do that? Indeed not! and they admit it in many instances, and finally give up from actual conviction that it is without their province. . . .

"The working man does not want charity. The class that is beneath the workingman, and does want charity dislikes the organized system, because it brings them down from a certain nobility all their own. . . ."

In conclusion, Miss Addams remarked that nevertheless charity must be dispensed in a systematic manner and should be placed on a basis where justice will prevail.

PD ("A Suggestive Question," *New York Times*, 10 Dec. 1897, SCPC, JAC; *JAPM*, 55:380).

1. Addams, "Diary [of Speeches], Nov. 1896–98."
2. Twenty-five dollars was apparently JA's usual fee in 1897. Sometimes she paid her own

travel expenses, and sometimes the host organization paid them or she lodged with her hostess. In Jan. she made speeches in Ypsilanti, Mich.; Toledo and Akron, Ohio; and St. Louis, earning a total of one hundred dollars. During her Feb. trip to the Boston area, she earned twenty-five dollars for her engagements at the Twentieth Century Club in Brookline and at Amesbury, Mass., but only ten dollars for her remarks in Lynn, Mass. She did not charge for the other appearances she made in the Boston area. Her tour to Clinton and Des Moines, Iowa, in Mar. netted fifty dollars for the two engagements. In Apr. her swing through Grand Rapids, Muskegan, and Grand Haven, Mich., brought in seventy-five dollars, and she also received twenty-five dollars for her appearance in Milwaukee, before the National Education Assn. In May she received a total of seventy-five dollars for appearances in Louisville, Ky.; Fort Wayne, Ind.; and Aurora, Ill. In June she did not charge RC for her missionary presentation, but did receive twenty-five dollars for speaking at the Freeport High School graduation. Although she made at least three speeches in July, the only one she received remuneration for was twenty-five dollars in Burlington, Iowa. She did not charge for the speech she made to the National Conf. of Charities and Correction. In Aug. the Woman's Assembly in Champaign, Ill., gave her ten dollars for her appearance at their gathering. In Sept. she received ten dollars for an appearance in Evanston, Ill., and in Oct. she earned another seventy-five dollars in three increments from appearances in Lafayette, Ind., and Chicago and Dixon, Ill. She lectured in Nashville, Tenn., and in several churches in Chicago during Oct. without charging any fee. Although she made several appearances in Nov., she was paid for only seven of them: River Forest, Ill., ten dollars; Danville, Ill., twenty-five dollars; Hyde Park, Ill., ten dollars; Madison, Wis., ten dollars; and Topeka and Lawrence, Kans., and Kansas City, Mo., twenty-five dollars each. In Dec. the Ethical Society of Philadelphia paid her for three appearances, ten dollars for one and twenty-five dollars each for the other two. Her free appearances were at the Dorcas Federal Labor Union in Chicago; Single Tax Club in Chicago; Political Equality League in Chicago; at Chicago Commons; at the CWC; the Pressman's Union; Congregational Church ministers' meeting, in Geneva, Ill.; in Jacksonville, Ill.; and in Girard, Kans., while she was visiting SAAH during Thanksgiving. She charged the Nineteenth Century Club of New York thirty-five dollars, but Swarthmore College paid her twenty-five dollars. She also appeared without fee in Montclair, N.J., at the Social Reform Club in New York City; Vassar College, Poughkeepsie, N.Y.; the Assn. of Working Women in Philadelphia; Bryn Mawr College, Pa.; and the West Side Ethical Society in Chicago.

3. She spoke on HH and social settlements in the following venues: First Baptist Church, Des Moines, Iowa; Topeka, Kans.; for the Federation of Clubs at the Athenaeum, Kansas City, Mo. She discussed social settlements and HH at Warren Memorial Church, Louisville, Ky.; Presbyterian Church, Girard, Kans.; and at RC, Ill.

4. She presented her ideas on the social obligations of citizenship at the First Congregational Church, Toledo, Ohio; in Des Moines, Iowa; at the Ethical Society of Philadelphia; in Topeka, Kans.; and with the Federation of Clubs at the Athenaeum, Kansas City, Mo.

5. Among those who heard a version of JA's speech on Tolstoy were the Single Tax Club of Chicago; Woman's Club, Madison, Wis.; Matheon Club, Chicago; University Club, Lake Forest, Ill.; a group of club women in Lafayette, Ind.; Hannah Lodge of Sinai Temple, Chicago; the Chicago Commons; Bryn Mawr College, Pa.; Beloit College, Wis.; and RC, Ill.

6. When asked by an interviewer for the *Chicago Chronicle* if her work at HH had "paid" or been a mistake, JA answered: "You ask me if it has paid," said Miss Addams. "We may as well challenge life itself. . . . [T]hese people were neither equipped for life nor were they at the edge of death. No one was paying any attention to them. And so we began. If I did not believe the work prospered, that it had been profitable I would quit today. The fact that I am going on with it is the best proof I can give that I have faith in it.

"Sometimes," said Miss Addams, "I get discouraged and blue, I suppose that comes in everyone's life. . . . But it is never for long. Surely it does them good. . . . When I get despondent

I have only to look at these who have come to depend on what they get here for their only relief from what is undesirable and unhappy. I know that they prize it, that it helps them, and so I am reassured" ("Talk with JA").

7. Among the newspapers that printed quotations from these remarks were the *Chicago Inter Ocean, Chicago Times-Herald, Hartford (Conn.) Courant, Waterbury (Conn.) American, Meriden (Conn.) Republican, New Haven (Conn.) Journal, New York Evening Post*, and *New York Public Opinion* (all SCPC, JAC; *JAPM*, 55:348, 349, 352–54, and 376).

8. Of JA's lecture, the *Chicago Daily Tribune* reported: "Miss Jane Addams spoke at the meeting which was held tonight and was accorded a reception such as was not given to any of the men or women who have thus far addressed the gathering" ("Talks by Teachers"). A Milwaukee newspaper reported: "It has been said of her that she is the 'embodiment of an idea,' that she holds audiences not by her voice, her face, her manner or her oratory, but by her subject. . . . She has the reputation of holding her audiences spellbound . . . giving only a plain, simple statement of facts in regard to her work" ([Jane Addams Addresses NEA], unknown evening newspaper, Milwaukee, 6 July 1897, SCPC, JAC; *JAPM*, 55:300). The *Grand Rapids Herald* on 25 July 1897 also quoted portions of JA's presentation.

9. "Foreign-Born Pupils in the Primary," presenting material extracted from the speech and appearing under JA's byline, appeared in the *School Journal* of New York City on 14 Aug. 1897.

10. A group of more than fifty Chicago women, led by the CWC and Judge Tuley, appealed to Chicago mayor Carter Harrison to appoint JA to the Chicago Board of Education. The news of their plea appeared in numerous Chicago newspapers throughout Mar. and early Apr. Harrison did not follow their suggestion. JA did serve as a member of the Chicago Board of Education, 1905–9.

11. The thesis of this presentation published in it entirety became one of the themes in many of JA's presentations for the remainder of the year. Among them were "Settlements vs Scientific Charity" at the National Conf. of Charities and Correction, Toronto, published as "Social Settlements," in the organization's *Proceedings* (1897); remarks to the Nineteenth Century Club of New York City; and a speech to the Ethical Society of Philadelphia.

12. Ernest Howard Crosby (1856–1907) was the son of Presbyterian minister Howard Crosby. He was educated at New York Univ. and Columbia Law School, from which he graduated in 1878. He became known in the United States for his steadfast and unquestioning devotion to Tolstoy and his promotion of Tolstoy's philosophy of nonresistance.

After practicing law for a time, Crosby was elected to the New York legislature, where he served from 1887 until 1889, when he was nominated by President Benjamin Harrison as a judge in the Court of the First Instance at Alexandria, Egypt. He resigned his lifetime position there in 1894 to return to the United States. On his way home, he detoured to Russia to meet Leo Tolstoy, whom he had discovered through Tolstoy's writings. It was a visit that led to an increasingly close friendship and a lifelong of correspondence between the two men. Crosby was a dedicated supporter of the single-tax philosophy and participated in movements that dealt with a number of reform issues, including child labor, immigrant education and protection, industrial arbitration, and civil liberties. He was primarily dedicated to Tolstoy's doctrine of nonresistance and supported pacifism and opposed imperialism, militarism, and war. He helped found the New York Social Reform Club and served as president of the New York Anti-Imperialists' League. Crosby wrote essays, poetry, and novels. Among his major works are *Plain Talk in Psalm and Parable* (1899), *Captain Jinks, Hero* (1902), and *Swords and Plowshares* (1902). He wrote numerous essays on Tolstoy and his philosophy during the late 1890s and into the early years of the 1900s. Crosby reported on his visit with his idol in "Two Days with Count Tolstoy," in the *Progressive Review* 2 (Aug. 1897): 407–22. Among JA's papers is a copy of Crosby's "The Plea of Labor from the Standpoint of a Russian Peasant," published in the *Arena* 17 (Jan. 1897): 312–22.

13. JA to Edward W. Ordway, 12 Nov. 1892, NYPL, Ordway; *JAPM*, 3:886.

14. JA to Edward W. Ordway, 22 Oct. 1897, NYPL, Ordway; *JAPM*, 3:864.

15. The *New York Mail and Express* reported on 8 Nov. 1897 that her topic would be "Why Is Systematic Charity Disliked?"

16. See Essay in the *International Journal of Ethics*, Apr. 1898, below.

17. JA also gave portions of this speech during her visit to Boston on 17 Feb. 1897. *Harper's Bazaar* 30, no. 10 (6 Mar. 1897): 186, quoted a portion of her remarks: "We must not boast . . . that women do not wreck railroads, since they have had no opportunity to do so. Women have not wrecked railroads and perverted legislature; and this not merely because they were women, but because they had no chance. When we have the ballot, we shall probably do many of the things that men do. . . . But if we insist on social equality and equality of consideration, we must take the consequences that go with them."

## Article in the *Hull-House Bulletin*

*In the June 1897 issue of the* Hull-House Bulletin, *Jane Addams described the settlement's Easter art exhibit. She reported, "It was more than ordinarily interesting and valuable because though, as usual, small, it included a choice little collection of handicraft work. It is the intention in future to devote part of the space to such an exhibit, with a view to arousing interest in beautiful handicraft and giving an opportunity to those who are interested to study it."[1] Among the items exhibited were "jewelry and dishes designed and wrought by Mr. C. R. Ashbee of London," which Addams described as having "the . . . interest of personality . . . attached."[2] This special exhibit, no doubt organized by Ellen Gates Starr, who, like C. R. Ashbee, was devoted to promoting art and handicraft, seemed to presage the development of an ever stronger art and handicraft focus at the settlement.*

*Although Ellen Starr left in October to spend a year studying a handicraft—specifically fine bookbinding—with T. J. Cobden-Sanderson at the Doves Bindery in London, she was part of the movement, along with Jane Addams, to found the Chicago Arts and Crafts Society at a meeting that took place, according to Jane Addams's diary, at 3:00 P.M. on 9 October 1897[3] at Hull-House. The Chicago Arts and Crafts Society was officially formed at the next meeting of potential members at Hull-House on 22 October 1897. Jane Addams and Ellen Gates Starr were among the first members. Addams was also in attendance 31 October 1897, when the society officially adopted a constitution and a young Frank Lloyd Wright,[4] supremely sure of himself and soon to be a world-famous architect, presented a paper that was titled "The Use of Machines."[5] Meetings of the organization were to continue every Sunday evening during November and December, and by the end of 1897 the Chicago Arts and Crafts Society had more than 120 members and was firmly established. The emphasis on developing a movement to promote and preserve handcrafted arts and artifacts was a primary influence on Jane Addams in her decision to establish the Labor Museum at Hull-House later in 1900.[6]*

## CHICAGO ARTS AND CRAFTS SOCIETY

Chicago, Ill. 1 Dec. 1897

An informal meeting was held at Hull-House in October, to discuss the advisability of forming a local arts and crafts society. At subsequent meetings, attended by an increasing number of sympathizers, the idea was farther discussed, and a society was formed with aims as stated in the following extract from the constitution:

To cultivate in its members, and through them in others, a just sense of beauty.

To call the attention of those engaged in the production of articles of every day use to the possibility of developing in these articles the highest beauty through a vital harmony with the conditions of production.

To influence the present movement toward manual training and art education.

To influence, as far as possible, the sources of the designs and decorations for all useful and ornamental work.

To recognize and encourage handicraft among our members, and through them in others, in order that the stimulation derived from this means may be a helpful factor in the development of those new ideas which present conditions, to wit, industrial organization and the machine, render necessary.

To consider the present state of the factories and the workmen therein, and to devise lines of development which shall retain the machine in so far as it relieves the workmen from drudgery and tends to perfect his product; but which shall insist that the machine no longer be allowed to dominate the workman and reduce his production to a mechanical distortion.

To hold exhibitions, and to found and maintain centers where the varius crafts may be carried on and developed on lines suggested by the society.

Meetings are to be held in the Hull-House Lecture Hall on the first and third Fridays of each month, and a paper dealing with some special craft will be read and discussed at each meeting. It is intended to hold an exhibition about the end of January, the exhibition to contain:

1. Good specimens of old work, for the sake of the stimulus to be obtained from them.
2. Specimens of modern work in pottery, glass, wood, metal, bookbinding, etc.

As far as possible with each exhibit will be given the name of the designers and maker. Local craftsmen who may have objects suitable for exhibition are requested to communicate with the secretary at Hull-House. The cooperation of all interested, both in the society and in the exhibition, is also requested.

PD (*HH Bulletin* 2, no. 8 [1 Dec. 1897]: 9; *JAPM*, 53:645).

1. 4; *JAPM*, 53:612.

2. *HH Bulletin* 2, no. 5 (June 1897): 4; *JAPM*, 53:612. Charles Robert Ashbee (1863–1942), English proponent of the Arts and Crafts movement in Great Britain and the United States,

architect, and designer, was born at Isleworth, the son of book collector and bibliographer of erotic literature Henry Spencer Ashbee (1834–1900) and his wife, Elisabeth Lavy, whom he wed in Germany in 1862 and from whom he was separated in 1893 after four children. "CRA," as Charles Robert Ashbee was known, attended Wellington College and King's College, Cambridge, 1883–86, and studied with architect George Frederick Bodley (1827–1907). During his residency at Toynbee Hall, May 1887–Mar. 1889, he established the Guild (1888) and School of Handicraft (1887), in London, and by 1890 had workshops in the East End and a retail outlet for the objects his guild produced in the West End on Brook St. In 1902 he moved his workshops to Chipping Campden in the Cotswolds, Gloucestershire, but by 1905 the craftsman-designed furnishings and metalwork for which his workshops became noted were being challenged for dominance in the crafts market by programs and artists associated with polytechnic institutes. In 1907–8, the Guild was liquidated; however, the school survived as the School of Arts and Crafts until World War I. Also a book publisher, between 1898 and 1910, Ashbee operated the Essex House Press and produced more than seventy titles in part using the two typeface styles, Endevour (1901) and Prayer Book (1903), that he designed. He became a friend of U.S. architect Frank Lloyd Wright and admired his work. He wrote the introduction for the German publication (1911) of *Frank Lloyd Wright: Ausgeführte Bauten*, published in Berlin by Verlegt Wasmuth. During World War I, Ashbee lectured on English literature at the university in Cairo and from 1918–22 was an adviser on civic affairs in Palestine. He returned to England, where he lived the remainder of his life.

There is no evidence in JA's 1896 diary that she met or saw Ashbee while she was in London; however, she must have learned of his commitment to the Arts and Crafts movement. On her return from Europe, she indicated that "Mr. Ashbee and his friends are endeavoring, by their Art and Crafts Guild, their lectures and writings, to cultivate the sense of the beautiful in our everyday lives, and to give art a principle to live up to. He is a follower of William Morris, and believes 'that the practical problems of art and the practical problems of industry are at present too disconnected, but they will not long be so, and then their bearing on each other will be direct and all-absorbing. An attempt must be made to get men, especially workmen, to feel the relationship between their work in life and their mental development.'

"Everywhere . . . there seemed to be a feeling that the time has come to do something" ("Miss Addams on London Social Reforms").

Ashbee visited HH for the first time in Dec. 1900. He considered Chicago a noisy but compelling environment, "a seethe" with humanity. And he saw HH as the epitome of the community. At HH, "the pot is nearly boiling." It "stirs & mixes the brew . . . its fame has gone out through all the earth & its words to the ends of the world." Ashbee saw the residents as a "[l]arge family" that did things in a "haphazard way," but yet he reported that the work that needed to be done was done: "each resident fits into his place, unobtrusively runs his club or his class, & gets a lot of gladness in life" (Ashbee, "Journals," 2:200–2). The two Chicagoans who most impressed Ashbee were Frank Lloyd Wright and JA. Of JA he wrote in part: "Jane Addams is to me one of the most wonderful women I have ever met. She is the embodiment of moral power. I never ~~met~~ <came across> any personality that was so 'convincing' as the artists say. The nearest I can place her is the head of a mediaeval abby. . . . [H]ow they idolize her here, men & women—they move to her magnetism <and humanity>! It is that that holds & controls as it always must" (Ashbee, "Journals," 2:206).

3. Addams, "Diary, 1897," 31 Oct.; *JAPM*, 29:369.

4. Frank Lloyd Wright (1867–1959), architect, interior designer, educator, writer, and art collector, was among the first members of the Chicago Arts and Crafts Society. He became a leader in developing the Prairie School of Architecture and throughout his life designed more than one thousand structures and completed at least five hundred works. He tried to design buildings that were in harmony with the environment, a philosophy that he called

organic architecture. In 1897 he had a studio in the Steinway Building in Chicago, as did the Pond brothers, architects for additions to the HH complex. He was related through his mother, Anna Lloyd Wright (1838/39–1923), to two of JA's friends and supporters of HH: Jenkin Lloyd Jones and Henry Demarest Lloyd.

5. "Sunday Evening Lectures," *HH Bulletin* 2, no. 7 (1 Nov. 1897): 1, *JAPM*, 53:629. Wright's speech at HH for the fledgling Chicago Arts and Crafts Society on 22 Oct. 1897 was a precursor for a similar presentation he gave before the same organization on 6 Mar. 1901, and to the Western Society of Engineers on 20 Mar. 1901, titled "The Art and Craft of the Machine." C. R. Ashbee met Wright in Chicago in Dec.1900, and wrote of him: "He threw down the glove to me in characteristic Chicagoan manner in the matter of Arts & Crafts and the creations of the machine. 'My God' said he, 'is machinery, & the art of the future will be the expression of the individual artist through the thousand powers of the machine, the machine, doing all those things that the individual workman cannot do, & the creative artist is the man that controls all this & understands it'" (Ashbee, "Journals," 2:224).

6. See Essay in the *Commons*, 30 June 1900, below.

## Article in the *Hull-House Bulletin*

*Almost from the beginning of the settlement, Jane Addams and Ellen Gates Starr were aware that their neighbors were fascinated by theater. Jane recalled in* Twenty Years at Hull-House: *"Our first Sunday evening in Hull-House, when a group of small boys sat on our piazza and told us 'about things around here,' their talk was all of the theater and of the astonishing things they had seen . . . it was difficult to discover the habits and purposes of this group of boys because they much preferred talking about the theater to contemplating their own lives." Jane Addams came to believe that "theater . . . appeared to be the one agency which freed the boys and girls from that destructive isolation of those who drag themselves up to maturity by themselves, and it gave them a glimpse of that order and beauty into which even the poorest drama endeavors to restore the bewildering facts of life."*[1]

*Even before 1896, when Jane Addams observed a children's theater program during her visit to Russia, theater had come to the settlement. The small stage, barely big enough for an upright piano and a chair or two, in the Hull home parlor-dining area featured dramatic readings as early as 1890, the same year that Ellen Starr began presenting a class in Shakespeare. These eventually became readings and led to the establishment of the Hull-House Shakespeare Club. When Jane added the new Gymnasium and Coffee House Building to the settlement in 1893, a stage with a proscenium arch graced one end and became the focus for productions presented by the Dramatic Section of the Hull-House Students' Association and by several social clubs.*[2] *Then, after Jane returned from her European trip in the fall of 1896, she appointed Hull-House resident Hervey White*[3] *to be in charge of dramatics at the settlement in the expectation that he would assist various social clubs with their dramatic presentations. However, his tenure was quickly overshadowed by that of Walter Gray Pietsch,*[4] *who led the initial development of*

*Hull-House theater until he left in 1900. He was replaced for an interim period by Hull-House resident George M. R. Twose,[5] and in October 1900 by Laura Dainty Pelham,[6] who led the Hull-House Dramatic Association during the early years of the twentieth century.*

Chicago, Ill. 1 Dec. 1897

## DRAMATICS

All dramatics at Hull-House are under the direction of Mr. Pietsch. Club officers are requested to consult with him in regard to plays. He will be at Hull-House every Wednesday evening, from 8 to 10, and will endeavor to coach each club at rehearsals at least every other week.

The Hull-House Dramatic Association has been formed and has a play in rehearsal. "A Scrap of Paper" will be presented by them during Christmas week.[7] The members of the Association have been selected by the Dramatic Committee from the several clubs of Hull-House and from among other people of Hull-House unattached to any club. There are still many vacancies in the Association and they will be filled from time to time as the members of the several clubs show their eligibility by reason of their good work. Everyone is urged to do his best, as Mr. Pietsch and the committee are endeavoring to raise the dramatic standard of all plays given at Hull-House. The Association now numbers sixteen and as its size is yet unlimited, there are plenty of places for those of good dramatic talent.

The Dramatic Committee, which governs the Association, is composed of five: Mr. Pietsch, chairman, Miss Watson,[8] secretary, Mr. Twose, Mr. White and Mr. Adams.[9]

PD (*HH Bulletin* 2, no. 8 [1 Dec. 1897]: 5–6; *JAPM*, 53:641–42).

1. 383–85.

2. Early in Jan. 1897, the Henry Learned Club presented *Poor Pillicoddy*, an 1877 one-act farce by John Maddison Morton (1811–91), which the *HH Bulletin* declared "a great success and showed early the persevering work of the actors" (2, no. 2 [1 Feb. 1897]: 6). Later in Apr., the club performed Shakespeare's *As You Like It* under the direction of Walter G. Pietsch (see n. 4). They performed it again on 22 May 1897, for an audience in Hubbard Woods, north of Chicago, for the benefit of the HH Country Club summer program. The *HH Bulletin* described the special event: "A very beautiful spot in the woods was selected for the stage, the wings and dressing rooms being formed out of bushes in which fresh boughs of apple blossoms had been twined. The audience came largely from Lakeside, Winnetka, Kenilworth, and Chicago, although other North Shore suburbs were represented" (2, no. 5 [June 1897]): 5–6). The HH Fourth of July Mandolin Club provided the music, which included the "HH Two-Step." The Henry Learned Club performed the play again at the People's Institute in Chicago on 10 June.

In Dec. 1896, the Lakeside Club performed a scene from Shakespeare's *Hamlet*. During that same month, on the tenth, the Drexel Club presented *A Regular Fix*. The Lowell Social Club staged *Tom Cobb or, Fortune's Toy*, a three-act farce by W. S. Gilbert (1836–1911), on 11

Actress Laura Dainty Pelham, seen here as Sincerity Weeks, the role she played in the early days of Hull-House productions of the melodrama *Mountain Pink*, helped found and successfully direct the group of talented neighborhood young people who became the Hull-House Players (private collection).

Feb. 1897. The *HH Bulletin* decided: "In selection . . . this play was perhaps the best of the season, for the humor was subtle and refined and the plot well sustained. This was the first full night play given by the club and showed the most careful work, enthusiasm and perseverance" (2, no. 3 [1 Mar. 1897]: 6). On 19 Feb. 1897, *Babes from the Woods*, a children's play, was presented, and on 20 Feb. members of the Friendship Club gave *Gringoire*, a French play written in 1866 by Théodore de Branville (1823–91).

3. Hervey White (1866–1944) was a HH resident when JA asked him to try to bring order out of the variety of plays offered by HH clubs. He also gave travel talks to groups at the settlement. He was born in New London, Iowa, to William Andrew and Martha Chandler White and raised by an aunt after his mother died. He worked his way through two years of college at the Univ. of Kansas and then received a scholarship from Harvard Univ., where he graduated in 1894. After traveling in Italy, he arrived at HH in 1896. There he wrote his first novel, *Differences*, published in 1899, the story of a love affair between a settlement worker and a widower. A second novel, *Quicksand*, was published to considerable acclaim in 1900 after he had left the settlement to found Byrdcliffe Arts and Crafts Colony in Woodstock, N.Y., with Ralph Radcliffe Whitehead (1854–1929) and Bolton Brown. The colony became a utopian community for noted artists and authors. Four years later, in 1904–5, he established the Maverick Colony, another communal effort that rented living quarters to artists, writers, actors, and musicians. There he created the Maverick Press, which printed some of his books as well as the works of other authors, and the *Wild Hawk* and *Plowshare* periodicals, which he edited. In order to support the colony financially, White and his friends created the Maverick Festivals in 1915, which included music and theatrical performances. These lasted until 1931 and predated the famous Woodstock Musical Festival of 1969 and those that followed. After the birth of two children, White's marriage to Vivian Bevans ended in divorce in 1908.

4. Walter Gray Pietsch (1875–1938) was the child of Florence Augusta Wells (1845–77) and Charles Francis Pietsch (1844–1920). He attended Chicago schools and graduated from Chicago Manual Training School in 1892. At Cornell, where he graduated in 1896, he was attracted to theater arts and writing, played the violin, and starred on the track team. When he returned to Chicago, he became a writer for the *Chicago Chronicle* and was soon associated with a variety of advertising agencies. When he died, he was president of Gale and Pietsch, Inc., which was located at 333 North Michigan Ave.

Pietsch became associated with HH shortly after his return to Chicago in 1896 and directed his first play, *As You Like It,* at the settlement in Apr. 1897. By Oct. 1897, JA named him director of dramatics at the settlement, a position he held until he retired in 1900. In the late summer and early fall of 1897, he formed the short-lived Marlowe Dramatic Club, which was merged with the HH Dramatic Assn., formed during Nov. 1897. Pietsch seemed to have influenced JA in 1898 to build a bigger theater with a larger stage in the new Coffee House and Theatre Building. He convinced her that although there could be many groups who did plays at HH, there needed to be one HH dramatic group that sought excellence in performance. In Jan. 1898, the HH Dramatic Assn. performed their *A Scrap of Paper*, and in the spring they offered *The Cricket on the Hearth*. By Apr. 1898, the group had a constitution, and they undertook their third production for the year, Jerome K. Jerome's one-act play *Sunset*. Pietsch worked hard to create a special group of players committed to a high standard of performance. By the end of 1898, there were sixteen active members of the HH Dramatic Assn., and they presented three one-act plays on 22 Dec. These were *Yellow Roses*, the *Morning Mail*, and *Lend Me Five Shillings*. Before he could direct a play in the new theater, Pietsch resigned as director of the HH Dramatic Assn. In June 1901, he married Amy Randolph Lake (1874–1923). The couple had three children, Walter Randolph (1902–74), Richard Francis (1904–2001), and Mary Wells (1908–93). Pietsch, who died of cancer and pneumonia, and his wife, who committed suicide, were buried in Graceland Cemetery, Chicago.

5. For a biographical note on George Mortimer Rendle Twose, see JA to MRS, [10 Oct. 1898], n. 7, below.

6. Laura Dainty Pelham (1849–1924), credited as one of the founders of the little theater movement in the United States, was born Sarah Elizabeth Mount in Southwick, Mass., the daughter of Dr. Charles T. and Maria H. Mount. She was educated in local schools. In Apr. 1870, at the Unity Church in Chicago, she wed Albert H. Dainty, who was also from Massachusetts and a carpet salesman, eventually for Marshall Field and Co. They lived in the same boardinghouse that Laura Mount, who identified herself in the 1870 census return as a teacher, called home in the Fourth Ward of Chicago. The couple had one child, a daughter named Emma Louise Dainty, born in June 1880, who became Mrs. Paul T. Gilbert (d. 1918). The Daintys divorced in 1884, primarily because Laura Dainty had not lived with her husband since the spring of 1880 and did not want to live with him. In the divorce proceeding, she indicated that they had "'drifted apart, and that the guilt was her own.' She said she wanted more liberty and preferred to stay away from home" ("Sundered Ties: Laura Dainty's Husband Granted a Divorce," *Chicago Daily Tribune*, 19 Oct. 1884). Although her husband had continued to provide money for her, she argued that she was able to support herself and did not want his help.

Beginning in 1871, Laura Dainty, sometimes termed the "pearl of the platform," became a famous reader, appearing through the Redpath Lyceum Bureau. Following that she traveled around the country, where she appeared onstage and successfully played in her own stock theater company. Beginning in 1877–78, her career took her away from Chicago for four months; during 1878–79, she was gone from the city for six months; in 1879–80, she was away from home for nine months. Newspapers, from Utah to Massachusetts where she appeared, sang her praises. In 1883 when she replaced Louise Sylvester in the part of Sincerity Weeks in *A Mountain Pink: Realistic Description of Life among the Moonshiners*, a melodrama by

Morgan Bates and Elwyn A. Barron, she gained instant stardom and was usually identified with that role after she formed her own stock company and toured in the play. "As Laura Dainty she was a great soubrette and famous in her speciality of Irish roles. As she proudly puts it, 'I played what were known as chambermaid parts. The chambermaid became a soubrette, and now the soubrette is an ingenue.' . . . Old time playgoers say her screams were . . . piercing and bloodcurdling, and with her blond wig and make-up, she looked . . . the simple Irish country lass" (Weil, "The HH Players," 20). Wherever she traveled, she always "'has given her spare days and evenings to the public institutions when she was within reach, and has read to the prisoners and insane in the States of Illinois, Michigan, Massachusetts, Nebraska and elsewhere,'" reported the *Lincoln (Neb.) Journal,* Apr. 1879 ("Sunshine in the Prison," *Laura Dainty. Humorous and Dramatic Recitations,* [3]). In 1889 she married Walter Fred Taunton Pelham (1861–1941), son of William Frederick Taunton, known by his stage name, Walter Pelham (d. 1907). He was an Englishman who brought his son with him as his manager when he came to the United States in 1882 to perform as a humorist. He had been a newspaperman and a printer and had directed a lyceum in Coventry, England. Fred Pelham followed in his father's footsteps and became an agent, 1887–92, and then a manager, 1893–97, for the Redpath Lyceum Bureau, which Laura helped run. Beginning in 1897, he became manager of the Central Lyceum Bureau of Chicago, and by 1900 Laura Dainty Pelham had organized her own booking agency, which existed for only a brief time, as the Laura Dainty Amusement Exchange. By 1906, when Laura Dainty Pelham went to live at HH as a resident, her marriage was over; however, Fred Pelham's death certificate in 1941 identified him as a widower whose wife, Laura Dainty Pelham, died in 1924.

Laura Dainty became involved with HH first through the HH Woman's Club, where by 1899 she was vice-president, and in 1900 she was elected to a four-year term as president. Beginning in 1905, she was once again named first vice-president of the club where she often was a speaker or gave dramatic readings. At HH she sometimes taught classes in parliamentary law. She became a leader in the People's Friendly Club at HH, once known as the Friendly Gardeners. The People's Friendly Club members were a blend of many different nationalities and families that met semimonthly, boasted a chorus, and held special gatherings on Christmas and New Year's Eve. Pelham helped organize the Women's Trade Union League at HH and served as president of the City Gardens Assn. During summers she often led group tours to Europe that were called Pelham European Tours.

Because of her experience and recognized skills as a performer, she was asked by JA to serve on the HH committee that was charged with the task of reorganizing the HH Dramatic Assn. when Walter Pietsch resigned. She quickly became the director of the program. With her leadership, the HH Dramatic Assn. blossomed and gained fame. The first play the association attempted was *A Mountain Pink*, presented on 10 Dec. 1900. More than one thousand people attended its three performances. Pelham recalled that "many people patronized us, the neighborhood was delighted, and at the close of the three night's 'run' we had two hundred dollars in our treasury and so vivid a sense of achievement that to do Gilbert's *Engaged*, which we chose for our second play, seemed a minor undertaking" (Pelham, "The Story of the HH Players," 251). To gain experience for her company, Pelham continued to present melodramas and light comedy, but by 1905–6 her selection of plays included more classical drama and plays associated with a display of contemporary social problems, "dramas of life, strong, sympathetic, and very real," in JA's words ("What the Theater at HH Has Done for the Neighborhood People," 285). JA viewed these plays as better for her neighbors than the melodramas they usually saw. JA believed theater at HH was a way to teach English, train young people in manners, reach people who were not readers, and connect the everyday lives of people with the wider world and with history.

Pelham also presented a number of premier performances of plays of well-known authors. For example, in 1911, the HH theater offered the American premier of John Galsworthy's drama *Justice*. However, these plays appealed more to the wealthy North Shore Chicagoans and theater critics of Chicago newspapers than the local neighborhood residents.

In 1910 the HH Dramatic Assn. changed its name to the HH Players. They gained a national reputation for excellent performances by an amateur group of actors. They also presented plays that were written by Irish playwrights. With an invitation from Ireland's Abbey Players in 1913, the HH Players made a European trip, with performances in Ireland and visits to England, France, and Holland. Returning to the United States, the HH Players continued to present plays under the direction of Pelham until her death, 22 Jan. 1924, from Bright's disease. Two days later, her funeral was held in Bowen Hall at HH. Among the attendees were representatives from the theater world, the Women's Trade Union League, City Gardens Assn., and the Woman's City Club. The HH Woman's Club helped to fund the Laura Dainty Pelham Cottage at Bowen Country Club, dedicated 25 May 1925. The North Shore Theater Guild gave performances at HH Theater on 5 and 6 Feb. 1924, in support of the Laura Dainty Pelham Memorial Fund.

7. *A Scrap of Paper* by Victorien Sardou (1831–1908), a French romance translated and adapted by John Palgrave Simpson (1807–87), was presented by the new HH Dramatic Assn. on 27 Dec. 1897.

8. Edith Saluda ("Luda") Watson Bartlett (1874–1966), was the daughter of Alexander R. and Saluda Van Buskirk Watson, who were married in Aug. 1867 and eventually had two children, George and Edith. Luda Watson was born in Eau Clair, Wis. Her mother died when she was only a few months old and her father when she was about fourteen. At that time, she became the ward of her father's employer, George Buffington, and was cared for primarily by his daughter Grace Kidder Atkinson in Eau Clair, where she was educated. She graduated from RC with an A.B. in 1893 and arrived at HH in Feb. 1896. She remained there as a resident for three and a half years, until she left the settlement to marry Frank Hart Bartlett (1871–1939) in Nov. 1899.

Her duties at HH were many and varied. In 1896 she was the director of the labor bureau for men and also began serving as the director for the Lakeside Club, a job she kept until 1898. Briefly in 1897, she was director of the Children's Building. During 1897 and 1898, she managed young people's clubs and arranged lectures and events for them. It was also during that time that she served as secretary, and then as treasurer, for the HH Dramatic Assn. When Luda Bartlett left the settlement in 1899, JA wrote to ask her if she would like to have her wedding at HH, but she declined. The residents at the settlement presented her with a desk and chair as a wedding gift.

The newlyweds lived for a while in Eau Clair before moving permanently, in Nov. 1900, to Drummond, Wis. There her husband eventually became the manager of the Rust-Owen Lumber Co. The Bartletts had two daughters: Elizabeth, who became Mrs. Walter Nordby and settled in Drummond, and Harriet, who became Mrs. Sig Anderson of DePere, Wis.

Luda Bartlett immediately created a number of clubs for women in her new community. Among them were the Dorcas Circle for young girls and the Priscilla Club for older women. She became active in the Cable Congregational Church, where she was soon a leader in the Sunday School. For fifty years, she served as the president of the Drummond School Board and was a leader in developing the Drummond High School as one of the first consolidated schools in northern Wisconsin. A member of the Wisconsin Federation of Women's Clubs, she successfully urged them to support wildlife conservation. She was an active leader in the Republican Party of Bayfield Co. and in the state of Wisconsin.

9. Mr. Adams seems to have been a volunteer who served until mid-1898 as a member of the committee overseeing the development of the HH Dramatic Assn., and he also became director of the Lowell Social Club for young people, which met weekly for entertainments and cultural events.

## Article in the *Chicago Times-Herald*

*On Sunday morning, 23 January 1898, Jane Addams spoke before the Ethical Culture Society gathered in Steinway Hall, Chicago. They heard a version of the speech that she had been giving for the past year about corruption in ward politics in Chicago and the need to elect reformers to the Chicago city council. Chicago was preparing for citywide municipal elections that would take place on 5 April 1898. Jane Addams reported to her sister Sarah Alice Haldeman that "the campaign has opened in full force," and she saw her speech as part of that effort, which she indicated "was a result of much deliberation."*[1]

*Chicago's* Times-Herald *and* Record *newspapers quoted large segments of the speech in their 24 January 1898 coverage of the event. The* New Unity *magazine summarized her presentation and reported that she "spoke a sane word, not only concerning the 'Johnny Powers' perplexity of the nineteenth ward of Chicago, but of corrupt politics everywhere."*[2] *William M. Salter of the Ethical Culture Society decided that the essay on which her speech was based "ought to be read & studied by everyone who wants to better things in the city" and asked for permission to have off-print copies of the article produced from the* International Journal of Ethics *when it was finally published.*[3] *After reading the account of her remarks in the* Chicago Times-Herald, *Jenkin Lloyd Jones wrote: "You have given the text upon which all political sermons on the coming campaign ought to be preached. Keep yourself in reserve for this work."*[4] *Even William Dillon, the editor of the Roman Catholic* New World, *wrote: "The address delivered by Miss Jane Addams of Hull House at Steinway Hall last Sunday morning, before the Chicago Society for Ethical Culture, is well worth careful perusal, and is eminently suggestive of useful thinking in regard to the true causes of the corruption of our municipal governments."*[5]

*Jane Addams followed her speech with sixteen speaking engagements in Chicago, downstate Illinois, Wisconsin, Michigan, and Ohio. Her subjects were a mix of the presentations that were part of her repertoire during the fall of 1897. From 27 February through 4 March 1898, Jane Addams made appearances in Grinnell, Iowa, for the Rand lectures at the local college and arrived back in Chicago on 5 March. She was immediately drawn into the campaign in the Nineteenth Ward. There were two candidates: the incumbent John Powers*[6] *and the independent and Republican Party coalition candidate Simeon W. Armstrong.*[7] *Armstrong was touted as a reform candidate by the fledgling Municipal Voters' League of Chicago, which campaigned to oust all of the aldermen they judged to be corrupt and taking bribes.*

HE WON'T BE REFORMED.
HULL HOUSE
JOBBER
GANG LEADER
The Bad Little Boy of the Nineteenth Ward Still Persists in Throwing Stones at Hull House.

Jane Addams and Hull-House tried to unseat the entrenched Nineteenth Ward "boodler" Alderman John Powers in 1898. There was considerable publicity about the campaign, and many hoped that the reformers associated with Hull-House would succeed. Former residents and volunteers returned to Hull-House to help in the campaign. Major Chicago newspapers took note of the contest, offering a number of cartoons like this one from the *Chicago Times-Herald*, 5 Mar. 1898. Powers still won.

## NOT TO BUDGE A BIT.

Chicago, Illinois — 6 March 1898

Miss Jane Addams returned from Iowa yesterday, after a week's absence, and found Hull House just where it was located a week ago. And all this despite "Johnny" Powers' threat to drive it from the nineteenth ward.

. . . She said last night that Hull House had so firm a foundation that it will continue in business for many years to come. . . .

"Political bossism in America has not reached that stage where one man can say who shall be and who shall not be his constituents."

This is her reply to Powers' declaration that he will have Hull House and all of its residents out of his ward within a specified time. This is her answer to Powers when he said that no one asked Miss Addams and her helpers to come to the nineteenth ward, and if they were to leave the ward would be able to get along just as well.

"There seems to me to be two reasons why Mr. Powers is trying to make the people believe Hull House is the heart and soul of the independent campaign," Miss Addams added. "He thinks that with some of the voters it will count against the independents to advertise their campaign as of 'petticoat' origin and backing. There is another reason of some significance, and that is the bringing in of religious partisanship. Hull House does not teach religion in any form. It receives aid from all denominations, and people of all creeds come here and get a welcome." . . .

"There is no personal motive in our siding with Simeon Armstrong and the independent party. It is all in and for public spirit, as it should be best directed. We have great faith in Mr. Armstrong, it is true, and have reasons to think he will win. . . . No one can pretend or plead ignorance of the political methods of the present alderman. They have been exposed time and again until they have become synonymous with political corruption.

"Hull House, however, is not the headquarters of the Armstrong campaign. . . . We simply wish the cause well and will help it along in every way that is honorable and just. I do not like to see neighbors quarreling, and we sincerely wish to soften hard and unfeeling partisanship. . . .

"We understand that much money is being spent by Powers in the ward to carry the election, but it strikes me that voters, who are appealed to repeatedly in the same way as Powers does and has been doing, cannot be depended upon, and may go to the polls and vote just opposite to what he wishes. His sort of political effort is passing out of vogue. It has had its day everywhere, in fact, and men are voting the way they please and the way they feel is right, though some may accept presents from one or both candidates at times. . . .

"In the present battle, the chances for this [independent party] side winning next April were never so good as they are right now."

PD (*Chicago Times-Herald*, 6 Mar. 1898).

1. [Feb. 1898], IU, Lilly, SAAH; *JAPM*, 3:953. See Essay in the *International Journal of Ethics*, Apr. 1898, below.
2. (27 Jan. 1898): 1073.
3. William M. Salter to JA, 23 Jan. 1898, SCPC, JAC; *JAPM*, 3:949. For the text of the essay he was referring to, see Essay in the *International Journal of Ethics*, Apr. 1898, below. Steinway Hall, located at 64 East Van Buren St., was demolished in 1990.
4. Jenkin Lloyd Jones to JA, MTS, Jones; *JAPM*, 3:951.
5. "Current Topics," *New World*, 29 Jan. 1898. In the same article, Dillon contended that the citizens in the Nineteenth Ward supported Powers because he supported them: "They vote for him because he is generous and open-handed, and because he has, on many occasions, and in many ways, acted the part of a friend in need to them or their neighbors. . . . The people of the Nineteenth ward who vote for Mr. Powers may not have very enlightened views on the subject of municipal government. Matters strictly personal may have more weight with them than abstract principles of right, but it is unjust to say that they are lovers of corruption. . . .

"In one respect, Miss Adams is certainly right. It will be necessary for reformers to get closer to the people before they can hope to contend with such men as Alderman Powers. . . . [I]t does involve the showing of human sympathy by a great many little acts of kindness,—with or without the spending of money,—which Alderman Powers has habitually done, and which, hitherto, the reformers have not done. Reform of this kind must prepare the way for the other kind."

William Dillon (1850–1935), born in Brooklyn, N.Y., educated in Ireland, and trained there as an attorney, returned to the United States in 1880 and settled initially in Colorado.

He moved to Chicago in 1893 and served as editor of the Roman Catholic archdiocesan newspaper, the *New World*, 1894–1902, after which he returned to the practice of law. He was the first dean of the Loyola Law School, 1907–16. He was married to Elizabeth Ratcliffe in Colorado in 1885, and they returned to retire there near Castle Rock in 1916.

6. The *Chicago Times-Herald*, which, along with the *Chicago Record*, favored the reform candidates throughout Chicago, offered the following description of John Powers on the day before the election: "Democrat: saloon-keeper, 243 Canal street and 170 Madison street; residence 79 Macalister place; . . . has uniformly voted for bad ordinances and taken a leading part in forcing through amendments and ordinances favorable to corporations and defeating compensation for franchises; during recent campaign has waged bitter warfare against all reform forces and enlisted the support of the most vicious element in ward; poses as 'the poor man's friend,' and maintains his position by pretense of charity, while attempting to drive from the ward the people who are endeavoring to improve its condition; vilifies and abuses his opponents, and sends gangs of roughs and hoodlums to their meetin[g]s; uses his official position to strengthen his own interests; opposed Gallagher's attempt to secure lower fares; his continuance in council would be a disgrace to the ward and a public calamity" ("Nineteenth Ward: Vote for Armstrong"). For a biographical note on John Powers, see Minutes of a HH Residents Meeting, 10 Dec. 1893, n. 13, above.

7. Of Simeon W. Armstrong, JA reported: "We have great faith in Mr. Armstrong, it is true, and have reasons to think he will win. He has lived for more than thirty years in the nineteenth ward, and is both well known and generally respected. He is of the same race, creed and political party as his opponent—the man who is seeking to return to the council for the sixth time. Any attempt to bring in party politics or religious and social questions is but an effort to confuse and conceal the real issues. We stand for honesty in public life as against dishonesty in public life" ("Not to Budge a Bit"). The *Chicago Times-Herald* described Armstrong as an "Independent; Indorsed by republican convention; lawyer, Reaper Block; residence 364 May street; born in Ireland, educated there and in Scotland; formerly laborer and porter in store; has reached his personal and professional position by his own efforts; after careful consideration was chosen by reform organizations as the most available candidate to redeem ward from misrule; a vote for Armstrong is a blow against gang leadership in the council; indorsed by [Municipal Voters'] league" ("Nineteenth Ward: Vote for Armstrong"). The *Chicago Record* quoted part of an Armstrong speech: "Mr. Powers wants to transfer the issue from his record to the Hull house. His record will not bear inspection, and he is aware of it. Co-existent with his official life property in the ward has depreciated in value, rents have gone down and people have moved from the ward. The only explanation is the filthy condition of the streets" ("Hurl Defiance at Ald. Powers").

In addition to raising funds to support their commitment to Armstrong, JA and the HH residents and volunteers devoted time to aiding their candidate through distributing political literature. "We began on Thursday afternoon [31 Mar. 1898]," wrote Alice Hamilton to her cousin Agnes on 3 Apr. 1898, "as soon as the new registration lists came in. . . . All the first evening it was addressing envelopes. I found that I did two hundred and eighty in three hours. That kept up until late Friday night [1 Apr. 1898] when the last of the twelve thousand was done. Then we adjourned to the dining-room and folded campaign literature. Mrs. Kelley and the men joined us at half past ten and we worked on till all hours of the night. Then Saturday morning [2 Apr. 1898] we went at it again. A good many volunteers came in and of course Miss Addams insisted on working, though she is still on the sick list" (Sicherman, *Alice Hamilton*, 120–21).

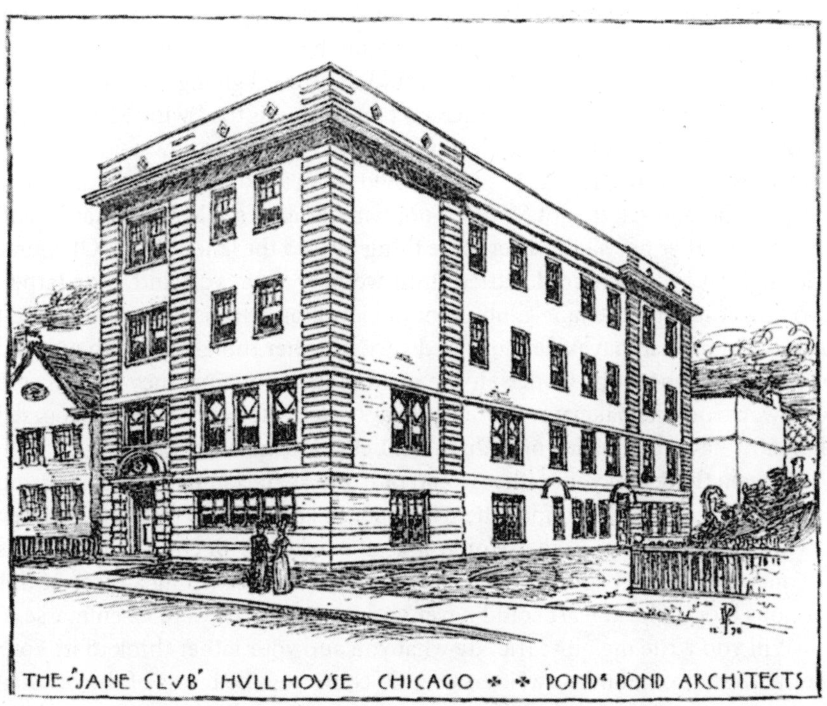


The new four-story Jane Club Building designed by the Pond brothers was opened in 1899 (*Commons* 5, no. 5 [or whole no. 37] [Sept. 1899]: 7).

## To Mary Rozet Smith

Hull-House 335 South Halsted Street Chicago [Ill.] March 23d 1898

Dearest

We have been having animated times over the Jane Club building.

Miss Culver came back from the south after a months meditation with a firm negative answer.[1] For the first time in her life however she proposed selling lots on the block. The old nursery lot 106 x ~~27~~ <26> 9/10 (106 ft deep ~~27~~ <26> 9/10 ft on Ewing St) she said she would sell at $12500 a foot, or as much land as we liked on Polk west of the Coffee House for $150 a ft.

I took lunch with your brother[2] and your Aunt[3] yesterday and we discussed the situation. Mr Pond thinks that we could build a very good club house, with an English basement and three stories, 90 ft east light[4] on the alley, ~~27~~<26> 9/10 south light[5] on Ewing St for $10000.00[.] This of course would be heated and lighted from our boiler house.

Your Aunt & brother Fred thought that she would put in $10000.00 which was about the sum the Jane Club proper would have cost on the other lot and I volunteered to see what Miss Culver would do toward giving the land. I had a long talk with her this morning. She says that she holds the Ewing St land at 150 a ft. has never sold a foot of it for lesser (the little Church[6] I know paid that) that at that price ~~27~~ <26 9/10> ft @ 150 a ft would be $4035.00. That she will donate the $1035.00 and sell the lot for 3000.00 I am going to see Mrs Wilmarth[7] and one or two other people, and get some thing toward the land if I can. Of course nothing can be considered settled until we hear from you and your father. Looking at it from the Jane Club point of view alone this is of course the best plan. The girls can have a laundry and various other things which they could n't have had <above the Coffee House> and at the same time they are only ten feet away from the bakery & it would always be easy to serve food. Of course I shall now have to fall back on Sidney Kent et al for the other building.[8]

Do you think that your father would rather have the family buy the land and own the <house> and the land. There is no special reason why it should be given to H.H. if the girls have the use of it. It is all perplexing of course, but there is the one advantage of someone else besides Miss Culver owning a piece of this precious block. She at least could never give it away to the U. of C. en masse.[9]

Will you write me quite frankly what you and your father think of it? Your brother has also doubtless written you. Of course by the terms of the original proposition for "the Smiths" there is nothing to bind the family to any thing since Miss C. won't play her part.[10]

Alice Kellogg has painted steadily for two days[11] with Mrs Rice[12] as a model dressed up in your clo. The picture is more beautiful all the time—I can scarcely wait to possess it really & truly.

Please give my best love to your mother. I do hope that she is getting better. Always yours

J.A.

P.S. The Nivers[13] are of course to receive my happiest messages—I tried so hard to get there to see you off but could n't make it without neglecting the guests at the critical moment of starting.

ALI (SCPC, JAC; *JAPM*, 3:1001–6).

1. JA may have expected Helen Culver to donate a piece of land in the HH block for a new Jane Club structure. See also JA to MRS, 20 Mar., 26 Mar., 29 Mar., and 6 Apr. 1898, SCPC, JAC; *JAPM*, 3:997–99, 1007–10, 1015–16, and 1031–32.

2. Charles Frederic ("Fred") Mather Smith. See Biographical Profiles: Smith, Mary Rozet (1868–1934), and Smith Family.

3. MRS's aunt Sarah Porter Smith. See Article in the *Chicago Inter Ocean*, 30 June 1892, n. 11, above.

4. JA may have meant to write "right" rather than "light."

5. JA may have meant to write "right" rather than "light."

6. JA was referring to the Ewing Street Church, of which she was a charter member. See also Two Essays in the *Forum*, Nov. and Oct. 1892, n. 97, above.

7. JA did ask Mary Wilmarth to help purchase the real estate on which the Jane Club could be built. On 26 Mar., JA reported to MRS: "Mrs Wilmarth will give another 1000.00 Mrs Foster whom I saw to day will probably give another 1000.00 She is considering it and will write. That leaves 1000 00 to be gotten and I will see Mr Higginson & Mrs McCormick about it" (SCPC, JAC; *JAPM*, 3:1008). See also Article in the *Chicago Inter Ocean*, 30 June 1892, n. 11, above.

When the Smith family provided the funding for the real estate as well as the Jane Club building, the gifts of Mrs. Wilmarth and Nancy Foster were transferred to support the development of the new Coffee House. Mr. Higginson's name does not appear among the list of donors for the Jane Club or the Coffee House, and the only McCormick whose name appears as a donor for the Coffee House is Stanley McCormick, who provided sixty-four hundred dollars toward that effort.

8. JA was also beginning to raise money to construct a new Coffee House Building. "We had 122 people to dinner yesterday & ten turned away with only 50 seats for all of them, but I am so anxious to get at least the Club settled and then I will tackle the other one," JA wrote to MRS on 26 Mar. 1898 (SCPC, JAC; *JAPM*, 3:1008–9). JA's fund-raising effort in support of the new structure began in earnest in 1899. Sidney Kent gave one thousand dollars to the effort.

9. JA recalled the 1895 attempt by the Univ. of Chicago to acquire HH through a Helen Culver gift. See JA to William Rainey Harper, 19 Dec. 1895, above.

10. JA had planned for the Smith family to give the Jane Club Building and for Helen Culver to provide the real estate on which to construct it.

11. "Alice Kellogg Tyler is doing a portrait of her [MRS] for me—I earned $200 00 in Grinnell this week and she is doing me one for 150.00. It is very big and beautiful," JA informed her sister SAAH (5 Mar. 1898, IU, Lilly, SAAH: *JAPM*, 3:987). See also headnote, Article in the *HH Bulletin*, Apr. and May 1898, below.

Alice Kellogg Tyler was delighted to be asked to undertake the MRS portrait for JA. "If you know how I have wanted to do something to add to your generously giving life—you would understand my delight when you asked me to paint Mary Smith for you—I am happy in the thought that it is artistically good. It really is, dear Miss Addams" (Alice Kellogg Tyler to JA, Wednesday, A.M. [1898?], SCPC, JAC; *JAPM*, 3:925).

12. This may have been Mrs. Mary Rice, who was responsible for holding a social for the HH Woman's Club on 31 Oct. 1900. She was an early and active member of the HH Woman's Club who lived at 35th St. and Ellis Ave., Chicago.

13. MRS and her parents may have been visiting in Baltimore. Cornelia Lee Post Niver (1866–1962) was a childhood friend of MRS. They met as teenagers in the spa that the Smith and Post families visited at the same time. Cornelia Post was married in 1893 to Edwin B. Niver (1863–1940), who was an Episcopal minister. He was born in Scott, N.Y., and attended Cazenovia Seminary in New York, 1882–84, and Amherst College, 1885. He became a member of the Board of Examiners, Civil Service Comm., Washington, D.C., 1885–90. From 1890 to 1892, he attended the Episcopal Theological Seminary, Cambridge, and was ordained in 1892. He became rector of St. Paul's in Providence, R.I., and served there until 1894, when he became assistant minister, 1894–97, and then beginning in 1897 the rector at Christ Church, Baltimore. Niver was a published author.

Cornelia Niver was active in the Woman's Civic League of Baltimore, where she served on the Smoke Abatement Com. and the Membership Com. The Nivers, who lived in Baltimore at 1014 St. Paul St. and later at 29 Warrenton St., had one child, who was named Charles Mather Smith Niver (b. 1891) after MRS's father. When Niver conducted the funeral service for MRS in 1934, he was associated with the College of Preachers, Cathedral Close, in Washington, D.C. Cornelia Post Niver received more than twelve thousand dollars from the estate of MRS.

## Essay in the *International Journal of Ethics*

*In April 1898, the scholarly* International Journal of Ethics *printed an essay by Jane Addams that stirred considerable comment among Chicago politicians and among progressive reformers throughout the United States. It was also noticed by John Powers, the Chicago alderman about whom the essay was written. It was a summary of the lessons Jane Addams had learned from her experiences while trying to encourage her Nineteenth Ward neighbors to elect a capable, honest, reform-minded alderman to replace the corrupt "boodler" Powers, who had ruled the ward for a number of years. Since at least 1897, she had been speaking about these issues in a variety of public forums, not only in Chicago, but also in New York and Philadelphia.*[1] *Her speech in Chicago for the Ethical Culture Society in January 1898*[2] *was the last before she submitted the essay to the journal.*[3] *By 9 February 1898, she knew that her essay titled "Ethical Survivals in City Immorality" would be published. When it was issued in April, it carried the title "Ethical Survivals in Municipal Corruption."*

*"I was very glad to get the copy of the Journal of Ethics containing the Powers article. I think it is the best thing you have ever done with the pen," wrote Robert A. Woods.*[4] *Up-and-coming social work leader and head of the Baltimore Charity Organization Society, Mary E. Richmond,*[5] *commented: "Just a line . . . to tell you how much our agents enjoyed your article in the Journal of Ethics. . . . I know of only one or two people in America and England who, out of ripe experiences have been able to give us so just and human a view of the movements of the public mind and conscience; in fact, there's no one else on this side the water, come to think of it."*[6]

*A second version of the essay was printed 2 April 1898 in* Outlook.[7] *The magazine editors gave credit for the original article to the* International Journal of Ethics *and indicated that a version of the essay was "read at a meeting in Chicago, and so reported by the Chicago daily papers as to stir the wrath of the Alderman described." The* Outlook *editors also reported: "We have selected those passages which show why the Alderman, who is the most obedient servant of the monopolies, holds a thus far impregnable position in a ward composed of the very poor. The situation presented is so far from confirming the conclusions of pessimists that it awakens new faith in the supremacy of human virtue, when that virtue manifests itself in constant neighborly kindness instead of annual political sermons."*[8]

### ETHICAL SURVIVALS IN MUNICIPAL CORRUPTION

Hull House, Chicago. [Ill.] April 1898

In submitting this paper on Ethical Survivals in Municipal Corruption, the writer is giving her own experience from an eight years' residence in a ward of Chicago which has, during all of that time, returned to the city council a notoriously corrupt politician. To say that all the men who vote for him are also

Jane Addams gave two different sittings to Alfred A. Cox during 1898. Although she wore the same dress for both sessions, for one sitting Jane Addams's hair was parted in the center. For the other sitting, her hair was not parted. By mid-1898, this photograph, especially, began appearing in publications, but the negative of it was often printed reversed. Here, the editors present it accurately (UIC, JAMC 00005 1437).

corrupt, or that they approve of his dealings, is manifestly unfair; but to find the motives from which the votes are cast is not an easy matter.

The status of the ethics attained by a given community is difficult to determine, and a newly-arrived resident is almost sure to make mistakes. He often fatuously attempts to correct public morals and change civic ideals without knowing the processes by which the present corrupt standards were obtained, and sometimes quite ignorant of the motives and temptations of those who naïvely hold those standards.

Living together as we do, within the narrow boundary of a Chicago ward, fifty thousand people of a score of different tongues and nationalities, the writer is much impressed with the fact that all that holds us together—Latin, Celt, Teuton, Jew, and Slav, as we are—is our intrinsic human nature,—the few basic experiences which we hold in common. Our social ethics have been determined much more by example than by precept, just as our religious life is largely determined by the biographies of the saints. As Stanley[9] points out, "the 'Acta Sanctorum' have been, after all, the main guide of the stumbling feet of thousands of Christians, the solace of darkened understandings, to whom the Credo has been but mysterious words." Or, in the scientific phrasing of Wundt,[10] "the conclusion is inevitable that the idea of morality is at first intimately connected with the person and personal conduct, and that its severance from this substrata is a very slow and gradual process." Granting, then, that morality develops far earlier in the form of moral fact than in the higher form of moral ideas, it becomes obvious that ideas only operate upon the popular mind through will and character, and that goodness has to be dramatized before it reaches the mass of men. Ethics as well as political opinions may be discussed and disseminated among the sophisticated by lectures and printed pages, but to the common people they can only come through example,—through a personality which seizes the popular imagination. The advantage of an unsophisticated neighborhood is, that the inhabitants do not keep their ideas as treasures; they are untouched by the notion of accumulating them, as one does knowledge or money, and frankly act upon those they have. The personal example promptly rouses to emulation. In a neighborhood where political standards are plastic and undeveloped, and where there has been little previous experiences in self-government, the office-holder himself sets the standard, and the ideas that cluster around him exercise a specific and permanent influence upon the political morality of his constituents. If his standard is low, it may be urged in his defence that he came into office with morals as plastic as those of his humbler neighbors, and that this plasticity has been seized upon and impressed by the cynical stamp of the corporations; but moral debauchery is nevertheless the result, and it will take years to change the impression if the stamp is once fairly set. No greater mistake could be made than to assume that politics is something off by itself which does not affect the common lot.

We must also take into consideration what his various neighbors have brought with them from their own countries, and remember that custom has a greater power of persistence than law or morality, and also that outward forms of conduct are apt to outlast the thought and feelings from which they sprang. Many Bohemians, for instance, have emigrated to this country, largely from the hope of getting away from Austrian oppression, both of the church and state. Their attitude towards the government under which they were born is one of distinct hostility. Some of the journalists and political leaders are so reactionary that to state that they are atheists and anarchists is in their minds to bid for popularity. Such men continually declare that both church and state pretend to protect in order that they may oppress, although they are living in a country in which both church and state are free institutions. Most of the Italians and even some of the Germans, in spite of all their love for the fatherland, have emigrated in order to escape service in the army. The Polish and Russian Jews, of course, have fled from persecution either active or threatened. The Irish bring with them the notion that the men who govern are rack-rent landlords; for centuries the substance of their forefathers was seized by rapacious landlords, who represented the governing class. It has long been regarded as legitimate for Irishmen to get as much as possible out of the English government, because they have been so grievously oppressed by it. Many a politician has come from Ireland, not only with the desire to feed at the public crib, but with a conviction that it is perfectly legitimate to do so, and it is the Irishmen who largely teach political methods to the others living in their vicinity, and who dramatize for them the aims and objects of civic government. It would be interesting to trace the effects of this old wrong of England against Ireland in the government of our American cities. The first Tammany ring,[11] for instance, showed in itself the stubbornness and power of a deep-rooted growth that certainly did not spring solely from New York soil. When we recall the heroic devotion and generous self-sacrifice of which the Irish race has always been capable, is it not clear that this sordidness and self-interest in regard to public affairs spring from their governmental experiences?

While the American-born people of the same community are putting forth a claim for a well-ordered democratic government, they at the same time shirk the responsibilities of self-governing citizens. The early enthusiasm for self-government was engendered by men who lived out their democratic principles. The impulse they gave was so energetic that it has outlived two generations of jobbery and office-vending, but the old impulse cannot always last, and we find little left of that old town meeting endeavor but patriotic phrases and a cloak of public spirit, under which American-born politicians too often hide office-seeking.

Nothing is more certain than that the quality which a heterogenous population, living in one of the less sophisticated wards, most admires is the quality of simple goodness; that the man who attracts them is the one whom they believe to be a good man. We all know that children long "to be good" with an intensity which they give to no other ambition. We can all remember that the earliest strivings of our childhood were in this direction and we venerated grown people because they had attained perfection.

Primitive people, such as the south Italian peasants who live in the Nineteenth Ward, are still in this stage. They want to be good, and deep down in their hearts they admire nothing so much as the good man. Abstract virtues are too difficult for their untrained minds to apprehend, and many of them are still simple enough to believe that power and wealth come only to good people.

The successful candidate, then, must be a good man according to the standards of his constituents. He must not attempt to hold up a morality beyond them, nor must he attempt to reform or change the standard. His safety lies in doing on a large scale the good deeds which his constituents are able to do only on a small scale. If he believes what they believe, and does what they are all cherishing a secret ambition to do, he will dazzle them by his success and win their confidence. There is a certain wisdom in this course. There is a common sense in the mass of men which cannot be neglected with impunity, just as there is sure to be an eccentricity in the differing and reforming individual which it is perhaps well to challenge. Any one who has lived among poorer people, cannot fail to be impressed with their constant kindness to each other; that unfailing response to the needs and distresses of their neighbors, even when in danger of bankruptcy themselves. This is their reward for living in the midst of poverty. They have constant opportunities for self-sacrifice and generosity, to which, as a rule, they respond. The human kindness which a poor man shows to his distressed neighbor is doubtless heightened by the consciousness that he himself may be in distress next week. The gruff and hearty good fellowship is not altogether unlike that of a frontier town. A man stands by his friend when he gets too drunk to take care of himself, when he loses his wife or child, when he is evicted for non-payment of rent, when he is arrested for a petty crime. It seems to such a man entirely fitting that his alderman should do the same thing on a larger scale,—that he should help a constituent out of trouble just because he is in trouble, irrespective of the justice involved.

The alderman, therefore, bails out his constituents when they are arrested, or says a good word to the police justice when they appear before him for trial; uses his "pull" with the magistrate when they are likely to be fined for a civil misdemeanor, or sees what he can do to "fix up matters" with the State's attorney, when the charge is really a serious one.

A gray-faced woman visited Hull House one morning and asked that her son be helped out of the city prison, because he was her last support. The alderman had always done it for her, but the boy had been arrested so often that even his patience, the most colossal she had ever known, had given way. One of her boys was in the penitentiary, and one of them in the reform school for a term of years, and if this one, her Benjamin, were sent up she would have no wages forthcoming. The alderman had bailed them out and spoken to the judges many times since they were little fellows. He had begun when her husband was still living, but he had kept on long after she was a widow, and when the boys were still too young to vote, which the neighbors all said was "mighty good of him." The mother had no notion of the indifference for law which this course had fostered in her sons; she was only in despair that her long-suffering and powerful friend had at last come to the position when he could no longer serve her and could only give his sympathy. It did not occur to any of those concerned that the sense of justice was thus slowly undermined and law-breaking encouraged.

Of a like blighting effect upon public morals was the alderman's action in standing by an Italian padrone of the ward when he was indicted for violating the Civil Service law.[12] The Commissioners had sent out notices to certain Italian day-laborers who were upon the eligible list that they were to report for work at a given day and hour. One of the padrones intercepted these notifications and sold them to the men for five dollars apiece, making also the usual bargain for a share of the wages. The padrone's entire arrangement followed the custom which had prevailed for years before the enactment of the Civil Service law.

Ten of the laborers swore out warrants against the padrone, who was convicted and fined seventy-five dollars. This sum was promptly paid by the alderman; and the padrone, assured that he would be protected from any further trouble, returned triumphant to the colony. The simple Italians were much bewildered by this show of a power stronger than that of the Civil Service law which they had trusted as they did that of Italy. This was one of the first violations of its authority, and various sinister acts have followed, until no Nineteenth Ward Italian feels quite secure in holding his job unless he is backed by the friendship of the alderman. According to the Civil Service law, a laborer has no right to a trial; many are discharged by the foreman, and find that they can be reinstated only upon the aldermanic recommendation. The alderman thus practically holds his old power over the laborers working for the city, and the popular mind is convinced that an honest administration of the Civil Service is impossible, and that it is but one more instrument in the hands of the powerful. It will be difficult to establish genuine Civil Service among these men who learn only by experience, to their minds it is "no good."

Because of simple friendliness, the alderman is expected to pay rent for the hard-pressed tenant when no rent is forthcoming, to find jobs when work is hard to get, to procure and divide among his constituents all the places which he can seize from the city hall. The alderman of the Nineteenth Ward at one time made the proud boast that he had two thousand six hundred people in his ward upon the public pay-roll. This, of course, included day-laborers, but each one felt under distinct obligations to him for getting the job. When we reflect that this is one-third of the entire vote of the ward, we realize that it is very important to vote for the right man, since there is, at the least, one chance out of three for a job.

If we recollect, further, that the franchise-seeking companies pay respectful heed to the applicants backed by the alderman, the question of voting for the successful man becomes as much an industrial as a political one. An Italian laborer wants a job more than anything else, and quite simply votes for the man who promises him one. It is not so different from his relation to the padrone, and, indeed, the two strengthen each other.

The alderman may himself be quite sincere in his acts of kindness. In certain stages of moral evolution, a man is incapable of unselfish action, the results of which will not benefit some one of his acquaintances; still more, of conduct that does not aim to assist any individual whatsoever; and it is a long step in moral progress to appreciate the work done by the individual for the community. An office-seeker may begin with the simple desire to alleviate suffering, and this may gradually change into the desire to put his constituents under obligations to him; but the action of such an individual becomes a demoralizing element in the community when a noble purpose is made the cloak for the satisfaction of lower impulses, and when the plastic morals of his constituents are thus formed to his own undeveloped standards.

While our political system has grown more and more complicated upon the basic assumption that the individual merges his interest in those of the community, and attains his own ends in terms of the common weal, such men living in the community are seeking solely their own advantage, and striving to obtain personal ends at the expense of the state. As the political system cannot change its direction, it brings the incongruity to the extreme limit of contradiction; a man holding office is known to the community to be there for the sake of "what there is in it;" or a candidate openly announces that his business affairs have gone badly; that he wants his chance at public office; that his opponent is now rich enough.

The alderman gives presents at weddings and christenings. He seizes these days of family festivities for making friends. It is easiest to reach people in the holiday mood of expansive good-will, but on their side it seems natural and kindly that he should do it. The alderman procures passes from the railroads when his constituents wish to visit friends or to attend the funerals of distant relatives; he buys tickets galore for benefit entertainments given for a widow or a consumptive in peculiar distress; he contributes to prizes which are awarded to the handsomest lady or the most popular man. At a church bazaar, for instance, the alderman finds the stage all set for his dramatic performance. When others are spending pennies he is spending dollars. Where anxious relatives are canvassing to secure votes for the two most beautiful children who are being voted upon, he recklessly buys votes from both sides, and laughingly declines to say which one he likes the best, buying off the young lady who is persistently determined to find out, with five dollars for the flower bazaar, the posies, of course, to be sent to the sick of the parish. The moral atmosphere of a bazaar suits him exactly. He murmurs many times, "Never mind; the money all goes to the poor," or "It is all straight enough if the church gets it," or "The poor won't ask too many questions." The oftener he can put sentiments of that sort into the minds of his constituents, the better he is pleased. Nothing so rapidly prepares them to take his view of money-getting and money-spending.

There is something archaic in a community of simple people in their attitude towards death and burial. Nothing so easy to collect money for as a funeral, and one involuntarily remembers that the early religious tithes were paid to ward off death and ghosts. At times one encounters almost the Greek feeling in regard to burial. If the alderman seizes upon festivities for expressions of his good-will, much more does he seize upon periods of sorrow. At a funeral he has the double advantage of ministering to a genuine craving for comfort and solace, and at the same time of assisting at an important social function. That curious feeling of remorse, which is an accompaniment of quick sorrow, that desire to "make up" for past delinquencies, to show the world how much, after all, we loved the person who has just died, is as natural as it is universal.

In addition to this, there is among the poor, who have few social occasions, a great desire for a well-arranged funeral, the grade of which almost determines their social standing in the neighborhood. The alderman saves the very poorest of his constituents from that awful horror of burial by the county; he provides carriages for the poor, who otherwise could not have them; for the more prosperous he sends extra carriages, so that they may invite more friends and have a longer procession; for the most prosperous of all there will be probably only a large "flower-piece." It may be too much to say that all the relatives and friends who ride in the carriages provided by the alderman's bounty vote for him, but they are certainly influenced by his kindness, and talk of his virtues during the long hours of the ride back and forth from the suburban cemetery. A man who would ask at such a time where all this money comes from would be considered sinister. They certainly do not discuss the alderman's corruption during the long ride. You cannot very well run a man down when you are sitting in a carriage provided by his generosity. The tendency to speak lightly of the faults of the dead and to judge them gently is transferred to the living, and many a man at such a time has formulated a lenient judgment of political corruption and has heard kindly speeches which he has remembered on election day. "Ah, well, he has a big Irish heart. He is good to the widow and the fatherless." "He knows the poor better than the big guns who are always about talking civil service and reform."

Indeed, what headway can the notion of civic purity, of honesty of administration, make against this big manifestation of human friendliness, this stalking survival of village kindness? The notions of the civic reformer are negative and impotent before it. The reformers give themselves over largely to criticisms of the present state of affairs, to writing and talking of what the future must be; but their goodness is not dramatic; it is not even concrete and human.

Such an alderman will keep a standing account with an undertaker, and telephone every week, and sometimes more than once, the kind of outfit he wishes provided for a bereaved constituent, until the sum may roll up into hundreds a year. Such a man understands what the people want, and ministers just as truly to a great human need as the musician or the artist does. I recall an attempt to substitute what we might call a later standard.

A delicate little child was deserted in the Hull House nursery. An investigation showed that it had been born ten days previously in the Cook County hospital, but no trace could be found of the unfortunate mother. The little thing lived for several weeks, and then, in spite of every care, died. We decided to have it buried by the county, and the wagon was to arrive by eleven o'clock. About nine o'clock in the morning the rumor of this awful deed reached the neighbors. A half dozen of them came, in a very excited state of mind, to protest. They took up a collection out of their poverty with which to defray a funeral. We were then comparatively new in the neighborhood. We did not realize that we were really shocking a genuine moral sentiment of the community. In our crudeness, we instanced the care and tenderness which had been expended upon the little creature while it was alive; that it had had every attention from a skilled physician and trained nurse; we even intimated that the excited members of the group had not taken part in this, and that it now lay with us to decide that the child should be buried, as it had been born, at the county's expense. It is doubtful whether Hull House has ever done anything which injured it so deeply in the minds of some of its neighbors. We were only forgiven by the most indulgent on the ground that we were spinsters and could not know a mother's heart. No one born and reared in the community could possibly have made a mistake like that. No one who had studied the ethical standards with any care could have bungled so completely.

The amount of sentiment among simple people is constantly underestimated. The songs which are most popular among them are those of reminiscent old age, in which the ripened soul calmly recounts and regrets the sins of his youth,—songs in which the wayward daughter is forgiven by her loving parents, in which the lovers are magnanimous and faithful through all vicissitudes. The tendency is to condone and forgive, and not to hold too rigidly to a standard. In the theatres it is the magnanimous man, the kindly reckless villain who is always applauded. So shrewd an observer as Samuel Johnson[13] once remarked that it was surprising to find how much more kindness than justice society contained.

The alderman of the Nineteenth Ward owns several saloons, one down town within easy access of the city hall, where he can catch the more important of his friends.[14] Here again he has seized upon an old tradition and primitive custom,—the good-fellowship which has long been best expressed when men drink together. The saloons offer a common meeting-ground, with stimulants enough to free the wits and tongues of the men who meet there.

Last Christmas,[15] our alderman distributed six tons of turkeys, and four or more tons of ducks and geese; but each luckless biped was handed out either by himself or one of his friends with a "Merry Christmas." Inevitably, some families got three or four apiece, but what of that? He had none of the nagging rules of the charitable societies, nor was he ready to declare that, because a man wanted two turkeys for Christmas, he was a scoundrel, who should never be allowed to eat turkey again.

Of course, there are those who see through the schemes. Some constituents merely suspect, others connive, and still others glory in the fact that they can thus "soak the alderman." The young man who fills his pockets with handfuls of cigars, giving a sly wink at his companions, takes a step downward to the position where he is willing to sell his vote to both parties, and then scratch his ticket as he pleases. Less than a year ago a man in ordinary conversation with the writer complained quite openly, and with no sense of shame, that he had sold his vote for only two dollars this year, and that he was awfully disappointed. The writer happened to know that his income during the nine months previous had been but twenty-eight dollars; that he was in debt thirty-two dollars; and she could well imagine the eagerness with which he had counted upon this source of revenue. The situation revealed once more the difficulty of attaining virtue by those hardest pressed in the industrial struggle; and in the revelation the writer felt the familiar grip that silences us all in the presence of temptations which have never been ours.

There is an old story which the writer has many times heard to the effect that a respectable candidate once tried to run against this popular alderman of ours, and was somewhat embarrassed by receiving an offer of help from the president of a large temperance society. He knew it would make him unpopular to be thus befriended, but he did not quite dare to refuse so moral a backing. The president and several of the members made a vigorous campaign, speaking in his behalf almost every night at the various meetings, and impressively asserting that, if the reform candidate were elected, he would soon have all the saloons of the ward closed at ten o'clock at night. The candidate ventured to protest once or twice that he had not thought of going to that extreme, but this protest so shocked the temperance orators that he at last gave it up. Such a campaign naturally made him very unpopular, and he lost heavily. On the day of the election he was surprised to see the president of the temperance society at the polls, openly working for his rival. He was quite nettled enough by that time to challenge him fiercely, only to receive the spirited reply, "I hope you weren't fool enough to think that I made those temperance speeches to help you along. I made them for the other man, and he is going in, too." Of what use to protest? The president was quite willing to retire, both from the society and from temperance, for he had received an office in the city hall.

The alderman's wisdom was again displayed in procuring from down town friends the sum of three thousand dollars wherewith to uniform and equip a boy's temperance brigade[16] which had been formed in the ward a few months before his campaign. Is it strange that the good leader, whose heart was filled with innocent pride as he looked upon these promising young scions of virtue, should decline to enter into a reform campaign? Of what use to suggest that uniforms and bayonets for the purpose of promoting temperance, bought with money contributed by a man who was the proprietor of a saloon and a gambling house, might perhaps confuse the ethics of the young soldiers? Why take the pains to urge that it was vain to lecture and march abstract virtues into them, so long as the champion boodler of the town was the man whom the boys recognized as the loyal and kind-hearted friend, the public-spirited citizen, whom their fathers enthusiastically voted for, and their mothers called the friend of the poor? So long as the actual and tangible success is thus embodied, marching, whether in kindergartens or brigades, does little to change this family ideal of goodness.

The question does, of course, occur to many minds, Where does the money come from with which to dramatize so successfully? The more primitive people accept the truthful statement of its sources without any shock to their moral sense. To their simple minds he gets it "from the rich," and so long as he again gives it out to the poor, as a true Robin Hood, with open hand, they have no objections to offer. Their ethics are quite honestly those of the merry-making foresters. The next less primitive people of the vicinage are quite willing to admit that he leads "the gang" in the city council, and sells out the city franchises; that he makes deals with the franchise-seeking companies; that he guarantees to steer dubious measures through the council, for which he demands liberal pay; that he is, in short, a successful boodler. But when there is intellect enough to get this point of view, there is also enough to make the contention that this is universally done; that all the alderman do it more or less successfully, but that the alderman of the Nineteenth Ward is unique in being so generous; that such a state of affairs is to be deplored, of course, but that that is the way business is run, and we are fortunate when a kind-hearted man who is close to the people gets a large share of the boodle; that he serves these franchised companies who employ men in the building and construction of their enterprises, and that they are bound in return to give jobs to his constituency. It is again the justification of stealing from the rich to give to the poor. Even when they are intelligent enough to complete the circle, and to see that the money comes, not from the pockets of the companies' agents, but from the street-car fares of people like themselves, it almost seems as if they would rather pay two cents more each time they ride than give up the consciousness that they have a big, warm-hearted friend at court who will stand by them in an emergency. The sense of just dealing comes apparently much later than the desire for protection and kindness. On the whole, the gifts and favors are taken quite simply, as an evidence of good and loving kindness, or are accepted as inevitable political measures.

The alderman is really elected because he is a good friend and neighbor. He is corrupt, of course, but he is not elected because he is corrupt, but rather in spite of it. His standard suits his constituents. He exemplifies and exaggerates the popular type of a good man. He has attained what his constituents secretly long for.

At one end of the ward there is a street of good houses, familiarly called "Con Row."[17] The term is perhaps quite unjustly used, but it is nevertheless universally applied because some of these houses are occupied by professional office-holders. This row is supposed to form a happy hunting ground of the successful politician, where he can live in prosperity, and still maintain his vote and influence in the ward. It would be difficult, I imagine, justly to estimate the influence which the successful and prominent alderman who lives here, has upon the ideals of the youth of the vicinity, to whose minds the path which leads to riches and success, to civic prominence and honor, is the path of the corrupt politician.

The writer remembers that when she was ten years old, the village schoolmaster told his little flock, without any mitigating clauses, that Jay Gould[18] laid the foundation of his colossal fortune by always saving bits of string; and that, as a result, every child in the village assiduously collected parti-colored balls of twine. It is needless to tell any Chicago boy who reads the newspapers that the most prominent alderman in Chicago is the keeper of a gambling house, and obtains large sums of money for services rendered in the council to the corporations; in short, that his success is founded upon law-breaking. One day the papers announce that he has been indicted for gambling, the next that he has been elected president of a great political organization. Even my village mind at the tender age of ten would, I think, have seen a connection which is certainly quite as close as Jay Gould's millions and bits of twine. A bright Chicago boy—not necessarily a Nineteenth Ward boy, but any boy in town—might well draw the inference that the path of the corrupt politician not only leads to civic honor, but to the glories of benevolence and philanthropy. This confusion was fortunately spared my infant mind in regard to Jay Gould, for we were never told that he was philanthropic.

We must also remember that the imitative impulse plays a important part in life, and that the loss of social estimation, keenly felt by all of us, is perhaps most dreaded by the humblest. It is doubtless true that freedom for individual conduct, the power to give only due weight to the opinions of one's neighbors, is one of the latest developments of civilization. A form of constraint, gentle but powerful, is afforded by the simple desire to do what others do, in order to share with them the approval of the community. Of course, the larger the number of people among whom an habitual mode of conduct obtains, the greater the constraint it puts upon the individual will. Thus it is that the great corruption of the city presses most heavily where it can least be resisted and is most likely to be imitated.

According to the same law, the positive evils of corrupt government are bound to fall heaviest upon the poorest and least capable. When the water of Chicago is foul, the prosperous buy water bottled at distant springs; the poor have no alternative but the typhoid fever which comes from using the city's supply. When the garbage contracts are not enforced, the well-to-do pay for private service; the poor suffer the discomfort and illness which are inevitable from a foul atmosphere. The prosperous business man has a certain choice as to whether he will treat with the boss politician or preserve his independence on a smaller income; but to an Italian day-laborer it is a choice between obeying the commands of a political boss or practical starvation. Again, a more intelligent man may philosophize a little upon the present state of corruption, and reflect that it is but a phase of our commercialism, from which we are bound to emerge; at any rate, he may solace himself with the ideals of literature and history; but the more ignorant man who lives only in the narrow present has no such resource, and slowly the conviction enters his mind that politics is a matter of favors and positions, that self-government means pleasing the boss and standing in with the gang. This slowly acquired knowledge he hands on to his family. During the month of February his boy may come home from school with rather incoherent tales about Washington and Lincoln, and the father may for the moment be fired to tell of Garibaldi, but such talk is only periodic, and the long year round the fortunes of the entire family, even to the opportunity to earn food and shelter, depend upon the boss.

This lowering of standards, this setting of an ideal, is perhaps the worst of the situation, for daily by our actions and decisions we not only determine ideals for ourselves, but largely for each other. We are all involved in this political corruption, and as members of the community stand indicted. This is the penalty of a democracy,—that we are bound to move forward or retrograde together. None of us can stand aside, for our feet are mired in the same soil, and our lungs breathe the same air.

During a campaign a year and a half ago, when a reform league put up a candidate[19] against our corrupt alderman, and when Hull House worked hard to rally the moral sentiment of the ward in favor of the new man, we encountered another and unexpected difficulty. Finding that it was hard to secure enough local speakers of the moral tone which we desired, we imported orators from other parts of the town, from the "better element," so to speak. Suddenly we heard it rumored on all sides that, while the money and speakers for the reform candidate were coming from the swells, the money which was backing our corrupt alderman also came from a swell source; it was rumored that the president of a street-car combination,[20] for whom he performed constant offices in the city council, was ready to back him to the extent of fifty thousand dollars; that he, too, was a good man, and sat in high places; that he had recently given a large sum of money to an educational institution, and was therefore as philanthropic, not to say good and upright, as any man in town; that our alderman had the sanction of the highest authorities, and that the lecturers who were talking were against corruption, and the selling and buying of franchises, were only the cranks, and not the solid business men who had developed and built up Chicago.

All parts of the community are bound together in ethical development. If the so-called more enlightened members of the community accept public gifts from the man who buys up the council, and the so-called less enlightened members accept individual gifts from the man who sells out the council, we surely must take our punishment together. There is the difference, of course, that in the first case we act collectively, and in the second case individually; but is the punishment of cynicism which follows the first any lighter or less far reaching in its consequences than the arousing of this imitative impulse which follows the second?

Another curious experience during that campaign was the difference of standards between the imported speakers and the audience. One man high in the council of the "better element," one evening, used as an example of the philanthropic politician an alderman of the vicinity recently dead, who was devotedly loved and mourned by his constituents. When the audience caught the familiar name in the midst of the platitudes, they brightened up wonderfully. But, as the speaker went on, they first looked puzzled, then astounded, and gradually their astonishment turned to indignation. The speaker, all unconscious of the situation, went on, imagining, perhaps, that he was addressing his usual audience, and totally unaware that he was perpetrating an outrage upon the finest feelings of the people who were sitting before him. He certainly succeeded in irrevocably injuring the chances of the candidate for whom he was speaking. The speaker's standard of ethics was upright dealing in positions of public trust. The standard of ethics held by his audience was, being good to the poor and speaking gently of the dead. If he considered them corrupt and illiterate voters, they quite honestly held him a blackguard.

If we would hold to our political democracy, some pains must be taken to keep on common ground in our human experiences, and to some solidarity in our ethical conceptions. Just because, in America, we have a wide difference in our traditions, customs, religion, and language, must we cherish our moral awakenings, our mutual compunctions, and strivings for better things. A strenuous moral appeal meets with a much surer response than one based upon prejudice or patriotism. Kinship of a common moral nature is the last and most comprehensive of all bases of union. The meaning of life is, after all, to search out and then to conform our activities to our new knowledge. And if we discover that men of low ideals and corrupt practice are forming popular political standards simply because such men stand by and for and with the people, then nothing remains but to obtain a like sense of identification before we can hope to modify ethical standards.

A neighborhood of less sophisticated people has one advantage that when a dramatized truth does reach them, it excites at the same time their hero worship, and their disposition to follow. They thus balance their opinions by their living, and if we could but dramatize "public spirit," it is conceivable that their big emotional ethics, just because it constantly results in activity, has in it a possibility for a higher and wider life than the ethics of those of us who are content to hold it merely as a possession. We may learn to trust our huge and uncouth democracy in its ethics, as we are coming to trust it in other directions, for by slow degrees the law emerges. "That conduct which opposes the ends of the common weal must finally give way to conduct which furthers those ends."

JANE ADDAMS.

PD (*International Journal of Ethics* 8 [Apr. 1898]: 273–91; *JAPM*, 46:843–62).

1. JA presented a version of what became "Ethical Survivals in Municipal Corruption" as early as 14 Feb. 1897 for a gathering of "Harvard professors, the daughters of Longfellow, and other distinguished people" at Mrs. Ole Bull's home in Cambridge, Mass., where one newspaper reported it as a "witty paper" ("JA Honored"). She revisited the topic for selected audiences during her Dec. 1897 lecture swing through the East, including Philadelphia at the Ethical Society and at the New York City Reform Club.

2. See headnote, Article in the *Chicago Times-Herald*, 6 Mar. 1898, above.

3. One manuscript version of what became "Ethical Survivals in Municipal Corruption" is extant in SCPC, JAC; *JAPM*, 46:815–38. Titled "Ethical Survivals in City Immorality," it is

a twenty-three-page carbon copy of the typed manuscript with autograph corrections and additions. It is likely an early draft of the essay that finally appeared in the *International Journal of Ethics*. Among its pages is a map of a portion of the Nineteenth Ward with a list of political leaders living in the area. It could have been, but was not, used as an illustration for a published presentation.

4. 28 Apr. 1898, SCPC, JAC; *JAPM*, 3:1060.

5. Mary Ellen Richmond (1861–1928) became a major force in the development of social case work and social work education. She was born to Henry and Lavinia Harris Richmond in Belleville, Ill., and after the death of her parents she was raised by her maternal grandmother and aunts in Baltimore. She graduated from Eastern Female High School and eventually became assistant treasurer with the COS of Baltimore in 1889, where she developed into a leader with the ability to explain the COS method. She took the Friendly Visitor process associated with the COS model and refined it until it became the preferred social work model. In a speech titled "The Need of a Training School in Applied Philanthropy" in *Proceedings of the National Conf. of Charities and Correction* (1898), Richmond argued for the professionalization of what had been for many a "life vocation of charity organization work" (181). She moved from Baltimore to become the head of the Philadelphia COS in 1900, and by 1909 she was director of the new Russell Sage Foundation, where she stayed for the remainder of her life. Her goal for the foundation was to support programs that improved social welfare in the United States. Among her notable publications were *Friendly Visiting among the Poor* (1899), *Social Diagnosis* (1917), and *What Is Social Case Work?* (1922).

Richmond came to disagree with JA about the efficiency of the settlement approach to helping the working poor. In a lecture given before the Social Science Club of the Woman's College, Baltimore, in early 1898, Richmond emphasized the need for good administration for helping the working poor and indicated that trying "to establish a college settlement" might be "unwise. The college or social settlement, when under competent management, seems to me the highest development of the charitable impulse. . . . But the higher the development and the more delicate the adjustment, the greater the chance of failure and wreck" (Richmond, *Long View*, 50).

The following statement made by JA while she was speaking to the Woman's Club of Springfield, Mass., reflected her position: "The chief difficulty now . . . is that we pay no attention to the poor and ignor our duties to those who have the hardest struggle for existence. The present-day attitude toward the social problem is to assume that there is no problem. How shall we find out what the problem is? The mere desire to do something is not enough; one must take an active part. Social reformers agree that no one has a right to change the condition of his fellow men unless he has shared their experience" ("Present-Day Attitude to Social Problems").

Two years later, in a speech before the Women's Conf. of the Society for Ethical Culture in Baltimore, Richmond indicated that she had not changed her mind about settlement methods. Responding to JA's position that the investigation of the working poor could be harmful to the person being investigated and the investigator, Richmond opined: "Miss Addams is somewhat influenced by her environment. Chicago is nothing but a great overgrown village, and it hasn't yet grown into a big city in its methods. It is far behind the times in its methods of charity, and only for a very few years has scientific investigation been known there. Investigation which seeks not to exact truth, but rather seeks to prove something favorable or unfavorable, is dishonest and always harmful" ("Pseudo-scientific Charity").

In 1922, on the fiftieth meeting of the National Conf. of Social Work, when JA and Mary Richmond were candidates for president, Mary Richmond was selected by the membership for the honor.

6. 11 May 1898, SCPC, JAC; *JAPM*, 3:1068–69.

7. "Why the Ward Boss Rules," *Outlook* 58 (2 Apr. 1898): 879–82.

8. "Why the Ward Boss Rules," *Outlook* 58 (2 Apr. 1898): 879.

9. JA was likely referring to Arthur Penrhyn Stanley. See *PJA*, 2:620, n. 12.

10. William Wundt (1832–1920), German physiologist and psychologist and a professor at Univ. of Leipzig, 1875–1917, believed that psychology should be based on experience. He was the author of numerous books on physiology, psychology, and ethics. Among the books in JA's library was Wundt's *Ethics: An Investigation of the Facts and Laws of the Moral Life*. It was translated from the second German edition by Edward Bradford Titchener, Julia Henrietta Gulliver, and Margaret Floy Washburn and published in New York by Macmillan, 1897–1901. The first volume, entitled *The Facts of the Moral Life*, was issued in 1897. These volumes are at UIC in the JAMC.

11. Tammany Hall was the New York political organization founded and known as the Society of St. Tammany in 1786 and incorporated in 1789 as the Tammany Society. It became the Democratic Party political machine and had a major part in controlling elections for the party in New York City and New York State from the 1790s into the twentieth century. Its power came from the large Irish community in New York in the 1800s and continued to grow as more and more immigrants entered the United States. Tammany Hall was ruled by an Irish boss from 1871 until the 1920s. He held his power through patronage and his ability to provide services that those newly arrived in this country needed. Tammany Hall was also associated with graft and political corruption. One of the most famous and notorious Tammany leaders was William M. ("Boss") Tweed (1823–78), who was not Irish and held forth primarily between 1858 and 1871, when he was finally arrested for his misuse of power.

12. "An Act to Regulate the Civil Service of Cities" was passed by the Illinois General Assembly and signed into law on 20 Mar. 1895. The Civil Service Comm. of the City of Chicago was organized and officially appointed 1 July 1895.

13. Samuel Johnson, known as Dr. Johnson (1707–84), was recognized for his English dictionary published in 1755, as the founder of the Literary Club, and for other published works, including poems, book reviews, essays, and novels.

Augustus H. Strong (1836–1921), who attended and later became president of the Rochester Theological Seminary, N.Y., used this Johnson quote on p. 297 of *Systematic Theology*, his principal theological work, originally published in 1886 with new editions through 1908. JA may have been familiar with the quote from that source.

14. In 1895 John Powers owned a saloon located at 243 South Canal St., just south of Van Buren St. (400 South) and west of the South Branch of the Chicago River. His second saloon was located at 170 East Madison St. (Later 165 West), between LaSalle and Wells streets, a short distance south of city hall.

15. Dec. 1897.

16. JA and HH were involved in three different aldermanic elections. The first took place in 1895 and resulted in a win of two hundred votes for Frank Lawler, a member of the HH Men's Club. He was tempted successfully to abandon his reform platform by Nineteenth Ward boss John Powers. In the second campaign, William J. Gleason ran against Powers and lost. In 1898, with JA actively engaged in the campaign as a speaker and fund-raiser, Simeon W. Armstrong tried unsuccessfully to defeat Powers. Alderman Powers certainly had the support of the Temperance Cadets that he had helped dress in the campaign of 1898. See JA to MRS, [3 Apr. 1898]; and Article in the *HH Bulletin*, Apr. and May 1898, both below.

17. Alderman Powers lived at 79 (later 1284) Macalister Place (later West Lexington St.), the area associated with "Con Row," which was referred to in the Holy Family Parish as "the Gold Coast of the District" (Mulkerins, *Holy Family Parish Chicago*, 941).

18. Jay Gould (1836–92), leading railroad developer, speculator, and financier who had developed a seventy-seven-million-dollar fortune by the time of his death, was noted for his unscrupulous methods. He became the archetypal "robber baron."

19. In the aldermanic campaign of 1896 in the Nineteenth Ward, William J. Gleason tried to unseat John Powers.

20. Alderman John Powers's backer was Charles Yerkes. See JA to SAAH, [22?] [June 1890], n. 3; and JA to Henry Demarest Lloyd, 22 Dec. 1895, nn. 2, 4, both above.

## To Mary Rozet Smith

Hull-House 335 South Halsted Street Chicago [Ill.] [3 Apr. 1898]

Dearest:

I have n't felt that your letters[1] were too fierce and I love you more than I ever did for in the midst of this horrible election and all the rest of it,[2] I find myself depending upon your moral fiber as never before—

I have recovered from my bowel attack but have developed a fine cold by going out too soon[3]—I shall be all right in a few days I fancy but just now it is a little trying to keep still. Mary Kenney[4] is so disappointed that you are not coming home while she is here—she almost wept about it. She is wearing your old blue dress yet altho it looks pretty shabby—she confided to me that she did hope you would give her the skirt & coat you were wearing in Boston, for she never had any money to spend on clothes for herself—which seems to be quite true. She spoke at the Arts & Crafts[5] the other evening in your fine green gown—Mrs Watson[6] was there and looked a little startled I think!

Mr Powers had a fine procession last evening led by the band of the Jesuit Ch. temperance cadets[7]—it has raised much talk in the neighborhood. He gave them a 1000.oo toward their <temperance> society in return for the favor. Is n't is[8] strange. There was a picture of your humble servant on a transparancy and others such as "No petticoat gov't for us" &c. We all stood out on the corner to see it, Mr Deknatel[9] carefully shielding me from public view.

Mrs Gernon goes abroad this week for the summer, & J. Lathrop sails April 30th.

I am so glad you are coming to H.H. for a mo.[10] I am saving Mr Moores[11] room for you. Sig Valerio[12] is back, Miss Johnson[13] has resigned and openings are happening rapidly! Give my love to the family. Always yours

J.A.

ALI (SCPC, JAC; *JAPM*, 3:977–79).

1. Unfortunately none of MRS's letters to JA during 1898 are known to be extant.

2. JA and the HH residents and volunteers were totally engaged in their battle to defeat John Powers as he attempted to retain his Nineteenth Ward aldermanic seat on the Chicago City Council. JA was raising money for the effort and speaking wherever she could for reform aldermanic candidates in Chicago, but especially for Simeon W. Armstrong, a Nineteenth Ward candidate for alderman. "The campaign really grows more cheerful day by day but we are suddenly swamped for funds," JA reported to MRS on 20 Mar. 1898. "The men insist that if we had a $1000.oo we would win. I sallied forth yesterday and got a 100.oo of it and will have to keep that up all week, charming prospect isn't it?" (SCPC, JAC; *JAPM*; 3:998). Six days later, on 26 Mar., JA wrote to MRS: "We are stranded flat, and altogether am much badgered by 'the campaign'—thank goodness it is most over" (SCPC, JAC; *JAPM*, 3:1009).

JA also found herself the target of scathing attacks for her reform stand. An example was a letter dated 17 Jan. 1898, from "A voter" in Chicago, who wrote in part: "God bless the Mother that brought such a son as John Powers into this world and taught him to be a good honest noble man. His hand is ever outstretched to assist the helpless, his pocket book ever open to the needy. . . . And now for a little advice to help you to defeat the good man you have so often tried to do without success of course I can speak very plain to you, as your highest ambition is to be recognized as capable of doing a man's work. When your maker created you, it was evidently a rush job as the most important part of the work was overlooked. Here then is your only resource Did it ever occur to you while on a tour of inspection, through alleyways old barns and such places where low depraved men with criminal records may be found (such a place a virtuous woman would be afraid to go.) You might for a small sum induce one of such men to sell you his pecker and balls. It would not be much loss to him, and will be your only chance to form yourself a man. You could then go before a board of examiners chosen from the 19th ward prove yourself capable of filling a man's place. You would then have the privelage of casting a vote, and should that bold bad Johnny Powers challenge you You could produce your pecker cast your vote, and probably defeat him. Untill you can do this you are a dead one" (SCPC, JAC; *JAPM*, 3:938–39, 941–43).

By "all the rest of it," JA may have been referring to raising money and support for the new Jane Club and the new combination theater and coffeehouse building. In addition, she may have meant international actions being taken by the U.S. government that eventually led to the Spanish-American War of 1898. Late in Apr., Robert Woods wrote to JA, "I wonder if you are managing to be patriotic about the war. . . . Perhaps your non-resistence faith could be sustained by knowing how Edward Atkinson carries out his doctrine of non-indifference and laissez-fair. He applies laissez-fair to socialistic legislation now on the statutes books; and refuses to oppose it" (28 Apr. 1898, SCPC, JAC; *JAPM*, 3:1060–1). Edward Atkinson (1827–1905) was a free-trade advocate and anti-imperialist who decried the policies of President William F. McKinley and Theodore Roosevelt. He became a founder of the American Anti-Imperialist League.

The battleship U.S.S. *Maine* exploded in the harbor at Havana, Cuba, on 15 Feb. 1898, and the United States expected the cause was sabotage and began preparing for war with Spain. Spanish possessions, including Cuba, Puerto Rico, and the Philippine Islands, where the indigenous population wanted their freedom from Spain, were once again in rebellion, and while Spain granted Puerto Rico its independence in 1897, it was not realized until 1898. After the explosion on the *Maine*, the U.S. Congress passed legislation supporting a buildup of the U.S. military, and on 28 Mar. a U.S. Naval Court of Inquiry found that the *Maine* was blown apart by a mine. That was followed on 21 Apr. by President McKinley ordering a blockade of Cuba. The United States declared war on 25 Apr.

3. On 3 Apr. 1898, the day before the aldermanic election in Chicago, JA wrote to MRS: "My cold is pretty bad and I am still staying in" (SCPC, JAC; *JAPM*, 3:1028). By 12 Apr., JA was still suffering: "I had a good visit at Cedarville but came back with my cold on my lungs and Dr Hamilton announces that I have bronchitis and will have to stay inside" ([12 Apr. 1898], SCPC, JAC; *JAPM*, 3:975–76).

4. Like other former HH residents, Mary Kenney O'Sullivan returned to Chicago as a volunteer to help with the election campaign of the HH candidate, Simeon W. Armstrong. She especially tried to encourage the Roman Catholic vote for Armstrong. "Miss Addams is more worried about it than I have ever seen her about anything except the Powers speech," wrote HH resident Alice Hamilton to her cousin Agnes ([Mar?] 1898, RS, HFP). JA reported to MRS in her letter of 20 Mar.: "Mary Kenney is an everlasting trump the way she is going into the Catholic opposition question. She has seen various dignitaries and has just gone out to Hoyne Ave to see Father Muldoon for the second time. As nearly as I can make out the opposition comes from the Jesuits, headed by Father Lambert, and the parish priests themselves are not in it and do not like it. Mary talked for a long time to Father Lambert and is sure that it is jealousy of H.H. and money obligations to Powers. . . . She cried when she came back from real grief" (SCPC, JAC; *JAPM*, 3:998–99). Hamilton reported that JA was

"bitterly disappointed over the result" and "does not think that the Catholic opposition will ever be active except if the House tries again to enter politics. Anyway the Church isn't at one upon the subject, for father Kelley told Mrs. O'Sullivan that Hull-House had done more good than any church in the ward. And Mr. Murray says that Father Lambert is being very severely criticized for allowing the temperance cadets to march" (Alice Hamilton to Agnes Hamilton, [Apr. 1898], RS, HFP).

5. It is likely that Mary O'Sullivan spoke to the Arts and Crafts Society of Chicago at HH during the last Friday of Mar.

6. Mrs. Watson was a member of the Arts and Crafts Society of Chicago who gave her address in 1897 as 319 S. Robey St., Chicago.

7. On 2 Apr. 1898, the people supporting John Powers for reelection as alderman held a rally beginning at 8:30 P.M. in the Nineteenth Ward. "Alderman John Powers overawed his foemen in the nineteenth ward last night with good music and brilliant red fire. He led 3,000 of his constituents through the streets and later received the wreath of victory in Garibaldi hall," wrote the *Chicago Chronicle* the next morning, 3 Apr. 1898. "The delegation from the Cook County Democracy swung into Harrison street from Halsted in the wake of a band. Alderman Powers was in the first row of silk-tied marchers and his presence aroused the greatest enthusiasm. . . . One sign that caused merriment was 'Armstrong and McKinley are together. They want the nation dishonored. Elect John Powers alderman And Cuba will be free. Hurrah for the Maine!!!' Father Mathew's cadets had a giant turkey for a mascot. The red fire did not scare the gobbler from his perch. A cartoon on Hull house, which has directed the opposition to Alderman Powers, aroused a great deal of amusement. . . . The alderman reiterated his promises for good government and received a great reception" ("Great Rally for Powers"). Alice Hamilton reported to her cousin Agnes, "Except for cheering loudly for Powers as they passed the house nobody did anything much, indeed I think it was only small boys who yelled 'Down with Hull-House.' Mr. Murray says that a good many mothers are very angry with Father Lambert for letting their boys who are Father Mathew's temperance boys march in a saloon keeper's parade" (Sunday, Apr. 3rd [1898], in Sicherman, *Alice Hamilton*, 121). On 4 Apr. 1898, the *Chronicle* pronounced that Powers and the Democrats would win in the Nineteenth Ward.

8. JA may have meant to write "it" instead of "is."

9. Frederick H. Dekantel. See JA to MRS, [12?] [Apr.1891], n. 13, above.

10. There is no evidence to indicate that MRS did lodge in HH for a month over the summer.

11. Ernest Carroll Moore.

12. Alessandro Mastro-Valerio was living in Daphne, Ala., but made frequent trips back to HH and the Italian neighborhood. His wife stayed in Chicago and remained associated with the settlement.

13. "The Condition of the district was so much better at the close of the three years that when, at the end of that time, she was removed from office a petition signed with an imposing array of names was sent to the city officials asking that she be retained and claiming that she had not only improved the general condition of the district, but had brought up the value of property in the district. During her term of office Miss Johnson began work at 6 o'clock in the morning, working regularly for eight hours a day. She had 12 teams under her charge. She asked no favors because she was a woman, but did her work as a man would have done it, inspecting personally the alleys and narrow streets in her district. She had two days vacation during the year—Fourth of July and Christmas. Her salary was $1,000 a year" ("Woman Garbage Inspector").

## To Mary Rozet Smith

Rockford Ill April 17" 1898

Dearie—

Miss Sutliffe[1] telegraphed me yesterday P.M. and I came out to the College. Esther is in a scrape. It is <not> nearly as serious as it sounds but it does sound very badly and is in this morning Star as badly as possible.[2] She is expelled of course, I will take her to Cedarville this afternoon and come back to Chicago tomorrow morning.

Can't you come over to dinner and attend the Jane Club meeting in the evening. I want so much that you should hear the girls talk about the Club house yourself, and I myself am sadly in need of your comfort—if you could stay all night it would be fine!

Poor Esther is cast down to the ground in grief, everybody writes in saying that she has done so well this year and has been really a good student but her career here is ended now.[3]

Do please come Monday[4]—

With love to the family Always yrs

Jane Addams

P.S. The Colvin girls were coming to dinner on Sunday—Could you call at the Virginia and explain to them.[5]

ALS (SCPC, JAC; *JAPM*, 3:1046–48).

1. Phebe Temperance Sutliff (1859–1955) was born in Warren, Ohio, one of six children of lawyer and active abolitionist Levi Sutliff and his wife, Phebe L. Marvin. She graduated from Vassar (B.A. 1880) and Cornell (M.A. 1890) and attended the Univ. of Zurich, Switzerland. Her positions before she became president of RC, 1896–1901, were principal, Hiram College, 1885–86, and professor of history and English literature at RS, 1887–89. During her tenure as president of RC, the school developed more rigorous academic programs. She left the school in 1901 to care for her mother in Warren, where she lived for the remainder of her life.

In Warren she began a career as a community activist. She was the founder and first president of the Warren branch of the AAUW. In addition, she helped organize the Warren Urban League, Visiting Nurse Assn., and Child Labor League. Her concern with immigrants led her to found an evening school for newcomers who were working toward citizenship. She organized political education sessions for women who had just received the vote, and in 1924 she became assistant secretary of the Democratic Party National Convention. Sutliff also served as a trustee of the Warren Public Library from 1938 until her death and was its first woman president.

Sutliff and JA worked together to improve RC. JA attempted to help her gain additional trustees to bring more financial support to the school, and she sent qualified and aspiring young women students to Rockford, Ill.

2. On 17 Apr. 1898, the *Rockford (Ill.) Evening Star* reported "Grief at the College. Escapade of Two Students Results in Dismissal. Occurred Friday Evening." Esther Margaret Linn and a classmate sneaked out of the college to meet "two well-known young men. What hour they intended coming back is not known," the *Star* continued, "but it was not until after the breakfast hour that they re-appeared. There was no hope for them to get in without detec-

tion, and they walked in with as brave an air as they could muster." They had not planned on an all-night adventure, but they were unable to return undetected as they had planned because a faculty member bolted the door they had planned to use to return. The newspaper also announced that one of the girls was a "relative" of "a prominent Chicago lady connected with Hull House, who is already identified with the college."

3. In responding to a letter, no longer known to be extant, from Phebe Sutliff about worries she had about Esther Margaret Linn, JA wrote on 18 Mar. 1898: "I want of course to sustain your decision in whatever you think best for Esther, and it will doubtless be the best arrangement to have no more visits outside, this year. I shall hope to find time commencement week for a talk with you about it. I had supposed all was going unusually well this <year> or I should have made an effort to come out to see you earlier—I should have made it the most important thing" (RC Archives; *JAPM*, 3:1312). For additional information on JA's troubled relationship with Esther Margaret Linn, see EGS [for JA] to SA, 8 Feb. [1895], n. 5, above. Soon JA had Esther enrolled in Morgan Park Academy, Chicago, and by the fall of 1898, Esther had become a junior college student at the Univ. of Chicago.

Esther Linn met Charles Baker Hulbert (1880–1939) at the Univ. of Chicago when both were students there in 1899. According to JA, Esther and Charlie were secretly married in Sept. 1900: "The foolish things meant to keep it a secret for six years until he finished his university and medical course. The inevitable thing happened." Esther became pregnant with the couple's first child. Although the university was willing to keep the marriage quiet so that Charles Hulbert could complete his initial degree, JA demanded a "prompt and public announcement" of the marriage and was relieved when the newspapers "implied no evil." JA also reported to Florence Kelley that she told Dr. Harper, "Academic morals had gone to the devil" (30 June 1901, Columbia Univ., Manuscript Dept., Kelley Family Papers; *JAPM*, 4:147–49). Esther and Charles left school, and neither ever graduated.

JA helped Charles find a job as the secretary of the Anthropology Com., beginning in 1889, and then the Anthropology Dept. of the 1903 Louisiana Purchase Exposition. She traveled with him to St. Louis on 12 and 13 July 1899 to help with his interview for the position and to advise on living quarters. She wrote to SAAH that she found their new nephew "open hearted and affectionate" (14 July 1901, IU, Lilly, SAAH; *JAPM*, 4:159), but to Florence Kelley she indicated that she found him at twenty-one years of age "a bright boy who has never earned fifty dollars in his life" (30 June 1901, Columbia Univ., Manuscripts Dept., Kelley Family Papers; *JAPM*, 4:149). The Hulberts settled in St. Louis, where their first child, Esther Louise (called Louise), was born 25 Oct. 1901. Eventually, they had three more children: Mary Addams Hulbert (1902–97), who never married; Eri Baker Hulbert (1905–55), who married Margaret ("Maggie") Hodges Brown; and Jane Addams Hulbert (1911–82), who married Richard Charles Ragle (1908–87). Louise married three times: Ashleigh Woodruff Brittain (1898–1971), in 1922; John Shedd Prescott (d. 1935), in 1934; and finally Richard Torchia (1898 in Italy–1973 in Mariposa, Calif.), in 1963. She died in 1984.

Charles Hulbert was the son of Ethelyn ("Etta") E. Spencer (1849–1926) and Eri Baker Hulbert (1841–1907), who was trained as a Baptist minister and became a professor of church history before becoming the first dean of the Univ. of Chicago Divinity School, 1892–1907. Although a "miler" on the Univ. of Chicago track team, Charles was not robust. He had typhoid fever in 1898–99, and then, at the time of the birth of Louise, he spent three months in a St. Louis hospital for what was diagnosed as amoebic dysentery. His recovery from that illness was difficult. By 1905, after the Louisiana Purchase Exposition closed, Charles Hulbert found a position as clerk and salesman for the Indian Curio Shop of the Fred Harvey restaurant at the Santa Fe Railroad train station in Albuquerque, N.M. The entire family moved west in 1905; however, by Dec. 1906, Charles Hulbert, who had been borrowing money from family and friends in order to make ends meet, returned to Chicago and began to search for new and better-paying employment. JA wanted the family back in Chicago and tried to help him search for well-paying employment; however, he chose not to accept a potential offer at the Western Electric Co. His father died in 1907, and Charles moved his family back to Chicago in the fall of 1907. In Jan. 1908, he and the three Hulbert children suffered through whooping cough together. His recovery took several months and was the most difficult. Between 1909 and 1910, he worked as a bookkeeper for the Chicago, Burlington & Quincy Railroad. He fell ill once again during the summer of 1910, and the problem was diagnosed as tuberculosis. He spent at least two months in a sanitarium located in Naperville, Ill. When he was discharged, the family retreated to the Lakeside, Mich., cabin that JA had given them, for what remained of the summer, and he continued to rest. On returning to Chicago, he began working for a real estate firm. He was extremely nervous and addicted to alcohol, for which he consulted a number of doctors. In the meantime, he started his own real estate firm, C. E. Hulbert and Co., where he served as a broker between building owners and business owners seeking space to rent, especially in Chicago's garment district to the west of the Chicago Loop, Wells St. to the Chicago River and Madison to Harrison streets.

During each major illness, beginning with the whooping cough in 1908, Charles Hulbert experienced an increasing amount of paralysis, first in his fingers and then in his left leg. As his health improved after each illness, the paralysis diminished. Then in 1913, he had a severe bout of paralysis, and finally his illness was diagnosed as multiple sclerosis. He continued to work, but with decreasing effectiveness, and Esther had to begin helping him. She recalled in her autobiographical statement, "[I]n 1917 when, I had 4 children (16, 15 12 & 5 years old) my husband in a wheel-chair from Multiple Sclerosis, we had no money & Charlie had not worked for some months & had been struggling with the fact that his disease would probably get worse as time went on. I had never been in business or even had a job of any kind. . . . But after talking things over we decided I must go in to business with him. . . . We decided I must go down, learn the business & do all the street business of making personal contacts with the business heads, showing space, talking prices—seeing owners & getting the space to rent etc. It was a hard job, indeed for me to go into these business places (manufacturing jobbing etc.) and talk to the head of the firm. . . . Many times I walked past the place several times before I would steel myself to go into a business place. . . . I remember well how very scared I was." She also recalled: "I was the first woman who had even tried the business which was considered one of the hardest renting businesses in Chicago" ("Autobiography of an Unknown," 15–16, JAPP, Hulbert). By 1922 she had become a full-fledged broker and partner in the business, located at suite 566 in the Insurance Exchange Building at 175 West Jackson St. As the paralysis in her husband's legs and arms progressed, Esther Hulbert became increasingly active in the business as well as her husband's caregiver at home. By 1927 Esther and Charles Hulbert had retired to Ft. Lauderdale, Fla., where she became a full-time caregiver. Before he died in July 1939, he was totally paralyzed by the disease. Esther then moved to Berkeley, Calif., where she lived with her daughters Louise and Mary, until her death.

In her partial autobiographical statement, Esther Hulbert recalled: "[T]he fact that my Mother died when I was 13 and Aunt Jane became my Guardian made a diff- in my life." She added that "Aunt Jane took me & my brothers in as her own children & was a wonderful Mother to us all" ("Autobiography of an Unknown," 1, 6). Throughout Esther's life with Charles Hulbert, JA maintained a surrogate mother–like relationship with the Hulberts. JA wrote an immediate note in reply to the telegram Charles Hulbert sent to JA announcing the birth of Louise: "I want to congratulate you and Esther with all my heart—and send my dearest love to the little daughter" (24 Oct. 1901, SCPC, JAC; *JAPM*, 4:222). JA wrote to Esther on 6 July 1915 just as she returned from Europe: "I find myself very anxious to see my family" (JAPP, Hulbert). No matter where JA traveled, she kept in touch by writing frequent notes to the Hulbert family. When JA died in 1935, Esther was surprised to discover that JA left her $4,373 in her will; she had anticipated that her brother Stanley would receive any funds remaining in JA's estate. Esther's brother James Weber Linn recalled that just before her death, JA reported to him: "[I]f there has been any heroism in our family, it has been Esther's" (James Weber Linn to Esther Linn Hulbert, 20 May 1935, UIC, JAMC, Hulbert).

4. 18 Apr. 1898.

5. Jessie and Katharine Colvin, daughters of William H. Colvin, lived at the Virginia Hotel, located at 78 Rush St. on Chicago's North Side. An 1892 Chicago guide reported that it was "[o]ne of the largest and most beautiful private and family hotels in the world" (Flinn, *Chicago . . . a Guide, 1892*, 358).

## Article in the *Hull-House Bulletin*

*The municipal election took place on 5 April 1898, and the next day Jane Addams reported to Mary Rozet Smith: "We are completely snowed under but curious to tell not so blue and harried as before election. . . . I got so blue yesterday that I brought your picture down from the studio and have it this minute over my mantel from which I get a surprising comfort—I do wish you were back."[1] Simeon W. Armstrong and his coalition of Republican and independent voters polled only 2,219 votes to John Powers's 5,450 votes.[2] Hull-House resident Alice Hamilton wrote to her cousin Agnes about Jane Addams's reaction shortly after the election was decided: "She . . . fully expected a larger vote for Armstrong."[3] Jane Addams wrote the following curt announcement and explanation of the election results in the combined April and May issue of the* Hull-House Bulletin.

Chicago, Ill. Apr. and May 1898

### THE ALDERMANIC CAMPAIGN

The aldermanic campaign which was carried on with great vigor in the Nineteenth Ward, resulted in the return to the city council of the man who has represented the ward for the last ten years. The issues of the campaign were clearly defined, and yet it is impossible to believe that they were fully understood by the majority of the voters.[4] One must assume that they cared so much for the personal favors and jobs within the gift of the alderman that they failed to see in his return to the council a menace to the best interests of the city. It will be a matter of growth and education, but the time must certainly come when the representative of the ward will stand for the higher interests of his constituents and of the city.

PD (*HH Bulletin* 3, nos. 4–5 [Apr. and May 1898]: 4; *JAPM*, 53:674).

1. SCPC, JAC; *JAPM*, 3:1031–32.
2. "Scenes at the Polls."
3. [Apr. 1898], RS, HFP.
4. JA announced the issues of the campaign on p. 6 of the Mar. 1898 issue of the *HH Bulletin*.
"1. We demand a municipal government composed of capable, honest men.
2. We demand a council which will serve, not corrupt corporations, but the people.
3. We demand that public moneys be expended for the benefit of the people.

4. We are unalterably opposed to the granting of long-term franchises.
5. We demand that no franchises or special privileges be granted without adequate compensation to the people.
6 We believe in laborers rather than in contractors.
7. We therefore demand that all laborers employed in city work be employed and paid by the city directly and not by or through agents or contractors.
8. We believe that all municipal employes should be selected on the ground of fitness rather than party affiliations.
9. Believing that well-paved, well-cleaned and well-lighted streets increase property values and conserve public health and morals, we demand that the nineteenth ward receive its just share of the public moneys annually expended for these purposes" (*JAPM*, 53:664).

## Article in the *Evening Gazette*

Terre Haute, Ind. 10 August 1898

TO GIVE A DRAMA.

HULL HOUSE CHICAGO TO PUT IN EFFECT SOME NEW PLANS.

Chicago Chronicle: Hull house is to give the west side a new theater, not a playhouse where the gay soubrette and the heavy villain in dyed mustache will thrill the shouting gallery with the gory lines of "The Terror of Rocky Gulch" and similar plays, but, instead, one where the young people of the neighborhood, centering about South Halsted and Polk street can find exercise for their dramatic talents. In fact, this theater, the construction of which [h]as just been made possible by the gifts of a number of generous women, will be the means of the opening up for Hull house of a new line of work among the cosmopolitan population of the district in which it stands.

The theater is going to be an elaborate structure. It will have a frontage of seventy-five feet on Polk street and will fill in all space between the present children's wing of the house and the alley on the west. The building will be forty-five feet deep and will have a total height of four stories.[1] The first floor will be used as a coffee-house and will take the place of the one which Hull house has now out-grown.[2] Above this floor will be the theater, which will be entered from a broad vestibule. The seating capacity of this home of amateur drama will [b]e exactly 396, almost evenly divided between the parquet and the bar[n]quet and the balcony.[3]

The stage, upon the plans for which the architects are now turning all their best efforts, will have a depth of twenty feet and a width of thirty-five feet.[4] The exterior walls of the building will be in brick and stone and will harmonize with the other structures constituting Hull house. The interior treatment of the coffee-house will be old English. That of the theater will be in harmony, but the general color scheme will be much lighter.

The new Coffee House and Theatre Building replaced the former Gymnasium and Coffee House Building on Polk Street, located on the right side of the drawing, in 1899. The Coffee House was located on the ground floor, and the auditorium with a much larger theatrical stage was on the second floor. Jane Addams celebrated its opening coincident with the recognition of the settlement's tenth anniversary in October 1899 (*Commons* 5, no. 5 [or whole no. 37] [Sept. 1899]: 7). The first Gymnasium and Coffee House, moved west on Polk Street, appears on the right side of the drawing.

A LONG-CHERISHED PLAN.

The building of this theater is the materialization of one of Miss Jane Addams' long-cherished plans. Long experience with the people with whom she had to work had shown that lessons could best be taught from the stage. There were many who would not read books, who could not give their attention to the ordinary lecturer, but who were constant attendants upon such dramatic entertainments as were afforded by the cheap vaudeville shows and theaters of the district.

Finally she decided to use the stage as an adjunct to her work, and accordingly the house gymnasium was provided with the necessary theatrical accessories[5] and a dramatic association was organized.[6] . . .

GIFTS ARE MADE.

Early in the spring of the present year Miss Addams determined that better provision should be made for this branch of her work during the coming year and finally told a number of the friends of the settlement of her elaborate plans. As a result one woman[7] pledged $5,000 and others[8] offered additional assistance until $12,000 had been raised. Miss Helen Culver tendered the use of the ground on Polk street for a term ending 1920 and Pond and Pond, who had designed the other buildings of the house, were ordered to begin the work of preparing the plan. They now have their designs so far advanced that the work of construction will begin by Sept. 1.

In speaking of her plans yesterday Miss Addams said: "Yes, we have decided to give the west side a new theater and it will be decidedly unique among the places of amusement of this section of the city. A number of our friends have aided us and before the winter has far advanced our dramatic association will have a new home. The young people around us have shown really remarkable dramatic ability. With our better facilities for the work we will enlarge its scope. Plays in Italian, Polish and in other languages of this district will be given[9] and I confidently believe that the results will be even more gratifying than even the most sanguine of us have yet dared to hope."

PD (*Terre Haute (Ind.) Evening Gazette*, 10 Aug. 1898, SCPC, JAC; *JAPM*, 55:448).

1. The *Chicago Chronicle*'s article, reprinted in the Terre Haute newspaper, was laudatory, hopeful, and, as it turned out, incorrect, insofar as the cost of the project and its construction time line. The former Gymnasium and Coffee House Building was saved and moved to a new location on Polk St., directly west of its previous location. By 1900 JA had raised the $19,203 necessary "[f]or moving the Hull House gymnasium sixteen ft west, providing greatly increased facilities for the baths and gymnasium. For adding another story to accomodate the shops and Labor Museum" (Addams, [Fund Raising Record], Jan. 1895–Jan. 1905; *JAPM*, 49:1787). Stanley McCormick gave by far the largest gift for the move and renovation of the structure designed by the Ponds and built in 1893 (see JA to MRS, 23 Mar. 1898, n. 7, above).

The new Coffee House and Theatre Building was completed in 1899. It was three stories tall and provided a home for the new and larger coffeehouse on the lower level, along with a renovated and larger kitchen area and a completely new theater on the second and third levels. It opened officially on Wednesday, 25 Oct. 1899. See Article in the *Commons*, 31 Oct. 1899, below.

2. Business in the old Coffee House was booming. See JA to MRS, 23 Mar. 1898, n. 7, above.

3. Louise de Koven Bowen provided $2,000 in 1901 so that a balcony could be added at the west end of the new theater.

4. For architects' plans of the combination Coffee House and Theatre dated 21 Oct. 1898, see UIC, JAMC, HH Assn.; and *JAPM*, Addendum 10:3. See also Article in the *Commons*, 31 Oct. 1899, n. 5, below.

5. At the start of the settlement in 1889, the only stage JA and EGS had for presentations was an alcove platform on the north side of the large drawing room–dining room near the entrance to the Hull home. The alcove stage was destroyed in 1899 when the new Coffee House and Theatre Building was constructed and the north side of the first floor of the original settlement building was renovated. "The workmen are in the hall now, tearing down the wall between the drawing room and hall," reported Alice Hamilton to her cousin Agnes. "You see our new building not only took away the alcove, but closed up the two back windows, which made the room very dark, so it is to be thrown into the hall by a big arch-way. We are to get into the next coffee-house through a door in the drawing room" (24 Feb. 1899, RS, HFP). When JA built the new gymnasium in 1893, she included a stage at one end of the facility that could then be treated as an auditorium.

6. JA created a committee to oversee the formation of a HH Dramatic Assn. (see also Article in the *HH Bulletin*, 1 Dec. 1897, above). When established, JA knew, the new program would require a proper theater.

7. JA soon discovered that $12,000 would purchase about half of the new building that she wanted. The actual cost of the new structure was $25,021.85. HH supporter Katherine Colvin provided the first $5,000.

8. Helen Culver also gave $5,000 in addition to providing the land rent-free on which the structure was built. Louise de Koven Bowen offered $3,500. Mary Wilmarth gave $1,657, and Nancy Foster, Mrs. K. S. Adams, and Anita McCormick Blaine donated $1,000 each. Among the male donors were F. W. Morgan, who contributed $1,564, and Sidney Kent and Allison V. Armour, each of whom gave $1,000. An assortment of smaller gifts ranging from $50 to $500 made up the remainder, with interest from the account adding $84.

9. "One of the most interesting entertainments of the year will be the Greek play which comes early in December. This is to be enacted by the Greeks resident in Chicago. Our colleges occasionally give Greek plays, but American students have been the actors. It is a unique experiment to have genuine Greeks portray Homer" (*HH Bulletin* 3, no. 12 [Nov. and Dec. 1899]: 2; *JAPM*, 53:720). *The Return of Odysseus*, a six-act play adapted from Homer's *Odyssey* by Mabel Hay Barrows (1873–1931), was presented on 6, 7, and 8 Dec. 1899 in the new theater. The first Greek play was so successful that a second, *The Ajax of Sophocles,* also adapted by Barrows, was presented in Dec. 1903.

Barrows was the daughter of reformers Samuel June and Isabel Chaplin Barrows. Born in Cambridge, Mass., she was a dramatic director and dancer. She owned the plays that she had adapted and the costumes in which they were to be presented and offered herself as the director who would help present them. "I should be very glad to give my services for the training and management, . . . and the use of my costume paid for," she wrote to JA. "My regular terms are $300. and all expenses. But I have always had such an intense interest in settlement life,—serving my apprenticeship at Denison House, . . . that I should count it a privilege, to give free service in this way" (22 Nov. 1898, SCPC, JAC; *JAPM*, 3:1214). Barrows wed Henry Raymond Mussey (1875–1940), a professor of economics at Columbia Univ. and Wellesley College, who became managing editor of the *Nation* (1918–20, 1929–30). Soon many of the ethnic groups in the neighborhood were using the theater for plays in their native languages, including Italian, Polish, and Russian.

## To Mary Rozet Smith

Hull-House 335 South Halsted Street Chicago [Ill.] Oct. 6" 1898

Dearie

Dont you think that you are treating your old love a little badly to be so soon "off" with H.H. and "on" with the new?[1]

My mind is filled with speculation as to what you are doing and never a word do I hear. Mr Taborski shot himself[2] last Saturday and the remaining three members of the family have been sleeping in my room since, we buried him out of the $100 <u>00</u> you left me, the cheapest "grave up" funeral we ever had for $37.<u>00</u>. We are now moving them, they are so frightened about going back to the same place, Sabrina[3] just saved her mother from being murdered. Mrs Lindahl has gone to her husband and we are getting poor distracted [Miss?] Kearnan off into the country.

Affairs have been lively I assure you and but for the quiet hour & a half in wh I am having my bust[4] done at the Lewis Institute,[5] there is little leisure. (The bust by the way in its present stage looks exactly like my Aunt Lydia[6] with her full sixty years)

The Tolstoy day was really quite brilliant altho a little incoherent[7]—I uttered not one sentence about him wh I had ever used before and I quite longed to have you hear how versatile I could be! Mr Yarros[8] was of course brilliant. Mrs Blackman[9] & her [son's?] wife asked to come to morrow to lunch is n't that getting on with a whilom enemy!

Please write me if only a word, I love you just the same and in a more <u>personal</u> and <u>individualistic</u> & <u>thorough</u> manner!! Always yrs

J.A—

Love to Miss Wald[10]

ALI (SCPC, JAC; *JAPM*, 3:1171–73).

1. MRS, who was seriously considering how to live more productively for the benefit of others, was spending a month with Lillian Wald to experience life at the Nurses' Settlement, also called the Henry Street Settlement, in New York City.

When JA and EGS were opening HH in Sept. 1889, Lillian D. Wald (1867–1940) had just become a probationary nursing student at the New York School of Nursing in New York City. Wald, a public health nurse who helped establish public health nursing throughout the United States, social reformer, and settlement house leader, was born in Cincinnati. She was the second of four children of Jewish immigrants Marcus D. ("Max") and Minnie Schwarz Wald. They had come to the United States in the late 1840s, and Max Wald became a dealer in optical goods. After living for a short time in Dayton, Ohio, the Wald family settled somewhat permanently in Rochester, N. Y., near other members of the Wald and Schwarz families.

Lillian Wald attended Miss Cruttenden's English-French Boarding and Day School until she was eighteen years old. While her family continued to groom her for a life as a wife and mother in the upper-middle-class Jewish society in Rochester, Lillian began to exert her independence and signal her hope for another kind of life. She found employment first as a clerk and a year later as an analyst for a financial firm.

As a youngster, she had dreamed of becoming a nurse for the physician she expected her favorite brother, Alfred, to be. Unfortunately, he did not become a physician and died unexpectedly while he was doing business in California in 1885. The idea of nursing was presented to her again when she became intrigued by the life and duties of the nurse who cared for her sister Julia during her first pregnancy. As a result, Lillian applied to the New York School of Nursing to become a student. She pronounced that she had "a good education" and that her "days were 'devoted to society,' study and housekeeping duties such as practical mothers consider essential to a daughter's education." She also admitted that she felt the "need of serious, definite work" and indicated that she was choosing nursing because she felt "a natural aptitude for it and because it has for years appeared to me womanly, congenial work" (Siegel, *Lillian Wald*, 15–16). Wald entered the nursing program and graduated in Mar. 1891.

For a year, 1891–92, Lillian was a staff nurse at the New York Juvenile Asylum in New York City, a job she found disheartening. Her experience with the poor, inadequate, sometimes cruel, and unfair treatment of the children in the facility probably helped establish her lifelong commitment to promoting the cause of child welfare in the United States.

Seeking more education, in the fall of 1892 she enrolled in the Woman's Medical College of New York. Once again, she found herself in the easy and comfortable company of other women who had similar hopes and goals and began to build firm and long-lasting friendships. Working in the college clinic, she became even more aware of the daily problems that immigrant women and their families faced. To help, she volunteered to teach a class for newly arrived immigrant women one morning each week on hygiene and home care at 267 Henry St. in the midst of New York City's Lower East Side. Appalled by what she discovered as she interacted with these women, she came to believe that it was time for her to give up study and act.

With Mary M. Brewster (1864–1901), who became Mrs. William Stone Booth in 1897, a nursing-school friend, she set out to live among the poor, discover the ill, and nurse them back to health in their own homes. To support her enterprise, she appealed to Mrs. Solomon Loeb and her son-in-law Jacob Schiff (1847–1920) for financial support. Between them they guaranteed $120 per month for living expenses and supplies for the two women. Those two supporters continued to provide help for Wald into the future and helped her attract to her program other financial angels, primarily from the New York Jewish society.

In the beginning, Lillian and Mary lived at the College Settlement on Rivington St. and, in the process, learned something about the settlement movement. At summer's end, the two women found their own rooms on the top floor of a six-floor walk-up at 27 Jefferson St. There they established themselves as visiting nurses under the auspices of the Board of Health, with badges announcing their position and special uniforms to distinguish themselves from other more expensive nursing services. Wald and Brewster charged only $0.10 for their visits. Soon other reformers and nurses began to offer them help and join their nursing effort. Among the early converts were Lavinia Lloyd Dock (1858–1956), who became a significant leader in the development of nursing in the United States, and Josephine Shaw Lowell (1843–1905), a reformer who helped found the New York COS and Consumers' League of New York and worked for woman suffrage.

The Visiting Nurse Service was well established by 1893 and continued to focus on providing an ever-increasing number of nursing services in the Lower East Side and in other neighborhoods in New York City. By 1895 Jacob Schiff had purchased a house at 265 Henry St., which he remodeled for Wald and her program. Soon Wald's financial supporters doubled the size of the lodging by adding to the first building the house next door at 267 Henry St., where Wald had once taught housekeeping and hygiene to newly arrived immigrants. In these two buildings, Wald and her coworkers lived and worked in social settlement–like cooperation. By 1900 Wald could count among her "family," as she called them, fifteen full-time nurses, most of whom became lifelong friends.

Wald's move from a primarily nursing service to include social settlement programs began in 1893 and slowly expanded, as she began to realize that the people she tended needed more than simple nursing help. By 1895 Wald and her helpers had created in the backyard of their houses one of the first play spaces for children of the Lower East Side of the city. In 1898 Wald was one of the founders of the Outdoor Recreation League, which helped establish the area's first neighborhood park. The nurses, led by Wald, gave testimony before various tenement-house commissions and helped to educate people about sanitation. In conjunction with the University and College settlements, Wald and the nurses participated in an investigation of dispossessed tenants in 1897. They worked for improved education and better schools and pushed the board of education to create an opportunity for children with physical and mental disabilities to have a classroom experience. They continued to expand their nursing programs, and toward the end of the 1890s Wald created the first convalescent home for workers, including women and children. She was also eventually successful in establishing the first public nurse program in public schools, when she convinced the New York City Board of Health to mandate the service.

Wald's Nurses Settlement became the Henry Street Settlement when it was incorporated on 27 Mar. 1903. It continued to expand its program as a neighborhood center committed to improving the civic, educational, and social aspects of life in the Lower East Side and as the

Nursing Service into other areas of New York City. By 1910 Wald was a major influence in establishing a department of nursing and health at the Teachers' College of Columbia Univ. She later convinced the Red Cross to establish a nursing program that became the Town and Country Nursing Service.

It is likely that JA and Wald met for the first time in Mar. 1898 when Wald and her friend Helen McDowell visited JA at HH and brought with them exhibits from the Henry Street Settlement for the Arts and Crafts Society Exhibition held at the Chicago Art Institute, 23 Mar.–15 Apr. 1898. MRS spent some time with Wald in Oct. 1898 to experience the work that the nurses were doing in their settlement, and JA visited in Nov. 1898. These times together cemented the lifetime friendship that blossomed among the three women. JA quickly added Wald to her network of progressive reformers associates and to those women she considered good personal friends.

After JA's initial visit to Henry Street, which took place coincident with a gathering of the Social Reform Club, of which Wald had been a member since 1894, to hear a plea from Aylmer Maude for help with the resettlement of the Doukhobors from Russia, Wald confided to JA: "I am tongue tied when deep feeling forces me but I am struggling between the longing to weep and the longing to say in more articulate language to you how much, how very much realizing you is to me." Wald wrote of "an everlasting debt to you that can never reimburse the world as it should. It may be of some little service to you that one small group has a deeper desire <than ever> to press its Service into and for a fairer society for having touched you. It isn't at all said as it should be but turn your perceptions here and know, that we want to be good and, like children looking up to you for guidance" (15 Nov. 1898, SCPC, JAC; *JAPM*, 3:1206–8).

During the next thirty-five years, Wald and JA often worked together for similar causes, some personal and others public. Wald provided access to sources for the brass trays and vessels with which JA enjoyed decorating her new HH dining room in 1899 and helped find items for the Labor Museum as well. By 1899 Wald had taken JA's nephew John Addams Linn, who was beginning work in New York City, under her wing. Both women tried unsuccessfully to find Florence Kelley appropriate work as chief factory inspector in New York. When Kelley became general secretary for the National Consumers' League in 1899, she became a resident at Henry Street, where she happily lodged until at least 1924. Wald and JA's mutual respect and love for Kelley became another part of the glue that bound the two women. They also had similar interests in child welfare, education, and housing; they shared ideas, applauded one another's settlement successes, visited one another's settlements, and shared vacations, sometimes in Maine and once in 1925 in Mexico, when Wald accompanied JA and MRS on the jaunt.

Although Wald was supportive of women and their efforts to use labor unions to secure equal treatment and wages with men workers, and was especially helpful during the shirtwaist workers' efforts in 1910–11, the Triangle Shirtwaist Factory Fire, and millworkers' strike in Lawrence, Mass., in 1912, her primary focus remained child welfare. Wald was a successful advocate for her Henry Street program, and as the settlement grew, her need for financial support increased. Her financial supporters made it clear to her that to keep their support for her Nursing Service and settlement, she needed to be very careful about her efforts on behalf of organized labor. At the same time, they applauded her commitment to child welfare.

In 1904 Wald, Kelley, and others were instrumental in founding the National Child Labor Com. with the goal of presenting the horrors of child labor to the public and working to enact state and federal legislation to end the practice. For the remainder of her life, her commitment to this effort never wavered. Wald, joined by JA, Kelley, and others, was successful in encouraging the creation of the U.S. Children's Bureau and helping to install Julia C. Lathrop as its first head.

When war came to Europe in 1914, both Wald and JA became leaders in efforts to support peace. Both feared the loss of social reform gains and progress, and both worked to prevent hostilities and, when that failed, hoped to keep the United States from entering the fighting. Wald and JA were two of the three people who called a group of reform leaders together at Henry Street to form an organization to oppose the U.S. entry into the war. One of the results of that meeting was the creation of the American Union against Militarism (AUAM), organized in 1916. Wald served as president of the executive board. In Jan. 1915, she joined JA in Washington, D.C., to help initiate the WPP. Throughout 1915 and even after the United States declared war on Germany on 6 Apr. 1917, Wald continued her antiwar work.

During World War I, Wald worked as head of the Com. on Nursing and Child Welfare for New York City to carry out the "Save the Baby Campaign" launched by the U.S. Children's Bureau. She also continued her work with the AUAM to carry out a program that continued quietly to oppose militarism and degradation of civil liberties. She opposed war, but she wanted to support her government. With the AUAM taking more radical positions with regard to the war effort than Wald was willing to take, she resigned from her leadership position and from membership in the organization, which eventually became the ACLU. She chose to try to influence positions about militarism and war after hostilities had ceased. Before war's end, Lillian Wald had been appointed chief of the Nurses Emergency Council, charged with dealing with the flu epidemic that raged in the United States and worldwide.

In the immediate aftermath of the war, Wald and many of her progressive reformer friends were attacked by leaders of the Red Scare. They were subjected to name-calling and finger-pointing by those who feared the spread of socialism and communism. Wald and JA and many of their friends found themselves investigated by their government and listed publicly by Archibald Stevenson of the U.S. Military Intelligence Bureau as one of sixty-two men and women identified as a "Who's Who in Pacifism" who had supposedly thwarted the war effort. New York State created the Lusk Com. in Jan. 1919 especially to target radicals in settlement houses and schools. Once again, Wald and JA were identified as trying to overthrow the government. Mrs. Elizabeth Dilling also identified Wald, as she had JA and Florence Kelley, as one of her "Who Is Who In Radicalism?" in her 1934 publication *The Red Network*. In the midst of these more than ten years of attacks, Wald went to Europe to attend an international conference on public health nursing, consulted for the Red Cross, and was appointed an adviser to the Child Welfare Division of the League of Nations. She also attended the conference of women in Zurich, Switzerland, in which the WILPF was formed.

Throughout the 1920s, Wald continued to develop the Henry Street Settlement and raise funds to keep it and the Nursing Service functioning. She also continued to support the cause of social reform where she could. She became vice-president of the American Assn. for Labor Legislation. She appealed for the release of Nicola Sacco and Bartolomeo Vanzetti, supported the independence movement in the Philippine Islands, and worked to abolish capital punishment. After visiting the new USSR to advise on public health issues, she became a member and officer of the American Society for Cultural Relations with Russia.

By the late 1920s, Lillian Wald's health had begun to fail. She resigned as head worker of Henry Street in 1933, yet remained as chairman of the settlement's board of directors. She spent more and more of her time in her home, "House-on-the-Pond," in Westport, Conn., which she had acquired in 1917. JA sometimes visited her there. A constant worry for Wald was the rise of Nazi Germany and its treatment of Jews. She took time to write the second volume of her autobiography, *Windows on Henry Street*, to accompany her first volume, *House on Henry Street*, first issued in 1915. She also provided the afterword to *Forty Years at HH*, the combination of JA's two previously published autobiographies, issued by Macmillan in 1935. It gave her an opportunity to offer a eulogy for JA. In it Wald recalled JA's commitment to world peace and to helping others as well as "her charm, her authority, her quick wit, her tolerance and generosity, her wisdom and charity. . . . Her humor, her gayety, her lack of pretense, her refusal to assume any role of greatness. . . . She had passionate beliefs, and power behind them to drive through to a goal, but she was never dogmatic in her conviction. She always held that she had more to learn and than to teach. . . . The last word on anything . . . never said" (456–58). Weakened by repeated illnesses, anemia, and heart problems, Wald died in Sept. 1940 from a cerebral hemorrhage. Numerous memorial services followed, ending with a public meeting in Carnegie Hall.

Wald received many honors during her lifetime and after her death. In 1912 she was selected to be the first president of the National Organization for Public Health Nursing. She was honored on her seventieth birthday with a special radio broadcast during which a number of distinguished leaders, including Franklin D. Roosevelt, praised her service and accomplishments, and she received a distinguished service award from New York City. Hundreds of people from her Henry Street neighborhood as well as her Westport, Conn., neighbors also gave greetings. A public playground near the Henry Street Settlement was dedicated to her in 1937. In 1947 a new low-income development was named the Lillian Wald Houses. She was honored in the Hall of Fame of New York Univ. in 1970 and in 1974 was among the first inductees in the new American Nurses Assn. Hall of Fame.

2. Frank Taborsky (1845?–98) and his wife, Sabina Polnany Taborsky, lived with their children at 105 Bunker St. (later 630 West Grenshaw). According to the *Chicago Record*: "After attempting to strangle his wife and children, Frank Taborsky, a shoemaker . . . blew out his brains with a double-barrel shotgun at 11 o'clock Saturday morning. Taborsky was in the habit of leaving his family for a week at a time mending shoes in the suburbs. Every Saturday he would come home, and, according to Mrs. Taborsky would beat and choke his family. Often he informed the mother that the family should die together. . . . Twice Mrs. Taborsky with her two children—Emma and Sabina—were cared for by neighbors. . . . Taborsky was indicted by the grand jury two weeks ago on a charge of assault with a deadly weapon, and with intent to kill" ("Killed Himself with a Gun," 3 Oct. 1898).

3. Sabina Taborsky (1885–1913) became a schoolteacher and died at age twenty-seven from pulmonary tuberculosis. Sabina's sister, Emma (b. 1887), and her mother were living at 5235 West Agatite St., on Chicago's North Side in 1920.

4. On 16 Nov. 1898, JA told SAAH: "Mrs Peck, Miss Culvers niece has been doing a bust of my head—In the course of her studies she tried one of pa from the various pictures which I had of him—It has come out very well indeed, and if she can make a few changes in the expression of the mouth, I shall be very well satisfied with it" (IU, Lilly, SAAH; *JAPM*, 3:1210). Unfortunately, JA was not pleased with the Peck bust. Almost a year later, during the period when she was sitting for her portrait to be painted by HH resident Carl Eric Olaf Lindin (1869–1942), she wrote to MRS: "The portrait comes on apace and there are some who like it very much, including G. Barnum who has been amusing me as I sit; I have tried my best to keep off that terrible 'Bust' feeling which I still have whenever I see Mrs Peck" (30 Aug. 1899, SCPC, JAC; *JAPM*, 3:1424–25).

Emily Ewing Peck (1855–1921) was born in Coldspring, N.Y., the daughter of Robert Finley and Aurelia Culver Ewing. Aurelia Culver and Helen Culver were sisters. Emily Ewing and her brother, Charles Hull Ewing, were niece and nephew of Helen Culver. Emily Ewing was an 1877 graduate of Oberlin College and two years later married fellow student John Fisher Peck (1853–1936), who received both his A.B. and A.M. from Oberlin and became principal of Oberlin Academy. She became interested in sculpture during a two-year visit in Europe in the 1890s when she studied in Geneva and in Paris, where she joined the studio of Auguste Rodin. She returned to Oberlin in 1896 and continued to practice her art. There she created perhaps her most noted surviving work, a statue of Giles W. Shurtleff, an Oberlin luminary. It was displayed at the Spear Library in Oberlin in 1898 before she moved to Chicago to continue studying and working. It was in Chicago that she produced clay busts of JA and William Rainey Harper. The sculpture of JA was never cast and does not survive. The Pecks had one son, Lyon Peck, who with his wife, Helen, had several children. Toward the end of her life, Emily Ewing Peck lived with Helen Culver in Florida and died there.

Carl Lindin, born in Sweden, arrived in the United States in 1887 and attended Chicago's Art Institute before he spent almost four years studying in Paris. Returning to Chicago in 1897, he became associated with HH, probably through his friendship with Arts and Crafts supporter and practitioner Hervey White, who was also a HH resident. During Lindin's association with the settlement, he painted a rendition of the Hull home as it might have looked in its surrounding landscape soon after it was built in 1856. Shortly after leaving the settlement, he presented a night-landscape painting to HH. "I did not hope that my moon-lights picture would give me so much joy again—for I had that in good measure when I painted the picture some three years ago" (Carl Lindin to JA, 30 Mar. 1899, SCPC, JAC; *JAPM*, 3:1320). JA responded: "I hope Mr White has told you how delighted all of the residents are with your generous gift to Hull-House. We care for the picture a very great deal" (JA to Carl Lindin, 28 Mar. 1899, SCPC, JAC; *JAPM*, 3:1318). Lindin married HH bookbinder Louise Hastings. Lindin and White were among the founders of the famous Arts and Crafts colony "Byrdcliffe," founded in 1902 in Woodstock, N.Y. For the remainder of Lindin's life, he was a painter, primarily of landscapes, and was connected with the Arts and Crafts colony. He helped found the Woodstock Artists Assn. and served as chairman of the board of the Woodstock Friends of Art, founded in 1932.

5. The Lewis Institute was chartered in 1895 and established with $1.6 million, made possible through the family estate of Stirling, Conn.–born Allen C. Lewis (1821–77) to provide training especially in various technical skills for students regardless of income, race, religion, or ethnicity. See also JA to EGS, 24 Jan. 1889, n. 7; and JA to MRS, 26 Aug. 1893, n. 8, both above.

6. Lydia Addams Albright, sister of JA's father, JHA.

7. Seven hundred members of the CWC gathered on 5 Oct. 1898 to initiate their new club rooms in Chicago's Fine Arts Building. JA was responsible for the special program presented as "Tolstoi as a Realist, Psychologist, Moralist, Writer, and Prophet." The speakers were Prof. Oscar Triggs of the Univ. of Chicago, whose subject title was "Peasantism," and Victor Yarros (see n. 8), whose speech was "Tolstoi as a Writer and Moralist." JA "told of the man from a personal standpoint. She talked of his early desire to do good and how he had always tried to live up to his youthful aspiration. She touched upon what he had accomplished for the whole in his living the simple life of the peasant and then gave anecdotes of her stay at his home" ("Women Talk of Tolstoi").

Oscar Lovell Triggs (1865–1930) was an instructor in English at the Univ. of Chicago, 1895–1903, but apparently lost his appointment when he promoted free love and socialism. He was a Walt Whitman scholar who produced an edition of *Leaves of Grass*. Active in, and associated with, the Arts and Crafts movement, he formed the Industrial Art League in 1899 and promoted the machine as a factor in design. He was the founder of the Saugatuck Press and editor of the *Bulletin of the Morris Society of Chicago*.

8. Victor S. Yarros (1865–1956) was born in Kiev, in the Ukraine, and immigrated to the United States. He met and married Russian immigrant Rachelle Slobodinsky (1869–1957) in New York in 1894, and by 1897 they had moved to Chicago. The Yarros couple adopted one child, a daughter. Victor became a lawyer, newspaper writer, speaker, editorial writer for the *Chicago Daily News*, and news and contributing editor for the *Literary Digest*. An influential anarchist, he was for a number of years a contributor to *Liberty*. Victor and Rachelle Yarros lived at HH, 1907–27. For a time, Victor Yarros practiced law with Clarence Darrow, and both authored *The Prohibition Mania* (1927), an answer to the rationale for Prohibition.

Victor S. Yarros was never selected for the Chicago *Who's Who* volumes, but his wife was. Rachelle Yarros supported the birth control and sex education movements in Chicago. Born in Berdechev in the Ukraine into a well-to-do family, she was well educated and through tutors achieved college-level studies. She left Russia for the United States when she was eighteen, and after two years in a Rahway, N.J., sweatshop she began her study of medicine as the first female student enrolled in the College of Physicians and Surgeons, Boston. She earned her M.D. in 1893 from the Woman's Medical College of Pennsylvania and interned at the New England Hospital for Women and Children, Boston.

After moving to Chicago with her husband, Rachelle Yarros became an instructor and then associate professor in clinical obstetrics at the College of Physicians and Surgeons of Chicago (later the Univ. of Illinois College of Medicine). Between 1898 and 1910, she was a teacher in its Dept. of Obstetrics and served the poor. She became more and more interested in women's health and in sexually transmitted diseases. While living at HH, Rachelle Yarros started Chicago's first birth control clinic, the second to be founded in the United States. The Mary Crane Nursery site associated with HH became one of the eight clinics that eventually served Chicago women. She worked through the CWC to promote birth control in Chicago, and in 1932 she offered a premarital counseling service.

Yarros helped found the American Social Hygiene Assn., was the first vice-president of the Illinois Social Hygiene League, and was president of the West Side branch of the Chicago Medical Society. She was active in the Illinois League of Women Voters and served as a special consultant to the U.S. Public Health Service.

The Yarros couple was very impressed with the early changes brought about in Russia by the creation of the Soviet Union, but after several visits there they became disillusioned with the social control aspects of the new government. Victor and Rachelle Yarros moved to Winter Park, Fla., in 1939, and then on to California, where Victor died in 1941. Rachelle continued to be as active as possible in support of the birth control and sexual education efforts there until her death.

9. JA's diary for 7 Oct. 1898 provides the following information: "Forward movement. Evening. Arts & Crafts dinner Bakers to dinner [Doris Ervin?] Straus Mr Thompson" (SCPC, JAC; *JAPM*, 29:444).

By 1911 the Forward Movement, formerly Epworth House, was located at Monroe and Loomis streets on the West Side of Chicago. Epworth House had been established on 1 Mar. 1893 under the auspices of the Methodist Episcopal Church to "study and improve the social, industrial and spiritual condition of the people in the congested districts of Chicago" (Woods and Kennedy, *Handbook of Settlements*, 49) and became independent May 1896. During the late 1890s, the Forward Movement had moved part of its program into the HH neighborhood. According to the description of its program in the *Handbook of Settlements*, the Forward Movement had a "[s]pecial interest . . . in public schools, seeking to socialize them as far as possible. In 1897 turned over kindergarten with an enrollment of 200, large cooking and sewing school, etc., to public school. A building was erected on Harrison between Halsted and Desplaines Streets especially for that purpose. . . . At present working on the problem of introducing moral and religious training into the public schools" (49).

10. See n. 1.

## To Mary Rozet Smith

Hull-House 335 South Halsted Street Chicago [Ill.] [10 Oct. 1898]

Darling

Your letter was delicious and almost made up for the long silence. The Taborskis departed Sat. and Mayor Jones and his wife[1] arrived <to take my room instead> Mr Spahr[2] of The Outlook is here and we are having a great feast of soul.

We tandemed[3] out to Winnetka yesterday and saw your family.[4] Your mother was more vigorous and <more> cheerful than I have seen her <before> this ~~entire~~ summer, your father less so perhaps but getting along—Miss Hill[5] and I are going out to dinner someday this week. The Arts & Crafts[6] opened brilliantly, Mr Twose[7] gave one of the most illuminating papers I ever heard. I am glad you are homesick for I certainly am, and even the portrait[8] fails to console me much—

I am going to Phila, for the evening of Nov. 12th The <American> Academy of Political & Social Sciences have a conference on Settlements, and asked me to give the leading address when Canon Barnett could n't come,[9] I tried in vain to work in Bro Woods[10] I am going north again to night.[11]

Bless you dearie—Ys

J.A.

Please urge Miss Wald to come to the Conference[12]

ALI (SCPC, JAC; *JAPM*, 3:1177–78).

1. JA had first invited the Jones couple for a visit in June. "We expect to entertain Mr & Mrs Webb for ten days beginning June 4" or 5th. I wish very much that Mrs Jones and yourself might plan to come at the same time" (JA to Samuel M. Jones, 20 May 1898, Toledo-Lucas Co., Ohio, Public Library, Local History Dept., Samuel M. Jones Collection; *JAPM*, 3:1077–78). Mayor Jones and his wife waited until Oct. for their visit.

Samuel Milton ("Golden Rule") Jones (1848–1904) was born in Ty Mawr, Wales. He emigrated to the United States with his parents when he was three years old and grew up in New York. When he was eighteen, he went to work in the Pennsylvania oil fields near Titusville. He advanced as a worker and then producer in the eastern oil fields of West Virginia, Ohio, and Indiana. By 1886 he settled in Lima, Ohio, and, after the death of his first wife, he married Helen W. Beach from Toledo, Ohio. They had three children.

In 1893 he invented a mechanical device that assisted in deep-well drilling and began manufacturing it through the Acme Sucker-Rod Co., which he founded in Toledo. He treated his employees with respect and introduced an assortment of employee benefits, including an eight-hour workday, profit sharing, paid vacations, a minimum wage, Christmas bonuses, and recreational facilities. His actions were the result of his belief in the "Golden Rule"—which became his sobriquet. In 1897 he was elected mayor of Toledo and instituted community social reforms that his initial Republican supporters rejected. Among them were establishing city parks and kindergartens; improving conditions for workers, including an eight-hour day and minimum wage; and fighting corruption. When his party refused to nominate him for mayor in 1899, he ran as an independent. He won in that and successive elections until his death in office.

JA became an early supporter of Mayor Jones. During the summer of 1897, he asked her to help with founding a social settlement in Toledo. He often invited her to speak in Toledo, and he visited HH and supported JA's work there. In addition, JA and Jones shared common progressive reform friends and appeared as speakers at the same reform conferences. In 1898 JA asked for his photograph to place with those of other progressive reform leaders in the settlement's octagon room. Shortly thereafter, Jones presented HH with a special piece of playground equipment called a "Giant Stride." The JA-Jones friendship continued throughout the life of Jones.

2. Charles Barzillai Spahr (d. 1904) was born in Ohio and graduated from Amherst College (1881). After studying in Leipzig, he completed his Ph.D. at Columbia Univ., where he lectured

for almost four years. He became an editorial writer on the *Commercial Advertiser* before he moved in 1886 to the *Outlook*, where he served as an editorial writer until 1904, when he left to become the editor of *Current Literature*. He was married to Jean Gurney Fine (see JA to MCAL, 13 Mar. 1889, n. 20, above), one of the founders of the College Settlement in New York City. The couple had five children. Colleagues at the *Outlook* recalled him as having "an expert knowledge in the field of economics, practical ability in applying that knowledge to current events, an inspiring and catholic sympathy for his fellow men, especially for the poor and the oppressed, . . . a passionate devotion to the truth as he sees the truth, and the power of clear statement and effective marshaling of facts and figures" ("Dr. Charles B. Spahr," *Outlook*, [30 Jan. 1904]: 253). Alice Hamilton concluded that he was in favor of the Spanish-American War "and in free silver and is tremendously combative" (Alice Hamilton to Agnes Hamilton, 11 Oct. 1898, RS, HFP).

3. By the late 1890s, bicycling had become a fad in the United States. During the summer of 1898, JA and a number of HH residents joined those who flocked to the pastime for exercise and recreation. On 3 July, JA reported to SAAH: "I rode twenty four miles on a tandem bicycle last evening and am quite in love with the new pleasure" (IU, Lilly, SAAH; *JAPM*, 3:1121). Of the same trip "riding a double bicycle," JA offered to MRS: "We had a charming ride home, the moon on the lake and the sense of swift motion combined make a memorable night of it. I suppose I will get used to it in time but at present it seems altogether delightful. We did n't talk any of the way and we did n't fall off. It took us a little more than two hours to reach H. H." (4 July 1898, SCPC, JAC; *JAPM*, 3:1122–23). Alice Hamilton, who was part of the party, also described the occasion for her cousin Agnes: "I think it will be the best thing in the world for" JA.

4. "This afternoon we three bicyclers, Mr. Ball, Miss Addams and Mrs. Kelley are going to Winnetka by train, taking our bicycles and the tandem with us. Then Miss Addams and Mrs. Kelley are going to the Smiths' for supper while we are going to the lake side where there is a farm house and a lovely Scotchwoman who gives us bread and butter and honey and eggs and lets us eat it on the bluff over-looking the lake" (Alice Hamilton to Agnes Hamilton, 3 July 1898 in Sicherman, *Alice Hamilton*, 125). MRS's parents also had a home in the Winnetka, north of Chicago. In the 1900 U.S. Census for Illinois, the Smith family is listed in both the Village of Winnetka in New Trier Twp. and in Chicago at 19 East Walton.

Frank H. Ball (1862?–1918) was the manual training director at HH and a resident, fall 1897 through May 1899. By the fall of 1899, George M. R. Twose (see n. 7) had replaced him. Frank H. Ball was born in Worcester, Mass., where he attended elementary school and then learned the foundry trade and then became head of the foundry operation for the Crampton Loom Works. Soon he was teaching foundry work at Worcester Polytechnic Institute. He moved into increasingly responsible positions, teaching manual training in Rindge Manual Training School in Cambridge, Mass., and then at the New York College for training teachers. While he was in New York, he began working with street children, teaching them skills that might help them find employment more easily. That interest led him to HH in Chicago, 1897–1900, where he directed the settlement's manual training program and at the same time taught manual training at the South Side Academy in the John Deweys' school that became part of the Univ. of Chicago Dept. of Education.

In 1900 Ball taught manual training to teachers in the Throop Polytechnic Institute in Pasadena, Calif., but soon became director of industrial education in Puerto Rico. After three years there, he settled in Cincinnati to supervise the community's industrial education program and remained for seven years. He then spent four years doing the same task in Pittsburgh, Pa., while he attended the Univ. of Pittsburgh (B.A. 1916), graduating at the same time as his daughter Katherine. During World War I, Ball became president of the Santa Barbara State Normal School of Manual Arts and Home Economics. There he had a disabling fall and died shortly after surgery to correct the injury.

5. JA's 1898 diary indicated that she went to Winnetka on 13 Oct. However, JA reported to MRS on 16 Oct.: "It rained tremendously the day Miss Hill and I had planned to go out to dinner and we went the next afternoon for a call" (SCPC, JAC; *JAPM*, 3:1181) .

Mary Dayton Hill (1871–1955) was born in New Brunswick, N.J., the daughter of John T. and Mary Elizabeth Dayton Hill. In 1896 she graduated from Bryn Mawr College. She arrived at HH as a volunteer by 1898 and became a resident. She served as director of the HH Shakespeare Club and taught hand weaving. Alice Hamilton recalled that she taught at the Dewey School at the Univ. of Chicago. The *HH Bulletin* for 1 Jan.–May 1901 identified her as director of the HH Labor Museum, opened Nov. 1900. It was at HH that Mary Hill met her husband, Gerard Swope (1873–1957), who at the time was employed at the Western Electric Co. in Chicago, and from June 1897 until the summer of 1899 he was also a resident at HH. They were married at St. Ignace, Mackinac, Mich., in 1901. On the occasion of their marriage, JA delivered an address on love and lauded the two young people, both so dedicated to progressive reform ([Address at the wedding of Gerard Swope and Mary Dayton Hill], [20 Aug. 1901], 10 pp., SCPC, JAC; *JAPM*, 46:1067–77; and 20 Aug. 1901, 3 pp., MIT, Swope). The Swopes remained lifelong friends of JA and the assortment of reformers that they met through HH, including Florence Kelley, Julia Lathrop, and Alice Hamilton. They made annual financial contributions to HH for the rest of their lives.

Gerard Swope, who eventually became president of General Electric Co., was born in St. Louis, the son of Isaac and Ida Cohn Swope. He was a graduate of MIT in electrical engineering and was employed shortly after graduation in 1896 by the Western Electric Co. in Chicago, where he began work pulling transformers apart for a salary of one dollar a day. During his almost five years in association with HH, he served as a volunteer in managing boys' clubs; taught algebra, electricity, and magnetism; served as the treasurer of the Men's Club; and took an active part in the Nineteenth Ward political campaign for alderman on behalf of the HH-supported reform candidate in 1898. While he was living at HH, he worked his way up in the Western Electric organization and in 1901 was sent to St. Louis to organize an office for the company there. By 1908 he was in New York, where he held increasingly significant leadership positions in the company. He served with the general staff of the army during World War I as assistant director of purchasing, storage, and traffic. After the war, Swope joined the General Electric Co. and by 1922 had become its president, a position he held until 1939 and again for two years during World War II. During his tenure, the company began designing and manufacturing electrical appliances for home use. He saw his company successfully through the Great Depression. His "Swope Plan" for stabilizing industry, proposed in 1931, placed emphasis on the responsibility of industry for preventing unemployment and for promoting unemployment insurance. Swope sent JA copies of his "Swope Plan" proposals (Swope to JA, 10 Dec. 1930, SCPC, JAC; *JAPM*, 21:1443–47). After his retirement from General Electric, he became the full-time chairman of the New York City Housing Authority. Swope was also associated with the development of the National Broadcasting Co. and RCA Victor Co. He became a leader in many cultural, civic, and philanthropic organizations. He received numerous honors for his achievements from universities and other countries.

Mary Hill Swope also lived a very active life after leaving HH. Mother of four children, she continued an interest in philanthropy in New York City with her work as a board member for the Henry Street Visiting Nurse Service and with Greenwich House. She joined JA and other reformers in working in the American peace movement during World War I, particularly as a member of the WILPF and the People's Mandate Com. to End War.

6. According to JA's diary, an Arts and Crafts Society of Chicago gathering was held on 7 Oct. 1898. It was likely the occasion JA was referring to.

7. George Mortimer Rendle Twose (1873–1924) was born in Plymouth, England, and came to the United States in 1886 (or 1890). In 1900 he became a U.S. citizen. By 1895 he was living in Chicago and had become associated with HH. According to JA's nephew and biographer

James Weber Linn, who knew Twose, he was "big bodied and bald and long in every feature . . . yet far from homely." Linn continued: "His tastes were fastidious, yet his indifferences to convention were colossal. . . . Almost everything bored him, except doing things for people . . . and painting" (Linn, *Jane Addams*, 213–14). He first appeared in the HH records directing, designing costumes and sets, and playing the part of the Knave of Hearts in Alfred Paxton's children's play *Rhymeland*, the HH Christmas play presented in Dec. 1895. It was presented on four separate occasions to audiences of two hundred invited guests in the HH gymnasium. He continued his association with the settlement by lecturing on 13 Feb. 1896 on London. He returned in the fall of 1896 to provide a series of lectures in the HH advanced educational classes that were offered for twelve weeks beginning in Sept. and continuing through Feb. 1897. His topic was architecture in relation to life and religion. In Dec. 1896, he presented "Old English Christmas" in the stereopticon lecture series, and he also began working with HH club members who were rehearsing plays. In Dec. 1897, the *HH Bulletin* reported that Twose was one of the members of the Dramatic Com., which JA appointed to govern the recently formed HH Dramatic Assn. He continued in that role into 1898, helping to design the evolving HH dramatic program in the late 1890s.

In 1897 he became certified to teach mechanical and architectural drawing in the Chicago public school system and began teaching in English High and Manual Training School for an annual salary of twelve hundred dollars. While in Chicago, he remained a schoolteacher. At HH in the fall of 1897, he began teaching mechanical drawing and elementary design one evening a week in the technical classes and was listed for the first time as a HH resident. He was also identified as the person at the settlement to whom all queries about manual training were to be directed. It was also in Oct. 1897 that he became a founder and first secretary of the Chicago Arts and Crafts Society. In the catalog of the initial arts society exhibit, Ella R. Waite exhibited a bookcase he designed. As a settlement resident, he became more active in its educational programs. In the fall of 1900, he presented public lectures on theories of creation and continued to hold classes in mechanical drawing. In Jan. 1901, he lectured on Egypt and continued with his mechanical drawing class throughout 1902. He was also identified as one of the fifteen members of the HH Dramatic Assn. and served as toastmaster for a Mar. banquet held by the Men's Club in which he became very active. In 1902 he was singled out for designing and producing scenery and costumes for the HH Dramatic Assn., and by 1904 he was identified as a stage manager for the dramatic association's presentations and took the character of Little John in Ben Jonson's *The Sad Shepherd*, presented at HH in 1904. Beginning in 1904 and through 1907, he continued to hold a class in mechanical drawing. In 1917 he was living in Chatham, N.Y., and during World War I he worked with the Wynne Bevan Ambulance Union. By 1920 his address was Austerlitz, N.Y. He died in New York City and was buried in St. Peter's Presbyterian Cemetery, Spencertown, N.Y.

8. Portrait of MRS that had been completed by Alice Kellogg Tyler. See JA to MRS, 23 Mar. 1898, n. 11, above.

9. JA, identified as "foremost representative of settlement work in America," presented a paper entitled "The Scope and Meaning of Social Settlements" before two hundred guests and members of the American Academy of Political and Social Science gathered in New Century Drawing Room on Saturday evening, 12 Nov. 1898. The next morning, she presented a version of her "Trades Unions and the Public Duty" essay to the Society of Ethical Culture of Philadelphia. For a version of the speech, see "Trades Unions and Public Duty," *American Journal of Sociology* 4, no. 4 (Jan. 1899): 448–62; and *JAPM*, 46:902–15.

10. Robert A. Woods.

11. JA planned to see MRS's parents in Winnetka, Ill.

12. Written on the right edge of p. 2 of the letter and perpendicular to the main body of text. This was a reference to the settlement conference that JA and other settlement leaders were planning to host in Chicago in the early part of 1899. Urging Lillian Wald to attend,

JA wrote: "We are n't arranging for any fine speaking and perhaps we will have a genuine 'Confluence' of people who are all interested in the same things—it really is helpful if it can be procured" (6 Dec. 1898, NYPL, Wald, Incoming; *JAPM*, 3:1248). See JA to Henrietta O. Barnett, 30 May 1899, below.

## To Mary Rozet Smith

Hull-House 335 South Halsted Street Chicago [Ill.] Oct. 21" 1898

My Dearie

How do you like my vulgar booming of the gentle brother?[1] He must have audiences at all hazards.[2] I am making other appointments for him over at the University. He said that I could say anything that was "decently true".

You are really falling in love with the Settlement are n't you?[3] it is fine but I do wish you would give us an uninterrupted chance some month, instead of coming in for one night and then going away—If you go to Baltimore[4] I think that I would rather have <eight> handles <for my chest of drawers> like those on my desk & bookcase than any present from New York—unless it was a brass pan for my fire place—

I sat in Mrs Potter Palmer's box at the Peace Jubilee[5] and otherwise exposed myself to its fascinations, but can do nothing but feel a lump in my throat over the whole thing—I have been really ~~blue~~ quite blue <not play blue but real depths> and will have to be more of a Tolstoyan or less of one right off! You got Mr Maude's dates did n't you? He comes Friday Oct 28" & stays until the next Wednesday.[6] My love to all the sisters who don't "venerate" me I am quite sure, but I dote on all of them for being so good to you—altho I know full well it is on your account, and not mine. I am going to take Laura[7] out to Winnetka to lunch some day, but she is so shy it is harder all the time to persuade her to do anything.

My undying & unfaltering love to you—Always yours

Jane Addams

P.S. I am so glad that you are coming home for Bro Maude I hardly dared hope you would!

ALS (SCPC, JAC; *JAPM*, 3:1185–87).

1. Aylmer Maude came to Chicago to see JA, visit HH, and to seek support for the Doukhobors. During Maude's visit with JA, she accepted membership on the committee established to secure funds and support for a colony of Doukhobortsi in the United States and Canada. Among other committee members were William Dean Howells, Ernest H. Crosby, and William Lloyd Garrison. According to the *New York Times*, "The committee has obtained options on lands in Oregon and Washington from the railroad companies . . . the members of the sect being permitted to occupy and cultivate the land for a time without immediate payment for its use. . . . About $150,000 will be needed to meet the expense of transporting the entire sect, and $20,000 has already been procured in England, while the Doukhobortsi have raised among themselves upward of $25,000. The purpose is to establish large colonies

devoted to agriculture" ("To Aid the Spirit Wrestlers," 13 Nov. 1898). JA helped Maude find speaking opportunities in Chicago in the hope of promoting his effort. He also visited St. Louis, Boston, Philadelphia, and New York City in his quest for support.

2. Aylmer Maude spoke at HH during his visit in Chicago, and Alice Hamilton reacted to his presentation in a letter to her cousin Agnes: "Imagine a man standing up in our gymnasium—which was crowded to its utmost—reading aloud passages from the Sermon on the Mount and telling us that that rule of life literally carried out was the only rational and sane rule. Wasn't it a novel experience for Hull-House. . . . And he does not accept Christ's teachings because they are inspired but because he has tried them and found them good. . . . He manages to interpret that part about divorces so that it does not forbid a man and wife to part if they do not love each other, but this seemed to me pretty much strained. You see he follows Tolstoy in repudiating all sexual relationships as belonging to lust, and he looks forward with calm philosophy to the ultimate extinction of the race through celibacy" (7 Nov. 1898, RS, HFP).

3. MRS was spending a month with Lillian D. Wald at the Nurses Settlement on Henry Street to learn what she could of its programs. See JA to MRS, 6 Oct. 1898, above.

4. JA may have assumed that MRS would visit Cornelia Niver, a childhood friend, who lived in Baltimore. See JA to MRS, 23 Mar. 1898, n. 13, above.

5. The Peace Jubilee was Chicago's celebration of the successful end of the short-lived Spanish-American War. Beginning on Sunday, 16 Oct., Chicago churches held special services of thanksgiving that culminated during the evening with a universal service in the Auditorium Theater, which could hold an audience of six thousand. "Thousands of lights dancing overhead, flags above them filling the sky, gay streamers fluttering from every building, everywhere light and bunting and the streets thronged with sightseers in holiday attire, marked the opening of Chicago's peace jubilee" ("City Ablaze with Golden Light"). President William F. McKinley was the star attraction of the week, attending many of the festivities, which included a reception on 17 Oct. followed by a bicycle parade during the evening. On Tuesday evening, Mrs. Potter Palmer created a peace jubilee ball, held at the Auditorium. Proceeds from the sale of thirty-four boxes from which attendees could watch the events, as well as from sales from individual tickets, went to a special fund created to aid the families of needy soldiers and sailors. JA was a guest of Mrs. Palmer in box 5, immediately next to box 4, which held President McKinley and his party. Wednesday, 19 Oct., was a special holiday so that everyone could see the peace parade, which was followed by a banquet in the Auditorium, where President McKinley was to speak and close the festivities.

6. 2 Nov. 1898.

7. JA was taking LSA to visit the parents of MRS in Winnetka.

## To Sarah Alice Addams Haldeman

Hull-House 335 South Halsted Street Chicago [Ill.] Dec. 31" 1898

My dear Alice

I have just come back from a little visit at Cedarville. The girls were both at home[1]—Esther is developing in many ways, among other things she is growing very pretty.

Harry's[2] mother[3] said that he had gone to St Louis on business and I could not tell what she knew of his whereabouts—

I am so sorry that you have had this worry again[4]—I cannot of course follow your motives and am indeed quite lost in regard to them. It is of course so personal in character that no one outside can be of any use, however willing—

I hope very much that your cold is better and that you are planning for a long visit north this summer. This year it is your turn and I feel that is only after some days of being together that I can get back into your mind in regard to this trouble. Weber[5] likes the bust[6] very much, I agree with you in regard to the head being narrow but not in regard to the eyes—

Miss Starr[7] has been at home for two weeks—her books are really very fine—she sends her love to you as does Mrs Kelley.

With much love to Marcet and yourself—Always your loving sister

Jane Addams

ALS (IU, Lilly, SAAH; *JAPM*, 3:1259–60).

1. Esther Margaret Linn and Sarah Weber Addams.
2. HWH.
3. AHHA.
4. It is likely that HWH, an alcoholic, had again disappeared for a time from the Haldeman household in Girard, Kans., and SAAH did not know where he had gone.
5. JWA.
6. JA is probably referring to the bust of JHA in her possession that Emily Ewing Peck had fashioned from photographs.
7. EGS was due back at HH by 1 Nov. from her year's study apprenticed to fine bookbinder T. J. Cobden-Sanderson at his Doves Bindery in England. This seems to indicate that she did not return to the settlement until mid-Dec. 1898.

## To Sarah Alice Addams Haldeman

203 N. Front St. Harrisburg, Pa. March 1st 1899

My dear Alice

Your letter was forwarded to me here where I find myself almost at the end of a two weeks lecturing tour.[1] I had a delightful sojourn in Boston[2] and from here go to Richmond Virginia,[3] after which to join Mary Smith at Columbia So Carolina[4] and we will reach Chicago about March 18th.[5]

I saw John Linn in New York,[6] he has a possible chance for a position there and in the mean time is doing good work and is looking very well.

I will try to get you an Atlantic[7] in Baltimore to morrow, I did not realize that you would have any difficulty about it.

My address at Columbia will be 829 Richland St Columbia So Carolina. It would be very nice indeed to have a letter there from you.[8] I seem to find little time for writing on these trips. I have consented to give twelve lectures at the University of Chicago next summer and am trying to get my material into shape;[9] I am going to make clear about $350.00 on this trip which is a great satisfaction and much relieves me financially.[10] Are n't you and Marcet coming to Chicago next summer,[11] I shall have to be in town quite steadily for six weeks after July 1st and I am sure you could be comfortable, or I could spend part of every week with you at Rockford.

Please give my love to Marcet and believe me always and forever your loving sister

Jane Addams

ALS (IU, Lilly, SAAH; *JAPM*, 3:1308–9).

1. The longest lecture tour that JA had yet undertaken began on 13 Feb. when she left Chicago for New York City. Before she left for Columbia, S.C., she spoke on nineteen different occasions. Her tour began on 14 Feb. in Aurora, N.Y., where she lectured at Wells College, and then went to Auburn Seminary and back to Wells College on 16 Feb. By the evening of 17 Feb., JA was back in New York City. On 18 Feb., she spoke in the afternoon in the Cambridge, Mass., Woman's Club and in Brighton, Mass., in the evening. She was once again at Mrs. Ole Bull's Sunday-afternoon social on the 19th and that evening at Denison House. On 20 Feb., she spoke at Science Hall of the Univ. of Vermont in Burlington, at 8:00 P.M., and the next day she appeared at Radcliffe College in the afternoon and the Episcopal Theological Seminary, Cambridge, in the evening. On the 22nd, she gave two speeches, one for the Consumers' League and one in the Old Public Library in its Municipal Lecture course. Her calendar for 23 Feb. identified her speaking engagement at the Woman's Club in Concord, Mass. From Saturday, 25 Feb., through the 27th, she spoke in Meadville, Pa. By 1 Mar., JA was in Harrisburg, Pa., where she appeared before the Harrisburg Civic Club. On 2 Mar., she was in Baltimore, where she made a presentation at the Johns Hopkins Training School for Nurses and the next day arrived in Richmond, Va., where she "had a charming visit . . . and quite lost . . . [her] heart to the old town." She spoke to the Woman's Club at 8:00 P.M. and then left by train at midnight to arrive in Columbia, S.C., shortly after noon the following day (JA to Julia C. Lathrop, 6 Mar. 1899, RC Archives, Lathrop; *JAPM*, 3:1311). Almost all of her lectures on this tour had as a focus the development of HH, its programs, and its role in the neighborhood it served; however, at the Old Public Library in Boston, she again returned to Tolstoy as her subject in remarks titled "The Life and Social Views of Tolstoi." See also JA to MRS, 13 Feb. 1899, SCPC, JAC; *JAPM*, 3:1295–97.

Unlike many well-known speakers of the day, JA was not represented by any lyceum group or agent. Requests for her appearance and participation came by mail, telephone, and telegram directly to her at HH, and JA or her surrogate responded to each one. JA set her own schedule. JA and her various secretaries, hired or volunteer (for example, Julia C. Lathrop, Frederick Deknatel, or Madeleine Wallin, or a relatively unknown resident, Eleanor H. Johnson, an 1894 Smith College graduate who taught various English-language and -literature classes at HH, 1895–97), made most of her travel arrangements. The organizations or individuals who invited her to appear usually reserved and paid for her board and lodging, sometimes in a private home or a social settlement house, but increasingly in hotels, where she could better manage her own private time. She usually traveled with a companion. In the 1890s, SAAH, Julia C. Lathrop, and MRS accompanied JA on speaking tours. As her fame as a speaker grew and her speaking fees increased, she often received a separate stipend for expenses.

JA was not shy about making her own arrangements for travel. To reach speaking engagements in Chicago, she most often used public transportation and, as the social mores of the day demanded, was usually accompanied by another friend or HH resident. With increasing frequency, especially after 1900, she was given the use of a private carriage or car. Except when she was garbage inspector for the Nineteenth Ward, JA never owned her own personal conveyance. Her travel away from Chicago was always by train, which at that time was the primary means of transportation between communities and regions throughout the United States. If she missed a rail connection, she simply selected another train that would get her to her destination. The only way to reach Europe was by boat. While in Europe, JA often changed her departure date and the ship on which she was sailing, made arrangements for train travel, and managed her luggage. In 1900, when returning from her duties as a juror at the Paris Exposition, she and MRS exchanged numerous letters in their effort to arrange to meet for a vacation in the East near the time she was to appear at the Chautauqua Assembly in New York. See especially the following: JA to MRS 27 June, 15 July, and 4 Aug. 1900, all SCPC, JAC; *JAPM*, 3:1597–1601, 1619–20, and 1626–29.

2. While she was in Boston, among the people she saw were Robert A. Woods, Helena S. Dudley, residents of Denison House, and Mrs. Ole Bull, all of whom she had seen on her previous visit in 1897.

3. See n. 1.

4. "I arrived here Saturday at noon, not in the least tired or worn out but in the best of spirits. The two good Smiths met me at the train, and we have been having a jolly visit ever since," JA wrote to Julia C. Lathrop on 6 Mar. 1899 (RC Archives, Lathrop; *JAPM*, 3:1309–10). MRS and Sarah Porter Smith, who still lived in Columbia, met the train.

5. JA's diary for 1899 indicated that she returned to HH during the weekend of 11 and 12 Mar. rather than on 18 Mar., when she attended the Every Day Club meeting at noon in Chicago. The Every Day Club met every two weeks on a Saturday at the Union League Club. It was composed of thirty-five women leaders who met to discuss some vital civic problem and consider what they could do to help solve it. JA and Julia C. Lathrop were members.

6. Through Lillian Wald, JA had arranged for her nephew, recently graduated from the Western Theological Seminary in Chicago, to get a job in New York City. JA wrote to Wald to thank her: "I do not know that I thanked you for all your kindness to my nephew including having him at dinner last night, he spoke with much feeling of all your goodness to him. He is so much better in every way that it was a great pleasure to see him and I do not in any way regret my trip to New York save that once more I put you to a great deal of trouble on my account" (18 Feb. 1899, NYPL, Wald, Incoming; *JAPM*, 3:1299–1300). John Addams Linn eventually became an assistant pastor at the Episcopal Church of St. Mary–the-Virgin, New York City, where he remained until 1902.

JA stopped in New York City to see John Addams Linn. She also hoped to meet with Theodore Roosevelt, who had become governor of New York. JA expected to lobby Roosevelt on behalf of Florence Kelley for the position as factory inspector of New York. Unfortunately, the appointment with the governor did not materialize. Kelley had already discovered that Roosevelt had "written Jacob Riis that while he Teddy has no prejudices, the community would object to an Altgeld appointee" in the position, and so Kelley had no chance at the job (Florence Kelley to MRS [for JA], 4 Feb. 1899, SCPC, JAC; *JAPM*, 3:1287–88). JA finally gave up her attempt to meet with Roosevelt.

7. The *Atlantic Monthly* magazine contained an article by JA entitled "The Subtle Problems of Charity" ([Feb. 1899]: 83:168–76; *JAPM*, 46:916–32), for which she received a fee of $130. Newspapers in cities—including New York City; Philadelphia; Buffalo and Rochester, N.Y.; Chicago; and Indianapolis—and a variety of church-related publications summarized or directed their readers to the article. The *New York Mail Express* described the presentation as "enlivened with many quaint and humorous experiences and incidents" ("February Magazines"). A similar article, condensed from the longer version that appeared in the *Atlantic Monthly*, appeared in Mar. 1899 in the *Outlook* 61 (11 Mar. 1899): 598–600. It was titled "The Charity Visitor's Perplexities."

8. "I have not heard from you for some time and hope that all is well with you," JA wrote to SAAH on 28 Mar. 1899 (IU, Lilly, SAAH; *JAPM*, 3:1317).

9. JA and Florence Kelley gave a series of lectures at the Univ. of Chicago over six weeks between 1 July and mid-Aug. See JA to MRS, 22 June 1899, n. 7, below.

10. JA kept a record of the fees she received from her speeches during 1899 in the back of her 1899 diary in the section labeled "Cash Account." It indicated that for her lecturing trip in Feb. and Mar., she made $385, less expenses of $85, for a total of $300 in Feb., and in Mar. on the same tour she made $50. JA did "clear" $350 on the lecture tour. Between 1899 and 1900, JA earned $1,700 from speaking and writings, almost twice as much as the $885 she had earned from 1898 to 1899.

11. SAAH and her daughter, Marcet, did visit in Chicago, Rockford, and Cedarville during the summer.

## Address before the Chicago Liberty Meeting

*On 30 April 1899, a group of citizens that included Jane Addams, who signed the call for the meeting, met at Chicago's Central Music Hall at 3:00 P.M. to protest President William A. McKinley's course of action in the Philippine Islands.[1] As a result of the peace treaty that settled the Spanish-American War, the United States had purchased the Philippine Islands from Spain for twenty million dollars. The treaty between the two warring powers was signed 10 December 1898 in Paris, and after heated argument not only in government circles, but among the American public, it was ratified by the U.S. Senate on 6 February 1899.*

*During the 1880s, a Filipino independence movement against Spanish rule had developed. Its leaders and adherents became allies of the United States against Spain with the expectation that at the successful conclusion of the war, America would support their claim to independence. When the United States chose to ignore a Philippine declaration of independence pronounced on 1 January 1899 and then moved to quell Filipino revolutionary hopes, one of the major results was the Filipino-American War, which lasted until July 1902. Another outcome was the Chicago Liberty Meeting, held as a public outcry against this U.S. foray into imperialism as a national policy and the specific treatment of the Filipino people.*

*The Central Anti-Imperialist League[2] in Chicago was formed, and Jane Addams became one of its vice-presidents. Among its first actions was the publication in 1899 of a selection of speeches from the meeting, the first of what the league called its "Liberty Tracts." Jane Addams was one of the speakers at the meeting, and her remarks were included in the publication. With this speech, Jane Addams became publicly identified as an anti-imperialist, pro-peace advocate—a stance that in future years became central to her personal philosophy and to her actions and activities.*

### DEMOCRACY OR MILITARISM

Chicago, Ill. 30 April 1899

No one of us who has been reared and nurtured in America can be wholly without the democratic instinct. It is not a question with any of us of having it or not having it; it is merely a question of trusting it or not trusting it. For good or ill we suddenly find ourselves bound to an international situation. The question practically reduces itself to this: Do we mean to democratize the situation? Are we going to trust our democracy, or are we going to weakly imitate the policy of other governments, which have never claimed a democratic basis?

The political code, we well as the moral law, has no meaning and becomes absolutely emptied of its contents if we take out of it all relation to the world and concrete cases, and it is exactly in such a time as this that we discover what we really believe. We may make a mistake in politics as well as in morals by forgetting that new conditions are ever demanding the evolution of a new morality, along old lines but in larger measure. Unless the present situation extends our nationalism into internationalism, unless it has thrust forward our patriotism into humanitarianism we cannot meet it.

We must also remember that peace has come to mean a larger thing. It is no longer merely absence of war, but the unfolding of life processes which are making for a common development. Peace is not merely something to hold congresses about and to discuss as an abstract dogma. It has come to be a rising tide of moral feeling, which is slowly engulfing all pride of conquest and making war impossible.

Under this new conception of peace it is perhaps natural that the first men to formulate it and give it international meaning should have been workingmen, who have always realized, however feebly and vaguely they may have expressed it, that it is they who in all ages have borne the heaviest burden of privation and suffering imposed on the world by the military spirit.

The first international organization founded not to promote a colorless peace, but to advance and develop the common life of all nations was founded in London in 1864 by workingmen and called simply "The International Association of Workingmen." They recognized that a supreme interest raised all workingmen above the prejudice of race, and united them by wider and deeper principles than those by which they were separated into nations. That as religion, science, art, had become international, so now at last labor took its position as an international interest. A few years later, at its third congress, held in Brussels in 1868, the internationals recommended in view of the Franco-German war, then threatening, that "the workers resist all war as systematic murder," and in case of war a universal strike be declared.

This is almost exactly what is now happening in Russia. The peasants are simply refusing to drill and fight and the czar gets credit for a peace manifesto the moral force of which comes from the humblest of his subjects. It is not, therefore, surprising that as long ago as last December, the organized workingmen of America recorded their protest against the adoption of an imperialistic policy.

In the annual convention of the American Federation of Labor, held that month in Kansas City, resolutions were adopted indorsing the declaration made by President Gompers in his opening address: "It has always been the hewers of wood and the carriers of water, the wealth producers, whose mission it has been not only to struggle for freedom, but to be ever vigilant to maintain the liberty of freedom achieved, and it behooves the representatives of the grand army of labor in convention assembled to give vent to the alarm we feel from the dangers threatening us and our entire people, to enter our solemn and emphatic protest against what we already feel; that, with the success of imperialism the decadence of our republic will have already set in."

There is a growing conviction among workingmen of all countries that, whatever may be accomplished by a national war, however high the supposed moral aim of such a war, there is one inevitable result—an increased standing army, the soldiers of which are non-producers and must be fed by the workers. The Russian peasants support an army of 1,000,000, the German peasants sow and reap for 500,000 more. The men in these armies spend their muscular force in drilling, their mental force in thoughts of warfare. The mere hours of idleness conduce mental and moral deterioration.

The appeal to the fighting instinct does not end in mere warfare, but arouses these brutal instincts latent in every human being. The countries with the large standing armies are likewise the countries with national hospitals for the treatment of diseases which should never exist, of large asylums for the care of children which should never have been born. These institutions as well as the barracks, again increase the taxation, which rests, in the last analysis upon producers, and, at the same time, withdraws so much of their product from the beneficent development of their national life. No one urges peaceful association with more fervor than the workingman. Organization is his only hope, but it must be kept distinct from militarism, which can never be made a democratic instrument.

Let us not make the mistake of confusing moral issues sometimes involved in warfare with warfare itself. Let us not glorify the brutality. The same strenuous endeavor, the same heroic self-sacrifice, the same fine courage and readiness to meet death, may be displayed without the accompaniment of killing our fellow men. With all Kipling's[3] insight he has, over and over, failed to distinguish between war and imperialism on the one hand and the advance of civilization on the other.

To "protect the weak" has always been the excuse of the ruler and tax-gatherer, the chief, the king, the baron; and now, at last, of "the white man."[4] The form of government is not necessarily the function itself. Government is not something extraneous, consisting of men who wear gold lace and sit on high stools and write rows of figures in books. We forget than an ideal government is merely an adjustment between men concerning their mutual relations towards those general matters which concern them all; that the office of an outside and alien people must always be to collect taxes and to hold a negative law and order. In its first attempt to restore mere order and quiet, the outside power inevitably breaks down the framework of the nascent government itself, the more virile and initiative forces are destroyed; new relations must in the end be established, not only with the handicap of smart animosity on the part of the conquered, but with the loss of the most able citizens among them

Some of us were beginning to hope that we were getting away from the ideals set by the civil war, that we had made all the presidents we could from men who had distinguished themselves in that war, and were coming to seek another type of man. That we were ready to accept the peace ideal, to be proud of our title as a peace nation; to recognize that the man who cleans a city is greater than he who bombards it, and the man who irrigates a plain greater than he who lays it waste. Then came the Spanish war, with its gilt and lace and tinsel, and again the moral issues are confused with exhibitions of brutality.

For ten years I have lived in a neighborhood which is by no means criminal, and yet during last October and November we were startled by seven murders within a radius of ten blocks. A little investigation of details and motives, the accident of a personal acquaintance with two of the criminals, made it not in the least difficult to trace the murders back to the influence of war. Simple people, who read of carnage and bloodshed easily receive its suggestions. Habits of self-control which have been but slowly and imperfectly acquired quickly break down under the stress.

Psychologists intimate that action is determined by the selection of the subject upon which the attention is habitually fixed. The newspapers, the theatrical posters, the street conversations for weeks had to do with war and bloodshed. The little children on the street played at war, day after day, killing Spaniards. The humane instinct, which keeps in abeyance the tendency to cruelty, the growing belief that the life of each human being—however hopeless or degraded, is still sacred—gives way, and the barbaric instinct asserts itself.

It is doubtless only during a time of war that the men and women of Chicago could tolerate whipping for children in our city prison, and it is only during such a time that the introduction in the legislature of a bill for the re-establishment of the whipping post could be possible. National events determine our ideals, as much as our ideals determine national events.

PD (*The Chicago Liberty Meeting Held at Central Music Hall, April 30, 1899*. Liberty Tracts, No. 1, Chicago: Central Anti-Imperialist League, 1899, 35–39; *JAPM*, 46:898–901).

1. Newspapers in Chicago and New York, including the *Chicago Inter Ocean* and the *Chicago Daily Tribune*, and the *New York Sun*, *World*, *Journal*, and *Times* covered the gathering. Univ. of Chicago professor J. Laurence Laughlin was most often quoted for this comment: "In the Philippines we are not merely hounding colored natives with the bloodhounds of ante-slavery days, but murdering them with rapid fire guns—'nigger hunting' it is grewsomely expressed. The flag there does not protect those over whom it floats. It is there the emblem of tyranny and butchery" ("Cried 'Treason!' to Prof. Laughlin"). Response to his statement from some voices in the audience was "Treason." Only one newspaper listed JA as one of the speakers; none covered her remarks.

James Laurence Laughlin (1850–1933) was an American economist who helped build the economics department at the Univ. of Chicago, 1892–1916; edited the *Journal of Political Economy*, 1892–1933; and helped create the Federal Reserve System.

2. The Central Anti-Imperialist League was officially formed in July 1899. Among its leaders were Henry Wade Rogers, William Kent, and Edwin Burritt Smith. The platform of the Central Anti-Imperialist League, Chicago, was as follows:

"1. The frank expression of honest convictions upon great questions of public policy is vital to the health and even to the preservation of representative government. . . .
2. We hold that the policy known as imperialism is hostile to liberty and tends toward militarism, an evil from which it has been our glory to be free. . . .
3. We honor our soldiers and sailors in the Philippine islands for their unquestioned bravery; and we mourn with the whole nation for the American lives that have been sacrificed. . . .
4. We earnestly condemn the policy of the present national administration in the Philippines. It is the spirit of '76 that our government is striving to extinguish in those islands; we denounce the attempt and demand its abandonment. . . .
5. We protest against the extension of American empire by Spanish methods, and demand the immediate cessation of the war against liberty, begun by Spain and continued by us. . . ." ("Platform [of the Central Anti-Imperialist League, Chicago]," *The Chicago Liberty Meeting Held at Central Music Hall, April 30, 1899*, [4]).

By late 1899, it had affiliated with the American Anti-Imperialist League, organized in 1898 in Boston.

3. JA, without doubt, knew Rudyard Kipling's poem "The White Man's Burden," which extolled the virtues of imperialism. It had been published in the Feb. 1899 *McClure's Magazine* as well as several newspapers. It was a defense of what Kipling saw as the positive aspects of imperialism, including planned development and economic progress. Rudyard Kipling (1865–1926), a celebrated English novelist and poet, was educated in India and was instrumental in bringing stories of that country's culture to the West through his famous *Jungle Book* series.

4. A reference to "The White Man's Burden" by Rudyard Kipling (see n. 3).

## To Henrietta O. Barnett

*Social settlement leaders began planning for a major gathering of settlement workers in 1898.[1] They considered a number of venues, including New York City and Boston, but in the end Jane Addams, Graham Taylor, and Chicago won the national event. Hull-House became the host site for the conference, which was held 15–17 May 1899. Henrietta and Samuel A. Barnett sent a formal letter to all of the attendees who came from settlements in Boston; New York; Cleveland and Cincinnati; San Francisco; Brooklyn; Philadelphia; Louisville, Kentucky; Des Moines, Iowa; Milwaukee, Racine, and Madison; Chicago, Freeport, and Le Claire, Illinois; and Omaha, Nebraska. Graham Taylor, who published a lengthy summary of the conference in the* Commons, *proclaimed, "The value of the conference was greatly enhanced by the fact that it had nothing to decide, could commit itself or its respective membership to no policy—in short, was in no sense legislative or judicial. It was for conference, purely and simply, and that result was thoroughly achieved."[2]*

*The major themes were the settlement in politics, economic relationships, education efforts, keeping settlement work personal rather than institutional, the value of publishing studies about the neighborhood while keeping the confidence of its citizens, and relationships with trade unions. Taylor recorded two of the salient points made by Jane Addams: "Miss Addams, in speaking of the unsatisfactory experience of Hull House in the politics of the 19th ward of Chicago, held that the settlement had no right to meddle in every other part of the community's life and ignore that in which the people were most interested. The corruption of politics was destroying the finest survivals of conscience among the new-come foreigners, and the settlement could not afford to ignore its most powerful enemy."*[3] *With regard to neighborhood studies: "Miss Addams wanted studies to be accurate, fair and in the service of truth only. 'No body objects to the truth,' said she, 'but they do object to exaggeration and distortion for the sake of effect. There is no use in picturing either the poor or the rich as better or worse than they are.'"*[4]

Hull-House 335 South Halsted Street Chicago [Ill.] May 30 1899

My dear Mrs Barnett

It was very good of you to send the letter which was really a great help to the Conference. It was printed and distributed to the various Settlements and I am sure will be of genuine value.[5]

The Conference itself was vital and on the whole encouraging. I am sure it proved that so far at least we have kept free from dogmatism and institutionalism. There were no "set speeches" but quite aside from that the tone of the discussion was strikingly simple and direct.

Some of the "residents" of course made one wince but I am really eagar to have you both come in 1900 and see that things are not so bad as we once feared.[6]

Won't you write me as your plans mature that we may know the approximate time when you will reach Chicago?[7]

I hope very much that you have quite recovered, it was so good of you to think of us in the midst of your convalesance. Miss Starr will be in London for the summer and perhaps will tell you of our latest plans and enlargments—[8] With affectionate greetings to Canon Barnett and yourself I am always faithfully yours

Jane Addams

ALS (UIC, JAMC, Barnett; *JAPM*, 3:1353–55).

1. Robert A. Woods corresponded with JA about plans for the upcoming conference: 17 May 1897; 23 May, 2 June, 5 June, and 10 June 1898, all SCPC, JAC; *JAPM*, 3:672–77, 1089–92, 1097–99, 1100–3, and 1108.

2. "Settlement Conference," *Commons* 6, no. 2 (June 1899): 7.

3. "Settlement Conference," *Commons* 6, no. 2 (June 1899): 10.

4. "Settlement Conference," *Commons* 6, no. 2 (June 1899): 12.

5. The letter from Canon Samuel A. Barnett and Henrietta Barnett was published in its entirety as "Letter to the Chicago Conference from the Rev. Canon and Mrs. S. A. Barnett," *Commons* 6, no. 2 (June 1899): 1–2. Among the cautions the Barnetts offered were the following: "A settlement, if it is to be true to its title, must keep within itself the characteristics

of the society from which it has been drawn. It is an off-shoot of cultivated life planted in the midst of industrial life. It must, therefore, be made up of persons who have had the advantages of culture, and they in their new home must keep around them the things such culture demands. A settlement must not be a social workshop. . . . [I]t may be further said that because a settlement is a microcosm of cultivated society its residents should represent various forms of opinion, religious and political. But as a settlement represents cultivated society in its care for the disinherited classes, there should be only one spirit. . . . A settlement is a growth and not an organization. . . . The capacity for helpfulness is the root from which settlements have sprung—the motive which has brought your conference together. It is deep in us all, and, existing even in the most degraded, should be recognized and freely used. No one has yet estimated the gold mine of social forces, both for healing and inspiration, which lie among those who have hitherto appeared themselves only to need help."

6. JA's comment may be in reference to the following admonition in the Barnett letter to the conference: "That a settlement should be the home of the residents, that the residents should be persons of varied interests and tastes, and that their activities should be free and spontaneous, are principles deeply affecting residents; but around all settlements there come by degrees other people who are veritable parts of the settlement, although not themselves settlers, and for them also tendencies have to be watched and directed. In England the dangers connected with volunteer workers is their (a) irregularity and (b) impatience of results" ("Letter to the Chicago Conference from Rev. Canon and Mrs. S. A. Barnett," 2).

7. Although the Barnetts hoped to visit the United States and Chicago soon, there is no evidence that they did.

8. JA expected EGS to report to the Barnetts about the new combination Coffee House and Theatre Building and about moving the current Gymnasium Building to the west of the new structure on Polk St. and redeveloping it as a place to promote Arts and Crafts enterprise and the Labor Museum.

## To Mary Rozet Smith

Hull-House 335 South Halsted Street Chicago [Ill.] May 31" 1899

Dearest

Your rediculous remark that you wanted moral reflections for your embarkation[1] drives me to pen the following!

That I have never known any one who so instinctively and steadily did the noble and right thing in all her relationships, as this dearest friend of mine. That we admire her for this most of all—that she simply does what the rest of us talk about. That my heart aches for the dearest friend of mine with all her dependent invalids and yet I love her for doing it. That in spite of all her remarks I am going to be homesick for her each day and the light of Chicago is different with her out of it.

For now and forever yours in the bonds of unchanging affection

Jane Addams

ALS (SCPC, JAC; *JAPM*, 3:1356–57).

1. MRS was taking her mother, Sarah Rozet Smith, and head of the HH music program Eleanor Smith, who was ill, to Europe for the summer.

## To Mary Rozet Smith

Hull-House 335 South Halsted Street Chicago [Ill.] June 22d 1899

Dearest

I keep missing you more and more and don't seem to get used to it. I fancy that the same is true of the Winnetka household altho I hope your father will feel better when the letters begin to come, the strain of not hearing has been hard on him. I have been out quite often and am going out to lunch today.[1] The Meads,[2] Mr Hooker and myself were out to dinner the other evening, and I am afraid that Mrs Mead was a little too lively for the quiet house hold and rather prostrated them. Polly[3] seems fairly cheerful and is perfectly devoted to your Aunt Sarah. Your father does n't seem strong enough to come to town as often as he had planned, but I think that that has been partly owing to his bad tooth.

The Commencement season is still on. I spoke at Armour yesterday,[4] to night I give the address at the Medill[5] and to morrow at the Dore[6] and then I am really at the end—it has been rather a long pull and made it impossible to get at the U. of C. lectures, Sister Kelley will have to pull us both through![7]

Last Sunday Miss Culver invited me to go bicycling with them to Riverside,[8] Mr Ewing[9] took me on the tandem. We ate lunch by the river, called on the Barnums[10] and really had quite a chummy day. When you think of an old lady of sixty nine riding twenty four miles, it seems really as if getting old were not such a burden.

The Blains School[11] site is still undecided. Col Parker[12] was here at the closing exercises of Mrs Putnam's class[13] and expressed himself as much pleased with the notion of putting it on the rest of the block, but so long as we hold on to the theatre and all the rest that will of course be almost impossible—

Mary Hill is going to stay for a few weeks and do some work at Rand and McNally's,[14] and curiously enough Mr Swope has decided not to leave until Sept 1st. It is going to make the summer much jollier to have them both here, and likewise interesting—

I continually add a little bit to my gym fund, am now up to $5500.00[15] and we are going ahead.

I inclose a note from Percival Chubb,[16] hoping that you will have time to look up the museum matter, at least for future ideas if not for purchases. The other cutting your father suggested my sending.[17]

We are all so anxious to know how your mother and E. Smith stood the journey—it is a long time to wait for the first letter. Give my love to them all—and most for you whom I love best. Ys

J—A—

ALI (SCPC, JAC; *JAPM*, 3:1368–72).

1. During the time that MRS, Eleanor Smith, and MRS's mother, Sarah Rozet Smith, were in Europe, JA and various HH residents made frequent day trips north to Winnetka, Ill., to

visit MRS's father, Charles Mather Smith; his sister, Sarah Porter Smith; and MRS's mother's relatives George H. and Josephine Mandeville Rozet. "Your first letter came yesterday morning and I assure you that it brought much pleasure and relief. I lunched at Winnetka and found that the two letters there had made the atmosphere a totally different one, and I believe that from now on with the letters coming things will be much better. There is one thing sure—you need never imagine that your 'being good to your family' is a made up mission—if there ever was a genuine and definite good performed you do it there!" (JA to MRS, 24 June 1899, SCPC, JAC; *JAPM*, 3:1373–74).

George Hollenbeck Rozet (1829?–1900) was born in Philadelphia, the only son of French merchant John Rozet and his wife, Mary Ann Laning, of Oswego, N.Y. Josephine Mandeville Rozet (1840?–99) was the daughter of Henry D. and Charlotte Schott Mandeville of Philadelphia. George Rozet was an 1848 graduate of the Univ. of Pennsylvania, studied law, and became interested in real estate. After serving as U.S. commissioner to Nicaragua, he returned to New Orleans and entered the cotton business. He arrived in Chicago in 1865. His Chicago residence was on LaSalle Ave. He was instrumental in helping the Roman Catholic church in Chicago acquire large tracts of land on Lake Shore Dr. As the representative of the Drexel family in Chicago (his sister had married into the Drexel family of Philadelphia), he helped to develop Drexel Blvd. in Chicago. He also donated a large section of Lake Michigan frontage property to the South Park Comm. of Chicago. The Rozet's son, John, died in 1883 (b. 1870), and two daughters survived them: Rebecca Mandeville (1863–1931) (who became Mrs. William Prescott Hunt Jr. in 1893) and Marie Josephine (1870–1933). See Biographical Profiles: Smith, Mary Rozet (1868–1934), and Smith Family, below.

2. George Herbert Mead (1863–1931) and his wife, Helen Kingsbury Castle (1860–1929), arrived in Chicago in 1894. George Herbert Mead was the son of Congregational minister Hiram and his wife, Elizabeth Storrs Billings Mead, educator and later president of Mt. Holyoke College, in South Hadley, Mass. After graduating from Oberlin College (A.B. 1883), he became a private tutor for the children of William James, 1883–97, and entered Harvard, where he received another M.A. in 1888. At the end of two years of study in Leipzig and Berlin, Germany, he returned to the United States with his bride and became an instructor in philosophy, 1891–93, and then an assistant professor, 1893–94, and colleague of John Dewey at the Univ. of Michigan. He followed Dewey to the Univ. of Chicago, where he was a faculty member for the remainder of his academic life.

Mead's scholarly interests centered around philosophy and social psychology. Along with his friend Dewey, he became one of America's leading pragmatist philosophers. He was also noted for his "attempt to show how the human self arises in the process of social interaction, especially by way of linguistic communication" (Cronk, "George Herbert Mead [1863–1931]").

Like the Deweys, the Meads became friends of JA and HH. The settlement, he said, "illustrates concretely how the community ought to form moral judgments" (Hogan, *Class and Reform*, 233). JA and Mead shared many reform ideas concerning education. As a member of the Municipal Voters' League, Mead became a founder in 1903 and president of the Chicago City Club. Between 1909 and 1911, he was the chairman of its Com. on Public Education, established to investigate the place of vocational education in Chicago schools. One of the results was *A Report on Vocational Training in Chicago and in Other States* (1912). Like JA he favored basic education for all boys and girls, with vocational education an option rather than a totally separate program. In 1916, again along with JA, he helped found the Public Education Assn. that promoted an appointed rather than an elected school board headed by a superintendent, business manager, and lawyer and included teacher tenure after three years of service. Mead also served as vice-president of the Illinois Progressive League and was a member of the Chicago Literary Club.

Shortly after Helen Castle Mead died, her husband and friends established the Helen Castle Mead Memorial Fund at the Univ. of Chicago for the purpose of "supporting some member of the colored race while engaged in original research in medicine or in advanced medical or nurses' training" (Helen Castle Mead Memorial Fund, Card). JA pledged and by 1931 had contributed seventy-five dollars to the fund.

3. Polly was Mary Ursula Smith, no relation to the Charles Mather Smith family, who was born in Ireland ca. 1859 and emigrated with her family to the United States ca. 1867. She was a servant in the Smith family from the time she was a teenager until the death of MRS in 1934. See Biographical Profiles, Smith, Mary Rozet (1868–1934), and Smith Family.

4. JA gave the commencement address at the Armour Institute at 3:00 P.M. on Wednesday, 21 June 1899.

5. The Joseph Medill High School conducted its graduation exercise at 8:00 P.M. on Thursday, 22 June 1899. The subject of JA's speech was the school's namesake, Joseph Medill (1823–99), friend of Abraham Lincoln, publisher and developer of the *Chicago Daily Tribune*, mayor immediately after the Chicago Fire of 1871, antislavery advocate, and philanthropist.

6. The HH neighborhood Doré school's commencement ceremony was held at the school at 8:00 P.M. on Friday, 23 June 1899.

7. No wonder JA was becoming concerned about the lectures that she and Florence Kelley had agreed to give at the Univ. of Chicago. The first was to be presented in two weeks by JA on 5 July 1899. In the meantime, JA had agreed to appearances at the CWC on 27 June and in Lake Forest, Ill., on 30 June. JA and Florence Kelley were to present twelve lectures each. JA's were given one on Wednesday and one on Friday afternoons in each of the next six weeks, with the final lecture on 11 Aug. JA wrote to Florence Kelley: "The new building and the moving of the gym—of which I have enough money if we omit the 3rd floor—have taken all my energies and I have n't begun a lecture" ([May–June?] [1899], NYPL, Kelley; *JAPM*, 3:1361). By 29 June 1899, JA indicated, "I have been doing my lectures on the type-writer until I have grown quite expert." However, she continued, "We are much as usual at H-H. some days are very wild . . . and down at the bottom of my mind conciousness that my lectures were not being done" (JA to MRS, SCPC, JAC; *JAPM*, 3:1380).

The lectures that JA and Kelley planned to offer were titled "Course of Lectures on Legalized and Non-Legalized Social Ethics." Students who attended their open lecture course could receive credit if they officially registered and took a final examination. The series of twelve lectures that JA gave was called "Contemporary Social Ethics." The introductory presentation was titled "Survivals and Intimations" and was JA's perspective on current attitudes on social issues. JA's next seven lectures were as follows: "July 7. As affecting Family Relationships. July 12. As affecting Domestic Service. July 14. As affecting Trades Unions. July 19. As affecting the Efforts of Model Employers. July 21. As affecting Educational Methods. July 26. As affecting City Politics. July 28. As affecting Charitable Efforts." She described the last four lectures as: "Aug. 2. The Individual Adjustment (Tolstoy). Aug. 4. Attempts at Group Adjustment (Croyden Commonwealth, the Labor Church). Aug. 9. Attempts at Group Adjustment (English and American Social Settlements). Aug. 11. The Trend" (Enclosure to JA to Richard T. Ely, 29 Sept. 1899, SHSW, Ely; *JAPM*, 3:1443). Of her Tolstoy lecture, JA typed to MRS: "I am giving a bran new Tolstoy you will be pleased to know" and she admitted that "We hear from various sources that" the lectures "are going very well and I will confess to quite liking it" (31 July 1899, SCPC, JAC; *JAPM*, 3:1398).

Florence Kelley spoke on 6, 11, 13, 18, 20, 25, and 27 July and on 1, 3, 8, and 10 in Aug. Among her topics were life, health, motherhood, childhood, education, skill, leisure, organization, the right to work, the rights of the buyer, the rights of the seller, and ethical gains through legislation.

JA confessed to MRS: "My first lecture at the U. of C. almost used me up and really didn't go very well. The second one however went off with much more spirit and I am beginning to feel the swing. I am rewriting all of them practically and quite enjoying it" ([18 July 1899], SCPC, JAC; *JAPM*, 3:1394–95). Of the whole experience, Gertrude Barnum reported to MRS:

"Lady Janes audiences have not been large but she has not lost any—rather gained on the whole" (16 Aug. 1899, SCPC, JAC; *JAPM*, 3:1411). See also JA to MRS, 25 July 1899, n. 5, below.

JA gave versions of her lectures at other places, most notably a series of six lectures in Davenport, Iowa, 21 and 28 Oct. and 4, 11, 18, and 25 Nov. 1899. A later and undated sixteen-page list of her lectures appeared as a syllabus titled *Democracy and Social Ethics: A Syllabus of a Course of Twelve Lectures*. In it JA suggested additional reading that students or listeners might find helpful for each lecture, and she also provided a summary statement for the topic of each lecture. Among the other venues for the lecture series 1899–1901 were the CWC, All Souls Unitarian Church in Chicago, and Iowa City, Keokuck, and Burlington, Iowa. JA's lectures were incorporated in several articles published in the scholarly and popular press, including the *Atlantic Monthly*, *International Journal of Ethics*, the *Commons*, and the *American Journal of Sociology*. More important, the lectures became the core of her first book, *Democracy and Social Ethics*.

Richard T. Ely, who wanted to publish a book from the lectures for his series in which *HH Maps and Papers* had appeared, approached JA about it shortly after the lectures were finished. She wrote back to him on 29 Sept. 1899: "For the book I had planned only the Introductory and the six illustrative lectures" (SHSW, Ely; *JAPM*, 3:1441). Ely wanted her to produce a manuscript quickly. "When do you think you will be able to finish your book? I much wish we could have it at an early day," he wrote to her on 6 Nov. 1899 (SCPC, JAC; *JAPM*, 3:1467). Ely continued to hound JA into 1900 about the book manuscript. On 13 Sept. 1900, JA wrote to Ely, "I hope to get at the book this winter, before Christmas if possible—I am tying to keep free of lecture engagements for that time. I am ashamed to have been so dilatory" (SHSW, Ely; *JAPM*, 3:1651). JA probably sent a version of what she planned for the book to Ely in the late spring of 1901. He visited her at HH over that summer to discuss the contents and its order. By Sept. 1901, JA was spending evenings and days until midafternoon working on the manuscript at the home of MRS and going to HH from 3:00 P.M. until 9:30 P.M. JA expected that she had captured the substance of her twelve original lectures in the introduction followed by six chapters: "Charitable Effort," "Filial Relations," "Household Adjustment," "Industrial Amelioration," "Educational Methods," and "Political Reform." The completed manuscript finally went to Ely in early Nov. 1901, and JA demanded to see galley proof before the page-proof stage. *Democracy and Social Ethics* was not published until Mar. 1902 in Ely's series Citizens' Library of Economics, Politics, and Sociology issued by Macmillan. JA, who followed her editor, Ely, to Macmillan, chose to remain a Macmillan author for the rest of her publishing life. This was the first book JA wrote, and it was an enormous success, judging by the complimentary notices it received. The book sold more than three thousand copies during the first year and remained in print through 1925. It was widely reviewed in general and scholarly journals and newspapers throughout the United States and England (for reviews and advertisements about the work, see SCPC, JAC, and *JAPM*, Addendum 11:1–199).

8. Riverside, Ill., was located on the Des Plaines River and approximately ten miles west of the Loop in downtown Chicago. It was designed in 1868 by famous landscape architect Frederick Law Olmsted, who laid out New York City's Central Park. Riverside began to attract residents during the 1870s and 1880s.

9. Charles Hull Ewing (1868–1954) was born in Randolph, Cattaragus Co., N.Y., to Aurelia Culver and Robert Finley Ewing. Aurelia Culver was an older sister of Helen Culver, and Charles Hull Ewing was therefore Helen Culver's nephew. Ewing was a graduate of Yale Univ. (A.B. 1893) and attended Northwestern Law School, 1893–94. He began his work career as manager of the Moorhead Stave Co., in Moorhead, Miss., 1895–96. Helen Culver brought him to Chicago to become manager of the Helen Culver Fund at the Univ. of Chicago (1896–1909) and to learn the real estate business that she managed. Culver's biographer Thomas W. Goodspeed reported that "Charles Hull Ewing . . . entered . . . [Culver's] office

and displayed such ability that she very soon began to transfer the burdens of the office to his younger shoulders. . . . For several years Mr. Ewing was a member of her family and gradually took over the care of the office" (Goodspeed, *Helen Culver*, 90–91). He invested in real estate in the Chicago area and in Florida. In 1906 he married Mary Everts of Minneapolis; the Ewings had two children, Katherine Everts Ewing Hocking and Helen Culver Ewing. They had homes in Lake Forest, Ill., and in Sarasota, Fla.

Ewing adopted many of his aunt Helen Culver's social and cultural interests. He was active in the Geographic Society of Chicago and served as its president, 1924–26, 1928–29, and established an endowment fund for the organization. He was also a member of the Royal Geographic Society of Persia and the Chicago Historical Society. He was a life member of the Art Institute of Chicago and the Field Museum of Natural History.

Ewing became a trustee at HH in place of Helen Culver on 19 Oct. 1920 and continued a close relationship with the settlement and with JA until her death. He made annual personal gifts to the settlement and supported special projects, including summer camps for HH children. He was often the person JA consulted about various financial holdings in the HH endowment fund. Through the years, the Ewing family became personal friends of JA and MRS.

10. William Henry and Clara Letitia Hyde Barnum were the parents of Belle, Gertrude, Edna, and Harry H. Barnum. Both Belle and Gertrude were volunteers at HH, and Gertrude became a resident. William H. Barnum (1840–1915) was an attorney and jurist who was born in Onondaga Co., N.Y., and moved with his parents to Belleville, Ill., where he grew up and met his wife. He attended schools in Michigan and was admitted to the Illinois Bar in 1862. He served as judge in the Circuit Court of Cook Co., 1879 to 1884. The Barnums moved to Riverside in the 1890s. See also JA to MRS, 15 Jan. 1895, n. 16, above.

11. Anita McCormick Blaine planned to provide funds to support the development of two laboratory schools in Chicago to help teachers learn how to teach the educational methods of Col. Francis Wayland Parker. See JA to MRS, 4 [, 5, and 6] Sept. 1895, n. 21, above.

12. It seems likely that Col. Francis Wayland Parker discussed placing one of the two training schools to be created by Anita McCormick Blaine near HH. In a letter to MRS about two weeks later, JA reported: "We take supper with Mrs Blaine this evening. I really think that the 'Slum School' has gone to the north side but that all the talk will probably result in a Dewey School for us" ([18 July 1899], SCPC, JAC; *JAPM*, 3:1395). There was no Dewey School for HH. See also JA to MRS, 4 [, 5, and 6] Sept. 1895, n. 24, above.

13. In 1897 Alice Putnam (see JA to SAAH, 8 Oct. 1889, n. 6, above) established the headquarters of her Chicago Froebel Assn. in the HH Children's House with the aim of providing training for those who would teach kindergarten. Among HH residents and volunteers who were part of her faculty were Eleanor Smith and Rose Gyles.

14. The Rand-McNally Co. was formed in 1856 by William Rand and Andrew McNally as a printing company that began by printing tickets and railroad timetables. By the last part of the nineteenth century, they were publishing maps and atlases. In 1877 the company initiated a trade department and in 1894 a textbook department.

15. In a letter to MRS dated 9 June 1899, JA reported that she had "$4500.00 enough to move it" (SCPC, JAC; *JAPM*, 3:1365). About two weeks later, JA indicated: "Money affairs has been moving slowly of late—I seem to have struck a dead line—we have almost six thousand however and have resolved to go ahead with the moving" (JA to MRS, [18 July 1899], SCPC, JAC; *JAPM*, 3:1395).

16. Chubb's note is not known to be extant.

17. The "cutting" enclosure is not known to be extant.

## To Mary Rozet Smith

Hull-House 335 South Halsted Street Chicago [Ill.] July 25 1899

Dearest:

Your letters are the most delightful thing about the summer and I bless you for each one.

Mrs Kelley and I dined at Winnetka this evening, your father is really very anxious about your Aunt Sarah who seems exactly as usual altho I think she felt the strain of the two invalids—Mr & Mrs Rozet[1]—a good deal. It is too bad that Dr Johnson[2] got to the scaring point just this summer for his letter said distinctly that there was no special change in her condition. Mr Taylor and Alice[3] went out with me last week and I made up my mind then that we must not have so many—it entertains your father of course, we really had a very good time—but he is distressed about your aunt through it all. He has planned so many times to come in to lunch but something has always prevented, he promised quite solemniny tonight for next Thursday—when Mrs Coonley and one or two other people are coming—

Alice and Marcet are here for two months[4] and just now Flora Guiteau is visiting me so that we have quite a family reunion. Sister Kelley was blooming when she came from N.Y. but is succumbing to the "Slum Climate" and has really been quite miserable.[5]

The Summer School[6] is so "full up" that we are turning people away—Mr Twose and his brother has been great acquisitions and have made it very gay.

Dr DeBey[7] came in today for news and really has a more cheerful diognosis on hand, I am happy to say. Please give my love to the lady. Helen Goodrich[8] is improving all of the time at Rockford and has given some charming recitals—she has apparently quite recovered from her maleria. G. Barnum is teaching the Music School straight through July and likes it immensly. The Coffee house is all finished but the floor and is very satisfactory[9]—my other fund is up to $6000.<u>00</u>[10]

Please give my love to your mother, and to the rest of the party in general—To<ward> the Head and the Heart of it, you know my sentiments which now and forever move unchanging—Always ys

J.A.

ALI (SCPC, JAC; *JAPM*, 3:1387–90).

1. See JA to MRS, 22 June 1899, n. 1, above.

2. Dr. Johnson may have been Dr. Frank Seward Johnson (1856–1922), who practiced at 2521 Prairie Ave. and was married in 1890 to Elizabeth B. Ayer, daughter of Edward E. Ayer (see *PJA*, 2:415). He was trained at Northwestern Univ., where he received his A.B., M.A., and medical degree from the Chicago Medical College, which eventually merged with Northwestern Univ. He then spent a year at the Univ. of Vienna and a year as an intern at Cook County Hospital. He became a professor and then dean of faculty at the Northwestern Medical School. He was consulting physician to Michael Reese, Mercy, and the Woman's hospitals.

The Johnsons also had a home in Lake Geneva, Wis., and in 1917 moved to Pasadena, Calif., where he died.

3. Graham Taylor and SAAH.

4. "I think it will be fine to have you here during the summer—it is what I have been hoping for all winter," JA wrote to SAAH, 19 May 1899. "The house is almost empty in August so that the question of room is easily settled and you know that a month is not too long but too short. . . .

"Summer School begins July 1st and runs for five weeks—I will see you in Rockford Commencement day June 13". I cannot get there until eleven o'clock because I speak in Davenport the night before. We can then talk over the Cedarville question. I should certainly go to the old house for part of the time. It is really much more peaceful than it used to be and much less danger of an explosion. Why not try it for a few days and then go to Weber?

"I cannot tell you how glad I am that you are coming" (IU, Lilly, SAAH; *JAPM*, 3:1348–50).

At the conclusion of the visit with SAAH and Marcet, JA reported to MRS: "Alice and Marcet leave this week, we have really had a very nice time the last of the visit and I am ashamed when I think of myself the first week" (14 Aug. 1899, SCPC, JAC; *JAPM*, 3:1405). Gertrude Barnum saw the relationship issues as well. "I don't think Mrs. Haldeman has been alto-gether easy—two more different individuals will hardly be found than she and her sister" (Gertrude Barnum to MRS, 16 Aug. 1899, SCPC, JAC; *JAPM*, 3:1413).

5. "Chicago was more horrid than I could have conceived possible," Florence Kelley wrote to MRS from New York City. "I fell ill two days after I arrived; and stayed ill until I reached Columbus, Ohio, . . . and entered upon a recovery which has completed itself here. I was so cross and so miserable all the time, that I made life even more miserable for the beloved Chief than the weather, her dear family, the trades unions, and her lecture course, all rolled into one long misery were doing without my diabolical help" (28 Aug. 1899, SCPC, JAC; *JAPM*, 3:1429–30). In a letter to MRS, Gertrude Barnum supported Florence Kelley's description of herself: "Mrs. Kelley has not been herself at all—her lectures were not prepared carefully & she got perfectly miserable over them. Margaret is so selfish & trying too & alto-gether Mrs. K—is really ill—nervous & prostrated. I am glad she goes back tomorrow. She was so well & happy when she came & will doubtless pick up again" (SCPC, JAC; *JAPM*, 3:1414–15). About Margaret Kelley, JA concluded, "Margaret is a handsome creature but her attitude when she found out her Semetic ancestry was pathetic, none the less so for its absurdity" (JA to MRS, 14 Aug. 1899, SCPC, JAC; *JAPM*, 3:1404).

6. Earlier in July, JA had reported to MRS: "The Summer School has only about fifty much to our sorrow" ([18 July 1899], SCPC, JAC; *JAPM*, 3:1394). But by 8 Aug. 1899, JA found, "The Summer School was full up to the very last, they had a commencement Sat. night in which the entire school appeared in caps and gowns, many of them took degrees. Mr Twose making a most magnificent Dean" (JA to MRS, SCPC, JAC; *JAPM*, 3:1400–1). In 1899 the HH Summer School at RC lasted from 1 July until 5 Aug., and according to the Nov. and Dec. *HH Bulletin*, the average attendance was eighty students, "the most successful in the history of the school" (3, no. 12:10; *JAPM*, 53:728)

7. Cornelia Bernarda de Bey (1865–1948), physician and social reformer, was born in Groningen, Netherlands, the daughter of religious leader and educational reformer Bernardus and Anje Schuringa de Beij. They emigrated with their family to Chicago in 1868, where the de Beij household became the center of the Dutch Reformed Church in Chicago. Cornelia de Bey, who Anglicized her last name slightly, graduated from the Cook County Normal School in 1889 and became a teacher and continued her education. Before becoming a homeopathic physician through study at the Hahnemann Medical College and Hospital, Chicago (M.D. 1895), she studied art at the Art Institute and at Northwestern Univ. She began to practice medicine in Chicago, which she continued until 1928, and also earned a reputation as an outspoken and decisive reformer with leadership qualities. In 1903, along

with HH residents, she participated in a two-day investigation of street-vending children; her territory was Englewood. In 1904 she helped settle a strike in the meatpacking industry and worked with JA, unsuccessfully, on a committee to try to arbitrate a teamsters strike in Chicago. Always interested in children and education, de Bey and JA were tapped by then reform Democratic mayor Edward F. Dunn (1853–1937), who served 1905–7, to become members of the Chicago Board of Education. The two women often worked together while they were on the board to improve the educational structure and opportunities for children in city schools. For example, both decried an experiment that promoted gender segregation in Chicago schools; they argued instead for smaller class sizes and more freedom for the teaching staff about methodology. de Bey was an ardent suffragist and, during World War I, a peace advocate. She also became a writer of short stories for children. After living briefly in California, beginning in 1940 she lived the remainder of her life in Grand Rapids, Mich.

8. Helen Goodrich served as a HH resident beginning in the fall of 1899. She was in charge of the settlement's Sunday concert program between 1901 and the fall of 1904. She was a music educator who participated in concerts as a soprano and gave recitals at HH beginning in 1897, continuing through 1904, and sang for HH Summer School students. In 1900 she joined Bertha Payne, head of the kindergarten training department of the Chicago Institute, Academic and Pedagogic, to present the music segment of the institute's course of study. While Payne discussed pedagogy, Goodrich suggested songs that teachers might use in the various grades from kindergarten through high school. Between 1901 and 1930, she taught music at the Francis W. Parker School.

9. JA was attempting to get her new combination Coffee House and Theatre Building completed, but a strike of mosaic workers, which began in Feb. 1899, caused a delay. On 24 June 1899, JA wrote to MRS: "The new Coffee house is very handsome with its black wood work, it is quite the most gorgeous room we have, and I quite share the Pond's enthusiasm" (SCPC, JAC; *JAPM*, 3:1373–77). Yet Gertrude Barnum reported to MRS on 16 Aug. 1899: "The building goes so slowly & is wearing her sadly yesterday a committee from the Building Trades Council waited upon her very courteously to tell her that the mosaic workers now at last engaged on the floor were 'each & all' scabs, & that the Union plasterers (also working) would have to be called off unless the others were" (SCPC, JAC; *JAPM*, 3:1412–13). JA's diary indicated that she met with mosaic workers later on 21 Aug., and the next day the strike ended. JA informed MRS: "We have been having a devilish time over a strike connected with the new building, I have been trying to arbitrate between two sets of men who are dying to shoot each other and I am feeling very foolish and ineffective" (22 Aug. 1899, SCPC, JAC; *JAPM*, 3:1419). By 30 Aug., JA told MRS: "The strike in regard to the floor has at last been adjusted by a ceramic mosaic floor; I am moved to state that the two sides in the struggle appeared about equally well or rather ill. Industrial Democracy comes on slowly in America" (30 Aug. 1899, SCPC, JAC; *JAPM*, 3:1425). On 29 Sept. 1899, JA reported to SAAH: "At last the mosaic floor is going down (ceramic instead of marble) and we hope to move into the entire building in ten days" (IU Lilly, SAAH; *JAPM*, 3:1444).

With the floor of the new building finally complete, JA turned her mind to decoration and wrote to ask Lillian Wald to do her "a favor. This time I am very anxious to have ten or twelve brass trays, the plain ones I think, of varying sizes avoiding the smallest and the huge ones. I have a scheme of decoration for the new coffee-house which I am at least anxious to try" (5 Sept. 1899, NYPL, Wald, Incoming; *JAPM*, 3:1431). JA also planned to purchase an Adalusian pitcher as her gift to the coffeehouse. "I am so fond of each new building that I usually make each one a Christening present" (JA to SAAH, 11 Sept. 1899, IU, Lilly, SAAH; *JAPM*, 3:1432). The building finally opened on 25 Oct. 1899. See Article in the *Commons*, 31 Oct. 1899, below.

10. JA had been struggling to raise sufficient funds to move and renovate the former Gymnasium and Coffee House Building and add a third story. When MRS offered to add

funds to what JA had already raised to make the project possible, JA responded: "Of course you can't pay the balance of the fund because it is yet too large for any single individual. I am afraid that G. Barnum told a too piteous tale, I am really all right" (8 Aug. 1899, SCPC, JAC; *JAPM*, 3:1400). By 29 July 1899, JA had increased her fund to $6,515. To correct what she seems to have told MRS in correspondence no longer extant, Gertrude Barnum wrote to MRS on 16 Aug. 1899 that JA was "within $1800.00 of money enough to the building" (SCPC, JAC; *JAPM*, 3:1412). By 11 Sept. 1899, JA announced: "We have just decided to give up moving and remodeling the gymnasium this fall. Prices of material are so high that it really becomes an extravagance altho we are going to be rather uncomfortable without it" (JA to SAAH, IU, Lilly, SAAH; *JAPM*, 3:1433). The total cost for the building was estimated to be $19,000. See Article in the *Evening Gazette*, 10 Aug. 1898, n. 1 above; and Article in the *Commons*, 31 Oct. 1899, below. The building was ready for occupancy at the end of 1901.

## To Florence Kelley

Hull-House 335 South Halsted Street Chicago [Ill.] Sept. 13th 1899

My dear Sister Kelley

Your letter cheered me very much and quite warmed my stoney old heart.[1] Please don't feel regrets about the summer,[2] it was the greatest pleasure in the world to have you back and nothing else counted. The cool weather is doing wonders for my temper,[3] so that I call myself restored. Margareat and I spent two days at Winnetka last week and had a really charming visit, the little lady blossemed under the drives and the evident devotion of her host.[4] Miss Gernon[5] and I went with her to the train and our hearts quite sank as she departed. She has been charming and you would be touched by all the nice things people are saying about her, my heart swells with vicarioious[6] pride. The "Trust Conference" opened to-day with much pomp.[7] Your President[8] made a good speech as did also Henry C. Adams[9] who with Mr Ely[10] is our guest. By the little man[11] wants to have our book, which Mr Small[12] has told him about, for a new series which he is undertaking for b Harpers;[13] he has left Crowell as being too slow.[14] Please write to <us> sometimes, I will do better.

With my love to your Mother and Ko,[15] I am always and forever yours

Jane Addams.

TLS (NYPL, Kelley; *JAPM*, 3:1434–35).

1. Florence Kelley's letter is not known to be extant.

2. See JA to MRS, 25 July 1899, n. 5, above. To MRS Florence Kelley wrote: "I'm wondering whether my faculties are not giving way—seeing that I have great trouble in inventing ways of keeping myself useful to my organization! I'm [to] go-to Saratoga week after next, to read a paper to the Amer. Social Sci. Ass'n. Perhaps I may get half an idea there. I did not get a decimal fraction of one in the University" (28 Aug. 1899, SCPC, JAC; *JAPM*, 3:1430).

3. On 4 Sept. 1899, JA wrote to MRS: "I have just come back from Cedarville where I had a very fine Sunday marred by a brief interview with Henry Haldeman. I am feeling better with all the world even including mosaic workers" (SCPC, JAC; *JAPM*, 3:1427). Sunday was 3 Sept. 1899.

4. JA and Margaret Kelley were visiting Henry Demarest Lloyd and his family at "Wayside" in Winnetka, Ill. The children of Kelley were particularly close to the Lloyds. From the time that the Kelley family moved to Chicago, the Kelley children often made their home with the Lloyds in Winnetka. Margaret Dana Kelley (1886–1905), Florence Kelley's second born, was about to return to Hillside Home School in Hillside, Wis., operated by two of Lloyd's cousins, Ellen and Jane Lloyd-Jones. Her board there was paid by MRS.

5. HH resident Maude Gernon.

6. The first part of the word "vicarious," which is misspelled, appears as the last word on the last line of the first page of the letter; a second part of the word "ious" is the first word at the beginning of the first line of p. 2 of the letter.

7. From 13 through 16 Sept. 1899, the Civic Federation of Chicago held the Chicago Conf. on Trusts, which JA attended as an observer. The goal of the federation was to educate leaders and the public on the issue of trusts. The federation believed that "upon no current topic was there so widespread and general an ignorance and confusion of ideas" (*Proceedings of the Chicago Conf. on Trusts*, 7). The *Chicago Record* agreed that the federation had achieved its goal of being inclusive: "All shades of opinion on the trust question seem to be represented" ("The Trust Conf. in Operation," 15 Sept. 1899). The organization expected "to hear the general subject discussed from all possible standpoints—from the view not only of the organizers of the combinations, but also from the workmen and customers of the industrial corporations" (*Proceedings of the Chicago Conf. on Trusts*, 7–8). Among the attendees were governors and delegates appointed by governors of various states as well as representatives of "leading commercial, industrial and labor organizations" and "students of economics from the various colleges and universities" in the region (*Proceedings of the Chicago Conf. on Trusts*, 5). In attendance were congressmen; former congressmen; former governors; judges and attorneys general; presidents of banks, railroads, and manufacturing and commercial organizations; and leaders in labor, educational, and agricultural interests. The *Chicago Record* reported that "some of the addresses . . . were trifling or flamboyant. . . . But there were others that represented careful study and deep thought . . . the conference has distinctly served to reveal how untenable is the extreme position on either side of the trust question" ("Influence of the Trust Conf.," 16 Sept. 1899).

8. John Graham Brooks (1846–1938), serving as first president of the newly formed National Consumers' League, had offered the post of corresponding secretary to Florence Kelley in Jan. 1899. She finally accepted the offer in Mar. 1899 and began working in New York City on 1 May 1899. When Brooks spoke at the trust conference, he was identified as a lecturer from the Univ. of Chicago. The *Chicago Inter Ocean* described him as "a scholarly man, known by his friends to be radical, believed by those who meet him casually to be a mild-mannered, extremely conservative dilettante. But he is not a dilettante. No slouch-hatted, blue-overalled socialist, was ever more wildly earnest than John Graham Brooks, the fashionably dressed, the fastidious, the well groomed. . . . He is one of the most successful of speakers" (17 Sept. 1899). JA heard him give a speech called "Are the New Combinations Socially Dangerous?"

John Graham Brooks was born in Aeworth, N.H., the son of Chapin Kidder and Parmelia Graham Brooks. He attended Oberlin College and Harvard Divinity School, from which he graduated in 1875. Ordained as a Unitarian minister, he held classes for workingmen in Roxbury, Mass. For a two-year period, he was an instructor at Harvard Univ. and moved to the Univ. of Chicago, where he served in the extension department. While there he gave a series of lectures at HH in Jan. and Feb. 1895. His subject was titled "Modern Socialism at Work." He also appeared in the Social Economic Conference hosted by HH and Chicago Commons that took place at both settlements in Dec. 1896. His lecture on Thursday 10 Dec. at HH was titled "The Fabian Movement." For several years, he was an investigator of strikes for the U.S. Dept. of Labor and eventually served as a lecturer at the Univ. of California. Among his published works are *The Social Unrest* (1903), *As Others See Us* (1908), and *Labor's Challenge*

According to a description by Alice Hamilton, it was during the construction of the Coffee House and Theatre Building that the first theatrical stage of the settlement located between the east and west parlors on the north side of the original Hull home was removed and when the wall between those rooms and the central stairwell was taken down to make the space one big area (*American Home Culture*, 338).

*to the Social Order* (1920). He was chosen as president of the American Social Science Assn., 1904.

9. Henry C. Adams, a faculty member at the Univ. of Michigan and identified as a statistician for the Interstate Commerce Comm., who received an ovation when he was introduced to begin the 3:00 P.M. session on the first day of the meeting, was charged with undertaking a "statement of the questions that arise in the consideration of the trust problem" (*Proceedings of the Chicago Conf. on Trusts*, 35).

10. Richard T. Ely attended the Chicago Conf. on Trusts as a delegate from the Univ. of Wisconsin, where he was a professor of political economy. He did not make a formal address at the meeting. The "little man" was Ely, who was the editor of the Library of Economics and Politics series that he developed for Thomas Y. Crowell and Co., in which *HH Maps and Papers,* published in 1895, became number 5. Ely was in the process of moving his series to another publisher (see n. 14). He took the opportunity of this HH visit to speak with JA about a book for the series based on the lectures that she had recently presented at the Univ. of Chicago. See JA to MRS, 22 June 1899, n. 7, above.

11. JA may have meant to write "By the way, the little man."

12. Albion Small was instrumental in providing the opportunity through the Univ. of Chicago extension program that became the six-week joint lectureship over the summer of 1899 for JA and Florence Kelley. See JA to MRS, 22 June 1899, n. 7, above.

13. JA, the likely typist of the letter, probably did not mean to insert a "b" between the words "for" and "Harpers."

14. Before JA had time to finish her manuscript for the book that she had agreed to do, Ely had moved his series from Thomas Y. Crowell to the Macmillan Co. See JA to MRS, 22 June 1899, n. 7, above.

15. Florence Kelley's mother was Caroline Bonsall Kelley (1828–1906), and Nicholas ("Ko") Kelley (1885–1968), was Florence Kelley's oldest child and her favorite.

## Article in the *Commons*

### TEN YEARS OF HULL HOUSE.

### Anniversary of the Most Noted American Settlement—New Building Opened—Events of Anniversary Day.

Chicago, Ill. 31 October 1899

The tenth anniversary of the founding of Hull House, Chicago, was observed informally on Wednesday, October 25,[1] by ceremonies whose informality only emphasized the notable history of which they were for the time being the climax. For not only was there a simple and happy gathering of old-time friends in the settlement in the evening, but there was also the gratifying fact of the completion and more or less formal opening of the new building on Polk street, with theater and coffee-house, a picture of which was printed in the last issue of THE COMMONS. From the exceedingly satisfactory account of the occasion contributed by a resident of Hull House to the Chicago Tribune[2] we summarize:

The first evidence of the significance of the day was in the slightly elaborated program and luncheon of the Woman's Club in the afternoon.[3] Last night the friends who have aided the efforts of Miss Addams and watched the growth of the movement met at an informal reception, and listened to a brief address by Miss Addams. Visitors were there from the settlement district, who during their years of residence in the Nineteenth Ward had been constant witnesses of the many reforms which the transformation of the old Hull mansion of 1856 to its present uses had secured for the neighborhood.

### THE NEW BUILDING

The new building[4] is expected to have far-reaching effect, and to this fact close attention was drawn. The lower floor has been made an extension of the coffee-house, recently built, and, as an initial step, is expected to supply the locality with a good, cheap restaurant. The auditorium on the upper floor, with its fully equipped stage,[5] will bring about a great development of dramatic presentations at Hull House, and many companies for the production of good plays are now being formed[6] by the resident teachers and Miss Addams. The hall will be used also for recitals and in connection with the university extension courses which have been outlined for the winter.

The new building is 75 feet long and 29 feet wide, its construction being marked chiefly by the peculiar arrangement of the windows, which admit light and air to every nook of the big coffee-room. From it direct entrance is afforded to the coffee-house proper, with its stained rafters and its rows of china mugs.[7]

Seats for 300 people are provided in the auditorium, which will relieve the gymnasium located above the old coffee-rooms of the handicap of conflicting entertainments which previously were accommodated here. The land on which the new building stands was donated by Miss Helen Culver and the construction expense of $25,000 was met by subscription.[8]

## "ANNIVERSARY DAY."

"Anniversary day" was characteristic of the every-day life of the settlement. The early morning brought the mothers and their children, the little ones being left to play about the little dining tables in the kindergarten. The coffee-house was as busy as ever at 7:30 o'clock. At 9 o'clock the nurses and workers hurried away to their duties as usual. The kindergarten training class of older boys and girls kept at its work in the afternoon, the children making for the play-grounds during the session of the Woman's Club of the settlement.

Each of the 160 members of the latter organization had invited a friend to hear the program of music and recitation. At the close there was a general meeting in the diningroom and a half-hour's discussion and gossip over luncheon. In the outer court groups of men chatted on the benches and watched the cable cars jangle by, dodged by Halsted street shoppers.

The evening reception brought the crowding of halls and rooms of all the settlement buildings.[9]

Aside from tracing the progress made by the settlement, Miss Addams was averse, as was Miss Starr, to discussing her own work. "Hull House," she said, "was started with the definite idea that it should be a social settlement. It was opened on the theory that the dependence of classes on each other is reciprocal, that the social relation is essentially a reciprocal relation. One of the motives constituting pressure toward the establishment of such a settlement was the desire to make the entire social organism democratic. 'Bossism' in politics causes scandal. Yet it goes on in society constantly without being challenged. Hull House has sought to relieve over-accumulation at one end of society and the destitution at the other. I believe there will be no wretched quarters in our cities when the conscience of each man is so touched that he prefers to live with the poorest of his brothren and not with the richest of them that his income will allow."

"What Hull House has accomplished speaks for itself," said Miss Addams, and with this keynote little time was spent in eulogy of the ten year's work.

PD (*Commons* 39 [31 Oct. 1899]: 9–10).

1. JA and the residents of HH received congratulations from the College Settlements Assn., whose members were located in New York City and Boston: "[T]he college settlements as-

After construction of the new Coffee House and Theatre Building, the Hull-House residents' dining room had to be reconfigured. The windows that had opened to the north were closed because the new building was built almost against the north side of the dining room. On the left back wall of this photograph of the room, a rendering of Jane Addams by Enella Benedict is displayed next to Benedict's oil painting of neighborhood child Edith Redding (1889–1959), who became Sister Sariel, B.V.M., a member of the Roman Catholic congregation, Sisters of Charity of the Blessed Virgin Mary. It is likely that these two portraits were created by or before 1900 when the settlement buildings were finally wired for electricity. Gas ceiling fixtures still hang from the ceiling in this photograph (SCPC photo 00387).

socn on our common decennial anniversary send to Hull House greeting and felicitations on the broad and far reaching work it has accomplished" (Telegram, Mabel G. Curtis to JA, 28 Oct. 1899, SCPC, JAC; *JAPM*, 3:1463).

2. "Entertained at HH" headed the article by the *Chicago Times Herald* on 26 Oct. 1899 about the HH anniversary. The *Chicago Daily Tribune*'s description, entitled "Fete Day at HH, Tenth Anniversary of the Settlement is Celebrated," was also published on 26 Oct. 1899.

3. The only surviving description of the HH Woman's Club meeting is in the *HH Bulletin* for Nov.–Dec. 1899, which indicated that on 25 Oct. the club simply held a social. No description of the events associated with the tenth anniversary celebration at HH was issued in the *HH Bulletin*.

4. See also Article in the *Evening Gazette*, 10 Aug. 1898, above.

5. See also Article in the *Evening Gazette*, 10 Aug. 1898, above. "The walls of the auditorium were of a dull, red brick, and its floor was level, without permanent seating. Judging from photographs, the proscenium stage was about twenty-five feet across, ten feet high, and suf-

ficiently deep for three wings and a backdrop. A dull red curtain hung from the proscenium, and above it read the inscription, 'Act well your part, there all the honor lies.'" In the early part of the twentieth century, among other things a gallery, a coat room, toilet facilities, an asbestos curtain, upgraded electrical wiring, and "an inclined floor with permanent opera seats" were added (Hecht, "HH Theatre: An Analytical and Evaluative History," 29–30). Murals on the side walls of the theater, one depicting Abraham Lincoln on a boat going down the Mississippi River by Chicago art student Bror Julius Olsson Nordfeldt (1878–1955), and one of Leo Tolstoy plowing a field by HH resident John Duncan, were added in 1903.

6. In addition to the HH Dramatic Assn., and the beginnings of ethnic theater at the settlement, many of the social clubs presented plays. See also Article in the *HH Bulletin*, 1 Dec. 1897; and Article in the *Evening Gazette*, 10 Aug. 1898, n. 9, both above.

7. Calling it "decidedly more pretentious than any other of the group to which it belongs," the *Chicago Times-Herald* of 9 July 1899 described the new HH coffee shop: "The furnishings of the new dining-room are to be in black oak. The ceiling shows the red and yellow tints of the tiling, and the flooring is all in colors to match. The roof shows heavy beams of the oak, black and polished, as are to be the tables, chairs and sideboards. The ornamental screen of the dark wood shelters the postoffice and the cashier's desk and behind the heavy carved doors are kitchen and serving rooms." The journalist who composed the description continued: "The serving-rooms are models of convenience. . . . The deep troughs for washing the dishes are bunched in the middle of the serving-room, and the tiers of shelves where they are placed for dining are so close to the troughs that the workers have but to turn and put each dish as she washes it on one. . . . The ice box is a marvel of convenience, with three doors, two small ones and one large one. The last has rarely to be opened except when the food is being put into it. For the smaller doors, one opens into the dining-room, from which the waitresses may get the milk and butter, the other into the kitchen and through it the cooks may get the small meals, which are all ready on sliding trays. The range is so close to the ice box that the cook has to take no more steps than do dishwashers at work in the center of the big room. A door admits from the private dining-room of the house to the new dining-room. . . . The demand for space for banquets was another factor entering into the building of this room and the hall above, no less than three college alumnae societies asking room this year for their social functions." The newspaper also pointed out that HH hoped to open other lunchrooms in the future near hospitals and schools in order to provide those populations "with cheap, wholesome luncheons" ("Fine New Addition to HH").

8. See also JA to MRS, 25 July 1899, n. 10, above.

9. The ceremony that evening took place in the new theater. In addition to JA, Mary Wilmarth spoke recalling the meeting at her home in 1889 when JA introduced the social settlement idea to her friends. Julia Lathrop addressed the crowd, and Helen Goodrich presented a vocal solo.

## Statement in the *St. Louis Post-Dispatch*

*The Second Boer War between Great Britain and the Dutch settlers, known as Boers, primarily in the Orange Free State and Transvaal, in Great Britain's Cape Colony in southern Africa began in October 1899 and continued until May 1902.*[1] *At stake was control of the two regions where diamonds and gold had recently been discovered.*[2] *Great Britain and the English, who had been defeated in their first attempt, 1880–81, to wrest control of those states,*[3] *were attempting once again to expand their authority over both Boer independent states. During the early phase of this second war, the Boers had the upper hand.*[4] *When the Boers successfully laid siege to garrisoned British troops, Great Britain responded by sending a contingent of three divisions to rescue their soldiers in peril and launch an offensive against the much smaller Boer force. Unsuccessful at first, the British added two more divisions of troops and encouraged volunteers to join their cause. Despite these increases in troop numbers by the British, a spectacular win for the Boers on 24 January 1900 in the Battle of Spion Kop left 350 British soldiers dead and 1,000 injured, while the Boers suffered fewer than 300 casualties. Many in Ireland and in Germany, and also immigrants from those two countries settled in the United States, felt sympathy for the outnumbered Boers defending their livelihood and independence.*

*This was the situation when a public meeting was called for the evening of 27 January 1900 in Chicago at the Central Music Hall by those who supported the idea of peace and also sympathized with the Boer cause.*[5] *From the estimated 3,000 people in attendance, the organizers expected to raise funds to assist the Boers through purchases of hospital equipment. Among the speakers were Mary H. Wilmarth, Jenkin Lloyd Jones, Clarence Darrow, and Jane Addams. Of Jane's speech, the* Chicago Times-Herald *reported, "Miss Jane Addams made an eloquent address and her remarks were listened to with rapt attention. No speaker received the greeting which she did and none seemed to make their statements any more effective."*[6] *Like the* Chicago Chronicle, *the* Chicago Times-Herald *reported a portion of her speech.*[7] *The* St. Louis Post-Dispatch *offered a later version of Jane's remarks and her perspective on the Boer War. This speech (later an essay) offered more evidence of Jane Addams's growing commitment to the movement against imperialism and war.*

## COMMERCIALISM DISGUISED AS PATRIOTISM AND DUTY.

Chicago, Ill. 27 Jan. 1900

It has been the time-honored custom to attribute unjust wars to the selfish ambition of rulers, who remorselessly sacrifice their subjects to satisfy their greed. But, as Lecky[8] has recently pointed out, it remains to be seen whether or no democratic rule will diminish war. Immoderate and uncontrolled desires are at the root of most national as well as individual crimes and a large number of people may be moved by unworthy ambitions quite as easily as a few. If a large body of people accustom themselves to the commercial view of life, to consider the extension of trade as the test of national prosperity, it becomes comparatively easy for mere extension of commercial opportunity to assume a moral aspect and receive the moral sanction.

In fact, unrestricted commercialism is an excellent preparation for governmental aggression. The nation accustomed to condone the questionable business methods of a rich man because of his success will find no difficulty in quickly obscuring the moral issues of a conquest because of a few splendid victories. A people which has become convinced that the opening of oil mines justifies ruthless private aggression becomes only too easily reconciled to ruthless national aggression when gold mines are concerned.

Our minds become polarized by passing events, so that we have a curious tendency to mold our opinions to those of our fellows. We bless and preach peace when all is peaceful; we justify and even uphold the necessity and beauty of war when war rages about us. It simply means that our religion and philosophy have no virility; that they tend to slip away from us; that they fail us when we need them most unless we make a distinct and concerted effort to hang on.

We cannot afford to let our minds drift at a time like this. If we ever mean to love mercy and do justly, now is the time to make the effort, when all our training and the current event pull us toward loving success and doing commercially. We even forget that civilization is an idea, a method of living, an attitude of respect toward all men. We actually come to believe in our confusion, that it is the opening of gold mines, the establishment of garrisons, the controlling of weaker men by brute force. It is mere sophistication to call it enlightment.

Let us see whither this tendency to condone the passing event is leading us. A little while ago England patted us on the back because we followed her methods of the conquest and government of remote and alien peoples.[9] We gave her the sincere admiration which imitation always implies.

It only remains for us now to cheer her on, to applaud her course in South Africa, in order to establish the ethics of dominion, the political and industrial control of one nation by another, as the accepted national ethics of the Anglo-Saxon. To establish this code is to admit that practically no progress has been made since the Persian Cyrus[10] or the Roman Cesar believed that a conquering nation had every right to enslave the conquered.

Each code had the enrichment and building up of the conquered nation for its avowed purpose; each had brute force for its method. They, too, persuaded themselves that the ignorant and weak should serve the wise and strong. They, too, said civilization was thus advanced. But the conception of modern democracy had never come to their understanding, but, having had this conception, it is worse for us to practice industrial exploitation by national force than for the Roman conqueror to make hopeless slavery the basis of his empire. The wisest of Roman emperors did not dream of internationalism as we have come to know it. We can forgive the Romans for extermination, believing, as they did, that civilization meant the extension of but one empire, but we must find some new ideal for ourselves if we are going to insist upon the rule of one race.

The Anglo-Saxon conqueror, like the Roman, leaves the conquered nations in the mines and plantations, that he may receive a steady stream of gold and sugar. He also gives in exchange superficial law and order, and commercial relations designed solely for his own advantage. To my mind the advance has not been great. At a time like this the difference between the civilizing Roman and the civilizing Anglo-Saxon seems very slight—the motives are almost identical, the methods differ but little. The results are justified by the same phrases; brutal commercialism, with a varnish of patriotism and morality.

The great pity of it all is that a war tends to fix our minds on the picturesque; that it seems so much more magnificent to do battle for the right than patiently to correct the wrong. A war throws back the ideals which the young are nourishing into the mold of those which the old should be outgrowing. We allure our young men not to develop but to exploit. We turn their imaginations from the courage and toil of industry to the bravery and endurance of war. We incite their ambitions not to irrigate, to make fertile and sanitary the barren plains of the savage, but to fill it with military posts and to collect taxes and tariffs.

I remember once making a feeble attempt to present the prosaic thing picturesquely. A gymnastic class of boys at Hull House were very eager to have military drill. At that time the Chicago alleys were very filthy—I won't tell whose administration it was in—at any rate. It was long ago, when we still had hopes of cleanliness and before the city hall had mathematically demonstrated that cleanliness is financially impossible. In that far-off time I persuaded these boys to drill with long, narrow, sewer spades, instead of bayonets. I made the simple argument that it was quite as noble to maneuver as if to clean the city in order to prevent disease and save life as it was to maneuver as if to charge into an enemy and kill our fellow men.

I found that if I sat by or handled the spade myself, talking lustily meanwhile of the dignity of human life and labor, the boys would keep at it, albeit somewhat shamefacedly. But if they were left without this stimulus for a single evening they pretended the spades were guns and went back to military tactics. I honestly doubt if now I could even get them to touch a spade, so besotted have we all become with the notion of military glory.

JANE ADDAMS

PD (*St. Louis Post-Dispatch*, 18 Feb. 1900; *JAPM*, 46:990–91).

1. The progeny of early Dutch settlers of South Africa moved or "trekked" farther north in the area managed by Great Britain to establish the independent Transvaal or South Africa Republic in 1852 and the Orange Free State in 1854 to distance themselves from British rule.

2. Diamonds had been discovered in Kimberly, Orange Free State, in 1866, and the gold mines were the result of the discovery of gold in 1886 in the Whitwatersrand area of the Transvaal.

3. The First Boer War, 1880–81, was an attempt by Great Britain to add the Transvaal and its diamond mines to Britain's Cape Colony. It ended unsuccessfully for the British with an armistice and finally a treaty.

4. War was declared 11 Oct. 1899, and the armies of the Transvaal and Orange Free State moved quickly on 12 Oct. to attack. The British leaders maintained that they went to war to gain appropriate rights for persons not of Dutch descent in the two states. A well-equipped and highly mobile Transvaal military laid siege to three British garrisons and kept the British soldiers contained in Ladysmith, Mafeking, and Kimberly, prompting the British to send reinforcements. While the British ultimately won the war, they employed guerrilla tactics that featured a "scorched earth" policy that included the destruction of crops and animals, land, and housing. They also interred women and children of the combatants in crowded, degrading, and unhealthy conditions in concentration camps.

5. The *Chicago Chronicle* reported, "The Meeting was arranged for by a committee of ladies and was presided over by Mrs. Mary H. Wilmarth. It was advertised as 'Anti-War and Pro-Boer Meeting'" ("The Call for Peace").

6. "Anti-war but Pro-Boer."

7. Portions of JA's remarks in the meeting of 27 Jan were quoted by the *Chicago Times-Herald*, 28 Jan. 1900, in its news story "Anti-war but Pro-Boer." The *Chicago Chronicle*, in a report of the meeting, published all of JA's speech in "The Call for Peace."

8. William Edward Hartpole Lecky (1838–1903), born near Dublin, educated in Ireland, became a priest in the Protestant Church of Ireland and a historian and author. JA may have been referring to his *Democracy and Liberty*, originally published in 1896 and reissued in 1899 shortly after Gladstone's death. In it he criticized four-time prime minister of Great Britain William E. Gladstone (1808–98) for his focus and tactics in promoting home rule for Ireland and both Great Britain and the United States for its drift toward socialism.

Charles Frederick Weller (1870–1957), who became a leader in peace organizations and founder of the World Fellowship of Faith (1929), reminded readers in a 27 Oct. 1927 issue of the *Chicago Record* that Leaky had warned about the abuses of "unwise charity," stating that "'the system of outdoor relief which prevailed in England prior to the reformation of 1830 has done more toward degrading and weakening the English people than any war or series of wars in which that country was ever engaged.'"

9. JA's reference to the Spanish-American War and its aftermath.

10. JA's reference is to other empire builders known to ancient history, namely, the Caesars of Rome, who built an empire between 600 BCE and 1400 CE, and Cyrus the Great (ca. 660 or 576–530 BCE), who created the first Persian Empire (550–330 BCE) during his reign that included lands on the continents of Asia, Africa, and Europe.

## Letter to the Editor

*In 1900 the campaign for alderman in the Nineteenth Ward of Chicago was once again under way, and John Powers was seeking reelection. Although Hull-House had chosen not to become involved in the fray, Jane Addams and Hull-House found themselves engaged. On 18 February 1900, James C. Denvir,[1] who served as secretary of the Nineteenth Ward Carter H. Harrison Club, announced his support of John Powers: "I understand that even Miss Jane Addams has decided to abandon her opposition to the Democratic idol of the ward. Last winter he introduced the ordinance granting free water to the settlement skating rink and I understand that other kindnesses shown Hull House have caused her to change her mind in regard to Alderman Powers. He has done more to help the poor people of this ward than all the other politicians put together."[2] Jane Addams sent an immediate response in the form of a letter to the editors of a great many of the Chicago daily newspapers.[3]*

### STILL OPPOSED TO POWERS.

Miss Addams Denies Statements Regarding Hull House.

Chicago, Ill. 20 February 1900

To the Editor: May I ask space in your columns for the denial of a statement which has been made repeatedly of late and which appeared in yesterday morning's issue of several papers? This statement is in effect that Mr. Powers, alderman of the Nineteenth ward, secured on behalf of Hull House the flooding of our playground, and that on account of this and "other kindnesses shown to Hull House" we have changed our attitude toward him and his candidacy.

I should not think it worth while to reply to these statements were it not evident that they are made to explain the fact that Hull House has not entered the present aldermanic campaign and that they are repeated because they have a certain campaign value. The statement that Mr. Powers obtained the flooding of the Hull House playground is absolutely untrue. The playground has been flooded each winter for the last five years, and no favor has been asked of Mr. Powers. We have on file at Hull House a letter from the mayor last December ordering the same public service to be performed this winter. Mr. Powers knew nothing about the matter until after the order had been presented to the fire department, our friend Mr. Walker,[4] corporation counsel, having kindly presented the matter to his honor.

I am sure I need not say it is precisely because we believe that the many small personal favors done in the ward by Mr. Powers blind the voters to their real rights and interests that Hull House has twice made a protest against the bossism which has complete political control of the Nineteenth ward. It is, perhaps, characteristic of Mr. Powers that he should imagine that alleged favors shown to Hull House could change its attitude, and this in spite of the fact that there are hundreds of constituents besides ourselves who resent his political dominion and who have never voted for him. It was at the request and with the backing of these men that Hull House twice gave its support to opposing candidates[5] and it is upon their information that there is no courage to undertake a campaign now that we have determined to allow this disheartenment to speak for itself, unobscured by any artificially fostered and hopeless candidacy. There is no hope of success, for Mr. Powers with his wealth and political methods could easily defeat an honest man.

Mr. Powers' resentment of "outside interference,"[6] as quoted yesterday morning, is manifestly absurd. Hull House has been in the ward ten years and has its property interests here as well as its social and educational interests, the latter founded upon a belief in the integrity of the citizens of the ward. It is needless to state that the pro[t]est of Hull House against a man who continually disregards the most fundamental rights of his constituents must be permanent, and that it is none the less sincere because this spring we have changed its expression.

JANE ADDAMS,
PRESIDENT OF HULL HOUSE ASSOCIATION

PD (*Chicago Evening Post*, 20 Feb. 1900, SCPC, JAC; *JAPM*, 46:992–93, 55:547).

1. James ("Jimmy") C. Denvir (1870–1974) was born in Chicago, the son of shoemaker William Denvir, who immigrated from Ireland with his wife and settled in the Nineteenth Ward of Chicago. He attended Doré public school and West Division High School before he became a student at the Metropolitan Business College. He did not marry Margaret Goodman until 1903. Denvir was an early member of the HH Men's Club. In 1896 he founded the *Standard Opinion*, an independent but decidedly Democratic Party–leaning weekly newspaper for

which he served as editor. It was published each Saturday, and by 1913 its circulation was forty-two thousand. By 1931 he had become active in Democratic Party politics, something that would be his calling for the remainder of his life. An unsuccessful candidate for Cook Co. commissioner in 1906, he became a member of the West Chicago Park Comm., 1911–17, and a presidential elector from Illinois for Woodrow Wilson in 1912. From 1919 he served as president of the Twenty-ninth Ward Democratic Organization, and in 1923 he became a member of the Cook County Civil Service Comm. and served as its president. From 1931 until 1935, he was chief assistant bailiff of the Municipal Court of Chicago. In 1932 he was a delegate to the Democratic Party Convention and helped nominate Franklin D. Roosevelt as a candidate for president of the United States. His wife, Margaret, died in 1936.

2. "To Vote for Powers."

3. Among Chicago periodicals in which JA's letter to the editor appeared were, in addition to the *Chicago Evening Post*, the *Chicago Record*, the *Chicago Times-Herald*, and the *Chicago Daily Tribune*. Her remarks were summarized by the *Chicago Inter Ocean*.

4. Charles M. Walker (1859–1920), Chicago Corporation Counsel, was born in Kentucky, the son of Samuel J. and Amanda Morehead Walker. He graduated from Yale Univ. (B.A. 1884) and studied law. He was admitted to the Illinois Bar in 1886 and practiced in Chicago until 1903. He served the Twenty-fourth Ward of Chicago as alderman, 1896–99, and was appointed corporation counsel for Chicago in 1899, reappointed in 1901. During his tenure, he handled many significant cases. Before the U.S. Supreme Court, he was successful in his suit against the Illinois Central Railroad, affirming title of the people to lands along the shore of Lake Michigan. Elected judge for the Circuit Court of Cook Co., in 1903, he was reelected in 1909 and 1915 and served until his death. In 1888 he married Harriet Warner, with whom he had four children.

5. JA and HH supported reform candidates William Gleason in 1896 and Simeon W. Armstrong in 1898. See Article in the *HH Bulletin*, Apr. 1896; Essay in the *International Journal of Ethics*, Apr. 1898; JA to MRS, [3 Apr. 1898]; and Article in the *HH Bulletin*, Apr. and May 1898, all above.

6. JA was responding to a comment by James C. Denvir, who pronounced that the Nineteenth Ward was "peculiar. It will submit to no outside interference. Even the mayor has been taught, to his cost, to keep his hands off" ("To Vote for Powers").

## To Sarah Alice Addams Haldeman

*For most of the 1890s, Paris had been getting ready for the Exposition Universelle it was to host 15 April through 12 November 1900. The Republic of France planned this world's fair as an opportunity for the countries around the world to commemorate the achievements of the past century and to celebrate the arrival of the twentieth century. It was to be an educational experience and one in which all peoples of the world could unite.*

*Like many other countries, the United States appointed a commission to oversee its participation. Ferdinand W. Peck*[1] *of Chicago, who had served on the commission that organized and promoted the World's Columbian Exposition of 1893, led the U.S. Commission. It was charged with creating a pavilion to represent the United States at the event and also with encouraging participation by individuals, businesses, and organizations representing the best that the United States had contributed to the world. All of the exhibits at the Exposition Universelle were to be judged and the best recognized by the Republic of France. This required a cadre of jurors who were to represent all of the countries of the world that had agreed to present exhibits at the exposition. To receive an appointment as a juror to the Exposition Universelle was an honor.*[2]

*Late in April 1900, Jane Addams wrote to Florence Kelley that she had received the following telegram from Bertha Honoré Palmer, a U.S. commissioner for the 1900 exposition: "Could you serve on Paris jury if appointed, think 500 dollars will be paid each juror." To which Jane replied: "Accept with pleasure if fee is attached, otherwise impossible." Jane wrote to Florence Kelley: "I am hoping that you are going—I know that you were invited as I was earlier. . . . Won't we have a lark!"*[3] *Although Florence Kelley ultimately did not go, Jane Addams became a juror and used her influence to assure that the National Consumers' League, headed by Kelley, received a gold medal for its exhibit at the exposition.*[4] *Jane's primary traveling companion was Julia Lathrop, who held no official position at the exposition.*

Hull-House 335 South Halsted Street Chicago [Ill.] [ca. 18 May 1900][5]

My dear Alice

I have been appointed a juror to Paris very suddenly and will sail Wed. May 23d, on the St Louis of the American Line.[6] The whole thing ought not to take more than six weeks and I will probably be back by the middle of July.[7] I am sorry to tear off so but there seems to be no help for it after ones name has gone in. The address will be c/o Munroe & Co 7 Rue Scribe Paris.[8]

The checks came yesterday and have been duly sent along.[9] Have you any commissions that I might execute? With love to Marcet Always yours

Jane Addams—

ALS (IU, Lilly, SAAH; *JAPM*, 3:1535).

1. Ferdinand Wythe Peck (1848–1924) was a wealthy Chicago businessman and philanthropist who had been instrumental in financing Chicago's Auditorium Theater.

2. France planned to have all of the exhibits judged by experts serving as jurors to establish their significance and to award prizes for those considered the best. In all there were 2,336 jurors. France was to name 1,421 jurors, primarily because it had the most exhibits. The United States received permission to name 95 jurors. Of those there were three women, and JA was one of them.

3. [May?] [1900], NYPL, Kelley; *JAPM*, 3:1536.

4. "An exhibit was also made and rewarded by a gold medal of the work of the National Assn. of Consumers' Leagues, with headquarters in New York, but with branches in the larger American cities. This association undertakes to inform interested purchasers who have become its members of the sanitary and industrial conditions under which certain articles are manufactured and sold, and a successful effort is being made to bring to bear the standard of better conditions, adopted by the conscientious consumers, as an actually modifying force in commercial affairs" (Addams, "Report on Institutions for the Mental and Moral Improvement of Workingmen [class 108]," *International Exposition at Paris*, 663).

5. According to the *Chicago Times Herald* on 21 May 1900, JA received her invitation on 18 May 1900. On the same date, in an article titled "Miss Addams to Go to Paris," the *Chicago*

*Daily Tribune* reported that her appointment as a juror was due to the resignation for family reasons of juror Clara de Graffenreid, assistant to Carroll D. Wright, commissioner of the Bureau of Labor Statistics in Washington, D.C.

6. The steam ship *St. Louis* of the American Line did leave from New York on Wednesday, 23 May, headed for Southampton in England, but JA was not on board. She actually sailed on the *Auguste-Victoria* of the Hamburg-American Line on Thursday, 24 May 1900.

7. JA did not return from Europe until the first week in Aug. 1900.

On 15 July 1900, JA's duties as a group juror complete, she reported to MRS: "I leave here for Oberammergau to morrow [16 July 1900]—get back on Friday [20 July 1900], reach London Sat [21 July 1900] at 4:55. Mr Maude meets me for supper & in the evening I am going to the Passmore Edwards Settlement. . . . I go to Bristol at noon Sunday [22 July 1900] & leave Tuesday A.M. [24 July 1900] for Plymouth. That will give me a glimpse of Devonshire. The Barnetts have written most affectionately as have the Maudes" (15 July 1900, SCPC, JAC; *JAPM*, 3:1620). Arriving back in the United States, JA reported to MRS that she and Julia Lathrop "were neither of us ill a minute and strange to say enjoyed the voyage. I was inclined to be impatient of course, but I slept & ate as if I had been in a sanitarium—neither was I sick crossing the channel—I may be a sailor yet—who knows!" (4 Aug. 1900, SCPC, JAC; *JAPM*, 3:1628). After two days at HH, JA set off for her speaking engagement at Chautauqua, N.Y., where she presented four lectures between 6 and 10 Aug. and met MRS for a ten-day vacation in the White Mountains, after which she returned to HH for the rest of the year. At Chautauqua, her subjects were titled "Democracy and Education," "Democracy and Industry," "Democracy and Domestic Service," and "Social Settlements." All of her speeches were published in the *Chautauqua Assembly Herald*, 25 (9, 10, 11, and 13 Aug. 1900); *JAPM*, 46:1002–10.

8. A bank in Paris.

9. JA was referring to financial matters associated with continuing to settle MCAL's estate.

## To Mary Rozet Smith

195 Rue de l'Université Chez Mme Chalmandrey
[Paris, France] [4?][1] [June 1900]

Dearest

We are well established in Paris in a charming little pension where we have bed, candles & breakfast for 7 fr each—The house is only around the corner from the American Commissioners office,[2] not three minutes walk from three different entrances to the Exposition & just across the bridge from the Social Economics building—[3] Paris is n't full as yet and nothing is easier to find than lodgings.

I have rec'd all sorts of documents & an enormous badge which admits me free any where our jury will not be organized until Wednesday P.M.[4] so that I have been here in ample time! To morrow there is a little log rolling committee meeting. I am to be made a vice pres't![5]

I lunched to day with Mrs Palmer[6] who unfolded many & devious plans. It appears that Woman with a large W. has not been properly recognized! and that of the American women appointed one has already been reduced by the ungallant Frenchmen to the place of substitute. I am bid stand firm for my rights &c.

J. Lathrop has been a treasure—Saturday[7] we shopped & recovered from the steamer—Sunday we viewed the Exposition somewhat & went to the Le Feté des Fleurs[8] in the afternoon—We had a very jolly afternoon—The Exposition & the park were simply filled with people—literally all the world was out, I never saw Paris so Parisian.

Prof Geddes[9] lectures three times a week—a course on the Sociology of Peace & War is going on now & we mean to take it beginning Wed—The Social Economics building is afloat with people whom between us we know—and it does not seem likely to be dull—altho there are moments when the sight seeing aspect comes over me with an overwhelming distaste.

We called on <u>Mrs Brodhead</u>[10] yesterday who was looking very well, but did not encourage us to think that she would return with us in July—she sent many greetings.

There are parts of the Exposition that are really very beautiful, one long vista which seems to me to surpass any one spot at the Worlds Fair—[11] It is built on both sides of the River & spreads out at both ends like a dumb bell. Being mixed with real buildings, & suggesting the other public buildings of Paris it is less unreal, more like a genuine, sure enough city—an enchanted one to be sure.

We are going to see Coquelin in Cyrano[12] to night & generally have our fling before the jury begins to sit on Wed.[13]

Do write to me, dear, about yourself and about the strike[14] concerning which I can hear never a word.

With love to your family I am always yrs.

J.A.

P.S. Mrs Brodhead was evidently very sorry to miss the wedding,[15] if we could have promised this at the end of July I think she would have come!

ALI and cover (SCPC, JAC; *JAPM*, 3:1574–78).

1. The editors have given the date of 4 June 1900 to this document primarily because JA's diary for June–Aug. 1900, the extent of her European visit in 1900, provides some evidence for this date. In a list of correspondents to whom she wrote after arriving, she listed a letter to MRS as the only piece of correspondence she produced on 4 June 1900 at the start of her visit in Paris. Her diary also indicates that JA went shopping on 2 June, when she purchased a parasol, four pairs of gloves, and books. She bought theater tickets on three separate days, 4, 5, and 6 June 1900. The cover associated with the correspondence has a 5 June 1900 postmark.

2. Ferdinand Wythe Peck's office was located near the exposition site at no. 20 ave. Rapp, Paris.

3. The Social Economics Building, located on the north side of the Seine River along the Quai de Billy, was a two-story structure that contained all of the exhibits on the first floor and meeting rooms on the second floor. The exhibits that JA was to judge were in this building.

4. JA was to be a member of the jury for class 108, identified as containing exhibits relating to the mental and moral improvement of workingmen. According to the *New York Times*, it was part of Group 16 composed of exhibits relating to social economy and hygiene. The jury was composed of ten Frenchmen, one German, and one American. Its task was to evaluate 264 exhibits. The Wednesday JA meant may have been 8 June 1900.

5. Being made a vice-president of her jury was indeed special. She was the only woman named as a vice-president on any of the juries associated with the exposition.

On 10 June 1900, JA wrote to MRS: "I hope there was n't a lot of stuff cabled to the Chicago Record the other day—A slate had been arranged by which I was vice pres't of my jury and therefore a member of the group jury. There had been a good deal of wire pulling in Mr Peck's office of which I knew nothing—If I need to stay much longer than the first plan involved I shall resign in favor of a substitute" (SCPC, JAC; *JAPM*, 3:1582). The jury for class 108 was to complete its work by 30 June 1900. Newspapers in the United States reported on 9 and 10 June that JA had been made a vice-president of her class jury. The *Chicago Record* did post an article that appeared in newspapers from Rochester, N.Y., to San Francisco: "Miss Adams is the only woman of any nationality to be appointed to any but a class jury. For a long time Prof. Gore has had the appointment in mind, and your correspondent was not surprised, accordingly, while the juries were sitting to receive a summons to go at once to French headquarters, where he arrived just in time to be present when Miss Addams achieved her success. The Frenchmen kept repeating 'but she is a woman and it never will do to have a woman in a group jury. That is unheard of.' For all the clamor, however, Dr. Gore remained firm, in spite of all the inducements held out to him not to press the matter. 'We really can't do this,' said the exposition authorities. 'We are ready to let the honor go to another American—a man. We would even give America the vice-presidency of still another great class, but really it would be impossible to have a woman serving on a superior jury!' Finally, however, the French weakened and they were the first to congratulate Miss Addams" (from the Paris correspondent for the *Chicago Record* and published in the Rochester, N.Y., *Union and Advertiser*, 11 June 1900, SCPC, JAC; *JAPM*, 55:579).

The jury system at the exposition was structured of class juries, composed of the first jurors to evaluate the exhibits placed in the class; followed by group juries, representing a related group of class juries; and finally by the superior jury, selected from among the commissioners-general of all of the countries having more than five hundred exhibits, officers of group juries, and "certain prominent persons" (Gore, "Report of the Juror in Chief," 25). As JA explained in the report of her activities: "The holding of an office in the class jury 108 made me a member of the Group Jury XVI, upon which I served from the 1st of July until the 15th. The work of the group jury was to consider the reports of all of the class juries within its group, to adjust the various awards, and in a general way to ratify and classify the previous work" (Addams, "Report on Institutions for the Mental and Moral Improvement of Workingmen [class 108]," 663–64). As a mathematician, Columbian Univ. professor and author James Howard Gore (1856–1939), juror in chief, reported: "The purpose of the group jury was to examine the list of exhibits placed 'hors concours'—out of the competition—to see if the reasons for this exclusion were adequate, and then to make a comparative study of the number of awards granted in the various classes. The purpose of this was to ascertain if one or more juries had been unusually severe or unduly lenient, in comparison with the others" (Gore, "Report of the Juror in Chief," 25).

The social economy and hygiene group jury on which JA served was composed of the following class juries: class 101, apprenticeship and protection of child labor; class 102, wages, industrial remuneration, and profit sharing; class 103, large and small industries, cooperative associations, and trade unions; class 104, farming, agricultural unions, and banks; class 105, protection of workers in factories; class 106, workingmen's dwellings; class 107, cooperative stores; class 108, institutions for the intellectual and moral development of workingmen; class 109, provident institutions; class 110, movements under public and private auspices for welfare of people; class 111, hygiene; and class 112, public and private charities.

By 16 June, the officers for JA's class jury had been selected: A. Le Roy Beaulieu (1842–1912) of France was president, and JA of the United States was vice-president. The reporter was E. O. Lani and the secretary Emaile Schmoll. They met four or five times each week, evaluated the exhibits, discussed their findings over lunch, and by the end of June reported their findings. They could award grand prizes and gold, silver, bronze, or honorable mention designations. All prizes were diplomas.

6. In an interview with a reporter for the *New York Tribune*, Bertha Honoré Palmer explained that she had brought the names of twelve women to Paris with her and campaigned for them to be selected as members of juries. She reported that "her best allies in the campaign to be one or two enthusiastic Frenchmen," and with their help she was able to get the attention of Alfred Picard (1844–1913), the commissioner-general and administrative leader of the exposition for the Republic of France. She received his support for three of the names and continued: "I had little hope of passing all my twelve names, and should have felt repaid if only one representative American woman had secured a place on a jury. It seemed to me of the greatest importance that women should be recognized on this jury. This Exposition is the greatest and most truly international that has occurred, and it comes just before the dawn of a century in which women are to take a new place in the industrial and economic world" ("Mrs. Palmer's Paris Work"). Besides JA, Mrs. Henrietta C. Oldberg of Washington, D.C., president of the Silk and Ramee Assn. of America, served as a juror in textiles, and Miss Annie Tolman Smith was a juror in education.

7. Likely 2 June 1900.

8. Le Fete des Fleurs, "the great floral carnival of the year," began at 2:00 P.M. on 2 June 1900. "The celebration is one of the established social affairs in Paris which Americans, as well as others, may enjoy. It is the event of the summer season, the French aristocracy, and even the representatives of the old Faubourg circles, have set upon it the stamp of approval. . . . [T]he Americans are allowed to come to it. With the exception of such affairs as this, the inner circle of French society is closed" ("In Parisian Society").

9. On 10 June, JA reported to MRS: "One meets a number of English & American people at Prof Geddes school, which has indeed but a humble and rather mixed up beginning but all the enthusiasm of its founder—He gave up the lectures on Peace & War just as I was enormously interested in them and this week lectures on pictures" (SCPC, JAC; *JAPM*, 3:1581).

Patrick Geddes (1854–1932), who became known as a pioneering town planner, was also a biologist, sociologist, and educator. He was born in Ballaster, Scotland, and attended Perth Academy. He was a student at the Royal College of Mines in London, 1874–78, where he worked with English biologist and influential Darwin advocate Thomas Henry Huxley (1825–95). From 1880 until 1888, Geddes lectured on zoology at Edinburgh Univ., and from 1888 until 1919 he was chair of botany at Univ. College, Dundee, Scotland. He became noted for his dedication to the scientific method and the significance that he placed on close observation to discover the important relationships among work, folk, and place. He advocated a survey that should include knowledge of the geology, geography, climate, economic life, and social institutions as necessary for town planning. Among his early attempts at civic improvement were efforts to renovate Edinburgh's Old Town. He moved his wife, Anna, and family into James Court and proceeded to improve the building and neighborhood in which he settled. He believed that gardens and green space were vital to urban living. He also believed that education was a key element in promoting social change and held that learning should incorporate physical activity, the emotions, and traditional educational methods. Between 1883 and 1903, he held Summer Meetings of Art and Science that were designed to help educate teachers and others in a wide array of subjects. Geddes lived in India from 1917 until 1924 and served as chair of sociology and civics at Bombay Univ., 1919–24. He also undertook planning projects in Jerusalem and in Colombo, Ceylon. From 1924 until his death, he established a home in Montpelier, France, where he began the Collège des Ecossais. He was a fellow of the Royal Society of Edinburgh, founder of the Edinburgh Social Union and the Franco-Scottish Society, as well as cofounder of Bombay Univ. Among his published works were *The Evolution of Sex* (1889), coauthored with J. A. Thomson, and *Cities in Evolution* (1915), both published in London.

JA and Geddes were already acquainted. He had visited HH in 1899 to promote membership in the International Assn. for the Advancement of Science, Art, and Education of which he served as secretary. JA was among the members of the organization, which was formed in Sept. 1899, in recognition of the fact that in "every field of human activity, the individuals and agencies engaged are more and more felt to be working in harmony. All are seen to be helping in the development of common civilization. . . . The great International Exhibitions and Congresses . . . are but an expression of this. To help this international movement, to extend its educational usefulness, to record and publish its results, and to further their practical applications, are the tasks of this Association" (International Assn. for the Advancement of Science, Art, and Education, *The Paris International Assembly of 1900*, 1). Geddes returned to Chicago in Feb. 1900. He spoke at HH and gave three lectures at the Univ. of Chicago before lecturing at the Univ. of Wisconsin to promote the organization. The association was composed of members from France, England, the United States, and other European countries. It helped guide visitors to the myriad exhibits and summarized discussions from the congresses, provided lectures about the exposition and an assortment of subjects associated with the exhibitions and congresses, helped members with travel plans, and held social gatherings at least weekly during the exposition. Geddes presented a weekly series of lectures, some of which JA attended (see also JA to MRS, 18 June 1900, below). JA's diary for her visit to Paris indicated that on 8 June, she purchased a ticket for "school" (Jun.–Aug. 1900:[44]; *JAPM*, 29:676). On 10 June, JA took tea with Geddes, and on Wednesday, 27 June, she had lunch with him. Geddes visited HH again in the early years of the twentieth century.

10. MRS had relatives in Paris, and JA visited with at least one of them. Her diary for June–Aug. 1900 while she was in Paris, had the following name and address on p. [5]: "Mrs. Rozet Broadhead, 12 Rue Pierre Charon" (*JAPM*, 29:657). Mrs. John Rozet Broadhead was the aunt of MRS.

11. JA was referring to the World's Columbian Exposition, Chicago, 1893.

12. JA's diary indicated that she did purchase theater tickets on 4 June. However, in her letter to MRS of 10 June, JA wrote: "We heard Sara last night in her play of Rostrands. She was as bewitching as ever to my mind & both J. Lathrop & I left her thearté with regret at 12.30 We heard Hanchel & Gretchel at the Opera Comique last week, are going to hear Cyrano and call our theatre going complete" (SCPC, JAC; *JAPM*, 3:1581). It is not clear exactly when JA saw Coquelin.

"Sara" was Sarah Bernhardt (1844–1923), whom JA had seen perform previously and who was in *Le Samaritain*, a play by French playwright and poet Edmond Rostand (1868–1918), in her own Théâtre Sarah-Bernhardt, which she had opened in 1899. The opera *Hansel & Gretel* was composed by Engelbert Humperdinck (1854–1921) between 1890 and 1892. Benoit Constant Coquelin (1841–1909), known as "Coquelin ainé" (Coquelin the eldest), was a world-famous French actor. Both Bernhardt and Coquelin appeared at the Paris Exposition in early versions of motion pictures accompanied by a synchronized sound recording. A comedic actor, Coquelin gained fame as Cyrano de Bergerac in the play by that title, also by Edmond Rostand.

13. It is likely that the members of JA's jury met initially on 6 June, because she knew that she would be named a vice-president by 8 June. However, according to the report that JA wrote about her activities as a class juror, the jurors met to organize for their work on 16 June.

14. During the 1890s, unions gained a great deal of control over the building industry in Chicago. Between 1893 and 1897, they accepted agreements to work only for Chicago Contractors' Assn. members, later adding material manufacturers to the agreement mix. In early 1900, contractors locked out unions, claiming that these agreements caused materials to be too costly. Lockouts and sympathy strikes were the result. When JA left for Paris at the end of May 1900, the dispute between the Chicago Contractors' Assn. and the Building Trades Council was still ongoing. Graham Taylor discovered that "[w]hile insisting upon

the disbanding of the Council, . . . [the Chicago Contractors' Assn.] resolutely insists upon maintaining its own association. While demanding the cessation of the sympathetic strike, it busily organized a sympathetic lock-out. While vigorously, and in part very justly, protesting against the interference of organized labor with the liberty of its contractors to purchase material from whom they pleased, it countenanced and abetted, if it did not organize, a boycott of building material producers against the employers of union labor allied with the Building Trades Council. Charging the men with refusing to keep their own agreement, in some instances at least, it locked them out for taking the Saturday half-holiday, which had been granted in their own agreement with them. While protesting against what may have been too great a limitation of the amount of daily work to be exacted, they failed sufficiently to recognize the complaint of the men against the 'rusher' being allowed to set the pace for a fair day's work" (Taylor, "Between the Lines in Chicago's Industrial Civil War," 3). In May 1900, Taylor was instrumental in promoting the 190 organizations that composed the Building Trades Council to nominate an investigating commission to try to settle the dispute. After that, Taylor reported,: "The daily press became more conciliatory in tone, demanding from both sides concessions necessary to a settlement" (Taylor, "Between the Lines in Chicago's Industrial Civil War," 4).

The battle between the contractors and union workmen continued after JA returned from Paris. On 1 Dec. 1900, when JA was speaking before an audience of almost seventy gathered by the Political Equality League, her remarks were presented by many of the largest Chicago newspapers for her stand on behalf of unions in the strike. She defended the sympathetic strike, saying that it "maybe ill advised, abominably managed, and entail much unnecessary suffering, but they are really altruistic and the basis of an unselfish attempt to uplift humanity" ("Jane Addams Defends Unions"). About unions' walking delegates, JA offered: "The walking delegate is the paid representative of the labor union, and no one will dispute the claim that the union has the same right to employ a representative as has a corporation to engage an attorney to look after its interests" ("Talks on 'Trade Unions'"). She also indicated that "an eight hour day is the maximum for efficient service. However . . . [t]here is nothing in the system which arbitrarily fixes the amount of work a man shall do for an average day's pay which keeps the exceptional man from rising. The unions seek to fix the minimum rate of wage, but there is nothing in the rule which prevents the contractors from paying more than the standard wages to an extraordinary man. This rule protects the weak without a[f]fecting the strong" ("Woman on Trade Unions"). JA was aware that the Building Trades Council was losing its battle with the contractors: "The alleged fact that the council was in the hands of men who misused their power is no argument for the dissolution of the council. The same reasoning would apply to the city council when it is in the hands of unscrupulous aldermen. Yet no one urges that institution be wiped out" ("Talks on 'Trade Unions'"). In her remarks, JA also continued to defend arbitration as the best way to solve labor disputes. The battle between the unions and the contractors would not be settled until 1901, when the unions lost their exclusive agreements with the members of the Chicago Contractors' Assn. and "acknowledged the supremacy of the contractors in the industry" (Schneirov, "Building Trades and Workers").

JA's public stance on the side of unions was criticized by some. After reading about her speech before the CWC in an article entitled "Defense of Unions," in the *Chicago Post,* Adolphus Clay Bartlett wrote to ask JA if "good workmen and whom I have for many years considered perfectly reliable are deceiving me when they say that a days work, as fixed by the Union, and which must not be exceeded, in some instances, can readily be performed by a skilled mechanic in three hours. I am trying to puzzle out how an 'exceptional man' can 'rise' under the rules of the Union." And he continued: "I am prompted to write this note (to which I ask only a brief response if you can spare the time for any reply) by criticism made by one of your lady friends, today, in my presence" (2 Dec. 1900, SCPC, *JAC; JAPM,* 3:1695). JA's

During her life, Jane Addams owned two different summer cottages. The first, shown above, was at Lakeside, Michigan (private collection). The second, and much grander, cottage was one Jane Addams shared with Mary Rozet Smith at Hulls Cove near Bar Harbor, Maine (Bar Harbor Historical Society, Maine).

response was in part: "Standing up for Trades Unions even from their historic and theoretic side, in the present crisis in Chicago, is much like preaching peace in time of war. If you preach peace in time of peace, you are called a Christian citizen but if you preach peace in time of war you are considered an unpatriotic citizen—but after all the time to extol the beauty of peace is at the moment when many people are forgetting it. . . . I have never aspired to be 'a leader' but I should recommend to anyone who did: to express his convictions as clearly as possible and not to be silent when those convictions happened to be unpopular in the community" (JA to Adolphus Clay Bartlett, [3 Dec. 1900], SCPC, JAC; *JAPM*, 3:1697–98, 1700). Bartlett followed with a rejoinder, writing in part: "My note did not repeat the lady's criticism to which I referred, but it was written because that criticism put it in my mind to write. She said in substance—'Jane Addams is no longer a safe leader to follow—she is becoming too socialistic in her tendencies.' Since the publication of excerpts from your paper or address, I have heard expressions from a number of gentlemen, some of whom were not directly interested in the labor questions, and without exception they deplored the state of mind into which you are, to them, apparently, drifting." And he continued: "To-day at a Committee Meeting, I sat beside a well known labor leader, a personal friend of Gompers and a strong advocate of Unions, who voluntarily said that conditions prevailing in Chicago are due to the unwarrantable rules and exactions of the local organizations. . . . At this time, when selfishness and love for rule are leading comparatively few men to dominate the situation, and force upon this community conditions which must result in anarchy, distress and crime, is it not the duty of every one who has at heart the real interest of the so-called laboring class, to fearlessly expose and criticize the acts which are responsible for this state of affairs, rather than to put these men upon the back, and attempt to apologize for their ruthless attack upon the rights of their fellow citizens? I know you will respond in the affirmative, and my only surprise (and that of others as well) is that you do not boldly and publically take that stand. . . . You exert a great influence, and can do much toward changing for the better the conditions now prevailing" (Bartlett to JA, 5 Dec. 1900, SCPC, JAC; *JAPM*, 3:1701–2).

15. JA was referring to the wedding of MRS's brother Francis ("Frank") Drexel Smith to Charlotte Sedgwick Silsbee, in the Episcopal Church of the Atonement in Edgewater, Ill., on 30 June 1900.

## To Mary Rozet Smith

Paris [France] June 18—1900

Dearest One

Both your letters about Mrs Stevens[1] have come and no one else has written.

It all seems so violent and dreadful and, altho we do not altogether confide it to each other, we both feel that we ought not to have come away. I am sure that every thing was done that could have been and I was so grateful that you wrote about the funeral.[2] I hoped that Dr Taylor would be asked. I thought about her most of the time between the two letters, one of which came on Friday and the other today—Monday.[3] It seems a long time from here, does n't it?

E. Smith's letter was not reassuring about you and I long for the time when we shall be established in a country spot—and you will see what a nurse I can be.[4]

The jury work is going on now quite rapidly and various things are developing that really interest me very much and make the undertaking seem worth while.[5]

I had a very nice talk with M. Desjardins[6] on Sunday, he is the man who founded "The Union of Moral Action," the school of morals people, Prof [Metier?] and three or four others have really been most suggestive and inspiring.

I speak at the Woman's Congress on Thursday[7] and we have found the Tenement House Congress that is going on this week very interesting.[8] Mr Hutchinson[9] & Mrs Cyrus McCormick[10] both represent our little Chicago Society[11] and have been very charming, we dine to night with the Coll *[text missing]*.[12]

Paris begins to seem human and friendly—more as London does to me. Mr Geddes School is n't going off with large numbers and the poor founder is quite discouraged—He gave a brilliant lecture on Paleotechnique yesterday.[13]

I hope little Miss Collson[14] will prove a valuable person, we must keep clear that the engagement is only for three months, until we see what arrangement can be made in the fall. I hope Miss Bowman[15] has arrived by this time and that there is no doubt in regard to Miss Bartlett.[16]

I know that you have been a saint all through the time of the trouble at H.H.[17] and I do hope that you have n't overdone. How does Winnetka seem this year and are you finding it possible to "lay low"—if you are not I do hope that you will plan to go some where else. I meant to send a little cadeau to Miss Silsbee[18] but think that I will bring it instead.

I am writing to Dr Yarros and to H.H. I have had waves of home sickness for you all. I was very grateful for the Lady Eleanor's[19] letter, will you please tell her with my best affections. My love to your father and mother, I do hope the latter has quite recovered. Always & forever yours

Jane Addams

J Lathrop[20] sends her love to you "a thousand times."

ALS (SCPC, JAC; *JAPM*, 3:1589–92).

1. Alzina Parsons Stevens, a labor reformer and HH resident, died while JA and Julia Lathrop were in Europe. JA wrote to MRS, perhaps anticipating the death of Mrs. Stevens: "I do hope that every thing will be done to make her comfortable and that she won't wait for my little Iowa lady to arrive, before she takes her vacation. If the end should come before I get back of course we would want H.H. to be considered her home and her place—she has made it so clear to me that she does n't want to have her sister put in charge of affairs" (10 June 1900, SCPC, JAC; *JAPM*, 3:1583). The funeral was conducted by Graham Taylor, who wrote of Stevens in the *Commons*: "Not only Hull House, but all the Chicago settlements, and the Woman's clubs in this and other cities, the Typographical Union here, and the Woman's Trades Unions everywhere, the juvenile Court, and the hundreds of families for whose delinquent children she has stood so wisely and so well—all these and many more besides, are in mourning for Mrs. Stevens" (Taylor, "The Death of Mrs. A. P. Stevens"). For a biographical note on Alzina Parsons Stevens, see JA to Richard T. Ely, 31 Oct. 1894, n. 10, above.

2. JA's letter from MRS about Stevens's funeral is not known to be extant.

3. The two letters JA mentions are not known to be extant.

4. Eleanor Smith's letter is not known to be extant. While JA was in Europe in June, MRS seems to have been the person that JA expected to keep her informed about events and issues at HH. On 15 July 1900, JA wrote to MRS: "You were very good to send the extra money to H.H. even the bills wait a little I can make them up in Sept. . . . Please don't make propositions to Miss Johnson about Mrs Stevens work until I see you" (SCPC, JAC; *JAPM*, 3:1619).

MRS's health was always a worry, for she had asthma and was often ill. MRS and JA did get away to the White Mountains for a ten-day vacation after JA returned from Europe in Aug (see JA to MRS, [4?] [June 1900], n. 7, above). By 1914 they had settled on taking their vacations together in the Hulls Cove area of Bar Harbor, Maine. Their home was near "Baymeath," the summer home owned by Louise de Koven Bowen. When they acquired the property, it was known as "Yulecraig." The house was torn down in 1986. They spent the summers there until 1932, when they sold the property.

5. JA may have shared her response to some of the things she saw in Paris that interested her in a speech that she gave before the Union Labor League at the University Settlement on 7 Sept. 1900. She described "trades unions in Paris working without contractors, and recognized as having a place in the business life of the city," and "cooperation in the place of antagonism and competition" as "the idea toward which the labor unions should work." She used as an example the fact that the Social Economics Building at the Paris exposition was constructed entirely by union laborers, but without the oversight of contractors.

Jane Addams also reported: "In the general department of social economy at the exposition there were many new and useful ideas to be gained. Each nation defined its scope differently, and some of them were devoted to exhibits of what we would class as philanthropies. Switzerland and Russia were devoted to exhibits of temperance societies. . . . The United States displayed a large number of exhibits illustrative of what is being done to ameliorate the conditions of working people. . . . The congress that brought together the many interesting people of different nationalities was one of the most valuable features in the department of social economics" ("Suggests Future of Unions").

6. Paul Desjardins (1859–1940), who founded the Union of Moral Action with some friends and his philosophy professor Jules Lagneau (1851–94) at the Lycée Michelet of Vanves in 1893, visited JA on 17 June 1900. He was a journalist and professor who taught in high schools and in colleges in France. He also worked for *Revue Bleue* and *Le Figaro*. Between 1910 and 1914, resuming in 1922, he held philosophical symposia, termed "Decades of Pontigny," of French intellectuals, who took up such issues as church and state, the rights of people, and education and work.

7. The Woman's Congress opened on 18 June, and JA spoke on the morning of the American day at the congress on 21 June 1900. An editorial in the *Chicago Times-Herald* on 24 June 1900 boasted: "It was America's day at the woman's congress at the exposition, and the feature of the programme was the address by Miss Jane Addams, who told the assembled delegates the remarkable story of the founding of the Hull House settlement in one of the darkest spots of Chicago" ("Parisians Cheer the Founder of HH"). On 25 June 1900, when she wrote MRS, JA offered no report of her own speech: "The Woman's Congress this week added much gaity to our Social Economics Building and May Wright Sewall's speeches in French in which libraté and solidarité flourished, covered us all with a reflected glory" (SCPC, JAC; *JAPM*, 3:1593). On 1 July 1900, the *Chicago Times-Herald* once again referred to JA's speech and indicated that the reaction to it was "a flattering ovation" and that it "was cheered" by those who heard it ([HH endeavors to make social intercourse], SCPC, JAC; *JAPM*, 71:1165).

8. The tenement house congress associated with the Paris exposition was held 18–21 June. In her letter of 25 June 1900 to MRS, JA also reported: "There is a very excellent inspiring housing exhibit here—the houses actually built so that one walks through them" (SCPC, JAC; *JAPM*, 3:1595).

In describing the attraction JA was to the French, especially the French men, journalist Alfred D. Cox reported that JA "was made the recipient of much attention from prominent people in France, and when she appeared and made a short address . . . it was conceded that she was among the most worthily notable of all the Americans who had this year crossed the Atlantic." He described her as "famous" because of her "social and economical studies" and with "[a]n earnestness, combined with a magnetic personality" that brought her success. "Her face is full of character," he reported, "and there is a fine quality about it that at once attracts. Within, there is a sadness, as if the depth of sorrow of which she has had to learn in her mission has left its indelible mark upon her" ("Men and Women of the Hour," 7).

9. Charles Lawrence Hutchinson was a member of the Exec. Com. of the City Homes Assn. and a member of the Model Tenement Sub-Com. of the Tenement Com. of the organization (n. 11). The Tenement Com. was charged with an "investigation of the problem which could be proceeded with during the summer; that the question of model tenements in all its bearings was another subject & could be profitably studied while the data was being collected on which action should be based; and that the general consideration of what conditions should be worked for and their relative importance and feasibility was a subject for study" (Minutes, Tenement Com., City Homes Assn., 5–6, SHSW, Blaine).

10. Nettie Fowler McCormick was a member of the Exec. Com. of the City Homes Assn.

11. The City Homes Assn. was organized Apr. 1900 with the goal of "the improvement of the physical conditions of life in Chicago, especially in the more thickly settled districts of the city" (City Homes Assn., n.d., [broadside], 1 p., SHSW, Blaine). It took over the work of the Improved Housing Assn., which had been operating since 1 and 2 Feb. 1897, when it was created as a result of the Improved Housing Conference that was organized by the Northwestern University Settlement, Bureau of Associated Charities, HH, and Chicago Commons. JA was a speaker at the gathering: "Miss Jane Addams, of Hull House, spoke of the growing sentiment in London against tenement houses in general and altogether, as such. She quoted Octavia Hill and others of the workers in London, in the opinion that tenement houses could be done away with. . . . Miss Addams spoke, too, of the movement under foot in London to make the tenements more attractive by interior decorations . . . for the common social room of the tenement" ("Bad Tenements").

The organization was most active 1900–10 and ceased to exist by 1914. Through its Investigative Com., led by JA, it considered the housing stock in three districts of Chicago: Near West Side, Northwest Side, and Lower West Side. The results of that study were published by the organization as *Tenement Conditions in Chicago* (1901) by Robert S. Hunter. According to the minutes of the Tenement House Com., JA was insistent that the organization also support the development of small parks and playgrounds and better city infrastructure. During her remarks titled "Civic Responsibility and the Tenement House" made at the Improved Housing Assn. gathering that took place on 22 Mar. 1900 at the Art Institute of Chicago, JA reported that "Chicago has no tenement house problem, for the sections of the city in which the tenement-houses are located are the healthiest, and diphtheria and scarlet fever seem to prefer the finest neighbors." She continued, "We have three kinds of . . . [tenements]; the small ill-drained house moved from somewhere else; the rear tenement, moved back to make way for a new house in front; and the house which covers the entire lot. But while in New York the occupants of tenements are 36 per cent of the population, in Chicago they are only 15 percent. Only 5 per cent here consist of whole families in one room each" ("No Tenement Problem Here"). JA could readily compare Chicago tenements with those in New York City because she had visited the New York City Tenement House Exhibition in Feb. 1900.

Wiles Robert S. Hunter (1874–1942) was born in Terre Haute, Ind., to W. R. and Caroline Fouts Hunter and graduated from Indiana Univ. (1896 A.B.). From 1896 until 1902, he was associated with the Chicago Bureau of Charities. After visiting Toynbee Hall during the summer of 1899, Hunter returned to Chicago, where he became a HH resident, 1899–1900, and an early member of the Chicago Small Parks Comm. Before he left Chicago to become head worker at the University Settlement, New York City, 1902–3, he attempted to start dental clinics for poor children and a lodging house for vagrants, as well as to initiate an antituberculosis campaign. In New York, he carried forward his antituberculosis campaign idea and worked, 1902–6, to secure legislation to abolish child labor in the state. In 1903 he married Carolina M. Phelps Stokes (1878?–1964). They had four children.

In 1900 he became associated with Chicago Homes Assn. and especially its Investigating Com., led by JA, for which he completed *Tenement Conditions in Chicago* (1901). It was a study conducted during the summer of 1900, with work on the report, its text, maps, and charts, completed between 1 Aug. and Oct. 1900. One of the three areas of Chicago selected for intense study was a portion of the HH neighborhood, the "Jewish and Italian district" bounded by Canal St. on the east, Fourteenth St. on the south, Halsted St. on the west, and Polk St. on the north, because it was seen "as typical of bad conditions throughout the city" (Hunter, *Tenement Conditions in Chicago*, 13–14).

Between 1905 and 1914, when Hunter resigned his New York position, he was a member of the Socialist Party and stood unsuccessfully for election to the New York Assembly. He became a lecturer on economics and English at the Univ. of California between 1918 and 1922 . In California he became a golf course designer of note and served as president of the Berkeley Comm. on Public Charities, 1921; as chairman of the English Speaking Union, Santa Barbara, 1929–30; and as a member of the Special Com. of the National Economic League on the Monetary Problem of the United States, 1934–38. He was the author of several works, including *Poverty* (1904), *Violence and the Labor Movement* (1914), and *Revolution* (1940). He died in Montecito, Calif.

12. A search of JA's diary, June–Aug. 1900, did not reveal with whom JA had dinner on the evening of 18 June 1900.

13. Geddes lectured on the coal mining industry at his school on 17 June 1900.

14. Mary E. Collson (1870–1953), who grew up in Iowa, was groomed by women who brought the Unitarian Church to towns in the Midwest and particularly Iowa, to follow in their footsteps. She attended the State Univ. of Iowa during the last years of the nineteenth century and then graduated from Meadville Seminary in Pennsylvania and took leadership of a Unitarian congregation in Ida Grove, Iowa. During the summer of 1900, Mary Collson became associated with HH and by Jan. 1901 was identified as "a resident probation office of the Juvenile Court" and a HH resident, "appointed to look after the boys and girls of the neighborhood who, through delinquency or dependency, have become wards of the court." In the "Office of the Juvenile Court," *HH Bulletin*, her job was described in the following way: "Some of these boys and girls need help in finding employment, others encouragement and sympathy to keep them steadily at work. When the children are of school age this officer seeks to work with parents and teachers and truant officers in securing school advantages for the children and in seeing that they make use of these advantages. Also when a child of the neighborhood is brought before the Judge of the Juvenile Court the probation officer, by investigating the immediate environment, is able to co-operate with the Judge in securing such action as will most benefit the child" (12–13).

The work was taxing, and by 1902 Mary Collson had moved to Boston and became identified with the Christian Science movement. For the next thirty years, she served as a leader in the church and had a career as a metaphysical therapist. Collson, who had become disillusioned with her faith, set out to expose it by writing a book about her experiences. She wrote to JA of her struggle and indicated: "I have lived broader and deeper because I met you" (20 Jan. 1934, SCPC, JAC; *JAPM*, 25:678). JA may have encouraged Collson's work, but no publisher would issue it. Collson died at eighty-three. Her only obituary was her death certificate, which listed her occupation as "doing housework at home" (Tucker, "A Biographer's Experience Using Photography," 4).

15. This may have been Wilhelmina Bowman. Financial records indicate that she was a HH volunteer in 1900.

16. This was likely Jessie Bartlett (1867–1926), sister of Ada Bartlett Taft, wife of Lorado Taft. She taught girls and boys sloyd at HH during the late 1890s. She was the daughter of Emily S. and Leavitt Bartlett and was living with her widowed mother in the Taft household in Rockville Twp., Ogle Co., Ill., in the summer of 1900 when the U.S. Census was taken. Ten years later, mother and daughter were living in Cook Co.

17. JA was probably referring to her own absence from HH over the summer when Alzina Parsons Stevens died, for she wrote to MRS, 25 June 1900, that "I am sorry H.H. seems so desolate, all the letters from there seem rather blue about it, and of course Mrs Stevens death has been a great sorrow and shock. I am going to devote myself to it next fall as never before—and lecture less" (SCPC, JAC; *JAPM*, 3:1595–96).

18. The French word *cadeau* translates as "gift." JA had apparently purchased a gift for Charlotte Silsbee, who was marrying Frank Smith, brother of MRS.

19. Eleanor Smith.

20. Julia Lathrop, who had accompanied JA to Paris, was about to travel on her own. JA reported to MRS in her 25 June 1900 letter that "J. Lathrop has been in Barbizon and Fountainbleau with some artists friends for three days and has just come back" (SCPC, JAC; *JAPM*, 3:1594). Lathrop also planned to visit Switzerland. "I am so anxious to have J. Lathrop take this little trip, for I feel that merely the month in Paris has n't been worth her coming over for" (JA to MRS, 29 June 1900, SCPC, JAC; *JAPM*, 3:1600). Lathrop may also have visited programs established in Germany and Belgium for managing mentally challenged adults.

## Essay in the *Commons*

*"I am very much interested in a plan we have for a labor museum," Jane Addams wrote to Lillian Wald in New York, and indicated that she expected to visit "a few schools and educators in New York" probably to further investigate her idea.*[1] *Before Jane left in May for the exposition in Paris, she developed the plan for the educational program that she envisioned. Graham Taylor published it in the 30 June 1900 issue of the* Commons *while she was out of the country. The program Jane Addams described was to be located on the ground floor of the former Gymnasium and Coffee House Building, which was moved to a site on Polk Street, several feet west of the site on which it was originally constructed.*[2] *The Labor Museum was opened initially on the second floor of the Butler Art Gallery Building beginning every Saturday evening at 8:00 P.M. in November 1900.*[3]

### SOCIAL EDUCATION OF THE INDUSTRIAL DEMOCRACY.

### Settlement Problems in Educational Work With Adults.

### LABOR MUSEUM AT HULL HOUSE.[4]

Chicago, Ill. 30 June 1900

After ten years of educational experience at Hull House, several distinct conclusions have been forced upon the residents. It has been found in offering classes in an industrial community certain concessions must be made. Working people cannot be held to regularity of hours and effort as children can. Many things conspire to make this impossible,—they are delayed by long hours of work or by "over-time" which may make attendance on a given evening utterly out of the question, by family cares, a delayed supper, a sick child, the necessity for shopping in the evening; and last, they are often waylaid by an irresistible desire for recreation and distraction which is almost the inevitable reaction from the long hours of dull factory work.

## ADAPTATION NEEDED MORE THAN DISCIPLINE.

The discipline which a child gets from regularity of attendance at school and being held to a given piece of work whether it is tasteful or not, is of course more than supplied to working people by the inexorable necessity of punctuality and regularity at work, which is often enforced by a system of fines, and by the fact that many of them are continually held to distasteful tasks.

To insist too rigidly upon the disciplinary aspect of education is simply to fail to recognize the situation. If the settlement holds that there must be regularity of attendance or no attendance at all, the result is a class in literature or history, composed of people who come regularly and study faithfully, but who represent the transfigured few in the vicinity, those who are capable of abstract mental effort, and who have more or less of the scholar's mental instinct. Hull House can point to flourishing classes of this kind, which have sustained an interest in a given subject for six and eight years, and from which the members have derived a very good imitation of college culture.[5]

We would by no means advocate the abandonment of these classes, but rather the enlargement and progressive development of them. Certainly the people who are capable of sustained mental effort should be fed and helped, as indeed they are by every "popular lecture," every reading room and "Extension" class in the city. In addition to these classes the residents are convinced that there is a distinct need for educational methods adapted to the situation, in which the majority of working people are placed. The present methods are either copied from those employed in teaching children and totally ignore a vast amount of experience which life is continually bringing to the usefully employed adult, or are copied from the colleges, which presuppose a previous training and a desire for persistent study on the part of the young people, whose very presence in the college is, to a certain extent, a guarantee of both.

## THE WORKERS' EXPERIENCE AND INTEREST AVAILABLE.

A settlement should certainly be able to use both methods when they are available, but should not be caught by a slavish imitation of either, simply because they are successful under other circumstances. The residents of a settlement should be able to utilize many facts and forces lying quite outside the range of books, should be able to seize affections and memories which are not available in schools for children or immature youth.

In the Italian colony immediately west of Hull House, for instance, may be found peasant women, who in Italy spun, wove and dyed and made the clothing for their families. Some of the older women still use the primitive form of distaff.

It will be possible by their help to illustrate the history of textile manufacture, to reveal the long human effort which it represents, to put into sequence and historic order the skill which the Italian colony contains, but which is now lost or despised.[6]

It may easily be observed that the spot which attracts most people at any exhibition or fair is the one where something is being done, so trivial a thing as a girl cleaning gloves or a man polishing metal almost inevitably attracts a crowd who look on with absorbed interest. The same thing is true of shop windows.

It is hoped that by utilizing this feature of interest, the actual carrying forward of the industrial processes, and by the fact that the explanation of each process or period will be complete in itself, may in a measure tend to make the teaching dramatic and so overcome the disadvantage of irregular attendance. It is also believed that when education process is connected with the materials of daily life, it will hold his interest and feed his thought as the present abstract and unconnected study utterly fails to do. At least an effort will be made to minister to the needs of people as they present themselves and to develop the life of cultivation from "things as they are."

## EDUCATIVE INTERPRETATION OF INDUSTRIES.[7]

Educators have failed to adjust themselves to the fact that cities have become great centers of production and manufacture, and manual labor has been left without historic interpretation or imaginative uplift. It has almost inevitably become dull and uninteresting.

There is no doubt that the life of the average laborer tends to be flat and monotonous, with nothing in his work to feed his mind or hold his interest. Little is done either in the schools or elsewhere to make him really intelligent in regard to the processes involved in his work or in regard to the material which he daily handles.

Workmen are brought in contact with existing machinery quite as abruptly as if the present set of industrial implements had been newly created. They handle the machinery day by day without any notion that each generation works with the gifts of the last and transmits this increased gift to the next. Few of the men who perform the mechanical work in the great factories have any apprehension of the fact that the inventions upon which the factory depends, the instruments which they use, have been slowly worked out by the necessities of the race, have been added to and modified until they have become a social possession and have an aggregate value which time and society alone can give them.[8]

A machine really represents the "seasoned life of man" preserved and treasured up within itself, quite as much as does a parish church or a market cross.

If the people who use machinery do not get a consciousness of historic continuity and human interest through that machinery, these same people will probably never get it at all—it is indeed their only chance.

To put all historic significance upon city walls and triumphal arches, is to teach history from the political and governmental side, which too often presents solely the records of wars and restrictive legislation, emphasizing that which destroys life and property rather than the processes of labor, which really create and conserve civilization. Fame and honor still largely cling to war and non-productive occupations, and there seems to be no way of changing this, unless we can make the materials and processes which form the daily experience of the workmen more interesting and increase their picturesqueness.

It is also believed that a study of industry and the material foundations of life will be the most natural mode of approach to the larger life of cultivation and learning.

## CREDIT DUE TO LABOR FROM LEARNING.

The business college man, or the man who goes through an academic course in order to prepare for a profession, comes to look on learning too much as an investment from which he will later reap the benefits in earning money. He does not connect learning with industrial pursuits, nor does he in the least lighten or illuminate those pursuits for those of his friends who have not "risen in life."

"It is as though nets were laid at the entrances to education, in which those who, by some means or other, escape from the masses bowed down by labor are inevitably caught" and held from substantial service to their fellows.

Our civilization is more than anything an industrial civilization, but we admire the men who accumulate riches and gather to themselves the results of industry, rather than the men who really carry forward industrial processes.

Apparently our democratic sentiment has not yet recovered industrial occupations from the deep distrust which slavery and the feudal organization of society have cast upon them.

Democracy claims for the workman the free right of citizenship, but does not yet insist that he shall be a cultivated member of society with a consciousness of his social and industrial value.

We fail to appreciate the patient performance of painful duty, the resignation in misfortune, forgiveness under injury, and quiet courage which goes to show the creative virtue there is in action itself. The manual worker in spite of all his drawbacks gets a great solace and comfort from the labor itself, but to that should be added the interest and stimulus which comes to the individual when he is able to see himself "in connection and co-operation with the whole."

## EDUCATIONAL MUSEUM OF LABOR.

The word "Museum" is purposely used in preference to "School," both because the latter is distasteful to grown-up people from its association with childish tasks, and because the former still retains some of the fascinations of the show.

The museum will be opened with five departments, which will present human progress as developed thro the laborer's efforts, and will be connected as closely as possible with the growth and history of Chicago and the development of its industries.

1. Metals with the copper of the Lake Superior region.

2. Wood with the lumber region of Wisconsin and Michigan.

3. Grain with the wheat and corn of Illinois and Indiana.

4 and 5. The books and textiles will be treated from the history of their own development, but connected so far as possible with the local conditions.

These five departments will contain specimens of the raw material and actual presentation of the processes to which that material is subjected. A history of the effect of the process upon the laborer will be given by informal lectures. Much stress will be laid upon the pictures and diagrams. So far as possible the historic presentation of the process will connect with the activities which have already centered about Hull House.

The department of wood will terminate in the shop for the carpentry and wood carving of Hull House guild.[9] The history of bookmaking will terminate in Miss Starr's own bindery,[10] to which will be added a printing shop. The history of textiles will correlate with the Hull House sewing, dressmaking and embroidery classes.

The grains will lead up to the Hull House bakery and cooking classes. A small blast furnace and forge will make possible a shop for metal work.[11]

As four Hull House shops[12] already exist, not merely for the sake of teaching, but primarily for the sake of producing, and include the activities of many people beside the Directors, so the shops will be enlarged upon these lines, and the historic background will be presented thro the people of the vicinity, whose training represents more primitive methods. These primitive methods in turn will be traced to the factories of the neighborhood, and the enlarged and developed tools rediscovered there, *i. e.* copper in the Western Electric, wood in the Box Factory, bread in the Bremner Bakery, textiles in the sweat shops, rug weaving, etc.

In illustration of the educational method in mind the *first* outlines of the departments of Metals and Textiles may be cited to show how it is hoped to correlate general history and literature with industrial processes.[13]

## METALS.

Maps of lakes and surrounding regions as known to the Indians. Indian methods of working copper compared with those of the mound builders. Maps of North America and the world, showing copper regions. Early discoveries of the lake regions—French explorers. Complete maps of the routes of Conti, LaSalle, Marquette, and Joliet, including the Mississippi valley. Establishment of Fort Dearborn.

Methods of mining copper employed by the first white man. Nationality of early emigrants and settlements which followed. Methods of transportation. Population of Chicago during this period. Map showing the development of the copper industry.

Specimens of crude ore—actual presentation of the processes. The ore submitted to a small blast furnace, smelted, rolled into sheet, shaped, annealed, etc. Maps showing districts in which metal has been discovered and worked. History of metal working and the effects of this craft upon civilization. Communities based upon metal industries.

Outline of Phœnician history as affected by metals, leading to explorations. Etruscans and their development of metals on the artistic side. Specimens of bronze coins, collections of copper and bronze coins, collections of copper and bronze ornaments and household utensils.

Medieval workers in metals, guilds, craftsmen and artists, such as Cellini. Product of guild spirit. Nurenberg. Peter Vischer.

Improvement of trade routes causing increase of trade. Workers become more scattered. Reunited under exploiting methods. Black country of England. Women and children used in mines, also for work at smithies and forges. Slow reform through labor legislation. Emergence from this state. Trades unions of metal workers in England and America. Pictures of modern mines and conditions of life in mining settlements.

Legends connected with metal workers:

The Nibelungen Lied and St. Dunstan.

In music—Handel's Harmonious Blacksmith, or Wagner's Siegfried.

In sculpture—Giotto's Tower. Music represented by a blacksmith striking metal on an anvil.

## TEXTILES.

Gradual development and preparation. Spinning and weaving of animal and vegetable fibres; soil and general climatic conditions necessary for their cultivation; effect of textile industries upon social organization.

Earliest weaving of branches and woody fibres in making of baskets, mats for sides of huts, etc. Method of lining baskets with clay and afterwards burning away the basket, leading to development of pottery and its earliest decorations, from impressions of baskets left. Use of various fibres in Pacific islands.

History and development of wool, linen and silk industries.

*Wool.* Map showing early wool-raising sections and general character of wool-raising countries.

Earliest wool-raising on grassy slopes and plains, first hand spinning—rough distaff and spindle, primitive looms, first crude scouring and dyeing, suggested reproduction of the processes and a comparison of the methods still employed by primitive peoples, such as the Navajo Indians, etc.

The effect of pastoral life, both in its nomad and more settled forms upon primitive culture; illustrated by pictures and related literature. Early Greek and Hebrew development taken as examples.

Medieval wool culture—the flocks of Spain and of England, the invention of the spinning wheel, the development of looms, the domestic system, the growth of organization among the weavers, traced to modern times.

Effect of the eighteenth century industrial revolution in England upon the weavers; first application of steam power to textile industry; the weavers hastily gather in large towns and factories; children prematurely put to work; persistence of many of the weavers in their homes, until driven out by starvation. Similar conditions now in the first application of steam sewing, much the same persistence among the "home workers" who sew in their own houses.

*Linen.* Map showing early districts. Cultivation of flax along the banks of the Nile. Early Egyptian pictures of flax spinning with distaff.

Medieval flax culture. American colonial period specifically emphasized, with its spinning wheels, processes of bleaching and dyeing, looms and embroideries.

Modern preparation of flax in Belgium, the outdoor retting in the river Lys, invention of retting tanks, controlling conditions. Irish culture and manufacture. Belgian and Irish lace-making and embroideries. Revival in Ireland of cottage industries.

Relation of the Hull House embroidery classes and the weaving and spinning of the Italian women in the neighborhood to general textile industries.

*Silk.* Earliest silk culture in the Orient. Silk trade of merchant caravans between India and southern Europe. Relation of silk carrying trade to discovery of America. Successful introduction and cultivation of silk worms in southern Europe.

Chinese and French silk manufacturers and embroideries.

Literature in relation to textile industries. Proverbs—Penelope. In music—Pastoral songs and symphonies.

PD (*Commons* 47 [30 June 1900]: 1–4; *JAPM*, 46:997–1001).

1. 15 Jan. 1900, NYPL, Wald, Incoming; *JAPM*, 3:1497–98.

2. On preparations associated with moving the former Gymnasium and Coffee House Building and replacing it with a new and larger Coffee House and Theatre Building, see Article in the *Evening Gazette*, 10 Aug. 1898, n. 1; and JA to MRS, 25 July 1899, n. 10, both above.

3. JA spoke about the development of the Labor Museum to the HH Arts and Crafts Society on 15 Feb. 1901. The Labor Museum did not move into its new quarters until the fall of 1901. Then it settled on the ground floor of the former Gymnasium and Coffee House Building with a weaving and spinning room, a space for laundry work and dyeing, equipment for cooking classes, a grain collection, benches for woodworking, forges and anvils for metalwork, and the beginning of a pottery exhibit. The second floor was given over to a print shop and EGS's bookbindery. The HH Labor Museum was described in *First Report for the Labor Museum at HH—1901–1902*, by JA, published by HH (UIC, JAMC, HH Assn., and SCPC, Balch; *JAPM*, 46:1078–88, 51:401–10.

4. A typescript with autograph notations of the article published by JA about the Labor Museum project in the *Commons*, 30 June 1900, is extant. See "First Outline of a Labor Museum at HH, Chicago," in the SHSW, Blaine; *JAPM*, 46:966–87, 51:378–98. In addition, portions of the same text appear in *First Report for the Labor Museum at HH—1901–1902*.

5. Almost from the beginning of HH, the founders had maintained a schedule of college-like courses on a variety of topics. See especially JA to AHHA, 3 June 1890; and Two Essays in the *Forum*, Nov. and Oct. 1892, both above.

6. The following text from JA's typescript was deleted from JA's published Article in the *Commons* (Addams, "First Outline of a Labor Museum at HH"; *JAPM*, 46:970–71, 51:381–82):

> Partly owing to the fact that undue stress in the schools is put upon the reading and speaking of English, partly because a rise in the social scale is only achieved by a commercial or professional position, and most of all because the simpler Italians who possess this skill are considered uncouth and un-American, the children and more ambitious young people look down upon them and are too often ashamed of their parents.
>
> Giving the older people a chance to use their skill that it may have a meaning and dignity, will, it is believed, tend to several distinct results:
>
> (a) Industrial processes themselves will be made more picturesque and be given a content and charm which is now laid upon the more barren life of business or solely upon recreation.
>
> (b) The young people who are forced to remain in the shops and factories, for with the most strenuous efforts, not all of them can become sales and shipping clerks, will have some idea of the material which they are handling, and it is hoped in time a consciousness of the social value of the work which they are performing.
>
> (c) The older people who are now at such a disadvantage because they lack certain superficial qualities which are too highly prized, will more easily attain the position in the community to which their previous life and training entitles them.

7. The following text from JA's typescript was deleted from this position in JA's article published in the *Commons*:

> The museum will, be kept a labor museum in contradistinction to a commercial museum.
>
> The attempt will be made to present history and human progress from the point of view of the laborer as civilization was developed through his efforts.
>
> The primitive notion of a city that it was a market place in which produce was exchanged, merely a meeting place for traders and merchants, still survives in our minds. Our schools still prepare our children almost exclusively for commercial and professional life. As the country boy dreams of leaving the farm for business in the city and imitates the traveling salesman in dress and manner, so the school boy in town hopes to be an 'office boy' and later a salesman or a clerk and looks upon work in a factory as the occupation of ignorant and unsuccessful men. The schools do little to really interest the child in the life of production or to excite his ambitions in he line of industrial occupations.

(Addams, "First Outline of a Labor Museum at HH," 5–6; *JAPM*, 46:972–73, 51:383–84).

8. The following text was deleted from JA's typescript at this position in her article published in the *Commons*: "We easily recognize the historic association in regard to ancient buildings, we say that 'generation after generation have stamped their mark upon them, have recorded their thoughts in them until they have become, "sacrosant," the property of all,' and yet this is even more true of the instruments of labor, which have been constantly held in human hands" (Addams, "First Outline of a Labor Museum at HH," 7; *JAPM*, 46:974, 51:385).

9. The HH Guild was another name for the HH Arts and Crafts Society.

10. The same issue of the *Commons* also printed a description of the HH Bookbindery by EGS. She described her rationale for studying and teaching fine bookbinding: "All modern life has been tending to separate the work of the mind and the work of the hands. One set of people work with their heads but produce nothing whatever with their hands. Another vast body work with their hands at very mechanical and uninteresting work, which does not in any way engage or develop the mind in its higher faculties. Both sets of people are living partial lives, not using all the powers God gave us. . . . So then it became necessary for me, if I were to act as I believed, to learn to make something worth making, and to do it as thoroughly well as I was able. I . . . selected books, being interested in them from several points of view. . . . I had thought, when I formed the intention of learning a craft, that I should teach it here at Hull House on the basis of the extension classes and the manual training. I have not been able to do this for several reasons: the implements and material are expensive; the time required to accomplish anything is too long for those who only give an evening or two or three evenings a week, and the amount of personal attention required by beginners precludes the possibility of anything but a small class . . . but by binding and ornamenting a few books as well as I can do it, and by teaching three private pupils as well as I can teach them," EGS believed she could reach her goal (Starr, "HH Bookbindery," *Commons* 47 [30 June 1900]: 5–6).

11. See n. 3.

12. An article titled "HH Shops" in the *HH Bulletin* 5 in 1902 described the shops as pottery, carpentry, printing, and bookbinding. It is likely that prior to 1902, instead of pottery, printing, and bookbinding, the shops that JA identified, besides woodworking, were sewing and weaving, baking or food preparation, as well as metal crafting.

13. In her typescript, JA included descriptions of how she planned to present the five industries she expected to feature; however, the *Commons* offered her notes for only two of them: metals and textiles. Omitted from the published article are JA's notes for wood and grain. For those notes, see Addams, "First Outline of a Labor Museum at HH," 5–7; *JAPM*, 46:982–84, 51:393–95).

## From Harris Weinstock

*By 1899 Jane Addams had won acclaim as the unchallenged leader of the social settlement movement in the United States. Increasing numbers of social settlements were being opened every year, primarily in urban settings. There were 6 settlements by 1891, and by 1900 there were 127 programs that identified themselves as settlements, located primarily in New York City, Boston, and Chicago,*[1] *but in other cities as well. The success of Hull-House along with Jane Addams's ability to describe what a settlement could be and relate a rationale for its development were key in the successful growth of the movement. Addams made hundreds of speeches about settlement work, many of which were reported in newspapers and periodicals throughout America.*[2] *Even after Jane Addams established a fee for her services as a speaker, she continued to speak pro bono for organizations in communities that planned to establish or further develop social settlements. She also helped establish local and national organizations to assist settlement leaders by promoting opportunities for them to gather, exchange views, and explore options for program and reform.*[3]

*A great many people sought Addams's advice and aid in developing social settlements. Emily Holmes asked her to come to Westminster House in Buffalo, New York, where she told Jane she expected her presence "will put your seal to give the world assurance of another settlement" similar to Hull-House.*[4] *Helena S. Dudley at Denison House in Boston wanted Jane to visit because she thought she would "put some of your spirit into our house."*[5] *A woman in Grand Rapids, Michigan, wanted Jane's advice about leaving money in her will to start a settlement.*[6] *Addams influenced the development of settlements in San Francisco and Berkeley; the Boston area; New York City and Buffalo; Baltimore; Cleveland, Cincinnati, and Toledo; Pittsburgh and Philadelphia; Milwaukee; Terra Haute, Indiana; and Louisville, Kentucky. She also gave advice and encouragement to a number of Chicago settlements, including the Chicago Commons,*[7] *on whose board of directors she sat until her death; the University of Chicago Settlement;*[8] *Maxwell Street Settlement;*[9] *Kirkland School Settlement;*[10] *and Helen Heath Settlement.*[11]

*The following letters seem to be evidence of the first opportunity that Jane Addams had to help create a social settlement for African Americans in Chicago. She investigated the planned Institutional Church and Social Settlement*[12] *that was being created by Rev. Reverdy C. Ransom*[13] *in Chicago, and she sent the one hundred dollars offered by Harris Weinstock*[14] *to Monroe N. Work*[15] *with her support. On Sunday, 31 October 1900, during the formal opening of the Institutional Church and Social Settlement, Jane Addams and Graham Taylor made welcoming remarks.*

Sacramento, Cal. Oct. 19, 1900

Dear Miss:—

I beg to enclose herewith a circular letter received from Mr. M. N. Work in behalf of the Colored Social Settlement of Chicago, as I do not know any thing about the responsibility of the parties engaged in the work or whether it is being established on proper lines, I beg to enclose herewith a check on the Bank of America for $100.00 in accordance with the proposition made in mine of Sept. 22nd, and would ask you to investigate into the character of the undertaking and the people who have charge thereof and if you find the effort a worthy and deserving one, I would ask you to turn over to them the enclosure with my best wishes for the success of their effort. If not, kindly advise me and meanwhile hold the check subject to my order. Thanking you in advance for the trouble this may give you, I beg to remain Sincerely yours,

H Weinstock

TLS (SCPC, JAC; *JAPM*, 3:1679).

ENCLOSURE

## M. N. Work to Harris Weinstock

The Institutional Church and Social Settlement
3825 Dearborn St.,

Chicago, [Ill.] Oct 15 1900

Dear Sir:

We are engaged in the work of the First Social Settlement ever established among colored people. We believe that this work reaches the very foundation of our people's need. We have gone forward in this work without asking aid, until now we find ourselves hampered in every department of our work for want of means. We find the people quite responsive to our efforts to better their condition, which makes us feel that we are at work on the right line. We hope you will pardon the liberty we have taken but we believe that of the many who are able to help, you are one to whom the need of this work will appeal.

We are trying to raise ($2,000), two thousand dollars to equip and run us for one year. Much of our work will remain at a standstill until a part of this is in hand. Our building is open for inspection every day and evening.

The more people we reach, the less will reach the police stations, reformatories and jails. I hope you will help us. Very respectfully yours,

M. N. Work.

TLS (SCPC, JAC; *JAPM*, 3:1680).

1. The counts come from Woods and Kennedy, *Handbook of Settlements* (1911).

2. Newspaper and periodical clippings files, 1892–1960, SCPC, JAC; *JAPM*, 55–71; and HH Scrapbooks; *JAPM*, Addendum 1A and 10 (see Article in *Good Housekeeping*, Nov. 1900, n. 1, below).

3. In 1894 JA hosted a group of leaders from the following social settlements as they met at HH to found the Chicago Federation of Settlements (which later became the Chicago Federation of Settlements and Neighborhood Houses [CFSNH]): HH, Northwestern University Settlement, Maxwell Street Settlement, the Forward Movement (which was incorporated as Epworth House in 1896), University of Chicago Settlement, and Chicago Commons. When the organization was incorporated in 1896, JA became one of its directors. JA also led planning efforts in 1897 and 1898 for a national conference of social settlement leaders and workers that took place at HH in May 1899. See JA to Henrietta O. Barnett, 30 May 1899, above. Woods and Kennedy in their *Handbook of Settlements* (1911) indicated that a number of "more or less informal national gatherings of settlement workers" had been held from time to time since the first and informal one at Plymouth, Mass., in 1892 (1).

4. Emily Holmes to JA, 24 Oct. 1894, SCPC, JAC; *JAPM*, 2:1582.

5. Helena S. Dudley to JA, 2 Nov. 1896, SCPC, JAC; *JAPM*, 3:487.

6. See Caroline W. Putnam to JA, 26 June 1897, SCPC, JAC; *JAPM*, 3:700.

7. See Graham Taylor to JA, 26 June 1897, above.

8. See Two Essays in the *Forum*, Nov. and Oct. 1892, n. 154, above.

9. The Maxwell Street Settlement was founded 11 Nov. 1893, at 185 (later 566 West) Maxwell St. by Jacob J. Abt (1868–1923), who became the first head resident, and by Jesse Lowenhaupt

"'to afford opportunity for personal fellowship and to be of some social service'" (Woods and Kennedy, *Handbook of Settlements*, 78).

10. See Cordelia Kirkland to JA, 15 Oct. [1896], SCPC, JAC; *JAPM*, 3:465–67 .

11. See Jenkin Lloyd Jones to JA, 19 Nov. 1895, MTS, Jones; JA to Jenkin Lloyd Jones, 21 Nov. 1895, UC, Jones; *JAPM*, 2:1805–6.

12. The Institutional Church and Social Settlement was incorporated in June 1900, at 3825 South Dearborn St., Chicago. With thirty-four thousand dollars from the African Methodist Episcopal Church (AME), under which authority it was created, the founder, Reverdy C. Ransom (see n. 13), was able to purchase the former Railroad Chapel of the Presbyterian Church to begin the program he envisioned to "meet and serve the moral, social, and industrial needs of people" (Ransom, *First Quadrennial Report of the Pastor and Warden of the Institutional Church and Social Settlement*, 6). The people he meant to help were the more than thirty thousand African Americans, a large number of whom were migrants from the southern states, who lived around the facility in Chicago's "black belt," which stretched "in a long, thin sliver of land, sandwiched between a well-to-do white neighborhood and that of the so-called 'shanty Irish'" (Drake and Cayton, *Black Metropolis*, 47) from immediately south of Chicago's downtown to the homes of the wealthier African Americans farther south. The Institutional Church and Social Settlement was officially opened on 21 Oct. 1900.

Between 1900 and 1904, when Ransom resigned, he created a spiritual and self-help settlement-like program that included day and after-school care for children, a kindergarten, sports program, literary clubs focusing on the writings of black authors, a penny savings bank, an employment agency, and job training programs. There were a sewing school, a kitchen garden program, catering classes, and opportunities to learn kindergarten work. In addition to helping provide safe milk for children, Ransom and his volunteers offered free coal, food, and clothing to those who were in dire need and could not pay. For spiritual life, there was Sunday School and church as well, but Ransom did not promote evangelism. His Sunday School began with approximately 150 students and his church with 100 followers. By 1904 that number of church members had increased to 300, with nearly 400 attending Sunday services.

Ransom also made attempts to improve conditions in his neighborhood, site of policy games, saloons, and prostitution. In the process, his life was threatened, and his church was once bombed after a Sunday service when no one was in the facility. His crusade drew positive recognition in the white community, and the Chicago police, who rarely came into the area to enforce laws, did arrest more than 100 policy makers in the Institutional Church and Social Settlement neighborhood. Leaders in other African American churches became convinced that Ransom's programs were taking the AME program too far away from the central spiritual mission of their faith; they seemed not to favor replicating or recognizing his successful program. By 1904, under pressure from the Illinois-Iowa Conf. in which he and his church were administratively located, he resigned.

Rev. James M. Townsend, who replaced him, dismantled a great many of the social outreach programs that Ransom had put in place. Townsend was followed in 1909 by Rev. Archibald J. Carey, who had been associated with the Quinn Chapel, Chicago, an AME church that competed with Ransom's program for members and visibility in the African American community. Quinn Chapel, organized in 1844, a leader in the abolitionist movement, carried on that tradition in support of African American social activism and was a powerful force in Chicago's burgeoning black communities. When Carey was named bishop in the AME Church in 1920, he left the Institutional Church and Social Settlement. Under his leadership, the church-settlement combination had become an AME church, with a traditional congregation. It survived into the mid-twentieth century.

13. Reverdy C. Ransom (1861–1959) was born in Flushing, Ohio, a small Quaker community. When he was five years old, his mother, Harriet, married George Ransom, and the family moved to Washington, Ohio, where he grew up and was educated. There he became an active member of the AME Church. He entered Wilberforce Univ. in 1881. After spend-

ing a semester at Oberlin College in 1882, he decided to become a minister. By 1883 he was licensed to preach in the AME Church, and by 1886 he graduated from Wilberforce Univ.

Between 1886 and 1893, when he attended the World's Parliament of Religions at the World's Columbian Exposition in Chicago, he served as pastor to a number of small community churches, many of which had memberships of no more than fifteen people. Influenced by social gospel writings and his own experiences with the poor African Americans he served, Ransom already believed that the AME organization should "serve as a center of the life of the people, and in that center the people may be educated" (Ransom, "Work of the Methodist Church in the Twentieth Century," 153).

In 1893 when he became pastor of St. John's AME Church in Cleveland, he began to put into practice his ideas for social and spiritual ministry. In addition to the usual church organizations and functions, he created special outreach activities, including infant education classes for mothers, a kindergarten, and social and educational organizations for children, women, and men, and then he added a YMCA program as well. By 1896 Ransom had been selected as a minister for Chicago's Bethel AME Church at 29th and Dearborn streets. With the support of significant black leaders, including physician Daniel Hale Williams; Ferdinand Lee Barnett (1852–1936), publisher of the *Conservator*, first of the African American newspapers published in Chicago; and his wife, antilynching advocate and reformer Ida Wells-Barnett (1862–1931), Ransom significantly increased Bethel's outreach to middle-class and migrant-class blacks, creating educational, training, and social programs that he hoped would lead to upward mobility for African Americans.

In 1900 Reverdy C. Ransom got an opportunity to develop fully his social outreach ideas. He was offered a chance to create the first black Institutional Church and Social Settlement in Chicago (see n. 12). Serving without salary, he and his second wife, Emma Connor Ransom, whom he met while serving a small country pastorate in Selma, Ohio, and their two sons settled in three rooms of the former Railroad Chapel in which the Institutional Church and Social Settlement was located and began to build their settlement program. They had the support of other settlement leaders in Chicago, including Jane Addams and Graham Taylor, and several wealthy white Chicago leaders, including Charles Hutchinson and Victor E. Lawson.

When Ransom left his Institutional Church and Social Settlement position, he assumed pastorates for the AME Church initially in New Bedford, Mass., and then the St. Charles AME Church, Boston, from 1905 until 1907, when he went to New York City's Bethel AME Church. He left that church in 1912 and became editor of the *A.M.E. Church Review*. From 1913 until 1924, he led the Church of Simon of Cyrene in New York City, a mission he started. Ransom ran unsuccessfully for a seat in the U.S. Congress in 1918, and in 1924 he became a bishop in the AME Church in Ohio, where he continued his long and creative career as a church leader to improve the spiritual and social life of African Americans through church participation and education.

14. Harris Weinstock (1854–1922) was a California merchant specializing in real estate. He was educated in public schools in New York and by 1872 was in business in San Francisco. He eventually became president of Weinstock Nicols Co., with offices in San Francisco, Los Angeles, and Oakland. California governors often appointed him to investigate special conditions affecting the state. In 1908 he was tapped to study labor laws and conditions in foreign countries; in 1912 to investigate Industrial Workers of the World free-speech disturbances in San Diego, Calif.; and in 1913 to consider European systems of rural credits. President Woodrow Wilson appointed him a member of the U.S. Industrial Relations Comm. in 1913, the same year that he became a member of the California Industrial Accident Comm. He also served as the marketing director for California, 1915 through at least 1920, and was a member of the board of the National Civic Federation. Weinstock wrote at least two books, served as a trustee for the State Library of California, and instituted the Barbara Felsenthal Weinstock lectureship of Morals of Trade at the Univ. of California.

15. Monroe Nathan Work (1866–1945), who became an important sociologist and creator of the Dept. of Records and Research at Tuskegee Institute, Ala., in 1908, was at the time he wrote this letter a student in the Sociology Dept. at the Univ. of Chicago. He had just published "Crime among the Negroes in Chicago," the first article by an African American scholar to appear in the *American Journal of Sociology* (6 Sept. 1900). He believed that education and facts would promote understanding among the races and that eventually prejudice would begin to disappear, an idea he held all of his life.

Work had been born of former slaves in Iredell Co., N.C., and grew up on a farm in Summer Co., Kans. At the age of twenty-three, he graduated third in his integrated high school class in Arkansas City, Kans. After trying his hand at teaching, homesteading, and preaching, he entered the Seminary at the Univ. of Chicago, but by 1898 he had transferred to the Sociology Dept. There he excelled. After graduating from the Univ. of Chicago (B.A. and M.A. 1903), he joined the faculty at Georgia State Industrial College, Savannah. While there he founded the Savannah Men's Sunday Club with a mission of improving living conditions in Savannah for African Americans.

Although he was associated with W. E. B. Du Bois in 1905 in the anti-Washington Niagara Movement, in 1908 he accepted a position offered by Booker T. Washington at Tuskegee. There he began to gather and organize materials especially about the African American experiences in the United States, focusing particularly on lynching statistics. Work began publishing material he gathered in the *Negro Year Book*, which he edited from 1912 until 1937, producing nine issues. He also compiled *A Bibliography of the Negro in Africa and America* that was issued in 1928, the same year he received the Harmon Award in Education.

## Article in *Good Housekeeping*

*By the end of the nineteenth century, Jane Addams and Hull-House had gained national, and even international, visibility, as a force for progress. If, in 1889, the "scheme" that she and Ellen Gates Starr set out to develop was known and admired primarily among reform-minded leaders, by 1900 Jane Addams's actions and the legend they inspired were reaching ordinary citizens in the United States. Her activities and speeches were regularly reported in newspapers. By 1895 not only were her public remarks presented verbatim in newspaper articles, but she was often pictured in sketches based on photographs. The comprehensive clipping collection now included with Addams's personal papers, composed of articles from daily newspapers and other periodicals, was started by Jane and Ellen in scrapbooks in 1889. It attests to the increasing coverage that Addams and her reform efforts inspired throughout the decade of the 1890s.*[1]

*In November 1900, and for the first of many times in the future, Jane Addams was lionized in a popular periodical directed specifically at women.*[2] Good Housekeeping, *with a circulation of fifty thousand in 1900, was one of the six major women's magazines published at that time in the United States.*[3] *In it its new editor, James Eaton Tower,*[4] *continued to publish a series of biographical treatments, "Women Who Have Made the World Better,"*[5] *and selected Jane Addams as the ninth woman to be featured.*

Sometime between 1899 and 1902, Jane Addams sat for a photographic study by Elizabeth B. Brownell (1860?–1909), who at that time may have shared a studio with her cousin photographer William B. Dyer in Chicago. Brownell, who became noted for her photographs of children, copyrighted this photograph in 1902, when it appeared in print for the first time. This study by Brownell became one of Jane Addams's favorite photographs. She had it reproduced to distribute to her admiring public (private collection).

## AMONG THE WORKERS [CONTINUING THE SERIES "WOMEN WHO HAVE MADE THE WORLD BETTER"] JANE ADDAMS, OF HULL HOUSE

Nov. 1900

To inquires concerning Jane Addams and her busy life at the head of the Hull House social settlement in Chicago, no answer could be more heartily indorsed in her own community or which would probably be a greater source of gratification to Miss Addams, herself, than the statement: She is neighbor to a portion of that great mass of human beings frequently referred to as "the common people." She aspires to no more exalted title.

Hull House, first and foremost, is a home; it is a home of wealth and beauty, a center of culture and refinement—and Jane Addams has been the presiding genius therein for eleven years. To her there is nothing incongruous in the fact that it is the only home of its kind in all that region, that only ugly tenements and squalid surroundings are to be seen from its windows—or were, until its own refining influence was felt in the neighborhood. It was one of the unexplainable mysteries to Jane Addams, in her girlhood, why all the homes of elegance and wealth should be confined to one portion of the city while the homes of barrenness and poverty should be huddled together in another locality. This condition of affairs sent a severe chill to her democratic heart. She, who always had valued her friends according to worth, not according to wealth, could see no reason for such a barrier dividing the rich and the poor. She applied herself to a study of the problem and perceived, back of this inequality of neighborhoods, an unjust pride, the mortal enemy of the most mutually helpful form of social intercourse. It has been Jane Addams's mission to extend to a densely crowded tenement community the advantages of a true "home atmosphere." To this woman there is nothing hopelessly sordid in the fact that the streets and alleys in her ward seem the natural habitat of filth and dirt. She rejoices that they are cleaner than they were yesterday.

Why has the success of her undertaking been so marked as to command a world's respectful attention and applause? Because her intentions have been so palpably genuine and because good faith has marked their fulfillment. She did not choose to make her home in Chicago's densest factory district from motives of magnificent condescension or because she believed herself appointed to uplift the destitute down-trodden. She is a woman of a different mold. Although she is looked upon by scores of the residents of the Nineteenth Ward as a veritable "angel in disguise," it is far from her thought to take any attitude regarding her environment save the democratic one of receiving as much help from her neighbors as she gives them. The impression which the visiting stranger invariably carries from an interview with Miss Addams is that he has talked with a plain, sensible, pleasant-faced woman, of broad views and warm sympathies, who finds life richly worth the living.

When asked to recall the reasons which prompted her to enter upon the problems of life hand in hand, as it were, with men and women of the laboring class, Miss Addams replied: "The question is hardly fair; at least it is a difficult one to answer. Do you not think the motives upon which we really base our actions are usually too deep and intricate to be definitely formulated? I cannot tell why, except that I have always cared for working people." And, herein, no doubt, lies the real secret of her influence, and herein may be found the real reason for the affectionate devotion of her "neighbors."

To obtain an adequate conception of the early purpose of the Hull House social settlement the reader should imagine himself, for the time being, in the shoes of a certain whole-souled young woman, the daughter of a democratic congressman,[6] as she stepped fresh from the halls of the Rockford college at Rockford, Illinois, some fourteen years ago.[7] Her name was Jane Addams. Before her mind's eye were the pictures of social inequality which had haunted her since childhood;[8] deep in her heart were sown the seeds of social democracy, the foundation upon which her own home had rested. She was bent upon a "finishing tour"[9] in Europe and possessed not only an absorbing ambition to become an earnest toiler in the world of helpful endeavor, but had at her command no inconsiderable fortune.[10] In company with a girl friend—Miss Ellen Gates Starr—she visited the principal cities of Europe and experienced keen delight in studying the great social institutions of the Old World. Her friend was no less enthusiastic than she. They found themselves in the most dingy and squalid quarters of London and of other cities; and it did not occur to them to regard themselves in the least degree as "ministering angels." Prompted by a love of democracy, they sought out these people from choice. It was during their visit at Toynbee Hall,[11] London, that they received the impulse which ripened in the founding of an institution which has been a boon to Chicago's poor people. A study of the results which were being obtained by the residents of this, the world's first social settlement, founded as a memorial to Arnold Toynbee by some of his Oxford friends, inspired them with a desire to kindle a little fire of "neighborliness" on their own account among that class of Chicagoans who, though poor in money, are not necessarily wholly devoid of riches of another kind. They came home with the avowed purpose, not of reforming the whole social system, but of doing their part in the actual demonstration of equality and democracy.

"Why," pondered Miss Addams, "do people continually strive to emulate and live among those who are far beyond them in means rather than cast their lots with those who are poorer than they?" She perceived in this too general tendency a social scourge whose evils were not to be counterbalanced by any amount of so-called "charity" on the part of kindly disposed persons having the time, money and inclination for philanthropic work. In an able lecture upon "Ethical Survivors in Municipal Corruption,"[12] Miss Addams seconds the sentiment expressed by Samuel Johnson[13] when he said: "It is surprising to find how much more kindness than justice society contains."

What course did Jane Addams pursue? She and her collaborator searched the poor tenement districts of Chicago for a locality which should exceed, if possible, all others in point of poverty and overcrowding. When they found it they decided to make their home therein. It so happened that, at the corner of Polk and Halsted streets, almost within a stone's throw of the spot they had selected, was an inviting old brick building, once the mansion of a Chicago pioneer, Charles J. Hull by name. The "old Hull house," as it was called, could not have been better adapted to the purposes of these young women had it been especially ordered, and delivered by magical process. It was about the only building in the neighborhood which escaped the big fire of '71 that started but a few blocks away.[14] This mute survivor of a pioneer grandeur, though in fairly good condition, would doubtless have fallen, at the sacrilegious hands of its shifting tenants, into a state of hopeless decrepitude, had not these energetic young women put new life into its every nook and cranny. The new tenants made no pretensions; they simply hired the upper floor and one room downstairs and, on a certain September day, 1889, established themselves comfortably therein.[15]

They did not publish the fact; neither did they enter upon a vigorous campaign of neighborhood reconstruction. They took up their abode as any other tenants would have done, the only difference being that they spared no money to make their home attractive. Besides this, they "cared for working people" and went about the establishment of a social settlement. When they invited to their rooms the children who had lived most of their short lives in the dirty streets and alleys of the neighborhood, it was surprising to watch them—the crowds that came. The building's office tenants soon moved elsewhere and the vacant space was immediately taken. When the association was incorporated, the settlement was given the permanent name, "Hull House."[16] The neighbors were invited to call and they became interested in literature and art. Science and mathematics, history and manual training, music and social entertainments were the lodestones which attracted scores of "neighbors" of various ages. The people who flock to Hull House for its social and educational privileges represent almost as many nationalities as there were different tongues among the workmen on the tower of Babel. This is one of the forms of "progress" for which Jane Addams's life stands.

The old mansion which sufficed years ago has been enlarged and is now the center of a group of buildings, each devoted to some department of Hull House work, and Miss Addams accepts her enlarged responsibilities as a matter of course. There is nothing of vital public importance to the Nineteenth Ward in which she does not take a personal interest. When she became the inspector of streets and alleys for her ward, the condition of the alleys underwent a marvelous change; and when she resigned this position it was with the knowledge that it was falling into equally competent hands.

Jane Addams has dared to raise her voice against corrupt city politics. She has not, thereby, obliterated these evils; but her methods have, at least, tended to educate the people to a point where they are beginning to have a conscience in the matter. She has not entered blindly into this feature of the work, ranting against corrupt politicians and their methods. Rather, she has taken the pains thoroughly to study into the subject from an ethical and practical standpoint, and the conclusions which she draws point to the fact that the corrupt methods employed are but the natural outcome of the regrettable conditions that exist; that the foreign poor people are not nearly so much alive to their moral starvation as to their physical wants, and that until the right sort of social intercourse shall have been developed to educate the moral and intellectual sensibilities, it were useless to attempt reform at the polls when votes are merchantable commodities or, possibly, represent material prosperity in the way of "jobs" for an indefinite time.

Miss Addams's efforts are directed toward the bringing about of a moral metamorphosis among the foreign settlements of the city, among people who have fled to America to escape oppression and who have, too often it is to be feared, the erroneous idea that their new-found liberty is simply a free license to benefit themselves personally at the expense of a beneficent government; a course which they had not, hitherto, been able to pursue, but a course which a long period of subjection to unjust rule had seemed, in their eyes, to render legitimate. It is not surprising, she infers, that, with moral perceptions greatly blunted by former national injustice the social and ethical perspective should seem strangely and hopelessly distorted. That these conditions are not incurable, however, is, the verdict of the average person who takes the trouble to examine into the methods employed and the measure of success achieved at the Hull House social settlement. One gathers the impression that the object for which Hull House stands and for which the residents are striving, is, by slow degrees, being brought about. That object is tersely stated in the charter: "To provide a center for a higher civic and social life; to institute and maintain educational and philanthropic enterprises, and to investigate and improve the conditions in the industrial districts of Chicago."

Jane Addams has earned during the past ten years a world-wide recognition, not only as an advanced thinker in the problems of social democracy, but as a leader in a substantial movement looking toward "philanthropic reform." What is even more pleasing to record she has become, as her "neighbors" will tell you, the best loved woman in Chicago.

PD (Milton B. Marks, "Among the Workers . . . Jane Addams, of HH," *Good Housekeeping* 31, no. 5 [Nov. 1900]: 213–16; *JAPM*, 55:604–6).

1. The clipping collection, 1892–1960, is located at SCPC, JAC; *JAPM*, 55–71. By 1895 JA was relying on a professional clipping service to gather articles in publications mentioning her name or that of HH. Articles were kept in scrapbooks and loose and organized roughly by year. Four of the scrapbooks that were kept to record HH and the activities of those associated with it survived and appear only in the microfilm edition of the Jane Addams Papers. The first volume, 1889–94, contained only clippings from publications; vol. 2, 1889–94, held publications primarily published by HH about its activities; vol. 3, 1895–97, contained both clippings and HH publications (all presented in *JAPM*, Addendum 10). HH publications, particularly playbills for ethnic theater at HH, spanned the period 1907–10 (presented in *JAPM*, Addendum 1A). A scrapbook relating to the fortieth anniversary celebration of the founding of HH is at UIC, JAMC; *JAPM*, Addendum 10.

2. In Jan. 1931, *Good Housekeeping*, presented JA as the first in its series "America's Twelve Greatest Women."

3. The others were *Pictorial Review*, *Woman's Home Companion*, *Ladies' Home Journal*, the *Delineator*, and *McCall's*.

In Oct. 1900, *Good Housekeeping* was sold by its previous owner, John Pettigrew, who had acquired it in 1898 from the estate of Clark W. Bryan, who founded it in 1885. In the fall of 1900, the Phelps Publishing Co. purchased it and began publishing it in Springfield, Mass. Numbers relating to its circulation in 1900 vary from 40,000 to 225,000 subscribers.

4. James Eaton Tower (1863–1947) was born in Groton, Mass., the son of James Edwin and Harriet Eaton Tower. After graduating from Amherst College, he became a journalist for the *Worcester (Mass.) Gazette* and by 1895 had become editor of the *Springfield (Mass.) Homestead*. In 1898 he joined the Phelps Publishing Co. as literary editor. Between 1900 and 1913, he was editor of *Good Housekeeping*, by then one of the Phelps periodicals. His article "Educated Women in Magazine Work," encouraging college graduates to consider a career in magazine publishing, appeared in Agnes Frances Perkins, *Vocations for the Trained Woman:*

*Opportunities Other than Teaching*, published by the Women's Educational and Industrial Union in Boston, 1910. He was editor of the *Designer*, New York, 1915–18, and managing editor of the *Delineator*, 1919–21, and *Pictorial Review*, 1922–23. He was also editor of *Springfield Present and Prospective, the City of Homes* (Springfield, Mass.: Pond and Campbell, 1905).

5. Elizabeth Palmer Peabody (1804–94), identified by *Good Housekeeping* as an educator, author, and philanthropist, was the eighth woman presented in the series. Her treatment appeared on pp. 29–32 in the Jan. 1900 issue of vol. 31.

Between June and Dec. 1899, seven other women were featured in the series. They were: Mary Lyon (1797–1849), educator and founder of Mount Holyoke Female Seminary; Lucy Stone (1818–93) feminist, abolitionist, and suffragist; Julia Knowlton Dyer (1829–1907), educator, club woman, and philanthropist; Celia Thaxter (1835–94), poet; Abby Hutchinson Patton (1929–92), singer, feminist, and reformer; Kate Sanborn (1839–1917), author, teacher, and lecturer; and Abby Morton Diaz (1821–1904), author and social reformer. All of these articles, as well as the article about Elizabeth Palmer Peabody, were written by Mary Sargent Neal Hopkins (d. 1924), born in Lynn, Mass., and the daughter of a shoe worker. She was a writer and produced articles for a number of periodicals, including the *Christian Herald*, *New England Kitchen Magazine*, and *Good Housekeeping*. Hopkins became known as "Merrie Wheeler" for her promotion of bicycling for women and for founding and serving as editor of *Wheelwoman*, beginning in 1895.

The author of the article about JA was Milton Bliss Marks (1878–1973), who was born in Illinois and died in Los Angeles. Marks was a Christian Science practitioner, and he lived at 4169 South Lake Ave., very near the First Church of Christ, Scientist, at 4017 South Drexel Blvd. In Apr. 1900, he married Jessie Hale Waterman, daughter of architect Harry Hale Waterman and his wife, Ida Viering Waterman. The Marks had one child, Josephine Hale Marks, born in 1901. Marks also wrote "How the Jane Club Keeps House," which was published in *Good Housekeeping* 33, no. 6 (Dec. 1901): 480–83.

The article about JA in the Nov. issue of the *Good Housekeeping* was accompanied by brief articles that were the result of a number of interviews with significant women in the United States. The women were Elizabeth Cady Stanton (1815–1902), social activist, abolitionist, and women's rights advocate; Elizabeth Barstow Stoddard (Mrs. R. H. ) (1823–1902), novelist, poet, and essayist; Adeline D. T. Whitney (1824–1906), poet and author; Mrs. Mary A. Livermore (1820–1905), journalist and women's rights advocate; and Mrs. C. M. Seymour-Severance (1820–1914), abolitionist, suffragist, and women's clubs founder.

6. JHA served in the Senate of the Illinois General Assembly, not in the U.S. Congress. See *PJA*, 1:466–79.

7. JA graduated from RFS on 19 June 1881.

8. For JA's early observation of "social inequality," see *PJA*, 1:28.

9. JA toured Europe twice before founding HH. On her first tour, likely the "'finishing tour'" JA mentioned, she was accompanied by her stepmother, AHHA, 1883–85. Her second tour of Europe took place in 1887–88.

10. On JA's "fortune," see *PJA*, 1:477–78; and *PJA*, 2:536–37.

11. EGS did not accompany JA on her first visit to Toynbee Hall, London, in 1888. EGS's first glimpse of Toynbee Hall came during her visit to England in 1892.

12. The correct title of that essay was "Ethical Survivals in Municipal Corruption." See Essay in the *International Journal of Ethics*, April 1898, above.

13. JA may have discovered the phrase she attributed to Samuel Johnson on p. 297 of Augustus Hopkins Strong's (1836–1921) popular theological work *Systematic Theology*, published in six different editions between 1886 and 1908. Strong was educated at Rochester Theological Seminary of which he later became president, 1872–1912. After graduating from Yale in 1857, he studied in Germany and in 1861 was ordained a pastor of the First Baptist Church of

Haverhill, Mass. His son, Charles Augustus Strong (1862–1940), a student of William James at Harvard, was a professor of psychology at the Univ. of Chicago, 1892–95.

14. The Great Chicago Fire of 8–11 Oct. 1871 was said to have started in a barn behind the frame home of Patrick and Catherine O'Leary at 137 (later 558 West) De Koven St., a few blocks to the east of the former Hull home on Halsted St. The conflagration destroyed three and a half square miles of the city.

15. Although it took several months to make the house suitable for their needs, JA and EGS identified 18 Sept. 1889 as the official start of their "scheme." They were the first two residents along with their housekeeper Mary Keyser.

16. While the identity "HH" came during the first year, the enterprise was not incorporated as HH Assn. until 1895. See Edwin Burritt Smith to JA, 2 Feb. 1895, above.

# BIOGRAPHICAL PROFILES

*Bowen, Louise de Koven*
*Lathrop, Julia Clifford*
*Smith, Mary Rozet and Smith Family*

## *Bowen, Louise de Koven (1859–1953)*

Louise de Koven Bowen, philanthropist, community leader, and self-styled "social worker," was born in Chicago, the only child of Helen Hadduck (1835–86) and John de Koven (1833–98), a successful banker. Helen Hadduck, her mother, was also an only child. Helen's parents were pioneer Chicago settlers Louisa Graves Hadduck (1816–94) and Edward Hiram Hadduck (1811–91). Hadduck, who arrived in Chicago in 1833, became an early leader in Chicago's development and the owner of real estate in what became the city's primary mercantile area.

Louise de Koven grew up the petted and privileged darling of her grandfather Hadduck. When beginning her autobiography, Louise wrote: "I was born an ugly baby. My Grandmother said so and she was a truthful woman . . . and when I looked in the glass I saw it was so! . . . People said I was a bright child but 'pity I was so pasty and peaked'" ("Autobiography of the Only Child of an Only Child," 1–2). When Hadduck sold the corner of Washington Street and Wabash Avenue (which became the site of Marshall Field and Company), he divided the proceeds between his daughter, Helen, and his granddaughter, Louise. "This was the first money I ever had," Louise reported, "and it gave me an annual income which I was allowed to spend as I chose" (Bowen, *Growing Up*, 9). She also understood that "someday I would inherit a fortune, and I was always taught that the responsibility of money was great, and that God would hold me accountable for the manner in which I used my talents" (Bowen, *Growing Up*, 51–52). When her mother died in 1886, Louise inherited another twenty million dollars.

Louise was a pupil in the Collegiate Department of Dearborn Seminary, a private girls' school in Chicago, and graduated in 1876 when she was sixteen years old. That same year, she convinced the superintendent of the Episcopal Sunday School at the Cathedral of St. James to place her in charge of a class of "boys of fourteen and sixteen years of age, very rough looking, and certainly very rough acting" (Bowen, *Growing Up*, 47). During the eleven years she managed the class, its membership grew to more than one hundred students. She offered them an opportunity for recreation, initially playing billiards in her home, but when they became too many for entertaining there, she found a clubhouse for them and thereby founded an early boys' club in Chicago. She sometimes helped her students find appropriate employment, and when she believed it was warranted, she provided financial assistance for their families: "I always had a very strong feeling that something must be done to put a family upon its feet and not just to give temporary aid" (Bowen, *Growing Up*, 52). During these early years at St. James, she also held classes in sewing and helped start a Kitchen Garden Association.

Louise de Koven and Joseph Tilden Bowen (1854–1911) were married in Chicago, 1 June 1886, shortly before Louise's mother died. Joseph Bowen was the son of William H. and Ednah B. Goodhue Bowen and was educated in the public schools of Providence, Rhode Island. He began his career representing Cheney and Brother, silk manufacturers of South Manchester, Connecticut, in New York and Chicago. In January 1890, he became the resident vice-president and manager of the City Trust, Safe Deposit, and Surety Company of Philadelphia in Chicago with an office in the Rookery. When that firm merged with the Metropolitan Surety Company of New York, he continued in the same capacity until ill health forced his retirement in January 1910. Between 1887 and 1892, the Bowens had four children: John de Koven (1887–1917); Joseph T. Jr. (1888–1977); Helen Hadduck (1890–1972), who became Mrs. William McCormick Blair; and Louise de Koven (1892–1961), who became Mrs. Mason Phelps, but eventually divorced her husband.

The Bowens built two family homes. In Chicago they constructed a forty-room house at 1430 Astor Street on Chicago's Near North Side. It became Louise's home for the remainder of her life. Jane Addams often visited her there and sometimes, especially after the death of Mary Rozet Smith, stayed there. During the fall of 1894 and the winter of 1895, the Bowens had a large and commodious summer home built in the small community of Hulls Cove, a little north of Bar Harbor, Maine. "Baymeath" (razed in 1980), as it was called, had thirty rooms on three floors, a swimming pool, a tennis court, and formal gardens. The name for the home derived from its location in a meadow ("meath," the Gaelic word for meadow) overlooking Frenchman's Bay. Louise and the de Koven family had summered in the Bar Harbor area, and Louise wanted her children to have a similar summer experience. She shared memories of these times in her book *Baymeath*, published privately in 1944 for friends and family. The Bowens maintained an assortment of nurses, nannies, maids, a chauffeur, and a gardener, many of whom moved with the family between the two residences. Jane Addams and Mary Rozet Smith also found the Bar Harbor area a favorite vacation destination and eventually purchased a large "cottage" called "Yulecraig" (razed in 1986) at Hulls Cove near Baymeath. Louise referred to the house as "a little place about half a mile from us. . . . A narrow path through the beautiful thick woods led to her place" (Bowen, *Baymeath*, 80).

For most of the 1890s and into the early 1900s, Louise Bowen was concerned primarily with the care of her children; however, she was determined to continue a civic life. She accepted membership on the Board of Managers of the Maurice Porter Memorial Hospital and eventually helped add a wing on the facility. After resigning her post there, she joined the Woman's Board of St. Luke's Hospital and soon was named vice-president. She later became president of the Woman's Board of Passavant Hospital. She also served as a board member of the Visiting Nurse Association and recalled that she was a member of the "nurses committee, interviewing and engaging nurses, talking to them of their duties, and trying to put a standard before them of what their work ought to be" (Bowen, *Growing Up*, 58). In 1906–7, Louise worked successfully to get visiting nurses assigned to public schools primarily to identify and help halt the spread of contagious diseases, reduce truancy, and help improve the health of children. By 1908–9, with the help of Jane Addams, who served on the Chicago Board of Education, 1905–9, the Chicago school system took over the school nurse program and expanded it.

It may well have been in 1891 that Jane Addams first asked Louise Bowen to become active at Hull-House. She declined because she was pregnant, but instead she recalled: "I remember giving some money to be used for the poor, the first donation I had ever made to Hull-House" (Bowen, *Growing Up*, 82).

When Louise did agree to become involved at Hull-House, the first task that Addams suggested to her was helping with the Hull-House Woman's Club. Louise joined the club in 1893 and reported that "for about seventeen years I filled some official position in the club" (*Growing Up*, 83). After first studying parliamentary procedure herself, she assisted club members in learning how to use it to conduct their meetings. By 1902 she was listed in the Hull-House Woman's Club annual as an honorary member of the club. Louise admitted that she honed her public speaking skills by addressing meetings of the Hull-House Woman's Club. Her subjects varied from flowers and gardening, to travel and descriptions of places she had visited, and to reform issues concerning children.

On 15 March 1905, Louise Bowen handed the keys to Jane Addams for the new Woman's Club Building that she and her husband had constructed for Hull-House on Polk Street. The largest room in the structure was known as Bowen Hall. Two years later, on 22 May 1907, she became president of the Hull-House Woman's Club. At that time, Laura Dainty Pelham, who had served for a number of years as club president, stepped down into the first vice-president chair. Louise Bowen served as president of the Woman's Club until 1910, when she refused to stand again for the office of president and again became vice-president.

Beginning in 1905, the Bowens provided the primary financing for the construction of another new Hull-House structure, the Boys' Club Building. That addition, also located on Polk Street, was formally dedicated on 12 January 1907. Helen Culver had provided the ground on which it was built and added an endowment for its upkeep.

By the end of the first ten years in the twentieth century, the Bowen family had become major financial supporters of Hull-House. After the death of her husband in 1911, Louise Bowen became more involved with Hull-House and continued to develop a special friendship with Jane Addams. In 1912, in honor of her husband, Louise provided the funding for the purchase of a seventy-two-acre property north of Chicago near Waukegan, Illinois, to be used as a summer camp for Hull-House. The Bowen Country Club, as it was known, became a major part of the settlement programs through the years. By 1895 Louise Bowen's financial support to the settlement stood at $387.36. Between 1895 and 1900, it increased to more than $4,000, often in $100.00 increments, providing for the summer camp fund, general settlement programs, building funds, and relief. In addition to the buildings and real estate that the Bowens gave Hull-House, before 1928 Louise Bowen had donated more than $500,000 to settlement operations, and by the time of her death she had added more than $1 million to what she had already given. In addition, she had secured hundreds of gifts from other Chicago friends for the settlement.

In 1903 Louise Bowen became a Hull-House trustee, replacing John Dewey. She remained on the Board of Trustees until her death. Bowen became treasurer in October 1907 and served until 25 October 1935, when, after the death of Jane Addams, she also became president of the Board of Trustees and held both offices. While continuing to serve as treasurer, she was made honorary president of the board in 1944 and remained in both roles until her death. In addition to her own major yearly financial support for the settlement, shortly after the death of Jane Addams, Bowen made a valiant effort to encourage gifts to the Jane Addams Memorial Fund, established in the hope of securing sufficient funds for Hull-House to generate interest income to equal what Addams "was accustomed to raise each year by her own efforts" (Linn, *Jane Addams*, 428).

Louise Bowen saw herself as the keeper of Jane Addams's legacy. As Addams's nephew James Weber Linn described her, she had a "sense of feudality in connection with Hull House, a consciousness that noblesse oblige" (*Jane Addams*, 144). Near the time of Bowen's eightieth birthday, a reporter for the *Chicago Daily News* captured her commitment to the settlement: "Every morning she is driven from the Bowen home on Astor street to Hull House on South Halsted, where she works vigorously all day long—conferring . . . , planning improvements, even overseeing the carpenters and bricklayers as they carry out their improvements for which she, nine times out of 10, has supplied the money" ("600 Friends to Pay Homage to Mrs. Joseph T. Bowen on Her 80th Birthday Feb. 27," 16 Feb. 1939).

The years immediately after Jane Addams's death were challenging ones for Hull-House; the settlement was faced with responding to increasingly rapid social changes and the challenges brought about in part by the Great Depression and World War II. With the death of Addams, the settlement had lost its symbol and its special identity with her celebrity. Bowen tried with an iron determination to manage the settlement successfully as she thought Jane would have done. She resigned the presidency of the Woman's City Club to spend more of her time and energy at Hull-House. As the chair of the board, she oversaw the settlement's development and growth with the help of three social workers who served successively as head residents. They were Adena Miller Rich (1888–1967), Charlotte Carr (1890–1956), and finally Russell W. Ballard (1917–71). Her relationship with them was often troubled as she sought to control the program, activities, and expenditures at the settlement. Although not a Hull-House founder, Louise Bowen became so identified with the settlement that when she died, Chicago newspapers touted her as a cofounder of Hull-House: "Mrs. Bowen was best known for her almost 60 years' association with Hull House, which she helped found" ("Mrs. Bowen, 94, Dies," *Chicago Daily Tribune*, 10 Nov. 1953).

Hull-House was not Louise Bowen's only philanthropic venture. Her commitment to sharing her leadership, organizational, and fund-raising skills with a number of civic and philanthropic enterprises was crucial to their success. Many of them were associated in some way with Jane Addams and the development of Hull-House. Although she did not join the Chicago Woman's Club until May 1911, she served as a member of the Juvenile Protective Committee that it spawned. She quickly became the committee's chair, helping to secure funds for parole officers. She also made vital connections in securing funding and support from Cook County political leaders for a detention center and court building for the Juvenile Court. When the Juvenile Court Committee was reconfigured as the Juvenile Protective League and then into the Juvenile Protective Association, Bowen remained in the leadership position.

At the start of the Juvenile Protective Association in January 1910, Bowen had two roles: president and chief fund-raiser. She carried those dual responsibilities almost continually into the 1940s. She saw the Juvenile Protective Association's goal as preventing the "exploitation of children" and seeking the "curtailment of organizations contributing to their delinquency" (Bowen, *Open Windows*, 144). In her positions, she became the spokesperson for the organization's efforts to investigate city conditions that led to juvenile delinquency, to publish findings, and to promote reform. She was a frequent public speaker on the behalf of the organization, and, using the research conducted by the employees and volunteers of the agency, she took credit for many of its publications, including *The Department Store Girl* (1911), *Five and Ten Cent Theaters* (1909 and 1911), *The Need of Recreation* (1912), *A Study of Public Dance Halls* (1912), *The Girl Employed in Hotels and Restaurants* (1912), *The Colored People of Chicago* (1913), *Boys in the County Jail* (1913), *A Study of Bastardy Cases* (1914), *Some Legislative Needs in Illinois* (1914), *The Road to Destruction Made Easy in Chicago* (1916), *The Straight Girl on the Crooked Path* (June 1916), and *The "Block System" of the Juvenile Protective Association of Chicago* (1916). All were widely circulated in pamphlet form and many published in Bowen's first book, *Safeguards of Youth at Work and at Play* (1914). They were meant to draw public attention of the problems of juvenile delinquency in the city. While she was closely associated with the Juvenile Court Committee, she also successfully promoted the establishment of a special Domestic Court and a Boys Court in Cook County.

Bowen also became president of the Woman's City Club and served in that capacity from 1914, when she resigned from her leadership role in the Hull-House Woman's Club, until 1924. With a citywide membership estimated to be at least five thousand, the Woman's City Club could provide a larger platform from which to influence politics in the city and thus be more able to affect reform. Bowen's goal was achieving woman suffrage and educating and registering women for voting, promoting citizenship education, and serving as a watchdog on political corruption and the implementation of municipal regulations and laws.

Louise Bowen was a dedicated supporter of woman suffrage and an active leader, along with Jane Addams, in organizations that worked to achieve voting power for women in national, state, and local elections. She served as vice-president of the Illinois Equal Suffrage Association, president of the Chicago Equal Suffrage Association, and an auditor for the National American Woman Suffrage Association. She had many opportunities to speak on behalf of woman suffrage. Her primary argument for it was that women were taxed without representation because they could not vote. After women won the vote, the Illinois Equal Suffrage Association was reorganized as the Illinois branch of the League of Women Voters, and Bowen served as a director. She opposed the Equal Rights Amendment to the U.S. Constitution because she feared its passage would cancel all of the protective legislation that still seemed vital for women in the workplace.

During World War I, regretful and disappointed by Jane Addams's leadership in establishing the women's peace movement, Louise Bowen chose to support the nation's war effort. Her friendship with Addams survived their differing choices, but, for a time, she was uncertain: "I know there was that horrid time of war," she wrote to Jane Addams in 1926, "when we differed so radically, but there never was a time when I did not respect your position although I know I was very horrid at times, but through it all there was only the hope that it was not going to make a difference in our friendship and I hope it has not. That I am not one of your peace flock doesn't make any difference" (26 Feb. 1926, SCPC, JAC; *JAPM*, 17:1505). When a Women's Committee of the National Council of Defense was formed, Louise Bowen became the leader of the Illinois Division. At the same time, she was chosen by Governor Frank O. Louden as a member—the only female member—of the Illinois Council of Defense. Serving in both capacities, she organized more than seven hundred thousand Illinois women to support the national war effort. They served as volunteers in hospitals and schools, held programs about food preservation, published wartime recipe books, provided speakers, held events to raise their own money, promoted war gardens, and provided instruction in child care.

Bowen also became more engaged politically after women received the vote. She helped form the Woman's Roosevelt Republican Club in June 1921 and served as its leader. She had decided "to devote a good deal" of her time to politics because she "considered politics the shortest road to good government" (Bowen, *Growing Up*, 208). She became very active in meeting with political leaders to promote her reform positions. After the war, she was named the woman fair price commissioner for Illinois by the U.S. Department of Justice. In 1924 the Republican National Committee appointed her associate Republican national committeewoman from Illinois. On behalf of the Illinois Republican Women's Club and the Woman's Roosevelt Republican Club, she became the driving force behind three successful Woman's World Fairs held in Chicago, 1925–27, to raise funds for charity and to promote the "multiplicity of occupations in which women had scored success" (Bowen, *Growing Up*, 220). She was also appointed to represent the United States at the Pan American Congress of Women, held in Baltimore in 1922.

Bowen also worked with the Chicago Council of Social Agencies, the agency that was engaged in combining all of the Chicago welfare organizations under one umbrella agency so that all could avoid duplication of effort and share information. For twelve years, she was a member and then chairman of the Lower North-Side District United Charities and met weekly to evaluate requests for assistance. She also served with Jane Addams for twenty-five years as a member of the board and then vice-president of the United Charities of Chicago. She spent twelve years on the Committee of Fifteen, whose goal was to eliminate vice in Chicago. Among Bowen's other board memberships were the Birth Control League, School of Civics and Philanthropy, and Illinois Training School for Nurses.

Louise Bowen, who began her public life as a reluctant public speaker, became a frequent and accomplished speaker; she could even take heckling in stride. Her published speeches and writings offer the texts of more than 125 public presentations on such topics as suffrage, juvenile delinquency, child welfare, and politics. In addition to *Speeches, Addresses, and Letters of Louise de Koven Bowen: Reflecting Social Movement in Chicago* in two volumes issued in 1937, Bowen authored other books, two of which were autobiographical: *Growing Up with a City* (1926) and *Open Windows* (1946). *Safeguards for Youth at Work and at Play* (1914) was based on Bowen's experiences with the Juvenile Court Committee and the Juvenile Protective Association. It presented her version of problems that young people faced in society. Jane Addams wrote the preface (vii–xiii) and reminded readers that the Juvenile Protective Association and its supporters had been working devotedly to gain recognition and legal status for the social reforms that were needed to positively affect the lives of children and youth in the city. It had taken time, Addams reported, for the public to recognize the issue as vital and immediate and stated that "public opinion has a curious trick of suddenly regarding as a living moral issue—vital and unappeasable—some old situation concerning which society has been indifferent for many years" (xi). Addams pronounced that "the basic safety of youthful health and morals must be secured by the civic authorities unless all the efforts of education and philanthropy, so constantly undertaken on behalf of city youth, are to be brought to nought" (ix) and found that the Juvenile Protective Association "has continually induced public authorities to assume new obligations" toward youth (xii).

Louise Bowen received numerous honors during her life. For all of her service to the medical community, she was recognized as a citizen-fellow of the Chicago Institute of Medicine. Along with Jane Addams, she received a master's of arts honorary degree from Knox College, Galesburg, Illinois, in 1934, and an L.H.D. degree from Tufts University, Medford, Massachusetts, in 1921. Bowen probably saw her long terms as presidents of the board of Hull-House Association, the Woman's City Club of Chicago, and the Juvenile Protective Association as honors, especially when those same organizations continued her in the position of honorary president of each board until her death.

On 26 February 1939, Louise Bowen's eightieth birthday, Hull-House Association, the Juvenile Protective Association, the Woman's City Club of Chicago, and United Charities, the organizations with which she had been most closely identified during her active civic life, hosted a birthday luncheon in her honor. Between six hundred and one thousand admirers and family members crowded into the Grand Ballroom at the Palmer House and heard her commitment to the civic and social improvement of Chicago extolled by five different speakers. Newspaper articles abounded. She was recognized as a practical leader who had a gift for organization. On 14 February 1939, in the *Chicago Daily News*, novelist and journalist Howard Vincent O'Brien (1888–1947) reported that her "best-known achievement" was that "she held up the arm of Jane Addams." She was also referred to as "indomitable" and a "dynamic dowager." A year later in a newspaper article, she was identified as the "first citizen of Chicago" and hailed for having "squeezed money out of the rich, and bullied decent laws out of the politicians" (Mayer, "First Citizen of Chicago").

By 1944 Louise Bowen had begun to relinquish her active public life. The small-in-stature, straight-backed woman with a very upright carriage, a droll sense of humor, and a twinkle in her eye also presented a no-nonsense directness that demanded attention. She was used to having her way, and so long as she produced progress and beneficial outcomes most of her contemporaries were willing to let her lead and did her bidding. She relished being in charge of any enterprise to which she lent her name, money, and power. Although she was not a college graduate, she was determined to make her mark in history. She was aware that her training in managing money was a valuable asset. In addition, she recognized that her inherited money gave her a freedom that others did not have. She could spend it for the purposes that she chose, including hiring her household chores done in her stead so that she could spend her time in civic affairs. She believed that because she "had no strings attached" and no "skeletons to hide," she also had a kind of freedom others did not have ("Clubs to Honor 'Indomitable' Mrs. Bowen Tomorrow").

In her remarks at the close of her eightieth birthday celebration, she reiterated that she had lived her life in public endeavor because that was what interested her and where she believed she could make a difference. "The older you grow," she said, "the more disgusted you become with how little you do. . . . I might have done more, but I have enjoyed it all hugely. . . . There is nothing so intensely interesting as public affairs. What is an afternoon at cards compared to activity where you can help people improve their lives and conditions?" (O'Brien, "All Things Considered"). "I've been down with the people most of the time," she said. "I like people, all kinds" (Kent, "Honor First Lady of Hull House"). In an article that appeared in the *Chicago Daily News*, 4 March 1939, Helen Cody Baker (1889–1948) reported in "Mrs. J. T. Bowen Social Pioneer" that Louise Bowen had a "long life of devotion to many good causes . . . indomitable courage of her tireless energy . . . warm heart and open mind . . . [and a] keen sense of social responsibility. All this is true. But the wonder is that it hasn't set her apart from us. No barrier, or wealth or social prestige or special privilege, has ever separated her from ordinary, ornery human beings. No pedestal could possibly be built on which she would feel at home. When she has something good her first impulse is to share it. When she sees something cruel her first impulse is to stop it. . . . Brave lady, gay lady, great lady; wise leader and loyal friends."

James Weber Linn, who knew Bowen because of her friendship with his aunt Jane Addams, reported that she was "accustomed to command, and to be obeyed" (*Jane Addams*, 142). She laughed at "everything except service and fineness; those two are the articles of her creed" (*Jane Addams*, 144). Linn recalled that Bowen was "[r]ooted in conservatism, a patriot of the old school, proud of her long record of 'Black Republicanism.'" And she "surveyed some of the activities, a few of the residents, and many of the visitors to Hull House with a severe though humorous eye. She liked things the way she liked them; and eccentric manifestations of radicalism she never liked. . . . To oddity of all sorts she opposed merely a kind of queenly acceptance. . . . Jane Addams herself, in Mrs. Bowen's view, might think strangely, but she could never do wrong" (*Jane Addams*, 143–44). Yet her inflexible and dogmatic positions, as well as her unwillingness by the 1940s to continue to use her own wealth to support social and civic enterprise as she had previously, made her pronouncements less powerful and acceptable. By her actions, she clearly wanted to improve the conditions under which all people, but especially children, in Chicago grew to maturity, yet she also still believed that a classless society was not and should not be possible. She seems to have tended her children and their families with much the same opinionated iron determination she accorded the social organizations that she led. Milton S. Mayer (1908–86), who knew her, wrote that her children, who wanted to take care of her after she reached eighty, were "[a]fraid of her and proud of her" (Mayer, "First Citizen of Chicago").

The relationship between Louise Bowen and Jane Addams evolved from one of philanthropist and fund-raiser to one of friendship, the bonds of which grew stronger throughout the years. In 1910 Addams stayed in the Bowen home to recover from a sever abscess on her face. When Joseph T. Bowen died, it was Jane who went to stay with Louise to help her deal with the loss and then, with Mary Rozet Smith, spent a portion of the summer of 1911 with Bowen at "Baymeath." Bowen also became one of the close personal friends that Addams relied upon increasingly for companionship and financial support, especially for Hull-House. Mary Rozet Smith and Jane Addams vacationed near the Bowen summer home, and the three women were often together there. Especially from the late 1920s until their deaths, Smith and Addams, and then Jane alone, spent time during the winter as the guests of Louise in the warmer climates of California and Arizona. After Mary Rozet Smith's death, JA found a home with Bowen on Astor Street.

Louise recalled that "Miss Addams was a very hard worker, and often when the excitement and responsibility of the House became so great she needed a rest, she visited me for months at a time" (*Open Windows*, 205–6). Louise asserted that the two friends had "many causes in common and so had good times together" (*Open Windows*, 206). Jane Addams never liked being alone, and, according to Bowen, she was often Jane's traveling companion. She also reported that sometimes when Jane became so tired she could not complete a speech, she would ask Bowen to continue it for her. Bowen recalled a time in New York when Addams was speaking and saw her come into the room and divulged to her audience, "I am feeling rather tired, and I see my friend, Mrs. Bowen from Chicago, has just come in, and she will be able to finish my speech" (*Open Windows*, 210). "This happened a great many times during my many years companionship with her" (*Open Windows*, 211). Bowen never seemed to achieve the easy friendship that Mary Rozet Smith enjoyed with Hull-House residents or with Jane Addams's network of reform-minded friends, like Florence Kelley, Alice Hamilton, or Mary Kenney O'Sullivan. In 1926 Bowen wrote to Addams to tell her that she considered her "one of the biggest blessings" in her life. "As I look back over our long friendship I realize what an inspiration you have always been to me, how proud I have been of your friendship and how much I have and do love you. . . . I am very Happy that you are my friend and though I have not told you so for a long time you must know that I love you most devotedly" (26 Feb. [1926], SCPC, JAC; *JAPM*, 17:1505). "For nearly half a century Jane Addams was an intimate friend of mine," she wrote in *Open Windows* (205). If Bowen had a heroine, it was likely Jane Addams.

Louise de Koven Bowen died of a stroke when she was ninety-four after surgery for cancer. She was buried in Graceland Cemetery in Chicago. Using her wealth, with her drive to achieve, her skill at organization, and her willingness to speak out and exert control in her search for a more just society as she saw it, Louise Bowen made a lasting mark on the history of Chicago and on social reform in the United States in the twentieth century.

## *Lathrop, Julia Clifford (1858–1932)*

Julia Clifford Lathrop, advocate for social justice, especially for women, children, and the mentally ill; first woman to direct a major division of the federal government, the Children's Bureau; educator; and one of the close, personal lifetime friends and colleagues of Jane Addams, was born in Rockford. She was the eldest child of William Lathrop (1825–1907) and his wife, Sarah Adeline Potter Lathrop (1836–1909). William, who was born in Genesee County, New York, was educated in Lima, New York, and read law in Attica, New York. He left New York for Rockford, Illinois, where he had relatives, passed the Illinois Bar in 1851, and shortly became Rockford city clerk and city attorney. At the same time, he began a "large and lucrative legal practice" (Church, *History of Rockford and Winnebago County, Illinois*, 335) with Mayor James L. Loop (d. 1865). In 1857 William Lathrop wed Sarah Adeline Potter, who had come to Rockford with her parents, Adeline Eells and Eleazer Hubbell Potter, from Medina, New York, in 1837. In 1854 she had graduated valedictorian of the first class of students at Rockford Female Seminary, where Jane Addams was a student from 1877–81. Adeline Lathrop became a cultural leader in her community and was active in Rockford Female Seminary affairs and at the Congregational church.

Julia Lathrop was eventually joined by five siblings, four of whom lived to maturity. They were Anna Hubbell (who became Anna Hubbell Lathrop Case) (see Robert A. Woods to JA, 20 June 1893, n. 10, above), Edward Potter (1863–1940), William Taggart (1868–1947), Robert (1870–1943), and Ruth Madge (1875–76). Julia helped her mother manage the younger Lathrop children and attended school in Rockford. There she was recalled as a "smart scholar" (Addams, *My Friend*, 35). According to Jane Addams, she was good at creating plays for the younger Lathrops, hated housework, but excelled at house decoration, and made "very good omelettes" (*My Friend*, 37). Life in the Lathrop home on Rockford Avenue was "quiet" and "restful" and of the "highest culture" (Addams, *My Friend*, 44). Julia's parents created an atmosphere that promoted tolerance, valued achievement, and demanded respect for the abilities of women. Both supported woman suffrage and increasing legal rights for women.

Like her mother before her, in 1876 Julia entered Rockford Female Seminary. After completing one year of school, and then taking special instruction in German and mathematics, she transferred to Vassar College in 1878. Her classmates there recalled her as a shy, retiring, serious, and quiet student. Julia Lathrop graduated in 1880. In her senior year, her sister Anna was her roommate. While Anna remained at Vassar, Julia returned to Rockford, where she spent the major part of the 1880s as a secretary in her father's law firm. She began to study law and invested in two Rockford companies that she helped to start.

It may have been during this period of her life that Julia Lathrop first met Jane Addams. As a former student of Rockford Female Seminary, Julia probably joined her mother for activities hosted by the school's alumnae association, the same events that Jane Addams also attended. William Lathrop, who might have known John Huy Addams through Republican Party politics, also knew his daughter Jane Addams. They were trustees for Rockford Female Seminary (later College) at the same time. He served on the Board of Trustees, 1876–1907, and as chairman of the Executive Committee, 1885–1907, and Jane Addams began her lifetime service as a board member in 1883. Julia may also have heard directly about Jane's social settlement "scheme" from Sarah Anderson, a favorite teacher at the Rockford Female Seminary and the European traveling companion with whom Jane and Ellen Gates Starr discussed their settlement idea before heading to Chicago. In March 1892, Lathrop agreed to become secretary for Anderson, who was then principal of Rockford College: "I will take the secretaryship for a year" (RC, Archives, Lathrop).

Julia Lathrop's involvement with Rockford College continued for the remainder of her life. At the same time that she returned to Hull-House as a resident in 1893, she became a member of the Rockford College Board of Trustees and served as its treasurer between 1895 and 1898, while her father and Jane Addams were continuing as members of the board. Julia Lathrop spoke in the Rockford Seminary and College lecture series: first on 17 November 1892, when her topic was social settlements, and later in May 1895 she presented a lecture on the work of the Illinois Board of Commissioners of State Charities. On 30 July 1901, a committee of the Board of Trustees that included Jane Addams offered Julia an opportunity to become the head of the school. She declined the offer, but did agree to serve another term as a trustee, 1901–5. Eventually, the bulk of her personal papers found their way to the archives of Rockford College.

Julia Lathrop first arrived at Hull-House in the early fall of 1890 when the settlement was barely one year old. She spent most of the next twenty years there as a resident. In December 1891, Jane Addams informed her sister Alice Haldeman that "Julia Lathrop is in charge, she has been here two months & is the best 'resident' we ever had. She will stay all winter" (28 Dec. 1891, IU, Lilly, SAAH; *JAPM*, 2:1296). During the 1890s, Jane Addams and Julia Lathrop had ample time and opportunity through their settlement activities to lay a firm foundation for what became their lifetime of friendship. Julia Lathrop, an intellectual peer, became a willing and able supporter of Jane Addams and the social reforms she fostered. She was the resident whom Jane most often turned to for companionship, for assistance, and for discussions about the development of the settlement. The two women were close in age, were both single in a time when most women their ages were married and mothers, and came from the same region of Illinois and from families with similar political and philosophical points of view. They were also members of the first generation of college women. They had similar intellectual interests and educational backgrounds, and both believed that social reform would develop from the knowledge of a needed change supported by facts gathered through investigation and presented in clear and compelling fashion to a reasonable and caring public. Both had a strong and enduring belief in the will of the people to right a social wrong and in the power of democracy. When Jane Addams received funds for the first Hull-House fellowship from the Chicago branch of what became the American Association of University Women, she chose Julia Lathrop to be its recipient. One of Julia's first undertakings at Hull-House was the Plato Club, which she launched and managed. Its membership was composed of older men who met on Sunday afternoons at the settlement from 4:00 P.M. until 6:00 P.M. to read and discuss philosophy.

In Chicago Julia Lathrop quickly became Jane Addams's regular assistant in settlement outreach and administration. In the beginning of her stay at Hull-House, Julia saw the settlement as an opportunity to enrich rather than to reform lives, but gradually her perspective changed. She often accompanied Jane on regular and special neighborhood expeditions. When no one in the neighborhood would come to the aid of a young unwed mother in labor, they comforted her and helped deliver her baby. At 3:00 A.M. one morning, responding to a request from an insurance company, Jane and Julia went to inspect horses that had been burned in a stable fire and saw to their destruction. In 1895, when Jane became the Nineteenth Ward garbage inspector, it was Julia who accompanied her on her early-morning inspection rounds before Amanda Johnson became Jane's assistant.

Julia Lathrop attended the first Hull-House Summer School at Rockford Seminary in 1891. In 1892 she managed the settlement in Chicago while Jane directed the second Hull-House Summer School at her alma mater and then took time to write the two seminal essays describing her settlement scheme that she delivered at the Summer School of Applied Ethics in Plymouth, Massachusetts. Julia accompanied Jane to the event and traveled with her to New York City, providing encouragement as Jane successfully negotiated with the *Forum* to publish both essays. The two women then spent ten days vacationing together in the White Mountains of New Hampshire.

In the winter of 1893–94, Chicago, and especially the Hull-House neighborhood, experienced a severe small-pox epidemic. Hull-House resident Florence Kelley, the newly appointed Illinois chief factory inspector, especially investigated the sweatshop industry, where the disease was prevalent and could be spread through infected clothing sold in stores throughout the city. Julia Lathrop helped Kelley with her investigations and supported Kelley and Hull-House in their campaign against sweatshop practices. Hull-House resident Andrew Alexander Bruce, who had come to the settlement primarily because of Lathrop's recommendation and served as attorney for Kelley, reported that during this small-pox epidemic, Lathrop and Kelley "'were risking their lives in the sweatshop districts of Chicago and were fearlessly entering the rooms and tenements of the west side and not merely alleviating the sufferings of the sick but preventing the sending abroad of the disease-infected garments to further contaminate the community. I saw these two women,'" he reported, "'do that which the health department of the great city of Chicago could not do. . . . Julia Lathrop, the diplomat, reasoned and cajoled, Mrs. Kelley, the fighter, asked me to file a mandamus suit to compel action'" (Addams, *My Friend*, 118). Through their Hull-House experiences, Florence Kelley and Julia Lathrop became lifelong personal friends deeply concerned about the lives of women and children. They were like-minded colleagues who consulted and supported one another in their various reform efforts.

It was also in 1893 that Julia Lathrop became a volunteer visitor in the Cook County Agent's office, with responsibility for visiting residents in the ten-block area around the settlement. What she discovered about the delivery of relief to those in need and the charitable institutional help available to them became the chapter entitled "Cook County Charities" that she wrote for *Hull-House Maps and Papers* (1895). She reported that the institutions designed to help the poor were mired in graft and local politics. She wrote that "the charities of Cook County will never properly perform their duties until politics are divorced from them" (*HH Maps and Papers*, 161). Julia was an outspoken supporter of the effort, led in part by Jane Addams and Hull-House, to establish an organized system for the distribution of relief in Chicago. In 1894 Julia reorganized the Hull-House relief effort when E. A. Waldo, who had been in charge, fell ill. In the process, she learned a great deal more about the acute day-to-day problems faced by the working poor.

With the encouragement of Jane Addams, Julia Lathrop wrote and spoke publicly about her settlement experiences. In May 1896, she published an article about the settlement in her alma mater's *Vassar Miscellany*. In "Hull House as a Sociological Laboratory," which was published in the National Conference of Charities and Correction *Proceedings*, 1894, Lathrop argued that the goal of the settlement was "to help make the 'undesirable quarter' a better place to live in and to gain both wisdom and render standing in the process" (314). Two years later, in "What the Settlement Work Stands For," also published in the *Proceedings* of the National Conference of Charities and Correction, she described the settlement as an attempt at a "realization of that idea of social democracy in whose image—this country was founded" (109–10).

On 1 July 1893, Julia Lathrop was appointed by reform governor John P. Altgeld to a five-year term as a member of the Illinois Board of State Commissioners of Public Charities. She became the first female to serve as a commissioner. Members of the board were authorized, and even required, to inspect "all the charitable and correctional institutions of the State" twice each year, discuss findings with the superintendent of each facility, and make recommendations for improvements. Julia visited the poorhouses and county farms in all of the 102 counties of Illinois. She was shocked by what she discovered, and she quickly became dedicated to improving conditions especially for the insane and for children.

Julia Lathrop set out to learn how other states and other countries managed similar institutions and populations and discovered that Illinois was seriously lagging behind in providing proper care for the poor and insane. She visited facilities and programs in several other states and even investigated programs in Scotland during a trip in 1898 and in Belgium, France, and Germany in 1900. She discovered more advanced and humane treatment options elsewhere, and she made a commitment to alter the situation in Illinois. She saw two immediate issues: first, management of the county poorhouses and farms was contracted annually to the lowest bidder and politics usually played an important role in the awarding of contracts, and, second, children were treated as adults and often grew up in conditions so deplorable that it led to hereditary pauperism. Lathrop became dedicated to removing the insane from county agencies to state institutions and to improving treatment and living facilities, preferring a cottage model to a hospital one. She also developed a lifetime commitment to removing children from institutions where they shared the same facilities with adults, and she favored foster homes for the children or, with special relief, returning them to their natural homes. As Jane Addams pointed out, Julia Lathrop had a "profound compassion for her helpless fellow man" and heartfelt feelings of responsibility for improving the conditions in which they lived (*My Friend*, 67). Lathrop's commitment to improved care for the mentally ill must have resonated with Jane Addams, whose brother, John Weber Addams, spent increasing amounts of time throughout his life in state-operated mental facilities.

Julia Lathrop also recognized that in order to remove politics from the management of state charities, there had to be "strong public opinion backing legislative and gubernatorial action" (Illinois, *Sixteenth Biennial Report of the Board of State Commissioners*, 1900, 374). In 1901 she resigned from the Board of Commissioners as a protest against political interference in the commission's membership and activities. While running for office, Richard Yates, who became governor, 1901–5, had promised to keep the state's charities safe from patronage interference. When he became governor, he forgot his election promise and appointed J. Mack Tanner, son of his predecessor as governor, as the secretary of the commission when that appointment was the prerogative of the commission itself. Lathrop was not idle during the four-year term of Governor Yates. In 1901 she successfully lobbied the Illinois General Assembly for the creation of a special school for troubled boys. It was located at St. Charles and opened in 1904. She also served as a member of the board of directors for the Illinois Children's Home and Aid Society, 1901–6.

While running for Illinois governor in 1904, candidate Charles Deneen announced that he would keep the promise that Governor Yates had abrogated. When Deneen became governor, 1905–9, he reappointed Lathrop to the commission, and she served during his first term. It was also in 1905 that the one book that Julia Lathrop wrote was published: *Suggestions for Visitors to County Poorhouses and to Other Charitable Public Institutions*. In it she argued for the power and importance of inspection of state charities by independent specialists. During her second term as a commissioner, she sought more help for children. She also served as chair of the committee on state supervision and administration for the National Conference of Charities and Correction. In 1905, due in part to her efforts, Illinois passed a law creating the Committee on the Visiting of Children that provided some funds for staff and supplies with a portion of the appointments made through the fledgling Illinois civil service system.

Julia Lathrop's concern for children also led to her participation in the campaign in Chicago to create the first Juvenile Court in the United States. Efforts to establish a court that treated children in a separate setting and with separate rules from adult offenders began as early as 1893–94 in the Chicago Woman's Club, where Julia became an active member in 1892. She knew from her own work with the Board of Commissioners that the laws relating to dependent and delinquent children were inadequate in Illinois. The Committee on Legislation of the Illinois State Conference of Charities, working with the Chicago Bar Association and representatives of the Chicago Woman's Club, drafted what became "An Act to Regulate the Treatment and Control of Dependent, Neglected and Delinquent Children," or the Juvenile Court Act. It was signed into law at the end of April 1899 and went into effect 1 July 1899. It created "a chancery tribunal to inquire into the condition of a given child, and, if he be found dependent, neglected, or delinquent, to order the most efficient means of alleviating or correcting that condition" (Illinois Juvenile Court Act [1899], sec. 1, quoted in Anderson, "The Good to Be Done," 88). Although in her letter of 30 October 1915 to the Chicago Woman's Club Lathrop gave Lucy Flower most of the credit for the legislation, both women lobbied actively and effectively for it at the Illinois General Assembly.

As chair of the Chicago Woman's Club probation committee, Lathrop favored developing a probation system as the primary means of discipline in preference to incarceration or special schooling. The court required probation officers who could continually review and assist children, influence their parents, improve neighborhoods, and remove temptations so that children could be kept from committing misdemeanors and other crimes. At the start of the court, Julia Lathrop contended, "The efficiency of the law depends upon the efficiency of the probation officers, and at present these officers must be either policemen or unpaid volunteers or paid volunteers" (Lathrop, "Report of the Joint [Probation] Committee of the Philanthropy and Reform Department," in Chicago Woman's Club, Minutes, 28 Apr. 1900, quoted in Anderson, "The Good to Be Done," 120). The Chicago Woman's Club's probation committee, led by Lathrop until 28 April 1900, when Lucy Flower assumed that role, furnished funds for three of the court's first six paid probation officers. One was Alzina P. Stevens, who was a resident at Hull-House. Unfortunately, she died shortly after her appointment. She was replaced by another Hull-House resident, Joseph B.

Riddle (1870–1942), who assumed responsibility for her 150 pending cases and eventually became director of boys' clubs at Hull-House.

After a year and a half of the court's operation, Lathrop reported: "It is easy to claim too much for the [Juvenile Court] Law." She stressed that the court "cannot work miracles—cannot turn evil into good *per se*—but it does make it possible for sincere and persistent people to bring a good force to bear upon neglected and wayward children which has been heretofore impossible" (*Juvenile Record* 2 [Apr. 1901]: 6, quoted in Anderson, "The Good to Be Done," 141). In September 1902, when the Chicago Woman's Club decided to spin off the probation committee as an independent organization to support the Juvenile Court, Julia Lathrop was chosen as chair of the agency that was to be known as the Juvenile Court Committee. One of its major tasks continued to be raising funds for the salaries of probation officers and for the recreation programs that the committee and court developed to help improve conditions in which children lived. The committee also managed the Juvenile Court's Detention Home, a lodging and school facility for children waiting assessment by the court. Louise de Koven Bowen was the chair and Lathrop vice-chair, primarily because the wealthy Bowen had more success raising funds.

Between 1906 and 1908 when the Juvenile Court Committee and the nascent Juvenile Protective Association combined their efforts, first as the Juvenile Court Committee and finally as the Juvenile Protective Association, Lathrop continued her participation as a member of the board of directors. She helped establish Hull-House (originally the site of Juvenile Protective League No. 5) as the headquarters for the combined Juvenile Court Committee and the Juvenile Protective Association. The new organization hoped "to prevent conditions and prosecute persons contributing to the dependence and delinquency of children . . . cooperate with the juvenile courts . . . and all other child-helping agencies" and "to promote the study of child problems" as well as to promote "public sentiment" for needed facilities to help children reach a responsible adulthood safely (Juvenile Protective League of Cook County, Petition for Incorporation, 13 Apr. 1906, UIC, JPA). Lathrop also helped develop the Juvenile Psychopathic Institute in 1909 and served initially as one of its three directors. It provided an opportunity for the Juvenile Court to separate those children who were ill from those who were simply misbehaving.

The need for training qualified workers, especially as probation officers, personnel for mental hospitals, and professional social workers, led Julia Lathrop to a new role. She became the first director of research and codirector with founder Graham Taylor of the Chicago Institute of Social Science. It had been created in 1903 as the Social Science Center for Practical Training in Philanthropic Dependency and Preventive Agencies to train professional social workers. In 1908, when the school was incorporated with Jane Addams among the trustees and with Julia Lathrop serving as vice-president as well as a trustee, its name was changed once again to the Chicago School of Civics and Philanthropy.

Lathrop's position was funded through a grant from the Russell Sage Foundation. With her assistant Sophonisba Breckinridge, a relatively new instructor in political economy at the University of Chicago, Lathrop began a study of juvenile delinquency in Chicago. At the same time, she pioneered in the development of a course of instruction for attendants of insane asylums with emphasis on occupational therapy. When Julia relinquished her position as director of research in order to devote her time to helping create the National Committee for Mental Hygiene (February 1909), she continued as a trustee, financial supporter, and lecturer for the school. It saddened her to see the school lose its independence in 1920 when it was absorbed by the University of Chicago and became the foundation for its graduate school of social work. She wrote to Edith Abbott, who was key in creating the arrangement: "I am sorry, but there is much to be said for the success you have achieved in gaining recognition as a graduate school. That is a genuine triumph which will descend in the history of education" (10 Aug. 1920, UC, Abbott).

Julia Lathrop also devoted her organizational skills to the Immigrants' Protective League, created in Chicago in 1908 and headquartered at Hull-House. From her settlement experience, she knew of the difficulties that immigrants faced in adjusting to life in the United States. Julia served as an active member of the league's board and helped establish its policies and public statements. She approved of the league's opposition to proposals for the registration of aliens because she believed it to be un-American and difficult to enforce. She also supported citizenship education and an easier naturalization process.

After the first White House Conference on the Care of Dependent Children, held in 1909, reform leaders, among them Julia Lathrop, Lillian Wald, Florence Kelley, and Jane Addams, reinitiated efforts to create a government entity to investigate the condition and promote the well-being of children in the United States. Legislation, which was introduced in successive U.S. Congresses beginning in 1906, was finally passed and signed into law 9 April 1912. It established the United States Children's Bureau "to investigate and report" upon matters relating to child welfare in the United States. Jane Addams and the leaders of the effort were adamant that the first head of the bureau, which was lodged in the Department of Commerce and Labor (and in the Department of Labor after the department was split in 1913), should be Julia Lathrop: "[W]e are all united on Miss Lathrop," Jane wrote to Lillian Wald on 12 April 1912. "It does seem to me a pity not to have a woman—and a very able one—in the position, and so much of Miss Lathrop's experience has naturally prepared her for a place of this sort. While I don't want to unduly urge her beyond any Eastern candidate, I am sure she would fill the place splendidly. No one who has not lived with her, year in and year out, can realize her splendid ability and absolutely clear mind. . . . Let's try hard for a woman first" (UC, Abbott; *JAPM*, 6:918). Julia Lathrop, who indicated that she would not seek the position, but would accept it if it were offered, became the first woman to head a federal government agency when

Republican president William A. Taft tapped her to lead what also became the first agency in any national government to be devoted to the well-being of children. Her appointment was continued by the next president, Democrat Woodrow Wilson.

Julia Lathrop served as chief of the United States Children's Bureau during its turbulent beginning years, 1912–21. She moved to Washington, D.C., and she and her sister Anna Case lived at the Ontario apartment complex at 2853 Ontario Road. Her first priority was to define a program that she could defend before the U.S. Congress and the public, one that was sustainable and one that could make a contribution to improvement in the condition and future of children in the United States. Lathrop began the new bureau with fifteen employees and an appropriation of $25,000, and when she left her position as chief nine years later, the bureau had two hundred employees with an appropriation of $350,000. She had long been an advocate for civil service, and she was adamant that bureau employees be recognized as professional civil servants.

In her new post, Julia Lathrop chose to investigate and publicize issues that reflected her own personal philosophy that children were "the ultimate treasure and resource of any people" and for that reason should be the "responsibility of the entire nation" (Lathrop, "Shall This Country Economize for or against Its Children?," 77). She believed that all children in a democracy had rights and should have the same opportunities. From her perspective, children need a traditional home, consisting of a nonworking mother and a breadwinner father, a place of safety in which they could grow up strong and healthy, and with access to appropriate education. Fathers were important members of the family, but mothers were vital to the well-being of children; they had to be protected.

The first topic the bureau investigated was infant welfare. Sophonisba Breckinridge reported that Lathrop's approach to investigation was "to select a subject in which there was not only a pressing need of investigation, but also a practical method of approach for this Bureau within the appropriation at its command. . . . The subject must be fundamental to social welfare, of popular interest, and serve a real human need; and from the practical standpoint it must be worked out a small bit at a time, and published in installments as each unit was finished. Although its full completion might require a considerable period, yet all the separate small inquiries when complete must furnish a certain composite picture of a social condition through typical communities existing through the country" ("International Aspect," 39–40; *JAPM*, 38:690–91). Lathrop established a program to promote birth registration so that there would be a method of establishing the number of children living in the United States and the bureau could begin to understand the size of the population it was charged with assisting. Between 1912 and 1918, the bureau conducted a series of studies on infant mortality in the expectation that what they learned could help in creating programs to moderate conditions. Through those studies, the Children's

Bureau correlated high infant mortality with low earning, poor housing, and a working mother with a large family.

Although Lathrop found that attention to children and their families at the state and local levels was more practical, she believed that there was a role for the U.S. Children's Bureau to play on the federal level. It could investigate nationwide problems as well as compare and contrast conditions among nations and report and agitate for needed and beneficial change. "The Bureau needs . . . the sternest statistical accuracy at base," she wrote, "because its appeal to the noblest human passion of pity must never be founded upon anything but truth, because it must guard against the easy charge of sentimentality and must be able to present its statements dispassionately with scientific candor and usefulness" (Lathrop, "The Children's Bureau," 319–20). The Children's Bureau gathered statistics on a wide variety of events and subjects affecting the lives of children and families in the United States and other countries. Among the specific topics the bureau investigated were costs associated with raising a child, costs in family budgets, the effect of war on the family and its ability to financially care for its children, childbirth mortality, child mortality, and maternity benefits in other countries. The ultimate goal was a set of standards for the care and development of children that could be promoted nationally. Lathrop chose to develop standards for three goals: improve maternal and child health care, protect children who had to work, and recommend better protection and alternatives for special needs children. Development of these standards became the hallmark of her effort at the Children's Bureau.

By the end of Lathrop's time in office, standards associated with improved care for women and children promoted maternal protection, including the creation of a public health system composed of prenatal care with testing and regular physician visits, an educational program about home delivery or hospital care, a free or partial-payment obstetrical program to be staffed by physicians, visiting nurses and midwives with care after delivery, and mother's pensions. The Sheppard-Towner Act, often referred to as the Maternity Act, which addressed almost all of these standards, was finally passed in 1921, shortly after Lathrop resigned her position because of poor health. It was meant to encourage states to develop programs for serving those women whose families existed on low incomes. It offered matching federal funds to states that hired physicians and nurses to educate and care for women and children in health clinics, that had a cadre of visiting nurses to educate and provide prenatal and postnatal care, that provided midwife training, and that provided families with nutrition and hygiene information. The legislation was the first federally funded social welfare program in the United States, and Lathrop was one of its primary architects.

Like Jane Addams, Julia Lathrop was an ardent advocate for the creation of mother's pensions and remained so all of her life. At a meeting of the Associated Charities of Minneapolis in early 1910, Julia remarked that one of progressive philanthropy's greatest problems was its failure "to initiate dignified methods of . . . pensioning families in which a good competent mother is . . . compelled to be breadwinner." She believed that the state could afford to pay and in time would do so ("The Responsibilities of the Newer Philanthropy"). She was unable to achieve this Children's Bureau standard during her lifetime. And although she argued for the need to create family economic standards that offered sufficient family income for "wholesome living conditions, and the abolition of racial discrimination" ("Standards of Child Welfare," *Annals*, 7), neither of those goals was reached while she was at the helm of the Children's Bureau. In 1919 she warned members of the National Conference of Charities and Correction of the difficulties that African Americans faced: "The welfare of the colored child is a nation-wide problem which no section can ignore with prudence or with honor" ("Presidential Address," 8).

The second issue addressed by the bureau was child labor. Lathrop was determined to protect children from premature employment and harsh labor conditions. Her primary objection to child labor was that she believed all children were entitled to a safe home and environment, education, and a chance for proper physical development. Like Florence Kelley, with whom she often worked on this effort, she supported compulsory school attendance and worked to achieve that goal by helping to develop and support laws providing for that outcome. She also favored a national law limiting child labor because almost all of the states had different laws and standards, and she believed that one national law would be more effective and easier to enforce. The bureau conducted studies about child labor and proposed and lobbied for legislation to establish standards. Two different laws that Lathrop, the Children's Bureau, and Julia's personal network of supportive progressive reformers helped draft were passed by the U.S. Congress. They were the Keating-Owen Act in 1916 and another similar law in 1919; however, both were declared unconstitutional by the U.S. Supreme Court. Lathrop came to believe that the only way to protect children from child labor was through a constitutional amendment. Among the standards that Lathrop and her staff promoted regarding the employment of children were age for employment of sixteen, limitations established for work conditions and hours of employment for young people up to the age of twenty-one, educational minimums such as the attainment to an eighth grade education in a school of nine months' duration, evidence that a child was physically capable of working, and work limited to eight hours a day and for adequate wages to support the child, and the child had to have a certificate of employment recognizing all of the conditions of employment.

The Children's Bureau continually sought ways to advertise its findings and activities. As the primary spokesperson for the bureau, Lathrop lectured publicly with increasing eloquence and wrote ably about the program for a variety of periodicals, from popular to professional and scholarly. She spent a great deal of time educating members of Congress about her program. She also appeared at hearings to promote and secure financial support for the bureau. She gave presentations to organizations like the National Association of Social Workers; Conference of Women's Community Council; National Education Association; the National Conference of Social Work; Academy of Political Science; National Conference of Charities and Correction; the General Federation of Women's Clubs; the International Conference on Child Welfare, 1918; International Conference of Women Physicians, 1919; and the International Conference of Working Women, 1919. Her speeches were published in the proceedings of various organizations, and her articles appeared in periodicals from the *Nation* and the *Woman Citizen* to the *American Journal of Sociology*, *Charities*, *Journal of Public Health*, *Survey*, *Illinois Voter*, *Journal of Home Economics*, *North American Review*, *Czechoslovak Review*, and *American Labor Legislation Review*. Lathrop wrote portions of the annual Children's Bureau reports and provided numerous introductions to Children's Bureau publications. Sometimes she was asked to provide introductions to the publications of others or to write chapters in combination studies like *The Child in the City* (1912), for which she provided "The Defective Child and the Juvenile Court," and *The Child, the Clinic and the Court* (1927), in which "The Background of the Juvenile Court in Illinois" appeared.

In addition to the detailed and statistical studies meant primarily for professional child care providers and social workers, under Lathrop's direction the bureau produced an assortment of pamphlets in simpler language about safe prenatal and postnatal care for mothers and best practices and child care for parents. One of the most popular was "Your Child from One to Six Years." Among other titles were "Is Your Child's Birth Recorded? If Not, Why Not?," "Why Drink Milk?," and "Are You Training Your Child to Be Happy?" The bureau held national campaigns to publicize important Children's Bureau findings and actions. For example, in 1916, the bureau partnered with the General Federation of Women's Clubs to create Baby Week, during which it engaged the public through publicity and events in an effort to share its findings and reduce infant mortality. More than twenty-one hundred communities participated in the program, which included a baby registration day, health conferences, baby exhibits, slide shows, posters and flags, and plays and speeches. The Children's Back to School Campaign, initiated in 1919, was an effort to stop children from leaving school for the higher wages of industrial work caused by the entry of the United States into World War I. For the Children's Year of 1919, every state but two formed committees composed primarily of women representing local committees, more than ten million people in all, to promote the activities on behalf of children and families.

Julia Lathrop knew at the beginning of her tenure that her organization and the social legislation that it hoped to encourage would meet opposition, but she also believed that eventually the facts that the Children's Bureau developed and presented would achieve the goals of a more secure childhood for the children of the United States. As Graham Taylor pointed out: "While politic in the best sense of the word, she was always direct in facing the issue. While tactful, she never compromised principles. In all exacting positions and situations she took her citizenship seriously. She was never impersonally official nor officially personal. . . . The nation's children and their mothers were her own heritage and hope in the American commonwealth" ("Julia Lathrop, Statesman," 5). Lathrop understood politics and bureaucratic infighting. She had great political skills, and she could enlist her inner circle of powerful progressive reformers to press for legislation and influence public officials. Her awareness of the political climate in which she found her organization led her to develop a program for the Children's Bureau that avoided controversial issues, like birth control, which she personally favored, and day care, which she did not support.

Lathrop also became adroit at beating back takeover attempts. Almost from the start of the bureau, the American Medical Association fought to wrest its leadership from Lathrop. Physicians believed that they, rather than social workers who had a social science approach to the welfare of children, should be in control of the bureau. Lathrop was successful in warning Congress that a change to the kind of focus the American Medical Association fostered would likely result in limiting the bureau to handling only sickness, diseases, and cures rather than addressing the root causes of those health problems. Other departments of the government also decried the existence of the bureau. Among them were the Bureau of Education and the Public Health Service. During World War I, the National Committee on Child Welfare, the medical section of the Council of National Defense, formed to coordinate all wartime activities of government agencies, tried to ignore the work that the bureau had already done with regard to birth registration and made an attempt to usurp that work of the bureau. They were unsuccessful. Lathrop also found herself subjected to personal attacks. This was the case especially after World War I, when many who had supported her and the bureau turned against her because of her progressive stance on many issues and her connection to progressive reformers who were denounced during the "Red Scare" era in the United States. Lathrop's outspoken views on compulsory education and the regulation of child labor also placed her in jeopardy because of the reaction of manufacturers who needed young labor for their businesses, especially during wartime.

Lathrop built friendships and support groups for her agency internationally. She spoke in Europe and often recruited leaders in child welfare there to participate in conferences in the United States. Beginning with her investigations of conditions in insane asylums, she visited most of the countries of Europe, investigated conditions in the Soviet Union, toured South and Latin Americas, and on her round-the-world tour with her sister Anna Case in 1910–11 visited Far Eastern countries, including India, Ceylon, China, and the Philippine Islands, where she investigated the school system. In the aftermath of the dislocations and misery of World War I, she helped plan the repatriation of thousands of children and was recognized for her leadership by Poland, where she was received with great appreciation, and in Czechoslovakia, where she consulted about the development of a child-care bureau and was honored with the Order of the White Lion. After presenting "Education of Women as Related to the Welfare of Children" for a session during the Second Pan-American Scientific Congress held Washington, D.C., in December 1915, Lathrop helped to organize a Women's Auxiliary Committee. It was charged with planning for a Women's Auxiliary Congress on child welfare to be held at the same time that the next Pan-American Scientific Congress was scheduled to take place in 1915 and 1916. Although the Auxiliary Congress was never held, members of the planning committee, working together, had an opportunity through correspondence to encourage the development of children's bureaus similar to that of the United States in various South American countries.

During the ten years between her retirement from the Children's Bureau and her death, Julia Lathrop lived primarily in a home that she and her widowed sister Anna Case built in Rockford, Illinois, on the shore of the Rock River. Between 1922 and 1924, Julia Lathrop was president of the Illinois League of Women Voters and eventually became vice-president and counselor in public welfare for the National League of Women Voters. "The League of Women Voters urges women to join and work in the parties of their choice," Lathrop wrote, "but first to have a choice based on something more than tradition or prejudice or sentiment. Only one way can an intelligent vote be made—the hard road of study and thought. . . . It cannot be done either by mere looking on—we must both study and take part. Nor can study and work be abstract. Study leads to decisions which we support by our work" ("Miss Lathrop's Own Words," 10). She believed that woman suffrage could bring untold power to women to affect policy, especially with regard to the welfare of children and their mothers and world peace. "Future historians are likely to hold that the most surprising and prophetic event in our [World] War [I] period was the quiet, world-wide enfranchisement of uncounted millions of women in countries differing as much in race, governments and traditions as Mexico, Canada, the United States, Lithuania, Czechoslovakia, and India. This enfranchisement creates a new world feeling among women, a new world power of unknown strength. It can mark the beginning of a new world peace if we work hard enough for just world politics" ("[Statement] from Defense Day and Patriots," 9).

In 1925 Julia Lathrop was appointed an assessor and member of the Advisory Committee of the Commission on the Welfare of Children and Young Persons of the League of Nations and served in that capacity until 1931. Lathrop's concern about parents being able to control and improve the conditions in which their children grew to maturity led her to help Vassar College create a School of Euthenics in 1924–25. She continued to work for legislation that would improve the lives of children throughout the world by speaking before groups who could help her cause and by lobbying before legislative bodies who could effect laws.

Lathrop's commitment to the international peace movement began in the founding days of the Woman's Peace Party and the Woman's International League for Peace and Freedom, 1914 and 1915. She strengthened those ties after her retirement from the Children's Bureau and became active in the National Council for the Reduction of Armaments. Her peace activities added to her reputation as a progressive reformer and resulted in her being labeled as a liberal, socialist, and communist during the early 1920s. Although Julia Lathrop was deceased by 1934 when Mrs. Elizabeth Dilling's *The Red Network* was published, she was identified in the section labeled "Who Is Who in Radicalism?" as a member of the American Civil Liberties Union, American Society for Cultural Relations with Russia, National Council for the Prevention of War, and National Consumers League and, among other things, as "one of Jane Addams' Hull House group" (299). She was also affiliated with the American Association of University Women, the Woman's Christian Temperance Union, National Association of Social Workers, National Conference of Social Work, and numerous other organizations that helped foster improved child welfare positions, immigrant protection, and peace.

Julia Lathrop was elected in 1917 as the first president of the National Council of Social Work. She also served as president of the National Conference of Charities and Correction in 1919. A member of a number of committees within national, state, and local reform organizations, Julia Lathrop became a trustee for the Elizabeth McCormick Fund, Chicago. On 15 April 1932, Julia Lathrop died unexpectedly after an operation in Rockford, Illinois, to remove a goiter. She was buried in the city's Greenwood Cemetery. As Lathrop and her friends had been devastated by the death of Florence Kelley the month before, Lathrop's many friends were doubly saddened by this death. A memorial service for Julia Lathrop was held on 22 May 1932 in Washington, D.C., under the auspices of the U.S. Department of Labor, the Children's Bureau, and the Women's Bureau. Prior to that, on 6 May 1932 a combined memorial service for Florence Kelley and Julia Lathrop was held at Hull-House, with Jane Addams presiding. There Andrew Alexander Bruce pronounced Lathrop "a soul which like the strings of a fine string harp could vibrate all emotions. Witty though she was, Julia Lathrop was one of the saddest of women, for the sorrow of others weighted heavily upon her. She used her fine sense of humor as a means, and not, as an end, to convey a point, to bridge a difficulty, and not for personal applause." He described her a "real gentlewoman" who exhibited "that sense of noblesse oblige which realized obligation and scorns a life of selfishness" ("Julia Lathrop in the Nineties," 17–18, 21; *JAPM*, 38:668–69, 672). Others that day recalled that Lathrop led by the force of her reasonableness and her calm judgment. She used her kind humor to make a point or cool an argument that had reached a breaking point. Another speaker remembered her ability to present a complete picture of a problem to be tackled and to follow that description with a reasonable and logical argument about how the problem could be solved.

At least two schools bear her name: a primary school in Rockford, Illinois, and a middle school in Santa Anna, California. A dormitory at Rockford College was also named for her. Lathrop Homes, a low-rise public housing project, one of the most successful ever built, was constructed in Chicago in 1934 and named in her honor. One of the most significant memorials was created when her longtime friend Jane Addams described their friendship and Lathrop's achievements in *My Friend, Julia Lathrop*, a biography published in 1935 after Addams herself had died. Along with a recitation of the significance of Lathrop's friendship for Addams, and a recounting of Lathrop's many contributions to progressive reform and the development of social work, Jane Addams tried to convey some of the personal traits that Lathrop exhibited that meant the most to her. She presented Lathrop as an "open minded inquirer . . . congenial, humorous, but never at the expense of others." She was someone who could be counted on for "absolute fairness and constructive helpfulness" (88). Lathrop had a "keen mind" given to "clear thinking" and a "remarkable capacity to evoke a sympathetic response from the most unpromising human mind" (167). She was the "most stimulating and great-hearted of friends," one who would "lend her whole mind, the endless resources of her rich experience to a given situation, which might be facing Hull-House or another group to which she held her allegiance" (169). Jane identified Julia as exhibiting profound compassion for the plight of those less fortunate and a heartfelt human sympathy for basic human needs. She saw her friend as an idealist who operated from a moral framework and believed in the goodness of all human beings. For Jane Addams, she was a friend who was "good all through" (191).

## *Smith, Mary Rozet (1868–1934), and Smith Family*

Mary Rozet Smith, philanthropist, was born on 23 December 1868 in Chicago, Illinois, at the home of her parents, Sarah Emily Rozet Smith (1839?–1903) and Charles Mather Smith (1831–1912), at 327 (later 60 East) Superior. According to Mary's great-nephew Richard Bull, she was a descendant of "Henry Smith a Protestant minister [who] fled Religious persecution in England and landed at Plymouth, Mass. in 1630" (27 Nov. 2001, JAPP, MRS Files). Henry and Dorothy Cotton Smith's progeny settled throughout Connecticut and New York, and Charles Mather Smith, Mary's father, was one of them. He was born in Ogdensburg, New York, a child of John Smith and Lucy Raney Bradner Smith. Among his siblings were John Bradner (1816–93), Sarah Porter (1819–1907), Frederick Lay (1824?–64), Lester P. (1827?–63), and George Cotton (1828–1915).

By the early 1850s, Charles Mather Smith had received his education in the St. Lawrence County, New York area, and with brother John Bradner and sister Sarah Porter journeyed to Chicago to join their brother George Cotton, who was establishing himself as a paper merchant and banker. George Smith had come to Chicago with his cousin Josiah H. Bradner of Dansville, New York, and a friend, William H. Warren. Together they organized Bradner-Warren and Company, as paper merchants. By 1852, after Warren left the partnership, the name of the company was changed to Bradner-Smith and Company and located in the city in a one-room shop at 12 (later near 324) LaSalle Street. Josiah H. Bradner died in 1857, the year that John Bradner Smith joined his brother George in the company. By January 1871, Charles Mather Smith had also come into the firm, bringing with him a bank credit line of one million dollars that helped to resurrect the firm after its offices and warehouses were destroyed in the Great Chicago Fire of 1871. Charles Mather's first job in Chicago had been as general freight agent for the Illinois Central Railroad, and by 1864 he was engaged with his brother George in the banking company George C. Smith and Brother (previously known under the title J. W. Drexel and Company). A few years later, George Cotton Smith retired from the Chicago businesses he had helped to develop, and he returned to the Wilkes-Barre, Pennsylvania, area, home of his wife, Elizabeth Virginia Laning Bradner Smith (1832–1910), who had been the first wife of his initial partner, Josiah H. Bradner. In 1873 Charles Mather Smith became president of Bradner-Smith and Company, which soon established its presence as one of the largest paper distributors in the Midwest.

In 1860 Charles Mather Smith married Sarah Emily Rozet, sister of George Hollenbeck Rozet (1829?–1900), who became a pioneer real estate developer in Chicago (see JA to MRS, 22 June 1899, n. 1, above). Sarah Emily Rozet was born in Philadelphia, Pennsylvania, the daughter of Mary Ann Laning Rozet (1807?–80) and French merchant John Rozet (1794?–1870). One of her two sisters became Mrs. John Broadhead and lived most of her life in Paris, where the Smith family sometimes visited. She was also related to the Drexel banking family through her other sister, Ellen B. Rozet, who became the wife of financier, banker, and founder of Philadelphia's Drexel University Anthony Joseph Drexel (1826–93). Despite their considerable financial and family connections in Pennsylvania, the young Smith couple settled permanently in Chicago near Rozet relatives, with whom they maintained a lifelong relationship. Besides Mary Rozet, Charles Mather Smith and Sarah Emily Rozet Smith had two sons who lived to maturity. They were Charles Frederic Mather (1863–1941), born in Chicago, and Francis Drexel (1874–1956), born in Englewood, Illinois.

Charles Frederic Mather Smith, called Fred, joined the Bradner-Smith firm in 1881. By the time he retired to Orange County, Florida, in 1930 to develop and operate a successful citrus business, he had served twenty years as the company's president, following his father. In July 1908, Fred and his first wife, Kathleen McDonald (1871?–1944), whom he wed in 1892 and with whom he had one child, Sara (or Sarah) Rozet Smith Bull Calvin (1893–1985), were divorced. In 1910 Kathleen McDonald Smith became the wife of Chicago attorney Charles H. Hamill (1868–1941). With his second wife, Grace Hamilton (b. 1884), of Denver, whom Smith wed in 1908, he had three more children: Grace Mary Smith

Debujaque Turner Matthiessen (b. 1909); Charles Mather Smith (b. 1910), who later called himself Charles M. Mather-Smith and wed three times; and Ann Rebecca Smith Baldwin Fischbeck (b. 1914).

Mary Rozet Smith's younger brother, Francis Drexel Smith, known in the family as Frank, had studied art in Chicago and New York. For health reasons, he finally settled in Colorado Springs and became an artist who was noted for his paintings of the Rocky Mountain country. He married Charlotte Silsbee (b. 1876) in June 1900. They had one child, Lyman Silsbee Smith, and were divorced in 1912, after which in 1914 Frank Smith married Edith Winslow Farnsworth of Colorado Springs, a wealthy miner's widow.

The Charles Mather Smith family seems to have lived a rather peripatetic existence in Chicago. The federal census taken in June 1870 recorded them, with Charles Mather Smith as head of household, living in Hyde Park, then a lakefront suburb located six miles south of Chicago's downtown business district. Brother John Bradner Smith and sister Sarah P. Smith were living at the same address. However, the Merchants' census of 1870, published in January 1871, lists the Charles M. Smith family as residing at 317 (later 46) East Superior Street. Family lore suggests that the Smiths left the city following the Great Fire of 8 October 1871. According to Mary Smith's nieces and nephews, the family's nursemaid delighted in relating her adventures helping the Smiths to safety along with what possessions they could gather. At the time, son Charles was nearly eight years old and Mary not quite three. Mary Ursula Smith, known as Polly, became associated with the Smith family early in her life, moving quickly from domestic servant to nursemaid status. Although she shared the family's surname, Polly was no relation. A Roman Catholic, she had emigrated from Ireland with her parents, James and Mary Smith, who by 1870 owned a farm worth two thousand dollars in the village of Ainsworth (later South Chicago) in Hyde Park township. It is likely that by the time of the 1870 census, Polly was "living out" as a domestic and contributing some of her wages to the support of four younger siblings. Although her name does not appear in the list of Smith family servants in the 1870 federal census return, Polly may have been in the process of being employed by the family. It was with the Smiths that she spent the remainder of her working life. By 1939, after caring for Mary Rozet Smith's great-nieces and great-nephews, Polly could boast that she had bathed three generations of Smith children. Although cemetery records place her age at eighty-nine, Smith family relatives believed her to be in her midnineties at the time of her death in 1948.

After the Great Chicago Fire, the Smiths established themselves in the village of Englewood, where their son Francis Drexel was born in 1874. Shortly thereafter, they once again moved east to Hyde Park to join many of Chicago's social elite who had reestablished themselves to the south of the city. According to Janet Hopkins Ayer (Mrs. B. F.), who was writing from firsthand experience, the "residents in Hyde Park were better off than most [after the Fire] as . . .

[they] had new and commodious homes, well-equipped stables and horses and carriages, which provided means of transportation" to the ruined city center. Mrs. Ayer recalled "lots of wholesome, inexpensive, harmless fun" that included public lectures, concerts, political gatherings, dancing classes, charades, "no balls but many dances," and dominoes, checkers, reading, spelling bees, and visiting (Kirkland, *Chicago Yesterdays*, 181–83). A great many of the entertainments centered around music. It is likely that the Smith children with their nanny shared those experiences.

Within a few years, the Smiths moved north, first to 536 (later 1414) Dearborn Street. From 1880 to 1887, they lived near the George Rozet family on LaSalle Street, occupying residences at 328 (later 942), 410 (later 1156) and 404 (later 1150) North LaSalle. In 1888 they settled at 19 (later 12) Walton Place, in a house that had been occupied until 1888 by the family of hardware merchant C. R. Larrabee, who came to Chicago from Ticonderoga, New York, in 1848. James Weber Linn, Jane Addams's nephew and biographer, described it as "a big square wooden castle, . . . huge, simple, four-square and nobly Chicagoan" ([Mary Rozet Smith] written for the *Chicago Daily News*, 23 Feb. 1924); however, photographic evidence indicates that most of the homes on Walton Place were brick. The structure may have been designed by Chicago architect Otto Matz and constructed after the Chicago Fire of 1871. It was the same three-story house with six bedrooms and three baths on the two upper floors, and quarters for four servants near the kitchen, in which Mary Smith lived the remainder of her life.

Mary Rozet Smith and her siblings seemed to have a fun-filled, carefree life in their new home on Walton Place. Polly sneaked cookies and special peppermint candies to the children, regaled them with stories of leprechauns and banshees, guided their play inside, and watched over them when they went for walks or rides. It may have been in part from Polly that Mary Smith developed her special love for children as well as her sense of fun and her storytelling ability that others remembered in her as an adult woman. Mary's great-niece Ellen Bull Sloan, who as a child was treated by Polly to baths with "a tub full of celluloid gold fish," recalled the following story that Polly recounted about Mary: "It was fun to know, for instance, that Aunt Mary, who was the most truly good person I've every known, was not always so perfect. When she let Uncle Frank, who was two or three years younger, carry her doll and he fell into a river with it Aunt Mary jumped in and rescued the doll. Polly rescued Uncle Frank," Mrs. Sloan also reported that Polly's "true position was best friend to all children" (12 Nov. 1985, JAPP, MRS Files).

Mary Smith was a student at Miss Kirkland's School for Girls in Chicago and may have been taught by Ellen Gates Starr. Like her brothers, she never attended college. Mary grew up a tall (at five feet, seven inches), slim, pretty young woman with gray eyes, light-brown hair, and a shy but pleasant, calm, and winning way about her. Her nephew Charles M. Mather-Smith recalled that "Mary Rozet Smith was a beautiful woman with beautiful curley hair and a lovely face and elegant body. She did not believe in people wearing any kind of make up" (24 Aug. 1985, JAPP, MRS Files). According to Addams's biographer and nephew James Weber Linn, she "traveled abroad with her father and mother extensively in her 'teens, and in 1890 found herself precisely in the situation that Jane Addams so gloomily analyzed as that of many young women in the 'eighties: 'She appreciated only too well that her opportunities had been fine and unusual, but she also knew that in spite of some facility and much good teaching she had no special talent. . . . She looked with positive envy upon those girl-hoods which had been filled with happy industry and extenuating obstacles'" (*Jane Addams*, 147). Likely in recognition of Mary's new place in society as a twenty-one-year-old young lady, in early February 1890 Mary and her mother, assisted by Jenny Dow, hosted a luncheon for about 130 guests at their Walton Place home, with rooms that were decorated with roses, lily of the valley, and maidenhair ferns and a mandolin orchestra for music. Her family and friends expected her to take her place among Chicago's social and cultural elite, and that she did, but on her own terms in a nontraditional fashion for the time in which she lived, guided by Jane Addams, and with the help of her family.

Mary first discovered Hull-House about the time of her twenty-first birthday. Jenny Dow, who had taken responsibility for developing and directing the settlement kindergarten, encouraged Mary to investigate the newly established social settlement venture. Jane Addams first recorded Mary Smith's presence at the settlement on 24 March 1890. She was identified as a member of the small Italian-language class that included Jane and Jenny and met on Monday afternoons at 2:30. Jane would later use a poem she may have written for Mary on the occasion of her twenty-fifth birthday (Addams, "A Retrospect," 3; *JAPM*, 45:1598) to describe her first glimpse of Mary:

One day I came into Hull House,
(No fairy whispered what was there)
And in the kindergarten room
~~A girl both tall and fair to see~~
There sat upon a childish chair
A girl both tall and fair to see
(To look at her gives one a thrill)
But I thought only would she be
Best fitted to lead club or drill?

The exciting settlement scheme and Jane's thoughtful and spirited dedication for helping those less fortunate quickly captured Mary Smith's attention and soon her commitment. She was searching for something appropriate to "do." Before the summer of 1890 began, Mary had taken the lead in Jane's attempt to establish a French night at Hull-House. On Monday, 12 May 1890, Jane Addams recorded in her diary that "Miss Smith [was] ready for a French eve. No French came but Mr. [Edward] Bideleux" ("Diary, 1889–90"; *JAPM*, 29:163). In mid-June 1890, Jane invited Mary to stay at Hull-House for a week with her friends Jenny Dow and Alice Trowbridge. All three accepted the invitation, and from that time forward Mary continued to participate in settlement activities. On 8 October 1890, she joined Jane, Ellen, Dr. Leila G. Bedell, and Julia Plato Harvey at dinner at the settlement. By 1891 Mary seems to have been comfortable with a supporting role at Hull-House. She began to introduce her family to Jane Addams and to direct the Smith family's financial patronage toward the settlement. In early February 1891, when Jane wrote to Mary reminding her to thank Charles Mather Smith for a program he gave one Sunday at Hull-House, Jane remarked to Mary that her "friendship has come to mean a great deal" (3 Feb. 1891, UIC, JAMC; *JAPM*, 2:1231).

The elder Smiths seemed to understand that Jane's friendship and Mary's connection with Hull-House had become a major part of their daughter's life. They began to treat Jane like another daughter. She was often in their home, and they invited her to travel with them, even to visit Smith relatives in Maryland, Pennsylvania, Colorado, and South Carolina. Jane established a warm and supportive father-daughter relationship with Charles Mather Smith. She consulted him frequently, and his son Fred after him, about Hull-House finances and real estate issues. Especially when Mary was away, Jane went often to Walton Place so that she could keep Mary informed about her parents. In 1902 when Mary took an ailing Eleanor Smith to Europe, Jane went almost daily to call on the Smiths and then accompanied them on a vacation to the New Jersey shore. Jane reported to Mary that the elder Smiths "filled . . . [her] with filial affections" (19 May 1902, SCPC, JAC; *JAPM*, 4:382).

In the beginning, Mary might have become a settlement resident herself, except for her fragile health and family responsibilities. Despite those issues, during the 1890s and the early 1900s she did serve at Hull-House as the director for two afternoon children's clubs: the Aloha-Vesperian Club of young girls interested in reading and embroidery in 1897–98 and the Young Folks' Literary Club, debate and reading for boys in 1902–3.

Health concerns plagued Mary throughout her life. She had a double mastectomy and in 1918 surgery to remove an abdominal tumor. Yet it was probably her own lifelong chronic asthma condition, exacerbated by allergies and by smoking cigarettes, which she refused to give up, that also kept her anchored in her own home and later in life gave her a "half-whisper" voice (Linn, [Mary Rozet Smith]). From time to time, especially when her asthma was aggravated by flu, bronchitis, or a cold, Mary left Chicago for a different climate, sometimes to the higher altitude of Colorado and sometimes to Smith relatives in Columbia, South Carolina.

Through Mary's dedication, devotion, and lifelong relationship with Jane Addams and with Hull-House, she became a crucial ingredient in the success of both. From the start of Mary's association with Hull-House, it was clear that her special early interest was the welfare of young children. She also seemed to understand that for those special programs, like the kindergarten and the Crêche, to succeed, the entire Hull-House enterprise needed continuing support. For the first five years of the settlement, with the exception of Jane Addams herself, Mary Smith and her family (including mother, father, brothers, Bradner-Smith and Co., and aunt Sarah Porter Smith) provided the most regular financial backing.

By the October 1891 to September 1892 financial year, Mary was pledging $100 annually, a little more than $2,709 in 2016 dollars. Instead of collecting the funds in small increments from friends, she simply paid the entire amount herself (in two $50 amounts in January and July). Mary's first major brick-and-mortar gift, presented in 1893, was $328 ($8,886 in 2016 dollars) to pave the front yard as a courtyard and to build a low wall in front of Hull-House. In 1899 Charles Mather Smith had the wall reconstructed and strengthened.

By 1893 Mary's parents, brothers Fred and Frank, as well as her aunt Sarah Porter Smith had joined her in providing regular monthly support for Hull-House. For the period 1891 until 1895, the Smiths gave more than $8,000 (in 2016 dollars the equivalent of $233,961), primarily to support the Hull-House Crêche, but also for general purposes, relief, the Hull-House Summer School, and to help provide fellowships for those residents and workers who needed financial help. From its beginning in 1893, the Hull-House Music School, led by Eleanor Smith (no relation to the Charles Mather Smith family), was funded largely by Mary and her family, perhaps because of Sarah Rozet Smith's interest in music. Mary, often identified as the founder of the Music School at the settlement, gave support to it throughout her life and shortly after the death of her mother presented a pipe organ to the settlement as a memorial to her. Mary forged a strong bond of friendship with Music School director Eleanor Smith, took her to Europe on at least two occasions, offered her a permanent residence in her Walton Place home, and provided for her lifelong financial security.

As the years went by, the entire Smith family, led by Mary, continued to make Hull-House a major recipient of their philanthropy. In 1910 members of the immediate Smith family, including Mary, gave $4,340 ($113,417 in 2016 dollars) of the annual and monthly donations of $18,629 ($486,831 in 2016 dollars), constituting about 23 percent of the funds expended for daily settlement operations. Beyond the Smith family's contribution of $1,800 ($47,039 in 2016 dollars) in 1910, Mary contributed at least $5,040 ($131,710 in 2016 dollars), $2,500 ($65,332 in 2016 dollars) of which was designated for the Hull-House endowment. The family's commitment varied from year to year, but they gave regularly.

In addition, Mary and members of her family supported Jane's development of the Hull-House physical plant. During the summer of 1895, Charles Mather Smith built and largely furnished the four-story brick forty-four-by-forty-four-foot Children's House or Children's Building (later renamed the Smith Building in his memory) at the southwest corner of Polk and Halsted streets. Among the other settlement construction projects to which the Smiths contributed were the electric plant (1898), the Coffee House and Theatre Building (1899), moving the former Hull-House gymnasium and adding baths and another story to the structure to accommodate the Labor Museum and shops (1900–1901), enlarging the boiler plant to heat all settlement buildings (1902), and developing the alley between Polk and Ewing streets (1903). They also erected the Men's Club on Halsted Street and helped with funds to construct the residents' apartments, on the northwest corner of Ewing and Halsted streets (1901–2). In 1898 Mary Smith's aunt Sarah Porter Smith gave $12,000 ($350,942 in 2016 dollars) to construct the brick four-story, twenty-six-bedroom Jane Club on Ewing Street, and although Jane Addams protested, Mary paid $2,000 ($58,490 in 2016 dollars) to purchase the real estate on which it was constructed. By 1906 the Smith family provided more than $4,500 ($121,909 in 2016 dollars) for a separate two-story Music School Building and the next year gave another $2,000 ($52,249 in 2016 dollars) to add a third story to it. Then, in 1910, the Smiths, including Mary, added approximately $18,000 ($470,394 in 2016 dollars) to the settlement endowment.

Extant Hull-House financial records indicate that over her lifetime, Mary Smith gave more than $151,476 ($4,429,943 in 2016 dollars) to Hull-House programs and endowment and added $25,000 ($455,559 in 2016 dollars) on her death in 1934. Mary also gave money directly to Jane for various special Hull-House and neighborhood-related needs that was never recorded in the settlement financial records. Other family contributions, alone, over the years, could easily have added another $100,000 (which would probably have equaled $1,500,000) or more to the total that Mary gave. In some years, the money to support pledges made by different Smith family members, including Mary, arrived at Hull-House in one check. Some of the checks were drawn on Bradner-Smith and Company. During the 1920s and 1930s, Mary, an astute businesswoman, served as a member of the Bradner-Smith and Company board when that successful and entirely family-owned business was one of the largest paper-distributing operations in the United States, boasting the largest paper warehouse in the world. Mary could also rely on real estate investments, especially those she helped purchase, sell, or manage through the Mather Smith Building Corporation, and she had access to moneys from at least one trust fund that had come to her through her mother's Rozet family. The Smith family's early and regular support for Hull-House was only one of the reasons that Jane Addams selected Mary as a member of the first Hull-House Association Board of Trustees when it was organized in 1895. Mary served as a trustee until her death.

By the mid-1890s, Jane and Mary had become best friends, and Mary had emerged as a pivotal helpmate for Jane, even more than a trusted confidant and convenient sounding board. "I have never known anyone who so instinctively and steadily did the noble and right thing in all relationships," Jane Addams told "this dearest friend of mine" (JA to MRS, 31 May 1899, SCPC, JAC; *JAPM*, 3:1356). Jane's reliance on Mary seemed to wax as her relationship with Ellen Gates Starr waned. Ellen Starr, who had to focus on earning a living, was not the leader or visionary that Jane was. She was highly emotional and prone to flashes of temper, impatient, decidedly judgmental, and sometimes as untactful as Jane was thoughtful of others, socially graceful, and diplomatic. The life interests and responsibilities of the two friends diverged. With the busy schedules Ellen and Jane were keeping soon after the settlement opened, there was little time to nurture the intellectual or emotional bond that they had shared in their younger days and as they were planning the settlement. Both women must have felt the widening gap in their relationship, as Jane moved into the limelight with Mary Smith increasingly at her elbow to provide the unconditional devotion and easy friendship that Jane required. Ellen developed her own separate interests, especially in fine bookbinding, making the fine arts more accessible to everyone, promoting the arts and crafts movement, actively supporting the cause of organized labor, and becoming more engaged in the Roman Catholic Church. Years later, Ellen confided to Jane that she believed that when she was a young woman, Jane had "overrated" her and "that it was inevitable that I should disappoint you. I think I have always—at any rate for a great many years—been thankful that ~~she~~ Mary came to supply what you needed. At all events, I thank God that I never was envious of her in any vulgar or ignoble way. One couldn't be of any one so noble and generous and in every way fair minded as she, & so humble; really self-depreciating. The way I did feel of others' gifts & graces & their just fruits which I know was a great trial to you" (EGS to JA, 12 Apr. 1935, SC, Starr; *JAPM*, 26:1325–26).

Mary came to provide the refuge of unqualified friendship, the emotional support, the "moral fiber" (JA to MRS, [Mar? 1898], SCPC, JAC; *JAPM*, 3:977), and venue for companionable relaxation that Jane required in order to keep up her pace of activity and manage her emerging public persona. When both Mary and Jane were in Chicago, they saw one another when their schedules permitted; they kept in touch initially by note or letter, but certainly by the mid-1890s by telephone. When one or the other was away from Chicago, they communicated primarily by letter. Only a portion of that correspondence survives. After Mary's death, Jane reviewed their correspondence and destroyed letters she believed contained information, especially concerning family issues, too personal to be seen by others. While more than 350 letters Jane wrote to Mary are extant, only a few that Mary wrote to Jane have survived (see introduction to *PJA*, 1).

In her early letters, Jane addressed Mary as "My dear friend" and "My dear Sister," but by the end of the 1890s the greetings were simply "Dearie" or "Darling." As Hull-House matured, so did their relationship. As spinsters, Jane and Mary developed their "Boston marriage" kinship in a time when women living together, even sleeping together, was not unusual. Jane Addams had grown up in her Cedarville home sharing a bed and bedroom with three sisters. "Addams and Smith began their relationship in the late nineteenth century, and had been raised by parents in Victorian America at a time when it was acceptable for young women friends to travel together, to share beds, to have deep friendships with sentimental correspondence, and to show a level of physical affection and tenderness strange to later generations" (Schultz, "Smith, Mary Rozet," *WBC*, 817). Though Jane and Mary traveled together beginning in the 1890s, they did not live together for large segments of time, except for vacations, until the early the 1920s. There is insufficient evidence to indicate that their relationship was actively lesbian, what Lillian Faderman in *Surpassing the Love of Men: Romantic Friendship and Love between Women from the Renaissance to the Present* described as women who "'if their personalities could be projected to our times . . . would [probably] see themselves as 'women-identified-women'" (190, as quoted in Schultz, "Smith, Mary Rozet," *WBC*, 817). Mary and Jane's relationship evolved in a sisterly and familial fashion, perhaps something like what Jane Addams may have hoped to maintain with her sisters: close, mutually supportive, and companionable.

During the late 1890s, Mary Smith was trying to determine her life's path. Much like Jane had a decade earlier, she struggled with her sense of responsibility to parents and family, her need to establish her own identity and occupation, and her compulsion to use her wealth wisely for the benefit of others. "You can never know," she wrote to Jane at Christmas, "what it is to me to have had you and to have you now—I only hope I am thankful enough. I'm given to turning sentimental at the season, as you know, and I feel quite a mush of emotion when I think of you. I have been having another bad time with my conscience (about my 'wealth') and I've been in the depths of gloom until yesterday when the sight and sound of you cheered me" (see MRS to JA, [Dec. 1896?], above). In the spring of 1897, Mary seriously considered, but ultimately rejected, the idea of adopting a Hull-House neighborhood child, born to Margaret Toomey. Mary also questioned the future of her friendship with Jane Addams. After the two women shared a lengthy heart-to-heart "confessional," Jane wrote to reassure Mary that "if you ever doubt my desire to be with you—I wish you could see at the bottom of my mind" (see JA to MRS, 21 Feb. 1897, above). Between 1897 and 1899, despite the fact that Jane did not want her to make the same mistakes in seeking a life's path that she had made prior to founding Hull-House, Mary attended classes at Chicago's Armour Institute in preparation for becoming a kindergarten teacher. Jane wrote to Mary, "That one cannot go to school with content [for?] at 28 one begins to grapple with the thing itself or is unhappy." And she continued, worried that Mary would shut her out, "I don't think 'withdrawing from the influence' is the most logical way of settling it. Of course 'everybody approves' just as they would approve your staying at home or any other <thing> which was conventional or approximated it—but the heart knowest its own bitterness—and if you would just let me guide you and love you and cooperate with you I know I could be of use" (see JA to MRS, [22 July 1897], above). As part of the "education" Jane may have hoped for, Mary was to live for a month at Hull-House. Instead, during September and October 1898, Mary spent time investigating Lillian Wald's Nurses Settlement in New York

City and became a close Wald friend. "Don't you think that you are treating your old love a little badly to be so soon 'off' with H.H. and on with the new?," teased Jane (see JA to MRS, 6 Oct. 1898, above). Whatever the outcome of Mary's search for a direction, by 1899 she finally chose the caregiving role for family, friends, and Hull-House, and Mary and Jane were firmly settled in what would be the remainder of a lifelong relationship. "There is one thing sure—" Jane commented, "you need never imagine that your 'being good to your family' is a made up mission—if there ever was a genuine and definite good performed you do it there!" (24 June 1899, SCPC, JAC; *JAPM*, 3:1373–74). Not too long before her death, Mary told a friend to both women that "because of Jane my life has been so full" (Rachelle S. Yarros to JA, 23 Feb. 1934, SCPC, JAC; *JAPM*, 25:857).

"It always appeared," wrote Mary's nephew Charles M. Mather-Smith, "that Jane Addams depended on Aunt Mary, not only for Financial backing but for help and advice" (26 Aug. 1985, JAPP, MRS Files). By the late 1890s, Jane was sharing her personal triumphs, disappointments, and fears as well as her family problems and Hull-House issues with Mary. Extant letters reveal that Jane kept Mary apprised of the health and financial situation of John Weber Addams and his shy wife, Laura. She also involved Mary in the lives of her nieces and nephews, especially the Linn children, for whom Jane acted as a surrogate mother; the young Stanley was often a guest at Mary's home, particularly when his aunt Jane had to be away. Jane kept Mary informed about her various reform efforts and the ever-evolving programs and improvements at Hull-House. When a new settlement building was in the development stage, Jane proudly announced her fund-raising achievements but also reported to Mary her failures with open dismay. As doubts appeared, Jane could count on Mary's supportive friendship to see her through. "It is surprising what power a written word from you has," Jane told Mary in a March 1898 letter (SCPC, JAC; *JAPM*, 3:975). In Mary's absence from Chicago during the Nineteenth Ward alderman election of March and April 1898, Jane wrote to tell her that she missed her and that seeing her portrait brought her comfort (see also introduction to Article in the *HH Bulletin*, Apr. and May 1898, above). Mary Rozet Smith and Jane Addams had recently posed for portraits by Alice Kellogg Tyler, a Hull-House artist in residence. Whereas Tyler depicted Mary as a gentlewoman of leisure clad in a lovely yellow dress and relaxing in a chair, she portrayed a slender Jane in restrained dark-gray garment standing with her hands clasped behind her back, a pose that conveyed power, determination, and authority. Yet as their correspondence reveals, formal portraits could be misleading. During a difficult time in February 1911 when Jane was by herself in New York City to speak before several organizations, each requiring a different speech, she confided in Mary that she was in "quite a fuss" before her speeches and in a state of collapse after them (3 Feb. 1911, SCPC, JAC; *JAPM*, 6:79). "I feel like an infant who has been learning to walk for the second time, and each speech has left me full of doubt concerning the next" (JA to MRS, [Feb. 1911], SCPC, JAC; *JAPM*, 6:70).

By 7 February, Jane was in such a dither that she told Mary that she feared her speaking days were over and it was a good thing that she had the settlement to fall back on. All of Jane's close friends and associates recognized the central role that Mary had assumed in Jane's personal life and loved her not only for herself, but also for her devotion to Jane. Florence Kelley, who addressed Mary in letters as "Dearly Beloved," wrote to her "The Lady misses you more than the uninitiated would think she had time for" (4 Feb. 1899, SCPC, JAC; *JAPM*, 3:1287). In Mary, Jane had found a nurse when she needed one, an unobtrusive and supportive traveling companion, a loyal confidante, generous financial support, a bright associate who could join her intellectual pursuits, someone with whom she could share her passion for reading and poetry, someone who shared her dedication to social justice, but mostly someone who would always be there for her with the unconditional love a family provided.

Mary had other philanthropic interests besides Hull-House and quietly pursued them. Many of them revolved around the welfare of children. She was an active supporter of the Maurice Porter Children's Hospital. When Florence Kelley's children were young, Mary's financial support for their schooling, with some incidentals and often transportation to see their mother, especially after Kelley moved to New York City, helped keep them in good schools and associated with the Lloyd children, and with the ability to see their mother. She also provided financial assistance for Margaret Toomey and her daughter, Jane, namesake of Jane Addams. Mary's nephew Charles M. Mather-Smith recalled that she made it possible for two bright and talented Jewish boys who had no means of their own to attend a university. Mary gave generously to the Chicago Babies Milk Fund and to the effort to develop free kindergartens for African American children in Chicago.

Mary joined the Chicago Woman's Club, where she was a member of the Education and the Philanthropy sections and beginning in 1920 a member of the board of managers of the Education section. She was also a member of the Woman's City Club and the Friday and Cordon clubs. She had served on boards of the Juvenile Protective Association and the Illinois Society for Mental Hygiene and was a member of the Tenement House Committee of the Chicago City Homes Association. Yet during this time, it was the cause of securing woman suffrage in Illinois that attracted Mary's active participation. In February 1911, she was identified by the *Chicago Daily Tribune* as one of the leaders at a gathering of Chicago reform notables invited to hear Mrs. Stanley McCormick speak about the need to organize in order to promote woman suffrage in Chicago. In response, Mary became an organizer and served as a board member or officer of the North Side branch of the Illinois Equal Suffrage Association until the organization disbanded in 1920. She passed out advisory ballots to secure a popular vote on woman suffrage during Chicago's preferential primary election in April 1912 and was quoted in the 14 April 1912 *Chicago Daily Tribune* about the experience: "Two young men whom I approached timidly were driven to a furious display of disapprobation and stamped upon the enlightening leaflets which I presented. This zeal in the annihilation of woman's pretensions really gave me a new sense of the importance of the 'movement.'" She helped to organize a concert by vocalist Mme. Ernestine Schumann-Heink on 19 November 1912 at Chicago's Orchestra Hall to support the educational efforts of her organization. In April 1913, as the organization changed its name to the Chicago Equal Suffrage Association, Mary was chosen as its president. Between 1913 and 1918, when she became recording secretary for the association, she hosted a number of ward meetings and a series of lectures in her home to educate and inform women voters. She also organized dinners and luncheons to recognize special achievements in Chicago connected with woman suffrage. As part of the effort to enlist support of trade unions and their memberships in the battle for woman suffrage, Mary worked with other wealthy Chicago women to support the Women's Trade Union League; they hosted special fund-raising events including dances and plays.

When women pickets, including Ellen Gates Starr, were arrested during the strike of Henrici waitresses in March 1914, Mary posted their bonds and then wrote to James J. Gleason, chief of the Chicago police, "asking him for information as to what the waitresses' union could do to keep within the law and at the same time present to the public their side of the dispute with Henrici's restaurant" (*Chicago Daily Tribune*, 4 Mar. 1914). On Lincoln's birthday in February 1919, she was a member of the Chicago delegation to the victory dinner in Washington, D.C., celebrating passage of the Nineteenth Amendment. When the League of Women Voters was organized in 1920, Mary, like her cousin Marie Josephine Rozet who had also participated in the Chicago Equal Suffrage Association, became an active member.

Almost from the beginning of Jane and Mary's friendship, travel together was a part of their companionship. In the summer of 1893, Mary's parents invited Jane to vacation with the family in New Jersey. Then in 1896, Jane sailed with Mary and the elder Smiths to Europe for the summer. The two young women spent time on their own in England and visited the Tolstoy family in Russia (see especially JA to EGS, 29 [and 30] May 1896; JA to Gertrude Barnum, 22 May [June] 1896; JA to MRS, 22 [24] June 1896; JA to MRS, [26 and] 27 June 1896; JA to MRS, 27 June 1896; JA to Gertrude Barnum, 25 July 1896; and JA to Aylmer Maude, [30 July 1896], all above). Later, they sometimes traveled together to the conferences, speaking engagements, or special functions that became a more frequent part of Jane's life. Mary served as companion, protector, and secretary. While they did not go together to the Paris Exposition of 1900 for which Jane was a juror for the United States, they did attend the 1904 World's Fair in St. Louis, Missouri. After Mary's abdominal surgery in 1918, Jane and Mary spent almost two months together in Estes Park, Colorado, while Jane watched over the recuperating patient. Although Mary belonged to the various peace organizations that Jane helped found, she accompanied Jane to very few national or international peace movement gatherings during World War I; however, she did go with Jane to the Woman's International League for Peace and Freedom meetings in Europe after 1920. Their 1923–24 world tour, underwritten by Mary, combined vacation with peace activities and planned lectures and appearances by Jane, who was by then a noted world figure. On other occasions, they also went to Europe, Egypt and the Near East, Mexico, and the West Indies, and although they visited Columbia, South Carolina, together on several occasions, both women ultimately preferred summer vacations in the U.S. Northeast.

Beginning in the 1890s, Jane Addams vacationed at Lakeside, Michigan, a resort about seventy-five miles from Chicago, which also attracted such Hull-House residents and friends as Dr. Alice Hamilton, Eleanor and Gertrude Smith, and Dr. Bayard Taylor Holmes and his family. Although Addams was granted the first membership certificate of the Chikaming County Club in 1912, by 1914 she and Mary Rozet Smith had purchased a two-story summer cottage called "Yulecraig" with a multitude of sleeping rooms at Hulls Cove, in the Bar Harbor, Maine, area near Louise de Koven Bowen's elegant vacation home "Baymeath." From that time until they sold it in 1932, they spent a portion of most summers there together. Family, old friends, and Hull-House residents came often as guests. Jane could find peace there and time to write at least one of her books. James Weber Linn recalled one visit when despite Mary's three or four servants, he found her "with a pail and a scrubbing-brush, cleaning the stone 'front steps' before luncheon" (Linn, [Mary Rozet Smith]). As Jane and Mary aged, they found winters in Chicago difficult and spent time, often with Louise de Koven Bowen, at the Biltmore Hotel near Scottsdale or in Tucson, Arizona.

Without Mary's financial help and that of their mutual friend Louise de Koven Bowen, Jane Addams would have found these vacations and style of living difficult if not impossible to achieve or maintain. During the early Hull-House years, Jane had spent a great deal of her financial resources on the development of settlement programs, and though she made money from her speaking engagements and from her books and articles, gradually she became accustomed to Mary's financial support. At Christmas in 1891, when Mary tried to give Jane money for a desk, Jane protested that her sisters had sent her money to purchase a desk, and she returned Mary's check. But soon after, Jane began to accept Mary's help. On 3 April 1898, Jane informed Mary: "I have ordered a dress from Miss Fay, not light blue I regret to say but a dark one—if you really like it I will be proud to have it from you" (SCPC, JAC; *JAPM*, 3:1028). When Mary offered to make it possible for Jane to have a salary at Hull-House, Jane responded: "I can't take the 25.oo a month because I don't need it and there is no use in my pretending not to take a salary and then to accept so much. I shall have to take it some time maybe but not yet. Besides the more money I have the more I spend. I gave twenty five dollars to the Dorcas [Federal Labor Union] for books upon my return home and committed another extravagance, which I will confess when I see you" (1 Mar. 1897, SCPC, JAC; *JAPM*, 3:593). Much later, after she had stayed with Mary "month after month," Jane admitted, "I am aghast [w]hen I think how much <money> you have spent on me and how much of every thing I have accepted like a greedy thing" (JA to MRS, 25 Aug. 1917, SCPC, JAC; *JAPM*, 11:143). Later in her life, Jane penned the following poem to Mary:

> The "mine" and "thine" of wedded folk
> Is often quite confusing
> And some times when they use the "ours"
> It sounds almost amusing.
>
> But you and I, may well defy
> Both married folk and single
> To do as well as we have done
> The "mine" and "thine" to mingle—
> ([Poem to Mary Smith], n.d., SCPC, JAC; *JAPM*, 45:1585)

The poem accompanied Jane's gift to Mary of a book by English essayist Charles Lamb. After the death of Mary's father in 1912, Jane became a more frequent guest in the Walton Place house, and by the mid-1920s she was there so often that she had her own bedroom. Mary's nephew Charles M. Mather-Smith, who lived in Mary's household during the 1920s, recalled that "Aunt Mary had two rooms and a bath on the second Floor on the left hand side and on the right hand side of the second Floor was a room for Aunt Mary's Friend (a Piano Teacher [Eleanor Smith]) with a Bath between another room for Aunt Mary's other Friend Jane Addams" (26 Aug. 1985, JAPP, MRS Files). There were usually four servants in the house, and every meal, breakfast, lunch, and dinner, was especially prepared and formally served in the dining room. "Although Aunt Mary never wore her religion on her shirt sleeves, she always prayed for other people and said grace at the table," Charles M. Mather-Smith reported (26 Aug. 1985, JAPP, MRS Files).

Despite the traditional courtesies observed in the Smith home whether on Walton Place in Chicago or at Hulls Cove in Bar Harbor, it was a lively place to be, particularly if you were one of the many children who visited. Mary especially enjoyed Florence Kelley's children, Jane's nieces and nephews, and the children of her own siblings. She included the children of close friends in special events and outings that she hosted. When Lyman Silsbee Smith's parents were fighting over who would have custody of him during their divorce proceedings, he lived with his aunt Mary, who invited Lyman's cousin Charles Mather to stay to keep him company. "Back in the middle 1920[s], Aunt Mary had me up to visit her and stay for a few weeks in her beautiful second home in Hulls Cove Maine across the bay from Bar Harbor," nephew Charles M. Mather-Smith recalled. "I was a young boy and she was always wonderful to me. She always made me feel special always" (26 Aug. 1985, JAPP, MRS Files). Mary provided gifts or checks on each child's birthday and at Christmas and made it possible for Jane Addams to do the same. Jane Addams "always gave me a Christmas or Birthday present like a pen or some little thing to go on my desk" wrote Charles M. Mather-Smith. "I always thought that Aunt Mary paid for them" (26 Aug. 1985, JAPP, MRS Files). Another Smith family friend, Edwina M. Lewis, recalled that "Mary Smith was very close & loyal to her own child hood friends and their children who often were included in the parties she arranged." Edwina Lewis's godfather, Charles Frederic, was Mary's brother, and Edwina often played with his daughter, Sara Rozet Smith, at the Smith home next door to MRS's home until the Charles Frederic Smiths divorced in 1908. Lewis remembered that Mary Smith "often planned lovely things for us when I visited Sara, . . . Trips to the circus, Miss Addams always with us—Trips to Hull House for Plays—one night Sara & I were invited to spend the night & Miss Addams let us sleep in her bed—I don't remember where she went for we had her room" (27 Aug. 1985, JAPP, MRS Files). James Weber Linn savored the memories of Christmas dinners at Mary's home "when he was a child; and so did his children when they were children; and how his grandchildren sat with round eyes and watched 'Miss Mary' carve the turkey, and laughed out suddenly at what she said, because all the older people around the ample table were laughing" (Linn, [Mary Rozet Smith]). Another "Aunt Mary" relative recalled a favorite Addams and Smith pastime, with or without children in attendance. It was called "'the poetry game.'" According to Mary's great-niece Ellen Sloan, "You write a question on the top of a sheet of paper, fold it over, and pass it to the next person, who writes a word and folds it over and passes it to a third person, who has to write a poem answering the question and containing the word" (12 Nov. 1985, JAPP, MRS Files).

Mary was charming and gracious. Noted for her essential gaiety and her ability to give others hope, assurance, and contentment, she had beauty, wit, integrity, a sense of responsibility, and practiced generosity as if she had made it the core of her life's work. "She cared for almost literally nothing except the content and welfare of others, and her own consciousness of the oddity, the quirkiness, of life." She loved being amused and being amusing. "A little preliminary chuckle, a born story-teller's straightening of the face, and she would offer some brief tale of yesterday or of forty years before, so delicious in its detachment that you never know which was its greater fascination, its matter or its manner," recalled Jane's nephew and biographer James Weber Linn, who knew Mary well ([Mary Rozet Smith]). "Social injustice, the cold or careless denial of opportunity to the poor, the weak, the unaccepted, drove her almost frantic, but never quite, for what with her utmost effort she could not alter, she could still make seem absurd with wit and laughter." Among her strengths, Linn identified her tolerance for "decisive thinkers," her "patience," her ability as a conversationalist, and her "brightness." Yet of all her attributes, "Love was her 'greatest thing in the world', and about all she asked for her devotion was that you should need it." Linn wondered, "[W]hat will many do, who were directly dependent on her for the daily kindness that makes life happy instead of a mere matter of indifference" ([Mary Rozet Smith]).

As Jane's health began to decline notably in the 1920s, Mary's personal and financial support meant even more. By 1930 Mary had arranged for a special fund to support Jane Addams. It was administered through the Northern Trust Company in Chicago. From 1930 through 1932, as the Great Depression gathered strength, the Northern Trust was to provide $4,500 to Jane Addams annually in equal monthly installments. Eleanor Smith and other close friends were also to receive yearly allowances. In 1933 the trust fund was renewed for another three years or until the death of Jane Addams and Eleanor Smith. Under this set of instructions, Jane Addams was to receive an annual stipend of $3,000 and Eleanor Smith $1,200. There was also provision that after Mary Smith's death, the net income of the trust was to be paid in equal portions to Jane and Eleanor, with the entire net income amount to the survivor of the two until her death, at which time the trust would be folded into Mary Rozet Smith's estate.

Mary Rozet Smith died on Thursday, 22 February 1934, from bronchial pneumonia. It was the day that Jane and Mary had planned to leave for a vacation with Louise de Koven Bowen in Phoenix, Arizona. According to Eleanor Smith, Mary had a bad cold in early February, and by Tuesday, 13 February, Mary had decided to recover in bed. Doctors were called in to consult when her temperature rose to 102 degrees; however, they were not overly concerned until Wednesday, 21 February, when they discovered that her entire right lung was infected with pneumonia. She grew rapidly worse, and though she seemed to rally early the next morning, Eleanor Smith recorded that "an unfavorable change came at 1 o'clock, and she died peacefully at 2" ([Death of Mary Rozet Smith], SCPC, JAC; *JAPM*, 25:913).

Jane Addams, whom Mary Smith had identified as a "docile patient" (MRS to Charles Hull Ewing, 13 Feb. 1934, UIC, JAMC, Hull-Culver; *JAPM*, 25:759), was lodged in her bedroom in Mary's home to "be kept perfectly quiet for several weeks" in the hope of complete recovery from a severe heart attack she had suffered on 9 February at Hull-House (Smith, Eleanor, [Death of Mary Rozet Smith], SCPC, JAC; *JAPM*, 25:913). Louise de Koven Bowen reported to Charles Hull Ewing that "the shock [Mary's death] was a terrible one to her [Jane] as she did not know until the day Mary died that she was so ill" (9 Mar. 1934, UIC, JAMC, Hull-Culver; *JAPM*, 25:1011). Mary's funeral was held on Monday, 26 February, at 11:00 A.M. in her home. A string trio and choir from the Hull-House Music School provided the music, and a close family friend, Rev. Edwin B. Niver, of Baltimore, conducted the service. Jane was forbidden from leaving her bed, which was moved close to the door of her bedroom so that she might hear the service, and Louise Bowen sat with her. Mary Smith's body was taken to Graceland Cemetery in Chicago and then quietly cremated on 26 February 1934. At a later date, according to Mary's niece, ninety-seven-year-old

Ann Mather-Smith Fischbeck (Ann Mather-Smith Fischbeck in a telephone conversation with Jane Addams biographer Lucy Knight, 15 Oct. 2011), Ann's sister Grace Mary Smith Turner and her husband, Allen, released the ashes into Lake Michigan from the bluff site of the Mather-Smith's summer house in Highland Park, north of Chicago. Family legend held that the site had been one of Mary Smith's favorite places.

Mary left an estate valued conservatively at $230,000 ($4,191,146 in 2016 dollars), composed primarily of Bradner-Smith and Company stock, her home valued at $30,000 ($546,671 in 2016 dollars), and interests in the Mather Smith Building Corporation; the Hollenback Estate of Wilkes-Barre, Pennsylvania; life insurance; the Ohio Kingsbury Trust; and investments in the First National Bank of Chicago and the Northern Trust Company of Chicago. Several of her oldest friends and all of her servants received small gifts and the faithful Polly a lifetime annuity of $1,000 annually. Hull-House received $25,000, and Jane and Eleanor received $5,000 ($91,112 in 2016 dollars) each in addition to their lifetime stipends from the trust Mary had established for them in 1930; however, the bulk of her estate was to be divided between her brothers and their children.

During February, March, and into April, condolence notes and letters poured in to Jane Addams and Hull-House from friends throughout the United States and abroad. Mary had long been associated with Jane Addams and Hull-House, and all who knew the settlement's women residents loved and admired Mary. Addams's close friends realized Mary's special significance and understood what the loss would be to Jane. Lillian Wald, ill at her Connecticut home, tried to describe her feelings for Mary. "I cannot bring up the outlines of any part of her. She has become suddenly elemental. Instead of her physically, I feel beauty—goodness—humor—devotion—wisdom & love—I want to see her too but though I try that, part of her eludes me. That sense of what made her the being that she was and that only—I have never known before with any one else" (Lillian Wald to JA, 23 Feb. 1934, SCPC, JAC; *JAPM*, 25:874–75). After the memorial service at Hull-House on 5 March, Louise Bowen wrote that "Hull-House is quite bereft, . . . not only because Mary partly supported the Music School and looked after her house on the [Bowen] Country Club grounds at Waukegan, but because she had some part in every department of Hull-House and was just adored by all the residents" (Louise de Koven Bowen to Charles Hull Ewing, 9 Mar. 1934, UIC, JAMC, Hull-Culver; *JAPM*, 25:1012). Ellen Gates Starr, who understood the kinship of Mary and Jane perhaps better than almost everyone else, wrote to Jane immediately: "I was quite unprepared. That journey to New York and out to Suffern to see me on a bitter cold day was too much. Of course Mary never spared herself. I could never think of a flaw in her character; or suggest any way in which she could have improved, really; perfect of her pattern,—and such a lovely pattern! Often when I have thought that one of you would have to finish the journey without the other after so many journeyings 'with Mary Smith beside me' I have been glad that nobody had to decide that" (23 Feb. 1934, SCPC, JAC; *JAPM*, 25:851–52). The phrase "with Mary Smith beside me" was a quote from a poem about Mary that Jane wrote: "But now I journey quite content / With Mary Smith beside me, / And thirty comes and forty too / But still no woes betide me." Jane Addams left no timely written record of her reaction to Mary's death; however, the 1935 anniversary of Mary's death did not pass unnoticed. College-aged Jane Addams Linn, Jane's niece who happened to be visiting Louise de Koven Bowen and Jane in February 1935 at the Biltmore Hotel in Phoenix, Arizona, wrote in her account of the visit: "[A]bout the middle of the week was the day on which Mary Smith had died just a year before. Aunt Jane missed her terribly. Probably not having her was the causes of Aunt Jane's unhappiness. On that day she and I drove to Phoenix where I picked out some flowers in an artistic little florists shop. . . . These flowers she took to Mrs. Bowen who in turn gave her some. Nothing was said all day on the subject but both of them were very quiet. Gee I felt sorry for Aunt Jane" ("At Arizona with Aunt Jane," 24–26). Following the death of Jane Addams in 1935, a Mary Rozet Smith Memorial Cottage was opened at the Hull-House Bowen County Club in Waukegan, Illinois. It continued as a vivid reminder of her life and generosity long after the Smith family home on Walton Place was sold and eventually demolished to make way for a new Ogden public school, built in 1952.

# *Bibliography*

This bibliography is divided into ten categories: (1) Manuscripts and Archives Collections; (2) Unpublished Documents, Clippings, and Individual Manuscripts; (3) Printed and Manuscript Sources of Genealogy and Vital Statistics, Government Records, Reports, and Returns; (4) Rare Book Collections; (5) Photograph Collections; (6) Directories, Published Minutes and Reports, Annuals, Catalogs, and Announcements; (7) Newspapers and Magazines; (8) General Internet Sources; (9) Newspaper, Journal, and Magazine Articles and Chapters from Books; and (10) Books. The most comprehensive presentation of the papers of Jane Addams is the eighty-two-reel microfilm edition of *The Jane Addams Papers*, edited by Mary Lynn McCree Bryan et al. (Ann Arbor, Mich.: University Microfilms International, 1985–86). A digital edition of the Jane Addams Papers, 1901–35, is in preparation at the Jane Addams Papers Project, Ramapo College, Mahway, New Jersey. For a bibliography of the writings and speeches of Jane Addams, consult Mary Lynn McCree Bryan, Nancy Slote, and Maree de Angury, *The Jane Addams Papers: A Comprehensive Guide* (Bloomington: Indiana University Press, 1996). For a full list of symbols for manuscript collections and repositories, see pages liv–lvii of this volume.

## *1. Manuscripts and Archives Collections*


Amherst College, Mass., Library, Archives and Special Collections
  Bayard Taylor Holmes Letters
Andover Newton Theological School, Newton Centre, Mass.
  Edwin A. Waldo Collection
  Trask Library, Archives and Special Collections
Art Institute of Chicago, Chicago Architects Oral History Project, Ernest R. Graham Study
  Center for Architectural Drawings, Department of Architecture
Baldwin County, Bay Minette, Ala., Department of Archives and History
Bar Harbor Historical Society, Bar Harbor, Maine

Beloit College, Wis., Library, Archives, Beloit

British Library, London, United Kingdom, Department of Manuscripts
- John Elliot Burns Papers

Cambridge Historical Society, Cambridge, Mass.
- Sara Bull Papers, 1830–1910

Cambridge University, Cambridge, United Kingdom, Kings College Library
- Charles Robert Ashbee Journals

Cedarville Area Historical Society, Cedarville, Ill.

Chicago Avenue Church, Chicago, Records

Chicago Board of Education, Archives
- Biographical Files
- School Files

Chicago History Museum, Chicago Historical Society
- C. H. Jordan Funeral Co. Records
- Charity Organization Society of the City of Chicago Records
- Chicago Commons Papers
- Chicago Woman's Club Records
- Citizens' Association of Chicago Records
- Civic Federation of Chicago Papers, 1894–98
- Crane-Lillie Papers
- George C. Sikes Collection
- Lorado Taft Papers
- Louise Hadduck de Koven Bowen Collection
- Mary Eliza McDowell Papers of the University of Chicago Settlement Records
- Municipal Voters League Papers, 1896–98
- Obituary File
- United Charities of Chicago Collection: Chicago Relief and Aid Society Records
- Visiting Nurse Association of Chicago

Chicago Public Library, Harold Washington Library Center, Special Collections
- Chicago Theological Seminary, Chicago, Archives
- Ewing Street, Chicago, File
- New England Congregational Church, Chicago, Records

Cincinnati Historical Society

Col. Robert R. McCormick Research Center, Cantigny Park, Wheaton, Ill.
- Robert R. McCormick Archives

Columbia University, New York, Libraries, Special Collections
- Kelley Family Papers

Congregational Library, Boston, Archives
- Biographical Files

Cook County, Chicago, Recorder
- Death Certificates
- Marriage Licenses

Cook County, Circuit Court, Chicago, Archives
- Divorce Records
- Probate Division, Records

Cornell University, Ithaca, N.Y.
- Library, Division of Rare and Manuscript Collections
- Wilbur Olin Atwater Papers

Duke University, Durham, N.C., Rare Book, Manuscript, and Special Collections Library
  H. J. Gow Diaries, 1896–97
Fourth Presbyterian Church, Chicago, Archives
Freeport, Ill., Public Library, Local History and Genealogy Collection
Garrett-Evangelical Theological Seminary, Evanston, Ill.
  Chicago Training School for City, Home, and Foreign Missions Records
Glenwood School for Boys, St. Charles, Ill., Archives
Harvard University, Cambridge, Mass.
  Alice Hamilton Papers
  Archives
Holiday Home Camp, Lake Geneva, Wis., and Chicago, Records, 1887–1987
Illinois Institute of Technology, Chicago, Archives, Lewis Institute Records
Illinois Secretary of State, State Archives, Springfield
  Corporation Records
  Death Index
  Marriage Index
Illinois State Historical Society, Library, Springfield
  George Schilling Papers
Indiana University, Bloomington, Lilly Library
  Mrs. Sarah Alice Haldeman Manuscripts
Jane Addams Papers Project, Fayetteville, N.C.
  Alice DeLoach Files
  Anna Hostetter Haldeman Addams File
  Louise Hadduck de Koven Bowen Files
  Mary Addams Hulbert Files
  Mary Rozet Smith Files
Kenilworth Historical Society, Ill., Miscellaneous Manuscripts and Errata
Lake Forest University, Ill., Archives, Lake Forest College Records
Library of Congress, Washington, D.C.
  Manuscripts Division
    McKim (Leonora Jackson and William Duncan McKim) Collection
  Music Division
    National Woman's Trade Union League Records
    William Dawson Johnson Papers
London Metropolitan Archives, Records of Toynbee Hall
Massachusetts Institute of Technology, Boston, Special Collections, Gerard Swope Collection
Meadville Lombard Theological School of Lombard College, Ill., Jenkin Lloyd Jones Papers
Newberry Library, Chicago
  Pullman Palace Car Company Archives
New York Public Library
  Edward W. Ordway Papers
  Florence Kelley Papers
  Lillian D. Wald, Incoming, Papers
  Nicholas Kelley Papers

Northwestern University, Evanston, Ill., Library, Special Collections, Julia Hintermeister Papers
Genealogical Collection
Graham Taylor Papers
Oberlin College, Ohio, Archives, John Henry Barrow Papers
Presbyterian Church in the U.S.A., Philadelphia
General Assembly Minutes
Synod of Illinois Minutes
Radcliffe College, Cambridge, Mass., Arthur and Elizabeth Schlesinger Library on the History of Women in America
Denison House Papers
Hamilton Family Papers
Mary Kenney O'Sullivan Papers
Richland County, Columbia, S.C., Probate Court Records
Rockford University, Ill., Howard Colman Library, Rockford College Archives
Anna Lathrop Case File
Board of Trustees Records
Julia C. Lathrop Papers
Lena C. Leland File
Presidents Papers
Rockford College Association of the Northwest Records
Sarah Anderson (Ainsworth) Papers
Rush University, Chicago, Library, Archives
Smith College, Northampton, Mass.
Archives, Biographical Files
Sophia Smith Collection, Ellen Gates Starr Papers
State Historical Society of Wisconsin, Madison
Anita McCormick Blaine Papers
City Homes Association Records
Cyrus H. McCormick Jr. Papers
Harold F. McCormick Papers
Henry Demarest Lloyd Papers
Nettie Fowler McCormick Papers
Richard T. Ely Papers
Swarthmore College, Pa., Swarthmore College Peace Collection
Emily Greene Balch Papers
Jane Addams Collection
Toledo-Lucas Co., Toledo, Ohio, Public Library
Local History Department
Samuel M. Jones Collection
Toynbee Hall, London, Barnett Research Center
Barnett Library and Archives Collection
University of Chicago, Joseph Regenstein Library
Albion W. Small Papers
Archives: Presidents' Papers, 1899–1925
Bayard Taylor Holmes Papers, 1880–95

Chicago Manual Training School Records
Chicago School of Civics and Philanthropy Papers
Frederick Taylor Gates Papers
George Ellsworth Hooker Collection
George Herbert Mead Papers
Jenkin Lloyd Jones Papers
Miscellaneous Manuscripts
Oscar Lovell Triggs Papers
William Rainey Harper Papers
William Vaughn Moody Papers, 1892–1925
University of Illinois at Chicago, Richard J. Daley Library, Special Collections
Adena Miller Rich Papers
Dame Henrietta O. Barnett Collection
Edith Saluda Watson Collection
Eleanor and Gertrude Smith Papers
Ellen Gates Starr Collection
Eric Hjorth Collection
Esther Loeb Kohn Papers
Haldeman-Julius Family Papers and Supplement
Hull-Culver Papers
Hull-House Association Records
Humpel-Zeman Collection
Illinois Humane Society Records
Jane Addams Memorial Collection
Juvenile Protective Association Papers
Louise Smith Papers
Madeleine Wallin Sikes Collection
Mary Hill Swope Papers, 1899–1933
Mrs. Karl Detzer (Dorothy Detzer) Collection
Rachelle and Victor Yarros Collection
Rose Marie Gyles File
Stanley Ross Linn, Family Papers
Sunset Club Records
University of Iowa, Iowa City, Special Collections, Hevey White Papers
University of Michigan, Ann Arbor
Bentley Historical Library, Michigan Historical Collections
Eliza Jane Read Sunderland Papers
Henry Carter Adams Papers
Pond Family Papers
Vertical File
University Library, Department of Rare Books and Special Collections
American Literary Manuscripts, Irving K. Pond, Letters
University of Southern Illinois, Carbondale, Special Collections Research Center
John Dewey Papers, 1858–1970
University of Warwick, England, Working Papers of John Trevor
Vassar College, Poughkeepsie, N.Y., Special Collections, Archives
Alumnae Association File, 1919–1944

Wellesley College, Mass., Wellesley College Library, Archives
Alumnae Biographical Files
Vida D. Scudder Papers
Wheaton College, Ill., Bill Graham Center Archives
Records of the Moody Church, Chicago
Woman's Union Missionary Society Records
Winnetka Historical Society, Ill.
Wisconsin, State of, Department of Health Services
Death Records
Mendota State Hospital Records
Yale University, New Haven, Conn., Sterling Memorial Library, Department of Manuscripts and Archives
Thomas Davidson Papers

## 2. *Unpublished Documents, Clippings, and Individual Manuscripts*

"A. A. McCormick, Ex-Editor and Alderman, Dies." *Chicago Daily Tribune*, 17 Nov. 1925.
"About a School Site." *Chicago Daily Tribune*, 19 July 1892.
Adams, Edwin Augustus, and [Caroline Amelia Plimpton] Adams, biographical notes. Congregational Library, Boston.
Addams, Jane. [Address at the Wedding of Gerard Swope and Mary Dayton Hill]. [20 Aug. 1901]. 10 pp., SCPC, JAC; *JAPM*, 46:1067–77; and 20 Aug. 1901, 3 pp., MIT, Swope.
———. Address Book, 1883–1898. H and ADS, 122 pp., SCPC, JAC; *JAPM*, 27:1150–1209.
———. "Anti-lynching Address." 12 Dec. 1899. TMs, A annotations, 3 pp. and attached A note. SCPC, JAC, *JAPM*, 46:957–61.
———. [Anti-lynching Address]. [12 Dec. 1899]. TMs carbon fragment, A annotations, 3 pp., SCPC, JAC; *JAPM*, 46:962–65.
———. [Birthday Poem to Alexandra Tolstoi]. [ca. 30 July 1934]. TMsI, A annotations, 2 pp., UIC, JAMC, Rich; *JAPM*, 49:398–400.
———. ["A Birthday Song for Mary"]. n.d. TMs. SCPC, JAC; *JAPM*, 45:1272.
———. [A Book That Changed My Life]. [1927]. TMsS carbon, A annotations, 4 pp., SCPC, JAC; *JAPM*, 48:852–56.
———. "Course: 'Divine Plan of Redemption' Fulfilled in the Old Testament [Remarks on Mrs. Humphrey's Lectures]." [ca. Feb 1889]. AMs, annotations, 28 pp., UIC, JAMC, Detzer; *JAPM*, 46:451–79.
———. "Diary, 1889–90." AD. SCPC, JAC; *JAPM*, 29:97–200.
———. "Diary, 1894–95." AD. SCPC, JAC; *JAPM*, 29:201–27.
———. "Diary, 1896." AD. SCPC, JAC; *JAPM*, 29:228–310.
———. "Diary [of speeches], Nov. 1896–1898." AD. SCPC, JAC; *JAPM*, 29:311–45.
———. "Diary, 1897." AD. SCPC, JAC; *JAPM*, 29: 346–75.
———. "Diary, 1897, 10–18 Feb." AD. SCPC, JAC; *JAPM*, 29:376–80.
———. "Diary, 1898." AD. SCPC, JAC; *JAPM*, 29:381–473.
———. "Diary, 1899." AD. SCPC, JAC; *JAPM*, 29:474–569.
———. "Diary, 1900." AD. SCPC, JAC; *JAPM*, 29:570–653.
———. "Diary, 1900, June–Aug." AD. SCPC, JAC; *JAPM*, 29:654–94.

———. "Ethical Survivals in City Immortality." [1897–Jan. 1898]. TMs carbon, A annotations, 23 pp., SCPC, JAC; *JAPM*, 46:815–38.

———. "First Outline of a Labor Museum at Hull-House, Chicago." [1900]. TMs carbon, A annotations, 20 pp. and title page. SHSW, Blaine; *JAPM*, 46:966–87, 51:378–98.

———. *First Report for the Labor Museum of Hull-House—1901–1902*. Chicago: printed for Hull-House Association, [1902?]. UIC, JAMC, Hull-House Association, and SCPC, Balch; *JAPM*, 46:1078–88, 51:401–10.

———. [Fund-Raising Record], "Book Used for Ten Years, 1895–1905." AMsS. 1 Jan. 1895–1 Jan. 1905, UIC, JAMC, Hull-House Association; *JAPM*, 49:1765–91.

———. "Hull-House: A Social Settlement." [1896, May]. PMs, AI annotations, 35 pp., SCPC, JAC; *JAPM*, 46:755–78.

———. "In Memoriam [William H. Colvin]." *Hull-House Bulletin*, 1 (15 Oct. 1896), UIC, JAMC, Hull-House Association; *JAPM*, 53:557, 55:197; Hull-House Scrapbook 3:96; *JAPM*, 46:779–80; Addendum 10:8ff.

———. [Introduction] to *What Then Must We Do?* by Leo Tolstoy. [Post–13 Oct. 1927]. Printed Ms, A annotations, 3 pp., SCPC, JAC; *JAPM*, 48:880–83.

———. [Introduction] to *What Then Must We Do?* by Leo Tolstoy. 13 Jan. 1928. TMsS carbon, A annotation, 6 pp., SCPC; *JAPM*, 48:927–33.

———. "Mary Catherine Addams Linn Estate Account Book." 1894–98. UIC, JAMC; *JAPM*, 27:883–944.

———. [A Modern Lear]. [ca. 1912?]. TMs, A annotations, SCPC, JAC; *JAPM*, 47:611–38.

———. "A Modern Tragedy." [1894?]. TMs carbon fragment with A annotations, 1 p., SCPC, JAC; *JAPM*, 46:589–90.

———. "A Modern Tragedy." [1895?]. TMs carbon, A annotations, 12 pp., SCPC, JAC; *JAPM*, 46:647–59.

———. "A Modern Tragedy: An Analysis of the Pullman Strike." [1896?]. TMs, A annotations, 15 pp., SCPC, JAC; *JAPM*, 46:722–37.

———. [Notes on Tolstoy and the Russian Revolution]. [1918?]. A and TMs, 10 pp., SCPC, JAC; *JAPM*, 47:1710–20.

———. "Outgrowths of Toynbee Hall." [3 Dec. 1891]. TMs, A and H annotations, 16 pp. with cover with AI note. JA's cover note dates the speech 1890. According to the Chicago Woman's Club Board minutes, JA delivered the speech on 3 Dec. 1891. SCPC, JAC; *JAPM*, 46:480–97.

———. *The Papers of Jane Addams*. Edited by Mary Lynn McCree Bryan et al. Microfilm edition, 82 reels. Sanford, N.C.: Microfilming Corporation of America; Ann Arbor, Mich.: University Microfilms International, 1985–86.

———. [Poem to Mary Rozet Smith]. [ca. 1900]. TMs carbon, 1 p., SCPC, JAC; *JAPM*, 46:988–98.

———. [Remarks on Tolstoi and the Russian Revolution]. [1918?]. TMsI carbon, A annotations, 15 pp., SCPC, JAC; *JAPM*, 47:1721–36.

———. "A Retrospect." [1896?]. A and TMs carbon, A annotations, SCPC, JAC; *JAPM*, 45:1595–99.

———. "The Russian Complication in the Light of Tolstoy's Teachings." [1918?]. A and TMs carbon, A annotations, 20 pp. and cover with note. SCPC, JAC; *JAPM*, 47:1737–58.

———. "See Sin in Each War." Address by Jane Addams at public meeting about the Boer War held 27 Jan. 1900. *Chicago Chronicle*, 28 Jan. 1900.

———. "Still Opposed to Powers [letter to the editor]." *Chicago Evening Post*, 20 Feb. 1900; *JAPM*, 55:549.

———. "Three Efforts of Contemporary Russia to Break through Current Abstractions." Aug. 1918. TMs carbon, A annotations, 18 pp. and title page with A note. SCPC, JAC; *JAPM*, 47:1759–78.

———. "To Bipps from J.A." [1926?]. AMsI, 1 p., SCPC, JAC; *JAPM*, 45:1600–2.

———. "Tolstoy and Gandhi." 20 Aug. 1931. TMs carbon, A annotations with attached A and T fragments, 20 pp., SCPC, JAC; *JAPM*, 48:1545–71.

———. "Tolstoy and Gandhi." 30 Aug. 1931. TMs carbon, A annotations and attached A and T fragment, 18 pp., SCPC, JAC; *JAPM*, 48:1572–94.

———. "Tolstoy and Gandhi." [30 Aug.?] [1931]. TMs carbon, A annotations and cover with AI note. SCPC, JAC; *JAPM*, 48:1595–1614.

———. "Tolstoy and Gandhi." 10 Nov. 1931. TMs carbon, A and H annotations, 9 pp., SCPC, JAC; *JAPM*, 48:1666–75.

———. [Tolstoy and the Russian Soldiers]. [1917?]. TMs, 4 pp., SCPC, JAC; *JAPM*, 47:1558–62.

———. ["To M. R. S.] [Dec. 1896?]. AMsI, 2 pp., SCPC, JAC; *JAPM*, 45:1584–86.

———. "To 'Sasha' Tolstoy—on Her Fiftieth Birthday—July 1st, 1934." [ca. 30 July 1934]. TMs, carbon, A annotation, 2 pp. and cover with A note, 18 pp., SCPC, JAC; *JAPM*, 49:394–97.

———. "Total Earnings." [Dec. 1934?]. A and TD. SCPC, JAC; *JAPM*, 27:1077.

———. [Tribute to Allen B. Pond], 24–32. In "Memorial Service for Allen B. Pond." City Club, Chicago, 21 Apr. 1929. Stenographer's Transcription, carbon. UM, BHL, Mich. Hist. Col. Pond; *JAPM*, 48:1155–64.

———. Will. 24 May 1934. TDS. UIC, JAMC; *JAPM*.

Addams, Jane, and Ellen Gates Starr. "Hull-House, a Social Settlement. An Outline Sketch." Chicago: Hull-House, [May 1896]: 207–30. PMI with A annotations by Jane Addams, 35 pp., SCPC, JAC; *JAPM*, 46:755–78. Reprinted from Hull-House Residents, *Hull-House Maps and Papers*. New York: Thomas Y. Crowell, 1895.

———. "Hull-House: A Social Settlement at 335 South Halsted St., Chicago. An Outline Sketch." 1 Jan. 1894. TMs carbon with A annotations, 26 pp., SCPC, JAC; *JAPM*, 46:591–617.

"Additions to Hull House." *Chicago Record*, [3?] Dec. 1894. Hull-House Scrapbook 1:60; *JAPM*, Addendum 10:6ff.

"Address by Jane Addams [Present-Day Attitude towards Social Problems]." *Milwaukee Sentinel*, 2 Apr. 1900. SCPC, JAC; *JAPM*, 55:571.

"Advocates Public Kitchen." Unidentified clipping, Feb. 1894. SCPC, JAC, *JAPM*, 55:19.

"After a Big Dinner." *Chicago Herald*, 22 Dec. 1893.

"Aim to Stop Strikes." *Chicago Record*, 15 May 1897.

"The Alabama Italian Colony." *Chicago Daily Tribune*, 14 June 1890.

"Aldermen Are Indorsed." *Chicago Chronicle*, 1 Apr. 1898.

"Alice Marion Rowland." Family Search, International Genealogical Index, www.familysearch.org.

"Alien Law Is the Issue." *Chicago Record*, 2 Apr. 1898.

"Allen B. Pond, Militant Citizen." *Chicago News*, 19 Mar. 1929. SCPC, JAC; *JAPM*, 68:117.
"Allison V. Armour, Noted Yachtsman." *New York Times*, 7 Mar. 1941.
"All Meet as Sisters." *Chicago Daily Tribune*, 2 Jan. 1895.
"Alpha Sorosis Club Meets [Ursula L. Harrison]." *Chicago Daily Tribune*, 1 May 1899.
"Amanda Johnson, Nineteenth Ward Sanitary Inspector." *Chicago Daily Tribune*, 17 Jan. 1895.
"Amanda Johnson Rites." *Wisconsin State Journal* (Madison), 25 June 1949.
"Amateur Photography." *Chicago Daily Tribune*, 10 Mar. 1889.
"An American Tee-To-Tum." *New York Times*, 22 Jan. 1893.
"Ample Room for All Pupils." *Chicago Daily Tribune*, 15 June 1910.
Anderson, Paul. "The Good to Be Done: A History of the Juvenile Protective Association 1898–1976." Ph.D. diss., University of Chicago, 1988.
"Anderson and Gough Proven Unfit for Attendants." *Chicago Daily Tribune*, 14 Aug. 1895.
"And Not Leave the Other Undone." *Advance* (Chicago), 20 Oct. 1892. Hull-House Scrapbook 1:22; *JAPM*, Addendum 10:6ff.
"Anna Lathrop (VC Class of 1883)." Vassar College, Special Collections, Archives, Alumnae Association Biographical Files, 1919–1944.
"Announcements. The Kenwood Kindergarten. . . ." *Chicago Daily Tribune*, 6 Sept. 1891.
"Another New Model Lodging-House." *London Daily News*, 15 Aug. 1895.
"Another Praiseworthy Gift." *Chicago Post*, 27 Dec. 1892. Hull-House Scrapbook 1:46; *JAPM*, Addendum 10:6ff.
"Anti-war but Pro-Boer." *Chicago Times-Herald*, 28 Jan. 1900. SCPC, JAC; *JAPM*, 55:543.
"Applause for Hardie. Crowd at the Auditorium." *Chicago Record*, 3 Sept. 1895.
Applegate, Roberta. "They Wear the Years Like Fine Clothes." *Miami Herald*, 11 Nov. 1961.
"Are Reform Aldermen for Sale?" *Chicago Inter Ocean*, 1 Apr. 1898.
"Are the New Combinations Socially Dangerous?" *Chicago Inter Ocean*, 17 Sept. 1899.
"Armstrong Is Confident." *Chicago Record*, 4 Apr. 1898.
"Art for the Masses." *Chicago Journal*, 27 May 1890. Hull-House Scrapbook 1:3; *JAPM*, Addendum 10:6ff.
"Articles of Association." [Lake Geneva, (Wis.), Fresh-Air Association]. In "Holiday Home Camp, 1887–1987." [Chicago: Holiday Home Camp Association, 1987], 1.
"Art [Locke, Josephine Carson]." *Chicago Daily Tribune*, 17 Sept. 1899.
"Art Matters in Chicago. Something about the Industrial Art Association." *Chicago Daily Tribune*, 18 Mar. 1888.
Ashbee, Charles Robert. "Journals," II (1900), X (1908), XVIII (1915), and XX (1916), Cambridge University, Cambridge, United Kingdom, Kings College Library, Charles Robert Ashbee Journals.
"Asks Hull House to Bring Proof. Mayor to Institute Inquiry on Charles against Sanitary Inspection." *Chicago Daily Tribune*, 15 Apr. 1903.
"Association of Collegiate Alumnae." *Woman's Journal* (Boston), 1 Nov. 1890.
"At Paris Fair Jurors Meet." *New York Times*, 24 May 1900. SCPC, JAC; *JAPM*, 55:576.

"Attack the Dividend. Pullman Strikers Aroused." *Chicago Record*, 16 May 1894.
"B. W. Firman, Oak Park, Dead." *Chicago Daily Tribune*, 6 June 1911.
"Babies' Milk Fund Grows." *Chicago Daily Tribune*, 29 Nov. 1910.
"Bad for Big Store Bill." *Chicago Daily Tribune*, 30 May 1897.
"Bad Tenements." *Chicago Commons* 1, no. 11 (Feb. 1897): 2.
Baker, Helen Cody. "Mrs. J. T. Bowen, Social Pioneer." *Chicago Daily New*, 4 Mar. 1939.
Ball, Mrs. Ernest W. "Leaders against Child Labor." *Chicago Daily Tribune*, 22 Oct. 1911.
Barnes, Clifford W. "Hull-House, Chicago." *Record of Christian Work*, Oct. 1893. Hull-House Scrapbook 1:43; *JAPM*, Addendum 10:6ff.
———. *Reminiscences of Clifford W. Barnes*. [Lake Forest, Ill.], 1942–43. TMs. CHM, CHS.
"[Barnes, Clifford Webster] Obituary." *Chicago Daily Tribune*, 19 Sept. 1944.
"Bay Oaks Home: 'The Nicest Place in the Whole U.S.A.'" *Miami Herald*, 18 Nov. 1962.
"Beauties of the Christian Home." *Chicago Daily Tribune*, 13 Sept. 1893.
Bedell, Leila G. "A Chicago Toynbee Hall." *Woman's Journal* (Boston) 20 (25 May 1889): 162.
Beedy, Mary E. "From the Archives: The Higher Education of Women, from the *Manchester Guardian*, January 18, 1873." *Guardian Review*, 17 Feb 2005.
"Believes Single Tax Will Be the Issue [Father Huntington's comments]." *Chicago Daily Tribune*, 1 Jan. 1890.
"[Benedict, Amzi] Obituary." *Chicago Daily Tribune*, 21 Apr. 1913.
"Betrayed by Tanner." *Chicago Times-Herald*, 6 Sept. 1897.
"Bid for the College Girls." *Chicago Daily Tribune*, 18 Feb. 1900. SCPC, JAC; *JAPM*, 55:546.
"Bill to Help the Child Laborers." *Chicago Daily Tribune*, 18 Feb. 1897.
"Bindery Girls' Meeting; The First Open Session of Their Union since Its Organization." *Chicago Daily Tribune*, 25 Aug. 1891.
"Biographical Note." Guide to the Oscar Lovell Triggs Papers, 1903, University of Chicago Library. www.lib.uchicago.edu/e/sere/findingaids/view.
"Biography of Rachelle and Victor Yarros." Rachelle and Victor Yarros Collection: An Inventory of its Records at the University of Illinois at Chicago, UIC, SC, Mss.
"Biography of Sara Thorp Bull." Guide to the Sara Bull Papers, 1830–1910. Cambridge (Mass.) Historical Society. www.cambridgehistory.org/library.
"Bishop-Elect Muldoon Talks of His Increased Work as If the Detail of an Archdiocese Were Only Play." *Chicago Daily Tribune*, 14 July 1901.
"Bits of Mexico Looms Larger on West Side." *Chicago Daily Tribune*, 24 Oct. 1937.
Blum, Betty J., comp. "Oral History of Lawrence Bradford Perkins." Compiled under the auspices of the Chicago Architects Oral History Project, the Ernest R. Graham Study Center for Architectural Drawings, Department of Architecture. Chicago: Art Institute of Chicago, 2000.
"Board of Conciliation Named." *Chicago Daily Tribune*, 8 May 1894.
"[Bogue, Lucy D.] Death Notice." *New York Times*, Dec. 6, 1953.
"[Bogue, Mrs. R. G.] Death Notices." *Chicago Daily Tribune*, 22 Jan. 1919.
"The Boss and His Machine." *Chicago Inter Ocean*, 3 Apr. 1898.
"Bound by Ties of Friendship; First Reception Given by the Bindery Girls' Protective Union." *Chicago Daily Tribune*, 1 May 1891.

"Bound to Educate Them; The Children Must Be Compelled to Attend School." *Chicago Daily Tribune*, 20 Jan. 1889.

Bowen, Louise de Koven. "Autobiography of the Only Child of an Only Child." AMs. (1912?). 24 pp., SCPC, JAC.

Bowen-Spencer, Michele Andrea. "The Institutional Church and Social Settlement, 1900–1904; Reverdy C. Ransom's Church for the Black Masses." Master's thesis, University of North Carolina at Chapel Hill, 1994.

Bowie, JoAnne W. "Alice D. Kellogg." 30 June 1982. Dup. TMs., 1 p., private collection.

"Brick-Makers Go Out." *Chicago Record*, 15 May 1894.

"British Writer Chicago's Critic." *Chicago Daily Tribune*, 6 Jan. 1903.

Brodlique, Eva H. "A Toynbee Hall Experiment in Chicago." *Chautauquan*, Sept. 1890. Hull-House Scrapbook 1:5; *JAPM*, Addendum 10:6ff.

"Brooks Classical School" [Advertisement]. *Chicago Daily Tribune*, 16 and 17 Sept. 1903.

[Browning Hall.] In "Epitome of General News." *Leicester Chronicle*, 11 July 1896.

Bruce, Josephine Beall Willson (1853–1923). "The Black Past: Remembered and Reclaimed." www.blackpast.org.

Brush, Mary Isabel. "Prominent Woman's Suffrage Workers Have Big Families: Duty of Motherhood Argument for Granting of the Ballot." *Chicago Sunday Tribune*, 3 Mar. 1912.

"Built for Children." *Chicago Journal American*, 12 Dec. 1895. Hull-House Scrapbook 3:30; *JAPM*, Addendum 10:8ff.

"[Bull, Mrs. Ole] Obituary." *New York Times*, 19 Jan. 1911.

Burgess, Wendy Kent. "This Beautiful Charity: Evolution of the Visiting Nurse Association of Chicago, 1889–1920." Dissertation for Ph.D. University of Wisconsin–Milwaukee, 1990. Ann Arbor, Mich.: University Microfilms International, 1990.

"Busy Day for Lady Aberdeen." *Chicago Daily News*, 2 Apr. 1897.

C. H. Jordan Funeral Co. "Day Book." 1896. CMH, CHS.

"C. J. Hull Is Dead." *Chicago Daily Tribune*, 14 Feb. 1889.

"C.L.S.C. Chronology." *Chautauquan* 37 (July 1903): 896.

"Call for Peace." *Chicago Chronicle*, 2 Feb. 1900. SCPC, JAC; *JAPM*, 55:544.

"Campaign Is Ended." *Chicago Inter Ocean*, 3 Apr. 1898.

"[Carpenter, George B.] Obituary." *Chicago Daily Tribune*, 12 Dec. 1912.

"[Carpenter, Mrs. Elizabeth Curtis] Obituary." *Chicago Daily Tribune*, 26 June 1905.

Carter, Sarah N. "Mr. Waldo among Friends." *Andover (Mass.) Townsman*, [Apr. 1894]. Andover Newton Theological School, Newton Centre, Mass., Trask Library, Archives and Special Collections.

Case, Anna Lathrop File, 1897–1944, RC, Archives.

Case, Anna Lathrop File, 1919–44, Vassar College, Special Collections, Archives, Alumnae Association Files, 1914–1944.

"Catalogue of the First Loan Collection of Paintings in the Butler Gallery, Hull House, June 20th to July 6th, 1891." Hull-House Scrapbook 2:6; *JAPM*, Addendum 10:7ff.

"[Chapman, Frederick L.] Obituary." *Chicago Daily Tribune*, 24 May 1925.

"Charity Organization." *Chicago Inter Ocean*, 5 Jan. 1892.

"Charity Organization Society. Good Results Accomplished by North Side Branch." *Chicago Daily Tribune*, 16 May 1888.

Charity Organization Society of the City of Chicago. "What Is Charity Organization?" Chicago: R. R. Donnelley and Sons, 1892. CHM, CHS.

*Charles F. Mather Smith v. Kathleen McDonald Smith*. Divorce Records, 1908. Circuit Court of Cook County, Clerk of Court, Archives. Circuit Court g-285 326.

"Charles Hamill, Outstanding as Lawyer, Is Dead." *Chicago Daily Tribune*, Aug. 11, 1941.

"Charter Member of Union League Dies [Luther W. McConnell]." *Chicago Daily Tribune*, 15 Jan. 1907.

"Cheer Jane Addams." *Chicago Record*, 22 June 1900.

"Chicago Academy, Henry H. Babcock, Principal" [Advertisement]. *Chicago Daily Tribune*, 3 and 18 Sept. 1881.

"Chicago at a Glance; Nineteenth and Twentieth Wards." *Chicago Daily Tribune*, 24 June 1900.

Chicago Avenue Church, Ill. Executive Committee. Minutes, 1885–1900. Chicago Avenue Church, Ill., Archives

Chicago Board of Education, Schools Files.

Chicago Bureau of Charities, Certificate of Incorporation, 7 May 1895. ISA, Corporation Records.

"Chicago Delegation at Victory Dinner." *Chicago Daily Tribune*, 4 Feb. 1919.

"Chicago Jane Club." *Chicago Herald*, 18 May 1894. Hull-House Scrapbook 1:52; *JAPM*, Addendum 10:6ff.

"Chicago Photographers 1847 through 1900 as Listed in Chicago City Directories." 1958. CHM, CHS.

Chicago Relief and Aid Society. Minutes, 1877–1901, vol. 2. CHM, CHS, United Charities of Chicago Collection.

"Chicago Tanners on Strike." *New York Times*, 31 Mar. 1897.

Chicago Training School for City, Home and Foreign Missions [Announcement]. 1889–90, 1893–94. Garrett-Evangelical Theological Seminary, Evanston, Ill., Chicago Training School for City, Home and Foreign Mission Records.

"Chicago Will Be Scene of Therapy Conference Soon." *Chicago Daily Tribune*, 31 Aug. 1919.

Chicago Woman's Club. "Annual Report of the Secretary, March 6, 1889." 9 pp., CHM, CHS, CWC Records.

———. Minutes. "Regular Meeting of the Board, April 10, 1889." 9 pp., CHM, CHS, CWS Records.

———. Minutes, 1876–1891. CHM, CHS, CWC Records.

"Chicago Women Protest against Mrs. Pankhurst's Deportation; Wire Washington: Say She Is Only a Political Offender." *Chicago Daily Tribune*, 19 Oct. 1913.

"Children's Concert by Wm. L. Tomlins' Free Singing Class, at Hull House Hall, May 4, 1895." Program PD, 4 pp., Hull-House Scrapbook 3:52; *JAPM*, Addendum 10:7ff.

"Christmas Entertainments." *Hull-House Bulletin* 2, no. 1 (Jan. 1897): 6, UIC, JAMC, Hull-House Association; *JAPM*, 53:573.

"Chubb and His Socialism." *Chicago Daily Tribune*, 27 Dec. 1889.

"Chubb's Exposition of English Socialism." *Chicago Daily Tribune*, 24 Dec. 1889.

"Church Aid for the Poor." *Chicago Record*, 30 July 1897.

Cierpik, Anne Felicia. "History of the Art Institute of Chicago from Its Incorporation on May 24, 1879, to the Death of Charles L. Hutchinson." Master's thesis, De Paul University, 1957.

"City Ablaze with Golden Light." *Chicago Record*, 17 Oct. 1898.

City Homes Association. Broadside, n.d. SHSW, Blaine.

———. Minutes of the Meetings of the Tenement Committee, May–Oct. 1900. SHSW, Blaine.

"City Worse than Constantinople." *Chicago Daily Tribune*, 21 Mar. 1896.

"Civic Federation Monthly Meeting." *Chicago Chronicle*, 2 May 1897. SCPC, JAC; *JAPM*, 55:264.

Civic Federation of Chicago. *By-laws and Certificate of Incorporation . . . 1894*. [Chicago: Eight-Hour Herald, 1894]. CHM, CHS.

———. *The Civic Federation of Chicago and Its Work*. [Chicago]: Wm. C. Hollister & Brothers, 12 Dec. 1895. CHM, CHS.

———. "Industrial Department." In *The Civic Federation of Chicago, First Annual Report*, 75–81. [Chicago], May 1895. CHM, CHS.

"[Clark, Elizabeth Keep] Death Notice." *Chicago Daily Tribune*, 17 Feb. 1934.

"[Clark, Elizabeth Keep] Obituary." *Evanston (Ill.) Review*, 22 Feb., 1934.

"[Clark, George Mark] Obituary." *Chicago Daily Tribune*, 6 Apr. 1924.

Clark, Herma. "When Chicago Was Young: The Visiting Nurses Began Work of Mercy." *Chicago Daily Tribune*, 17 July 1938.

"Clean the Streets." *Chicago Daily Tribune*, 28 Mar. 1892.

"Clubs of Working Girls." *Chicago Daily Tribune*, 13 Oct. 1891. Hull-House Scrapbook 1:12; *JAPM*, Addendum 10:6ff.

"Clubs to Honor Indomitable Mrs. Bowen Tomorrow." *Chicago Daily Tribune*, 26 Feb. 1939.

"Club Women Urge Naming of New Parental School for Mrs. Alzina P. Stevens." *Chicago Times-Herald*, 22 June 1900.

Cole, George E. "19th Ward." 23 Mar. 1896. TMs. CHM, CHS, Citizens Association of Chicago Records, in Municipal Voters' League Papers, 1896–98.

"College Days Are Over [George Springer]." *Chicago Daily Tribune*, 20 June 1890.

"A College for Teachers." *Chicago Daily News*, 3 Oct. 1898.

"College for Teachers Open." *Chicago Daily News*, 1 Oct. 1898.

[College Settlement]. *New York World*, 16 June 1889. Hull-House Scrapbook 1:1; *JAPM*, Addendum 10:6ff

"College Settlement Survey." Hull-House Scrapbook 2:28½; *JAPM*, Addendum 10:7ff; *JAPM*, 54:661–77.

"Colonies for Labor." *Chicago Record*, 2 May 1894.

"Colored Club Women Entertained at Hull House." *Chicago Times-Herald*, 18 Aug. 1899.

"Colored Men's Sunday Club." *Times Herald*, 24 Oct. 1897. SCPC, JAC; *JAPM*, 55:329.

Commission on Chicago Historical and Architectural Landmarks. *Jane Addams' Hull-House and Dining Hall*. Chicago: Commission on Chicago Historical and Architectural Landmarks, 1974.

"Compositors Have a Dance." *Chicago Inter Ocean*, 22 Nov. 1893.

"Compulsory School Law Defective." *Chicago Record*, 20 June 1900.

"Congress of Labor. Formally Opened to Discuss Pressing Problems." *Chicago Inter Ocean*, 27 Aug. 1893.

Congress of Social Settlements, World's Columbian Exposition, Chicago. Committee on Settlements. Minutes, 7 May and 1 June 1893. HD. SCPC, JAC; *JAPM*, 41:986–98.

"Constitution of Hull-House Woman's Club." Chicago: Pioneer, 1898. UIC, JAMC, Hull-House Association; *JAPM*, 51:2–7.

"The Convention of Housekeepers." *Chicago Daily Tribune*, 23 Oct. 1892.

Cooley, Helen H. *Statement of the Civil Achievements of the Chicago Woman's Club Prepared at the Request of the Building Committee by the President of the Club*. [1915]. CHM, CHS, CWC Records.

Coonley, Mary L. Marriage License. 18 Apr. 1892. #180353 Cook County, Ill., County Recorder.

"[Coonley-Ward, Lydia Arms Avery] Obituary." *Chicago Daily Tribune*, Feb. 1924.

"Counts 75,000 Names. Strength of Voters' League." *Chicago Record*, 3 Mar. 1898.

"Course of Six Lectures on Physics." Hull-House College Extension Program. 1892. PD. Hull-House Scrapbook 2:18; *JAPM*, Addendum 10:7ff.

Cox, Alfred D. "Men and Women of the Hour: Settlement Worker Wins the French." *Saturday Evening Post*, 173, no. 5 (4 Aug. 1900): 7. SCPC, JAC; *JAPM*, 55:589.

"Crazed by Poverty." *Chicago Record*, 17 May 1894.

Crescent, Jacob. "A Guide to the Charles Hull Ewing Papers." University of Florida, George A. Smathers Libraries, Special and Area Studies Collections. www.library.ufl.edu.

"Cried 'Treason' to Prof. Laughlin." *New York Journal*, 1 May 1899. SCPC, JAC; *JAPM*, 55:507.

"Criticism of Church Methods." *Indianapolis Journal*, 30 Nov. 1898. SCPC, JAC; *JAPM*, 55:477.

"Crowds on All Sides." *Chicago Record*, 17 Oct. 1898.

Curlin, Eva V. "The Day in Altruria." *San Francisco Chronicle*, 4 Feb. 1894. Hull-House Scrapbook 1:47; *JAPM*, Addendum 10:6ff.

"Current Topics." *New World*, 29 Jan. 1898.

"D. D. Healy as a Czar." *Chicago Daily Tribune*, 31 Aug. 1895.

"Daniel O. Eshbaugh Dead." *New York Times*, 2 Oct. 1898.

"Dante School." TMs, n.d. CBE, School Files.

"[Day, William Horace] Obituary." *Chicago Daily Tribune*, 17 Mar. 1942.

"[Day, William Horace] Obituary." *New York Times*, 17 Mar. 1942.

[Day nurseries for colored children]. *Chicago Daily Tribune*, 26 May 1918.

"Dearborn Alumnae Elects Officers. It Also Takes Charge of the Hull House Dispensary." *Chicago Daily Tribune*, 29 Jan. 1894.

"Dearborn School Graduates Meet. Alumnae of Chicago's First Seminary Have Luncheon and Elect Officers." *Chicago Daily Tribune*, 18 Jan. 1914.

"Death of a Noted Surgeon. Roswell G. Bogue Departs after a Useful Life." *Chicago Daily Tribune*, 9 Dec. 1893.

"Death of L. J. M'Cormick." *Chicago Daily News*, 20 Feb. 1900.

"Death of Michael O'Brien." *Chicago Daily Tribune*, 29 Dec. 1901.

"Death of Mrs. Joseph Medill." *Chicago Daily Tribune*, 2 Oct. 1894.

"Deaths [Edith Nason]." *American Journal of Nursing* 13 (May 1913): 650–51.

"Defense of Unions." *Chicago Post*, Dec. 1900. SCPC, JAC; *JAPM*, 55:609.

"[Deknatel, Frederick H.] Death Notices." *Chicago Daily Tribune*, 17 Apr. 1949.

"Democracy in Social Life Coming." *Religio-Philosophical Journal*, 29 Mar. 1893. Hull-House Scrapbook 1:21½; *JAPM*, Addendum 10:6ff.
"The Depression of 1893." Vassar College. projects.vassar.edu.
"Difficulties in the Way of a New City Party." *New World*, 18 Jan. 1896.
"Directors of Banks." *Chicago Daily Tribune*, 10 Jan. 1893.
"Doing a Good Work." *Chicago Times-Herald*, 5 July 1895. Hull-House Scrapbook 3:14; *JAPM*, Addendum 10:8ff.
"Dore School." TMs, n.d. CBE, School Files.
Dow, Jenny. "The Chicago Toynbee Hall." *Unity*, 15 Mar. 1890. Hull-House Scrapbook 1:2; *JAPM*, Addendum 10:6ff.
"Dr. Charles B. Spahr." *Outlook* (30 Jan. 1904): 253.
"Dr. Goss Suffers Physical Breakdown." *Cincinnati Commercial Tribune*, 25 Sept. 1912.
"Dr. Josephine Milligan, Leader in Health, Civil Reforms, Passes Away." *Jacksonville (Ill.) Daily Journal*, 29 Aug. 1946.
"Dr. Rogers Resigns." *Chicago Record*, 13 June 1900.
"Dramatics." *Hull-House Bulletin* 2, no. 2 (1 Feb 1897): 6, UIC, JAMC, Hull-House Association; *JAPM*, 53:584.
"Dramatics." *Hull-House Bulletin* 2, no. 3 (1 Mar. 1897): 6, UIC, JAMC, Hull-House Association; *JAPM*, 53:595.
"Dramatics." *Hull-House Bulletin* 2, no. 5 (June 1897): 5–6, UIC, JAMC, Hull-House Association; *JAPM*, 55:613–14.
"[Dudley, Emelius Clark] Obituary." *Chicago Daily Tribune*, 2 Dec. 1928.
"Dunning a County Disgrace." *Chicago Times-Herald*, 13 Aug. 1895.
"The Dunning Committee's Report." *Chicago Inter Ocean*, 31 Aug. 1895.
"The Dunning Investigation." *Chicago Daily Tribune*, 21 Aug. 1895.
"The Dunning Investigation." *Chicago Daily Tribune*, 1 Sept. 1895.
"The Duty of the Church." *New York Times*, 17 Dec. 1898. SCPC, JAC; *JAPM*, 55:486.
"E. P. Bailey, Active Banker at 82, Is Dead." *Chicago Daily Tribune*, 29 Mar. 1925.
"E. Stewart, 79, Dies; Noted Statistician." *New York Times*, 14 Oct. 1936.
Eaton, Isabel, 1884–1937. SC, Archives, Biographical Files.
"Economic Conference." *Commons* 2, no. 5 (Sept. 1897): 6.
"Editorial [Economic Conference, Chicago]." *Chicago Daily Tribune*, 22 May 1888.
"Editorial [Jane Addams and Nineteenth Ward Politics]," from the *Northwestern Christian Advocate. New Unity*, 10 Feb. 1898:1120–21.
"Editorial [Jane Addams Chosen as a Juror, Paris Exposition, 1900]." *Commons* 47 (June 1900): 7.
"Educating the Waifs. The Good Work of the Industrial Art Association." *Chicago Daily Tribune*, 27 Nov. 1887.
"Education and Social Economy." *New York Times*, 17 June 1900.
"Edward F. Bideleux." Unidentified tear sheet from an unidentified source, n.d. Kenilworth, Ill., Historical Society.
Edwards, Carole. "Locke School Named for Pioneer Art Teacher." *Chicago Tribune West News*, 16 Mar. 1967.
"Edwin A. Waldo Found." Unknown newspaper article, [6 Apr. 1894]. Andover Newton Theological School, Newton Centre, Mass., Trask Library, Archives and Special Collections.

"Elder Coquelin Dies of Acute Embolism." *New York Times*, 28 Jan. 1909.

"Eleanor and Gertrude Smith Papers": A Guide. UIC, JAMC. www.uic.edu/depts/lib/specialcoll.

"Elect Good Aldermen." *Chicago Record*, 4 Apr. 1898.

"The Election Tuesday." *Chicago Chronicle*, 3 Apr. 1898.

"Eliza Allen Sarr." *Chicago Evening Post*, 5 July 1890.

"Eliza Jane Read Sunderland Papers, 1865–1910." UM, BHL, Finding Aids. quod.lib.umich.edu/cgi/f/findaid.

"Ellen G. Starr's Trial on Today." *Chicago Daily Tribune*, 4 Mar. 1914.

"Employment of Minors." *Chicago Times-Herald*, 26 Apr. 1895.

"Entertained at Hull House." *Chicago Times-Herald*, 26 Oct. 1899.

"Equal Suffrage Association Has Day of Rejoicing." *Chicago Daily Tribune*, 25 Jan. 1918.

Evans, Elizabeth Gardiner. "Interesting People I Have Known—Florence Kelley, Always a Pioneer." *Springfield (Mass.) Republican*, 16 Sept 1934.

———. "Mary Kenney O'Sullivan; Labor Leader, Factory Inspector, Citizen." *Springfield (Mass.) Sunday Union and Republican*, 12 Feb. 1933.

"Ewing Street." Chicago, 7 Aug. 1894. TMs, 2 pp. Chicago Theological Seminary, Ewing Street File.

"F. H. Deknatel [Obituary]." *Chicago Herald American*, 16 Apr. 1949.

"Factory and Workshop Inspection Law [for the State of Illinois]." 1894. Hull-House Scrapbook 2:41; *JAPM*, Addendum 10:7ff.

Farnsworth, Doug. "Men of Early Oconto County: Descendants of George Farnsworth, 1825–1913." Oconto County, Wis., WIGenWeb Project, 11 pp.

"[Farnsworth, Jane Worthington] Obituary." *Chicago Daily Tribune*, 24 Aug. 1921.

"February Magazines." *New York Mail Express*, 23 Jan. 1897. SCPC, JAC; *JAPM*, 55:493.

"Feeding the Hungry." *Chicago Inter Ocean*, 22 Dec. 1893.

"Fete Day at Hull House, Tenth Anniversary of the Settlement Is Celebrated." *Chicago Daily Tribune*, 26 Oct. 1899.

"Few Pupils Crowded Out." Unidentified newspaper clipping, [Sept.?] 1892. Hull-House Scrapbook 1:22½; *JAPM*, Addendum 10:6ff.

"Finding-Aid for the Horace Elisha Scudder Papers (MSS100)." Washington University, St. Louis, Olin Library, Department of Special Collections.

"Fine New Addition to Hull House." *Chicago Times-Herald*, 9 July 1899.

"Finishes Its Work. Subcommittee to Submit Its Report on Specific Charges [at Dunning]." *Chicago Inter Ocean*, 30 Aug. 1895.

"Flags Fail to Aid Girl Pickets." *Chicago Daily Tribune*, 5 Mar. 1914.

"[Fletcher, Margaretta Stuart West] Obituary." *Chicago Daily Tribune*, 20 Mar. 1942.

"[Fletcher, Margaretta Stuart West] Obituary." *Talk* (Winnetka, Ill.), 26 Mar. 1942.

"Florence Kelley, Humanitarian, Dies." *New York Times*, 17 Feb. 1932.

"Foes to Suffrage Meet." *Chicago Daily Tribune*, 20 Nov. 1898.

"For an Industrial Conference: Civic Federation Making Plans for a Discussion of Arbitration." *Chicago Daily Tribune*, 30 Sept. 1894.

"For an Italian Hospital." *Chicago Daily Tribune*, 11 Apr. 1890.

"For Better Scavenger Service." *Chicago Daily Tribune*, 29 June 1892.

"For Church Unity; Ministers Discuss Christian Union and Cooperation." *Chicago Daily Tribune*, 11 Oct. 1893.

"Former Chief of GE Dies in New York." *Salt Lake Tribune*, 21 Nov. 1957.
"Former Geneseo Man Serves Hull House 45 Years." *Geneseo (Ill.) Republican*, Jan. 1940.
"For Sweet Charity [*Chicago Daily News* Fresh-Air Fund]." *Chicago Daily News*, 14 June 1892.
"For Systematic Charity." *New York Times*, 10 Dec. 1897.
"Forty Kindergarten Graduates; Young Women Receive Their Diplomas at the Woman's Club." *Chicago Daily Tribune*, 19 June 1895.
"For Working Children." *Hull-House Bulletin* 2, no. 3 (1 Mar. 1897): 6. UIC, JAMC, Hull-House Association; *JAPM*, 53:594.
"Fourth of July; American Celebrations in London." *Lloyd's Weekly (*London), 5 July 1896.
"4 Youths Hold Up Factory." *Chicago Daily Tribune*, 7 Dec. 1912.
"[Fox, Dr. Harriet Magee Fox] Obituary." *Chicago Daily Tribune*. 24 Apr. 1911.
"Frederic Harrison." National Archives, Learning Curve. www.spartacus.schoolnet.co.uk/TUharrison.htm.
"Frederick H. Deknatel [Obituary]." *Chicago Daily News*, 18 Apr. 1949.
"[French, William Merchant Richardson] Obituary." *Chicago Daily Tribune*, 4 June 1914.
"Friendly Visiting." *Chicago Record*, 1 Oct. 1897.
Frothingham, James. "The Toynbee Idea." *Interior*, 7 July 1890. Hull-House Scrapbook 1:4; *JAPM*, Addendum 10:6ff.
Fryar, Annie. Marriage License, 11 Oct. 1895. Cook County, Ill., Recorder.
"Funeral of Dr. Roswell G. Bogue." *Chicago Daily Tribune*, Dec. 11, 1893.
"Funeral of L. J. McCormick." *Chicago Daily News*, 22 Feb. 1900.
"Funeral of Miss Scammon." *Chicago Daily Tribune*, 25 May 1898.
"Funeral of Mrs. A. P. Stevens." *Chicago Post*, 4 June 1900.
"Funeral of Mrs. Joseph Medill." *Chicago Daily Tribune*, 5 Oct. 1894.
"Funeral of William H. Colvin." *Chicago Daily Tribune*, 10 July 1896.
"G. Cotton Smith Dies Suddenly." *Wilkes-Barre (Pa.) Record*, 30 Nov. 1915.
"Gallery of Local Celebrities: No. XLVII. Dr. Ralph N. Isham." *Chicago Daily Tribune*, 16 Dec. 1900.
"Gallery of Local Celebrities: No. LXIII, Eliphalet Wickes Blatchford." *Chicago Daily Tribune*, 21 Apr. 1901.
"[Garrot, Erasmus] Obituary." *Chicago Daily Tribune*, 20 Apr. 1898.
"[Garrot, Erasmus] Obituary." *Chicago Times-Herald*, 20 Apr. 1898.
"Gen. A. C. M'Clurg Dies in Florida." *Chicago Daily Tribune*, 16 Apr. 1901.
"General Stiles Is Dead. Prominent Chicagoan Passes Away While Asleep." *Chicago Daily Tribune*, 18 Jan. 1895.
"George Armour, 80, Collector, Is Dead." *New York Times*, 9 June 1936.
"George Clark, Head of Stove Concern, Dies." *Chicago Daily Tribune*, 6 Apr. 1924.
"George Farnsworth, Pioneer, Dies of Paralytic Stroke." *Chicago Daily Tribune*, 27 June 1913.
"George H. Rozet Dead." *Chicago Daily Tribune*, 16 Nov. 1900.
"Gerard Swope, 84, Ex-G.E. Head, Dies." *New York Times*, 21 Nov. 1957.
"Gives It a Million." *Chicago Sunday Tribune*, 15 Dec. 1895.
"Gleanings in Local Fields: Bindery Girls to Give an Entertainment." *Chicago Daily Tribune*, 27 Sept. 1891.

"Gleanings in Local Fields: [Working Woman's Club]." *Chicago Daily Tribune*, 2 July 1890.

Gleason, William. "The Objects of the [Municipal Voters'] League Are the Following . . . ," [Mar. 1896]. TMsS Citizens Association of Chicago Records, Box 20, in Municipal Voters' League Papers, 1896–98. CHM, CHS.

Glenwood School for Boys. Board of Trustees. Minutes, 1897. Glenwood School for Boys, St. Charles, Ill.

"Glimpse into Hull House." *Churchman*, 30 July 1892. Hull-House Scrapbook 1:25; *JAPM*, Addendum 10:6ff.

"Gompers to Attend Ball." *Chicago Daily Tribune*. 29 Oct. 1913.

"Good in Labor Unions." *Chicago Journal-Herald*, 2 Dec. 1900. SCPC, JAC; *JAPM*, 55:608.

"Gospel for Anarchists. Christianity in Its Shirt-Sleeves Working in 'Little Hell.'" *Chicago Daily Tribune*, 3 Feb. 1889.

"Gov. Tanner's Double-Dealing." *Chicago Times-Herald*, 7 Sept., 1897.

Gow, H. J. "Diaries 1896 Sept. 28–1897 June 13." 2 vols. Duke University, Rare Book, Manuscript, and Special Collections Library.

"[Grady, Michael R.] Death Notices." *Chicago Daily Tribune*, 30 July 1916.

"Grand Jury the Only Remedy." *Chicago Times-Herald*, 13 Aug. 1895.

"Grant Collegiate Institute" [Advertisement]. *Chicago Daily Tribune*, Aug. 31 1897.

"Great Rally for Powers." *Chicago Chronicle*, 3 Apr. 1898.

"Grief at the College." *Rockford (Ill.) Evening Starr*, 17 Apr. 1898.

"Grim Want in the Model Town." *Chicago Mail*, 25 May 1894.

"Guide to the Bayard Taylor Holmes Papers, 1888–1925." UC, Crerar Manuscript 91.

"Guide to the George Ellsworth Hooker City Planning, Transportation and Housing Collection, 1882–1932." University of Chicago Library, 2007. www.lib.chicago.edu.

"Guide to the Hervey White Papers, 1913–1931." University of Iowa, Special Collections, #MSC0724. 20 Aug. 2012. lib.uiowa.edu/collguides/?MSC0724.

Haldeman, Sarah Alice Addams. "[Record Book of Copies of Letters and Articles Kept by Sarah Alice Addams Haldeman]." 1889. Copies of Jane Addams letters made by Sarah Alice Addams Haldeman and PD. SC, Starr.

"[Hamill, Katharine Lyon] Obituary." *Chicago Daily Tribune*, 27 Aug. 1964.

Harper, William R., John Dewey, and Henry H. Belfield. "Circular to the Alumni, Patrons, and Other Friends of the Chicago Manual Training School." July 1901, PD. UC, Archives, Chicago Manual Training School Records.

"Harriet Stone." In *Class of 1888 Record Book*, Wellesley College, 1900, p. 21. Wellesley College, Wellesley College Archives.

[Harrison, Mrs. Ursula L., portrait]. *Graphic News* (Chicago) (Feb. 1888): 313.

"Harshness Was Used. The Condition at Dunning." *Chicago Record*, 10 Sept. 1895.

"[Harvey, Julia Plato] Obituary." *Chicago Daily Tribune*, 24 July 1918.

"[Harvey, Julia Plato] Obituary." *Geneva (Ill.) Republican*, 26 July 1918.

"Hattie Simmons, Widow of Park President, Dies." *Chicago Daily Tribune*, 17 Nov. 1931.

"[Hay, William A.] Obituary." *Chicago Daily Tribune*, 17 Dec. 1902.

"Health Appeals Pass Unheeded." *Chicago Daily Tribune*, 3 June 1903.

"Health Inquiry Is On." *Chicago Daily Tribune*, 5 May 1903.

Heaton, Eliza Putnam. "A Women's Toynbee Hall." *Kansas City (Mo.) Journal*, [19?] [Apr. 1889].

Hecht, Stuart Joel. "Hull-House Theatre: An Analytical and Evaluative History." Ph.D. diss., Northwestern University, 1983.

"Helen Castle Mead Memorial Fund." Card, [1930]. SCPC, JAC; *JAPM*, 27:1129–30.

"Help Appealed For. Women's Clubs' Emergency Association Needs Money." *Chicago Inter Ocean*, 26 Feb. 1894.

"Henrietta Octavia Weston Rowland." Family Search International Genealogical Index. www.familysearch.org.

Herndon, Emily. "The Spectator [on Hull House]." *Christian Union,* 27 Aug. 1892. Hull-House Scrapbook 1:23; *JAPM*, Addendum 10:6ff.

"He Will Not Act: Pullman Ignores the Efforts of Jane Addams on Behalf of Arbitration: She Makes Final Appeal." *Chicago Mail*, 1 June 1894.

Hibbert, Mary Jo. "Hull House and the Press: A Study in Journalistic Representation, 1889 through 1896." A paper submitted to the ACM Seminar, Lawrence University, Appleton, Wis., 13 Dec. 1973, TMs.

"[Hintermeister, Julia M. E] Obituary." *Chicago Daily Tribune*, 19 Feb. 1918.

"Holiday Home Camp, 1887–1987." Second printing of the original publication. Published by the Holiday Home Camp, [Chicago, 1987].

["Hollister, Dr. John Hamilcar] Obituary." *Chicago Daily Tribune*, 4 Nov. 1911.

"Home for Working Women." *Chicago Daily Tribune*, 4 June 1890.

"Home for Working Women." *Chicago Daily Tribune*, 4 Apr. 1891.

"Home Has Its Day." *Chicago Daily Tribune*, 20 May 1893.

"Home Men Get Work." *Chicago Daily Tribune*, 2 Sept. 1893.

"Honors for Students." *Chicago Record*, 2 Apr. 1897.

Hooker, George E. *Hull House Recreation Guide*. "A List of Pleasant Places for Nineteenth Warders to Go. Arranged in Order of Cost for Round Trip." Published by Hull-House, Chicago, [July 1896], PD. Hull-House Scrapbook 3:95; *JAPM*, Addendum 10:8ff.

———. "Social Economic Conference." *Hull-House Bulletin* 2, no. 1 (Jan. 1897): 6. UIC, JAMC, Hull-House Association; *JAPM*, 53:573.

"Household Help." *Union Signal*, 4 Feb. 1892. Hull-House Scrapbook 1:11; *JAPM*, Addendum 10:6ff.

"Housekeepers in Conference. The Abolition of Servant Girls Discussed by Progressive Women." *Chicago Times-Herald,* 25 Oct. 1892.

"How Boys Are Reformed [Ursula L. Harrison]." *Chicago Daily Tribune*, 10 May 1891.

"How Dr. Harper Wins." *Chicago Daily Tribune*, 19 Jan. 1896.

Howe, Mary Ware (Mrs. Michael Straus). "Wellesley College Alumnae Association 1942 Biographical Record." 22 Oct. 1941, miscellaneous clippings. Wellesley College, Wellesley College Archives, Biographical Files.

"How He Holds Power." *Chicago Times-Herald*, 24 Jan. 1898. SCPC, JAC; *JAPM*, 55:411.

"How to Drain Roads." *Chicago Daily Tribune*, 19 Oct. 1893.

"How to Own a Ward." *Chicago Record*, 24 Jan. 1898.

"How to Reform Dunning." *Chicago Inter Ocean*, 2 Sept. 1895.

"How Toynbee Hall Is Conducted." *Chicago Daily Tribune*, 18 June 1891. Hull-House Scrapbook 1:7½; *JAPM*, Addendum 10:6ff.

"How Would You Elevate the Masses?" *Advance* (Chicago), 18 Feb 1892, 133. Hull-House Scrapbook 1:14; *JAPM*, Addendum 10:6ff.

"How You Are Robbed." *Chicago Record,* 30 June 1897.

Hulbert, Louise. "Autobiography of an Unknown." [1951?]. AmsS, 6 pp., JAPP, Hulbert.

"Hull House." *Altruistic Review*, Springfield, Ohio, Oct. 1890.

"Hull House." *Chicago Record*, 2 Dec. 1896.

"Hull House." *Illinois Christian World*, Nov. 1892. Hull-House Scrapbook 1:26; *JAPM*, Addendum 10:6ff.

"The Hull House." *Interior*, Chicago, 28 Apr. 1892. Hull-House Scrapbook 1:18; *JAPM*, Addendum 10:6ff.

"Hull House. The American Toynbee Hall. Interview with Miss Addams." *London Daily News*, 3 June 1896.

Hull-House, Chicago. Account Book, Oct. 1894–May 1895. UIC, JAMC, Hull-House Association; *JAPM*, Addendum 3:4ff.

———. Cash Book 1 Jan. 1894–30 June 1895. AD. UIC, JAMC, Hull-House Association; *JAPM*, Addendum 3:3ff.

———. "Hull-House Acc't Oct 1st 1891." AD in hand of Jane Addams, Oct. 1891–Oct. 1893. UIC, JAMC, Hull-House Association; *JAPM*, Addendum 3:1ff.

———. Hull House Residents, "Residents Meetings Reports." 2 vols. 1893–95, 1896. HMsS by various secretaries. UIC, JAMC, Hull-House Association; *JAPM*, 50:331–424.

———. Hull-House Scrapbooks. 3 vols. 1889–97. H and PD [scrapbook of clippings and documents]. UIC, JAMC, Hull-House Association; *JAPM*, Addendum 10. The scrapbooks have been dismantled and the materials they contained refiled. The scrapbook format appears only in the microfilm edition of the Jane Addams papers.

———. Lease between Jane Addams and Helen Culver, 10 May 1892, UIC, JAMC, HH Assn.; *JAPM*, 49:1335–36.

"Hull House a Social Settlement . . . Weekly Program Lectures, Clubs, Classes, Etc. March 1st 1892." [Chicago: Hull-House, 1892]. Hull-House Scrapbook 2:13½; *JAPM*, Addendum 10:7ff.

Hull-House Association, Chicago. By-laws, 1895. UIC, JAMC, HH Assn., *JAPM*, 49:125–28, 1005–7, 1022–24, 1050–53.

———. Certificate of Incorporation, 30 Mar. 1895. Illinois Secretary of State, Corporation Department, Box 702, No. 32966.

"Hull House Bureau." *Chicago Post*, 23 Jan. 1892. Hull-House Scrapbook 1:14; *JAPM*, Addendum 10:6ff.

"Hull House Chicago." *Syracuse (N.Y.) Post,* 3 Mar. 1896; *JAPM*, 55:159.

"[Hull-House endeavors to make social intercourse]." *Chicago Times-Herald,* 1 July 1900. SCPC, JAC; *JAPM*, 71:1165.

"Hull House Gets a $25,000 Bequest from Co-Founder." *Chicago Daily Tribune*, 9 Mar. 1934.

"Hull House in Chicago." *Springfield (Mass.) Republican*, June 1892. Hull-House Scrapbook 120; *JAPM*, Addendum 10:6ff.

"Hull House Kitchen Opened." *Chicago Inter Ocean*, 24 Aug. 1893.

Hull House Men's Club. Constitution. Jan. 1893. TMs. Hull-House Scrapbook 2:47; *JAPM*, Addendum 10:7ff.

"Hull-House Music School." Brochure. [1935?]. 2 pp., UIC, JAMC.

"[Hull-House] Thursday Lectures and Concerts." In "Hull-House College Extension

Classes." [Chicago: Hull-House, Sept. 1891]. Hull-House Scrapbook 2:7; *JAPM*, Addendum 10:7ff.
"Hull House to Have a New Auditorium Seating 400 People." *Chicago Daily Tribune*, 7 Aug. 1898.
"Hull House Wedding Reception." *Chicago Times-Herald*, 7 Feb. 1897.
"Hull House . . . Weekly Programme of Lectures Clubs Classes Etc. January 1891." [Chicago: Hull-House. 1891]. HD. Hull-House Scrapbook 2:5; *JAPM*, Addendum 10:7ff.
"Hull House Work in Chicago: [a review of *Hull House Maps and Papers*]." *New York Times*, 16 June 1895.
"Human Drones and Parasites. They Are Discussed by the Sunset Club—the Speeches." *Chicago Daily Tribune*, 11 Apr. 1890.
"Hurl Defiance at Ald. Powers." *Chicago Record*, 3 Mar. 1898.
"[Hutchinson, Dr. Edward B.] Obituary." *Chicago Daily Tribune*, 21 Feb. 1951.
"Illinois Industrial Training-School Affairs." *Chicago Daily Tribune*, 21 May 1890.
[Illinois League of Women Voters holds annual state convention]. *Chicago Daily Tribune*, 18 Nov. 1923.
"Immigration and Chicago." *Chicago Times-Herald*, 2 Feb. 1897.
"Impetus Given Suffrage Cause." *Chicago Daily Tribune*. 24 Dec. 1911.
"Industrial Arts for the Boys. More about the Work of the Industrial Art Association." *Chicago Daily Tribune*, 28 Nov. 1887.
"Industrial Home." *Chicago Daily Tribune*, 7 July 1882.
"Industrial School." *Chicago Daily Tribune*, 2 Oct. 1879.
"Influence of the Trust Conference." *Chicago Record*, 16 Sept. 1899.
"In Labor Circles." *Chicago Record*, 6, 10, 11 May 1897.
*In Memoriam. Jessie Bross Lloyd, September 27, 1844–December 29, 1904*. [Chicago: H. G. Adair], [1905?].
"In Memoriam [Mary E. Beedy]." *Yellow Springs (Ohio) News*, 6 May 1910.
"In Memoriam [Rose M. Gyles]." [1949]. PD, Card. UIC, JAMC, Gyles.
"In Memory of Mrs. Joseph Medill." *Chicago Daily Tribune*, 8 Oct. 1894.
"In Parisian Society." *Chicago Record*, 16 June 1900.
"In the Butler Gallery." *Chicago Daily Tribune*, 31 May 1891. Hull-House Scrapbook 1:7; *JAPM*, Addendum:6ff.
"In the Fight to Stay: Manufacturers' Association Refuses to Arbitrate." *Chicago Daily Tribune*, 22 Mar. 1896.
"In the 19th Ward." *Chicago Record*, 22 Mar. 1898.
"In the Society World [Edward J. McGeeney]." *Chicago Daily Tribune*, 22 June 1899.
"In the Theatrical World. Plays That Will Be Seen at the Various Houses This Week." *Chicago Daily Tribune*, 17 Mar. 1890.
"Invaded the Sunset Club." *Chicago Times*, 5 Feb. 1892. SCPC, JAC; *JAPM*, 55:11.
"Irish Village Snarl." *Chicago Daily Tribune*, 28 Nov. 1892.
"Isabelle Stone, '89." Unidentified clipping. Wellesley College, Wellesley College Archives, Biographical Files.
"Is a Merit Victory." *Chicago Daily Tribune*, 19 Feb. 1899.
"Is Deaf to Appeal: Pullman Relief Committee Meets with Rebuff: Lyman Gage Has No Sympathy with the Strikers: Says He Will Not Give a Cent: Thinks Pullman Is a

Dream and Its Plutocrat a Saint: Calls Strikers Lazy Loafers." *Chicago Times*, 7 June 1894.

"[Isham, Katharine Snow] Obituary." *Chicago Daily Tribune*, 24 Feb. 1913.

"Is Stabbed with a Trowel." *Chicago Chronicle*, 13 June 1900.

"Italians of the Patch." *Chicago Daily Tribune*, 24 July 1887.

"Italy's Progress Here." *Chicago Daily Tribune*, 19 Dec. 1886.

"It Is Doing a Good Work [Lincoln Park Sanitarium]." *Chicago Daily News*, 1 July 1892.

"J. Bradner Smith Passes Away." *Chicago Daily Tribune*, 7 May 1893.

"J. Young Scammon Leaves $250." *Chicago Daily Tribune*, 26 Mar. 1890.

"Jacob A. Riis, Reformer, Dead." *New York Times*, 27 May 1914.

"James Samuel Windeatt." broadway.cas.sc.edu.

[Jane Addams Addresses National Education Association]. Unidentified evening newspaper, Milwaukee, 6 July 1897. SCPC, JAC; *JAPM*, 55:300.

"Jane Addams at Mansfield House." *Chicago Commons* 1, no. 4 (July 1896): 13.

"Jane Addams Defends Unions." Unidentified Chicago newspaper, 2 Dec. 1900. SCPC, JAC; *JAPM*, 55:608.

"Jane Addams Has Returned. She Has Been Inspecting the Scavenger System of New York." *Chicago Daily News*, 8 May 1895.

"Jane Addams Honored." Unidentified newspaper clipping, [19?] Feb. 1897. SCPC, JAC; *JAPM*, 55:245.

[Jane Addams] in "Roundabout Notes." *Hackney Express and Shoreditch Observer* (London), 6 June 1896.

"Jane Addams Is for Arbitration." *Chicago Chronicle*, 2 Dec. 1900. SCPC, JAC; *JAPM*, 55:608.

"Jane Addams Is Ill." *Chicago Daily Tribune*, 12 Sept. 1895.

"Jane Addams Is Ill." *Chicago Times-Herald*, 12 Sept. 1895. SCPC, JAC; *JAPM*, 55:104.

"Jane Addams Is Pleased." *Chicago Times-Herald*, 7 Aug. 1900. SCPC, JAC; *JAPM*, 55:589.

"Jane Addams Wears a Star." *Chicago Record*, 25 Apr. 1895. Hull-House Scrapbook 3:2: *JAPM*, Addendum 10:8ff.

Jane Club, Hull-House, Chicago. "Articles of Incorporation." June 1895. P and AD. UIC, JAMC, Hull-House Association; *JAPM*, 51:364.

———. "Constitution and By-laws of the Jane Club." [1895]. PD. UIC, JAMC, Hull-House Association; *JAPM*, 51:345–50.

"Jane Club's New Home." *Chicago Daily News*, 2 Apr. 1898.

"Jane Club's New Home." *Chicago Daily Tribune*, 14 Aug. 1898.

"Jaunts to the Country [Ursula L. Harrison]." *Chicago Daily Tribune*, 5 July 1888.

"Jean F. Spahr Dies; Welfare Worker." *New York Times*, 26 Sept. 1935.

"Jefferson Park College, Chicago" [Advertisement]. *Chicago Daily Tribune*, 20 Sept. 1908.

Jenkins, Robert E. "The Mission of the Sunday School." Unidentified publication clipping, [1894?]. Hull-House Scrapbook 1:55; *JAPM*, Addendum 10:6ff.

"John McLaren." *Chicago Daily Tribune*, 27 July 1916. In Edinburgh Residents in U.S. Newspapers, www.angelfire.com/ct2/corstorphine/chicagodeaths.html.

"John S. Coonley, Business, Civic Leader, Is Dead." *Chicago Daily Tribune*, 13 Feb. 1933.

Johnson, Amanda. Death Certificate, 24 June 1949. Wisconsin Department of Health Services, Wisconsin Vital Records Services, Death Records.

Jones, Katharine A. "The Working Girls of Chicago." *Review of Reviews*, New York, Sept. 1891. Hull-House Scrapbook 1:10; *JAPM*, Addendum 10:6ff.

Josephine Carson Locke File. CBE, Biographical Files.

"Jubilee in the Public Schools." *Chicago Daily Tribune*, 19 Oct. 1898.

"Jubilee Week." *Chicago Record*, 15 Oct. 1898.

"Keeps His Divorce a Secret by Omission of Initials." *Chicago Daily Tribune*, 20 Nov. 1908.

"Keir Hardie Is Here." *Chicago Inter Ocean*, Aug. 31, 1895.

Kelley, Florence to John McLaren, Trustee of the Lewis Estate. ALS, 19 July 1894. 3 pp., ITT, Archives, Lewis Institute Records.

Kellogg, Emily A. "Hull House." *Union Signal*, 22 Jan. 1891. Hull-House Scrapbook 1:6; *JAPM*, Addendum 10:6ff.

"Kenilworth Hall. Mrs. Babcock's Kenilworth School" [Advertisements]. *Chicago Daily Tribune*, 6 June 1891, 15 Aug. 1891, 2 Sept. 1899, 5 Oct. 1899, 1 Aug. 1903, 25 Aug. 1903.

Kenney, Mary E. "Organization of Women." *Age of Labor*, 1 Jan. 1893. Hull-House Scrapbook 1:27; *JAPM*, Addendum 10:6ff.

Kent, Carlton. "Honor First Lady of Hull House." *Sunday Chicago Times*, 25 Feb. 1940.

Kent, William. "Letter to the Chicago Times." *Chicago Times*, 13 Feb. 1893.

"Killed Himself with a Gun." *Chicago Record*, 3 Oct. 1898.

Knobe, Bertha Damaris. "Light-Houses of Chicago." *Union Signal*, 26 July 1894. Hull-House Scrapbook 1:56; *JAPM*, Addendum 10:6ff.

Kramer, Julia W. "Jane Addams at the World's Columbian Exposition, 1893." Chicago, n.d. Dup. Ms, 12 pp.

"Labor to Assist Children." *Chicago Daily Tribune*. 22 Mar. 1903.

"The Ladies Branch of the Oxford House." *Times* (London), 19 Dec. 1896.

"The Ladies' Page." *Illustrated London News*, 29 Aug. 1896:278.

"Lady Is the Orator." *Chicago Inter Ocean*, 2 Apr. 1897.

"The Lady of the House." *Chicago Inter Ocean*, 25 Mar. 1892. Hull-House Scrapbook 1:19a; *JAPM*, Addendum 10:6ff.

Landau, Deborah. "The Paradox of a Social Settlement: Jane Addams' Hull-House—Residents, Regulations and Internal Organizations, 1889 to 1900." An Honors essay. 11 May 1977. TMs, 72 pp.

"Langdon, James Robbins." In *America's Successful Men of Affairs: The United States at Large*. Vol. 2. Edited by Henry Hall. New York. *New York Tribune*, 1896.

"Last Rites for Enella Benedict Held at Hull-House." *Hull-House Bulletin*, 10 (13 Apr. 1942). UIC, JAMC, HH Assn.

Lathrop, Julia. "The Responsibilities of the Newer Philanthropy." Speech before the Associated Charities of Minneapolis, 18–19 Jan. 1910. RC, Archives, Lathrop.

"Lauds Labor Unions." *Chicago Inter Ocean*, 2 Dec 1900. SCPC, JAC; *JAPM*, 55:609.

*Laura Dainty: Humorous and Dramatic Recitations*. 1879–80. Chicago: Redpath Lyceum Bureau, [1879?]. PD. UIC, JAMC, Eric Hjorth Collection.

Learned, Henry B. "Hull House, Chicago." *Unitarian* (Boston), Sept. 1893.

"The Leather Trade." *Chicago Record*, 26 July 1897.

"Lecture at Hull House on Ireland's Cottage Industries." *Chicago Daily Tribune*, 6 Nov. 1892.
"A Lecture on Abraham Lincoln." *Times* (London), 7 Oct 1895.
"Lecture on Tolstoi." *Chicago Post*, 2 Oct. 1897.
"Lena C. Leland [obituary]." *The Rockford Alumna* 1 (May 1923). RC, Archives.
"Letter from Mrs. Lila Peabody Cragin. Read by Mrs. Cynthia Barber Cheney." *Alumnae Chronicle* (Northfield, Mass.), Dec. 1911.
"Like Hercules' Task." *Chicago Daily Tribune*, 25 Apr. 1895.
Linn, James Weber. [Mary Rozet Smith]. *Chicago Daily News*, 25 Feb. 1934.
Linn, Jane Addams. "At Arizona with Aunt Jane." "Diary, Feb. 1935." UIC, JAMC.
Linn, Mary Catherine Addams. Cook County, Ill., Circuit Court, Probate Records, Document 34, p. 307. 12 Jul. 1894–22 Sept. 1897. P and ADS. *JAPM*, 27:882.
———. Records of the Estate of Mary Catherine Addams Linn, 12 July 1894–22 Sept. 1897. Cook County, Ill., Circuit Court, Probate Records; *JAPM*, 27:733–944.
Linn, Myra. "The Story of My Mother, Harriet Melissa Youmans and My Father, Francis Wayland Reynolds." La Sierra, Calif.: privately printed, [1969].
"Little Sisters of the Poor." *Chicago Times*, 26 Aug. 1877.
"A Local Toynbee Hall." *Chicago Inter Ocean*, 20 June 1891. Hull-House Scrapbook 1:8; *JAPM*, Addendum 10:6ff.
"London Settlements." *Chicago Commons* 1, no. 7 (Oct. 1896): 12–13.
"[Looseveldt, Camille] Obituary." *Chicago Daily News*, 16 Mar. 1908.
"Lord Rectorship of Glasgow University." *Glasgow Herald*, Scotland, 3 Nov. 1894.
"Lyman J. Gage's Denial." *Chicago News*, 7 June 1894.
"The Main Cause of Poverty." *Chicago Daily Tribune*, 25 Dec. 1889.
"Many Bids Opened." *Chicago Inter Ocean*, 23 Mar. 1895.
"Many Mourn Noted Artist [Alice Kellogg Tyler]." *Chicago Chronicle*, 16 Feb. 1900.
"Many Women Asking for Aid." *Chicago Daily Tribune*, 25 Jan. 1894.
Marks, Nora. "Industrial School at Norwood. What It Is and How It Is Managed—Its Inmates." *Chicago Daily Tribune*, 15 Jan. 1889.
———. "Two Women's Work." *Chicago Daily Tribune*, 19 May 1890. Hull-House Scrapbook 1:2; *JAPM*, Addendum 10:6ff.
———. "With a Truant Officer; a Glimpse of the Workings of the Compulsory Education Law." *Chicago Daily Tribune*, 2 Feb. 1889.
"Mary M'Dowell Will Disposes of $3,000 Estate." *Chicago Daily Tribune*, 6 Nov. 1936.
"Mary O'Sullivan Dies in Medford." *Daily Boston Globe*, 19 Jan. 1943.
"Mass Meeting This Afternoon." *Chicago Chronicle*, 8 Mar. 1896. Hull-House Scrapbook 3:69; *JAPM*, Addendum 10:8ff.
"Mather-Smith Dies; Ex-Head of Paper Firm." *Chicago Daily Tribune*, 29 Oct. 1914.
"[Matz, Evelyn] Obituary." *Chicago Daily Tribune*, 15 Aug. 1958.
"[Matz, Otto Hermann] Obituary." *Chicago Daily Tribune*, 10 Mar. 1919.
"Max Platz Succumbs to Death." *Chicago Daily Tribune*, 26 Feb. 1894.
"May Aid the Tanners." *Chicago Record*, 21 May 1897.
Mayer, Milton S. "First Citizen of Chicago." *Chicago Daily News*, 20 Feb. 1940.
"The Mayor's Civil-Service Pledge." *Chicago Daily News*, 26 Apr. 1895.
"[McClurg, Alexander Caldwell] Obituary." *Chicago Daily Tribune*, 16 Apr. 1901.
"[McConnell, Jane Binney] Death Notices." *Chicago Daily Tribune*, 15 Dec. 1892.

"[McGeeney, E. J.] Obituary." *Chicago Daily Tribune*, 28 Mar. 1908.
"[McGeeney, Mrs. Mary Agnes] Obituary." *Chicago Daily Tribune*, 24 Dec. 1941.
"McKim (Leonora Jackson and William Duncan McKim) Collection." Guides to Special Collections in the Music Division of the Library of Congress. Washington, D.C., 1998, 36 pp. lcweb2.loc.gov/service/music/eadxmlmusic/eadpfmunic/mu2005.wp.0053.pd.
"Men and Things." *Unity* (27 July 1893): 252. Hull-House Scrapbook 1:40; *JAPM*, Addendum 10:6ff.
"Men at Trust Meet." *Chicago Inter Ocean*, 17 Sept. 1899.
Mendota, Wisconsin State Hospital, Records, 1915–1927, Wisconsin Department of Health Services, Mendota State Hospital Records.
Merriam, Mildred. "Hull House and Its Founder." *Munci (Ind.) Times*, 17 July 1900. SCPC, JAC; *JAPM*, 55:584.
"Methodists to Help Boys." *Chicago Daily Tribune*, 19 Nov. 1901.
"[Milligan, Dr. Josephine] Obituary." *New York Times*, 29 Aug. 1946.
"[Milligan, Josephine] Obituary." *Chicago Daily Tribune*, 29 Aug. 1946.
"Miss A[d]dams after Powers." *Chicago Chronicle*, 20 Feb. 1900. SCPC, JAC; *JAPM*, 55:548.
"Miss Addams a Good Model." Unidentified newspaper clipping, [Oct?] 1895. Hull-House Scrapbook 3:24; *JAPM*, Addendum 10:8ff.
"Miss Addams as Scavenger." *Topeka (Kans.) Journal*, 28 May 1895. Hull-House Scrapbook 3:7; *JAPM*, Addendum 10;8ff.
"Miss Addams as Scavenger." *Woman's Journal* (Boston) 26 (13 Apr. 1895): 113.
"Miss Addams at Mansfield House." *Chicago Commons* 1, no. 4 (July 1896): 13.
"Miss Addams Goes to Paris." *Chicago Daily Tribune*, 21 May 1900. SCPC, JAC; *JAPM*, 55:576.
"Miss Addam's Ideas on Co-operative Housekeeping." *Pittsburgh Bulletin*, 24 Feb. 1900. SCPC, JAC; *JAPM*, 55:556.
"Miss Addams Lectures." *Philadelphia Times*, 6 Dec. 1897. SCPC, JAC; *JAPM*, 55:379.
"Miss Addams Loses." *Chicago Daily Tribune*, 23 Mar. 1895.
"Miss Addams on London Social Reforms." *Chicago Inter Ocean*, 27 Sept. 1896.
"Miss Addams' Promotion." *Chicago Daily Tribune*, [9?] June 1900. SCPC, JAC; *JAPM*, 55:578.
"Miss Addams' Remedy for Poverty." *Chicago Post,* 16 Nov. 1900. SCPC, JAC; *JAPM*, 55:597.
"Miss Addams Speaks on College Settlement Ideas." *Boston Transcript*, 13 Feb 1897. SCPC, JAC; *JAPM*, 55:243.
"Miss Amanda Johnson, Nineteenth Ward Sanitary Inspector." *Chicago Daily Tribune*, 17 Jan. 1898.
"Miss Brooks' School for Girls" [Advertisement]. *Chicago Daily Tribune*, Aug. 29, 1890.
"Miss Culver Is Modest." *Chicago Daily News*, 16 Dec. 1895.
"Miss Culver's Christmas Gift to the University of Chicago." *Chicago Daily Tribune*, 16 Dec. 1895.
"Miss Culver's Rich Gift." *Chicago Daily Tribune*, 16 Dec. 1895.
"Miss Harington [obituary]." *Times* (London), 8 Oct. 1936.

"Miss Jane Addams." *Buffalo (N.Y.) Courier,* 28 Mar. 1896. SCPC, JAC; *JAPM* 55:157.
"Miss Jane Addams at Canning Town." *East Ham Express* (London), 20 June 1896.
"Miss Jane Addams Honored at the Paris Exposition." *San Francisco Chronicle*, 11 June 1900. SCPC, JAC; *JAPM*, 55:579.
"Miss Jane Addams in London." *Chicago Post*, 17 June 1896.
"Miss Jane Addams Lectures." *Chicago Inter Ocean*, 15 Jan. 1900. SCPC, JAC; *JAPM*, 55:540.
"Miss Johnson Made Inspector." *Chicago Daily Tribune*, 17 May 1896.
"Miss Mary Rozet Smith." *New York Times*, 24 Feb. 1934.
"Mistakes in Settlement Work." *New York Evening Telegram*, 3 Mar. 1900. SCPC, JAC; *JAPM*, 55:562.
"Mlle. Rhea, Actress, Dead." *New York Times*, 23 May 1899.
"Model Lodging House Not Moved." *Chicago Daily Tribune*, 2 Sept. 1898.
"Money for Strikers." *Chicago Inter Ocean*, 28 May 1894.
"Mourned as Dead; The Rev. Edward A. Waldo Heard from at Last." *Boston Herald*, [7] Feb. 1902.
"Mr. Asquith on Social Settlements." *London Morning Post,* 22 Nov. 1895.
"Mr. Hull's Millions." *Chicago Times*, 22 Feb. 1889.
"Mr. [William E. ] Burns and the *New World.*" *New World,* 14 Dec. 1895.
"Mrs. A. P. Stevens Dead." *Chicago Daily Tribune*, 5 June 1900.
"Mrs. Alzina Parsons Stevens." *New York Mail and Express*, 4 June 1900.
"Mrs. Bowen, 94, Dies." *Chicago Daily Tribune*, 10 Nov. 1953.
"Mrs. Corbin on Voting." *Chicago Daily Tribune*, 15 Dec. 1899.
"Mrs. Dainty Loses a Husband." *New York Times*, 19 Oct. 1884.
"Mrs. E. A. Paul." *New York Times*, 10 Oct. 1897.
[Mrs. E. A. Paul's Appointment as Inspector of Street Cleaning]. *Outlook* 57, no. 6 (9 Oct. 1897): 351–52.
"Mrs. Emily Peck's Burial Today from Hull House." *Chicago Daily Tribune*, 8 May 1921.
"Mrs. Frank Deknatel Dies Suddenly." *Chicago Record*, 2 June 1897.
"Mrs. Geo. Cotton Smith Dead." *Columbia (S.C.) State*, 15 May 1910.
"Mrs. Gerard Swope Is Dead at Age of 84; Active in Hull House, Welfare Work Here." *New York Times*, 29 Oct. 1955.
"Mrs. Henry H. Babcock's School for Young Ladies & Children" [Advertisements]. *Chicago Daily Tribune*, 21 Aug. 1882; 14 Sept. 1886; 21 Sept. 1888; 17 Sept. 1889; 1 Oct. 1890.
"Mrs. Humphrey Ward at Home." *Wheeling (W. Va.) News*, 6 Nov. 1898. SCPC, JAC; *JAPM*, 55:463.
"Mrs. Kathleen MacDonald Hamill [Obituary]." *Chicago Daily Tribune*, 3 Feb. 1944.
"Mrs. Mary C. Hollis Dead." *Chicago Daily Tribune*, 13 Oct. 1912.
"Mrs. Morrison Re-elected Head of Suffrage Assn." *Chicago Daily Tribune*, 30 Apr. 1918.
"Mrs. Palmer Is Honored." *Chicago Chronicle*, 13 Feb. 1900.
"Mrs. Palmer's Paris Work." *New York Tribune*, 1 July 1900. SCPC, JAC; *JAPM*, 55:582.
"Mrs. Sophia Rogers Durfee." *Chicago Daily Tribune*, 9 Feb. 1900.
"Mrs. Terrell Is Again President." *Chicago Times-Herald*, 16 Aug. 1899.

"Mrs. Trout's News Year Message to the New Voters." *Chicago Daily Tribune*, 29 Dec. 1913.

"Mrs. Ursula L. Harrison Starts for Denver to Take Charge of the State Industrial School." *Chicago Daily Tribune*, 11 Mar. 1898.

"Mrs. Whitman Is Dead; Member of Pioneer Family." *Chicago Daily Tribune*, 3 Feb. 1932.

"Mrs. Wickes Sues for a Divorce." *New York Times*, 2 Nov. 1894.

[Muldoon]. In "Parish New Notes: Cathedral." *New World*, 3 and 10 Dec. 1892.

"Multitude of Improvements for Chicago Postoffice." *Chicago Times-Herald*, 30 June 1900. SCPC, JAC; *JAPM*, 55:580.

Mumford, John. [Florence Kelley Interview]. *New York Herald and Tribune*, 9 Nov. 1924.

Mumford, Manly W. "The Old Family Fire." Delivered to the Chicago Literary Club, 27 Jan. 1997. www.chilit.org/MUMFORD2.HTM.

Municipal Voters' League [of Chicago]. "Nineteenth Ward—Thomas Gallagher." In "The Municipal Campaign of 1897—Official Records of . . . Aldermen," 7. CHM, CHS, Citizens' Association of Chicago Collection, Municipal Voters' League of Chicago Records, 1896–98.

———. "Official Records of Retiring Aldermen." The Municipal Campaign, 5 Apr. 1898. Chicago: Municipal Voters' League, 1898. CHM, CHS, Citizens' Association of Chicago Collection, Municipal Voters' League of Chicago Records, 1896–98.

Murphy, Mary E. "Bill of Divorce" from Matthew Murphy. 24 May 1895. Cook County, Circuit Court, Archives, Divorce Records.

"[Murphy, Matthew] Death Notices." *Chicago Daily Tribune*, 24 Dec. 1924.

"[Murphy, Matthew] Obituary." *Chicago Daily Tribune* 25 Dec. 1924.

"Must Show Authority. Strikers Are Pullman's Reason for Closing Calumet Lake." *Chicago Times*, 6 June 1894.

"National Banks Elect Officers." *Chicago Daily Tribune*. Jan. 15, 1890.

"Need One Day's Rest in Seven." *Chicago Daily Tribune*, 30 Sept. 1893.

Nelli, Humbert Steven. "The Role of the 'Colonial' Press in the Italian-American Community of Chicago, 1886–1921." Ph.D. thesis, University of Chicago, 1965.

"New Auxiliary Bishop for Chicago Diocese [Rev. P. J. Muldoon]." *Chicago Daily Tribune*, 13 July 1901.

"The New Child Labor Law." *Chicago Record*, 2 July 1897.

"New Church for Negroes." *Chicago Daily Tribune*, 22 Oct. 1900.

New England Congregational Church (Chicago). *Record Books, 1853–1940* [list of members]. Chicago Theological Seminary, Archives, New England Congregational Church, Chicago.

"New Hull House Annex." *Chicago Times-Herald*, 19 July 1895. Hull-House Scrapbook 3:17; *JAPM*, Addendum 10:8ff.

"New School Seeks Pupils." *Chicago Chronicle*, 23 Feb. 1900.

"New School's Plans Told. Chicago Institute, Psychologic and Pedagogic, May Open Its Doors July 1." *Chicago Daily News*, 22 Feb. 1900.

"News of Woman's Clubs." *Chicago Daily Tribune*, 14 May 1899.

"Nicholas Kelley, Lawyer, Is Dead." *New York Times*, 29 Oct. 1965.

"The Nineteenth Century Club." *New York Times*, 17 Feb. 1893.

"Nineteenth Ward: Vote for Armstrong." *Chicago Times-Herald*, 4 Apr. 1898.

Nineteenth Ward Improvement Club, Chicago. "Constitution." UIC, JAMC, Hull-House Association; *JAPM*, 51:625.

"Nineteenth Ward's Crowning Glory." *Chicago Daily Tribune*, 10 Oct. 1897.

"90 Flee 2 Fires in Flat Building; Hunt Firebug. Third Blaze Destroys Settlement." *Chicago Daily Tribune*, 3 Mar. 1930.

Niver, Edwin B. "Remarks at the Funeral of Mary Rozet Smith." TMs, 2 pp., UIC, JAMC.

"Noble Charity Work." *Chicago Post*, 1 Feb. 1893. Hull-House Scrapbook 1:28; *JAPM*, Addendum 10:6ff.

"No Future for Social-Reform Bosses." *Chicago Inter Ocean*, May 17, 1889.

"Normal School Exercises." *Chicago Evening Post*, 16 June 1894.

"Noted Clergyman and Religious Writer Dies." Unidentified newspaper clipping. [7 May 1930?]. Cincinnati Historical Society.

"No Tenement Problem Here." *Chicago Inter Ocean*, 23 Mar. 1900. SCPC; JAC; *JAPM*, 55:565.

"Not to Budge a Bit." *Chicago Times-Herald*, 6 Mar. 1898.

"Novel Charity Work." *Chicago Post*, 1 Feb. 1893.

O'Brien, Howard Vincent. "All Things Considered." *Chicago Daily Tribune*, 14 Feb. 1939.

"O'Brien in Arrears." *Chicago Daily Tribune*, 31 Mar. 1893.

"Officer of the Juvenile Court." *Hull-House Bulletin* 4, no. 4 (1 Jan.–1 May 1901): 12–13. UIC, JAMC, Hull-House Association; *JAPM*, 53:767–68.

"Of Interest to the Gentler Sex." *Chicago Daily Tribune*, 22 Mar. 1897. SCPC, JAC; *JAPM*, 55:248.

"Of Interest to Women [re: Bertha Payne]." *Chicago Daily Tribune*, 14 Nov. 1895.

"Old Dearborn Seminary." *Chicago Daily News*, 18–19 Jan. 1889.

Onahan, Mary Josephine. "A Social Settlement." *Citizen*, [1894?]. Hull-House Scrapbook 1:61; *JAPM*, Addendum 10:6ff.

"Opening of Chautauqua Assembly Season." *New York Times*, 2 July 1893.

"Opening of 'Children's House.'" *Chicago Daily Tribune*, 16 Dec. 1895.

"Opening the Tee-To-Tum." *New York Times*, 24 Mar. 1893.

O'Sullivan, Mary Kenney. "Address by Mrs. Mary K. O'Sullivan of the Bookbinders Union," [1905]. TMs. LC, NWTUL.

O'Sullivan, Mary Kenney. "Autobiography of Mary Kenney O'Sullivan." [1930?]. TMs. RS, O'Sullivan.

"Our Boston Letter: The Cool Reasoning at Plymouth." *Springfield (Mass.) Republican*. Hull-House Scrapbook 1:21; *JAPM*, Addendum, 10:6ff.

"Outlet for Faculties: The Subjective Necessity of a Social Settlement." *Boston Herald*, 29 July 1892. Hull-House Scrapbook 1:21; *JAPM*, Addendum 10:6ff.

"Oxford House in Bethnal Green." *Jackson's Oxford Journal* (London), 18 May 1895.

["P. R. Buchanan"]. *Guardian* (London), 19 Mar. 1890.

"Palmer, Charles Harvey." *Twenty-fifth Anniversary Report of the Class of 1889*. HUA.

[Paris correspondent of the *Chicago Record*]. untitled article. *Rochester (N.Y.) Union and Advertiser*, 11 June 1900. SCPC, JAC; *JAPM*, 55:579.

"Parisians Cheer the Founder of Hull House." *Chicago Times-Herald*, 14 June 1900. SCPC, JAC; *JAPM*, 55:579.

"Pass Her through Fire. Theosophists Cremate the Remains of Their Sister [Meri Topelius]." *Chicago Daily Tribune*, 30 Jan. 1896.

"Pays Tribute to William H. Colvin." *Chicago Daily Tribune*, 9 July 1896.

Pelham, Laura Dainty. "Short Stories about Clever People Whom You Ought to Know." Chicago: Hollister Brothers Printers for the Laura Dainty Amusement Exchange, 1900. Private collection.

"Permanent Organization Formed." *Chicago Times*, 28 May 1894.

"Petition for a New School." *Hull-House Bulletin* 2, no. 6 (Oct. 1897): 6. UIC, JAMC, Hull-House Association; *JAPM*, 53:624.

"Philanthropy Won't Do." *Philadelphia Sun*, 27 Feb. 1900. SCPC, JAC; *JAPM*, 55:558.

"Philip W. Ayres, Forester, Was 84." *New York Times*, 5 Nov. 1945.

"Pick Mrs. Dixon as Woman's Club Vice President." *Chicago Daily Tribune*, 2 May 1920.

"Picks Out Its Men; Municipal Voters' League Issues Its Annual Report." *Chicago Daily Tribune*, 3 Apr. 1897.

"Pictures Lent to the Poor." *New York Times*, 25 Mar. 1896. Hull-House Scrapbook 3:69; *JAPM*, Addendum 10:8ff.

"Pioneer Patron of Hull House, Mary Smith, Dies." *Chicago Daily Tribune*, 24 Feb. 1934.

"Pioneer Surgeon Dead in Chicago." *Chicago Daily Tribune*, 29 May 1904.

"Plan for a Race." *Chicago Times-Herald*, 18 Aug. 1899.

"Plan for College Extension Classes at the Hull House. Summer Term, Beginning 5 June 1893." Hull-House Scrapbook 2:29½; *JAPM*, Addendum 10:7ff.

"Plan League Benefit for Easter Week." *Chicago Daily Tribune*, 24 Mar. 1915.

"Plan of National Federation [for grade school teachers]." *Chicago Daily Tribune*, 5 July 1895.

"Plans for the Jane Club." *Chicago Daily Tribune*, 14 Aug. 1898.

"Plans for the Poor." *Chicago Record*, 6 Sept. 1894. Hull-House Scrapbook 1:58; *JAPM*, Addendum 10:6ff.

"Plans of the New School of Pedagogy." *Chicago Herald*, 5 July 1899.

"Platform [of the Central Anti-Imperialist League, Chicago]." In *The Chicago Liberty Meeting Held at Central Music Hall, April 30, 1899*, 4. Liberty Tract No. 1 (1894).

"The Plymouth School." *Boston Transcript*, [5?] Aug. 1892. Hull-House Scrapbook 1:22; *JAPM*, Addendum 10:6ff.

"Polk Street Primary School." CBE, School Files.

Pond, Allen B. "Personal Philanthropy." *Plymouth Review*, Nov. 1890. Hull-House Scrapbook 1:5; *JAPM*, Addendum 10:6ff.

"Poor House Chocks Her." *Kansas City (Mo.) Star*, 25 Nov. 1897. SCPC, JAC; *JAPM*, 55:369.

Porter, Mary H. "A Home on Halsted St." *Advance* (Chicago), 11 July 1889. Hull-House Scrapbook 1:1; *JAPM*, Addendum 10:6ff.

"Predict Death to Fireman; Marshall Field & Co. Manager Told of Approaching Demise." *Chicago Daily Tribune*, 8 June 1911.

Presbyterian Church in the U.S.A. General Assembly. Minutes, 1889–1900. Presbyterian Historical Society.

———. Synod of Illinois. Minutes, 1889–1900. Presbyterian Historical Society.

"Present-Day Attitude to Social Problems." *Springfield (Mass.) Republican*, 8 Mar. 1900. SCPC, JAC; *JAPM*, 55:564.

"President Healy's Statement. Claims to Have Reformed Many of the Abuses at Dunning." *Chicago Times-Herald*, 13 Aug 1895.

"President's Guarded Language." *Chicago Daily Tribune*, 17 Oct. 1898.

"Primaries or Leagues?" *Chicago Chronicle*, 2 Apr. 1898.

"Prods for the Lazy; Civil Federation Hot after Chicago Garbage Contractors." *Chicago Daily Tribune*, 7 Sept. 1894.

*Programme of the Department of Labor* [for the World's Columbian Exposition]. Chicago: W. B. Conkey, 1890.

"Progress of Woman." *Chicago Record*, 19 June 1900.

Pryor, Mary P., and Luz Elena Montenegro. "Index to the Julia Lathrop Papers." [2006]. TMs, 16 pp., RC, Archives.

"Pseudo-scientific Charity. Miss Richmond of Baltimore in Mistakes of Organized Investigators and Reformers." *New York Sun*, 23 Jan. 1900. SCPC, JAC; *JAPM*, 55:541.

"Public Farewell to Loved Bishop [Muldoon]." *Chicago Daily Tribune*, 13 Dec. 1908.

"Public School Drawings at the Art Institute [of Chicago]." *Arts* 4 (Sept. 1895): 78–79.

"Public Speaking Course for Women Begins Today." *Chicago Daily Tribune*. 5 Jan. 1914.

"'Pull' Cripples Health Bureau; Witnesses Say Complaints Are Useless and Inspectors Are Moved If They Report Violations." *Chicago Daily Tribune*, 6 June 1903.

"Pullman Hides Hovels." *Chicago Times*, 26 May 1894.

"The Pullman Industrial Community." *Chicago Record*, 16 May 1894.

"Pullman Is Stubborn: Flatly Refuses to Arbitrate with Striking Employees." *Chicago Times*, 2 June 1894.

Pullman Palace Car Co., Secretary Office: Strike Scrapbooks, 1894–1897. Newberry Library, Chicago, Pullman Palace Car Co. Archives. Scrapbooks, 1865–1947, Series 03.

"Pullman Relief Committee Withdraws." Unidentified newspaper, 13 June 1894. Newberry Library, Pullman Palace Car Co. Archives, Chicago Pullman Secretary, Scrapbook 1894–95, Series 03.

"Pullman's Men Go Out." *Chicago Record*, 12 May 1894.

"Pullman Strike." *Chicago Record*, 12 May 1894.

"Quinn Chapel." Early Chicago, Dusable to Obama: Chicago's Black Metropolis—WTTW. www.wttw.com.

"R. Whitman, 88, Retired Dean of Lawyers, Dies." *Chicago Daily Tribune*, 24 Dec. 1949.

"Ready to Arbitrate: American Railway Union's Offer: Willing to Submit Its Grievances against the Pullman Company to the Civic Federation." *Chicago Herald*, 2 June 1894.

"Reception to Miss A[d]dams." *Boston Herald*, 17 Feb. 1897. SCPC, JAC; *JAPM*, 55:243.

["Record Book of Copies of Letters and Articles"]. [1889–92]. SC, Starr.

"Relief Work Begun." *Chicago Record*, 18 May 1894.

"A Remembrance of Dr. Anna E. Blount." Nineteenth Century Charitable Association, 30 Jan. 2012. www.19thcenturyclub.com/index.php?pr=dr-anna-e-blount.

"Report on Child Labor." *Chicago Daily Tribune*, 20 May 1897.

"Reports of Good Work by Women [sewing rooms]." *Chicago Daily Tribune*, 11 Jan. 1894.

"Reports on Dunning." *Chicago Inter Ocean*, 1 Sept 1895.

"Resolutions on the Death of Mrs. Alzina Parsons Stevens by the Hull-House Women's Club." *Hull-House Bulletin* 4, no. 3 (Autumn 1900): 13. UIC, JAMC, Hull-House Association; *JAPM*, 53:752.

"Retrospective Glance at the Woman's Congress." *New York Evening Telegraph*, 9 July 1900. SCPC, JAC; *JAPM*, 55:584.

"Reunion of the Pullmans." *Chicago Daily News*, 18 Aug. 1902.

"Rev. Edwin A. Adams, D.D." *Missionary Herald*, May 1927, p. 207.

"Revenge for Saloonkeeper O'Brien." *Chicago Daily Tribune*, 28 July 1892.

Rice, Rebecca. "Students of Antioch in Chicago." *Antiochian* (Yellow Springs, Ohio), May 1888.

Rich, Adena Miller. "Julia Lathrop and the League of Women Voters." 6 May 1932. TMsI, 15 pp., SCPC, JAC.

"Rites Tomorrow for F. D. Keyser, Hull House Aid." *Chicago American*, 23 May 1961.

"Rockefeller to Give $1,000,000." *New York Times*, 21 Mar. 1900.

Ruegamer, Lana. "The Paradise of Exceptional Women: Chicago Women Reformers, 1863–1893." Ph.D. diss., Indiana University, 1982.

Russell, John. "Art View: An Art School That Also Taught Life." *New York Times*, 19 Mar. 1989.

"The Salvation Army." *London Morning Post*, 13 Jan. 1896.

"A Salvation Army Shelter for Women in Whitechapel." *London Graphic*, 27 Feb. 1892.

"[Sammons, Frederick Harrington Cruikshank] Obituary." *Chicago Daily Tribune*, 8 Sept. 1917.

Särkkä, Timo. "Hobson's Imperialism: A Study in Lake-Victorian Political Thought." Jyväskylä Studies in Humanities, no. 118. Ph.D. diss., University of Jyväskylä, 2009.

"Saved by the Needle; Emergency Relief Association Saves Many Women." *Chicago Daily Tribune*, 4 Jan. 1894.

"Say There's Nothing to Arbitrate." *Chicago Daily Tribune*, 17 Apr. 1892.

"Scenes at the Polls." *Chicago Chronicle*, 6 Apr. 1898.

Schilling, George. "[Mary Kenney]." 1 Aug. 1902. TMsS. ISHL, Schilling.

Schmidt, Heinie. "It's Worth Repeating; One of the Light Brigade [Henry Gyles]." *High Plains Journal* (Dodge City, Kans.), 2 Jun 1949.

Schultz, Rima Lunin. "Hull-House after Jane Addams; Revisiting the Social Settlement as Wonen's Space, 1889–1935." Paper for the Newberry Seminar on Women and Gender. Chicago: 5 Dec. 2008. TMs, 26 pp.

"The Schumann-Heink Concert." *Chicago Daily Tribune*, 10 Nov. 1912.

"Schumann-Heink to Sing; Suffrage Will Benefit." *Chicago Daily Tribune*, 14 Nov. 1912.

"[Sears, Laura Raymond Davidson]. Obituary." *Chicago Daily Tribune*, 4 Apr. 1930.

"[Sears, Nathaniel Clinton] Obituary." *Chicago Daily Tribune*, 8 May 1934.

"Seek Pulpit Aid." *Chicago Times* and *Eight Hour Herald*, 29 May 1894.

Segur, Rosa L. "Mrs. A. P. Stevens." *Toledo (Ohio) Times*, 10 June 1900.

"Service to Honor the Memory of Eleanor Smith Founder of Hull-House Music School June 15, 1858–June 30, 1942, Held at Hull-House Saturday, October 3, 1942." 1942. TMs. UIC, JAMC.

"Settlement Conference." *Commons* 6, no. 2 (June 1897): 7, 9–13.

"She Gave Up Her Home." *Chicago Journal*, 17 May 1890. Hull-House Scrapbook 1:2; *JAPM*, Addendum 10:6ff.

"She Labors for the People." *Boston Daily Globe*, 21 Feb. 1899.

Silke, Lucy S. "Josephine-Carson-Locke." 27 Jan. 1926. TMs, 3 pp. CBE, Biographical Files.

"[Simmons, Francis T.] Obituary." *Chicago Daily Tribune*, 6 July 1920.

"Single Tax League Discussion." *Chicago Daily Tribune*, 30 Aug. 1893.

"Sir John Gorst on Social Questions; Universities and the Poor." *Aberdeen Weekly Journal* (Scotland), 3 Nov. 1894.

Sive-Tomashefsky, Rebecca Anne. "Jane Addams and Mary Smith: The Single Woman and the Societal Claim." Master's thesis, UIC, 1974. TMs, 53 pp., private collection.

"600 Friends to Pay Homage to Mrs. Joseph T. Bowen on Her 80th Birthday, Feb. 27." *Chicago Daily Tribune*, 16 Feb. 1939.

"Slot-Machine Gas . . . Transfers Miss Johnson." *Chicago Record*, 28 June 1897.

"'Sloyd,' the New Swedish Educational Device, Will Be Introduced by Miss Meri Toppelius of Sloyd Institute, Chicago" [Advertisement]. *Chicago Daily Tribune*, 14 July 1891.

"Sloyd [at the Bay View Summer University, Bay View, Mich.]" [Announcement]. *Chicago Daily Tribune*, 14 July 1891.

"Sloyd Institute—Now Open at 188 Madison-St" [Advertisement]. *Chicago Daily Tribune*, 13 Sept. 1890.

"[Smith, Edwin Burritt] Obituary." *Chicago Daily Tribune*, 9 May 1906.

[Smith, Mary]. In "Judges' Good Nature Impressive." *Chicago Daily Tribune*, 14 Apr. 1912.

Smith, Mary Rozet. Records of the Estate of Mary Rozet. Cook County, Ill., Circuit Court, Archives, Probate Records.

"[Smith, Mrs. Charles Mather] Obituary." *Chicago Daily Tribune*, 27 Mar. 1903.

"Snare for Workmen." *Chicago Times*, 19 May 1894.

Snively, Julie. "Letters Paint Rockford's Past; Dr. Lena C. Leland's Writings to a Friend Describe the City as It Was at the Dawn of the 20th Century." *Rockford (Ill.) Register Star*. n.d. RC, Archives, Lena C. Leland File.

"Social Awakening in London." *Decatur (Ill.) Daily Review*, 31 May 1892.

"Socialism." *Chicago Daily Tribune*, 28 Dec. 1889.

"Socialism and Nationalism. Tommy Morgan's People Object to Having Their Creed Sugar-Coated." *Chicago Daily Tribune*, 30 Dec. 1889.

"Socialism in England." *Chicago Daily Tribune*, 23 Dec. 1889.

"Socialist Sunday School in Chicago. Its History, Its Curriculum, Its Effectiveness." *New York Volks-Zeitung*, 28 July 1889.

"A Social Settlement." *Boston Transcript*, 30 July 1892. Hull-House Scrapbook 1:21; *JAPM*, Addendum 10:6ff.

"Social Settlements." *Churchman*, New York, 24 Nov. 1892. Hull-House Scrapbook 1:22; *JAPM*, Addendum 10:6ff.

"The Social Test." *Public Opinion*, 29 Mar. 1900. SCPC, JAC; *JAPM*, 55:567.

"Society Divides a Family [Kathleen McDonald and Charles Frederick Mather Smith]." *Chicago Daily Tribune*, 3 May 1908.

"Solving the Problem: Working Men and Women Learning to Help Themselves." *Chicago Daily Tribune*, 1 Nov. 1891.

"Songs of the People." *Chicago Record*, 21 Nov. 1895. Hull-House Scrapbook 3:28; *JAPM*, Addendum 10:8ff.
"Sparks from the Wires: [Alessandro Mastro-Valerio]." *Chicago Daily Tribune*, 11 Dec. 1893.
"The Spectator." *Christian Union* (New York), 27 Aug. 1892. Hull-House Scrapbook 1:23; *JAPM*, Addendum 10:6ff.
"[Springer, Milton C.] Obituary." *Chicago Daily Tribune*, 27 Dec. 1890.
"[Stalbus, Anna Bauer] Death Notices." *Chicago Daily Tribune*, 2 Apr. 1944.
Stalbus, Michael J. Marriage License. 11 May 1896. Cook County, Ill., Recorder, Marriage Licenses.
[Statement by Edwin A. Waldo]. N.p., n.d. Andover Newton Theological School, Newton Centre, Mass. Trask Library, Archives and Special Collections.
"[Stehman, Dr. Henry B.] Obituary." *Chicago Daily Tribune*, 18 Feb. 1918.
"Step for a Pullman School." *Chicago Chronicle*, 16 Feb. 1900.
Stone, Isabelle. "General Information [biographical data], 55452." N.d., 3 pp., Wellesley College Archives, Alumnae Biographical Files.
*The Story of a Play; Realistic Description of Life among the Moonshiners: A Mountain Pink*. Pamphlet. Chicago: R. R. Donnelley & Sons [1878?].
"Street Cleaning Is Inexpensive." *Chicago Daily Tribune*, 21 June 1895.
"The Strike at Pullman." *Chicago Herald*, 26 June 1894.
"Strikers Go Back to Work." *Chicago Daily News*, 22 May 1897.
"Strikers Stand Fast." *Chicago Record*, 14 May 1894.
"Studies at Hull House." Unidentified newspaper clipping, [1892?]. Hull-House Scrapbook 1:17; *JAPM*, Addendum 10:6ff.
"Suffering of Pullman Strikers." *Chicago Record*, 18 May 1894.
"Suffrage Body Plans Luncheon." *Chicago Daily Tribune*, 29 Oct 1915.
"Suffragists Plan Fall Work." *Chicago Daily Tribune*, 3 May 1912.
"A Suggestive Question." *New York Times*, 10 Dec. 1897. SCPC, JAC; *JAPM*, 55:380.
"Suggests Future of Unions." *Chicago Daily Tribune*, 9 Sept. 1900. SCPC, JAC; *JAPM*, 55:590.
"Suggests School for Suffragist Speakers." *Chicago Daily Tribune*, 8 Apr. 1912.
"Sunday Evening Lectures." *Hull-House Bulletin* 2, no. 7 (1 Nov. 1897): 1. UIC, JAMC, Hull-House Association; *JAPM*, 53:629.
"Sundered Ties: Laura Dainty's Husband Granted a Divorce." *Chicago Daily Tribune*, 19 Oct. 1884.
"Sunset Club Dinner." *Chicago Daily Tribune*, 22 Dec. 1893.
"Sure of Victories." *Chicago Chronicle*, 3 Apr. 1898.
"Sure to Make Gains." *Chicago Chronicle*, 4 Apr. 1898.
"Susannah Parrish Wharton." Family Search, International Genealogical Index, 9 Mar. 2011. www.familysearch.org.
"Sweep Streets; Leave Dirt." *Chicago Daily Tribune*, 24 Mar. 1903.
Swing, David. "A New Social Movement." *Chicago Evening Journal*, 8 June 1889. Hull-House Scrapbook 1:1; *JAPM*, Addendum 10:6ff.
"Syllabus for a Course in Electricity." Hull-House College Extension Program. Hull-House Scrapbook 2:8; *JAPM*, Addendum 10:7ff.
"Syllabus for a Course of Six Lectures on Physics." Hull-House College Extension Program. Hull-House Scrapbook 2:18; *JAPM*, Addendum 10:7ff.

"T. H. Wickes Dies Suddenly." *New York Times*, 29 Mar. 1905.

T. W. H. "Women and Me: On the Advantages of Candor." *Harper's Bazaar* (6 Mar. 1897).

"Talked of Chicago's Idle." *Chicago Times*, 22 Feb. 1893.

"Talk Equal Rights." *Chicago Inter Ocean*, 7 Nov. 1897. SCPC, JAC; *JAPM*, 55:348.

"Talks by Teachers." *Chicago Daily Tribune*, 3 July 1897. SCPC, JAC; *JAPM*, 55:304.

"Talks on 'Trade Unions.'" *Chicago Journal*, 1 Dec. 1900. SCPC, JAC; *JAPM*, 55:607.

"Talk with Jane Addams." *Chicago Chronicle*, [Apr. 1897]. SCPC, JAC; *JAPM*, 55:297.

"Tee-To-Tum." *Chicago Inter Ocean*, 31 July 1892.

"The Tee-To-Tum." *Ogden (Utah) Standard*, 12 Dec. 1891.

"Tells Ministers of Hull House." *Advance* (Chicago), 23 May 1894. SCPC, JAC; *JAPM*, 55:16.

"Their Work Is Done. Various Subcommittees Submit Their Reports on Dunning." *Chicago Inter Ocean*, 31 Aug. 1895.

"They Decry Equal Suffrage. Members of Illinois Association Issue a Manifesto Arguing against Extending the Right to Vote." *Chicago Daily Tribune*, 18 Jan. 1900.

"They Uphold the Strikers." *Chicago Daily Tribune*, 19 Apr. 1892.

"They Will Propose Arbitration." *Chicago Daily Tribune*, 16 Apr. 1892.

"They Won Fame Both Sides of the Atlantic [Walter and Fred Pelham]." *Lyceumite and Talent* 5, no. 1 (June 1911): 20–21.

"Thinks the Criticism Is Unjust." *Chicago Daily Tribune*, 5 May 1895.

"Thomas Y. Crowell." *New York Times*, 30 July 1915.

"Thomas Y. Crowell Publishers Records. An Inventory of Its Records at Syracuse University." Syracuse University, Library, Finding Aids. library.syr.edu/digital/guides.

"Thousands at Service of Thanks." *Chicago Daily Tribune*, 17 Oct. 1898.

"To Abolish Sweat Shops." *Chicago Daily Tribune*, 9 Mar. 1896. Hull-House Scrapbook 3:70; *JAPM*, Addendum 10:8ff.

"To Aid Sick and Wounded Boers." *New York Tribune*, 13 Jan. 1900. SCPC, JAC; *JAPM*, 55:540.

"To Aid Slum Sister; Plans of the Woman's Club." *Chicago Record*, 1 Apr. 1897.

"To Aid the Negro." *Chicago Times-Herald*, 15 Aug. 1899.

"To Aid the Spirit Wrestlers." *New York Times*, 13 Nov. 1898.

"To Convert the Rich; Socialism and the Church before the Economic Conference." *Chicago Daily Tribune*, 30 Dec. 1889.

"To-Day's Municipal Election." *Chicago Times-Herald*, 5 Apr. 1898.

Todd, Arthur J. "Tribute to Enella Benedict, Delivered at Her Funeral Services at Hull-House on April 11, 1942." [Apr. 1892]. Dup. Ms. UIC, JAMC, Rich.

"To Give a Drama." *Terre Haute (Ind.) Evening Gazette*, 10 Aug. 1898.

"To Help Seamstresses." *Chicago Record*, 6 Sept. 1894. Hull-House Scrapbook 1:58; *JAPM*, Addendum 10:6ff.

"To Lecture on Donegal." *Chicago Daily Tribune*, 16 Nov. 1892.

"To Lift Her Race." *Chicago Times-Herald*, 13 Aug. 1899.

Tomlins, William L. "People's Songs. Hull-House Prize Competitions." 1 May 1895. Hull-House Scrapbook 3:55; *JAPM*, Addendum 10:8ff.

[Toomey, Maggie, Obituary]. *Juneau County (Wis.) Chronicle*, 4 Feb. 1897.

"To Speak at Paris Fair." *Chicago Times-Herald*, 21 May 1900. SCPC, JAC; *JAPM*, 55:576.

"To Stop All Strikes." *Chicago Daily Tribune*, 28 Sept. 1894.
"To Stop Sweatshops." *Chicago Inter Ocean*, 21 Feb. 1893. Hull-House Scrapbook 1:34; *JAPM*, Addendum 10:6ff.
"Tour of the Alleys." *Chicago Daily Tribune*, 4 May 1895.
"To Vote for Powers." *Chicago Inter Ocean*, 19 Feb. 1900. SCPC, JAC; *JAPM*, 55:547.
"A Training Class of Irish Girls in Art Embroidery." *Chicago Daily Tribune*, 12 Aug. 1888.
"Tribulations of Chicago." *New York Times*, 5 Sept. 1897.
"Trouble at Pullman." *Chicago Record*, 8–9 May 1894.
Trowbridge, Harriet H. Death Certificate #18680. Cook County, Ill., Recorder.
"True Democracy and Social Ethics." *Philadelphia Press*, 26 Feb. 1900. SCPC, JAC; *JAPM*, 55:557.
"The Trust Conference in Operation." *Chicago Record*, 15 Sept. 1899.
"Twelve Jolly Bachelors in a Bunch." *Chicago Record*, [Jan. 1895]. Hull-House Scrapbook 3:9; *JAPM*, Addendum 10:8ff.
"Two Die [Julia A. Beveridge], Three Injured in Five Street Crashes." *Chicago Daily Tribune*, 21 June 1919.
"Two Great Meetings." *Milwaukee Sentinel*, 8 July 1897. SCPC, JAC; *JAPM*, 55:309–10.
"Two Reports from Dunning." *Chicago Inter Ocean*, 3 Sept. 1895.
"Two Thousand Tanners Are Out." *Chicago Daily Tribune*, 17 Feb. 1897.
"Uncle Sam's Birthday Party." *Chicago Times*, 5 July 1890.
Underwood, B. F. "A Valuable Institution." *Religio-Philosophical Journal* (Nov. 1892). Hull-House Scrapbook 1:21½; *JAPM*, Addendum 10:6ff.
"Union Girls Give a May Party." *Chicago Daily Tribune*, 7 May 1892.
"Union Women Will Give Ball Saturday Evening." *Chicago Daily Tribune*, 28 Oct., 1913.
"University Intelligence [Oxford House]." *Jackson's Oxford Journal* (London), 19 May 1900.
"University of Chicago; Mrs. Nancy S. Foster Makes Another Handsome Gift to the Institution." *Chicago Inter Ocean*, 12 Feb. 1893.
"University Settlements in East London." *London Daily News*, 1 Mar. 1895.
"Unlikeness to Lear." *Chicago Daily News*, 5 May 1895.
Valerio, J. M. "A Rose Is a Rose When Ir Recalls Patti." *Chicago Daily Tribune*, 14 Dec. 1939.
"Vassar." *Boston Herald*, 19 Feb. 1893.
"Vassar College." *New York Times*, 19 Feb. 1893.
"The Verestchagin Exhibit." *Chicago Tribune*, 3 Feb. 1889.
"Viewing the Canvases." *Chicago Daily Tribune*, 2–3 Feb 1889.
Visiting Nurse Association of Chicago. "General Rules." Chicago: Visiting Nurse Association of Chicago, n.d. CHM, CHS, Visiting Nurse Association of Chicago Records.
———. [Invitation to Theodore Thomas Concert]. 3 Dec. 1894. PD, CHM, CHS.
———. "Rules for Nurses, Visiting Nurse Association of Chicago." Chicago: Visiting Nurse Association of Chicago, n.d. CHM, CHS, Visiting Nurse Association of Chicago Records.
"Voluntary Probation Officers." *Chicago Daily Tribune*, 19 Nov. 1901.
Vosswinkel, Laura. "Government Response to the Pullman Strike." History 185: Seminar Late Nineteenth Century. Professor Yohn, Spring 2001, 32 pp.

"W. H. Colvin Is Dead." *Chicago Times-Herald*, 8 July 1896.
"W. H. Colvin's Will Filed." *Chicago Daily Tribune*, 14 July 1896.
"Wage War on Dirt." *Chicago Daily Tribune*, 22 Mar. 1895.
Waldo, Edwin A. File, Andover Newton Theological School, Newton Centre, Mass., Trask Library, Archives and Special Collections.
"Ward Politics Made Honest." *Chicago Record*, 12 Mar. 1898.
"War on Dirty Places." *Chicago Daily Tribune*, 3 May 1895.
"Wealthy Women Rip 'False Front' from Their Ward. Find Tenements Back of Lake Shore Drive." *Chicago Daily Tribune*, 13 June 1917.
"Weaving in Donegal." *Chicago Inter Ocean*. 6 Nov. 1892. Hull-House Scrapbook 1:24; *JAPM*, Addendum 10:6ff.
"Weddings. Wallin–Sikes." *Chicago Chronicle*, 4 Feb. 1897.
"The Week of Jubilee." *Chicago Daily Tribune*, 16 Oct. 1898.
Welch, Jeannette Cora. Wellesley College, Wellesley College Archives, Alumnae Biographical Files.
Weller, Charles. "Friendly Visiting." *Chicago Record*, 1 Oct. 1897.
———. "[The sloth which Chicago and some cities manifest . . .]." *Chicago Record*, 20 Oct. 1897.
"[Weston, Olive E.] Death Notices." *Chicago Daily Tribune*, 1 Sept. 1918.
"West Side Deal Realty Feature." *Chicago Daily Tribune*. 1 July 1913.
"What a Patient Saw." *Chicago Times-Herald*, 13 Aug. 1895.
"What a Police Matron Should Be." *Chicago Daily Tribune*. 22 Aug. 1891.
"What Irish Peasants Are Doing." *Chicago Daily Tribune*, 10 Nov. 1892.
"Where Filth Is King." *Chicago Daily Tribune*, 26 July 1885.
"Whitewashed." *Chicago Record*, 10 Sept. 1895.
"Why Churches Fail." *Chicago Evening Post*, 21 Nov. 1898. SCPC, JAC; *JAPM*, 55:474.
"Why Servants Are Scarce." *Chicago Daily Tribune*, 1 Mar. 1896.
"Why the Church Fails to Reach the Workmen." *Chicago Daily Tribune*, 29 Nov. 1898.
"Will Exhibit Fine Laces." *Chicago Daily Tribune*, 7 Aug. 1892.
"William Bross Dead." *Chicago Daily Tribune*, 28 Jan. 1890.
"William Dawson Johnson Papers; A Finding Aid," prepared by Patrick Kerwin and Lia Apodoca, Library of Congress, Manuscript Division, 2005, encoded by Jennifer Eidson, 2010. hdl.loc.gov.
"William Dillon, Loyola's First Law Dean, Buried." *Chicago Daily Tribune*, 1 Apr. 1935.
"William H. Colvin." *Chicago Times-Herald*, 8 July 1896. SCPC, JAC; *JAPM*, 55:190.
"Will Keep Mrs. Kelley in Office." *Chicago Record*, 29 May 1897.
"Will Nose about Alleys." *Chicago Daily News*, 1 May 1895.
"Will Not Arbitrate; Federation of Labor Is Strongly Opposed to the Idea." *Chicago Inter Ocean*, 14 Dec. 1893.
Will of Elizabeth V. Smith. Richland County, S.C., Probate Court Records.
"Will Turn Out for Powers." *Chicago Chronicle*, 2 Apr. 1898.
"Will Work in the Slums [Addison Alvord Ewing]." *New York Times*, 18 Mar. 1897.
"Winter Resident Has Passed Away; George Cotton Smith Dies in Pennsylvania." *Columbia (S.C.) State*, 1 Dec. 1915.
"With Modest Grace; Description of a Ball at Hull House Settlement." *Chicago Inter Ocean*, 4 Dec. 1893.

"With Spring Comes Talk of Vacation Days." *Chicago Daily Tribune*, 16 Mar. 1933.

"Woman as Worker. Her Condition Discussed at the Labor Congress. Servant Girl Problem." *Chicago Inter Ocean*, 30 Aug. 1893.

"Woman Garbage Inspector." *Baltimore Sun*, 1 Mar. 1900.

"A Woman on Labor Unions." *State Register* (Des Moines, Iowa), 11 Dec. 1900. SCPC, JAC, *JAPM*, 55:611.

"Woman on Trade Unions." *Chicago Daily Tribune*, 2 Dec. 1900. SCPC, JAC; *JAPM*, 55:607. "Woman Plunges 4 Floors to Her Death in Hospital [Valerio]." *Chicago Daily Tribune*, 17 Dec. 1944.

"Woman's Board. Room 48 M'Cormick Block." *Interior*, 7, 14, and 21 Feb. 1889.

"A Woman's Congress in Paris." *New York Times*, 8 July 1900. SCPC, JAC; *JAPM*, 55:584.

"Woman's Work at Hull House." *Buffalo (N.Y.) Courier*, 28 July 1895. Hull-House Scrapbook 3:14; *JAPM*, Addendum 10:8ff.

"Woman's Work at Paris Fair." *Chicago Daily Tribune*, 6 June 1900.

"Women and Clean Streets." *Chicago Herald*, 26 Apr., 1895.

"Women Declare War." *Chicago Inter Ocean*, 16 Dec. 1892. Hull-House Scrapbook 1:26; *JAPM*, Addendum 10:6ff.

"Women Doing Good Work; Sewing Rooms Continue Successful—More Money Needed." *Chicago Daily Tribune*, 11 Jan. 1894.

"Women in Wartime." *Chicago Daily Tribune*, 29 Jan. 1918.

"Women of the Every Day Club." *Chicago Times-Herald*, 15 Jan. 1899. SCPC, JAC; *JAPM*, 55:493.

"Women Out of Work." *Chicago Inter Ocean*, 17 Dec. 1893.

"Women Talk of Tolstoi." *Chicago Chronicle*, 6 Oct. 1898.

"Women to Be Turned Out." *Chicago Daily News*, 26 Feb. 1894.

"Women to Meet in Four Halls." *Chicago Daily Tribune*. 2 Mar. 1914.

"Won for Reform." *Chicago Record*, 6 Apr. 1898.

Woolfolk, Ada S. Wellesley College, Wellesley College Archives, Alumnae Biographical Files.

"The Working Girls of Chicago." *Review of Reviews*, Sept. 1891. Hull-House Scrapbook 1:11; *JAPM*, Addendum 10:6ff.

"Working Papers on Rev. John Trevor (1855–1930), Founder of the Labour Church." Collection description, MSS.143. Reference Code TRV, 1892–1968. University of Warwick, England. dscalm.warwick.ac.uk.

"Work of the Police Matrons." *Chicago Daily Tribune*, 8 Jan. 1887.

"Work of Two Women." *Chicago Times*, 3 July 1890. Hull-House Scrapbook 1:2; *JAPM*, Addendum 10:6ff.

"Work of Women's Clubs." *Chicago Daily Tribune*, 13 July 1899.

"A Worthy Appointment [Alessandro Mastro-Valerio]." *Chicago Inter Ocean*, 13 Jan. 1889.

["A Writer in the *Living Church*, of Chicago"], originally published in the *Independent* and reissued in *Unity*, 27 July 1893, p. 252. Hull-House Scrapbook 1:40; *JAPM*, Addendum 10:6ff.

"Young Ones at Work: Those at Hull House Are Helping the Civic Federation; Intend to Have Clean Alleys." Unidentified newspaper clipping, [June 1895]. Hull-House Scrapbook 3:9; *JAPM*, Addendum 10:8ff.

## *3. Printed and Manuscript Sources of Genealogy and Vital Statistics, Government Records, Reports, and Returns*

Addams Family Genealogy Files, JAPP.

Alabama, State of. Baldwin County, Marriage Bond Records.

Anderson, Marian, comp. *De Kalb County, Illinois, Index to Death Register I: January 1878–June 1903*. Sycamore, Ill.: Genealogical Society of De Kalb County, Ill., 1982.

Atwater, W. O., and A. P. Bryant. *Dietary Studies in Chicago in 1895 and 1896: Conducted with the Cooperation of Jane Addams and Carolina L. Hunt, of Hull House*. Bulletin No. 55, U.S. Department of Agriculture, Office of Experiment Stations. Washington, D.C.: GPO, 1898; *JAPM*, 54:678–754.

Banks, Olive. *The Biographical Dictionary of British Feminists*. Vol. 1, *1800–1930*. New York: New York University Press, 1985.

Beaver, I. M. *History and Genealogy of the Bieber, Beaver, Biever, Beeber Family*. Reading, Pa.: I. M. Beaver, 1939.

Benedict, Elwyn Ellsworth. *The Genealogy of the Benedicts in America*. N.p.: [E. Benedict, ca. 1969].

Benedict, Henry Marvin. *The Genealogy of the Benedicts in America*. Albany, N.Y.: J. Munsell, 1870.

*Biographical Directory of the United States Congress, 1774–Present*. biogide.congress.gov/biosearch.

Blatchford, Eliphalet Wickes. *Blatchford Memorial II: A Genealogical Record of the Family of Rev. Samuel Blatchford, D. D., with Some Allied Families*. Chicago: privately printed, 1912.

Bogue, Virgil T. *Bogue and Allied Families*. Holly, Mich.: Herald, [1944].

Cedarville, Ill. Cemetery Index to Burial Records, 1850–1994. N.d. HMs, 64 pp., CAHS.

*Centennial List of Mayors, City Clerks, City Attorneys, City Treasurers, and Aldermen Elected by the People of the City of Chicago, from the Incorporation of the City on March 4, 1837, Arranged in Alphabetical Order, Showing the Years during Which Each Official Held Office*. Compiled by Frederick Rex. Chicago: Municipal Reference Library, [1937].

Chicago Board of Education. *Public Schools of the City of Chicago: Forty-fourth Annual Report of the Board of Education for the Year Ending June 24, 1898*. Chicago: Board of Education, 1898.

Chicago City Directories, 1892–95.

*Chicago Daily News Almanac and Year-Book*, 1890–1901. Chicago Daily News, 1890–1901.

Chicago Department of Development and Planning. *The People of Chicago: Who We Are and Who We Have Been; Census Data on Foreign Born, Foreign Stock and Race, 1837–1970; Mother Tongue Addendum, 1910–1970*. Duplicated D, 1976.

Chicago Department of Health. *Biennial Report of the Department of Health of the City of Chicago for the Year 1904–05*. Chicago: Cameron Amberg, 1906.

Congregational and Christian Churches. *The Year-Book of the Congregational and Christian Churches*. Vol. 53 as *Congregational Year Book*. New York and Dayton, Ohio: Executive Committee of the General Council of the Congregational and Christian Churches, 1930.

Cook County, Ill., Circuit Court Records, 1895–96.

Cutter, William Richard, ed. *Genealogical and Personal Memories Relating to the Families of the State of Massachusetts*. Vol. 2. New York: Lewis Historical, 1910.

Edwards, Richard, [comp.] *Chicago Census Report, and Statistical Review*. Chicago: Richard Edwards, 1871.

Fink, Gary M., ed. *Biographical Dictionary of American Labor Leaders*. Westport, Conn.: Greenwood Press, 1974.

*General Catalogue of the Officers and Graduates of the University of Wisconsin, 1849–1902*. Compiled by David B. Frankenburger. Madison: University of Wisconsin, 1902.

*General Catalogue, Presbyterian Theological Seminary, Chicago, Lane Seminary Affiliated*. Chicago: Presbyterian Theological Seminary, 1959.

Gore, James H. "Report of the Juror in Chief." In *Report of the Commissioner-General for the United States to the International Universal Exposition, Paris, 1900*, 5:3–14. 56th Cong., 2nd sess., Senate Doc. No. 232. Washington, D.C.: GPO, 1901.

Haldeman Family Genealogy Files, JAPP.

Herringshaw, Thomas William. *Herringshaw's Encyclopedia of American Biography of the Nineteenth Century*. Chicago: American Publishers Association, 1898.

Hopper, Orion Cornelius. *Biographical Catalogue of Princeton Theological Seminary, 1815–1954*. Princeton, N.J.: Theological Seminary of the Presbyterian Church, 1955.

Hunt, Caroline L. "Food." In *U.S. Commissioner of Labor, Ninth Special Report: The Italians in Chicago; A Social and Economic Study*, 44–50. Washington, D.C.: GPO, 1897; *JAPM*, 54:784–88.

Illinois. Cook County, City Board of Health. Death Certificates.

———. *Report of the Board of State Commissioners of Public Charities to the State of Illinois*. 13th–16th, 19th, and 21st biennial reports. Springfield, Ill., 1894, 1896, 1898, 1900, 1906, 1910.

Illinois, State of. Board of Health. *Eleventh Report [Being for the Year Ended December 31, 1888*. Springfield, Ill.: R. W. Rokker, 1892.

———. *Official Register of Physicians*. Springfield, Ill.: H. W. Rokker, 1894.

———. *Official Register of Physicians and Midwives in Illinois, 1884*. Springfield, Ill.: H. W. Rokker, 1884.

———. *Official Register of Physicians and Midwives Now in Practice to Whom Certificates Have Been Issued by the State Board of Health, 1877–1886*. Springfield, Ill.: H. W. Rokker, 1886.

Illinois, State of. Secretary of State. *Blue Book*, 1906–35. Springfield, Ill., 1906–35.

Illinois, State of. State Archives. "Illinois Public Domain Land Sales from the 1st Half of the 19th Century." ISA, Land Records Databases.

———. "Pre-1916 Illinois Statewide Death Index." And Illinois Statewide Death Index, 1916–50. www.cyberdriveillinois.com.

Illinois, State of. State Archives and Illinois Department of Public Health. "Database of Illinois Death Certificates, 1916–1950." www.cyberdriveillinois.com.

Illinois, State of. State Archives and Illinois State Genealogical Society. "Illinois Statewide Marriage Index, 1763–1900." www.cyberdriveillinois.com.

Intercollegiate Community Service Association. [*Report*]. Dec. 1919.

Iowa, State of. Deaths and Burials, 1850–1990.

———. Marriages, 1802–1992.

———. State Census Returns, 1885.

Jordan, John Woolf. *Genealogical and Personal History of the Allegheny Valley Pennsylvania.* Vol. 1. New York: Lewis Historical, 1912.

Kansas, State of. State Census Returns, Crawford County, 1895.

Kelley, Florence. *First Annual Report of the Factory Inspectors of Illinois for the Year Ending December 15, 1893*. Springfield: H. W. Rokker, 1894.

———. *First Special Report of the Factory Inspectors of Illinois, on Small-Pox in Tenement House Sweat-Shops of Chicago, July 1, 1894*. Springfield: H. W Rokker, 1894.

———. *Second Annual Report of the Factory Inspectors of Illinois for the Year Ending December 15, 1894*. Springfield: Ed. F. Hartman, 1895; *JAPM*, 54:161–280, 283–347.

Keyser Family Vertical File, Geneseo (Ill.) Public Library.

Linn Family Files, JAPP.

Linn Family Vertical File, Geneseo (Ill.) Public Library.

Martin, Elizabeth Wyant. "Esther Margaret Linn and Charles Eri Hulbert." Family History Library, prepared by Jonathan Peter Harris.

"Master List, Carroll County [Ill.] Cemeteries." Carroll County Genealogy Society, n.d., Mimeograph, Carroll County, Ill.

May, Samuel P. *The Descendants of Richard Sares (Sears) of Yarmouth, Mass., 1688–1888*. Albany, N.Y.: J. Munsell's Sons, 1890.

Military Order of the Loyal Legion of the United States. Commandery of the State of Illinois. *Memorials of Deceased Companions of the Commandery of the State of Illinois, Military Order of the Loyal Legion of the United States*. Vol. 2, *1901–12*. Chicago: [Military Order of the Loyal Legion of the United States. Commandery of the State of Illinois], 1923.

Minnesota, State of. Deaths and Burials, 1935–1900.

———. Death Records, 1866–1916.

Montague, W. L, comp. and ed. *Biographical Record of the Alumni and Non-graduates of Amherst College (Classes '72–'96) 1871–96*. Vol. 2. Amherst, Mass.: Carpenter and Morehouse, 1901.

Murray, Alexander S. *Who's Who in Mythology*. New York: Bonanza, 1989.

*National Cyclopaedia of American Biography.* Current vol. G, 1943–46. New York: J. T. White, 1946.

*New Zealand Journal of the Department of Labor for the Year 1897.* Wellington, New Zealand: John Mackay, 1897.

North Carolina, State of. Death Certificate Records.

Ohio, State of. Department of Health. Index to annual deaths, 1958–2002. Ohio Department of Health, Columbus.

———. Division of Vital Statistics. Death certificates and index, 20 Dec. 1908–31 Dec. 1953. State Archives Series 3084. [Columbus]: Ohio Historical Society.

———. Marriages, 1880–1958.

*Prominent Women of Illinois, 1885–1932*. Chicago: Illinois Woman's Press Association, 1932.

Reed, William F. *The Descendants of Thomas Durfee of Portsmouth, R.I.* 2 vols. Washington, D.C.: Gibson Brothers, 1902–5.

*Report of the Commissioner-General for the United States to the International Exposition, Paris.* Report to the 56th Cong., 2nd sess., Senate. Document No. 232. Washington, D.C.: GPO, 1901.

*Report on the Chicago Strike of June–July, 1894 by the United States Strike Commission.* Washington, D.C.: GPO, 1895.

*Report on the Manufacturing Industries in the United States at the Eleventh Census: 1890.* Pt. 2. Washington, D.C.: GPO, 1895.

Seller, Maxine Schwartz. *Women Educators in the United States, 1820–1993: A Bio-bibliographical Sourcebook.* Westport, Conn.: Greenwood Press, 1994.

Stephenson County, Ill. County Clerk. Records relating to the Addams and Haldeman families.

Stephenson County, Ill. Recorder. Records relating to the Addams and Haldeman families.

Stephenson County [Ill.] Genealogical Society. *Cemetery Inscriptions, Stephenson County, Illinois.* Vol. 5, *Freeport City Cemetery, Freeport, Ill.* Freeport, Ill: Stephenson County Genealogical Society, [1992].

Stiles, Henry Reed. *The Stiles Family in America: Genealogies of the Connecticut Family.* Jersey City, N.J.: Doan and Pilson, 1895.

Trowbridge, Mason. *Family Annals.* [West Cornwall, Conn.]: privately printed, 1958.

United States. Census Returns.

Illinois, 1850, 1860, 1870, 1880, 1900, 1910, 1920, 1930.

Indiana, 1850, 1870.

Iowa, 1880, 1900.

Kansas, 1880, 1900.

Maryland, 1930, 1940.

Massachusetts, 1870, 1900, 1910, 1920.

Nebraska, 1880.

Pennsylvania, 1870, 1880, 1900, 1910, 1920.

Vermont, 1850, 1900, 1910, 1920.

Wisconsin, 1860, 1870, 1880, 1900, 1910, 1920.

———. Immigration Records.

———. Passport Records.

U.S. Department of Interior. Commissioner of Labor. *Fourth Annual Report, 1888: Working Women in Large Cities.* Washington, D.C.: GPO, 1889.

———. *The Italians in Chicago: A Social and Economic Study; Ninth Special Report.* Washington, D.C.: GPO, 1897; *JAPM*, 54:761–973.

U.S. Department of Labor. Children's Bureau. *Annual Reports of the Chief: Children's Bureau to the Secretary of Labor, 1st–9th.* Washington, D.C.: GPO, 1913–21.

Waterman, Richard, Jr. *The Social Economy Exhibit, Paris Exposition of 1900.* [Boston?]: Commonwealth of Massachusetts for the Department of Education and Social Economy for the U. S. Commission to the Paris Exposition of 1900.

Wright, Carroll D. *Seventh Special Report: The Slums of Baltimore, Chicago, New York, and Philadelphia.* Washington, D.C.: GPO, 1894.

### *4. Rare Book Collections*

Cedarville Area Historical Society, Cedarville, Ill.
Rare Book Room, Colman Library, Rockford University, Rockford, Ill.
Swarthmore College Peace Collection, Jane Addams Collection, Swarthmore, Pa.
University of Illinois at Chicago, Jane Addams Memorial Collection.

### *5. Photograph Collections*

Andover Theological Seminary, Newton, Mass.
Art Institute of Chicago
Bar Harbor Historical Society, Maine
Beloit College, Archives, Wis.
Chicago Museum of History, Chicago Historical Society, Photographs
Chicago Public Library, Harold Washington Library Center, Special Collections
Congregational Library, Boston
Harvard University, Radcliffe Institute, Schlesinger Library, Cambridge, Mass.
Illinois Institute of Technology, Chicago
Jane Addams Papers Project, DeLoach Files, Fayetteville, N.C.
Jane Addams Papers Project, Hulbert Files, Fayetteville, N.C.
Library of Congress, Prints and Photographs Division, Washington, D.C.
National Portrait Gallery, London
Oshkosh Public Museum, Wis.
Radcliffe College, Schlesinger Library, Cambridge, Mass.
Rockford University, Howard Colman Library, Archives, Rockford, Ill.
Smith College, Archives, Northampton, Mass.
Somerville College, Oxford, England
Swarthmore College, Swarthmore College Peace Collection, Pa.
University of Chicago
University of Florida, Library, Gainesville
University of Illinois at Chicago, Jane Addams' Hull-House Museum
University of Illinois at Chicago, Jane Addams Memorial Collection, Photographs
University of Michigan, Bentley Historical Library, Ann Arbor
Victoria and Albert Museum, London
Winnetka Historical Society, Ill.
Yale University, Manuscripts and Archives, New Haven, Conn.

### *6. Directories, Published Minutes and Reports, Annuals, Catalogs, and Announcements*

Addams, Jane, and Ellen Gates Starr. *Hull-House, a Social Settlement at 335 South Halsted St., Chicago. An Outline Sketch*. Chicago: privately printed, 1 Feb. 1894, 31 pp. and photographs. SCPC, JAC; *JAPM*, 46:618–42.

All Souls Church (Chicago). *All Souls Church, Eleventh Annual, 1894*. Chicago: [All Souls Church], [1894].

———. *Ten Years of Church Life. The Tenth Annual of All Souls Church, Chicago*. Chicago: [All Souls Church], 1893.

American Board of Commissioners for Foreign Missions. *Annual Report*, 1868–1930.
*The American Physician and Surgeon Blue Book, 1919*. Chicago: American Blue Book, 1919.
Armour Institute. *Integral* [yearbook]. 1896/97–1900/01.
*Armour Mission, Chicago*. [Chicago: Armour Mission, 1895].
*The Book of Chicagoans*. Chicago: A. N. Marquis, 1905, 1911, 1917, 1930, 1936.
*Catalogue and Directory of Officers, Alumni, and Former Students* [of Wabash College]. Crawfordsville, Ind.: Wabash College, 1923.
*Catalogue of the University of Wisconsin, 1887–88*. Madison: University of Wisconsin, 1888.
Charity Organization Society of Chicago. *Annual Report*, 1896, 1888. CMH.
*The Chicago Blue Book of Selected Names of Chicago and Suburban Towns*. Chicago: Chicago Directory, 1890.
Chicago Bureau of Charities. *Annual Report*, 5th, 6th, and 7th, 1898–1901.
Chicago City Directories, 1857–1905.
*Chicago Daily News Almanac and Year-Book*, 1890–1901. Chicago Daily News, 1890–1901.
Chicago Historical Society. *Annual Report*, 1919.
*Chicago Medical Blue Book 1921*. Chicago, 1921.
Chicago Relief and Aid Society. *Annual Report to the Common Council of the City of Chicago*. Chicago: various printers, 1888–1901.
Chicago Training School for City, Home and Foreign Missions. *Annual Announcement, 1889/90–1895/96*. [Chicago: The School, 1889–95].
———. *Annual Reports*, 9th, 10th, and 11th. 1894/95–1896/97. [Chicago: The School, 1895–97].
Chicago Woman's Club. *1885–86, 1891/92–1903/-04 Announcements*.
———. *Forty-second Annual Announcement 1918–19*. [Chicago]: Chicago Woman's Club, [1918].
———. *Fifty-fourth Annual Announcement 1930–31*. [Chicago]: Chicago Woman's Club, [1930].
Civic Federation of Chicago, *First Annual Report*. Chicago: R. R. Donnelly and Sons, 1895.
*Columbia City Directory, 1891*. Charleston, S.C.: Southern Directory, 1891.
Congregational and Christian Churches. *The Year-Book of the Congregational and Christian Churches*. Vol. 53 as *Congregational Year Book*. New York and Dayton, Ohio: Executive Committee of the General Council of the Congregational and Christian Churches, 1930.
Dearborn Female Seminary. *Dearborn Female Seminary*. Annual catalogs, 1859–1870, 1875–76, 1901–2. Chicago: various printers, 1859–70, 1901, CHM, CHS.
*Directory of Directors in the City of Chicago*. Chicago: Audit Company of New York, 1902.
*Directory of the Physicians, Druggists and Dentists of Chicago*. Chicago: A. B. Judson, [1886]. CHM, CHS.
*The Elite Directory and Club List of Chicago*, 1885–86, 1887–88. Chicago: Elite, 1885 and 1887.
Evanston, Ill. *City Directory*, 1903–5.

Ferry Hall, Lake Forest University. *Annual Register Fourteenth and Fifteenth*, 1882–83, 1883–84. Chicago: J. J. Spalding, 1883; Spalding and Keefer, 1884. LFC, Archives.

———. *Catalogue of Ferry College for Young Ladies and Ferry Hall Seminary for the Academic Year, 1887–88*. Chicago: Clark and Longley, 1888. LFC, Archives.

Fortnightly [Club] of Chicago. *Annuals*. [Chicago]: [Fortnightly Club of Chicago], 1884–85, 1891. CHM, CHS.

*General Catalogue, Presbyterian Theological Seminary, Chicago, Lane Seminary affiliated*. Chicago: Presbyterian Theological Seminary, 1959.

*General Catalogue of Oberlin College, 1833–1908*. Oberlin College, Ohio, [1920?].

*General Catalogue of the Officers and Graduates of the University of Wisconsin, 1849–1902*. Compiled by David B. Frankenburger. Madison: University of Wisconsin, 1902.

Girton School, Winnetka, Ill. *Girtonian*, 1907, 1909, 1910, 1911–16. North Shore Country Day School, Winnetka, Ill.: Winnetka Historical Society.

Glossop, Frank. *Glossop's Street Guide Strangers' Directory and Hotel Manual of Chicago*. 12th ed. Chicago: Frank Glossop, 1888.

Hafner, Arthur W., ed. *Directory of Deceased American Physicians, 1804–1929*. 2 vols. Chicago: American Medical Association, 1993.

*Hand-Book of Chicago's Charities*. Compiled by John Visher. Published by the Illinois Conference of Charities and Correction. Chicago: Edwin M. Colvin, 1892.

Harvard University. *Twenty-fifth Anniversary Report of the Class of 1889*. Cambridge, Mass.: Harvard University, 1914.

Harvard University Class of 1894. *Twenty-fifth Anniversary Report, 1894–1919*. Norwood, Mass.: privately printed for the Plimpton Press, [1919?].

*Hoye's Kansas City Directory*. Kansas City, Mo.: Hoye's, 1882, 1899, 1902.

Hull-House Woman's Club. *Year Book*, 1902–10. CHM, CHS, Bowen; 1911–12, RC, Archives; 1922–35, UIC, JAMC; *JAPM*, 51:27–294.

*Hull-House Year Book, 1906–1907, 1910, 1913, 1916, 1921, 1925, 1929, 1931, 1935*. Chicago: Hull-House Association, UIC, JAMC, Hull-House Association; *JAPM*, 53:875–1497.

*Illinois Industrial Training School for Boys at Norwood Park, Cook Co., Ill., for the Year Ending May 15, 1888. First Annual Report*. Chicago, [1888?].

Kingsley House, Pittsburgh, *Annual Reports*, 1894, 1895, 1896. Pittsburgh: various printers, 1894–96.

Kirkland School. *Announcements*, 1883–84, 1885–86, 1886–87, 1887–88, 1889–90. [Chicago: Kirkland School Association], [1883–90]. CHM, CHS.

Kirkland [School] Association. *Annual Report*, 1st–3rd (1891/92–1895/96). Chicago: [Kirkland School Association], 1892?–95? CHM, CHS.

Lake Forest College *Yearbook*. Chicago, 1903. LFC.

Lake Forest University. *Annual Register*, 1878–79, 1886–87. Chicago: J. J. Spalding, 1879; Lake Forest University, 1879, 1887. LFC.

*Lakeside Annual Directory of the City of Chicago, 1874–1914*. Chicago: Chicago Directory.

McDonald, J. Newton. *McDonald's Medical Directory of Chicago, Milwaukee, Minneapolis and St. Paul*. Chicago: J. N. McDonald, Nov. 1890.

*Minutes of the Annual Session of the Congregational Churches and Ministers of the State of Iowa*, 66th–67th annual sessions, 1906–7.

Montague, W. L. *Biographical Record of Amherst College Graduates and Non-graduates, 1871–96*. Amherst, Mass.: Carpenter and Morehouse, 1901.

Municipal Voters' League. *Official Records of Retiring Aldermen*. Chicago: Municipal Voters' League, 1897–98.

North End Club, Chicago. *Annual Announcements*, 1898–99, 1902–3. CHM, CHS.

*Plan of Re-Numbering City of Chicago*. Chicago: Chicago Directory, 1909.

*Polk's Kansas City (Mo.) Directory*. Kansas City, Mo.: Gate City Directory, 1930.

Presbyterian Church in the U.S.A. General Assembly. *Minutes*, 1889–1930.

Presbyterian Theological Seminary, Chicago. *General Catalogue*. Chicago: Presbyterian Theological Seminary, 1939.

*Proceedings of the Chicago Conference on Trusts . . . Held September 13th, 14th, 15th, 16th, 1899*. Edited by Franklin H. Head. Chicago: Civic Federation of Chicago, 1900.

Ransom, Reverdy C. *First Quadrennial Report of the Pastor and Warden of the Institutional Church and Social Settlement*. Presented to the Twenty-second Session of the General Conference and to the Connectional Trustees of the African Methodist Episcopal Church. Quinn Chapel, Chicago, May 1904.

*Report of the Chicago Relief and Aid Society . . . for the Sufferers by the Chicago Fire*. Cambridge, Mass.: Riverside Press for the Chicago Relief and Aid Society, 1874.

*Reversed Directory of the Elite of Chicago*. Chicago: H. A. Pierce, 1889.

Rockford College, Rockford, Ill. *Annual Report of the President, 1905–1906*. [Rockford, Ill.: Clark Co. Press, 1906]. RC, Archives.

———. *Annual Report to the Board of Trustees, 1891–1896*. RC, Archives.

———. *Forty-sixth Annual Catalogue, 1896–1897*. Rockford, Ill.: Horner, 1897. RC, Archives.

———. *Fifty-fourth Official Circular, 1904–1905*. Chicago: P. F. Pettibone, 1905. RC, Archives.

———. *Fifty-fifth Official Bulletin, 1905–1906: Announcements for 1906–1907*. Rockford, Ill.: Clark Co. Press, [1906]. RC, Archives.

Rockford Seminary, Rockford, Ill. *Thirty-fifth Annual Catalogue of the Officers and Students, 1885–1886*. RC, Archives.

———. *Thirty-ninth Annual Catalogue of the Officers and Students, 1889–1890*. Rockford, Ill.: Gazette Printing House, 1890. RC, Archives.

Scott, E. C., comp. *Ministerial Directory of the Presbyterian Church, U.S., 1861–1941*. Austin, Tex.: Von Boeckmann–Jones, 1942.

Scott, Frank William, ed. *The Semi-centennial Alumni Record of the University of Illinois*. Vol. 1. Chicago: R. R. Donnelley and Sons, for University of Illinois Alumni Association, 1918.

*Second Chicago Photographic Salon, October 1 to 20, 1901*. Chicago: Chicago Society of Amateur Photographers and the Art Institute of Chicago, 1901.

*Social Register Chicago, 1929*. New York: Social Register Association, 1928.

*Social Register Chicago, 1934*. New York: Social Register Association, 1933.

*Social Register Chicago, 1935*. New York: Social Register Association, 1934.

*Social Service Directory, Chicago, 1930*. Chicago: Chicago Council of Social Agencies, 1930.

*Souvenir Musical Directory of Chicago . . . 1891–92*. [Chicago, 1892].

Stowe, Andrew David, ed. *Stowe's Clerical Directory of the American Church 1920–21*. Minneapolis: Andrew David Stowe, 1920.

University of Chicago. *Annual Register, 1896–1900, 1903–5*. Chicago: University of Chicago Press, 1897–1900, 1903–6. UC, Archives.

University School for Girls, Chicago. *Announcements*, 1897–1900, 1903–9, 1929–30. CHM, CHS.

University School for Girls, Chicago. *Castanon* [yearbook], 1917 and 1919. CHM, CHS.

University School for Girls, Chicago. *Catalogue*, 1889/1900–1919/30. Chicago: The School, 1899–1929. CHM, CHS.

Visiting Nurse Association. *Annual Report, 4th, 5th, 10th, 11th, 12th, 15th*. Visiting Nurse Association, 1894, 1895, 1900, 1902, 1904. Various publishers. CHM, CHS.

*Walsh's Directory of the City of Columbia for 1899*. Charleston, S.C.: Wm. H. Walsh, 1899.

*The Wellesley Legenda for A. D. 1892. [Boston*]: Senior Class of Wellesley College, 1892.

Whalen, Chas. J. *Biennial Report of the Department of Health of the City of Chicago for the Years 1904–1905*. Chicago: City of Chicago, 1906.

Woman's Christian Temperance Union, Chicago. *Thirteenth Annual Report of the Central Woman's Christian Temperance Union, Chicago, Illinois, for the Year Ending March 17, 1887*. [Chicago, 1887].

World's Columbian Exposition, 1893. Board of Lady Managers. *Approved Official Minutes, 1st–6th Session of the Board of Lady Managers*. 4 vols. Chicago: Rand, McNally, 1891–94.

*Year-Book of the Congregational and Christian Churches*. New York and Dayton, Ohio: Executive Committee of the General Council of the Congregational and Christian Churches, 1930.

## *7. Newspapers and Magazines*

*Aberdeen Weekly Journal* (Scotland), 1894.

*Andover (Mass.) Townsman*, 1894.

*Antiochian* (Yellow Springs, Ohio), 1888.

*Armour Mission Visitor* (Chicago), Dec. 1886–Nov. 1897.

*Arts*, 1895.

*Atlantic Monthly*, 1898–1900.

*Baltimore Sun*, 1900.

*Bird-Lore* (Audubon Societies, Chicago), 1907–18.

*Blackwood's Edinburgh Magazine* (Scotland), 1894.

*Boston Daily Globe*, 1899.

*Boston Herald*, 1892–1902.

*Boston Transcript*, 1892.

*Buffalo (N.Y.) Courier*, 1895–96.

*Charities and the Commons*, 1905–9.

*Charities Review*, 1891–1905.

*Chautauquan*, 1892–1903.

*Chautauqua Assembly Herald*, 1900.

*Chicago Chronicle*, 1896–1907.
*Chicago Daily News*, 1889–1900.
*Chicago Daily Tribune*, 1857–1987.
*Chicago Evening Journal*, 1889.
*Chicago Herald*, 1892–95.
*Chicago Herald-Record*, 1901–14.
*Chicago Inter Ocean*, 1889–1900.
*Chicago Journal*, 1900.
*Chicago Mail*, 1894–95.
*Chicago News*, 1929.
*Chicago Post*, 1890–1932.
*Chicago Record*, 1893–1901.
*Chicago Times*, 1889–95.
*Chicago Times-Herald*, 1895–1901.
*Columbia (S.C.) State*, 1890–1900.
*Commons* (Chicago), 1896–1905.
*Commons Index*, vols. 1–10, *April 1896–October 1895*. Compiled by Harriet R. Peck. Chicago: Training Center, National Federation of Settlements and Neighborhood Centers, 1964. Duplicated D.
*Dawn*, 1889–91.
*Decatur (Ill.) Daily Review*, 1892.
*East Ham Express* (London), 1896.
*Elgin (Ill.) Advocate*, 1881.
*Elgin (Ill.) Daily Courier*, 1887, 1915.
*Every Saturday* (Elgin, Ill.), 1897.
*Geneva (Ill.) Republican*, 1918.
*Glasgow Herald* (Scotland), 1894–96.
*Good Housekeeping*, 1898–1900.
*Graphic News* (Chicago), 1888.
*Guardian* (London), 1890.
*Hackney Express and Shoreditch Observer* (London), 1896.
*Hull-House Bulletin*, 1896–1906, UIC, JAMC, Hull-House Association; *JAPM*, 53:502a–873.
*Illustrated London News*, 1896.
*Inland Architect and News Record*, 1890–1900.
*Interior*, 1889–1900.
*Jackson's Oxford Journal* (London), 1895–1900.
*Juneau County (Wis.) Chronicle*, 1897.
*Kansas City (Mo.) Star*, 1897.
*Lancet* (London), 1872.
*Leicester Chronicle* (England), 1896.
*Light and Life for Women*, 1889–1900.
*London Daily News*, 1894–96.
*London Graphic*, 1892.
*London Morning Post*, 1895–96.
*Manchester Review* (England), 2005.

*Miami Herald*, 1961–62.
*Milwaukee Sentinel*, 1897–1900.
*Missionary Herald*, 1927.
*Munci (Ind.) Times*, 1900.
*New World* (Chicago), 1892–1900.
*New York Evening Telegram*, 1900.
*New York Mail and Express*, 1900.
*New York Sun*, 1900.
*New York Times*, 1880–1960.
*New York Tribune*, 1900.
*New York Volks-Zeitung*, 1899.
*New York World*, 1889.
*Ogden (Utah) Standard*, 1891.
*Outlook*, 1893–99.
*Pen and Scissors* [of the Chicago Avenue Church], vols. 1 and 2, Chicago, 1888–89.
*Philadelphia Press*, 1900.
*Plymouth Review*, Feb. 1889.
*Popular Science Magazine*, 1889–91.
*Public Opinion*, 1892–1900.
*Rochester (N.Y.) Union and Advertiser*, 1900.
*Rockford (Ill.) Collegian*, 1893–96.
*Rockford (Ill.) Evening Star*, 1898.
*Rockford (Ill.) Female Seminary Magazine*, 1889–93.
*Rockford (Ill.) Register Star*.
*San Francisco Chronicle*, 1900.
*Saturday Evening Post* (Chicago Lawn), 1893–96.
*Springfield (Mass.) Republican*, 1892.
*St. Louis Post-Dispatch*, Mo., 1900.
*Sunday Magazine* (London), 1889.
*Survey*, 1909–35.
*Syracuse (N.Y.) Post*, 1896.
*Talk* (Winnetka, Ill.), 1942.
*Terre Haute (Ind.) Evening Gazette*, 1898.
*Times* (London), 1896–1900.
*Toledo (Ohio) Times*, 1900.
*Toynbee Hall Record*, 1888–93.
*Union Signal*, 1886–92.
*Unity*, 1889–96.
*Wheeling (W.Va.) News*, 1898.
*Wisconsin State Journal* (Madison), 1949.
*Woman's Journal* (Boston), 1888–95.
*Yellow Springs (Ohio) News*, 1910.

## *8. General Internet Sources*

Ancestry. www.ancestry.com.
Answers. www.answers.com.
Blackpast. www.blackpast.org.

*Britannica Online Encyclopedia*. www.britannica.com.
British Museum. www.britishmuseum.org.
*Columbia Electronic Encyclopedia*. education.yahoo.com/reference/encyclopedia/.
*Dictionary of Art Historians*. www.dictionaryofarthistorians.org.
Family Search. Church of Jesus Christ of the Latter Day Saints. www.familysearch.org.
Find-a-Grave. findagrave.com.
Fodor's Travel. www.fodor.com.
*Internet Encyclopedia of Philosophy*. www.iep.utm.edu/.
National Archives. www.nationalarchives.gov.uk/education.
Poetry Foundation. www.poetryfoundation.org/.
*Saint Petersburg Encyclopedia*. www.encspb.ru/.
Salvation Army. www.salvationarmy.org.
Spartacus Educational. www.spartacus.schoolnet.co.uk/index.html.
*Stanford Encyclopedia of Philosophy*. plato.stanford.edu/Plato/Stanford.edu.
*Wikipedia*. wikipedia.com.

## *9. Newspaper, Journal, and Magazine Articles and Chapters from Books*

Abbott, Edith. "Julia Lathrop and Professional Education for Social Work." *Illinois Voter* 12, pt. 2 (June 1932): 8.
"Abel, Mary Hinman." Feeding America. digital.lib.msu.edu.
"About the Doukhobors." Union of Spiritual Communities of Christ. www.uscedoukhobors.org.
Adams, James M., comp. "A List of Illinois Place Names." *Illinois Libraries* 50 (Apr.–May 1968): iii–vi, 275–596.
Adams, Mrs. Elizabeth Livingston Steele. "The Palette Club." In *Official Catalogue of the Illinois Woman's Exposition Board*, 45–47, 56. Chicago: W. B. Conkey, 1893.
Addams, Jane. Address. "Funeral Services for Mary Hawes Wilmarth at Hubbard Woods, Illinois, August 30, 1919." PD, RC. JAPM, 48:102–13.
———. [Address at the commencement exercises at Western Reserve College for Women]. In "The Commencement." *College Folio* 2 (June 1894): 129–31; *JAPM*, 46:643–46.
———. "Address by Miss Jane Addams [on Jessie Bross Lloyd]." In *In Memoriam: Jessie Bross Lloyd, September 27, 1844–December 29, 1904*, 41–43. [Chicago: H. G. Adair Printing], [1905?]; *JAPM*, 46:1297–99, 1300–1304.
———. [Address on "How Would You Uplift the Masses?"]. In "[Report of] The Sunset Club, Chicago, Forty-second Meeting, Held at the Grand Pacific, Thursday Eve., February 4, 1892," 10–13. UIC, Sunset; *JAPM*, 46:498–502.
———. [Address on "How Would You Uplift the Masses?"]. In Sunset Club, Chicago, [*Year Book*] (1891–92): 118–21. UIC, Sunset.
———. [Address on "What Shall We Do for Our Unemployed?"]. In Sunset Club, Chicago, [*Year Book*] (1893–94): 81–82. UIC, Sunset; *JAPM*, 46:567–69.
———. "Alice Kellogg Tyler." In *The Excellent Becomes the Permanent*, 51–58. New York: Macmillan, 1932.
———. "The Art-Work Done by Hull-House, Chicago." *Forum* 19 (July 1895): 614–17; *JAPM*, 46: 717–21.

———. "A Belated Industry." *American Journal of Sociology* 1 (Mar. 1896): 536–50; *JAPM*, 46:743–51.

———. "A Belated Industry." *Journal of Home Economics* 11 (Aug. 1919): 355–64.

———. "A Book That Changed My Life." *Christian Century* 44 (13 Oct. 1927): 1196–98; *JAPM*, 48:876–79.

———. "The Charity Visitor's Perplexities." *Outlook* 61 (11 Mar. 1899): 598–600.

———. "Christmas Fellowship." *Unity* 42 (22 Dec. 1898): 308–9; *JAPM*, 46:895–97.

———. "Claim on the College Woman." *Rockford Collegian* 23 (June 1895): 59–63; *JAPM*, 46:711–16.

———. "The College Woman and the Family Claim." *Commons* 3 (Sept. 1898): 3–7; *JAPM*, 46:863–68.

———. "Commercialism Disguised as Patriotism and Duty." *St. Louis Post-Dispatch*, 18 Feb. 1900, sec. 4, 4; *JAPM*, 46:990–91.

———. "Count Tolstoy." *Chautauqua (N.Y.) Assembly Herald* 27 (11 July 1902): 5, 8; *JAPM*, 46:1119–21.

———. "Democracy and Domestic Service." *Chautauqua (N.Y.) Assembly Herald* 25 (11 Aug. 1900): 7; *JAPM*, 46:1007–8.

———. "Democracy and Education." *Chautauqua (N.Y.) Assembly Herald* 25 (9 Aug. 1900): 2; *JAPM*, 46:1002–3.

———. "Democracy and Industry." *Chautauqua (N.Y.) Assembly Herald* 25 (10 Aug. 1900): 7; *JAPM*, 46:1004–6.

———. "Democracy or Militarism." In *The Chicago Liberty Meeting Held at Central Music Hall, April 30, 1899*, by Central Anti-Imperialist League, 35–39. Liberty Tracts, No. 1. Chicago: Central Anti-Imperialist League, 1899; *JAPM*, 46:898–901.

———. "Discussion [on the 'After-care of Recovered and Convalescent Insane Patients']." National Conference of Charities and Correction, *Proceedings* (1897): 464–66; *JAPM*, 46:781–84.

———. "Domestic Service and the Family Claim—Address by Jane Addams of Illinois." In *The World's Congress of Representative Women*, edited by May Wright Sewall, 2:626–31. Chicago: Rand, McNally, 1894; *JAPM*, 46:570–76.

———. "Ethical Survivals in Municipal Corruption." *International Journal of Ethics* 8 (Apr. 1898): 273–91; *JAPM*, 46:843–62.

———. "'The Excellent Becomes the Permanent' [Julia C. Lathrop]." *Illinois Voter* 12, pt. 2 (June 1932): 3.

———. "Extracts of a Letter to Aylmer Maude." *Humane Review* 3 (June 1902): 216–17; *JAPM*, 3:435.

———. "Foreign-Born Children in the Primary Grades." *Journal of Proceedings and Addresses* (National Education Association) 36 (1897): 104–12; *JAPM*, 46:785–94.

———. "Foreign-Born Pupils in the Primary." *School Journal* 55 (14 Aug. 1897): 113. SCPC, JAC; *JAPM*, 55:319.

———. "A Function of the Social Settlement." *Annals of the American Academy of Political and Social Science* 13 (May 1899): 323–45; *JAPM*, 46:933–56.

———. "Growth of the Corporate Consciousness." *Illinois Conference of Charities Proceedings* (1897): 40–42; *JAPM*, 46:795–98.

———. "The Housing Problem in Chicago." *Annals of the American Academy of Political and Social Science* 20 (July 1902): 99–107.

———. "How Would You Uplift the Masses?," 10–13. In Minutes, Sunset Club. *Sunset Club Year Book*, 1891–92. UIC, Sunset; *JAPM*, 46:498–502.
———. "Hull-House." *Atlantic Monthly* 43 (Feb. 1899): 163.
———. "Hull-House, Chicago: An Effort toward Social Democracy." *Forum* 14 (Oct. 1892): 226–41; *JAPM*, 46:503–19.
———. "Hull-House, Chicago: An Effort toward Social Democracy." *Freeport (Ill.) Daily Journal*, 18 Nov. 1892, [2].
———. "Hull-House and Ald. Powers." *Chicago Record*, 20 Feb. 1900, 4.
———. "Hull-House as a Type of College Settlement." *Wisconsin State Conference of Charities and Correction Proceedings* (1894): 97–115; *JAPM*, 46:577–88.
———. "[Hull-House] Still Opposed to Powers." *Chicago Evening Post*, 20 Feb. 1900, 3; *JAPM*, 46:992–93, 55:549.
———. "[In Memoriam: William H. Colvin]." In "Golden Rule Men." *Commons* 1 (Oct. 1896): 2–3.
———. Introduction to *What Then Must We Do?* by Leo Tolstoy, vii–xiii. Translated by Aylmer Maude. London: Oxford University Press for Tolstoy Society, 1934; *JAPM*, 49:299–303.
———. "Judge Murray F. Tuley." In *The Excellent Becomes the Permanent*, 73–80. New York: Macmillan, 1932.
———. "Labor Museum at Hull House." *Current Literature* 29 (Oct. 1900): 423–24.
———. "Lecture on Tolstoi." *Chicago Post*, 2 Oct. 1897. SCPC, JAC; *JAPM*, 55:324–25.
———. "Mary Hawes Wilmarth." In *The Excellent Becomes the Permanent*, 97–109. New York: Macmillan, 1932.
———. "A Modern Lear." *Survey* 29 (2 Nov. 1912): 131–37; *JAPM*, 47:611–46.
———. "A Modern Lear: A Parenthetical Chapter." In *Satellite Cities: A Study in Industrial Suburbs*, edited by Graham Taylor, 68–90. New York: D. Appleton, 1915.
———. "A New Impulse to an Old Gospel." *Forum* 14 (Nov. 1892): 345–58; *JAPM*: 520–34.
———. "Nineteenth Ward School Notes." *Hull-House Bulletin* 1 (Jan. 1896): 8; *JAPM*, 53:510.
———. "The Objective Value of a Social Settlement." In *Philanthropy and Social Progress*, 27–56. New York: Thomas Y. Crowell, 1893; *JAPM*, 46:535–51.
———. "The Object of Social Settlements." *Union Signal* 22 (5 Mar. 1896): 148–49; *JAPM*, 46:752–54.
———. "Poor House Shocks Her." *Kansas City (Mo.) Star*, 25 Nov. 1897. SCPC, JAC; *JAPM*, 55:369.
———. "Prefatory Note." In *Hull-House Maps and Papers*, by Residents of Hull House, vii–viii. Crowell's Library of Economics and Politics, no. 5. New York: Thomas Y. Crowell, 1895; *JAPM*, 46:683–85.
———. "The Problem of Domestic Service Viewed Scientifically." *Review of Reviews* 12 (May 1896): 604–5.
———. "Report on Institutions for the Mental and Moral Improvement of Workingmen (Class 108)." In *Report of the Commissioner-General for the United States to the International Exposition, Paris,* 5: 654–64. Report to the 56th Cong., 2nd sess., Senate. Document No. 232. Washington, D.C.: GPO, 1901.
———. "Rockford Seminary Endowment." In *Memorials of Anna P. Sill, First Principal*

*of Rockford Female Seminary, 1849–1889*, 70–75. Rockford, Ill.: Daily Register Electric, 1889; *JAPM*, 46:447–50.

———. "The Settlement." *Illinois State Conference of Charities and Correction Proceedings* (1896): 54–58; *JAPM*, 46:738–42.

———. "The Settlement as a Factor in the Labor Movement." In *Hull-House Maps and Papers*, by Residents of Hull House, 183–204. Crowell's Library of Economics and Politics, no. 5. New York: Thomas Y. Crowell, 1895.

———. "Significance of Organized Labor." *International Association of Machinists Monthly Journal* 10 (Sept., 1898): 551–52; *JAPM*, 46:869–70A.

———. "Social Education of the Industrial Democracy: Settlement Problems in Educational Work with Adults: Labor Museum at Hull House." *Commons* [5] (30 June 1900): 17–20; *JAPM*, 46:997–1001.

———. "Social Relations." In *The Sunday Problem: Papers Presented at the International Congress on Sunday Rest, Chicago, Sept. 28–30, 1893*, 28–29. New York: Baker and Taylor, 1894.

———. "Social Settlement." *Chautauqua (N.Y.) Assembly Herald* 25 (13 Aug. 1900): 2; *JAPM*, 46:1009–10.

———. "The Social Settlement and University Extension." *Review of Reviews* 20 (July 1899): 93.

———. "Social Settlements." *National Conference of Charities and Correction Proceedings* (1897): 338–46; *JAPM*, 46:805–14.

———. "Social Settlements: A Three Years' Test." *Union Gospel News*, 28 Mar. 1895; *JAPM*, 46:704–6.

———. "Social Settlements: A Three Years' Test." *Union Gospel News*, 11 Apr. 1895; *JAPM*, 46:707–10.

———. "The Social Test." *Public Opinion* 28 (29 Mar. 1900): 398; *JAPM*, 46:994–96.

———. "The Subjective Necessity for Social Settlements." In *Philanthropy and Social Progress*, 1–26. New York: Thomas Y. Crowell, 1893; *JAPM*, 46:552–66.

———. *The Subjective Value of a Social Settlement*. Off print, n.p., [1892?]. 16 pp., RC.

———. *The Subjective Value of Social Settlements*. Off print, n.p., [1892?]. 13 pp., private collection.

———. "The Subtle Problems of Charity." *Atlantic Monthly* 43 (Feb. 1899): 163–78; *JAPM*, 46:916–32.

———. "Testimony of Jane Addams [on the Pullman Strike]." In *Report on the Chicago Strike of June–July, 1894, by the United States Strike Commission, Appointed by the President July 26, 1894, under the Provisions of Section 6 of Chapter 1063 of the Laws of the United States Passed October 1, 1888, with Appendices Containing Testimony, Proceedings and Recommendations*, by United States Strike Commission, 645–48. S. Ex. Doc., No. 7 (Serial set 3276), 53rd Cong., 3rd sess., 1895; *JAPM*, 46:699–703.

———. "Tolstoy, Prophet of Righteousness." *Unity* 102 (10 Sept. 1928): 11–12; *JAPM*, 48:1068–70.

———. "Tolstoy and Gandhi." *Christian Century* 48 (25 Nov. 1931): 1485–88; *JAPM*, 48:1676–80.

———. "Tolstoy and the Russian Soldiers." *New Republic* 12 (29 Sept. 1917): 240–42; *JAPM*, 47:1563–66.

———. "Tolstoy's Theory of Life." *Chautauqua (N.Y.) Assembly Herald* 27 (14 July 1902): 2–3; *JAPM*, 46:1122–24.

———. "Trades Unions and Public Duty." *American Journal of Sociology* 4 (Jan. 1899): 448–62; *JAPM*, 46:902–15.

———. "Trades Unions and Public Duty." *Railroad Trainmen's Journal 16* (Dec. 1899): 1070–86.

———. "A Visit to Tolstoi." *Woman's Journal* 41 (3 Dec. 1910): 221; *JAPM*, 47:71.

———. "A Visit to Tolstoy." *McClure's Magazine* 36 (Jan. 1911): 295–302; *JAPM*, 47:124–32.

———. "What Peace Means." *Unity* 43 (4 May 1899): 178.

———. "What Shall We Do for Our Unemployed?" In *The Meetings of 1893–94 and a List of the Members to January 1895*, 80–82. Chicago: Sunset Club, 1895. UIC, Sunset; *JAPM*, 46:567–69.

———. "What the Theater at Hull-House Has Done for the Neighborhood People." In "The Third Monthly Conference," 284–86. *Charities* 8, no. 13 (29 Mar. 1902); *JAPM*, 46:1094–97.

———. "Why Servants Are Scarce." *Chicago Tribune*, 1 Mar. 1896, 42.

———. "Why the Ward Boss Rules." *Outlook* 58 (2 Apr. 1898): 879–82.

———. "With the Masses." *Advance* (Chicago), 18 Feb 1892, 133.

———. "Woman's Work for Chicago." *Municipal Affairs* 2 (Sept. 1898): 502–8; *JAPM*, 46:871–75.

———. "The Workingwoman's Need of the Ballot." *Public Opinion* 23 (9 Dec. 1897): 749. SCPC, JAC; *JAPM*, 46:839–40, 55:376.

Addams, Jane, and Harry Sands Grindley. *A Study of the Milk Supply of Chicago*. University of Illinois Agricultural Experiment Station Circular, No. 13. Urbana: [University of Illinois], Dec. 1898. 18 pp., UIC, JAMC; *JAPM*, 46:876–94.

Addams, Jane, and Ellen Gates Starr. "Outline Sketch Descriptive of Hull House." In *Hull-House Maps and Papers*, by Residents of Hull House, 205–30. Crowell's Library of Economics and Politics, no. 5. New York: Thomas Y. Crowell, 1895; *JAPM*, 46:660–82.

"Alderman John Powers': Home Bombed by Political Rivals." Chicago Crime Scene Project. chicagocrimescenes.blogspot.com.

"Alfred Picard—Minister of the Marine, 1908–1909." www.globalsecurity.org.

Alter, Sharon Z. "Bowen, Louise deKoven." *WBC*.

"Andrews, Elisha Benjamin." Brunoniana. www.brown.edu.

"Atkinson, Edward." A Taste for Science. exhibits.mannlib.cornell.edu.

"Auditorium Theatre, Chicago." www.auditoriumtheatre.org.

"B. F. C. Costelloe, 1855–1899: A Biographical Note." www.euppublishing.com.

"Bacher, Otto Henry." *The Encyclopedia of Cleveland History*. ech.case.edu/cgi/article .ph?:d=BOH.

Baker, Ray S. "The Civic Federation of Chicago." *Outlook* (27 July 1893): 132–33.

Ball, Sidney. "Moral Aspects of Socialism." *International Journal of Ethics* 6 (1896): 291–322.

———. "The Socialist Ideal." *Economic Review* 9 (1899): 425–49.

"Ball, Sidney." In *Dictionary of British Educationists*, by Richard Aldrich and Peter Gordon. London: Woburn Press, 1989.

Barnett, Samuel A., and Henrietta Barnett. "Letter to the Chicago Conference from the Rev. Canon and Mrs. S. A. Barnett." *Commons* 6, no. 2 (June 1899): 1–2.

Barnum, Gertrude. "At the Shirtwaist Factory: A Story." *Ladies' Garment Worker* (June 1910): 4.

———. "'Button, "Button, Who's Got the Button?': The Strike at Muscatine, Iowa." *Survey* 26 (May 1911): 253–55.

———. "A Hungarian Girl's Impressions of America: A True Story Told by a White Good Striker." *Outlook* 104 (17 May 1913): 111–16.

———. "The Pittsburgh Convention and Women Unionists." *Charities and the Commons* 15, no. 14 (6 Jan. 1906): 441–42.

———. "A Story with a Moral." *Weekly Bulletin of the Clothing Trades* (20 Nov. 1908): 6.

———. "Women in the American Labor Movement." *American Federationist* 22 (Sept. 1915): 731–33.

Bartelme, Mary M. "A Judge Speaks." *Illinois Voter* 12, pt. 2 (June 1932): 7.

Bedell, Leila G. "A Chicago Toynbee Hall." *Woman's Journal* (Boston) 20 (25 May 1889): 162.

———. "Similar but Not Identical." *Woman's Journal* (Boston) 20 (21 July 1889): 231.

"Beloiter Was First Male Resident of Hull House." *Beloit College Magazine* (Spring 2003): 6.

Biehler, Dawn Day. "Flies, Manure, and Window Screens: Medical Entomology and Environmental Reform in Early-Twentieth-Century US Cities." *Journal of Historical Geography* 36 (2010): 68–78.

"Biography of George Mortimer Pullman." Orleans County, N.Y., Biographies. www.onlinebiographies.info/ny/orle.

"Biography of John Atkinson Hobson." Liberal Democrat History Group. liberalhistory.org.uk.

Birtwell, Charles W. "Home Libraries." In "The Care of Dependent, Neglected, and Wayward Children." *Proceedings*, International Congress of Charities, Correction and Philanthropy, 2nd sess. (June 1893): 144–51.

Blaugrund, Annette, with Joanne W. Bowie, eds. "Alice D. Kellogg: Letters from Paris, 1887–1889." *Archives of American Art Journal* 28 (1988): 11–19.

Booth, Charles. "The Unemployed." Chap. 5 in vol. 1 of *Labour and Life of the People*. London: Williams and Norgate, 1889.

Bowie, Joanne Wiemers. "Kellogg Tyler, Alice deWolf." *WBC*, 468–70.

Breckinridge, Sophonisba. "International Aspect of Miss Lathrop's Work." *Illinois Voter* 12, pt. 2 (June 1932): 9.

"Brief Sketch of the Life and Work of Henry Homes Babcock." *Bulletin of the Chicago Academy of Sciences* 2 (1891): vi–viii.

Brodlique, Eva H. "A Toynbee Hall Experiment in Chicago." *Chautauquan* 11 (Sept. 1890): 746–47. Hull-House Scrapbook 1:5; *JAPM*, Addendum 10:6ff.

"The Brotherhood Church: A Brief History." www.thebrotherhoodchurch.org.

Brown, Victoria. "Advocate for Democracy." In *Pullman Strike and the Crisis of the 1890s: Essays on Labor and Politics*, edited by Richard Schneirov, Shelton Stromquist, and Nick Slavatore, 130–58. Urbana: University of Illinois Press, 1999.

Bruce, Andrew Alexander. "Julia Lathrop in the Nineties." *Illinois Voter* 12, pt. 2 (June 1932): 4.

Bush, Mertica MacCrea. "Hull-House Labor Museum." *Craftsman* 8, no. 2 (Nov. 1907): 229–30; *JAPM*, 51:452–53.

Caldwell, Thekla Ellen. "Nettie Fowler McCormick." *WBC*, 551–54.
Carter, Heath W. "Scab Ministers, Striking Saints: Christianity and Class Conflict in 1894." *American Nineteenth Century History* 11, no. 3 (Sept. 2010): 321–49.
"Charles Columbus Arnold, Obituary." *Hamilton Alumni Review* 6 (Mar. 1939): 170–71.
"Charles D. Hamill." In *Biographical Dictionary and Portrait Gallery of Representative Men of Chicago, Milwaukee, and the World's Columbian Exposition*, 199–200. Chicago and New York: American Biographical, 1892.
"Chicago." *American Nineteenth Century History* 11 (Sept. 2010): 321–49.
"Chicago Lockout Events." *Commons* 48 (15 July 1900): 3.
"Christmas Entertainments." *Hull-House Bulletin* 2, no. 1 (Jan. 1897): 6.
"The Clarion Scouts." Working Class Movement Library. www.wcml.org.uk.
"C.L.S.C. Chronology." *Chautauquan* 37 (July 1903): 896.
Cobb, John Storer. "Swinburne Island." In *Quartercentury of Cremation in North America*, 88–89. Boston: Knight and Millet, 1901.
Colson, Ethel M. "A Home in the Tenements." *Junior Munsey* 10 (Apr. 1901): 28–30.
Connelley, Willima E. "Henry J. Gyles." In vol. 4 of *A Standard History of Kansas and Kansans*. Chicago: Lewis, 1918.
Cronk, George. "George Herbert Mead (1863–1931)." *Internet Encyclopedia of Philosophy*. www.iep.utm.edu/mead.
Crosby, Ernest Howard. "The Plea of Labor from the Standpoint of a Russian Peasant." *Arena* 17 (Jan. 1897): 312–22.
———. "Two Days with Count Tolstoy." *Progressive Review* 2 (Aug. 1897): 407–22.
Crowl, Rev. Theodore. "Hull-House." *Presbyterian Messenger* (1894): [555]3. Hull-House Scrapbook 1:46; *JAPM*, Addendum 10:6ff.
Cummings, Edward. "Weak Points in the Settlement Method." *Quarterly Journal of Economics* 6, no. 3 (Apr. 1892): 257–79.
Davis, Anne. "The Protector of Children." *Illinois Voter* 12, pt. 2 (June 1932): 6.
"Department of Social Policy and Social Work." University of Oxford. www.spi.ox.ac.uk.
Dewey, Alice C. "Dewey, Harriet Alice Chipman." In *Historical Dictionary of Women's Education in the United States*, edited by Linda Eisenmann, 130–32. Westport, Conn.: Greenwood Press, 1998.
Dewey, John. "The School as Social Center." *Elementary School Teacher* 3 (Oct. 1902): 73–86.
Dewey, John, and Evelyn Dewey. "The School as Social Settlement." In *Schools of Tomorrow*, 205–28. London: J. M. Dent and Son, 1915.
Dodge, Mrs. Arthur M. "The Development of the Day Nursery Idea." *Outlook* (1 May 1897): 61–67.
"Dorothea Lummis." In *American Women*, edited by Frances E. Willard and Mary A. Livermore, 2:478. New York: Mast, Crowell and Kirkpatrick, 1897.
Downey, Dennis B. "The Congress on Labor at the 1893 World's Columbian Exposition." *Journal of the Illinois State Historical Society* 76 (1983): 131–38.
"Dr. F. A. McGrew." In *History of La Porte County, Indiana, and Its Townships, Towns and Cities*, by Jasper Packard. LaPorte, Ind.: S. E. Taylor, 1990.
Eaton, Isabelle. "Hull-House and Its Distinctive Features." *Smith College Monthly* 1, no. 7 (Apr. 1894): 1–10.

———. "Receipts and Expenditures of Cloakmakers in Chicago, Compared with Those of That Trade in New York." In *Hull-House Maps and Papers*, by Residents of Hull House, 79–88. Crowell's Library of Economics and Politics, no. 5. New York: Thomas Y. Crowell, 1895.

———. *A Special Report on Domestic Service*. In *The Philadelphia Negro: A Social Study*, by W. E. B. Du Bois. Philadelphia: University of Pennsylvania, 1899.

"An Economic Conference." *Outlook* 53 (26 Dec. 1896): 1190.

"Edward Caird." Gifford Lectures. www.giffordlectures.org.

"Edward Caird (1835–1908)." *Internet Encyclopedia of Philosophy*. www.iep.utm.edu.

"Elegy Written in a Country Churchyard." Thomas Gray Archive, a Collaborative Digital Collection. University of Oxford, 2000–2010. www.info@thomasgray.org.

Elrod, Pamela G. "Smith, Eleanor Sophia." *WBC*, 810–12.

Farmer, J. David. "Overcoming All Obstacles: The Women of the Académie Julian; An Exhibition Organized by the Dahesh Museum." *Newsletter of the California Art Club*. www.californiaartclub.org.

Ffrench, Florence. "Frances A. Root." In *Music and Musicians in Chicago*, by Florence Ffrench, 178–79. Chicago: Florence Ffrench, 1899.

Flanagan, Nina. "Hervey White: Brief Life of a Maverick Impresario, 1866–1944." *Harvard Magazine*, July–Aug. 2006. harvardmagazine.com/206/07/hervey-white.html.

"Francis Herbert Stead, Robert Browning Hall and the Fight for Old Age Pensions." www.infed.org/thinkers.

Fraser, W. Lewis. "Open Letters: American Artists Series; Alice D. Kellogg." *Century Magazine* 45 (Jan. 1893): 478.

F[rederic]. W. S[anders]. "The World's Fair Congress of Social Settlements." *Unity* 31 (27 July 1893): 251–52. Hull-House Scrapbook 1:40; *JAPM*, Addendum 10:6ff. Also published in *Pratt Institute Monthly* 2, no. 1 (Sept. 1893): 18–19.

"Fred Fischbeck." In *The Industrial Interests of Chicago*, by S. S. Schoff. Chicago: Knight and Leonard, 1873.

Funchion, Michael F. "Irish Chicago: Church, Homeland, Politics, and Class—the Shaping of an Ethnic Group, 1870–1900." In *Ethnic Chicago: A Multicultural Portrait*, by Melvin G. Holli and Peter d'A. Jones, 57–92. 4th ed. Grand Rapids, Mich.: William B. Eerdmans, 1995.

Ganz, Cheryl R. "Benedict, Enella." *WBC*, 75–77.

Garnett, Mrs. Charles. "In Whitechapel." In *Sunday Magazine*, edited by Rev. Benjamin Waugh, 703–6. London: Isbister, 1889.

Gavit, John P. "Mary E. McDowell—a Settlement Worker." *Commons*, no. 21 (Jan. 1898): 1–2.

Goodspeed, Thomas Wakefield. "Helen Culver." In *The University of Chicago Biographical Sketches*, by Thomas W. Goodspeed, 2:37–99. Chicago: University of Chicago, 1925.

Gurteen, S. Humphreys. "Methods of Charity Organization: Paper." In *The Proceedings of the Seventh Church Congress in the Protestant Episcopal Church in the United States, Providence, R.I., 25–28 October 1881*. New York: Thomas Whittaker, 1881.

Hale, E. E. "Home Rule in Cities." *Cosmopolitan* 16 (Apr. 1894): 735–38.

Hamilton, Alice. "Jane Addams, Gentle Rebel." *Political Affairs* (Mar. 1960): 33–35.

———. "Jane Addams of Hull House." *Social Service* 27, no. 1 (June–Aug. 1953): 12–15.

Hamm, Elizabeth C. "Jennette Perry Lee, 1886." *Smith Alumnae Quarterly* 43 (Feb. 1952).

Hard, William. "Chicago's Five Maiden Aunts." *Everybody's Magazine* 62 (May 1906): 481–89.

Hardy, A. S. "Last Impressions." *Cosmopolitan* 16 (Dec. 1893): 199.

"Harry Sands Grindley." In "Record of the Proceedings of the Forty-seventh Annual Meeting of the American Society of Animal Production." *Journal of Animal Science* 15 (Jan. 1956): 334–35.

Hart, Alice M. "The Trades and Professions Underlying the Home." In *The World's Congress of Representative Women*, edited by May Wright Sewall, 578–89. Chicago and New York: Rand, McNally, 1894.

Hendricks, Walter. "Historical Sketch of Armour Institute of Technology." *Armour Engineer and Alumnus* 2, no. 4 (May 1937): 34–40, 70, 72.

Herndon, Emily. "Hull-House: A Swept-Out Corner of Chicago." *Christian Union* 45 (20 Feb. 1892): 351.

Holbrook, Agnes Sinclair. "Hull-House." *Wellesley Magazine* 2, no. 4 (Jan. 1894): 171–80.

———. "Map Notes and Comments." In *Hull-House Maps and Papers*, by Residents of Hull House, 3–23. Crowell's Library and Economics and Politics, no. 5. New York: Thomas Y. Crowell, 1895.

"Holiday Home Camp." www.holidayhomecamp.org.

"The Home Club: A Social Settlement Appointee [Amanda Johnson]." *Outlook* 59, no. 6 (11 June 1898): 401.

Hooker, George. "Social Economic Conference." *Hull-House Bulletin* 2, no. 1 (Jan. 1897): 6.

———. "Social Feeling in Great Britain." *Outlook* 54, no. 16 (Oct. 1896): 685–86.

———. "Tom Mann, the English Labor Agitator, at Home." *Outlook* (7 Sept. 1895): 382–83.

"Housing Problem in London." *Charities* 5, no. 6 (7 July 1900): 6–7.

"Housing Question for Working Women." In "The Common Welfare." *Survey* 22 (11 Sept. 1909): 799–800.

"Hull House." In the Literary Department of *Rockford (Ill.) Female Seminary Magazine* 20 (Oct. 1892): 129–32.

"Hull-House—a Social Settlement." *Confectioner, Baker and American Caterer* (1 July 1894): 8–9. Hull-House Scrapbook 1:53; *JAPM*, Addendum 10:6ff.

"Hull House Mourns Passing of Miss de Nancrede." *Hull House Octagon* 1 (June 1936): [3].

"Hull-House Shops." *Hull-House Bulletin* 5, no. 2 (Semi-annual 1902): 11; *JAPM*, 53:800.

"In Memoriam: Helen Culver: Philanthropist." *Bulletin* (Geographic Society of Chicago) 67 (Mar. 1926): 3.

"In Memoriam Mrs. Alzina Parsons Stevens." *Hull-House Bulletin* 4, no. 3 (Autumn 1900): 13; *JAPM*, 53:752.

"Interview with Eleanor Smith." *Journal of Social Music* 1, no. 4 (Jan. 1909): 113–14.

"Israel Newton Stiles." In vol. 5 of *Appleton's Cyclopaedia of American Biography*, edited by J. G. Wilson and J. Fiske. New York: D. Appleton.

James, Belle L. "The Story of the Chicago Training School." *Bulletin* (Chicago Training School) 48 (Apr.–June 1945): 9.

James, Edward T. "Leonora O'Reilly." In *Papers of the Women's Trade Union League and Its Principal Leaders: Guide to the Microfilm Edition*, edited by Edward T. James, 211–18. Published for the Schlesinger Library, Radcliffe College. Woodbridge, Conn.: Research Publications, 1981.

"James Keir Hardie." www.scotlandvacations.com.

Johnson, Amanda. "Clean Streets and Alleys." In *The Sunset Club, Chicago, Meetings of 1898–99*, 227. Chicago: Chicago Sunset Club, 1899. UIC, Sunset.

"Julia Lathrop." *Vassar Encyclopedia*. vcencyclopedia.vassar.edu/alumni/julia-lathrop.html.

Kelley, Florence. "Aims and Principles of the Consumers' League." *American Journal of Sociology* 5 (Nov. 1899): 289–304.

———. "Child Labor Law." *American Journal of Sociology* 3 (Jan. 1898): 490–501.

———. "Description and Work of Hull-House." *Living Age* 218 (9 July 1898): 138.

———. "An Effective Child-Labor Law." *Annals of the American Academy* 21, no. 3 (May 1903): 96–103.

———. "Efficiency in Factory Inspection." In *The Child in the City*, 278–86. A series of papers presented at the conferences held during the Chicago Child Welfare Exhibit. Chicago: Department of Social Investigation, Chicago School of Civics and Philanthropy, 1912.

———. "Hull-House." *New England Magazine* 13 (22 Feb. 1896): 327; 18 (July 1898): 550–66.

———. "I Go to Work." *Survey Graphic* 58 (1 June 1927): 271–74, 301.

———. "Illinois Child Labor Law." *American Journal of Sociology* 3 (Jan. 1898): 490–501.

———. "The National Federation of Consumers' Leagues." *Independent* 51 (14 Dec. 1899): 353–55.

———. "On Some Changes in the Legal Status of the Child since Blackstone." *International Review* (Aug. 1882): 83–98.

———. "The Street Trader under Illinois Law." In *The Child in the City*, 290–301. A series of papers presented a the conferences held during the Chicago Child Welfare Exhibit. Chicago: Department of Social Investigation, Chicago School of Civics and Philanthropy, 1912.

———. "The Sweating System." In *Hull-House Maps and Papers*, by Residents of Hull House, 27–45. Crowell's Library of Economics and Politics, no. 5. New York: Thomas Y. Crowell, 1895.

———. "The United States Supreme Court and the Utah Eight-Hour Law." *American Journal of Sociology* 4 (July 1898): 21–34.

———. "The Working Boy." *American Journal of Sociology* 2 (Nov. 1896): 358–68.

Kelley, Florence, and Alzina P. Stevens. "Wage-Earning Children." In *Hull-House Maps and Papers*, by Residents of Hull-House, 49–76. Crowell's Library of Economics and Politics, no. 5. New York: Thomas Y. Crowell, 1895.

Kelley, Nicholas. "Early Days at Hull House." *Social Service Review* 28, no. 4 (Dec. 1954): 424–29.

Kellogg, Emily A. "Hull-House." *Union Signal*, 22 Jan. 1891. Hull-House Scrapbook 1: 6; *JAPM*, Addendum 10:6ff.

Kenney, Mary E., "Organization of Working Women." In *The World's Congress of Representative Women*, edited by May Wright Sewall, 871–74. Chicago and New York: Rand, McNally, 1894.

"King's Daughters' History." Norfolk City Union, Norfolk, Va. www.kingsdaughters.org/history.

Kirkland, Joseph. "The Poor in Great Cities, IV: Among the Poor of Chicago." *Scribner's Magazine* 12, no. 1 (July 1892): 3–27.

Knight, Louise W. "Rice, Harriet Alleyne." *WBC*, 740–42.

Knobe, Bertha Damaris. "Light-Houses of Chicago." *Union Signal*, 26 July 1894. Hull-House Scrapbook 1: 56; *JAPM*, Addendum 10:6ff.

Kohn, Esther L. "A Challenge to the League." *Illinois Voter* 12, pt. 2 (June 1932): 12.

Krouse, Agate, and Harry Krouse. "Educated Daughters and Sisters: Three Graduates Comment." In *They Came to Learn, They Came to Teach, They Came to Stay*, by Marian J. Swoboda and Audrey J. Roberts, 95–105. Vol. 1, *University Women: A Series of Essays*. Office of Women, University of Wisconsin, 1980. digital.library.

"The Labor Museum." *Chautauquan* 37 (Sept. 1903): 439–40; *JAPM*, 51:60–61.

Lannon, Frances. "Toynbee [née Atwood], Charlotte Maria." *Oxford Dictionary of National Biography*, www.oxforddnb.com/view/printable/48428. Oxford University Press, 2004–11.

Larrabee, W. H. "Correspondence: 'What Shall We Do with the Dago?'" *Popular Science Monthly* 38 (Feb. 1891): 553–54.

Lathrop, Julia C. "Background of the Juvenile Court in Illinois." In *The Child, the Clinic, and the Court*, 290–97. New York: New Republic, 1925.

———. "The Children's Bureau." *American Journal of Sociology* 18 (Nov. 1912): 318–30.

———. "The Children's Bureau." *Proceedings of the National Conference of Charities and Correction* (1912): 30–33.

———. "The Cook County Charities." In *Hull-House Maps and Papers*, by Residents of Hull-House, 143–61. Crowell's Library of Economics and Politics, no. 5. New York: Thomas Y. Crowell, 1895.

———. "The Defective Child in the City." In *The Child in the City*, edited by Sophonisba P. Breckinridge, 224–27. Chicago: Department of Social Investigation, the Chicago School of Civics and Philanthropy, 1912.

———. "Federal Safeguards of Child Welfare." *Annals of the American Academy of Political and Social Science* 121 (Sept. 1925): 96–107.

———. "The Highest Education for Women." *Journal of Home Economics* 8 (Jan. 1916): 1–8.

———. "Hull House." In *Vassar Miscellany* (May 1896): 366–71; *JAPM*, 55:70–72.

———. "Hull House as a Sociological Laboratory." *Proceedings of the National Conference of Charities and Correction* (1894): 313–18.

———. "Income and Infant Mortality." *American Journal of Public Health* 9 (Apr. 1919): 1–6.

———. Introduction to *The Delinquent Child and the Home*, by Sophonisba P. Breckinridge and Edith Abbott, 1–10. New York: Charities Publication Committee, 1912.

———. "Miss Lathrop's Own Words." *Illinois Voter* 12, pt. 2 (June 1932): 10.

———. "Presidential Address: Child Welfare Standards a Test of Democracy." In *Proceedings of the National Conference of Charities and Correction* (1919): 5–9.

———. "Provision for the Care of the Families and Dependents of Soldiers and Sailors." In *Proceedings of the Academy of Political Science* (1918): 140–51.

———. "Public Protection of Maternity." *American Labor Legislation Review* 7 (Mar. 1917): 27–35.

———. "Social Settlements in the United States." *University Extension World* 3 (Apr. 1894): 1101–11.

———. "Standards of Child Welfare." *Annals of the American Academy of Political and Social Science* 98 (Nov. 1921): 1–8.

———. "The Transition from Charities and Corrections to Social Work, 1873–1923. And Then?" *Proceedings of the National Conference of Social Work* (1923): 199–203.

———. "What the Settlement Work Stands For." *Proceedings of the National Conference of Charities and Correction* (1896): 106–10.

Learned, Henry B. "Hull-House." *Lend a Hand* (Boston) 10 (May 1893): 318.

———. "Social Settlements in the United States." *University Extension World* 7, no. 4 (Apr. 1894): 102–11.

"Letter to the Chicago Conference from Rev. Canon and Mrs. S. A. Barnett." *Commons* 6, no. 2 (June 1899): 1–2.

"Lewis Arington, Private." www.lindapages.com.

"The Lewis Institute in Chicago." *Outlook* (26 Sept. 1896): 581.

Lloyd, Henry Demarest. "Strikes and Lockouts." In *Twenty-third Meeting*, by Chicago Sunset Club, 1–5. Chicago: Chicago Sunset Club, 1890. UIC, Sunset.

Luther, Jessie. "The Labor Museum at Hull-House." *Commons* 7, no. 10 (May 1902): 1–13; *JAPM*, 51:415–27.

Maclean, Annie Marion. "Homes for Working Women in Large Cities." *Charities Review* 9 (July 1899): 215–28.

"Marchmont Hall." UCL Bloomsbury Project. www.ucl.ac.uk/bloomsbury-project.

"Mary Ward and the Passmore Edwards Settlement." www.infed.org.

[Mass meeting was held in Central Music Hall, Chicago]. *Outlook* 53, no. 12 (21 Mar. 1896): 503.

Mastro-Valerio, Alessandro. "Italians." In *Reports of the Industrial Commission on Immigration . . . United States. Industrial Commission*. Vol. 15, *Reports of the Industrial Commission*. Washington, D.C.: GPO, 1900–1902.

———. "Remarks upon the Italian Colony in Chicago." In *Hull-House Maps and Papers*, by Residents of Hull-House, 131–39. Crowell's Library of Economics and Politics, no. 5. New York: Thomas Y. Crowell, 1895.

Maude, Aylmer. "A Talk with Miss Jane Addams and Leo Tolstoy." *Humane Review* 2 (Oct. 1902): 203–18.

"May Abraham." In *Women in Ireland, 1800–1918: A Documentary History*, by Maria Luddey, 209. Reprint, Cork: Cork University Press, 1999.

McBryde, M. M. "The Penny Provident Fund." *Charities Review* 1 (Apr. 1892): 280–82.

McCaffrey, Lawrence J. "Preserving the Union, Shaping a New Image: Chicago's Irish Catholics and the Civil War." In *At the Crossroads: Old Saint Patrick's and the Chicago Irish*, edited by Ellen Skerrett, 53–68. Chicago: Loyola Press, 1997.

McCree, Mary Lynn. "Bowen, Louise deKoven." *NAW* 4.

McDowell, Mary. "Social Settlements . . . a Descriptive Definition." *Commons* 49 (Aug. 1900): 5.

McK., W. McC. "Etchings by Otto H. Bacher Memorial Exhibition." *Bulletin of the Cleveland Museum of Art* 8, no. 3 (Mar. 1921): 47–50.
Meriam, Lewis. "A Great Bureau Chief." *Illinois Voter* 12, pt. 2 (June 1932): 7.
"Michael Reese Hospital." *American Jewess* 2, no. 1 (Oct. 1895): 28–35.
Miller, Alice. "Hull-House." *Charities Review* 1, no. 4 (Feb. 1892): 167–73. Hull-House Scrapbook 1:16a; *JAPM*, Addendum 10:6ff.
"Miss Addams as Scavenger." *Woman's Journal* (Boston) 26 (13 Apr. 1895): 113.
"Miss Addams at Mansfield House." *Chicago Commons* 1, no. 4 (July 1896): 13.
Moffatt, Warneford. "Club-House for Unmarried Working Men." In *Blackwood's Edinburgh Magazine* (Scotland) 156 (Nov. 1894): 701–13.
Monroe, Lucy. "A Circulating Picture Gallery, Hull-House." *Current Literature* 19 (Jan. 1896): 46.
Moore, Dorothea. "A Day at Hull-House." *American Journal of Sociology* 2 (Mar. 1897): 629–40.
Moore, Ernest C. "Social Value of the Saloon." *American Journal of Sociology* 3 (July 1897): 1–12.
Morgan, Appleton. "What Shall We Do with the 'Dago'?" *Popular Science Monthly* 38 (Dec. 1890): 172–79.
"Mrs. Nancy Smith Foster." *University* [of Chicago] *Record* 6 (7 Dec. 1901): 281–83.
Muncy, Robin. "Lathrop, Julia Clifford." *WBC*, 490–92.
"Municipal Progress: The Chicago Victory." *Outlook* 53, no. 16 (18 Apr. 1896): 715.
"Necrology: 1883, Mrs. Charles B. Spahr." *Smith Alumnae Quarterly* 27 (Nov. 1935): 67.
"Newspapers in the Illinois State Historical Library." *Illinois Libraries* 70 (Mar.–Apr. 1988): 131–268.
O'Day, Rosemary. "Aves, Ernest Harry (1857–1917)." In *Oxford Dictionary of National Biography*. Oxford: Oxford University Press, 2004.
Oehler, Carolyn Henninger. "Lucy Jane Rider Meyer." *WBC*, 587–89.
"Panic of 1893." www.conservapedia.com.
"Passmore Edwards Settlement." UCL Bloomsbury Project. www.ucl.ac.uk.
Patterson, Charles Brodie. "Ernest Howard Crosby: A Biographical Sketch." In *Libertarian Labyrinth*. libertarian-labyrinth.org.
Pelham, Laura Dainty. "The Story of the Hull-House Players." *Drama* 22 (May 1916): 249–62.
Perkins, Frances. "My Recollections of Florence Kelley." *Social Service Review* 28, no. 1 (Mar. 1954): 12–19.
"Petition for a New School." *Hull-House Bulletin* 2, no. 6 (Oct. 1897): 6.
Potter, E. T. "A Study of Some New York Tenement House Problems." *Charities Review* 1, no. 3 (Jan. 1892): 129–40.
Prothero, Stephen. "Hinduphobia and Hinduphilia in U.S. Culture." www.bu.edu/religion/files/pdf/Hinduphobia_and_Hinduphilia.pft.
Ralph, Julian. "Chicago's Gentle Side." *Harper's Magazine* 87 (July 1893): 286–98.
Ransom, Reverdy C. "Work of the Methodist Church in the Twentieth Century." *A.M.E. Church Review* 18 (Oct. 1901): 152–53.
"A Remembrance of Dr. Anna E. Blount." Nineteenth Century Charitable Association. www.19thcenturyclub.com.
"Report of the Children's Selection Com. [Lake Geneva Fresh-Air Association]." In

*Holiday Home Camp*, 13. Lake Geneva, Wis.: Lake Geneva Fresh Air Association, [1987].

"Rev. P. J. Muldoon." In *Biographical History of the American Irish in Chicago*, edited by Charles Ffrench, 186–89. Chicago and New York: American Biographical, 1897.

Rich, Adena M. "Miss Lathrop and the Illinois League [of Women Voters]." *Illinois Voter* 12, pt. 2 (June 1932): 11.

Richmond, Mary E. "The Need of a Training-School in Applied Philanthropy." In *Proceedings of the National Conference of Charities and Correction*, edited by Isabel C. Barrows, 181–86. Boston: Geo. H. Ellis, 1898.

Rothschild, Piper Wentz. "Porter, Julia Foster." *WBC*, 711–13.

"Samuel Eddy Barrett." In *Memorials of Deceased Companions of the Commandery of the State of Illinois, Military Order of the Loyal Legion of the United States*, 91–94. Vol. 2, *1901–12*. Chicago: Military Order of the Loyal Legion of the United States, Commandery of the State of Illinois, 1923.

"Samuel M. Jones Biography." Teaching Cleveland. www.teachingcleveland.org.

Sargent, D. A. "The System of Physical Training at the Hemenway Gymnasium." In *Physical Training: A Full Report of the Papers and Discussions of the Conference Held in Boston in November 1889*, edited by Isabel C. Barrows, 62–86. Boston: Press of George H. Ellis, 1899.

Schlesinger, Arthur, Jr. "Who Was Henry A. Wallace: The Story of a Perplexing and Indomitable Naive Public Servant." *Los Angeles Times*, 12 Mar. 2000. www.cooperativeindividualism.org.

Schneiderhan, Erik. "Jane Addams and Charity Organization in Chicago." *Journal of the Illinois State Historical Society* 100 (Winter 2007–8): 299–327.

Schneirov, Richard. "Building Trades and Workers." *EC*, 101.

"The School House, an Educational Center for the People." In *Forty-fourth Annual Report of the Board of Education for the Year Ending June 24, 1898*, 96–109. Chicago: Board of Education, 1898.

"The School House for the People." In *Forty-third Annual Report of the Board of Education for the Year Ending June 25, 1897*, 69–75. Chicago: Board of Education, 1897.

Schultz, Rima Lunin. "Smith, Mary Rozet." *WBC*, 817–19.

Scott, Anne Firor. "Saint Jane and the Ward Boss." *American Heritage* 12 (Dec. 1960): 12–17, 94–99.

Scudder, Vida D. "We Pay Tribune to Two Distinguished Members of the Class of 1884: Helen Rand Thayer, Who Died April 14, 1935." *Smith Alumnae Quarterly* 26 (May 1935): 254–55.

Shaw, Albert. "Necrology: Elgin R. L. Gould." *Johns Hopkins Alumni Magazine* 4 (1915): 82–84.

Shively, Charles. "Leonora O'Reilly." *NAW* 2.

"Short History of the Kremlin." www.moscow.info.

"Sidney Ball and Barnett House, Whitechapel—a Druitt Contemporary." forum.casebook.org.

Silkenat, David. "Workers in the White City: Working Class Culture at the World's Columbian Exposition of 1893." *Journal of the Illinois State Historical Society* 104, no. 4 (2011): 266–300.

"Sir Arthur Fairbairn, Bart." *Silent Worker* 28 (Nov. 1915): 34.

Skerrett, Ellen. "The Irish of Chicago's Hull-House Neighborhood." *Chicago History* 30 (Summer 2001): 22–63.
Slatter, John. "Our Friends from the East: Russian Revolutionaries and British Radicals, 1852–1917." *History Today* 53, no. 10 (Oct. 2003). www.historytoday.com.
"Smith, Francis Drexel." In *National Cyclopaedia of American Biography*, 44:609.
Smith, Mark K. "Francis Herbert Stead, Browning Hall and the Fight for Old Age Pensions." In *The Encyclopaedia of Informal Education*. www.infed.org/thinkers/herbert_stead_browning_hall_pensions.htm.
Smith, T. Guilford. "Stephen Humphreys Gurteen." *Charities Review* 8 (Sept. 1898): 364–67.
"Smolny Cathedral." www.saint-petersburg.com.
Solomon, Barbara Miller. "Balch, Emily Greene." *NAW* 4.
"Solon Robinson." www.crownprint.net.
"Songs for the Hull House Quarter Century." *Survey* 33, no. 23 (6 Mar. 1915): 597.
"St. Basil's Cathedral." www.moscow/info.
"St. Margaret's House Settlement: History." www.stmargaretshouse.org.uk.
"St. Paul's Episcopal Church, 1837." *2010 Historic Episcopal Churches Engagement Calendar*. Swarthmore, Pa.: National Episcopal Historians and Archivists, 2009.
Starr, Ellen Gates. "Art and Labor." In *Hull-House Maps and Papers*, by Residents of Hull-House, 165–79. Crowell's Library of Economics and Politics, no. 5. New York: Thomas Y. Crowell, 1895.
———."Hull-House Book Bindery." *Commons* 47 (30 June 1900): 5–6.
———. "Hull House (Chicago)." In *Encyclopedia of Social Reform*, edited by William D. P. Bliss. New York: Funk and Wagnalls, 1897.
Start, Sandra M. "Newspapers in the Illinois Historical Library." *Illinois Libraries* 73 (Apr. 1999): 301–442.
[Stead, W. T.] "The Civic Life of Chicago." *Review of Reviews* 8 (Aug. 1893): 178–82. Hull-House Scrapbook 1:42d–f; *JAPM*, Addendum 10:6ff.
Stevens, Alzina Parsons. "Hull-House in Civic Movements." *Public Opinion* 26 (6 Mar. 1899): 333.
———. "Life in a Social Settlement, Hull-House, Chicago." *Self-Culture Magazine* 9, no. 1 (Mar. 1899): 42–51.
Stone, Melville E. "The Higher Life of Chicago." *Outlook* 53, no. 8 (22 Feb. 1896): 326–31.
Sunderland, Eliza R. "Hull House, Chicago: Its Work and Workers." *Unitarian* (Sept. 1893): 400–402. Hull-House Scrapbook 1:42a–c; *JAPM*, Addendum 10:6ff.
Sweet, William. "Bosanquet, Bernard." In *Stanford Encyclopedia of Philosophy*. 15 June 1977, rev. 8, Jan. 2008. www.plato.stanford.edu/entries/bosanquet.
Swift, Morrison I. "The Working Population of Cities, and What the Universities Owe Them." *Andover Review* 13, no. 78 (June 1890): 589–613.
Taylor, Graham. "Between the Lines in Chicago's Industrial Civil War." *Commons* 45 (30 Apr. 1900): 1–5.
———. "The Death of Mrs. A. P. Stevens." *Commons* 47 (30 June 1900): 7.
———. "Jane Addams: The Great Neighbor." *Survey Graphic* 24, no.7 (July 1935): 339–41, 368.
———. "Julia Lathrop, Statesman." *Illinois Voter* 12, pt. 2 (June 1932): 5.

———. "Settlement Conference: American Social Workers in Session at the Hull House." *Commons* 6, no. 2 (June 1899): 7, 9–13.
———. "Social Propaganda." *Commons* 1, no. 4 (July 1896): 2–3.
Tello, Jean C. "Flower, Lucy Louisa Coues." *WBC*, 273–76.
"Testimony of Jane Addams." In *Report on the Chicago Strike of June–July, 1894, by the United States Strike Commission*, 645–48. Washington, D.C.: GPO, 1895.
"They Talk for Charity." Unidentified Chicago newspaper, [Nov 1896], SCPC, JAC; *JAPM*, 55:219.
"They Won Fame Both Sides of the Atlantic." *Lyceumite and Talent* 5 no. 1 (June 1911): 20–21.
Thompson, Mary Harris. "The Chicago Hospital for Women and Children." In *In Memoriam Mary Harris Thompson*, 43–59. Chicago: Mary Harris Thompson Hospital of Chicago for Women and Children Board of Managers, 1896.
"A Tribute to Jean Fine Spahr 1883, Who Died on September 25, 1935." *Smith Alumnae Quarterly* 27 (Nov. 1935): 14.
Tucker, Cynthia Grant. "A Biographer's Experience Using Photography." www.uuhhs.org.
Twose, George M. R. "The Coffee Room at Hull House." *House Beautiful* 7, no. 2 (Jan. 1900): 107–9.
"Uncle Sam's Birthday." *Chicago Times*, 5 July 1890.
Vandercreek, Drew. "1892–95: 1893 Chicago's World Fair." Illinois during the Gilded Age. dig.lib.niu.edu.
Wade, Louise C. "Kelley, Florence." *NAW* 2.
———."Lathrop, Julia Clifford." *NAW* 2.
Washburne, Marion Foster. "A Labor Museum." *Craftsman* 6, no. 6 (Sept. 1904): 441–50; *JAPM*, 51:570–80.
Weil, Elsie F. "The Hull-House Players." *Theatre Magazine* (Sept. 1913): xix–xxii. In *100 Years at Hull-House*, by Mary Lynn Bryan and Allen F. Davis. Bloomington: Indiana University Press, 1990.
West, Max. "Chicago's Other Half. Maps and Papers of Hull-House." *Dial* 18 (16 Apr 1895): 239.
Whitten, David O. "The Depression of 1893." EH, *Net Encyclopedia*. eh.net/encyclopedia.
[Wilke's Victoria Home for Working Men, London]. Magisterial Case: *Charles J. Logsdon v. Edward Trotter*. In *Magisterial Cases Reprinted from Vol. 64 "The Justice of the Peace," 1900*, edited by C. E. Allan, 5:201–8. London: Shaw and Sons, 1901.
"William J. Ohahan, 1836–1919." *Journal of the Illinois State Historical Society*, 636–53. www.jstor.org/stable/40194518.
Wilson, Mark R. "Western Electric Co." *EC*.
Wischnewetzky, Florence Kelley. "A Decade of Retrogression." *Arena* 1 (Aug. 1891): 365–72.
———. "The Need of Theoretical Preparation for Philanthropic Work." In *The Need and Opportunity for College-Trained Women in Philanthropic Work*, by Helen H. Backus, 15–26. New York: New York Association of Collegiate Alumnae, 1887.
"The Women's Congresses." *Unity* (22 June 1893): 172–73.
"Won for Reform." *Chicago Chronicle*, 6 Apr. 1898.
Work, Monroe Nathan. "Crime among the Negroes of Chicago." *American Journal of Sociology* 6 (Sept. 1900): 204–23.

"Work, Monroe Nathan (1866–1945)." Black Past Remembered and Reclaimed: An Online Reference Guide to African American History. www.blackpast.org.

"The World in 1898: The Spanish-American War; Chronology." www.loc.gov/rr/hispanic.

"World's Congresses." World's Columbian Exposition: World's Congresses. xroads.virginia.edu.

Zeman, Josefa Humpal. "The Bohemian People in Chicago." In *Hull-House Maps and Papers*, by Residents of Hull-House, 115–28. Crowell's Library of Economics and Politics, no. 5. New York: Thomas Y. Crowell, 1895.

———. "Hull-House." In *Ženské Listy*. Chicago: Dubna, 1896.

Zeublin [Zueblin], Charles. "The Chicago Ghetto." In *Hull-House Maps and Papers*, by Residents of Hull-House, 91–111. Crowell's Library of Economics and Politics, no. 5. New York: Thomas Y. Crowell, 1895.

## *10. Books*

Adams, Stephen B., and Orville R. Butler. *Manufacturing the Future: A History of Western Electric*. New York: Cambridge University Press, 1999.

Addams, Jane. *Democracy and Social Ethics*. New York: Macmillan, 1902. A reprint edition with introduction by Charlene Haddock Seigfried. Urbana: University of Illinois Press, 2002.

———. *Democracy and Social Ethics: A Syllabus of a Course of Twelve Lectures*. Chicago: Press of Hollister Brothers, [1899?].

———. *The Excellent Becomes the Permanent*. New York: Macmillan, 1932.

———. *Forty Years at Hull-House*. With an afterword by Lillian D. Wald. New York: Macmillan, 1935.

———. *Jane Addams on Education*. Edited by Ellen Condliffe Lagemann. Classics in Education, no. 51. New York: Teachers College Press, Columbia University. 1985.

———. *The Jane Addams Reader*. Edited by Jean Bethke Elshtain. New York: Basic Books, 2002.

———. *Long Road of Woman's Memory*. New York. Macmillan, 1926. Reprint, Urbana: University of Illinois Press, 2002.

———. *My Friend, Julia Lathrop*. New York: Macmillan, 1935.

———. *A New Conscience and an Ancient Evil*. New York: Macmillan, 1912.

———. *Newer Ideals of Peace*. Chautauqua Home Reading Series. New York: Macmillan, 1907. Reprint, Chautauqua, N.Y.: Chautauqua Press, 1907.

———. *Peace and Bread in Time of War*. New York: Macmillan, 1922.

———. *The Selected Papers of Jane Addams*. Vol. 1, *Preparing to Lead, 1860–81*. Edited by Mary Lynn McCree Bryan, Barbara Bair, and Maree de Angury. Urbana: University of Illinois Press, 2003.

———. *The Selected Papers of Jane Addams*. Vol. 2, *Venturing into Usefulness, 1881–88*. Edited by Mary Lynn McCree Bryan, Barbara Bair, and Maree de Angury. Urbana: University of Illinois Press, 2009.

———. *Twenty Years at Hull-House, with Autobiographical Notes*. Chautauqua Home Reading Series. New York: Macmillan, 1910. Reprint, Chautauqua, N.Y.: Chautauqua, 1911. A new edition of *Twenty Years at Hull-House*. Introduction by James Hurt. Urbana: University of Illinois Press, 1990.

Addams, Jane, and Florence Kelley. *Course of Lectures on Legalized and Non-legalized Social Ethics*. Chicago: Press of Hollister Brothers, [1899]. Enclosure to Jane Addams to Richard T. Ely, 29 Sept. 1899, SHSW, Ely; *JAPM*, 3:1441–43.

Adelman, William J. *Haymarket Revisited*. Published by the Illinois Labor History Society. Terre Haute, Ind.: Moore Langen, 1976.

Aldrich, Richard, and Peter Gordon. *Dictionary of British Educationists*. London: Woburn Press, 1989.

Alger, J. G. *The New Paris Sketch Book: Manners, Men, Institutions*. 2nd ed. London: W. H. Allen, 1889.

Allen, Frank Charles. *A Critical Edition of Robert Browning's "Bishop Blougram's Apology."* Salzburg Studies in English Literature under the Direction of Professor Erwin A. Stürzl. Romantic Reassessment, edited by Dr. James Hogg. Salzburg, Austria: Institut für Englische Sprache und Literatur, Universität Salzburg, 1976.

Allswang, John M. *A House for All Peoples: Ethnic Politics in Chicago, 1890–1936*. Lexington: University Press of Kentucky, 1971.

Amberg, Mary Agnes. *Madonna Center*. Chicago: Loyola University Press, 1976.

*American Heritage College Dictionary*. 3rd ed. Boston: Houghton Mifflin, 1993.

Andreas, A. T. *History of Chicago from the Earliest Period to the Present Time*. 3 vols. Chicago: A. T. Andreas, 1884–86.

Angle, Paul M., ed. *The Great Chicago Fire*. Chicago: Chicago Historical Society, 1946.

Arey, Leslie B. *Northwestern University Medical School, 1859–1959: A Pioneer in Educational Reform*. Evanston, Ind.: Northwestern University, 1959.

*Armour Mission, Chicago*. [Chicago: Armour Mission, 1895].

Arpee, Edward. *Lake Forest Illinois: History and Reminiscences, 1861–1961*. Chicago: R. R. Donnelly and Sons for the Rotary Club of Lake Forest, 1963.

Bachin, Robin F. *Building the South Side*. Chicago: University of Chicago Press, 2004.

Badger, Reid. *The Great American Fair: The World's Columbian Exposition & American Culture*. Chicago: Nelson Hall, 1979.

Baedeker, Karl. *Great Britain*. 3rd ed. Leipsic: Karl Baedeker, 1894.

———. *London and Its Environs*. London: Dulau, 1885.

———. *Russland*. Leipsic: Karl Baedeker, 1888.

Baldwin, Keturah E. *The AHEA Saga*. Washington, D.C.: American Home Economics Association, 1949.

Ball, Oona Howard. *Sidney Ball: Memories and Impressions of "an Ideal Don."* Oxford: Basil Blackwell, 1923.

Banks, Charles, and Marshall Everett. *American Home Culture and Correct Customs of Polite Society*. Chicago: Henry Neil, 1902.

Banks, Olive. *The Biographical Dictionary of British Feminists*. Vol. 1, *1800–1930*. New York: New York University Press, 1985.

Baring, Evelyn. *Political and Literary Essays, 1908–1913*. London: Macmillan, 1913.

Barnett, Henrietta O. *Canon Barnett: His Life, Work, and Friends*. 2 vols. London: John Murray, 1918.

Barrett, Mary X., and Philip L. Keister, eds. *History of Stephenson County, 1970*. Freeport, Ill.: County of Stephenson, 1972.

Barrows, John Henry, ed. *The World's Parliament of Religions*. 2 vols. Chicago: Parliament, 1893.

Barrows, Mary Eleanor. *John Henry Barrows: A Memoir*. Chicago: F. H. Revell, 1904.

Baynor, Ronald H., and Timothy J. Meagher, eds. *The New York Irish*. Baltimore: Johns Hopkins University Press, 1996.

Beadle, Muriel. *The Fortnightly of Chicago: The City and Its Women, 1873–1973*. Chicago: H. Regnery, [1973].

Beauman, Katherine Bentley. *Women and the Settlement Movement*. New York: St. Martin's Press, 1996.

Becker, L. K. *A History of Elgin Academy of Northwestern University*. Elgin, Ill.: The Academy, 1906.

Beckner, Earl R. *A History of Labor Legislation in Illinois*. Chicago: University of Chicago Press, 1929.

Beckwith, Albert Clayton. *History of Walworth County, Wisconsin*. Indianapolis: B. E. Bowen, 1912.

Bellamy, Joyce M., John Saville, Keith Gildart, David Howell, Neville Kirk, and David E. Martin, eds. *Dictionary of Labour Biography*. 12 vols. London and Basingstoke: Macmillan Press and Pelgrave Macmillan, 1972–2005.

*Bench and Bar of Chicago: Biographical Sketches*. [Chicago: American Biographical, 1883?].

Bermant, Chaim. *London's East End: Point of Arrival*. New York: Macmillan, 1975.

Besant, Walter. *East London*. London: Chatto & Windus, 1903.

*Bibliography of College, Social, University and Church Settlements*. 4th ed. New York: College Settlements Association, 1900.

*The Biographical Dictionary and Portrait Gallery of Representative Men of Chicago, Minnesota Cities and the World's Columbian Exposition*. Chicago: American Biographical, 1892.

*Biographical Encyclopedia of Illinois of the Nineteenth Century*. Philadelphia: Galaxy, 1875.

*Biographical Record of Ogle County, Illinois*. Chicago: S. J. Clark, 1899.

*Biographical Sketches of the Leading Men of Chicago, Photographically Illustrated*. Chicago: Wilson, Pierce, 1876.

Bishop, Edward. *Blood & Fire! The Story of William Booth & the Salvation Army*. Chicago: Moody Press, 1965.

Bisno, Abraham. *Abraham Bisno Union Pioneer*. Madison: University of Wisconsin Press, 1967.

Blair, Karen. *The Clubwoman as Feminist: True Womanhood Redefined, 1868–1914*. New York: Holmes and Meier, 1980.

Blatchford, Eliphalet Huntington. *Letters, Journals and Memories of E. Huntington Blatchford*. Edited by his sister, Frances May Blatchford. Chicago: privately printed, 1920.

Bliss, William D. P. *The Encyclopedia of Social Reform*. New York: Funk and Wagnalls, 1897.

Boardman, Philip. *Patrick Geddes: Maker of the Future*. Chapel Hill: University of North Carolina Press, 1944.

Bogart, Ernest Ludlow, and Charles Manfred Thompson. *Industrial State, 1870–1893*. Vol. 4 of *Centennial History of Illinois*. Springfield: Illinois Centennial Commission, 1920.

Bonner, Thomas Neville. *Medicine in Chicago, 1850–1950: A Chapter in the Social and Scientific Development of the City*. 2nd ed. Urbana: University of Illinois Press, 1991.

Booth, Charles, ed. *Life and Labour of the People in London*. 17 vols. 3rd ed. London and New York: Macmillan, 1902–3.

Boris, Eileen. *Art and Labor: Ruskin, Morris, and the Craftsman Ideal in America*. Philadelphia: Temple University Press, 1986.

Bowen, Louise de Koven. *Baymeath*. Chicago: privately printed by Ralph Fletcher Seymour, 1944.

———. *Growing Up with a City*. New York: Macmillan, 1926.

———. *Open Windows*. Chicago: Ralph Fletcher Seymour, 1946.

———. *Safeguards for Youth at Work and at Play*. New York: Macmillan, 1914.

———. *Speeches, Addresses, and Letters of Louise deKoven Bowen: Reflecting Social Movements in Chicago*. 2 vols. Edited by Mary E. Humphrey. Ann Arbor, Mich.: Edwards Brothers, 1937

Bregstone, Philip P. *Chicago and Its Jews: A Cultural History*. [Chicago]: privately published, 1933.

Brener, Carol B. *The Founders of the Woodstock Artists Association*. Exhibition catalog. Kingston, N.Y.: Artco Printing for Woodstock Artists Association, 2000.

Briggs, Asa, and Anne Macartney. *Toynbee Hall: The First Hundred Years*. London: Routledge and Kegan Paul, 1984.

Briggs, Martha T., and Cynthia H. Peter. *Guide to the Pullman Company Archives*. Chicago: Newberry Library, 1995.

Brown, Elizabeth Read. *A Union List of Newspapers Published in Michigan Based on the Principal Newspaper Collections in the State with Notes Concerning Papers Not Located*. Ann Arbor: University of Michigan, Department of Library Science, 1954.

Brown, James. *The History of Public Assistance in Chicago, 1833–1893*. Chicago: University of Chicago Press, 1941.

Brown, Victoria Bissell. *The Education of Jane Addams*. Philadelphia: University of Pennsylvania Press, 2004.

Browne, Waldo R. *Altgeld of Illinois: A Record of His Life and Work*. New York: B. W. Huebsch, 1924.

Bryan, Mary Lynn McCree, and Allen F. Davis. *One Hundred Years at Hull-House*. Bloomington: Indiana University Press, 1990.

Bryan, Mary Lynn McCree, et al., eds. *The Jane Addams Papers* [guide to the microfilm edition of *The Jane Addams Papers*]. Ann Arbor, Mich.: University Microfilms International, 1985.

Bryan, Mary Lynn McCree, Nancy Slote, and Maree de Angury. *The Jane Addams Papers: A Comprehensive Guide*. Bloomington: Indiana University Press, 1996.

Buechler, Steven M. *The Transformation of the Woman Suffrage Movement: The Case of Illinois, 1850–1920*. New Brunswick, N.J.: Rutgers University Press, 1986.

Burg, David F. *Chicago's White City of 1893*. Lexington: University Press of Kentucky, 1976.

Bush, Gregory W. *Lord of Attention: Gerald Stanley Lee & the Crowd Metaphor in Industrializing America*. Amherst: University of Massachusetts Press, 1991.

Campbell, Mrs. N. W. *Forty Years: A Historical Sketch of the Woman's Presbyterian*

*Board of Missions of the Northwest.* [Chicago: Woman's Presbyterian Board of Missions of the Northwest, 1911?].

Candeloro, Dominic. *Chicago's Italians: Immigrants, Ethnics, Americans.* Making of America Series. Charleston, S.C.: Arcadia, 2003.

Carsel, Wilfred. *A History of the Chicago Ladies' Garment Workers' Union.* Chicago: Normandie House, 1940.

Carson, Mina. *Settlement Folk: Social Thought and the American Settlement Movement, 1885–1930.* Chicago: University of Chicago Press, 1990.

*Centennial History of Lakeside [Mich.].* N.p.: Village of Lakeside Association, 1974.

Chapman, J. Wilbur. *Life and Work of D. L. Moody.* N.p.: W. E. Scull, 1900.

*Chicago and Its Resources Twenty Years after, 1871–1891: A Commercial History Showing the Progress and Growth of Two Decades from the Great Fire to the Present Time.* Chicago: Chicago Times, 1892.

*The Chicago Liberty Meeting Held at Central Music Hall, April 30, 1899.* Chicago: Central Anti-Imperialist League, 1899.

*The Chicago Literary Club: The First Hundred Years, 1874–1974.* Chicago: Chicago Literary Club, 1974.

Chicago Training School for City, Home and Foreign Missions. "Sixtieth Anniversary, Chicago Training School, 1885–1945." *Bulletin* 48, nos. 1–2 (Jan.–Mar., Apr.–June).

Church, Charles A. *History of Rockford and Winnebago County, Illinois.* Rockford, Ill.: New England Society of Rockford, 1900.

Cimbala, Paul A., and Randall M. Miller. *Against the Tide: Women Reformers in American Society.* New York: Praeger, 1997.

*Cincinnati Social Settlement.* www.ebooksread.com.

Cipriani, Lisi, comp. *Italians in Chicago and the Selected Directory of the Italians in Chicago.* 1933–38. Chicago: L. Cipriani, [1933].

Clapp, Elizabeth J. *Mothers of All Children: Women Reformers and the Rise of Juvenile Courts in Progressive Era America.* University Park: Pennsylvania State University Press, 1998.

Clarke, Ida Clyde, ed. *Women of Today, International.* 3 vols. New York: Women's New Service and Women of Today Press, 1924, 1925, 1928–29.

Clayton, John. *Illinois Fact Book and Historical Almanac, 1673–1968.* Carbondale: Southern Illinois University Press, 1970.

Cohen, Saul B., ed. *Columbia Gazetteer of the World.* 3 vols. New York: Columbia University Press, 1998.

Coit, Stanton. *Neighborhood Guilds: An Instrument of Social Reform.* London: Swan Sonnenschein, 1891.

Colcord, Joanna C., and Ruth Z. S. Mann, eds. *The Long View: Papers and Addresses by Mary E. Richmond.* New York: Russell Sage Foundation, 1930.

Collini, Stefan. *Liberalism and Sociology: L. T. Hobhouse and Political Argument in England, 1880–1914.* Cambridge: Cambridge University Press, 1979.

*Columbia Encyclopedia.* 5th ed. New York: Columbia University Press, 1993.

*Combined 1871 Combination Atlas Map of Stephenson County, Ill., 1913 Standard Atlas and 1894 Plat Book.* 1913. Reprint, Evansville, Ind.: Whippoorwill Publications for the Stephenson County Genealogical Society, 1986.

Comings, L. J. Newcomb, and Martha M. Albers. *A Brief History of Baldwin County.* Fairhope, Ala.: Baldwin County Historical Society, 1928, fourth printing, 1971.
Committee of Nineteen, International Kindergarten Union. *Pioneers of the Kindergarten in America.* New York: Century, 1924.
Connelley, William E. *A Standard History of Kansas and Kansans.* 5 vols. Chicago: Lewis, 1918.
Converse, Florence. *The Story of Wellesley.* Boston: Little, Brown, 1915.
Conway, Jill Ker. *The First Generation of American Women Graduates.* New York: Garland, 1987.
Cook, Chris, et al., comps. *Sources in British Political History.* 5 vols. London: Macmillan Press for British Library of Political and Economic Science, 1975–78.
Cook, David, and Linda Cook. *John F. Carlson and Artists of the Broadmoor Academy.* Denver: David Cook Fine Art, Oct. 1999.
Coonley, Lydia Avery, et al. *Singing Verses for Children.* New York: Macmillan, 1897.
Cooper, John Milton, Jr. *Walter Hines Page, the Southerner as American.* Chapel Hill: University of North Carolina Press, 1977.
Cox, Henry Joseph, and John Howard Armington. *The Weather and Climate of Chicago.* Geographic Society of Chicago, Bulletin no. 4. Chicago: University of Chicago Press, 1914.
Croly, Mrs. J. C. *The History of the Woman's Club Movement in America.* New York: Henry G. Allen, 1898.
Crosby, Ernest Howard. *Golden Rule Jones.* Chicago: Public, 1906.
———. *Tolstoy and His Message.* New York: Funk and Wagnalls, 1904. JA's personal library.
Cushing, Helen Grant, and Adah V. Morris, eds. *Nineteenth Century Readers' Guide to Periodical Literature, 1890–1899.* 2 vols. New York: H. W. Wilson, 1944.
Cuthbertson, William C. *The Genesis of Girard.* Fort Scott, Kans.: Sekan Publications for Friends of Historic Girard, 1993.
Danforth, I.[saac] N.[ewton]. *The Life of Nathan Smith Davis, A.M., M.D., LL.D., 1817–1904.* Chicago: Cleveland Press, 1907.
Darrow, Clarence. *The Story of My Life.* New York: Charles Scribner's Sons, 1934.
Davis, Allen F. *American Heroine: The Life and Legend of Jane Addams.* New York: Oxford University Press, 1973.
———. *Spearheads for Reform: The Social Settlements and the Progressive Movement, 1890–1914.* New York: Oxford University Press, 1967.
Davis, Allen F., and Mary Lynn McCree. *Eighty Years at Hull-House.* Chicago: Quadrangle Press, 1969.
Davis, David J., ed. *History of Medical Practice in Illinois.* Vol. 2, *1850–1900.* Chicago: Illinois State Medical Society, 1955.
Day, Richard Ellsworth. *Bush Aglow: The Life Story of Dwight Lyman Moody, Commoner of Northfield.* Philadelphia: Judson Press, 1936.
Debs, Eugene Victor. *Walls and Bars.* Chicago: Socialist Party, 1927.
Deegan, Mary Jo. *Jane Addams and the Men of the Chicago School, 1892–1918.* New Brunswick, N.J.: Transaction Books, 1988.
DeGregorio, William A. *The Complete Book of U.S. Presidents.* New York: Dembner Books, 1984.

Denker, Ellen Paul, Robert Edwards, Heidi Nasstrom Evans, Nancy E. Green, Cheryl Robertson, and Tom Wolf. *Byrdcliffe: An American Arts and Crafts Colony*. Ithaca, N.Y.: Herbert F. Johnson Museum of Art, Cornell University, 2004.

Dent, J. M. *Memoirs, 1849–1926*. With some additions by Hugh R. Dent. London: J. M. Dent and Sons, 1928.

Destler, Chester McArthur. *Henry Demarest Lloyd and the Empire of Reform*. Philadelphia: University of Pennsylvania Press, 1963.

Deutsch, Albert. *The Mentally Ill in America: A History of Their Care and Treatment from Colonial Times*. 2nd rev. ed. New York: Columbia University Press, 1949.

Dewey, John. *The School and Society: Being Three Lectures*. Chicago: University of Chicago Press, 1911.

Dick, Charles, L. D. Dearborn, John William Fay, and James E. Homans, eds. *The Cyclopaedia of American Biography*. 8 vols. New enlarged ed. of *Appleton's Cyclopaedia of American Biography*, originally edited by James Grant Wilson and John Fiske. 1886. Reprint, New York: Press Association, Compilers, 1915 and 1918.

*Dictionary of American Biography*. 22 vols. New York: Charles Scribner, 1963.

Dilling, Elizabeth. *The Red Network*. Kenilworth, Ill.: The Author, 1936.

Diner, Steven. *A City and Its Universities: Public Policy in Chicago, 1892–1919*. Chapel Hill: University of North Carolina Press, 1980.

Diver, V. H. *The "Black Hole"; or, The Missionary Experience of a Girl in the Slums of Chicago, 1891–1892*. [Chicago: Baptist Missionary Training School], 1893.

Dougall, Lily. *Beggars All: A Novel*. London: Longmans, Green, 1893.

Drabble, Margaret, ed. *The Oxford Companion to English Literature*. 5th ed. Oxford: Oxford University Press, 1985.

Drake, St. Clair, and Horace R. Cayton. *Black Metropolis: A Study of Negro Life in a Northern City*. New York: Harcourt, Brace, 1945.

Du Bois, W. E. B. *The Philadelphia Negro, a Social Study*. With *A Special Report on Domestic Service* by Isabel Eaton. No. 14, Series Political Economy and Public Law. Philadelphia: University of Pennsylvania, 1899.

Dudley, Emilius C. *The Medicine Man: Being the Memoirs of Fifty Years of Medical Progress*. New York: J. H. Sears, 1927.

Duffus, R. L. *Lillian Wald: Neighbor and Crusader*. New York: Macmillan, 1938.

Duis, Perry R. *The Saloon: Public Drinking in Chicago and Boston, 1880–1920*. Urbana: University of Illinois Press, 1983.

Dunwiddie, Mary. *A History of the Illinois State Nurses' Association, 1901–1935*. [Chicago?]: Illinois State Nurses' Association, 1937.

Duster, Alfreda M., ed. *Crusade for Justice: The Autobiography of Ida B. Wells*. Chicago: University of Chicago Press, 1970.

Dye, Nancy Schrom. *As Equals and as Sisters: Feminism, Unionism, and the Women's Trade Union League of New York*. Columbia: University of Missouri Press, 1980.

Eagle, Mary Kavanaugh Oldham. *The Congress of Women Held in the Woman's Building: World's Columbian Exposition, Chicago, U.S.A., 1893*. Philadelphia: International, 1895.

Eaton, Edward Dwight. *Historical Sketches of Beloit College, with Chapters by Members of the Faculty*. New York: A. S. Barnes, 1928.

*Edinburgh Residents in U.S. Newspapers*. www.angelfire.com.

Edlund, Lawrence L. *The Apollo Musical Club of Chicago: A Historical Sketch*. Chicago: The Club, 1946.

*Edward B. Butler, 1853–1928*. Chicago: privately printed by R. R. Donnelly Sons, 1929.

Eliot, George. *Romola*. London: Oxford University Press, 1949.

Elshtain, Jean Bethke. *Jane Addams and the Dream of American Democracy*. New York: Basic Books, 2002.

Ely, Richard T. *Ground under Our Feet: An Autobiography*. New York: Macmillan, 1938.

———. *Socialism: An Examination of Its Nature, Its Strength and Its Weakness, with Suggestions for Social Reform*. New York: Thomas Y. Crowell, 1894.

*Encyclopedia Britannica*. 11th ed. Cambridge: Cambridge University Press, 1911.

*Encyclopedia Britannica: A New Survey of Universal Knowledge*. Chicago: William Benton, 1966.

Ewen, David. *The New Encyclopedia of the Opera*. New York: Hill and Wang, 1971.

*Eyewitness Travel Guides: Paris*. New York: Dorling Kindersley, 1993.

Fanning, Charles. *Finley Peter Dunne and Mr. Dooley: The Chicago Years*. Lexington: University Press of Kentucky, 1978.

Farrell, John C. *Beloved Lady: A History of Jane Addams' Ideas on Reform and Peace*. Baltimore: Johns Hopkins Press, 1967.

Federal Writers' Project, Ill. *Illinois: A Descriptive and Historical Guide*. Compiled and written by the Federal Writers' Project of the Works Projects Administration for the State of Illinois. Sponsored by Henry Horner, governor. Chicago: A. C. McClurg, 1939.

Ffrench, Florence. *Music and Musicians in Chicago*. Chicago: Ffrench, 1899.

Fink, Gary M., ed. *Biographical Dictionary of American Labor Leaders*. Westport, Conn.: Greenwood Press, 1974.

*Firman Congregational Church and Firman House: A Center of Friendliness*. [Chicago]: Chicago City Missionary Society, [ca. 1917?]

[First Presbyterian Church]. *Centennial Celebration, Nov. 8–15, 1942*. [Freeport, Ill.: First Presbyterian Church, 1942].

Flinn, John J. *Chicago: The Marvelous City of the West; A History, an Encyclopedia, and a Guide, 1892*. Chicago: Standard Guide, [1892].

Frank, Henriette Greenebaum, and Amalie Hofer Jerome, comps. *Annals of the Chicago Woman's Club for the First Forty Years of Its Organization, 1876–1916*. Chicago: Chicago Woman's Club, 1916.

Frankford, Roberta. *Collegiate Women: Domesticity and Career in Turn-of-the-Century America*. New York: New York University Press, 1977.

Fried, Albert, and Richard M. Elman eds. *Charles Booth's London: A Portrait of the Poor at the Turn of the Century, Drawn from His "Life and Labour of the People in London."* New York: Pantheon Books, 1968.

Fry, Paul E. *Generous Spirit: The Life of Mary Fry*. Cedarville, Ill.: Cedarville Area Historical Society, third printing, 2003.

———. *The Story of a Parish: St. Joseph, Freeport, Illinois, 1862–2012*. For the St. Joseph History Committee. Freeport, Ill.: Freeport Press, Summer 2012.

Fulwider, Addison L. *History of Stephenson County, Illinois*. Chicago: S. J. Clarke, 1910.

Garvey, Timothy J. *Public Sculptor: Lorado Taft and the Beautification of Chicago*. Urbana: University of Illinois Press, 1988.

Gaston, Paul M. *Man and Mission: E. B. Gaston and the Origins of the Fairhope Single Tax Colony*. Montgomery, Ala.: Black Belt Press, 1993.

[George B. Carpenter & Son]. *1840–1940: The First Hundred Years*. [Privately printed, ca. 1940]. CHM, CHS.

Getz, Gene A. *MBI: The Story of Moody Bible Institute*. Chicago: Moody Press, 1969.

Gilbert, Paul, and Charles Lee Bryson. *Chicago and Its Makers*. Chicago: Felix Mendelsohn, 1929.

Gileman, Agness Geneva, and Gertrude Marcella Gilman. *Who's Who in Illinois: Women-Makers of History*. Chicago: Eclectic, 1927.

Ginger, Ray. *Altgeld's America*. New York: New Viewpoints, 1973.

Ginzberg, Lori D. *Women and the Work of Benevolence: Morality, Politics, and Class in the Nineteenth-Century United States*. New Haven, Conn.: Yale University Press, 1990.

Glenwood School for Boys, Glenwood, Ill. *Fifty Years of Boy-Building, 1887–1937*. Glenwood, Ill.: The School, 1937.

Goldmark, Josephine. *Impatient Crusader: Florence Kelley's Life Story*. Urbana: University of Illinois Press, 1953.

Goodsell, Fred Field. *You Shall Be My Neighbor*. Boston: American Board of Commissioners for Foreign Missions, 1959.

Goodspeed, Rev. E. J. *A Full History of the Wonderful Career of Moody and Sankey in Great Britain and America*. New York: Henry S. Goodspeed, 1877.

Goodspeed, Thomas Wakefield. *Helen Culver*. Reprinted from *University Record* 9 (Jan. 1923).

———. *A History of the University of Chicago*. Chicago: University of Chicago Press, 1916.

Graham, Abbie. *Grace H. Dodge: Merchant of Dreams*. New York: Woman's Press, 1926.

Grant, Madeleine P. *Alice Hamilton: Pioneer Doctor in Industrial Medicine*. London, New York, and Toronto: Abelard-Schuman, 1967.

Green, Nancy E., ed. *Byrdcliffe: An American Arts and Crafts Colony*. Ithaca, N.Y.: Herbert F. Johnson Museum of Art, Cornell University, 2004.

*The Green Street Congregational Church, Golden Jubilee, 1888–1938*. Chicago: Green Street Congregational Church, 1938.

Gregor-Dellin, Martin. *Richard Wagner: His Life, His Work, His Century*. Translated by J. Maxwell Brownjohn. New York: Harcourt, Brace, Jovanovich, 1983.

Grossman, James R., Ann Durkin Keating, and Janice L. Reiff, eds. *The Encyclopedia of Chicago*. Chicago: University of Chicago Press, 2004.

*Grove's Dictionary of Music and Musicians*. American supplement. New edition with new material. New York: Macmillan, 1928.

Gurteen, S. Humphreys. *What Is Charity Organization?* Buffalo, N.Y.: Bidelow Brothers, 1881.

Gustason, Harriett. *Looking Back: From the Pages of the "Journal-Standard" [Freeport, Ill.]*. Vol. 1, *1982–1895*. Freeport, Ill.: Stephenson County Historical Society, 1994.

Hafner, Arthur W., ed. *Directory of Deceased American Physicians, 1804–1929*. 2 vols. Chicago: American Medical Association, 1993.

Halsey, John J., ed. *A History of Lake County, Illinois*. [Chicago]: Roy S. Bates, 1912.

Hamilton, Alice. *Exploring the Dangerous Trades: The Autobiography of Alice Hamilton, M. D.* Boston: Little, Brown, 1943.

Hanscom, Elizabeth Deering, and Helen French Greene. *Sophia Smith and the Beginnings of Smith College.* Northampton, Mass.: Smith College, 1925.

Hanson, J. W., ed. *The World's Congress of Religions.* Chicago: Louis Benham, 1894.

Harrison, Gilbert A. *A Timeless Affair: The Life of Anita McCormick Blaine.* Chicago: University of Chicago Press, 1979.

Hart, Hastings H. *Preventive Treatment of Neglected Children.* Vol. 4 of *Correction and Prevention.* Edited by Charles Richmond Henderson. New York: Russell Sage Foundation Charities Publication Committee, 1910.

Hart, James D., ed. *The Oxford Companion to American Literature.* London: Oxford University Press, 1941.

Hartley, Elizabeth Kennedy. *Social Work and Social Reform: Selected Women Social Workers and Child Welfare Reforms, 1877–1932.* Ph.D. diss., University of Pennsylvania, 1985. Ann Arbor, Mich.: University Microfilms International, 1991.

Hartnoll, Phyllis, ed. *The Oxford Companion to the Theatre.* 4th ed. New York: Oxford University Press, 1983.

Harvey, Sir Paul, ed. *The Oxford Companion to English Literature.* 4th ed. rev. London: Oxford University Press, 1967.

Havestock, Mary Sayre, Jeannette Mahoney Vance, and Brian L. Meggitt. *Artists in Ohio, 1787–1900: A Biographical Dictionary.* Kent, Ohio: Kent State University Press, 2000.

Head, Franklin H., ed. *Chicago Conference on Trusts: Speeches, Debates, Resolutions, List of the Delegates, Committees, Etc., Held September 13th, 14th, 15th, 16th, 1899.* Chicago: Civic Federation of Chicago, 1900.

Helfrich, G. W., and Gladys O'Neil. *Lost Bar Harbor.* Camden, Maine: Down East Books, 1982.

Henderson, C. R. *Social Elements, Institutions, Character, Progress.* New York: Charles Scribner's Sons, 1906.

———. *Social Settlements.* New York: Lentilhon, 1899.

Hendrick, Burton J. *The Life and Letters of Walter H. Page.* 3 vols. Garden City, N.Y.: Doubleday, Page, 1926.

Higinbotham, H. N. *Report of the President to the Board of Directors of the World's Columbian Exposition.* Chicago: Rand, McNally, 1895.

Hill, Caroline M., comp. *Mary McDowell and Municipal Housekeeping.* Chicago: privately printed, [1937?].

Hill, Mary A. *Charlotte Perkins Gilman: The Making of a Radical Feminist, 1860–1896.* Philadelphia: Temple University Press, 1980.

Hill, William Thomson. *Octavia Hill.* London: Hutchinson, 1956.

*Historical Encyclopedia of Illinois and History of Ogle County.* 2 vols. Chicago: Munsell, 1909.

*History of Medicine and Surgery and Physicians and Surgeons of Chicago.* Chicago: Biographical, 1922.

*History of Winnebago County, Illinois, Its Past and Present.* Chicago: H. F. Kett, 1877.

Hogan, David John. *Class and Reform: School and Society in Chicago, 1880–1930.* Philadelphia: University of Pennsylvania Press, 1985.

Holber, Harriet Wells, Caroline A. Potter Brazee, Nellie Rose Caswell, Catharine Waugh McCullough, and Mabel Walker Herrick, comps. and eds. *Jubilee Book: Commemorating the Fiftieth Anniversary of the Graduation of the First Class, 1854–1904*. Rockford, Ill.: Alumnae Association of Rockford College, 1904.

Holli, Melvin G., and Peter d'A. Jones. *Ethnic Chicago: A Multicultural Portrait*. 4th ed. Grand Rapids, Mich.: William B. Eerdmans, 1995.

Horowitz, Helen Lefkowitz. *Culture and the City: Cultural Philanthropy in Chicago from the 1880s to 1917*. Lexington: University Press of Kentucky, 1976.

Horton, Isabelle. *The Builders: A Story of Faith and Works*. Chicago: Deaconess Advocates, 1910.

———. *High Adventures: Life of Lucy Rider Meyer*. New York: Methodist Book Concern, [1928].

Houghton, Walter R., ed. *Neely's History of the Parliament of Religions and Religious Congresses of the World's Columbian Exposition*. Chicago: Frank Tennyson Neely, 1893.

Howatt, John. *Notes on the First One Hundred Years of Chicago School History*. Chicago: John Howatt, 2nd printing, 1946.

Howe, Sondra Wieland. *Women Music Educators in the United States: A History*. Lanham, Md.: Scarecrow Press, 2014.

Howes, Durward, ed. *American Women: The Official Who's Who among the Women of the Nation*. 1935–40. 3 vols. Los Angeles: American Publications, 1935, 1937, 1939.

Hoy, Suellen. *Ellen Gates Starr: Her Later Years*. Chicago: Chicago History Museum, 2010.

Hull, Charles J. *Reflections from a Busy Life*. Chicago: Knight and Leonard, 1881.

*Hull-House Maps and Papers*. See Residents of Hull-House. *Hull-House Maps and Papers*.

Humphrey, Zephine. *Recollections of My Mother*. New York: F. H. Revell, 1912.

Hunt, Caroline L. *The Life of Ellen H. Richards*. Boston: Whitcomb & Barrows, 1912.

Hunter, Robert. *Tenement Conditions in Chicago*. Chicago: City Homes Association, 1901.

Hurlbut, Jesse Lyman. *The Story of Chautauqua*. New York: G. P. Putnam's Sons, 1921.

*Illinois: A Descriptive and Historical Guide*. Compiled and written by Federal Writers' Project of the Work Projects Administration for the State of Illinois. American Guide Series. Chicago: A. C. McClurg, 1939.

*The Illinois Building and . . . Exhibits Therein: At the World's Columbian Exposition, 1893*. Chicago: John Morris, [1893].

*Illinois Guide & Gazetteer*. Prepared for the Illinois Sesquicentennial Commission. Chicago: Rand McNally, 1969.

*Illustrated Freeport*. Originally published by Freeport Journal, 1896. Reprint sponsored by Stephenson County Genealogical Society, Freeport, Ill. Mt. Vernon, Ind.: Windmill, 2000.

*Industrial Chicago*. Vol. 6, *Bench and Bar*. Chicago: Goodspeed, 1896.

*In Memoriam Mary Harris Thompson*. Chicago: Mary Thompson Hospital of Chicago for Women and Children Board of Managers, 1896.

International Association for the Advancement of Science, Art, and Education. *The Paris International Assembly of 1900*. Paris: École Internationale de'l'Exposition, [1900].

*In the Foot-Prints of the Pioneers of Stephenson County, Illinois*. Freeport, Ill.: Pioneer, 1900. Reprint, Evansville, Ind.: Whippoorwill, 1988.

*Italians in Chicago*. Compiled by Rose Ann Rabiola and Christina West Wells. [Chicago]: Italians in Chicago Project, University of Illinois at Chicago, [1981?].

Jackson, Shannon. *Lines of Activity: Performance, Historiography, Hull-House Domesticity*. Ann Arbor: University of Michigan Press, 2004.

James, Edward T., ed. *Papers of the Women's Trade Union League and Its Principal Leaders*. Woodbridge, Conn.: Research Publications, 1981.

James, Edward T., Janet Wilson James, and Paul S. Boyer, eds. *Notable American Women, 1607–1950*. 3 vols. Cambridge, Mass.: Harvard University Press, 1971.

*James Bronson Reynolds, March 17, 1896–January 1, 1924: A Memorial*. New York: University Settlement, 1927.

Jenkins, Paul B. *The Book of Lake Geneva*. Chicago: Published for the Chicago Historical Society by the University of Illinois Press, 1922.

Johnson, Alexander. *Adventures in Social Welfare*. Fort Wayne, Ind.: Fort Wayne Printing, May, 1923.

Johnson, Allen, Dumas Malone, and Harris E. Starr, eds. *Dictionary of American Biography*. Vols. 1–20, 1929. Reprint. New York: Charles Scribner's Sons, 1937.

Johnson, Allen, Dumas Malone, Harris E. Starr, Robert Schuyler, Edward T. James, and John A. Garraty, eds. *Dictionary of American Biography*. 24 vols. New York: Simon and Schuster, 1952.

Johnson, Rossiter. *A History of the World's Columbian Exposition Held in Chicago in 1893*. 2 vols. New York: Appleton, 1897, 1898.

Jones, M. Katharine, comp. *Bibliography of College, Social and University Settlements*. New York: College Settlements Association, [1895].

Joslin, Katherine. *Jane Addams: A Writer's Life*. Urbana: University of Illinois Press, 2004.

Kaplan, Wendy. *The Art That Is Life: The Arts and Crafts Movement in America, 1875–1920*. Boston: Little, Brown/Museum of Fine Arts, 1987.

Kauffman, Horace G., and Rebecca H. Kauffman, eds. *Historical Encyclopedia of Illinois*. 2 vols. Chicago: Munsell, 1909.

Kaufman, Martin, Stuart Galishoff, and Todd L. Savitt, eds. *Dictionary of American Medical Biography*. 2 vols. Westport, Conn.: Greenwood Press, 1984.

Kaufman, Stuart B., Peter J. Albert, and Grace Palladino, eds. *The Samuel Gompers Papers*. Vol. 4, *1895–98*. Urbana: University of Illinois Press, 1991.

Keil, Hartmut, and John B. Jentz, eds. *German Workers in Chicago: A Documentary History of Working-Class Culture from 1850 to World War I*. Urbana: University of Illinois Press, 1988.

Kelley, Florence. *The Autobiography of Florence Kelley: Notes of Sixty Years*. Edited by Kathryn Kish Sklar. Chicago: Charles H. Kerr, for the Illinois Labor History Society, 1986.

———. *The Selected Letters of Florence Kelley, 1869–1931*. Edited by Kathryn Kish Sklar and Beverly Wilson Palmer. Urbana: University of Illinois Press, 2009.

Kelly, Howard A. *A Cyclopedia of American Medical Biography Comprising the Lives of Eminent Deceased Physicians and Surgeons from 1610 to 1910*. 2 vols. Philadelphia: W. B. Saunders, 1912.

Kelly, Howard A., and Walter L. Burrage. *Dictionary of American Medical Biography: Lives of Eminent Physicians of the United States and Canada*. New York: D. Appleton, 1928. Reprint, Boston: Milford House, 1971.

*Kenilworth: First Fifty Years*. Kenilworth, Ill.: Village of Kenilworth, 1947.

Kent, Elizabeth T. *William Kent, Independent: A Biography*. N.p.: [Elizabeth T. Kent, 1950].

Kett, Joseph F. *The Pursuit of Knowledge under Difficulties: From Self-Improvement to Adult Education in America, 1750–1990*. Stanford, Calif.: Stanford University Press, 1994.

Kilner, Colleen Browne. *Joseph Sears and His Kenilworth*. Kenilworth, Ill.: Kenilworth Historical Society, 1969.

Kirkland, Caroline. *Chicago Yesterdays: A Sheaf of Reminiscences*. Chicago: Daughaday, 1919.

Knight, Louise W. *Citizen Jane Addams and the Struggle for Democracy*. Chicago: University of Chicago Press, 2005.

Koenig, Rev. Msgr. Harry C., ed. *A History of the Parishes of the Archdiocese of Chicago*. 2 vols. Published in observance of Centenary of the Archdiocese 1980. Sponsored by His Eminence, John Cardinal Cody. Chicago: Archdiocese of Chicago, 1980.

Kogan, Herman, and Lloyd Went. *Chicago: A Pictorial History*. New York: E. P. Dutton, 1958.

Lagemann, Ellen Condliffe. *A Generation of Women: Education in the Lives of Progressive Reformers*. Cambridge, Mass.: Harvard University Press, 1979.

Lasch-Quinn, Elisabeth. *Black Neighbors: Race and the Limits of Reform in the American Settlement House Movement, 1890–1945*. Chapel Hill: University of North Carolina Press, 1993.

Lash, Christopher. *New Radicalism in America, 1889–1963: The Intellectual as a Social Type*. New York: Alfred A. Knopf, 1965.

Leonard, John William, ed. *Woman's Who's Who of America, 1914–15*. New York: American Commonwealth, 1914.

Leroy, Rev. A. *History of the Little Sisters of the Poor*. London: Burns, Oates, and Washbourne, 1925.

Lewis, Lloyd, and Henry Justin-Smith. *Chicago: The History of Its Reputation*. New York: Harcourt, Brace, 1929.

*"Liberty" Costumes for Ladies and Children*. Series V, *Spring and Summer Designs*. London and Paris: Liberty, 1896.

Lillie, Mary Prentice. *Frances Crane Lillie (1869–1958), a Memoir*. N.p.: privately printed, [1969?]. CHM, CHS.

———. *Moon Out of the Well: Reminiscences*. N.p.: privately printed, [1970?]. CHM, CHS

Lindsey, Almont. *The Pullman Strike*. Chicago: Phoenix Books, University of Chicago Press, 1964.

Linn, James Weber. *Jane Addams A Biography*. New York: D. Appleton–Century, 1938. New edition with an introduction by Anne Firor Scott. Urbana: University of Illinois Press, 2000.

Lissak, Rivka Shpak. *Pluralism and Progressives: Hull House and the New Immigrants, 1890–1919*. Chicago: University of Chicago Press, 1989.

Lloyd, Caro. *Henry Demarest Lloyd, 1847–1903. A Biography*. 2 vols. New York: G. P. Putnam's Sons, 1912.

Lloyd, Henry Demarest. *Man, the Social Creator*. Edited by Jane Addams and Anne Withington. New York: Doubleday, Page, 1906.

———. *Men, the Workers*. Edited by Caroline Stallbohm and Anne Withington. New York: Doubleday, Page, 1909.

Lockyer, Herbert. *All the Miracles of the Bible*. Grand Rapids, Mich.: Zondervan, 1961.

Macdonald, J. Ramsay. *Margaret Ethel MacDonald*. London: George Allen and Unwin, 1930.

MacLeish, Archibald. *Martha Hillard MacLeish (1856–1947)*. Geneva, N.Y.: privately printed, 1949.

Mairet, Philip. *Pioneer of Sociology: The Life and Letters of Patrick Geddes*. London: Lund Humphries, 1957.

Mallon, James Joseph. *Toynbee Hall: Past and Present*. Reprinted from *Britain To-Day*, nos. 100 and 101. Oxford: Oxford University Press, [1944?].

Mann, Cutis, Edward Russo, and Melinda Garvert. *Springfield Entertainment: A Pictorial History*. St. Louis: G. Bradley, 1998.

Mann, Tom. *Tom Mann's Memoirs*. London: Labour, 1923.

Marciniak, Virginia, ed. *The Illinois Humane Society, 1869 to 1979*. River Forest, Ill.: Rosary College Graduate School of Library Science, 1981.

Marilley, Suzanne M. *Woman Suffrage and the Origins of Liberal Feminism in the United States, 1820–1920*. Cambridge, Mass.: Harvard University Press, 1996.

*Marquis Hand-Book of Chicago*. Chicago: A. N. Marquis, 1885.

*Martha Hillard MacLeish (1856–1947)*. Geneva, N.Y.: privately printed by W. F. Humphrey Press for Archibald MacLeish, 1949.

Martin, Theodora Penny. *The Sound of Our Own Voices: Women's Study Clubs, 1860–1910*. Boston: Beacon Press, 1987.

Maude, Aylmer. *Life of Tolstoy*. New York: Dodd, Mead, 1910.

———. *A Peculiar People: The Dukhobórs*. New York: Funk and Wagnalls, 1904.

Mayer, Harold M., and Richard C. Wade. *Chicago: Growth of a Metropolis*. Chicago: University of Chicago Press, 1969.

Mazzini, Giuseppe. *An Essay on the Duties of Man Addressed to Workingmen*. New York: Funk and Wagnalls, 1898.

McCaffrey, Lawrence J., Ellen Skerrett, Michael F. Funchion, and Charles Fanning. *The Irish in Chicago*. Urbana: University of Illinois Press, 1987.

McCarthy, Kathleen D., ed. *Lady Bountiful Revisited: Women, Philanthropy, and Power*. New Brunswick, N.J.: Rutgers University Press, 1990.

———. *Noblesse Oblige: Charity and Cultural Philanthropy in Chicago, 1849–1929*. Chicago: University of Chicago Press, 1982.

McCausland, Clare. *An Element of Love: A History of the Children's Memorial Hospital of Chicago, Illinois*. Chicago: Children's Memorial Hospital, 1981.

McCormick, Cyrus. *The Century of the Reaper*. Boston and New York: Houghton Mifflin, 1931.

McDonald, Edward L. *Golden Jubilee History of the Diocese of Rockford*. N.p.: Wladsmith Illustrators, 1958.

McGovern, Rev. James J., ed. *The Life and Letters of Eliza Allen Starr*. Chicago: Lakeside Press, 1905.

———. *Souvenir of the Silver Jubilee in the Episcopacy of His Grace the Most Rev. Patrick Augustine Feeham, Archbishop of Chicago, 1890*. Chicago: privately printed, 1891.
McLaughlin, John Gerard. *Irish Chicago*. Images of America Series. Charleston, S.C.: Arcadia, 2003.
Meacham, Standish. *Toynbee Hall and Social Reform, 1880–1914: The Search for Community*. New Haven, Conn.: Yale University Press, 1987.
Meites, Hyman L., ed. *History of the Jews of Chicago*. Chicago: Chicago Jewish Historical Society and Wellington, 1990.
Merwood-Salisbury, Joanna. *Chicago, 1890: The Skyscraper and the Modern City*. Chicago: University of Chicago Press, 2009.
Meyer, Mary S., comp. *History of the Lake View Woman's Club, 1893–1918*. [Chicago: Lake View Woman's Club, 1918].
Montgomery, Caroline Williamson, comp. and ed. *Bibliography of College, Social, University and Church Settlements . . . Chicago, Illinois, for the College Settlements Association*. 4th ed. Rev. ed. New York: College Settlements Association, 1900.
Morantz-Sachez, Regina. *Sympathy and Science: Women Physicians in American Medicine*. New York: Oxford University Press, 1985.
Morford, Henry. *Morford's Short-Trip Guide to Europe Comprising Tours in England, Scotland, Ireland, Wales, France, Holland, Belgium, Germany, Austria, Switzerland, Italy, Spain &c. with Hints for Russia, Sweden, the East, &c.: A Collection of Travels' Phrases in French and German and Skeleton Tours in America*. New York: Sheldon, 1872.
*Moscow*. London: D. K., 1998.
*Moscow and St. Petersburg*. 5th ed. New York: Fodor's, 2002.
Mottier, Charles H. *Biography of Roswell B. Mason*. Chicago: Western Society of Engineers, 1938.
Mulkerins, Brother Thomas M., S.J. *Holy Family Parish Chicago: Priests and People*. Edited by Joseph J. Thompson. Chicago: Universal Press, 1923.
Muncy, Robyn. *Creating a Female Dominion in American Reform, 1890–1935*. New York: Oxford University Press, 1991.
*The Municipal Herald of Chicago*. Chicago: John C. Sterchie, 1896.
Murolo, Priscilla. *The Common Ground of Womanhood: Class, Gender, and Working Girls' Clubs, 1884–1928*. Urbana: University of Illinois Press, 1997.
*The National Cyclopedia of American Biography: Being the History of the United States as Illustrated in the Lives of the Founders, Builders, and Defenders of the Republic, and of the Men and Women Who Are Doing the Work and Molding the Thought of the Present Time*. 63 vols. Clifton, N.J.: James T. White, 1892–96.
Nelli, Humbert Steven. *Italians in Chicago, 1880–1930: A Study in Ethnicity*. New York: Oxford University Press, 1970.
Nelson, Bruce C. *Beyond the Martyrs: A Social History of Chicago's Anarchists, 1870–1900*. New Brunswick, N.J.: Rutgers University Press, 1988.
Nelson, C. Hjalmar, comp. and ed. *Sinnissippi Saga: A History of Rockford and Winnebago County, Illinois*. Mendota, Ill.: Published for Winnebago County Illinois Sesquicentennial Committee by Wayside Press, 1968.
Nelson, C. Hjalmar, Joan Surrey, Isy Nelson, Leona Carlson, and Betty Asprooth, eds. *Rockford College: A Retrospective Look*. Rockford, Ill.: C. Hjalmar Nelson and Rockford College, 1980.

Newton, Joseph Fort. *David Swing Poet-Preacher*. Chicago: Unity, Abraham Lincoln Centre, 1909.

Northwestern University Medical School, Chicago. *Dedication of the Montgomery Ward Building*. Chicago, 1927.

Norton, William Bernard. *The Founding of the Chicago Training School for City, Home and Foreign Missions*. Chicago: J. Watson, [1916?].

Nuzum, Kay. *A History of Baldwin County* [Alabama]. 3rd ed. Fairhope, Ala.: Eastern Shore, [1971].

*100 Years, Our First Century of Services: Saint Anthony Hospital*. Chicago: The Hospital, 1997.

Osborne, Georgia L., comp. *Brief Biographies of the Figurines on Display in the Illinois State Historical Library*. Springfield, Ill.: State of Illinois, 1932.

Otis, Philo Adams. *The First Presbyterian Church, 1833–1913: A History of the Oldest Organization in Chicago*. Rev. ed. Chicago: F. H. Revell, 1913.

Palmer, John M., ed. *The Bench and the Bar of the Illinois: Historical and Reminiscent*. 2 vols. Chicago: Lewis, 1899.

Palmer, R. R. *Rand McNally Atlas of World History*. Chicago: Rand McNally, 1957.

Peebles, James C. *A History of Armour Institute of Technology*. [Chicago: Illinois Institute of Technology, 1955?].

Pegram, Thomas R. *Partisans and Progressives: Private Interests and Public Policy in Illinois, 1870–1922*. Urbana: University of Illinois Press, 1992.

Pence, Cheryl. *Newspapers in the [Illinois State] Historical Library*. Springfield: Illinois State Library, Office of the Secretary of State, 1994.

Perkins, Helen M. *A Preliminary Checklist for a Bibliography on Jane Addams*. Compiled . . . under the Direction of the Rockford Area Jane Addams Centennial Committee, Dr. Mildred F. Berry, Chairman. Rockford, Ill.: [Rockford Area Jane Addams Centennial Committee], 30 Apr. 1960.

*Philanthropy and Social Progress*. New York: Thomas Y. Crowell, 1893.

*Picturesque Chicago and Guide to the World's Fair*. Baltimore: R. H. Woodward, 1892.

Pierce, Bessie L. *History of Chicago*. 3 vols. Chicago: University of Chicago Press, 1937, 1940, 1957.

Pimlott, J[ohn]. A[lfred]. R[alph]. *Toynbee Hall: Fifty Years of Social Progress, 1884–1934*. London: J. M. Dent and Sons, 1935.

*Pioneers of the Kindergarten in America*. Authorized by the International Kindergarten Union and prepared by the Committee of Nineteen. New York: Century, 1924.

Polacheck, Hilda Satt. *I Came a Stranger: The Story of a Hull-House Girl*. Edited by Dena J. Polacheck Epstein. Urbana: University of Illinois Press, 1989.

*The Poor in Great Cities: Their Problems and What Is Doing to Solve Them*. New York: Charles Scribner's Sons, 1895.

Porter, Mary H. *Eliza Chappell Porter: A Memoir*. Chicago and New York: F. H. Revell, 1892.

Profiles of the Principals of Rockford Seminary and Presidents of Rockford College, 1847–1947. Rockford, Ill.: Rockford College, 1947.

Radar, Benjamin G. *The Academic Mind and Reform: The Influence of Richard T. Ely in American Life*. Lexington: University Press of Kentucky, 1966.

Randall, Frank A. *History of the Development of Building Construction in Chicago*. Urbana: University of Illinois Press, 1949.

Randall, Mercedes M. *Improper Bostonian: Emily Greene Balch*. New York: Twayne, 1964.

*Random House Dictionary of the English Language*. 2nd ed. New York: Random House, 1987.

Ransom, Reverdy C. *First Quadrennial Report of the Pastor and Warden of the Institutional Church and Social Settlement*. Presented to the Twenty-second Session of the General Conference and the Connectional Trustees of the African Methodist Episcopal Church. Quinn Chapel. Chicago, May 1904.

Reeling, Viola Crouch. *Evanston: Its Land and Its People*. Evanston, Ill.: Fort Dearborn Chapter, Daughters of the American Revolution, 1928.

Regnery, Henry. *The Cliff Dwellers: A History of a Chicago Cultural Institution*. Evanston, Ill.: Chicago Historical Bookworks, 1990.

Residents of Hull-House. *Hull-House Maps and Papers*. Crowell's Library of Economics and Politics, no. 5. New York: Thomas Y. Crowell, 1895. Another edition with an introduction by Rima Lumin Schultz. Urbana: University of Illinois Press, 2007.

Reynolds, Marcus T. *The Housing of the Poor in American Cities: The Prize Essay of the American Economic Association for 1892*. College Park, Md.: McGrath, 1969.

Richmond, Mary E. *The Long View: Papers and Addresses*. Edited by Joanna Colcord and Ruth Z. S. Mann. New York: Russell Sage Foundation, 1930.

Robinson, Elisha. *Robinson's Atlas of the City of Chicago, Illinois*. 5 vols. New York: E. Robinson, 1886. Microfilm, CHM.

*Rockford Today: Historical, Descriptive, Biographical, Illustrated*. Rockford, Ill.: Clark Company Press for the Rockford Morning Star, 1903.

Roderick, Stella Virginia. *Nettie Fowler McCormick*. Rindge, N.H.: Richard R. Smith, 1956.

Rolfe, W. J. *A Satchel Guide for the Vacation Tourist in Europe: A Compact Itinerary of the British Isles, Belgium and Holland, Germany and the Rhine, Switzeland, France, Austria and Italy*. Boston: Houghton Mifflin 1897.

Root, George Frederick. *The Story of a Musical Life: An Autobiography*. Cincinnati: John Church, 1891.

Rossiter, Johnson. *A History of the World's Columbian Exposition Held in Chicago in 1893*. 2 vols. New York: Appleton, 1897–98.

Russell, Nellie Naomi. *Gleanings from Chinese Folklore*. Compiled by Mary H. Porter. New York: F. H. Revell, [1915].

*Russia, Ukraine and Belarus*. 2nd ed. Melbourne: Lonely Planet, 2000.

Scarborough, Elizabeth, and Laurel Futurmoto. *Untold Lives: The First Generation of American Women Psychologists*. New York: Columbia University Press, 1989.

Schaack, Michael. *Anarchy and Anarchists*. Chicago: F. J. Schulte, 1889.

Schiavo, Giovanni E. *The Italians in Chicago: A Study in Americanization*. Chicago: Italian American, 1928.

Schneer, Jonathan. *Ben Tillett: Portrait of a Labour Leader*. Urbana: University of Illinois Press, 1982.

Schneirov, Richard. *Labor and Urban Politics: Class Conflict and the Origins of Modern Liberalism in Chicago, 1864–97*. Urbana: University of Illinois Press, 1998.

Schneirov, Richard, Shelton Stromquist, and Nick Salvatore, eds. *The Pullman Strike and the Crisis of the 1890s: Essays on Labor and Politics*. Urbana: University of Illinois Press, 1999.

Schofield, Ann. *"To Do & to Be."* Boston: Northeastern University Press, 1997.

Schultz, Rima Lunin, and Adele Hast, eds. *Women Building Chicago, 1790–1990: A Biographical Dictionary.* Bloomington: Indiana University Press, 2001.

Schulze, Franz, Rosemary Cowler, and Arthur H. Miller. *Thirty Miles North: A History of Lake Forest College, Its Town, and Its City of Chicago.* Lake Forest, Ill.: Lake Forest College, distributed by University of Chicago Press, 2000.

Scott, Florence Dolive, and Richard Joseph Scott. *Daphne [Alabama]: A History of Its People and Their Pursuits as Some Saw It and Others Remember It.* Bay Minette, Ala.: Lavender Press, 2003.

Scroggs, Marilee Munger. *A Light in the City: The Fourth Presbyterian Church of Chicago.* Chicago: The Church, 1990.

Scudder, Vida Dutton. *Father Huntington: Founder of the Order of the Holy Cross.* New York: E. P. Dutton, 1940.

———. *On Journey.* New York: E. P. Dutton, 1937.

Seigfried, Charlene Haddock. *Pragmatism and Freminism: Reweaving the Social Fabric.* Urbana: University of Illinois Press, 1996.

Seller, Maxine Schwartz, ed. *Women Educators in the United States, 1820–1993: A Bio-bibliographical Sourcebook.* Westport, Conn.: Greenwood Press, 1994.

Sewall, May Wright. *The World's Congress of Representative Women.* Chicago and New York: Rand, McNally, 1894.

Shane, Martha P., ed. *Papers of Emily Greene Balch, 1875–1961: Guide to the Scholarly Resources Microfilm Edition.* Wilmington, Del.: Scholarly Resources, 1988.

Shannon, David A., ed. *Beatrice Webb's American Diary, 1898.* Madison: University of Wisconsin Press, 1963.

Shaw, Lloyd. *Prominent Democrats of Illinois: A Brief History.* Chicago: Democrat, 1899.

Shepherd, Massey Hamilton, Jr. *History of St. James Church, Chicago.* [Chicago]: privately printed, 1934.

Sicherman, Barbara. *Alice Hamilton: A Life in Letters.* A Commonwealth Fund Book. Cambridge, Mass.: Harvard University Press, 1984.

———. *Well-Read Lives: How Books Inspired a Generation of American Women.* Chapel Hill: University of North Carolina Press, 2010.

Sicherman, Barbara, and Carol Hurd Green, eds. *Notable American Women: The Modern Period.* Cambridge, Mass.: Belknap Press of Harvard University Press, 1980.

Siegel, Beatrice. *Lillian Wald of Henry Street.* New York: Macmillan, 1983.

Signor, Isaac C., ed. *Landmarks of Orleans County, New York.* Syracuse, N.Y.: D. Mason, 1894.

Sinkevitch, Alice, ed. *AIA Guide to Chicago.* 2nd ed. A Harvest Original. Orlando: Harcourt, 2004.

Skerrett, Ellen, and Mary Lesch, eds. *Chief O'Neill's Sketchy Recollections of an Eventual Life in Chicago: Francis O'Neill.* Evanston, Ill.: Northwestern University Press, 2008.

Sklar, Kathryn Kish. *Florence Kelley and the Nation's Work: The Rise of Women's Political Culture, 1830–1900.* New Haven, Conn.: Yale University Press, 1995.

Slonimsky, Nicholas, rev. *Baker's Biographical Dictionary of Musicians.* 8th ed. New York: Schirmer Books, 1992.

Smith, Carl. *Urban Disorder and the Shape of Belief: The Great Chicago Fire, the Haymarket Bomb, and the Model Town of Pullman*. Chicago: University of Chicago Press, 1995.

Smith, David Lee. *Community Renewal Society, 1882–1982. 100 Years of Service*. Chicago: Community Renewal Society. Distributed by Chicago Review Press, 1982.

Smith, Eleanor. *The Eleanor Smith Music Course, Book Three*. New York: American Book, 1908.

———. *Hull House Songs*. Chicago: Clayton F. Summy, [1915].

———. *The Modern Music Series: Primer*. New York: Silver, Burdett, 1901.

———. *The Modern Music Series: Second Book*. New York: Silver, Burdett, 1901.

Smith, Henry Justin, and Lloyd Lewis. *Chicago: The History of Its Reputation*. New York: Harcourt, Brace, 1929.

Smith, Richard Norton. *The Colonel: The Life and Legend of Robert T. McCormick, 1880–1955*. Boston and New York: Houghton Mifflin, 1997.

Smith-Rosenberg, Carroll. *Disorderly Conduct: Visions of Gender in Victorian America*. New York: Oxford University Press, 1985.

Sperry, F. M., comp. *A Group of Distinguished Physicians and Surgeons of Chicago*. Chicago: J. H. Beers, 1904.

Spinka, Matthew, ed. *A History of Illinois Congregational and Christian Churches*. Chicago: Congregational and Christian Conference of Illinois, 1944.

*St. Petersburg*. New York: Alfred A. Knopf, 1995.

*St. Petersburg*. Rev. ed. London: Dorling Kindersley Travel Guides, 2000.

Staley, Eugene. *History of the Illinois State Federation of Labor*. Chicago: University of Chicago Press, 1930.

Starr, Eliza Allen. *The Life and Letters of Eliza Allen Starr*. Edited by Rev. James J. McGovern. Chicago: Printed at the Lakeside Press, 1905.

Starr, Herbert W., and J. R. Hendrickson, eds. *The Complete Poems of Thoms Gray: English, Latin, and Greek*. Oxford: Oxford University Press, 1966.

Stead, William T. *If Christ Came to Chicago!* Chicago: Laird and Lee, 1894.

Stebner, Eleanor J. *The Women of Hull House: A Study in Spirituality, Vocation, and Friendship*. Albany: State University of New York Press, 1997.

Stedman, Edmund, and Thomas L. Stedman, eds. *The Complete Pocket-Guide to Europe*. New York: William R. Jenkins, 1899.

Stone, Marie Kirchner, ed. *Between Home and Community: Chronicle of the Francis W. Parker School, 1901–1976*. Chicago: Francis W. Parker School, 1976.

Storr, Richard J. *Harper's University: The Beginnings*. Chicago: University of Chicago Press, 1966.

Strelsky, Katharine, and Catherine Wolkonsky, eds. *Out of the Past, Alexandra Tolstoy*. New York: Columbia University Press, 1981.

*The Sunday Problem: Papers Presented at the International Congress on Sunday Rest, Chicago, Sept. 28–30, 1893*. New York: Baker and Taylor, 1894.

Swan, David, and Terry Tatum, eds. *The Autobiography of Irving K. Pond. The Sons of Mary and Elihu*. Oak Park, Ill.: Hyoogen Press, 2009.

Swift, Lindsay. *Brook Farm: Its Members, Scholars, and Visitors*. London: Macmillan, 1904.

*Taber's Encyclopedia Medical Dictionary*. 15th ed. Philadelphia: F. A. Davis, 1981.

Talbot, Marion, and Lois Kimball Mathews Rosenberry. *The History of the American*

*Association of University Women, 1881–1931*. Boston and New York: Houghton Mifflin, 1931.

Talmadge, Thomas E. *Architecture in Old Chicago*. Chicago: University of Chicago Press, 1941.

Taylor, Graham. *Chicago Commons through Forty Years*. Chicago: Chicago Commons Assn., 1936.

———. *Pioneering on Social Frontiers*. Chicago: University of Chicago Press, 1930.

Taylor and Francis Group, Cathy Hartley, and Susan Leckey. *A Historical Dictionary of British Women*. New York: Routledge, 2003.

Tebbel, John. *An American Dynasty: The Story of the McCormicks, Medills and Pattersons*. New York: Doubleday, 1947.

———. *The Marshall Fields: A Study in Wealth*. New York: E. P. Dutton, 1947.

Thompson, Oscar. *The International Cyclopedia of Music and Musicians*. Edited by Bruce Boble. 10th ed. New York: Dodd, Mead, 1975.

Tillier, Alan, main contributor. *Eyewitness Travel Guides: Paris*. London, New York, Stuttgart: Dorling Kindersley, 1993.

Tolstoy, Alexandra. *I Worked for the Soviet*. New Haven, Conn.: Yale University Press, 1934. Gift to JA from Alexandra Tolstoy, UIC, JAMC.

Tolstoy, Leo. *Christianity and Patriotism*. Chicago: Open Court, 1905. JA gift to SCPC, JAC.

———. *The Christian Teaching*. Translated by V. Tchertkoff. New York: Frederick A. Stokes, [1898] with JA signature. UIC, JAMC.

———. *A Great Iniquity: Count Tolstoy's Letter to "the Times."* Translated by V. Tchertkoff and I. F. M. Manchester: Ancoats Brotherhood, 1906. UIC, JAMC.

———. *My Confession and the Spirit of Christ's Teaching*. Translated from the Russian. New York: Thomas Y. Crowell, 1887.

———. *Toil*. Translated from Russian by B. Tseyline and Amedee Pages and from French by James E. Alvord. Chicago: Charles H. Sergel, 1890. Jane Addams gift to SCPC, JAC.

———. *The Tsar's Coronation as Seen by "De Monto Alto" Resident in Moscow*. Translated by Aylmer Maude. London and Croydon: Brotherhood, 1896.

———. *What I Believe*. Translated by Constantine Popoff. London: Elliot Stock, 1885. A gift from Mary Rozet Smith to Jane Addams, n.d. UIC, JAMC.

———. *What Then Must We Do?* Translated by Aylmer Maude with an introduction by Jane Addams (1934), with Jane Addams signature. UIC, JAMC.

———. *What to Do?* A new and authorized translation from the unabridged Russian manuscript. London: Walter Scott, [1888?]. A gift from Mary Rozet Smith to Jane Addams, Aug. 1896. UIC, JAMC

Trevelyan, Janet Penrose. *The Life of Mrs. Humphry Ward*. London: Constable, [1923?]

Tsuzuki, Ghushighi. *Tom Mann, 1856–1941: The Challenges of Labour*. Oxford: Clarendon Press, 1991.

Tucker, Cynthia Grant. *A Woman's Ministry: Mary Collson's Search for Reform as a Unitarian Minister*. Philadelphia: Temple University Press, 1984.

*A Twentieth Century History and Biographical Record of Crawford County, Kansas, by Home Authors*. Chicago: Lewis, 1905.

Vaillant, Derek. *Sounds of Reform: Progressivism & Music in Chicago, 1873–1935*. Chapel Hill: University of North Carolina Press, 2003.

Ver Berkmoes, Ryan. *Moscow*. Melbourne: Lonely Planet, Aug. 2000.

Vincent, John Heyl. *The Chautauqua Movement*. Boston: Chautauqua Press, 1886.

Vitrano, Steven P. *An Hour of Good News: The Chicago Sunday Evening Club, a Unique Preaching Ministry*. Chicago: Chicago Sunday Evening Club, 1974.

Wade, Louise C. *Graham Taylor, Pioneer for Social Justice, 1851–1938*. Chicago: University of Chicago Press, 1964.

Wade, Stuart C., and W. S. Wrenn. *"The Nut Shell": The Ideal Pocket Guide to the World's Fair and What to See There*. Chicago: A. J. Burton, 1893.

Wald, Lillian S. *The House on Henry Street*. New York: Henry Holt, 1915.

———. *Windows on Henry Street*. Boston: Little, Brown, 1934.

Waldrop, Frank C. *McCormick of Chicago*. Englewood Cliffs, N.J.: Prentice Hall, 1966.

Wanamaker, John. *Wanamaker's Paris Guide*. Philadelphia, New York, and Paris: John Wanamaker, 1900.

Ward, Mrs. Humphry. *A Writer's Recollections*. New York: Harper and Brothers, 1918.

Webb, Beatrice Potter. *My Apprenticeship*. New York: Longmans, Green, 1926.

———. *Our Partnership*. Edited by Barbara Drake and Margaret I. Cole. New York: Longmans, Green, [1948].

Webber, Frederick Roth. *A History of Preaching in Britain and America*. 3 vols. Milwaukee: Northwestern, 1952–57.

*Webster's Biographical Dictionary*. Springfield, Mass.: G. and C. Merriam, 1943, 1972.

*Webster's New Geographical Dictionary*. Springfield, Mass.: Merriam-Webster, 1988.

*Webster's Third International Dictionary of the English Language*. Springfield, Mass.: G. and C. Merriam, 1981.

Weimann, Jeanne Madeline. *The Fair Women: The Story of the Woman's Building, World's Columbian Exposition, Chicago, 1893*. Chicago: Academy Chicago, 1981.

Wells, Ida M. *Crusade for Justice*. Chicago: University of Chicago Press, 1970.

Wells, Mildred White, ed. *Unity in Diversity: The History of the General Federation of Women's Clubs*. Washington, D.C.: General Federation of Women's Clubs, 1953.

Wendt, Lloyd. *"Chicago Tribune": The Rise of a Great American Newspaper*. Chicago: Rand McNally, 1979.

Wendt, Lloyd, and Herman Kogan. *Lords of the Levee*. Indianapolis and New York: Bobbs-Merrill, 1943.

*Who's Who at Bar Harbor and New Port*. Salem, Mass.: Salem Press, 1917.

*Who's Who in Chicago*. [1905, 1911, 1917, 1926, 1931, 1936]. Chicago: A. N. Marquise, 1905, 1911, 1917, 1926, 1931, 1936.

*Who Was Who in America*. 7 vols. Chicago: Marquis-Who's Who, 1981.

*Who Was Who in America, 1607–1896: A Component Volume of Who Was Who in American History*. Chicago: Marquis, 1963.

Whyte, Frederic. *The Life of W. T. Stead*. 2 vols. New York and Boston: Houghton Mifflin, [1925].

Willard, Frances E. *A Classic Town: The Story of Evanston*. Chicago: Woman's Temperance Publishing Association, 1891.

———. *Glimpses of Fifty Years: The Autobiography of an American Woman*. Chicago: Woman's Temperance Publication Association and H. J. Smith, 1889.

Williams, [Melissa Pierce], and [Thomas] McCormick. *Alice Kellogg Tyler*. Kansas City, Mo.: Williams and McCormick, Fall 1987.

———. *Alice Kellogg Tyler, 1866–1900: Private Works*. Kansas City, Mo.: Williams and McCormick, [1987].

Wilson, Howard E. *Mary McDowell Neighbor*. Chicago: University of Chicago Press, 1928.

Wilson, Otto, and Robert South Barrett. *Fifty Years' Work with Girls, 1883–1933*. Alexandria, Va.: National Florence Crittenton Mission, 1933.

Wise, Winifred E. *Jane Addams of Hull-House*. New York: Harcourt, Brace, 1935.

Withey, Henry F. *Biographical Dictionary of American Architects (Deceased)*. Los Angeles: Hennessey and Ingalls, 1970.

Wolfmeyer, Ann, and Mary Burns Gage. *Lake Geneva, Newport of the West, 1870–1920*. Vol. 1. [Lake Geneva, Wis.]: Lake Geneva Historical Society, 1976.

*Woman's Who's Who of America, 1914–1915*. Edited by John William Leonard. New York: American Commonwealth, 1914.

Wood, David Ward, ed. *History of the Republican Party and Biographies of Its Supporters: Illinois Volume*. Chicago: Lincoln, 1895.

Wood, Mary I. *The History of the General Federation of Women's Clubs, for the First Twenty-two Years of Its Organization*. Northwood, Mass.: Northwood Press for the History Department, General Federation of Women's Clubs, New York, 1912.

Woods, Eleanor H. *Robert A. Woods: Champion of Democracy*. Boston and New York: Houghton Mifflin; Cambridge: Riverside Press, 1929.

Woods, Robert A., ed. *Americans in Process: A Settlement Study by Residents and Associates of the South End House; North and West Ends, Boston*. Boston and New York: Houghton, Mifflin, 1903.

———. *English Social Movements*. New York: C. Scribner's Sons, 1891.

———. *The Neighborhood in Nation-Building: The Running Comment of Thirty Years at the South End House*. Boston and New York: Houghton Mifflin, 1923.

Woods, Robert A., and Albert J. Kennedy. *Handbook of Settlements*. New York: Charities Publication Committee for the Russell Sage Foundation, 1911.

———. *The Settlement Horizon: A National Estimate*. New York: Russell Sage Foundation, 1922.

Wright, Frank Lloyd. *Augefuhrte Bauten*. With an introduction by C. R. Ashbee. Berlin: Verlegt Bei Ernst Wasmuth A. G., 1911.

Yeaxlee, Basil A., comp. *Settlements and Their Outlook: An Account of the First International Conference of Settlements, Toynbee Hall, London, July 1922*. London: For the Continuation Committee of the International Conference of Settlements by P. S. King and Son, 1922.

Zueblin, Charles. *A Decade of Civic Development*. Chicago: University of Chicago Press, 1905.

# Index

# Index of Works by Jane Addams

## Books



## Speeches, Essays, Comments, and Articles

## *Poems and Songs*



## *Works Edited by Jane Addams*

MARY LYNN MCCREE BRYAN, retired editor of the Jane Addams Papers, Department of History, Duke University, led the team editors in producing the first two volumes of this edition of *The Selected Papers of Jane Addams* and the microfilm edition of the Jane Addams Papers as well as *The Jane Addams Papers: A Comprehensive Guide*. She is also coeditor, with Allen F. Davis, of *100 Years at Hull-House* and former curator of the Jane Addams Hull-House at the University of Illinois at Chicago.

MAREE DE ANGURY has retired from the Jane Addams Papers Project for which she served as assistant to the editor for almost thirty years and is a member of the editorial team that produced *The Jane Addams Papers: A Comprehensive Guide*. She also served as a business officer at the University of North Carolina, Wilmington, from which she is now retired.

RICHARD R. SEIDEL, librarian, noted Chicago researcher, and historiographer, was the founding archivist of the Chicago School Board Archives and guided the development of the Episcopal Diocese of Chicago Archives, now named in his memory. For a number of years, he helped identify reference materials useful to the Jane Addams Project, and he conducted special research in Chicago and throughout the Midwest for volume 3 of *The Selected Papers of Jane Addams*.

ELLEN SKERRETT, a historian of Chicago and its neighborhoods, has been the Chicago-based researcher for the Jane Addams Papers Project since 2006. She was associate editor of the University of Illinois at Chicago website "Urban Experience in Chicago and Its Neighborhoods, 1889–1963" and served in the same capacity in the development of the initial website for the Jane Addams Papers Project.

The University of Illinois Press
is a founding member of the
Association of American University Presses.

---

Text designed by Copenhaver Cumpston
Composed in 10.5/12.5 Minion
with Burlington display
by Jim Proefrock
at the University of Illinois Press
Jacket illustration: Jane Addams, 1895.
Photo by Alfred A. Cox.
Manufactured by Sheridan Books, Inc.

University of Illinois Press
1325 South Oak Street
Champaign, IL 61820-6903
www.press.uillinois.edu